SOMETHING ABOUT THE AUTHOR®

Something about
the Author *was named
an* **"Outstanding
Reference Source,"**
*the highest honor given
by the American
Library Association
Reference and Adult
Services Division.*

ISSN 0276-816X

sOMeTHING ABOUT THe AUTHOR®

**Facts and Pictures about Authors
and Illustrators of Books for Young People**

volume 223

GALE
CENGAGE Learning™

Detroit • New York • San Francisco • New Haven, Conn • Waterville, Maine • London

Something about the Author, Volume 223

Project Editor: Lisa Kumar

Permissions: Kimberly Potvin

Imaging and Multimedia: Kimberly Potvin, John Watkins

Composition and Electronic Capture: Amy Darga

Manufacturing: Rhonda Dover

Product Manager: Mary Onorato

Gale, Cengage Learning
27500 Drake Rd.
Farmington Hills, MI, 48331-3535

LIBRARY OF CONGRESS CATALOG CARD NUMBER 62-52046

ISBN-13: 978-1-4144-6126-7
ISBN-10: 1-4144-6126-7

ISSN 0276-816X

This title is also available as an e-book.
ISBN-13: 978-1-4144-6455-8
ISBN-10: 1-4144-6455-X
Contact your Gale, Cengage Learning sales representative for ordering information.

Printed in Mexico
1 2 3 4 5 6 7 15 14 13 12 11

Contents

Authors in Forthcoming Volumes vii

Introduction ix

SATA Product Advisory Board xi

Illustrations Index 193

Author Index 229

A

Agard, John 1949- 1

Alexander, Jill S. 1964- 6

Alexander, Jill Shurbet
   See Alexander, Jill S. 6

Austen, Catherine 1965- 7

B

Baker-Smith, Grahame 9

Barnett, Mac 10

Barrett, Angela 1955- 12

Bass, Hester 1956- 16

Björkman, Steve 18

Blessing, Charlotte 22

Byars, Betsy 1928- 23

C

Carman, Bill
   See Carman, William 34

Carman, William 34

Caswell, Deanna 35

Cecil, Randy 1968- 36

Chapman, Linda 1969- 39

Chocolate, Debbi 1954- 40

Chocolate, Deborah H. Newton
   See Chocolate, Debbi 40

Coverly, Dave 1964- 43

Cusimano, Maryann K.
   See Love, Maryann Cusimano 118

D

Douglas, Allen 45

Dunkle, Clare B. 1964- 45

Dusíková, Maja 1946- 48

E

Edwardson, Debby Dahl 51

F

Ferrari, Michael 53

Ferrari, Michael J.
   See Ferrari, Michael 53

Forler, Nan 54

Franco, Betsy 55

Franson, Leanne 1963- 61

G

Gauch, Sarah 66

Gavin, Jamila 1941- 66

Glass, Andrew 1949- 71

Gréban, Quentin 1977- 75

Gritton, Steve 77

H

Haddon, Mark 1962- 78

Hapka, C.A.
   See Hapka, Catherine 82

Hapka, Catherine 82

Hapka, Cathy
   See Hapka, Catherine 82

Hemingway, Edith M. 1950- 86

Hemingway, Edith Morris
   See Hemingway, Edith M. 86

Higgins, Dalton 87

Holt, Kimberly Willis 1960- 89

I

Idle, Molly Schaar 94

Impey, Rose 1947- 95

K

Ketteman, Helen 1945- 101

Kilaka, John 1966- 106

Kulak, Jeff 1984(?)- 108

L

Ladwig, Tim 1952- 110

Ladwig, Timothy
   See Ladwig, Tim 110

Lee, Cora 112

Long, Ethan 1968(?)- 114

Love, Maryann Cusimano 118

M

Martini, Angela 1972(?)- 121

Mazo, Michael 122

Meadows, Daisy
   See Chapman, Linda 39

Milgrim, David 123

Mohanty, Raja 128

Munro, Roxie 1945- 128

N

Norman, Geoffrey 135

O

Oldland, Nicholas 1972- 135

Ostow, Micol 1976- 136

P

Patterson, Valerie O. 140

Perkins, Dan
   See Tomorrow, Tom 175

Perry, John 1967- 141

Pignataro, Anna 1965- 142

Pogue, Carolyn 1948- 144

R

Reed, Amy 1979- 146

Reef, Catherine 1951- 147

Riddle, Tohby 1965- 153

Roberts, Ken 1946- 156

Rubel, David 1961- 159

S

Sauer, Tammi 1972- 162

Schon, Nick 1955- 164

Silvano, Wendi 1962- 164

Sonnenblick, Jordan 1969- 165

Spengler, Margaret 169

Suma, Nova Ren 170

T

Teevee, Ningeokuluk 1963- 173

Tidholm, Anna-Clara 1946- 174

Tomorrow, Tom 1961- 175

V

Verroken, Sarah 1982- 178

W

Wadsworth, Ginger 1945- 179

Walker, Anna 185

Wehrman, Vicki 185

Wharton, Thomas 1963- 186

White, Lee 188

Authors in Forthcoming Volumes

Below are some of the authors and illustrators that will be featured in upcoming volumes of *SATA*. These include new entries on the swiftly rising stars of the field, as well as completely revised and updated entries (indicated with *) on some of the most notable and best-loved creators of books for children.

*Rudine Sims Bishop ▮ A highly respected scholar and educator, Bishop has produced the notable nonfiction works *Shadow and Substance: Afro-American Experience in Contemporary Children's Fiction* and *Free within Ourselves: The Development of African-American Children's Literature.* Her books for young readers include the biography *Presenting Walter Dean Myers* and *Bishop Daniel Alexander Payne: Great Black Leader,* the latter of which examines the life of a noted nineteenth-century educator, author, and theologian.

Glen Dakin ▮ Demonstrating his versatility as a writer, Dakin has created comics and written books compiling facts, character profiles, plot synopses, and assorted trivia about popular television series and films. He has also written comedy sketches for television and radio programming produced in his native England. While continuing to juggle these varied projects, Dakin also turns to fantasy fiction in his "Candle Man" adventure-novel series, which includes *The Society of Unrelenting Vigilance* and *The Society of Dread.*

*Kathleen Gear ▮ Gear and her husband, W. Michael Gear, are the coauthors of a popular series of novels that follow the tribes of prehistoric North America. Their "First North Americans" series, which includes the novels *People of the Wolf, People of the Fire, People of the Moon,* and *People of the Thunder,* feature detailed descriptions of an ancient way of life that are enriched by Kathleen Gear's training as an archeologist.

Tim Hopgood ▮ British author and artist Hopgood was inspired to create his first book for children after contemplating his family's couch, and the lumpy, old-fashioned sofa stars in his self-illustrated picture book *Our Big Blue Sofa.* Hopgood has continued to pair whimsical stories and original art in several other picture books, among them *A Dog Called Rod, Here Comes Frankie!, Wow! Said the Owl,* and *Tip Tap Went the Crab,* the last of which earned Hopgood a Kate Greenway Award nomination.

Josh Lieb ▮ Lieb is a television producer and writer whose professional credits include a four-year stint as executive producer of the popular *Daily Show with Jon Stewart,* which airs on the Comedy Central cable network. In 2007 his trade union went on a prolonged strike. With free time on his hands and no idea how long the Writer's Guild strike would last, Lieb planned the outline and first four chapters of what would become the quirky teen novel *I Am a Genius of Unspeakable Evil and I Want to Be Your Class President.*

*Jim Murphy ▮ An award-winning author, Murphy writes on a variety of topics, among them sports, transportation, inventions, dinosaurs, animal life, mechanical devices, and historical figures. In addition, Murphy has created picture books as well as historical fiction, contemporary realistic fiction, and a collection of horror stories for teen readers. A prolific writer, he is perhaps best known for his books on U.S. military history, such as *Inside the Alamo* and *The Crossing: How George Washington Saved the American Revolution.*

*Mark Podwal ▮ In addition to his career as a physician and educator, Podwal is an accomplished author and artist whose works have been exhibited and recognized internationally. His creative work includes designing a medal for the U.S. Holocaust Memorial Council and creating a tapestry for a prominent synagogue in New York City, posters for Lincoln Center, and ceramics for the Metropolitan Museum of Art. Podwal has also written and/or illustrated books that focus on the events, symbols, and stories that inform his own Jewish faith and history, such as *Jerusalem Sky: Stars, Crosses, and Crescents,* and *Golem: A Giant Made of Mud.*

Guadalupe Rivera Marin ▮ The daughter of noted Mexican muralist and sculptor Diego Rivera and Rivera's second wife, Rivera Marin grew up to become a professor of law. In addition to writing several books in her field, she has also shared her memories of her famous family in the books *Un rio dos Riveras: Vida de Diego Rivera 1886-1926, Diego el Rojo,* the bilingual picture book *My Papá Diego and Me: Memories of My Father and His Art,* and a cookbook and memoir about her famous stepmother titled *Frida's Fiestas: Recipes and Reminiscences of Life with Frida Kahlo.*

Suza Scalora ▮ A highly regarded commercial photographer based in New York City, Scalora's work has a wide following. She has also gained recognition for the haunting and evocative photographs she crafts and collects in books such as *The Fairies: Photographic Evidence of the Existence of Another World* and *Evidence of Angels,* the latter a collaboration with novelist Francesca Lia Block. Scalora chooses to explore her interest in the supernatural, especially the presence of angels, in many of her written works.

Andrew Zuckerman ▮ Zuckerman is a photographer and filmmaker who creates still photographs that allow readers to perceive his subjects in a new way: in isolation. Since his first book, *Creature,* introduced his unique technique through its images of dozens of the world's animals, Zuckerman has also narrowed his focus to capture the many varieties within a species in his colorful photographs for *Birds* and celebrated the insights of the world's most influential elders in a multi-volume project that begins with *Wisdom.*

Introduction

Something about the Author (*SATA*) is an ongoing reference series that examines the lives and works of authors and illustrators of books for children. *SATA* includes not only well-known writers and artists but also less prominent individuals whose works are just coming to be recognized. This series is often the only readily available information source on emerging authors and illustrators. You'll find *SATA* informative and entertaining, whether you are a student, a librarian, an English teacher, a parent, or simply an adult who enjoys children's literature.

What's Inside *SATA*

SATA provides detailed information about authors and illustrators who span the full time range of children's literature, from early figures like John Newbery and L. Frank Baum to contemporary figures like Judy Blume and Richard Peck. Authors in the series represent primarily English-speaking countries, particularly the United States, Canada, and the United Kingdom. Also included, however, are authors from around the world whose works are available in English translation. The writings represented in *SATA* include those created intentionally for children and young adults as well as those written for a general audience and known to interest younger readers. These writings cover the entire spectrum of children's literature, including picture books, humor, folk and fairy tales, animal stories, mystery and adventure, science fiction and fantasy, historical fiction, poetry and nonsense verse, drama, biography, and nonfiction. Obituaries are also included in *SATA* and are intended not only as death notices but also as concise overviews of people's lives and work. Additionally, each edition features newly revised and updated entries for a selection of *SATA* listees who remain of interest to today's readers and who have been active enough to require extensive revisions of their earlier biographies.

Autobiography Feature

Beginning with Volume 103, many volumes of *SATA* feature one or more specially commissioned autobiographical essays. These unique essays, averaging about ten thousand words in length and illustrated with an abundance of personal photos, present an entertaining and informative first-person perspective on the lives and careers of prominent authors and illustrators profiled in *SATA*.

Two Convenient Indexes

In response to suggestions from librarians, *SATA* indexes no longer appear in every volume but are included in alternate (odd-numbered) volumes of the series, beginning with Volume 57.

SATA continues to include two indexes that cumulate with each alternate volume: the Illustrations Index, arranged by the name of the illustrator, gives the number of the volume and page where the illustrator's work appears in the current volume as well as all preceding volumes in the series; the Author Index gives the number of the volume in which a person's biographical sketch, autobiographical essay, or obituary appears in the current volume as well as all preceding volumes in the series.

These indexes also include references to authors and illustrators who appear in *Gale's Yesterday's Authors of Books for Children*, *Children's Literature Review*, and *Something about the Author Autobiography Series*.

Easy-to-Use Entry Format

Whether you're already familiar with the *SATA* series or just getting acquainted, you will want to be aware of the kind of information that an entry provides. In every *SATA* entry the editors attempt to give as complete a picture of the person's life and work as possible. A typical entry in *SATA* includes the following clearly labeled information sections:

PERSONAL: date and place of birth and death, parents' names and occupations, name of spouse, date of marriage, names of children, educational institutions attended, degrees received, religious and political affiliations, hobbies and other interests.

ADDRESSES: complete home, office, electronic mail, and agent addresses, whenever available.

CAREER: name of employer, position, and dates for each career post; art exhibitions; military service; memberships and offices held in professional and civic organizations.

MEMBER: professional, civic, and other association memberships and any official posts held.

AWARDS, HONORS: literary and professional awards received.

WRITINGS: title-by-title chronological bibliography of books written and/or illustrated, listed by genre when known; lists of other notable publications, such as plays, screenplays, and periodical contributions.

ADAPTATIONS: a list of films, television programs, plays, CD-ROMs, recordings, and other media presentations that have been adapted from the author's work.

WORK IN PROGRESS: description of projects in progress.

SIDELIGHTS: a biographical portrait of the author or illustrator's development, either directly from the biographee—and often written specifically for the *SATA* entry—or gathered from diaries, letters, interviews, or other published sources.

BIOGRAPHICAL AND CRITICAL SOURCES: cites sources quoted in "Sidelights" along with references for further reading.

EXTENSIVE ILLUSTRATIONS: photographs, movie stills, book illustrations, and other interesting visual materials supplement the text.

How a *SATA* Entry Is Compiled

SATA editors examine a wide variety of published sources to gather information for an entry. Biographical and bibliographic sources are consulted, as are book reviews, feature articles, published interviews, and material sometimes obtained from the biographee's family, publishers, agent, or other associates. Whenever possible, the author or illustrator is sent a copy of the entry to check for accuracy and completeness.

Entries that have not been verified by the biographees or their representatives are marked with an asterisk (*).

Contact the Editor

We encourage our readers to examine the entire *SATA* series. Please write and tell us if we can make *SATA* even more helpful to you. Give your comments and suggestions to the editor:

Editor
Something about the Author
Gale, Cengage Learning
27500 Drake Rd.
Farmington Hills MI 48331-3535

Toll-free: 800-877-GALE
Fax: 248-699-8070

Something about the Author Product Advisory Board

The editors of *Something about the Author* are dedicated to maintaining a high standard of excellence by publishing comprehensive, accurate, and highly readable entries on a wide array of writers for children and young adults. In addition to the quality of the content, the editors take pride in the graphic design of the series, which is intended to be orderly yet inviting, allowing readers to utilize the pages of *SATA* easily and with efficiency. Despite the longevity of the *SATA* print series, and the success of its format, we are mindful that the vitality of a literary reference product is dependent on its ability to serve its users over time. As literature, and attitudes about literature, constantly evolve, so do the reference needs of students, teachers, scholars, journalists, researchers, and book club members. To be certain that we continue to keep pace with the expectations of our customers, the editors of *SATA* listen carefully to their comments regarding the value, utility, and quality of the series. Librarians, who have firsthand knowledge of the needs of library users, are a valuable resource for us. The *Something about the Author* Product Advisory Board, made up of school, public, and academic librarians, is a forum to promote focused feedback about *SATA* on a regular basis. The nine-member advisory board includes the following individuals, whom the editors wish to thank for sharing their expertise:

something ABOUT the AUThOR

AGARD, John 1949-

Personal

Born 1949, in British Guiana (now Guyana); immigrated to England, 1977; partner of Grace Nichols (a poet); children: one daughter. *Education:* Attended Roman Catholic secondary school in Georgetown, British Guiana (now Guyana).

Addresses

Home—Lewes, East Sussex, England.

Career

Poet, playwright, and children's writer. *Guyana Sunday Chronicle,* sub-editor and feature writer, until 1977; Commonwealth Institute, London, England, touring lecturer. South Bank Centre, London, writer-in-residence, 1993; British Broadcasting Corporation, writer-in-residence for Windrush project, 1998; National Maritime Museum, Greenwich, England, writer-in-residence, 2007. Also worked as an actor and a performer with a jazz group.

Awards, Honors

Poetry prize, Casa de la Amèricas (Cuba), 1982, for *Man to Pan;* Other Award, Children's Rights Workshop, 1986, for *Say It Again, Granny!;* Nestlé Smarties Book Prize shortlist, 1987, for *Lend Me Your Wings;*

John Agard (Photograph by Phil Taylor. Reproduced by permission of Bloodaxe Books, Ltd.)

Nestlé Smarties Book Prize Bronze Award, 1995, for *We Animals Would Like a Word with You;* Paul Hamlyn Award for Poetry, 1997; Children's Poetry Bookshelf

1

Best Anthology selection, Poetry Society, 2000; Cholmondeley Award, 2003; British Book Awards Decibel Writer of the Year shortlist, 2007, for *We Brits;* Poetry Award, Centre for Literacy in Primary Education, 2009, for *The Young Inferno.*

Writings

JUVENILE AND YOUNG-ADULT POETRY

I Din Do Nuttin and Other Poems, illustrated by Susanna Gretz, Bodley Head (London, England), 1983.

Say It Again, Granny!: Twenty Poems from Caribbean Proverbs, illustrated by Susanna Gretz, Bodley Head (London, England), 1986.

The Calypso Alphabet, illustrated by Jennifer Bent, Henry Holt (New York, NY), 1989.

(Editor) *Life Doesn't Frighten Me at All,* Heinemann (London, England), 1989, Henry Holt (New York, NY), 1990.

Go Noah, Go!, illustrated by Judy Brown, Hodder & Stoughton (London, England), 1990.

Laughter Is an Egg, illustrated by Alan Rowe, Viking (London, England), 1990.

(With partner Grace Nichols) *No Hickory, No Dickory, No Dock: A Collection of Caribbean Nursery Rhymes,* illustrated by Cynthia Jabar, Viking (London, England), 1991, published as *No Hickory, No Dickory, No Dock: Caribbean Nursery Rhymes,* Candlewick Press (Cambridge, MA), 1994.

Grandfather's Old Bruk-a-down Car, illustrated by Kevin Dean, Bodley Head (London, England), 1994.

(Editor, with Grace Nichols, and contributor) *A Caribbean Dozen: Poems from Caribbean Poets,* illustrated by Cathie Felstead, Candlewick Press (Cambridge, MA), 1994, published as *A Caribbean Dozen: A Collection of Poems,* Walker Books (Boston, MA), 1995.

(With others) *Another Day on Your Foot and I Would Have Died,* illustrated by Colin McNaughton, Macmillan (London, England), 1996.

(Editor) *Why Is the Sky?,* illustrated by Andrzej Klimowski, Faber & Faber (London, England), 1996.

We Animals Would Like a Word with You, illustrated by Satoshi Kitamura, Bodley Head (London, England), 1996.

Get Back, Pimple!, Viking (London, England), 1996.

From the Devil's Pulpit, Bloodaxe Books (Newcastle upon Tyne, England), 1997.

Hello New! New Poems for a New Century, illustrated by Lydia Monks, Orchard (London, England), 2000.

Points of View with Professor Peekaboo, illustrated by Satoshi Kitamura, Bodley Head (London, England), 2000.

Come Back to Me, My Boomerang, illustrated by Lydia Monks, Orchard (London, England), 2001.

(Editor, with Grace Nichols) *Under the Moon and over the Sea: A Collection of Caribbean Poems,* illustrated by Christopher Corr, Candlewick Press (Cambridge, MA), 2002.

Einstein, the Girl Who Hated Maths, illustrated by Satoshi Kitamura, Hodder Wayland (London, England), 2002.

Hello H20, illustrated by Satoshi Kitamura, Hodder Wayland (London, England), 2003.

(Editor, with Grace Nichols) *From Mouth to Mouth: Oral Poems from around the World,* illustrated by Annabel Wright, Walker (London, England), 2004.

Half-caste and Other Poems, Hodder (London, England), 2004.

Wriggle Piggy Toes, illustrated by Jenny Bent, Frances Lincoln (London, England), 2005.

The Young Inferno, illustrated by Satoshi Kitamura, Frances Lincoln (London, England), 2008.

Contributor to *Inside Out: Children's Poets Discuss Their Work,* edited by JonArno Lawson, Walker (London, England), 2008.

CHILDREN'S FICTION

Letters for Lettie and Other Stories, illustrated by Errol Lloyd, Bodley Head (London, England), 1979.

Dig away Two-Hole Tim, illustrated by Jennifer Northway, Bodley Head (London, England), 1981.

Lend Me Your Wings, illustrated by Adrienne Kennaway, Little, Brown (Boston, MA), 1987.

The Emperor's Dan-Dan, illustrated by Alison Forsyth, Hodder & Stoughton (London, England), 1992.

Oriki and the Monster Who Hated Balloons, illustrated by Jenny Stowe, Longman (Harlow, England), 1994.

The Monster Who Loved Telephones, illustrated by Jenny Stowe, Longman (Harlow, England), 1994.

The Monster Who Loved Cameras, illustrated by Jenny Stowe, Longman (Harlow, England), 1994.

The Monster Who Loved Toothbrushes, illustrated by Jenny Stowe, Longman (Harlow, England), 1994.

(With Korky Paul) *Brer Rabbit, the Great Tug-o-War,* Barron's Educational Series (Hauppauge, NY), 1998.

(With Bob Cattell) *Butter-finger,* illustrated by Pam Smy, Frances Lincoln (London, England), 2006.

(With Bob Cattell) *Shine on, Butter-finger,* illustrated by Pam Smy, Frances Lincoln (London, England), 2007.

(With Bob Cattell) *Big City Butter-finger,* illustrated by Pam Smy, Frances Lincoln (London, England), 2010.

Some of Agard's work has been translated into Welsh.

OTHER

Shoot Me with Flowers (poetry), illustrated by Marilyn Agard, privately printed (Guyana), 1974.

Man to Pan: A Cycle of Poems to Be Performed with Drums and Steelpans, Casa de las Américas (Havana, Cuba), 1982.

Limbo Dancer in the Dark (poetry), privately printed, 1983.

Limbo Dancer in Dark Glasses (poetry), Greenheart, 1983.

Livingroom, Black Ink Collective (London, England), 1983.

Mangoes and Bullets: Selected and New Poems, 1972-84, Pluto Press (London, England), 1985.

(With others) *Wake Up, Stir About: Songs for Assembly* (traditional tunes), arranged by Barrie Carson Turner, illustrated by Peter Kent, Unwin Hyman (Cambridge, MA), 1989.

Lovelines for a Goat-born Lady (poetry), Serpent's Tail (London, England), 1990.

A Stone's Throw from Embankment: The South Bank Collection (poetry), Royal Festival Hall (London, England), 1993.

The Great Snakeskin (children's play), illustrated by Jill Newton, Ginn (Aylesbury, England), 1993.

(Editor) *Poems in My Earphone*, Longman (Harlow, England), 1995.

Weblines (poetry), illustrated by Satoshi Kitamura, Bloodaxe Books (Newcastle upon Tyne, England), 2000.

We Brits (poetry), Bloodaxe Books (Tarset, England), 2006.

Clever Backbone (poetry), Bloodaxe Books (Tarset, England), 2009.

Alternative Anthem: Selected Poems, Bloodaxe Books (Tarset, England), 2009.

Petrushka (children's play), produced in London, England, at Little Angel Theatre, 2009.

Work represented in anthologies, including *Border Country: Poems in Progress,* edited by David Hart, Wood Wind Publications (Birmingham, England), 1991; and *Grandchildren of Albion,* edited by Michael Horovitz, New Departures (Piedmont, Bisley, Stroud, Gloucester, England), 1992. Contributor of poetry to periodicals, including *Poetry Review.*

Sidelights

John Agard is a poet, anthologist, playwright, and children's author whose writing is infused with the Caribbean rhythms of his homeland in South America. Now living in England, Agard is regarded as a performance poet because his work is most powerful when read aloud. However, with the publications of such books as *Lend Me Your Wings, We Animals Would Like a Word with You,* and *Come to Me, My Boomerang,* he has also earned a solid readership; his vocal rhythms, combined with an affinity for word play, puns, and jokes, are appealing to children of all ages.

Agard's stories are sometimes retellings or revisions of folk tales and are enlivened by his own sense of the comic and his appreciation for the absurd. His poems concern the elements of everyday life common to children everywhere, made unique by the poet's tendency toward Caribbean dialect and whimsical humor. Geared for beginning readers, *The Calypso Alphabet* is full to the brim with exotic new words and concepts embedded in the musical ambience of Caribbean idiom and illustrated by Jennifer Brent with the colors, people, and landscapes that epitomize life in the West Indies. *I Din Do Nuttin and Other Poems* retains the idiomatic flavor of Agard's verse, and here his rhymes describe the ordinary events and people common to all children. Another collection, *Grandfather's Old Bruk-a-down Car,*

explores the relationships between people and the objects they hold dear, while *Laughter Is an Egg* contains rhymes and riddles for the young reader who welcomes the challenge of a mystery.

Lest a reader presume that Agard's sole objective as a poet is to entertain, a *Junior Bookshelf* reviewer of *Laughter Is an Egg* emphasized that Agard's poetry reveals "a serious man" dedicated to the often difficult art of crafting exceptional poetry. Even in rhymes intended for children Agard uses his work as a vehicle for his thoughts on topical issues and trends. *No Hickory, No Dickory, No Dock: A Collection of Caribbean Nursery Rhymes,* which he wrote with his partner, fellow Guyanese poet Grace Nichols, contains poems compelling in their musicality, according to a *Kirkus Reviews* contributor. In *We Animals Would Like a Word with You* he questions, in lyrical rhyme, the way people treat the world's animals. In her review of *We Animals Would Like a Word with You* for the *Times Educational Supplement,* Josephine Balmer commented that Agard "subverts and invents," ultimately producing "the best that poetry can offer."

Cover of Agard's adult poetry collection **Weblines,** *featuring colorful graphic illustrations by Satoshi Kitamura.* (Bloodaxe Books, 2000. Illustration © 2000 by Satoshi Kitamura. Reproduced by permission.)

Dig away Two-Hole Tim is set in Guyana, where Agard was born and raised, and introduces young readers to the colorful English dialect of the West Indies. More a captioned picture book than a continuous narrative, it tells the story of an unintentionally mischievous boy preoccupied with holes: digging, cutting, exploring, or simply pondering holes. *The Emperor's Dan-Dan* is a Caribbean-style versification of the story of the emperor's new clothes, replete with appropriate dialect and featuring the trickster Anancy as the emperor's tailor. Another of Agard's stories is *Brer Rabbit, the Great Tug-o-War,* in which the great American trickster matches wits with Rhino and Hippo, luring them into a competition that none can win.

Geared for older students, *Points of View with Professor Peekaboo* addresses a range of contemporary issues, from the majesty of the natural world to the increasing degradation of the environment to the question of genetic identity. Although some reviewers faulted the volume for its uneven poetic quality, in the *Times Educational Supplement* John Mole cited the work as an "often funny, inventive" collection. In *Half-Caste and Other Poems* Agard examines themes of identity, politics, and diversity. In "Checking Out Me History," for example, the poet explores the immigrant experience, while "The Giant with a Taste for Mongrel Blood" concerns racism. The collection is not entirely devoted to serious matters, however; Agard also displays his playful side in such works as "Poetry Jump Up" and "Punctuating the Silence," which celebrate the joys of language. "By turns playful and sincere, buoyant and thoughtful, his humanism is the thread that runs throughout these selections," commented Marilyn Taniguchi in *School Library Journal.* Hazel Rochman, writing in *Booklist,* praised the volume's "witty, colloquial voice and rhythmic beat," and *Horn Book* critic Jennifer M. Brabander similarly noted that several of the poems in *Half-Caste and Other Poems* "are written in a Caribbean patois that has a distinctive presence both aloud and on the page."

Agard received the Centre for Literacy in Primary Education (CLPE) Poetry Award for *The Young Inferno,* a contemporary take on *The Divine Comedy,* the fourteenth-century masterpiece by Italian poet Alighieri Dante. Featuring haunting artwork by Satoshi Kitamura, *The Young Inferno* concerns the adventures of a teenaged protagonist who describes, in verse, his descent into Hell accompanied by the legendary storyteller Aesop. During their journey, the duo encounters all manner of sinners, including drunk drivers, scientists, and politicians, as they search for the narrator's "Good Fairy," Beatrice. "The narrative poems in this short book are accessible and have important things to say about the state of the human race," Heather M. Campbell remarked in *School Library Journal.* Although a *Publishers Weekly* reviewer believed that *The Young Inferno* would be best appreciated by readers familiar with Dante's epic, the critic added that "its potential to ignite curiosity about the original should not be underestimated."

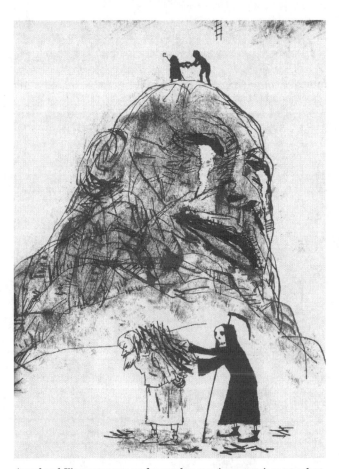

Agard and Kitamura team up for another creative entertainment, adapting a classical story in the picture book **The Young Inferno.** *(Frances Lincoln Books, 2008. Illustration copyright © 2008 by Satoshi Kitamura. Reproduced by permission.)*

In addition to his prolific and successful career as an author, Agard has worked toward popularizing the work of talented Caribbean poets, especially among young readers in England and North America. Working with Nichols, he compiled *A Caribbean Dozen: Poems from Caribbean Poets,* in which they introduce the work of thirteen Caribbean poets from around the world, amplifying their poems by adding photographs and personal background narratives from each poet included. The collection was well received by critics, John Mole reporting in the *Times Educational Supplement* that "even the weakest of [the selections] . . . are joyously enthusiastic." "Most of the entries here speak directly to the child's own world," Bettina Berch noted in *Belles Lettres,* and *Books for Keeps* contributor Morag Styles called *A Caribbean Dozen* "a great treat" suitable for readers as young as primary-school age.

Agard and Nichols have also served as coeditors of *Under the Moon and over the Sea: A Collection of Caribbean Poems,* an anthology featuring verse by Alan Smith, Agnes Maxwell-Hall, Valerie Bloom, and Faustin Charles, among other writers. Divided into five sections, each illustrated by a different artist, the volume contains works by more than thirty poets and delves into an eclectic array of topics that include island folk-

lore, the sea, Caribbean cuisine, natural disasters, and immigration. A critic in *Kirkus Reviews* described *Under the Moon and over the Sea* as "a lively mix of rhythms, stories, and descriptions that illuminate the geography and culture of the region, while providing a variety of linguistic and visual delights," and Kathleen Whalin maintained in *School Library Journal,* maintained that Agard and Nichols "have once again created an exuberant tribute to one of the world's enchanted places." In the words of a *Black Issues Book Review* contributor, the volume "is a rhythmic treasure trove of island experiences. Its lyrical patois and visuals make this book a delight to read."

Agard's work as an editor also includes *Why Is the Sky?* Reflecting his characteristic serious-minded focus, the work addresses the sometimes imponderable questions children ask. "It is a richly seasoned stew," wrote a *Junior Bookshelf* reviewer, drawn from every corner of the world and from the ages. The poetry comes from Shakespeare and from the Bible; also represented are twentieth-century poets such as Langston Hughes and Helen Dunmore. The selections are intended for young readers, although adult poetry is included as well. Linda Saunders described *Why Is the Sky?* in *School Librarian* as "an excellent collection of poetry. . . . There is something here for every child."

Biographical and Critical Sources

BOOKS

Contemporary Poets, Gale (Detroit, MI), 2001.
Dictionary of Literary Biography, Volume 347, *Twenty-first-Century "Black" British Writers,* Gale (Detroit, MI), 2009.
St. James Guide to Children's Writers, 5th edition, St. James Press (Detroit, MI), 1999.

PERIODICALS

Black Issues Book Review, March-April, 2003, review of *Under the Moon and over the Sea: A Collection of Caribbean Poems,* p. 66.
Booklist, March 15, 1991, review of *Life Doesn't Frighten Me at All,* p. 1742; May 1, 1995, Hazel Rochman, review of *No Hickory, No Dickory, No Dock: A Collection of Caribbean Nursery Rhymes,* p. 1576; October 15, 2005, Hazel Rochman, review of *Half-caste and Other Poems,* p. 44.
Books for Keeps, January, 1988, review of *Say It Again, Granny! Twenty Poems from Caribbean Proverbs,* p. 16; July, 1991, review of *Laughter Is an Egg,* p. 11; November, 1992, review of *Go Noah, Go!,* p. 17; May, 1993, review of *The Calypso Alphabet,* pp. 8-9; September, 1994, Morag Styles, review of *A Caribbean Dozen,* p. 88; March, 1997, M. Styles, review of *We Animals Would Like a Word with You,* p. 23; May,

1997, review of *Another Day on Your Foot and I Would Have Died,* pp. 24-25; January, 1998, review of *Why Is the Sky?,* p. 20; May, 1998, Elaine Moss, review of *Brer Rabbit, the Great Tug-o-War,* p. 6; March, 2001, review of *Points of View with Professor Peekaboo,* p. 24.
English Journal, April, 1991, Elizabeth A. Belden and Judith M. Beckman, review of *Life Doesn't Frighten Me at All,* p. 84.
Guardian (London, England), January 20, 2007, Jeremy Noel-Tod, review of *We Brits,* p. 18.
Growing Point, March, 1983, review of *I Din Do Nuttin and Other Poems,* p. 4040; July, 1986, review of *Say It Again, Granny!,* p. 4654.
Horn Book, January-February, 2006, Jennifer M. Brabander, review of *Half-caste and Other Poems,* p. 94.
Instructor, August, 2001, "Jump into Shape Poetry," p. 54.
Junior Bookshelf, June, 1980, review of *Letters for Lettie and Other Stories,* p. 123; February, 1982, review of *Dig away Two-Hole Tim,* p. 12; August, 1983, review of *I Din Do Nuttin and Other Poems,* pp. 156-157; August, 1990, review of *Laughter Is an Egg,* p. 172; April, 1991, review of *Go Noah, Go!,* pp. 53-54; February, 1993, review of *The Emperor's Dan-Dan,* p. 9; February, 1995, review of *Grandfather's Old Bruk-a-down Car,* p. 14; August, 1996, review of *Get Back, Pimple!,* p. 153; October, 1996, review of *Why Is the Sky?,* pp. 189-190.
Kirkus Reviews, April 15, 1989, review of *Lend Me Your Wings,* p. 619; May 15, 1995, review of *No Hickory, No Dickory, No Dock,* p. 706; April 15, 2001, review of *Weblines,* pp. 550-551; December 15, 2002, review of *Under the Moon and over the Sea,* p. 1844; November 1, 2005, review of *Half-caste and Other Poems,* p. 1181; June 1, 2009, review of *The Young Inferno.*
London Review of Books, December 5, 1985, Blake Morrison, review of *Mangoes and Bullets: Selected and New Poems, 1972-84,* pp. 14-15.
Observer (London, England), October 26, 1997, Helen Dunmore, review of *From the Devil's Pulpit,* p. 15.
Publishers Weekly, November 24, 1989, review of *The Calypso Alphabet,* p. 70; June 5, 1995, review of *No Hickory, No Dickory, No Dock,* p. 64; July 23, 2001, review of *Weblines,* p. 69; January 13, 2003, "Rhyme Time," review of *Under the Moon and over the Sea,* p. 62; July 27, 2009, review of *The Young Inferno,* p. 63.
School Librarian, February, 1991, Pauline Long, review of *Go Noah, Go!,* p. 17; November, 1992, Celia Gibbs, review of *The Emperor's Dan-Dan,* p. 138; November, 1994, Vivienne Grant, review of *Grandfather's Old Bruk-a-down Car,* p. 160; February, 1997, review of *Why Is the Sky?,* p. 41; November, 1997, review of *From the Devil's Pulpit,* p. 220; autumn, 1998, Vivienne Grant, review of *Brer Rabbit, the Great Tug-o-War,* p. 129; spring, 2001, review of *Points of View with Professor Peekaboo,* p. 42.
School Library Journal, September, 1982, Marilyn Payne Phillips, review of *Dig away Two-Hole Tim;* July, 1989, Carolyn Caywood, review of *Lend Me Your Wings,* p. 61; April, 1990, Marilyn Iarusso, review of

The Calypso Alphabet, p. 86; August, 1990, Annette Curtis Klause, review of *Life Doesn't Frighten Me at All,* p. 166; August, 1995, Barbara Osborne Williams, review of *No Hickory, No Dickory, No Dock,* pp. 131-132; February, 2003, Kathleen Whalin, review of *Under the Moon and over the Sea,* p. 126; June, 2005, Elaine Lesh Morgan, review of *Wriggle Piggy Toes,* p. 102; January, 2006, Marilyn Taniguchi, review of *Half-caste and Other Poems,* p. 145; August, 2009, Heather M. Campbell, review of *The Young Inferno,* p. 118.

Times Educational Supplement, February 16, 1990, Gerard Benson, review of *Life Doesn't Frighten Me at All,* p. 67; July 13, 1990, Kevin Crossley-Holland, review of *Laughter Is an Egg,* p. 28; June 14, 1991, Charles Causley, review of *No Hickory, No Dickory, No Dock,* p. 25; February 5, 1993, James Riordan, review of *The Emperor's Dan-Dan,* p. R10; November 11, 1994, Gillian Clarke, review of *Grandfather's Old Bruk-a-down Car,* p. R7; December 2, 1994, John Mole, review of *A Caribbean Dozen,* p. A14; September 22, 1995, J. Mole, review of *Poems in My Earphone;* March 8, 1996, p. X; Jill Pirrie, review of *Get Back, Pimple!,* p. II; December 13, 1996, Josephine Balmer, review of *We Animals Would Like a Word with You;* January 19, 2001, J. Mole, review of *Points of View with Professor Peekaboo,* p. 20.

Times Literary Supplement, January 18, 1991, Giles Foden, review of *Lovelines for a Goat-born Lady,* p. 18; July 27, 2001, Paula Burnett, review of *Weblines,* p. 23.

Wilson Library Bulletin, November, 1990, Cathi MacRae, review of *Life Doesn't Frighten Me at All,* p. 129.

ONLINE

Contemporary Writers in the UK Web site, http://www.contemporarywriters.com/ (December 15, 2010), "John Agard."

OTHER

Roots and Water (videotape series), Films for the Humanities and Sciences, 2000.*

* * *

ALEXANDER, Jill S. 1964-
(Jill Shurbet Alexander)

Personal

Born 1964, in TX; married; children: one son. *Education:* Baylor University, B.A. (English), 1992. *Hobbies and other interests:* Country music, cooking, travel.

Addresses

Home—Tyler, TX. *Agent*—Michael Bourret, Dystel & Goderich Literary Management, One Union Sq. W., Ste. 904, New York, NY 10003.

Career

Author and educator. Former teacher of high-school English and Spanish; full-time writer.

Member

Society of Children's Book Writers and Illustrators (North Texas chapter).

Awards, Honors

Lone Star Reading List inclusion, Amelia Walden Award finalist, National Council of Teachers of English Assembly on Literature for Adolescents, and Best Books for Young Adults designation, American Library Association, all 2010, all for *The Sweetheart of Prosper County.*

Writings

The Sweetheart of Prosper County, Feiwel & Friends (New York, NY), 2009.
Paradise, Feiwel & Friends (New York, NY), 2010.

Adaptations

The Sweetheart of Prosper County was adapted for audiobook, read by Suzy Jackson, Recorded Books, 2009.

Sidelights

In her writing, East Texas native Jill S. Alexander draws on her experiences growing up in a small town, and she has been fascinated with people's life stories since working as a truck-stop waitress during junior high. Her first novel, *The Sweetheart of Prosper County,* finds a young teen determined to break free of an overprotective mother and show up a local bully, while a talented drummer falls for the lead singer in her country rock band in *Paradise.* "I love people—especially the quirky ones," Alexander noted in a Macmillan Web site interview. "Real people inspire me."

In *The Sweetheart of Prosper County* Alexander introduces readers to Austin Gray, a fifteen year old who has been sheltered by her widowed mom ever since her father died in a tragic car accident. Unfortunately, Mom's reach has not extended to school, where Dean Ottmer has been Austin's constant tormentor for years. Dean's taunting has become worse now that they are both in high school, and Austin is determined to find a way to end it. Setting her sights on a role in her town's upcoming Christmas parade, the teen realizes that a bantam rooster named Charles Dickens may be her key to success. And she may be right, as a baby chick and participation in the Future Farmers of America yields Austin more than she expected, including new friends and a growing sense in what determination can accomplish. Praising Alexander's story, Kelley Siegrist wrote in her

School Library Journal review that *The Sweetheart of Prosper County* benefits from "strong-willed female characters" and treats readers to "a refreshing picture of teen angst, with realistic dialogue." In *Booklist* Frances Bradburn made special note of the story's "memorable" secondary characters, predicting that Alexander's "substantive, enjoyable coming-of-age novel . . . will speak to rural and urban readers alike."

Biographical and Critical Sources

PERIODICALS

Booklist, August 1, 2009, Frances Bradburn, review of *The Sweetheart of Prosper County,* p. 61.
Bulletin of the Center for Children's Books, Karen Coats, review of *The Sweetheart of Prosper County,* p. 144.
Kirkus Reviews, August 1, 2009, review of *The Sweetheart of Prosper County.*
Publishers Weekly, October 5, 2009, review of *The Sweetheart of Prosper County,* p. 50.
School Library Journal, September, 2009, Kelley Siegrist, review of *The Sweetheart of Prosper County,* p. 150.

ONLINE

Jill S. Alexander Home Page, http://jillsalexander.com (November 14, 2010).
Jill S. Alexander Web log, http://jillatex.livejournal.com (December 15, 2010).
Macmillan Web site, http://us.macmillan.com/ (December 15, 2010).*

*   *   *

ALEXANDER, Jill Shurbet
See ALEXANDER, Jill S.

*   *   *

AUSTEN, Catherine 1965-

Personal
Born December 26, 1965, in Newcastle, New Brunswick, Canada; married Geoff Quaile; children: Sawyer, Daimon. *Education:* Attended Queen's University and York University. *Hobbies and other interests:* Yoga, quilting, canoeing.

Addresses
Home—Quebec, Canada. *E-mail*—info@catherineausten.com.

Career
Author. Worked for environmental organizations, c. 1990s; freelance writer, 2000—.

Catherine Austen (Photograph by Melinda Vallillee. Reproduced by permission.)

Member
Canadian Children's Book Centre, Society of Children's Book Writers and Illustrators, Canadian Society of Children's Authors, Illustrators, and Performers, Quebec Writers' Federation.

Awards, Honors
Book of the Year for Children Award finalist, Canadian Library Association, and Quebec Writers' Federation Prize for Children's and Young Adults' Literature, both 2010, both for *Walking Backward.*

Writings

Walking Backward (novel), Orca Book Publishers (Victoria, British Columbia, Canada), 2009.
My Cat Isis, illustrated by Virginie Egger, Kids Can Press (Toronto, Ontario, Canada), 2011.

Contributor of short stories to literary journals.

Sidelights
Catherine Austen, an award-winning Canadian writer, examines loss, grief, and faith in *Walking Backward,* her debut novel for middle graders. *Walking Backward* centers on Josh, a twelve year old who is struggling to cope with his heartache following the death of his mother, a university professor who accidentally crashed her automobile into a tree after discovering that a snake was riding in the car's passenger compartment. Josh's father offers little support, instead focusing his attention on building a machine that will allow him to go back in time and prevent the accident from ever occurring. The preteen soon must step in and caretake his younger brother when the little boy's suffering begins mani-

Cover of Austen's middle-grade novel **Walking Backward,** *which focuses on a preteen dealing with a parent's sudden death.* (Orca Books Publishers, 2009. Cover artwork by Dreamstime. Reprinted with permission of the publisher.)

fested itself in a series of bizarre behaviors. At the recommendation of a psychiatrist, Josh begins recording his own thoughts and feelings in a journal, and this writing allows him to ponder the mourning rituals of various religions and, eventually, begin to make sense of the devastating event that has shattered his family.

"Throughout his emotional journey, Josh's voice is both natural and believable," remarked Joanie Terrizzi in a *School Library Journal* review of *Walking Backward.* Ruth Latta noted in the *Canadian Review of Materials* that Austen "made an inspired choice in choosing the journal as a narrative device," and Toronto *Globe & Mail* critic Donna Bailey Nurse wrote that "recording one's emotions proves integral to plot development" and helps the boy "articulate his despair and confusion." A contributor in *Kirkus Reviews* described *Walking Backward* as "an elegantly crafted volume of lasting power," and Nurse concluded that Austen's "writing cuts straight to the heart. She delivers a wise, rich novel, wonderfully compelling for children and adults alike."

Biographical and Critical Sources

PERIODICALS

Canadian Review of Materials, September 4, 2009, Ruth Latta, review of *Walking Backward.*
Globe & Mail (Toronto, Ontario, Canada), November 19, 2009, Donna Bailey Nurse, review of *Walking Backward.*
Kirkus Reviews, September 15, 2009, review of *Walking Backward.*
Quill & Quire, December, 2009, Shaun Smith, review of *Walking Backward.*
School Library Journal, February, 2010, Joanie Terrizzi, review of *Walking Backward,* p. 104.

ONLINE

Catherine Austen Home Page, http://www.catherineausten. com (December 1, 2010).
Catherine Austen Web log, http://catherineausten.word press.com (December 1, 2010).

B

BAKER-SMITH, Grahame

Personal

Married; wife's name Linda; children: three. *Education:* Studied at Berkshire College of Art and Design.

Addresses

Home and office—Bath, England. *Agent*—Stacey Endress, Illustration Ltd., 23 Ohio St., Maplewood, NJ 07040.

Career

Illustrator and author. Commercial illustrator since 1980s; Shooting Stars (card company), founder. *Exhibitions:* Work included in group show at Illustration Cupboard, London, England, 2010.

Awards, Honors

Kate Greenaway Medal shortlist, 2010, for *Leon and the Place Between.*

Writings

SELF-ILLUSTRATED

Jo-Jo's Journey, Bodley Head (London, England), 1994.
George's Magic Day, Hodder (London, England), 2005.

ILLUSTRATOR

Margery Williams, *The Velveteen Rabbit; or, How Toys Become Real,* Bodley Head (London, England), 1996.
Angela McAllister, *Leon and the Place Between,* Templar Books (Somerville, MA), 2009.

Sidelights

British illustrator Grahame Baker-Smith was shortlisted for the prestigious Kate Greenaway Medal in 2010 for his work on *Leon and the Place Between,* a tale of the fantastic by Angela McAllister. Baker-Smith, who began his career as a freelance illustrator in the 1980s, works in a variety of traditional media, such as acrylic, gouache, and pen-and-ink, and also incorporates digital collage techniques into his projects, which include advertising designs, album covers, and posters. The tools he uses, Baker-Smith noted in a *Creative Boom* interview with Alison Vellacott, "are just gateways to my imagination—which is the most important medium of all!"

Baker-Smith developed an interest in the creative arts at a young age, he recalled to Victoria Pearce in an *Illustration Web.com* interview. "As far back as I can remember I always loved the printed image," he commented. "I used to endlessly copy the artwork in American comics such as the Fantastic Four, Spiderman, X-Men." Baker-Smith was particularly influenced by such renowned illustrators as Jack Kirby, John Buscema, Steve Ditko, and Gene Colan. "To me, these artists were on a sort of mythical plane—through them I could visit other worlds and other dimensions, places of sheer imagination . . .," he told Vellacott. "I knew then I wanted to have a life of drawing and dreaming."

To pursue his dream of becoming an illustrator, Baker-Smith spent four years teaching himself to draw while living in a small bedsit—a rented room—in Oxford, England; he often spent his meager earnings on art supplies instead of basic necessities. He later enrolled in a graphics course at the Berkshire College of Art and Design in Reading, where he received two years of credit for his efforts in Oxford. In 1984, Baker-Smith began submitting his work to publishers and advertising agencies, eventually landing projects for Singapore Airlines, Motorola, and EMI, among other companies. He also produced a pair of self-illustrated children's book, *Jo-Jo's Journey* and *George's Magic Day,* and contributed artwork to a new version of *The Velveteen Rabbit; or, How Toys Become Real* by Margery Williams.

McAllister's *Leon and the Place Between* follows a boy's extraordinary voyage to an ethereal otherworld.

Grahame Baker-Smith's illustration projects include creating the art for Angela McAllister's **Leon and the Place Between.** (Illustration copyright © 2008 by Grahame Baker-Smith. Reproduced by permission of Candlewick Press, Somerville, MA.)

While enjoying a magic show, Leon volunteers for a disappearing act performed by the mystical Abdul Kazam, who transports the youngster to the "place between," where magician's props and audience members await until they are summoned back to the stage. "Baker-Smith's moody, gold-filigreed digital pictures, . . . conjure up the excitement of surrendering to suspended disbelief," a critic in *Publishers Weekly* observed, and Meg Smith noted in *School Library Journal* that the digital collages in *Leon and the Place Between* offer "richness and depth; majestic purple backgrounds dominate, and swirling golden lines support the dynamic, fluid spreads."

Baker-Smith lives with his wife, Linda, an illustrator, and their three children in Bath, where he keeps a home studio that also serves as a family room. "Work and life have always been one thing to me, not something I go to or return from, just part of me, part of the total," he told Pearce, describing his studio as "a wonderful place to think and dream."

Biographical and Critical Sources

PERIODICALS

Kirkus Reviews, July 1, 2009, review of *Leon and the Place Between.*

Publishers Weekly, August 3, 2009, review of *Leon and the Place Between,* p. 44.
Quill & Quire, August, 1994, review of *Jo-Jo's Journey,* p. 35.
School Library Journal, September, 2009, Meg Smith, review of *Leon and the Place Between,* p. 128.

ONLINE

Creative Boom E-zine, http://www.creativeboom.co.uk/ (May 26, 2010), Alison Vellacott, "Grahame Baker-Smith."
Directory of Illustration Web site, http://www.directory ofillustration.com/ (December 15, 2010), "Grahame Baker-Smith."
Illustration Web.com, http://www.illustrationweb.com/ (December 15, 2010), Victoria Pearce, interview with Baker-Smith.*

*   *   *

BARNETT, Mac

Personal

Born in CA.

Addresses

Home—Northern CA. *E-mail*—mac@macbarnett.com.

Career

Author and educator. 826LA (nonprofit writing and education center), Los Angeles, CA, member of board of directors.

Awards, Honors

One Hundred Titles for Reading and Sharing inclusion, New York Public Library, 2009, for *The Case of the Case of Mistaken Identity.*

Writings

Billy Twitters and His Blue Whale Problem, illustrated by Adam Rex, Disney/Hyperion Books (New York, NY), 2009.
Guess Again!, illustrated by Adam Rex, Simon & Schuster Books for Young Readers (New York, NY), 2009.
Oh No!; or, How My Science Project Destroyed the World, illustrated by Dan Santat, Disney Hyperion Books (New York, NY), 2010.
(With Eli Horowitz) *The Clock without a Face* (novelty board-game book), illustrated by Scott Teplin and Adam Rex, McSweeney's, 2010.
Extra Yarn, illustrated by Jon Klassen, Balzer & Bray (New York, NY), 2011.

Work included in anthology *Funny Business,* edited by Jon Scieszka, 2010.

"BRIXTON BROTHERS" SERIES

The Case of the Case of Mistaken Identity, illustrated by Adam Rex, Simon & Schuster Books for Young Readers (New York, NY), 2009.
The Ghostwriter Secret, illustrated by Adam Rex, Simon & Schuster Books for Young Readers (New York, NY), 2010.

Sidelights

California native Mac Barnett's books for children include the picture books *Billy Twitters and His Blue Whale Problem* and *Guess Again!* as well as the beginning chapter books *The Case of the Case of Mistaken Identity* and *The Ghostwriter Secret,* all illustrated by illustrator Adam Rex. Barnett also teams up with artist Dan Santat in *Oh No!; or, How My Science Project Destroyed the World,* a story about a science-fair robot that runs amuck, unstoppable because its wiz-kid cre-

Mac Barnett teams up with artist Adam Rex to create his "Brixton Brothers" mystery series, including The Case of the Case of Mistaken Identity. (Illustration copyright © 2009 by Adam Rex. Reprinted with permission of Simon & Schuster Books for Young Readers, an imprint of Simon & Schuster Children's Publishing Division.)

ator has armed it with city-destroying capabilities. While Barnett "packs wicked humor into economical, comic book-style lines," a *Publishers Weekly* contributor added of *Oh, No!* that the artist's colorful cartoon art "pay[s] homage to old monster movies."

Barnett's picture books are playful affairs, full of whimsical connections and quirky scenarios. In *Billy Twitters and His Blue Whale Problem,* for example, a typically untidy young boy receives an unusual punishment when he neglects to clean his room: his parents present him with a full-sized blue whale. Although cleaning his room was onerous, taking his new pet with him everywhere is truly trying, especially when the whale destroys his classroom and requires more seawater than Billy can possibly collect. A *Kirkus Reviews* writer dubbed *Billy Twitters and His Blue Whale problem* as "definitely funny and slyly subversive."

Described by *School Library Journal* contributor Laura Butler as "an especially fun book to share," the interactive *Guess Again!* presents readers with a sequence of short rhyming clues, each clue paired with a picture that hints at the surprising solution to be found with a turn of the page. Reviewing the book, a *Kirkus Reviews* critic noted the combination of Barnett's "rollicking riddles unexpected answers" and Rex's humorously detailed and realistic paintings, while a *Publishers Weekly* critic found the pairing of author and illustrator particularly effective. "Rex's *Mad* magazine-style artwork . . . is the perfect choice for Barnett's high-concept" story, the critic concluded of *Guess Again!*

In *The Case of the Case of Mistaken Identity,* the first volume in Barnett's "Brixton Brothers" mystery series, seasoned readers meet a twelve year old who turns into an amateur detective after a trip to the local library. Steve's social-studies assignment has forced him to research the girlish subject of American needlework. When he suffers the humiliation of requesting a book on quilting, the preteen is drawn into a plot that involves gun-wielding ninjas, librarian spies, and the mysterious superspy Mr. E. A fan of the "Hardy Boys" and "Baily Brothers" books, Steve has the sleuthing savvy to stay one step ahead of danger, and his own investigation plays out in a "fast-moving plot [that] is sure to hold readers' attention," according to *School Library Journal* contributor Mairead McInnes. Describing *The Case of the Case of Mistaken Identity* as a "coolly hysterical sendup" of child-detective series fiction, a *Kirkus Reviews* writer also praised "Rex's tongue-in-cheek black-and-white illustrations." In *Booklist* Carolyn Phelan deemed the book a "a fine start" to Barnett's own "Brixton Brothers" series, adding that the author "adds a level of humor" to the genre "that will sometimes have readers laughing out loud."

Biographical and Critical Sources

PERIODICALS

Booklist, October 15, 2009, Carolyn Phelan, review of *The Case of the Case of Mistaken Identity,* p. 63.

Kirkus Reviews, May 1, 2009, review of *Billy Twitters and His Blue Whale Problem*; September 1, 2009, review of *The Case of the Case of Mistaken Identity*; August 1, 2009, review of *Guess Again!*; April 15, 2010, review of *The Clock without a Face.*

Publishers Weekly, May 18, 2009, review of *Billy Twitters and His Blue Whale Problem,* p. 52; August 31, 2009, review of *Guess Again!,* p. 58; April 26, 2010, review of *The Clock without a Face,* p. 108; May 10, 2010, review of *Oh, No! (or, How My Science Project Destroyed the World),* p. 44.

School Library Journal, August, 2009, Laura Butler, review of *Guess Again!,* p. 69; March, 2010, Mairead McInnes, review of *The Case of the Case of Mistaken Identity,* p. 151.

ONLINE

Mac Barnett Home Page, http://macbarnett.com (November 14, 2010).

Mac Barnett Web log, http://www.macbarnett.blogspot. com (December 2, 2010).*

*   *   *

BARRETT, Angela 1955-

Personal

Born August 23, 1955, in Essex, England; daughter of Donald (an insurance broker) and Dinah Patricia (a secretary and homemaker) Barrett. *Education:* Maidstone College of Art, B.F.A., 1977; Royal College of Art, M.F.A., 1980. *Politics:* "Liberal." *Hobbies and other interests:* Needlework, reading, walking, dressmaking, stage design.

Addresses

Home—London, England. *Agent*—A.P. Watt Ltd., 20 John St., London WC1N 2DR, England.

Career

Illustrator. *Exhibitions:* Solo shows include Thomas Williams Fine Art, London, England, 2000, Illustration Cupboard, London, 2007, and Illustration Cupboard, London, 2009-10. Work also exhibited in group shows at galleries, museums, and other venues, including AOI, 1976, 1977, 1978; National Theatre, London, 1977; Barbican, London, 1983; Bratislava Biennial of Illustration, 1983; Michael Parkin Fine Art, 1984; Clarendon Gallery, London, 1985; On the Wall Gallery, 1985; Folio Society, 1986; Markswood Gallery, Essex, England, 1988; Royal College of Art, London, 1989, 1994; Commonwealth Institute, London, 1989; Chris Beetles, 1990; Newport Museum and Art Gallery, Newport, England, 1991-92; Victoria & Albert Museum, London, 1992; and British Council exhibition, 2002.

Member

Art Workers Guild.

Angela Barrett (Photograph by Chris Brown. Reproduced by permission.)

Awards, Honors

Kurt Maschler Award runner-up, 1984, for *The Woman in the Moon, and Other Tales of Forgotten Heroines;* Mother Goose Award runner-up, 1984, for *The King, the Cat, and the Fiddle;* Nestlé Smarties Book Prize, 1988, for *Can It Be True?;* W.H. Smith Illustration Award, British Book Trust, 1991, for *The Hidden House;* Kate Greenaway Medal shortlist, 1993, for *Beware, Beware,* and 2009, for *The Snow Goose;* Rattenfanger literature prize, 1994, for translation of *The Witches and the Singing Mice;* International Board on Books for Young People (IBBY) Honor List selection, 2000, for *The Emperor's New Clothes;* Parents' Choice Award recommendation, 2010, for *The Night Fairy.*

Illustrator

Frances Hodgson Burnett, *The Secret Garden,* new edition, Octopus Books (London, England), 1983.

Yehudi Menuhin and Christopher Hope, *The King, the Cat and the Fiddle,* Holt, Rinehart & Winston (New York, NY), 1983.

Hans Christian Andersen, *The Wild Swans,* translation by Naomi Lewis, Bedrick Books (New York, NY), 1984.

Susan Hill, *Through the Kitchen Window,* Hamish Hamilton (London, England), 1984.

James Riordan, *The Woman in the Moon, and Other Tales of Forgotten Heroines,* Hutchinson (London, England), 1984, Dial (New York, NY), 1985.

Susan Hope, *The Dragon Wore Pink,* Atheneum (New York, NY), 1985.

Lis Marks, *Ghostly Towers,* Octopus Books (London, England), 1985, Dial (New York, NY), 1986.

Susan Hill, *Through the Garden Gate,* Hamish Hamilton (London, England), 1986.

Graham Rose, *The Sunday Times Gardeners' Almanac,* Roger Houghton (London, England), 1986.

Susan Hill, *Can It Be True?,* Viking Kestrel (New York, NY), 1988.

Hans Christian Andersen, *The Snow Queen,* translation and introduction by Naomi Lewis, Henry Holt (New York, NY), 1988.

Proud Knight, Fair Lady: The Twelve Laïs of Marie de France, translation by Naomi Lewis, Viking Kestrel (New York, NY), 1989.

Martin Waddell, *The Hidden House,* Walker (London, England), 1989, Philomel (New York, NY), 1990.

Susan Hill, editor, *Walker Book of Ghost Stories,* Walker Books (London, England), 1990, published as *The Random House Book of Ghost Stories,* Random House (New York, NY), 1991.

Josephine Poole, reteller, *Snow White,* Hutchinson (London, England), 1991, Random House (New York, NY), 1992.

Jenny Nimmo, *The Witches and the Singing Mice,* Dial (New York, NY), 1993.

Susan Hill, *Beware, Beware,* Candlewick Press (Cambridge, MA), 1993.

Geraldine McCaughrean, reteller, *Orchard Book of Stories from the Ballet,* Orchard Books (London, England), 1994, published as *The Random House Book of Stories from the Ballet,* Random House (New York, NY), 1994.

Angela McAllister, *The Ice Palace,* Putnam (New York, NY), 1994.

Voltaire, *Candide; or, Optimism,* translation by Doctor Christopher Thacker, Libanus Press (Marlborough, England), 1996.

Hans Christian Andersen, *The Emperor's New Clothes,* translated by Naomi Lewis, Candlewick Press (Cambridge, MA), 1997.

Josephine Poole, *Joan of Arc,* Knopf (New York, NY), 1998.

Naomi Lewis, compiler, *Rocking Horse Land, and Other Classic Tales of Dolls and Toys,* Candlewick Press (Cambridge, MA), 2000.

Andrew Matthews, reteller, *The Orchard Book of Shakespeare Stories,* Orchard (London, England), 2001, published as *The Random House Book of Shakespeare Stories,* Random House (New York, NY), 2003.

Sharon Darrow, *Through the Tempests Dark and Wild: A Story of Mary Shelley, Creator of "Frankenstein,"* Candlewick Press (Cambridge, MA), 2002, Walker Books (London, England), 2003.

Josephine Poole, *Anne Frank,* Knopf (New York, NY), 2005.

Max Eilenberg, *Beauty and the Beast,* Candlewick Press (Cambridge, MA), 2006.

(With others) *Princes and Princesses: Seven Tales of Enchantment,* Orchard Books (London, England), 2007.

Paul Gallico, *The Snow Goose,* Hutchinson (London, England), 2007, Knopf (New York, NY), 2008.

Tim Binding, *Sylvie and the Songman,* David Fickling Books (New York, NY), 2008.

Laura Amy Schlitz, *The Night Fairy,* Candlewick Press (Cambridge, MA), 2010.

Also illustrator of book covers for novels by A.S. Byatt and Nancy Mitford, published by Viking Penguin, and for books published by Gollancz, Faber & Faber, Arrow, and Macmillan. Contributor of illustrations to books and periodicals.

Sidelights

Angela Barrett is a British illustrator whose award-winning paintings are known for their evocative, curious, and sometimes amusing details, delighting and bewitching picture-book audiences. "There is a stillness and a quiet atmospheric intensity to her illustrations which appeal across a wide range of understanding," Joanna Carey remarked in the London *Guardian.* "She doesn't simplify things—on the contrary, she both assumes and respects the intelligence of her readers—and her richly allusive work, full of detail and symbolism, invites and rewards as much time and investigation as you care to give it."

Born in Essex, England, in 1955, Barrett began drawing at an early age, influenced by the books she read as a child. "One of the earliest was a book of Russian fairy stories illustrated with black and white pictures, which were very dark and full of forests," she recalled to Madelyn Travis on the Booktrust Children's Books Web site. "When I was reading books I was always thinking, 'That would make a cracking picture.'" Although her parents suggested that she attend secretarial school, Barrett enrolled at the Maidstone College of Art and later earned a master's degree from the Royal College of Art in London.

Barrett often chooses stories with an element of mystery or a hint of the darker side of things. "Atmospheric, dark and intricately detailed, her style is particularly suited to stories from the past: fairy tales, ghost stories, retellings of Shakespeare," Travis observed. An early example is Martin Waddell's *The Hidden House,* in which a man creates three dolls to keep him company, then inexplicably moves away, never to return. The dolls, who in Barrett's incarnation contribute a "haunting and strangely animating presence" in the story, according to a contributor to *Publishers Weekly,* observe their surroundings as flora and fauna take over the house. Eventually though, a new family moves in and restores all to order.

Likewise, Barrett's illustrations for Susan Hill's *Walker Book of Ghost Stories*—published in the United States as *Random House Book of Ghost Stories*—"are occa-

Barrett's detailed and imaginative illustrations bring to life the tales in Naomi Lewis's **Rocking Horse Land, and Other Classic Tales of Dolls and Toys.** (Illustration © 2000 by Angela Barrett. Reproduced by permission of A.P. Watt, Ltd. on behalf of Angela Barrett.)

sionally Gorey-esque and always fittingly portentous," a *Publishers Weekly* reviewer observed, referencing illustrator Edward Gorey. Hill's original story *Beware, Beware* features another example of this aspect of Barrett's work. Here the illustrator provides much of the eerie tone to a lyrical story about a girl who dares herself to go out into the woods just to find out what is out there. "Barrett's dramatic use of color, texture, and light creates a captivating and haunting atmosphere," observed Heide Piehler in *School Library Journal.*

Barrett has illustrated a number of classic fairy tales with great success, according to critics. In Josephine Poole's new edition of the Brothers Grimm tale *Snow White,* the result is "exquisite," remarked a *Publishers Weekly* reviewer, calling the collaboration between Poole and Barrett "an exemplary marriage of illustration and narrative." Whereas in *Snow White,* Barrett's strongly colored paintings emphasize the contrasting extremes of good and evil, the "gentle watercolor and pencil" illustrations she contributes to Naomi Lewis's retelling of Hans Christian Andersen's "The Snow Queen" capture what a reviewer in *Publishers Weekly* described as "an ageless fairy-tale realm" in which "a frisson of danger lingers beneath her flower-filled images." Barrett's illustrations set Lewis's retelling of

Andersen's *The Emperor's New Clothes* in pre-World War I Europe, where a fashion-obsessed court is surrounded by equally foppish dogs that present the artist with numerous opportunities for visual humor. "The illustrations, incorporated into a design of exceptional cleverness and wit, are spectacular," contended Ann A. Flowers in her *Horn Book* review of the work.

Max Eilenberg's retelling of *Beauty and the Beast* offers a sly take on the original in its story about a selfless young woman who offers herself to a lonely, tortured creature in order to save her father. "Barrett's paintings are exquisitely dreamy and delicate, and most suggestive when the shadow of the Beast looms in the background behind the joyful, innocent heroine," Amanda Craig stated in the London *Times.* A critic in *Publishers Weekly* also complimented the book's art, writing that "each of the artist's vignettes offers viewers a small assortment of delicacies." Kirsten Cutler, reviewing *Beauty and the Beast* for *School Library Journal,* noted that Barrett's "effective use of light and shadow communicates the shifting moods" of Eilenberg's evocative story.

First published shortly after the Battle of Dunkirk in World War II, Paul Gallico's *The Snow Goose* tells the story of a hunchback's love for a beautiful girl and of the injured snow goose who brings the two together. Working in pencil, "Barrett approaches the story with a softness that matches the tone," a contributor maintained in *Kirkus Reviews.* Nancy Menaldi-Scanlan wrote in *Horn Book* that the illustrations in this new edition of *The Snow Goose* "perfectly complement the tale's serious nature, capturing the spareness of the landscape and the intensity of the characters' feelings."

Barrett's illustrations have also graced the pages of a number of picture-book biographies. The life of Joan of Arc, the fifteenth-century teen who went to war for France at the behest of an angel of God and was burned at the stake by her enemies, is the subject of Poole's *Joan of Arc.* Here, Barrett's paintings capture the historic and spiritual importance of Joan's actions, according to a contributor to *Publishers Weekly.* "Aflame with premonitory fires and flooded with the emotion of battle," the critic wrote, these images "sear the imagination with their horror and beauty." Likewise, *Horn Book* critic Mary Burns remarked favorably upon Barrett's contributions, describing them as "dramatic, full-color illustrations that unfold like a gorgeous pageant."

In *Through the Tempests Dark and Wild: A Story of Mary Shelley, Creator of "Frankenstein"* Sharon Darrow offers a fictionalized look at Shelley's adolescence, focusing on her time in Scotland with the Baxter family, who served as her caretakers after she was sent away by her disinterested father and harsh stepmother. Some believe that Shelley's creative instincts first blossomed in Scotland, where she was treated to fireside stories of supernatural creatures and haunted lovers. Barrett's watercolor illustrations for Darrow's tale "set

the archetypal outsider story against wild, dark views of the Scottish landscape," observed Hazel Rochman in *Booklist,* and Beth Tegart noted in *School Library Journal* that "the pictures draw readers into a melancholy and emotional world."

Barrett and Poole join forces once again on *Anne Frank,* dubbed "a potent combination of atmospheric illustrations and evocative text," by London *Guardian* reviewer Kate Agnew. Poole offers a concise retelling of Anne's brief life, set against the background of Adolf Hitler's rise to power and the persecution of the Jews. "Spreads are dominated by Barrett's realistically rendered paintings done in subdued tones," Teri Markson commented in *School Library Journal,* and *Horn Book* critic Martha V. Parravano described the pictures in *Anne Frank* as "stark and formal, yet immediate," adding that they possess "a fairy-tale remove that serves to heighten emotion."

Among her many illustration projects, Barrett has provided artwork to *The Random House Book of Stories from the Ballet,* a collection of tales by Geraldine McCaughrean that explores the narratives behind such celebrated ballets as *Swan Lake, Coppelia,* and *The Nutcracker.* Barrett's pictures contribute "a nineteenth-century, old-fashioned look" to the volume, according to Kay McPherson in a *School Library Journal* review of the book. Working again with Lewis, she brings to life stories about toys in *Rocking Horse Land, and Other Classic Tales of Dolls and Toys.* Lewis's collection has an innate appeal for children, remarked Anne Knickerbocker in *School Library Journal.* "What makes this book special, however, are [Barrett's] detailed illustrations peppered throughout the stories," the critic added.

In Angela McAllister's *Ice Palace,* one of several fantasy tales illustrated by Barrett, a father's stories work to cool the fevered brow of his young daughter during a hot, dry summer. Barrett's illustrations, "serene watercolors, in blues and greens tinged with soft violets, capture ephemeral dreamscapes," according to a reviewer for *Publishers Weekly.* Another illustration project, Tim Binding's surreal novel *Sylvie and the Songman,* concerns the strange goings-on surrounding a girl and her composer father as they come under the power of the malevolent Songman who hopes to control the world's music. "Barrett's mostly spare, elegant drawings haunt the pages" of this book, reported a *Kirkus Reviews* contributor. In *The Night Fairy,* a work by Laura Amy Schlitz, a tiny wingéd creature loses its ability to fly and must learn to survive in a foreign environment: a giant's garden. "Beautifully composed, [Barrett's] . . . artwork combines subtle use of color with a keen observation of nature that's reminiscent of Beatrix Potter's work," Carolyn Phelan remarked in her review of *The Night Fairy* for *Booklist.*

Biographical and Critical Sources

PERIODICALS

Booklist, January 1, 1992, Carolyn Phelan, review of *Snow White,* p. 832; August, 1993, Hazel Rochman, review of *The Witches and the Singing Mice,* p. 2067; November 1, 1993, Hazel Rochman, review of *The Snow Queen,* p. 521; November 15, 1993, Carolyn Phelan, review of *Beware, Beware,* p. 631; October 15, 1994, Mary Harris Veeder, review of *The Ice Palace,* p. 437; August, 1998, Ilene Cooper, review of *Joan of Arc,* p. 2001; March 1, 2001, Stephanie Zvirin, review of *Joan of Arc,* p. 1280; June 1, 2003, Hazel Rochman, review of *Through the Tempests Dark and Wild: A Story of Mary Shelley, Creator of "Frankenstein,"* p. 1793; June 1, 2005, Hazel Rochman, review of *Anne Frank,* p. 1797; December 1, 2006, Hazel Rochman, review of *Beauty and the Beast,* p. 50; June 1, 2009, Ian Chipman, review of *Sylvie and the Songman,* p. 66; January 1, 2010, Carolyn Phelan, review of *The Night Fairy,* p. 81.

Books for Keeps, November, 2001, Quentin Blake, interview with Barrett.

Guardian (London, England), July 5, 2005, Kate Agnew, review of *Anne Frank,* p. 5; September 9, 2006, Joanna Carey, "Running with Wolves," profile of Barrett, p. 20.

Horn Book, November-December, 1989, Mary M. Burns, review of *Proud Knight, Fair Lady: The Twelve Laïs of Marie de France,* p. 781; September-October, 1990, Hanna B. Zeiger, review of *The Hidden House,* p. 595; March-April, 1992, Ann A. Flowers, review of *Snow White,* p. 214; September-October, 1993, Ann A. Flowers, review of *The Witches and the Singing Mice,* p. 611; January-February, 1994, Ann A. Flowers, review of *Beware, Beware,* p. 64; January-February, 1996, Mary M. Burns, review of *The Random House Book of Stories from the Ballet,* p. 92; November-December, 1997, Ann A. Flowers, review of *The Emperor's New Clothes,* p. 688; September-October, 1998, Mary M. Burns, review of *Joan of Arc,* p. 623; November-December, 2005, Martha V. Parravano, review of *Anne Frank,* p. 740; March-April, 2010, Robin L. Smith, review of *The Night Fairy,* p. 72.

Kirkus Reviews, July 15, 2005, review of *Anne Frank,* p. 795; November 15, 2006, review of *Beauty and the Beast,* p. 1173; September 1, 2007, review of *The Snow Goose;* July 1, 2009, review of *Sylvie and the Songman.*

New Statesman, December 21, 1984, Michael Rosen, review of *The Woman in the Moon, and Other Tales of Forgotten Heroines,* p. 49.

New York Times Book Review, July 9, 1989; November 16, 1997, Francine Prose, review of *The Emperor's New Clothes,* p. 57.

Observer (London, England), February 11, 2007, Kate Kellaway, review of *Beauty and the Beast,* p. 23.

Publishers Weekly, July 29, 1983, review of *The King, the Cat, and the Fiddle,* p. 70; August 2, 1985, review of *The Woman in the Moon, and Other Tales of Forgot-*

ten Heroines, p. 66; January 22, 1988, Penny Kaga-
noff, review of *Through the Garden Gate,* p. 99; August 26, 1988, review of *The Snow Queen,* p. 84; April
27, 1990, review of *The Hidden House,* p. 61; August
30, 1991, review of *The Random House Book of Ghost
Stories,* p. 84; November 8, 1991, review of *Snow
White,* p. 63; August 2, 1993, review of *The Witches
and the Singing Mice,* p. 81; September 6, 1993, review of *Beware, Beware,* p. 94, and review of *The
Snow Queen,* p. 96; October 24, 1994, review of *The
Ice Palace,* p. 61; July 7, 1997, review of *The Emper-
or's New Clothes,* p. 67; July 13, 1998, review of
Joan of Arc, p. 77; November 20, 2000, "Toy Stories," p. 70; June, 2003, Beth Tegart, review of
Through the Tempests Dark and Wild, p. 158; May
23, 2005, review of *Anne Frank,* p. 78; November 20,
2006, review of *Beauty and the Beast,* p. 58.

School Library Journal, Susan H. Patron, review of *The
Wild Swans,* p. 67; February, 1986, Denise A. Anton,
review of *The Woman in the Moon, and Other Tales
of Forgotten Heroines,* p. 89; August, 1986, Trev
Jones, review of *The Dragon Wore Pink,* p. 83; Octo-
ber, 1988, Susan Hepler, review of *Can It Be True?,*
p. 34; November, 1988, Helen Gregory, review of *The
Snow Queen,* p. 99; September, 1989, Jeanne Marie
Clancy, review of *Proud Knight, Fair Lady,* p. 282;
July, 1990, Judith Gloyer, review of *The Hidden
House,* p. 65; January, 1992, Linda Boyles, review of
Snow White, p. 106; August, 1993, Joy Fleishhacker,
review of *The Witches and the Singing Mice,* p. 166;
February, 1994, Susan Scheps, review of *The Snow
Queen,* p. 76, and Heide Piehler, review of *Beware,
Beware,* p. 86; October, 1994, Patricia Lothrop Green,
review of *The Ice Palace,* p. 125; December, 1995,
Kay McPherson, review of *The Random House Book
of Stories from the Ballet,* pp. 120-121; November,
1997, Marilyn Iarusso, review of *The Emperor's New
Clothes,* p. 76; September, 1998, Shirley Wilton, review of *Joan of Arc,* p. 196; April, 2001, Anne Knick-
erbocker, review of *Rocking Horse Land, and Other
Classic Tales of Dolls and Toys,* p. 115; June, 2003,
Beth Tegart, review of *Through the Tempests Dark
and Wild,* p. 158; September, 2005, Teri Markson, review of *Anne Frank,* p. 195; December, 2006, Kristen
Cutler, review of *Beauty and the Beast,* p. 121; December, 2007, Nancy Menaldi-Scanlan, review of *The
Snow Goose,* p. 128; October, 2009, Sue Giffard, review of *Sylvie and the Songman,* p. 120; April, 2010,
Sarah Polace, review of *The Night Fairy,* p. 139.

Times (London, England), January 13, 2007, Amanda
Craig, "Having a Perfectly Beastly Time," p. 15.

Times Literary Supplement, August 18, 1989, Nicole Irving, review of *Proud Knight, Fair Lady,* p. 905.

ONLINE

Booktrust Children's Books Web site, http://www.booktrust
childrensbooks.org.uk/ (December 1, 2010), Madelyn
Travis, interview with Barrett.

British Library Web site, http://www.bl.uk/ (October 8,
2003), Bridget McKenzie, interview with Barrett.

Candlewick Press Web site, http://www.candlewick.com/
(December 20, 2010), "Angela Barrett."*

BASS, Hester 1956-

Personal

Born 1956, in GA; married Clayton Bass (an artist);
children: two. *Education:* Simmons College, B.A.; studied acting at HB Studio (New York, NY).

Addresses

Home—AL. *E-mail*—hester@hesterbass.com.

Career

Author and educator. Radio and television advertising
copywriter/voice talent, actress, and singer, c. 1980s;
storyteller, c. 1990s.

Member

Society of Children's Book Writers and Illustrators, Authors Guild.

Awards, Honors

Orbis Pictus Award for Outstanding Nonfiction for Chil-
dren, National Council of Teachers of English, Southern
Independent Booksellers Alliance Children's Book
Award, Best Children's Books selection, Bank Street

Hester Bass (Photograph by S & S Photography. Reproduced by permission.)

Bass's picture book The Secret World of Walter Anderson *is brought to life in watercolor paintings by award-winning artist E.B. Lewis.* (Illustration copyright © 2009 by E.B. Lewis. Reproduced by permission of Candlewick Press, Somerville, MA.)

College of Education, Choices selection, Cooperative Children's Book Center, and Notable Social Studies Trade Books for Young People designation, National Council for the Social Studies/Children's Book Council, all 2010, all for *The Secret World of Walter Anderson.*

Writings

So Many Houses, illustrated by Alik Arzoumanian, Children's Press (New York, NY), 2006.
The Secret World of Walter Anderson, illustrated by E.B. Lewis, Candlewick Press (Somerville, MA), 2009.

Sidelights

Hester Bass profiles a most unusual American artist in *The Secret World of Walter Anderson,* a picture-book biography that received an Orbis Pictus award for Out-

standing nonfiction for children. Anderson, a twentieth-century painter who spent his last seventeen years living a mostly solitary existence on Horn Island off the coast of Mississippi, earned recognition for his intense, vibrant, and energetic depictions of wildlife, done in a variety of media. "I find Anderson's art and writings, like nature itself, endlessly refreshing and wanted to share his story in the same way that one wants to tell friends about a fabulous restaurant or an engaging film," Bass remarked in a *Seven Impossible Things before Breakfast* online interview. "There were many books about Anderson for adults, but almost nothing for children. In workshops, writers are often told to 'write the story that only you can write.' I took that advice to heart, and was compelled to tell the story of Walter Anderson."

A native of Georgia, Bass loved to read as a child, in particular the works of Beatrix Potter and A.A. Milne. She earned a degree in communications from Boston's

Simmons College, then worked in television and radio advertising while also singing in a rock band. Bass later ventured to New York City where she delivered singing telegrams and studied acting. In New York she met her husband, artist Clayton Bass, who at one point was director of the Walter Anderson Museum of Art in Ocean Springs, Mississippi. During the 1990s Bass began working as a storyteller there and sharing tales of Anderson's life with museum visitors. "Some of his adventures sound like mythology, but they're true, and the children were fascinated," she noted in her interview. "Fidgety kids would relax into the tale of a man who drew with crayons as expertly as he did with ink, who rode a bicycle but didn't drive a car, who occasionally ate what washed up on the beach, and made friends with the animals on Horn Island."

Born in 1903, in New Orleans, Louisiana, Walter Anderson was immersed in the arts from an early age. He graduated from the Pennsylvania Academy of the Fine Arts, then began working at Shearwater Pottery, founded in 1928 by his brother Peter on the family's property in Ocean Springs, Mississippi. Diagnosed with mental illness in the 1930s, Anderson spent time at a series of hospitals before rejoining his wife and children at Oldfields in Gautier, Mississippi, where he produced a wide range of artworks. In 1947 he moved back to Ocean Springs to live alone in a cottage at Shearwater, while his family lived nearby. He began spending weeks at a time on nearby Horn Island, twelve miles offshore in the Gulf of Mexico, bringing only his art supplies and the barest of necessities. In his quest to capture the island's flora and fauna and working primarily in watercolor, he endured harsh weather and primitive accommodations, usually spending his nights asleep beneath his rowboat. Anderson was extremely prolific yet very private throughout his lifetime, and the majority of his drawings and paintings were discovered in his cottage following his death in 1965.

In *The Secret World of Walter Anderson* Bass focuses on the artist's Horn Island years, emphasizing his devotion to both art and nature. *Booklist* critic Andrew Medlar stated that the author "clearly has a passion for Anderson's art . . . and her biographical text is fluid and gentle," and a *Kirkus Reviews* critic described the work as "a gorgeous chronicle of a versatile southern American artist." Praising the "simple language and quirky details" in the picture-book biography, as well as commending E.B. Lewis's light-filled illustrations, Barbara Auerbach wrote in *School Library Journal* that "Bass makes an eccentric, unknown subject exciting and accessible to children."

Biographical and Critical Sources

PERIODICALS

Booklist, August 1, 2009, review of *The Secret World of Walter Anderson,* p. 65.

Kirkus Reviews, August 1, 2009, review of *The Secret World of Walter Anderson.*

School Library Journal, September, 2009, Barbara Auerbach, review of *The Secret World of Walter Anderson,* p. 138.

ONLINE

Hester Bass Home Page, http://www.hesterbass.com (December 1, 2010).

Seven Impossible Things before Breakfast Web log, http://blaine.org/sevenimpossiblethings/ (September 30, 2009), interview with Bass and E.B. Lewis.

*　　*　　*

BJÖRKMAN, Steve

Personal

Married; children: three. *Education:* Attended college.

Addresses

Home—Aliso Viejo CA. *Agent*—Vince Kamin, 400 W. Erie, Chicago, IL 60610. *E-mail*—stevebjorkman@sbcglobal.net.

Career

Illustrator, beginning c. mid-1970s, including advertising/editorial, children's books and greeting cards. Art teacher and presenter at schools, churches, and youth camps.

Writings

SELF-ILLUSTRATED

Good Night, Little One, WaterBrook Press (Colorado Springs, CO), 1999.

The Flyaway Kite, WaterBrook Press (Colorado Springs, CO), 2000.

Supersnouts!, Holiday House (New York, NY), 2004.

ILLUSTRATOR

Jonathan Etra, *Aliens for Breakfast,* Random House (New York, NY), 1988.

Ellen Levine, *I Hate English!,* Scholastic (New York, NY), 1989.

Edith Baer, *This Is the Way We Go to School: A Book about Children around the World,* Scholastic (New York, NY), 1990.

Jonathan Etra and Stephanie Spinner, *Aliens for Lunch,* Random House (New York, NY), 1991.

Greg Johnson, *If I Could Ask God One Question—,* Tyndale House (Wheaton, IL), 1991.

Jean Marzollo, *In 1492,* Scholastic (New York, NY), 1991.

Todd Temple, *How to Become a Teenager Millionaire,* T. Nelson (Nashville, TN), 1991.

Susan Saunders, *Tyrone Goes to School,* Dutton Children's Books (New York, NY), 1992.

Joyce K. Ellis, editor, *The One-Minute Bible for Kids: From the New International Version of the Bible,* Garborg's (Bloomington, MN), 1993.

Ruth Belov Gross, *A Book about Your Skeleton,* Scholastic (New York, NY), 1994.

Jean Marzollo, *In 1776,* Scholastic (New York, NY), 1994.

George Shannon, *Seeds,* Houghton Mifflin (Boston, MA), 1994.

Stephanie Spinner, *Aliens for Dinner,* Random House (New York, NY), 1994.

Edith Baer, *This Is the Way We Eat Our Lunch: A Book about Children around the World,* Scholastic (New York, NY), 1995.

George Shannon, *Heart to Heart,* Houghton Mifflin (Boston, MA), 1995.

Jeff Brown, *Flat Stanley,* HarperTrophy (New York, NY), 1996.

Jeff Brown, *Invisible Stanley,* HarperTrophy (New York, NY), 1996.

Jeff Brown, *Stanley and the Magic Lamp,* new edition, HarperCollins (New York, NY), 1996.

Bobbie Katz, *Germs! Germs! Germs!,* Scholastic (New York, NY), 1996.

L.J. Sattgast, *When the World Was New,* Gold 'n' Honey Books (Sisters, OR), 1996.

Louise Borden, *Thanksgiving Is—,* Scholastic (New York, NY), 1997.

Melody Carlson, *The Ark That Noah Built,* Gold 'n' Honey Books (Sister, OR), 1997.

Melody Carlson, *A Tale of Two Houses,* Gold 'n' Honey Books (Sisters, OR), 1998.

Bobbi Katz, *Lots of Lice,* Scholastic (New York, NY), 1998.

Jennifer Rees Larcombe, *The Terrible Giant,* Crossway Books (Wheaton, IL), 1999.

Edith Tarbescu, *Bring Back My Gerbil!,* Scholastic (New York, NY), 1999.

Melody Carlson, *The Lost Lamb,* Crossway Books (Wheaton, IL), 1999.

Melody Carlson, *The Other Brother,* Crossway Books (Wheaton, IL), 1999.

Bobbi Katz, *Make Way for Tooth Decay,* Scholastic (New York, NY), 1999.

Jennifer Rees Larcombe, *The Baby in the Basket,* Crossway Books (Wheaton, IL), 1999.

Jennifer Rees Larcombe, *The Boy Who Ran Away,* Crossway Books (Wheaton, IL), 1999.

Jennifer Rees Larcombe, *The Man Who Was Not Tall Enough,* Crossway Books (Wheaton, IL), 1999.

Jennifer Rees Larcombe, *Lost in Jerusalem!,* Crossway Books (Wheaton, IL), 2000.

Jennifer Rees Larcombe, *The Walls That Fell down Flat,* Crossway Books (Wheaton, IL), 2000.

Rachel Vail, *Mama Rex and T Lose a Waffle,* Scholastic (New York, NY), 2000.

Rachel Vail, *Mama Rex and T Shop for Shoes,* Scholastic (New York, NY), 2000.

Eve Bunting, *Dear Wish Fairy,* Scholastic (New York, NY), 2000.

Melody Carlson, *Farmer Brown's Field Trip,* Crossway Books (Wheaton, IL), 2000.

Melody Carlson, *It's Not Funny, I Lost My Money,* Crossway Books (Wheaton, IL), 2000.

Jennifer Rees Larcombe, *The Best Boat Ever Built,* Crossway Books (Wheaton, IL), 2000.

Jennifer Rees Larcombe, *Danger on the Lonely Road,* Crossway Books (Wheaton, IL), 2000.

Melody Carlson, *A Treasure beyond Measure,* Crossway Books (Wheaton, IL), 2001.

Rachel Vail, *Mama Rex and T: The Horrible Play Date,* Scholastic (New York, NY), 2002.

Rachel Vail, *Mama Rex and T: Homework Trouble,* Scholastic (New York, NY), 2002.

Cari Meister, *Skinny and Fats, Best Friends,* Holiday House (New York, NY), 2002.

Carol Wallace, *One Nosy Pup,* Holiday House (New York, NY), 2005.

Renee Riva, *Izzy the Lizzy,* WaterBrook Press (Colorado Springs, CO), 2005.

Renee Riva, *Guido's Gondola,* WaterBrook Press (Colorado Springs, CO), 2005.

Stuart J. Murphy, *Same Old Hankie,* HarperCollins (New York, NY), 2005.

Stuart J. Murphy, *Same Old Horse,* HarperCollins (New York, NY), 2005.

Kay Arthur, *Bible Prophecy for Kids: Revelation 1-7,* Harvest House (Eugene, OR), 2006.

Peggy Post and Cindy Post Senning, *Emily's Everyday Manners,* HarperCollins (New York, NY), 2006.

Cynthia Leitich Smith and Greg Leitich Smith, *Santa Knows,* Dutton Children's Books (New York, NY), 2006.

Kay Arthur and Janna Arndt, *A Sneak Peek into the Future,* Harvest House (Eugene, OR), 2007.

Carol Wallace, *The Santa Secret,* Holiday House (New York, NY), 2007.

Jeff Foxworthy, *Dirt on My Shirt,* HarperCollins Children's Books (New York, NY), 2008.

Peggy Post and Cindy Post Senning, *Emily's Christmas Gifts,* HarperCollins (New York, NY), 2008.

Kay Arthur and Janna Arndt, *Fast-forward to the Future,* Harvest House (Eugene, OR), 2008.

Judy Cox, *Puppy Power,* Holiday House (New York, NY), 2008.

Carol Wallace, *Easter Bunny Blues,* Holiday House (New York, NY), 2009.

Bill Cochran, *My Parents Are Divorced, My Elbows Have Nicknames, and Other Facts about Me,* HarperCollins (New York, NY), 2009.

Peggy Post and Cindy Post Senning, *Emily Post's Table Manners for Kids,* HarperCollins (New York, NY), 2009.

Jeff Foxworthy, *Silly Street,* HarperCollins (New York, NY), 2009.

Alyson Heller, *Soccer Day,* Aladdin Paperbacks (New York, NY), 2009.

Alyson Heller, *Let's Go Skating!* ("After School Sports Club" series), Aladdin (New York, NY), 2009.

Cindy Post Selling and Peggy Post, *Emily's New Friend,* HarperCollins (New York, NY), 2010.

Jeff Foxworthy, *Hide!!!,* Beaufort Books (New York, NY), 2010.

Carol Wallace, *The Pumpkin Mystery,* Holiday House (New York, NY), 2010.

Alyson Heller, *Time for T-ball* ("After School Sports Club" series), Aladdin (New York, NY), 2010.

Alyson Heller, *Touchdown!* ("After School Sports Club" series), Simon Spotlight (New York, NY), 2010.

Marty Nystrom, *Zack, You're Acting Zany!: Playful Poems and Riveting Rhymes,* Standard Pub. (Cincinnati, OH), 2010.

ILLUSTRATOR; "WEEBIE ZONE" SERIES

Stephanie Spinner and Ellen Weiss, *Gerbilities,* Harper Collins (New York, NY), 1996.

Stephanie Spinner and Ellen Weiss, *Sing, Elvis, Sing!,* Harper Collins (New York, NY), 1996.

Stephanie Spinner and Ellen Weiss, *Bright Lights, Little Gerbil,* HarperCollins (New York, NY), 1997.

Stephanie Spinner and Ellen Weiss, *Born to Be Wild,* HarperCollins (New York, NY), 1997.

Björkman's illustration projects include creating the entertaining line art in Sing, Elvis, Sing! *by Stephanie Spinner and Ellen Weiss.* (Harper-Trophy, 1996. Illustration © 1996 by Steve Björkman. Reproduced by permission.)

Stephanie Spinner and Ellen Weiss, *The Bird Is the Word,* HarperCollins (New York, NY), 1997.

Stephanie Spinner and Ellen Weiss, *We're Off to See the Lizard,* HarperCollins (New York, NY), 1998.

Adaptations

I Hate English by Ellen Levine was adapted as a short film by Nutmeg Media, 2007.

Sidelights

Steve Björkman is an illustrator whose work has been paired with picture-book texts by authors ranging from Stuart J. Murphy and Jean Marzollo to Judy Cox and George Shannon, and even stand-up comedian Jeff Foxworthy. Known for mixing line drawings with touches of watercolor to produce endearing images full of humor, Björkman is also the official illustrator of the gerbil-centered "Weebie Zone" chapter books by Stephanie Spinner and Ellen Weiss. In addition to his illustration work, Björkman has also created the original picture books *Good Night, Little One, The Flyaway Kite,* and *Supersnouts!* the last which pits two thieves against a trio of watchdog pigs. Dubbing Björkman's humorous story a "farmyard free-for-all," a *Kirkus Reviews* writer added that the "loosely drawn, exuberantly brushed watercolors" in *Supersnouts!* capture the story's "fundamental daffiness," and in *Publishers Weekly* a critic cited the story's "absurd action," "jazzy watercolor" illustrations, and preponderance of "porky puns."

Although Björkman originally intended to pursue a career as a high-school English teacher, he took a side path that led to book illustration. In addition, his artwork has appeared in advertisements and magazine illustrations as well as on greeting cards that he creates with his brother, Carl Björkman, and markets through Recycled Paper Greetings. "While the illustration keeps me busy, the English teacher part of me still creeps out. I enjoy doing school visits and occasional teaching, using my drawing as I speak, for churches and youth camps," the California-based author/artist noted on his home page.

As an illustrator, Björkman has contributed his animated drawings to many books for children. In *Puppy Power,* a beginning reader by Judy Cox in which a third grader learns the importance of fair play, the artist's "expressive black-and-white illustrations . . . sustain . . . the mood" of Cox's "realistic" tale, according to Laura Scott in *School Library Journal,* and his "jaunty loose watercolors add to the overall effect" of Cari Meister's *Skinny and Fats, Best Friends,* "especially the amusing expressions on the animal's faces."

In *My Parents Are Divorced, My Elbows Have Nicknames, and Other Facts about Me* Björkman's "colorful cartoons add to the upbeat nature" of Bill Cochran's story about a child dealing with a parental split-up "and make a serious subject a little easier to swallow," according to *School Library Journal* critic Maura Bresna-

Steve Björkman creates the art to illuminate Linda Granfield's picture-book civics lesson in **America Votes.** (Illustration copyright © 2003 by Steve Björkman. Reproduced by permission.)

han. "With their sprays of color and hectic lines," Björkman's ink and watercolor images for Rachel Vail's *Mama Rex and T: The Horrible Play Date* "practically define the book's big word: rambunctious," according to a *Kirkus Reviews* writer.

Björkman's creative collaboration with Foxworthy has resulted in the picture books *Dirt on My Shirt, Silly Street,* and *Hide!!!,* all of which draw on Foxworth's hometown country roots. In *Dirt on My Shirt,* for example, Björkman "punches up" Foxworth's rhyming text about friends and family "with plentiful illustrations in a cheery cartoon style," according to a *Publishers Weekly* contributor. In *School Library Journal* Catherine Threadgill also cited the story's upbeat text and added that the illustrator "peppers every page with tykes and friendly suburban wildlife in perpetual states of pop-eyed delight." Another rural-themed tale, Elizabeth Spurr's *Farm Life,* features a cast of animal characters that are depicted by the artist in what a *Publishers Weekly* contributor described as "zesty watercolors hedged about with quick, free-flowing pen strokes."

Biographical and Critical Sources

PERIODICALS

Booklist, September 15, 1995, Linda Ward-Callaghan, review of *This Is the Way We Eat Our Lunch: A Book about Children around the World,* p. 174; January 1, 1997, Shelley Towsend-Hudson, review of *Gerbilitis,* p. 862; February 1, 1997, Carolyn Phelan, review of *Germs, Germs, Germs!,* p. 950; February 1, 2002, Carolyn Phelan, review of *Safari Park,* p. 944; September 15, 2003, Carolyn Phelan, review of *America Votes: How Our President Is Elected,* p. 223; January 1, 2005, GraceAnne A. DeCandido, review of *The Guide to Good Manners for Kids,* p. 854; April 1, 2009, Carolyn Phelan, review of *Emily Post's Table Manners for Kids,* p. 35.

Horn Book, November-December, 2006, Roger Sutton, review of *Santa Knows,* p. 693.

Kirkus Reviews, August 1, 2002, review of *Skinny and Fats,* p. 1137; January 15, 2003, review of *Farm Life,* p. 147; February 1, 2004, review of *Supersnouts!,* p. 129; July 1, 2004, review of *Mama Rex and T: The Horrible Play Date,* p. 964; April 1, 2008, review of *Puppy Power;* November 1, 2008, review of *Emily's Christmas Gifts;* May 15, 2009, review of *My Parents Are Divorced, My Elbows Have Nicknames, and Other Facts about Me.*

Publishers Weekly, July 29, 1996, review of *Gerbilitis,* p. 89 September 2, 2002, review of *Skinny and Fats, Best Friends,* p. 76; January 20, 2003, review of *Farm Life,* p. 80; March 29, 2004, review of *Supernouts!,* p. 62; September 25, 2006, review of *Santa Knows,* p. 71; March 17, 2008, review of *Dirt on My Shirt,* p. 70.

School Library Journal, August, 2002, Nancy A. Gifford, review of *Safari Park,* p. 178, and Linda Beck, review

of *So You Want to Be a Teenager?*, p. 216; December, 2003, Dona Ratterree, review of *America Votes*, p. 168; May, 2004, Marge Loch-Wouters, review of *Supersnouts!*, p. 102; October, 2006, Maureen Wade, review of *Santa Knows*, p. 101; April, 2007, Barbara Auerbach, review of *I Hate English!*, p. 66; June, 2008, Laura Scott, review of *Puppy Power*, p. 100, and Catherine Threadgill, review of *Dirt on My Shirt*, p. 122; October, 2008, Lisa Falk, review of *Emily's Christmas Gifts*, p. 98; May, 2009, Maura Bresnahan, review of *My Parents Are Divorced, My Elbows Have Nicknames, and Other Facts about Me*, p. 72; July, 2009, Julie Roach, review of *Silly Street*, p. 72; November, 2009, Maura Bresnahan, review of *Emily Post's Table Manners for Kids*, p. 135.

ONLINE

Steve Björkman Home Page, http://www.stevebjorkman. com (December 2, 2010).*

* * *

BLESSING, Charlotte

Personal

Born in Copenhagen, Denmark; immigrated from Kenya to United States, 2005; married (husband an outdoor educator); children: one son, one daughter. *Education:* B.A. (education); School for International Training, M.A. (international and intercultural management), 1997. *Hobbies and other interests:* Hiking, bicycling, reading, writing.

Addresses

Home—Seattle, WA. *E-mail*—chekabaraka@yahoo.com.

Career

Author and administrator. Worked in Africa, beginning 1986; held educational positions in Africa for fifteen years, including School for International Training, Kenya, academic director, 1995-2005; Colorado College, Colorado Springs, director of international programs; Lakeside School, Seattle, WA, director of global education. *Abroad View* magazine, member of editorial board. Presenter at schools.

Writings

New Old Shoes, illustrated by Gary R. Phillips, Pleasant Street Press (Raynham, MA), 2008.

Contributor of stories and articles to periodicals, including *Abroad View*, *Caffeine Society*, *Faces*, *Frontiers Journal*, *Highlights for Children*, and *Stepping Stone*.

Charlotte Blessing (Photograph by Miles Blessing. Reproduced by permission.)

Sidelights

With her focus on promoting cross-cultural understanding and a global perspective, Charlotte Blessing has devoted her career to creating opportunities for U.S. college students as well as those in middle school and high school to immerse themselves in a new culture through international education programs. She believes that it is when interacting with people of difference that students begin to develop a new and expanded perspective on other cultures. Blessing herself has lived and worked around the world, and her experiences in the African nations of Ghana, Kenya, Morocco, Rwanda, South Africa, Tanzania, and Uganda continue to inspire her work as an educator. These experiences have also inspired Blessing's work as a writer, including her picture book *New Old Shoes*.

As Blessing explained on her home page, while in Kenya "I enjoyed visiting the many second-hand clothing and shoe markets in the city and rural towns. As I checked out shoes of all kinds, I would begin to imagine where they had come from and who had worn them before." In *New Old Shoes* she relates one possible scenario, which is narrated by a pair of bright red sneakers. After being well worn by an American boy who plays outside much of the time, the sneakers are donated to charity. From the United States, they travel to East Africa, where a second boy enjoys them as much

as the first boy had while playing soccer in his small village. When the sneakers once again are discarded, they find yet another home, this time with a girl who needs strong, rubber-soled shoes during her long daily walk to school. The red sneakers find their ultimate home as part of a scarecrow guarding a farmer's field.

Blessing's "text and [Gary R. Phillips'] illustrations work well together to portray the stark contrast between First-and Third-World countries," wrote a _Kirkus Reviews_ contributor of _New Old Shoes,_ and _Booklist_ critic Carolyn Phelan praised it as a "simple, accessible story." Reviewing the book for _School Library Journal,_ Kate Neff dubbed its story "touching" and predicted that Blessing's tale will inspire young readers to "think about how they can help other youngsters around the world." In an endnote to _New Old Shoes_ Soles4Souls founder Wayne Elsey provides information about ways that children can act on that inspiration.

Biographical and Critical Sources

PERIODICALS

Booklist, September 1, 2009, Carolyn Phelan, review of _New Old Shoes,_ p. 100.
Kirkus Reviews, August 15, 2009, review of _New Old Shoes._
School Library Journal, August, 2009, Kate Neff, review of _New Old Shoes,_ p. 70.

Blessing takes readers on an international journey in her picture book **New Old Shoes,** _illustrated by Gary R. Phillips._ (Illustration copyright © 2009 by Gary R Phillips. Reproduced by permission of Pleasant Street Press.)

ONLINE

Charlotte Blessing Home Page, http://www.charlotteblessing.com (November 14, 2010).
Colorado College Web site, http://www.coloradocollege.edu/ (November 14, 2010), Leslie Weddell, "Get to Know Charlotte Blessing."

*   *   *

BYARS, Betsy 1928-

Personal

Born August 7, 1928, in Charlotte, NC; daughter of George Guy (a cotton mill executive) and Nan (a homemaker) Cromer; married Edward Ford Byars (a professor of engineering), June 24, 1950; children: Laurie, Betsy Ann, Nan, Guy. _Education:_ Attended Furman University, 1946-48; Queens College (Charlotte, NC), B.A., 1950. _Hobbies and other interests:_ Gliding, flying airplanes, reading, traveling, music, needlepoint, crosswords.

Addresses

Home—Seneca, SC.

Career

Children's book author.

Awards, Honors

Book of the Year selection, Child Study Association of America, 1968, for _The Midnight Fox,_ 1969, for _Trouble River,_ 1970, for _The Summer of the Swans,_ 1972, for _The House of Wings,_ 1973, for _The Winged Colt of Casa Mia_ and _The Eighteenth Emergency,_ 1974, for _After the Goat Man,_ 1975, for _The Lace Snail,_ 1976, for _The TV Kid,_ and 1980, for _The Night Swimmers;_ Notable Book selection, American Library Association, 1969, for _Trouble River,_ 1972, for _The House of Wings,_ 1974, for _After the Goat Man,_ 1977, for _The Pinballs,_ 1981, for _The Cybil War,_ 1982, and for _The 2,000-Pound Goldfish;_ Lewis Carroll Shelf Award, 1970, for _The Midnight Fox;_ Newbery Medal, 1971, for _The Summer of the Swans;_ National Book Award finalist, 1973, for _The House of Wings;_ Outstanding Book selection, _New York Times,_ 1973, for _The Winged Colt of Casa Mia_ and _The Eighteenth Emergency_ 1979, for _Good-bye Chicken Little,_ and 1982, for _The 2,000-Pound Goldfish;_ Dorothy Canfield Fisher Memorial Book Award, Vermont Congress of Parents and Teachers, 1975, for _The Eighteenth Emergency;_ Child Study Children Book Award, Child Study Children's Book Committee at Bank Street College of Education, 1977, Hans Christian Andersen Honor List selection for Promoting Concern for the Disadvantaged and Handicapped, and Georgia Children's Book Award, both 1979, Charlie May Simon Book Award, Arkansas Elementary School Council, Sur-

Betsy Byars (Reproduced by permission.)

rey School Book of the Year Award, Surrey School Librarians of Surrey, British Columbia, Mark Twain Award, Missouri Association of School Librarians, William Allen White Children's Book Award, Emporia State University, and Young Reader Medal, California Reading Association, all 1980, Nene Award runner up, 1981, 1983, and Golden Archer Award, Department of Library Science of the University of Wisconsin—Oshkosh, 1982, all for *The Pinballs; Boston Globe/Horn Book* fiction honor selection, and Best Book of the Year selection, *School Library Journal*, both 1980, and American Book Award for Children's Fiction (hardcover), 1981, all for *The Night Swimmers;* International Board on Books for Young People Award, 1982, for *The 2,000 Goldfish* (in translation); Children's Choice selection, International Reading Association, 1982, Tennessee Children's Choice Book Award, Tennessee Library Association, 1983, and Sequoyah Children's Book Award, 1984, all for *The Cybil War;* Parents' Choice Award for literature, Parents' Choice Foundation, 1982, and Mark Twain Award, 1985, both for *The Animal, the Vegetable, and John D. Jones;* Parents' Choice Award for literature, 1985, South Carolina Children's Book Award, 1987, and William Allen White Children's Book Award, and Maryland Children's Book Award, both 1988, all for *Cracker Jackson;* Parents' Choice Award

for literature, 1986, for *The Not-Just-Anybody Family;* Regina Medal, Catholic Library Association, 1987; Charlie May Simon Award, 1987, for *The Computer Nut;* Edgar Allan Poe Award, Mystery Writers of America, 1992, for *Wanted . . . Mud Blossom;* Texas Bluebonnet Award, and Sunshine State Young Readers Award, both 1998, both for *Tornado;* Nevada Young Readers Award, 1998, for *Tarot Says Beware;* Book of the Year selection, Bank Street College of Education, 2004, for *The SOS File,* 2006, for *Boo's Dinosaur;* (with Betsy Duffey and Laurie Myers) Choice selection, Cooperative Children's Book Center, and Book of the Year selection, Bank Street College of Education, both 2007, both for *Dog Diaries.*

Writings

JUVENILE FICTION

Clementine, illustrated by Charles Wilton, Houghton (Boston, MA), 1962.

The Dancing Camel, illustrated by Harold Berson, Viking (New York, NY), 1965.

Rama, the Gypsy Cat, illustrated by Peggy Bacon, Viking (New York, NY), 1966.

(And illustrator) *The Groober,* Harper (New York, NY), 1967.

The Midnight Fox, illustrated by Ann Grifalconi, Viking (New York, NY), 1968.

Trouble River, illustrated by Rocco Negri, Viking (New York, NY), 1969.

The Summer of the Swans, illustrated by Ted CoConis, Viking (New York, NY), 1970, reprinted, Puffin (New York, NY), 2004.

Go and Hush the Baby, illustrated by Emily A. McCully, Viking (New York, NY), 1971.

The House of Wings, illustrated by Daniel Schwartz, Viking (New York, NY), 1972.

The Eighteenth Emergency, illustrated by Robert Grossman, Viking (New York, NY), 1973.

The Winged Colt of Casa Mia, illustrated by Richard Cuffari, Viking, 1973.

After the Goat Man, illustrated by Ronald Himler, Viking (New York, NY), 1974.

(And illustrator) *The Lace Snail,* Viking (New York, NY), 1975.

The TV Kid, illustrated by Richard Cuffari, Viking (New York, NY), 1976.

The Pinballs, Harper (New York, NY), 1977.

The Cartoonist, illustrated by Richard Cuffari, Viking (New York, NY), 1978.

Good-bye Chicken Little, Harper (New York, NY), 1979.

The Night Swimmers, illustrated by Troy Howell, Delacorte (New York, NY), 1980.

The Cybil War, illustrated by Gail Owens, Viking (New York, NY), 1981.

The Animal, the Vegetable, and John D. Jones, illustrated by Ruth Sanderson, Delacorte (New York, NY), 1982.

The 2,000-Pound Goldfish, Harper (New York, NY), 1982.

The Glory Girl, Viking (New York, NY), 1983.

The Computer Nut, illustrated with computer graphics by son, Guy Byars, Viking (New York, NY), 1984.

Cracker Jackson, Viking (New York, NY), 1985.

The Golly Sisters Go West, illustrated by Sue Truesdell, Harper (New York, NY), 1986.

Beans on the Roof, illustrated by Melodye Rosales, Delacorte (New York, NY), 1988.

Hooray for the Golly Sisters, illustrated by Sue Truesdell, Harper (New York, NY), 1990.

Seven Treasure Hunts, Harper (New York, NY), 1991.

Coast to Coast, Delacorte (New York, NY), 1992.

McMummy, Viking (New York, NY), 1993.

The Golly Sisters Ride Again, illustrated by Sue Truesdell, HarperCollins (New York, NY), 1994.

(Compiler) *Growing up Stories,* illustrated by Robert Geary, Kingfisher (New York, NY), 1995, published as *Top Teen Stories,* Kingfisher (Boston, MA), 2004.

My Brother, Ant, illustrated by Marc Simont, Viking (New York, NY), 1996.

Tornado, HarperCollins (New York, NY), 1996.

The Joy Boys, illustrated by Frank Remkiewicz, Delacorte (New York, NY), 1996.

A Bean Birthday, Macmillan (New York, NY), 1996.

Ant Plays Bear, illustrated by Marc Simont, Viking (New York, NY), 1997.

Me Tarzan, illustrated by Bill Cigliano, HarperCollins (New York, NY), 2000.

(With daughters Betsy Duffey and Laurie Myers) *My Dog, My Hero,* Holt (New York, NY), 2000.

Little Horse, illustrated by David McPhail, Holt (New York, NY), 2002.

Keeper of the Doves, Viking (New York, NY), 2002.

(With Betsy Duffey and Laurie Myers) *The SOS File,* illustrated by Arthur Howard, Henry Holt (New York, NY), 2004.

Little Horse on His Own, illustrated by David McPhail, Henry Holt (New York, NY), 2004.

Boo's Dinosaur, illustrated by Erik Brooks, Henry Holt (New York, NY), 2006.

(With Betsy Duffey and Laurie Myers) *Dog Diaries: Secret Writings of the WOOF Society,* illustrated by Erik Brooks, Holt (New York, NY), 2007.

Boo's Surprise, illustrated by Erik Brooks, Henry Holt (New York, NY), 2009.

(With Betsy Duffey and Laurie Myers) *Cat Diaries: Secret Writings of the MEOW Society,* illustrated by Erik Brooks, Holt (New York, NY), 2010.

Contributor to anthologies, including *Scary Stories to Read When It's Dark,* SeaStar Books, 2000. Byars' works have been translated into several languages.

"BLOSSOM FAMILY" SERIES

The Not-Just-Anybody Family, illustrated by Jacqueline Rogers, Delacorte (New York, NY), 1986, reprinted, Holiday House (New York, NY), 2008.

The Blossoms Meet the Vulture Lady, illustrated by Jacqueline Rogers, Delacorte (New York, NY), 1986, reprinted, Holiday House (New York, NY), 2008.

The Blossoms and the Green Phantom, illustrated by Jacqueline Rogers, Delacorte (New York, NY), 1987, reprinted, Holiday House (New York, NY), 2008.

A Blossom Promise, illustrated by Jacqueline Rogers, Delacorte (New York, NY), 1987, reprinted, Holiday House (New York, NY), 2008.

Wanted . . . Mud Blossom, Delacorte (New York, NY), 1991, reprinted, Holiday House (New York, NY), 2008.

"BINGO BROWN" SERIES

The Burning Questions of Bingo Brown, illustrated by Cathy Bobak, Viking (New York, NY), 1988.

Bingo Brown and the Language of Love, illustrated by Cathy Bobak, Viking (New York, NY), 1989.

Bingo Brown, Gypsy Lover, Viking (New York, NY), 1990.

Bingo Brown's Guide to Romance, Viking (New York, NY), 1992.

"HERCULEAH JONES" MYSTERY SERIES

The Dark Stairs, Viking (New York, NY), 1994.

Tarot Says Beware, Viking (New York, NY), 1995.

Dead Letter, Viking (New York, NY), 1996.

Death's Door, Viking (New York, NY), 1997.

Disappearing Acts, Viking (New York, NY), 1998.

King of Murder, Viking (New York, NY), 2006.

The Black Tower, Viking (New York, NY), 2006.

OTHER

The Moon and I (autobiography), J. Messner (New York, NY), 1991.

Author of afterword to *The Five Little Peppers and How They Grew* by Margaret Sidney, Dell (New York, NY), 1985; author of preface to *For Reading out Loud* by Margaret M. Kimmel, Dell (New York, NY), 1987. Contributor of articles to periodicals, including *Saturday Evening Post,* *TV Guide,* and *Look.*

Byars' manuscripts are housed at Clemson University, South Carolina.

Adaptations

The following were adapted as episodes of *ABC Afterschool Special,* ABC-TV: "Pssst! Hammerman's After You," adapted from *The Eighteenth Emergency,* 1973; "Sara's Summer of the Swans," adapted from *The Summer of the Swans,* 1974; "Trouble River," 1975; "The Winged Colt," adapted from *The Winged Colt of Casa Mia,* 1976; "The Pinballs," 1977; and "Daddy, I'm Their Mamma Now," adapted from *The Night Swimmers,* 1981. *The Lace Snail* was adapted as a filmstrip with cassette by Viking; numerous works have been adapted as audiobooks.

Sidelights

Betsy Byars is one of the most popular and versatile authors of contemporary realistic fiction for middle-school readers. Winner of the Newbery Medal, the

American Book Award, and the Edgar Allan Poe Award, among numerous other honors, Byars is consistently lauded for creating adventurous works that blend humor and sympathy to address the universal emotions of childhood. Concentrating on themes of maturation and relationships with family, peers, and animals, Byars frequently portrays the growth of respect and understanding between child and adult characters. "Writing about children under stress, she uses her wit to grapple unsentimentally with subjects ordinarily considered too painful for young readers," Elizabeth Segal commented in the *Dictionary of Literary Biography*. "Her energy and enjoyment of life, together with her belief in the sensitivity and resilience of ordinary children, endow her books with a fundamental hopefulness."

Byars came relatively late to her writing career. "In all of my school years . . . not one single teacher ever said to me, 'Perhaps you should consider becoming a writer,'" she told interviewer Elizabeth Segel in *Children's Literature in Education*. "Anyway, I didn't want to be a writer. Writing seemed boring. You sat in a room all day by yourself and typed. If I was going to be a writer at all, I was going to be a foreign correspondent like Claudette Colbert in *Arise My Love*. I would wear smashing hats, wisecrack with the guys, and have a byline known round the world."

The author married Edward Byars after graduating from college, in 1950. They had been married for five years and had two daughters when Ed decided that he needed a Ph.D. degree to continue in his career. The family packed up its belongings and moved to Illinois for the next two years. Byars soon discovered that the other wives living in her neighborhood either worked or were in school. "The highlight of my day was the arrival of the grocery truck after lunch," she later wrote in an essay for the *Something about the Author Autobiography Series* (SAAS). So she got herself a second-hand typewriter—"so old I had to press the keys down an inch to make a letter"—and began to write. "I thought it couldn't be as hard as people say it is. I thought probably the reason professional writers claim it's so hard is because they don't want any more competition."

Although she wrote "constantly" for the next two years, successful writing proved more difficult than she had anticipated. "My first sale was a short article to the *Saturday Evening Post* and I got seventy-five dollars for it. I was elated. I had known all along there was nothing to writing. Seven months passed before I sold a second article.

"I was learning what most other writers have learned before me—that writing is a profession in which there is an apprenticeship period, oftentimes a very long one. In that, writing is like baseball or piano playing. You have got to practice if you want to be successful."

Byars' early books, including *Clementine, The Dancing Camel, Rama, the Gypsy Cat,* and *The Groober,* received a somewhat cool reception from critics. Of her

next publication Byars remarked in *Something about the Author Autobiography Series:* "The first book that turned out the way I had envisioned it was *The Midnight Fox. . . .* I look on *The Midnight Fox* as another turning point of my career. It gave me a confidence I had not had before. I knew now that I was going to be able to do some of the things I wanted to do, some of the things I had not had the courage and skill to try. For this reason, and others, it remains my favorite of my books."

With *The Midnight Fox* and *Trouble River* Byars began utilizing humor and realistic details in her stories. *Trouble River* tells the story of Dewey Martin, a twelve year old who is left alone with his grandmother on the frontier during his mother's lying-in. Although Dewey and his dog successfully drive off a hostile Indian, the boy knows that the man will return so he takes his grandmother on his raft down Trouble River to safety. As Margaret F. O'Connell remarked in the *New York Times Book Review* remarked: "Byars has a talent for plot and dialogue that makes her low-keyed story a skillful portrayal of the growing respect between a

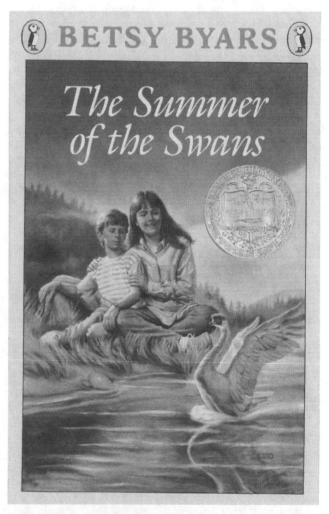

Cover of Byars' award-winning, middle-grade adventure **The Summer of the Swans,** *featuring artwork by Lino Saffioti.* (Illustration copyright © 1991 by Lino Saffioti. Used by permission of Viking Penguin, a division of Penguin Books USA, Inc.)

young boy and an old woman." In *The Midnight Fox* Tom is left to spend the summer at his Aunt Millie and Uncle Fred's farm while his parents take a bicycle tour of Europe. Tom is bored and lonely until he begins searching the woods and fields around the farm for the beautiful black fox that he has only glimpsed. When the fox steals one of Aunt Millie's turkeys, however, Uncle Fred decides to hunt it down, and Tom must defy his uncle in order to rescue the wild creature he has come to respect.

The Summer of the Swans grew out of Byars' experiences telling stories to a Brownie troop of mentally challenged children, augmented by some additional research. In this work, Sara, an unhappy adolescent, takes her mentally challenged younger brother to see six swans that have alighted on a lake near their home. Charlie is mesmerized by the birds and goes in search of them on his own late that night, quickly becoming lost. Sara's agonized search for her brother changes her perspective on many of the things that had been making her unhappy. In *Children's Literature in Education*, I.V. Hansen described Byars' protagonist in *The Summer of the Swans* as "a character rich in teenage humour and genuine compassion."

Byars was awarded the Newbery Medal in 1971 for *The Summer of the Swans,* an experience, she wrote in *SAAS,* that "literally changed my life overnight. Up until this time I had had a few letters from kids. Now we had to get a bigger mailbox. I got tapes, questionnaires, invitations to speak, invitations to visit schools, requests for interviews. For the first time in my life, I started feeling like an author."

In Byars' young-adult novel *The House of Wings* Sammy is left with his grandfather, a virtual stranger, in a rundown cabin in Ohio, while his parents travel on to Detroit to try to find work there. Sammy's anger at being abandoned sends him running off into the woods followed closely by his grandfather, but the chase is brought to an abrupt end when the two discover an injured whooping crane. A relationship develops as they work together to nurse the bird back to health. In *The Eighteenth Emergency,* "Mouse" Fawley must face one of the many emergencies for which he and his friend Ezzie have prepared: the wrath of the school bully, Marv Hammerman. Mouse successfully avoids Marv until, influenced by studying medieval chivalry in his English class, he decides to do the honorable thing and face the consequences of insulting the other boy. Hansen called *The Eighteenth Emergency* "a wry, sometimes uproariously humorous story . . . in which the medieval vision Mouse has slips easily into its fabric."

In *After the Goat Man* an elderly man returns to the cabin home he was forced to give up when the state decided to build a highway on his land. Three children—the cool Ada; Harold, who is overweight and rueful; and Figgy, the old man's grandson, whose fears are overwhelming without his magic rabbit foot—come to

the old man's rescue and learn something about themselves in the process. As Alice Bach wrote in her *New York Times Book Review* of *After the Goat Man:* "Never losing control of her material (and God knows a fat kid, an uprooted old man and a puny boy scared silly could be prime candidates for a pile of damp Kleenex in the hands of a lesser writer), Byars remains a dispassionate craftsman, weaving a sturdy homespun tale with the simple words of plain people."

The Pinballs remains one of Byars' most highly acclaimed works. The "pinballs" of the title are three children who have been abandoned or abused and have come to live one summer with the same foster parents. Together they help each other come to feel that they are not merely pinballs but have some control over their lives. As Ethel L. Heins remarked in *Horn Book,* "The stark facts about three ill-matched, abused children living in a foster home could have made an almost unbearably bitter novel; but the economically told story, liberally spiced with humor, is something of a tour de force." Writing in *School Library Journal,* Helene H. Levene called *The Pinballs* "engrossing."

With *Good-bye Chicken Little* Byars once again explores a serious topic by focusing on individuality, a theme that runs through several of her fictional works. When Jimmie "Chicken" Little's Uncle Pete takes a dare to walk across a frozen river and falls through and drowns, Jimmie worries that he did not try hard enough to save him. When Jimmie's mother plans a festive Christmas party a few days later, the boy is offended until he realizes that she knows better than he how to honor her unique brother. Byars focuses on parental irresponsibility in *The Night Swimmers,* a story about three children who are left alone every evening while their father pursues his dream: a career singing country music. They often swim secretly in a nearby private swimming pool, but when the youngest child is nearly drowned, the eldest child is finally relieved of responsibility for their welfare. Elaine Moss concluded in the *Times Literary Supplement* that "in *The Night Swimmers* [Byars] has written a short novel that makes the reader hold his breath, cry and laugh; not for one moment are the emotions disengaged."

In *The 2,000-Pound Goldfish* a boy creates imaginary horror films to distract himself from the insecurity and lack of love in his own life. George A. Woods remarked in the *New York Times Book Review* that the book shows "an exceptionally skillful blending of fantasy and reality." Byars depicts another outcast in *The Glory Girl,* which centers on Anna, the only nonmusical member of a family of gospel singers. In the story, Anna is befriended by her uncle Newt, an ex-convict. In *The Computer Nut,* Byars joined forces with her son, Guy Byars, who provides the computer graphics that illustrate his mother's story of a girl who gets a message from a space alien via her home computer.

With *Cracker Jackson* Byars takes on the serious subject of spousal abuse with what critics noted is a char-

Byars crafts a story for younger readers in **My Brother, Ant,** *a chapter book featuring artwork by Marc Simont.*

acteristic blend of realism and humor. The title character, eleven-year-old Jackson, is called Cracker only by Alma, his former babysitter. Alma now has a husband and small child, and now the boy begins to suspect that her husband, Billy Ray, is beating her. Jackson now enlists his friend Goat in a desperate rescue attempt that Lillian Gerhardt characterized in *School Library Journal* as leading to "some of the most harrowing but hilarious moments in the book." Byars reintroduces Jackson and Goat in *The Seven Treasure Hunts,* a humorous tale that critics called lighthearted for its episodic plot and adventurous action. Audrey Laski, writing in the *Times Educational Supplement,* remarked of Byars that "nobody writing in America for this age range is as good."

With *The Not-Just-Anybody Family* and its sequels Byars again addresses the importance of individuality. In *The Not-Just-Anybody Family* the reader is introduced to the poor and eccentric Blossom clan, whose members always seem to be getting into trouble. Katherine Duncan-Jones, writing in the *Times Literary Supplement,* dubbed it "a tough, entertaining American urban romance, in the best tradition of stories about

children carrying more than adult responsibilities and almost magically winning the day." Like several other reviewers, Susan Kenney commented in the *New York Times Book Review* that some of the events depicted in *The Not-Just-Anybody Family* might seem frightening to younger readers. "Tragicomedy would be a truer description of what goes on here," Kenney wrote, then concluded: "Funny-ha-ha maybe not; well worth reading, certainly yes."

In the second volume of "Blossom Family" series, *The Blossoms Meet the Vulture Lady,* Junior gets caught in his own coyote trap and is rescued by the dreaded Mad Mary, a homeless woman who lives in a cave and eats road kill. "This is a lively, likable family, handled lightly but surely by an author known for her ability to write believable dialogue and present the desires of her characters with humor and understanding," wrote Sara Miller in *School Library Journal.* In *The Blossoms and the Green Phantom* Junior Blossom is depressed by his failure to interest anyone in the flying saucer he has made. His mother takes time out from searching for her father, Pap, who has disappeared, to rally the family around the boy. In a review in *School Library Journal,* Dudley B. Carlson called *The Blossoms Meet the Vulture Lady* "a story about love in its many forms. Like Byars' best, it is rock-solid and full of chuckles, and it lingers in the mind."

In the fourth book about the Blossoms, *A Blossom Promise,* the family is struck by disaster on several fronts, culminating in a mild heart attack suffered by Pap. Billed as the last in the series, the book elicited much praise from critics, who commented that fans of the series will miss the Blossom family. As Kristiana Gregory wrote in the *Los Angeles Times Book Review,* "This is the final, bittersweet volume in the Blossom Family Quartet, bittersweet only because the cast is so memorably quirky that you hate to say goodbye."

To appease "Blossom Family" fans, Byars published *Wanted . . . Mud Blossom* as a fifth installment in the series. The story takes place one weekend when the family is plagued by the disappearance of Mad Mary, now a family friend, as well as the loss of the hamster entrusted to Junior by his class. In the latter case, the family dog, Mud, is suspected, and many critics praised the children's mock trial of Mud Blossom.

In *The Golly Sisters Go West* and *Hooray for the Golly Sisters* Byars introduces two women whose ignorance and exuberance lead them into and out of all sorts of adventures as they sing and dance their way westward across North America during the mid-1800s. Set up as collections of stories for young readers, the books garnered praise for their humor and accessibility. A reviewer for the *Bulletin of the Center for Children's Books* remarked that Byars makes a virtue of the simple vocabulary of books for beginning readers, "spoofing the choppy style with dialogue in which the childlike sisters echo each other." Also for young readers is *Beans*

on the Roof, which introduces each of its characters through the poem he or she composes while sitting on the roof of the house. According to a *Publishers Weekly* critic, "In the simplest language and a natural, unadorned style, Byars has created an easy-to-read chapter book that is humorous and realistic."

Beginning in the late 1980s, Byars wrote a series of books centering on the lovesick adventures of a preteen named Bingo Brown. In the first installment, *The Burning Questions of Bingo Brown,* Bingo learns that even though his love for Melissa is returned, not everyone is so lucky, as his teacher, the suicidal Mr. Markham, proves. A reviewer for the *Bulletin of the Center for Children's Books* concluded: "This is a story that children are going to get a lot out of and love, while adults appreciate both craft and content." In *Bingo Brown and the Language of Love* Melissa has moved away, inspiring many costly long-distance phone calls between the two. Byars' universally loved protagonist must also contend with the odd behavior of his parents and the attentions of a physically well-developed classmate. Fannie Flagg reviewed *Bingo Brown and the Language of*

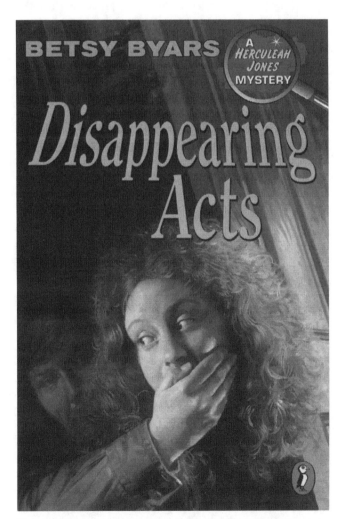

Byars' "Herculeah Jones" mystery novels include **Disappearing Acts,** *featuring artwork by Robert Sabin.* (Copyright © 2000 by Robert Sabin. Used by permission of Puffin Books, a division of Penguin Young Readers Group, a member of Penguin Group (USA) Inc. All rights reserved.)

Love for the *New York Times Book Review,* writing that, "if there is such a thing as a typical American kid, Bingo Brown is it. He is funny and bright and lovable without being precocious, and Betsy Byars has demonstrated a special creative genius in pulling off this delicate balancing act."

The adventures of Bingo continue in *Bingo Brown, Gypsy Lover,* in which Melissa tells Bingo that he resembles the hero in the romantic novel she is reading. As Christine Behrmann wrote in *School Library Journal,* "Bingo continues to grow . . . in each book, and here he progresses from slightly cocky self-preoccupation to vulnerable concern for others." This volume was followed by *Bingo Brown's Guide to Romance,* in which Bingo records his misadventures with Melissa, who is back in town, in the hope that his baby brother will be spared similar travails of his troubles when the time comes for him to fall in love. A reviewer for the *Bulletin of the Center for Children's Books* concluded: "More episodic than cohesive, this is nevertheless keen-eyed and better-written than most series titles."

Byars turns her attention to the mystery genre with her "Herculeah Jones" series for middle-grade readers. Herculeah is a teenage sleuth whose parents also investigate crimes. In *The Dark Stairs* the first volume in the series, the plucky heroine and her loyal sidekick, Meat, unravel the strange goings-on at a decaying mansion. Here Byars "offers genre fans genuine suspense as well as some laugh-out-loud comedy," wrote *Booklist* critic Stephanie Zvirin. In *Tarot Says Beware* Herculeah and Meat look into the murder of a fortune teller, and according to *School Library Journal* contributor Patricia A. Dollisch, "the story is well plotted and the characters are nicely rounded." A famous mystery writer becomes the prime suspect in a series of gruesome murders in *King of Murder,* the sixth "Herculeah Jones" novel. "With its twisty conclusion and short, exciting chapters," Tina Zubak remarked in *School Library Journal,* "this story will grab even reluctant readers." *The Black Tower,* a suspenseful series installment about a disturbing family secret, "delivers breathless adventure moderated by amiable comedy," Zvirin commented.

Byars is also the author of *Coast to Coast,* in which Birch convinces her grieving grandfather to take one last trip in his antique airplane before he sells it, the girl's hope being that the flight will raise the man's spirits in the wake of his wife's death. "The details about flying will draw readers in, as will the loving story of friendship over the generations," wrote Judy Fink in *Voice of Youth Advocates.* A reviewer for the *Bulletin of the Center for Children's Books* concluded of *Coast to Coast:* "It's an episodic trip, but one worth taking."

Illustrated by Marc Simont, *My Brother, Ant* and *Ant Plays Bear* are books for early readers. Although young Anthony, known as Ant, finds innumerable ways to an-

noy his big brother—scribbling on a homework assignment and imagining "monsters" that live under the bed—the older sibling, who narrates the episodes, never loses his patience. The four stories about the pair contained in *My Brother, Ant* "are full of homespun warmth and easy-going humor," commented a *Publishers Weekly* contributor. "A great story teller and a great illustrator are at their very best in this tender, funny, easy-to-read chapter book," *Booklist* reviewer Hazel Rochman declared about in discussing the same title.

Byars teams up with her daughters, Betsy Duffey and Laurie Myers, to write several short-story collections with a canine focus. *My Dog, My Hero* offers eight tales designed as entries in the "My Hero" essay contest, in which contestants are asked to explain their canines' most outstanding attributes. "Drama, humor, excitement, and love fuel these short, well-written stories," Ellen Mandel noted in *Booklist*. In *The SOS File,* the students in Mr. Magro's class can earn extra credit by describing their responses to distressing situations. "Some tales are poignant, others are humorous," Maria B. Salvadore commented in *School Library Journal,* and Shelle Rosenfeld noted in *Booklist* that the students' essays "will inspire thought and discussion about the different kinds of crises that may touch our lives."

In *Dog Diaries: Secret Writings of the WOOF Society* Byars and her daughters present readers with a most unusual club: a gathering of story-loving canines who share tales of notable dogs from around the globe. Known as the WOOF (Words of Our Friends) Society, the group meets in an abandoned building where the members regale one another with an eclectic array of stories, including the tale of Abu, a royal dog of ancient Egypt, and Tidbit, a star of the Grand Old Opry. "Some of the stories are touching while others are humorous," a contributor noted in *Kirkus Reviews,* and *School Library Journal* critic Terrie Dorio predicted that "readers will enjoy seeing the world from a canine's perspective." A companion volume, *Cat Diaries: Secret Writings of the MEOW Society,* contains tales from the WOOF Society's feline counterpart, the MEOW (Memories Expressed in Our Writing) Society. "The book has a few standout tales," wrote *School Library Journal* reviewer Beth Cuddy, citing as one example the adventures of Go Go, a cat whose school visit turns chaotic.

Little Horse and *Little Horse on His Own,* also for beginning readers, are fantasies about a tiny horse no bigger than a kitten. In the first title, the pint-sized creature is terrified when it loses its mother and has to fend for himself in a strange world that is full of hazards, including streams, birds, and a dog. Luckily for Little Horse, a boy comes along to take care of it. "Young horse lovers will delight in the idea of a real horse they could hold in their hands and will enjoy the small creature's adventures," Louise L. Sherman wrote in *School Library Journal,* speaking about the former title. In *Little Horse on His Own,* the tiny creature sets out to

find his family, even though the world is still a very dangerous place for someone so small. "Byars masterfully conveys Little Horse's naive perspective," Marilyn Taniguchi explained in *School Library Journal.* "The prose is clear and uncluttered, and the action moves crisply." The "brief, action-packed chapters will please horse fanciers ready to advance beyond traditional easy readers," Jennifer Mattson wrote in her *Booklist* review of *Little Horse on His Own.*

The middle-grade novel *Keeper of the Doves,* set during the 1890s, is told from the point of view of the youngest child in a family of five daughters. Amen McBee ("Amie' for short) is a born poet who writes her first work at the age of six. In addition to her four older sisters—Abigal, Augusta, and twins Annabella and Arabella—and her parents, the McBee household also includes Mr. Tominski, a reclusive man whom their father allows to live in the chapel on the family's estate; and Aunt Pauline and Grandmama, who help care for the girls while their fragile mother copes with her latest pregnancy. Byars's story of the joys and tragedies that come to this family over several years was widely praised by critics. Byars writes "in a prose that ripples

Cover of Byars' middle-grade historical novel **Keeper of the Doves,** *featuring artwork by Kamil Vojnar.* (Copyright © 2002 by Kamil Vojnar. Used by permission of Viking Children's Books, a division of Penguin Young Readers Group, a member of Penguin Group (USA) Inc. All rights reserved.)

with clarity and sweetness and an underlying evolution of spirit," declared a *Kirkus Reviews* contributor, and a *Publishers Weekly* critic concluded that "the snippets of Amie's and her family's lives add up to an exquisitely complete picture."

An imaginative young girl is the focus of *Boo's Dinosaur,* an early chapter book by Byars. Unable to convince her older brother, Sammy, to play with her, Boo creates an imaginary friend—a lovable and energetic dinosaur—to keep her company. Although Sammy grows a bit perturbed by his sibling's antics, he shows his true colors when a terribly disappointed Boo must say goodbye to her new companion. Byars' concise text allows youngsters "to see themselves both in Boo's plays for attention and Sammy's desire for some peace and quiet," Adrienne Furness observed in *School Library Journal.* A critic in *Kirkus Reviews* also praised the work, calling *Boo's Dinosaur* a "reassuring tale of sibling love for new readers." In a sequel, *Boo's Surprise,* the exuberant girl makes the acquaintance of a baby dinosaur after she finds an enormous egg hatching in her backyard. "The successful balance between fantasy and realism creates a satisfying chapter-book selection," a contributor remarked in *Kirkus Reviews* in discussing the further adventures of Byars' likeable sibling characters.

In her highly acclaimed autobiography *The Moon and I* Byars traces her development as a writer, starting with her childhood encounter with the huge black snake that she nicknamed Moon. A *Publishers Weekly* critic called the writer's memoir "an appealingly idiosyncratic narrative that seamlessly weaves together the Newbery winner's life and art," while Phyllis Graves, writing in *School Library Journal,* deemed *The Moon and I* as "very special nonfiction that truly entertains as it informs."

Byars is often commended as a thoughtful and original writer who creates fresh, convincing characterizations, skillful portrayals of human interaction, vibrant images, and deceptively simple prose. While occasional critics have found her conclusions contrived, Byars remains well regarded as a compassionate explorer of the social and moral issues confronting her audience. Jennifer FitzGerald described her in *School Library Journal* as "preeminent among authors" due to her ability to "combine unstinted awareness with a remarkable rollicking sense of humor, dispelling despair and self-pity without ignoring pain."

"I used to think, when I first started writing, that writers were like wells," Byars wrote in her *SAAS* essay, "and sooner or later we'd use up what had happened to us and our children and our friends and our dogs and cats, and there wouldn't be anything left. We'd go dry and have to quit. I imagine we would if it weren't for that elusive quality—creativity. I can't define it, but I have found from experience that the more you use it, the better it works."

Biographical and Critical Sources

BOOKS

Beacham's Guide to Literature for Young Adults, Volume 3, Beacham Publishing (Osprey, FL), 1990.

Byars, Betsy, *The Moon and I,* J. Messner (New York, NY), 1991.

Byars, Betsy, autobiographical essay in *Something about the Author,* Volume 108, Gale (Detroit, MI), 2000.

Carpenter, Humphrey, and Mari Prichard, *The Oxford Companion to Children's Literature,* Oxford University Press (Oxford, England), 1984.

Children's Literature Review, Gale (Detroit, MI), Volume 1, 1976, Volume 16, 1989.

Contemporary Literary Criticism, Volume 35, Gale (Detroit, MI), 1985.

Dictionary of Literary Biography, Volume 52: *American Writers for Children since 1960: Fiction,* Gale (Detroit, MI), 1986.

Drew, Bernard A., *The One Hundred Most Popular Young Adult Authors,* Libraries Unlimited (Englewood, CO), 1996.

Hopkins, Lee Bennett, *More Books by More People,* Citation Press (New York, NY), 1974.

Kingman, Lee, editor, *Newbery and Caldecott Medal Books, 1966-1975,* Horn Book (Boston, MA), 1975.

St. James Guide to Young-Adult Writers, 2nd edition, St. James Press (Detroit, MI), 1999.

Silvey, Anita, editor, *Children's Books and Their Creators,* Houghton Mifflin (Boston, MA), 1995.

Twentieth-Century Children's Writers, St. Martin's Press (New York, NY), 1978, pp. 215-217.

Usrey, Malcolm, *Betsy Byars,* Twayne (New York, NY), 1995.

Ward, Martha E., and others, *Authors of Books for Young People,* 3rd edition, Scarecrow Press (Metuchen, NJ), 1990.

PERIODICALS

Book September, 2000, Kathleen Odean, review of *Me Tarzan,* p. 86.

Booklist, January 15, 1993, Ilene Cooper, interview with Byars, pp. 906-907; August, 1994, Stephanie Zvirin, review of *The Dark Stairs,* p. 2042; July, 1995, Stephanie Zvirin, review of *Tarot Says Beware,* p. 1878; January 1, 1996, Hazel Rochman, review of *My Brother, Ant* p. 828; June 1, 1996, Ilene Cooper, review of *Dead Letter,* p. 1716; September 15, 1996, Carolyn Phelan, review of *Tornado,* p. 238, and Kristi Beavin, review of *The Dark Stairs,* p. 264; March 1, 1997, Stephanie Zvirin, review of *Death's Door,* p. 1162; September 1, 1997, Hazel Rochman, review of *Ant Plays Bear,* p. 116; February 15, 1998, Barbara Baskin, review of *The Golly Sisters Ride Again,* p. 1027; March 1, 1998, Stephanie Zvirin, review of *Disappearing Acts,* p. 1134; March 1, 2000, Debra McLeod, review of *The Summer of the Swans,* p. 1255; January 1, 2001, Ellen Mandel, review of *My Dog, My Hero,* p. 954; March 15, 2002, Gillian Engberg,

review of *Little Horse,* p. 1255; October 1, 2002, Ilene Cooper, review of *Keeper of the Doves,* p. 322; June 1, 2004, Shelle Rosenfeld, review of *The SOS File,* p. 1725; July, 2004, Anna Rich, review of *Keeper of the Doves,* p. 1857; September 1, 2004, Jennifer Mattson, review of *Little Horse on His Own,* p. 120; October 15, 2006, Stephanie Zvirin, review of *The Black Tower,* p. 44; August, 2007, Suzanne Harold, review of *Dog Diaries: Secret Writings of the WOOF Society,* p. 73; September 15, 2009, Hazel Rochman, review of *Boo's Surprise,* p. 60.

Bulletin of the Center for Children's Books, July-August, 1981, Zena Sutherland, review of *The Cybil War,* p. 209; June, 1982, Zena Sutherland, review of *The Animal, the Vegetable, and John D. Jones,* pp. 183-184; January, 1985, review of *The Computer Nut,* p. 81; March, 1986, review of *The Not-Just-Anybody Family,* p. 123; October, 1986, review of *The Blossoms Meet the Vulture Lady,* pp. 22-23; November, 1986, review of *The Golly Sisters Go West,* p. 44; April, 1987, review of *The Blossoms and the Green Phantom,* p. 143; November, 1987, review of *A Blossom Promise,* p. 44; April, 1988, review of *The Burning Questions of Bingo Brown,* pp. 151-152; November, 1988, review of *Beans on the Roof,* pp. 66-67; June, 1989, review of *Bingo Brown and the Language of Love,* p. 244; June, 1990, review of *Bingo Brown, Gypsy Lover,* p. 234; October, 1990, review of *Hooray for the Golly Sisters,* p. 23; April, 1991, review of *The Seven Treasure Hunts,* pp. 185-186; March, 1992, review of *The Moon and I,* p. 77; June, 1992, review of *Bingo Brown's Guide to Romance,* p. 256; December, 1992, review of *Coast to Coast,* p. 107; June, 1994, review of *The Golly Sisters Ride Again,* p. 314.

Children's Literature in Education, winter, 1982, Elizabeth Segel, interview with Byars; spring, 1984, I.V. Hansen, "A Decade of Betsy Byars' Boys," pp. 3-11.

Horn Book, August, 1971, Betsy Byars, "Newberry Award Acceptance Speech"; February, 1971, Ethel L. Heins, review of *The Summer of the Swans,* pp. 53-54; August, 1977, Ethel L. Heins, review of *The Pinballs,* p. 437; September-October, 1986, Ann A. Flowers, review of *The Not-Just-Anybody Family,* p. 588; July-August, 1990, Nancy Vasilakis, review of *Bingo Brown, Gypsy Lover,* p. 453; January-February, 1991, Carolyn K. Jenks, review of *Horray for the Golly Sisters!,* p. 63; November-December, 1994, Elizabeth S. Watson, review of *Tarot Says Beware,* p. 730; July-August, 1996, Hanna B. Zeiger, review of *My Brother, Ant,* pp. 459-460; November-December, 1996, Maeve Visser Knoth, review of *Tornado,* p. 732; July-August, 1997, Martha A. Parravano, review of *Ant Plays Bear,* pp. 450-452; May-June, 1998, Elizabeth S. Watson, review of *Disappearing Acts,* p. 341; May-June, 2000, review of *Me Tarzan,* p. 309; May-June, 2002, Betty Carter, review of *Little Horse,* p. 325; September-October, 2002, Joanna Rudge, review of *Keeper of the Doves,* p. 567.

Kirkus Reviews, March 15, 2002, review of *Little Horse,* p. 407; July 15, 2002, review of *Keeper of the Doves,* p. 1028; May 1, 2004, review of *The SOS File,* p. 439; August 15, 2004, review of *Little Horse on His Own,* p. 803; September 15, 2006, review of *Boo's*

Dinosaur, p. 948; May 1, 2007, review of *Dog Diaries;* June 15, 2009, review of *Boo's Surprise.*

Los Angeles Times Book Review, January 31, 1988, Kristiana Gregory, "The Blossom Quartet Ends," p. 7.

New York Times Book Review, September 14, 1969, Margaret F. O'Connell, review of *Trouble River,* p. 30; February 28, 1971, Josh Greenfield, review of *The Summer of the Swans,* p. 22; October 13, 1974, review of *The Eighteenth Emergency,* p. 54; December 15, 1974, Alice Bach, review of *After the Goat Man,* p. 8; November 30, 1982, George A. Woods, review of *The 2,000-Pound Goldfish,* August 4, 1985, Mary Louise Cuneo, review of *Cracker Jackson,* p. 2; June 15, 1986, Susan Kenney, review of *The Not-Just-Anybody Family,* p. 38; April 2, 1989, review of *The Burning Questions of Bingo Brown,* p. 26; October 8, 1989, Fannie Flagg, review of *Bingo Brown and the Language of Love,* p. 34; December 15, 1991, Elizabeth Ann-Sachs, review of *Wanted . . . Mud Blossom,* p. 29.

Publishers Weekly, May 24, 1985, review of *The Glory Girl,* p. 70; June 14, 1985, review of *Cracker Jackson,* p. 72; September 25, 1987, review of *A Blossom Promise,* p. 111; April 8, 1988, review of *The Burning Question of Bingo Brown,* p. 95; September 30, 1988, review of *Beans on the Roof,* p. 69; May 12, 1989, review of *Bingo Brown and the Language of Love,* p. 294; May 11, 1990, review of *Bingo Brown, Gypsy Lover,* p. 260; January 25, 1991, review of *Bingo Brown and the Language of Love,* p. 59; April 12, 1991, review of *The Seven Treasure Hunts,* p. 58; July 19, 1991, review of *Wanted . . . Mud Blossom,* p. 56; April 20, 1992, review of *The Moon and I,* p. 58; May 18, 1992, review of *Bingo Brown's Guide to Romance,* p. 71; October 12, 1992, review of *Coast to Coast,* pp. 79-80; August 16, 1993, review of *McMummy,* p. 105; July 18, 1994, review of *The Dark Stairs,* p. 246; January 15, 1996, review of *My Brother, Ant,* p. 462; May 22, 2000, review of *Me Tarzan,* p. 93; October 16, 2000, "Putting on the Dog," p. 78; August 19, 2002, review of *Keeper of the Doves,* p. 90; May 17, 2004, review of *The SOS File,* p. 50.

School Librarian, March, 1986, Betsy Byars, "Spinning Straw into Gold," pp. 6-13.

School Library Journal, May, 1985, Lillian Gerhardt, review of *Cracker Jackson,* p. 87; May, 1986, Connie C. Rockman, review of *The Not-Just-Anybody Family,* pp. 88-89; September, 1986, Jennifer FitzGerald, "Challenge the Pressure to Conform: Byars and Kerr," pp. 46-47; November, 1986, Sara Miller, review of *The Blossoms Meet the Vulture Lady,* p. 86; December, 1986, Nancy Palmer, review of *The Golly Sisters Go West,* p. 122; May, 1987, Dudley B. Carlson, review of *The Blossoms and the Green Phantom,* p. 96; November, 1987, Amy Kellman, review of *A Blossom Promise,* pp. 103-104; May, 1988, Ellen Fader, review of *The Burning Question of Bingo Brown,* pp. 95-96; November, 1988, Trev Jones, review of *Beans on the Roof,* p. 84; July, 1989, Martha Rosen, review of *Bingo Brown and the Language of Love,* pp. 81-82; November, 1989, Helene H. Levene, review of *The Pinballs,* pp. 70-71; January, 1990, review of *The 2,000-Pound*

Goldfish, p. 56; June, 1990, Christine Behrmann, review of *Bingo Brown, Gypsy Lover,* p. 117; September, 1990, Sharon McElmeel, review of *Hooray for the Golly Sisters!,* p. 194; June, 1991, Martha Rosen, review of *The Seven Treasure Hunts,* p. 74; July, 1991, review of *Wanted: Mud Blossom,* p. 72; April, 1992, Phyllis Graves, review of *The Moon and I,* p. 130; September, 1994, Ellen Fader, review of *The Dark Stairs,* p. 214; August, 1995, Patricia A. Dollisch, review of *Tarot Says Beware,* p. 139; July, 2000, Janet Gillen, review of *Me Tarzan,* p. 68; April, 2002, Louise L. Sherman, review of *Little Horse,* p. 101; October, 2002, Caroline Ward, review of *Keeper of the Doves,* p. 158; November, 2003, Carol Fazioli, review of *The Moon and I,* p. 81; June, 2004, MaryAnn Karre, review of *Keeper of the Doves,* p. 73, Maria B. Salvatore, review of *The SOS Files,* p. 103; September, 2004, Marilyn Taniguchi, review of *Little Horse on His Own,* p. 154; June, 2006, Tina Zubak, review of *King of Murder,* p. 148; September, 2006, Adrienne Furness, review of *Boo's Dinosaur,* p. 160; December, 2006, Krista Tokarz, review of *The Black Tower,* p. 134; June, 2007, Terrie Dorio, review of *Dog Diaries,* p. 92; April, 2010, Beth Cuddy, review of *Cat Diaries: Secret Writings of the MEOW Society,* p. 121.

Signal, January, 1982, Nancy Chambers, "Writing for Children," pp. 3-10.

Times Educational Supplement, January 30, 1987, Audrey Laski, "Paper Tapestry."

Times Literary Supplement, July 18, 1980, Elaine Moss, "Dreams of a Surrogate Mother," review of *The Night Swimmers,* p. 806; June 20, 1986, Katherine Duncan-Jones, "Down at Ditch Level," p. 691.

Voice of Youth Advocates, August-October, 1986, review of *The Not-Just-Anybody Family,* p. 140; December, 1986, review of *The Blossoms Meet the Vulture Lady,* p. 213; April, 1987, review of *The Blossoms and the Green Phantom,* p. 29; December, 1987, review of *A Blossom Promise,* p. 46; August, 1991, review of *Wanted . . . Mud Blossom,* p. 168; December, 1992, Judy Fink, review of *Coast to Coast,* p. 301.

Washington Post Book World, May 14, 1978, Paula Fox, "A Room of His Own," pp. 1, 4.

ONLINE

Betsy Byars Home Page, http://www.betsybyars.com (December 20, 2010).

Random House Web site, http://www.randomhouse.com/ (December 20, 2010) "Betsy Byars."

OTHER

A Talk with Betsy Byars (DVD) Good Conversations (Scarborough, NY), 1995.*

C

CARMAN, Bill
See CARMAN, William

* * *

CARMAN, William
(Bill Carman)

Personal

Born in Seoul, Korea; married. *Education:* Attended De Anza College; Brigham Young University, B.F.A. (visual communications/illustration), M.F.A. (painting). *Hobbies and other interests:* Reading, hiking, fishing, walking his two pugs, mini-wiener dog, and large python.

Addresses

Home—Boise, ID. *Office*—Department of Art, Boise State University, 1910 University Dr., Boise, ID 83725. *E-mail*—bcarman@boisestate.edu.

Career

Educator, illustrator, and author. Ford Aerospace, Palo Alto, CA, designer/illustrator, 1981-83; freelance illustrator, beginning 1983; Louis Saekow Design, Mountain View, CA, designer/illustrator, 1983-84; Quantum Advertising, Orem, UT, art director, 1984-85; Brigham Young University, Provo, UT, 1986-91; LucasArts Entertainment, San Rafael, CA, design and illustration consultant, 1991; Avid Publications, Cupertino, CA, design and illustration consultant, 1991-92. Brigham Young University, Provo, member of adjunct faculty, 1990-91; Cardinal Stritch University, Milwaukee, WI, assistant professor, 1992-98, and chair of art department, 1995-98; Boise State University, Boise, ID, assistant professor, 1998-2001, associate professor, 2001-06, currently professor of illustration. *Exhibitions:* Work included in numerous juried exhibitions, beginning 1988, and at University of Texas El Paso Gallery of Art; Do-

lores Chase Fine Arts, Salt Lake City, UT; Springville Museum of Art, Springville, UT; Kohler-Clark Gallery, Milwaukee, WI; Abbey Lane Gallery, Creede, CO; Edgewood Orchard Gallery, Fish Creek, WI; Leftbank Gallery, Salt Lake City; Basement Gallery, Boise, ID; Clackamas College, Portland, OR; University of Idaho, Moscow; Society of Illustrators exhibitions, New York, NY; Portland Community College, Portland; and Favorite Things Gallery, Alhambra, CA.

Awards, Honors

Award in publication illustration category, Case Council for Advancement and Support of Education, gold medal, 2000, 2005, silver medal, 2001, 2007, bronze medal, 2006; Idaho Press Club Award, 2003; Director's Award, National Small Works (Greenwich, CT), 2008; numerous awards from juried art shows.

Writings

(Self-illustrated) *What's That Noise?,* Random House (New York, NY), 2002.
(Illustrator) Kate Saunders, *The Little Secret,* Feiwel & Friends (New York, NY), 2009.

Work included in annuals, including *Spectrum: The Best in Contemporary Fantastic Art, American Illustration, 3x3,* and *Illustrators.* Contributor to periodicals, including *Arche, Boise Weekly, DPI, Idaho Arts Quarterly, Imagine FX, Stripolis,* and *Utne Reader.*

Sidelights

William Carman is an illustrator and designer whose detailed, surreal images are crafted from pencil, pen, and paint onto both traditional textured paper to copper sheeting and other interesting surfaces that speak to him. While Carman devotes much of his time to teaching at Boise State University, his work also appears in advertising, promotion, and other visual media as well

as in gallery exhibition. In 2002 he produced his first original self-illustrated picture book, *What's That Noise?,* and has contributed fantastical spot-art and cover illustrations to Kate Saunders' middle-grade fantasy *The Little Secret.*

A bedtime story that *Booklist* critic Cynthia Turnquest recommended "for kids who can't help wondering about that monster under the bed," *What's That Noise?* introduces a brave young boy who is awakened in the night by an unusual sound. Determined to find the source of the noise without his parents' help, the independent-minded lad leaves the safety of his bed and ventures into the dark hall, eventually locating the sound's source in a surprising place. In Carman's illustrations readers can share the boy's wild imaginings, which range from a backyard U.F.O. landing to multi-eyed monsters and even a hungry, long-clawed bear. The author/illustrator "showcases a flair for visual drama," noted a *Kirkus Reviews* critic, citing the off-kilter perspectives and dusky-toned "renditions of lurid imaginings" that fill each page Carman's storybook. Noting the story's "haunting illustrations and cool atmosphere," a *Publishers Weekly* contributor praised the "technical skill and careful pacing" exhibited in *What's That Noise?,* while *School Library Journal* critic Marianne Saccardi asserted that the combination of fantastical art and pared-down text in *What's That Noise?* produces "just the right amount of suspense and a surprise ending."

Biographical and Critical Sources

PERIODICALS

Booklist, September 15, 2002, Cynthia Turnquest, review of *What's That Noise?,* p. 238; May 15, 2009, Carolyn Phelan, review of *The Little Secret,* p. 55.

Kirkus Reviews, June 1, 2002, review of *What's That Noise?;* June 15, 2009, review of *The Little Secret.*

Publishers Weekly, June 17, 2002, review of *What's That Noise?,* p. 63; July 13, 2009, review of *The Little Secret,* p. 57.

School Library Journal, August, 2002, Marianne Saccardi, review of *What's That Noise?,* p. 148; August, 2009, Nancy Saunders Menaldi-Scanlan, review of *The Little Secret,* p. 114.

ONLINE

Bill Carman Web log, http://billcarman.blogspot.com/ (November 27, 2010).

Boise State University Web site, http://www.boisestate.edu/ (November 14, 2010), "Bill Carman."

*   *   *

CASWELL, Deanna

Personal

Born in TN; married Jeff Caswell (a math teacher); children: Nate, Callie, Zach. *Education:* B.S. (chemistry); M.A. (family therapy).

Addresses

Home—Collierville, TN. *Agent*—Steven Malk, Writer's House, 21 W. 26th St., New York, NY 10010.

Career

Educator and author. Former lab technician; has worked as a nanny and teacher.

Writings

First Ballet, illustrated by Elizabeth Matthews, Disney/ Hyperion (New York, NY), 2009.

Train Trip, illustrated by Dan Andreasen, Disney/Hyperion (New York, NY), 2010.

Sidelights

When she is not tending to the family chickens, working in the garden, cooking and baking, or mothering her three children, Tennessee native Deanna Caswell writes. An advocate of urban homesteading, which encourages suburban families to be as self-sufficient as those of

Deanna Caswell focuses on a favorite topic of many young girls in her picture book **First Ballet,** *featuring artwork by Elizabeth Matthews.*

generations past, Caswell also enjoys writing for children. Her debut picture book, *First Ballet,* is the result of both her own writing and her efforts to connect with and learn from other writers.

In *First Ballet* Caswell tells a rhyming story about a special outing taken by a little girl and her grandmother. Wearing their best "going out" clothes, granddaughter and grandmother venture into town. and are impressed by the grandeur of the city auditorium. When the curtains open onto the first scene of the magical "Nutcracker," they are carried away into the art of the ballet. Featuring illustrations by Elizabeth Matthews, *First Ballet* pairs briefly worded "rhyming couplets and captivating" art, according to *Booklist* critic Gillian Engberg, the reviewer recommending Caswell's story as a good selection for reading to "young children headed off to the theater for the first time."

Biographical and Critical Sources

PERIODICALS

Booklist, November 1, 2009, Gillian Engberg, review of *First Ballet,* p. 61.
Kirkus Reviews, October 1, 2009, review of *First Ballet.*
Publishers Weekly, October 12, 2009, review of *First Ballet,* p. 47.
School Library Journal, December, 2009, Maryann H. Owen, review of *First Ballet,* p. 78.

ONLINE

Deanna Casewell Home Page, http://deannacaswell.com (November 14, 2010).
Little House in the Suburbs Web log, http://littlehouseinthesuburbs.com/ (December 15, 2010), "Deanna Caswell."*

*   *   *

CECIL, Randy 1968-

Personal

Born 1968. *Education:* Rhode Island School of Design, degree.

Addresses

Home and office—Houston, TX. *E-mail*—Ran9000@aol.com.

Career

Children's author and illustrator.

Awards, Honors

Christopher Award, 2003, for *The Ugly Princess and the Wise Fool* by Margaret Gray; Wanda Gag Book Award, for *My Father the Dog* by Elizabeth Bluemle; American Library Association Notable Book designation, for *One Is a Snail, Ten Is a Crab* by April Pulley Sayre.

Writings

SELF-ILLUSTRATED

One Dark and Dreadful Night, Holt (New York, NY), 2004.
Gator, Candlewick (Cambridge, MA), 2007.
Duck, Candlewick (Cambridge, MA), 2008.

ILLUSTRATOR

Emilie Poulsson, *Baby's Breakfast,* Holt (New York, NY), 1996.
Dian Curtis Regan, *Dear Dr. Sillybear,* Holt (New York, NY), 1997.
Susan Lowell, *Little Red Cowboy Hat,* Holt (New York, NY), 1997.
Victoria Stenmark, *The Singing Chick,* Holt (New York, NY), 1999.
Eric A. Kimmel, *The Runaway Tortilla,* Winslow Press (Delray Beach, FL), 2000.
Larry Weinberg, *The Forgetful Bears,* Golden Books (New York, NY), 2000.
Susan Lowell, *Dusty Locks and the Three Bears,* Holt (New York, NY), 2001.
Margaret Gray, *The Ugly Princess and the Wise Fool,* Holt (New York, NY), 2002.
Sarah Wilson, *Big Day on the River,* Holt (New York, NY), 2003.
April Pulley Sayre, *One Is a Snail, Ten Is a Crab: A Counting by Feet Book,* Candlewick (Cambridge, MA), 2003.
David Elliott, *And Here's to You!,* Candlewick (Cambridge, MA), 2004.
Margaret Gray, *The Lovesick Salesman,* Holt (New York, NY), 2004.
David Martin, *We've All Got Bellybuttons!,* Candlewick (Cambridge, MA), 2005.
Elizabeth Bluemle, *My Father the Dog,* Candlewick (Cambridge, MA), 2006.
Phyllis Root, *Looking for a Moose,* Candlewick (Cambridge, MA), 2006.
Elizabeth Bluemle, *How Do You Wokka-wokka?,* Candlewick Press (Somerville, MA), 2009.
James Howe, *Brontorina,* Candlewick Press (Somerville, MA), 2010.

Sidelights

Author and illustrator Randy Cecil has always been fascinated by picture books. In fact, he submitted his first work for publication—a book of mazes he created with

his brother—when he was seven or eight years old. Although this initial submission generated his first rejection letter, Cecil continued to pursue his interest with the goal of becoming a picture-book artist. In 1996 his efforts were rewarded when his illustrations appeared alongside Emilie Poulsson's text in *Baby's Breakfast.* Since then, Cecil has not only provided illustrations for a number of authors, but has written and illustrated several books of his own.

Cecil's first independent picture-book project, *One Dark and Dreadful Night,* borrows from fairy tales and melodrama to poke fun at gothic tales featuring "unfortunate events," according to a *Kirkus Reviews* contributor. In the story, Maestro Von Haughty, director of the Wayward Orphans Theatre, plans to stage three short plays full of terror and misfortune. Featuring questionable casting choices that find Lilly Riley-Hood playing a fairy princess and Jack's giant cast as a huge bunny who rescues Hansel and Gretel, the show does not come off with the fear factor Von Haughty had hoped for. Cecil "signals the ensuing mayhem with his lively, joke-packed illustrations," observed a *Publishers Weekly* contributor. The *Kirkus Reviews* critic dubbed *One Dark and Dreadful Night* "a hysterical addition to any fractured-fairytale collection."

A carved wooden alligator goes exploring and strays away from its home on an amusement park carousel in *Gator.* When Gator arrives at a nearby zoo, children be-

Randy Cecil's self-illustrated Gator *follows a curious animal on a magical adventure.* (Copyright © 2007 by Randy Cecil. Reproduced by permission of Candlewick Press, Inc., Cambridge, MA.)

gin to follow it home, and the carousel miraculously begins to work again once the carved creature returns. "Cecil creates a fine sense of place in a series of well-composed oil paintings featuring stylized characters," wrote Carolyn Phelan in *Booklist,* and a *Kirkus Reviews* contributor predicted that the author/illustrator's "mini-adventure will leave readers warmed."

A companion volume to *Gator, Duck* focuses on a painted wooden duck living on the same amusement park carousel, as it dreams of the promise that life a real duck could hold. While roaming from its merry-go-round perch, the wooden duck meets a lost ducking and the two immediately bond. While Duck teaches the young foundling many things about being a duck, it cannot teach the art of flight because its wooden wings are immobile. Ultimately, the duckling matures and flies away for the winter, but when it returns it gives Duck a special gift in Cecil's touching story. Enriched by the author/illustrator's oil paintings in smoky tones of green, brown, and gold, *Duck* treats readers to what *School Library Journal* contributor Mary Jean Smith described as "a beautifully realized friendship story with a happy ending." A *Kirkus Reviews* writer also praised Cecil's story, calling it "equally affecting on literal and metaphorical levels." The author/illustrator "captures nuances of feeling in body angles and poses," the critic added.

Many books featuring Cecil's art treat readers to modern twists on traditional fairy tales. Susan Lowell's *Little Red Cowboy Hat* retells the story of Little Red Riding Hood in an Old West setting, and here Cecil "contributes flat, angular gouache illustrations of desert scenes," according to a contributor to *Publishers Weekly.* Ilene Cooper, reviewing the same title for *Booklist,* wrote that the illustrations "have a cartoon edge that is full of humor." Of *Dusty Locks and the Three Bears,* another fairy tale by Lowell that is reset in the Old West, *Booklist* critic Hazel Rochman wrote that "Cecil's bright acrylic gouache pictures extend the rhythm of the words with a rugged western landscape."

The misadventures of a curious chick are brought to life by Cecil in *The Singing Chick,* a story by Victoria Stenmark in which "colorful, comical, and carefree illustrations" "suit the story and have solid child appeal," according to *Booklist* reviewer Shelley Townsend-Hudson. In Margaret Gray's Christopher Award-winning *The Ugly Princess and the Wise Fool* "Cecil's illustrations convey the ridiculous state of affairs" in a land far, far away, according to Sharon Grover in *School Library Journal.* Diane Foote, writing for *Booklist,* said of the same title that "Cecil's cartoony artwork fits the fun to a T." More silliness is afoot in his illustrations for Elizabeth Bluemle's *How Do You Wokka-Wokka?,* an "infectious burst of movement, rhythm, and rhyme" that is enlivened by "sketchy, full-color" paintings of the story's multicultural cast, according to *School Library Journal* contributor Marge Loch-Wouters.

Cecil's illustrations capture the fun in Elizabeth Bluemle's picture-book story **How Do You Wokka-Wokka?** (Illustration copyright © 2009 by Randy Cecil. Reproduced by permission of Candlewick Press, Somerville, MA.)

Cecil has also illustrated counting books, concept books, and other original tales. For April Pulley Sayre's *One Is a Snail, Ten Is a Crab: A Counting by Feet Book* the illustrator "covers every inch of the spreads with scratchy-textured, tropically-hued oils," according to a *Publishers Weekly* contributor. Louise L. Sherman noted in *School Library Journal* that "Cecil's googly-eyed snails, sports-minded crabs, and other animals add a touch of humor." In David Martin's concept book *We've All Got Bellybuttons!* Cecil provides "happily goofy oil illustrations [that] are perfectly matched" by Martin's text, according to *School Library Journal* reviewer Loch-Wouters.

And Here's to You! was marketed to young children as well as to teens due to author David Elliott's optimistic message. "Cecil's full-bleed illustrations reflect all [the author's] . . . unfettered exuberance," wrote a *Kirkus Reviews* writer, and Andrea Tarr noted in *School Library Journal* that his "effervescent, entertaining cartoons, done in oils, perfectly complement the narrative." Observant readers of *Looking for a Moose,* a collaboration between Cecil and well-known writer Phyllis Root, "will notice the stray antler and muzzle that appear throughout the illustrations," advised a *Kirkus Reviews* contributor, and in the pages of James Howe's *Brontorina* the story of a dinosaur who dreams of dancing the ballet are captured in "arresting oil paintings" that "show up well from a distance," according to *Booklist* critic Phelan.

Biographical and Critical Sources

PERIODICALS

Booklist, April 15, 1997, Ilene Cooper, review of *Little Red Cowboy Hat,* p. 1436; March 15, 1999, Shelley Townsend-Hudson, review of *The Singing Chick,* p. 1336; July, 2001, Hazel Rochman, review of *Dusty Locks and the Three Bears,* p. 2014; November 15, 2002, Diane Foote, review of *The Ugly Princess and the Wise Fool,* p. 597; June 1, 2003, Gillian Engberg, review of *Big Day on the River,* p. 1788; January 1, 2005, Carolyn Phelan, review of *The Lovesick Salesman,* p. 858; May 15, 2006, Randall Enos, review of *My Father the Dog,* p. 48; October 1, 2006, Connie Fletcher, review of *Looking for a Moose,* p. 60; February 1, 2007, Carolyn Phelan, review of *Gator,* p. 48; February 1, 2008, Ilene Cooper, review of *Duck,* p. 48; September 1, 2009, Shelle Rosenfeld, review of *How Do You Wokka-Wokka?,* p. 98; May 15, 2010, Carolyn Phelan, review of *Brontorina,* p. 40.

Horn Book, May, 1999, review of *The Singing Chick,* p. 323.

Kirkus Reviews, May 1, 2003, review of *One Is a Snail, Ten Is a Crab: A Counting by Feet Book,* p. 683; March 15, 2004, review of *And Here's to You!,* p. 268; July 15, 2004, review of *One Dark and Dreadful Night,* p. 682; October 15, 2004, review of *The Lovesick Salesman,* p. 1006; January 1, 2005, review of *We've All Got Bellybuttons!,* p. 54; April 1, 2006, review of *My Father the Dog,* p. 342; July 15, 2006, review of *Looking for a Moose,* p. 729; January 15, 2007, review of *Gator,* p. 71; December 15, 2007, review of *Duck;* February 1, 2009, review of *The Three Little Tamales;* July 1, 2009, review of *How Do You Wokka-Wokka?*

Publishers Weekly, March 3, 1997, review of *Little Red Cowboy Hat,* p. 75; May 21, 2001, review of *Dusty Locks and the Three Bears,* p. 107; October 28, 2002, review of *The Ugly Princess and the Wise Fool,* p. 71; April 28, 2003, review of *One Is a Snail, Ten Is a Crab,* p. 69; August 9, 2004, review of *One Dark and Dreadful Night,* p. 250; May 8, 2006, review of *My Father the Dog,* p. 64; September 18, 2006, review of *Looking for a Moose,* p. 53; March 5, 2007, review of *Gator,* p. 60; January 28, 2008, review of *Duck,* p. 67; July 6, 2009, review of *How Do You Wokka-Wokka?,* p. 50.

School Library Journal, October, 2000, Ruth Semrau, review of *The Runaway Tortilla,* p. 148; July, 2001, Adele Greenlee, review of *Dusty Locks and the Three*

Bears, p. 96; October, 2002, Sharon Grover, review of *The Ugly Princess and the Wise Fool,* p. 111; April, 2003, Kathleen Kelly MacMillan, review of *Big Day on the River,* p. 144; July, 2003, Louise L. Sherman, review of *One Is a Snail, Ten Is a Crab,* p. 117; May, 2004, Andrea Tarr, review of *And Here's to You!,* p. 109; December, 2004, Teri Markson, review of *The Lovesick Salesman,* p. 146; February, 2005, Marge Loch-Wouters, review of *We've All Got Bellybuttons!,* p. 107; July, 2006, Piper L. Nyman, review of *My Father the Dog,* p. 68; October, 2006, Kara Schaff Dean, review of *Looking for a Moose,* p. 124; March, 2007, Catherine Callegari, review of *Gator,* p. 156; March, 2008, Mary Jean Smith, review of *Duck,* p. 155; August, 2009, Marge Loch-Wouters, review of *How Do You Wokka-Wokka?,* p. 70.

ONLINE

Randy Cecil Home Page, http://www.randycecil.com (December 2, 2010).*

*   *   *

CHAPMAN, Linda 1969-
(Daisy Meadows, a joint pseudonym)

Personal

Born 1969, in England; married; children: has daughters. *Hobbies and other interests:* Training dogs, horses.

Addresses

Home—Leicestershire, England.

Career

Author of books for children. Former stage manager; drama teacher; Working Partners, Ltd., staff writer beginning 1998.

Writings

FOR CHILDREN

Bright Lights, illustrated by Angie Thompson, Puffin (London, England), 2003.
Centre Stage, Penguin (London, England), 2004.
(With Steve Cole) *Genie Us,* Red Fox (London, England), 2008, published as *Be a Genie in Six Easy Steps,* Harper (New York, NY), 2009.
(With Steve Cole) *Genie and the Phoenix,* Red Fox (London, England), 2009, published as *The Last Phoenix,* Harper (New York, NY), 2010.
Loving Spirit, Penguin (New York, NY), 2010.

Also coauthor, with Narinder Dhami, Sue Bentley, and Sue Mongredien under the joint pseudonym Daisy Meadows, of the eighteen-book "Rainbow Magic" reader series, illustrated by Georgie Ripper.

"UNICORN MEADOWS" SERIES

The Magic Spell, illustrated by Biz Hull, Scholastic (New York, NY), 2002.
Dreams Come True, illustrated by Biz Hull, Scholastic (New York, NY), 2002.
Flying High, illustrated by Biz Hull, Scholastic (New York, NY), 2002.
Starlight Surprise, illustrated by Biz Hull, Scholastic (New York, NY), 2003.
A Special Friend, illustrated by Biz Hull, Puffin (London, England), 2003.
Stronger than Magic, illustrated by Biz Hull, Puffin (London, England), 2003.
A Touch of Magic, illustrated by Biz Hull, Puffin (London, England), 2003, Scholastic (New York, NY), 2005, illustrated by Ann Kronheimer, Puffin (London, England), 2005.
A Winter Wish, illlustrated by Biz Hull, Puffin (London, England), 2004.
Snowy Dreams, illustrated by Ann Kronheimer, Puffin (London, England), 2005, Scholastic (New York, NY), 2007.
The Secret Treasury (omnibus), illustrated by Ann Kronheimer, Puffin (London, England), 2006.
Twilight Magic, illustrated by Ann Kronheimer, Puffin (London, England), 2006, Scholastic (New York, NY), 2008.
Friends Forever, illustrated by Ann Kronheimer, Puffin (London, England), 2006, Scholastic (New York, NY), 2008.
Rising Star, illustrated by Ann Kronheimer, Puffin (London, England), 2006.
Moonlight Journey, illustrated by Ann Kronheimer, Puffin (London, England), 2007.
Keeper of Magic, illustrated by Ann Kronheimer, Puffin (London, England), 2007.
Starry Skies, illustrated by Ann Kronheimer, Puffin (London, England), 2007.

"STARDUST FOREST" SERIES

Magic by Moonlight, illustrated by Biz Hull, Puffin (London, England), 2004.
Magic in the Air, illustrated by Angie Thompson, Puffin (London, England), 2005.
Believe in Magic, illustrated by Biz Hull, Puffin (London, England), 2005.
Stolen Magic, illustrated by Biz Hull, Puffin (London, England), 2005.
Shadows of Magic, illustrated by Angie Thompson, Puffin (London, England), 2007.
Magic Secrets, illustrated by Angie Thompson, Puffin (London, England), 2007.
Midnight Magic, illustrated by Angie Thompson, Puffin (London, England), 2008.
Lucy's Magic Journal, illustrated by Angie Thompson, Puffin (London, England), 2008.

"MERMAID FALLS" SERIES

Mermaid Island, illustrated by Dawn Apperley, Puffin (London, England), 2005.

Mermaid Fire, illustrated by Dawn Apperley, Puffin (London, England), 2005.

Not Quite a Mermaid, illustrated by Dawn Apperley, Puffin (London, England), 2006.

Mermaid Treasure, illustrated by Dawn Apperley, Puffin (London, England), 2006.

Mermaid Wish, illustrated by Dawn Apperley, Puffin (London, England), 2006.

Mermaid Party, illustrated by Dawn Apperley, Puffin (London, England), 2006.

Mermaid Surprise, illustrated by Dawn Apperley, Puffin (London, England), 2007.

Mermaid Tricks, illustrated by Dawn Apperley, Puffin (London, England), 2008.

Mermaid Rescue, illustrated by Dawn Apperley, Puffin (London, England), 2008.

Mermaid Promise, illustrated by Dawn Apperley, Puffin (London, England), 2008.

"UNICORN SCHOOL" SERIES

The Surprise Party, illustrated by Ann Kronheimer, Puffin (London, England), 2007.

First Class Friends, illustrated by Ann Kronheimer, Puffin (London, England), 2007.

The Treasure Hunt, illustrated by Ann Kronheimer, Puffin (London, England), 2007.

The Pet Show, illustrated by Ann Kronheimer, Puffin (London, England), 2008.

The School Play, illustrated by Ann Kronheimer, Puffin (London, England), 2008.

Team Magic, illustrated by Ann Kronheimer, Puffin (London, England), 2009.

"SKY HORSES" SERIES

Cloud Magic, Puffin (London, England), 2009.
The Eye of the Storm, Puffin (London, England), 2009.
The Royal Foal, Puffin (London, England), 2009.
The Whispering Tree, Puffin (London, England), 2009.

"SKATING SCHOOL" SERIES

Amber Skate Star, Puffin (London, England), 2010.
Blue Skate Dreams, Puffin (London, England), 2010.
Diamond Skate Forever, Puffin (London, England), 2010.
Emerald Skate Promise, Puffin (London, England), 2010.
Pink Skate Party, Puffin (London, England), 2010.
Ruby Skate Secrets, Puffin (London, England), 2010.
Sapphire Skate Fun, Puffin (London, England), 2010.
Scarlet Skate Magic, Puffin (London, England), 2010.
Silver Skate Surprise, Puffin (London, England), 2010.
Topaz Skate Sparkle, Puffin (London, England), 2010.
Violet Skate Friends, Puffin (London, England), 2010.
White Skate Wishes, Puffin (London, England), 2010.

Biographical and Critical Sources

PERIODICALS

Booklist, May 15, 2009, Andrew Medlar, review of *Be a Genie in Six Easy Steps,* p. 54.

Kirkus Reviews, August 1, 2009, review of *Be a Genie in Six Easy Steps.*

School Library Journal, December, 2009, Caitlin Augusta, review of *Be a Genie in Six Easy Steps,* p. 108.

ONLINE

Linda Chapman Home Page, http://www.lindachapman author.co.uk (November 14, 2010).

Puffin Web site, http://www.puffin.co.uk/ (December 5, 2010), "Linda Chapman's Circle of Magic."*

*   *   *

CHOCOLATE, Debbi 1954-
(Deborah H. Newton Chocolate)

Personal

Born January 25, 1954, in Chicago, IL; daughter of Steve (a mailman) and Alma L. Newton; married Robert Chocolate, Sr. (an accountant) December 31, 1980; children: Robert, Jr., Allen Whitney. *Education:* Spelman College, B.A., 1976; Brown University, M.A., 1978; attended School of the Art Institute of Chicago. *Religion:* Baptist. *Hobbies and other interests:* Reading, traveling, playing basketball, collecting baseball cards.

Addresses

Home—Chicago, IL. *Agent*—Jane Jordan Browne, 410 S. Michigan Ave., Ste. 724, Chicago, IL 60605. *E-mail*—DebbiChocolate@hotmail.com.

Career

Author and educator. Riverside Publishing Company, Chicago, IL, editor, 1978-90; Triton College, River Grove, IL, English instructor, 1990-92; Columbia College, Chicago, former member of faculty. Oak Park Public Schools, writing workshop leader at Youth Author's Conference, 1985-95; AYA African Arts Festival, storyteller, 1990-91; freelance writer. Affiliated with Illinois Young Author's Conference, Illinois State Board of Education, 1992, 1995, 1997.

Member

Children's Reading Roundtable of Chicago.

Awards, Honors

Brown University fellowship, 1976-78; grant from City of Chicago Cultural Arts grant, 1991, 1992; Parent's Choice Award, 1993, for *Talk, Talk;* Pick of the Lists selection, American Booksellers Association, 1994, for *Imani in the Belly;* Notable Book selection, Children's Book Council, 1995, for *On the Day I Was Born.*

Writings

NEATE to the Rescue!, illustrated by Melodye Rosales, Just Us Books (East Orange, NJ), 1992.
Elizabeth's Wish, Just Us Books (East Orange, NJ), 1994.

Debbi Chocolate (Reproduced by permission.)

On the Day I Was Born, illustrated by Melodye Rosales, Scholastic, Inc. (New York, NY), 1995.

A Very Special Kwanzaa, Scholastic, Inc. (New York, NY), 1996.

Kente Colors, illustrated by John Ward, Walker & Co. (New York, NY), 1996.

The Piano Man, illustrated by Eric Velasquez, Walker & Co. (New York, NY), 1998.

Pigs Can Fly!: The Adventures of Harriet Pig and Friends, illustrated by Leslie Tryon, Cricket Books (Chicago, IL), 2004.

El Barrio, illustrated by David Diaz, Henry Holt (New York, NY), 2009.

UNDER NAME DEBORAH H. NEWTON CHOCOLATE

Kwanzaa, illustrated by Melodye Rosales, Children's Press (New York, NY), 1990.

My First Kwanzaa Book, illustrated by Cal Massey, Scholastic, Inc. (New York, NY), 1992.

Spider and the Sky God: An Akan Legend, illustrated by Dave Albers, Troll Publications (Mahwah, NJ), 1993.

Talk, Talk: An Ashanti Legend, illustrated by Dave Albers, Troll Publications (Mahwah, NJ), 1993.

Imani in the Belly, illustrated by Alex Boies, BridgeWater Books (New York, NY), 1994.

Sidelights

Debbi Chocolate is an author, storyteller, and educator who draws from her own cultural history as an African

American in many of her books for younger readers. In addition to dealing with the Kwanzaa holiday in the nonfiction picture books *Kwanzaa, My First Kwanzaa Book,* and *A Very Special Kwanzaa,* which were published under her full name Debbie H. Newton Chocolate, Chocolate has also produced fictional stories such as *The Piano Man, Pigs Can Fly!: The Adventures of Harriet Pig and Friends,* as well as the bilingual picture book *El Barrio.* "My purpose is always the same," she noted of her career as a children's author: "I write to entertain. And, more often than not, I write to share my vision of life's hope, its beauty and its promise."

Raised in Chicago as the youngest of five children, Chocolate inherited her love of books and reading from her mother. "By the time I was seven, when I wasn't reading, painting, or drawing, I was busy recreating my mother's childhood memories of the theater into my own stories," the author recalled on her home page. Although her creativity ranged from writing to painting, filmmaking, and music, Chocolate found that the course of her life pulled her toward creating books for children. While working as an editor of a children's book publisher "I read so many books that I found it easy to sit down and create my own storybook," she explained. "The first book I wrote was published right away. The publisher said they had been looking for a book just like the one I'd written. I felt very lucky."

In *My First Kwanzaa Book* Chocolate guides young readers through the seven days of Kwanzaa, which lasts from December 26th through New Year's Day. The book illustrates such traditions as lighting candles, dressing in African clothing, and gift-giving between family and friends. Through Chocolate's words and illustrator Cal Massey's creative images, *My First Kwanzaa Book* "effectively conveys the spirit of the holiday," commented Jane Marino, a reviewer for *School Library Journal.* Writing in the *Bulletin of the Center for Children's Books,* Roger Sutton deemed *My First Kwanzaa Book* "a pleasant introduction to the holiday."

Chocolate also features African-enriched themes in *On the Day I Was Born* and *Kente Colors,* both of which depict the symbolism and beauty of African heritage. Prompted by Alex Haley's television version of *Roots, On the Day I Was Born* celebrates the arrival of an African-American baby. The grown-up boy narrates the story, recalling the warmth and love expressed by his family on his special day. *School Library Journal* contributor Barbara Osborne Williams praised the colorful illustrations by Melodye Rosales that "complement the text," calling the book "an excellent collaboration."

One Day I Was Born also describes the symbolic use of the kente cloth, a colorful African textile, during childhood. Presented with a special kente at birth, the young narrator tells readers that he must save this cloth to celebrate his twelfth birthday. This traditional fabric is the subject of *Kente Colors* as well. Through Chocolate's rhythmic text and vivid colors, children learn how kente

cloth is utilized in West African culture and what each color within its design signifies. *School Library Journal* contributor Carol Jones Collins praised *Kente Colors* as "the first [children's book] to convey an understanding of kente cloth's history and cultural significance."

Chocolate captures the spirit of two folktales in her picture-book retellings *Spider and the Sky God: An Akan Legend* and *Imani in the Belly*. In *Spider and the Sky God* the spider Ananse announces that he can present the Sky God with species that are much larger than him. Although it seems utterly impossible, Ananse achieves this feat with the help of his wife. In retelling this trickster tale taken from the West African Akan culture, Chocolate adds "a nice combination of narrative patterns, colloquial speech, and descriptions of a genius web spinner," according to a *Wilson Library Bulletin* contributor.

Imani in the Belly is Chocolate's retelling of a Swahili folktale. Imani is a grieving mother whose children have been swallowed by a lion. After receiving guidance from her own mother in a dream, Imani risks her life by entering the lion's stomach and saves her children and several others by starting a fire inside the creature's belly. Advocating spirituality and faith, *Imani in the Belly* is an "exuberant retelling" of an old story, according to a *Publishers Weekly* contributor.

Both *NEATE to the Rescue!* and *Elizabeth's Wish* introduce a club composed of members Naimah, Elizabeth, Anthony, Tayesha, and Eddie (or NEATE). *NEATE to the Rescue!* focuses on Naimah Jackson as her mother, Shannon Gordon, campaigns to maintain her seat on the local city council. Mrs. Gordon's opponent is a prejudiced ex-police officer whose son happens to be challenging Naimah for student council president. NEATE members inadvertently imperil Mrs. Gordon's chances when they confront supporters of her opponent and end up in jail. Ultimately, however, Naimah and her friends regroup and facilitate a plan to encourage people to vote for her mother. *Booklist* contributor Quraysh Ali praised *NEATE to the Rescue!* as a "positive" book with characters who have "clearly defined personalities."

Elizabeth's Wish centers on Elizabeth's entrance into a citywide music competition. Other sub-plots surrounding NEATE members include prejudice, a local Vietnamese refugee shelter's possible closure, a father/son conflict, and a debate on rap versus heavy-metal music. Praising the "natural" dialogue in *Elizabeth's Wish*, *School Library Journal* contributor Elaine E. Knight dubbed Chocolate's book "emotionally satisfying."

Inspired by the musical talent that has woven itself throughout her own family history, Chocolate's picture book *The Piano Man* features a young narrator's story about her grandfather, who played piano and danced in vaudeville during the first decades of the twentieth century. As he got older, the man worked as a piano tuner,

but continued to share his music with his family and friends. The book's "heartening slice of African-American family history . . . is refreshingly short on role-modeling and long on joy and visual glamour," wrote *Horn Book* contributor Roger Sutton, praising Chocolate's relaxed and "unassuming" narration. Grandfather's colorful life is captured in detailed paintings by Eric Velasquez, whose "subtle characterization of faces gives warmth and individuality to the main characters," according to *Booklist* critic Carolyn Phelan. According to a *Publishers Weekly* critic, *The Piano Man* treats readers to a "lively and affectionate tribute" to a beloved relative that "may well prompt discussions of the nation's history as well as family roots."

Featuring artwork by Leslie Tryon, *Pigs Can Fly!* is an easy reader that finds the spunky Harriet Pig determined to help others in four simple stories. The likeable pig helps a friend overcome a fear of heights while also taking her first flight ever. In other tales she enters a swimming race against a goose and makes a new but tiny friend. "Harriet is a likable, outgoing character whose antics are sure to evoke giggles from readers," predicted Lynn K. Vanca in *School Library Journal*, and in *Booklist* Lauren Peterson recommended *Pigs Can Fly!* as "a good choice for new readers ready for more challenge."

In *El Barrio* an Hispanic boy shares the many things that make his city neighborhood a magical place to live, from holiday celebrations for Cinco de Mayo and La Dia de los Muertos to the colorful murals, bright lights, and constant bustle of busy people that energize the streets. Brought to life in brightly colored folk-style artwork by award-winning illustrator David Diaz, Chocolate's rhyming text calls forth simple but colorful imagery; "simply by calling upon these images as treasure" her story encourages children to life in Hispanic neighborhoods "that their neighborhood . . . is both normal and special," observed to *School Library Journal* contributor Nina Lindsay.

"What do I like most about being a writer?," Chocolate once commented. "Meeting children who love to read, and who have enjoyed reading books that I have written. For those who want to be writers, my advice is to keep reading. Reading is what makes a writer."

Biographical and Critical Sources

PERIODICALS

Booklist, March 15, 1993, Quraysh Ali, review of *NEATE to the Rescue!,* p. 1319; February 15, 1996, Hazel Rochman, review of *Kente Colors,* p. 1023; February 15, 1998, Carolyn Phelan, review of *The Piano Man,* p. 1018; May 1, 2004, Lauren Peterson, review of *Pigs Can Fly!: The Adventures of Harriet Pig and Friends,* p. 1561.

Bulletin of the Center for Children's Books, February, 1993, Roger Sutton, review of *My First Kwanzaa Book,* p. 171.

Horn Book, March-April, 1998, Roger Sutton, review of *The Piano Man,* p. 211.

Publishers Weekly, October 3, 1994, review of *Imani in the Belly,* p. 69; February 12, 1996, review of *Kente Colors,* p. 77; November 24, 1997, review of *The Piano Man,* p. 73.

School Library Journal, October, 1992, Jane Marino, review of *My First Kwanzaa Book,* p. 38; January, 1996, Barbara Osborne Williams, review of *On the Day I Was Born,* p. 77; June, 1996, Carol Jones Collins, review of *Kente Colors,* p. 114; May, 2004, Lynn K. Vanca, review of *Pigs Can Fly!,* p. 108; March, 2009, Nina Lindsay, review of *El Barrio,* p. 107.

Wilson Library Bulletin, September, 1993, review of *Spider and the Sky God: An Akan Legend,* p. 87.

ONLINE

Debbi Chocolate Home Page, http://www.debbichocolate.com (November 29, 2010).

Family Cares Web site, http://www.familycares.org/ (November, 2004), interview with Chocolate.*

*   *   *

CHOCOLATE, Deborah H. Newton
See CHOCOLATE, Debbi

*   *   *

COVERLY, Dave 1964-

Personal

Born 1964, in Ann Arbor, MI; married; wife's name Chris; children: Alayna, Simone. *Education:* Eastern Michigan University, B.S. (philosophy and imaginative writing), 1987; Indiana University, M.A. (creative writing), 1992.

Addresses

Home and office—Ann Arbor, MI. *Agent*—(Syndication) c/o Creators Syndicate, 5777 W. Century Blvd., Ste. 700, Los Angeles, CA 90045; (Books) Melissa Chinchillo, Fletcher & Company, 78 5th Ave., Fl. 3, New York, NY 10011. *E-mail*—speedbumpcomic@comcast.net.

Career

Cartoonist and illustrator. Worked as an art director for a public relations firm; *Battle Creek Enquirer,* Battle Creek, MI, editorial cartoonist; *Herald-Times,* Bloomington, IN, editorial cartoonist, 1990-95. *Exhibitions:* Work has been exhibited in Kilkenny Castle, Kilkenny,

Dave Coverly (Photograph by Scott Stewart. Reproduced by permission.)

Ireland, Wisconsin Rapids Cultural Center, and Kalamazoo Institute of Arts, Kalamazoo, MI, and included in private collections.

Member

National Cartoonists Society.

Awards, Honors

National awards for cartoon in *Indiana Daily Student;* first prize, *Boston Comic News* cartooning contest, 1993; Reuben Award for Best Newspaper Panel, National Cartoonists Society, 1995 and 2003, both for "Speed Bump"; Reuben Award for Best Greeting Cards, 1998; Reuben Award for Outstanding Cartoonist of the Year, 2009.

Writings

SELF-ILLUSTRATED

Caution Speed Bump: A Collection of Cartoon Skidmarks, Andrews McMeel (Kansas City, MO), 2000.

Speed Bump: Cartoons for Idea People, ECW Press (Toronto, Ontario, Canada), 2004.

Just One %$#@ Speed Bump after Another . . ., ECW Press (Toronto, Ontario, Canada), 2005.
Ten Things You Should Never Do during a Soccer Game, Henry Holt (New York, NY), 2011.

Creator of "Speed Bump" comic strip, syndicated, 1994—. Contributor of cartoons to periodicals, including *New Yorker, Parade,* and *Road & Track.*

ILLUSTRATOR

Charles Monagan, *How to Get a Monkey into Harvard: An Impractical Guide to Fooling the Top Colleges,* Black Cat (New York, NY), 2007.
Jim Tobin, *Sue MacDonald Had a Book,* Henry Holt (New York, NY), 2009.

Contributor to periodicals, including *Esquire, New Yorker, New York Times, Saturday Evening Post,* and *USA Today.*

Sidelights

Dave Coverly received the prestigious Reuben Award for Outstanding Cartoonist of the Year in 2009 for "Speed Bump," a nationally syndicated comic strip that presents an off-kilter look at the minutiae of everyday life. Created in 1994, "Speed Bump" appears in more than 400 newspapers and Web sites, including the *Washington Post, Chicago Tribune, New Orleans Times-Picayune,* Toronto *Globe & Mail,* and the *Arizona Republic.* The cartoon, which received Reuben awards for Best Newspaper Panel in 1995 and 2003, has drawn comparisons to Gary Larson's classic comic "The Far Side." Describing the philosophy behind "Speed Bump," Coverly observed on his home page: "Basically, if life were a movie, these would be the outtakes."

In addition to his work as a cartoonist, Coverly has provided the illustrations for *Sue MacDonald Had a Book,* Jim Tobin's humorous tale for children. A wacky revisioning on the popular song "Old MacDonald Had a Farm," the picture book concerns a literary-minded youngster who sets off in pursuit of the five vowels after they extricate themselves from the book she is reading. Liberated from the confines of their pages, the alphabetic escape artists flee to the far corners of the globe, sending Sue on a journey from Maine to Kath-

mandu. "Coverly's cartoon-like illustrations complement the text nicely," a *Kirkus Reviews* critic noted, and a *Publishers Weekly* reviewer wrote of *Sue MacDonald Had a Book* that the artist "draws the vowels with Krazy Kat noses, googly eyes and miniature hands and feet." In their debut work for young readers, Tobin and Coverly "create a fun song parody and a wry rescue story," Hazel Rochman stated in *Booklist.*

As a representative of the National Cartoonists Society, Coverly has traveled extensively with the United Service Organizations (USO), drawing cartoons for injured and active-duty U.S. troops around the world. A recent trip took him, along with nine other cartoonists, to forward operating bases in Iraq, including Basra and Baghdad.

Biographical and Critical Sources

PERIODICALS

Booklist, July 1, 2009, Hazel Rochman, review of *Sue MacDonald Had a Book,* p. 69.
Kirkus Reviews, June 15, 2009, review of *Sue MacDonald Had a Book.*
Publishers Weekly, June 15, 2009, review of *Sue MacDonald Had a Book,* p. 48.
Saturday Evening Post, March-April, 2005, Ted Kreiter, "Funny at Any Speed," p. 40.
School Library Journal, June, 2009, Mary Jean Smith, review of *Sue MacDonald Had a Book,* p. 101.

ONLINE

Cartoonist Studio Web site, http://www.thecartooniststudio. com/ (December 1, 2010), "Dave Coverly."
Creators Syndicate Web site, http://www.creators.com/ (December 1, 2010), "Dave Coverly."
Dave Coverly Home Page, http://www.speedbump.com (December 1, 2010).

*   *   *

CUSIMANO, Maryann K.
See LOVE, Maryann Cusimano

D

DOUGLAS, Allen

Personal
Male. *Education:* Syracuse University, degree.

Addresses
Home—Rochester, NY. *Agent*—Peter Lott, Lott Representatives, P.O. Box 3607, New York, NY 10163. *E-mail*—allen@allendouglasstudio.com.

Career
Illustrator. Freelance artist, beginning c. 1995.

Awards, Honors
Numerous awards for art from juried exhibitions.

Illustrator
Lucille Recht Penner, *Monsters,* Random House (New York, NY), 2009.

Biographical and Critical Sources

PERIODICALS

Kirkus Reviews, July 1, 2009, review of *Monsters.*

ONLINE

Allen Douglas Home Page, http://www.allendouglasstudio. com (November 14, 2010).*

*   *   *

DUNKLE, Clare B. 1964-

Personal
Born June 11, 1964, in Fort Worth, TX; daughter of William E. (an engineer) and Mary (an English professor) Buckalew; married Joseph R. Dunkle (an engi-

Clare B. Dunkle (Photograph by Joseph R. Dunkle. Reproduced by permission.)

neer), August 23, 1986; children: Valerie M., Elena T. *Education:* Trinity University (San Antonio, TX), B.A. (Russian), 1985; Indiana University, M.L.S., 1989. *Politics:* "Independent." *Religion:* Roman Catholic.

Addresses
Home—San Antonio, TX. *E-mail*—clare@claredunkle. com.

Career
Writer, educator, and librarian. Trinity University, San Antonio, TX, associate professor and librarian, 1990-99; freelance author, beginning 2001.

Awards, Honors
Mythopoeic Fantasy Award for Children's Literature, 2004, for *The Hollow Kingdom;* Best Fiction for Young Adults nomination, American Library Association, 2011, for *The House of Dead Maids.*

Writings

MIDDLE-GRADE NOVELS

By These Ten Bones, Henry Holt (New York, NY), 2005.
The Sky Inside, Atheneum Books for Young Readers (New York, NY), 2008.
The Walls Have Eyes (sequel to *The Sky Inside*), Atheneum Books for Young Readers (New York, NY), 2009.
The House of Dead Maids, illustrated by Patrick Arrasmith, Henry Holt (New York, NY), 2010.

"HOLLOW KINGDOM" NOVEL TRILOGY

The Hollow Kingdom, Henry Holt (New York, NY), 2003.
Close Kin, Henry Holt (New York, NY), 2004.
In the Coils of the Snake, Henry Holt (New York, NY), 2005.

Adaptations

The Hollow Kingdom was adapted as an audiobook, read by Jenny Sterlin, Recorded Books, 2003. *Close Kin* was adapted as an audiobook, read by Sterlin, Recorded Books, 2004. *The Sky Inside* was adapted as an audiobook, read by Brace Turk, Listening Library, 2008.

Sidelights

Texas-based writer Clare B. Dunkle is the author of the "Hollow Kingdom" fantasy trilogy, as well as of other middle-grade novels featuring dark fantasy and science fiction. Focusing on two orphaned sisters who are drawn from their homes in Regency England into a fantasy world fraught with cultural tensions between elves, dwarves, and goblins, Dunkle's "Hollow Kingdom" trilogy includes *The Hollow Kingdom, Close Kin,* and *In the Coils of the Snake.* Cementing her skill in creating spine-tinging stories, her novel *The House of Dead Maids* taps into Emily Brontë's classic *Wuthering Heights* in a stale that envisions the early life of Heathcliff and his haunted home from the point of view of a young servant named Tabby Aykroyd. Reviewing the novel in *Booklist,* Daniel Kraus wrote of *The House of Dead Maids* that it "channel[s]. . . Brontë's gothic atmosphere" into a young-adult novel "more thoroughly soaked in ghostly mayhem" than the classic novel that inspired it. Commending the book's literary roots, *School Library Journal* contributor Kathryn Kosiorek concluded that "Dunkle has incorporated real people . . . , fictional characters . . . , and the ancient Druidic practice of human sacrifice into a tense tale of supernatural doings."

Dunkle started writing fiction in 2001, during her husband's six-year job relocation to Germany and while her daughters attended a German boarding school as a way to immerse themselves in a new culture. "For the first time in my adult life, I had no full-time work to do," the former librarian explained to *Smart Writers Journal* online interviewer Roxyanne Young, "and my brain promptly took a holiday. At the end of a week, I complained to my husband Joe that I was wasting all my time daydreaming. 'Write it down for me,' Joe said, so I did, sending each chapter off to the girls in a letter. . . . Nothing else got done that summer, let me tell you!" As Dunkle later explained to a *Publishers Weekly* interviewer, penning the fantasy fiction that would become the "Hollow Kingdom" allowed her to "focus on what happens when an ugly old man has a relationship with a beautiful young woman. . . . We find it unacceptable, because we think love depends on chemistry. But it's worth telling our teens that love depends on respect, generosity, self-sacrifice and allowing the other person room for growth."

With their parents both dead, teenage sisters Kate and Emily are sent to a remote English estate called Hallow Hill, where they will live with their great aunts and an unpleasant cousin. When she believes that Emily has been kidnapped by goblins who live in the region's underground, Kate agrees to marry the goblin king Marak,

Cover of Dunkle's young-adult novel **The Sky Inside,** *featuring artwork by Sammy Yuen, Jr.* (Illustration copyright © 2008 by Sammy Yuen, Jr. Reprinted with the permission of Atheneum Books for Young Readers, an imprint of Simon & Schuster Children's Publishing Division.)

who must take a human wife. Like Persephone, Kate will be forced to live underground forever, but she makes the sacrifice in order to save her sister. Despite his age and ghastly appearance, Marak soon proves to be an oddly attractive companion, and when the goblin kingdom is threatened by a powerful sorcerer, Kate discovers the depth of her true feelings for the king. With the help of the elvin Seylin and her snake-like attendant Charm, the teen goes in search of the sorcerer and the goblins he has enslaved.

Praising *The Hollow Kingdom* as "a luminously polished fantasy that starts off strong and just gets better," a *Publishers Weekly* reviewer added that Dunkle remains true to the inspiration of Victorian novels as well as to "archetypal themes about love and death" while also providing a captivating romance, evil villains, and surprising plot twists. "Kate is surely a heroine to be reckoned with," added *School Library Journal* reviewer Bruce Anne Shook, "and girls will relate to her predicament."

Close Kin, the second volume of the "Hollow Kingdom" trilogy, focuses on Kate's sister, Emily, and her search for Seylin, who has fallen in love with her. In addition, the tragic elf woman Sable mourns the ruin of her culture, partly the result of goblin aggression. The third volume, *In the Coils of the Snake,* brings the remnants of the elven population into contact with the goblins again, thirty years later, as human Miranda and elven Arianna attempt to adapt to goblin culture while war again looms. Noting Dunkle's focus on the intolerances exhibited among the different fantasy folk, Farida S. Dowler added in *School Library Journal* that *Close Kin* "draws readers into a multifaceted world of strong, compelling individuals." Calling *In the Coils of the Snake* a "satisfying conclusion" to Dunkle's fantasy trilogy, *Booklist* critic Jennifer Mattson predicted that "followers of the series will revel in this . . . final opportunity to lose themselves in Dunkle's distinctive, intriguingly disquieting vision."

In addition to her "Hollow Kingdom" novels, Dunkle has also written several stand-alone novels. In *By These Ten Bones,* which mixes romance, werewolves, and medieval mystery, a beautiful Scottish lass named Maddie learns that Paul, the handsome but mute woodcarver she loves, is somehow linked to the evil presence that is haunting her village. "Dunkle creates a menacing atmosphere for this chillingly good tale," concluded a *Publishers Weekly* contributor, while in *School Library Journal* Joel Shoemaker wrote that the "moody setting" and "age-old theme of self-sacrifice" provide *By These Ten Bones* with "a romantic and mysterious air" that will transfix readers. While noting the elements of "grisly horror" that salt Dunkle's story, Mattson concluded in *Booklist* that teens "with a taste for fantasy rooted in folklore and history . . . will happily roam the mist-shrouded Highlands of Dunkle's latest creation."

Both *The Sky Inside* and *The Walls Have Eyes* take place in a future where suburbs have become giant, domed refuges that protect humans from an inhospitable atmosphere. Ruled by a totalitarian government, these suburbs are connected by railways that provide all the food and material goods required. With robots to perform all work, humans are left to spend their time as mindless observers: even their children are genetically engineered. When thirteen-year-old Martin Glass gets a robot dog named Chip for his birthday, he begins to pay attention to the world around him. For instance, his little sister Cassie is unusually curious, like other test-tube babies of her generation, and these so-called "Wonder Babies" are attracting the hostility of grownups. When Cassie is taken from the suburb by a government official, Martin decides to track her down, even though leaving the safety of his suburb is frightening. In Dunkle's well-wrought dystopia, Martin's adventure "will leave readers reflecting on their own media-deluged lives," according to Mattson, and "ponder looming questions about scientific ethics, human rights, and the push-pull between security and freedom." A *Kirkus Reviews* writer recommended *The Sky Inside* as "a compelling shift from the expected" sci-fi fare, while Lisa Marie Williams praised the novel's young protagonists as "well-rounded and thought-provoking characters filled with imagination and real emotions."

Martin's story continues in *The Walls Have Eyes* as the thirteen year old attempts to rescue his parents from the confines of their suburb and help them make a life in the beautiful but uncontrolled world outside. While the boy's mother is up to the adventures, his spineless father risks their family's safety, and soon superdog Chip may be the only thing saving them from government capture. "In a genre populated by gifted, destined and otherwise special child protagonists, Martin's . . . normality is a breath of fresh air," wrote a *Kirkus Reviews* contributor in appraising *The Walls Have Eyes,* and in *Booklist* Carolyn Phelan cited Dunkle's skill in sustaining a "vivid sense of imminent danger" throughout her future-Earth fantasy.

Dunkle once told *SATA:* "Although I have been telling myself stories all my life, I never actually wanted to write books at all; in fact, the last thing I wrote before *The Hollow Kingdom* was a short story in seventh-grade creative writing class. For decades, my daydreams belonged exclusively to me, and I felt no desire to share them. But in June of 2001, my husband asked me to write him a story, and that got me hooked. Now I can't seem to stop writing.

"Because I have had to bring my stories out of this intensely private daydream life into the light of day, I am very aware of books as communication. My books belong to readers just as much as they do to me. I try to find something in each story that I myself want to explore, some experience that will make me grow as a person, and I hope that readers will be able to grow through the stories as well. In the 'Hollow Kingdom'

trilogy I have been exploring ideas of prejudice and race or cultural identity that became particularly important to me once we moved to Germany and I saw my own daughters adapting themselves successfully to a culture that was quite foreign to me.

"My early ideas of fantasy were strongly influenced by J.R.R. Tolkien and Lloyd Alexander, but they were influenced as well by myth and folklore from all over the world. Now that I write fiction, I have abandoned reading fiction altogether. I find so much richness in nonfiction to bring to my writing, from folklore and history to essays and memoirs. The truth really is stranger than anything we can dream up."

Biographical and Critical Sources

PERIODICALS

Booklist, November 15, 2003, Jennifer Mattson, review of *The Hollow Kingdom,* p. 608; October 1, 2004, Jennifer Mattson, review of *Close Kin,* p. 322; May 1, 2005, Jennifer Mattson, review of *By These Ten Bones,* p. 1580; January 1, 2006, Jennifer Mattson, review of *In the Coils of the Snake,* p. 92; May 15, 2008, Jennifer Mattson, review of *The Sky Inside,* p. 60; July 1, 2009, Carolyn Phelan, review of *The Walls Have Eyes,* p. 58; August 1, 2010, Daniel Kraus, review of *The House of Dead Maids,* p. 47.

Bulletin of the Center for Children's Books, February, 2004, Janice Del Negro, review of *The Hollow Kingdom,* p. 227; December, 2004, Timnah Card, review of *Close Kin,* p. 165.

Kirkus Reviews, October 1, 2003, review of *The Hollow Kingdom,* p. 1223; September 15, 2004, review of *Close Kin,* p. 913; April 15, 2005, review of *By These Ten Bones,* p. 472; January, 2008, review of *The Sky Inside;* July 1, 2009, review of *The Walls Have Eyes.*

Kliatt, November, 2006, Janet Julian, review of *The Hollow Kingdom,* p. 28.

Locus, January, 2004, Carolyn Cushman, review of *The Hollow Kingdom,* p. 29; November, 2004, Carolyn Cushman, review of *Close Kin,* p. 31.

Publishers Weekly, November 17, 2003, review of *The Hollow Kingdom,* p. 66; June 6, 2005, review of *By These Ten Bones,* p. 66.

School Library Journal, December, 2003, Bruce Anne Shook, review of *The Hollow Kingdom,* p. 149; May, 2004, Sarah Flowers, review of *The Hollow Kingdom,* p. 92; October, 2004, Farida S. Dowler, review of *Close Kin,* p. 161; June, 2005, Joel Shoemaker, review of *By These Ten Bones,* p. 156; October, 2005, Beth L. Meister, review of *In the Coils of the Snake,* p. 158; May, 2008, Lisa Marie Williams, review of *The Sky Inside,* p. 122; July, 2008, Karen T. Bilton, review of *The Sky Inside,* p. 59; November, 2009, Walter Minkel, review of *The Walls Have Eyes,* p. 104; November, 2010, Kathryn Kosiorek, review of *The House of Dead Maids,* p. 112.

Voice of Youth Advocates, April, 2004, Stacy Dillon, review of *The Hollow Kingdom,* p. 58; December, 2004, Stacy Dillon, review of *Close Kin,* p. 402; August, 2008, Christina Fairman, review of *The Sky Inside,* p. 257.

ONLINE

Clare B. Dunkle Web site, http://www.claredunkle.com (December 4, 2010).

Mythopoeic Society Web site, http://www.mythsoc.org/ (December, 2004), "Clare B. Dunkle: Award Acceptance Remarks."

Smart Writers Journal Online, http://www.SmartWriters.com/ (October, 2003), Roxyanne Young, interview with Dunkle.*

*   *   *

DUSÍKOVÁ, Maja 1946-

Personal

Born 1946, in Piešt'any, Czechoslovakia (now Slovakia). *Education:* Studied art in Bratislava, Czechoslovakia (now Slovakia).

Addresses

Home—Florence, Italy. *E-mail*—majadusikova@yahoo.com.

Career

Illustrator.

Illustrator

Rolf Krenzer, *Die Geschichte vom Weihnachtsglöckchen,* Bohem Press (Zurich, Switzerland), 1994.

Dorothea Lachner, *Ein Geschenk vom Nikolaus,* NordSüd Verlag (Zurich, Switzerland), 1994, translated by J. Alison James as *The Gift from Saint Nicholas,* North-South Books (New York, NY), 1995.

Peter Grosz, *Alina, Aluna und die zwölf Monatsbrüder,* NordSüd Verlag (Zurich, Switzerland), 1996.

Dorothea Lachner, *Du warst es! sagte Berberitz,* NordSüd Verlag (Zurich, Switzerland), 1997.

Jacob and Wilhelm Grimm, *Rapunzel,* NordSüd Verlag (Zurich, Switzerland), 1997, translated by Anthea Bell as *Rapunzel: A Fairy Tale,* North-South Books (New York, NY), 1997.

Antonie Schneider, *Leb wohl, Chaja!,* NordSüd Verlag (Zurich, Switzerland), 1998, translated by J. Alison James as *Good-bye, Vivi!,* North-South Books (New York, NY), 1998.

Joseph Mohr, *Stille Nacht, heilige Nacht,* NordSüd Verlag (Zurich, Switzerland), 1999, translation published as *Silent Night, Holy Night: A Christmas Carol,* North-South Books (New York, NY), 1999.

Antonie Schneider, *Sankt Martin und der kleine Bär,* NordSüd Verlag (Zurich, Switzerland), 2000.

Friedrich Recknagel, *Sarah's Weide,* NordSüd Verlag (Zurich, Switzerland), 2001, translated by Anthea Bell as *Sarah's Willow,* North-South Books (New York, NY), 2002.

Udo Weigelt, *Stimmt das alles was man hört?,* NordSüd Verlag (Zurich, Switzerland), 2001, translated by J. Alison James as *What Lies on the Other Side?,* North-South Books (New York, NY), 2002.

Rolf Krenzer, *The Christmas Bell,* Gingham Dog Press (Columbus, OH), 2003.

Moritz Petz, *Monstermädchen Mona,* NordSüd Verlag (Zurich, Switzerland), 2004, translated by J. Alison James as *Mona the Monster Girl,* North-South Books (New York, NY), 2004.

Antonie Schneider, *Advent Storybook: Twenty-four Stories to Share before Christmas,* translated by Marisa Miller, North-South Books (New York, NY), 2005.

Hans Christian Andersen, *Die Prinzessin auf der Erbse,* NordSüd Verlag (Zurich, Switzerland), 2007.

Johanna Spyri, *Heidi,* North-South Books (New York, NY), 2009.

Antonie Schneider, *Kleiner Löwe, willst du den König sehen?,* Berlin Verlag (Berlin, Germany), 2009.

Felix Salten, *Bambi,* NordSüd Verlag (Zurich, Switzerland), 2011.

Sidelights

Maja Dusíková, a highly regarded illustrator of children's books, has gained recognition for her warm, emotion-filled watercolor artwork. A native of Czechoslovakia who now lives and works in Florence, Italy, Dusíková is perhaps best known for her holiday fare, which includes a line of popular Advent calendars. Although most of her works have been published abroad, several books featuring her art have been released in the United States in English translation, among them *Good-bye, Vivi!* by Antonie Schneider, Dorothea Lachner's *The Gift from Saint Nicholas,* and *Sarah's Willow* by Friedrich Recknagel.

The Gift from Saint Nicholas was the first of Dusíková's illustration projects to be translated into English. The work centers on snowbound youngsters Anna and Misha, who ask Saint Nicholas to clear a path so they can visit their grandfather. To their surprise, the saint instead leaves a mysterious package in the village square, prompting an unexpected reunion as the townsfolk shovel their way to the gift. *Booklist* critic Lauren Peterson observed that Dusíková's illustrations "convey the warmth and spirit of the season," and a *Publishers Weekly* reviewer commented that her "tranquil watercolors" for Lachner's tale captures "the timelessness—and the irresistible appeal—of Saint Nicholas legends."

In *Silent Night, Holy Night: A Christmas Carol* Dusíková offers a visual portrait of the holiday classic composed by Joseph Mohr, a nineteenth-century Austrian priest. According to *Booklist* contributor Susan Dove Lempke, "the watercolors nicely capture the sense of peace found in the song's words." Rolf Krenzer's *The Christmas Bell,* a Nativity story, focuses on Rachel, a

shepherd's daughter who, after discovering a silver bell, realizes that she has been chosen for a special purpose. Dusíková's "watercolor pictures glow with light," Hazel Rochman noted in her *Booklist* review of this work, while a critic in *Kirkus Reviews* praised the "soft focus and muted colors" to be found in the art for *The Christmas Bell.*

Two young children learn to cope with loss after the death of their grandmother's pet canary in Schneider's *Good-bye, Vivi!,* and here Dusíková's images, "painted in soft, warm colors, visually complement the lyrical narrative," according to April Judge in *Booklist.* Another story of hope, Recknagel's *Sarah's Willow,* depicts a girl's efforts to nurture a sapling after her favorite tree is felled. The artist "offers gentle-toned watercolors of affectionate scenes," commented Gay Lynn Van Vleck in reviewing this European import for *School Library Journal.*

An allegorical tale, Udo Weigelt's *What Lies on the Other Side?* concerns a young fox that grows curious about life across the stream. With encouragement from his new friend, Raccoon, who lives on the opposite riverbank, Fox summons the courage to visit unknown territory. Be Astengo, writing in *School Library Jour-*

Maja Dusíková's illustration projects include Friedrich Recknagel's **Sarah's Willow,** *a book originally published in German.* (Copyright © 2002 by NordSud Verlag AG, CH-8005 Zurich, Switzerland. Used with permission of North-South Books, Inc., New York.)

nal, applauded Dusíková's work for Weigelt's story, stating that her "naturalistic watercolors of forest scenes and animals create a warm, pleasant atmosphere, inviting readers into the story." Dusíková has also contributed the illustrations to a picture-book version of Johanna Spyri's classic 1880 novel *Heidi,* about a young girl who is sent to live with her reclusive grandfather in his mountain cabin. "Dusíková taps into the emotional core of this tale," a critic in *Kirkus Reviews* stated, and Shelle Rosenfeld noted in *Booklist* that the "colorful, soft illustrations depict Heidi in the idyllic, Alpine landscapes and upscale mansions, filled with period details."

Biographical and Critical Sources

PERIODICALS

Booklist, November 1, 1995, Lauren Peterson, review of *The Gift from Saint Nicholas,* p. 476; August, 1997, review of *Rapunzel: A Fairy Tale,* p. 1903; January 1, 1999, April Judge, review of *Good-Bye, Vivi!,* p. 890; September 1, 1999, Susan Dove Lempke, review of *Silent Night, Holy Night; A Christmas Carol,* p. 149; December 15, 2003, Hazel Rochman, review of *The Christmas Bell,* p. 753; September 1, 2009, Shelle Rosenfeld, review of *Heidi,* p. 97.

Kirkus Reviews, November 1, 2003, review of *The Christmas Bell,* p. 1317; November 1, 2005, review of *Advent Storybook: Twenty-four Stories to Share before Christmas,* p. 1196; September 15, 2009, review of *Heidi.*

New York Times Book Review, November 16, 1997, Maud Lavin, review of *Rapunzel.*

Publishers Weekly, September 18, 1995, review of *The Gift from Saint Nicholas,* p. 102.

School Library Journal, October, 1995, Jane Marino, review of *The Gift from Saint Nicholas,* p. 38; January, 1999, Ann Cook, review of *Good-Bye, Vivi!,* p. 102; October, 1999, Susan Patron, review of *Silent Night, Holy Night,* p. 69; May, 2002, Gay Lynn Van Vleck, review of *Sarah's Willow,* p. 125; September, 2002, Be Astengo, review of *What Lies on the Other Side?,* p. 208; December, 2009, Kathy Piehl, review of *Heidi,* p. 92.*

E-F

EDWARDSON, Debby Dahl

Personal

Born in MN; married; children: seven. *Education:* Colorado College, B.A., 1974; Vermont College of Fine Arts, M.F.A., 2005. *Religion:* Christian.

Addresses

Home—Barrow, AK. *E-mail*—debby.dahl.edwardson@gmail.com.

Career

Author and educator. Teacher of writing courses through Writers.com/Writers on the Net and Ilisagvik College. Worked variously as a nurse's aide, waitress, pipeline worker, radio reporter, public-relations writer, college director, and school-board president.

Member

Society of Children's Book Writers and Illustrators, Authors Guild.

Awards, Honors

Notable Books for a Global Society designation, International Reading Association (IRA), Notable Social Studies Trade Books for Young People, National Council for the Social Studies/Children's Book Council, and Children's Picture Book award, Independent Publisher Book Awards, all 2004, all for *Whale Snow;* Best Fiction for Young Adults designation, American Library Association, and Notable Books for a Global Society designation, and *Booklist* Top-Ten Historical Novels for Youth and Top-Ten First Novels for Youth selections, all 2010, all for *Blessing's Bead.*

Writings

Whale Snow, illustrated by Annie Patterson, Charlesbridge/Talewinds (Watertown, MA), 2003.

Debby Dahl Edwardson (Reproduced by permission.)

Blessing's Bead (novel), Farrar, Straus & Giroux (New York, NY), 2009.

Author's work has been translated into Iñupiaq and Korean.

Sidelights

In works like *Whale Snow,* an award-winning picture book, and *Blessing's Bead,* a critically acclaimed young-

adult novel, Debby Dahl Edwardson offers readers a look at Alaska's Iñupiaq (Eskimo) culture. A native of Minnesota who has lived for some three decades in Barrow, Alaska, the northernmost city in North America, Edwardson notes that her experiences in the "Last Frontier" have shaped her literary efforts. "As many writers do, I write what I know, and through knowing it in my own way, make it my own, something both very old and very new at the same time," the author stated on the Macmillan Web site.

In *Whale Snow* a young Iñupiaq boy learns the significance of his community's customs and traditions after his father's whaling crew catches the first bowhead of the season. According to a *Publishers Weekly* critic, "the story strikes an appropriate balance between a child's inquisitive delight and his respectful discoveries about his heritage," and *School Library Journal* reviewer Susan Marie Pitard described *Whale Snow* as "an intriguing glimpse into another culture."

Blessing's Bead grew from an interview Edwardson conducted with an elderly Yupik woman who shared

Cover of Debby Dahl Edwardson's fantasy novel Blessing's Bead, *which focuses on native Alaskan culture.* (Farrar, Straus & Giroux, 2009. Jacket photograph by Cindy Schults. Reproduced by permission of Farrar, Straus & Giroux.)

painful memories of her decades-long separation from friends and family. The work features two interconnected plotlines: the first, set in 1917 during a devastating influenza epidemic, concerns a young Iñupiaq woman who leaves her village—and her beloved sister—to marry a visiting Siberian; the second focuses on a contemporary fourteen year old named Blessing who discovers a treasured blue bead that belonged to her grandmother, the only family member to survive the epidemic. Reviewing Edwardson's first novel, *Horn Book* contributor Joanna Rudge Long praised "the authentic imagery, details, and language that pervade this memorable story," and a *Publishers Weekly* reviewer deemed *Blessing's Bead* "a fascinating portrait of a family's rich history." "It's the Nutaaqs' rhythmic, indelible voices—both as steady and elemental as the beat of a drum or a heart—that will move readers most," predicted *Booklist* critic Gillian Engberg in reviewing the novel.

"What I love most about writing is that wonderful alchemy that turns words on a page into complete worlds, places that become so real we can smell the trees and hear the voices," Edwardson told *Cynsations* online interviewer Cynthia Leitich Smith. "I especially like it when a character jumps right off the page and says or does something that takes me, the writer, by surprise. This is the part of writing that most excites me."

Biographical and Critical Sources

PERIODICALS

Booklist, August, 2003, Carolyn Phelan, review of *Whale Snow,* p. 1988; October, 2009, Gillian Engberg, review of *Blessing's Bead.*

Horn Book, November-December, 2009, Joanna Rudge Long, review of *Blessing's Bead,* p. 667.

Kirkus Reviews, October 1, 2009, review of *Blessing's Bead.*

Publishers Weekly, June 23, 2003, review of *Whale Snow,* p. 66; November 23, 2009, review of *Blessing's Bead,* p. 57.

School Library Journal, December, 2003, Susan Marie Pitard, review of *Whale Snow,* p. 112; November, 2009, Alison Follos, review of *Blessing's Bead,* p. 104.

ONLINE

Cynsations Web log, http://cynthialeitichsmith.blogspot.com/ (November 16, 2009), Cynthia Leitich Smith, interview with Edwardson.

Debby Dahl Edwardson Home Page, http://www.debbydahledwardson.com (December 1, 2010).

Macmillan Web site, http://us.macmillan.com/ (December 1, 2010), "Debby Dahl Edwardson."

FERRARI, Michael
(Michael J. Ferrari)

Personal

Born December 3, in Columbus, IN; married; children: two daughters, one son. *Education:* Attended Wright State University, 1982-83, and Cleveland State University, 1983-84; Ohio State University, B.F.A. (photography and cinema) 1988; California State University, Los Angeles, M.A. (English literature and creative writing), 2002.

Addresses

Home—OH.

Career

Educator and writer. Film and video editor in Los Angeles, CA, for sixteen years; script reader, 2000; WB Television Network, senior editor, 2000-04; Southwestern Academy, English teacher, 2004-06; legal proofreader, 2006-08; teacher of screenwriting at Cleveland State University, beginning 2008, and Oberlin College, 2009-10.

Awards, Honors

Delacorte Yearling Prize, 2007, for *Born to Fly*.

Writings

Born to Fly, Delacorte Press (New York, NY), 2009.

Sidelights

Michael Ferrari worked on the West Coast as a film editor for several years before making a career change and returning to his home state of Ohio. Armed with a master's degree in English, Ferrari spent several years teaching at the middle-school level before taking a job in the film studies department at Cleveland State University. He credits a question from one of his young students with inspiring his first book, *Born to Fly*. The student, a girl, asked Ferrari for reading suggestions: stories that had adventures in which girls, rather than boys, were the ones who managed to overcome the odds and save the day. Because Ferrari could not think of an appropriate story, he decided to write one, and when he wove in his knowledge of World War II fighter planes, *Born to Fly* was the result.

Praised by a *Publishers Weekly* critic as a "high-flying, nail-biting historical adventure that is uplifting and just good fun," *Born to Fly* introduces readers to an eleven-year-old girl with unconventional dreams. For Bird McGill, it is taking too long to grow up: she cannot wait until she is old enough to become a pilot. Bird's

love of flying has come from her dad, an airline mechanic who allows her to help pilot the small propeller airplanes that he repairs in a local hangar at their small Rhode Island airport. Since Japan bombed the U.S. Naval Base at Pearl Harbor, Bird's dad has joined the Air Force and gone overseas, and now the town's small airfield has become a training ground. In addition to being without her flying partner, Bird also finds herself thrown together with a new student, a Japanese-American boy named Kenji Fujita, who has come to live with his Uncle Tomo since being released from one of the U.S. government's internment camps. Although many locals suspect Kenji of being a spy, Bird becomes his friend, and when the two preteens discover a real threat to the safety of their coastal town they must work hard to find an adult who believes them.

Born to Fly "is chock-full of both action and theme," asserted Betty Carter in her *Horn Book* review of Ferrari's novel, noting that Bird's pivotal flight in a P-40 Warhawk fighter jet shows her to be the hero the author intended. "Bird's first-person voice is convincing," noted a *Kirkus Reviews* writer, and in *School Library*

Cover of Michael Ferrari's history-themed novel* Born to Fly, *featuring cover art by Allen Douglas. (Jacket art © 2009 by Allen Douglas; jacket design © 2009 by Marci Senders. Reproduced by permission of Random House Children's Books, a division of Random House, Inc.)

Journal Kim Dare dubbed *Born to Fly* an "action-packed" example of "first-rate historical fiction."

Biographical and Critical Sources

PERIODICALS

Booklist, May 15, 2009, Monika Schroder, review of *Born to Fly,* p. 40.
Horn Book, November-December, 2009, Betty Carter, review of *Born to Fly,* p. 670.
Kirkus Reviews, June 15, 2009, review of *Born to Fly.*
Publishers Weekly, July 13, 2009, review of *Born to Fly,* p. 57.
School Library Journal, August, 2009, Kim Dare, review of *Born to Fly,* p. 102.

ONLINE

Michael Ferrari Home Page, http://michaeljferrari.com (November 14, 2010).*

* * *

FERRARI, Michael J.
See FERRARI, Michael

* * *

FORLER, Nan

Personal

Born in Elmira, Ontario, Canada; married Kevin Coates (a teacher and musician); children. *Education:* University degrees (music and education). *Hobbies and other interests:* Music, movies and plays, traveling, spending time with family.

Addresses

Home—Waterloo, Ontario, Canada. *E-mail*—nanforler@ rogers.com.

Career

Author and educator. Elementary-school teacher in Canada, beginning c. late 1980s.

Awards, Honors

Top Ten Canadian Children's Picture Books selection, Ontario Library Association, and Shining Willow Award nomination, Saskatchewan Young Readers' Choice Awards, both 2010, both for *Bird Child.*

Writings

R. Murray Schafer: A Canadian Voice, privately published (Waterloo, Ontario, Canada), 1987.

Bird Child, illustrated by François Thisdale, Tundra Books (Toronto, Ontario, Canada), 2009.
Winterberries and Appleblossoms: Reflections and Flavors of a Mennonite Year, illustrated by Peter Etril Snyder, Tundra Books (Toronto, Ontario, Canada), 2011.

Contributor to books, including *All Together Now,* Scholastic Canada (Toronto, Ontario, Canada), 2010.

Author's work has been translated into Braille.

Sidelights

Writer and educator Nan Forler lives in Ontario, Canada, where her experiences as an elementary-school teacher inspired her to write the picture book *Bird Child.* Reviewing Forler's fiction debut in *School Library Journal,* Lucinda Snyder Whitehurst dubbed *Bird Child* a "lyrical combination of realism and fantasy [that] defies expectation."

Brought to life in colorful illustrations by François Thisdale, Forler's story introduces Eliza, a young elementary-school student who has been raised with a strong self-image. In contrast to the resilience Eliza has gained through her mother's encouragement, new student Lainey is emotionally crushed by the taunting of several classroom bullies. A small, thin child who, in her oversized hand-me-down clothing seems all elbows and knees, Lainey reminds Eliza of a bird, and as the teasing continues Lainey gradually loses her interest even in her favorite subject: art. Although she is also petite for her age, Eliza decides to take an active role in helping her new friend and, in addition to bravely confronting the schoolyard bullies, she also finds a way to metaphorically share her belief in her own possibilities with her friend.

Calling *Bird Child* "a beautiful book with a somber tone," Whitehurst added praise for Thisdale's "dramatic, mixed-media" art, which add a dreamlike element to the story. In *Booklist* Kay Weisman wrote that the picture book is "lyrically written and conveys an astute awareness of children and bullying." While a *Kirkus Reviews* writer maintained that the richly toned images—digitized meldings of photographs, paintings, and line drawings—"add layers of context" to Forler's tale, *Resource Links* contributor reviewer Lorie Battershill asserted that the author's "word choices approach the finely tuned standard of poetry." Keith McPherson agreed, writing in his review of *Bird Child* for the *Canadian Review of Materials* that "Forler's use of highly evocative similes and thickly descriptive language helps the reader step into the story, re/imagine and weave their own experiences into the story, and become personally engaged with Eliza's struggles and triumphs."

Bird Child, my first published picture book, is the story of a tiny, bird-like girl who stands up for a friend who is being bullied in the schoolyard," Forler told *SATA.* "Eliza is a child who appears frail and powerless, yet she finds her voice and makes a difference as an active bystander.

Nan Forler's story in **Bird Child** *is captured in artwork by François* **Thisdale.** (Tundra Books, 2009. Reproduced with permission of the publisher.)

"The bystander, the person who witnesses a bullying incident, is the character in the scene whom we often forget, yet the bystander has more power than we sometimes imagine. Doing nothing further empowers the bully; speaking up can change the life of a victim. Standing up for injustice and speaking up when someone is treated unfairly are themes that are close to my heart—maybe because I am a teacher and know the difficulties of dealing with a bully, maybe because I am a mother and hear the heartbreaking stories of classmates, or maybe because I am a writer.

"The writer's role is very much like the role of the bystander. A bystander sees what others do not, or choose not, to see. A bystander acts as a voice for the voiceless. So too, as a writer, my job is to be the 'other' character in the scene, to watch and listen, to notice something unnoticed, to speak up and be heard. A writer brings a voice to that which would otherwise be left unspoken."

Biographical and Critical Sources

PERIODICALS

Booklist, November 1, 2009, Kay Weisman, review of *Bird Child,* p. 51.

Canadian Review of Materials, September 25, 2009, Keith McPherson, review of *Bird Child.*
Kirkus Reviews, July 1, 2009, review of *Bird Child.*
Resource Links, October, 2009, Lorie Battershill, review of *Bird Child,* p. 1.
School Library Journal, September, 2009, Lucinda Snyder Whitehurst, review of *Bird Child,* p. 120.

ONLINE

Nan Forler Home Page, http://www.nanforler.com (November 27, 2010).
Tundra Books Web site, http://www.tundrabooks.com/ (November 27, 2010), "Nan Forler."

*   *   *

FRANCO, Betsy

Personal

Married Douglas Franco; children: James, Thomas, David. *Education:* Stanford University, B.A.; Lesley College, M.Ed. *Hobbies and other interests:* Swing dancing.

Addresses

Home—CA. *E-mail*—franco.betsy@gmail.com.

Career

Writer and editor for children and adults; creator of educational materials. Actor; member of Suburban Squirrel comedy troupe and Studio-33 Actor's Collective.

Member

Authors Guild, Society of Children's Book Writers and Illustrators.

Awards, Honors

Arizona Book Award for Best Educational Book, for *Math Poetry;* Northern California Book Award nomination, and Northern California Independent Booksellers Award for Best Illustrated Children's Book, both 2009, both for *Zero Is the Leaves on the Tree* illustrated by Shino Arihara; Best Books selection, Bank Street College of Education, 2010, for *Pond Circle;* Lee Bennett Hopkins Poetry Award Honor designation, 2010, for *A Curious Collection of Cats.*

Writings

Japan, illustrated by Jo Supancich, Evan-Moor (Monterey, CA), 1993.

Betsy Franco (Photograph by Jim Warren. Reproduced by permission.)

Mexico, illustrated by Jo Supancich, Evan-Moor (Monterey, CA), 1993.

Russia, illustrated by Jo Supancich, Evan-Moor (Monterey, CA), 1993.

India, illustrated by Jo Supancich, Evan-Moor (Monterey, CA), 1994.

Nigeria, illustrated by Jo Supancich, Evan-Moor (Monterey, CA), 1994.

China, illustrated by Jo Supancich, Evan-Moor (Monterey, CA), 1994.

Brazil, illustrated by Cheryl Kirk Noll, Evan-Moor (Monterey, CA), 1995.

South Korea, illustrated by Cheryl Kirk Noll, Evan-Moor (Monterey, CA), 1995.

Italy, illustrated by Susan O'Neill, Evan-Moor (Monterey, CA), 1995.

(With Michael Verne) *Quiet Elegance: Japan through the Eyes of Nine American Artists,* Charles E. Tuttle (Boston, MA), 1997.

Sorting All Sorts of Socks, illustrated by Sheila Lucas, Creative Publications (Mountain View, CA), 1997.

Fourscore and Seven, Good Year Books (Glenview, IL), 1999.

Grandpa's Quilt, illustrated by Linda A. Bild, Children's Press (New York, NY), 1999.

Write and Read Math Story Books, Scholastic (New York, NY), 1999.

Unfolding Mathematics with Unit Origami, Key Curriculum, 1999.

Shells, illustrated by Kristin Sorra, Children's Press (New York, NY), 2000.

Why the Frog Has Big Eyes, illustrated by Joung Un Kim, Harcourt, Brace (San Diego, CA), 2000.

Caring, Sharing, and Getting Along, Scholastic (New York, NY), 2000.

Thematic Poetry: On the Farm, Scholastic (New York, NY), 2000.

Twenty Marvelous Math Tales, Scholastic (New York, NY), 2000.

Thematic Poetry: Neighborhoods and Communities, Scholastic (New York, NY), 2000.

Thematic Poetry: Creepy Crawlies, Scholastic (New York, NY), 2000.

201 Thematic Riddle Poems to Build Literacy, Scholastic (New York, NY), 2000.

Thematic Poetry: All about Me!, Scholastic (New York, NY), 2000.

The Tortoise Who Bragged: A Chinese Tale with Trigrams, illustrated by Ann-Marie Perks, Stokes Publishing (Sunnyvale, CA), 2000.

My Pinkie Finger, illustrated by Margeaux Lucas, Children's Press (New York, NY), 2001.

Instant Poetry Frames for Primary Poets, Scholastic (New York, NY), 2001.

Fifteen Wonderful Writing-Prompt Mini-Books, Scholastic (New York, NY), 2001.

Clever Calculator Cat, illustrated by Ann-Marie Perks, Stokes Publishing (Sunnyvale, CA), 2001.

Funny Fairy Tale Math, Scholastic (New York, NY), 2001.

Thematic Poetry: Transportation, Scholastic (New York, NY), 2001.

Clever Calculations about Cats and Other Cool Creatures (teacher resource), Stokes Publishing (Sunnyvale, CA), 2001.

Adding Alligators and Other Easy-to-Read Math Stories, Scholastic (New York, NY), 2001.

Five-Minute Math Problem of the Day for Young Learners, Scholastic (New York, NY), 2001.

Twelve Genre Mini-Books, Scholastic (New York, NY), 2002.

Instant Math Practice Pages for Homework—or Anytime!, Scholastic (New York, NY), 2002.

Six Silly Seals, and Other Read-Aloud Story Skits, Teaching Resources, 2002.

Amazing Animals, illustrated by Jesse Reisch, Children's Press (New York, NY), 2002.

Pocket Poetry Mini-Books, Scholastic (New York, NY), 2002.

Silly Sally, illustrated by Stacey Lamb, Children's Press (New York, NY), 2002.

Jake's Cake Mistake, illustrated by Paul Harvey, Scholastic (New York, NY), 2002.

(With Claudine Jellison and Johanna Kaufman) *Subtraction Fun,* Pebble Books, 2002.

(With Denise Dauler) *Math in Motion: Wiggle, Gallop, and Leap with Numbers,* Creative Teaching Press, 2002.

Many Ways to 100, Yellow Umbrella Books (Mankato, MN), 2002.

A Bat Named Pat, illustrated by Bari Weissman, Scholastic (New York, NY), 2002.

Time to Estimate, Yellow Umbrella Books (Mankato, MN), 2002.

Marvelous Math Word Problem Mini-Books, Scholastic (New York, NY), 2002.

What's Zero?, Yellow Umbrella Books (Mankato, MN), 2002.

Going to Grandma's Farm, illustrated by Claudia Rueda, Children's Press (New York, NY), 2003.

Word Families: Guess-Me Poems and Puzzles, Scholastic (New York, NY), 2003.

Mathematickles!, illustrated by Steven Salerno, Margaret K. McElderry Books (New York, NY), 2003.

Amoeba Hop, illustrated by Christine Lavin, Puddle Jump Press, 2003.

Alphabet: Guess-Me Poems and Puzzles, Scholastic (New York, NY), 2003.

Counting Our Way to the 100th Day!: 100 Poems and 100 Pictures to Celebrate the 100th Day of School, illustrated by Steven Salerno, Margaret K. McElderry Books (New York, NY), 2004.

Conversations with a Poet: Inviting Poetry into K-12 Classrooms, Richard C. Owen (Katonah, NY), 2005.

Birdsongs: A Backwards Counting Book, illustrated by Steve Jenkins, Margaret K. McElderry (New York, NY), 2006.

Math Poetry: Linking Language and Math in a Fresh Way, Good Year Books (Tucson, AZ), 2006.

Summer Beat, illustrated by Charlotte Middleton, Margaret K. McElderry Books (New York, NY), 2007.

Bees, Snails, and Peacock Tails: Shapes—Naturally, illustrated by Steve Jenkins, Margaret K. McElderry Books (New York, NY), 2008.

Instant Poetry Frames: Neighborhood and Community, Scholastic Teaching Resources (New York, NY), 2008.

A Curious Collection of Cats, illustrated by Michael Wertz, Tricycle Press (Berkeley, CA), 2009.

Messing around on the Monkey Bars, and Other School Poems for Two Voices, illustrated by Jessie Hartland, Candlewick Press (Somerville, MA), 2009.

Metamorphosis: Junior Year (young-adult novel), illustrated by son Tom Franco, Candlewick Press (Somerville, MA), 2009.

Pond Circle, illustrated by Stefano Vitale, Margaret K. McElderry Books (New York, NY), 2009.

Zero Is the Leaves on the Tree, illustrated by Shino Arihara, Tricycle Press (Berkeley, CA), 2009.

A Dazzling Display of Dogs, illustrated by Michael Wertz, Tricycle Press (Berkeley, CA), 2011.

Double Play, illustrated by Doug Cushman, Tricycle Press (Berkeley, CA), 2011.

Author of numerous workbooks, easy-level readers, easy mathematics resource books, and science resource books.

EDITOR

You Hear Me?: Poems and Writing by Teenage Boys, Candlewick Press (Cambridge, MA), 2000.

Things I Have to Tell You: Poems and Writing by Teenage Girls, photographs by Nina Nickles, Candlewick Press (Cambridge, MA), 2001.

(With Annette Ochoa and Traci Gourdine) *Night Is Gone, Day Is Still Coming: Stories and Poems by American Indian Teenagers and Young Adults,* Candlewick Press (Cambridge, MA), 2003.

Falling Hard: 100 Love Poems by Teens, Candlewick Press (Cambridge, MA), 2008.

Adaptations

Metamorphosis: Junior Year was adapted for audiobook, read by James Franco and David Franco, Brilliance Audio, 2010, and was produced on the stage by the Palo Alto Children's Theatre, 2011.

Sidelights

Betsy Franco's many projects for children range widely across the educational and entertainment spectrums, from beginning readers and books that use games and projects to teach basic skills to picture books to teen fiction to edited anthologies of poetry by young adults. In many of her books for younger children, such as *Mathematickles!, Counting Our Way to the 100th Day!: 100 Poems and 100 Pictures to Celebrate the 100th Day of School,* and *Zero Is the Leaves on the Trees,* she teams up with talented artists to confront one of her first—and favorite—challenges: finding ways to make learning fun. As she noted on her home page, "I particularly love to show how exciting, sassy, and creative math can be." Other books, such as *A Curious Collection of Cats, Pond Circle,* and the teen novel *Metamorphosis: Junior Year,* showcase more of Franco's creative vision and highlight her skillful use of words.

Although she has gained prominence as an author, Franco initially studied to be a fine artist. When her children were born, however, she realized that she could not spare the time needed for her visual art, so she channeled her creativity into writing. During the early 1990s she produced several works of culturally based nonfiction, then gradually expanded into other educational works, mixing information and concepts into engaging and rhyming texts. Honing in on mathematics in books such as *Clever Calculator Cat* and *Many Ways to 100,* Franco has helped young readers sharpen their math skills through activities and riddles, while *Zero Is the Leaves on the Tree* uses nature to explain a concept that is sometimes difficult for young children to comprehend. Illustrated with gouache paintings by Shino Arihara, *Zero Is the Leaves on the Tree* moves beyond the perfunctory definition of zero as "nothing" and "reveals instead that zero is an absence that is observable, countable, and meaningful," according to *Horn Book* critic Tanya D. Auger.

With its lighthearted approach, Franco's *Mathematickles!* incorporates common math signs such as plus, minus, and parentheses into word poems dealing with the four seasons and the outdoor world. Noting Steven Salerno's colorful artwork for the book, a *Publishers Weekly* critic praised *Mathematickles!* as a "nimble brain teaser" that "elevates basic mathematical concepts plus wordplay to the level of inspiration." Franco and Salerno also collaborate on *Counting Our Way to the 100th Day!*, which *Booklist* contributor Gillian Engberg recommended for its pairing of Franco's "whimsical arithmetic exercises" and "reassuring" verses with Salerno's "stylish, cheerful gouache paintings."

Franco's poetry collection* Messing around on the Monkey Bars and Other School Poems for Two Voices *features artwork by Jessie Hartland. (Illustration copyright © 2009 by Jessie Hartland. Reproduced by permission of Candlewick Press, Somerville, MA.)

In addition to mathematical concepts, Franco also encourages children to consider their role in the natural world as they encounter the cycle of seasons, various animals, and changing weather. In *Summer Beat* she uses alliteration and rhyme to chronicle the many activities that fill up a child's summer vacation. *Pond Circle* allows readers to explore the interconnectedness of plants and animals in a pond ecosystem, the journey from algae to nymph to beetle to bullfrog and beyond all captured in the blues and greens of Stefano Vitale's oil paintings. Enhanced by Charlotte Middleton's digitally enhanced art, *Summer Beat* serves up "an energetic tribute to the sensations of summer," according to a *Kirkus Reviews* contributor, while *Pond Circle* was

praised by *School Library Journal* contributor Kathleen Kelly MacMillan as "a clear, child-friendly look at ecology" that provides a "straightforward depiction of the food chain" in Franco's rhyming text. Citing the book's usefulness in both science lessons and storyhour, Gillian Engberg added in *Booklist* that Franco's verses in *Pond Circle* "scan with an irresistible beat that will invite participation."

In *Birdsongs,* a picture book featuring cut-paper collages by award-winning artist Steve Jenkins, Franco "spins a nature lesson in lucid language," according to *Booklist* contributor GraceAnne A. DeCandido. "The writing is lyrical and engaging," wrote Teresa Pfeifer in

School Library Journal, the critic concluding that the "lavishly illustrated" *Birdsongs* "will engender a love for birds and an awareness of their unique music." Another collaboration with Jenkins, *Bees, Snails, and Peacock Tails: Shapes—Naturally,* introduces readers to the amazing designs of Mother Nature, from the rounded curve of a puffer fish and the complex spiral of a snail shell to the geometric repetition found in a honeybee's hive. Praising Franco's "lively" rhymes in *Bees, Snails, and Peacock Tales,* a *Kirkus Reviews* writer also ranked Jenkins' collages as "stunning."

Inspired by the poet's own two felines, Franco's *A Curious Collection of Cats* is illustrated in single-color block prints by Michael Wertz. In this unusual work—which has been obediently followed by the companion volume *A Dazzling Display of Dogs*—Franco crafts thirty-two "concrete" poems: poems that are typeset on the page in the shape of the thing that they represent. Showcasing both free verse and poetic forms such as haiku and limerick, the poems capture cats of all sorts, from pudgy, purring, lap-snugglers to friskier felines that are known for twitching tails, pouncing, and biting. Praising *A Curious Collection of Cats* as "an ideal match of subject and form," Susan Dove Lempke added in *Horn Book* that both Franco and Wertz "convey the silliness of cats and their humans without ever being silly themselves."

Based on Roman poet Ovid's lengthy narrative poem of the same name, Franco's mixed-verse novel *Metamorphosis* captures the experiences of an artistic high-school junior who lives at the effect of others: his parents, his brilliant but drug-addicted sister Thena, and classmates whom he compares to the classical characters Orpheus, Psyche, Cupid, Midas, and Proserpina, among others. Framed as Ovid's texts, Facebook entries, and journal writings, *Metamorphosis* combines what a *Kirkus Reviews* contributor described as both "prose entries in realistic teenspeak" and "beautifully crafted poems," the text highlighted by line drawings created by Franco's son Tom Franco during his own high-school years. While Anthony C. Doyle noted in *School Library Journal* that the novel's references to classic mythology might be lost on some readers, Ovid's adolescent need to rebel against parental overprotection and his feelings of abandonment and loss "will resonate with many young adults." In *Booklist* Hazel Rochman predicted of *Metamorphosis* that Franco's "wry combination of contemporary technology and archetypes will appeal to [techno-savvy] teens."

The poetry Franco collects in her anthologies *You Hear Me?: Poems and Writing by Teenage Boys, Things I Have to Tell You: Poems and Writing by Teenage Girls, Night Is Gone, Day Is Still Coming: Stories and Poems by American Indian Teenagers and Young Adults,* and *Falling Hard: 100 Love Poems by Teens* reveals the authentic voices of contemporary teens wrestling with typical issues, feelings, and challenges. *You Here Me?,*

her first edited anthology was inspired by her own teenage sons and includes frank and honest verses on topics ranging from homosexuality and dating to self-image, family and neighborhood issues, aspirations, and creativity. Sharon Korbeck, reviewing the work for *School Library Journal,* cited the book's "fresh approach to hearing what today's youths have to say." In *Booklist* Rochman wrote that the poems have "more urgency than many YA novels," and concluded of *You Here Me?* that "many teens will recognize their search for themselves" within its pages.

A companion volume, *Things I Have to Tell You,* collects the poetry of teenage girls. A *Horn Book* reviewer wrote of this book that, "varying in tone, style, and degree of polish," the verses collected in *Things I Have to Tell You* "convey moments of strength and weakness, of anger, fear, and joy, commanding our attention from beginning to end."

Cover of the verse anthology **You Hear Me?,** *featuring work by teen poets that was selected and edited by Franco.* (Copyright © 2000 by Candlewick Press. Reproduced by permission of the publisher Candlewick Press, Inc., Cambridge, MA.)

The combined voices of both young men and young women are represented in Franco's *Night Is Gone, Day Is Still Coming* and *Falling Hard,* the first a collection of Native-American voices and the second a reflection of the ups and downs of first love. In her *School Library Journal* review of *Night Is Gone, Day Is Still Coming,* Sharon Korbek observed of the book's contributors: "Whether they feel oppressed, cheated, or inspired, these young people write from the depths of their souls." Noting the emotional "energy" captured by the diverse poems in *Falling Hard, New York Times Book Review* contributor Katie Roiphe added that a reading of Franco's anthology "brings back the intensity and bewilderment of those first few forays into what you might at the time have thought of as love."

In an online interview for *Teenreads,* Franco had some advice for aspiring authors. "You have things to say that no one else can say," she commented. "Just don't give up. Half of being a writer is being stubborn and believing in yourself, not so much in a self-esteem way, but knowing you have something to say. . . . In my case, I found I had to write all kinds of different types of books to make a living, from poetry to nonfiction, from adults to young children. Work very hard." "Just know that it may take as much creativity to make a living as a writer as it takes to do the writing itself," Franco added. "But, think about it. In every generation some people get to be writers. Why not you?"

Biographical and Critical Sources

PERIODICALS

Booklist, October 1, 2000, Hazel Rochman, review of *You Hear Me?: Poems and Writing by Teenage Boys,* p. 330; August, 2004, Gillian Engberg, review of *Counting Our Way to the 100th Day!: 100 Poems and 100 Picture to Celebrate the 100th Day of School,* p. 1947; January 1, 2007, GraceAnne A. DeCandido, review of *Birdsongs: A Backwards Counting Book,* p. 114; May 15, 2007, Carolyn Phelan, review of *Summer Beat,* p. 53; March 15, 2009, Hazel Rochman, review of *A Curious Collection of Cats,* p. 62; May 15, 2009, Kathleen Isaacs, review of *Messing around on the Monkey Bars, and Other School Poems for Two Voices,* p. 36; June 1, 2009, Gillian Engberg, review of *Pond Circle,* p. 76; September 1, 2009, Hazel Rochman, review of *Metamorphosis: Junior Year,* p. 84; September 15, 2009, Carolyn Phelan, review of *Zero Is the Leaves on the Tree,* p. 62.

Bulletin of the Center for Children's Books, May, 2007, Deborah Stevenson, review of *Birdsongs,* p. 366; September, 2007, Hope Morrison, review of *Summer Beat,* p. 22.

Horn Book, May, 2001, review of *Things I Have to Tell You: Poems and Writing by Teenage Girls,* p. 343; July-August, 2003, Susan Dove Lempke, review of *Mathematickles!,* p. 472; May-June, 2009, Susan Dove Lempke, review of *A Curious Collection of Cats,* p. 314; July-August, 2009, Danielle J. Ford, review of *Pond Circle,* p. 407, and Nina Lindsay, review of *Messing around on the Monkey Bars, and Other School Poems for Two Voices,* p. 436; November-December, 2009, review of *Zero Is the Leaves on the Tree,* p. 653.

Kirkus Reviews, June 1, 2003, Betsy Franco, review of *Mathematickles!,* p. 803; July 1, 2003, review of *Night Is Gone, Day Is Still Coming: Stories and Poems by American Indian Teens and Young Adults,* p. 912; June 15, 2004, review of *Counting Our Way to the 100th Day!,* p. 576; December 1, 2006, review of *Birdsongs,* p. 1220; May 1, 2007, review of *Summer Beat;* July 15, 2008, reviews of *Zero Is the Leaves on the Tree* and *Bees, Snails, and Peacock Tails;* October 15, 2008, review of *Falling Hard;* May 15, 2009, review of *Pond Circle;* June 15, 2009, review of *Messing around on the Monkey Bars, and Other School Poems for Two Voices;* September, 2009, review of *Metamorphosis.*

New York Times Book Review, April 12, 2009, Katie Roiphe, review of *Falling Hard,* p. 14.

Publishers Weekly, June 16, 2003, review of *Mathematickles!,* p. 70; December 11, 2006, review of *Birdsongs,* p. 68; June 22, 2009, review of *Pond Circle,* p. 45.

School Library Journal, October, 2000, Sharon Korbeck, review of *You Hear Me?,* p. 183; May, 2001, Sharon Korbeck, review of *Things I Have to Tell You,* p. 164; August, 2003, Sharon Korbeck, review of *Night Is Gone, Day Is Still Coming,* p. 184; July, 2004, Lisa Gangemi Kropp, review of *Counting Our Way to the 100th Day!,* p. 93; September, 2006, Cris Reidel, review of *Conversations with a Poet: Inviting Poetry into K-12 Classrooms,* p. 252; January, 2007, Teresa Pfeifer, review of *Birdsongs,* p. 94; May, 2007, Gloria Koster, review of *Summer Beat,* p. 91; September, 2008, Ellen Heath, review of *Bees, Snails, and Peacock Tails,* p. 164; December, 2008, Ann Nored, review of *Falling Hard,* p. 147; April, 2009, Teresa Pfeifer, review of *A Curious Collection of Cats,* p. 147; May, 2009, Kathleen Kelly MacMillan, review of *Pond Circle,* p. 78; September, 2009, Grace Oliff, review of *Zero Is the Leaves on the Tree,* p. 141; November, 2009, Shawn Brommer, review of *Messing around on the Monkey Bars, and Other School Poems for Two Voices,* p. 94; December, 2009, Anthony C. Doyle, review of *Metamorphosis,* p. 118.

Voice of Youth Advocates, October, 2001, review of *Things I Have to Tell You,* p. 308.

ONLINE

Betsy Franco Home Page, http://www.betsyfranco.com (December 5, 2010).

Candlewick Press Web site, http://www.candlewick.com/ (December 5, 2010), "Betsy Franco."

Teenreads.com, http://www.teenreads.com/ (December 12, 2003), interview with Franco.

FRANSON, Leanne 1963-

Personal
Born August 7, 1963, in Regina, Saskatchewan, Canada; daughter of Hilding Otto (an urban planner) and Elaine Helene (a nurse) Franson; children: Benjamin Taotao. *Education:* Attended University of Saskatchewan, 1981-82; Concordia University, B.F.A. (with distinction), 1985, additional study, 1986-88; attended Banff School of Fine Arts, 1988-89. *Politics:* "Leftist/socialist." *Religion:* "Questioning agnostic." *Hobbies and other interests:* Cartooning, ceramics, literature, weightlifting.

Addresses
Home and office—4323 Parthenais, Montréal, Québec H2H 2G2, Canada. *E-mail*—inkspots@videotron.ca.

Career
Freelance illustrator, 1991—. *Exhibitions:* Flemington Gallery, Australia; Gabrielle Roy Library, Quebec City, Quebec, Canada; Galerie 303, Montreal, Quebec, Canada.

Member
Society of Children's Book Writers and Illustrators, Picture Book Artists Association, Association des Illustrateurs et Illustratrices du Québec (member of board of directors, 1992-93), Regroupment des Artistes en Arts Visuels du Québec.

Awards, Honors
Governor General's Award nomination for illustration of French children's literature, Canada Council, and Prix Saint-Exupéry (Paris, France), both 1997, and Prix Alvine-Bélisle for best children's book, Quebec Librarians' Association, 1998, all for *L'urson qui voulait une Juliette* by Jasmine Dube.

Illustrator

FICTION

Linda Brousseau, *Marelie de la mer,* Éditions Pierre Tisseyre (Montréal, Québec, Canada), 1993, translated by David Homel as *Marina's Star,* J. Lorimer (Toronto, Ontario, Canada), 1997.

Linda Brousseau, *Le vrai père de Marelie,* Éditions Pierre Tisseyre (Montréal, Québec, Canada), 1995.

Eleanor Allen, *Ghost from the Sea,* A. & C. Black (London, England), 1995.

Daniel Defoe, *Robinson Crusoe,* abridged and translated by Carmen Marois, Graficor (Boucherville, Québec, Canada), 1996.

The Little Red Hen, Ginn (Aylesbury, England), 1996.

Mark Twain, *Tom Sawyer,* abridged and translated by Michèle Marineau, Graficor (Boucherville, Québec, Canada), 1996.

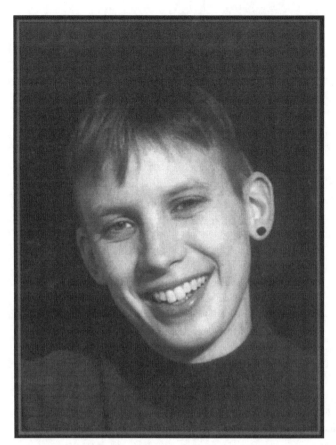

Leanne Franson (Photograph by Colleen Ayoup. Reproduced by permission.)

Mark Twain, *Huckleberry Finn,* abridged and translated by Carmen Marois), Graficor (Boucherville, Québec, Canada), 1997.

Cass Hollander, *On a Hot Day,* Rigby Educational Publishing (New York, NY), 1997.

Louisa May Alcott, *Les quatres filles du docteur March,* abridged and translated by Michèle Marineau, Graficor (Boucherville, Québec, Canada), 1997.

Anne Legault, *Une fille pas comme les autres,* Éditions de la courte échelle (Montréal, Québec, Canada), 1997.

Jasmine Dube, *L'ourson qui voulait une Juliette,* Éditions de la courte échelle (Montréal, Québec, Canada), 1997.

Jack London, *Croc-blanc,* abridged and translated by Michèle Marineau, Graficor (Boucherville, Québec, Canada), 1997.

Agathe Genois, *Adieu vieux lézard!,* Éditions Héritage (Saint-Lambert, Québec, Canada), 1998.

Anne Legault, *Une première pour Étamine Léger,* Éditions de la courte échelle (Montréal, Québec, Canada), 1998.

Manjusha Pawagi, *The Girl Who Hated Books,* Second Story Press (Toronto, Ontario, Canada), 1998, Beyond Words Publishing (Hillsboro, OR), 1999.

Ulana Snihura, *I Miss Franklin P. Shuckles,* Annick Press (Toronto, Ontario, Canada), 1998.

Leslie Ellen, *Quackers, the Troublesome Duck,* Modern Curriculum Press (Parsippany, NJ), 1998.

Judy Nayer, *Best Wishes for Eddie,* Modern Curriculum Press (Parsippany, NJ), 1998.

Judy Nayer, *The Lost and Found Game,* Modern Curriculum Press (Parsippany, NJ), 1998.

James R. MacClean, *The Great Riddle Mystery,* Modern Curriculum Press (Parsippany, NJ), 1998.

Linda LaRose, *Jessica Takes Charge,* Annick Press (Toronto, Ontario, Canada), 1998.

Rhea Tregebov, *What-If Sara,* Second Story Press (Toronto, Ontario, Canada), 1999.

Anne Legault, *Un message d'Étamine Léger,* Éditions de la courte échelle (Montréal, Québec, Canada), 1999.

Éric Gérard, *Drôle de singe!,* Éditions Michel Quintin (Waterloo, Québec, Canada), 1999.

Maurice Therrien, *Eloise et le cadeau des arbres,* Éditions Michel Quintin (Waterloo, Québec, Canada), 1999.

Cécile Gagnon, *Le chien de Pavel,* Soulières Éditeur (Saint-Lambert, Québec, Canada), 2000.

Lucie Bergeron, *Bout de comète!,* Québec Amérique (Montréal, Québec, Canada), 2000.

Nicole M.-Boisvert, *Crapule le chat,* Éditions Michel Quintin (Waterloo, Québec, Canada), 2000.

Sylvie Desrosiers, *Au revoir, Camille!,* Éditions de la courte échelle (Montréal, Québec, Canada), 2000.

Maurice Therrien, *Eloise et le vent,* Éditions Michel Quintin (Waterloo, Québec, Canada), 2000.

Peter Marlowe, *The Trailer Park Princesses,* Annick Press (Toronto, Ontario, Canada), 2000.

Veronika Martenova Charles, *Don't Open the Door!,* Stoddart Kids (Toronto, Ontario, Canada), 2000.

Judith Ross Enderle and Stephanie Jacob Gordon, *School Stinks!,* Scholastic (New York, NY), 2001.

David A. Adler, *Andy Russell, NOT Wanted by the Police!,* Harcourt (New York, NY), 2001.

Ken Roberts, *The Thumb in the Box,* Douglas & McIntyre (Toronto, Ontario, Canada), 2001.

Veronika Martenova Charles, *Don't Go into the Forest!,* Stoddart Kids (Toronto, Ontario, Canada), 2001.

Yvon Brochu, *Sauvez Henri!,* Dominque et Cie. (Saint-Laurent, Québec, Canada), 2001.

Sylvie Desrosiers, *Le concert de Thomas,* Éditions de la courte échelle (Montréal, Québec, Canada), 2001.

Andrée-Anne Gratton, *Simon et Violette,* Éditions Pierre Tisseyre (Montréal, Québec, Canada), 2001.

Andrée-Anne Gratton, *Le mystère des nuits blanches,* Éditions Pierre Tisseyre (Montréal, Québec, Canada), 2001.

Sylvie Desrosiers, *Ma mère est une extraterrestre,* Éditions de la courte échelle (Montréal, Québec, Canada), 2002.

Michelle Poploff, *Pyjama Party!,* Scholastic (New York, NY), 2002.

Cécile Gagnon, *Justine et le chien de Pavel,* Soulières Éditeur (Saint-Lambert, Québec, Canada), 2003.

Sylvie Desrosiers, *Je suis Thomas,* Éditions de la courte échelle (Montréal, Québec, Canada), 2003.

Andrée-Anne Gratton, *Simon, l'as du ballon,* Éditions Pierre Tisseyre (Montréal, Québec, Canada), 2004.

Raymond Plante, *Un canard entre les canines,* Éditions de Boreal (Montréal, Québec, Canada), 2004.

Andrée-Anne Gratton, *Un espion dans la maison,* Éditions Pierre Tisseyre (Montréal, Québec, Canada), 2004.

Maureen Hull, *Rainy Days with Bear,* Lobster Press (Montreal, Quebec, Canada), 2004.

David A. Adler, *It's a Baby, Andy Russell!,* Harcourt (New York, NY), 2005.

Raymond Plante, *La vedette de la ronflette!,* Éditions de Boreal (Montréal, Québec, Canada), 2005.

Chantal Blanchette, *Les chaussettes de Julien,* Éditions Pierre Tisseyre (Montréal, Québec, Canada), 2005.

Raymond Plante, *Le chaud manteau de Léo,* Éditions de Boreal (Montréal, Québec, Canada), 2006.

Cécile Gagnon, *Justine et Sofia,* Soulières Éditeur (Saint-Lambert, Québec, Canada), 2006.

Sylvie Desrosiers, *L'audition de Thomas,* Éditions de la courte échelle (Montréal, Québec, Canada), 2006.

Louise-Michelle Sauriol, *Les aventures du Géant Beaupré,* Éditions des Plaines (Saint-Boniface, Manitoba, Canada), 2006.

Ken Roberts, *Thumb on a Diamond,* Groundwood Books (Toronto, Ontario, Canada), 2006.

Nathalie Bertrand, *Les pieds dans les plats,* Éditions du Renouveau Pédagogique (Saint-Laurent, Québec, Canada), 2007.

Andrée-Anne Gratton, *Mission chocolat pour Simon,* Éditions Pierre Tisseyre (Montréal, Québec, Canada), 2007.

Nadine Poirier, *Au voleur!,* Bayard Jeunesse Canada (Montréal, Québec Canada), 2008.

Cécile Gagnon, *Justine au pays de Sofia,* Soulières Éditeur (Saint-Lambert, Québec, Canada), 2008.

Andrée-Anne Gratton, *Simon et Zizou,* Éditions Pierre Tisseyre (Montréal, Québec, Canada), 2008.

Frieda Wishinsky, *Far from Home,* Maple Tree Press (Toronto, Ontario, Canada), 2008.

Frieda Wishinsky, *Lost in the Snow,* Maple Tree Press (Toronto, Ontario, Canada), 2008.

Frieda Wishinsky, *All Aboard!,* Maple Tree Press (Toronto, Ontario, Canada), 2008.

Ken Roberts, *Thumb and the Bad Guys,* Groundwood Books (Toronto, Ontario, Canada), 2009.

Geneviève Mativat, *La sonate des chatouilles,* Éditions Hurtubise (Montréal, Québec, Canada), 2009.

Jean-François Somain, *Le beret vert,* Soulières Éditeur (Saint-Lambert, Québec, Canada), 2009.

Andrée-Anne Gratton, *Simon est amoureux,* Éditions Pierre Tisseyre (Montréal, Québec, Canada), 2009.

"RIPLEY'S BELIEVE IT OR NOT!" SERIES BY MARY PACKARD

Big Book Special Edition, Scholastic (New York, NY), 2001.

World's Weirdest Critters, Scholastic (New York, NY), 2001.

Amazing Escapes, Scholastic (New York, NY), 2001.

Creepy Stuff, Scholastic (New York, NY), 2001.

Bizarre Bugs, Scholastic (New York, NY), 2001.

Odd-inary People, Scholastic (New York, NY), 2001.

Weird Science, Scholastic (New York, NY), 2001.

Wild and Deadly, Scholastic (New York, NY), 2001.

Blasts from the Past, Scholastic (New York, NY), 2001.

Awesome Animals, Scholastic (New York, NY), 2002.

World's Weirdest Gadgets!, Scholastic (New York, NY), 2002.

X-traordinary X-tremes, Scholastic (New York, NY), 2003.

Weird Weird World, Scholastic (New York, NY), 2004.

OTHER

Double Take Listening and Speaking 3 (textbook), Oxford University Press (Oxford, England), 1996.
Team Up 6 Manual (textbook), Éditions du Renouveau Pédagogique (Montreal, Quebec, Canada), 1997.
(And author of text) *Assume Nothing: Evolution of a Bi-dyke* (graphic novel), Slab-O-Concrete, 1997.
(And author of text) *Don't Be a Crotte! Teaching through Trauma* (graphic novel), Slab-O-Concrete, 1999.
(And author of text) *Don't Be a Crotte! Don't Be a Crotte!* (graphic novel), Slab-O-Concrete, 2004.

Contributor of editorial illustrations to periodicals, including *Zellers Magalog* and *Today's Parent.*

Sidelights

A critically acclaimed illustrator based in Montreal, Quebec, Canada, Leanne Franson has provided the artwork for dozens of children's books, including titles by Veronika Martenova Charles, David A. Adler, Mary Packard, and Ken Roberts. Franson's pictures, done in both India ink and transparent acrylic ink, have garnered praise for their simplicity and eloquence, as well

Franson's illustration projects include David A. Adler's chapter book **Andy Russell, Not Wanted by the Police.** (Illustration copyright © 2001 by Leanne Franson. Houghton Mifflin Harcourt Publishing Company, 2001. Reproduced with permission.)

as their ability to evoke strong emotions. In the pages of Linda LaRose's *Jessica Takes Charge,* for instance, Franson's illustrations "economically capture the moods of mingled drama and comedy," according to *Quill & Quire* reviewer Gwyneth Evans.

Rainy Days with Bear, a work by Maureen Hull, centers on a toy bear's imaginative response to being stuck indoors on a rainy day. "The illustrations are a powerful force in plot development," Linda Berezowski commented in her review of the book for *Resource Links.* "They visually inform the reader of details beyond the text." In the pages of Ulana Snihura's *I Miss Franklin P. Shuckles* a youngster learns the true meaning of friendship after she ostracizes an awkward-looking neighbor. "Stylized and highly expressive . . . paintings surround the text on each page, faithfully representing the narrative action and elaborating on it with a number of clever motifs," noted Bridget Donald in a *Quill & Quire* review.

Franson and Charles have joined forces on a pair of works designed to send chills down readers' spines, *Don't Open the Door!* and *Don't Go into the Forest!* In the former, three boys spend the night trading scary tales about disobedient children. "Franson's pen-and-ink drawings add comic emphasis to the text and highlight some gory details," remarked *Quill & Quire* reviewer Laurie Mcneill. The latter work also features a trio of horrific stories, including one about the ghoulish Berbalangs of Filipino myth. Reviewing *Don't Go into the Forest!,* Evette Signarowski maintained in *Resource Links* that Franson "is able to invoke suspense through simple line drawings."

Franson has also contributed artwork to Adler's "Andy Russell" series of chapter books. In *Andy Russell, NOT Wanted by the Police!* the young protagonist investigates the strange goings-on at a vacationing neighbor's house. "Friendly black-and-white drawings, humorous text, and a cast of likable characters" make the book worth reading, Helen Rosenberg stated in *Booklist.* Both new addition to the Russell family and a meddling aunt complicate Andy's life in *It's a Baby, Andy Russell!* "Enlivened with full-page cartoon illustrations," wrote *School Library Journal* critic Jennifer Cogan, Adler's story makes it "a friendly and funny book for reluctant and transitional readers."

Roberts depicts the absurdities of life in a small Canadian town in his "Thumb" series of middle-grade novels. Narrated by Leon "Thumb" Mazzei, a resident of New Auckland, British Columbia, *The Thumb in the Box* follows the humorous chain of events that occurs after the remote—and road-less—fishing village receives a new fire truck from the Canadian government. Franson's full-page illustrations "combine elements of whimsy and nostalgia," Donald remarked. A follow-up, *Thumb on a Diamond,* concerns the efforts of nine schoolchildren to get a taste of big-city life, and *Thumb and the Bad Guys* centers on Leon's attempts to solve a

Ken Roberts' middle-grade novel **Thumb and the Bad Guys** *benefits from Franson's engaging illustrations.* (Copyright © 2009 by Ken Roberts. Reprinted with permission of Groundwood Books Limited, www.groundwoodbooks.com.)

puzzling mystery. Michele Shaw, writing in *School Library Journal,* reported that "Franson's black-and-white graphic-style illustrations enhance the suspense."

Franson once told *SATA:* "As an illustrator of children's books, I am inspired by the vision of small children cuddled next to Mommy or big brother, at bedtime, sharing a cozy story session, or pulling out a new book from the library shelf with excitement, or carrying a favorite book around under the arm, sticky with peanut butter. I have extremely fond memories of all the above moments in my young life, and I am fueled by the possibility of playing such a role in the memories of future readers.

"I think my favorite part of illustrating books is when I take a new script to the corner café and sit down with a café au lait to read it for the first time. The thrill of a new story is compounded by the thrill of being one of the first to get a chance to see it and imagine the scenes and characters brought to life by the author. At that point, all is possible. Often my imagination is fired up so that the sketch process occurs almost automatically in my head.

"Then comes the work part: getting the characters down on paper. Sometimes the expressions and mannerisms are the easiest part, as I imagine them in their world,

and more down-to-earth things such as hair color and clothing styles seem quite arbitrary and difficult to pin down. After that is the whole collaborative process with the author and art director, where all our imaginations collide. The author imagined her kid sister who has freckles and is a bit plumper; the art director needs the color red to stand out on the page. Finally it is all worked through, and the final characters emerge. At that point they take on their own lives and must stay in character and 'look' for the entire book. This is less fun for me, but it is exciting to see the original formless sketches become fleshed out.

"When I send off the final artwork, it is like the book disappears from my life and control, and it is sometimes hard for me to disengage. For instance, with *Jessica Takes Charge* the main subject for me was the shadows. For weeks and even months after the book was out of my hands, I was still hooked on studying shadows, coming up with shadow monster ideas.

"The second most exciting part of doing a book is receiving the finished book from a courier at my front door, especially if it has a shiny, glossy, hard cover. It's like fresh candy. It's amazing that my lowly drawings come back as a *real* book! Also, there is some of the excitement of opening that new book package that I experienced when I was four or five, and we received 'Cat in the Hat' books from a book club.

"I am particularly drawn to books where the child protagonists are real. They have full ranges of emotions, are often troubled but strong, vulnerable but proactive. As a child, I was crazy about black-and-white drawings, often of alternative and magical worlds closed to adults; for example, Pauline Baynes in the *Chronicles of Narnia,* Beth and Joe Krush in the 'Gone-Away Lake' books, and Marguerite de Angeli's *The Door in the Wall.* I also loved Maurice Sendak, Beatrix Potter (such child-friendly sizes!), and Ernest H. Shepard's Pooh. As for characters, I was also inspired by Laura Ingalls Wilder, Pippi Longstocking, and the Borrowers. More recently I admire Stephane Jorish, Marie-Louis Gay, Raymond Briggs, and Ralph Steadman. I only wish I had as much time now to revel in the wonders of the children's section of the library as I did when I was five or ten."

Biographical and Critical Sources

PERIODICALS

Booklist, November 1, 1999, Ilene Cooper, review of *The Girl Who Hated Books,* p. 540; April 15, 2001, Ilene Cooper, review of *Don't Open the Door!,* p. 1568; October 15, 2001, Helen Rosenberg, review of *The Thumb in the Box,* p. 392; January 1, 2002, Helen Rosenberg, review of *Andy Russell, NOT Wanted by*

the Police, p. 855; May 15, 2005, Carolyn Phelan, review of *It's a Baby, Andy Russell,* p. 1656; June 1, 2006, Carolyn Phelan, review of *Thumb on a Diamond,* p. 72.

Horn Book, September, 2001, Martha V. Parravano, review of *The Thumb in the Box,* p. 593; May-June, 2006, Roger Sutton, review of *Thumb on a Diamond,* p. 327; September-October, 2009, Roger Sutton, review of *Thumb and the Bad Guys,* p. 575.

Kirkus Reviews, September 15, 2001, review of *Andy Russell, NOT Wanted by the Police,* p. 1352; July 1, 2009, review of *Thumb and the Bad Guys.*

Quill & Quire, February, 1998, Bridget Donald, review of *I Miss Franklin P. Shuckles;* May, 1999, Gwyneth Evans, review of *Jessica Takes Charge;* December, 2000, Laurie Mcneill, review of *Don't Open the Door!;* May, 2001, Bridget Donald, review of *The Thumb in the Box;* March, 2004, Gwyneth Evans, review of *Rainy Days with Bear.*

Resource Links, April, 1999, review of *Jessica Takes Charge,* p. 4; June, 2001, Evette Signarowski, review of *Don't Go into the Forest!,* p. 9; October, 2001, Johal Jinder, review of *The Thumb in the Box,* p. 19; December, 2004, Linda Berezowski, review of *Rainy Days with Bear,* p. 4; October, 2009, Moira Kirkpatrick, review of *Far from Home,* p. 8; February, 2010, Carolyn Cutt, review of *Thumb and the Bad Guys,* p. 11.

School Library Journal, September, 2001, Karen Scott, review of *Don't Open the Door!,* p. 184; January, 2002, Debbie Feulner, review of *Andy Russell, NOT Wanted by the Police,* p. 89; January, 2002, Laura Scott, review of *Don't Go into the Forest!,* p. 95; March, 2005, Jennifer Cogan, review of *It's a Baby, Andy Russell,* p. 164; August, 2006, Maria B. Salvadore, review of *Thumb on a Diamond,* p. 128; October, 2009, Michele Shaw, review of *Thumb and the Bad Guys,* p. 102.

ONLINE

Annick Press Web site, http://www.annickpress.com/ (December 1, 2010), "Leanne Franson."

Leanne Franson Home Page, http://leannefranson.com (December 1, 2010).*

G

GAUCH, Sarah

Personal
Married; children: two. *Education:* Attended college.

Addresses
Home—Cairo, Egypt.

Career
Journalist and author. Correspondent journalist based in Cairo, Egypt, beginning 1989.

Writings
Voyage to the Pharos, illustrated by Roger Roth, Viking (New York, NY), 2009.

Contributor to numerous periodicals, including *Business Week, Christian Science Monitor,* and *Newsweek.*

Biographical and Critical Sources

PERIODICALS

Booklist, October 1, 2009, Carolyn Phelan, review of *Voyage to the Pharos,* p. 48.
Kirkus Reviews, August 15, 2009, review of *Voyage to the Pharos.*
School Library Journal, October, 2009, Lucinda Snyder Whiteburst, review of *Voyage to the Pharos,* p. 92.*

*　　*　　*

GAVIN, Jamila 1941-

Personal
Born August 9, 1941, in Mussoorie, Uttar Pradesh, India; immigrated to England; daughter of Terence (a retired Indian civil servant) and Florence Jessica (a teacher) Khushal-Singh; married Barrie Gavin (a television producer), 1971 (divorced, 1990); children: Rohan Robert, Indra Helen. *Education:* Trinity College of Music, L.T.C.L. (piano performance and drama instruction); studied piano in Paris; attended Hochschul für Musik, Berlin, Germany. *Politics:* Labour Party.

Addresses
Home—Stroud, England. *Agent*—Jacqueline Korn, David Higham Associates, 5-8 Lower John St., Golden Square, London W1R 4HA, England.

Career
Freelance writer and lecturer. British Broadcasting Corporation (BBC), London, England, radio studio manager, then television production assistant, 1964-71. Member, Stroud Town Council; member of advisory committee, Cheltenham Literary Festival. Writer and co-director, Taynton House Children's Opera Group; affiliated with Children's Drama Group, Niccol Center, Cirencester.

Member
PEN, West of England Writers, Writers Guild.

Awards, Honors
London *Guardian* Award, runner-up, 1993, for *The Wheel of Surya; Guardian* Award special runner-up, and Carnegie Medal nomination, both 1995, both for *The Eye of the Horse;* Whitbread Children's Book Award, 2000, for *Coram Boy.*

Writings

"SURYA" SERIES

The Wheel of Surya, Methuen (London, England), 1992.

Jamila Gavin (Photograph by Anthony Moth. Reproduced by permission.)

The Eye of the Horse, Methuen (London, England), 1994.
The Track of the Wind, Methuen (London, England), 1997.

"GRANDPA CHATTERJI" SERIES

Grandpa Chatterji, illustrated by Mei-Yim Low, Methuen (London, England), 1993.
Grandpa's Indian Summer, illustrated by Mei-Yim Low, Methuen (London, England), 1995.

OTHER

The Magic Orange Tree and Other Stories, illustrated by Ossie Murray, Methuen (New York, NY), 1979.
Double Dare and Other Stories, illustrated by Simon Willby, Methuen (New York, NY), 1982.
Kamla and Kate (short stories), illustrated by Thelma Lambert, Methuen (New York, NY), 1983.
Digital Dan, illustrated by Patrice Aitken, Methuen (New York, NY), 1984.
Ali and the Robots, illustrated by Sally Williams, Methuen (New York, NY), 1986.
Stories from the Hindu World, illustrated by Joanna Troughton, Macdonald (London, England), 1986, Silver Burdett (Morristown, NJ), 1987.
The Hideaway, illustrated by Jane Bottomley, Methuen (New York, NY), 1987.

(Reteller) *Three Indian Princesses: The Stories of Savitri, Damayanti, and Sita,* illustrated by Govinder Ram, Methuen (New York, NY), 1987.
The Singing Bowls, Methuen (New York, NY), 1989.
I Want to Be an Angel, Methuen (New York, NY), 1990.
Kamla and Kate Again (short stories), illustrated by Rhian Nest-James, Methuen (New York, NY), 1991.
Deadly Friend, Heinemann (London, England), 1994.
A Fine Feathered Friend, illustrated by Carol Walters, Heinemann (London, England), 1996, illustrated by Dan Williams, Crabtree Pub. (New York, NY), 2002.
The Mango Tree, illustrated by Rhian Nest-James, Heinemann (London, England), 1996.
Presents, illustrated by Rhian Nest-James, Heinemann (London, England), 1996.
Who Did It?, illustrated by Rhian Nest-James, Heinemann (London, England), 1996.
The Wormholers, Methuen (New York, NY), 1996.
Grandma's Surprise, illustrated by Rhian Nest-James, Heinemann (London, England), 1996.
Our Favourite Stories: Children Just like Me Storybook, Dorling Kindersley (London, England), 1997, published as *Children Just like Me: Our Favorite Stories from around the World,* Dorling Kindersley (New York, NY), 1997.
Out of India: An Anglo-Indian Childhood (memoir), Pavilion (London, England), 1997.
Forbidden Memories, illustrated by Mark Robertson, Mammoth (London, England), 1998.
Someone's Watching, Someone's Waiting, illustrated by Anthony Lewis, Mammoth (London, England), 1998.
Monkey in the Stars (also see below), illustrated by Anthony Lewis, Mammoth (London, England), 1998.
Star Child on Clark Street, Cambridge University Press (Cambridge, England), 1998.
Ali and the Robots, Methuen (London, England), 1999.
Coram Boy, Mammoth (London, England), 2000, Farrar, Straus (New York, NY), 2001.
The Turning Point, Collins (London, England), 2001.
Fox, Methuen (London, England), 2001.
Monkeys in the Stars (play; adapted from the novel), Samuel French (New York, NY), 2001.
Danger by Moonlight, Walker Books (London, England), 2002.
The Bow of Shiva: The Story of Rama and Sita, Collins (London, England), 2002.
Coming Home: A Story about Divali, Hodder Wayland (London, England), 2002.
Totally Crushed! (based on the television series), Egmont (London, England), 2002.
The Blood Stone, Egmont (London, England), 2003, Farrar, Straus & Giroux (New York, NY), 2005.
Walking on My Hands: Out of India—The Teenage Years (autobiography), Hodder & Stoughton (London, England), 2007.
The Robber Baron's Daughter, Egmont Children's Books (London, England), 2008, published as *See No Evil,* Farrar, Straus & Giroux (New York, NY), 2009.

Also author of the books *The Temple by the Sea,* Ginn; *The Demon Drummer,* Pavillion; *Pitchou; The Girl Who Rode on a Lion,* Ginn; *Forbidden Dreams,* Mammoth; *All Aboard,* Heinemann; *A Singer from the Desert,* Pavillion; *Forbidden Clothes,* Methuen; and *Just Friends,* Mammoth. Contributor to educational publications by Heinemann Educational (Exeter, NH), 1996.

Also author of the musical *The Green Factor,* music by Nigel Stephenson.

Adaptations

The Demon Drummer was adapted as a play produced at the Cheltenham Literary Festival, 1994; *Grandpa Chatterji* was adapted for television, 1996; a six-part adaptation of *The Wheel of Surya* was broadcast on BBC-TV, 1996; *Coram Boy* was adapted for the stage by Helen Edmundson and produced in London and New York, NY, 2007.

Sidelights

Jamila Gavin brings her understanding of the special concerns of children with a multicultural heritage to many of her stories and novels for young readers. Born in India of an Indian father and a British mother, Gavin has focused on her Indian heritage in her autobiographies *Out of India: An Anglo-Indian Childhood* and *Walking on My Hands: Out of India—The Teenage Years,* as well as in novels such as *Three Indian Princesses: The Stories of Savitri, Damayanti, and Sita* and her highly praised epic "Surya" trilogy that begins with *The Wheel of Surya.* In addition to her novels and short fiction for middle-school readers, Gavin, who has worked in television and in theater for many years, has also authored plays for younger viewers. Several of her works have been adapted for broadcast on British television. "I began writing to be published, rather than for fun, in 1979, when I realized how few books for children reflected the multicultural society in which they lived," Gavin once explained. "As someone of mixed Indian and British origins, I wanted to see my mirror image, and felt that every child, no matter what their race or color, was entitled to see their mirror image."

Among Gavin's first books is *Kamla and Kate,* a collection of short stories featuring a young girl named Kate who gains a best friend when six-year-old Kamla and her family move from India to Kate's boy-dominated street. While engaging together in tasks and activities common to young British children, Kate joins her new friend in celebrating the Indian Festival of Light, or Diwali. The book reflects the author's belief that "people with different customs and beliefs [need] to find common ground" while also celebrating their differences, according to Margery Fisher in *Growing Point.* The two best friends return in *Kamla and Kate Again,* a second collection of stories that *School Librarian* contributor Julie Blaisdale cited as showing "with sensitivity and understanding" the many ways in which young people can "share in and celebrate a diversity of cultural influences."

Several other books by Gavin are steeped in Indian culture and tradition. In *The Singing Bowls* a mixed Anglo-Indian teen named Ronnie delves into the mystery surrounding three wooden bowls said to have mystical properties rooted in Tibetan history. The sixteen year old hopes that the bowls can help him locate his Indian father, who disappeared ten years before. While noting that the writing is "slightly uneven," a *Junior Bookshelf* reviewer praised *The Singing Bowls* for evoking "the dust, heat and beauty of India" and presenting a "revealing and thought-provoking" portrait of the multi-layered generations that make up Indian society.

Indian culture also plays a significant role in *Grandpa Chatterji,* a collection of stories about sisters Sanjay and Neeta, who get to know their Indian grandfather when he takes a long-awaited trip from his home in Calcutta. A man of traditional, old-fashioned values, "Grandpa Chatterji is a wonderful character . . . with his warmth and enthusiasm for life," according to *School Librarian* contributor Teresa Scragg. A *Junior Bookshelf* reviewer similarly noted that Gavin's "charming" book paints the portrait of a family with strong ties to two diverse cultures "and offers the hope that its members will draw the best from both." In *Children Just like Me: Our Favorite Stories from around the World* Gavin brings together folk tales from all over the world and includes corresponding geographical and cultural information for each story in her book. A reviewer for *Publishers Weekly* deemed the work an "unusually successful" project that presents information in an "engagingly personal way," and Chris Brown noted in *School Librarian* that Gavin's "straightforward storytelling" *Children Just like Me* in provides both observations and commentary without intruding on the pace of each story.

First published in England in 1992, *The Wheel of Surya* begins Gavin's "Surya" trilogy. Taking place in a small Indian village in the Punjab on the eve of India's war for independence, the novel follows the adventures of Marvinder and Jaspal Singh, after their mother decides to bring the family to England and join her husband, Govind, who has been absent for many years in an effort to further his education. During the trip, the children's mother and grandmother both die, but the siblings remain determined to find the father whom they hardly remember. With little money, Marvinder and Jaspal find their way to Bombay and stow away aboard an ocean liner bound for England. When at last they find Govind, he is not at all the person they expected to find—he has married an Irishwoman and has a son—and the two children must adjust to both a new family and a new culture. In a review of *The Wheel of Surya* for *School Librarian,* Linda Saunders praised Gavin for "the power of her descriptions and her portrayal of two different societies." A *Junior Bookshelf* critic called the novel "a tribute to the stubbornness of children the world over whose instinct is for survival first and prosperity second."

In the sequels to *The Wheel of Surya—The Eye of the Horse* and *The Track of the Wind—*readers continue to

follow the adventures of Marvinder and her brother, Jaspal. *The Eye of the Horse* finds the children's father released from jail after a conviction for dealing in stolen goods. Abandoned by his Irish wife, Govind gathers his children together and returns to his native India, which is now free of British domination. The story threads in and out of many historic events during the 1940s, including the death of Mahatma Gandhi and the religious and political turmoil that troubled India during that decade. In a review for *Books for Your Children,* Val Bierman dubbed *The Eye of the Horse* a "powerful book of betrayal, sadness and anger" that also reveals the "power of healing and forgiveness." In a *School Librarian* review, Peter Hollindale praised Gavin's tale as "an immensely readable, exciting story."

In *The Track of the Wind* Marvinder and Jaspal now struggle to understand the country they had once fled in search of their father. Through Jaspal's efforts to study India's history, and Marvinder's personal struggles as she is married off to a kindly but serious man named Bahadur, Gavin once again "encompasses all manner of clashes between East and West," Susan Hamlyn noted in *School Librarian.* The "Surya" trilogy covers over a quarter century of events in India and England, beginning from the period leading up to World War II and ending with the partition of India and Pakistan in the late 1940s. Characterizing the trilogy as a "rich weave of history, geography, myth and religion," Adrian Jackson wrote in *Books for Keeps* that its final book is full of "striking scenes" and reflects the darker tones of its characters as they finally face the reality of their almost-adult lives.

Other novels by Gavin range more widely in their focus, among them the time-travel fantasy *The Wormholers* the historical novel *Coram Boy,* and the contemporary adventure *The Robber Baron's Daughter.* In *The Wormholers* a boy witnesses his step-sister disappear through a crack in the floor and ultimately joins her in a strange world where time runs backward as well as sideways. As Gavin once told *SATA,* the novel "represents my exploration of the inner world, but inspired by the glorious theories and astro-physical world of the physicist Stephen Hawking. That is the joy of writing; that there are so many doors waiting to be opened and be a source of inspiration."

Gavin turns from fantasy to history in her award-winning novel *Coram Boy,* which is set in mid-eighteenth-century England. Meshak is the mentally ill son of Otis Gardiner, an evil man who, for a price, promises to take unwanted infants to London's Coram Foundling Hospital but actually murders them or sells them. Although Meshak is forced to aid his father's awful work, he knows that it is wrong. When his father is called to take the newborn child of Melissa, a kindly young woman whom Meshak admires, the boy finds a way to save the infant's life and place it in the care of the hospital. Named Aaron, the infant grows up and reveals a gift for music, whereupon he becomes the stu-

Cover of Gavin's award-winning novel **Coram Boy,** *featuring artwork by Victor Ambrus.* (Farrar, Straus & Giroux, 2001. Illustration © 2001 by Victor Ambrus. Reproduced by permission.)

dent of composer George Frederic Handel. Meanwhile, neither Melissa nor Aaron's father, Alexander, know that their son is alive, but when Meshak recognizes the relationship between Aaron and Alexander, he is determined to reunite this family. Writing in *School Library Journal,* Kristen Oravec cited the mix of "mystery, romance, horror, and adventure" in *Coram Boy,* while Paula Rohrlick referenced the factual basis of Gavin's novel in her *Kliatt* review. Explaining that the Coram Foundling Hospital was established by a British sea captain in 1741 to care for foundlings from all classes of society, and that there really was said to be such a person as the murderous "Coram Man," Rohrlick wrote that Gavin's "complex plot" rewards teen readers with "a rich Gothic tale for lovers of historical fiction." Describing *Coram Boy* as "Dickensian in the richness of its tale," *Booklist* critic GraceAnne A. DeCandido also praised Gavin's melodramatic stew of "good and evil characters" and "impossible coincidences." "This is the stuff of high melodrama," asserted a *Kirkus Reviews* writer, "and readers of the genre who will be swept along by the theatrics will not be disappointed."

Gavin takes readers back to the 1600s and a tour through Europe and the Mogul Empire in *The Blood*

Stone. The tour is that of Fillipo Veroneo, the twelve-year-old son of jeweler Geronimo Veroneo. Veroneo has been imprisoned by his greedy and vilent brother in law, Bernardo Pagliarin, and held in Hindustan (now Afghanistan). To release his father, who he has never met, Fillipo must bring Pagliarin a valuable diamond called the Ocean of the Moon, and his dangerous journey is aided by gifts of magic, valuable friends, and his ability to pass through some of the most powerful kingdoms of the era. Noting Gavin's use of "sumptuous, cinematic detail," Engberg dubbed *The Blood Stone* "an accomplished, lyrical, high-reaching novel that will stay with readers," while a *Kirkus Reviews* writer observed that the author's "rich prose punctuated by changes of tense and person create[s] a dreamlike atmosphere." In *School Library Journal,* Renee Steinberg described the villainous Pagliarin as appropriately one-dimensional and added that "Gavin has created fascinating, multidimensional characters whose actions and motives remain suspicious through much of the story." A "compelling" saga, according to *Horn Book* contributor Vicky Smith, *The Blood Stone* is "a gorgeously detailed" story that "gives such places as Damascus, Basra, and Kabul their full cultural and historical due."

First published as *The Robber Baron's Daughter, See No Evil* finds twelve-year-old Antoinetta living a cloistered world in her family's London mansion. Then her Eastern European-born teacher Miss Kovachev suddenly disappears, leaving behind a journal written in Bulgarian. Nettie finds herself able to translate her teacher's entries into vivid dreams that focus on Eastern European girls who are brought to England to work like slaves in factories until they die. When Nettie realizes that her own family's affluence may be a direct result of such slavery, she knows she must break from her parents and right this wrong, in the process gaining help from a surprising source. Praising *See No Evil* as a "well-written novel" in her *School Library Journal* review, Susan W. Hunter cited Gavin's use of "descriptive language, atmosphere, and lots of intrigue," while Gillian Engberg wrote in *Booklist* that the author's "evocative mystery" captures Nettie's "archetypal loss of innocence" in "masterful detail" and "indelible characters, settings, and moods." While a *Publishers Weekly* contributor dubbed Nettie "infuriatingly naive" at times, *See No Evil* benefits from both a "rich sense of setting" and a "shocking" conclusion, the critic added.

Biographical and Critical Sources

BOOKS

Gavin, Jamila, *Out of India: An Anglo-Indian Childhood,* Pavilion (London, England), 1997.

Gavin, Jamila, *Walking on My Hands: Out of India—The Teenage Years* Hodder & Stoughton (London, England), 2007.

PERIODICALS

Booklist, December 15, 2001, GraceAnne A. DeCandido, review of *Coram Boy,* p. 722; December 15, 2005, Gillian Engberg, review of *The Blood Stone,* p. 39; May 1, 2009, Gillian Engberg, review of *See No Evil,* p. 39.

Books for Keeps, November, 1997, Jill Bennett, review of *Children Just like Me: Our Favorite Stories from around the World,* p. 21; November, 1997, Adrian Jackson, review of "Surya Trilogy," p. 27.

Books for Your Children, spring, 1995, Val Bierman, review of *The Eye of the Horse,* p. 12.

Bulletin of the Center for Children's Books, September, 1997, Pat Mathews, review of *Children Just like Me,* p. 10.

Horn Book, September-October, 2005, Vicky Smith, review of *The Blood Stone,* p. 577.

Growing Point, May, 1983, Margery Fisher, review of *Kamla and Kate,* p. 4089.

Journal of Adolescent and Adult Literacy, February, 2002, Carol Grantham, review of *Coram Boy,* p. 437; November, 2005, Fatma Haidara, review of *The Blood Stone,* p. 246.

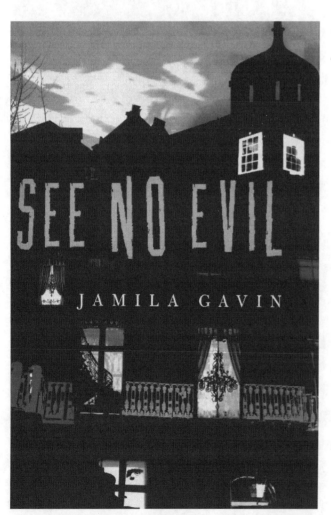

Cover of Gavin's spine-tingling middle-grade novel See No Evil, *featuring artwork by Wendy Birch.* (Jacket art by Wendy Birch ©2008 by Egmont UK, Ltd. Reproduced with permission of Farrar, Straus & Giroux.)

Junior Bookshelf, October, 1989, review of *The Singing Bowls,* p. 237; August, 1992, review of *The Wheel of Surya,* p. 153; June, 1993, review of *Grandpa Chatterji,* pp. 96-97.

Kirkus Reviews, September 15, 2001, review of *Coram Boy,* p. 1358; November 1, 2005, review of *The Blood Stone,* p. 1184; May 1, 2009, review of *See No Evil.*

Kliatt, May, 2005, Paula Rohrlick, review of *Coram Boy,* p. 24.

New York Times Book Review, January 15, 2006, review of *The Blood Stone,* p. 19.

Publishers Weekly, April 28, 1997, review of *Children Just like Me,* p. 77; November 28, 2005, review of *The Blood Stone,* p. 52; June 15, 2009, review of *See No Evil,* p. 51.

School Librarian, November, 1991, Julie Blaisdale, review of *Kamla and Kate Again,* p. 144; November, 1992, Linda Saunders, review of *The Wheel of Surya,* pp. 157-158; August, 1993, Teresa Scragg, review of *Grandpa Chatterji,* p. 108; November, 1994, Peter Hollindale, review of *The Eye of the Horse,* p. 165; February, 1997, Celia Gibbs, review of *Fine Feathered Friend,* p. 24; August, 1997, Chris Brown, review of *Children Just like Me,* p. 145; spring, 1998, Susan Hamlyn, review of *The Track of the Wind,* p. 48.

School Library Journal, November, 2001, Kristen Oravec, review of *Coram Boy,* p. 154; December, 2005, Renee Steinberg, review of *The Blood Stone,* p. 147; July, 2009, Susan W. Hunter, review of *See No Evil,* p. 82.

ONLINE

Achuka Web site, http://www.achuka.com/ (October, 2000), interview with Gavin.

Jamila Gavin Home Page, http://www.jamilagavin.co.uk (December 7, 2010).*

*   *   *

GLASS, Andrew 1949-

Personal

Born 1949. *Education:* Attended Temple University and School of Visual Arts (New York, NY).

Addresses

Home—New York, NY. *E-mail*—andgls@yahoo.com.

Career

Author and illustrator.

Awards, Honors

Newbery Honor Book designation, American Library Association, 1983, for *Graven Images* by Paul Fleischman, and 1984, for *The Wish Giver* by Bill Brittain; Spur Award for storytelling, Western Writers of America, 2002, for *The Legend of Strap Buckner* by Connie Nordhielm Wooldridge.

Writings

FOR CHILDREN; SELF-ILLUSTRATED

Jackson Makes His Move, Warne (New York, NY), 1982.

My Brother Tries to Make Me Laugh, Lothrop (New York, NY), 1984.

Chickpea and the Talking Cow, Lothrop (New York, NY), 1987.

Charles T. McBiddle, Doubleday (New York, NY), 1993.

Folks Call Me Appleseed John, Doubleday (New York, NY), 1995.

The Sweetwater Run: The Story of Buffalo Bill Cody and the Pony Express, Doubleday (New York, NY), 1996.

A Right Fine Life: Kit Carson on the Santa Fe Trail, Holiday House (New York, NY), 1997.

Bad Guys: True Stories of Legendary Gunslingers, Sidewinders, Fourflushers, Drygulchers, Bushwhackers, Freebooters, and Downright Bad Guys and Gals of the Wild West, Doubleday (New York, NY), 1998.

Bewildered for Three Days: As to Why Daniel Boone Never Wore His Coonskin Cap, Holiday House (New York, NY), 2000.

Mountain Men: True Grit and Tall Tales, Doubleday (New York, NY), 2001.

The Wondrous Whirligig: The Wright Brothers' First Flying Machine, Holiday House (New York, NY), 2003.

ILLUSTRATOR

George E. Stanley, *Crime Lab,* Avon Books (New York, NY), 1980.

Nancy Etchemendy, *The Watchers of Space,* Avon Books (New York, NY), 1980.

Bill Brittain, *Devil's Donkey,* Harper (New York, NY), 1981.

Catherine E. Sadler, adapter, *The Adventures of Sherlock Holmes,* four volumes, Avon Books (New York, NY), 1981.

Elizabeth Charlton, *Terrible Tyrannosaurus,* Elsevier/Nelson (New York, NY), 1981.

Theodore Taylor, *The Battle of Midway Island,* Avon Books (New York, NY), 1981.

Theodore Taylor, *H.M.S. Hood vs. Bismarck: The Battleship Battle,* Avon Books (New York, NY), 1982.

Robert Newton Peck, *Banjo,* Alfred A. Knopf (New York, NY), 1982.

Natalie Savage Carlson, *Spooky Night,* Lothrop (New York, NY), 1982.

Paul Fleischman, *Graven Images: Three Stories,* Harper & Row (New York, NY), 1982.

Marilyn Singer, *The Fido Frame-Up,* Warne (New York, NY), 1983.

Theodore Taylor, *Battle in the English Channel,* Avon Books (New York, NY), 1983.

Joan Lowery Nixon, *The Gift,* Macmillan (New York, NY), 1983.

Bill Brittain, *The Wish Giver: Three Tales of Coven Tree,* Harper & Row (New York, NY), 1983.

Natalie Savage Carlson, *The Ghost in the Lagoon,* Lothrop (New York, NY), 1984.

Marilyn Singer, *A Nose for Trouble,* Holt (New York, NY), 1985.

Natalie Savage Carlson, *Spooky and the Ghost Cat,* Lothrop (New York, NY), 1985.

Natalie Savage Carlson, *Spooky and the Wizard's Bats,* Lothrop (New York, NY), 1986.

Marilyn Singer, *Where There's a Will, There's a Wag,* Holt (New York, NY), 1986.

Bill Brittain, *Dr. Dredd's Wagon of Wonders,* Harper & Row (New York, NY), 1987.

Beverly Major, *Playing Sardines,* Scholastic (New York, NY), 1988.

Natalie Savage Carlson, *Spooky and the Bad Luck Raven,* Lothrop (New York, NY), 1988.

Susan Beth Pfeffer, *Rewind to Yesterday,* Delacorte (New York, NY), 1988.

Susan Beth Pfeffer, *Future Forward,* Delacorte (New York, NY), 1989.

Natalie Savage Carlson, *Spooky and the Witch's Goat,* Lothrop (New York, NY), 1989.

Robert D. San Souci, *Larger than Life: John Henry and Other Tall Tales,* Doubleday, 1991.

Bill Brittain, *Professor Popkin's Prodigious Polish,* HarperCollins (New York, NY), 1991.

David Gifaldi, *Gregory, Maw, and the Mean One,* Clarion Books (New York, NY), 1992.

Tom Birdseye, reteller, *Soap! Soap! Don't Forget the Soap: An Appalachian Folktale,* Holiday House (New York, NY), 1993.

Karen Hesse, *Lavender,* Holt (New York, NY), 1993.

Susan Whitcher, *Real Mummies Don't Bleed: Friendly Tales for October Nights,* Farrar, Straus & Giroux (New York, NY), 1993.

Susan Mathias Smith, *The Booford Summer,* Clarion Books (New York, NY), 1994.

Tom Birdseye and Debbie Holsclaw Birdseye, adapters, *She'll Be Comin' round the Mountain,* Holiday House (New York, NY), 1994.

Al Carusone, *Don't Open the Door after the Sun Goes Down: Tales of the Real and Unreal,* Clarion Books (New York, NY), 1994.

Tololwa M. Mollel, reteller, *Ananse's Feast: An Ashanti Tale,* Clarion Books (New York, NY), 1996.

Susan Whitcher, *The Key to the Cupboard,* Farrar, Straus & Giroux (New York, NY), 1996.

Emily Herman, *Liza and the Fossil,* Hyperion (New York, NY), 1996.

Bethany Roberts, *Monster Manners: A Guide to Monster Etiquette,* Clarion Books (New York, NY), 1996.

Eric A. Kimmel, reteller, *Easy Work!: An Old Tale,* Holiday House (New York, NY), 1998.

Alan Schroeder, reteller, *The Tale of Willie Monroe,* Clarion Books (New York, NY), 1999.

Tynia Thomasie, *Cajun Through and Through,* Little, Brown (New York, NY), 2000.

Eric A. Kimmel, *Grizz!,* Holiday House (New York, NY), 2000.

Gregory Maguire, *Crabby Cratchitt,* Clarion Books (New York, NY), 2000.

Connie Nordhielm Wooldridge, reteller, *The Legend of Strap Buckner: A Texas Tale,* Holiday House (New York, NY), 2001.

Kathy Price, *The Bourbon Street Musicians,* Clarion Books (New York, NY), 2002.

Eric A. Kimmel, *The Erie Canal Pirates,* Holiday House (New York, NY), 2002.

Connie Nordhielm Wooldridge, *Thank You Very Much, Captain Ericsson!,* Holiday House (New York, NY), 2005.

Tracie Vaughn Zimmer, *Sketches from a Spy Tree* (poetry), Clarion Books (New York, NY), 2005.

Dan Bernstein, *The Tortoise and the Hare Race Again,* Holiday House (New York, NY), 2006.

Maxine Rose Schur, *Gullible Gus,* Clarion Books (New York, NY), 2009.

Also illustrator of *The Glass Ring,* by Mary Kennedy, Dandelion Press.

Sidelights

A respected illustrator who has been commended for his versatile approach to children's books, Andrew Glass has provided the artwork to such highly regarded children's books as *The Legend of Strap Buckner: A Texas Tale* by Connie Nordhielm Wooldridge, Dan Bernstein's *The Tortoise and the Hare Race Again,* and Maxine Rose Schur's *Gullible Gus.* In addition, Glass has produced a number of self-illustrated titles, among them *The Wondrous Whirligig: The Wright Brothers' First Flying Machine,* often drawing on U.S. history for inspiration.

Published in 1982, Glass's self-illustrated debut *Jackson Makes His Move* features a raccoon artist, rendered by Glass in pencil and watercolor. When Jackson realizes that he is no longer inspired by the country around him, and when he tires of his realistic paintings, he heads for the busy, chaotic city. There, instead of painting what he sees, he paints what he feels, and the resulting works are large and abstract. According to *School Library Journal* critic Kenneth Marantz, Glass's illustrations help young readers "come to grips with some of the rationale of such movements as Abstract Expressionism."

My Brother Tries to Make Me Laugh serves as an example of the author-illustrator's penchant for whimsy. In crayon-colored illustrations, Glass portrays alien siblings traveling to Planet Earth on their spaceship. Odeon, a bright purple alien with a snout and stalk-eyes, attempts to get his sister to laugh to break up the monotony of a long journey. "How could this miss?" asked a critic in a review of the picture book for the *Bulletin of the Center for Children's Books.*

Another of Glass's works recalls the classic children's story "Tom Thumb." In *Chickpea and the Talking Cow* a tiny boy named Chickpea is swallowed up by his father's cow. Despite his misfortune, the boy is determined to make his father rich by speaking from within the cow and tricking the emperor into believing that the cow can talk. According to Patricia Dooley in *School*

Library Journal, "everyone should enjoy" the book's line-and-wash illustrations, which are "warm, fuzzy, and light-struck."

Glass adopts a cartoon style highlighted with earth tones and bright blues to create illustrations for his retelling *Folks Call Me Appleseed John.* Narrated by John Chapman—also known as Johnny Appleseed—the book tells of winter travels and adventures. A *Publishers Weekly* critic remarked that Glass's text has a "rough-hewn tone," and that the "homespun, almost unfinished appearance" of his illustrations "express a variety of moods."

Glass has produced several other works on figures from American history and folklore. *Bad Guys: True Stories of Legendary Gunslingers, Sidewinders, Fourflushers, Drygulchers, Bushwhackers, Freebooters, and Downright Bad Guys and Gals of the Wild West* profiles such figures as Jesse James, Wild Bill Hickok, Calamity Jane, Billy the Kid, and Belle Starr. With "wit and finesse," according to a *Publishers Weekly* reviewer, Glass provides "appropriately hyperbolic caricatures of these likable lawbreakers." Also, noted John Peters in *Booklist,* he manages to portray their quirks "without ennobling them."

A much ennobled figure is at the center of *Bewildered for Three Days: As to Why Daniel Boone Never Wore His Coonskin Cap.* Mixing history and fiction, the story has frontiersman Boone explaining to a portrait painter why he does not wear such a cap; it turns out that as a boy, he bonded with a mother raccoon and her babies while hiding from pursuers in a hollow log. "Glass tells the tale in an amiable, folksy way, and the dappled oil-paint art reflects the humor," commented *Booklist* contributor Peters. In *School Library Journal* Steven Engelfried remarked that Glass's "impressionistic oil paintings are well suited to the tall-tale genre," concluding that *Bewildered for Three Days* is both "lively and fast paced."

Mountain Men introduces readers to other denizens of the frontier, including Jim Bridger, Mike Fink, and Kit Carson, put their histories into perspective by discussing both the Louisiana Purchase and the Lewis and Clark expedition. Glass "tells fascinating stories based on real facts" that also reflect the mountain men's tendency to embellish, noted a reviewer for *Children's Digest.* In *Booklist,* GraceAnne A. DeCandido observed that "the pictures are as full of color and exaggeration as the text," but the exclusion of Sacajawea from the segment on Lewis and Clark was regretable. In *School Library Journal* Engelfried expressed concern that some younger children might have trouble distinguishing fact from fiction in Glass's text, but nonetheless praised the story's "energetic narrative" and "vibrant paintings." Much of the appeal of *Mountain Men* results from "embracing both history and legend," Engelfried concluded.

The Wondrous Whirligig, another book written and illustrated by Glass, takes true events from the childhood of Orville and Wilbur Wright and weaves them into a

Andrew Glass introduces young readers to the achievements of the Wright brothers in his self-illustrated picture book The Wondrous Whirligig. (Copyright © 2003 by Andrew Glass. Reproduced by permission of Holiday House, Inc.)

tall tale. Fascinated by a whirligig their father gives them, the two young brothers decide to build a whirligig big enough to life them into the sky. Other family members help as young Orv and Wil construct their flying machine and the boys are cheered them on even when their first attempts fail. In her *Horn Book* review of *The Wondrous Whirligig,* Betty Carter concluded that Glass "wraps the wonder of discovery and invention into an energetic tale that celebrates small joys while hinting of larger ones." Carolyn Phelan in *Booklist* commented that the "spirited tale" captures the many qualities "that helped the Wright brothers succeed."

Glass has also illustrated stories for other authors, including the books in the "Spooky" series by Natalie Savage Carlson. Ann A. Flowers commented in *Horn Book* on the varied techniques Glass incorporates into his illustrations, dubbing the art for *Spooky and the Ghost Cat* "vibrant" and "textured," while describing the illustrations for *Spooky Night* as "crosshatched" and "shadowy." In a review of *Spooky and the Wizard's Bats,* a critic in *Kirkus Reviews* noted that Glass captures the "essence of . . . Halloween without being trite." Susan H. Patron in *School Library Journal* found the illustrations for the same book to be "dramatic and colorful."

The award-winning *The Legend of Strap Buckner,* a piece of Western folklore retold by Wooldridge, concerns a Texan so large and strong he can knock folks down without trying. Eventually Strap's ego swells so much that he picks a fight with the Devil himself. Glass's artwork for this tall tale "captures the humor" of the text, with "bright, colorful appeal and action," related Mary Elam in *School Library Journal.* Glass and Wooldridge also collaborate on *Thank You Very Much, Captain Ericsson!,* a fictionalized biography of the nineteenth-century engineer and inventor who brought the world such technological innovations as the steam-powered locomotive and the screw propeller, and who is perhaps best known for designing the U.S.S. *Monitor,* the first ironclad warship. A *Publishers Weekly* reviewer applauded Glass's contributions, stating that "his ink-and-watercolor wash illustrations combine the spunk of editorial cartooning with the visceral punch of visual storytelling."

In *The Bourbon Street Musicians,* a Cajun-flavored retelling of "The Bremen Town Musicians" by Kathy Price, a quartet of aging barnyard animals hope to escape their cruel owners by pooling their musical talents and heading to New Orleans. "Glass uses oil crayons to fill the oversized pages with marvelous images of the animals and their wacky actions," Judith Constantinides noted in *School Library Journal. New York Times Book Review* contributor Stephen Sigmund also praised the work, stating that *"The Bourbon Street Musicians* combines pictures and words to capture the dreamy feel of southern Louisiana, and Andrew Glass's illustrations, thick and vivid with the bayou night, are the book's best asset." In Tracie Vaughn Zimmer's *Sketches from a Spy Tree,* a poetry collection, a preteen reflects openly and honestly on her father's absence, her eccentric neighbors, and her mother's plans to remarry, among other topics. "Glass's multimedia illustrations" for this book "are as varied as Anne Marie's subjects and her very natural emotions," observed a critic in *Kirkus Reviews,* and in *School Library Journal,* Lee Bock applauded the "delightfully energized illustrations that complement the subject and mood of each poem well."

Dan Bernstein's humorous tale *The Tortoise and the Hare Race Again* presents the next chapter in the well-known saga. Humiliated by his loss in the original race and subject to constant taunts by his neighbors, Hare longs for another chance to race against Tortoise, who has quickly grown tired of the adulation heaped upon him. Realizing that his furry adversary will likely only repeat the same mistakes, however, Tortoise concocts a scheme ensuring that both parties will be pleased with the race's outcome. "Glass's scenes of disheveled-looking animals in rumpled clothing create an appropriately comic setting for this Aesopian sequel," maintained a contributor in *Kirkus Reviews.* In another folksy tale, Schur's *Gullible Gus,* an impossibly naïve cowboy ventures to the town of Fibrock, where he hopes to learn the difference between truth and fiction. Once there Gus meets Hokum Malarkey, a terrific spinner of yarns whose tall tales spellbind the gentle cowpoke. According to *School Library Journal* reviewer Nancy Baumann, "Glass's bright oil crayon cartoons fit the exaggerated storytelling style to a tee."

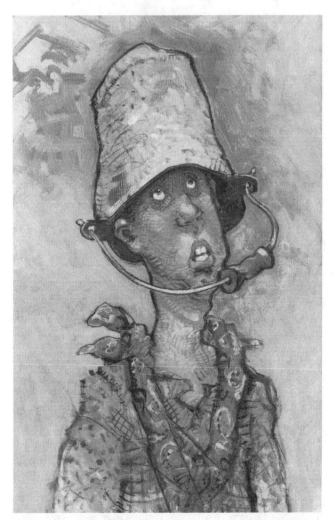

Glass's cartoon art is a highlight of Maxine Rose Schur's elementary-grade novel **Gullible Gus.** (Illustration copyright © 2009 by Andrew Glass. Reprinted by permission of Clarion Books, an imprint of Houghton Mifflin Harcourt Publishing Company. All rights reserved.)

Biographical and Critical Sources

PERIODICALS

Booklist, October 15, 1998, John Peters, review of *Bad Guys: True Stories of Legendary Gunslingers, Sidewinders, Fourflushers, Drygulchers, Bushwhackers, Freebooters, and Downright Bad Guys and Gals of the Wild West,* p. 414; September 1, 2000, John Peters, review of *Bewildered for Three Days: As to Why Daniel Boone Never Wore His Coonskin Cap,* p. 122; August, 2001, GraceAnne A. DeCandido, review of *Mountain Men: True Grit and Tall Tales,* p. 2109; September 15, 2003, Carolyn Phelan, review of *The Wondrous Whirligig: The Wright Brothers' First Fly-*

ing Machine, p. 244; August, 2005, Carolyn Phelan, review of *Sketches from a Spy Tree,* p. 2032; August 1, 2009, Randall Enos, review of *Gullible Gus,* p. 69.

Bulletin of the Center for Children's Books, October, 1984, review of *My Brother Tries to Make Me Laugh,* p. 25.

Children's Digest, October, 2001, review of *Mountain Men,* p. 14.

Horn Book, October, 1982, review of *Spooky Night,* pp. 508-509; March-April, 1986, Ann A. Flowers, review of *Spooky and the Ghost Cat,* p. 190; November-December, 2003, Betty Carter, review of *The Wondrous Whirligig,* p. 729.

Kirkus Reviews, September 15, 1986, review of *Spooky and the Wizard's Bat,* p. 1443; February 1, 1993, review of *Charles T. McBiddle,* p. 146; September 1, 2003, review of *The Wondrous Whirligig,* p. 1124; June 15, 2005, review of *Sketches from a Spy Tree,* p. 693; July 1, 2005, review of *Thank You Very Much, Captain Erickson!,* p. 745; March 1, 2006, review of *The Tortoise and the Hare Race Again,* p. 226; June 15, 2009, review of *Gullible Gus.*

New York Times Book Review, May 19, 2002, Stephen Sigmund, review of *The Bourbon Street Musicians,* p. 22.

Publishers Weekly, July 10, 1995, review of *Folks Call Me Appleseed John,* p. 58; October 19, 1998, review of *Bad Guys,* p. 80; August 8, 2005, review of *Thank You Very Much, Captain Ericsson!,* p. 234.

School Library Journal, May, 1982, review of *Jackson Makes His Move,* pp. 52-53; December, 1986, Susan H. Patron, review of *Spooky and the Wizard's Bats,* p. 81; October, 1987, Patricia Dooley, review of *Chickpea and the Talking Cow,* pp. 111-112; August, 1995, p. 134; October, 2000, Steven Engelfried, review of *Bewildered for Three Days,* p. 125; June, 2001, Steven Engelfried, review of *Mountain Men,* p. 170; September, 2001, Mary Elam, review of *The Legend of Strap Buckner: A Texas Tale,* p. 222; May, 2002, Judith Constantinides, review of *The Bourbon Street Musicians,* p. 143; November, 2003, Harriett Fargnoli, review of *The Wondrous Whirligig,* p. 95; August, 2005, Marianne Saccardi, review of *Thank You Very Much, Captain Ericsson,* p. 120; August, 2005, Lee Bock, review of *Sketches from a Spy Tree,* p. 140; April, 2006, Suzanne Myers Harold, review of *The Tortoise and the Hare Race Again,* p. 96; December, 2009, Nancy Baumann, review of *Gullible Gus,* p. 91.

ONLINE

Andrew Glass Home Page, http://andrewglassbooks.com (December 5, 2010).*

*   *   *

GRÉBAN, Quentin 1977-

Personal

Born March 25, 1977, in Brussels, Belgium. *Education:* Attended Institut Saint-Luc.

Addresses

Home—Brussels, Belgium.

Career

Author and illustrator. *Exhibitions:* Work exhibited at Bologna Children's Book Fair, 1999, 2000.

Awards, Honors

Saint-Exupéry Award, 2000.

Writings

SELF-ILLUSTRATED

Nestor, Mijade (Namur, Belgium), 2000, Mondo Publishing (New York, NY), 2001.

Suzette, Mijade (Namur, Belgium), 2001.

Tu es un grand garçon, Nestor!, Mijade (Namur, Belgium), 2003.

Un cadeau pour Léa, Mijade (Namur, Belgium), 2005.

Mommy, I Love You, Milk & Cookies Press (New York, NY), 2005.

Dis papa . . . pourquoi les zèbres ne font-ils pas du patin à roulettes?, Mijade (Namur, Belgium), 2006.

Zéphir, Mijade (Namur, Belgium), 2006.

Jusqu'ici, tout va bien!, Mijade (Namur, Belgium), 2007.

La véritable histoire des trois petits cochons, Mijade (Namur, Belgium), 2007.

La route des pastèques, Mijade (Namur, Belgium), 2008.

Mais pourquoi les loups sont-ils si mechants?, Mijade (Namur, Belgium), 2009.

ILLUSTRATOR

André Dehant, Michèle Bertrand, Christine Loutre, and Danielle l'Oiseau, *L'arc-en-ciel,* Editions Erasme (Namur, Belgium), 1999.

André Dehant, Michèle Bertrand, Christine Loutre, and Danielle l'Oiseau, *Qui va hiberner?,* Editions Erasme (Namur, Belgium), 1999.

Dominique Blaizot, *Monsieur lapin et le toboggan rouge,* Mijade (Namur, Belgium), 1999.

Tanguy Gréban, *Capucine,* Mijade (Namur, Belgium), 2000.

Jutta Langreuter, *Clémentine et Mimosa,* Mijade (Namur, Belgium), 2001.

Laurence Bourguignon, *Olga,* Mijade (Namur, Belgium), 2002.

Tanguy Gréban, *Capucine, la petite sorcière,* Mijade (Namur, Belgium), 2002.

Jutta Langreuter, *Les trois petits cuisiniers,* Mijade (Namur, Belgium), 2003.

Annie Caldirac, *Nounours Grognon,* Mijade (Namur, Belgium), 2003.

Tanguy Gréban, *Sarah So Small,* Milk & Cookies Press (New York, NY), 2004.

Antonie Schneider, *Du bist die liebste kleine Maus!,* Nord-Süd Verlag (Zurich, Switzerland), 2004, translated by J. Alison James as *The Dearest Little Mouse in the World,* North-South Books (New York, NY), 2004.

Nadine Walter, *Les commandes de Liselotte,* Mijade (Namur, Belgium), 2004.

Claire Bouiller, *Un loup dans le potager,* Mijade (Namur, Belgium), 2004.

Moritz Petz, *Ich freu mich so auf dich!,* Nord-Süd Verlag (Zurich, Switzerland), 2005, translated by J. Alison James as *Wish You Were Here,* North-South Books (New York, NY), 2005.

Isabelle Maquoy, *Mélie,* Mijade (Namur, Belgium), 2005.

Madeleine Mansiet, *Les plus belles légendes de France,* Lipokili (Trois-Ponts, Belgium), 2005.

Hans Christian Andersen, *Poucette,* Mijade (Namur, Belgium), 2006.

Tanguy Gréban, *Capucine au pays des rêves,* Mijade (Namur, Belgium), 2006.

Hans Christian Andersen, *L'intrépide petit soldat de plomb,* Mijade (Namur, Belgium), 2007.

Reina Ollivier, *Het verhaal van de drie biggetjes,* Mijade (Namur, Belgium), 2007.

Hans Christian Andersen, *Thumbelina,* adapted by Sindy McKay, translated by Elizabeth Bell, Treasure Bay (San Anselmo, CA), 2007.

The Brothers Grimm, *Blanche-Neige,* Mijade (Namur, Belgium), 2007, published as *Snow White,* North-South Books (New York, NY), 2009.

Un bébé, bientôt . . ., Office de la naissance et de l'enfance (Brussels, Belgium), 2008.

Muriel Molhant, adaptor, *La petite sirène,* Mijade (Namur, Belgium), 2008.

Carlos Collodi, *Pinocchio,* North-South Books (New York, NY), 2010.

Work featuring Gréban's art has been translated into German, Dutch, Hungarian, Greek, and Korean.

Sidelights

Belgian illustrator Quentin Gréban has provided the artwork for dozens of children's books, including *Wish You Were Here,* a story of friendship by Moritz Petz, and *Snow White,* a version of the classic fairy tale by the Brothers Grimm. Born in Brussels in 1977, Gréban studied at the Institut Saint-Luc. He has earned recognition for his sensitive and evocative watercolor illustrations, influenced by the work of Rébecca Dautremer, Arthur Rackham, and Edmund Dulac.

Gréban has enjoyed a successful collaboration with his brother, Tanguy Gréban, the author of *Sarah So Small,* among other works. In *Sarah So Small,* a young girl shrinks to the size of a mouse after swallowing a magic pearl that her father pilfered from Hazel, a witch. To her amazement, Sarah soon discovers that she can now converse with animals, and she joins forces with a host of creatures to visit Hazel's laboratory. "Charming, delicate watercolor illustrations . . . do much to enhance this original story," Carol Ann Wilson noted in

School Library Journal. Gréban's "precise lines and muted shades of parchment and sky blue create a lovable cast of characters," remarked Gillian Engberg in *Booklist.*

In *The Dearest Little Mouse in the World,* a work by Antonie Schneider, a sweet-natured rodent befriends a huge, frightening dog that she passes each day on the way to mouse school. According to *School Library Journal* critic Suzanne Myers Harold, "the animals' faces are expressive and entertaining." Companionship is also the focus of Petz's *Wish You Were Here,* a "strikingly visualized work," according to a contributor in *Publishers Weekly.* While Hedgehog takes a vacation to the shore, he keeps in touch with his best friend, Mouse, by exchanging letters delivered by via seagull. Upon his return, Hedgehog fails to connect with Mouse at the train station, prompting the duo to alter their future travel plans. The "tender artwork serves to move the story along," wrote Blair Christolon in *School Library Journal,* and the *Publishers Weekly* reviewer stated that Gréban's "paintings are by turns austere and voluptuous, evocative and elusive."

Gréban also contributed to Sindy McKay's interactive, read-aloud version of Hans Christian Andersen's beloved *Thumbelina.* The work, which follows the adventures of a tiny girl who marries a fairy prince, features two strands of text: longer passages are meant to be

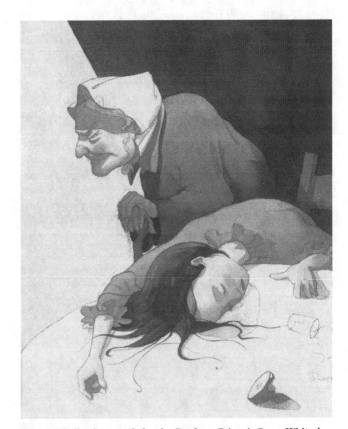

Quentin Gréban's artwork for the Brothers Grimm's **Snow White** *has reached American readers in an English-language translation.* (North-South Books, 2002. Copyright © by NordSud Verlag AG, CH-8005 Zurich, Switzerland. Used with permission of North-South Books, Inc., New York.)

read by adults, while the simpler sentences are designed for beginning readers. "Gréban has preserved the delicate fairy-tale setting of the story while emphasizing its emotional transitions," Marian Drabkin commented in *School Library Journal*. The artist earned further praise for his efforts on *Snow White,* which hews closely to the Grimm Brothers' original. A contributor in *Kirkus Reviews* applauded "the illustrator's pictures of the satisfyingly individual seven dwarfs—one bespectacled, some clean-shaven, others bearded," and Margaret Bush reported in *School Library Journal* that Gréban's "clear, nicely articulated characters are most appealing in the varied personalities of the dwarfs and the old women who are the disguised queen."

During his career, Gréban has produced a number of self-illustrated tales, including *Mommy, I Love You.* This work focuses on Suzette, a young ladybug who, finding herself lost, sketches a picture of her mother that she displays to a host of creatures. Although the animals compliment Suzette's artistic talents, they appear to misunderstand her plea for help, at least until the tiny bug receives a surprise visit from a friendly face. "Gréban's soft watercolor illustrations capture the tiny insect's wide-eyed fear and sadness," Linda Ludke maintained in *School Library Journal.*

Biographical and Critical Sources

PERIODICALS

Booklist, January 1, 2005, Gillian Engberg, review of *Sarah So Small,* p. 869; October 1, 2005, Julie Cummins, review of *Wish You Were Here,* p. 65.

Kirkus Reviews, October 1, 2009, review of *Snow White.*

Publishers Weekly, September 12, 2005, review of *Wish You Were Here,* p. 68.

School Library Journal, October, 2004, Carol Ann Wilson, review of *Sarah So Small,* p. 114; January, 2005, Suzanne Myers Harold, review of *The Dearest Little Mouse in the World,* p. 98; April, 2005, Linda Ludke, review of *Mommy, I Love You,* p. 98; December, 2005, Blair Christolon, review of *Wish You Were Here,* p. 119; January, 2008, Marian Drabkin, review of *Thumbelina,* p. 80; November, 2009, Margaret Bush, review of *Snow White,* p. 92.

ONLINE

Mijade Web site, http://www.mijade.be/ (December 20, 2010), "Quentin Gréban."*

* * *

GRITTON, Steve

Personal

Born in Los Angeles, CA; married; wife's name Lyssa; children: two. *Education:* California State University at Fullerton, B.F.A. (illustration). *Hobbies and other interests:* Basketball, digital art, cartoons and comic books.

Addresses

Home—Issaquah, WA. *E-mail*—steve@stevegritton. com.

Career

Educator and author. Elementary-school teacher in WA, beginning 2003. Presenter at schools and libraries.

Writings

(Self-illustrated) *The Trouble with Sisters and Robots,* Albert Whitman (Morton Grove, IL), 2009.

Biographical and Critical Sources

PERIODICALS

Kirkus Reviews, August 1, 2009, review of *The Trouble with Sisters and Robots.*

School Library Journal, October, 2009, Linda Ludke, review of *The Trouble with Sisters and Robots,* p. 94.

ONLINE

Steve Gritton Home Page, http://www.stevegritton.com (November 14, 2010).

Steve Gritton Web log, http://stevegritton.blogspot.com (November 29, 2010).*

H

HADDON, Mark 1962-

Personal

Born 1962, in Northampton, England; married Sos Eltis (an educator); children: two sons. *Education:* Merton College, Oxford, B.A., 1981; Edinburgh University, M.A., 1984. *Hobbies and other interests:* Marathon canoeing, abstract painting.

Addresses

Home—Oxford, England. *Agent*—Aitken Alexander Associates, 18-21 Cavaye Pl., London SW10 9PT, England.

Career

Novelist, poet, playwright, artist, cartoonist, and illustrator. Formerly assisted patients with multiple sclerosis and autism; worked variously at a theater box office and in a mail-order business; illustrator and cartoonist for periodicals; creator of and writer for children's television series *Microsoap*. Teaches creative writing at Arvon Foundation and Oxford University.

Awards, Honors

Smarties Prize shortlist, 1994, for *The Real Porky Philips;* British Booktrust Teenage Prize, *Guardian* Children's Fiction Prize, and Art Seidenbaum First Fiction Award, *Los Angeles Times* Book Prize, all 2003, Whitbread Book of the Year Award, South Bank Show Literature Award, Commonwealth Writers Prize Best First Book Award, Waterstone's Literary Fiction Award, McKitterick Prize, W.H. Smith Children's Book of the Year designation, Dolly Gray Children's Literature Award, Council for Exceptional Children, Alex Award, American Library Association, and Grand Prix, Sankei Children's Book Awards (Japan), all 2004, all for *The Curious Incident of the Dog in the Night-Time;* Gold Award, New York Television Festival, two British Academy of Film and Television Arts (BAFTA) awards, and

Mark Haddon (Photograph by Ian West/EPA/Landov. © 2004 by Landov LLC. Reproduced by permission. All rights reserved.)

Royal Television Society Best Children's Drama Award, all 1999, and Prix Jeunesse (Germany), 2000, all for *Microsoap;* BAFTA Children's Award nomination for Best Drama, 2005, for *Fungus and the Bogeyman;* BAFTA Award nomination for Best Single Drama, 2008, for *Coming down the Mountain;* Costa Novel Award shortlist, 2006, for *A Spot of Bother.*

Writings

FOR CHILDREN

(And illustrator) *Gilbert's Gobstopper*, Hamish Hamilton (London, England), 1987, Dial Books for Young Readers (New York, NY), 1988.

(And illustrator) *Toni and the Tomato Soup*, Harcourt Brace (San Diego, CA), 1988.

A Narrow Escape for Princess Sharon, Hamish Hamilton (London, England), 1989.

Gridzbi Spudvetch!, Walker (New York, NY), 1993.

Titch Johnson, Almost World Champion, illustrated by Martin Brown, Walker (New York, NY), 1993.

(And illustrator) *The Real Porky Philips*, A. & C. Black (London, England), 1994.

(And illustrator) *Baby Dinosaurs at Home*, Western Publishing (New York, NY), 1994.

(And illustrator) *Baby Dinosaurs at Playgroup*, Western Publishing (New York, NY), 1994.

(And illustrator) *Baby Dinosaurs in the Garden*, Western Publishing (New York, NY), 1994.

(And illustrator) *Baby Dinosaurs on Vacation*, Western Publishing (New York, NY), 1994.

Secret Agent Handbook, illustrated by Sue Heap, Walker (London, England), 1994.

The Sea of Tranquility, illustrated by Christian Birmingham, Harcourt Brace (San Diego, CA), 1996, published as *Footprints on the Moon*, Candlewick Press (Somerville, MA), 2009.

The Ice Bear's Cave, illustrated by David Axtell, Collins (London, England), 2002.

Ocean Star Express, illustrated by Peter Sutton, Collins (London, England), 2002.

(And illustrator) *Boom!* (based on *Gridzbi Spudvetch!*), David Fickling Books (London, England), 2009, David Fickling Books (New York, NY), 2010.

SELF-ILLUSTRATED; "AGENT Z" SERIES

Agent Z Meets the Masked Crusader, Bodley Head (London, England), 1993.

Agent Z Goes Wild, Bodley Head (London, England), 1994.

Agent Z and the Penguin from Mars, Red Fox (London, England), 1995.

Agent Z and the Killer Bananas, Red Fox (London, England), 2001.

OTHER

The Curious Incident of the Dog in the Night-Time (novel), Doubleday (New York, NY), 2003.

The Talking Horse and the Sad Girl and the Village under the Sea (poetry), Picador (London, England), 2005, Vintage Books (New York, NY), 2006.

A Spot of Bother (novel), Doubleday (New York, NY), 2006.

Coming down the Mountain (teleplay), British Broadcasting Corporation (BBC), 2007.

Polar Bears (play; produced in London, England, 2010), Methuen Drama (London, England), 2010.

Also author of episodes for children's television series, including *Microsoap* and *Starstreet;* contributor to screenplay adaptation of *Fungus and the Bogeyman*, by Raymond Briggs. Creator of comic strip "Men—A User's Guide" contributor to periodicals, including *New Statesman, Spectator, Guardian*, London *Sunday Telegraph*, and *Private Eye*.

Adaptations

Agent Z Meets the Masked Crusader was adapted for television, 1996; *The Curious Incident of the Dog in the Night-Time* was adapted as an audiobook by Recorded Books, 2003, and was optioned for film.

Sidelights

A talented and versatile writer, Mark Haddon is best known for his Whitbread Award-winning novel *The Curious Incident of the Dog in the Night-Time*, a quirky novel about an autistic boy who investigates the murder of his neighbor's dog. In addition, the acclaimed British author has enjoyed a successful career as a writer and illustrator of children's books, a screenwriter for popular British children's television programs, and a poet and playwright. "I'm really lucky in that I can do lots of different things," Haddon remarked to London *Guardian* interviewer Hadley Freeman, adding: "I really like the idea of being a bit unpredictable. I'm known for being a nice, easy-going person with a straightforward exterior. So I think a bit of me wants to be sort of sly and devious."

Born in England in 1962, Haddon began his writing career in the mid-1980s, after working a variety of part-time jobs and earning an advanced degree from Edinburgh University. His 1987 children's book, *Gilbert's Gobstopper*, introduces his inventive mix of humor and adventure as it follows a boy's lost jawbreaker as it travels through sewer pipes, enters the ocean, is found by a fisherman, and even takes a trip into outer space. Praising the book's narrator—the gobstopper itself—Carolyn Polese commented in a *School Library Journal* review that Haddon's "irreverent entertainment will tickle many a funnybone."

In *Boom!*, a greatly revised and expanded version of his 1993 work, *Gridzbi Spudvetch!*, middle schoolers Jim and Charlie unravel a devious plot by their teachers—actually malevolent aliens in disguise—to repopulate their dying planet by kidnapping science-fiction fans. The boys' investigation takes them to a number of far-flung locales, including Scotland's Isle of Skye and the planet of Plonk. The book "manages to be both a send-up and a celebration of classic sci-fi," Sarah Ellis noted in her review of *Boom!* for *Horn Book,* and Chris Shoemaker observed in *School Library Journal* that readers "will appreciate the simple and engaging tale."

Haddon combines adventure and humor in his "Agent Z" series for children that includes *Agent Z and the Penguin from Mars* and *Agent Z and the Killer Bananas.* The Agent Z of the title actually refers to a group of three boys: Jenks, Ben, and Barney. They assume the secret-agent identity as part of their club, then get involved in one goofy adventure after another. In one volume they take advantage of Mr. Sidebottom's obsession with UFO's by concocting an alien plot using a penguin and some aluminum foil, while in another they make a mock film about killer bananas. Reviewers generally had high praise for the "Agent Z" stories, *School Librarian* contributor Alicen Geddes-Ward dubbing *Agent Z Meets the Masked Crusader* a "witty, tight and brilliantly funny book." Adrian Jackson, writing in *Books for Keeps,* similarly felt that *Agent Z and the Penguin from Mars* is "a real hoot of a story, wildly imagined."

Although many of his stories feature humor and quirky child protagonists, Haddon's books *The Real Porky Philips* and *Titch Johnson, Almost World Champion* show a decidedly more sensitive side. Praised by *Books for Keeps* critic Gill Roberts as "powerful, poignant and pertinent," *The Real Porky Philips* is about a young, sensitive, overweight boy who finds the courage to finally assert his real personality after he has to play the role of a genie in the school play. *Titch Johnson, Almost World Champion* has a similar theme about self-confidence. Here, Titch, who seems to possess the sole talent of being able to balance a fork on his nose, gains a better appreciation of himself after successfully organizing a fundraising event.

Haddon both explores the rich world of dreams and imagination in both *The Sea of Tranquility* and *Ocean Star Express.* In the former, the author draws on his childhood fascination with mankind's first landing on the moon in 1969. The boy in the tale has a picture of the solar system on his wall and he fantasizes about what it would be like to be an astronaut. Within the storyline Haddon includes unusual facts about the actual landing: for example, the footprints left on the Moon's surface will remain visible for millions of years because of the lack of any wind or rain. Carolyn Boyd, writing in *School Librarian,* predicted that *The Sea of Tranquility* "will appeal to those who remember the first moon landing and to young readers who will marvel at it." To celebrate the fortieth anniversary of the Apollo 11 mission, *The Sea of Tranquility* was re-released as *Footprints on the Moon.* A *Publishers Weekly* reviewer complimented the "spare, emotive story," and Maura Bresnahan predicted in *School Library Journal* that audiences "will identify with the boy's interest in the solar system, particularly the Moon."

Ocean Star Express, by comparison, is not as grounded in reality. Here a boy named Joe is becoming bored during his summer holiday when Mr. Robertson, the owner of the hotel where Joe's family is staying, invites him to see his train set. No ordinary toy, apparently, the train takes Joe and its owner on a magical ride around the world in what a *Kirkus Reviews* contributor called a "sweet and simple story that young train enthusiasts will enjoy."

After writing over a dozen books for children, Haddon branched out into more complex themes with *The Curious Incident of the Dog in the Night-Time.* In this novel the narrator, fifteen-year-old Christopher Boone, suffers from a disorder known as Asperger's syndrome, a type of autism that prevents him from accurately perceiving and interpreting other people's emotions. Christopher's school counselor assigns the teen the task of writing a book, and Christopher starts writing when he discovers the body of a dead poodle named Wellington. A lover of dogs, as well as a fan of Sherlock Holmes detective stories, Christopher decides to search for Wellington's killer, and this quest becomes the subject of his writing assignment. While Christopher is very logical, he is unable to understand the emotions of the people around him, so his story is told in a matter-of-fact manner. In his novel Haddon also brings to life Christopher's personal quirks: for example, the teen has an aversion to being touched, and he hates the colors brown and yellow. On the other hand, he is brilliant at math, loves puzzles, and has a photographic memory. According to *Book* contributor Beth Kephart, Haddon is "pitch perfect here in his presentation of the disorder, while at the same time developing Christopher as a true character, not a type."

Although his teen narrator struggles with autism, Haddon told *Powells.com* interviewer Dave Weich that *The Curious Incident of the Dog in the Night-Time* is "not just a book about disability." "Here's a character whom if you met him in real life you'd never, ever get inside his head. Yet something magical happens when you write a novel about him. You slip inside his head, and it seems like the most natural thing in the world." As a *Publishers Weekly* critic put it, *The Curious Incident of the Dog in the Night-Time* "brims with touching, ironic humor," yet "treats its protagonist with sensitivity; it is also 'told' in a unique and compelling literary voice." Writing in *Newsweek,* David Noonan similarly noted that "what makes the book so involving and unforgettable isn't the deft plot, it's Christopher's voice—the flat, funny, deeply moving sound of a human being who simply doesn't know what love, or any other emotion, is."

Another novel geared for older readers, *A Spot of Bother* is a dark comedy that centers on a dull British retiree who convinces himself that he has cancer. *USA Today* critic Donna Freydkin wrote of this book that the author "makes the routine minutiae of day-to-day life appealing and often hilarious." "I am really interested in eccentric minds," Haddon told Rosie Barcroft in the London *Independent.* "It's rather like being fascinated by how cars work. It's really boring if your car works all the time. But as soon as something happens you get the bonnet up. If someone has an abnormal or dysfunctional state of mind, you get the bonnet up."

An "eccentric mind" is also at the heart of Haddon's teleplay *Coming down the Mountain,* a British Broadcasting Corporation production. An intense family drama, *Coming down the Mountain* centers on Ben, a teenager with Down's syndrome, and his disconsolate older brother, David, whose hatred for Ben borders on homicidal. "It's not just a film about Down's syndrome," Haddon stated to James Rampton in an interview in the London *Independent.* "It's about the way in which a family can be thrown by the different needs of different children. That's a state common to many families. These characters may seem odd at first, but I think they come alive when you find aspects of them that chime with your own life."

Despite his immense success, Haddon is not content to rest on his laurels. "What keeps you writing is that you don't ever enter a place that feels like home at last," he remarked to Carole Cadwalladr in the London *Observer.* "You're still going uphill. There's still a little glowing light in the distance that you're trying to get to. I was writing something recently and I was chuckling at something I'd written, and my wife looked across and said, 'Do you think that real writers do that?' And I didn't even notice it was funny at first, because I still think, 'Oh, one day I'll be a real writer.'"

Biographical and Critical Sources

PERIODICALS

Atlanta Journal-Constitution, June 29, 2003, John Freeman, "Whodunit Unveils Autistic Boy's Mind," p. D2; October 26, 2003, Greg Changnon, "Teen 'Rain Man' Confronts Canine and Other Mysteries," p. F3.

Book, January-February, 2003, Adam Langer, "The New Houdini: Mark Haddon," p. 43; July-August, 2003, Beth Kephart, review of *The Curious Incident of the Dog in the Night-Time,* p. 76.

Booklist, April 1, 2003, Kristine Huntley, review of *The Curious Incident of the Dog in the Night-Time,* p. 1376; January 1, 2004, Mary McCay, review of *The Curious Incident of the Dog in the Night-Time,* p. 890.

Bookseller, January 24, 2003, "A Young Detective Obsessed by Detail," p. 29.

Books for Keeps, July, 1993, Adrian Jackson, review of *Gridzbi Spudvetch!,* p. 28; May, 1994, Steve Rosson, review of *The Real Porky Philips,* p. 8; July, 1995, Adrian Jackson, review of *Agent Z and the Penguin from Mars,* p. 12; September, 1995, Gill Roberts, review of *The Real Porky Philips,* p. 12.

Books for Your Children, summer, 1994, S. Williams, review of *The Real Porky Philips,* p. 13.

British Book News, March, 1988, Judith Elkin, review of *Gilbert's Gobstopper,* p. 13.

Daily Telegraph (London, England), March 27, 2010, Mark Haddon, "The Curious Incident of the Play in the Spring-time," p. 14; April 7, 2010, Charles Spencer, review of *Polar Bears,* p. 29.

Daily Variety, April 8, 2010, David Benedict, review of *Polar Bears,* p. 3.

Economist, May 24, 2003, review of *The Curious Incident of the Dog in the Night-Time,* p. 85.

Entertainment Weekly, June 20, 2003, Ken Tucker, review of *The Curious Incident of the Dog in the Night-Time,* p. 76.

Growing Point, July, 1989, review of *Toni and the Tomato Soup,* p. 5197.

Guardian (London, England), May 29, 2006, Hadley Freeman, interview with Haddon; August 26, 2006, Patrick Ness, review of *A Spot of Bother,* p. 15.

Horn Book, July-August, 2010, Sarah Ellis, review of *Boom!,* p. 107.

Independent (London, England), June 6, 2003, Nicholas Tucker, review of *The Curious Incident of the Dog in the Night-Time,* p. 15; August 30, 2007, James Rampton, review of *Coming down the Mountain;* March 31, 2010, Rosie Barcroft, "The Curious Incident of the Novelist Turned Playwright," p. 14.

Junior Bookshelf, June, 1993, review of *Gridzbi Spudvetch!,* p. 105; August, 1993, review of *Titch Johnson, Almost World Champion,* p. 135.

Kirkus Reviews, January 1, 2003, review of *Ocean Star Express,* p. 60; April 15, 2003, review of *The Curious Incident of the Dog in the Night-Time,* p. 557; July 15, 2006, review of *A Spot of Bother,* p. 691.

Library Journal, May 1, 2003, David Hellman, review of *The Curious Incident of the Dog in the Night-Time,* p. 155; January, 2004, Michael Adams, review of *The Curious Incident of the Dog in the Night-Time,* p. 184; September 1, 2006, Donna Bettencourt, review of *A Spot of Bother,* p. 136.

Liverpool Echo (Liverpool, England), August 23, 2010, Janet Tansley, review of *Boom!,* p. 11.

Magpies, September, 1996, Margaret Philips, review of *The Sea of Tranquility,* p. 28.

New Statesman, April 26, 2010, Andrew Billen, review of *Polar Bears,* p. 52.

Newsweek, September 8, 2003, David Noonan, "'Allowed to Be Odd'," p. 50.

New York Times Book Review, June 15, 2003, Jay McInerney, "The Remains of the Dog," p. 5; September 7, 2006, Janet Maslin, review of *A Spot of Bother,* p. E11.

Observer (London, England), March 28, 2010, Carole Cadwalladr, interview with Haddon, p. 5; April 11, 2010, Susannah Clapp, review of *Polar Bears,* p. 30.

People, September 18, 2006, Kyle Smith, review of *A Spot of Bother,* p. 51.

Publishers Weekly, May 13, 1988, review of *Gilbert's Gobstopper,* p. 273; April 25, 1994, reviews of *Baby Dinosaurs at Home, Baby Dinosaurs on Vacation, Baby Dinosaurs at Playgroup,* and *Baby Dinosaurs in the Garden,* all p. 75; September 16, 1996, review of *The Sea of Tranquility,* p. 82; July 1, 2002, John F. Baker, "Obsessed by Sherlock Holmes," p. 14; April 7, 2003, review of *The Curious Incident of the Dog in the Night-Time,* p. 42; April 3, 2006, review of *The Talking Horse and the Sad Girl and the Village under the Sea,* p. 41; July 17, 2006, review of *A Spot of Bother,* p. 134; May 4, 2009, review of *Footprints on the Moon,* p. 48; April 26, 2010, review of *Boom!,* p. 109.

Reading Teacher, October, 1989, review of *Gilbert's Gobstopper,* p. 56.

School Librarian, August, 1989, Joyce Banks, review of *A Narrow Escape for Princess Sharon,* p. 104; August, 1993, Julie Blaisdale, review of *Gridzbi Spudvetch!,* and Caroline Axon, review of *Titch Johnson, Almost World Champion,* both p. 109; November, 1993, Alicen Geddes-Ward, review of *Agent Z Meets the Masked Crusader,* p. 155; February, 1997, Carolyn Boyd, review of *The Sea of Tranquility,* p. 19; August, 2001, review of *Agent Z and the Killer Bananas,* p. 136; summer, 2002, review of *Ocean Star Express,* pp. 74-75.

School Library Journal, September, 1988, Carolyn Polese, review of *Gilbert's Gobstopper,* p. 160; October, 1989, Susan H. Patron, review of *Toni and the Tomato Soup,* p. 84; September, 1994, Linda Wicher, reviews of *Baby Dinosaurs at Home, Baby Dinosaurs at Playgroup, Baby Dinosaurs in the Garden,* and *Baby Dinosaurs on Vacation,* all p. 185; September, 1996, John Peters, review of *The Sea of Tranquility,* p. 178; October, 2003, Jackie Gropman, review of *The Curious Incident of the Dog in the Night-Time,* p. 207; June, 2009, Maura Bresnahan, review of *Footprints on the Moon,* p. 90; May, 2010, Chris Shoemaker, review of *Boom!,* p. 114.

Spectator, May 17, 2003, Nicholas Barrow, "It Ain't Necessarily So," p. 65; April 17, 2010, Lloyd Evans, review of *Polar Bears,* p. 46.

Times (London, England), October 1, 2005, Neel Mukherjee, "The Curious Incident of the Bestseller and the Poet," p. 17; April 8, 2010, Benedict Nightingale, review of *Polar Bears,* p. 52.

USA Today, September 5, 2006, Donna Freydkin, review of *A Spot of Bother,* p. D6.

ONLINE

Contemporary Writers in the UK Web site, http://www.contemporarywriters.com/ (December 20, 2010), "Mark Haddon."

Mark Haddon Home Page, http://www.markhaddon.com (December 20, 2010).

Powells.com, http://www.powells.com/ (June 24, 2003), Dave Weich, "The Curiously Irresistible Literary Debut of Mark Haddon."*

*   *   *

HAPKA, C.A.
See HAPKA, Catherine

*   *   *

HAPKA, Catherine
(C.A. Hapka, Cathy Hapka)

Personal

Female. *Hobbies and other interests:* Horseback riding, gardening, music, animals.

Addresses

Home—Lincoln University, PA.

Career

Writer.

Writings

Mickey's Walt Disney World Adventure, illustrated by Scott Tilley and Philippe Harchy Studios, Golden Books (Racine, WI), 1997.

(Adaptor) *Walt Disney's Cinderella: Party Clothes, a Dress-up Book,* Golden Books (Racine, WI), 1997.

(Adaptor as Cathy Hapka) *Walt Disney's Snow White and the Seven Dwarfs: Apple Pie, a Counting Book,* illustrated by Steve Slawich and Don Williams, Golden Books (Racine, WI), 1997.

(Adaptor) *Disney's The Lion King: How Simba Met Timon and Pumbaa,* illustrated by Robbin Cuddy, Golden Books (New York, NY), 1998.

(Compiler) *Disney's Add a Little Magic: Words of Inspiration,* Disney Press (New York, NY), 1999.

(Adaptor) *Disney's Five-minute Bedtime Stories: A Magical Collection of Disney Tales,* illustrated by Design Rights International, Mouse Works (New York, NY), 2000.

(Under name Cathy Hapka) *Fool's Gold* ("Woody's Roundup" series), Disney Press (New York, NY), 2000.

(Under name Cathy Hapka) *Showdown at the Okeydokey Corral* ("Woody's Roundup" series), Disney Press (New York, NY), 2000.

(Adaptor) *Disney's Atlantis, the Lost Empire: A Read-aloud Storybook,* Random House (New York, NY), 2001.

(Adaptor) *Monsters, Inc.,* Random House (New York, NY), 2001.

(Adaptor as Cathy Hapka) *A Friend in Rain,* Puffin Books (New York, NY), 2002.

Bubbles and the Opposite Potion, illustrated by Christopher Cook, Scholastic (New York, NY), 2002.

(Adaptor) *Diego's Journey,* HarperEntertainment (New York, NY), 2002.

(Adaptor) *Disney's Lilo and Stitch,* Random House (New York, NY), 2002.

(Under name Cathy Hapka) *Oasis,* Random House (New York, NY), 2002.

Stuart Little 2: The Joke Book, HarperFestival (New York, NY), 2002.

(Adaptor as Cathy Hapka) *Treasure Planet: Read-aloud Storybook,* Random House (New York, NY), 2002.

(Adaptor) *Big Bad Flea,* HarperFestival (New York, NY), 2003.

(As C.A. Hapka) *Tale of the Toa* ("Bionicle Chronicles" series), Scholastic, Inc. (New York, NY), 2003.

(As C.A. Hapka) *Beware the Bohrok* ("Bionicle Chronicles" series), Scholastic, Inc. (New York, NY), 2003.

(As C.A. Hapka) *Makuta's Revenge* ("Bionicle Chronicles" series), Scholastic, Inc. (New York, NY), 2003.

Christmas Princess, illustrated by April Rousch, Playhouse Pub. (Akron, OH), 2003.

(Adaptor with others) *Disney's Family Story Collection, Volume II: 75 More Fables for Living, Loving, and Learning,* Disney Press (New York, NY), 2003.

(Adaptor) *Disney's Piglet's Big Movie*, illustrated by Mario Cortes and others, Random House (New York, NY), 2003.

(Adaptor) *Disney's The Jungle Book 2: A Read-aloud Storybook*, illustrated by Judith Clarke and others, Random House (New York, NY), 2003.

(Under name Cathy Hapka) *My Sparkle Purse Book*, Playhouse Pub. (Akron, OH), 2003.

Peter Pan: The Joke Book, HarperFestival (New York, NY), 2003.

(Adaptor) *Sinbad and Marina*, DreamWorks/Puffin Books (New York, NY), 2003.

(Adaptor) *The Fortune Donut*, HarperFestival (New York, NY), 2003.

To the Rescue, illustrated by April Roush, Playhouse Pub. (Akron, OH), 2003.

(Adaptor) *Walt Disney's Sleeping Beauty: A Read-aloud Storybook*, Random House (New York, NY), 2003.

(Adaptor) *A Little Fishy*, HarperFestival (New York, NY), 2004.

Ballerina Bear, illustrated by Jim and Kara Valeri, HarperFestival (New York, NY), 2004.

(Adaptor) *Doggone It*, HarperFestival (New York, NY), 2004.

Friends Furever, illustrated by Jim and Kara Valeri, HarperFestival (New York, NY), 2004.

Pretend and Play Kitty, illustrated by Hector Borlasca, Playhouse Pub. (Akron, OH), 2004.

Pretend and Play Princess, illustrated by Hector Borlasca, Playhouse Pub. (Akron, OH), 2004.

Princess Bear, illustrated by Jim and Kara Valeri, HarperFestival (New York, NY), 2004.

Talent Show, illustrated by Jim and Kara Valeri, HarperFestival (New York, NY), 2004.

Becoming the Thing, HarperKidsEntertainment (New York, NY), 2005.

(Under name C.A. Hapka) *Bionicle Chronicles Collection*, Scholastic (New York, NY), 2005.

(Under name Cathy Hapka) *Dreamer: Inspired by a True Story*, Scholastic (New York, NY), 2005.

(Adaptor) *Fantastic Four: The Movie Storybook*, HarperKidsEntertainment (New York, NY), 2005.

Fantastic Four: The Cosmic Storm, HarperKidsEntertainment (New York, NY), 2005.

(With Ellen Titlebaum) *How Not to Babysit Your Brother*, illustrated by Debbie Palen, Random House (New York, NY), 2005.

My Little Doctor Bag Book, illustrated by Paul Sharp, Playhouse Pub. (Akron, OH), 2005.

(Under name Cathy Hapka) *Lost: Endangered Species*, Hyperion (New York, NY), 2005.

(Under name Cathy Hapka) *Pardon My French* ("Students across the Seven Seas" series), Speak (New York, NY), 2005.

Pretend and Play Superhero, illustrated by Hector Borlasca, Playhouse Pub. (Akron, OH), 2005.

(With Peter Bollinger and Michael Koelsch) *The Search for Kong*, HarperKidsEntertainment (New York, NY), 2005.

A Mammoth Mix-up, HarperKidsEntertainment (New York, NY), 2006.

Curious George's Dinosaur Discovery, illustrated by Anna Grossnickle Hines, Houghton Mifflin (Boston, MA), 2006.

(Under name Cathy Hapka) *Dancing*, Playhouse Pub. (Akron, OH), 2006.

(Under name Cathy Hapka) *Lost: Secret Identity*, Hyperion (New York, NY), 2006.

Margret and H.A. Rey's Merry Christmas, Curious George, illustrated by Mary O'Keefe Young, Houghton Mifflin (Boston, MA), 2006.

(Adaptor) *New in the Barn* (novelization; based on *Charlotte's Web* by E.B. White), HarperEntertainment (New York, NY), 2006.

Show-off ("Wildfire" series), Disney Press (New York, NY), 2006.

(Adaptor) *The Last Stand: Beast Chooses Sides*, illustrated by Steven E. Gordon, HarperKidsEntertainment (New York, NY), 2006.

(Adaptor) *The Last Stand: Teaming Up*, illustrated by Boyd Kirkland, HarperKidsEntertainment (New York, NY), 2006.

(Adaptor) *The Perfect Word* (novelization; based on *Charlotte's Web* by E.B. White), HarperEntertainment (New York, NY), 2006.

A Good King Is Hard to Find, HarperTrophy (New York, NY), 2007.

(With Steve E. Gordon and Kanila Tripp) *Barry's Buzzy World*, HarperTrophy (New York, NY), 2007.

(With Charles Grosvenor) *Cera's Shiny Stone*, HarperTrophy (New York, NY), 2007.

Changing Tides ("Gates Family Mystery" series), Disney Press (New York, NY), 2007.

Friends and Foes, HarperTrophy (New York, NY), 2007.

(With Ellen Titlebaum) *How Not to Start Third Grade*, illustrated by Debbie Palen, Random House (New York, NY), 2007.

Racing Away ("Wildfire" series), Disney Press (New York, NY), 2007.

Riding Lessons ("Wildfire" series), Disney Press (New York, NY), 2007.

(With Mike Sullivan and Michael Koelsch) *Shrek the Halls*, HarperCollins Childrens Books (New York, NY), 2007.

The Lost Lunch Mystery, illustrated by Richard Torrey, Scholastic (New York, NY), 2007.

Triple the Trouble, HarperTrophy (New York, NY), 2007.

(With Alice Alfonsi) *Wildcat Spirit* ("High-school Musical" series), Disney Press (New York, NY), 2007.

(Adaptor) *Time Warp Trio: South Pole or Bust (an Egg)*, illustrated by Lisa Rao, HarperCollins (New York, NY), 2007.

Track Record ("Wildfire" series), Disney Press (New York, NY), 2007.

(Adaptor) *Batman's Friends and Foes*, HarperTrophy (New York, NY), 2008.

(Under name Cathy Hapka) *French Kissmas* ("Students across the Seven Seas" series), Speak (New York, NY), 2008.

Go West, Disney Press (New York, NY), 2008.

(Adaptor) *I Am Batman*, HarperTrophy (New York, NY), 2008.

(Adaptor) *Igor: Movie Novelization,* Simon Spotlight (New York, NY), 2008.

In the Spotlight ("High-School Musical" series), Disney Press (New York, NY), 2008.

Kung Fu Panda: The Movie Storybook ("Kung Fu Panda" series), HarperEntertainment (New York, NY), 2008.

Po's Crash Course ("Kung Fu Panda" series), HarperTrophy (New York, NY), 2008.

Meet the Masters ("Kung Fu Panda" series), HarperEntertainment (New York, NY), 2008.

Midnight Ride ("Gates Family Mystery" series), New York Disney Press 2008.

Royal Champions: An Enchanted Stables Storybook, Disney Press (New York, NY), 2008.

Friends 4 Ever? ("High-school Musical" series), Disney Press (New York, NY), 2008.

The Lonely Dinosaur, HarperTrophy (New York, NY), 2008.

Uncharted ("Gates Family Mystery" series), Disney Press (New York, NY), 2008.

(Under name Cathy Hapka) *Animalia's Talent-O-Topia,* Grosset & Dunlap (New York, NY), 2009.

(Adaptor) *Battle of the Smithsonian: To the Rescue!* (based on a screenplay by Robert Ben Garant and Thomas Lennon), HarperCollins Childrens Books (New York, NY), 2009.

Larry's Friends and Foes, HarperCollins Childrens Books (New York, NY), 2009.

(Adaptor) *Princess Protection Program: The Movie Storybook,* Disney Press (New York, NY), 2009.

Forever Free ("Gates Family Mystery" series), New York Disney Press 2009.

Roaring In ("Gates Family Mystery" series), Disney Press (New York, NY), 2009.

Wild Hearts ("Jonas" series), Disney Press (New York, NY), 2009.

Off the Charts ("Jonas" series), Disney Press (New York, NY), 2009.

(Adaptor) *About Face,* Disney Press (New York, NY), 2010.

(Adaptor) *Meet the Dragons* ("Meet the Dragons" reader series), illustrated by Justin Gerard and Charles Grosvenor, Harper (New York, NY), 2010.

Hiccup the Hero ("Meet the Dragons" reader series), HarperCollins (New York, NY), 2010.

Prince of Persia: Crisis in Alamut, Disney Press (New York, NY), 2010.

Prince of Persia: The Road to Sardis, Disney Press (New York, NY), 2010.

Prince of Persia: Young Dastan, Disney Press (New York, NY), 2010.

(Adaptor) *Santa Buddies: The 2-in-1 Junior Novel,* Disney Press (New York, NY), 2010.

(Adaptor) *Shrek Forever After: The Movie Storybook,* illustrated by Larry Navarro, Price Stern Sloan (New York, NY), 2010.

(Adaptor) *Three's a Crowd,* Disney Press (New York, NY), 2010.

Yatimah, illustrated by Ruth Sanderson, Random House (New York, NY), 2010.

Blue and Friends ("Rio" reader series), HarperCollins (New York, NY), 2011.

Learning to Fly ("Rio" reader series), HarperCollins (New York, NY), 2011.

(With Georgina Bloomberg) *The A Circuit,* Bloomsbury Children's (New York, NY), 2011.

"WALT DISNEY'S MINNIE MYSTERIES" SERIES

The Butterscotch Bandit, Golden Books (Racine, WI), 1997.

The Dognapper, Golden Books (New York, NY), 1997.

The Flower Prowler, Golden Books (New York, NY), 1998.

The Noisy Attic, Golden Books (New York, NY), 1998.

Disney Minnie Mysteries, Random House (New York, NY), 2004.

"KICKING AND SCREAMING" SERIES

My Dad, the Coach, HarperKidsEntertainment (New York, NY), 2005.

The Comeback Kids, HarperKidsEntertainment (New York, NY), 2005.

"STAR POWER" SERIES

Supernova, Aladdin Paperbacks (New York, NY), 2004.

Always Dreamin', Aladdin Paperbacks (New York, NY), 2004.

Never Give Up, Aladdin Paperbacks (New York, NY), 2004.

Together We Can Do It, Aladdin Paperbacks (New York, NY), 2004.

Blast from the Past, Aladdin Paperbacks (New York, NY), 2004.

Someday, Some Way, Aladdin Paperbacks (New York, NY), 2005.

Star Bright, Aladdin Paperbacks (New York, NY), 2005.

Over the Top, Aladdin Paperbacks (New York, NY), 2005.

"ROMANTIC COMEDIES" SERIES

Something Borrowed, Simon Pulse (New York, NY), 2008.

The Twelve Dates of Christmas, Simon Pulse (New York, NY), 2008.

Love on Cue, Simon Pulse (New York, NY), 2009.

At First Sight, Simon Pulse (New York, NY), 2010.

"PONY SCOUTS" BEGINNING-READER SERIES

Really Riding!, illustrated by Anne Kennedy, HarperCollins (New York, NY), 2009.

Pony Crazy, illustrated by Anne Kennedy, HarperCollins Childrens Books (New York, NY), 2009.

At the Show, illustrated by Anne Kennedy, Harper (New York, NY), 2011.

Back in the Saddle, illustrated by Anne Kennedy, Harper (New York, NY), 2011.

"HORSE DIARIES" NOVEL SERIES

Elska, illustrated by Ruth Sanderson, Random House (New York, NY), 2009.

Yatimah, illustrated by Ruth Sanderson, Random House (New York, NY), 2011.

Sidelights

Sometimes publishing her work under the names Cathy Hapka and C.A. Hapka, Catherine Hapka is a prolific writer whose stories for children range from picture books and easy-reader retellings to chapter-book series and young-adult novels. In addition to working as a ghost-writer on established fiction series, Hapka has also created several series of her own, including the "Star Power" books for preteens and the "Romantic Comedies" novels for slightly older readers. Living on a small farm in rural Pennsylvania along with horses, goats, chickens, and cats, she particularly enjoys writing about horses, which have been her passion for many years. Both her "Pony Scouts" books and her contributions to the "Horse Diaries" series are designed to appeal to preteen girls with a similar passion for horses. Praising Hapka's "Horse Diaries" installment *Elska,* *Horn Book* contributor Robin L. Smith wrote that the dappled mare's narration of its experiences from birth to its time in the care of a girl named Amma in Iceland

Catherine Hapka's horse story **Elska** *allows readers to travel to prehistoric Iceland via Ruth Sanderson's evocative art.* (Illustration copyright © 2009 by Ruth Sanderson. Used by permission of Random House Children's Books, a division of Random House, Inc.)

circa 1000 B.C. is enriched with Icelandic words and features enough horse facts to make it "perfect for the intended primary-grade horse-loving audience." Dubbing the unusual setting in *Elska* "dynamic" and the illustrations by Ruth Sanderson "beautiful," Hazel Rochman predicted in *Booklist* that Hapka's "cozy and exciting adventure will draw a wide audience."

Hapka focuses on rock music in her "Star Power" series, in which a teen pop singer's high-profile life also has its share of adventure. In *Supernova* readers meet fourteen-year-old Star Calloway, a singer whose hit songs have earned her fans throughout the world. Although Star lives a magical life as she travels from place to place, she also worries over the whereabouts of her mom, dad, and younger brother, who she has not heard from since they disappeared during a vacation months before. As the girl tries to remain optimistic about the return of her family, she suffers another loss when a music rival steals her beloved pug dog, Dudley Do Wrong. *Always Dreamin'* finds Star at the center of a media battle when her offhanded comment about another pop diva is misquoted, while *Together We Can Do It* finds her in Sweden where local gossip has it that she is spending her off-stage time with a handsome Swedish singer named Sven. Switzerland is the setting of *Blast from the Past,* as a new friend named Samantha seems to know more about Star's family than she should. Other novels in the "Star Power" series include *Over the Top* and *Never Give Up,* the latter which finds Star touring Italy when news come that her parents may have been located. Reviewing the first two novels in Hapka's middle-grade series for *School Library Journal,* Tina Zubak likened their upbeat stories to "candy-coated popcorn that some teens will gobble up." A *Publishers Weekly* critic predicted of *Supernova* that "the star-studded hoopla . . . will appeal to kids who like their reading lite and bouncy."

Biographical and Critical Sources

PERIODICALS

Booklist, February 15, 2009, Hazel Rochman, review of *Elska,* p. 82.

Horn Book, July-August, 2009, Robin L. Smith, review of *Elska,* p. 425.

Publishers Weekly, June 14, 2004, review of *Supernova,* p. 64.

School Library Journal, August, 2004, Tina Zubak, reviews of *Supernova* and *Always Dreamin'* both p. 123; July, 2007, Gloria Koster, review of *Time Warp Trio: The High and the Flighty,* p. 84.

ONLINE

HarperCollins Web site, http://www.harpercollins.com/ (December 15, 2010).*

HAPKA, Cathy
See HAPKA, Catherine

*   *   *

HEMINGWAY, Edith M. 1950-
(Edith Morris Hemingway)

Personal
Born 1950, in Miami, FL; father a flight engineer; married; children: Daniel, Katie. *Education:* Attended Guilford College; Appalachian State University, degree; Spalding University, M.F.A., 2004. *Hobbies and other interests:* Kayaking, playing mountain dulcimer, gardening, hiking.

Addresses
Home—MD. *E-mail*—edie@ediehemingway.com.

Career
Author and educator. Teacher of special education in Loudoun County, VA; Frederick High School, Frederick, MD, member of guidance department; Hood College, Frederick, academic advisor; Carroll Community College, Westminster, MD, coordinator of admissions and academic advisor; creative writing teacher, 2004—.

Member
Authors Guild, Society of Children's Book Writers and Illustrators (regional advisor), Children's Book Guild of Washington, DC.

Awards, Honors
Parents' Choice Gold Award, 2009, and Best Children's Book designation, Bank Street College of Education, 2010, both for *Road to Tater Hill.*

Edith M. Hemingway (Photograph by Douglas Hemingway. Reproduced by permission.)

Writings

NOVELS

(With Jacqueline Cosgrove Shields, under name Edith Morris Hemingway) *Broken Drum,* White Mane Publishing (Shippensburg, PA), 1996.
(With Jacqueline Cosgrove Shields, under name Edith Morris Hemingway) *Rebel Hart,* White Mane Publishing (Shippensburg, PA), 2000.
Road to Tater Hill, Delacorte Press (New York, NY), 2009.

Contributor to *Summer Shorts: A Short Story Anthology,* Blooming Tree Press.

Sidelights
Edith M. Hemingway draws upon her memories of summers spent in rural North Carolina in *Road to Tater Hill,* a middle-grade novel that offers "a universal drama of childhood grief," according to *Booklist* critic Hazel Rochman. "The writing of the novel has been a long and winding personal road for me . . . and began as an autobiographical incident," Hemingway remarked to *Class of 2K9* online interviewer Fran Cannon Slayton. "Like my character, Annie, I spent my childhood summers at my grandparents' home in the mountains of North Carolina and enjoyed many of the same pastimes—blackberry picking on Tater Hill, building dams in the creek, swinging on the rope in the barn, reading many of the same books. It's also the place where my own baby sister was born prematurely and died."

Set in 1963, *Road to Tater Hill* focuses on Annie Winter, a ten year old who is spending the summer at her grandparents' home in the Appalachian Mountains. With her father, a member of the U.S. Air Force, stationed overseas, Annie turns to an elderly recluse for support when her baby sister dies at birth and her mom becomes deeply depressed. The preteen must decide if she can continue this new friendship, however, when she learns that her helpful confidante, Miss Eliza, has a disturbing past that includes a thirty-year prison sentence for the murder of her abusive husband. Hemingway's "characters and setting are finely drawn," maintained *School Library Journal* reviewer Nancy P. Reeder, the critic dubbing *Road to Tater Hill* a "well-written and enjoyable novel."

Biographical and Critical Sources

PERIODICALS

Booklist, July 1, 2009, Hazel Rochman, review of *Road to Tater Hill,* p. 61.

Cover of Hemingway's middle-grade novel Road to Tater Hill, *which is set in the Appalachian Mountains during the early 1960s.* (Jacket photograph by Eva Kolenko. Jacket design © 2009 by Angela Carlino. Reproduced by permission of Random House Children's Books, a division of Random House, Inc.)

Bulletin of the Center for Children's Books, October, 2009, Deborah Stevenson, review of *Road to Tater Hill,* p. 65.

Kirkus Reviews, August 15, 2009, review of *Road to Tater Hill.*

School Library Journal, December, 2009, Nancy P. Reeder, review of *Road to Tater Hill,* p. 120.

ONLINE

Class of 2K9 Web log, http://community.livejournal.com/classof2k9/ (September 10, 2009), Fran Cannon Slayton, interview with Hemingway.

Edith M. Hemingway Home Page, http://www.ediehemingway.com (December 1, 2010).

* * *

HEMINGWAY, Edith Morris
    See HEMINGWAY, Edith M.

HIGGINS, Dalton

Personal

Born in Toronto, Ontario, Canada. *Education:* York University, B.A. (English literature/mass communications; with honours); Centennial College, diploma (book and magazine publishing; graduate study at University of the West Indies (Jamaica).

Addresses

Home—Toronto, Ontario, Canada. *E-mail*—daltonhiggins@gmail.com.

Career

Journalist, broadcast personality, and pop-culture critic. BPM TV, former host and writer for *Urban Groove* (television series); commentator on numerous television programs. Producer of documentary films, including *More than a Haircut,* 2009. Harbourfront Centre, music programmer; Web-content provider. Juror for Canadian music awards, including Juno awards, Echo Prize, and Honey Jam. Public speaker.

Awards, Honors

Canadian National Magazine Award.

Writings

(With Tony Young) *Much Master T: One VJ's Journey,* foreword by Shaggy, ECW Press (Toronto, Ontario, Canada), 2002.

(With Greg Smith) *Hip Pop,* Rubicon/Harcourt Canada (Oakville, Ontario, Canada), 2004.

Hip Hop World ("Groundwood Guides" series), Groundwood Books (Berkeley, CA), 2009.

Fatherhood 4.0, Insomniac Press (Canada), 2010.

Contributor to periodicals, including *Now, Saturday Night, Toronto Star, Quill & Quire, The Source, Urb,* and *Vibe.*

Sidelights

Considered his country's top expert on hip-hop culture, Canadian journalist and media personality Dalton Higgins is also a music programmer, pop-culture critic, and author. His book *Hip Hop World* introduces teens to the roots and global expansion of hip hop, a musical form that originated in New York City's black community and mixes rap, graffiti art, breakdancing, and the manual manipulation of recorded music. Higgins also shares his expertise as coauthor of two other music-related books: *Hip Hop* and *Much Master T: A VJ's Journey,* the latter which he wrote with Canadian urban-music producer Tony "Master T" Young. Continuing his study of modern culture, he has also produced *Fatherhood 4.0,* which

Dalton Higgins (Photograph by Shiloh Bell-Higgins. Reproduced by permission.)

presents interviews, poetry, essays, and other writings that shed a light on the role of black fathers in an increasingly high-technology, multi-media age.

Part of the "Groundwood Guides" series, *Hip Hop World* is geared to readers interested in the cultural phenomenon that is hip hop. From the first use of the term in the 1970s by a rapper named Space Cowboy, Higgins chronicles the music's adoption by an evolving counterculture rooted in inner-city gang violence, racial and sexual disparities, and the showy "bling" signifying material wealth. In North America, Public Enemy, Lil' Wayne, Jay-Z, and Eminem are among the genre's best-known performers: while their music has become less popular in recent years, Higgins maintains that hip hop continues to migrate throughout the world, echoing the voice of teens and others who live outside the placid "social norm" as represented by modern media. By this assertion—that hip hop is linked to social-justice movements in Asia, Australia, and the Middle East—"Higgins's arguments and examples are sure to cause debate," according to *School Library Journal* contributor Matthew L. Moffett. Calling *Hip Hop World* an "excellent" resource, Moffett added that the book encourages "fans both new and old [to] . . . look at this art form in a serious, critical way," while in the *Canadian Review of Materials* Joanne Peters commended the breadth of facts presented regarding the growth of the many-faceted hip-hop culture by noting that "it speaks to Higgins' skill as a writer that he packs so much information into such a small volume." In *Booklist* Gillian Engberg explained that Higgins "is upfront about his biases and beliefs" and asserted that his "personal candor will only add to the book's appeal." Describing *Hip Hop World* as a well-researched mix of "academic treatise" and music journalism, a *Kirkus Reviews* critic predicted that Higgins' "pithy, unapologetically political narrative . . . is sure to engage readers."

Biographical and Critical Sources

PERIODICALS

Booklist, November 1, 2009, Gillian Engberg, review of *Hip Hop World*, p. 56.

Canadian Review of Materials, October 9, 2009, Joanne Peters, review of *Hip Hop World*.

Kirkus Reviews, September 15, 2009, review of *Hip Hop World*.

Quill & Quire, October, 2009, Alessandro Porco, review of *Hip Hop World*.

Rescource Links, February, 2010, Lesley Little, review of *Hip Hop World*, p. 38.

School Library Journal, November, 2009, Matthew L. Moffett, review of *Hip Hop World*, p. 146.

Voice of Youth Advocates, February, 2010, Lynne Farrell Stover, review of *Hip Hop World*, p. 526.

ONLINE

Dalton Higgins Web log, http://daltonhiggins.wordpress.com (November 14, 2010).

National Speakers Bureau Web site, http://nsb.com/ (December 4, 2010), "Dalton Higgins."

Cover of Higgins' Hip Hop World, which takes a global view of urban hip-hop culture. (Copyright © 2009 by Dalton Higgins. Reprinted with permission of Groundwood Books Limited, www.groundwoodbooks.com.)

HOLT, Kimberly Willis 1960-

Personal

Born September 9, 1960, in Pensacola, FL; daughter of Julian Ray (a data processing manager) and Brenda (a teacher) Willis; married Jerry William Holt (director of Amarillo CVC), February 23, 1985; children: Shannon. *Education:* Attended University of New Orleans, 1978-79, and Louisiana State University, 1979-81.

Addresses

Office—P.O. Box 20135, Amarillo, TX 79114. *Agent*—Flannery Literary Agency, 114 Wickfield Ct., Naperville, IL 60563.

Career

Author of books for children. Radio news director, 1980-82; worked in advertising and marketing, 1982-87; interior decorator, 1987-93; writer, 1994—. Mitchell-Willis Scholarship, founder. Presenter at schools and libraries; speaker at state and national conferences.

Awards, Honors

Boston Globe/Horn Book Award for Fiction, 1998, and American Library Association (ALA) Notable Book selection and Top Ten Best Books for Young Adults selection, both 1999, all for *My Louisiana Sky;* National Book Award for Young People's Literature, 1999, for *When Zachary Beaver Came to Town;* Dorothy Canfield Fisher Award finalist, Rebecca Caudill Reader's Book Award finalist, and other state book award nominations, all c. 2001, all for *Dancing in Cadillac Light;* ALA Notable Book and Best Books for Young Adults selections, Parent's Choice Gold Award, Best Children's Book designation, Bank Street College of Education, Notable Book for a Global Society designation, and Books for the Teen Age selection, New York Public Library, all c. 2003, all for *Keeper of the Night;* CYBILS Award finalist, 2006, for *Waiting for Gregory;* Literary Merit Award, Louisiana Library Association, Cooperative Children's Book Center Choices selection, and Charlie May Simon Children's Book Award nomination, all c. 2007, all for *Part of Me;* Oppenheim Gold Toy Award, 2007, for *Skinny Brown Dog;* One Hundred Titles for Reading and Sharing selection, New York Public Library, 2010, for *The Water Seeker.*

Writings

YOUNG-ADULT NOVELS

My Louisiana Sky, Holt (New York, NY), 1998.
Mister and Me, Putnam (New York, NY), 1998.
When Zachary Beaver Came to Town, Holt (New York, NY), 1999.

Dancing in Cadillac Light, Putnam (New York, NY), 2001.
The Water Seeker, Henry Holt (New York, NY), 2010.

PICTURE BOOKS

Waiting for Gregory, illustrated by Gabi Swiatkowska, Holt (New York, NY), 2006.
Skinny Brown Dog, illustrated by Donald Saaf, Henry Holt (New York, NY), 2007.
The Adventures of Granny Clearwater and Little Critter, illustrated by Laura Huliska-Beith, Henry Holt (New York, NY), 2010.

"PIPER REED" CHAPTER BOOK SERIES

Piper Reed, Navy Brat, illustrated by Christine Davenier, Holt (New York, NY), 2007.
Piper Reed, the Great Gypsy, illustrated by Christine Davenier, Henry Holt (New York, NY), 2008.
Piper Reed Gets a Job, illustrated by Christine Davenier, Henry Holt (New York, NY), 2009.
Piper Reed: Into the Wild, illustrated by Christine Davenier, Henry Holt (New York, NY), 2010.

OTHER

Part of Me: Stories of a Louisiana Family, Holt (New York, NY), 2006.

Adaptations

Holt's novels have been adapted as audiobooks.

Sidelights

Kimberly Willis Holt writes poignant coming-of-age fiction for young readers, and her novels and short stories hum with the sleepy rhythms of small-town life. Since publishing her first novel, *My Louisiana Sky,* in

Kimberly Willis Holt (second from left) earned the 1999 National Book Award for Young People's literature for her novel My Louisiana Sky. (Photograph courtesy of Diane Bondareff, AP Images.)

1994, Holt has continued to expand her focus, moving from the American South west to Texas, and including picture books as well as the anthology *Part of Me: Stories of a Louisiana Family* in her list of published works. In the process, she has won a number of awards, including two American Library Association citations and a prestigious National Book Award for Young People's Literature, the last for her novel *When Zachary Beaver Came to Town.* Holt's fiction has been praised for its realistic depiction of life in the rural South, as well as for the iconoclastic yet sympathetic characters she creates within her fictional world.

Holt was born in 1960, in Pensacola, Florida, the site of a large naval base. Her father worked for many years as a chef for the U.S. Navy, and her mother was a teacher. Julian Willis's job took the family to several far-flung places, including France and the Pacific Ocean territory of Guam. They also lived in a number of American states, but always made Forest Hill, Louisiana, their spiritual home. Holt's grandmother lived there, and the future author loved spending time in a place where her roots ran so deep. She began to consider writing as a career at the age of twelve, when she read Carson Mc-Cullers's 1940 novel *The Heart Is a Lonely Hunter.* "It was just life-changing because of the characters," she later told *School Library Journal* writer Kathleen T. Horning. "That was the first time I read a book where the characters seemed like real people to me."

As a teen and young adult, Holt had always envisioned a life as an author, but never pursued it in earnest due to the discouraging comments of a former English teacher. Instead, she studied broadcast journalism at the University of New Orleans and Louisiana State University, but left school in 1981 to work as a news director for a radio station. The work was far from challenging, however, and so she took another job at the station selling advertising time. She also worked as an interior decorator for six years before thinking about writing for publication.

Around 1994, Holt—by then married and raising her daughter Shannon—moved to Amarillo, Texas, for her husband's job. In the sudden isolation, she turned her free time to writing for children. "I didn't know a soul there and I thought, 'If I'm ever going to do it, this is the time,'" she told Horning. The result was *My Louisiana Sky,* which was published in 1998. Set in a small town in central Louisiana, the story was inspired by a memorable incident that occurred when Holt was nine years old. She had been traveling through rural Louisiana with her parents, and saw a woman carrying groceries walking on the side of the road. "This lady looked strange to me," Holt recalled in the interview with Horning. "She just had a different look about her on her face and I mentioned her to my mom and my mom said, 'That lady's mentally retarded and her husband is mentally retarded and they have a lot of kids.' It haunted me for the rest of my life."

Twelve-year-old Tiger Ann Parker is the unlikely heroine of *My Louisiana Sky,* which takes place in 1957 in a town called Saitter. Tiger does well in both school and athletics, but feels a certain degree of social ostracism because of her parents. Her father, who works in a local plant nursery, cannot even do simple math and Tiger's mother is even more developmentally challenged. The preteen knows that some townspeople view the family as odd and are of the opinion that the Parkers should have never been allowed to marry and start a family. Fortunately, Tiger also lives with her astute, practical grandmother, who helps the girl face the teasing of others. Things begin to change in sleepy Saitter, however: Tiger's baseball-playing pal surprises her with a kiss one day, and then her beloved grandmother dies. The girl's sophisticated aunt comes to Saitter in the midst of the crisis, and offers to take Tiger with her to live in the city of Baton Rouge. Tiger is torn between staying with her parents, who love her dearly, and going with the glamorous Dorie Kay and experiencing a world of new opportunities far from the town's small-mindedness. When a natural disaster strikes, she begins to realize the more positive aspects of life in Saitter.

Betsy Hearne, reviewing *My Louisiana Sky* for the *Bulletin of the Center for Children's Books,* wrote that in Tiger Holt creates a character "with a distinctive voice" as well as "a credible resolution showing Tiger's values to be as strong as her family ties." In her *School Library Journal* review, Cindy Darling Codell asserted that "Holt has nicely portrayed the rhythms, relationships, and sometimes harsh realities of small-town life." Marilyn Bousquin, reviewing the novel for *Horn Book,* found that Holt "eases the action along with a low-key, unpretentious plot, never resorting to over-dramatization or sentimentality in developing her uncannily credible characters." In *Booklist* Hazel Rochman opined that "all the characters, including Tiger's parents, are drawn with warmth but no patronizing reverence," while a *Publishers Weekly* critic asserted that in *My Louisiana Sky* Holt "presents and handles a sticky dilemma with remarkable grace."

The plot of Holt's National Book Award-winning *When Zachary Beaver Came to Town* originated with another memorable event in the author's life. At age thirteen, she went to the Louisiana state fair and paid two dollars to see a youth billed as "the fattest boy in the world." He sat in a small trailer and, in a manner somewhat out of character for the shy Holt, she asked him several questions about himself. He answered them, but he was understandably a bit surly about it. Years later, Holt met another woman who recalled meeting the boy and also eating her lunch with him. In Holt's story, the action takes place in the fictional small town of Antler, Texas, during the summer of 1971, when young teens Toby and Cal watch the trailer bearing Zachary Beaver, "the world's fattest teenaged boy," drive into town. The boys dream of life outside of Antler, and when they visit the 643-pound Zachary they ask him numerous questions. Zachary seems to possess an oddly encyclopedic know-

ledge of the world, but relies on his legal guardian—who disappears shortly after Zachary's trailer arrives in the parking lot of the local Dairy Maid. In their sleuthing, Toby and Cal discover one of Zachary's secrets, and they help him fulfill a dream while also coming to terms with their own limited reality.

In *When Zachary Beaver Came to Town* "Holt tenderly captures small-town life and deftly fills it with decent characters who ring true," wrote Linnea Lannon in her *New York Times Book Review* appraisal. "Picturesque images . . . drive home the point that everyday life is studded with memorable moments," stated a *Publishers Weekly* contributor also in praise of the award-winning work.

Set in the late 1960s, in the small town of Moon, Texas, *Dancing in Cadillac Light* follows the story of Jaynell Lambert, an eleven-year-old tomboy whose life changes after her independent-minded grandfather comes to stay with her family. While Grandpap's behaviors seem odd to the girl—he lets the low-class Pickens family live in his old house free of charge, pays cash for a gaudy, green 1962 Cadillac, and shuffles around town with no destination in mind—Jaynell finds her views about character and the meaning of poverty changing after the old man's passing. Calling *Dancing in Cadillac Light* "a solid page-turner," *School Library Journal* reviewer Wiliam McLoughlin added that the story clearly showcases Holt's "remarkable gift for creating endearingly eccentric characters as well as witty dialogue rich in dialect and idiom." Jaynell is enjoyable and serves as a "spunky and tough" narrator, in the opinion of a *Publishers Weekly* contributor, the critic adding that *Dancing in Cadillac Light* "captures a child's sense that time stretches endlessly before her."

Thirteen-year-old Isabel Moreno is center stage in *Keeper of the Night*. Living on the island of Guam with her family, Isabel must still learn to cope with tragedy and her troubled siblings after her mother commits suicide and the family starts to come apart. Noting that Isabel "comes through as a thoroughly believable eighth grader" in Holt's story, Kathleen Isaacs described *Keeper of the Night* as "a beautifully written description of sorrow and recovery that should appeal to a wide audience." *Kliatt* contributor Michele Winship dubbed the novel an engaging coming-of-age tale.

In *The Water Seeker* readers are taken back to the 1830s, where Missouri-born Amos Kincaid has a rough start to life. Although his mother has died in childbirth, father Jake must be away from home due to his work as a trapper. Raised predominately by relatives, Amos survives several illnesses and works hard while growing up, and the difficulties continue once Jake returns with news that he will lead a pioneer party to Oregon and plans to take Amos with him. Discovering that they share a talent for dowsing (locating where water flows underground), father and son build a close relationship that is supported by other characters, such as Jake's

Cover of Holt's middle-grade novel **Keeper of the Night,** *featuring artwork by Fabian Negrin.* (Illustration copyright © 2005 by Fabian Negrin. Reproduced by permission of Laurel-Leaf, an imprint of Random House Children's Books, a division of Random House, Inc.)

Native-American wife, family members, and fellow travelers. *The Water Seeker* "serves up an absorbing, atmospheric epic of intertwined lives on America's western frontier," according to a *Publishers Weekly* contributor, while in *School Library Journal* Cristi Esterle deemed the novel "a well-developed character study" that is enriched by vivid descriptions of "the hars and often deadly" trip to Oregon's Willamette Valley. In *Booklist* Gillian Engberg noted that the "moving, palpable sense of pioneer life" Holt creates in her novel is told in "graceful prose that occassionally reads like poetry."

Geared for younger readers, *Mister and Me* won praise for its depiction of a time and place that had long passed. The book's protagonist, Jolene Johnson, knows no other world except the sometimes-challenging, segregated South of the World War II era. An African-American child, Jolene lives with her widowed mother and grandfather in a Louisiana logging town. Life be-

gins to change a bit too quickly for the girl when Mister Leroy Redfield, a logger new to town, starts courting Jolene's mom. Dealing with a rival for her busy mother's affection makes Jolene miss her deceased father even more. Although the girl attempts to rid the man from their lives, her strategies only backfire. When her mother and grandfather leave on a hurried trip to New Orleans, Jolene is left with Leroy for caretaking, and a truce between the two leads to a new beginning in their ongoing relationship. Lynda Short, writing in *School Library Journal,* called *Mister and Me* a "touching short novel" that depicts Jolene's coming to terms with the presence of a "man whose love and patience allow her to expand her notion of family." A *Publishers Weekly* review wrote that "the warmth and love in the Johnson household envelops the novel," and Kay Weisman noted in *Booklist* that Holt's "heartfelt story is filled with richly developed characters who deal with all-too-real problems."

Upper-elementary-grade readers are the focus of Holt's "Piper Reed" series, which includes *Piper Reed, Navy Brat, Piper Reed, the Great Gypsy, Piper Reed Gets a Job,* and *Piper Reed, Campfire Girl.* Brought to life in humorous ink drawings by Christine Davenier, the first book in the series finds nine-year-old Piper and her two sisters sad about the prospect of moving away from school friends and relatives when their father, a Navy aircraft mechanic, is transferred to a Navy base in Pensacola, Florida, during the middle of the school year. Although the trip is especially hard for older sister Tori, Piper is quick to discover positive things about the move, such as the family's new puppy, Bruna, and the chance to make new friends when she starts her Gypsy Club. Piper plans to win the pet show at her newly formed Gypsy Club, but Bruna does not cooperate by learning her tricks in *Piper Reed, the Great Gypsy.* Piper's determination to earn enough money to build a Gypsy Club clubhouse inspires her to scout out money-making ideas in *Piper Reed Gets a Job,* and a trip into the wild is the focus of *Piper Reed, Campfire Girl.* Praising Piper as "an irrepressible character struggling with dyslexia," *School Library Journal* contributor Terrie Dorio added that in *Piper Reed: Navy Brat* the fourth grader's "upbeat individuality shines," and a *Kirkus Reviews* writer noted that her "lively imagination, wholesomeness and moments of 'sister magic' are likable and believable." Reviewing *Piper Reed Gets a Job* in *School Library Journal,* Elizabeth Swistock recommended Holt's series to "fans of Clementine or Judy Moody," two other popular preteen heroines, while *Horn Book* contributor Robin L. Smith called Holt's fictional family "loving without being cloying, strong without being perfect, and optimistic without seeming unbelievable."

In addition to novels, Holt has also authored several picture books. In *Waiting for Gregory,* which feature paintings by Polish-born artist Gabi Swiatkowska, a young girl eagerly awaits the birth of her baby cousin. After Iris asks various relatives factual questions about childbirth, she finds that everyone gives her a different answer in Holt's amusing tale. Reviewing *Waiting for Gregory* in *Booklist,* Hazel Rochman wrote that Holt's mix of the everyday and the magical . . . captures the longing, mystery, and joy" of childhood, while a *Kirkus Reviews* writer concluded that her "child's-eye take on the passage of time is concrete and comforting" to young readers.

Skinny Brown Dog finds a stray dog with white spots adopting a small-town baker named Benny, who grudgingly is won over by the pup's doggy charm. Another picture-book by Holt, *The Adventures of Granny Clearwater and Little Critter,* is illustrated in fabric collage by Laura Huliska-Beith and follows the travels of a grandma and grandson after they tumble out of the back of the family's covered wagon and become stranded in the Wild West. Featuring multimedia artwork by Donald Saaf, *Skinny Brown Dog* was cited by *School Library Journal* contributor Kirsten Cutler for its "humorous details and happy ending," while a *Kirkus Reviews* writer praised the story's "unassuming text" as "nicely structured and paced." *Booklist* critic Ian Chipman dubbed *The Adventures of Granny Clearwater and Little Critter* "bursting at the seams with Old West zaniness," and in *School Library Journal* Donna Atmur described it as both "a wonderful tall tale" and "a rip-roaring yarn."

When asked by *School Library Journal* interviewer Horning about the eccentricity of her characters, Holt replied: "I'm attracted to people like that. I like the flaws in people. . . . And I also love the people that seem normal on the surface and then they're really not. I find that a high compliment when people say that they think my characters are eccentric or quirky, because I guess that's what I love about life."

Biographical and Critical Sources

PERIODICALS

Booklist, April 15, 1998, Hazel Rochman, review of *My Louisiana Sky,* p. 1438; November 15, 1998, Kay Weisman, review of *Mister and Me,* p. 590; January 1, 2000, review of *When Zachary Beaver Came to Town,* p. 820; February 1, 2001, Hazel Rochman, review of *Dancing in Cadillac Light,* p. 1053; February 1, 2006, Hazel Rochman, review of *Waiting for Gregory,* p. 55; September 1, 2006, Carolyn Phelan, review of *Part of Me: Stories of a Louisiana Family,* p. 128; July 1, 2008, Carolyn Phelan, review of *Piper Reed, the Great Gypsy,* p. 67; April 15, 2010, Gillian Engberg, review of *The Water Seeker,* p. 58; November 1, 2010, Ian Chipman, review of *The Adventures of Granny Clearwater and Little Critter,* p. 72.

Bulletin of the Center for Children's Books, June, 1998, Betsy Hearne, review of *My Louisiana Sky,* p. 364; March, 2001, review of *Dancing in Cadillac Light,* p. 263; August, 2006, Karen Coats, review of *Waiting*

for Gregory, p. 502; November, 2006, Karen Coats, review of *Part of Me,* p. 127; September, 2010, Elizabeth Bush, review of *The Water Seeker,* p. 25.

Horn Book, July-August, 1998, Marilyn Bousquin, review of *My Louisiana Sky,* p. 489; November, 1999, Marilyn Bousquin, review of *When Zachary Beaver Came to Town,* p. 741; March, 2001, Susan P. Brabander, review of *Dancing in Cadillac Light,* p. 207; May-June, 2003, Lauren Adams, review of *Keeper of the Night,* p. 349; November-December, 2006, Christine M. Heppermann, review of *Part of Me,* p. 713; September-October, 2007, Robin Smith, review of *Piper Reed, Navy Brat,* p. 578; September-October, 2008, Robin L. Smith, review of *Piper Reed, the Great Gypsy,* p. 588; September-October, 2009, Martha V. Parravano, review of *Piper Reed Gets a Job,* p. 564.

Kirkus Reviews, May 1, 2003, review of *Keeper of the Night,* p. 677; April 1, 2006, review of *Waiting for Gregory,* p. 348; August 15, 2006, review of *Part of Me,* p. 843; July 1, 2007, review of *Piper Reed, Navy Brat;* May 15, 2007, review of *Skinny Brown Dog;* July 1, 2009, review of *Piper Reed Gets a Job.*

Kliatt, May, 2003, Michele Winship, review of *Keeper of the Night,* p. 10; September, 2006, Claire Rosser, review of *Part of Me,* p. 13.

New York Times Book Review, December 19, 1999, Linnea Lannon, review of *When Zachary Beaver Came to Town;* April 9, 2006, review of *Waiting for Gregory,* p. 21.

Publishers Weekly, May 4, 1998, review of *My Louisiana Sky,* p. 213; August 31, 1998, review of *Mister and Me,* p. 76; November 1, 1999, review of *When Zachary Beaver Came to Town,* p. 85; January 29, 2001, review of *Dancing in Cadillac Light,* p. 90; May 12, 2003, review of *Keeper of the Night,* p. 68; April 24, 2006, review of *Waiting for Gregory,* p. 59; July 17, 2006, review of *Part of Me,* p. 158; May 28, 2007, review of *Skinny Brown Dog,* p. 60; July 30, 2007, review of *Piper Reed, Navy Brat,* p. 82; April 26, 2010, review of *The Water Seeker,* p. 109.

School Library Journal, July, 1998, Cindy Darling Codell, review of *My Louisiana Sky,* pp. 95-96; November, 1998, Lynda Short, review of *Mister and Me,* p. 122; February, 2000, Kathleen T. Horning, "Small Town Girl," pp. 43-45; March, 2001, William McLoughlin, review of *Dancing in Cadillac Light,* p. 250; May, 2003, Kathleen Isaacs, review of *Keeper of the Night,* p. 153; March, 2006, Marianne Saccardi, review of *Waiting for Gregory,* p. 194; September, 2006, Melissa Moore, review of *Part of Me,* p. 208; May, 2007, Elizabeth Willoughby, review of *Part of Me,* p. 74; June, 2007, Kirsten Cutler, review of *Skinny Brown Dog,* p. 107; August, 2007, Terrie Dorio, review of *Piper Reed, Navy Brat,* p. 81; August, 2009, Elizabeth Swistock, review of *Piper Reed Gets a Job,* p. 77; July, 2010, Christi Esterle, review of *The Water Seeker,* p. 90; September, 2010, Donna Atmur, review of *The Adventures of Granny Clearwater and Little Critter,* p. 126.

Texas Monthly, December, 1999, Mike Shea, review of *When Zachary Beaver Came to Town,* p. 34.

Voice of Youth Advocates, August, 1998, Lynn Evarts, review of *My Louisiana Sky,* p. 202; April, 2001, Diane Tuccillo, review of *Dancing in Cadillac Light,* p. 42; June, 2003, review of *Keeper of the Night,* p. 405; April, 2007, Lisa A. Hazlett, review of *Part of Me,* p. 50.

ONLINE

Kimberley Willis Holt Home Page, http://www.kimberly willisholt.com (December 15, 2010).

Kimberley Willis Holt Web log, http://whatsnewwithkim berly.blogspot.com (December 15, 2010).*

I

IDLE, Molly Schaar

Personal
Born in CA; married; children: two sons. *Education:* Arizona State University, B.F.A. (drawing).

Addresses
Home—Tempe, AZ. *E-mail*—molly@idleillustration. com.

Career
Author and illustrator of children's books. DreamWorks Feature Animation Studio, former fine-line animator; animation artist for PBS Kids. Presenter at schools. *Exhibitions:* Work included in Original Art Show, Society of Illustrators, New York, NY, 2008.

Awards, Honors
Juried Portfolio Competition winner, Society of Children's Book Writers and Illustrators, 2010.

Writings

SELF-ILLUSTRATED

Emma's Gift, Abingdon Press (Nashville, TN), 2003.
Heads Up: The Story of One Quarter ("In God We Trust" series), Abingdon Press (Nashville, TN), 2004.
If I Had a Nickel . . . ("In God We Trust" series), Abingdon Press (Nashville, TN), 2005.
Pennies from Heaven ("In God We Trust" series), Abingdon Press (Nashville, TN), 2006.
Brother, Can You Spare a Dime? ("In God We Trust" series), Abingdon Press (Nashville, TN), 2007.
Nighty Night, Noah, Abingdon Press (Nashville TN), 2008.
Nighty Night, Baby Jesus: A Noisy Nativity, Abingdon Press (Nashville TN), 2009.

Molly Schaar Idle (Reproduced by permission.)

ILLUSTRATOR

Jeannie St.-John Taylor, *Penguin's Special Christmas Tree,* Lobster Press, 2007.
He's Got the Whole World in His Hands, Zonderkidz (Grand Rapids, MI), 2008.
Lynn Gordon, *Circus Fantastico: A Magnifying Mystery,* Andrews McMeel (Kansas City, MO), 2010.
Santa's Workshop, Andrews McMeel (Kansas City, MO), 2011.

Sidelights
Arizona-based artist and author Molly Schaar Idle started her career working in the animation department at DreamWorks Studios, and her book illustration continues to reflect her roots in film. In addition to creating colorful images for stories by other writers, Idle has created a number of original picture books, among them *Emma's Gift, Pennies from Heaven, Penguin's Special Christmas Tree,* and the holiday bedtime tale *Nighty Night, Baby Jesus: A Noisy Nativity.*

Several of Idle's original stories focus on close-knit families, among them *Emma's Gift,* which finds a young girl missing her beloved grandmother over the holidays. Her "In God We Trust" books, which include *Heads Up: The Story of One Quarter, If I Had a Nickel, Pennies from Heaven,* and *Brother, Can You Spare a Dime?,* describe the lives of children who remain rich even in economically challenging times because of a wealth of loving friends and family. The richness of the Christian faith, with its many biblical tales, is the basis for both *Nighty Night, Baby Jesus* and *Nighty Night, Noah,* the latter which teaches alphabet and counting skills as well as a classic bedtime prayer in which Noah says goodnight to each and every creature on his ark. All the creatures of the barnyard meet the infant Jesus in *Nighty Night, Baby Jesus,* and here Idle's depiction of creatures such as Goat and Sheep and Cat "are reminiscent of Disney cartoons" due to the artist's use of "saturated colors and rounded shapes," according to *School Library Journal* critic Eva Mitnick. Noting the book's appeal to the toddler set, a *Kirkus Reviews* writer made special note of the prose in the bedtime tale by calling Idle's "rhyming text . . . short and pleasant without being saccharine."

As an illustrator, Idle's colorful artwork has brought to life stories by Jeannie St.-John Taylor and Lynn Gordon, as well as of the well-known American spiritual "He's Got the Whole World in His Hands." In Taylor's story for *Penguin's Special Christmas Tree,* which finds a dapper bird hoping to win Santa's approval of his tree-decorating skills, Idle's vividly colored images gain special energy through their "movement" and her ability to "manipulate . . . perspective in comical ways," according to *Resource Links* critic Isobel Lang, while Eva Mitnick wrote in *School Library Journal* that the "color-saturated" illustrations Idle crafts for *Penguin's Special Christmas Tree* "are whimsical."

Idle's colorful, stylized art captures the gentle story in her self-illustrated picture book Nighty, Night, Baby Jesus. *(Abingdon Press, 2009.* Copyright © 2009 by Molly Schaar Idle. Reprinted with permission.)

Biographical and Critical Sources

PERIODICALS

Kirkus Reviews, September 15, 2009, review of *Nighty Night, Baby Jesus: A Noisy Nativity.*
Resource Links, December, 2007, Isobel Lang, review of *Penguin's Special Christmas Tree,* p. 12.
School Library Journal, October, 2007, Eva Mitnick, review of *Penguin's Special Christmas Tree,* p. 104; October, 2009, Eva Mitnick, review of *Nighty Night, Baby Jesus,* p. 81.

ONLINE

Molly Schaar Idle Home Page, http://www.idleillustration. com (November 14, 2010).

*   *   *

IMPEY, Rose 1947-

Personal

Born June 7, 1947, in Northwich, Cheshire, England; daughter of William Hall and Ella McVinnie; married Graham Impey; children: Rachel, Charlotte. *Education:* Attended Northumberland College of Education. *Hobbies and other interests:* Swimming, reading.

Addresses

Home—Birstall, Leicester, England.

Career

Author of children's books. Formerly worked as a bank clerk; primary school teacher in Leicester, England; former reader for a publishing company. Presenter at schools.

Awards, Honors

National Book League Children's Books of the Year designation, 1986, for *Who's a Clever Girl, Then?,* 1987, for *The Girls' Gang,* 1989, for *A Letter to Father Christmas, Desperate for a Dog,* and *Scare Yourself to Sleep,* and 1990, for *The Ankle Grabber; Who's a Clever Girl, Then?* named to Public Lending Right list of one hundred most-borrowed books, 1987; Smarties Prize shortlist, British Book Trust, 1988, for *Desperate for a Dog;* Sheffield Children's Book Award, Sheffield Library Services, 1991, for *Joe's Café;* Prix Versele de litterature enfantine, Belgian League of Families, 1991, for French version of *Scare Yourself to Sleep..*

Writings

FOR CHILDREN

Who's a Clever Girl, Then?, illustrated by André Amstutz, Heinemann (London, England), 1985, published as

Who's a Bright Girl?, Barron's (Hauppauge, NY), 1989, reprinted under original title, Crabtree (New York, NY), 2003.

The Girls' Gang, illustrated by Glenys Ambrus, Heinemann (London, England), 1986.

The Not-So-Clever Genie, illustrated by André Amstutz, Heinemann (London, England), 1987.

A Letter to Father Christmas, illustrated by Sue Porter, Orchard (London, England), 1988, published as *A Letter to Santa Claus,* Delacorte (New York, NY), 1989.

Houdini Dog, illustrated by Jolyne Knox, A. & C. Black (London, England), 1988, published as *Desperate for a Dog,* illustrated by Jolyne Knox, Dutton (New York, NY), 1988.

Teddy's Story, illustrated by Sue Porter, Heinemann (London, England), 1988.

Rabbit's Story, illustrated by Sue Porter, Little Mammoth (London, England), 1988.

You Herman, Me Mary!, illustrated by André Amstutz, Heinemann (London, England), 1989.

Instant Sisters, Orchard (London, England), 1989.

Revenge of the Rabbit, illustrated by André Amstutz, Orchard (London, England), 1990.

My Mom and Our Dad, illustrated by Maureen Galvani, Viking Kestrel (New York, NY), 1990.

No-Name Dog, illustrated by Jolyne Knox, Dutton (New York, NY), 1990.

Trouble with the Tucker Twins, illustrated by Maureen Galvani, Viking (New York, NY), 1990.

Who's Afraid Now?, Longman/British Broadcasting Corporation Books (London, England), 1991.

Joe's Café, illustrated by Sue Porter, Little, Brown (New York, NY), 1991.

Magical Tales from Toyland, illustrated by Sue Porter, Treasure (Los Angeles, CA), 1991.

First Class, illustrated by Sue Porter, Orchard (London, England), 1992, published as *Our Class,* 2001.

Precious Potter, Orchard (London, England), 1994.

More Dog Trouble, illustrated by Jolyne Knox, Collins (London, England), 1994.

Fireballs from Hell, HarperCollins (London, England), 1996.

Sir Billy Bear and Other Friends, illustrated by Ian Beck, Collins (London, England), 1996.

Feather Pillows, illustrated by Robin Bell Corfield, Picture Lions (London, England), 1997.

Holly's Puppies, illustrated by Jolyne Knox, Collins (London, England), 1998.

Stella's Staying Put, illustrated by Shoo Rayner, Orchard (London, England), 1998.

(Adapter) *J.M. Barrie's Peter Pan and Wendy,* illustrated by Ian Beck, Orchard (London, England), 1998.

The Animal Crackers Joke Book, illustrated by Shoo Rainer, Orchard (London, England), 2001.

My Scary Fairy Godmother, Orchard (London, England), 2005.

Hothouse Flower, Orchard (London, England), 2006.

One Man Went to Mow, illustrated by Chris Mould, Hodder Children's (London, England), 2007.

Pandora's Box, A. & C. Black (London, England), 2007.

Introducing Scarlett Lee, Orchard (London, England), 2008.

Six Feet Deep, Orchard (London, England), 2009.

Rachel and the Refuseniks, Orchard (London, England), 2010.

Ten Little Babies, illustrated by Nicola Smee, Orchard (London, England), 2011.

Impey's books have been translated into Danish, Gaelic, German, and Spanish.

RETELLER

The Ladybird Book of Fairy Tales, illustrated by John Dyke and others, Ladybird (London, England), 1980.

The Pied Piper of Hamelin, illustrated by Richard Hook, Ladybird (London, England), 1985.

Orchard Book of Fairy Tales, illustrated by Peter Bailey, Orchard (London, England), 1992, portions published as *Cinderella and The Sleeping Beauty, Rapunzel and Rumpelstiltskin, Hansel and Gretel and The Princess and the Pea,* and *Jack and the Beanstalk and The Three Wishes,* all 2001, and *Hansel and Gretel,* 2002.

Read Me a Fairy Tale: A Child's Book of Classic Fairy Tales, Scholastic (New York, NY), 1993.

"TWICE UPON A TIME" SERIES

Bad Boys and Naughty Girls, illustrated by Peter Bailey, Orchard (London, England), 1999.

Greedy Guts and Belly Busters, illustrated by Anthony Lewis, Orchard (London, England), 1999.

If Wishes Were Fishes, illustrated by John Eastwood, Orchard (London, England), 1999.

Silly Sons and Dozy Daughters, illustrated by Peter Bailey, Orchard (London, England), 1999.

Ugly Dogs and Slimy Frogs, illustrated by Peter Bailey, Orchard (London, England), 1999.

Bad Bears and Good Bears, illustrated by Priscilla Lamont, Orchard (London, England), 2000.

Hairy Toes and Scary Bones, illustrated by Hilda Offen, Orchard (London, England), 2000.

I-Spy, Pancakes and Pie, illustrated by Anthony Lewis, Orchard (London, England), 2000.

Knock, Knock! Who's There?, illustrated by Louise Voce, Orchard (London, England), 2000.

Over the Stile and into the Sack, illustrated by Hilda Offen, Orchard (London, England), 2000.

Runaway Cakes and Skipalong Pots, illustrated by Priscilla Lamont, Orchard (London, England), 2000.

Sneaky Deals and Tricky Tricks, illustrated by Louise Voce, Orchard (London, England), 2000.

"BADDIES" SERIES

Baked Bean Queen, illustrated by Sue Porter, Heinemann (London, England), 1986.

The Demon Kevin, illustrated by Sue Porter, Heinemann (London, England), 1986.

Tough Teddy, illustrated by Sue Porter, Heinemann (London, England), 1986.

The Bedtime Beast, illustrated by Sue Porter, Heinemann (London, England), 1987.

The Little Smasher, illustrated by Sue Porter, Heinemann (London, England), 1987.

The Toothbrush Monster, illustrated by Sue Porter, Heinemann (London, England), 1987.

"CREEPIES" SERIES

The Flat Man, illustrated by Moira Kemp, Barron's (Hauppauge, NY), 1988, reprinted, Gingham Dog Press (Columbus, OH), 2004.

Scare Yourself to Sleep, illustrated by Moira Kemp, Barron's (Hauppauge, NY), 1988, reprinted, Gingham Dog Press (Columbus, OH), 2004.

Jumble Joan, illustrated by Moira Kemp, Barron's (Hauppauge, NY), 1989, reprinted, Gingham Dog Press (Columbus, OH), 2004.

The Ankle Grabber, illustrated by Moira Kemp, Barron's (Hauppauge, NY), 1989, reprinted, Gingham Dog Press (Columbus, OH), 2004.

The Midnight Ship, illustrated by Moira Kemp, Mathew Price (Sherborne, Dorset, England), 2004, reprinted, Mathew Price Limited (Dallas, TX), 2010.

The Flying Vampire, illustrated by Moira Kemp, Mathew Price (Sherborne, Dorset, England), 2004, reprinted, Mathew Price Limited (Dallas, TX), 2010.

"BEST IN THE WORLD" SERIES

A Birthday for Bluebell, the Oldest Cow in the World, illustrated by Shoo Rayner, Orchard (London, England), 1993, reprinted, 2008.

Tiny Tim, the Longest Jumping Frog in the World, illustrated by Shoo Rayner, Orchard (London, England), 1993.

Hot Dog Harris, the Smallest Dog in the World, illustrated by Shoo Rayner, Orchard (London, England), 1993.

Too Many Babies, the Largest Litter in the World, illustrated by Shoo Rayner, Orchard (London, England), 1993.

Phew, Sydney! the Sweetest Smelling Skunk in the World, illustrated by Shoo Rayner, Orchard (London, England), 1994.

A Fortune for Yo-Yo, the Richest Dog in the World, illustrated by Shoo Rayner, Orchard (London, England), 1994.

Sleep Sammy, the Sleepiest Sloth in the World, illustrated by Shoo Rayner, Orchard (London, England), 1994.

Rhode Island Roy, the Roughest Rooster in the World, illustrated by Shoo Rayner, Orchard (London, England), 1995.

Welcome Home, Barney, the Loneliest Bat in the World, illustrated by Shoo Rayner, Orchard (London, England), 1995.

Pipe down Prudle!, illustrated by Shoo Rayner, Orchard (London, England), 1995.

We Want William, Wisest Worm in the World, illustrated by Shoo Rayner, Orchard (London, England), 1995.

Long Live Roberto, the Most Royal Rabbit in the World, illustrated by Shoo Rayner, Orchard (London, England), 1997.

A Medal for Poppy, the Pluckiest Pig in the World, illustrated by Shoo Rayner, Orchard (London, England), 1998.

Open Wide Wilbur! the Most Welcoming Whale in the World, illustrated by Shoo Rayner, Orchard (London, England), 2003.

"MONSTER AND FROG" SERIES

Monster and Frog at Sea, illustrated by Jonathan Allen, Collins (London, England), 1994.

Monster and Frog Mind the Baby, illustrated by Jonathan Allen, Collins (London, England), 1994.

Monster's Terrible Toothache, illustrated by Jonathan Allen, Collins (London, England), 1994, illustrated by Russell Ayto, Orchard (London, England), 2006.

Monster and Frog Get Fit, illustrated by Jonathan Allen, Collins (London, England), 1994, illustrated by Russell Ayto, Orchard (London, England), 2006.

Monster and Frog and the All-in-Together Cake, illustrated by Russell Ayto, Orchard (London, England), 2006.

Monster and Frog and the Big Adventure, illustrated by Russell Ayto, Orchard (London, England), 2006.

"POTBELLY" SERIES

Potbelly and the Haunted House, illustrated by Keith Brumpton, Orchard (London, England), 1996.

Potbelly Needs a Job, illustrated by Keith Brumpton, Orchard (London, England), 1996.

Potbelly in Love, illustrated by Keith Brumpton, Orchard (London, England), 1996.

Potbelly's Lost His Bike, illustrated by Keith Brumpton, Orchard (London, England), 1996.

"SLEEPOVER CLUB" SERIES

The Sleepover Club at Frankie's, Collins (London, England), 1997, published as *The Sleepover Club at Laura's,* HarperCollins (New York, NY), 1997

The Sleepover Club at Lindsey's, HarperCollins (New York, NY), 1997.

The Sleepover Club at Rosie's, HarperCollins (New York, NY), 1997.

The Sleepover Club at Fliss's, Collins (London, England), 1997, published as *The Sleepover Club at Felicity's,* HarperCollins (New York, NY), 1997.

The Sleepover Club at Kenny's, HarperCollins (New York, NY), 1997.

"TJ" SERIES; FOR BEGINNING READERS

TJ's Sunflower Race, illustrated by Anna Currey, Hodder (London, England), 1999.

TJ and the Baby Bird, illustrated by Anna Currey, Hodder (London, England), 1999.

TJ's Accident, illustrated by Anna Currey, Hodder (London, England), 1999.

TJ and the Great Snail Show, illustrated by Anna Currey, Hodder (London, England), 1999.

"TITCHY WITCH/WANDA WITCH" SERIES

Titchy Witch and the Disappearing Baby, illustrated by Katharine McEwen, Orchard (London, England), 2003.

Titchy Witch and the Birthday Broomstick, illustrated by Katharine McEwen, Orchard (London, England), 2003.

Titchy Witch and the Stray Dragon, illustrated by Katharine McEwen, Orchard (London, England), 2003, published as *Wanda Witch and the Stray Dragon,* illustrated by Katharine McEwen, Scholastic, (New York, NY), 2003.

Titchy Witch and the Frog Fiasco, illustrated by Katharine McEwen, Orchard (London, England), 2003, published as *Wanda Witch and Too Many Frogs,* illustrated by Katharine McEwen, Scholastic (New York, NY), 2006.

Titchy Witch and the Bully Boggarts, illustrated by Katharine McEwen, Orchard (London, England), 2003.

Titchy Witch and the Wobbly Fang, illustrated by Katharine McEwen, Orchard (London, England), 2003, published as *Wanda Witch and the Wobbly Fang,* Scholastic (New York, NY), 2006.

Titchy Witch and the Get-better Spell, illustrated by Katharine McEwen, Orchard (London, England), 2003.

Titchy Witch and the Magic Party, illustrated by Katharine McEwen, Orchard (London, England), 2003.

"SCOUT AND ACE" SERIES

Kippers for Supper, illustrated by Ant Parker, Orchard (London, England), 2004.

Kissing Frogs, illustrated by Ant Parker, Orchard (London, England), 2004.

Stuck on Planet Gloo, illustrated by Ant Parker, Orchard (London, England), 2004.

Flying in a Frying Pan, illustrated by Ant Parker, Orchard (London, England), 2004.

Talking Tables, illustrated by Ant Parker, Orchard (London, England), 2005.

Three Heads to Feed, illustrated by Ant Parker, Orchard (London, England), 2005.

A Cat, a Rat, and a Bag, illustrated by Ant Parker, Orchard (London, England), 2005.

The Scary Bear, illustrated by Ant Parker, Orchard (London, England), 2005.

"PIRATE PATCH"

Pirate Patch and the Gallant Rescue, illustrated by Nathan Reed, Orchard (London, England), 2008.

Pirate Patch and the Black Bonnet Attack, illustrated by Nathan Reed, Orchard (London, England), 2008.

Pirate Patch and the Message in a Bottle, illustrated by Nathan Reed, Orchard (London, England), 2008.

Pirate Patch and the Abominable Pirates, illustrated by Nathan Reed, Orchard (London, England), 2008.

Pirate Patch and the Chest of Bones, illustrated by Nathan Reed, Orchard (London, England), 2009.

Pirate Patch and the Five-Minute Fortune, illustrated by Nathan Reed, Orchard (London, England), 2009.

Pirate Patch and the Great Sea Chase, illustrated by Nathan Reed, Orchard (London, England), 2009.

Pirate Patch and the Treasure Map, illustrated by Nathan Reed, Orchard (London, England), 2009.

"NIPPER MCFEE" SERIES

In Trouble with Great Aunt Twitter, illustrated by Melanie Williamson, Orchard (London, England), 2010.

In Trouble with Growler Grimes, illustrated by Melanie Williamson, Orchard (London, England), 2010.

In Trouble with Bertie Barker, illustrated by Melanie Williamson, Orchard (London, England), 2010.

In Trouble with Mrs Lulu Lamb, illustrated by Melanie Williamson, Orchard (London, England), 2010.

In Trouble with Mrs McFee, illustrated by Melanie Williamson, Orchard (London, England), 2011.

In Trouble with Primrose Paws, illustrated by Melanie Williamson, Orchard (London, England), 2011.

In Trouble with P.C. Poodle, illustrated by Melanie Williamson, Orchard (London, England), 2011.

In Trouble with Susie Soapsuds, illustrated by Melanie Williamson, Orchard (London, England), 2011.

Adaptations

Who's Afraid Now? was recorded on cassette. Impey's "Sleepover Club" series was adapted as a television series in Australia.

Sidelights

A former teacher in her native England, Rose Impey never expected to be a writer, and it was not she was raising the first of her two children that she started to set pen to paper in earnest. Impey began by retelling fairy tales, and she took her research very seriously. In the years since, her work has expanded far beyond fairy tales, and includes original stories such as *Who's a Clever Girl, Then?, Desperate for a Dog, Joe's Café,* and *One Man Went to Mow . . . ,* as well as her books in the "Animal Crackers," "Sleepover Club," "Creepies," "Titchy Witch," "Scout and Ace," and "Nipper McFee" series, among others. Janice Del Negro, writing in *Booklist,* complimented the prolific Impey for developing a "conversational style that lends itself to reading aloud."

Impey's first original title, *Who's a Clever Girl, Then?,* was very well received, and was named to the British National Book League's list of children's books of the year. Impey once told *SATA* how she got the idea for the book: It "was contrived when one of my daughters asked for help on a story for a school assignment. I outlined a plot to her: A little girl, on her way to school,

gets kidnapped by a gang of pirates. They want her to do the housework while they go off having adventures. But because she's a clever little girl she tricks the pirates and ends up captain of the ship. 'What do you think of that?' I asked triumphant. 'Rubbish,' she replied. 'Honestly, Mum. That wouldn't make a story.' I could hardly ignore the challenge so I wrote it to prove her wrong. The story was accepted immediately and I've just kept on writing ever since."

As a teacher, Impey has often focused her talents on creating stories that engage beginning readers. Along these lines, the tales in her "Creepies" series, illustrated by Moira Kemp, are designed to cause shivers up and down the spines of children who are still wrestling with reading. Her first book in this series is *The Flat Man,* in which a young boy imagines that a monster known as the Flat Man is trying to crawl into his bed. Each noise that the boy hears he attributes to the Flat Man. Two cousins are featured in *Scare Yourself to Sleep,* which finds the pair camping out in the back yard. Their imaginations begin to run away with them, especially when one of their little brothers decides to "help" in the scaring. In *The Ankle Grabber* a father must convince his

Jake and his pirate band take a girl on board to do the cooking, cleaning, and sewing in Rose Impey's **Who's a Clever Girl, Then?,** *illustrated by André Amstutz.* (Illustration © 1985 by André Amstutz. Published by Egmont UK Ltd., London. Used with permission.)

daughter that there is no invisible swamp under her bed, but she refuses to leave her bed until Dad scares the sword monster away. Reviewing two other books in the "Creepies" series, *The Midnight Ship* and *The Flying Vampire,* Lindsey Fraser noted in the London *Guardian* that Impey's "mini-dramas, narrated in the first person, are outstanding read-alouds."

Impey once told *SATA* about adult reactions to her series: "I've written a number of scary stories which are very popular with children but have met with some resistance from adults. My view is that those adults who are made uncomfortable by scary stories are the ones who as children were either unable to or prevented from working through their own childhood fears. Unfortunately, because of this they go on to make it hard for their own children to work on theirs. I'm a great believer in working through things. I think that may well be why I'm a writer."

Other series by Impey's are not so scary. Her contributions to the "Sleepover Club" series focus on five girls who spend their sleep-overs dealing with issues such as friendship, boys, and teenaged life. Reviewing the series, which was eventually expanded by other authors and also inspired a much-watched television show that aired in both Australia and the United Kingdom, Shelle Rosenfeld noted in *Booklist* that Impey's "lively cast" and "often-humorous narrative" will encourage readers to "look forward to future installments." In all of her series stories, Impey has continued to treat young children to the adventures of engaging characters, among them Monster and Frog, Potbelly the pig, Pirate Patch, Nipper McFee, and Titchy Witch—the last known as Wanda Witch to U.S. readers.

Impey once told *SATA* how she became a writer: "I left grammar school at sixteen feeling I had no talent for anything other than enjoying myself and having a good time. After some pretty dreadful career advice I ended up working in a bank! Banks are not places where people generally enjoy themselves and have a good time. I was soon terribly depressed and knew I had to get out—even if that meant going back to school for a while. I then trained as a primary teacher which suited me better than banking but still wasn't entirely right for me.

"I loved reading to classes and would have been happy spending the whole day doing that (in fact I sometimes did) and this is clearly where the desire to write began. I still spend a lot of time visiting schools, reading my work to children, and when I am writing I have a strong sense of audience. I identify far more easily with storytellers than authors and I think this is evident in the way I write.

"I'm frequently asked why I write so much about girls, don't I like boys? Well, of course I do. But the fact is I am a girl, or I was; I have two sisters, two daughters,

and most of my friends are female. Girls are what I know about; it isn't surprising I choose to write about what I know best, most of the time.

"Although I don't always write realistic stories, much of my material comes from real life, either from my time as a teacher or from my own family life. What I think I do well is to see the humour potential in a seemingly small event or anecdote and exaggerate it and elaborate on it until it makes a story. One of the most familiar cries in my household is, 'Oh mum, you do exaggerate.' And I do, but that's okay. If it makes a good story anything goes."

Biographical and Critical Sources

PERIODICALS

Booklist, January 15, 1994, Janice Del Negro, review of *Read Me a Fairy Tale: A Child's Book of Classic Fairy Tales,* p. 926; November 1, 2009, Shelle Rosenfeld, review of *The Sleepover Club,* p. 49.

Guardian (London, England), February 25, 2003, Lindsey Fraser, review of *A Medal for Poppy, the Pluckiest Pig in the World,* p. 61; July 6, 2004, Lindsey Fraser, reviews of *The Midnight Ship* and *The Flying Vampire,* both p. 11.

Kirkus Reviews, May 1, 2009, review of *One Man Went to Mow. . . .*

School Library Journal, January, 1992, Lauralyn Persson, review of *My Mom and Our Dad,* p. 92; February, 1994, Donna L. Scanlon, review of *Read Me a Fairy Tale,* p. 94; January, 2005, Marilyn Taniguchi, review of *The Ankle Grabber,* p. 94; August, 2006, Susan Lissim, review of *Wanda Witch and the Wobbly Fang,* p. 90.

Times Educational Supplement, October 30, 1992, Nicholas Tucker, review of *Orchard Book of Fairy Tales,* p. 7B.

ONLINE

Hodder Children's Books Web site, http://www.hodder childrens.co.uk/ (December 15, 2010).*

K

KETTEMAN, Helen 1945-

Personal

Born July 1, 1945, in Augusta, GA; daughter of Jack (a physician) and Mary Helen (a teacher) Moon; married Charles Harry Ketteman, Jr. (an accountant), 1969; children: William Gregory, Mark David. *Education:* Young Harris College, A.A., 1965; attended Georgia Southern College, 1965-66; Georgia State University, B.A., 1968.

Addresses

Home—Sanibel Island, FL.

Career

Writer. Teacher at high-school and elementary levels; also taught at Southern Methodist University.

Awards, Honors

Best Children's Books of the Year selection, Bank Street College of Education, 1993, for *The Year of No More Corn;* Best Books of the Year listee, *Boston Globe,* 1995, for *Luck with Potatoes;* Pick of the Lists designation, American Booksellers Association, 1998, for *I Remember Papa;* Wanda Gag Honor Book designation, 2010, for *The Three Little Gators.*

Writings

Not Yet, Yvette, illustrated by Irene Trivas, Albert Whitman (Morton Grove, IL), 1992.

Aunt Hilarity's Bustle, illustrated by James Warhola, Simon & Schuster (New York, NY), 1992.

The Year of No More Corn, illustrated by Robert Andrew Parker, Orchard Books (New York, NY), 1993.

One Baby Boy: A Counting Book, illustrated by Maggie Flynn-Staton, Simon & Schuster (New York, NY), 1994.

The Christmas Blizzard, illustrated by James Warhola, Scholastic (New York, NY), 1995.

Luck with Potatoes, illustrated by Brian Floca, Orchard Books (New York, NY), 1995.

Grandma's Cat, illustrated by Marsha Lynn Winborn, Houghton Mifflin (Boston, MA), 1996.

Bubba, the Cowboy Prince: A Fractured Texas Tale, illustrated by James Warhola, Scholastic (New York, NY), 1997.

Heat Wave, illustrated by Scott Goto, Walker (New York, NY), 1998.

I Remember Papa, illustrated by Greg Shed, Dial (New York, NY), 1998.

Shoeshine Whittaker, illustrated by Scott Goto, Walker (New York, NY), 1999.

Armadillo Tattletale, illustrated by Keith Graves, Scholastic (New York, NY), 2000.

Mama's Way, illustrations by Mary Whyte, Dial (New York, NY), 2001.

Armadilly Chili, illustrated by Will Terry, Albert Whitman (Morton Grove, IL), 2004.

The Great Cake Bake, illustrated by Matt Collins, Walker (New York, NY), 2005.

Waynetta and the Cornstalk: A Texas Fairy Tale, illustrated by Diane Greenseid, Albert Whitman (Morton Grove, IL), 2007.

Swamp Song, illustrated by Ponder Goembel, Marshall Cavendish (New York, NY), 2009.

The Three Little Gators, illustrated by Will Terry, Albert Whitman (Morton Grove, IL), 2009.

Goodnight, Little Monster, illustrated by Bonnie Leick, Marshall Cavendish (New York, NY), 2010.

Contributor to periodicals, including *Spider* and *Highlights for Children.*

Adaptations

Bubba the Cowboy Prince was adapted as a musical by Nancy Cassaro and Randall Thropp, with music by Matthew Cassaro, Samuel French (New York, NY), 2007.

Sidelights

Helen Ketteman is known for spinning tall tales and introducing rambunctious protagonists in picture books such as *Heat Wave, Armadilly Chili,* and *Waynetta and the Cornstalk: A Texas Fairy Tale.* Ketteman weaves stories of simple folk and larger-than-life figures, often spicing her writing with a dash of playful humor. "It's my hope that when a child finds and reads one of my books—even a reluctant reader—he'll like it, he'll have fun with it, and make time to read another book," the author stated on her home page. "I write so that children will read. And once they start, who knows where it'll take them?"

Several of Ketteman's titles, such as *The Christmas Blizzard, Mama's Way,* and *The Year of No More Corn,* reflect a nostalgia for bygone days and are rich with the sights and sounds of rural America. Reviewing *Mama's Way,* a story about a single, hardworking mother who, despite her lack of money, manages to make her sixth-grade daughter's dream come true, was praised by *Booklist* reviewer Shelley Townsend Hudson as a "celebration of old-fashioned values," while in *Publishers Weekly* a reviewer noted that Ketteman's story "ably outlines both the friction and the underlying love between mother and daughter."

Ketteman's first book, *Not Yet, Yvette,* tells of a girl who waits impatiently while she and her dad prepare a surprise birthday party for her mother. Together this African-American father and daughter vacuum, dust, and bake. Excited by the preparations, young Yvette must repeatedly be cautioned by her father that it is not yet time for the celebration. "In this homey picture book, excitement and anticipation run high for a girl

Helen Ketteman mixes fairy-story humor with a Wild-West setting in **Bubba the Cowboy Prince,** *featuring illustrations by James Warhola.* (Illustration copyright © 1997 by James Warhola. Reproduced by permission of Scholastic, Inc.)

and her father," according to a reviewer in *Publishers Weekly*, the critic adding: "It would be hard to find more likable party givers . . . who aptly illustrate just how much fun giving can be." *Booklist* contributor Carolyn Phelan predicted that *Not Yet, Yvette* "will appeal to any child old enough to enjoy secrets and surprises," while a *Kirkus Reviews* contributor noted that Ketteman's "simple story is deftly conveyed in natural-sounding dialogue" and, with its accompanying illustrations by Irene Trivas, "nicely reflect[s] this black family's warm pleasure in each other's company."

Fashion foibles are put on display in *Aunt Hilarity's Bustle*, a "funny story about a heroine with plenty of spark," according to Michelle M. Strazer writing in *School Library Journal*. Unable to find a high-fashion bustle in the backwater town of Willow Flats, Aunt Hilarity determines to make one herself. Her initial creation, made out of a hay-filled grain sack, has fleas; when Hilarity uses paint rags as stuffing for a bustle, these scraps of cloth quickly catch fire when she backs too close to a candle flame. A bystander spills a glass of punch onto her bustled backside to extinguish the flames, but unfortunately much of the punch drenches Mrs. Anna Belle Prather, precipitating a food fight of gargantuan proportions. Finally a chicken-wire frame provides support for the dress Hilarity wears to a Christmas party, but when the wire begins to unravel, the woman is forced to don the Christmas tree. *Aunt Hilarity's Bustle* "is bound to be a winner with the preschool set and with early readers," commented *Booklist* reviewer Sheilamae O'Hara.

Beanie and his grandfather are at opposite ends of the age cycle in *The Year of No More Corn*. Neither can help out with the corn planting on the family farm this year: one is too young and the other too old. Instead, Old Grampa tells Beanie of the dreadful year 1928 when local farmers had to plant and replant their corn crop because of weather conditions, and Old Grampa himself finally resorted to planting corn kernels carved out of wood. He grew a forest of corncob-bearing trees from such ingenuity and saved the day. *Booklist* reviewer Phelan applauded Ketteman's wild tall tale, noting "its well-written text and accessible story and artwork." A *Publishers Weekly* reviewer commented that "Ketteman spins her tall tale in a pleasingly folksy deadpan style, her vivid descriptions bringing the old man's outrageous account to life until the reader, like Beanie, would like nothing better than to believe every word." A *Kirkus Reviews* critic concluded that *The Year of No More Corn* is a "lively, likable tall tale."

The Yuletide season is at the center of Ketteman's *The Christmas Blizzard*, a "tale taller than the Empire State Building," according to a reviewer for *School Library Journal*. The winter of 1922 saw weather so crazy, according to Maynard Jenkins, that the North Pole became a slush pond and Santa had to pull up stakes and set up shop at narrator Maynard's hometown of Lizzard, Indiana. Although cold, there was no snow in Liz-

zard until a visit to a local weather spell-caster made the suitable climactic corrections. *The Christmas Blizzard* "is a fun-filled story with more hyperbole than a Christmas turkey has stuffing," a critic wrote in the *School Library Journal*. "Ketteman's rollicking original tall tale has a true Christmasy flavor," noted a reviewer for *Publishers Weekly*, while in *Booklist* Kay Weisman recommended the book as an "appealing choice for holiday read-alouds or for older children learning to write their own tall tales."

Weather goes to other extremes when a passing heat wave gets snagged on a weather vane at a Kansas farm in Ketteman's *Heat Wave*. In fact, it gets so hot on the farm that the corn in the fields starts popping and the cattle are almost cooked. Finally it is left to the young girl of the farm—who has repeatedly been told that girls cannot farm—to save the family by planting iceberg lettuce to cool things off. A critic writing in *Publishers Weekly* called *Heat Wave* a "rollicking original tall tale that would do Paul Bunyan proud." Lee Bock, in a *School Library Journal* review, also praised Ketteman's "rollicking American tall tale," noting that while "things go from bad to worse," "younger children will enjoy the prescribed exaggeration and silliness, and older children might well be encouraged to create their own."

Farming again provides a venue for a tall tale in *Luck with Potatoes*, in which giant potatoes pop out of the

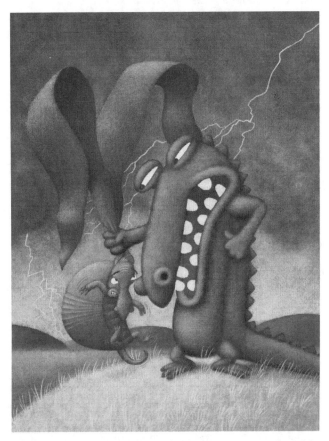

Ketteman teams up with illustrator Keith Graves to create the quirky Western tale Armadillo Tattletale. *(Albert Whitman & Company, 2000. Reproduced by permission of the publisher.)*

Featuring Greg Shed's nostalgic paintings, Ketteman's **I Remember Papa** *captures a close relationship between father and son.* (Illustration copyright © 1998 by Greg Shed. All rights reserved. Used by permission of Dial Books for Young Readers, a division of Penguin Young Readers Group, a member of Penguin Group (USA) Inc., 345 Hudson St., New York, NY 10014.)

earth at a farm where there was never any luck before. One huge potato fills the bed of the farmer's pick-up truck, and several cause earthquakes as they grow. In fact, the tubers are so big that the farmer, Clemmon Hardigree, starts sawing them into planks to sell to the local lumber company. "Ketteman has a firm grasp on the humor and stylistic elements of the tall tale," noted Janice Del Negro in a *Booklist* review. "Her narrative voice is bemused yet down-to-earth, retaining its laconic style even as the situation becomes more and more outlandish." *Horn Book* contributor Ann A. Flowers called Ketteman's creation a "cheerful story," while Virginia Opocensky, writing in *School Library Journal,* cautioned young readers: "Don't miss the fun!"

Ketteman revises the famous Cinderella fairy tale in *Bubba, the Cowboy Prince: A Fractured Texas Tale,* one of her most popular stories. A Texas cowboy serves as something of a Cinderella stand-in, and the Prince Charming of the story—or rather *Princess* Charming—is Miz Lurleen, a rich and feisty young cowgirl who decides it is time to find a husband and throws a ball in order to do so. Poor Bubba is overworked and under-appreciated by his step-dad and no-account stepbrothers, Milton and Dwayne, but manages, Cinderella-like, to attend Lurleen's ball courtesy of his fairy god-cow. "Ketteman wisely leaves the [Cinderella] plot

unchanged," noted Lauren Peterson in *Booklist,* "but the story has a distinct western flair and a humorous tall-tale feel." A *Kirkus Reviews* contributor remarked that this "Cinderella parody features the off-the-wall, whang-dang Texas hyperbole of Ketteman," while a *Publishers Weekly* critic joined in the linguistic fun: "Rustler lingo and illustrations chock-ablock with Texas kitsch make this ranch-spun Cinder-fella a knee-slappin' tale. . . . Just the ticket for buckaroos lookin' fer a good read."

An armadillo is at the heart of both *Armadillo Tattletale* and *Armadilly Chilli.* In *Armadillo Tattletale* the creature's habit of eavesdropping and then spreading gossip makes Armadillo a persona non grata among the local critters until they finally find a way to cure him of his bad habit of listening in on private conversations. In *Armadilly Chili* Miss Billy Armadilly decides to mix up some of her special-recipe chili for a passel of friends. However when she passes out her list of ingredients— beetles, a peck of hot peppers, and even a piece of prickly pear cactus—excuses abound on dinner night. In *Booklist* Julie Cummins described *Armadilly Chili* as "a surefire hit for the lap-sit crowd," while a *Kirkus Reviews* writer noted that Ketteman's story "is . . . guaranteed to warm the bones on a cold night."

More mischief is served up in *The Great Cake Bake,* as well as in Ketteman's counting book *One Baby Boy,* in which the baby in question performs a series of rather naughty deeds that introduce, in rhyme, the numbers from one to ten. In *The Great Cake Bake* a young woman with more imagination than cooking savvy is nonetheless determined to win the local July 4th cake-baking contest. With the town mayor as her judge, she tries several ill-conceived cakes, and when contest-day arrives the disaster her cake causes is balanced by the announcement that she will become a judge from now on. Dubbing the story a "lightly amusing tale," *Booklist* reviewer GraceAnne A. DeCandido called special attention to illustrator Matt Collins's use of "vivid colors" in his "hyperrealistic" art for Ketteman's tale.

In *Grandma's Cat,* a book written from a child's point of view, a little girl visiting her grandmother tries to make a friend of an aloof cat. The girl has no idea how to go about her task; she makes the cat hiss and spit at her by treating it roughly and pulling its tail. Finally the kindly grandmother intervenes, showing her granddaughter how to befriend the animal. *Grandma's Cat* "will appeal to the many children whose ideas of befriending animals work better in their dreams than in reality," commented *Booklist* reviewer Phelan, the critic adding that Ketteman's "story reads aloud well, making this a good choice for storytime." Christina Linz, writing in *School Library Journal,* noted that *Grandma's Cat* "is delightfully told in brief, rhymed sentences that make a charming group or individual read-aloud, yet are simple enough for beginning readers to try on their own." A reviewer for *Publishers Weekly* wrote that "Ketteman delivers a full roller coaster of emotion with

an economy of words." The same reviewer went on: "Her rhythmic, rhyming (mostly) couplets speak to every child who has tried desperately to express fondness for a pet."

Another family story forms the core of *I Remember Papa,* in which young Audie saves his allowance for months in hopes of buying a baseball mitt. He gets his chance one Saturday when he and his dad take the morning train to the city to see a Cincinnati Reds game. While shopping before gametime, Audie finds the perfect baseball glove while his dad finds a pair of new work boots. They make plans to return to the store and purchase them after the game. When Audie loses his money in the stands, his dad sacrifices his new boots to buy his son the prized mitt. Christine A. Moesch called *I Remember Papa* a "warm story set in the past" in her *School Library Journal* review, noting that her retelling "is warm without being treacly." *Booklist* contributor Weisman predicted that "baseball fans will appreciate this rich family story," while a *Kirkus Reviews* critic concluded that "the theme at the center of the story is the hallowed relationship between father and son in a bygone era, fondly remembered."

Ketteman returned to the Lone Star State in *Waynetta and the Cornstalk,* a "fractured, feminist version of Jack and the Beanstalk," asHazel Rochman noted in *Booklist.* A plucky cowgirl, Waynetta lives with her mother on a makeshift Texas ranch, where a summer-long drought threatens their livelihood. Forced to sell their last longhorn, Waynetta exchanges the creature for some magic corn which produces an enormous cornstalk. Upon climbing to the top, the youngster discovers an enormous ranch owned by a thieving giant who, years earlier, pilfered three treasures from Waynetta's mother. With the surprising help of the giant's wife, the scrappy heroine manages to restore her family's fortunes. According to *School Library Journal* reviewer Kirsten Cutler, a host of "exaggerative characters accompany the rich Texan parlance that peppers this amusing read-aloud."

The rag-snapping hero of *Shoeshine Whittaker* discovers the town of Mudville and thinks he has found the perfect place to ply his trade. Freshly shined boots are quick to lose their luster on the soggy streets of this aptly named town, however, and Shoeshine's satisfaction guarantee soon gets him into trouble. Quick thinking and a creative solution save the day, however. "Ketteman's colorful yarn is all twang and swagger, sheer catnip to read-aloud enthusiasts," declared a *Publishers Weekly* reviewer in a review of *Shoeshine Whittaker.*

A humorous story by Ketteman pairs with Will Terry's quirky illustrations in the picture book **Armadilly Chili.** (Albert Whitman & Company, 2004. Reproduced by permission of the publisher.)

A work told in verse, Ketteman's *Swamp Song* offers a lighthearted look at the toe-tapping antics of such creatures as the wood stork, the pygmy rattler, and the river otter as they fill their swampy home with a raucous wall of noise. "Ketteman sets a you-can't-help-but-chant-it verse pattern that incorporates a different onomatopoeic sound for each animal," a contributor noted in *Kirkus Reviews,* and Mary Jean Smith predicted in *School Library Journal* that young readers will be "creating their own cacophony of swamp sounds as they learn about the inhabitants of this habitat." In another tale of the swamp, *The Three Little Gators,* Ketteman presents her version of "The Three Little Pigs." Despite warnings from their mother to beware of the Big-Bottomed Boar, two young alligators construct their new homes from sand and sticks; the flimsy shelters are quickly destroyed with a few wiggles from their adversary's rather prominent backside. The gators are forced to retreat to the site of their brother's home, a stone structure that they hope proves invulnerable. *School Library Journal* critic Susan E. Murray praised the Southern-fried take on a familiar tale, stating that "Ketteman's retelling, including a sassy Texas twang, makes the story hilarious and bright."

A bedtime tale, *Goodnight, Little Monster* depicts a fuzzy young creature's nightly rituals, which includes snacking on worm juice and beetle bread, brushing his fangs, and slipping into bed with a slimy companion. "Cute, with just the right amount of ick," observed a reviewer in *Publishers Weekly.*

Ketteman once told *SATA:* "I believe children should be exposed to books early and often. If children learn at an early age that books can be fun and entertaining, I think the battle with television and video games can be won. Readers that are created early will be lifelong readers."

Biographical and Critical Sources

PERIODICALS

Booklist, February 15, 1993, Sheilamae O'Hara, review of *Aunt Hilarity's Bustle,* p. 1067; September 15, 1993, Carolyn Phelan, review of *The Year of No More Corn,* p. 158; September 15, 1995, Kay Weisman, review of *The Christmas Blizzard,* p. 170; October 1, 1995, Janice Del Negro, review of *Luck with Potatoes,* p. 326; April 1, 1996, Carolyn Phelan, review of *Grandma's Cat,* p. 1372; December 1, 1997, Lauren Peterson, review of *Bubba, the Cowboy Prince: A Fractured Texas Tale,* p. 641; March 15, 1998, Kay Weisman, review of *I Remember Papa,* p. 1249; December 15, 2000, Kelly Milner Halls, review of *Armadillo Tattletale,* p. 827; February 15, 2001, Shelley Townsend Hudson, review of *Mama's Way,* p. 1140; June 1, 2004, Julie Cummins, review of *Armadilly Chili,* p. 1742; June 1, 2005, GraceAnne A. DeCandido, review of *The Great Cake Bake,* p. 1821; May 15, 2007, Hazel Rochman, review of *Waynetta and the Cornstalk: A Texas Fairy Tale,* p. 48.

Bulletin of the Center for Children's Books, November, 2000, review of *Armadillo Tattletale,* p. 108.

Horn Book, January-February, 1996, Ann A. Flowers, review of *Luck with Potatoes,* pp. 64-65.

Kirkus Reviews, February 1, 1992, review of *Not Yet, Yvette,* p. 186; August 1, 1993, review of *The Year of No More Corn,* p. 1003; November 1, 1997, review of *Bubba, the Cowboy Prince,* p. 1646; January 15, 1998, review of *I Remember Papa,* p. 114; February 15, 2004, review of *Armadilly Chili,* p. 180; February 1, 2007, review of *Waynetta and the Cornstalk,* p. 124; August 1, 2009, review of *Swamp Song.*

Publishers Weekly, February 24, 1992, review of *Not Yet, Yvette,* p. 53; March 15, 1992, Carolyn Phelan, review of *Not Yet, Yvette,* p. 1388; July 26, 1993, review of *The Year of No More Corn,* p. 70; September 18, 1995, review of *The Christmas Blizzard,* p. 100; April 15, 1996, review of *Grandma's Cat,* p. 67; November 17, 1997, review of *Bubba, the Cowboy Prince,* p. 61; December 15, 1997, review of *Heat Wave,* p. 58; November 15, 1999, review of *Shoeshine Whittaker,* p. 66; January 29, 2001, review of *Mama's Way,* p. 89; July 5, 2010, review of *Goodnight, Little Monster,* p. 42.

Reading Today, August, 2001, Lynne T. Burke, review of *Mama's Way,* p. 30.

School Library Journal, May, 1992, Barbara Osborne Williams, review of *Not Yet, Yvette,* p. 90; February, 1993, Michelle M. Strazer, review of *Aunt Hilarity's Bustle,* pp. 72-73; October, 1995, review of *The Christmas Blizzard,* p. 38, and Virginia Opocensky, review of *Luck with Potatoes,* p. 105; May, 1996, Christina Linz, review of *Grandma's Cat,* p. 93; March, 1998, Lee Bock, review of *Heat Wave,* p. 182; June, 1998, Christine A. Moesch, review of *I Remember Papa,* p. 112; March, 2001, Rosalyn Pierini, review of *Mama's Way,* p. 214; May, 2004, Mary Elam, review of *Armadilly Chili,* p. 133; May, 2005, Linda M. Kenton, review of *The Great Cake Bake,* p. 86; April, 2007, Kirsten Cutler, review of *Waynetta and the Cornstalk,* p. 108; June, 2009, Susan E. Murray, review of *The Three Little Gators,* p. 109; August, 2009, Mary Jean Smith, review of *Swamp Song,* p. 78; September, 2010, Catherine Callegari, review of *Goodnight, Little Monster,* p. 128.

PERIODICALS

Helen Ketteman Home Page, http://helenketteman.com (December 1, 2010).*

* * *

KILAKA, John 1966-

Personal

Born November 4, 1966, in Sumbawanga, Tanzania. *Education:* Studied at Village Museum (Dar es Salaam, Tanzania).

Addresses

Home—P.O. Box 14333, Dar es Salaam, Tanzania. *E-mail*—john@kilaka.com.

Career

Artist, author, and storyteller. Storyteller and presenter of Tinga Tinga art workshops to schools and other groups. *Exhibitions:* Works have been exhibited in Botswana, the Czech Republic, Denmark, England, France, Germany, Kenya, South Africa, Sweden, Switzerland, and Tanzania.

Awards, Honors

Blauen Brillenschlangen, and Katolischer Jugendbuchpreis, both 2002, and Peter Pans Silverstar Award, Göteborg Book Fair, 2004, all for *Fresh Fish;* Ragazzi Award and New Horizon Award, both Bologna Book Fair, both 2005, and White Ravens Award selection, 2006, all for *True Friends;* Rattenfänger literature prize selection, 2010, for *The Amazing Tree.*

Writings

Frische Fische, Baobab Children's Book Fund (Switzerland), 1997, translated as *Fresh Fish: A Tale from Tanzania,* Groundwood Books (Berkeley, CA), 2005.

Ubucuti bw'imbeba n'inzovu, Éditions Bakame (Kigali, Rwanda), 2004, translated by Shelley Tanaka as *True Friends: A Tale from Tanzania,* Groundwood Books (Berkeley, CA), 2006.

The Amazing Tree, Groundwood Books (Berkeley, CA), 2009.

Author's works have been published in several languages, including German, Swedish, and Kinyarwanda.

Sidelights

Born in a village in southwestern Tanzania, John Kilaka demonstrated a talent for art when he enrolled in primary school at age ten. After eight years of schooling, which he completed while also helping his parents farm

John Kilaka's African-themed art pairs with his folk-style story of friendship in the picture book **The Amazing Tree.** (Copyright © 2009 by NordSud Verlag AG, CH-8005 Zurich, Switzerland. Used with permission of North-South Books, Inc., New York.)

and hunt food for the family, Kilaka moved to Dar es Salaam, where he studied with noted Tingatinga artist Peter Martin. While earning renown as an artist in his native Tanzania, he began to focus on children's illustration in the mid-1990s. Kilaka's first book, written in German and published by Switzerland-based Baobab Children's Book Fund, was 1997's *Frische Fische,* which features the artist's unique stylized line drawings and use of flat, jewel-toned hues.

Published in English as *Fresh Fish: A Tale from Tanzania, Frische Fische* focuses on Sokwe, a chimpanzee who is also a successful fisherman. Returning one day with his catch, he meets greedy Dog, who hopes to steal the tasty fish but is given only one. When Sokwe travels to the market the next day, Dog and several other friends join him. Again Dog attempts to steal Sokwe's catch, and this time he successfully makes off with a basket of fish, although he is observed and followed. During a trial by Sokwe's friends, Dog is accorded a just punishment and eventually atones for his crime. *Fresh Fish* "serves as a showcase for Kilaka's charming illustrations," according to a *Publishers Weekly* contributor. Writing that Kilaka's "striking paintings depict the landscape and indigenous animals of Africa," *School Library Journal* critic Barbara Auerbach added that the "colorful clothing, music, and dance" depicted in the book's art "capture its spirit."

Elephant and Rat are the stars of Kilaka's picture book *True Friends: A Tale from Tanzania.* Clever and diligent, Rat knows the art of making fire and also works hard to store enough food to last through times of drought and hardship. Elephant is lazy, however, and hopes to get through hard times by counting on Rat's generosity rather than his own efforts. When he offers Rat a place to store food at his house, Rat accepts the offer, but is locked away from his food store when a drought comes. Fortunately, Elephant eventually encounters a mishap that brings Rat to his side, and he learns to value and reciprocate his friend's unconditional loyalty. "Typical of Tanzanian storytelling," *True Friends* "has an inviting leisure," noted *Horn Book* contributor Anita Burkam, the critic adding that Kilaka's "lively pace sustains reader attention." Featuring animals wearing brilliant patterned kanga cloths, the "richly colored" and "graphically stylized" images "add a real sense of place to the story," concluded Genevieve Gallagher in her *School Library Journal* reveiw of the book.

In *The Amazing Tree,* Kilaka's third picture book, a drought finds all the animals hungry and hoping to harvest fruit from a tall tree. Not sure how to get the fruit to fall, several groups of animals ask advice of wise Tortoise. Unfortunately, when the wise one instructs them in the proper magic word to use, it is forgotten in the confusion that follows. Fortunately, tiny Rabbit eventually makes another trip to Tortoise and back, and is able to remember the word where Elephant, Giraffe, Zebra, and other large animals have failed. While not-

ing that the original story's multiple translations (from Kinyarwanda to German to English) give the text a "wooden formality," a *Kirkus Reviews* critic praised Kilaka's brightly colored and patterned, "smoothly finished paintings." Also offering praise for the artist's "eye-catching, stylized illustrations," Mary Jean Smith added in *School Library Journal* that *The Amazing Tree* is "a solid choice" for lessons on Africa.

Kilaka continues to travel throughout his native Tanzania, visiting villages on foot or by bicycle and listening to local stories that use animal characters to address issues of relationships, community traditions, and human emotions. In addition to bringing tales to life in his paintings and illustrations, he also passes them along to other audiences in his own storytelling, performing before audiences in Europe as well as Africa.

Biographical and Critical Sources

PERIODICALS

Horn Book, July-August, 2006, Anita L. Burkam, review of *True Friends: A Tale from Tanzania,* p. 457.
Kirkus Reviews, August 1, 2009, review of *The Amazing Tree.*
Publishers Weekly, May 23, 2005, review of *Fresh Fish: A Tale from Tanzania,* p. 77.
School Library Journal, June, 2005, Barbara Auerbach, review of *Fresh Fish,* p. 138; May, 2006, Genevieve Gallagher, review of *True Friends,* p. 114; October, 2009, Mary Jean Smith, review of *The Amazing Tree,* p. 112.

ONLINE

John Kilaka Home Page, http://www.kilaka.com (November 14, 2010).*

*   *   *

KULAK, Jeff 1984(?)-

Personal

Born c. 1984, in Canada. *Education:* Attended University of New South Wales, 2005; University of Alberta, B.A. (design), 2007.

Addresses

Home—Montreal, Quebec, Canada. *E-mail*—jeffkulak@ gmail.com.

Career

Graphic designer and illustrator. *Exhibitions:* Work exhibited at Latitude 53 Gallery, Edmonton, Alberta, Canada.

Illustrator

Emma Hooper, *Alphabet Boys,* privately published, 2007.
John Crossingham, *Learn to Speak Music: A Guide to Creating, Performing, and Promoting Your Songs,* Owlkids Books (Toronto, Ontario, Canada), 2009.

Contributor to periodicals, including *Beatrouge, Canadian Journal of Sociology, Explore, Momentum, Montreal Mirror, Notebook, SEE, Unlimited, Uppercase, VUE,* and *Quill & Quire.*

Biographical and Critical Sources

PERIODICALS

Booklist, November 1, 2009, Ilene Cooper, review of *Learn to Speak Music: A Guide to Creating, Performing, and Promoting Your Songs,* p. 57.

Publishers Weekly, November 2, 2009, review of *Learn to Speak Music,* p. 53.

Quill & Quire, October, 2009, Gary Butler, review of *Learn to Speak Music.*

Resource Links, February, 2010, Ann Ketcheson, review of *Learn to Speak Music,* p. 37.

School Library Journal, November, 2009, Tracy Weiskind, review of *Learn to Speak Music,* p. 128.

ONLINE

Jeff Kulak Home Page, http://www.jeffkulak.com (November 14, 2010).*

L

LADWIG, Tim 1952-
(Timothy Ladwig)

Personal

Born 1952; married; wife's name Leah; children: three. *Education:* Wichita State University, degree; studied painting and drawing in Rome, Italy.

Addresses

Home—Wichita, KS. *Office*—Urban Ministry Institute, Wichita World Impact Complex, 3701 E. 13th St., Wichita, KS 67208. *E-mail*—tim@timladwig.com.

Career

Illustrator and minister. Former associate art director for an advertising studio in Wichita, KS; art director and illustrator for publishing company in New York, NY, for two years; freelance illustrator for eight years; World Impact, community minister in Wichita, Los Angeles, CA, and Newark, NJ, for seventeen years; World Impact Urban Ministry Institute, Wichita, graphic artist, beginning 2002.

Awards, Honors

Gold Medallion Award finalist, c. 1993 for *Psalm Twenty-three,* and 1996, for *Probity Jones and the Fear Not Angel;* Pick of the Lists designation, American Booksellers Association, 1993, for *Psalm Twenty-three,* and 1997, for *Silent Night.*

Illustrator

Psalm Twenty-three, African American Family Press (New York, NY), 1993, new edition, Eerdmans Books (Grand Rapids, MI), 1997.

Francis Thompson, *The Hound of Heaven,* McCracken Press (New York, NY), 1993.

Eleanor Farjeon, *Morning Has Broken,* new edition, Eerdmans Books (Grand Rapids, MI), 1996.

Walter Wangerin, Jr., *Probity Jones and the Fear Not Angel,* Augsburg Press (Minneapolis, MN), 1996.

Margaret Hodges, *Silent Night: The Song and Its Story,* Eerdmans Books (Grand Rapids, MI), 1997.

Lisa McCourt, *Chicken Soup for Little Souls: The Braids Girl,* Health Communications (Deerfield Beach, FL), 1998.

(As Timothy Ladwig) Walter Wangerin, Jr., *Mary's First Christmas,* Zondervan (Grand Rapids, MI), 1998.

(As Timothy Ladwig) Walter Wangerin, Jr., *Peter's First Easter,* Zonderkidz (Grand Rapids, MI), 2000.

The Lord's Prayer, Eerdmans Books (Grand Rapids, MI), 2000.

Mary Quattlebaum, *The Shine Man: A Christmas Story,* Eerdmans Books (Grand Rapids, MI), 2001.

Nancy White Carlstrom, *What Does the Sky Say?,* Eerdmans Books (Grand Rapids, MI), 2001.

Walter Wangerin, Jr., *Angels and All Children: A Nativity Story in Words, Music, and Art,* music by Randy Courts, Augsburg (Minneapolis, MN), 2002.

Nikki Grimes, *When Daddy Prays,* Eerdmans Books (Grand Rapids, MI), 2002.

Amy Hill Hearth, *The Delany Sister Reach High,* Abingdon Press (Nashville, TN), 2002.

Virginia Kroll, *Especially Heroes,* Eerdmans Books (Grand Rapids, MI), 2003.

Ellen Yeomans, *Jubilee,* Eerdmans Books (Grand Rapids, MI), 2004.

Lisa McCourt, *Chicken Soup for Little Souls: The Greatest Gift of All,* Health Communications (Deerfield Beach, FL), 2004.

John M. Neale, *Good King Wenceslas,* Eerdmans Books (Grand Rapids, MI), 2005.

Jeannine Q. Norris, *Tonight You Are My Baby: Mary's Christmas Gift,* HarperCollins (New York, NY), 2008.

(As Timothy Ladwig) Virginia Kroll, *Saying Grace: A Prayer of Thanksgiving,* Zonderkidz (Grand Rapids, MI), 2009.

Carole Boston Weatherford, *The Beatitudes: From Slavery to Civil Rights,* Eerdmans Books (Grand Rapids, MI), 2010.

Sidelights

A former community minister, illustrator Tim Ladwig has provided the artwork for a number of religious-themed children's books, among them *When Daddy Prays* by Nikki Grimes and *The Beatitudes: From Slavery to Civil Rights* by Carole Boston Weatherford. Ladwig's artistic career was born out of a near tragedy: when he was eight years old, he lost his eye in an accident. During his recovery, while he was adjusting to life with an artificial eye, Ladwig came to realize "that sight was to be used to the fullest," as he later remarked in an interview for the Eerdmans Web site. "Almost as soon as I came home from the hospital, I began to draw and paint. It was both something I enjoyed doing and something that bubbled out from inside—and something that my parents couldn't have kept from bubbling out even if they tried. (They were, in fact, great encouragers.)"

Ladwig's first illustration project, *Psalm Twenty-three,* appeared in 1993 and was reissued four years later. The work, featuring text from a well-known Bible passage, follows a day in the life of two African-American children who experience joy and comfort in spite of their bleak surroundings. Writing in *Booklist,* Hazel Rochman stated that Ladwig's "pictures make extraordinary

Tim Ladwig contributes his detailed paintings to Nancy White Carlstrom's picture book **What Does the Sky Say?** (Eerdmans Books for Young Readers, 2001. Illustration copyright 2001 by Tim Ladwig. Reproduced by permission.)

use of light and perspective, showing that the children are being watched with loving attention." A similar work, *The Lord's Prayer,* concerns a father and daughter's efforts to assist an elderly neighbor. According to *School Library Journal* critic Carolyn Jenks, the characters are "depicted in strong, realistic watercolor-and-acrylic pictures."

Ladwig also contributed the illustrations to *Morning Has Broken,* a lyrical work inspired by Psalm 118:24. Although perhaps best known in its incarnation as a popular song released by Cat Stevens in the 1970s, *Morning Has Broken* was actually a children's hymn written by Eleanor Farjeon in 1931. Ladwig earned praise for crafting what *Booklist* contributor Shelley Townsend-Hudson described as the "bold and richly colored illustrations" that accompany Farjeon's text. Nancy White Carlstrom's *What Does the Sky Say?,* another work inspired by a Bible passage, celebrates the joys of nature. Here "Ladwig's watercolor illustrations are breathtaking," Be Astengo remarked in *School Library Journal.*

Ladwig's artwork has also graced the pages of several works featuring a holiday theme. *Probity Jones and the Fear Not Angel,* a tale by Walter Wangerin, Jr., focuses on a youngster's miraculous Christmas vision. *Booklist* critic Ilene Jones stated that Ladwig's illustrations "featuring a joyful African American family and a haunting dark-skinned angel . . . will stay with readers and listeners." Set during the Great Depression of the 1930s, Mary Quattlebaum's *The Shine Man: A Christmas Story* extols the virtues of a generous spirit. Ladwig's "watercolor with acrylic illustrations feature dramatic perspectives," a critic noted in a *School Library Journal* of this work. *Silent Night: The Song and Its Story,* a work by Margaret Hodges, explores the history of the popular Christmas song. According to Cooper, "Ladwig's glowing paintings have a holiday spirit that complements the information-packed text."

African-American characters continue to appear frequently in Ladwig's artwork. Set in 1962, Virginia Kroll's *Especially Heroes* examines racism through the eyes of a young girl. Her "Ladwig's large, realistic paintings are dramatic in their use of light and shadow," reported Karen Land in *School Library Journal.* A collection of verse, *When Daddy Prays* by Nikki Grimes, explores the loving bond between a father and son. "Bold, strong pictures match the poetry and anchor the writing in an everyday world," a contributor maintained in *Kirkus Reviews.* Carole Boston Weatherford depicts the African-American struggle for freedom and equality in *The Beatitudes.* Writing in *Booklist,* Courtney Jones applauded "Ladwig's elegant watercolors" for this book and *School Library Journal* reviewer Barbara Elleman cited *The Beatitudes* for its "inspired, richly hued, expressive illustrations."

Ladwig's illustration projects include creating art for Carole Boston Weatherford's **The Beatitudes from Slavery to Civil Rights.** (Illustration © 2010 by Tim Ladwig. Reproduced by permission of William. B. Eerdmans Publishing Co. All rights reserved.)

Biographical and Critical Sources

PERIODICALS

Booklist, January 15, 1995, Hazel Rochman, review of *Psalm Twenty-three,* p. 925; October 1, 1996, Shelley Townsend-Hudson, review of *Morning Has Broken,* p. 337; December 15, 1996, Ilene Cooper, review of *Probity Jones and the Fear Not Angel,* p. 734; September 1, 1997, Ilene Cooper, review of *Silent Night: The Song and Its Story,* p. 141; October 1, 1997, Hazel Rochman, review of *Psalm Twenty-three,* p. 324; October 1, 2000, GraceAnne A. DeCandido, review of *The Lord's Prayer,* p. 360; July, 2001, Denise Wilms, review of *What Does the Sky Say?,* p. 2017; September 1, 2001, Ilene Cooper, review of *The Shine Man: A Christmas Story,* p. 121; March 1, 2002, Hazel Rochman, review of *When Daddy Prays,* p. 1138; February 1, 2003, Carolyn Phelan, review of *Especially Heroes,* p. 996; March 15, 2004, Ilene Cooper, review of *Jubilee,* p. 1312; October 15, 2005, Karin Snelson, review of *Good King Wenceslas,* p. 51; February 1, 2010, Courtney Jones, review of *The Beatitudes: From Slavery to Civil Rights,* p. 56.

Kirkus Reviews, January 1, 2002, review of *When Daddy Prays,* p. 46; August 15, 2009, review of *Saying Grace;* December 15, 2009, review of *The Beatitudes.*

Publishers Weekly, September 30, 1996, review of *Probity Jones and the Fear Not Angel,* p. 92; February 21, 2000, Elizabeth Devereaux, review of *Peter's First Easter,* p. 55; September 24, 2001, review of *The Shine Man,* p. 53; January 27, 2003, review of *The Delany Sisters Reach High,* p. 259, and review of *Especially Heroes,* p. 260.

School Library Journal, January, 2001, Carolyn Jenks, review of *The Lord's Prayer,* p. 120; October, 2001, review of *The Shine Man,* p. 68; December, 2001, Be Astengo, review of *What Does the Sky Say?,* p. 118; April, 2002, Patricia Pearl Dole, review of *When Daddy Prays,* p. 132; October, 2002, Susan Patron, review of *Angels and All Children: A Nativity Story in Words, Music, and Art,* p. 64; February, 2003, Dorothy N. Bowen, review of *The Delany Sisters Reach High,* p. 131; April, 2003, Karen Land, review of *Especially Heroes,* p. 130; July, 2004, Carolyn Janssen, review of *Jubilee,* p. 90; March, 2010, Barbara Elleman, review of *The Beatitudes,* p. 145.

ONLINE

Eerdmans Web site, http://www.eerdmans.com/ (March, 2004), interview with Ladwig.
Timothy Ladwig Home Page, http://www.timladwig.com (December 1, 2010).

*   *   *

LADWIG, Timothy
See LADWIG, Tim

*   *   *

LEE, Cora

Personal

Born in Ashcroft, British Columbia, Canada. *Education:* Attended University of British Columbia, Simon Fraser University, and British Columbia Institute of Technology (degrees in biochemistry and biotechnology).

Addresses

Home—Vancouver, British Columbia, Canada.

Career

Writer, editor, and researcher. Formerly worked as a research associate and geochemical analyst; freelance consultant and scientific writer for pharmaceutical and biotechnology industries. Canadian Association for Girls in Science, Vancouver chapter coordinator.

Awards, Honors

(With Gillian O'Reilly) Best Books for Kids and Teens selection, Canadian Children's Book Centre, Science in Society Book Award finalist, both 2007, and Science

Communications Award in children's category, American Institute of Physics, 2009, all for *The Great Number Rumble;* Science in Society Book Award honorable mention, 2009, for *The Great Motion Mission.*

Writings

(With Gillian O'Reilly) *The Great Number Rumble: A Story of Math in Surprising Places,* illustrated by Virginia Gray, Annick Press (Toronto, Ontario, Canada), 2007.

The Great Motion Mission: A Surprising Story of Physics in Everyday Life, illustrated by Steve Rolston, Annick Press (Toronto, Ontario, Canada), 2009.

Sidelights

Born and raised in Canada, Cora Lee followed her childhood fascination with science into a career as a researcher in the field of biochemistry and geochemistry.

From there she turned to writing and editing scientific literature, a field she has continued to pursue from her home in Vancouver, British Columbia. During her education and career, Lee became very aware of the need for more women to be represented in the sciences, and this inspired her to volunteer with the Canadian Association for Girls in Science, which supports the interest of girls aged seven through sixteen who are interested in the fields of science, mathematics, technology, and engineering. She has also pursued a similar goal through her authorship of the award-winning children's books *The Great Number Rumble: A Story of Math in Surprising Places* and *The Great Motion Mission: A Surprising Story of Physics in Everyday Life.*

Coauthored with Gillian O'Reilly and illustrated by Virginia Gray, *The Great Number Rumble* is geared for children from grades four through six and weaves science theory, history, and fact into an entertaining story. Jeremy and his schoolmates are glad when the local school leaders decide to stop teaching math in public school. When the schools in Jeremy's town ban math,

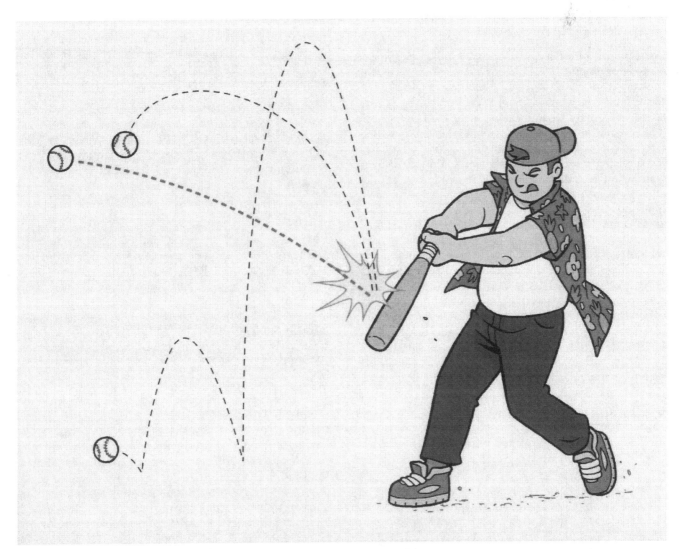

Cora Lee creates an entertaining mix of science and story in **The Great Motion Mission,** *a novel featuring illustrations by Steve Rolston.* (Annick Press, 2009. Reproduced by permission of the publisher.)

there are loud cheers from the kids. Although many teachers agree with this decision, Jeremy's friend Sam is quick to question the curriculum change. During a debate with the director of education, Sam shows that math is involved everywhere, from sports to art to nature, to architecture and construction. Along with Sam's clearly stated arguments, the book also includes sidebars that introduce chaos theory, Fibonacci numbers, and other mathematical abstractions as well as biographies of famous mathematicians from Pythagoras the Greek to Andrew Wiles, the British mathematician who in 1994 proved Fermat's Last Theorem.

In her *Resource Links* review of *The Great Number Rumble*, Claire Hazzard cited the coauthors' "lively style," while Etta Kaner predicted in *Quill & Quire* that teachers will find *The Great Number Rumble* "a useful resource to help make math an exciting experience for their students." According to *Canadian Review of Materials* contributor Thomas Falkenberg, O'Reilly and Lee's book reveals "the surprising places in which mathematical ideas can be found in nature, sport, the arts, music, and other places of human living," and as such it "will be experienced by the curious student reader as a gold mine."

Lee turns to physics in *The Great Motion Mission*, a companion book to *The Great Number Rumble* that is illustrated by Steve Rolston. This time a physics research building proposed by the local university is protested by Jeremy's opinionated Uncle Liam because it will be built on the site of the summer fair grounds. Jeremy surprises his uncle when he supports the prophysics stance of exchange student Audrey, a science whiz who does a thorough job of showing how physics affects everything from a baseball pitch to music to transportation. Citing Rolston's child-friendly cartoon art and the "dynamism" of Lee's story, Mavis Holder added in *Resource Links* that *The Great Motion Mission* "could be a great introduction to an esoteric subject and . . . a huge motivator for middle school students." Featuring extensive sidebars as well as a glossary and suggestions for further study, Lee's book "introduces a complicated field of study in a lighthearted way," according to a *Kirkus Reviews* critic, while in *Canadian Review of Materials* Katarin MacLeod described the characters' discussions of real-world physics as "true, accurate and age appropriate."

Biographical and Critical Sources

PERIODICALS

Canadian Review of Materials, April 13, 2007, Thomas Falkenberg review of *The Great Number Rumble: A Story of Math in Surprising Places*; February 26, 2010, Katarin MacLeod, review of *The Great Motion Mission: A Suprising Story of Physics in Everyday Life.*

Kirkus Reviews, October 1, 2009, review of *The Great Motion Mission.*

Quill & Quire, May, 2007, Etta Kaner, review of *The Great Number Rumble.*

Resource Links, April, 2007, Claire Hazzard, review of *The Great Number Rumble,* p. 31 December, 2009, Mavis Holder, review of *The Great Motion Mission,* p. 24.

School Library Journal, June, 2007, Ann Joslin, review of *The Great Number Rumble,* p. 150; January, 2010, Maren Ostergard, review of *The Great Motion Mission,* p. 123.

Voice of Youth Advocates, April, 2010, Heather Pittman, review of *The Great Motion Mission,* p. 82.

ONLINE

Annick Press Web site, http://www.annickpress.com/ (December 1, 2010), "Cora Lee."*

* * *

LONG, Ethan 1968(?)-

Personal

Born c. 1968, in PA; married (divorced); second wife's name Heather; children: (first marriage) Katherine; (second marriage) Cooper, Carson. *Education:* Ringling School of Art and Design, degree, 1991.

Addresses

Home and office—Orlando, FL. *Agent*—Nicole Tugeau, Tugeau 2 Children's Artist Representatives, 2231 Grandview Ave., Cleveland Heights, OH 44106. *E-mail*—ethan@ethanlong.com.

Career

Illustrator, author, animator, and educator. Creator of animated films, including *Farm Force: Send in the Clones,* Nicktoons, 2005, *Dead Stuntman,* and *Tasty Time with Ze Fronk.* Instructor at schools, including LeMoyne Art Foundation, Tallahassee, FL; has served as artist-in-residence. Commercial clients include Nickelodeon Studios, Scholastic, and Barnes & Noble. *Exhibitions:* Work included in shows staged by Society of Illustrators Los Angeles and Society of Illustrators New York.

Awards, Honors

Certificate of Merit, Society of Illustrators New York, 1994; Certificate of Merit, Society of Illustrators Los Angeles, 2002, 2003; Children's Choice designation, International Reading Association (IRA), 2004, for *Stinky Smelly Feet* by Margie Palatini; Nextoons Film Festival Viewer's Choice Award, 2005, for *Farm Force* (animated film); National Parenting Publications Award Honor designation, 2005, for *Tickle the Duck!;* ADDY Awards in District Gold, 2004, and District Silver and Local Silver, 2005; Charlie Award, Florida Magazine

Ethan Long (Photograph by Spencer Freeman. Reproduced by permission.)

Association, 2006; Best Children's Book of the Year designation, Bank Street College of Education, and IRA/Children's Book Council Choice designation, both 2008, both for *Drooling and Dangerous* by Mary Amato; Comic Strip Superstar Competition semifinalist, 2009; Moonbeam Children's Book Award, Independent Publisher Online, 2009, for *The Zombie Nite Café* by Merrily Kutner; numerous state award nominations.

Writings

SELF-ILLUSTRATED

Tickle the Duck!, Little, Brown (New York, NY), 2006.
Stop Kissing Me, Little, Brown (New York, NY), 2007.
Have You Been Naughty or Nice?, Little, Brown (New York, NY), 2009.
Duck's Not Afraid of the Dark!, Little, Brown (New York, NY), 2009.
One Drowsy Dragon, Orchard Books (New York, NY), 2010.
Bird and Birdie in A Fine Day, Tricycle Press (Berkeley, CA), 2010.

Chamelia, Little, Brown (New York, NY), 2011.
The Croaky Pokey, Holiday House (New York, NY), 2011.

Author and illustrator of "Landfill" (weekly cartoon).

ILLUSTRATOR

Jason Eaton, *The Day My Runny Nose Ran Away,* Dutton Children's Books (New York, NY), 2002.
Esther Hershenhorn, *The Confessions and Secrets of Howard J. Fingerhut,* Holiday House (New York, NY), 2002.
Tom Birdseye, *Oh Yeah!,* Holiday House (New York, NY), 2003.
Mary Amato, *Snarf Attack, Underfoodle, and the Secret of Life: The Riot Brothers Tell All,* Holiday House (New York, NY), 2004.
Margie Palatini, *Stinky Smelly Feet: A Love Story,* Dutton Children's Books (New York, NY), 2004.
Ann Whitford Paul, *Mañana, Iguana,* Holiday House (New York, NY), 2004.
Elizabeth Spurr, *Halloween Skyride,* Holiday House (New York, NY), 2005.
Teddy Slater, *The Best Thanksgiving Ever!,* Scholastic (New York, NY), 2005.
Karen M. Stegman-Bourgeois, *Trollerella,* Holiday House (New York, NY), 2006.
Mary Amato, *Drooling and Dangerous: The Riot Brothers Return!,* Holiday House (New York, NY), 2006.
Teddy Slater, *The Spookiest Halloween Ever!,* Scholastic (New York, NY), 2006.
Ann Whitford Paul, *Fiesta Fiasco,* Holiday House (New York, NY), 2007.
Merrily Kutner, *The Zombie Nite Café,* Holiday House (New York, NY), 2007.
David Elliott, *One Little Chicken: A Counting Book* Holiday House (New York, NY), 2007.
Jan Carr, *Greedy Apostrophe: A Cautionary Tale,* Holiday House (New York, NY), 2007.
Mary Amato, *Stinky and Successful: The Riot Brothers Never Stop,* Holiday House (New York, NY), 2007.
Teddy Slater, *The Luckiest St. Patrick's Day Ever!,* Scholastic (New York, NY), 2007.
Ann Whitford Paul, *Count on Culebra: Go from 1 to 10 in Spanish,* Holiday House (New York, NY), 2008.
D.L. Garfinkle, *Fine Feathered Four Eyes,* Mirrorstone (Renton, WA), 2008.
D.L. Garfinkle, *Fowl Language,* Mirrorstone (Renton, WA), 2008.
Bob Longe, *No Boredom Allowed!: Nutty Challenges and Zany Dares,* Sterling (New York, NY), 2008.
Matt Rissinger and Philip Yates, *Nuttiest Knock-knocks Ever,* Sterling (New York, NY), 2008.
D.L. Garfinkle, *Poultry in Motion,* Wizards of the Coast (Renton, WA), 2008.
David Elliott, *Wuv Bunnies from Outers Pace,* Holiday House (New York, NY), 2008.
Grace Maccarone, *Bunny Race,* Scholastic, Inc. (New York, NY), 2009.
J. Patrick Lewis, *Countdown to Summer: A Poem for Every Day of the School Year,* Little, Brown (New York, NY), 2009.

Alicia Potter, *Fritz Danced the Fandango,* Scholastic, Inc. (New York, NY), 2009.

Kenn Nesbitt, *My Hippo Has the Hiccups, and Other Poems I Totally Made Up,* Sourcebooks/Jabberwocky (Naperville, IL), 2009.

Mary Amato, *Take the Mummy and Run: The Riot Brothers Are on a Roll,* Holiday House (New York, NY), 2009.

Ann Whitford Paul, *Tortuga in Trouble,* Holiday House (New York, NY), 2009.

Harriet Ziefert, *You and Me: We're Opposites,* Blue Apple Books (Maplewood, NJ), 2009.

Steve Bertman, *Funny Mummy,* Sterling (New York, NY), 2010.

Laurie Lawlor, *Muddy as a Duck Puddle, and Other American Similes,* Holiday House (New York, NY), 2010.

Chris Pallatto and Ron DeFazio, *The Summer Camp Survival Guide: Cool Games, Camp Classics, and How to Capture the Flag,* Sterling (New York, NY), 2010.

Kenn Nesbitt, *The Tighty Whitey Spider,* Sourcebooks/Jabberwocky (Naperville, IL), 2010.

Sidelights

In addition to his work as an animator, cartoonist, and educator, Ethan Long has gained a following among picture-book readers. His brightly colored, quirky cartoon illustrations, with their round-eyed characters, have graced the pages of a sea of humorous books that includes Mary Amato's "Riot Brothers" series, Marge Palatini's *Stinky Smelly Feet: A Love Story,* Karen M. Stegman-Bourgeois's *Trollerella,* Jan Carr's *Greedy Apostrophe: A Cautionary Tale,* and Harriet Zieffert's *You and Me: We're Opposites.* Long's art also takes

Cover of Long's self-illustrated picture book Tickle the Duck, *in which readers can test the patience of a testy but feathery fowl.* (Little, Brown & Company, 2006. Illustration © 2006 by Ethan Long. Reproduced by permission.)

center stage in several animated films, as well as in his original picture books. In *Tickle the Duck!* he introduces a somewhat confrontational duck whose constant demands and determination echo those of a demanding child, while a pantheon of equally ridiculous creatures star in *One Drowsy Dragon, Bird and Birdie in A Fine Day, Chamelia,* and *The Croaky Pokey.*

Born in Pennsylvania, Long was busy drawing by age three. He spent much of his childhood in Camp Hill, then moved with his family to Connecticut in his mid-teens. After high-school graduation Long enrolled at the Ringling School of Art and Design, a decision that took him south to Sarasota, Florida. Now married and the father of three, he continues to make his home in the Sunshine state. Despite his training and talent, on his home page Long modestly credited many of his ideas to his children and his family's cats, the aptly named Barnum and Bailey.

The art for Jason Eaton's 2002 picture book *The Day My Runny Nose Ran Away* was Long's first published work, marking the start of a prolific career that has included illustrating texts by David Elliott, Teddy Slater, Tom Birdseye, Kenn Nesbitt, Ann Whitford Paul, and Palatini. In Birdseye's *Oh Yeah!,* which finds two young campers confronting their fears of the dark, Long's warm-toned "colored-pencil and acrylic" images "burst with energy . . . and feature jagged edges and the deliciously menacing imagined threats" of the story's young protagonists, according to *School Library Journal* contributor Marge Loch-Wouters. "The expressions on Long's bright and quirky punctuation people will delight . . . listeners," predicted Jayne Damron in her *School Library Journal* review of Carr's *Greedy Apostrophe,* while his "bright, stylized art" for Palatini's *Stinky Smelly Feet* inspired a *Kirkus Reviews* writer to note that the "pop-eyed animals" populating Palatini's tale of a duck with personal problems contribute "hysterical detail." The illustrator's "vibrant cartoon illustrations in watercolors and gouache [also] propel the text" of *Mañana, Iguana,* according to *School Library Journal* critic Mary Elam in a review of the first of several Paul-Long collaborations.

Amato's "Riot Brothers" series, about rambunctious sibling troublemakers Wilbur and Orville, is a perfect outlet for Long's quirky art. His "playful cartoon illustrations extend the fun" of the brothers' debut in *Snarf Attack, Underfoodle, and the Secret of Life: The Riot Brothers Tell All,* according to *Booklist* reviewer Ed Sullivan, while Roger Leslie concluded in the same periodical that Long's cartoon drawings "add significantly to the . . . humor" featured in the siblings' return in *Drooling and Dangerous.* Gracing the pages of *Stinky and Successful: The Riot Brothers Never Stop,* his "lively cartoon illustrations" add to the "clever fun" of an April Fools' Day adventure, according to *School Library Journal* contributor Amanda Moss, while in *Take the Mummy and Run: The Riot Brother Are on a Roll* the combination of "goofy, good natured fun" and "zany

cartoon drawings" add up to what Madigan McGilli-cuddy dubbed an "uproariously funny" story in the same periodical.

Long's first original picture book, *Tickle the Duck!*, has its roots in a duck character that belligerently asserted itself in Long's animated film *Farm Force: Send in the Clones,* a pilot for a cartoon series produced by Nickel-odeon Studios. After seeing award-winning author/illustrator Mo Willems' books featuring a surly pigeon, Long decided to stop fighting the fowl's persistent efforts to take center stage in the film and gave the duck its own story. According to Lana Berkowitz in the *Houston Chronicle,* Long's daughter Katie also "provided inspiration for the story. When she was a toddler, Long says, Katie would tell him to stop tickling her, but then she'd want more."

Tickle the Duck! was published in 2006 as a board book designed for toddlers. To create an interactive element, Long incorporates actual fluffy spots on the body of his cranky character, à la perennial board-book favorite *Pat the Bunny.* In the sequel, *Stop Kissing Me!,* Long includes a sound chip that captures the smootches that pass between the temporarily upbeat Duck and the perturbed pink poodle that finds itself the object of Duck's affection.

Duck returns include *Duck's Not Afraid of the Dark!,* and this time Long's curmudgeonly quacker is nervous about going to bed in the dark. Fortunately, the interactive board book is supplied with a light switch that toddlers can flip and click whenever Duck demands. *Have You Been Naughty or Nice?* finds Duck preparing to bribe Santa Claus with a plate of cookies . . . if only he could stop eating them himself. As Duck's dilemma plays out in Long's cartoon tale, readers are left reassured by the "earnest apology," their pre-Christmas jitters vanquished, according to a *Publishers Weekly* critic.

In the three short stories in *Bird and Birdie in A Fine Day,* Long follows the antics of blue-feathered Bird and bright yellow Birdie, who are good friends despite their very different personalities. From greeting each other at the start of the day to hunting for food to settling into the nest at night, Long's "fetching" characters are rendered in simple line and pastel-toned images that "will hit the right note" with young children, according to *Booklist* critic Randall Enos. A *Publishers Weekly* contributor remarked on the "upbeat and simple" sequential tales Long pairs with his cartoon art, while in *School Library Journal* Rachel G. Payne recommended *Bird and Birdie in A Fine Day* as an effective "introduction to the comic-strip format for the younger set."

Dubbed a "catchy counting tale" by a *Publishers Weekly* contributor, *One Drowsy Dragon* is a book that parents of young children can relate to. In the story, a sleepy dragon has put on his night cap and has his teddy bear at the ready, prepared for some sleep. But then comes one young dragon, banging on a metal cup. With the

Long's illustration projects include capturing the antics of mischievous middle schoolers in Mary Amato's **Take the Mummy and Run: The Riot Brothers Are on a Roll.** (Illustration copyright © 2009 by Ethan Long. Reproduced by permission of Holiday House, Inc.)

turn of the page, the sleepy dragon is accosted by two dragonlings who are playing a battle game, complete with sound effects. Soon three, four, five dragons, and so on crowd the pages of Long's story, as the nighttime noise level continues to rise. Storytime listeners "will appreciate the bouncy beat" of the text, as well as the artist's cartoon illustrations of "very oblivious and raucous dragons," predicted the *Publishers Weekly* writer, while Steven Engelfried wrote in *School Library Journal* that the "big round eyes and slightly goofy expressions" that Long gives to his cartoon characters "seem equal parts dragon and child."

Creating full-color illustrations for a picture-book project requires about twelve months, according to Long, who adds that he can complete the line drawings for a chapter book in less than half that time. Another twelve months is required for planning, which includes the months needed to create characters and draw them in various poses. In addition to pen-and-ink drawings, Long also uses several other media, including digital. Although much of his work involves creating poster art and illustrations for commercial clients, he gets the greatest satisfaction illustrating for children, and he expands this through his work visiting schools.

Biographical and Critical Sources

PERIODICALS

Booklist, October 15, 2002, John Peters, review of *The Day My Runny Nose Ran Away,* p. 411; July, 2004, Ed Sullivan, review of *Snarf Attack, Underfoodle, and*

the Secret of Life: The Riot Brothers Tell All, p. 1841; November 1, 2004, Connie Fletcher, review of *Mañana, Iguana,* p. 493; May 15, 2006, Roger Leslie, review of *Drooling and Dangerous: The Riot Brothers Return,* p. 44; May 15, 2007, Shelle Rosenfeld, review of *Fiesta Fiasco,* p. 51; November 15, 2007, Julie Cummins, review of *One Little Chicken: A Counting Book,* p. 50; February 15, 2008, Linda Perkins, review of *Count on Culebra: Go from One to Ten in Spanish,* p. 84; May 1, 2009, Ilene Cooper, review of *Tortuga in Trouble,* p. 88; February 15, 2010, Hazel Rochman, review of *Muddy as a Duck Puddle, and Other American Similes,* p. 79; March 1, 2010, Randall Enos, review of *Bird and Birdie in A Fine Day,* p. 76.

Bulletin of the Center for Children's Books, February, 2006, Elizabeth Bush, review of *Tickle the Duck!,* p. 273.

Houston Chronicle, November 28, 2005, Lana Berkowitz, "Don't Goose This Duck!," "STAR" section, p. 1.

Horn Book, March-April, 2009, Joanna Rudge Long, review of *Tortuga in Trouble,* p. 184.

Kirkus Reviews, September 15, 2002, review of *The Day My Runny Nose Ran Away,* p. 1388; July 15, 2003, review of *Oh Yeah!,* p. 961; May 1, 2004, review of *Stinky Smelly Feet,* p. 446; September 15, 2004, review of *Mañana, Iguana,* p. 917; May 1, 2006, review of *Drooling and Dangerous,* p. 453; August 15, 2006, review of *Trollerella,* p. 852; August 1, 2007, review of *The Zombie Nite Café*; May 1, 2008, review of *Wuv Bunnies from Outers Pace*; April 1, 2009, review of *Fritz Danced the Fandango;* May, 2009, review of *You and Me.*

Library Journal, September, 2007, Judith Constantinides, review of *The Zombie Nite Café,* p. 168.

Publishers Weekly, August 26, 2002, review of *The Day My Runny Nose Ran Away,* p. 68; April 26, 2004, review of *Stinky Smelly Feet,* p. 65, and *Snarf Attack, Underfoodle, and the Secret of Life,* p. 66; October 15, 2007, review of *One Little Chicken,* p. 59; March 17, 2008, review of *Count on Culebra,* p. 69; May 11, 2009, review of *You and Me: We're Opposites,* p. 52; October 26, 2009, review of *Have You Been Naughty or Nice?,* p. 54; February 8, 2010, review of *Muddy as a Duck Puddle, and Other American Similes,* p. 50; March 29, 2010, review of *Bird and Birdie in A Fine Day,* p. 56; July 19, 2010, review of *One Drowsy Dragon,* p. 126.

School Library Journal, September, 2002, Mary Elam, review of *The Day My Runny Nose Ran Away,* p. 189; August, 2003, Marge Loch-Wouters, review of *Oh Yeah!,* p. 122; June, 2004, Marge Louch-Wouters, review of *Stinky Smelly Feet,* p. 116; July, 2004, Jean Lowery, review of *Snarf Attack, Underfoodle, and the Secret of Life,* p. 66; September, 2004, Mary Elam, review of *Mañana, Iguana,* p. 176; August, 2005, Wendy Woodfill, review of *Halloween Sky Ride,* p. 106; September, 2006, Martha Topol, review of *Trollerella,* p. 185; October, 2006, Kristine M. Casper, review of *Drooling and Dangerous,* p. 102; May, 2007, Linda M. Kenton, review of *Fiesta Fiasco,* p. 106; July, 2007, Jayne Damron, review of *Greedy Apostro-*

phe: A Cautionary Tale, p. 73; September, 2007, Judith Constantinides, review of *The Zombie Night Café,* p. 168; October, 2007, Amanda Moss, review of *Stinky and Successful: The Riot Brothers Never Stop,* p. 106; December, 2007, Mary Jean Smith, review of *One Little Chicken,* p. 88; October, 2008, Joanna K. Fabicon, review of *Wuv Bunnies from Outers Pace,* p. 106; February, 2009, Catherine Callegari, review of *Tortuga in Trouble,* p. 82; May, 2009, Marge Loch-Wouters, review of *Fritz Danced the Fandango,* p. 86, and Lee Bock, review of *My Hippo Has the Hiccups, and Other Poems I Totally Made Up,* p. 97; June, 2009, Madigan McGillicuddy, review of *Take the Mummy and Run: The Riot Brothers Are on a Roll,* p. 77, and Marilyn Taniguchi, review of *Countdown to Summer: A Poem for Everyday,* p. 144; August, 2009, Margaret R. Tassia, review of *You and Me,* p. 87; March, 2010, Grace Oliff, review of *Muddy as a Duck Puddle, and Other American Similes,* p. 142; April, 2010, Rachel G. Payne. review of *Bird and Birdie in A Fine Day,* p. 134; June, 2010, Lauralyn Persson, review of *The Tighty Whitey Spider,* p. 90; July, 2010, Steven Engelfried, review of *One Drowsy Dragon,* p. 64, and Donna Cardon, review of *The Summer Camp Survival Guide: Cool Games, Camp Classics, and How to Capture the Flag,* p. 103.

Tallahassee Democrat, July 20, 2006, Mark Hinson, "Driven to Draw."

ONLINE

Ethan Long Home Page, http://www.ethanlong.com (December 5, 2010).*

* * *

LOVE, Maryann Cusimano (Maryann K. Cusimano)

Personal

Born in Buffalo, NY; married; husband's name Richard; children: Maria, Ricky, Ava. *Education:* St. Joseph's University, B.A; University of Texas, M.A.; Johns Hopkins University, Ph.D.

Addresses

Office—Department of Politics, Catholic University of America, 620 Michigan Ave. N.E., Washington, DC 20064. *E-mail*—mcusimanolove@comcast.net.

Career

Author, political consultant, and educator. Catholic University of America, Washington, DC, associate professor of international relations. Consultant to Georgetown University's Institute for the Study of Diplomacy; member of U.S. Catholic Bishops' International Justice and Peace Committee and Communications Committee of Jesuit Refugee Services; member of advisory board of Catholic Peacebuilding Network. Frequent speaker on international affairs issues.

Member

Women in International Security (former member of governing board), American Political Science Association Society (founder of political psychology section), Society of Children's Book Writers and Illustrators, Authors Guild.

Awards, Honors

Named Teacher of the Year, Catholic University of America; Pew Faculty fellowship for teaching, Harvard University; U.S. Naval Academy Center for Military Ethics fellow, 2002-03; Joseph R. Crapa fellow, U.S. Commission on International Religious Freedom; Institute for Policy Research fellow, Catholic University of America; Catholic Press Award for Best Columnist, 2009.

Writings

FOR CHILDREN

(As Maryann K. Cusimano) *You Are My I Love You,* illustrated by Satomi Ichikawa, Philomel Books (New York, NY), 2001.

You Are My Miracle, illustrated by Satomi Ichikawa, Philomel Books (New York, NY), 2005.

Alphaducks, Price Stern Sloan (New York, NY), 2007.

Holiducks, Price, Stern Sloan (New York, NY), 2007.

Sleep, Baby, Sleep, illustrated by Maria van Lieshout, Philomel Books (New York, NY), 2009.

You Are My Wish, illustrated by Satomi Ichikawa, Philomel Books (New York, NY), 2010.

OTHER

(As Maryann K. Cusimano) *Beyond Sovereignty: Issues for a Global Agenda,* Bedford/St. Martins (Boston, MA), 2000, 4th edition, Wadsworth Publishing (Belmont, CA), 2009.

Member of editorial board of Rowman & Littlefield's "New Millennium" book series. Columnist for *America* magazine.

Sidelights

A recognized authority on international relations, Maryann Cusimano Love is also the author of several well-received picture books. Love, a professor at the Catholic University of America who serves on the Catholic Peacebuilding Network, the U.S. Catholic Bishops' International Justice and Peace Committee, and other organizations, notes that her literary efforts for young readers help her maintain a positive outlook, even when she is confronted with the serious issues involved in her work. "If it weren't for the children's writing, I probably would not be able to continue to write and teach

on such heavy topics as war, refugees, and trafficking in women and children," she noted on her home page, adding: "Children's writing helps restore the balance, and reminds me of the hope and wonder in life. I also occasionally get to write a story with a happy ending."

Even as a youngster, Love enjoyed writing stories. She completed her first book at the age of seven and later bound her own books, using yarn to stitch the spines. At the age of ten she convinced her mother to enroll her in a writing course at Villanova University that was taught by celebrated authors Jan and Stan Berenstain. "I was by far the youngest there," Love recalled, "but I loved meeting writers and learning about the craft." An avid reader, Love often visited her public library, devouring works by such beloved authors as A.A. Milne, Charlotte Zolotov, Ezra Jack Keats, and Maurice Sendak. As a teen she turned her attention to classic fare written by Katherine Paterson, Madeleine L'Engle, John Steinbeck, and Ernest Hemingway.

Interestingly, Love's first picture book, *You Are My I Love You,* was written before she had children. While driving to work one morning, Love began pondering her work with inner-city parents and their children. She remarked on her home page that "there appeared this lovely verse in my head: 'I am your parent; you are my

Maryann Cusimano Love captures the bedtime ritual of nature's creatures in her picture book **Sleep, Baby, Sleep,** *featuring artwork by* **Maria van Lieshout.** (Illustration copyright © 2009 by Maria van Leishout. Reproduced with permission of Penguin Young Readers Group.)

child. I am your quiet place, you are my wild.'" As soon as she parked her car in the university lot, Love began scribbling furiously. "Students gave me odd looks streaming past on their way to class," she recalled, "but I wanted to capture the magic song that was playing in my head about the ying/yang of the adult/child relationship, the parent providing stability and constant love, the child bringing mischief and wonder."

You Are My I Love You marked the first collaboration between Love and illustrator Satomi Ichikawa. In the work, a mother teddy bear plays with and comforts her baby during a busy day of activities. Love's debut work "offers reassurances about a mother's watchful presence when her child begins to explore," Connie Fletcher noted in *Booklist,* and *School Library Journal* contributor Genevieve Ceraldi called *You Are My I Love You* "an appealing choice for bedtime sharing."

Love and Ichikawa have also teamed on the companion volumes *You Are My Miracle* and *You Are My Wish.* The former, a celebration of Christmas, earned praise from a contributor in *Kirkus Reviews* who noted that "the sentiments of tender love and care shine through in both text and illustrations." The latter, described as "a gentle love song for grandparents to share with their grandchildren" by *School Library Journal* reviewer Judith Constantinides, depicts a grandmotherly bear enjoying a fun-filled day with an energetic cub. "Grandparents today (aging baby boomers) are more active and involved in their grandchildren's lives than ever before," Love noted, "so I wanted to write a book celebrating the simple joys of gardening, picnics, children's story books, and shared naps."

Adapted from a Mother Goose rhyme, Love's bedtime tale *Sleep, Baby, Sleep* encourages youngsters to experi- ence the joys of life, to seek challenges, and to follow their dreams. "Love's language lulls using a rhyme scheme and syllabic stresses that establish a comforting cadence," observed a *Kirkus Reviews* critic, and Laura Butler, writing in *School Library Journal,* called *Sleep, Baby, Sleep* "simultaneously reassuring and celebratory."

Biographical and Critical Sources

PERIODICALS

Booklist, May 1, 2001, Connie Fletcher, review of *You Are My I Love You,* p. 1688.
Kirkus Reviews, November 1, 2005, review of *You Are My Miracle,* p. 1195; September 15, 2009, review of *Sleep, Baby, Sleep.*
Publishers Weekly, June 18, 2007, review of *Alphaducks,* p. 57.
School Library Journal, May, 2001, Genevieve Ceraldi, review of *You Are My I Love You,* p. 114; December, 2009, Laura Butler, review of *Sleep, Baby, Sleep,* p. 79; March, 2010, Judith Constantinides, review of *You Are My Wish,* p. 116.

ONLINE

Berkley Center for Religion, Peace & World Affairs Web site, http://berkleycenter.georgetown.edu/ (July 6, 2010), Susan Hayward, interview with Love.
Catholic University of America Web site, http://www.cua. edu/ (December 1, 2010), "Maryann Cusimano Love."
Maryann Cusimano Love Home Page, http://maryannlove. com (December 1, 2010).*

M

MARTINI, Angela 1972(?)-

Personal

Born c. 1972; married; husband's name Kyle; children.

Addresses

Home—Brooklyn, NY. *E-mail*—am@angelamartini.com.

Career

Illustrator and cartoonist. Creator of "Katbot" Web comic, c. 2000.

Illustrator

Tracey West, *Say My Name!: A Guide to Fashion Tees,* Grosset & Dunlap (New York, NY), 2002.

Patti Kelley Criswell, *A Smart Girl's Guide to Friendship Troubles: Dealing with Fights, Being Left Out, and the Whole Popularity Thing,* American Girl (Middleton, WI), 2003.

Robin Wasserman, *Oops!: I Did It (Again)!,* Scholastic (New York, NY), 2003.

Julie Williams, *A Smart Girl's Guide to Starting Middle School: Everything You Need to Know about Juggling More Homework, More Teachers, and More Friends!,* American Girl (Middleton, WI), 2004.

Rosanne Golosi, *Best Friends Forever!,* Scholastic (New York, NY), 2005.

Deordre Bligh, *Perfect World: I Was Soooo Embarrassed!,* Scholastic (New York, NY), 2005.

Shawn K. Stout, *Fiona Finkelstein, Big-time Ballerina!!,* Aladdin (New York, NY), 2009.

Shawn K. Stout, *Fiona Finkelstein Meets Her Match!!,* Aladdin (New York, NY), 2010.

Apryl Lundsten, *A Smart Girl's Guide to Parties: How to Be a Great Guest, a Happy Hostess, and Have Fun at Any Party,* American Girl (Middleton, WI), 2010.

Contributor to periodicals, including *American Cheerleader, Girls' Life, Ms., National Geographic Kids, New York Daily News, Seventeen,* and the *Wall Street Journal.*

Sidelights

Angela Martini has a fresh, upbeat illustration style that fits well with tuned-in young teens who are interested in improving their social skills, fashion I.Q., and enjoying an upbeat story. In addition to highlighting the pages of nonfiction books such as Patti Kelley Criswell's *A Smart Girl's Guide to Friendship Troubles: Dealing with Fights, Being Left Out, and the Whole Popularity Thing,* Julie Williams' *A Smart Girl's Guide to Starting Middle School: Everything You Need to Know about Juggling More Homework, More Teachers, and More Friends!,* and Apryl Lundsten's *A Smart Girl's Guide to Parties: How to Be a Great Guest, a Happy Hostess, and Have Fun at Any Party,* Martini's art brings to life stories by Shawn K. Stout, Deordre Bligh, and Rosanne Golosi. Her artwork is also a feature of the humorous Web comic "Katbot," which follows the adventures of an alien kitty from the planet Katatonia that is mistakenly assigned to live with a do-nothing family in small-town Long Island when it is sent to Earth to study teen culture.

Published by American Girl, *A Smart Girl's Guide to Friendship Troubles* gives pointers on speaking one's mind or giving advice without hurting feelings, riding the highs and lows of popularity, knowing when to involve parents, and other tricky interpersonal skills. Similar in approach, *A Smart Girl's Guide to Starting Middle School* offers advice on scheduling after-school activities, cementing friendships, and dealing with the teasing that sometimes escalates into bullying. Although Kim Donius questioned the usefulness of the information in *A Smart Girl's Guide to Starting Middle School,* she added in *School Library Journal* that Martini's "colorful cartoons" help to combat the book's "dry contents."

One of several elementary-grade novels by Stout that feature an upbeat fourth grader, *Fiona Finkelstein, Big-time Ballerina!!* deals with the subject of stage fright, while *Fiona Finkelstein Meets Her Match!!* finds the nine year old competing with classmate Milo by starting a rival school club. In *School Library Journal* Kate

Neff wrote that Martini's illustrations for *Fiona Finkelstein, Big-time Ballerina!!* "give Fiona and company a sweet look that is simple and charming."

Biographical and Critical Sources

PERIODICALS

Booklist, September 15, 2009, Shelle Rosenfeld, review of *Fiona Finkelstein, Big-time Ballerina!!,* p. 54.
Kirkus Reviews, August 15, 2009, review of *Fiona Finkelstein, Big-time Ballerina!!*
Publishers Weekly, June 14, 2004, review of *A Smart Girl's Guide to Starting Middle School: Everything You Need to Know about Juggling More Homework, More Teachers, and More Friends!,,* p. 64.

School Library Journal, October, 2004, Kim Donius, review of *A Smart Girl's Guide to Starting Middle School,* p. 196; January, 2010, Kate Neff, review of *Fiona Finkelstein, Big-time Ballerina!!,* p. 82.

ONLINE

Angela Martini Home Page, http://www.angelamartini.com (November 14, 2010).

*   *   *

MAZO, Michael

Personal

Born in Moscow, Russia; son of Nina Kostina (founder of a nonprofit adoption agency); immigrated to United

Michael Mazo's folk-style story Brothers *is brought to life in art by Russian designer Michael Soloviov.* (Tundra Books, 2009. Reproduced with permission of the publisher.)

States; married; children. *Education:* Brandeis University, B.A.; Yale University, M.A.

Addresses

Home—Middleburg, VA.

Career

Author and nonprofit executive. Frank Foundation Child Assistance International (non-profit), vice president; Leaves of Grass Vineyards, Middleburg, VA, owner.

Writings

Elephant Bill (pop-up book), illustrated by Michael Soloviov, Inky Press (Nazareth, Belgium), 2008.
Brothers, illustrated by Michael Soloviov, Tundra Books (Plattsburgh, NY), 2009.

Sidelights

Michael Mazo emigrated from his birthplace in Russia to the United States when his mother, Nina Kostina, moved to Washington, DC, and began her work facilitating the adoptions of needy children throughout the world. In addition to now serving as the vice president of Kostina's Frank Foundation Child Assistance International, Mazo has teamed up with a friend, Russian artist and theatrical designer Michael Soloviov, to create two children's books: the pop-up book *Elephant Bill* and the picture book *Brothers.*

Inspired by Nicholas and Gula, bull terriers that have lived with Mazo's family for several years, *Brothers* finds doggie stand-ins Julius and William taking on the role of young rival siblings. Julius, the narrator, is also the older pup, and William annoys him through his constant efforts to best his older brother. Although William the Upstart is always a personality to be reckoned with, Julius the Elder is impressed by the younger dog's exuberance and energy. Together with Mazo's wordy text, which includes what a *Publishers Weekly* critic described as "screenplay-sharp lines" that draw on history, the arts, and even international politics in their references, Soloviov's "postmodern ironic" illustrations are set against an inky black backdrop, according to the critic. A *Kirkus Reviews* writer also cited the "stylishly" rendered cartoon illustrations in *Brothers,* predicting that adults in particular will enjoy the book's wry humor. Mazo's "formal prose," which Shelle Rosenfeld noted in *Booklist* is "often addressed to the reader" in a humorously stilted fashion, combines with Soloviov's "over-the-top visuals [to] elevate the everyday scenarios [in *Brothers*] to epic proportions."

Biographical and Critical Sources

PERIODICALS

Booklist, December 1, 2009, Shelle Rosenfeld, review of *Brothers,* p. 41.
Kirkus Reviews, October 1, 2009, review of *Brothers.*

Publishers Weekly, November 2, 2009, review of *Brothers,* p. 50.

ONLINE

Open Book Toronto Web site, http://www.openbooktoronto. com/ (November 17, 2009), interview with Mazo.*

*   *   *

MEADOWS, Daisy
See CHAPMAN, Linda

*   *   *

MILGRIM, David

Personal

Born September 12, in CA; married; wife's name Kyra; children: Wyatt. *Education:* San Diego State University, degree; attended Parson's School of Design.

Addresses

Home—Wakefield, RI. *Agent*—Jan Collier Represents, P.O. Box 470818, San Francisco, CA 94147-0818; jan@ jan-collier.com. *E-mail*—david@davidmilgrim.com.

Career

Writer and illustrator. Worked as a graphic designer, 1984-89; freelance illustrator and author.

Awards, Honors

International Reading Association/Children's Book Council Children's Choice selection, for *Cows Can't Fly; Parenting* magazine Best Books of the Year selection, for *See Pip Point;* Cooperative Children's Book Council Choice selection, for *Swing Otto Swing!*

Writings

SELF-ILLUSTRATED PICTURE BOOKS

Why Benny Barks, Random House (New York, NY), 1994.
Dog Brain, Viking (New York, NY), 1996.
Here in Space, Bridgewater Books (Mahwah, NJ), 1997.
Cows Can't Fly, Viking (New York, NY), 1998.
My Friend Lucky, Atheneum (New York, NY), 2002.
Thank You, Thanksgiving, Clarion Books (New York, NY), 2003.
Time to Get up, Time to Go, Clarion Books (New York, NY), 2006.
Young MacDonald, Dutton (New York, NY), 2006.
Another Day in the Milky Way, Putnam (New York, NY), 2007.

My Dog, Buddy, Scholastic (New York, NY), 2008.
Amelia Makes a Movie, Putnam (New York, NY), 2008.
Santa Duck, G.P. Putnam's Sons (New York, NY), 2008.
Best Baby Ever, G.P. Putnam's Sons (New York, NY), 2009.
How You Got So Smart, G.P. Putnam's Sons (New York, NY), 2010.
Santa Duck Gets Some Help, G.P. Putnam's Sons (New York, NY), 2010.
Eddie Gets Ready for School, Cartwheel Books (New York, NY), 2011.

"OTTO THE ROBOT" SERIES

See Otto, Atheneum (New York, NY), 2002.
Ride Otto Ride!, Atheneum (New York, NY), 2002.
See Pip Point, Atheneum (New York, NY), 2003.
Swing Otto Swing!, Atheneum (New York, NY), 2004.
See Santa Nap, Atheneum (New York, NY), 2004.

ILLUSTRATOR

Carol Carrick, *Patrick's Dinosaurs on the Internet,* Clarion Books (New York, NY), 1999.
Josephine Page, *Little Lamb's Christmas,* Cartwheel Books (New York, NY), 2003.
Kes Gray, *My Mum Goes to Work,* Hodder (London, England), 2006.

Marilyn Singer, *I'm Getting a Checkup,* Clarion Books (New York, NY), 2009.

Sidelights

Writer and illustrator David Milgrim specializes in creating picture books that engage the attention of even the most distractible beginning readers. In addition to his popular series about Otto the robot and his animal friends, Milgrim treats children to a generous helping of quirky humor in his self-illustrated stories *Amelia Makes a Movie, Best Baby Ever, Santa Duck,* and *How You Got So Smart* as well as in his artwork for other's stories. "For children who are just beginning to read," Carolyn Phelan wrote in *Booklist,* "Milgrim's Otto books . . . offer the unbeatable combination of simple words and funny stories." Reviewing his illustrations for Marilyn Singer's *I'm Getting a Checkup,* a *Kirkus Reviews* writer wrote that Milgrim's "digitally rendered oil spreads utilize nimble lines" and his "characters' smiling expressions add comfort and warmth to the potentially anxiety-producing subject" of Singer's story.

See Otto, Ride Otto Ride!, Swing Otto Swing!, See Pip Point, and *See Santa Nap* chronicle the adventures of a robot from another planet whose spaceship has run out of fuel, forcing him to land on Earth. Using a vocabulary of just twenty-one words, the first book follows the protagonist as he lands in a jungle and, after running

David Milgrim's unique illustration style pairs well with Carol Carrick's text for **Patrick's Dinosaurs on the Internet.** (Illustration copyright © 1999 by David Milgrim. All rights reserved. Reprinted by permission of Clarion Books, an imprint of Houghton Mifflin Company.)

afoul of a rhinoceros, makes friends with two cheerful monkeys. "Though the limited vocabulary imposes its own restraints," a commentator in *Kirkus Reviews* wrote of *See Otto,* "Milgrim uses visual humor with a touch of irony to craft a real story with enough action to appeal to new readers."

In *Ride Otto Ride!* the robot goes for a ride on Peanut the elephant's back, but as more and more animal friends pile on, Peanut grows tired and cannot walk anymore. Working together, Otto and the others build a wagon for the pachyderm and pull Peanut to the watering hole where everyone can go for a swim. Nancy A. Gifford, reviewing the book for *School Library Journal,* explained that, "flowing much like a 'Dick and Jane' primer with added humor," *Ride Otto Ride!* "will appeal to fledgling readers." Reviewing the first two "Otto" books for *Booklist,* Phelan described Milgrim's series as "an appealing option for children just beginning to read and feeling as hopeful and adventurous as Otto."

In *Swing Otto Swing!* Otto attempts to swing through the trees on jungle vines, just like his monkey friends Flip and Flop can. However, the metallic and far-more-weighty Otto keeps falling. Only when he builds himself a hanging vine equipped with a seat can Otto swing in the air with the busy monkeys. Martha V. Parravano, writing in *Horn Book,* found that *Swing Otto Swing!* "contains humor, suspense, and a satisfying narrative arc." According to a *Kirkus Reviews* writer, in his picture book "Milgrim provides clean illustrations, full of movement and with wildly varying perspectives that render words almost unnecessary to the understanding of the narrative."

Milgrim turns to the holiday season in *See Santa Nap,* which finds Santa Claus vacationing at an island locale following a typically exhausting Christmas. Joining the bearded one on his holiday, Otto and his animal pals cannot resist playing with their new gifts. Their loud and rambunctious ways, prevent Santa from catching up on his sleep until Otto comes up with the perfect solution: he uses his new fishing rod to hoist the jolly old elf into a tree house. A contributor in *Horn Book* applauded the book's combination of the "simplest of easy-reader texts" and "action-packed" art and a critic in *Kirkus Reviews* stated that Milgrim exhibits "a deft touch with his humorous illustrations full of quirky characters and slapstick comedy."

The humor Milgrim brings to his "Otto" stories can also be found in his other original self-illustrated tales. In *Dog Brain,* for instance, he introduces Sneakers, a dog that does not want to perform such demeaning tricks as rolling over or fetching. Sneakers pretends not to understand its owner's commands when tricks are requested; when told to get off the furniture or stay out of the pool, Sneakers also pretends not to understand and continues to do as it pleases. Even though the boy in the family has caught on to the dog's game, his parents

A tiny mouse gets carried away with fun in Milgrim's engaging self-illustrated toddler tale See Pip Point. (Copyright © 2003 by David Milgrim. Reprinted with the permission of Simon Spotlight, an imprint of Simon & Schuster Children's Publishing Division.)

refuse to believe that Sneakers is faking it. Stephanie Zvirin, in a *Booklist* review of *Dog Brain,* wrote that "Milgrim's illustrations are outrageous" and the story's "dry humor and the popularity of the subject, dogs, ultimately prevail."

Milgrim creates a fantasy tale in *Cows Can't Fly,* the story of a boy who draws a picture of flying cows, only to be informed by his father that it cannot be: only birds can fly. When the boy's drawing is blown by the wind into a cow pasture, the resident bovines are inspired to attempt the art of flight and soon begin to frolic in the air. "Appealing to the dreamer, the artist, and the anarchist in every child," Phelan noted, "this picture book will be great fun to read aloud."

In *My Friend Lucky* Milgrim presents a series of opposites as listed by a little boy who uses his dog, Lucky, to demonstrate them. These opposites are enunciated in extremely simple couplets and illustrated by spare black-line drawings on a field of white, with color reserved for the main characters themselves. In many cases, the demonstration of opposing concepts involves witty distinctions: for example, "Lucky's big" finds the dog looking down at a caterpillar, while "Lucky's small" shows him gazing up at a horse. To illustrate "Lucky's loud," the dog barks while the narrator tries to do his homework; in the converse the dog is still barking, but now the narrator has donned earmuffs.

Noting that in *My Friend Lucky* "the interplay of text and illustration has more subtlety and wit than most books of opposites," Carolyn Phelan added in *Booklist* that "there's no mistaking the meanings of the paired images." Kay Bowes, reviewing the same book for *School Library Journal,* dubbed the title "a gentle concept book about opposites," and a *Publishers Weekly* reviewer similarly described the picture book as "mild-mannered." A *Kirkus Reviews* critic characterized Milgrim's work as "a splendid primer in the art of visual irony" as well as "a love story" of a boy and his dog.

Time to Get up, Time to Go, a self-illustrated work told in verse, follows a young boy and his favorite stuffed doll through a busy day. Waking early, the preschooler feeds breakfast to his "baby" and then heads off to the playground before the pair enjoys a dip in a neighbor's wading pool. The youngster also delights in shopping for his companion, cooking it meals, nursing it back to health, and reading it stories. Although several picture books feature a male protagonist playing with a doll, Christine M. Heppermann observed in *Horn Book* that "the matter-of-factness with which Milgrim treats his character's actions . . . makes [*Time to Get up, Time to Go*] . . . stand out." Linda Staskus, writing in *School Library Journal,* praised "the minimal text, in which not a word is wasted," and a *Kirkus Reviews* writer observed that "the gentle rhymes will satisfy the youngest listeners and help set the stage for bedtime." Other reviewers complimented Milgrim's artwork, a *Publishers Weekly* writer stating that he "has a keen eye for detail . . . and a savvy sense of composition."

Milgrim spoofs a favorite children's song in *Young MacDonald.* A technologically gifted, lab-coated farm boy constructs a mysterious device that allows him to recombine the barnyard animals into humorously bizarre new creatures. When the lad places a horse and a pig in his gizmo, for instance, he creates a "hig" that bellows "Oink-Neigh." He also produces a "cowl" (cow-owl) that plays polo, a "doose" (donkey-goose) that skateboards, a "shicken" (sheep-chicken) that swims, and a "muck" (mouse-duck) that flies planes. The scientist becomes a victim of his own success, however, when he accidentally steps onto the platform with his pet dog. "The lyrics are great fun and have lots of wordplay," Staskus wrote of *Young MacDonald,* and Phelan stated that "the clean lines and flat colors of the digitally assisted artwork brim with energy and comedy."

Silliness is also given free rein in *Another Day in the Milky Way.* After Monty wakes up one morning, he discovers that his life has been turned upside down: his mother has three heads, his dog sports pink stripes, and his friends dress in horse costumes. Following the advice of a donkey named Tulip, Monty must consult with a mountaintop guru in order to find his way back to his real home. "The first-person narrative reads like a child relating a dream, complete with abrupt transitions

and surreal events," remarked *School Library Journal* reviewer Suzanne Myers Harold, and Parravano noted of *Another Day in the Milky Way* that "cheerful cartoon illustrations . . . indulge completely in the offbeat while retaining a simplicity of shape and composition that will appeal" to young readers.

Milgrim focuses on an aspiring actress in *Amelia Makes a Movie,* in which a little girl asks her younger brother Drew to help her produce her cinematic debut. Although Amelia plans to do it all—write the script, arrange lighting and costumes, paint the backdrops, and direct and star in the lead—Drew has ideas of his own, and after the siblings learn to work together they create a story that entertains the whole family. Predicting that *Amelia Makes a Movie* will inspire other children to experiment with movie-making, Krista Hutley added in *Booklist* that the "quirky signature illustrations" in Milgrim's story "add humorous details" that reinforce the loving relationship between brother and sister. A *Publishers Weekly* recommended *Amelia Makes a Movie* as "an entertaining and practical how-to" for "the YouTube generation," and in *School Library Journal* Julie R. Ranelli recommended the book's mix of "appealing cartoon" art and simple rhyming text as "a good choice for beginning and reluctant readers."

Child development is Milgrim's focus in both *Best Baby Ever* and *How You Got So Smart.* A chronicle of hand-

Milgrim profiles the life style of the young and clever in his humorous self-illustrated picture book How You Got So Smart. (Copyright © 2010 by David Milgrim. Reproduced with permission of G.P. Putnam's Sons, a division of Penguin Young Readers Group.)

ily accomplished firsts, *Best Baby Ever* follows an infant as it shows its first smile, first laugh, and first word, begins to crawl, then walk, and eventually leaves its doting parents for its first ride to school. In addition to the child's firsts, Mom and Dad experience firsts of their own, which Milgrim captures in all their ridiculous humor in his digital cartoon art. "Many parents will certainly relate to the adoring adults" in *Best Baby Every,* according to *Booklist* contributor Abby Nolan, while in *School Library Journal* Julie Roach recommended the story's comedic mix of "simple yet exaggerated cartoon art" and "deadpan text."

No longer a baby, the young boy in *How You Got So Smart* is motivated by a child's universal curiosity, tenacity, and optimism. With his love of donuts and his belief in the world's limitless wonders, Milgrim's young hero spends his time playing, listening and watching, questioning, and expressing his own thoughts and ideas about how things work. With its theme that "play is a form of education," according to *Booklist* critic Kara Dean, *How You Got So Smart* eschews time spent in front of televisions or computer screens and instead "celebrates kids being kids." A *Publishers Weekly* contributor described the work as a "breezy yet tender celebration of childhood achievements," and Julie Roach commended the "comical cartoon illustrations" Milgrim crafts to "bring humor to the [book's] enthusiastic text."

Milgrim presents a holiday story in *Thank You, Thanksgiving.* A little girl goes to the store on Thanksgiving Day to buy some whipped cream for the family's pumpkin pie, and along the way she thanks all the things around her that she enjoys and appreciates, including her warm boots, the rabbits in the park, and the clouds above. A critic for *Publishers Weekly* called *Thank You, Thanksgiving* a "visually playful outing." "Milgrim helps young children recognize the blessings in their daily lives," Zvirin pointed out in her review of the colorfully illustrated work.

Like *See Santa Nap,* which starred Otto the robot, *Santa Duck* allows Milgrim to once again cause mischief with Christmas traditions. In the story, Nicholas Duck decides to clarify his gift list to Santa in person, but along the way he is mysteriously enlisted by the "Jolly Old Elf" to collect the wishes of the animals he meets on his way to the North Pole. While recording the many gift lists of others, Nicholas Duck forgets to add his own, but readers know to trust in Santa's savvy as Milgrim's story plays out. Illustrated in the author/illustrator's characteristic digitized ink and pastel art, *Santa Duck* features a holiday story "infusing humor and deftly revealing personality," according to *Horn Book* contributor Martha V. Parravano. In *School Library Journal* Maureen Wade also praised the "charming" art in *Santa Duck,* noting that Milgrim's use of both text and speech balloons "move the story along at a brisk pace." In *Kirkus Reviews* a critic predicted that *Santa Duck* "has the potential to become a read-it-over-and-over favorite."

Milgrim treats readers to an upbeat holiday story in his self-illustrated **Thank You, Thanksgiving.** (Copyright © 2003 by David Milgrim. All rights reserved. Reprinted by permission of Clarion Books, an imprint of Houghton Mifflin Company.)

Biographical and Critical Sources

PERIODICALS

Booklist, September 1, 1996, Stephanie Zvirin, review of *Dog Brain,* p. 144; November 1, 1997, Carolyn Phelan, review of *Here in Space,* p. 467; August, 1998, Carolyn Phelan, review of *Cows Can't Fly,* p. 2015; December 1, 1999, John Peters, review of *Patrick's Dinosaur's on the Internet,* p. 709; April 15, 2002, Carolyn Phelan, review of *My Friend Lucky,* p. 1408; September 15, 2002, Carolyn Phelan, review of *Ride Otto Ride!,* p. 241; February 1, 2003, Carolyn Phelan, review of *See Pip Point,* p. 1001; September 1, 2003, Stephanie Zvirin, review of *Thank You, Thanksgiving,* p. 135; July, 2004, Carolyn Phelan, review of *Swing Otto Swing!,* p. 1852; April 15, 2006, Carolyn Phelan, review of *Young MacDonald,* p. 54; February 15, 2007, Carolyn Phelan, review of *Another Day in the Milky Way,* p. 84; February 1, 2008, Krista Hutley, review of *Amelia Makes a Movie,* p. 47; May 15, 2009, Abby Nolan, review of *Best Baby Ever,* p. 43; October 15, 2009, Hazel Rochman, review of *I'm Getting a Checkup,* p. 54; March 15, 2010, Kara Dean, review of *How You Got So Smart,* p. 47.

Canadian Review of Materials, January 2, 2004, Dave Jenkinson, review of *Little Lamb's Christmas.*

Horn Book, May-June, 2004, Martha V. Parravano, review of *Swing Otto Swing!,* p. 334; November-December, 2004, review of *See Santa Nap,* p. 662; March-April, 2006, Christine M. Heppermann, review of *Time to Get up, Time to Go,* p. 176; January-February, 2007, Martha V. Parravano, review of *Another Day in the*

Milky Way, 59; November-December, 2008, Martha V. Parravano, review of *Santa Duck,* p. 650.

Kirkus Reviews, November 1, 2001, review of *My Friend Lucky,* p. 1553; August 1, 2002, review of *See Otto,* p. 1138; February 1, 2003, review of *See Pip Point,* p. 236; April 15, 2004, review of *Swing Otto Swing!,* p. 398; November 1, 2004, review of *See Santa Nap,* p. 1052; February 1, 2006, review of *Young MacDonald,* p. 134; April 1, 2006, review of *Time to Get up, Time to Go,* p. 352; August 15, 2006, review of *My Mum Goes to Work,* p. 841; January 15, 2008, review of *Amelia Makes a Movie;* November 1, 2008, review of *Santa Duck;* June 1, 2009, review of *Best Baby Ever;* August 1, 2009, review of *I'm Getting a Checkup.*

Publishers Weekly, August 19, 1996, review of *Dog Brain,* p. 65; May 25, 1998, review of *Cows Can't Fly,* p. 89; September 6, 1999, review of *Patrick's Dinosaur's on the Internet,* p. 102; December 10, 2001, review of *My Friend Lucky,* p. 68; September 22, 2003, review of *Thank You, Thanksgiving,* p. 65; April 3, 2006, review of *Time to Get up, Time to Go,* p. 73; June 19, 2006, review of *Young MacDonald,* p. 62; January 15, 2007, review of *Another Day in the Milky Way,* p. 51; March 17, 2008, review of *Amelia Makes a Movie,* p. 68; March 15, 2010, review of *How You Got So Smart,* p. 50.

Reviewer's Bookwatch, November, 2004, Kimberly Hutmacher, review of *Thank You, Thanksgiving.*

San Francisco Chronicle, October 26, 2003, Regan McMahon, review of *Thank You, Thanksgiving,* p. M6.

School Library Journal, February, 2002, Kay Bowes, review of *My Friend Lucky,* p. 108; March, 2003, Nancy A. Gifford, review of *Ride Otto Ride!,* p. 199; September, 2003, Janet M. Bair, review of *Thank You, Thanksgiving,* p. 185; July, 2004, Bethany L.W. Hankinson, review of *Swing Otto Swing!,* p. 83; April, 2006, Linda Staskus, review of *Time to Get up, Time to Go,* p. 112; May, 2006, Linda Staskus, review of *Young MacDonald,* p. 95; February, 2007, Suzanne Myers Harold, review of *Another Day in the Milky Way,* p. 92; April, 2008, Julie R. Ramelli, review of *Amelia Makes a Movie,* p. 117; October, 2008, Maureen Wade, review of *Santa Duck,* p. 97; July, 2009, Julie Roach, review of *Best Baby Ever,* p. 66; November, 2009, Lynn K. Vanca, review of *I'm Getting a Checkup,* p. 97; May, 2010, Julie Roach, review of *How You Got So Smart,* p. 89.

Tribune Books (Chicago, IL), February 18, 2007, Mary Harris Russell, review of *Another Day in the Milky Way,* p. 7; May 13, 2007, Maria Pontillas, review of *Young MacDonald,* p. 6.

ONLINE

Children's Literuature Web site, http://www.childrenslit. com/ (October 26, 2006), Marilyn Courtot, "David Milgrim."

David Milgrim Home Page, http://www.davidmilgrim.com (December 5, 2010).*

MOHANTY, Raja

Personal

Born in India. *Education:* Indian Institute of Technology Bombay, B.S. (technology), M.A. (design); MSU Baroda, Ph.D.

Addresses

Home—Mumbai, India. *Office*—Industrial Design Centre, Indian Institute of Technology, Powai, Mumbai 400076, India. *E-mail*—rajam@ittb.ac.in.

Career

Educator, author, and filmmaker. Industrial Design Centre, Mumbai, India, assistant professor of visual communication. Freelance designer and illustrator; lecturer.

Writings

(With Sirish Rao) *The Circle of Fate,* illustrated by Radhashyam Raut, Tara Publishing (Chennai, India), 2009.

Biographical and Critical Sources

PERIODICALS

Booklist, May 15, 2008, Janice Del Negro, review of *The Circle of Fate,* p. 131.

ONLINE

Industrial Design Centre Web site, http://www.idc.iitb.ac. in/ (November 27, 2010), "Raj Mohanty."

Tara Publishing Web site, http://www.tarabooks.com/ (November 27, 2010), "Raja Mohanty."*

*   *   *

MUNRO, Roxie 1945-

Personal

Born September 5, 1945, in Mineral Wells, TX; daughter of Robert Enoch (an automotive shop owner and boat builder) and Margaret (a librarian) Munro; married Bo Zaunders (a writer and photographer), May 17, 1986. *Education:* Attended University of Maryland, 1963-65, Maryland Institute College of Art, 1965-66, and Ohio University, 1969-70; University of Hawai'i, B.F.A., 1969, graduate work, 1970-71. *Hobbies and other interests:* Travel, reading.

Addresses

Home—New York, NY. *Office*—43-01 21st St., Studio No. 340, Long Island City, NY 11101. *E-mail*—roxie@roxiemunro.com.

Career

Roxie (dress company), Washington, DC, dress designer and manufacturer, 1972-76; television courtroom artist in Washington, DC, 1976-81; freelance artist, beginning 1976. Presenter at schools. *Exhibitions:* Work included in Original Art Exhibit, Society of Illustrators, New York, NY, and group shows staged at New York Public Library, New York, NY; Detroit Institute of Arts, Detroit, MI; High Museum, Atlanta, GA; Boston Atheneum, Boston, MA; Corcoran Gallery of Art, Washington, DC; Victoria & Albert Museum, London, England; Art Gallery of Ontario, Toronto, Ontario, Canada; Fine Arts Museum of San Francisco, San Francisco, CA, and others. Solo shows staged at Foundry Gallery, Washington, DC; Delaware Museum of Art; Zimmerli Museum, Rutgers University, Rutgers, NJ; Gotham Book Mart, New York, NY; Marin-Price Gallery, Chevy Chase, MD; Simie Maryles Gallery, Provincetown, MA; and Michael Ingbar Gallery of Architectural Art, Sigrid Freundorfer Gallery, and Denise Bibro Fine Arts, all New York, NY. Works included in numerous private and public collections.

Member

New York Artists' Equity, Society of Children's Book Writers and Illustrators.

Awards, Honors

Yaddo painting fellowship, 1980; Best Illustrated Children's Books citation, *New York Times,* and Best Children's Books citation, *Time,* both 1985, both for *The Inside-Outside Book of New York City;* Best Book selection, *School Library Journal,* 1996, for *The Inside-Outside Book of Libraries,* 2001, for *Feathers, Flaps, and Flops;* Bank Street College of Education Best Books designation, 1997, for *The Inside-Outside Book of Washington, DC,* 1998, for *Crocodiles, Camels, and Dugout Canoes* by Bo Zaunders, 2003, for *Gargoyles, Girders, and Glass Houses* by Zaunders, and *Doors,* and 2008, for *Mazeways;* Notable Children's Trade Book in the Field of Social Studies designation, National Council on the Social Studies/Children's Book Council, 2003, for *Gargoyles, Girders, and Glass Houses* by Zaunders; National Parenting Publications Family Honors Award, 2006, for *Ranch;* Bronze Medal for interactive children's books, Independent Publishers IPPY Awards, 2006, for *The Wild West Trail Ride Maze;* Children and Young Adult Bloggers Literary Award nomination in nonfiction category, 2010, for *EcoMazes.*

Writings

SELF-ILLUSTRATED

Color New York, Arbor House (New York, NY), 1985.

The Inside-Outside Book of New York City, Dodd (New York, NY), 1985, revised edition, SeaStar Books (New York, NY), 2001.

The Inside-Outside Book of Washington, DC, Dutton (New York, NY), 1987.

Christmastime in New York City, Dodd (New York, NY), 1987.

Blimps, Dutton (New York, NY), 1989.

The Inside-Outside Book of London, Dutton (New York, NY), 1989.

The Inside-Outside Book of Paris, Dutton (New York, NY), 1992.

The Inside-Outside Book of Texas, SeaStar Books (New York, NY), 2001.

Mazescapes, SeaStar Books (New York, NY), 2001.

Doors, SeaStar Books (New York, NY), 2003.

Amazement Park, Chronicle Books (San Francisco, CA), 2005.

The Wild West Trail Ride Maze, Bright Sky Press (Albany, TX), 2006.

Circus, Chronicle Books (San Francisco, CA), 2006.

Mazeways: A to Z, Sterling Publishing (New York, NY), 2007.

Rodeo, Bright Sky Press (Albany, TX), 2007.

Go! Go! Go!: With More than Seventy Flaps to Uncover and Discover, Sterling (New York, NY), 2009.

Amazement Park, Sterling Publishing (New York, NY), 2009.

Inside-Outside Dinosaurs, Marshall Cavendish Children (Tarrytown, NY), 2009.

Desert Days, Desert Nights, Bright Sky Press (Houston, TX), 2010.

Ecomazes: Twelve Earth Adventures, Sterling (New York, NY), 2010.

Hatch!, Marshall Cavendish Children's (New York, NY), 2011.

Contributor of illustrations to periodicals, including *New Yorker, Washington Post, U.S. News & World Report, Gourmet, Historic Preservation,* and *New Republic.*

Author's works have been translated into Chinese, Dutch, French, Italian, and Japanese.

ILLUSTRATOR

Kay D. Weeks, *The Great American Landmark Adventure,* National Park Service and American Architectural Foundation (Washington, DC), 1982.

Diane Maddex, *Architects Make Zigzags: Looking at Architecture from A to Z,* Preservation Press (Washington, DC), 1986.

Kay D. Weeks, *American Defenders of Land, Sea, and Sky,* National Park Service (Washington, DC), 1996.

Julie Cummins, *The Inside-Outside Book of Libraries,* Dutton (New York, NY), 1996.

Bo Zaunders, *Crocodiles, Camels, and Dugout Canoes: Eight Adventurous Episodes,* Dutton (New York, NY), 1998.

Bo Zaunders, *Feathers, Flaps, and Flops: Fabulous Early Fliers,* Dutton (New York, NY), 2001.

Raymond D. Keene, *Learn Chess Fast: The Fun Way to Start Smart and Master the Game,* Bright Sky Press (Albany, TX), 2001.

Joseph Siano, editor, *The New York Times What's Doing around the World,* Lebhar-Friedman (New York, NY), 2001.

Bo Zaunders, *Gargoyles, Girders, and Glass Houses: Magnificent Master Builders,* Dutton (New York, NY), 2003.

Bo Zaunders, *The Great Bridge Building Contest,* Harry N. Abrams (New York, NY), 2004.

Michael P. Spradlin, *Texas Rangers: Legendary Lawmen,* Walker & Co. (New York, NY), 2008.

Sidelights

Author and illustrator of the popular "Inside-Out" series, which focus on a selection of well-known cityscapes, Roxie Munro is an inveterate city watcher.

Munro is also an artist with a unique visual sensibility, making her detailed ink-and-watercolor illustrations for her "Inside-Outside" series, as well as for her picture books *Amazement Park, Rodeo,* and *Circus,* unique interactive experiences for young readers. "There's a wonderfully obsessive quality to her views," wrote Sam Swope in a review of Munro's *The Inside-Outside Book of New York City,* "as if she can't stop herself from capturing each water tower and skylight, each arch and colonnade."

Born in Mineral Wells, Texas, in 1945, Munro once told *SATA,* "Unlike many children's book creators, I don't have a lot of specific memories of my childhood. I remember mainly sensuous impressions: water running across rocks in a ditch, the dried fall leaves, the splash of waves across a boat's bow." Growing up in a small, rural town, much of Munro's spare time was

In Amazement Park *Roxie Munro treats readers to an assortment of mazes guaranteed to challenge even the most experienced maze afficionado.*
(Chronicle Books, 2005. Illustration © 2005 by Roxie Munro. Reproduced by permission.)

spent "reading and daydreaming." Her parents encouraged their children to engage in independent, creative activities: drawing, making their own toys, and reading. The family also traveled a good deal together, and in annual vacations to the Northeast, South, and West Munro gained a familiarity with urban as well as rural America.

Munro's love of art inspired many early successes. In first grade she won a county art competition; in high school she was editor of the school yearbook and was also named "most talented" in her class. After studying art at the University of Maryland, the Maryland Institute College of Art, the University of Hawai'i, and Ohio State University, Munro established a business as a dress designer, marketing her fashions to small boutiques in Washington, DC. She then freelanced for several years as a courtroom artist, working for newspapers and television. In 1981, Munro moved to New York City and continued her career as a freelance illustrator. Among her successes, she has created cover art for over a dozen issues of the prestigious *New Yorker* magazine, a periodical known for its distinctive covers.

Approaching book publishers, Munro was asked to come up with ideas for children's books, and *The Inside-Outside Book of New York City* was born. In this witty pictorial, Munro tells the story of the city visually, taking unique vantage points on well-known sites. For the Statue of Liberty, for instance, she looks not only at its exterior, but also from the inside out at the city. There are views of the inside of the New York Stock Exchange and of busy traffic. Other landmarks viewed from both outside and inside include St. Patrick's Cathedral and the animal cages at the Bronx Zoo. Munro looks through windows, behind bars, and even across theater footlights to get an intimate view of the city.

Winner of a *New York Times* Best Illustrated Children's Book Award in 1985, *The Inside-Outside Book of New York City* inaugurated a series of similar books, spanning the globe from London to Paris, revealing the mysteries of the prehistoric world in *Inside Outside Dinosaurs,* and bringing to life the culture of Munro's home state of Texas. *The Inside-Outside Book of Texas* features pictures "ranging from the dramatic . . . to the mundane," according to a *Publishers Weekly* critic. Among the various sites and topics covered are a skyline of Dallas, ranch hands at chow time, the Texas Stadium (home of the Dallas Cowboys football team), the Lyndon B. Johnson Space Center in Houston, and various wildlife scenes. "Bright, cheerful colors invite the eye," noted *School Library Journal* contributor Ruth Semrau, and a *Horn Book* reviewer wrote that Munro not only introduces young readers to landmarks of the state, "but also cleverly stretches the definitional boundaries of inside and outside."

Extending her view skyward, Munro's *Mazescapes* invites readers to find their way through interconnected aerial mazes of cities and the countryside using any of six punch-out cars provided with the book. Alison Kastner, writing in *School Library Journal,* predicted that older fans of the "Where's Waldo" books who are looking for "something a little more challenging will find it in Munro's brightly colored and intricate paintings." The challenge the illustrator poses here is to find the way to the zoo and back home again through maze-like renderings of towns, cities, and countryside. Peter D. Sieruta observed in a *Horn Book* review that *Mazescapes* contains "the kind of dizzyingly detailed artwork that sends adults running for the Dramamine yet almost always entrances kids."

Other maze books include *Mazeways: A to Z,* which contains an alphabet's worth of entrances, and a tour through Earth's varied ecosystems titled *EcoMazes: Twelve Earth Adventures.* In *Mazeways* Munro incorporates each letter into a large-format illustration and then hides objects beginning with that letter in her complex art to encourage readers to hunt and seek. Featuring over 350 hidden animals—all of which can be tracked by a key to their location at the back of the book—*EcoMazes* also provides factual information about plants, weather, and other characteristics of the many different habitats on earth. In *Booklist* Carolyn Phelan recommended *Mazeways* as "a bright, enticing book to challenge fans of the 'Where's Waldo' and 'I Spy' series," while John Peters praised *EcoMazes* in *School Library Journal* as an "engrossing" picture book in which Munro's "finely and accurately detailed" illustrations will add to readers' "understanding of the natural world."

With over fifty flaps for readers to lift, *Doors* allows readers to enter everything from a country barn to a city fire station before traveling off-planet to an orbiting space station through Munro's colorful art. Readers are transported to the Wild West in *Rodeo,* which Joy Fleishhacker commended in *School Library Journal* for its "clear, concise text and clever" Western-themed art. Dirigibles are given the Munro treatment in *Blimps,* a book done with "accurate and complete detail," according to a reviewer in the *New Advocate.* "The fun thing here was the research," Munro noted while discussing *Blimps* in *Children's Book Illustration and Design.* "I got a three-hour ride in a blimp over Manhattan, and in England visited the biggest blimp-making factory in the world."

A group of clowns guides readers through the hide-and-seek and lift-the-flap challenges in *Circus,* while other amusements await readers in *Amazement Park* and *Go! Go! Go!: With More than Seventy Flaps to Uncover and Discover.* A collection of twelve mazes depicted in "cartoon art [that] is eye-catching and colorful," according to *School Library Journal* critic Julie Roach, *Amazement Park* features "intricate, colored-ink illustrations [that] beguile the eye with their exquisite attention to detail," in the opinion of a *Kirkus Reviews* contributor. Transportation is Munro's focus in *Go! Go! Go!,* as the action speeds up from hot-air balloons to bicycles to

Munro continues to treat reader to her tangle of tantalizing mazes in her self-illustrated **Mazeways A to Z.** (Copyright © 2007 by Roxie Munro. Reproduced by permission of Sterling Publishing.)

horses, race cars, and fire engines. Citing the "wonderfully energetic sense of motion" that emanates from each page of *Go! Go! Go!*, Lynn K. Vanca commended Munro's "careful planning" in her *School Library Journal* review, and *Horn Book* contributor Betty Carter predicted that rapt "toddlers [will be] on their stomachs studying each page."

As an illustrator, Munro has also worked with a variety of writers, including her husband, Swedish photographer, artist, and writer Bo Zaunders. Illustrating his *Crocodiles, Camels, and Dugout Canoes: Eight Adventurous Episodes,* her illustrations add "even more liveliness" to the text, according to *Booklist* contributor Susan Dove Lempke. A reviewer for *Publishers Weekly* also commended the book-sized gathering of travelers and explorers, noting that the couple's enthusiasm "shine[s] through the pages of this absorbing picture book."

A second husband-and-wife collaboration, *Feathers, Flaps, and Flops: Fabulous Early Fliers,* depicts the exploits of some early aviators in seven sketches, while

Gargoyles, Girders, and Glass Houses: Magnificent Master Builders focuses on seven architects who tackled building projects in which "enormous obstacles . . . would have daunted less courageous, less obsessive geniuses," according to *Horn Book* critic Sally P. Bloom. In *School Library Journal,* Louise L. Sherman praised Munro's "fine illustrations" in *Feathers, Flaps, and Flops,* and a *Horn Book* reviewer wrote that the book's "playful perspective is a Roxie Munro hallmark."

Munro's "captivating" illustrations for *Gargoyles, Girders, and Glass Houses,* in introducing readers to the works of Mimar Koca Sinan, Antoni Gaudi, and others, "provides clear visual reference" and reflect the "grandeur and the subtle details" included in Zaunders' text, according to *School Library Journal* critic Steven Engelfried. Citing the illustrator's "use of unusual perspectives" and "well-chosen details," Carolyn Phelan concluded in her *Booklist* review that Munro's art depicts monumental works of architecture as "within the scale of human use and understanding."

Working with Michael P. Spradlin, Munro's artwork for *Texas Rangers: Legendary Lawmen* draws on the Texas root that she has also tapped in her books *Rodeo, Ranch,* and *The Wild West Trail Ride Maze.* In her cartoon art, she brings to life Spradlin's picture-book history of the Texas Rangers, which were formed in 1823, when the area was still part of a newly independent Mexico. Although Spradlin minimizes what Madeline J. Bryant characterized in *School Library Journal* as the state's "violent and somewhat reckless" history, Munro's colorful images of famous Texas lawmen will "entice youngsters and keep them turning the pages." A *Kirkus Reviews* writer praised *Texas Rangers* as a "handsome tribute" to the men that helped to bring law to the "wildest parts of the Wild West," and Randall Enos concluded his *Booklist* review of Spradlin's history by noting that Munro's "abundant" art "provide[s] competent visual support to the facts."

Characterizing her illustration work as "developing from perception," Munro once explained to *SATA* that it is also "very visual, spatial. Ideas develop from a kind of active seeing. When I walk down a street, ride a bus, or go up an escalator, I FEEL the changing space. I see patterns, paintings everywhere. My mind organizes reality. I'll notice two gray cars, a red car, a black car, and two more red cars—aha!—a pattern."

Biographical and Critical Sources

BOOKS

Children's Book Illustration and Design, edited by Julie Cummins, Library of Applied Design (New York, NY), 1992.

Children's Books and Their Creators, edited by Anita Silvey, Houghton Mifflin (New York, NY), 1995.

PERIODICALS

Booklist, October 15, 1996, Carolyn Phelan, review of *The Inside-Outside Book of Libraries,* p. 426; October 15, 1998, Susan Dove Lempke, review of *Crocodiles, Camels, and Dugout Canoes: Eight Adventurous Episodes,* p. 420; April 1, 2001, Gillian Engberg, review of *The Inside-Outside Book of Texas,* p. 1475; November 1, 2004, Carolyn Phelan, review of *Gargoyles, Girders, and Glass Houses: Magnificent Master Builders,* p. 498; December 1, 2004, Carolyn Phelan, review of *The Great Bridge-Building Contest,* p. 672;; August, 2007, Carolyn Phelan, review of *Mazeways: A to Z,* p. 80; January 1, 2008, Randall Enos, review of *Texas Rangers: Legendary Lawmen,* p. 72; September 1, 2009, Carolyn Phelan, review of *Inside-Outside Dinosaurs,* p. 95; June 1, 2010, Courtney Jones, review of *EcoMazes: Twelve Earth Adventures,* p. 89.

Bulletin of the Center for Children's Books, October, 1996, Elizabeth Bush, review of *The Inside-Outside Book of Libraries,* p. 53; January, 2005, Elizabeth Bush, review of *Gargoyles, Girders, and Glass Houses,* p. 233.

Horn Book, March-April, 1992, Ellen Fader, review of *The Inside-Outside Book of Paris,* p. 221; September-October, 1996, Roger Sutton, review of *The Inside-Outside Book of Libraries,* p. 611; January-February, 1999, review of *Crocodiles, Camels, and Dugout Canoes,* p. 85; May-June, 2001, review of *The Inside-Outside Book of Texas,* p. 350; July-August, 2001, review of *Feathers, Flaps, and Flops: Fabulous Early Fliers,* p. 480; September-October, 2001, Peter D. Sieruta, review of *Mazescapes,* p. 577; November-December, 2004, Susan P. Bloom, review of *Gargoyles, Girders, and Glass Houses,* p. 732; May-June, 2005, Peter D. Sieruta, review of *Amazement Park,* p. 311; July-August, 2009, Betty Carter, review of *Go! Go! Go!,* p. 412.

Kirkus Reviews, November 15, 2004, review of *Gargoyles, Girders, and Glass Houses,* p. 1095; April 1, 2005, review of *Amazement Park,* p. 422; October 15, 2006, review of *Circus,* p. 1076; August 1, 2007, review of *Mazeways;* January 1, 2008, review of *Texas Rangers;* July 1, 2009, review of *Inside-Outside Dinosaurs.* July-August, 2009, Betty Carter, review of *Go! Go! Go!,* p. 412.

New Advocate, winter, 1990, review of *Blimps,* p. 69.

New York Times Book Review, May 20, 2001, Sam Swope, "Oz on the Hudson," p. 30.

Publishers Weekly, November 29, 1991, review of *The Inside-Outside Book of Paris,* p. 50; August 19, 1996, review of *The Inside-Outside Book of Libraries,* p. 65;

Cover of Circus, *which features Munro's unique interactive mix of text and art.* (Illustration © 2006 by Roxie Munro. Used by permission of Chronicle Books, LLC, San Francisco. Visit ChronicleBooks.com.)

August 31, 1998, review of *Crocodiles, Camels, and Dugout Canoes,* p. 76; February 26, 2001, review of *The Inside-Outside Book of Texas,* p. 88; July 30, 2001, review of *Mazescapes,* p. 86; October 15, 2007, review of *Rodeo,* p. 63.

School Library Journal, August, 1996, Nancy Menaldi-Scanlan, review of *The Inside-Outside Book of Libraries,* p. 134; November, 1998, Patricia Manning, review of *Crocodiles, Camels, and Dugout Canoes,* p. 144; June, 2001, Ruth Semrau, review of *The Inside-Outside Book of Texas,* p. 140; July, 2001, Louise L. Sherman, review of *Feathers, Flaps, and Flops,* p. 101; August, 2001, Alison Kastner, review of *Mazescapes,* p. 171; September, 2004, John Sigwald, review of *Ranch,* p. 190; December, 2004, Steven Engelfried, review of *Gargoyles, Girders, and Glass Houses,* p. 172; March, 2005, Edith Ching, review of *The Great Bridge-Building Contest,* p. 205; May, 2005, Julie Roach, review of *Amazement Park,* p. 112; December, 2006, Maryann H. Owen, review of *Circus,* p. 110; September, 2007, Mary Hazelton, review of *Mazeways,* p. 185; December, 2007, Joy Fleishhacker, review of *Rodeo,* p. 113; April, 2008, Madeline J. Bryant, review of *Texas Rangers,* p. 138; June, 2009, Lynn K. Vanca, review of *Go! Go! Go!,* p. 96; November, 2009, Patricia Manning, review of *Inside-Outside Dinosaurs,* p. 96; June, 2010, John Peters, review of *EcoMazes,* p. 89.

Time, December 23, 1985, Stefan Kanfer, review of *The Inside-Outside Book of New York City,* p. 62.

ONLINE

Roxie Munro Home Page, http://www.roxiemunro.com (December 5, 2010).*

N-O

NORMAN, Geoffrey

Personal

Born in AL; married; children: Brooke, one other daughter. *Hobbies and other interests:* Mountain climbing, outdoor sports.

Addresses

Home—Dorset, VT. *E-mail*—info@vermonttiger.com.

Career

Editor, journalist, and author. *Esquire* (magazine), former contributing editor; *Forbes* FYI, former editor at large; Vermont Tiger (Web site), currently editor in chief.

Writings

Midnight Water (novel), Avon (New York, NY), 1985.
The Orvis Book of Upland Bird Shooting, Winchester Press, 1985.
Alabama Showdown: The Football Rivalry between Auburn and Alabama, Henry Holt (New York, NY), 1986.
Bouncing Back: How a Heroic Band of POWs Survived Vietnam, Pocket Books (New York, NY), 1992.
(With Leigh Perkins) *A Sportsman's Life: How I Built Orvis by Mixing Business and Sport,* Atlantic Monthly Press (Boston, MA), 1999.
Two for the Summit: My Daughter, the Mountains, and Me, Dutton (New York, NY), 2000.
Inch by Inch: A Novel of Breast Cancer and Healing, Lyons Press, 2003.
Riding with Jeb Stuart: Hunting Adventures with an English Pointer, Lyons Press, 2005.
Stars above Us, (picture book), illustrated by E.B. Lewis, Putnam's (New York, NY), 2009.

Contributor to periodicals, including *American Spectator, Men's Journal, National Geographic, National Geographic Adventurer, Outside, Smithsonian, Sports Illustrated,* and the *Wall Street Journal.*

"MORGAN HUNT" ADULT MYSTERY SERIES

Sweetwater Ranch, Dell (New York, NY), 1992.
Blue Chipper, Morrow (New York, NY), 1992.
Deep End, Avon (New York, NY), 1995.

Biographical and Critical Sources

PERIODICALS

Booklist, September 15, 2009, Carolyn Phelan, review of *Stars above Us,* p. 65.
Kirkus Reviews, August 15, 2009, review of *Stars above Us.*
School Library Journal, October, 2009, Mary Jean Smith, review of *Stars above Us,* p. 100.

ONLINE

Vermont Tiger Web site, http://www.vermonttiger.com/ (December 5, 2010), "Geoffrey Norman."*

*   *   *

OLDLAND, Nicholas 1972-

Personal

Born 1972, in Canada; son of John (a company cofounder) and Alice (an artist and company cofounder) Oldland. *Education:* Mount Allison University (New Brunswick, Canada), B.F.A.

Addresses

Home—Montreal, Quebec, Canada.

Career

Creative director, textile designer, and author. Worked as a commercial artist and filmmaker; Hatley (apparel company), coowner and creative director.

Awards, Honors

Blue Spruce Award shortlist, Ontario Library Association, 2011, for *Big Bear Hug*.

Writings

Big Bear Hug, Kids Can Press (Toronto, Ontario, Canada), 2009.

Making the Moose out of Life, Kids Can Press (Toronto, Ontario, Canada), 2010.

Author's work has been translated into French.

Sidelights

When Nicholas Oldland joined his two brothers in taking over the family business, he was able to use both his business acumen and the creative talents he inherited from his mom, artist and company founder Alice Oldland. Alice was a painter, and she and husband John adapted her designs for aprons that they sold in their family-run gift store. That store eventually grew to become Hatley, a Canadian-based apparel company that has retail stores in both the United States and Canada. Now the creative director of Hatley, Oldland devised the graphic images of moose, bears, ducks, dogs, cows, and pigs that decorate the distinctive flannel used in the company's line of children's pajamas. His decision to create a picture book for children that could accompany his cozy flannels to bed was the inspiration behind Oldland's first picture book, *Big Bear Hug*.

Canadians' love for their native wildlife is captured in Nicholas Oldland's self-illustrated picture book **Bib Bear Hug.** (Illustration © 2000 by Nicholas Oldland. Reproduced by permission of Kids Can Press Ltd., Toronto, Ontario, Canada.)

In *Big Bear Hug* readers are transported to Canada's northern forest and the home of a big brown bear. Although the bear is big and strong, it is actually gentle in nature, and loves to hug the creatures that it meets. It also loves to hug trees, so when a logger comes and threatens Bear's beloved forest, the creature must find a way to save the trees without reverting to its natural bear-like state and using fear to get its way. Reviewing *Big Bear Hunt* for *School Library Journal*, Julie Roach noted that Oldland's "sweet but deadpan text paired with the [author's] almost slapstick cartoon art makes for an entertaining conservation story." The "stylized" illustrations in the book "play sly comic foil to the earnest text," wrote a *Publishers Weekly* contributor, and Gwyneth Evans commented in *Quill & Quire* that Oldland's digital images and use of a "limited colour palette keep the focus on the . . . story, and make for an attractive and appealing book." Also in praise of Oldand's tale, a *Kirkus Reviews* writer dubbed *Big Bear Hug* "a treat for the tree hugger in all of us."

Biographical and Critical Sources

PERIODICALS

Children's Bookwatch, October, 2009, review of *Big Bear Hug*.

Kirkus Reviews, August 1, 2009, review of *Big Bear Hug*.

Publishers Weekly, October 5, 2009, review of *Big Bear Hug*, p. 46.

Quill & Quire, October, 2009, Gwyneth Evans, review of *Big Bear Hug*.

School Library Journal, October, 2009, Julie Roach, review of *Big Bear Hug*, p. 100.

ONLINE

Hatley Company Web site, http://www.hatleystore.com/ (November 21, 2010), "Nicholas Oldland."

Kids Can Press Web site, http://www.kidscanpress.com/ (December 15, 2010), "Nicholas Oldland."*

*   *   *

OSTOW, Micol 1976-

Personal

Born April 29, 1976; daughters of Meier (an attorney) and Carmen (a social worker) Ostow; married Noah Harlan (a film producer and writer), December, 2009. *Ethnicity:* "Puerto Rican and Jewish." *Education:* Tufts University, B.A.; Vermont College of Fine Arts, M.F.A. (writing for children and young adults), 2009. *Religion:* Jewish. *Hobbies and other interests:* Reading, running, watching inappropriate quantities of bad TV.

Addresses

Home—New York, NY. *E-mail*—micol@micolostow.com.

Career

Writer and editor. Simon & Schuster, New York, NY, editor in trade nonfiction, then young-adult division. Creator of *Fireplace in a Box* and *Executive Desk Gong,* for Running Press, 2003. Workshop teacher for Media Bistro.

Writings

FOR YOUNG ADULTS

(Compiler with Steven Brezenoff) *The Quotable Slayer* (based on television series *Buffy the Vampire Slayer*), Simon Pulse (New York, NY), 2003.
30 Guys in 30 Days, Simon Pulse (New York, NY), 2005.
Westminster Abby ("Students across the Seven Seas" series), Speak (New York, NY), 2005.
Changeling Places (based on television series *Charmed*), Simon Spotlight Entertainment (New York, NY), 2005.
Ultimate Travel Games, Price, Stern, Sloan, 2006.
House of Shards (based on *Buffy the Vampire Slayer* television series), Simon Spotlight (New York, NY), 2006.
Emily Goldberg Learns to Salsa, Razorbill (New York, NY), 2006.
(With husband Noah Harlan) *Mind Your Manners, Dick and Jane,* Grosset & Dunlap (New York, NY), 2006.
Gettin' Lucky, Simon Pulse (New York, NY), 2007.
Crush du Jour, Simon Pulse (New York, NY), 2007.
Popular Vote, Scholastic, Inc. (New York, NY), 2008.
GoldenGirl ("Bradford" series), Simon Pulse (New York, NY), 2009.
Fashionista ("Bradford" series), Simon Pulse (New York, NY), 2009.
So Punk Rock (and Other Ways to Disappoint Your Mother, illustrated by brother David Ostow, Flux (Woodbury, MN), 2009.
(With Noah Harlan) *Up over down Under* ("Students across the Seven Seas" series), Speak (New York, NY), 2010.
Family, Egmont (New York, NY), 2011.

Also author (uncredited) of young-adult novels based on television series, including *Once More, with Feeling,* 2001, and *American Dreams,* and for novel series, including "Fearless" and "Camp Confidential." Contributor to anthologies, including *First Kiss (then Tell),* edited by Cylin Busby, Bloomsbury (New York, NY), 2008.

Sidelights

Micol Ostow began her writing career as an editor with a major New York publisher, but soon found her niche in writing for teens. Known for their likeable heroines and entertaining plots, Ostow's novels include *30 Guys in 30 Days, Emily Goldberg Learns to Salsa, Fashionista,* and *So Punk Rock (and Other Ways to Disappoint Your Mother.* Reviewing her teen romance *30 Guys in*

Cover of Micol Ostow's young-adult novel **Westminster Abby,** *featuring artwork by Yuko Sugimoto.*

30 Days as "tastefully written," *Kliatt* contributor Annette Wells predicted that older teens "will love this cleverly constructed novel" about a college freshman who decides to overcome her shyness by talking to a different guy each day for a month. Praising Ostow's chronicle of the adventures of a Manhattan high-school senior spending a multicultural summer in Puerto Rico, *Booklist* critic Hazel Rochman wrote that *Emily Goldberg Learns to Salsa* mixes the heroine's "fast, funny, present-tense narrative" with lighthearted romance in a tale touching on "issues of tradition, feminism, friendship, and loyalty."

After graduating from Tufts University, Ostow hired on with Simon & Schuster, where she worked as an editor. Describing her move to author as "a very organic" process in an online interview with *NYC24* contributor Catherine Shu, she explained that she started as a ghostwriter for novelizations of popular ongoing series such as *Buffy the Vampire Slayer, Charmed,* and *Fearless,* some published under house pseudonyms.

Ostow focuses on the ups and downs of teen romance in the novels in *Gettin' Lucky, Crush du Jour,* and *Popular Vote.* Las Vegas teen Cass Parker is determined to get past the fact that her best friend has linked up with handsome Jesse on the sly in *Gettin' Lucky,* and talented cook Laine finds her own romance threatened by a conniving colleague in *Crush du Jour.* Set during an election year, *Popular Vote* focuses on sixteen-year-old Erin as she goes against her father's campaign for mayor to advocate for the survival of a local landmark, even though her activism may also threaten her relationship with her political-minded boyfriend. Relieved that *Gettin' Lucky* avoids the typical plotline of "Nice Girls vs. Mean Girls," Amelia Jenkins added in *School Library Journal* that "Cass's narration sounds like a real teen without getting bogged down in trendy slang."

Ostow has made several contributions to the ongoing "Students across the Seven Seas" series, which focuses on teens visiting exotic locations. *Westminster Abby* centers around sixteen-year-old Abby, who is in London for the summer now that her parents have uncovered her lies about boyfriend James. When Abby meets up with the charming Ian the two strike up a fun relationship, at least until two-timing James appears in London, hoping to rekindle their relationship. A collaboration between Ostow and her husband, Noah Harlan, *Up over Down Under* takes readers to Melbourne, Victoria, Australia, where Eliza Ritter is hoping that an environmental education program will lead to interactions with attractive guys. Meanwhile, Green-minded Billie Echols arrives in Washington, DC, hoping to make a difference but finding controversy instead. Calling *Westminister Abby* "as much a travel book as a romance," Ilene Cooper added in *Booklist* that "Ostow does a good job of fitting all the sights, sounds, and smells into the story." Catherine Ensley, writing in *School Library Journal,* also enjoyed the novel, commenting that, while "light in conflict," *Westminister Abby* "will appeal to teens . . . whose lives are similarly sheltered and somewhat economically privileged."

The first of Ostow's "Bradford" novels, *GoldenGirl* introduces Spencer Grace Kelly, a Philadelphia teen from a wealthy family whose life revolves around best friends Madison, Regan, and Paige and boyfriend Tyler. Although Spencer and company have been secure in their top respectability ranking at Bradford Prep, things go into flux when two new students threaten to expose unpleasant aspects of Spencer and Paige's pasts. In *Fashionista* it is Madison who has secrets that she wants to keep hidden, secrets that involve a late-night tryst with Tyler and some local shoplifting. Told as a sequence of blog posts, *Fashionista* was described by *School Library Journal* critic Erin Carrillo as "a tamer alternative to the books in Cecily von Ziegesar's 'Gossip Girl' series" despite the story's references to "underage drinking, some sex (though not explicit), and mentions of drug use."

Praised by *Booklist* critic Courtney Jones as "a rollicking, witty, and ultra-contemporary book that drums on the funny bone and reverberates through the heart," *So Punk Rock (and Other Ways to Disappoint Your Mother* finds Ostow working alongside her brother, artist David Ostow. In the graphic novel, four juniors at New Jersey's Leo R. Gittleman Jewish Day School decided to pursue the quintessential teen dream and form their own rock band. Fueled by his love of ska music—and his dream of attracting the attention of the lovely Sari Horowitz—Ari Abramson connects with Yossi, Jonas, and Reena and forms The Tribe. While his parents grow increasingly concerned over his lack of concern over the upcoming SAT exams that will make or break his application to Brandeis, sixteen-year-old Ari is pulled off track by The Tribe's growing fame and internal drama. Describing *So Punk Rock (and Other Ways to Disappoint Your Mother* as "a witty study of Jewish day-school culture," Erin Carillo added in *School Library Journal* that the cartoon "doodles" contributed by David Ostow "are some of the funniest parts of the book." Ostow's "pitch-perfect dialogue pairs seamlessly with [her brother's] . . . black-and-white panels,"

Ostow teams up with her brother, illustrator David Ostow, to create the tongue-in-cheek teen advice manual So Punk Rock (and Other Ways to Disappoint Your Mother). *(Llewellyn Publications, 2009. Art © 2009 David Ostow. Reproduced by permission.)*

agreed a *Kirkus Reviews* writer, the critic citing the novel for "successfully balanc[ing Jewish] . . . culture with teen experience."

Biographical and Critical Sources

PERIODICALS

Booklist, August, 2005, Ilene Cooper, review of *Westminster Abby,* p. 2016; December 15, 2006, Hazel Rochman, review of *Emily Goldberg Learns to Salsa,* p. 43; June 1, 2009, Courtney Jones, review of *So Punk Rock (and Other Ways to Disappoint Your Mother,* p. 66.

Bulletin of the Center for Children's Books, March, 2007, Karen Coats, review of *So Punk Rock (and Other Ways to Disappoint Your Mother,* p. 305.

Kirkus Reviews, October 15, 2006, review of *Emily Goldberg Learns to Salsa,* p. 1076; June 1, 2009, review of *So Punk Rock (and Other Ways to Disappoint Your Mother.*

Kliatt, July, 2005, Annette Wells, review of *30 Guys in 30 Days,* p. 24; September, 2006, Claire Rosser, review of *Emily Goldberg Learns to Salsa,* p. 16.

School Library Journal, June, 2005, Catherine Ensley, review of *Westminster Abby,* p. 167; January, 2007, Barbara Auerbach, review of *Emily Goldberg Learns to Salsa,* p. 136; July, 2007, Amelia Jenkins, review of *Gettin' Lucky,* p. 107; September, 2009, Erin Carrillo, review of *Fashinista,* p. 169; November, 2009, Erin Carillo, review of *So Punk Rock (and Other Ways to Disappoint Your Mother,* p. 116.

Voice of Youth Advocates, December, 2006, Sherry York, review of *Emily Goldberg Learns to Salsa,* p. 430August, 2009, Geri Diorio and Lucy Freedman, review of *So Punk Rock (and Other Ways to Disappoint Your Mother,* p. 230.

ONLINE

Micol Ostow Home Page, http://www.micolostow.com (December 2, 2010).

NYC24 Web site, http://www.nyc24.org/ (April 11, 2005), Catherine Shu, interview with Ostow.*

P

PATTERSON, Valerie O.

Personal

Born in FL; married to a cartographer. *Education:* Earned law degree; Hollins University, M.F.A., 2008.

Addresses

Home—Leesburg, VA. *Agent*—Sarah Davies, Greenhouse Literary Agency, Washington, DC. *E-mail*—valopttrsn@verizon.net.

Career

Author, attorney, and educator. Works as a government attorney; teacher of political science and creative writing. Member of The Writers's Center.

Member

Society of Children's Book Writers and Illustrators, Mystery Writers of America, Sisters in Crime, Women's National Book Association, Authors Guild, Northern Virginia Writers.

Awards, Honors

Society of Children's Book Writers and Illustrators work-in-progress grant; Agatha Award nominee for Best Children/Young Adult, 2009, for *The Other Side of Blue.*

Writings

The Other Side of Blue, Clarion Books (Boston, MA), 2009.

Sidelights

In her debut novel, *The Other Side of Blue,* Valerie O. Patterson explores a teenager's complicated relationship with her mother, an artist who plans to remarry only

Valerie O. Patterson (Photograph by Anne Lord. Reproduced by permission.)

months after her husband's death. Set on the Caribbean island of Curaçao, *The Other Side of Blue* focuses on Cyan, a confused and angry fifteen year old who decides to investigate the mysterious circumstances surrounding her father's drowning. "I have long been intrigued by art, mother-daughter relationships, and the ocean," Patterson remarked in a *Children's Literature*

Comprehensive Database online interview with Emily Griffin. "The character of Cyan came to me first. Then came the mystery of the absent father. I did not have a fully developed plot before I began writing. For me it was the sound of Cyan's voice, which was so not my own, that drove me to explore the story further, to find out what happened."

The Other Side of Blue opens as Cyan and her mother return to Curaçao, their annual family vacation site, for the first time since the family tragedy. Still grieving the loss of her father, Cyan also struggles to cope with her feelings toward her picture-perfect future stepsister, thirteen-year-old Kammi, a budding artist who has also been invited to the island. Determined to learn the truth behind her father's boating accident, Cyan enters an un-likely relationship with Mayur, a manipulative neighbor boy who claims to have knowledge of the incident. *Booklist* critic Gillian Engberg offered praise for Cyan's "memorable first-person voice," and a contributor in *Kirkus Reviews* stated of *The Other Side of Blue* that Paterson's "artful writing and beautiful imagery com-bine to create a study . . . of grief." Although some re-viewers noted the leisurely pace of Patterson's work, Suzanne Gordon remarked in *School Library Journal* that, "for readers who like contemplative, realistic prob-lem books, this novel may still be a match."

"Sometimes people ask me whether I start with a char-acter or a plot idea," Patterson commented to *SATA* in discussing her writing process. "Usually, I start when a character—often with a distinctive voice from the be-ginning—enters my consciousness. Once I envisioned two girl cross-country runners meeting on a bridge, and I wrote a whole novel on how they arrived at that point. I'm interested in interactions between characters and the main character's interior life, which sometimes means I have to be careful about external plot elements and ratcheting up tension. My advice to others who are starting to write is 1) read the types of books you want to write, 2) keep writing, even if it's ten minutes a day, and 3) NEVER give up on your dream."

Biographical and Critical Sources

PERIODICALS

Booklist, October 15, 2009, Gillian Engberg, review of *The Other Side of Blue,* p. 62.
Bulletin of the Center for Children's Books, November, 2009, Deborah Stevenson, review of *The Other Side of Blue,* p. 122.
Kirkus Reviews, September 1, 2009, review of *The Other Side of Blue.*
Publishers Weekly, October 19, 2009, review of *The Other Side of Blue,* p. 55.
School Library Journal, October 19, 2009, Suzanne Gor-don, review of *The Other Side of Blue,* p. 118.
Voice of Youth Advocates, December, 2009, Ann T. Reddy-Damon, review of *The Other Side of Blue,* p. 413.

Cover of Valerie O. Patterson's young-adult novel **The Other Side of Blue,** *which focuses on a teen's attempt to cope with a parent's death.*
(Copyright © 2009 by Valerie O. Patterson. Reprinted by permission of Clarion Books, an imprint of Houghton Mifflin Harcourt Publishing Company. All rights reserved.)

ONLINE

Children's Literature Comprehensive Database, http://www.childrenslit.com/ (December 1, 2010), Emily Griffin, interview with Patterson.
Greenhouse Literary Agency Web site, http://greenhouseliterary.com/ (December 1, 2010), interview with Patterson.
Valerie O. Patterson Home Page, http://www.valerieopatterson.com (December 1, 2010).

*   *   *

PERKINS, Dan
See TOMORROW, Tom

*   *   *

PERRY, John 1967-

Personal

Born 1967; married; children: two daughters. *Educa-tion:* College degree.

Addresses

Home—Ann Arbor, MI.

Career

Author. Worked in advertising for ten years; formerly worked in advertising media sales in Detroit and Ann Arbor, MI.

Writings

The Book That Eats People, illustrated by Mark Fearing, Tricycle Press (Berkeley, CA), 2009.

Sidelights

John Perry worked for ten years in advertising, a career that gave him an edge when he came up with an idea for his first picture book. Years later, while living in Ann Arbor, Michigan, Perry became a father and decided to be the stay-at-home parent to his two daughters. Staying at home allowed his creativity full rein, and Perry was fleshing out his concept for a new television program when the idea for *The Book That Eats People* suddenly revealed itself, "in a dream," as the author later told *AnnArbor.com* writer Leah Dumouchel.

Imaginatively crafted and designed, *The Book That Eats People* is chock full of pencil doodles, drawings, photographs, newspaper clippings, and other cut-and-paste

John Perry spins a quirky story of biblio-barbarism in **The Book That Eats People,** *featuring artwork by Mark Fearing.* (Illustration copyright © 2009 by Mark Fearing. Reproduced by permission of Random House Children's Books, a division of Random House, Inc.)

ephemera, as well as colorful illustrations by Mark Fearing that help establish the book's maniacal threat. In what *School Library Journal* contributor Marge Loch-Wouters characterized as a "tale of tongue-in-cheek terror" recounted by a "breathless narrator," Perry describes the tendency for the paperbound tome to suddenly consume those who turn its pages, particularly children with sticky fingers. Rather than readers consuming its story, the book consumes readers, laying wait on a library shelf, or on a nightstand for an unsuspecting victim. Although Perry's tale ends with the offending volume safely out of circulation, readers are left holding the selfsame work in their hands, making *The Book That Eats People* perfect for "readers who love monsters and a good scare," according to Loch-Wouters. "Fearing's Photoshopped collages and cartoon illustrations have a suitably menacing aspect," noted a *Kirkus Reviews* writer, recommending the work as a gift perfect "for frenemies," and a *Publishers Weekly* critic urged of the "irresistible" story: "Read it. Carefully."

Biographical and Critical Sources

PERIODICALS

Kirkus Reviews, September 1, 2009, review of *The Book That Eats People.*
Publishers Weekly, October 12, 2009, review of *The Book That Eats People,* p. 47.
School Library Journal, November, 2009, Marge Loch-Wouters, review of *The Book That Eats People,* p. 86.

ONLINE

AnnArbor.com, http://www.annarbor.com/ (August 10, 2009), Leah DuMouchel, "A Book with Bite."*

*   *   *

PIGNATARO, Anna 1965-

Personal

Born 1965, in Australia; married; children: Isabella. *Education:* Attended art college (Melbourne, Victoria, Australia).

Addresses

Home—Melbourne, Victoria, Australia.

Career

Artist, illustrator, and graphic designer. Worked as an art teacher; muralist. *Exhibitions:* Work included in private collections in Australia and elsewhere.

Awards, Honors

Crichton Award for Children's Book Illustration, 1998, for *I'm in the Sky and I Can't Come Back* by Holly Young Huth; Picture Book of the Year shortlist, Children's Book Council of Australia (CBCA), 1999, and YABBA Children's Choice shortlist, 2000, both for *The Staircase Cat* by Colin Thompson; Notable Book designation, CBCA, 2000, for *Unknown* by Thompson, 2002, for *Waiting for Mum* by Helen Lunn, 2003, for *Little Red Bear* by Penny Matthews, 2004, for *The Great Big Animal Ask* by Libby Hathorn, 2005, for *Once upon a Time in the Kitchen* by Carol Odell, 2007, for *Stephen's Music* by Sofie Laguna, 2008, for *Brave Little Penguin,* 2009, for *Sun* by Natalie Jane Prior.

Writings

SELF-ILLUSTRATED

Always, Scholastic Australia (Gosford, New South Wales, Australia), 2006, published as *Mama, How Long Will You Love Me?,* Cartwheel Books/Scholastic (New York, NY), 2006.

The Friends of Apple Street, Lothian (South Melbourne, Victoria, Australia), 2006.

Brave Little Penguin, Scholastic Australia (Gosford, New South Wales, Australia), 2008.

Together, Scholastic Australia (Lindfield, New South Wales, Australia), 2009, published as *Mama, Will You Hold My Hand?,* Cartwheel Books (New York, NY), 2010.

Papa's Little Penguin, Scholastic Australia (Lindfield, New South Wales, Australia), 2009.

Pignataro's books have been translated into Chinese, French, Korean, Japanese, and Romanian.

SELF-ILLUSTRATED; "PRINCESS AND FAIRY" SERIES

Princess and Fairy, Scholastic Australia (Gosford, New South Wales, Australia), 2007, Alfred A. Knopf (New York, NY), 2009.

A Very Sparkly Christmas, Scholastic Australia (Gosford, New South Wales, Australia), 2008.

Most Charming Flower Girls, Scholastic Australia (Gosford, New South Wales, Australia), 2009.

Princess and Fairy, Friends Forever, Scholastic Australia (Gosford, New South Wales, Australia), 2009.

Twinkly Ballerinas, Scholastic Australia (Gosford, New South Wales, Australia), 2010.

ILLUSTRATOR

Holly Young Huth, *I'm in the Sky and I Can't Come Back,* Allen & Unwin (St. Leonards, New South Wales, Australia), 1997.

Errol Broome, *Quicksilver,* Allen & Unwin (St. Leonards, New South Wales, Australia), 1997.

Colin Thompson, *The Staircase Cat,* Hodder Headline (Sydney, New South Wales, Australia), 1998.

Gillian Rubinstein, *The Mermaid of Bondi Beach,* Hodder Children's Books (Rydalmere, New South Wales, Australia), 1999.

Colin Thompson, *Unknown,* Hodder Children's (Rydalmere, New South Wales, Australia), 1999, Walker & Co. (New York, NY), 2000.

Rachel Flynn, *Whisper Wild, Freedom Child,* Viking (Ringwood, Victoria, Australia), 2000.

Romie Claridge, *Uncle Albert's Seal,* Roland Harvey (Melbourne, Victoria, Australia), 2001.

Colin Thompson, *No Place like Home,* Hodder Headline Australia (Sydney, New South Wales, Australia), 2001.

Venero Armanno, *The Very Super Adventures of Nic and Naomi,* Lothian Books (South Melbourne, Victoria, Australia), 2002.

Anna Pignataro features the color pink in her girl-friendly picture books Princess and Fairy ***and its companions.*** (Illustration copyright © 2007 by Anna Pignataro. Reproduced by permission of Random House Children's Books, a division of Random House, Inc.)

Gael Cresp, *Fish for Breakfast,* Benchmark (Montrose, Victoria, Australia), 2002.

Ian Bone, *Dancing Night, Tonight,* Scholastic Australia (Sydney, New South Wales, Australia), 2002.

Nigel Gray, *Delightful Delilah,* Lothian (Port Melbourne, Victoria, Australia), 2002.

Helen Lunn, *Waiting for Mum,* Scholastic Australia (Linfield, New South Wales, Australia), 2002.

Esther Takac, *Loni and the Moon,* Lothian (South Melbourne, Victoria, Australia), 2003.

Phil Cummings, *The Tobbley Twins,* Lothian (South Melbourne, Victoria, Australia), 2003.

Penny Matthews, *Little Red Bear,* Scholastic Australia (Linfield, New South Wales, Australia), 2003.

Libby Hathorn, *The Great Big Animal Ask,* Lothian (South Melbourne, Victoria, Australia), 2004.

Rosanne Hawke, *The Collector,* Lothian (South Melbourne, Victoria, Australia), 2004.

Margaret Campbell, *All Dressed Up,* Lothian (South Melbourne, Victoria, Australia), 2005.

Carol Odell, *Once upon a Time in the Kitchen: Recipes and Tales from the Children's Classics,* Citrus Press (Broadway, New South Wales, Australia), 2005, published as *Once upon a Time in the Kitchen: Recipes and Tales from Classic Children's Stories,* Sleeping Bear Press (Ann Arbor, MI), 2010.

Gillian Bouras, *Aphrodite Alexandra,* Lothian (Sydney, New South Wales, Australia), 2007.

Sofie Laguna, *Stephen's Music,* Lothian (Sydney, New South Wales, Australia), 2007.

Natalie Jane Prior, *Sun* ABC Books (Sydney, New South Wales, Australia), 2008, Kane/Miller (La Jola, CA), 2009.

Natalie Jane Prior, *Star* ABC Books (Sydney, New South Wales, Australia), 2008.

Susanne Gervay, *Ships in the Field,* Ford Street Publishers, 2011.

Sidelights

While growing up, Australian illustrator and author Anna Pignataro fell in love with illustrated stories, especially the tales of Enid Blyton and the artwork of noted nineteenth-century illustrator Arthur Rackham. After graduating from art college, she spent several years traveling through Europe and elsewhere, gaining inspiration from the great works of Western art. Her detailed watercolor images have appeared in dozens of books for children, and Pignataro has also written the self-illustrated stories *Always, Together,* and *Papa's Little Penguin,* as well as a series of girl-friendly picture books about the bunny friends Princess and Fairy. In a review of her illustrations for Colin Thompson's *Unknown,* a picture book about a shy little shelter dog that ultimately saves the day, *School Library Journal* critic Holly Belli dubbed the book "charming" on the strength of Pignataro's evocative "watercolor-and-ink paintings."

Princess and Fairy is the first book in a series that includes *Most Charming Flower Girls, Princess and Fairy, Friends Forever,* and *Twinkly Ballerinas.* With its bubble-gum pink cover, *Princess and Fairy* introduces Pignataro's popular bunny characters as they make a list of what they need to attend a ball honoring the birthday of the queen of Fairyland. During the bunnies' shopping spree, Princess and Fairy become more and more bedraggled, and in her collage illustrations the author/artist conceals the sought-for objects within what a *Kirkus Reviews* writer described as "intricately detailed double-page" illustrations. Each page is edged in a decorative border that contains Pignataro's multimedia art, showcasing her use of pencil, pen, water color, and collage elements. Noting the effective pairing of "visual sophistication" and a "sunny story," a *Publishers Weekly* predicted that *Princess and Fairy* is "sure to sit on the top of the favorites pile."

Biographical and Critical Sources

PERIODICALS

Booklist, May 1, 2000, John Peters, review of *Unknown,* p. 1680.

Children's Bookwatch, July, 2010, review of *Once upon a Time in the Kitchen: Recipes and Tales from the Children's Classics.*

Kirkus Reviews, July 1, 2009, review of *Princess and Fairy;* November 1, 2009, review of *Sun.*

Publishers Weekly, September 21, 2009, review of *Princess and Fairy,* p. 55.

School Library Journal, July, 2000, Holly Belli, review of *Unknown,* p. 88.

ONLINE

Anna Pignataro Home Page, http://www.annapignataro. com (December 15, 2010).

Scholastic Web site, http://www.scholastic.com.au/ (December 15, 2010), "Anna Pignataro."*

*   *   *

POGUE, Carolyn 1948-

Personal

Born 1948, in Canada; married Bill Phipps. *Religion:* Protestant.

Addresses

Home—Calgary, Alberta, Canada. *E-mail*—info@carolynpogue.ca.

Career

Writer, editor, and workshop presenter. Art of Peace (children's art camp), Calgary, Alberta, Canada, cofounder. Writer in residence; presenter at schools, li-

braries, conferences, and religious groups. Member, Child Well-being Initiative, Raffi's Child Honouring advisory council.

Member

Writers' Union of Canada, Writers' Guild of Alberta, Young Alberta Book Society.

Awards, Honors

YMCA Peace Medal nomination, 2000, 2009; Alberta Centennial Medal, 2005, for peace writing and activism; W.O. Mitchell Calgary Book Prize shortlist, 2010, for *Gwen*.

Writings

The Weekend Parent: Learning to Live without Full-time Kids, Western Producer Prairie Books (Saskatoon, Saskatchewan, Canada), 1990.

Mother's Children; and Other Plays, Playing for Life (Edmonton, Alberta, Canada), 1992.

(Editor) *Treasury of Celebrations: Create Celebrations That Reflect Your Values and Don't Cost the Earth,* Northstone (Kelowna, British Columbia, Canada), 1996.

Language of the Heart: Rituals, Stories, and Information about Death, Northstone Publishing (Kelowna, British Columbia, Canada), 1997.

A Creation Story, illustrated by Chao Yu, ParseNip Press (Spruce Grove, Alberta, Canada), 1998.

Part-time Parent: Learning to Live without Full-time Custody, Northstone (Saskatoon, Saskatchewan, Canada), 1998.

A New Day: Peacemaking Stories and Activities, United Church Publishing House (Toronto, Ontario, Canada), 2005.

Remember Peace, illustrated by Ed Carswell, Connections (Courtney, British Columbia, Canada), 2005.

After the Beginning, illustrated by Margaret Kyle, Copperhouse (Kelowna, British Columbia, Canada), 2006.

Seasons of Peace: A Teaching Resource, foreword by Lois M. Wilson, Connections Pub. (Courtenay, British Columbia, Canada), 2007.

A World of Faith: Introducing Spiritual Traditions to Teens, Copperhouse (Kelowna, British Columbia, Canada), 2007.

Gwen, Sumach Press (Toronto, Ontario, Canada), 2009.

Contributor to *United Church Observer.*

Author's work has been translated into Chinese.

Adaptations

The Weekend Parent was adapted as a sound recording, CNIB (Toronto, Ontario, Canada), 1996.

Sidelights

"Writing for children, teens and adults is an adventure," Carolyn Pogue told *SATA.* "When a story comes to me, I need to figure out if it wants to be told in dramatic form, short story, nonfiction, or fiction. One story arrived as a musical for young people, another as a picture book, and yet another as YA nonfiction. I've also written two colouring books.

"I believe that words are so powerful they can change the world. It is fun and exciting to use word tools to help re-imagine a world I want to leave for my grandchildren—and yours!"

Biographical and Critical Sources

PERIODICALS

Canadian Review of Materials, March 19, 2010, Ruth Latta, review of *Gwen.*

Kirkus Reviews, September 1, 2009, review of *Gwen.*

ONLINE

Carolyn Pogue Home Page, http://www.carolynpogue.ca (November 21, 2010).

R

REED, Amy 1979-

Personal

Born 1979, in Seattle, WA; married. *Education:* Attended Reed College; Academy of Art University, degree (film); New College of California, M.F.A.

Addresses

Home—Oakland, CA. *E-mail*—amy_lynn_reed@yahoo.com.

Career

Writer.

Awards, Honors

Several awards for short fiction; YALSA/American Library Association Quick Picks for Reluctant Young-Adult Readers nomination, 2011, for *Beautiful.*

Amy Reed (Photograph by Erika Hart. Reproduced by permission.)

Writings

Beautiful, Simon Pulse (New York, NY), 2009.
Clean, Simon Pulse (New York, NY), 2011.

Contributor of short fiction to periodicals, including *Contrary, Fiction,* and *Kitchen Sink.*

Sidelights

Amy Reed's first novel for teens was based on "Under the Wall," a short story that the Seattle-born writer originally published in *Fiction* magazine. Released in 2009 as *Beautiful,* Reed's compelling story follows a young woman as she breaks with the rules and traditions that have guided her life, only to find herself slipping into a world that may never let her go.

Set in western Washington, where Reed grew up, *Beautiful* focuses on Cassie, a pretty thirteen year old who feels overlooked in her small home town on Bainbridge Island. When her parents relocate to a Seattle suburb, the seventh grader decides to reinvent herself and enters her new school with a new attitude that shows her willingness to do whatever it takes to fit in. Alex, a member of a popular clique of partiers, befriends Cassie, sensing the new girl's compliance, and the attention of a popular boy named Ethan makes Cassie feel special. Soon these new relationships draw the girl into a culture where unsupervised parties spring up spontaneously, last all night, and involve drinking, drugs, stealing, and sex. Only when Alex's troubled half-sister Sarah arrives and looks to Cassie for help in dealing with her abusive father does the teen realize that her lifestyle choices are not leading her to the life she really wants. In *Kirkus Reviews* a critic described *Beautiful* as "a roadmap to a dark but realistic underworld of young . . . teens drift-

Cover of Amy Reed's novel Beautiful, *in which a small-town girl is pulled into the fast-paced world of affluent urban teens.* (Simon & Schuster Children's Publishing Division, 2009. Jacket photograph © copyright 2009 by Michael Frost. Reproduced with permission of Michael Frost.)

ing from one unsavory experience to another," while a *Voice of Youth Advocates* critic praised Reed's prose as "lonely, haunting, sensuous, and oddly beautiful."

Biographical and Critical Sources

PERIODICALS

Booklist, October 15, 2009, Daniel Kraus, review of *Beautiful,* p. 58.

Bulletin of the Center for Children's Books, November, 2009, Deborah Stevenson, review of *Beautiful,* p. 125.

Kirkus Reviews, September 1, 2009, review of *Beautiful.*

School Library Journal, December, 2009, Amy S. Pattee, review of *Beautiful,* p. 130.

Voice of Youth Advocates, August, 2010, review of *Beautiful.*

ONLINE

Amy Reed Home Page, http://www.amyreedfiction.com (November 21, 2010).

REEF, Catherine 1951-

Personal

Born April 28, 1951, in New York, NY; daughter of Walter H. Preston, Jr. (an advertising executive) and Patricia Preziosi (a teacher); married John W. Reef (a photographer), March 13, 1971; children: John Stephen. *Education:* Washington State University, B.A., 1983. *Hobbies and other interests:* Reading, music, handicrafts.

Addresses

Home and office—College Park, MD.

Career

Author of books for children. *Taking Care* (health education newsletter), Reston, VA, editor, 1985-90; freelance writer, beginning 1990.

Member

Society of Children's Book Writers and Illustrators, Children's Book Guild (Washington, DC).

Awards, Honors

Joan G. Sugarman Children's Book Award, 1994-95, Notable Children's Trade Book in the Field of Social Studies selection, National Council for the Social Studies/Childrens Book Council (NCSS/CBC), and New York Public Library Books for the Teen Age selection and 100 Titles for Reading and Sharing selection, all 1996, all for *Walt Whitman;* Notable Children's Book selection, American Library Association (ALA), and New York Public Library Books for the Teen Age selection, both 1997, both for *John Steinbeck;* Society of School Librarians International Honor Book selection, and New York Public Library Books for the Teen Age selection, both 1997, both for *Black Explorers;* New York Public Library Books for the Teen Age selection, 2000, for *Africans in America;* Notable Children's Trade Book in the Field of Social Studies selection, NCSS/CBC, 2001, for *Paul Laurence Dunbar;* New York Public Library 100 Titles for Reading and Sharing selection, and Sydney Taylor Award, Association of Jewish Libraries, both 2001, and New York Public Library Books for the Teen Age selection, National Jewish Book Award finalist, and Bank Street College of Education Best Children's Books of the Year designation, all 2002, all for *Sigmund Freud;* Society of School Librarians International Honor Book designation, 2002, for *Childhood in America;* Recommended Title, American Council of Teachers of English, New York Public Library Books for the Teen Age selection, and Bank Street College of Education Best Children's Books of the Year designation, all 2003, all for *This Our Dark Country;* Kansas State Reading Circle recommendation, and Cooperative Children's Book Center Choice designation, both 2006, both for *Alone in the World;* New York Pub-

Catherine Reef (Photograph by John Reef. Reproduced by permission.)

lic Library Books for the Teen Age selection, 2007, and YALSA Best Books for Young Adults selection, 2008, both for *E.E. Cummings: A Poet's Life;* Golden Kite Honor Book designation, 2010, for *Ernest Hemingway: A Writer's Life.*

Writings

Washington, DC, Dillon Press (New York, NY), 1990.

Baltimore, Dillon Press (New York, NY), 1990.

Albert Einstein: Scientist of the Twentieth Century, Dillon Press (New York, NY), 1991.

Arlington National Cemetery, Dillon Press (New York, NY), 1991.

Monticello, Dillon Press (New York, NY), 1991.

Ellis Island, Dillon Press (New York, NY), 1991.

Rachel Carson: The Wonder of Nature, Twenty-first Century Books (New York, NY), 1992.

Henry David Thoreau: A Neighbor to Nature, Twenty-first Century Books (New York, NY), 1992.

Jacques Cousteau: Champion of the Sea, Twenty-first Century Books (New York, NY), 1992.

Gettysburg, Dillon Press (New York, NY), 1992.

Mount Vernon, Dillon Press (New York, NY), 1992.

Benjamin Davis, Jr., Twenty-first Century Books (New York, NY), 1992.

Colin Powell, Twenty-first Century Books (New York, NY), 1992.

Buffalo Soldiers, Twenty-first Century Books (New York, NY), 1993

Civil War Soldiers, Twenty-first Century Books (New York, NY), 1993.

Eat the Right Stuff: Food Facts, Twenty-first Century Books (New York, NY), 1993.

Stay Fit: Build a Strong Body, Twenty-first Century Books (New York, NY), 1993.

Think Positive: Cope with Stress, Twenty-first Century Books, 1993.

Black Fighting Men: A Proud History, Twenty-first Century Books (New York, NY), 1994.

The Lincoln Memorial, Dillon Press (New York, NY), 1994.

Ralph David Abernathy, Dillon Press (New York, NY), 1995.

The Supreme Court, Dillon Press (New York, NY), 1995.

Walt Whitman, Clarion Books (New York, NY), 1995.

John Steinbeck, Clarion Books (New York, NY), 1996.

Black Explorers, Facts on File (New York, NY), 1996.

Africans in America: The Spread of People and Culture, Facts on File (New York, NY), 1999.

Working in America: An Eyewitness History, Facts on File (New York, NY), 2000, new edition, 2007.

George Gershwin: American Composer, Morgan Reynolds (Greensboro, NC), 2000.

Paul Laurence Dunbar: Portrait of a Poet, Enslow (Berkeley Heights, NJ), 2000.

A. Philip Randolph: Union Leader and Civil Rights Crusader, Enslow (Berkeley Heights, NJ), 2001.

Sigmund Freud: Pioneer of the Mind, Clarion Books (New York, NY), 2001.

Childhood in America: An Eyewitness History, Facts on File (New York, NY), 2002.

This Our Dark Country: The American Settlers of Liberia, Clarion Books (New York, NY), 2002.

William Grant Still: African-American Composer, Morgan Reynolds (Greensboro, NC), 2003.

Alone in the World: Orphans and Orphanages in America, Clarion Books (New York, NY), 2005.

Poverty in America, Facts on File (New York, NY), 2006.

E.E. Cummings: A Poet's Life, Clarion Books (New York, NY), 2006.

Education and Learning in America, Facts on File (New York, NY), 2009.

Ernest Hemingway: A Writer's Life, Clarion Books (Boston, MA), 2009.

African Americans in the Military, Facts on File (New York, NY), 2010.

African-American Writers, Facts on File (New York, NY), 2010.

Sidelights

Catherine Reef is a nonfiction writer for children and young adults whose biographies, social histories, health books, and descriptions of famous buildings and monuments both inform and entertain their readers. Notable among her biographical subjects are the writers E.E. Cummings, Ernest Hemingway, John Steinbeck, and

Walt Whitman, the scientists Albert Einstein and Sigmund Freud, and outstanding African Americans such as former U.S. General Colin Powell and poet Paul Laurence Dunbar. Addressing the spirit of place in America, Reef has also written about such historical monuments as Monticello, Mount Vernon, and the Lincoln Memorial; focused on the nation's cultural landscape in *Education and Learning in America* and *Africans in America: The Spread of People and Culture;* and honored the African-American military contribution in *Buffalo Soldiers, Civil War Soldiers,* and *African Americans in the Military.*

Reef once commented about her childhood: "I grew up in Commack, New York, a flat, spreading Long Island town, during the 1950s and 1960s. It was a town where most people lived in clean, new split-level or ranch houses on treeless land that had been farmers' fields. My house was different. I lived in one of Commack's few old houses, a place with carved woodwork and a yard full of trees. That backyard seemed enormous, and it beckoned my friends and me to imaginative play. There was an ancient apple tree, bent-over and climber-friendly, where we acted out stories of loss and rescue. There was a sky-high pine tree from which a tire hung on a rope. We often would swing, heads leaning back and faces pointing up through the branches, and imagine that we could fly.

Cover of Reef's illustrated biography **Walt Whitman,** *featuring artwork by* **Wendell Minor.** (Illustration copyright © 1995 by Wendell Minor. Reprinted by permission of Clarion Books, an imprint of Houghton Mifflin Harcourt Publishing Company. All rights reserved.)

"Sometimes I played indoors on my bedroom floor with my dolls and stuffed animals lined up in front of me. The game was school, and it could last for hours. The dolls and toys were the pupils, and I was their teacher. If there ever was an energetic teacher, I was she! I planned lessons and lectured to my students on science and geography. I taught them to form letters and numbers, and to add and subtract. I made all of their textbooks and work sheets by hand, and I completed every assignment for everyone in my class. Then I corrected all of the work and handed it back."

Such childhood games fostered an early love of reading in Reef, as she once explained. "I read to my class, too, because I loved to read stories and poems. Literature never meant more to me than when I was a child. Dr. Seuss's books were among my early favorites, and I read them so often that I committed them to memory. I loved the poems of English fiction writer and playwright A.A. Milne and turned my favorites into songs. I delighted in the silly, unreal characters of American journalist and playwright L. Frank Baum's 'Oz' stories. Books brought scenes and characters to life in my imagination. They expressed wonder, love, humor, and sorrow. They taught me that language is a powerful tool. Words are an artist's medium. Like clay, they can be molded into something beautiful."

From a love of reading, it was a short jump to experimenting with writing. "I also wrote poems and stories of my own," Reef once remarked. "Some high-school boys I knew printed a small newspaper. How proud I was when they published one of my stories—the all-but-forgotten 'I Am a Dishwasher'! I kept on reading and writing as I got older, but I developed other interests as well. As a teenager I loved to draw with pastels, pencils, and charcoal. I acted in two school plays. I listened to music for hours at a time. I learned to knit and sew."

However, Reef was about to learn the truth of the old adage "Jack of all trades, master of none." "By the time I reached college, I had so many interests that I couldn't decide what to do—and so I did nothing," she once recalled. "I felt bored with college and left after my first classes ended. I took a job as a secretary and soon got married. Then, nearly a decade later, when I was twenty-eight years old and the mother of a young son, I decided that I wanted an education. I was finally ready to go to college. I still didn't know what to choose as a major, or main subject of study, but this time I didn't worry about it. I took classes in a variety of subjects, and I developed even more interests than I already had. I studied history, psychology, anthropology, and science. I also took courses in literature and writing, and I found that I liked writing best of all. Creating with the English language offered greater possibilities and deeper satisfaction than working with pastels or yarn or fabric. I realized, too, that my many interests stem from the fact that I love to learn—and so writing was right up my alley.

"I never became the classroom teacher that I pretended to be as a child, but I work as a teacher through my writing. For five years I wrote a newsletter about health for adults called *Taking Care.* My articles gave people information they needed to stay healthy. It was an interesting job that taught me a lot, but I wanted to do something more. When I tried writing a book for children, I liked it right away. Here was something that would enable me to keep on learning—about all kinds of subjects—for the rest of my life. By writing children's books, I could remain a teacher and share what I had learned with a very important group of readers."

Reef began her writing career with *Washington, DC,* a "brief history and description of the nation's capital with emphasis on the federal government and its buildings," as Margaret C. Howell described the book in *School Library Journal.* She followed this early portrait with other books dealing with monuments, memorials, and buildings. In *Mount Vernon,* Reef tells the story of General George Washington and his famous home. Reviewing several books in the "Places in American History" series, including *Mount Vernon, School Library Journal* critic Pamela K. Bomboy called them "attractive and informative glimpses of the past." Reviewing Reef's *Arlington National Cemetery* and *Monticello,* Susan Nemeth McCarthy noted in the same periodical that they would be useful "as supplements to encyclopedia information for reports," while Joyce Adams Burner deemed Reef's *The Lincoln Memorial* a "clearly written and well-illustrated" introduction to a famous American landmark. In other books, such as *The Supreme Court* and *Ellis Island,* Reef also blends history with architecture and even tour information to introduce young readers to some of the famous places in U.S. history.

"To me, one of the best parts of writing nonfiction is doing the necessary research," Reef once explained. "I feel lucky to spend my time gathering information on the lives and work of famous people, learning about life in years gone by, talking with scientists and historians, and traveling to historic places. Writing lets me learn in other ways as well. As I organize and evaluate the facts that I have gathered, I gain insights into human nature and my own beliefs. I better understand the time in which I live by understanding times gone by. As I write, I continue to learn about using the language. I continue to become a more competent, more creative writer."

Reef has written several biographies dealing with writers, composers, scientists, military figures, and civic leaders. An early work, *Albert Einstein: Scientist of the Twentieth Century,* was described as "a smooth and balanced integration of Einstein's life and accomplishments" by *School Library Journal* contributor Tatiana Castleton. Another twentieth-century intellectual revolutionary is presented in *Sigmund Freud: Pioneer of the Mind,* and a *Horn Book* contributor noted that here Reef "depicts a complex, brilliant, and human man"

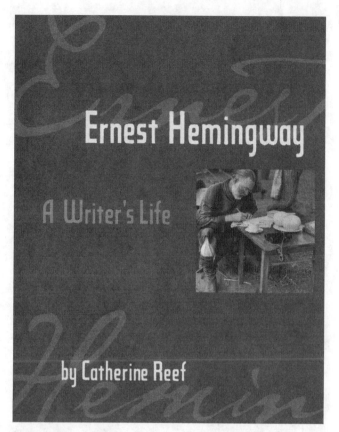

Reef introduces a new generation of readers to the life of a great twentieth-century American author in her illustrated biography Ernest Hemingway: A Writer's Life.

and "presents his seminal ideas and the objections, refinements and alternatives to them . . . [with] admirable clarity."

In *John Steinbeck* Reef chronicles the life and works of the Nobel Prize-winning author of such fiction classics as *The Grapes of Wrath* and *East of Eden.* "Reef captures the quintessential twentieth-century American writer," observed a reviewer in appraising this work for *Booklist.* A *Publishers Weekly* contributor called *John Steinbeck* a "thoughtful story" and as "nonjudgmental and upbeat as Steinbeck himself strove to be," while *Horn Book* critic Mary M. Burns dubbed it "an accessible introduction to a significant literary figure" despite the "somewhat sporadic" documentation.

Walt Whitman follows the life of the nineteenth-century bard who is best known for his verse collection *Leaves of Grass.* Burns described Reef's biography of the former U.S. poet laureate as "handsomely produced" and a "thoughtfully composed introduction to Whitman's work and life that neither sensationalizes nor diminishes the controversial aspects of his oeuvre." A writer for *Publishers Weekly* predicted that even readers already familiar with Whitman "will find much to ponder in this forthright biography."

Reef continues to examine noted U.S. literary figures in *E.E. Cummings: A Poet's Life* and *Ernest Hemingway:*

A Writer's Life, both of which focus on writers who gained renown in the early part of the twentieth century. In her discussion of the life of Massachusetts-born Edward Estlin Cummings, who turned from the poetry traditions he studied during his Harvard years to create controversial imagist and free-verse poems that often shocked the literary establishment, she "makes it clear that the king of experimental poetry was deeply grounded in the very structure he subverted," according to *Horn Book* contributor Betsy Hearne. In *School Library Journal* Elaine Fort Weischedel praised the balanced approach in Reef's well-illustrated biography, calling *E.E. Cummings* an "engaging and informative chronicle" of a "talented and unconventional artist."

A very different character is presented in *Ernest Hemingway,* as Reef sets out to introduce middle-grade students to the author of such acclaimed novels as *A Farewell to Arms, The Old Man and the Sea,* and *For Whom the Bell Tolls.* Beginning his career as a journalist, Hemingway was inspired by both his many travels and his troubled personal relationships, and the biographer discusses both his "iconic prose style" and the "connection between art and life" that underscores each of his works, according to *Horn Book* critic Jonathan Hunt. "Teens jaded by too much classroom analysis" of Hemingway's works "will come away from Reef's thorough, skillfully constructed biography with fresh interest in and appreciation for this American legend," predicted *Booklist* critic Gillian Engbert, and a *Kirkus Reviews* writer deemed *Ernest Hemingway* "a memorable portrait of the writer and his times."

Reef turns to musicians in *George Gershwin: American Composer* and *William Grant Still: African-American Composer.* Creator of the opera *Porgy and Bess* and the symphonic *Rhapsody in Blue,* among other well-known pieces, Gershwin comes alive in Reef's biography because "the writing gives a sense of [his] personality, his family, and his times," according to *Booklist* reviewer Carolyn Phelan. In her study of Still she highlights a man who overcame the setbacks of poverty and prejudice to succeed in creating his own style of classical and operatic form from traditional blues, jazz, and black folk music. Still was a composer, arranger, and director who also played several instruments, and little was written about him previous to the publication of Reef's book. In both *George Gershwin* and *William Grant Still* Reef includes sources, a list of compositions, and a bibliography.

Movers and shakers in ecology and the environment are dealt with in other biographies from Reef. *Rachel Carson: The Wonder of Nature* takes a look at the author of *Silent Spring,* who took aim at the ill-effects of the widely used pesticide DDT. In *Henry David Thoreau: A Neighbor to Nature* Reef introduces the great nineteenth-century nonconformist and writer whose *Walden* presents the classic vision of living the simple life. Reviewing both these titles in *School Library Journal,* Burner wrote that Reef's "nicely drawn and organized

biographies . . . convey their subjects' personal philosophies, politics, and actions in a highly readable manner." In *Jacques Cousteau: Champion of the Sea* Reef plumbs the depths of the man who explored the ocean's underworld using diving inventions he himself created. "The story this book begins will continue to be written by the generations to come," wrote James H. Wandersee in *Science Books and Films,* the critic noting that Cousteau "is one champion of the biosphere whom every child should learn to know."

"I have always been interested in the human side of history," Reef once commented. "I prefer to read about how people lived and thought in the past than to memorize dates or pore over accounts of battles. I try, in my books, to bring the human stories in history to life. When I write about a famous person, whether it's George Washington . . . or French oceanographer Jacques Cousteau, I try to give a complete portrait of the person. I emphasize not just his or her outstanding accomplishments, but his or her activities outside of public life as well—how the person played as a child, what he or she was like as a parent, what kinds of hobbies the person enjoyed."

Additionally, Reef has penned a number of biographies of eminent African Americans. Looking at military men, she wrote *Benjamin Davis, Jr.* and *Colin Powell.* In the latter, she traces the future secretary of state's life from his South Bronx youth to his rise to chairman of the U.S. military's Joint Chiefs of Staff in a narrative "simply phrased and clearly organized," according to a critic for *Kirkus Reviews.* In *Ralph David Abernathy* Reef's look at that civil-rights leader "fills a void," according to Kay McPherson in *School Library Journal.* In *Paul Laurence Dunbar: Portrait of a Poet* Reef profiles a black writer whose life ended early because of tuberculosis. Janet Woodward, reviewing this biography in *School Library Journal,* noted its service as an "accessible introductory biography of this African American writer," a man who ultimately influenced the works of Langston Hughes and Maya Angelou, among others.

Reef writes more broadly about African Americans in several of her books. In *Civil War Soldiers* and *Buffalo Soldiers* she details the military contributions of black soldiers during and after the U.S. Civil War, while in *Black Fighting Men* she gives an overview of African Americans in the military. Reviewing *Civil War Soldiers* and *Buffalo Soldiers* in *School Library Journal,* David A. Lindsey noted that these "concise works," written in "clear, interest-holding prose . . . bring to life two little-known aspects of American history." *Booklist* contributor Janice Del Negro called the same two titles "engagingly written."

In *Black Fighting Men* Reef chronicles the acts of fourteen black soldiers in the major conflicts the United States has fought, from the American Revolution to the Gulf War. "Reef's appreciation for her subjects comes through loud and clear," wrote a critic for *Kirkus Re-*

views. *African Americans in the Military* contains alphabetically arranged entries profiling more than 125 men and women of color who served during wartime, including nurses, soldiers, and chaplains. Reef includes their biographies and a bibliography and Web sites for further reading.

Sociology is the focus of several books by Reef, among them *Alone in the World: Orphans and Orphanages in America, Africans in America, Poverty in America,* and *Working in America.* Blending general history with individual accounts, *Africans in America* follows the history of Africans in America from the slave trade through emancipation and northern migration to the present. In *Poverty in America,* which *School Library Journal* contributor Linda Greengrass described as a "valuable resource," Reef tracks the causes and effects of both absolute and relative poverty as it has existed in the United States both in rural farming communities and mining areas and industrialized cities. *Africans in America* is "written with clarity and depth," according to *Booklist* critic Hazel Rochman, the critic recommending Reef's account as an "excellent account of the 'African diaspora.'"

In *Alone in the World,* which was described as "exhaustively detailed" by *Horn Book* contributor Ed Sullivan, Reef provides a history of the changing attitudes toward the treatment of orphaned children in the United States. She begins in 1729 with the founding of the first orphans' home in New Orleans and notes that children often lived in filthy crowded institutions and almshouses, where they sometimes shared quarters with criminals and the mentally ill. During the century that followed attention was paid to providing safer and more appropriate refuge. Homes for the children of soldiers who died in the U.S. Civil War were opened, and in 1909 a White House conference concluded that widowed and deserted mothers should be given support so that the children could remain with them. Reef concludes with a discussion of contemporary problems that exist in the United States as a result of the increasing numbers of neglected, abused, and homeless children. Included are archival photographs and prints. Sullivan concluded by writing that *Alone in the World* "offers a perceptive look at American society's evolving views of childhood."

"I like to think about the many young people I've never met who will gain knowledge and pleasure from my books," Reef once remarked. "But I also write for another person: the girl who climbed the crooked apple tree and read out loud to her dolls. I get to know her better as I think about what she would like to read; at the same time, I get a deeper understanding of the woman I am today."

Biographical and Critical Sources

PERIODICALS

Booklist, August, 1993, Janice Del Negro, reviews of *Buffalo Soldiers* and *Civil War Soldiers,* both p. 2056; April 1, 1997, review of *John Steinbeck,* p. 1305; February 15, 1999, Hazel Rochman, review of *Africans in America: The Spread of People and Culture,* p. 1058; February 15, 2000, Carolyn Phelan, review of *George Gershwin: American Composer,* p. 1110; July, 2004, review of *African Americans in the Military,* p. 1860; November 15, 2006, Gillian Engberg, review of *E.E. Cummings: A Poet's Life,* p. 44; June 1, 2009, Gillian Engberg, review of *Ernest Hemingway: A Writer's Life,* p. 82.

Horn Book, September-October, 1995, Mary M. Burns, review of *Walt Whitman,* pp. 622-623; September-October, 1996, Mary M. Burns, review of *John Steinbeck,* p. 624; July-August, 2001, review of *Sigmund Freud: Pioneer of the Mind,* p. 475; July, 2003, Carolyn Phelan, review of *William Grant Still: African-American Composer,* p. 1880; July-August, 2005, Ed Sullivan, review of *Alone in the World: Orphans and Orphanages in America,* p. 489; November-December, 2006, Betsy Hearne, review of *E.E. Cummings,* p. 736; September-October, 2009, Jonathan Hunt, review of *Ernest Hemingway,* p. 583.

Kirkus Reviews, July 1, 1992, review of *Colin Powell,* p. 854; May 15, 1994, review of *Black Fighting Men,* p. 705; October 15, 2006, review of *E.E. Cummings,* p. 1078; June 1, 2009, review of *Ernest Hemingway.*

Kliatt, September, 2004, Anthony Pucci, review of *John Steinbeck,* p. 42.

Library Journal, June 15, 2007, Katherine Mossman, review of *Poverty in America,* p. 100.

New York Times Book Review, August 12, 2001, Patricia McCormick, review of *Sigmund Freud.*

Publishers Weekly, May 8, 1995, review of *Walt Whitman,* p. 298; May 6, 1996, review of *John Steinbeck,* p. 82.

School Library Journal, April, 1990, Margaret C. Howell, review of *Washington, DC,* p. 137; December, 1991, Tatiana Castleton, review of *Albert Einstein: Scientist of the Twentieth Century,* p. 127; March, 1992, Susan Nemeth McCarthy, reviews of *Arlington National Cemetery* and *Monticello,* both p. 250; May, 1992, Joyce Adams Burner, reviews of *Henry David Thoreau: A Neighbor to Nature* and *Rachel Carson: The Wonder of Nature,* both p. 126; August, 1992, Pamela K. Bomboy, review of *Mount Vernon,* pp. 171-172; August, 1993, David A. Lindsey, reviews of *Buffalo Soldiers* and *Civil War Soldiers,* both p. 201; August, 1994, Joyce Adams Burner, review of *The Lincoln Memorial,* p. 166; October, 1995, Kay McPherson, review of *Ralph David Abernathy,* p. 150; September, 2000, Janet Woodward, review of *Paul Laurence Dunbar: Portrait of a Poet,* p. 254; September, 2003, Carol Jones Collins, review of *William Grant Still,* p. 236; June, 2005, Ginny Gustin, review of *Alone in the World,* p. 186; March, 2007, Elaine Fort Weischedel, review of *E.E. Cummings,* p. 234; August, 2007, Linda Greengrass, review of *Poverty in America,* p. 72; August, 2009, Vicki Reutter, review of *Ernest Hemingway,* p. 126.

Science Books and Films, August-September, 1992, James H. Wandersee, review of *Jacques Cousteau: Champion of the Sea,* p. 173.

ONLINE

Catherine Reef Home Page, http://catherinereef.com (December 15, 2010).
Children's Book Guild of Washington, DC Web site, http://www.childrensbookguild.org/ (December 15, 2010), "Catherine Reef."*

*   *   *

RIDDLE, Tohby 1965-

Personal

Born May 31, 1965, in Sydney, New South Wales, Australia; son of Edgerton Harold (an engineer) and Jasmine (a psychologist) Riddle; married; children: two daughters, one son. *Education:* Sydney College of the Arts, B.A. (visual arts), 1985; Sydney University, bachelor's degree (architectural science), 1991.

Addresses

Office—P.O. Box 275, Katoomba, New South Wales 2789, Australia. *Agent*—Fiona Inglis, Curtis Brown Australia, P.O. Box 19, Level 1, 2 Boundary St., Paddington NSW 2021 Australia; Jill Grinberg, Jill Grinberg Literary Management, 244 5th Ave., Fl. 11, New York NY 10001. *E-mail*—admin@tohby.com.

Career

Author and illustrator. Freelance cartoonist and illustrator, 1986—; writer and illustrator of picture books, 1988—. Former editor of *School* magazine.

Awards, Honors

May Gibbs fellowship, 2002; Picture Book of the Year, Children's Book Council of Australia (CBCA), 1997, and Ena Noël Award, International Board on Books for Young People, 2000, both for *The Tip at the End of the Street;* CBCA Picture Book of the Year shortlist, 1998, and New South Wales Premier's Literary Award shortlist, 1999, both for *The Great Escape from City Zoo;* Best Designed Children's Picture Book Highly Commended citation, Australian Publishers Association Design Awards, 2000, CBCA Picture Book of the Year Honor Book designation, and Environment Award, Wilderness Society of Australia, both 2001, all for *The Singing Hat;* Best Designed Illustrated Book Highly Commended citation, Australian Publishers Association Design Awards, 2003, for *What's the Big Idea?;* CBCA Picture Book of the Year shortlist, and Queensland Premier's Literary Award shortlist, both 2006, both for *Irving the Magician;* Patricia Wrightson Prize for Children's Literature, and Eve Pownall Award for Information Books Honor Book designation, CBCA, both 2009, and Best Designed Children's Nonfiction Book Highly Commended citation, Australian Publishers Association Design Awards, all for *The Word Spy* by

Tohby Riddle (Photograph by Michael Small. Reproduced by permission.)

Ursula Dubosarsky; Patricia Wrightson Prize shortlist, Western Australia Premier's Literary Awards shortlist, CBCA Picture Book of the Year shortlist, and CJ Picture Book Award finalist, all 2009, and Best Designed Children's Picture Book citation, Australian Publishers Association Book Design Awards, all for *Nobody Owns the Moon.*

Writings

SELF-ILLUSTRATED

Careful with That Ball, Eugene!, Pan Books (Sydney, New South Wales, Australia), 1989, Orchard (New York, NY), 1991.
A Most Unusual Dog, Macmillan (South Melbourne, Victoria, Australia), 1992, Gareth Stevens (Milwaukee, WI), 1994.
Arnold Z. Jones Could Really Play the Trumpet, Hodder & Stoughton (Sydney, New South Wales, Australia), 1993.
The Royal Guest, Hodder & Stoughton (Sydney, New South Wales, Australia), 1993.
Fifty Fairies You Ought to Know About, Angus & Robertson (Pymble, New South Wales, Australia), 1995.
The Tip at the End of the Street, Angus & Robertson (Pymble, New South Wales, Australia), 1996.
Captain James Cook: The Adventures of the Endeavour, Weldon Kids (Warriewood, New South Wales, Australia), 1996.

The Great Escape from City Zoo, HarperCollins (Pymble, New South Wales, Australia), 1997, Farrar, Straus (New York, NY), 1999.

The Singing Hat, Penguin Australia (Ringwood, Victoria, Australia), 2000, Farrar, Straus (New York, NY), 2001.

What's the Big Idea? (cartoon collection), Penguin Australia (Camberwell, Victoria, Australia), 2003.

Irving the Magician, Penguin Australia (Camberwell, Victoria, Australia), 2005.

Dog and Bird See the Moon, Penguin Australia (Camberwell, Victoria, Australia), 2007.

Pink Freud (cartoon collection), Penguin Australia (Camberwell, Victoria, Australia), 2007.

Nobody Owns the Moon, Penguin Australia (Camberwell, Victoria, Australia), 2008.

Dog and Bird Water the Garden, Penguin Australia (Camberwell, Victoria, Australia), 2009.

Dog and Bird Follow a Butterfly, Penguin Australia (Camberwell, Victoria, Australia), 2009.

Dog and Bird and the Caterpillar, Penguin Australia (Camberwell, Victoria, Australia), 2010.

My Uncle's Donkey, Penguin Australia (Camberwell, Victoria, Australia), 2010.

Contributor of cartoons to periodicals, including *Sydney Morning Herald*'s *Good Weekend* magazine.

ILLUSTRATOR

Leonie Young and Avril Janks, *Ansett Explorer B: Explore Australia with Ansett,* Weldon Kids (Willoughby, New South Wales, Australia). 1989

Leonie Young and Avril Janks, *I Wish I'd Sailed with Captain Cook,* Weldon Kids (Willoughby, New South Wales, Australia), 1993.

Leonie Young and Avril Janks, *I Wish I'd Flown the Atlantic with Amelia Earhart,* Weldon Kids (Sydney, New South Wales, Australia), 1994.

Leonie Young and Avril Janks, *Amelia Earhart: Alone across the Ocean,* Weldon Kids (Warriewood, New South Wales, Australia), 1996.

June Loves, *My Guardian Angel,* HarperCollins (Pymble, New South Wales, Australia), 1997.

Margaret Wild, *Pat the Cat and Sailor Sam,* SOLO Books (Norwood, South Australia, Australia), 2003.

Ursula Dubosarsky, *The Word Spy,* Penguin Australia (Camberwell, Victoria, Australia), 2008, published as *The Word Snoop,* Dial Books (New York, NY), 2009.

Ursula Dubosarsky, *The Return of the Word Spy,* Penguin Australia (Camberwell, Victoria, Australia), 2010.

OTHER

(Adapter, with Michael Verde) *Caught in a Trap: Boggled* (novelization of animated television series *Li'l Elvis Jones and the Truckstoppers*), illustrated by Peter Viska, HarperCollins (Pymble, New South Wales, Australia), 1998.

(Adapter) *Little Memphis PTD; and, Wandering Star* (novelization of animated television series *Li'l Elvis Jones and the Truckstoppers*), HarperCollins (Pymble, New South Wales, Australia), 1998.

The Lucky Ones (young-adult novel), Penguin Books (Camberwell, Victoria, Australia), 2009.

Sidelights

Trained as an architect, Australian cartoonist Tohby Riddle has created self-illustrated picture books, provided artwork for stories by other authors, penned a highly regarded young-adult novel, and even served as the editor of a children's magazine. As Riddle noted in a *Reading Time* essay, much of his success in these varied endeavors is that, "whatever the project is, I'm simply preoccupied with making an idea work in whatever medium and format suits that idea (and rarely with an audience in mind). To that end, I find there are universal principles—usually pertaining to beauty that are applied to any of these endeavours. Principles such as rhythm, timing, harmony and proportion—whether to do with the words or the pictures."

Although his works often feature silly plots that appeal to a young child's sense of humor, Riddle also weaves in themes and cultural references designed to resonate with adults. In fact, Herborn reported, "One of his goals is to create books that can be a shared experience for both children and the adults who read to them." *The Great Escape from City Zoo,* for example, combines a kid-friendly plot about a flamingo, elephant, anteater, and turtle trying to hide out in the big city with adult-oriented visual references to black-and-white jail-break movies set during the 1920s, when this still-famous zoo-break supposedly occurred. After going "over the wall," the animals don the uniforms of various human professions—including a sailor and a chef—and try to "blend in" while walking around town and enjoying such typical human activities as watching a movie and going to a museum.

Riddle's cartoon-style graphic art captures the exuberance of his picture-book story in **The Singing Hat.** (Copyright © 2000 by Tohby Riddle. Reproduced by permission of Farrar, Straus & Giroux, a division of Farrar, Straus & Giroux, LLC.)

"Much of the humor of the book comes from the contrast between the deadpan narrative and the pictures," wrote *Booklist* critic Susan Dove Lempke, in a review of *The Great Escape from City Zoo.* There is also humor in the visual references to Roaring Twenties pop culture: when the four animals go to a movie, King Kong is on the screen; the museum they visit features works by Surrealist painters Giorgio de Chirico and René Magritte. Eventually, three of the four are recaptured and returned to the zoo, but the flamingo remains free. The final pages, which feature "unconfirmed sightings" of the flamingo, "will likely prompt laughter across the board," a critic predicted in *Publishers Weekly:* instead of the actual flamingo, Riddle's pictures feature the ubiquitous plastic flamingo lawn ornament, the sign on top of a Flamingo casino, and something that appears to be the Loch Ness monster.

The Singing Hat has a more serious message than *The Great Escape from the City Zoo,* but Riddle still makes the most of incongruous situations in his story's illustrations. A single father named Colin Jenkins falls asleep under a tree and awakens to find that a bird has built a nest and laid an egg atop his head. "It's an absurd situation that appeals to the pre-school mind," Lucy Clark wrote in the *Daily Telegraph,* but the message of the book is very sophisticated. At his daughter's urging, Mr. Jenkins allows the bird to stay, but this decision has an ever-increasing impact on his life. He loses his job and some of his friends, and then he and his daughter are forced to move. Despite these setbacks, Mr. Jenkins also discovers a great satisfaction in helping the endangered bird survive. *The Singing Hat* appeals to a diverse audience, offering language somewhat above the level of the typical picture book, both in vocabulary (Mr. Jenkins' situation is described as a "conundrum") and in syntax. Some of the visual gags might also go over the heads of young readers: for example, Mr. Jenkins' boss's dialogue consists of word balloons full of stock quotes. Nonetheless, *School Library Journal* critic Jeanne Clancy Watkins predicted that Riddle's book will be "a great discussion starter for thoughtful readers."

In *My Uncle's Donkey,* another self-illustrated tale, Riddle draws humor from an absurdly fascinating living arrangement. In the work, a young narrator describes the antics of his uncle's unusual housemate, a most amiable donkey who enjoys playing the piano, reading the newspaper, and cartwheeling across the living room floor. Tali Lavi in *Magpies* commented that the narrative "serves mostly as a comic counterpoint to the illustrations which are populated with whimsy, cultural references, and complexity," and Meg Sorensen maintained in the *Sydney Morning Herald* that the work "leaves the reader with an intriguing question and the seductive scent of a world where cohabiting with a donkey whose socks coordinate with your bathrobe seems a thoroughly sensible thing to do." In the words of *Reading Time* contributor Lynne Babbage, with *My Uncle's Donkey* "Riddle has created another funny, entertaining yet meaningful book."

Riddle has also contributed the illustrations to works by other writers, including *The Word Spy* by Ursula Dubosarsky. Published in the United States as *The Word Snoop,* the work offers a playful look at the history of the English language, discussing such topics as the evolution of the alphabet, palindromes and onomatopoeia, and the origins of knock-knock jokes. "Riddle's cartoons provide humorous flourishes as well as drive home certain points," a critic stated in *Publishers Weekly* and a *Kirkus Reviews* contributor noted that the illustrations "enhance the playful nature of this thoroughly engaging, well-crafted primer." Dubosarsky has also released a companion volume, *The Return of the Word Spy,* which focuses on grammar. "Providing a great support are illustrations by Tohby Riddle, which, like Dubosarsky's writing, are humorous, remarkably concise and informative," Angie Schiavone observed of the work in the *Sydney Morning Herald.*

In addition to his books for younger readers, Riddle has also released a young-adult novel titled *The Lucky Ones.* Set in the 1980s in Sydney, Australia, *The Lucky Ones* explores the relationship between Tom, a sensitive and philosophical art student, and Tom's best friend Cain, a maverick whose impulsive behavior leads to trouble. "With language and imagery both beautiful and deceptively simple," Meredith Capp noted in *Reading Time,* "Riddle has created a novel that evolves slowly, quietly." According to Schiavone, "There are shades of Jack Kerouac's *On The Road,* perhaps because of the characters' casual drifting through life, their apathetic recklessness and love of poetry and rock'n'roll, and the way all this affects the pace and tone of the story. There's a strong sense, too, that the story is real: a guide to Riddle as a teenager. But ultimately the impression of veracity is simply a result of truly evocative writing."

"From an early age, I was encouraged to draw," Riddle once told SATA. "In the sunniest room in the house, I would sit on the floor where my mother would provide me with reams of butcher's paper and a box of crayons. Then I would claim, crayon in hand, that the next drawing would be a masterpiece. Very soon I learned that masterpieces don't come so easily, but although the crayon in my hand is now a pen, I continue to try.

"I was schooled until the age of eleven at a Rudolf Steiner school where . . . painting, drawing, and other forms of creativity were actively encouraged. This entailed illustrating everything you learned from mythology to mathematics. I suppose the idea was to stimulate both the left and the right hemispheres of the brain during learning.

"Later, I studied painting at Sydney College of the Arts. I enjoyed painting, but as a medium to communicate ideas I began to wonder if it could compete in the face of such media as television, film, magazines, and books. I felt painting was tending to reach an increasingly smaller audience in contemporary culture and wondered

Riddle's illustration projects include creating the amusing art found in Ursula Dubosarsky's book **The Word Snoop.** (Illustration copyright © 2008 by Tohby Riddle. Reproduced with permission of Dial Books, a member of the Penguin Group (USA) Inc.)

about my options. I think I was also too lazy to make stretchers for my canvases. After graduating from art college, I found myself moving toward the immediacy and accessibility of illustrating and decided that a picture book would be the ideal vehicle for an illustrator. As an unknown, I figured that the best opportunity to illustrate a picture book would be to write the story as well. So far this has worked for me, and since I tend to conceive picture-book ideas in words and pictures simultaneously (which I find creates special opportunities for the relationship between image and text), I can now think of no better way of working.

"My concerns as a picture-book creator are based on the premise that one can never overestimate the natural intelligence of children. I target this intelligence with ideas that I hope neither patronize nor moralize, but stimulate the child's mind."

Biographical and Critical Sources

PERIODICALS

Advertiser (Adelaide, South Australia, Australia), August 16, 1997, review of *The Great Escape from City Zoo*, p. A19.

Booklist, January 1, 2000, Susan Dove Lempke, review of *The Great Escape from City Zoo*, p. 937; February 15, 2001, Ilene Cooper, review of *The Singing Hat*, p. 1141; May 15, 2010, Hazel Rochman, review of *Basil's Birds*, p. 42.

Courier-Mail (Brisbane, Queensland, Australia), June 21, 1997, review of *The Great Escape from City Zoo*, p. 8; August 15, 1998, review of *The Great Escape from City Zoo*, p. 8; August 11, 2001, Cindy Lord, review of *The Singing Hat*, p. M06.

Daily Telegraph (Surry Hills, New South Wales, Australia), November 11, 2000, Lucy Clark, review of *The Singing Hat*, p. G10.

Horn Book, July-August, 1991, Lolly Robinson, review of *Careful with That Ball, Eugene!*, p. 450; September-October, 2009, Jonathan Hunt, review of *The Word Snoop*, p. 580.

Kirkus Reviews, June 15, 2009, review of *The Word Snoop*.

Magpies, May, 2009, Kevin Steinberger, review of *The Lucky Ones;* September, 2009, James Rory, "Know the Author/Illustrator: Tohby Riddle," p. 8; September, 2010, Tali Lavi, review of *My Uncle's Donkey*.

New York Times Book Review, May 20, 2001, Jane Margolies, review of *The Singing Hat*, p. 29.

Publishers Weekly, January 11, 1991, review of *Careful with That Ball, Eugene!*, p. 100; September 20, 1999, review of *The Great Escape from City Zoo*, p. 87; February 19, 2001, review of *The Singing Hat*, p. 89; July 6, 2009, review of *The Word Snoop*, p. 53.

Reading Time, August, 2009, Meredith Capp, review of *The Lucky Ones*, p. 39; November, 2009, Tohby Riddle, "Writing for Everyone," p. 9; February, 2010, Kaye Throssell, reviews of *Dog and Bird Water the Garden* and *Dog and Bird Follow a Butterfly*, both p. 17; November, 2010, Lynne Babbage, review of *The Lucky Ones*, p. 26.

School Library Journal, May, 1991, JoAnn Rees, review of *Careful with That Ball, Eugene!*, p. 83; July, 2001, Jeanne Clancy Watkins, review of *The Singing Hat*, p. 87; September, 2009, Geri Diorio, review of *The Word Snoop*, p. 180.

Sydney Morning Herald (Sydney, New South Wales, Australia), October 19, 2008, Daniel Herborn, "Attic Dreaming," p. 12; May 2, 2009, Angie Schiavone, review of *The Lucky Ones*, p. 32; June 26, 2010, Angie Schiavone, review of *Return of the Word Spy*, p. 41; October 19, 2010, Meg Sorensen, review of *My Uncle's Donkey*.

ONLINE

Penguin Australia Web site, http://www.penguin.com.au/ (December 1, 2010), "Tohby Riddle."

Tohby Riddle Home Page, http://www.tohby.com (December 1, 2010).*

*   *   *

ROBERTS, Ken 1946-

Personal

Born 1946, in CA; dual U.S./Canadian citizen; married Jo-Anne Westerby; children: four. *Education:* University of California, Los Angeles, bachelor's degree; McMaster University. M.A.; University of Western Ontario, M.A.

Addresses

Home—Brantford, Ontario, Canada. *Office*—Hamilton Public Library, 55 York Blvd., Hamilton, Ontario L8N 4E4, Canada. *E-mail*—robetshpl@me.com.

Ken Roberts (Reproduced by permission.)

Career

Librarian, author, and educator. Hamilton Public Library, Hamilton, Ontario, Canada, chief librarian until 2011. Has taught at University of British Columbia, Simon Fraser University, and University of Lethbridge. Storyteller-in-residence for Vancouver School Board, Vancouver, British Columbia, Canada.

Awards, Honors

CanPro award for television writing; Christie Book Award finalist; Canadian Children's Book of the Year finalist; Governor General's Award for Children's Literature shortlist, 1994, for *Past Tense;* Outstanding Service Award, Canadian Public Library Association, 2001; President's Award for Exceptional Achievement for Hamilton Public Library System, Ontario Library Association, 2002.

Writings

FICTION

Crazy Ideas, Groundwood Books (Vancouver, British Columbia, Canada), 1984.

Pop Bottles, Douglas & McIntyre (Vancouver, British Columbia, Canada), 1987.

Hiccup Champion of the World, Douglas & McIntyre (Vancouver, British Columbia, Canada), 1988.

(With Loretta Castellarin) *Spike,* J. Lorimer (Toronto, Ontario, Canada), 1988, published as *Degrassi Junior High: Spike,* 2006.

(With Loretta Castellarin) *Stephanie Kaye,* J. Lorimer (Toronto, Ontario, Canada), 1988, published as *Degrassi Junior High: Stephanie Kaye,* 2006.

Nothing Wright, Groundwood Books (Toronto, Ontario, Canada), 1991.

Past Tense, Douglas & McIntyre (Toronto, Ontario, Canada), 1994.

Also co-author of *Suspect,* a comedic play for adults.

"THUMB" SERIES

The Thumb in the Box, illustrated by Leanne Franson, Douglas & McIntyre (Toronto, Ontario, Canada), 2001.

Thumb on a Diamond, illustrated by Leanne Franson, Groundwood Books (Toronto, Ontario, Canada), 2006.

Ken Roberts, *Thumb and the Bad Guys,* illustrated by Leanne Franson, Groundwood Books (Toronto, Ontario, Canada), 2009.

NONFICTION

Exploring Altona with Rachel, photographs by Chuck Heath, Douglas & McIntyre (Vancouver, British Columbia, Canada), 1986.

Exploring Vancouver with Francisco, photographs by Chuck Heath, Douglas & McIntyre (Vancouver, British Columbia, Canada), 1986.

Exploring Red Deer with Paula, photographs by Chuck Heath, Douglas & McIntyre (Vancouver, British Columbia, Canada), 1986.

Exploring Regina with Jarrod, photographs by Chuck Heath, Douglas & McIntyre (Vancouver, British Columbia, Canada), 1986.

Exploring Kentville with Billy, photographs by Chuck Heath, Douglas & McIntyre (Vancouver, British Columbia, Canada), 1986.

Freedom within Boundaries: A Scrapbook of Ideas for Fostering Story Creation Skills in Young People, Vancouver School Board (Vancouver, British Columbia, Canada), 1987.

Pre-school Storytimes, Canadian Library Association (Ottawa, Quebec, Canada), 1987.

Jacques Cartier, Grolier (Toronto, Ontario, Canada), 1988.

Sidelights

An award-winning librarian, writer, and educator, Ken Roberts is the author of the "Thumb" middle-grade novel series, which follows the humorous goings-on in the small, remote Canadian fishing village of New Auckland, British Columbia. "The village in the 'Thumb' books is the star of the series," Roberts told *Horn Book* interviewer Roger Sutton. "The unique setting gives me the chance to tilt the world just a little bit so I can follow the effect."

Roberts began his literary career in 1984 with the publication of *Crazy Ideas,* which drew comparisons to the works of popular Canadian young-adult author Gordon Korman. *Crazy Ideas* follows the efforts of Christine, a junior in high school, to promote her wacky invention, a do-it-yourself demolition kit. The success of Christine's project creates a problem for Mr. Hopman, the owner of a lucrative demolition company who wants his business to remain profitable. According to Nancy E. Black in the *Canadian Review of Materials,* readers "will surely appreciate the humour involved in the creation of crazy ideas."

Set in Vancouver, British Columbia, during the Great Depression of the 1930s, Roberts's novel *Pop Bottles* concerns twelve-year-old Will, who discovers a treasure trove of glass bottles—worth two cents apiece—buried in his front yard. When a local bully tries to pilfer some of the bottles, Will challenges him to a paddleball competition. Jo Anna Burns Patton, writing in the *Canadian Review of Materials,* offered praise for the author, citing *Pop Bottles* as "another example of [Roberts'] . . . excellent storytelling skill and his ability to create characters who come alive for young readers."

A jinxed fifth grader is the unlucky protagonist of *Nothing Wright.* Trouble seems to follow Noel "Nothing" Wright everywhere he goes: alarm clocks fail to ring in his presence, and drivers are sure to encounter a series of red lights when Noel comes along for a ride. The youngster's streak of bad luck intrigues classmate Emma, who decides to study Noel in hopes of finding a solution to his dilemma. Dave Jenkinson applauded the work in the *Canadian Review of Materials,* calling it "fast-paced, light, humorous reading."

With *The Thumb in the Box* Roberts introduces readers to his fictional Canadian town. Narrated by Leon "Thumb" Mazzei, a resident of New Auckland, the novel centers on the villagers' reactions to some surprising news: they will soon receive a new fire truck from the Canadian government, a most unusual gift for a town without roads. The author's "extensive experience shows in his prose style, which has touches of extravagance but is knit together by a strong sense of control," as Bridget Donald remarked in a review of the novel for *Quill & Quire.* In *Booklist* Helen Rosenberg predicted that the "humor and insight" of *The Thumb in the Box* "will appeal even to the most reluctant readers."

In *Thumb on a Diamond,* the second work in the series, Leon and friend Susan help a group of their classmates earn a trip to the city of Vancouver by fielding a baseball team, even though none of them have ever played the game. "The country-mice-in-the-city theme is very funny," Sutton remarked in his *Horn Book* review of *Thumb on a Diamond,* and Maria B. Salvadore wrote in *School Library Journal* that the "characters are appealing and the plot unfolds naturally to create a satisfying and plausible story."

Bored with the dull pace of life in New Auckland and influenced by a host of detective films, Leon decides to ferret out a mystery in *Thumb and the Bad Guys.* When a series of bizarre events occur in town, Leon and Susan cast suspicion on Ms. Weatherly, a new teacher who wears a wig and excessive make-up, and Kirk McKenna, a fisherman known for his spitting prowess. Writing in *School Library Journal,* Michele Shaw complimented the "blend of creepiness, mystery, and humor," and Sutton maintained that both Roberts and his energetic protagonist "are adept at creating adventure from the slimmest of means."

Cover of Ken Roberts' middle-grade novel Thumb and the Bad Guys, *featuring illustrations by Leanne R. Franson.* (Copyright © 2009 by Ken Roberts. Reprinted with permission of Groundwood Books, Ltd., www.groundwoodbooks.com.)

Biographical and Critical Sources

PERIODICALS

Booklist, October 15, 2001, Helen Rosenberg, review of *The Thumb in the Box,* p. 392; June 1, 2006, Carolyn Phelan, review of *Thumb on a Diamond,* p. 72.

Canadian Review of Materials, January, 1985, Nancy E. Black, review of *Crazy Ideas;* November, 1987, Jo Anna Burns Patton, review of *Pop Bottles;* March, 1992, Dave Jenkinson, review of *Nothing Wright;* March 17, 2006, Shelly Tyler, review of *The Thumb in the Box;* June 9, 2006, Shelly Tyler, review of *Thumb on a Diamond.*

Horn Book, September, 2001, Martha V. Parravano, review of *The Thumb in the Box,* p. 593; May-June, 2006, Roger Sutton, review of *Thumb on a Diamond,* p. 327; September-October, 2009, Roger Sutton, review of *Thumb and the Bad Guys,* p. 575.

Kirkus Reviews, July 1, 2009, review of *Thumb and the Bad Guys.*

Quill & Quire, May, 2001, Bridget Donald, review of *The Thumb in the Box.*

Resource Links, October, 2001, Johal Jinder, review of *The Thumb in the Box,* p. 19; February, 2010, Carolyn Cutt, review of *Thumb and the Bad Guys,* p. 11.

School Library Journal, August, 2006, Maria B. Salvadore, review of *Thumb on a Diamond,* p. 128; October, 2009, Michele Shaw, review of *Thumb and the Bad Guys,* p. 102.

ONLINE

MyHamilton Web site, http://www.myhamilton.ca/ (December 1, 2010), "Ken Roberts."

Horn Book Online, http://www.hbook.com/ (August, 2009), Roger Sutton, interview with Roberts.

*   *   *

RUBEL, David 1961-

Personal

Born 1961; married; wife's name Julia; children: one son, one daughter. *Education:* Columbia University, degree, 1983. *Hobbies and other interests:* Cooking.

Addresses

Home—Chatham, NY. *E-mail*—david@davidrubel.net.

Career

Historian, author, publisher, and speaker. Pacific News Service, correspondent, c. mid-1980s; HarperCollins (publisher), New York, NY, former assistant editor; freelance writer beginning c. 1989; Agincourt Press, Chatham, NY, president, editor, and publisher, beginning 1990. Host of "What's for Dinner?" (biweekly radio program), Northeast Public Radio, 2002-07. Speaker at numerous schools and institution, including at National Archives, Washington, DC.

Member

American Book Producers Association (president, 1994-96).

Writings

NONFICTION

Fannie Lou Hamer: From Sharecropping to Politics, introduction by Andrew Young, Silver Burdett Press (Englewood Cliffs, NJ), 1990.

Elvis Presley: The Rise of Rock and Roll, Millbrook Press (Brookfield, CT), 1991.

How to Drive an Indy Race Car, photography by Edward Keating, J. Muir Publications (Santa Fe, NM), 1992.

(Compiler) *Webster's 21st-Century Chronology of World History, 3000 BC-1993,* Thomas Nelson (Nashville, TN), 1993.

Scholastic Encyclopedia of the Presidents and Their Times, Scholastic Reference (New York, NY), 1994.

Science, Scholastic Reference (New York, NY), 1995.

The United States in the Twentieth Century ("Scholastic Timelines" series), Scholastic Reference (New York, NY), 1995.

The United States in the Nineteenth Century ("Scholastic Timelines" series), Scholastic Reference (New York, NY), 1996.

Mr. President: The Human Side of America's Chief Executives, Time-Life Books (Alexandria, VA), 1998.

Scholastic Atlas of the United States, Scholastic Reference (New York, NY), 2000.

(With Allen Weinstein) *The Story of America: Freedom and Crisis from Settlement to Superpower,* Dorling Kindersley (New York, NY), 2002.

The Coming Free: The Struggle for African-American Equality, Dorling Kindersley (New York, NY), 2005.

If I Had a Hammer: Building Homes and Hope with Habitat for Humanity, Candlewick/Agincourt Press (New York, NY), 2009.

EDITOR

(With Russell Shorto and J. Matthew Gallman) *The Civil War Chronicle: The Only Day-by-Day Portrait of America's Tragic Conflicts as Told by Soldiers, Journalists, Politicians, Farmers, Nurses, Slaves, and Other Eyewitnesses,* introduction by Eric Foner, Crown (New York, NY), 1998.

The Reading List: Contemporary Fiction: A Critical Guide to the Complete Works of 110 Authors, Henry Holt (New York, NY), 1998.

(With James M. McPherson) *"To the Best of My Ability": The American Presidents,* Dorling Kindersley (New York, NY), 2000.

(With Douglas Brinkley) *World War II: The Axis Assault, 1939-1942,* Holt (New York, NY), 2003.

(With Douglas Brinkley) *World War II: The Allied Counteroffensive, 1942-1945,* Holt (New York, NY), 2004.

The Bedside Baccalaureate, Sterling (New York, NY), 2008.

Sidelights

David Rubel focuses on U.S. history and politics in his research and talks, and he strives to make that history accessible to young readers in his work as an author and editor. Unlike many nonfiction writers for young people, Rubel is respected for his scholarship and professionalism, skills that have gained him the collaboration of such noteworthy historians as Joseph J. Ellis, Eric Foner, and James M. McPherson. Among Rubel's works are *"To the Best of My Ability": The American Presidents, The Story of America: Freedom and Crisis from Settlement to Superpower, The Coming Free: The Struggle for African-American Equality,* and *If I Had a Hammer: Building Homes and Hope with Habitat for Humanity.* Coauthored with Allen Weinstein, *The Story of America* was described by a *Publishers Weekly* critic as "an anthology of our nation's favorite stories." "With

its lively storytelling and thorough coverage of our nation's first five centuries," the critic added, Rubel and Weinstein's volume "truly is a treasury."

After graduating from Columbia University in 1983, Rubel drew on his experience in college journalism to work as a news correspondent for the Pacific News Service, where he covered current news and popular culture. After entering publishing as an editorial assistant at New York City-based HarperCollins, he moved on to freelance writing and founded his own publishing house, Agincourt Press, in 1990. Six years later, he relocated to Chatham, New York, where he has continued to focus on books relating to American history while also speaking at schools and institutions as well as on television and radio.

In *Scholastic Encyclopedia of the Presidents and Their Times, Mr. President: The Human Side of America's Chief Executives,* and the edited anthology *"To the Best of My Ability",* Rubel focuses primarily on the history of the American presidency. Joined by Pulitzer-Prize-winning historian McPherson as co-editor, Rubel collects essays by noted presidential scholars in *"To the Best of My Ability",* producing well-illustrated profiles on forty-two U.S. presidents that "capture the essence of the individual, his major accomplishments, and the issues he faced," according to *Library Journal* critic Thomas J. Baldino. The volume also includes a discussion of each of the nation's presidential campaigns and the issues that inspired the nation's vote, as well as a transcript of each relevant inaugural address. Designed as a resource for elementary-school students, *Scholastic Encyclopedia of the Presidents and Their Times* presents basic information in an encyclopedia format, presenting young historians with what a *Booklist* critic described as an "attractive" resource that presents "concise information in an easy-to-read format."

Rubel focuses on the civil-rights movement in *The Coming Free,* a well-illustrated history of the fight for racial equality that occurred in the United States during the mid-twentieth century. In his book, he highlights the lives of civil-rights activists such as the Reverend Martin Luther King, Jr., Medgar Evers, Huey P. Newton, and the outspoken boxer Muhammad Ali. In addition to over 500 illustrations, Rubel also includes transcripts of speeches, articles, and interviews that capture the memories and experiences of the men, women, and children who experienced the movement first hand.

Rubel draws on his own experiences and wide-ranging research in writing *If I Had a Hammer,* a profile of the organization known as Habitat for Humanity. From the 1976 origins of the Georgia-based nonprofit founded by Millard Fuller, he discusses Habitat's mission, its many work projects around the world, and the unique relationship the organization cultivates between its community of volunteer builders and the families that ultimately benefit from these volunteer efforts. "Especially eye-opening are vignettes about projects in developing

Former U.S. President Jimmy Carter is among the many volunteers profiled in David Rubel's inspiring work **If I Had a Hammer: Building Homes and Hope with Habitat for Humanity.** (Candlewick, 2009. Photograph of Jimmy Carter by Gregg Pachkowksi. Reproduced with permission of Habitat for Humanity International.)

countries, where Habitat strives to reconcile modern building methods with local customs," noted a *Publishers Weekly* critic, while in *Booklist* Hazel Rochman noted the organization's melding of "technology and faith." Featuring an introduction by former U.S. president and Habitat for Humanity activist Jimmy Carter, *If I Had a Hammer* shares a "powerful message that will inspire many readers," according to Rochman. Rubel profiles the globe-spanning charity "enthusiastically and in clear, simple terms," noted *School Library Journal* critic Margaret Auguste, while a *Kirkus Reviews* writer maintained that the author's retelling of "the stories of the people involved . . . make the most compelling reading."

Biographical and Critical Sources

PERIODICALS

Booklist, July, 1994, review of *Scholastic Encyclopedia of the Presidents and Their Times,* p. 1978; November 1, 1996, review of *The United States in the Nineteenth Century,* p. 540; November 15, 2002, Gilbert Taylor, review of *The Story of America: Freedom vand Crisis from Settlement to Superpower,* p. 567; October 1, 2003, Gilbert Taylor, review of *World War II: The*

Axis Assault, 1939-1942, p. 297; December 15, 2003, Gilbert Taylor, review of *World War II: The Allied Counteroffensive, 1942-1945,* p. 724; December 1, 2009, Hazel Rochman, review of *I Had a Hammer: Building Homes and Hope with Habitat for Humanity,* p. 54.

Kirkus Reviews, November 1, 2005, review of *Scholastic Encyclopedia of the Presidents and Their Times*; September 15, 2009, review of *If I Had a Hammer.*

Library Journal, July, 2000, Thomas J. Baldino, review of *"To the Best of My Ability": The American Presidents,* p. 116; November 15, 2002, Daniel Liestman, review of *The Story of America,* p. 85; September 15, 2005, Edward G. McCormack, review of *The Coming Free: The Struggle for African-American Equality,* p. 75.

Publishers Weekly, October 23, 2000, review of *The Civil War Chronicle: The Only Day-by-Day Portrait of America's Tragic Conflicts as Told by Soldiers, Journalists, Politicians, Farmers, Nurses, Slaves, and Other Eyewitnesses,* p. 64; September 16, 2002, review of *The Story of America,* p. 60; October 12, 2009, review of *If I Had a Hammer,* p. 51.

School Library Journal, February, 2001, John Palmer, review of *Scholastic Atlas of the United States,* p. 114; November, 2009, Margaret Auguste, review of *If I Had a Hammer,* p. 135.

ONLINE

David Rubel Home Page, http://www.davidrubel.net (November 21, 2010).

S

SAUER, Tammi 1972-

Personal

Born 1972, in KS; married Ron Sauer; children: Julia, Mason. *Education:* Kansas State University, B.S. (elementary education). *Hobbies and other interests:* Skiing, reading, attending baseball games, spending time with family and friends.

Addresses

Home—Edmund, OK. *E-mail*—tksauer@aol.com.

Career

Educator and author. Former teacher of prekindergarten, middle school, and summer school; elementary-school library media specialist for two years. Freelance writer; presenter at schools, libraries, book festivals, and reading and writing conferences.

Awards, Honors

Oklahoma Book Award finalist, 2006, and Buckaroo Book Award nomination, 2010, both for *Cowboy Camp;* NAPPA Gold Award, and ABC Best Book for Children selection, both 2009, Chicago Public Library Best of the Best selection, and Oklahoma Book Award, both 2010, and Buckaroo Book Award nomination, 2011, all for *Chicken Dance;* Scholastic Parent and Child Best Book of the Year selection, 2010, for *Mostly Monsterly.*

Writings

Cowboy Camp, illustrated by Mike Reed, Sterling (New York, NY), 2005.
Chicken Dance, illustrated by Dan Santat, Sterling (New York, NY), 2009.
Mostly Monsterly, illustrated by Scott Magoon, Simon & Schuster/Paula Wiseman Books (New York, NY), 2010.

Tammi Sauer (Photograph by Tori North. Reproduced by permission.)

Mr. Duck Means Business, illustrated by Jeff Mack, Simon & Schuster/Paula Wiseman Books (New York, NY), 2011.
Bawk and Roll, illustrated by Dan Santat, Sterling (New York, NY), 2011.
Me Want Pet, illustrated by Bob Shea, Simon & Schuster/ Paula Wiseman Books (New York, NY), 2012.
Oh Nuts, illustrated by Dan Krall, Bloomsbury Children's Books (New York, NY), 2012.
Princess-in-Training, illustrated by Joe Berger, Houghton Mifflin Harcourt (New York, NY), 2012.

Sidelights

Born and raised in Kansas, Tammi Sauer worked as a teacher for several years before beginning her career as a children's author. Now living in Oklahoma, she shares her upbeat humor in stories such as *Cowboy Camp, Chicken Dance, Mostly Monsterly,* and *Bawk and Roll.*

Dubbing *Mostly Monsterly* "a fun and delightful read" about a little monster who bravely reveals her kind and loving side to her sharp-clawed monster friends, Kim T. Ha added in *School Library Journal* that Sauer's "simple, repetitive" text adds up to a "well-paced story" that is brought to life in Scott Magoon's digital art.

In *Cowboy Camp* Sauer introduces Avery, a little boy whose dream has been to ride the range as a cowboy. When he arrives at Cowboy Camp, however, things do not go as planned. Avery cannot stand the grub, is allergic to horses, and gets rope burn. Just when he thinks things cannot get any worse, Black Bart shows up and tries to put a stop to Cowboy Camp, and it is up to Avery to save the day. Praising the "expressive paintings" that Mike Reed contributes to the story, *Booklist* critic Carolyn Phelan went on to note of *Cowboy Camp* that in Avery "Sauer creates an unlikely yet likable hero." Also recommending the picture book, Polly K. Korbata predicted in *School Library Journal* that *Cowboy Camp* will be "appreciated" by young readers who "share . . . Avery's concerns about not fitting in."

Raised on a farm in rural Middle America, Sauer was surrounded by barnyard animals, and her knowledge of poultry is evident in *Chicken Dance*. Hens Marge and Lola, the feathered stars of Sauer's adventure, will do anything to acquire tickets to hear barnyard-music sensation Elvis Poultry, and they now enter a local talent show where two tickets to the concert are first prize. While watching the ditsy hens vainly search for a talent worth showing, the farmyard ducks smugly criticize, certain that first prize will be theirs. As she captures the energetic squawk and flutter that ultimately wins the day, Sauer contributes what a *Kirkus Reviews* writer praised as a "zippy narrative [that] features punchy dialogue and witty interactions," as well as a healthy dose of silliness. In *Booklist* Kay Weisman also praised Sauer's "broad humor," adding that Dan Santat's colorful digitized art in *Chicken Dance,* "comically extends Sauer's droll text." A *Publishers Weekly* contributor remarked on her success in "both embracing and spoofing the against-all-odds genre."

Illustrated by Jeff Mack, *Mr. Duck Means Business* features a different cast of barnyard characters. Mr. Duck is perfectly content living a life of solitude on his pond. When the other animals mistakenly think they have been invited for a swim, Mr. Duck goes a little haywire until he realizes that sometimes a little commotion can be a good thing. A *Kirkus Reviews* writer stated that "Sauer's dour and disciplined duck and his rhyming hissy fits will most definitely entertain" young children, while *School Library Journal* contributor Barbara Ellerman praised the "clever use of language" in a "pleasing" story that "offers a viable avenue for discussion about how sometimes compromise is the best way to go."

Sauer loved to write even as a child, and she began to view it has a possible career in college, when a professor suggested that she had the talent needed to write for children and teens. On her home page, she encourages others in the field to keep their eyes open for ideas. "Learn everything you can about the craft," Sauer advised. "Interact with other writers. Read as much as possible. Find a critique partner who takes writing as seriously as you do. Believe in yourself and never give up." "I couldn't imagine a more rewarding career," Sauer also told *SATA*. "And the fan mail from kids? It's unbeatable."

Biographical and Critical Sources

PERIODICALS

Booklist, February 15, 2006, Carolyn Phelan, review of *Cowboy Camp,* p. 101; August 1, 2009, Kay Weisman, review of *Chicken Dance,* p. 77; July 1, 2010, Abby Nolan, review of *Mostly Monsterly,* p. 67.

Kirkus Reviews, July 1, 2009, review of *Chicken Dance*; December 1, 2010, review of *Mr. Duck Means Business.*

Publishers Weekly, July 20, 2009, review of *Chicken Dance,* p. 139.

School Library Journal, March, 2006, Polly K. Kotarba, review of *Cowboy Camp,* p. 201; September, 2009, Barbara Elleman, review of *Chicken Dance,* p. 133;

A farmyard tale with musical overtones comes to life in Dan Santat's art for Sauer's picture book Chicken Dance. (Illustration © 2009 by Dan Santat. Reproduced by permission of Sterling Publishing Co., Inc.)

August, 2010, Kim T. Ha, review of *Mostly Monsterly,* p. 86; January, 2011, Barbara Elleman, review of *Mr. Duck Means Business.*

ONLINE

Tammi Sauer Home Page, http://www.tammisauer.com (November 21, 2010).
Tammi Sauer Web log, http://tamarak.livejournal.com (December 5, 2010).

*   *   *

SCHON, Nick 1955-

Personal

Born 1955, in London, England; married; children: three. *Education:* College degree.

Addresses

Home—Wheathampstead, England. *E-mail*—schon1@mac.com.

Career

Illustrator and cartoonist. Art director in Frankfurt, Germany, 1977-83, and London, England, 1983-99; freelance illustrator. Juror, D&AD Students Awards, 2002, AOI Awards, 2005.

Awards, Honors

Cannes Gold award, shortlist, and certificates; International Advertising Awards Campaign of the Year honor; Campaign Press silver and bronze awards; British Television Awards; Creative Circle bronze award; New York International Ad Festival honor; Bavarian Art Directors Club silver honor; Sheffield Children's Book Award Commended designation, 2008, for *The Monkey with a Bright Blue Bottom* by Steve Smallman.

Writings

Steve Smallman, *The Monkey with a Bright Blue Bottom,* Good Books (Intercourse, PA), 2009.

Biographical and Critical Sources

PERIODICALS

Kirkus Reviews, September 15, 2009, review of *The Monkey with a Bright Blue Bottom.*
Publishers Weekly, October 19, 2009, review of *The Monkey with a Bright Blue Bottom,* p. 50.

ONLINE

Nick Schon Home Page, http://www.nickschonillustrator.com (November 21, 2010).*

*   *   *

SILVANO, Wendi 1962-

Personal

Born 1962, Salt Lake City, UT; married; husband's name Eddy; children: Nicole Natalie, Liliana, David, Keaton. *Education:* University of Utah, B.A. (early childhood education). *Hobbies and other interests:* Hiking, playing piano, reading.

Addresses

Home—Grand Junction, CO. *E-mail*—wsilvano@hotmail.com.

Career

Educator and author. Teacher of preschool and elementary school for eleven years. Presenter at schools.

Member

International Reading Association (Colorado chapter), Society of Children's Book Writers and Illustrators.

Awards, Honors

Children's Choice Award, 2002, for *Just One More;* Children's Choice Award, 2009 for *Turkey Trouble;* Ed-Press Award for Excellence in Children's Magazine Fiction, Paul A. Witty Short Story Award, IRA, *Highlights for Children* Humorous Fiction Contest, winner, all for "Talbot's Tub Trouble."

Writings

Just One More, illustrated by Ricardo Gamboa, All About Kids (San Jose, CA), 2002.
Hey Diddle Riddle, illustrated by Tad Hills, Little Simon (New York, NY), 2003.
Counting Coconuts/Contado cocos, illustrated by Marty Granius, Raven Tree Press (Green Bay, WI), 2004.
What Does the Wind Say?, illustrated by Joan M. Delehanty, NorthWord (Minnetonka, MN), 2006.
Turkey Trouble, illustrated by Lee Harper, Marshall Cavendish Children (Tarrytown, NY), 2009.

Also author of educational readers for Continental Press, including *Good Morning Duck and Goose, Duck and Goose Have a Picnic, Duck and Goose in the Rain, Duck and Goose Play with Frog, Duck and Goose Give a Party, Little Duck and Little Goose,* and *Duck and Goose and the Perfect Puddle.*

Sidelights

As a former preschool and elementary teacher who has also raised five children of her own, Colorado author Wendi Silvano mixes a bit of learning in each of her books for young people. Some, like *Counting Coconuts/ Contado cocos,* focus on counting and basic math skills, while *What Does the Wind Say?* employs a rhyming question-and-answer format to highlight elements of nature that are reflected in Joan M. Delehanty's ink-and-watercolor art. *Hey Diddle Riddle,* with its humorous twist on well-known nursery rhymes, is just for fun, while in *Turkey Trouble* a sly but silly bird pretends to be a horse, a cow, a sheep, a pizza-delivery man—anything but poultry in order not to become the main course in Farmer Jake's Thanksgiving feast. Illustrated with "comical watercolor" art by Lee Harper, *Turkey Trouble* also benefits from a "clever, filled-with-wordplay text," according to *School Library Journal* critic Mary Hazelton, and Julie Cummins predicted in *Booklist* that readers who enjoy Silvano's "clever and comical tale" will "very likely request pizza for Thanksgiving dinner, too."

Silvano's husband is of Peruvian descent, and the author has a great familiarity with the geography and history of that region of South America through her travels there. Her bilingual concept book *Counting Coconuts/ Contado cocos* is set in the Peruvian Amazon, where a monkey is helped by its jungle friends in using set theory to count his coconuts quickly. In *Just One More* Silvano once again returns to Peru, this time taking readers to a small town high in the Andes Mountains where a boy named Hector awaits a bus. After Hector boards the bus and takes a seat, the vehicle becomes more and more crowded with each successive stop as people, packages, suitcases, vegetables, and livestock of all shapes and sizes come steadily crowding in. Captured in watercolor art by Ricardo Gamboa, *Just One More* also benefits from Silvano's "rhythmic, repetitive" text, making it "an ideal read-aloud" according to *School Library Journal* critic Shawn Brommer.

Biographical and Critical Sources

PERIODICALS

Booklist, September 1, 2009, Julie Cummins, review of *Turkey Trouble,* p. 102.
Kirkus Reviews, August 15, 2009, review of *Turkey Trouble.*
Publishers Weekly, January 26, 2004, review of *Hey Diddle Riddle: A Silly Nursery Rhyme,* p. 256; September 21, 2009, review of *Turkey Trouble,* p. 56.
School Library Journal, September, 2002, Shawn Brommer, review of *Just One More,* p. 206; October, 2009, Mary Hazelton, review of *Turkey Trouble,* p. 106.

ONLINE

Wendi Silvano Home Page, http://www.wendiwrite.com (November 21, 2010).

*   *   *

SONNENBLICK, Jordan 1969-

Personal

Born 1969; married; children: two.

Addresses

Home—P.O. Box 20070, Lehigh Valley, PA 18002-0070. *E-mail*—jordansonnenblick@rcn.com.

Career

Writer. Teacher in New Jersey and Pennsylvania.

Awards, Honors

Rebecca Caudill Award, and Maud Hart Lovelace Award, both 2005, both for *Drums, Girls & Dangerous Pie;* Best Book for Young Adults nomination, American Library Association, 2006, and Book Sense Pick for Teens, and Premio Cento (Italy), all for *Notes from the Midnight Driver.*

Writings

YOUNG-ADULT NOVELS

Drums, Girls & Dangerous Pie, DayBue Publishing, 2004, Scholastic (New York, NY), 2005.

Wendi Silvano tells a story of nature and family in her gentle picture book What Does the Wind Say, *featuring artwork by Joan W. Delehanty.* (Northword Press, 2006. Reproduced by permission of Cooper Square Publishing.)

Notes from the Midnight Driver, Scholastic (New York, NY), 2006.

Zen and the Art of Faking It, Scholastic (New York, NY), 2007.

Dodger and Me, Feiwel & Friends (New York, NY), 2008.

Dodger for President, Feiwel & Friends (New York, NY), 2009.

After Ever After (sequel to *Drums, Girls & Dangerous Pie*), Scholastic Press (New York, NY), 2010.

Dodger for Sale, Feiwel & Friends (New York, NY), 2010.

Contributor to periodicals, including *Horn Book* and *School Library Journal.*

Adaptations

Zen and the Art of Faking It was adapted for audiobook, read by Mike Chamberlain, Listening Library, 2008. *Dodger and Me* was adapted for audiobook, read by William Dufris, Brilliance Audio, 2009.

Sidelights

Jordan Sonnenblick, a former middle-school teacher, has written several novels about teenagers facing serious problems in their lives. Despite his focus on realis-

Cover of Jordan Sonnenblick's 2004 novel Drums, Girls & Dangerous Pie, *featuring artwork by Istvan Banyai.* (Cover art copyright © by Istvan Banyai. Reproduced by permission of Scholastic, Inc.)

tic situations in books that include *Drums, Girls & Dangerous Pie, Zen and the Art of Faking It,* and *After Ever After,* Sonnenblick's stories are full of humor and warmth. Writing in *Kliatt,* Claire Rosser noted that "Sonnenblick describes family life with great skill, and the frequently humorous anecdotes are entertaining, even when the basic story is grim."

Sonnenblick was teaching eighth-grade English in New Jersey when he wrote *Drums, Girls & Dangerous Pie.* One of his students had a younger brother with cancer and asked for recommendations as to books she could read to help her through the situation. When Sonnenblick realized that there was nothing suitable available, he decided to write a book on the subject himself. He credits his own high-school English teacher, author Frank McCourt, with spurring him on. Sonnenblick told Melissa Jenco in the Arlington Heights, Illinois, *Daily Herald:* "He was a huge inspiration for me because, when his first book came out, I thought, well, he could do it, he's a person, I know him. If he can write a book, I can write a book."

Sonnenblick did two weeks of research and ten weeks of writing before his manuscript for *Drums, Girls & Dangerous Pie* was finished. "For those twelve weeks," he later recalled to online interviewer Cynthia Leitich Smith for *Cynsations,* "life was a whirl of teaching all day, parenting all evening, and then writing from the time the kids went to bed until I finally collapsed into bed myself." Although his publisher, DayBue Publishing, went out of business three weeks after *Drums, Girls & Dangerous Pie* was released, the novel attracted good reviews and was reprinted by Scholastic, which has continued to be Sonnenblick's publisher.

Drums, Girls & Dangerous Pie introduces thirteen-year-old Steven Alper, whose passion in life is playing the drums in his school band. When Steven's little brother Jeffrey develops leukemia, life changes for the whole family. The boys' mother leaves her job as a teacher, their father withdraws emotionally, and Steven himself has a hard time keeping up with his schoolwork. The whole family spends most of its time taking care of five-year-old Jeffrey and making sure he gets to the hospital for his treatments. In the course of the novel, Steven develops the strength and maturity needed to help his little brother through his ordeal.

"Somehow," wrote Cheryl Stritzel McCarthy in her review of *Drums, Girls & Dangerous Pie* for the Cleveland *Plain Dealer,* "Steven's narration retains a down-to-earth sense of humor and regular middle-school angst." A *Kirkus Reviews* critic noted that, not only is Sonnenblick's story "real and raw and heart-rending, he made it hysterically funny as well." Ilene Cooper concluded in *Booklist* that "Sonneblick shows that even in the midst of tragedy, life goes on, love can flower, and the one thing you can always change is yourself." Summing up *Drums, Girls & Dangerous Pie, Detroit Free Press* contributor Cassandra Spratling called it "a richly textured, finely told tale."

Featuring cover art by Istvan Banyai, Sonnenblick's Notes from the Midnight Driver *focuses on a teen whose car accident changes his life.*
(Cover art copyright © 2006 by Istavan Banyai. Reproduced by permission of Scholastic, Inc.)

A sequel to *Drums, Girls & Dangerous Pie, After Ever After,* finds Jeffrey in eighth grade and dealing with the aftereffects of his many years of radiation treatments. Although his cancer is in remission, Jeffrey has been left with a new difficulty: focusing his attention enough to keep up with class. Fortunately, his friend Tad also suffered ill effects from chemotherapy, and he is now in a wheelchair. Jeffrey is able to keep things in perspective, although troubles at home and his worries about impressing a certain girl in his class provide some stressful moments for the preteen. Writing that "Sonnenblick imbues Jeffrey['s first-person narration] with a smooth, likable, and unaffected voice," *Booklist* contributor Ian Chipman dubbed *After Ever After* "irresistible reading." In *Horn Book* Claire E. Gross cited the author's "trademark combination of sarcasm and shameless heartstring-pulling," as well his "gift for comic exaggeration and snappy dialogue," and Terri Clark praised the book in *School Library Journal* as "a solid" novel "that will leave an emotional, uplifting imprint on readers." Praising Sonnenblick's story in *Publishers Weekly,* a reviewer predicted that *After Ever After* will help "readers . . . understand the toll cancer takes on victims and everyone around them."

Notes from the Midnight Driver was also inspired by Sonnenblick's teaching experience. In the novel, teenager Alex Gregory gets drunk on vodka and steals his mother's car with the intent to visit his father and tell him off (his parents are divorced). When Alex ends up driving the vehicle up on his neighbor's front lawn, he vehemently denies being responsible for the accident. Sentenced in court to serve one hundred hours of community service at the Johnson Nursing Home, he is assigned to be a companion to Solomon Lewis, a grumpy senior. At first, Sol is a sarcastic nuisance, but over time Alex realizes that there is wisdom beneath the man's crotchety surface. Through Sol, Alex learns about taking responsibility, comes to terms with his own troubled life, learns the value of his girlfriend Laurie, and comes to an understanding of his divorced parents.

"*Drums, Girls & Dangerous Pie* was remarkable in its intertwining of pain and wit," wrote James Blasingame in the *Journal of Adolescent & Adult Literacy.* "and *Notes from the Midnight Driver* adds a few more layers of humor, pathos, and passion. This book is touching, hysterical, and insightful, sometimes even on the same page." Similarly, *Horn Book* critic Gross described Alex's first-person narrative as "riddled with enough hapless confusion, mulish equivocation, and beleaguered deadpan humor to have readers nodding with recognition, sighing in sympathy, and gasping with laughter—often on the same page."

In *Zen and the Art of Faking It,* Chinese teenager San Lee once again finds himself the new kid in school. Poor, and with a parent in jail, San wants to be accepted. When he correctly answers questions about Zen in his world history class, his classmates assume that he is a Zen master who has deep insights into life. Although San's popularity quickly rises, especially with a girl he has a crush on, he knows that the popularity is all based on a wild lie. Worse still, it is a lie that is uncomfortably similar to the one that put San's conman father in prison. In a *Publishers Weekly* review of *Zen and the Art of Faking It* a critic wrote that the story's "lighter moments take a basic message about the importance of honesty and forgiveness and treat it with panache." Writing in *Kliatt,* Paula Rohrlick dubbed Sonnenblick's story "wildly funny," adding that "San and his predicament are a delight."

Focusing on younger readers, Sonnenblick crafts a humorous fantasy in *Dodger and Me* and its sequels. When Willie Ryan takes a shortcut through the woods on his way home from a baseball game, he finds a magic lamp. Emerging from the lamp, a giant blue chimpanzee named Dodger promises to grant Willie three wishes. Trouble ensues, however, when Dodger's effort to grant the wishes he has promised make things worse for Willie rather than better. A critic for *Kirkus Reviews* called *Dodger and Me* "over the top, short on logic and often quite silly." Carolyn Phelan wrote in *Booklist* that Sonnenblick's "humor will draw kids—especially Dodg-

er's off-the-wall dialogue and the outlandish predicaments that result when he decides to 'help.'"

Dodger and Willie return for further adventures in *Dodger for President* and *Dodger for Sale*. The invisible blue chimpanzee once again comes to the rescue—sort of—in the first book, as Willie and friend Lizzie hope to win the top spots in their election for fifth-grade government. In *Dodger for Sale* the chimp's magical home turf is threatened when a group of developers plans to tear down the woods where Willie first discovered his magic lamp. While Willie and Lizzie mobilize the student council to help stop the developers, magic is unleased and soon Willie's sister is abducted by some unusual little kidnappers. Reviewing *Dodger for President* in *Booklist*, Ian Chipman concluded that the story's "outlandish tone should please . . . fans" of the first "Dodger" novel, while Lauralyn Persson remarked on the "ironic silliness and mild gross-out humor" in Sonnenblick's tale. Along with the author's characteristic humor, *Dodger for Sale* "offers realistic relationships and an environmental message," according to *School Library Journal* critic Laurie Slagenwhite.

Cover of Sonnenblick's young-adult novel Zen and the Art of Faking It, *featuring artwork by Marc Tauss.* (Jacket photo/illustration copyright © 2007 by Marc Tauss. Reproduced by permission of Scholastic, Inc.)

Biographical and Critical Sources

PERIODICALS

ALAN Review, winter, 2006, Jim Blasingame, "Venturing into the Deep Waters: The Work of Jordan Sonnenblick."

Booklist, September 15, 2005, Cooper Ilene, review of *Drums, Girls & Dangerous Pie,* p. 63; October 1, 2006, Frances Bradburn, review of *Notes from the Midnight Driver,* p. 52; October 1, 2007, Ilene Cooper, review of *Zen and the Art of Faking It,* p. 68; March 15, 2008, Carolyn Phelan, review of *Dodger and Me,* p. 50; April 15, 2009, Ian Chipman, review of *Dodger for President,* p. 38; December 15, 2009, Ian Chipman, review of *After Ever After,* p. 39.

Daily Herald (Arlington Heights, IL), November 30, 2007, Melissa Jenco, "Author Tells Students What Inspired Books," p. 1.

Detroit Free Press, November 23, 2005, Cassandra Spratling, review of *Drums, Girls & Dangerous Pie.*

Horn Book, January-February, 2006, Claire E. Gross, review of *Drums, Girls & Dangerous Pie,* p. 89; September-October, 2006, Claire E. Gross, review of *Notes from the Midnight Driver,* p. 597; November-December, 2007, Christine M. Heppermann, review of *Zen and the Art of Faking It,* p. 686; March-April, 2010, Claire E. Gross, review of *After Ever After,* p. 73.

Journal of Adolescent & Adult Literacy, November, 2006, James Blasingame, review of *Notes from the Midnight Driver,* p. 238.

Kirkus Reviews, September 1, 2005, review of *Drums, Girls & Dangerous Pie,* p. 983; September 15, 2006, review of *Notes from the Midnight Driver,* p. 968; September 1, 2007, review of *Zen and the Art of Faking It;* April 15, 2008, review of *Dodger and Me;* June 1, 2009, review of *Dodger for President;* January 1, 2010, review of *After Ever After.*

Kliatt, September, 2005, review of *Drums, Girls & Dangerous Pie,* p. 15; November, 2006, review of *Notes from the Midnight Driver,* p. 15; September, 2007, Paula Rohrlick, review of *Zen and the Art of Faking It,* p. 18.

Plain Dealer (Cleveland, OH), October 9, 2005, Cheryl Stritzel McCarthy, review of *Drums, Girls & Dangerous Pie,* p. H5.

Publishers Weekly, December 12, 2005, review of *Drums, Girls & Dangerous Pie,* p. 68; September 18, 2006, review of *Notes from the Midnight Driver,* p. 55; September 28, 2006, Jennifer M. Brown, interview with Sonnenblick; October 8, 2007, review of *Zen and the Art of Faking It,* p. 55; January 4, 2010, review of *After Ever After,* p. 48.

School Library Journal, October, 2004, Joel Shoemaker, review of *Drums, Girls & Dangerous Pie,* p. 178; October, 2006, Shannon Seglin, review of *Notes from the Midnight Driver,* p. 173; October, 2007, Heather E. Miller, review of *Zen and the Art of Faking It,* p. 164; June, 2008, Miranda Doyle, review of *Dodger and Me,* p. 150; September, 2009, Karen T. Bilton, review of *Dodger and Me,* p. 61; August, 2009, Lauralyn

Persson, review of *Dodger for President,* p. 114; January, 2010, Terri Clark, review of *After Ever After,* p. 114; May, 2010, Laurie Slagenwhite, review of *Dodger for Sale,* p. 124.

ONLINE

Book Page, http://www.bookpage.com/ (October, 2006), Heidi Henneman, "Self-serving Students Inspire a Teacher's Teen Novel."
Cynsations Web log, http://cynthialeitichsmith.blogspot. com/ (December 22, 2005), Cynthia Leitich Smith, interview with Sonnenblick.
Jordan Sonnenblick Home Page, http://www.jordanson nenblick.com (December 7, 2010).*

*   *   *

SPENGLER, Margaret

Personal

Born in CA; married Kenneth Spengler (an illustrator and author); children: Matthew. *Education:* Art Center of Pasadena (now Art Center College of Design), B.A. (advertising).

Addresses

Home—Sacramento, CA. *E-mail*—margaret@spengler creations.com.

Career

Illustrator and designer. Worked as an art director in advertising, New York, NY; freelance graphic designer and illustrator; *Sacramento Bee,* Sacramento, CA, designer and illustrator.

Awards, Honors

Numerous design and illustration awards.

Illustrator

Cindy Chang, compiler, *The Joy of Reading,* Andrews McMeel (Kansas City, MO), 1997.
Rob and Amy Spence, *Clickety Clack,* Viking (New York, NY), 1999.
Betty Schwartz, adaptor, *Old MacDonald Had a Farm,* Little Simon (New York, NY), 2000.
Anne Akers Johnson, *The Treasure Hunt Book,* Klutz (Palo Alto, CA), 2000.
Heather Tekavec, *Storm Is Coming!,* Dial Books for Young Readers (New York, NY), 2002.
Toni Buzzeo, *Dawdle Duckling,* Dial Books for Young Readers (New York, NY), 2003.
Toni Buzzeo, *Little Loon and Papa,* Dial Books for Young Readers (New York, NY), 2004.
Heather Tekavec, *What's That Awful Smell?,* Dial Books for Young Readers (New York, NY), 2004.

Margaret Spengler (Photograph by Kenneth Spengler. Reproduced by permission.)

Toni Buzzeo, *Ready or Not, Dawdle Duckling,* Dial Books for Young Readers (New York, NY), 2005.
Karma Wilson, *Animal Strike at the Zoo, It's True!,* HarperCollins (New York, NY), 2006.
Dorthea DePrisco, *Three Little Caterpillars,* Piggy Toes Press (Inglewood, CA), 2006.
Kenneth Spengler, *Little Red Hen Gets Help,* Harcourt (Orlando, FL), 2007.
Danielle Steel, *The Happiest Hippo in the World,* HarperCollins (New York, NY), 2009.

Contributor to periodicals.

Sidelights

Margaret Spengler began her career at a New York City advertising agency, where she worked as an art director. Born in northern California and a graduate of the Art Center of Pasadena, Spengler relocated to the East coast to accept this job. However, the pull of the west eventually prompted her to return to California, where she now lives and works as an illustrator and graphic designer. Her brightly colored, digitized pastel artwork is a feature of a range of picture-book stories, including tales written by Toni Buzzeo, Heather Tekavec, Karma Wilson, and her husband, artist/author Kenneth Spengler. Reviewing one of Spengler's first illustration projects, Amy and Rob Spence's *Clickety Clack, Booklist* critic Lauren Peterson noted the "visual excite-

ment" created by the artist's use of "bright colors and unusual perspectives" and a *Publishers Weekly* critic cited the images' "deeply saturated colors" and "puckish sensibility."

Pairing Spengler's art with a story by Telavek, *Storm Is Coming!* takes readers to a farmyard, where Dog gathers Cat, Duck, and the larger animals into the barn to keep out of the way of an unknown creature called Storm. Also by Telavek, *What's That Awful Smell?* finds the animals concerned about a bad smell that is now emanating from the barn. They assume it is caused by a little piglet and take steps to clean the tiny piggy until Cat arrives and reveals the source of the odor. Spengler's use of "unusual perspectives and expressive details" in *Storm Is Coming!* "enhance both the scary and humorous aspects of this clever tale," wrote Lauren Peterson in her *Booklist* review, and *School Library Journal* critic Susan Hepler praised the book's "pleasantly rounded cartoon creatures, rendered in cheerfully colored pastels." In *What's That Awful Smell?* Spengler's "shiny pastel" illustrations "emphasize the animals' noses to comic effect," wrote *Horn Book* contributor Martha V. Parravano, while a *Kirkus Reviews* writer hailed her for giving Telavek's story a cast of "big-nosed, dot-eyed, rattled-looking livestock."

Spengler has created illustrations for several bird-centered stories by Buzzeo, among them *Dawdle Duckling*, *Ready or Not, Dawdle Duckling*, and *Little Loon and Papa*. Children's independence is the focus of *Dawdle Duckling*, the story of a Mama Duck that must constantly keep track of her curious offspring. *Ready or Not, Dawdle Duckling* finds the duckling family spending a day at the beach, where Dawdle makes some unusual friends when out of range of Mama Duck's view. Reviewing *Dawdle Duckling* in *Booklist*, Ilene Cooper enjoyed Spengler's depiction of the ducklings in dapper straw hats and added that the book's "smile-provoking pastel illustrations put the characters front and center." Joy Fleishhacker wrote in *School Library Journal* that Spengler's illustrations for *Dawdle Duckling* "have a dreamy quality that matches the text's even tempo," while thr "intense, sunny pastels" she uses in her art for *Ready or Not, Dawdle Duckling* "match the atmosphere" of Buzzeo's upbeat tale, according to *Booklist* critic Connie Fletcher.

A relationship between a parent and an exuberant child is also the focus of *Little Loon and Papa*, but here Buzzeo and Spengler focus on teaching rather than supervision. Papa Loon is attempting to teach Little Loon how to dive under water. However, while Papa is under the water demonstrating the skill, Little Loon swims off to shore where it encounters several new friends and a small adventure. Calling the book "appealing," Linda Staskus added in *School Library Journal* that Spengler's "jewel-toned" pastel art "evoke[s] the splendor of the north wood," and a *Publishers Weekly* critic wrote of *Little Loon and Papa* that the artist's "warm pastels capture the cheeky [little] loon's every emotion."

Biographical and Critical Sources

PERIODICALS

Booklist, July, 1999, Lauren Peterson, review of *Clickety Clack,* p. 1955; March 1, 2002, Lauren Peterson, review of *Storm Is Coming!,* p. 1144; May 15, 2003, Ilene Cooper, review of *Dawdle Duckling,* p. 1669; March 1, 2005, Connie Fletcher, review of *Ready or Not, Dawdle Duckling,* p. 1202.

Horn Book, July-August, 2004, Martha V. Parravano, review of *What's That Awful Smell?,* p. 442.

Kirkus Reviews, December 15, 2001, review of *Storm Is Coming!,* p. 1763; November 15, 2002, review of *Dawdle Duckling,* p. 1689; January 1, 2004, review of *What's That Awful Smell?,* p. 42; May 1, 2004, review of *Little Loon and Papa,* p. 438; January, 2005, review of *Ready or Not, Dawdle Duckling,* p. 49; May 1, 2006, review of *Animal Strike at the Zoo: It's True!;* August 1, 2009, review of *The Happiest Hippo in the World.*

Publishers Weekly, May 17, 1999, review of *Clickety Clack,* p. 78; February 11, 2002, review of *Storm Is Coming!,* p. 187; November 18, 2002, review of *Dawdle Duckling,* p. 58; May 17, 2004, review of *Little Loon and Papa,* p. 49; August 24, 2009, review of *The Happiest Hippo in the World,* p. 61.

School Library Journal, March, 2002, Susan Hepler, review of *Storm Is Coming!,* p. 204; April, 2003, Joy Fleishhacker, review of *Dawdle Duckling,* p. 116; April, 2004, Linda Ludke, review of *What's That Awful Smell?,* p. 126; June, 2004, Linda Staskus, review of *Little Loon and Papa,* p. 103; March, 2005, Susan Weitz, review of *Ready or Not, Dawdle Duckling,* p. 168; June, 2006, Wanda Meyers-Hines, review of *Animal Strike at the Zoo: It's True!,* p. 130.

ONLINE

Margaret Spengler Home Page, http://www.margaretspengler.com (November 21, 2010).

*   *   *

SUMA, Nova Ren

Personal

Born in NY. *Education:* Antioch College, B.A. (writing and photography); Columbia University, M.F.A. (fiction).

Addresses

Home—New York, NY. *Agent*—Michael Bourret, Dystel & Goderich Literary Management, One Union Square W., Ste. 904, New York, NY 10003. *E-mail*—nova@novaren.com.

Career

Author and editor. Former assistant at a literary agency; member of editorial and production staff for book and comics publishers; copyeditor and ghostwriter.

Awards, Honors

New York Foundation for the Arts fellowship; Mac-Dowell Colony fellowship; Yaddo fellowship.

Writings

Dani Noir, Aladdin (New York, NY), 2009.
Imaginary Girls, Dutton (New York, NY), 2011.

Uncredited author of over a dozen other books for children. Contributor to literary journals, including *Gulf Coast, LIT, Orchid,* and *Small Spiral Notebook.*

Sidelights

A graduate of Columbia University's master's program in writing, Nova Ren Suma worked as a ghost writer and produced over seventeen books before releasing her first novel under her own name. Drawing on the author's love of the black-and-white "noir" films of the 1940s and 1950s, *Dani Noir* is geared for a preteen audience, while Suma's second novel, *Imaginary Girls,* addresses older teen readers in its story of the complex and potentially destructive relationship between two teen sisters.

For the thirteen-year-old protagonist of *Dani Noir,* summer in her small town promises nothing but heat and boredom, but then she discovers a local cinema's film series. Called "Summer of Noir," the series guarantees Danielle at least temporary and intermittent escapes from the heat as well as from the drama surrounding her divorced parents. To her surprise, the girl is soon hooked by the beauty of leading ladies like Rita Hayworth, Barbara Stanwick, Ida Lupino, and Lana Turner. In addition, the passionate crimes that are slowly revealed in each film, cloaked in lies and shrouded in intrigue, capture Dani's young imagination with their reassuring distinction between good and menacing evil. By framing her own life as a noir film, the girl's world is divided cleanly between villains and victims, and the arrival in town of a mysterious young woman allows her to take on the classic detective role. But unsettling doubts make Dani wonder whether real life is quite that simple.

As Kitty Flynn noted in a *Horn Book* review, Suma's young heroine "is a believably flawed character" whose "authentic" narration reveals her feelings of anger and loss as well as her desire for excitement. Although the film noir genre may not be familiar to contemporary tweens, Suma interjects references to social networking and technology that "contrast pleasingly with [noir's] . . . old-fashioned timelessness," according to a *Kirkus Reviews* writer. Also reviewing *Dani Noir,* a *Publishers Weekly* contributor praised Suma's fiction debut, citing the book's "expert balance of the realities of teenaged life, humor and intrigue."

Cover of Nova Ren Suma's young-adult novel **Dani Noir,** *which mixes 1940s crime movies and a teen's family mystery.* (Aladdin, 2009. Jacket design by Lisa Vega. Reproduced with permission of Simon & Schuster Children's Division.)

"There's this thing that happens when you get the inspiration to write," Suma explained in discussing the writing life with a Simon & Schuster online interview. "A push of motivation or an idea comes at the most inconvenient moment, like when you're seconds from falling asleep, or in the shower, or about to step out the door. . . . There's always something that needs doing, and the writing always seems like it can wait. You wait for another tomorrow, and another, and that's how books don't get written. So don't keep putting it off—if you really want to write a book, get to work today."

Biographical and Critical Sources

PERIODICALS

Booklist, November 1, 2009, Ilene Cooper, review of *Dani Noir,* p. 59.
Bulletin of the Center for Children's Books, November, 2009, Deborah Stevenson, review of *Dani Noir,* p. 130.

Horn Book, November-December, 2009, Kitty Flynn, review of *Dani Noir,* p. 688.

Kirkus Reviews, August 15, 2009, review of *Dani Noir.*

Publishers Weekly, September 14, 2009, review of *Dani Noir,* p. 47.

School Library Journal, December, 2009, Susan W. Hunter, review of *Dani Noir,* p. 134.

Voice of Youth Advocates, October, 2009, Summer Hayes, review of *Dani Noir,* p. 323.

ONLINE

Nova Ren Suma Home Page, http://novaren.com (November 21, 2010).

Nova Ren Suma Web log, http://novaren.wordpress.com (December 6, 2010).

Simon & Schuster Web site, http://authors.simonand schuster.com/ (December 5, 2010), interview with Suma.*

T

TEEVEE, Ningeokuluk 1963-

Personal

Born May 27, 1963; daughter of Joanasie (a community leader) and Kanajuk Salomonie; married Simeonie Teevee (a musician).

Addresses

Home—Cape Dorset, Nunavut, Canada.

Career

Artist and author. Employee of municipal government in Cape Dorset, Nunavut Territory, Canada. *Exhibitions:* Work exhibited at Dorset Fine Arts, Toronto, Ontario, Canada, 2004-10.

Awards, Honors

Governor General's Literary Award finalist for Children's Illustration, Canada Council for the Arts, and Alcuin Society Book Design Award honorable mention, both 2009, Choices selection, Cooperative Children's Book Center, Best Books for Kids and Teens selection, Canadian Children's Book Centre, and Outstanding International Books honor listee, U.St. Board on Books for Young People, all 2010, all for *Alego.*

Writings

Qanutuinnarli isumasuungguviit?/What If?, Baffin Divisional Board of Education (Iqaluit, Northwest Territories, Canada), 1990.
(Self-illustrated) *Alego,* (bilingual edition), translated by Nina Manning-Toonoo, Groundwood Books (Toronto, Ontario, Canada), 2009.

Sidelights

An Inuit artist, Ningeokuluk Teevee is the author and illustrator of *Alego,* a finalist for Canada's Governor General's Literary Award. Teevee, who lives and works in Cape Dorset, an artist's haven on the southwest tip of Baffin Island, has earned recognition for her colorful and expressive lithograph prints that reflect the stories and legends of the Inuit culture.

Published in both Inuktitut and English, *Alego,* Teevee's critically acclaimed title for young readers, is based on the artist's childhood memories of growing up in the Arctic. The work centers on the title character, a young Inuit girl who joins her grandmother for a clam-digging

Canadian-born Inuit artist Ningeokuluk Teevee shares a story set in her native Northwest Territories in her self-illustrated picture book **Alego.** (Groundwood Books, 2009. Reproduced by permission of Groundwood Books Ltd., www.groundwoodbooks.com.)

expedition. Walking along the beach at low tide, Alego discovers a host of amazing creatures, including kinquit (sea lice), aggaujaq (starfish), and, of course, ammuu-majuit (clams). According to a critic in *Kirkus Reviews,* "Teevee illustrates the outing in a naïve style that reflects its simplicity," and Lauralyn Persson, writing in *School Library Journal,* similarly observed that *Alego*'s "unadorned text is suited to the primitive and childlike pictures," which are rendered in graphite and colored pencil. Writing in *Quill & Quire,* Nathan Whitlock also offered praise for *Alego,* stating: "At first glance, Teevee's . . . illustrations resemble those of a child, but closer scrutiny reveals subtler levels of sophistication and composition."

Biographical and Critical Sources

PERIODICALS

Canadian Review of Materials, January 8, 2010, Gail de Vos, review of *Alego.*

Kirkus Reviews, September 1, 2009, review of *Alego.*

Quill & Quire, December, 2009, Nathan Whitlock, review of *Alego.*

Resource Links, February, 2010, Anne Burke, review of *Alego,* p. 60.

School Library Journal, November, 2009, Lauralyn Persson, review of *Alego,* p. 90.

ONLINE

Canada House Gallery Web site, http://www.canadahouse.com/ (December 20, 2010), "Ningeokuluk Teevee."

Dorset Fine Arts Web site, http://www.dorsetfinearts.com/ (December 20, 2010), "Ningeokuluk Teevee."

Spirit Wrestler Gallery Web site, http://www.spiritwrestler.com/ (December 20, 2010), "Ningeokuluk Teevee."*

*　　*　　*

TIDHOLM, Anna-Clara 1946-

Personal

Born January 7, 1946, in Stockholm, Sweden; married Thomas Tidholm (a writer). *Education:* University degree (literature).

Addresses

Home—Arbra, Sweden. *E-mail*—anna-clara@tidholm. se.

Career

Comic artist, illustrator, and author of books for children. Former journalist.

Awards, Honors

Elsa Beskow medal, 1986; Deutscher Jugendliteraturpreis, 1992; Astrid Lindgren prize, 1997; Augustpriset, 2002, for *Adjö, herr Muffin* by Ulf Nilsson.

Writings

SELF-ILLUSTRATED

Tillbaks till Naturen, Bonnier (Stockholm, Sweden), 1970.

Sagan om pannkakan (collected comics), Gidlunds, 1982.

Jätten och ekorren, 1985.

Kanin med Nedhängande Öron (collected comics), Korpen, 1985.

Knacka på, Alfabeta (Stockholm, Sweden), 1992, reprinted, 2009, translated by MaryChris Bradley as *Knock! Knock!,* MacKenzie Smiles (San Francisco, CA), 2009.

Ut och gå, Alfabeta (Stockholm, Sweden), 1993.

Hitta på, Alfabeta (Stockholm, Sweden), 1993.

Varför då, Alfabeta (Stockholm, Sweden), 1994.

Ture blåser bort, Alfabeta (Stockholm, Sweden), 1995.

Ture sitter och tittar, Alfabeta (Stockholm, Sweden), 1996.

Lilla Grodan, Alfabeta (Stockholm, Sweden), 2000.

Lite sjuk, Alfabeta (Stockholm, Sweden), 2002.

Hela natten, Alfabeta (Stockholm, Sweden), 2002.

Pappan som försvann och andra berättelser barn och vuxna, Alfabeta (Stockholm, Sweden), 2003.

Hanna huset hunden, Alfabeta (Stockholm, Sweden), 2004.

Alla får åka med, Alfabeta (Stockholm, Sweden), 2004.

Ett fall för Nalle, Alfabeta (Stockholm, Sweden), 2004.

Läsa bok, Alfabeta (Stockholm, Sweden), 2006.

En liten stund, Alfabeta (Stockholm, Sweden), 2006.

Apan fin, Alfabeta (Stockholm, Sweden), 2010.

Contributor to periodicals, including *399, Aftonbladet, Dagens Nyheter, Fönstret, Galago, Steget,* and *Utslag.*

ILLUSTRATOR

Mats Arvidsson, *Bolaget, Pluttarna och Moskrogafolket,* Bonnier (Stockholm, Sweden), 1970.

Thomas Tidholm, *Universums Historia* (collected comics), Morkullan, 1988.

Thomas Tidholm, *Jims vinter,* Alfabeta (Stockholm, Sweden), 1988.

Thomas Tidholm, *Förr i tiden i skogen,* Alfabeta (Stockholm, Sweden), 1993.

Thomas Tidholm, *Ture skottar snö,* Alfabeta (Stockholm, Sweden), 1997.

Thomas Tidholm, *Alla Djuren,* Alfabeta (Stockholm, Sweden), 1998.

Thomas Tidholm, *Balladen om Marjan o Rolf,* Alfabeta (Stockholm, Sweden), 1998.

Lisa Berg Ortman, *Se ut,* Alfabeta (Stockholm, Sweden), 1999.

Sonja Hulth, *Flickan Som Bara Ville Läsa,* Alfabeta (Stockholm, Sweden), 2000.

Thomas Tidholm, *Åke-boken,* Alfabeta (Stockholm, Sweden), 2001.

Lilian Edvall, translated by Elisabeth Kallick Dyssengaard as *The Rabbit Who Longed for Home,* R&S Books (New York, NY), 2001.

Ulf Nilsson, *Adjö, herr Muffin,* Bonnier Carlsen (Sweden), 2002.

Solja Krapu, *Jag behöver lillbrorsan,* Alfabeta (Stockholm, Sweden), 2002.

Thomas Tidholm, *Jolanta,* Alfabeta (Stockholm, Sweden), 2002.

Per Gustavsson, *Väck inte den björn som sover,* Alfabeta (Stockholm, Sweden), 2004.

Thomas Tidholm, *När vi fick Felix,* Alfabeta (Stockholm, Sweden), 2005.

Thomas Tidholm, *Snälla barn,* Alfabeta (Stockholm, Sweden), 2007.

Kristina Lindström, *Flickornas historia,* Alfabeta (Stockholm, Sweden), 2007.

Gun Jacobson, *Nelly packar,* Alfabeta (Stockholm, Sweden), 2008.

Gunn Jacobson, *Simons anka,* Alfabeta (Stockholm, Sweden), 2008.

Gunn Jacobson, *Snuttefilm: fem snuttefilmer för de små barn* (omnibus), Alfabeta (Stockholm, Sweden), 2008.

Thomas Tidholm, *En som du inte känner,* Alfabeta (Stockholm, Sweden), 2010.

Biographical and Critical Sources

PERIODICALS

Booklist, September 15, 2001, Gillian Engberg, review of *The Rabbit Who Longed for Home,* p. 230.

Kirkus Reviews, September 1, 2009, review of *Knock! Knock!*

School Library Journal, November, 2001, Sarah O'Neal, review of *The Rabbit Who Longed for Home,* p. 119; May, 2009, Gloria Koster, review of *Knock! Knock!,* p. 90.

ONLINE

Anna-Clara Tidholm Home Page, http://anna-clara.tidholm.se/ (December 5, 2010).

Barensbibliotek Web site, http://www.barensbibliotek.se/ (December 15, 2010), "Anna-Clara Tidholm."

Lambiek Web site, http://www.lambiek.net/ (October 19, 2007), "Anna-Clara Tidholm."*

*   *   *

TOMORROW, Tom 1961-
(Dan Perkins)

Personal

Born April 5, 1961, in Wichita, KS.

Addresses

Home—New Haven, CT. *E-mail*—tom.tomorrow@gmail.com.

Career

Cartoonist, animator, and author. Public speaker.

Awards, Honors

Media Alliance Meritorious Achievement Award, 1993; James Madison Freedom of Information Award, Society of Professional Journalists 1995; Robert F. Kennedy Award for Excellence in Journalism, 1998, 2003; Professional Freedom and Responsibility Award, Association for Education in Journalism and Education, 2000; James Aronson Award for Social Justice Journalism, 2001, *Altweekly* Awards, second place, 2005, third place, 2006.

Writings

SELF-ILLUSTRATED

The Very Silly Mayor, IG Publishing (Brooklyn, NY), 2009.

CARTOON ANTHOLOGIES

Greetings from This Modern World, St. Martin's Press (New York, NY), 1992.

Tune in Tomorrow, St. Martin's Press (New York, NY), 1994.

The Wrath of Sparky, St. Martin's Griffin (New York, NY), 1996.

Penguin Soup for the Soul, St. Martin's Griffin (New York, NY), 1998.

When Penguins Attack!, introduction by Dave Eggers, St. Martin's Griffin (New York, NY), 2000.

The Great Big Book of Tomorrow: A Treasury of Cartoons, St. Martin's Griffin (New York, NY), 2003.

Hell in a Handbasket: Dispatches from the Country Formerly Known as America, J.P. Tarcher/Penguin (New York, NY), 2006.

The Future's So Bright I Can't Bear to Look, Nation Books (New York, NY), 2008.

Too Much Crazy, foreword by Michael Moore, 2010.

Author and illustrator of comic "This Modern World," beginning late 1980s and syndicated to over 100 periodicals, including *American Prospect, Economist, Esquire, Mother Jones, New Yorker, New York Times, Spin, U.S. News & World Report,* and *Village Voice,* and to Web sites, including Salon.com.

ILLUSTRATOR

Peter Phillips and Project Censored, *Censored 2000: The Year's Top 25 Censored Stories,* Seven Stories/Turnaround (New York, NY), 2000.

Also illustrator of book covers and album art.

Sidelights

Creator of "This Modern World," a cartoon feature of alternative newspapers across the country and Web sites that include Salon.com and *Truthout,* Tom Tomorrow is well known for his satirical depictions of U.S. politics and culture. In addition to collecting his many cartoons into book-length anthologies such as *Penguin Soup for the Soul* and *The Great Big Book of Tomorrow: A Treasury of Cartoons,* Tomorrow has also channeled his wry humor and cartoon characters Sparky the Wonder Penguin and a Boston terrier known as Blinky the Very Nice Dog into the picture book *The Very Silly Mayor,* which is published by Brooklyn-based current affairs publisher IG. Describing Tomorrow (a pen name for artist Dan Perkins) as "an unabashed Leftie," *Booklist* contributor Gordon Flagg noted of *The Great Big Book of Tom Tomorrow* that, while the book's "retro look draws readers in," the cartoonist's "acerbic humor keeps them coming back, and his wry intelligence just might make them think."

A feature of *The Very Silly Mayor* is Tomorrow's original pastiche of digitally created riffs on mid-twentieth-century cartoon and advertising art and his drawings based on contemporary news photographs, all rendered in flat black lines and comic-book colors. In the picture-book tale, a grinning politician decides to wield absolute power after he is elected city mayor. His new laws include dressing city policemen in clown costumes and arming firefighters with hoses full of sticky peanut butter. When city residents Sparky and Binky hear about the mayor's proclamations, they are astounded that no one is criticizing them. Ultimately, Sparky shows his political savvy by working within the system and signing on to assist rather than fight the absurdly misguided city leader. "While children can appreciate the absurdities, adults are most likely to chuckle at the satire" in Tomorrow's first children's book, according to a *Publishers Weekly* contributor. In *Kirkus Reviews* a critic concluded that the "silliness and the bright, flat cartoon art" in *The Very Silly Mayor* present a "lesson in the . . . necessity of questioning authority" that will appeal to readers of all ages.

Tom Tomorrow casts several of his quirky comic-book characters in his self-illustrated picture book **The Very Silly Mayor.** (IG Publishing, 2009. Copyright © 2009 by Dan Perkins. Reproduced by permission.)

Biographical and Critical Sources

BOOKS

Rall, Ted, *Attitude: The New Subversive Political Cartoonists,* NBM (New York, NY), 2002, pp. 28-33.

PERIODICALS

Booklist, September 15, 1994, Gordon Flagg, review of *Tune in Tomorrow,* p. 98; August, 2003, Gordon Flagg, review of *The Great Big Book of Tom Tomorrow,* p. 1942.

Kirkus Reviews, September 1, 2009, review of *The Very Silly Mayor.*

Publishers Weekly, July 29, 1996, review of *The Wrath of Sparky,* p. 83; September 14, 1998, review of *Penguin Soup for the Soul,* p. 52; October 5, 2009, review of *The Very Silly Mayor,* p. 46.

ONLINE

Tom Tomorrow Home Page, http://thismodernworld.com (November 25, 2010).

V-W

VERROKEN, Sarah 1982-

Personal
Born 1982, in Belgium; immigrated to New Zealand. *Education:* Master in Visual Arts degree (illustration), 2006.

Addresses
Home—Wellington, New Zealand. *E-mail*—suzie.wafer@gmail.com.

Career
Author, illustrator, and graphic designer. *Exhibitions:* Works exhibited in Knokke-Heist library, Belgium, 2010.

Awards, Honors
Illustrator's Award, City of Hasselt, Belgium, 2006, Boekenpauw award nomination, and Plantin Moretus award, both 2008, and Kids and Young Jury Flanders selection, 2009, all for *Boos*.

Writings

(Self-illustrated) *Boos,* Clavis (Amsterdam, Netherlands), 2007, translated as *Feeling Sad,* Enchanted Lion Books (Brooklyn, NY), 2009.
(Illustrator) Dirk Derom, *Pigeon and Pigeonette,* Enchanted Lion Books (Brooklyn, NY), 2009.

Illustrations included in poetry anthologies, including *Ik wil een naam van chocala,* edited by Ted van Lieshout, Querido (Amsterdam, Netherlands), 2010.

Author's work has been translated into Japanese and Korean.

Sidelights
During her final year of art school, graphic designer and illustrator Sarah Verroken created the illustrated story that would eventually be published as *Boos.* Winner of several awards in Verroken's native Belgium, *Boos* has also been translated into English as *Feeling*

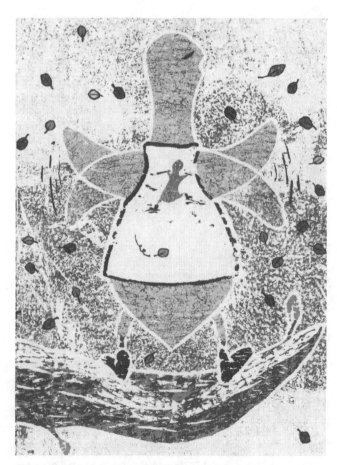

Belgian author and artists Dirk Derom and Sarah Verroken team up on the engaging picture book **Pigeon and Pigeonette,** *which inspires readers to hold onto their dreams.* (Copyright © 2009 by Enchanted Lion Books. Reproduced by permission of the publisher.)

Sad. The story highlights the power of an optimistic attitude and features Verroken's unique woodcut art, which also incorporates pen and ink, paint, and digital manipulation.

In *Feeling Sad* Duck is taking a walk with her favorite toy. As the sun clouds over and the rain falls on a grey world, Duck becomes despondent. However, when she encounters the encouraging words of a peppy little frog, Duck's day begins to brighten and color returns to her world. Verroken's "control of line and color easily communicate Duck's emotional journey," observed a *Kirkus Reviews* writer in appraising the "deceptively simple" story in *Feeling Sad.* Calling the picture book "outstanding," Anne Beier added in her *School Library Journal* review that the author/illustrator's "spare text underscores" the "bold" and "charming, folk-art-like illustrations" that bring her story to life.

Verroken now lives in New Zealand, but she returned to Belgium to oversee the publication of her next illustration project, *Pigeon and Pigeonette,* at a family-owned small press. Written in English by fellow Belgian Dirk Derom, *Pigeon and Pigeonette* resonates with another uplifting message: hold onto your dreams and never giving up. In the story, Pigeonette is too small to fly south with her friends so must stay at her summer home throughout the winter months. When she meets an older, stronger pigeon who has been forced to remain behind because of blindness, the two become friends and ultimately find a way to follow their flock south. Verroken's "bold woodcuts and limited color palette convey the setting of the woods throughout the seasons," observed *School Library Journal* contributor Stacy Dillon in a review of *Pigeon and Pigeonette,* while a *Kirkus Reviews* critic predicted that, with the benefit of the artist's "rich, blogly colored woodblock prints," Derom's "quirky tale will beguile" young picture-book audiences.

Biographical and Critical Sources

PERIODICALS

Children's Bookwatch, October, 2009, review of *Pigeon and Pigeonette.*

Kirkus Reviews, May 15, 2009, review of *Feeling Sad*; September 1, 2009, review of *Pigeon and Pigeonette.*

School Library Journal, August, 2009, Anne Beier, review of *Feeling Sad,* p. 86; November, 2009, Stacy Dillon, review of *Pigeon and Pigeonette,* p. 76.

ONLINE

Sarah Verroken Home Page, http://sarahverroken.com (November 21, 2010).

Sarah Verroken Web log, http://sarahverroken.blogspot.com (December 15, 2010).*

WADSWORTH, Ginger 1945-

Personal

Born May 7, 1945, in San Diego, CA; daughter of Hal G. (a writer) and Dorothea A. (an art teacher) Evarts; married Bill Wadsworth (an accountant and financial advisor for an engineering firm), June 4, 1967; children: Mark, Dan. *Education:* University of California, Davis, B.A. (English and American history), 1967. *Politics:* Democrat. *Hobbies and other interests:* Gardening with California native plants, western history, hiking, camping, bird watching, photography, travel, reading.

Addresses

Home and office—2 Fleetwood Court, Orinda, CA 94563-4004. *E-mail*—plumepal@aol.com.

Career

Elementary school teacher and teacher's aide in Walnut Creek and Orinda, CA, 1982-86; writer, 1986—. Former owner of a book store in Napa, CA. Active volunteer with local library; presenter at schools.

Member

Society of Children's Book Writers and Illustrators, Authors Guild, Western Writers of America, Women Writing the West, Audubon Society, Nature Conservancy, Yosemite Association, John Burroughs Association, California Historical Society.

Awards, Honors

Notable Children's Trade Book in the Field of Social Studies selection, National Council for the Social Studies/ Children's Book Council (NCSS/CBC), Best Book in Social Studies designation, Social Studies Librarians International (SSLI), and Distinguished Book designation, Association of Children's Librarians of Northern California, all 1990, all for *Julia Morgan, Architect of Dreams;* Nature Books for Young Readers selection, John Burroughs Association, 1992, for *John Muir, Wilderness Protector;* Best Book in Science (secondary) selection, Social Studies Librarians International, 1992, for *Rachel Carson, Voice for the Earth;* Notable Children's Trade Book in the Field of Social Studies designation, NCSS/CBC, 1994, for *Along the Santa Fe Trail,* and 2004, for *Benjamin Banneker, Pioneering Scientist;* third-place award for illustrated nonfiction, New York Book Show, 1997, and Books for the Teen Age designation, New York Public Library, 1998, both for *John Burroughs, the Sage of Slabsides;* Spur Award for juvenile nonfiction, Western Writers of America, Distinguished Book designation, Association of Children's Librarians of Northern California, Will Award finalist, Women Writing the West, and finalist for PEN Center Literary Award, all 2004, all for *Words West: Voices of Young Pioneers; Smithsonian* magazine Best Books selection, 2009, for *Camping with the President.*

Ginger Wadsworth (Reproduced by permission.)

Writings

JUVENILE BIOGRAPHIES

Julia Morgan, Architect of Dreams, Lerner Publications (Minneapolis, MN), 1990.

Rachel Carson, Voice for the Earth, Lerner Publications (Minneapolis, MN), 1992.

John Muir, Wilderness Protector, Lerner Publications (Minneapolis, MN), 1992.

(Adaptor) *Along the Santa Fe Trail: Marion Russell's Own Story,* illustrated by James Watling, Albert Whitman (Morton Grove, IL), 1993.

Susan Butcher, Sled Dog Racer, Lerner Publications (Minneapolis, MN), 1994.

Laura Ingalls Wilder: Storyteller of the Prairie, Lerner Publications (Minneapolis, MN), 1997.

John Burroughs, the Sage of Slabsides, Clarion Books (New York, NY), 1997.

Laura Ingalls Wilder ("On My Own" series), illustrated by Shelly O. Haas, Carolrhoda Books (Minneapolis, MN), 2000.

(Editor) *Words West: Voices of Young Pioneers,* Clarion Books (New York, NY), 2003.

Benjamin Banneker: Pioneering Scientist ("On My Own" series), illustrated by Craig Orback, Carolrhoda Books (Minneapolis, MN), 2003.

The Wright Brothers, Lerner Publications (Minneapolis, MN), 2004.

Cesar Chavez ("On My Own" series), Carolrhoda Books (Minneapolis, MN), 2005.

Annie Oakley, Lerner Publications (Minneapolis, MN), 2006.

Work included in anthology *Explore, Invitations to Literacy,* Houghton (Boston, MA), 1996.

Author's books have been translated into Japanese, Korean, Chinese, and Danish.

OTHER

Tomorrow Is Daddy's Birthday, illustrated by Maxie Chambliss, Caroline House/Boyds Mills Press (Honesdale, PA), 1994.

Giant Sequoia Trees, photographs by Frank J. Staub, Lerner Publications (Minneapolis, MN), 1995.

One on a Web: Counting Animals at Home, illustrated by James M. Needham, Charlesbridge (Watertown, MA), 1997.

Desert Discoveries, illustrated by John Carrozza, Charlesbridge (Watertown, MA), 1997.

Tundra Discoveries, illustrated by John Carrozza, Charlesbridge (Watertown, MA), 1999.

One Tiger Growls: A Counting Book of Animal Sounds, illustrated by James M. Needham, Charlesbridge (Watertown, MA), 1999.

River Discoveries, illustrated by Paul Kratter, Charlesbridge (Watertown, MA), 2002.

Wooly Mammoths, Carolrhoda Books (Minneapolis, MN), 2006.

Camping with the President, illustrated by Karen Dugan, Calkins Creek (Honesdale, PA), 2009.

Survival in the Snow, illustrated by Craig Orback, Millbrook Press (Minneapolis, MN), 2009.

Up, Up, and Away, illustrated by Patricia J. Wynne, Charlesbridge (Watertown, MA), 2009.

Contributor to *Writers in the Kitchen,* compiled by Tricia Gardella, Boyds Mills Press, 1998; *Idiot's Guide to Publishing Children's Books,* Alpha Books, 2001; and *ABC's of Writing for Children,* comprised by Elizabeth Koehler-Pentacoff, Quill Driver Books, 2003.

Adaptations

Rachel Carson: Voice for the Earth was adapted as an audiobook, Audio Bookshelf, 1996.

Sidelights

Ginger Wadsworth is, as she has pointed out, "a third-generation writer." Not only was her father, Hal G. Evarts, Jr., a writer, but so was his father before him, and all three generations have sought to capture aspects of the American West in their prose. Biographies form the core of Wadsworth's published work, and most of these concern either prominent Western figures or environmentalists, and sometimes—as in the case of naturalist John Muir—both.

The subject of Wadsworth's first book, *Julia Morgan, Architect of Dreams,* is most famous for her design of Hearst Castle, the San Simeon, California, home that

served as a playground for newspaper magnate William Randolph Hearst and his many celebrity guests during the early twentieth century. This structure alone constituted the work of a lifetime—"Morgan devoted 27 years to creating a setting for [Hearst's] life," explained Cathy Simon in the *New York Times Book Review*—but the architect also managed to design some seven hundred other buildings, ranging from churches to libraries to private residences. Working as she did in the early years of the twentieth century, Morgan was a ground-breaking figure for women in the field of architecture, but she did not tend to be outspoken about her abilities. In fact, she was reserved about disclosing the facts of her life, which may be why the first biography of her, Sara Holmes Boutelle's *Julia Morgan, Architect,* did not appear until 1988, some thirty years after Morgan's death. Wadsworth's book followed two years later and distinguished itself as "a lively read," in the words of Deborah Stevenson in the *Bulletin of the Center for Children's Books.* "It should be an inspiration," wrote Rosilind von Au in *Appraisal,* "to young women who feel called to scientifically oriented careers, such as architecture, where women are not in great number."

Rachel Carson, Voice for the Earth examines the life of the woman whose books *Silent Spring* and *The Sea around Us* are credited with spawning the environmental movement of the late twentieth century. Carolyn Phelan, writing in *Booklist,* commented favorably on "Wadsworth's competent research, writing, and source notes." *Appraisal* contributor Kathryn L. Harvis called *Rachel Carson* "a well-done, laudatory effort by an author who obviously has done her homework." Comparing Wadsworth's effort to other biographies, *School Library Journal* contributor Pat Katka maintained that it "stands up well" and "is more visually appealing than most."

Long before Carson, there was John Muir, the naturalist who founded the Sierra Club and, in the 1800s, started the movement to conserve the nation's vast natural resources that would ultimately lead to the establishment of the National Parks system. Wadsworth's biography *John Muir, Wilderness Protector* captures the life of this famed naturalist, while *Camping with the President* focuses on a 1903 excursion Muir took with then-U.S. President Theodore Roosevelt. Calling Wadsworth's profile of Muir "far superior to any series biographies about the naturalist," Judith Walker added in *Appraisal* that *John Muir, Wilderness Protector* is particularly timely given "the resurgence of interest in the environmental movement."

A nature lover and outdoorsman, Teddy Roosevelt remains known for his forceful advocacy of set-aside wild lands and his establishment of the U.S. Forest Service in 1905 under the management of Gifford Pinchot. With illustrations by Karen Dugan, *Camping with the President* describes a visit to the west made by the president and Muir as they explored the region that would eventually become Yosemite National Park. In-

cluding quotes from the two men, Wadsworth captures the controversy surrounding the early conservation movement, as lumber and land interests, as well as incursions from the transcontinental railroads, threatened millions of acres of Western wilderness. The author's use of detail places her book somewhere between a picture book and a social-studies resource, according to a *Kirkus Reviews* writer, and "Wadsworth's research is sound, her writing sprightly and her information interesting." Paired with the author's "well-written, lively account" of this pivotal four-day journey, *Camping with the President* features "intricately rendered watercolors" by Dugan that capture the region's "stunning vistas and wildlife," according to *Booklist* critic Shelle Rosenfeld.

In contrast to her fact-based books, Wadsworth takes a more interpretive approach in *Along the Santa Fe Trail: Marion Russell's Own Story.* The book is an adaptation of a pioneer's recollections and was written when Russell was eighty years old. As Julie Corsaro noted in *Booklist,* whereas Russell herself wrote from the perspective of an adult, Wadsworth utilizes the viewpoint of the seven-year-old Marion. The book, Corsaro concluded, "deserves a place in large regional or pioneer [library] collections."

Pioneer children are also the subject of several other books by Wadsworth. Intended for middle-grades students, *Words West: Voices of Young Pioneers* mixes excerpts from the journals, diaries, and letters of children who traveled westward with their families together with Wadsworth's own explanations of the subject. The text is accompanied by period photographs and engravings,

Featuring archival documents, **Words West** *captures the hardships, challenges, optimism, and lust for adventure that characterized nineteenth-century America.* (Cover illustration by G.E. Anderson. Reprinted by permission of Clarion Books, an imprint of Houghton Mifflin Harcourt Publishing Company. All rights reserved.)

as well as maps and an extensive bibliography. Critics praised the volume for presenting so vividly the experience of being a young pioneer, with its delights as well as its perils—at its best, riding in a wagon across the prairie, watching the scenery go by day and singing around a campfire by night, was much more fun than sitting in a schoolroom for the young travelers. "This book will be a valuable addition to large collections of Western history because of its unique primary-source material," Ginny Gustin concluded in *School Library Journal,* while a *Kirkus Reviews* contributor wrote that Wadsworth's "clear prose and . . . passion for her subject" make *Words West* "a model of fine history writing."

Survival in the Snow, which Wadsworth wrote as part of the "On My Own History" series, features realistic paintings by Craig Orback that bring to life the journey of a young man attempting to cross the Rocky Moun-

tains by wagon train in 1844. For Moses Schallenberger, the 2,000-mile journey reaches its most difficult stage in the midst of winter, as he must pass several frigid months alone in a rustic cabin after others in his party decide to risk the harsh conditions and continue on to California. Although Moses is not part of the ill-fated Donner party, which would take that same route only a few years later, Wadsworth discusses that historic trek as part of the history of the westward movement she includes in her afterword. Reviewing *Survival in the Snow* for *Booklist,* Carolyn Phelan praised the author's use of "concrete details" in capturing the story's drama, noting that she "puts a human face on the sometimes-anonymous image of the pioneer" in her tale of one teen's determination and bravery.

In *Laura Ingalls Wilder: Storyteller of the Prairie* Wadsworth profiles a much more famous pioneer woman. The facts of the biography, several reviewers noted,

Wadsworth's family centered picture book Tomorrow Is Daddy's Birthday *features engaging artwork by Maxie Chambliss.* (Boyds Mills Press, Inc., 1994.

will be familiar to anyone who has read Wilder's novels, which chronicle her story in a fictionalized form. Nonetheless, Wilder leaves out a painful chapter about her loss of an infant baby boy, which Wadsworth reports. Pat Mathews, writing in the *Bulletin of the Center for Children's Books,* maintained that *Laura Ingalls Wilder* is "a fine contribution to any biography collection," with its inclusion of Little House addresses, a bibliography, a map called "Laura's Tracks," a list of sources and an index, and "twelve readable chapters." Adele Greenlee, writing in *School Library Journal,* also praised *Laura Ingalls Wilder* as a "readable biography."

Wadsworth has also written other well-received biographies. *Susan Butcher, Sled Dog Racer* describes an athlete who, like Julia Morgan, competed as a woman in a man's world, in Butcher's case, the grueling Iditarod sled-dog race through Alaska and Canada. *John Burroughs, the Sage of Slabsides* tells the life story of a figure who occupied a place similar to that of John Muir in the history of American naturalism. John Burroughs, whose woodland hideaway in New York state was called Slabsides, rejected the urban life of the late nineteenth and early twentieth centuries. Some of the era's most distinguished figures—among them President Theodore Roosevelt, poet Walt Whitman, and automaker Henry Ford—became his friends. Wadsworth's biography, observed Marilyn Fairbanks in *School Library Journal,* is "written with a familiar, almost intimate tone." *Horn Book* reviewer Mary M. Burns called it "an accessible, respectable, and respectful treatment . . . aimed at young nature buffs, for whom little else about this significant individual is readily available." A *Kirkus Reviews* commentator called Wadsworth's book "a capable biography," noting that it "offers a good sense of Burroughs's gregarious personality."

Wadsworth has also written fiction and other works for a younger audience. Her picture book *Tomorrow Is Daddy's Birthday* introduces a young narrator named Rachel, who is so excited about the gift she plans to give her father that she cannot resist telling everyone she knows. Patricia Pearl Dole, writing in *School Library Journal,* called the book "an enjoyable story of family giving and sharing." *One Tiger Growls: A Counting Book of Animal Sounds* is also geared for young children, but not quite as young as the usual counting-book audience. Twenty animals are presented, from one tiger growling, through llamas um-m-m-m-m-ming and sea lions ork-ork-orking, all the way to twenty frogs ribbiting. Each two-page spread features a single animal, depicted realistically in its natural habitat, and Wadsworth's inclusion of a paragraph detailing scientific facts about the animal represented makes the book a potentially useful teaching tool. "There's not enough information for report writers," Kay Weisman commented in *Booklist,* but *One Tiger Growls* is perfect for "sophisticated browsers who may be almost ready for research."

Tundra Discoveries and *River Discoveries* also share information about wildlife with young listeners and readers. The former book follows various Arctic inhabitants, including caribou, musk oxen, foxes, lemmings, and ground squirrels, through a year, month by month. Watercolor paintings by John Carrozza depict the animals going about their lives, while graphs on each page visually display information about the weather in that month, such as the number of hours of daylight versus darkness and the average temperature. As in *Tundra Discoveries,* each page of *River Discoveries* focuses on much-asked questions to help keep children engaged. *River Discoveries* uses a similar format, but only takes readers through a single day, rather than an entire year in the life of a waterway. The animals featured in this volume live both in the river—catfish, trout, river otters, water beetles—and near it—blackbirds, raccoons, mountain lions, and moose, for example. The "attractive visuals together with the focused facts will engage many young naturalists," wrote *Booklist* reviewer Ellen Mandel in her appraisal of *Tundra Discoveries,* while Catherine Andronik concluded in *Booklist* that *River Discoveries* "offers children an attractive, informative introduction to riparian ecology."

Nature also takes center stage in *Up, Up, and Away,* a picture book by Wadsworth that features detailed multimedia artwork by Patricia J. Wynne. In a text that Phelan characterized in *Booklist* as "simply told with well-chosen words and phrases," Wadsworth described the short life of a garden spider as its destined role in nature prompts it to float away from its predatory fellow hatchlings, construct the delicate web that will trap its food, find a mate and lay eggs, and ultimately die. Noting the book's focus on the construction of the spider's complex web, *School Library Journal* contributor Patricia Manning added that the author's "clear, simple text" is matched by Wynne's "bright-hued" and detailed water-color images. A *Kirkus Reviews* writer also recommended Wadsworth's story, dubbing *Up, Up, and Away* "good preparatory material for a shared reading of [E.B. White's childhood classic] *Charlotte's Web.*"

Biographical and Critical Sources

PERIODICALS

Appraisal, spring-summer, 1991, Rosilind Von Au, review of *Julia Morgan, Architect of Dreams,* pp. 49-50; autumn, 1992, Kathryn L. Harvis, review of *Rachel Carson, Voice for the Earth,* pp. 38-39; winter, 1993, Judith A. Walker, review of *John Muir,* pp. 52-53.

Booklist, June 1, 1992, Carolyn Phelan, review of *Rachel Carson, Voice for the Earth,* p. 1761; August, 1992, Mary Romano, review of *John Muir, Wilderness Protector,* pp. 2003; January 15, 1994, Julie Corsaro, review of *Along the Santa Fe Trail: Marion Russell's Own Story,* p. 928; March 15, 1997, Carolyn Phelan, review of *John Burroughs, the Sage of Slabsides,* p. 1241; February 1, 1999, Kay Weisman, review of *One Tiger Growls: A Counting Book of Animal Sounds,* p.

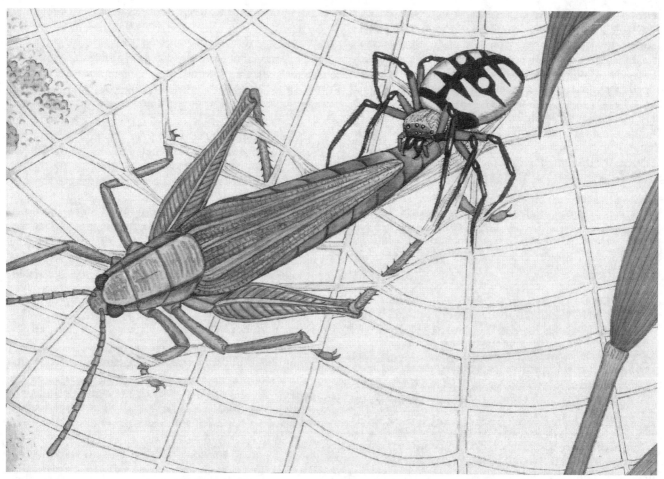

Wadsworth turns from nonfiction to storytelling in her nature-themed picture book Up, Up, and Away, *featuring artwork by Patricia J. Wynne.* (Illustration copyright © 2009 by Patricia J. Wayne. Reproduced by permission of Charlesbridge Publishing, Inc. All rights reserved.)

978; September 1, 1999, Ellen Mandel, review of *Tundra Discoveries,* p. 136; September 15, 2002, Catherine Andronik, review of *River Discoveries,* p. 230; May 1, 2005, Hazel Rochman, review of *Cesar Chavez,* p. 1583; February 15, 2009, Carolyn Phelan, review of *Survival in the Snow,* p. 85; August 1, 2009, Carolyn Phelan, review of *Up, Up, and Away,* p. 75; September 15, 2009, Shelle Rosenfeld, review of *Camping with the President,* p. 53.

Bulletin of the Center for Children's Books, December, 1990, Deborah Stevenson, review of *Julia Morgan, Architect of Dreams,* p. 104; May, 1997, review of *John Burroughs, the Sage of Slabsides,* pp. 336-37; September, 1997, Pat Mathews, review of *Laura Ingalls Wilder: Storyteller of the Prairie,* p. 30.

Horn Book, July-August, 1992, Ellen Fader, review of *Rachel Carson, Voice for the Earth,* pp. 471-472; July-August, 1997, Mary M. Burns, review of *John Burroughs, the Sage of Slabsides,* pp. 478-479.

Journal of Adolescent and Adult Literacy, November, 2004, review of *Words West: Voices of Young Pioneers,* p. 268.

Kirkus Reviews, February 1, 1997, review of *John Burroughs, the Sage of Slabsides,* p. 229; February 15, 1997, p. 307; July 1, 2002, review of *River Discoveries,* p. 964; October 1, 2003, review of *Words West,* p. 1232; June 1, 2009, review of *Up, Up, and Away*; August 15, 2009, review of *Camping with the President.*

New York Times Book Review, March 17, 1991, Cathy Simon, review of *Julia Morgan, Architect of Dreams,* p. 27.

Publishers Weekly, August 9, 1993, review of *Along the Santa Fe Trail,* p. 479; February 1, 1999, review of *One Tiger Growls,* p. 83.

School Library Journal, February, 1991, Jeanette Larson, review of *Julia Morgan, Architect of Dreams,* p. 101; July, 1992, Pat Katka, review of *Rachel Carson, Voice for the Earth,* p. 88; September, 1992, Kathleen Odean, review of *John Muir, Wilderness Protector,* p. 271; December, 1993, Sally Bates Goodroe, review of *Along the Santa Fe Trail,* p. 108; November, 1994, Patricia Pearl Dole, review of *Tomorrow Is Daddy's Birthday,* p. 92; April, 1997, Adele Greenlee, review of *Laura Ingalls Wilder,* p. 162; May, 1997, Marilyn Fairbanks, review of *John Burroughs, the Sage of Slabsides,* p. 151; May, 2000, Kathleen Simonetta, review of *Laura Ingalls Wilder,* p. 165; August, 2002, Barbara L. McMullin, review of *River Discoveries,* p. 181; December, 2003, Ginny Gustin, review of *Words West,* p. 175; September, 2009, Patricia Manning, review of *Up, Up, and Away,* p. 149.

ONLINE

Ginger Wadsworth Home Page, http://www.gingerwads worth.com (December 5, 2010).

WALKER, Anna

Personal

Born in Australia; married; children: three.

Addresses

Home—Melbourne, Victoria, Australia.

Career

Artist and graphic designer. Illustrator and author of books for children, beginning 2007.

Writings

SELF-ILLUSTRATED

I Love Birthdays, Scholastic Australia (Lindfield, New South Wales, Australia), 2008.

I Love Holidays, Scholastic Australia (Lindfield, New South Wales, Australia), 2008.

I Love My Mum, Puffin (Camberwell, Victoria, Australia), 2008, published as *I Love My Mom,* Simon & Schuster Books for Young Children (New York, NY), 2010.

I Love to Dance, Puffin (Camberwell, Victoria, Australia), 2008, Simon & Schuster Books for Young Readers (New York, NY), 2011.

I Love to Sing, Puffin (Camberwell, Victoria, Australia), 2008, Simon & Schuster Books for Young Readers (New York, NY), 2011.

Froggy Green, Puffin (Camberwell, Victoria, Australia), 2008, Kane/Miller (La Jolla, CA), 2009.

Funny Face, Kane/Miller (Tulsa, OK), 2009.

I Love Christmas, Simon & Schuster Books for Young Readers (New York, NY), 2009.

I Love My Dad, Puffin (Camberwell, Victoria, Australia), 2009, Simon & Schuster Books for Young Readers (New York, NY), 2010.

I Don't Believe in Dragons, Scholastic Australia (Lindfield, New South Wales, Australia), 2010.

I Love My Grandpa, Scholastic Australia (Lindfield, New South Wales, Australia), 2010.

I Love My Grandma, Scholastic Australia (Lindfield, New South Wales, Australia), 2010.

I Love Vacations, Simon & Schuster Books for Young Readers (New York, NY), 2011.

I Love Easter, Scholastic Australia (Lindfield, New South Wales, Australia), 2011.

ILLUSTRATOR

Maria Farrer, *Santa's Aussie Holiday,* Scholastic Press (Gosford, New South Wales, Australia), 2007.

Karl Yeomans, *The Miggy Tree,* Klaussen Publishing (South Yarra, Victoria, Australia), 2007.

Jane Godwin, *Little Cat and the Big Red Bus,* Penguin Viking (Camberwell, Victoria, Australia), 2008.

Emma Quay, *Let's Play House: A Book about Imagination,* Scholastic Australia (Lindfield, New South Wales, Australia), 2009, Dial Books for Young Readers (New York, NY), 2011.

Emma Quay, *Yummy Ice Cream: A Book about Sharing,* Scholastic Australia (Lindfield, New South Wales, Australia), 2009, Dial Books for Young Readers (New York, NY), 2011.

Emma Quay, *Jump over the Puddle,* Scholastic Australia (Lindfield, New South Wales, Australia), 2009, published as *Puddle Jumping: A Book about Bravery,* Dial Books for Young Readers (New York, NY), 2011.

Emma Quay, *Lets Go Camping,* Scholastic Australia (Gosford, New South Wales, Australia), 2010.

Emma Quay, *Birthday Surprise,* Scholastic Australia (Gosford, New South Wales, Australia), 2010.

Emma Quay, *Dotty Sprinkles,* Scholastic Australia (Lindfield, New South Wales, Australia), 2010.

Jane Godwin, *All through the Year,* Penguin (Camberwell, Victoria, Australia), 2010.

Emma Quay, *Sleep Tight: A Book about Bedtime,* Dial Books for Young Readers (New York, NY), 2011.

Biographical and Critical Sources

PERIODICALS

Kirkus Reviews, September 15, 2009, review of *I Love Christmas;* November 1, 2009, review of *Funny Face.*

Magpies, November, 2008, Annette Dale Meiklejohn, review of *Little Cat and the Big Red Bus,* p. 30; March, 2009, Liz Derouet, review of *Funny Face,* p. 26; July, 2009, Liz Derouet, review of *Friends for Keeps,* p. 26.

Publishers Weekly, March 22, 2010, review of *I Love My Mom,* p. 68.

School Library Journal, October, 2009, Maureen Wade, review of *I Love Christmas,* p. 84; March, 2010, Gay Lynn Van Vleck, review of *I Love My Dad,* p. 135.

ONLINE

Anna Walker Home Page, http://www.annawalker.com.au (November 21, 2010).

Anna Walker Web log, http://annawalker.com.au (December 10, 2010).*

*　　　*　　　*

WEHRMAN, Vicki

Personal

Married Richard Wehrman (an illustrator and designer); children. *Education:* Washington University (St. Louis, MO), B.F.A.

Addresses

Home—East Bloomfield, NY. *E-mail*—vwehrman@rochester.rr.com.

Career

Illustrator of children's books.

Illustrator

Bruce Lansky, *Sweet Dreams: Bedtime Poems, Songs, and Lullabies,* Meadowbrook Press (Deephaven, MN), 1996.

Linda Andersen, *Love Adds the Chocolate,* WaterBrook Press (Colorado Springs, CO), 2000.

Brenda Ehrmantraut, *Night Catch,* Bubble Gum Press (Jamestown, ND), 2005.

Tami Lehman-Wilzig, *Hanukkah around the World,* Kar-Ben Pub. (Minneapolis, MN), 2009.

Sidelights

Based in upper New York State, Vicki Wehrman is an artist and designer whose work has appeared in picture books as well as in advertising, on book covers, and in magazines. With her use of bright colors, soft-edged and stylized shapes, and folk-art sensibility, Wehrman captivates young children with each image, encouraging viewers to explore its details. Her illustrations projects include *Sweet Dreams: Bedtime Poems, Songs, and Lullabies* by Bruce Lansky, Linda Andersen's *Love Adds the Chocolate,* Brenda Ehrmantraut's *Night Catch,* and Tami Lehman-Wilzig's *Hanukkah around the World.*

In Lehman-Wilzig's *Hanukkah around the World* young children learn the history of the best-known Jewish holiday and the traditions that have developed around it throughout history and around the world. Enriching Lehman-Wilzig's collection of history, stories, and recipes, Wehrman creates maps, illustrations, and other visual elements that *School Library Journal* critic Teri Markson described as "densely colored" and "appealing," while in *Kirkus Reviews* a contributor wrote that the artist's "soft muted paintings" for *Hanukkah around the World* contribute an "instructional element" due to the artist's well-researched detail.

Biographical and Critical Sources

PERIODICALS

Booklist, December 1, 2009, Kay Weisman, review of *Hanukkah around the World,* p. 40.

Kirkus Reviews, September 15, 2009, review of *Hanukkah around the World.*

Publishers Weekly, October 19, 2009, review of *Hanukkah around the World,* p. 52.

School Library Journal, October, 2009, Teri Markson, review of *Hanukkah around the World,* p. 81.*

* * *

WHARTON, Thomas 1963-

Personal

Born 1963, in Grande Prairie, Alberta, Canada; son of a utilities manager; married; wife's name Sharon; children: three. *Education:* University of Alberta, B.A., M.A.; University of Calgary, Ph.D., 1998.

Addresses

Home—Edmonton, Alberta, Canada. *Office*—Department of English and Film Studies, University of Alberta, Edmonton, Alberta T6G 2R3, Canada. *E-mail*—twharton@ualberta.ca.

Career

Author and educator. University of Alberta, Edmonton, Alberta, Canada, assistant professor of English and film studies; also taught at Grant MacEwan College and Athabasca College.

Awards, Honors

Grand Prize and Banff National Park Award, Banff Mountain Book Festival, 1995, Commonwealth Writers' Prize for Best First Book (Canada and Caribbean division), and Henry Kreisel Award, Alberta Book Awards, both 1996, and Boardman Tasker Prize in Mountain Literature shortlist, and Grant MacEwan College Book of the Year, both 1998, all for *Icefields;* Sunburst Award for Canadian Fantasy shortlist, Governor General's Award for Fiction shortlist, and Rogers Writers' Trust Fiction Prize finalist, all 2001, and Grant MacEwan Author's Award shortlist, and Georges Bugnet Award for Fiction, Alberta Book Awards, both 2002, all for *Salamander;* Sunburst Award for Canadian Fantasy shortlist, and Writers' Guild of Alberta Award for Short Fiction, both 2005, and IMPAC-Dublin Prize shortlist, 2006, all for *The Logogryph;* Ruth and Sylvia Schwartz Children's Book Awards shortlist, 2008, for *The Shadow of Malabron.*

Writings

Icefields, NeWest Press (Edmonton, Alberta, Canada), 1995, Washington Square Press (New York, NY), 1996.

Salamander, McClelland & Stewart (Toronto, Ontario, Canada), 2001, Washington Square Press (New York, NY), 2002.

The Logogryph, Gaspereau Press (Kentville, Nova Scotia, Canada), 2004.

The Shadow of Malabron (first book in "Perilous Realm" trilogy), Doubleday Canada (Toronto, Ontario, Canada), 2008, Candlewick Press (Somerville, MA), 2009.

Sidelights

In *The Shadow of Malabron,* his first novel for young adult audiences, Canadian writer Thomas Wharton offers "a well-constructed quest in the style of [J.R.R.] Tolkien and [Philip] Pullman," observed *Booklist* critic Cindy Welch. Wharton, who teaches English at the Uni-

versity of Alberta, has garnered attention for his challenging, inventive, and haunting adult titles, including *Icefields,* which earned him the Commonwealth Writers' Prize, and *Salamander.* Discussing his love of crafting complex, imaginative narratives, Wharton told *Quill & Quire* interviewer Helen Metella: "I kind of delight in being the creator of a world where I can say, 'This is my world and I can do as I please.'"

Born and raised in Grand Prairie, Alberta, Canada, a flourishing agricultural center, Wharton moved to the small town of Jasper as a teenager and the change proved difficult. "I got very, very shy and had a complete crisis of confidence," he recalled to Metella. Wharton turned to books—particularly adventure tales and fantasies—and journal writing as a way to cope with his feelings of isolation. "I was trying to work through these feelings of loneliness with words—writing as therapy," he stated.

Literature also played a pivotal role in altering Wharton's career path. After first studying art and design at the University of Alberta, he ultimately earned a degree in biological sciences, but working as a medical lab technician failed to fire his imagination. "Then I picked up [James Joyce's novel] *Ulysses,*" he told Metella. "One summer, working as a lab tech, I sat and read that

Cover of Thomas Wharton's middle-grade fantasy novel The Shadow of Malabron, *featuring artwork by Tim Jessell.* (Illustration copyright © 2009 by Tim Jessell. Reproduced by permission of Candlewick Press, Somerville, MA.)

whole book. Then I went to the library and got an annotated guide to help me understand it, and I reread it and made notes in the margin. By the time I was halfway through, I realized, 'I'm going back into English.' The inventiveness and energy of the prose in that book totally revitalized me."

Enrolling in a creative-writing course taught by visionary Canadian writer Rudy Wiebe, Wharton began composing a series of tall tales set in Alberta. These pieces formed the basis for *Icefields,* a prize-winning work in which Wharton demonstrates "a fine sense of description, dialogue that is as spare as the landscape and a subtle hand with narrative," according to a *Publishers Weekly* contributor. He followed that title with *Salamander,* a book that examines the storytelling process, and *The Logogryph,* an experimental work.

In *The Shadow of Malabron,* the first work in his "Perilous Realm" trilogy, Wharton introduces Will Lightfoot, a teenager who enters the Perilous Realm, a mysterious otherworld where all stories originate. While trying to locate an exit from the Perilous Realm, a land filled with golems, wizards, dragons, and other fantastic creatures, Will meets Rowen, a resourceful young woman, and her grandfather Pendrake, a toymaker turned loremaster who believes that Will may be the key in an ongoing struggle with the Night King Malabron. As they journey through the region pursued by Lotan, one of Malabron's soldiers, Will, Rowen, and Pendrake join forces with a host of other colorful characters, including Finn, a knight errant, and Shade, a talking wolf. "The Realm's metaphysics are unusual and intriguing: stories are both concept and substance, with the power to trap, seduce and liberate," Megan Honig noted in her review of *The Shadow of Malabron* for *School Library Journal.* A critic in *Kirkus Reviews* also praised the work, predicting that readers who appreciate folklore "will be delighted by Wharton's twisting of the tropes and tales of myth and legend."

Biographical and Critical Sources

PERIODICALS

Booklist, February 15, 2010, Cindy Welch, review of *The Shadow of Malabron,* p. 78.
Canadian Review of Materials, September 12, 2008, Ronald Hore, review of *The Shadow of Malabron.*
Geographical, March, 1997, review of *Icefields,* p. 62.
Kirkus Reviews, September 15, 2009, review of *The Shadow of Malabron.*
New Statesman, April 8, 2002, Francis Gilbert, review of *Salamander,* p. 54.
Papers of the Bibliographical Society of Canada, fall, 2002, Gillian Fenwick, review of *Salamander,* p. 126.
People, December 2, 1996, Emily Mitchell, review of *Icefields,* p. 29.
Publishers Weekly, August 19, 1996, review of *Icefields,* p. 62; October 19, 2009, review of *The Shadow of Malabron,* p. 53.

Quill & Quire, May, 2001, Helen Metella, review of _Salamander;_ September, 2008, Maureen Garvie, review of _The Shadow of Malabron._

Resource Links, October, 2001, review of _Salamander,_ p. 56.

School Library Journal, November, 2009, Megan Honig, review of _The Shadow of Malabron,_ p. 124.

ONLINE

NeWest Press Web site, http://www.newestpress.com/ (December 1, 2010), "Thomas Wharton."

Thomas Wharton Web log, http://logogryph.blogspot.com (December 1, 2010).

University of Alberta Web site, http://www.ualberta.ca/ (December 1, 2010), "Thomas Wharton."*

*   *   *

WHITE, Lee

Personal

Married; wife's name Lisa; children: one. _Education:_ Art Center College of Design, B.F.A. (illustration; with honors), 2003. _Hobbies and other interests:_ Skateboarding, snowboarding.

Addresses

Home and office—Portland, OR. _E-mail_—l.white@leewhiteillustration.com.

White's illustration projects include his colorful updated version of the well-known tale "Little Red Riding Hood." (Illustration © 2009 by Lee White. Reproduced with permission of Lee White, www.leewhiteillustration.com.)

Career

Graphic designer and illustrator. Art Institute of Portland, Portland, OR, teacher, beginning 2008. _Exhibitions:_ Works have been exhibited at galleries, including Every Picture Tells a Story, Santa Monica, CA, 2004, and Nucleus Gallery, Los Angeles, CA, 2010.

Illustrator

PICTURE BOOKS

Simon T. Ribke, _I'll Do It Later,_ Children's Press (New York, NY), 2005.

Martha Peaslee Levine, _Stop That Nose!,_ Marshall Cavendish (New York, NY), 2006.

Elle Olson-Brown, _Hush, Little Digger,_ Tricycle Press (Berkeley, CA), 2006.

Jacqueline Davies, _The House Takes a Vacation,_ Marshall Cavendish (New York, NY), 2006.

Devin Scillian, _Brewster the Rooster,_ Sleeping Bear Press (Farmington Hills, MI), 2007.

John Nedwidek, _Ducks Don't Wear Socks,_ Viking (New York, NY), 2008.

Carole Boston Weatherford, _The Library Ghost,_ Upstart Books (Fort Atkinson, WI), 2008.

Barbara Odanaka, _A Crazy Day at the Critter Café,_ Margaret K. McElderry Books (New York, NY), 2009.

Sally M. Walker, _Druscilla's Halloween,_ Carolrhoda Books (Minneapolis, MN), 2009.

Lee White (Photograph courtesy of Lee White.)

Contributor to periodicals, including *Ladybug*.

Sidelights

Portland, Oregon artist Lee White creates illustrations for book covers, posters, and magazines as well as for children's picture books. Whether working in pen, ink wash, water color, acrylics, oils, alkyds, or digitally, White adds another level of entertainment to each text he brings to life, from the story of a shortsighted foul in Devian Scillian's *Brewster the Rooster* to Sally M. Walker's holiday-themed tale bout a crackle-boned witch trying to do her part in frightening trick-or-treaters in *Druscilla's Halloween*. Reviewing *Druscilla's Halloween* in *School Library Journal*, Catherine Callegari noted the illustrator's ability to effectively gauge his audience, writing that White's "atmospheric spreads have just the right amount of spookiness and ample touches of humor."

While earning his B.F.A. at the prestigious Pasadena-based Art Center College of Design, White experimented with various media and styles while also drawing on his previous work as a graphic designer. "The big lesson I learned at Art Center is the value of really hard work," he told online interviewer Amy Baskin. "I learned how to fully finish a project. That last 10 or 20 percent of an illustration is the most difficult and requires a huge amount of dedication. I learned that almost anything can be made better with a few more hours work and a strong cup of coffee." A trip to New York City and a year of building and shopping his portfolio led to his first illustration project, Simon T. Ribke's 2006 picture book *I'll Do It Later*.

In *Brewster the Rooster* White's "exaggerated illustrations heighten the humor of [Scillian's] . . . whimsically rhymed story," wrote Julie Cummins in her *Booklist* review of a more-recent White project while *School Library Journal* critic Mary Elam cited the use of a "bold palette of soft-focus warm colors" to bring to life Brewster's antic farmyard. *Hush, Little Digger*, a story by Elle Olson-Brown that casts a steam shovel as the dozy recipient of a "Hush Little Baby"-type rhyme, features oil and colored-pencil images that "perk up the verses" and make the book a "fun, lively choice for . . . storytimes," according to *School Library Journal* contributor Lynn K. Vanca. In *Kirkus Reviews* a contributor agreed, recommending the "cartoon vibrancy and nimble, witty tidbits" of visual humor in White's illustrations for Olson-Brown's rhyming text.

The opportunity to create the illustrations for Jacqueline Davies' *The House Takes a Vacation* presented White with an unusual task: Find a way to give a house legs. In the story, the Petersons' family home decides that if its residents deserve a vacation, their house does as well. Soon the upper floors of the structure are suspended over its foundation on thin, wobbly legs, and a day at the beach is at hand. Paired with Davies' pun-filled text, White's "large oil and colored pencil illustrations blend vivid colors and flowing shapes to create an impressionistic mood," according to *School Library Journal* critic Judith Constantinides, while Kitty Flynn wrote in *Horn Book* that the "spirited" images in *The House Takes a Vacation* capture the story's "kooky premise and characters." Another quirky tale, *A Crazy Day at the Critter Café*, also benefits from White's contribution as his use of "colorful splotches" and "muted, colorful backgrounds" highlight what a *Kirkus Reviews* writer described as the "disheveled environment" in Barbara Odanaka's "rollicking read-aloud."

White's art captures the fun in Ellen Olson-Brown's boy-friendly bedtime book **Hush, Little Digger.** (Copyright © 2006 by Lee White. Used with permission of Tricycle Press, an imprint of Random House Children's Books, a division of Random House, Inc.)

Animals take over human tasks in Lee's art for Barbara Odanaka's high-energy picture book A Crazy Day at the Critter Café. (Illustration copyright © 2009 Lee White. Margaret K. McElderry Books, 2009. Reprinted by permission of Simon & Schuster Children's Publishing Division.)

Biographical and Critical Sources

PERIODICALS

Booklist, April 1, 2006, Carolyn Phelan, review of *Hush, Little Digger,* p. 45; July 1, 2007, Julie Cummins, review of *Brewster the Rooster,* p. 63; June 1, 2008, Abby Nolan, review of *Ducks Don't Wear Socks,* p. 86; May 1, 2009, Julie Cummins, review of *A Crazy Day at the Critter Café,* p. 85; September 15, 2009, Carolyn Phelan, review of *Druscilla's Halloween,* p. 63.

Horn Book, May-June, 2007, Kitty Flynn, review of *The House Takes a Vacation,* p. 263.

Kirkus Reviews, February 15, 2006, review of *Stop That Nose!,* p. 185; April 15, 2006, review of *Hush, Little Digger,* p. 413; February 15, 2007, review of *The House Takes a Vacation;* March 1, 2008, review of *Ducks Don't Wear Socks;* May 1, 2009, review of *A Crazy Day at the Critter Café.*

Publishers Weekly, August 31, 2009, review of *Druscilla's Halloween,* p. 56.

School Library Journal, April, 2006, Suzanne Myers Harold, review of *Stop That Nose!,* p. 110; June, 2006; Lynn K. Vanca, review of *Hush, Little Digger,* p. 139;

May, 2007, Judith Constantinides, review of *The House Takes a Vacation,* p. 90; August, 2007, Mary Elam, review of *Brewster the Rooster,* p. 90; May, 2008, Maura Bresnahan, review of *Ducks Don't Wear Socks,* p. 104; June, 2009, Marge Loch-Wouters, review of *A Crazy Day at the Critter Café,* p. 97; September, 2009, Catherine Callegari, review of *Brewster the Rooster,* p. 136.

ONLINE

Amy Baskin Web log, http://amy-basking.blogspot.com/ (March 30, 2010), Amy Baskin, interview with White.

Lee White Home Page, http://www.leewhiteillustration. com (December 6, 2010).

Lee White Web log, http://leewhiteillustration.blogspot.com (December 6, 2010).*

Illustrations Index

(In the following index, the number of the *volume* in which an illustrator's work appears is given *before* the colon, and the *page number* on which it appears is given *after* the colon. For example, a drawing by Adams, Adrienne appears in Volume 2 on page 6, another drawing by her appears in Volume 3 on page 80, another drawing in Volume 8 on page 1, and so on and so on. . . .)

YABC

Index references to *YABC* refer to listings appearing in the two-volume *Yesterday's Authors of Books for Children,* also published by Gale, Cengage Learning. *YABC* covers prominent authors and illustrators who died prior to 1960.

A

Aas, Ulf *5:* 174
Abbe, S. van
See van Abbe, S.
Abel, Raymond *6:* 122; *7:* 195; *12:* 3; *21:* 86; *25:* 119
Abelliera, Aldo *71:* 120
Abolafia, Yossi *60:* 2; *93:* 163; *152:* 202
Abrahams, Hilary *26:* 205; *29:* 24, 25; *53:* 61
Abrams, Kathie *36:* 170
Abrams, Lester *49:* 26
Abulafia, Yossi *154:* 67; *177:* 3
Accardo, Anthony *191:* 3, 8
Accornero, Franco *184:* 8
Accorsi, William *11:* 198
Acs, Laszlo *14:* 156; *42:* 22
Acuna, Ed *198:* 79
Adams, Adrienne *2:* 6; *3:* 80; *8:* 1; *15:* 107; *16:* 180; *20:* 65; *22:* 134, 135; *33:* 75; *36:* 103, 112; *39:* 74; *86:* 54; *90:* 2, 3
Adams, Connie J. *129:* 68
Adams, John Wolcott *17:* 162
Adams, Lynn *96:* 44
Adams, Norman *55:* 82
Adams, Pam *112:* 1, 2
Adams, Sarah *98:* 126; *164:* 180
Adams, Steve *209:* 64
Adamson, George *30:* 23, 24; *69:* 64
Addams, Charles *55:* 5
Addison, Kenneth *192:* 173
Addy, Sean *180:* 8; *222:* 31
Ade, Rene *76:* 198; *195:* 162
Adinolfi, JoAnn *115:* 42; *176:* 2; *217:* 79
Adkins, Alta *22:* 250
Adkins, Jan *8:* 3; *69:* 4; *144:* 2, 3, 4; *210:* 11, 17, 18, 19
Adler, Kelynn *195:* 47
Adler, Peggy *22:* 6; *29:* 31
Adler, Ruth *29:* 29
Adlerman, Daniel *163:* 2
Adragna, Robert *47:* 145
Agard, Nadema *18:* 1
Agee, Jon *116:* 8, 9, 10; *157:* 4; *196:* 3, 4, 5, 6, 7, 8
Agre, Patricia *47:* 195
Aguirre, Alfredo *152:* 218
Ahl, Anna Maria *32:* 24
Ahlberg, Allan *68:* 6, 7, 9; *165:* 5; *214:* 9
Ahlberg, Janet *68:* 6, 7, 9; *214:* 9

Aicher-Scholl, Inge *63:* 127
Aichinger, Helga *4:* 5, 45
Aitken, Amy *31:* 34
Ajhar, Brian *207:* 126; *220:* 2
Akaba, Suekichi *46:* 23; *53:* 127
Akasaka, Miyoshi *YABC 2:* 261
Akib, Jamel *181:* 13; *182:* 99; *220:* 74
Akino, Fuku *6:* 144
Alain *40:* 41
Alajalov *2:* 226
Albert, Chris *200:* 64
Alborough, Jez *86:* 1, 2, 3; *149:* 3
Albrecht, Jan *37:* 176
Albright, Donn *1:* 91
Alcala, Alfredo *91:* 128
Alcantará, Felipe Ugalde *171:* 186
Alcorn, John *3:* 159; *7:* 165; *31:* 22; *44:* 127; *46:* 23, 170
Alcorn, Stephen *110:* 4; *125:* 106; *128:* 172; *150:* 97; *160:* 188; *165:* 48; *201:* 113; *203:* 39; *207:* 3
Alcott, May *100:* 3
Alda, Arlene *44:* 24; *158:* 2
Alden, Albert *11:* 103
Aldridge, Andy *27:* 131
Aldridge, George *105:* 125
Aldridge, Sheila *192:* 4
Alejandro, Cliff *176:* 75
Alex, Ben *45:* 25, 26
Alexander, Ellen *91:* 3
Alexander, Lloyd *49:* 34
Alexander, Martha *3:* 206; *11:* 103; *13:* 109; *25:* 100; *36:* 131; *70:* 6, 7; *136:* 3, 4, 5; *169:* 120
Alexander, Paul *85:* 57; *90:* 9
Alexeieff, Alexander *14:* 6; *26:* 199
Alfano, Wayne *80:* 69
Aliki
See Brandenberg, Aliki
Alko, Selina *218:* 2
Allamand, Pascale *12:* 9
Allan, Judith *38:* 166
Alland, Alexandra *16:* 255
Allen, Gertrude *9:* 6
Allen, Graham *31:* 145
Allen, Jonathan *131:* 3, 4; *177:* 8, 9, 10
Allen, Joy *168:* 185; *217:* 6, 7
Allen, Pamela *50:* 25, 26, 27, 28; *81:* 9, 10; *123:* 4, 5
Allen, Raul *207:* 94
Allen, Rowena *47:* 75

Allen, Thomas B. *81:* 101; *82:* 248; *89:* 37; *104:* 9
Allen, Tom *85:* 176
Allender, David *73:* 223
Alley, R.W. *80:* 183; *95:* 187; *156:* 100, 153; *169:* 4, 5; *179:* 17
Allison, Linda *43:* 27
Allon, Jeffrey *119:* 174
Allport, Mike *71:* 55
Almquist, Don *11:* 8; *12:* 128; *17:* 46; *22:* 110
Aloise, Frank *5:* 38; *10:* 133; *30:* 92
Alsenas, Linas *186:* 2
Alter, Ann *206:* 4, 5
Althea
See Braithwaite, Althea
Altschuler, Franz *11:* 185; *23:* 141; *40:* 48; *45:* 29; *57:* 181
Alvin, John *117:* 5
Ambrus, Victor G. *1:* 6, 7, 194; *3:* 69; *5:* 15; *6:* 44; *7:* 36; *8:* 210; *12:* 227; *14:* 213; *15:* 213; *22:* 209; *24:* 36; *28:* 179; *30:* 178; *32:* 44, 46; *38:* 143; *41:* 25, 26, 27, 28, 29, 30, 31, 32; *42:* 87; *44:* 190; *55:* 172; *62:* 30, 144, 145, 148; *86:* 99, 100, 101; *87:* 66, 137; *89:* 162; *134:* 160
Ames, Lee J. *3:* 12; *9:* 130; *10:* 69; *17:* 214; *22:* 124; *151:* 13; *223:* 69
Amini, Mehrdokht *211:* 119
Amon, Aline *9:* 9
Amoss, Berthe *5:* 5
Amstutz, André *152:* 102; *214:* 11, 16; *223:* 99
Amundsen, Dick *7:* 77
Amundsen, Richard E. *5:* 10; *24:* 122
Ancona, George *12:* 11; *55:* 144; *145:* 7; *208:* 13
Anderson, Alasdair *18:* 122
Andersen, Bethanne *116:* 167; *162:* 189; *175:* 17; *191:* 4, 5; *218:* 20
Anderson, Bob *139:* 16
Anderson, Brad *33:* 28
Anderson, Brian *211:* 8
Anderson, C.W. *11:* 10
Anderson, Carl *7:* 4
Anderson, Catherine Corley *72:* 2
Anderson, Cecil *127:* 152
Anderson, David Lee *118:* 176
Anderson, Derek *169:* 9; *174:* 180
Anderson, Doug *40:* 111
Anderson, Erica *23:* 65
Anderson, G.E. *223:* 181

Anderson, Laurie *12:* 153, 155
Anderson, Lena *99:* 26
Anderson, Peggy Perry *179:* 2
Anderson, Sara *173:* 3
Anderson, Scoular *138:* 13; *201:* 6
Anderson, Susan *90:* 12
Anderson, Tara *188:* 132; *211:* 115
Anderson, Wayne *23:* 119; *41:* 239; *56:* 7; *62:* 26; *147:* 6; *202:* 4, 5
Andreasen, Daniel *86:* 157; *87:* 104; *103:* 201, 202; *159:* 75; *167:* 106, 107; *168:* 184; *180:* 247; *186:* 9; *212:* 101; *220:* 110, 111; *221:* 56
Andrew, Ian *111:* 37; *116:* 12; *166:* 2
Andrew, John *22:* 4
Andrews, Benny *14:* 251; *31:* 24; *57:* 6, 7; *183:* 8
Andrews, Vaughn *166:* 28
Anelay, Henry *57:* 173
Angel, Marie *47:* 22
Angelo, Valenti *14:* 8; *18:* 100; *20:* 232; *32:* 70
Anglund, Joan Walsh *2:* 7, 250, 251; *37:* 198, 199, 200
Anholt, Catherine *74:* 8; *131:* 7; *141:* 5
Anholt, Laurence *141:* 4
Anno, Mitsumasa *5:* 7; *38:* 25, 26, 27, 28, 29, 30, 31, 32; *77:* 3, 4; *157:* 10, 11
Antal, Andrew *1:* 124; *30:* 145
Antram, David *152:* 133
Apostolou, Christy Hale
  See Hale, Christy
Apple, Margot *33:* 25; *35:* 206; *46:* 81; *53:* 8; *61:* 109; *64:* 21, 22, 24, 25, 27; *71:* 176; *77:* 53; *82:* 245; *92:* 39; *94:* 180; *96:* 107; *152:* 4, 5; *162:* 192, 194; *173:* 44; *214:* 21, 22, 23, 24
Appleyard, Dev *2:* 192
Aragones, Sergio *48:* 23, 24, 25, 26, 27
Araneus *40:* 29
Arbo, Cris *103:* 4; *220:* 4, 5
Archambault, Matt *85:* 173; *138:* 19, 20; *143:* 33; *145:* 144; *179:* 103; *187:* 7; *219:* 2
Archer, Janet *16:* 69; *178:* 156
Ardizzone, Edward *1:* 11, 12; *2:* 105; *3:* 258; *4:* 78; *7:* 79; *10:* 100; *15:* 232; *20:* 69,178; *23:* 223; *24:* 125; *28:* 25, 26, 27, 28, 29, 30, 31,33, 34, 35, 36, 37; *31:* 192, 193; *34:* 215, 217; *60:* 173; *64:* 145; *87:* 176; *YABC 2:* 25
Arena, Jill *176:* 49
Arenella, Roy *14:* 9
Argemi, David *197:* 2
Argent, Kerry *103:* 56; *138:* 17; *158:* 134
Arihara, Shino *201:* 98
Arisman, Marshall *162:* 50
Armer, Austin *13:* 3
Armer, Laura Adams *13:* 3
Armer, Sidney *13:* 3
Armitage, David *47:* 23; *99:* 5; *155:* 4
Armitage, Eileen *4:* 16
Armstrong, George *10:* 6; *21:* 72
Armstrong, Shelagh *102:* 114
Armstrong-Ellis, Carey *185:* 196
Arno, Enrico *1:* 217; *2:* 22, 210; *4:* 9; *5:* 43; *6:* 52; *29:* 217, 219; *33:* 152; *35:* 99; *43:* 31, 32, 33; *45:* 212, 213, 214; *72:* 72; *74:* 166; *100:* 169
Arnold, Alli *187:* 40, 41
Arnold, Andrew *219:* 155; *221:* 155
Arnold, Caroline *174:* 5
Arnold, Emily *76:* 7, 9, 10
Arnold, Katya *115:* 11; *168:* 2, 3
Arnold, Tedd *116:* 14; *133:* 152; *160:* 5; *208:* 24, 25, 26, 176
Arnosky, Jim *22:* 20; *70:* 9, 10, 11; *118:* 3, 5; *160:* 8, 10; *189:* 5, 7, 8, 9, 10; *217:* 11, 12, 13, 14
Arnsteen, Katy Keck *105:* 97; *116:* 145
Arsenault, Isabelle *207:* 7
Arrowood, Clinton *12:* 193; *19:* 11; *65:* 210
Artell, Mike *89:* 8

Arting, Fred J. *41:* 63
Artzybasheff, Boris *13:* 143; *14:* 15; *40:* 152, 155
Aruego, Ariane *6:* 4
Aruego, José *4:* 140; *6:* 4; *7:* 64; *33:* 195; *35:* 208; *68:* 16, 17; *75:* 46; *93:* 91, 92; *94:* 197; *109:* 65, 67; *125:* 2, 3, 4, 5; *127:* 188; *143:* 25; *178:* 17, 19, 74; *188:* 166; *202:* 164
Arzoumanian, Alik *177:* 12; *194:* 115
Asare, Meshack *86:* 9; *139:* 19
Ascensios, Natalie *105:* 139
Asch, Frank *5:* 9; *66:* 2, 4, 6, 7, 9, 10; *102:* 18, 19,21; *154:* 12
Ashby, Gail *11:* 135
Ashby, Gil *146:* 4
Ashby, Gwynneth *44:* 26
Ashley, C.W. *19:* 197
Ashmead, Hal *8:* 70
Ashton, Tim *211:* 204
Aska, Warabe *56:* 10
Assel, Steven *44:* 153; *77:* 22, 97
Astrop, John *32:* 56
Atene, Ann *12:* 18
Atherton, Lisa *38:* 198
Atkinson, Allen *60:* 5
Atkinson, J. Priestman *17:* 275
Atkinson, Janet *86:* 147; *103:* 138
Atkinson, Mike *127:* 74
Atkinson, Wayne *40:* 46
Attard, Karl *196:* 22, 23
Attebery, Charles *38:* 170
Atwell, Debby *150:* 6
Atwood, Ann *7:* 9
Aubrey, Meg Kelleher *77:* 159
Auch, Herm *173:* 7, 8
Auch, Mary Jane *173:* 7
Augarde, Steve *25:* 22; *159:* 7; *210:* 43, 44
Austerman, Miriam *23:* 107
Austin, Margot *11:* 16
Austin, Robert *3:* 44
Austin, Virginia *81:* 205; *127:* 221
Auth, Tony *51:* 5; *192:* 18
Avendano, Dolores *158:* 74
Avedon, Richard *57:* 140
Averill, Esther *1:* 17; *28:* 39, 40, 41
Avilés, Martha *218:* 6
Axeman, Lois *2:* 32; *11:* 84; *13:* 165; *22:* 8; *23:* 49; *61:* 116; *101:* 124
Axtel, David *155:* 110
Ayer, Jacqueline *13:* 7
Ayer, Margaret *15:* 12; *50:* 120
Ayers, Alan *91:* 58; *107:* 169
Ayliffe, Alex *95:* 164
Ayto, Russell *111:* 5; *112:* 54; *206:* 7, 8; *213:* 56
Azarian, Mary *112:* 9, 10; *114:* 129; *117:* 171; *137:* 163; *171:* 4, 5; *181:* 161; *188:* 128

B

B.T.B.
  See Blackwell, Basil T.
Baasansuren, Bolormaa *216:* 40
Babbitt, Bradford *33:* 158
Babbitt, Natalie *6:* 6; *8:* 220; *68:* 20; *70:* 242, 243; *194:* 8, 9
Baca, Maria *104:* 5
Bacchus, Andy *94:* 87
Bacha, Andy *109:* 169
Bachelet, Gilles *196:* 18
Bachem, Paul *48:* 180; *67:* 65; *144:* 206
Back, Adam *63:* 125
Back, George *31:* 161
Backes, Nick *190:* 72
Backhouse, Colin *78:* 142
Bacon, Bruce *4:* 74
Bacon, Paul *7:* 155; *8:* 121; *31:* 55; *50:* 42; *56:* 175; *62:* 82, 84
Bacon, Peggy *2:* 11, 228; *46:* 44

Baek, Matthew J. *169:* 95; *202:* 8
Baer, Julie *161:* 2
Baicker-McKee, Carol *177:* 15; *180:* 215
Bailey, Peter *58:* 174; *87:* 221; *194:* 12
Bailey, Sheila *155:* 11
Baker, Alan *22:* 22; *61:* 134; *93:* 11, 12; *146:* 6, 7, 10
Baker, Charlotte *2:* 12
Baker, Garin *89:* 65
Baker, Jeannie *23:* 4; *88:* 18, 19, 20
Baker, Jim *22:* 24
Baker, Joe *82:* 188; *111:* 55; *124:* 70; *197:* 73
Baker, Keith *179:* 6, 7; *222:* 36
Baker, Leslie *112:* 214; *132:* 103, 246; *180:* 74, 246
Baker-Smith, Grahame *223:* 10
Baldacci, Rudy *184:* 9
Baldridge, Cyrus LeRoy *19:* 69; *44:* 50
Baldus, Jackie *216:* 81
Baldus, Zachary *152:* 231; *187:* 60
Balet, Jan *11:* 22
Balian, Lorna *9:* 16; *91:* 16
Balit, Christina *102:* 24; *159:* 9; *162:* 118, 119; *212:* 2, 3
Ballantyne, R.M. *24:* 34
Ballis, George *14:* 199
Balouch, Kristen *176:* 11
Baltzer, Hans *40:* 30
Banbery, Fred *58:* 15
Bancroft, Bronwyn *216:* 42
Banfill, A. Scott *98:* 7; *112:* 59
Bang, Molly *24:* 37, 38; *69:* 8, 9, 10; *111:* 7,9, 10, 11; *140:* 11; *158:* 37, 38, 39; *195:* 3; *215:* 11, 12, 13, 14
Banik, Yvette Santiago *21:* 136
Banks, Erin Bennett *211:* 12
Banner, Angela
  See Maddison, Angela Mary
Bannerman, Helen *19:* 13, 14
Banning, Greg *202:* 98
Bannon, Laura *6:* 10; *23:* 8
Bantock, Nick *74:* 229; *95:* 6
Banyai, Istvan *185:* 209; *193:* 14, 16; *209:* 155; *223:* 166, 167
Baptist, Michael *37:* 208
Baracca, Sal *135:* 206
Baranaski, Marcin *182:* 113
Barasch, Lynne *126:* 16; *186:* 15
Barbarin, Lucien C., Jr. *89:* 88
Barbour, Karen *96:* 5; *74:* 209; *170:* 16
Bare, Arnold Edwin *16:* 31
Bare, Colleen Stanley *32:* 33
Barger, Jan *147:* 11
Bargery, Geoffrey *14:* 258
Barkat, Jonathan *149:* 177; *164:* 254; *181:* 106; *184:* 186; *196:* 11; *198:* 148
Barker, Carol *31:* 27
Barker, Cicely Mary *49:* 50, 51
Barkley, James *4:* 13; *6:* 11; *13:* 112
Barks, Carl *37:* 27, 28, 29, 30, 31, 32, 33, 34
Barling, Joy *62:* 148
Barling, Tom *9:* 23
Barlow, Gillian *62:* 20
Barlow, Perry *35:* 28
Barlowe, Dot *30:* 223
Barlowe, Wayne *37:* 72; *84:* 43; *105:* 5
Barnard, Bryn *88:* 53; *13:* 55; *169:* 13; *193:* 194
Barneda, David *206:* 11
Barner, Bob *29:* 37; *128:* 33; *136:* 19, 20; *177:* 27
Barnes, Hiram P. *20:* 28
Barnes, Tim *137:* 28
Barnes-Murphy, Rowan *88:* 22
Barnett, Charles II *175:* 150
Barnett, Ivan *70:* 14
Barnett, Moneta *16:* 89; *19:* 142; *31:* 102; *33:* 30, 31, 32; *41:* 153; *61:* 94, 97
Barney, Maginel Wright *39:* 32, 33, 34; *YABC 2:* 306

Barnum, Jay Hyde *11:* 224; *20:* 5; *37:* 189, 190
Baron, Alan *80:* 3; *89:* 123
Barr, George *60:* 74; *69:* 64
Barragán, Paula S. *134:* 116; *186:* 158; *216:* 43, 44, 197
Barrall, Tim *115:* 152
Barraud, Martin *189:* 38
Barrauds *33:* 114
Barrer-Russell, Gertrude *9:* 65; *27:* 31
Barret, Robert *85:* 134
Barrett, Angela *40:* 136, 137; *62:* 74; *75:* 10; *76:* 142; *144:* 137; *145:* 14; *223:* 14
Barrett, Jennifer *58:* 149
Barrett, John E. *43:* 119
Barrett, Moneta *74:* 10
Barrett, Peter *55:* 169; *86:* 111
Barrett, Robert *62:* 145; *77:* 146; *82:* 35
Barrett, Ron *14:* 24; *26:* 35
Barron, John N. *3:* 261; *5:* 101; *14:* 220
Barrow, Ann *136:* 27
Barrows, Walter *14:* 268
Barry, Ethelred B. *37:* 79; *YABC 1:* 229
Barry, James *14:* 25
Barry, Katharina *2:* 159; *4:* 22
Barry, Robert E. *6:* 12
Barry, Scott *32:* 35
Barshaw, Ruth McNally *203:* 9
Bartenbach, Jean *40:* 31
Barth, Ernest Kurt *2:* 172; *3:* 160; *8:* 26; *10:* 31
Bartholomew, Caty *208:* 153
Bartholomew, Marie *200:* 66
Bartlett, Alison *101:* 88; *165:* 93; *209:* 51
Barton, Byron *8:* 207; *9:* 18; *23:* 66; *80:* 181; *90:* 18, 19, 20, 21; *126:* 29, 30
Barton, Harriett *30:* 71
Barton, Jill *129:* 108; *135:* 120; *145:* 185, 189; *184:* 177
Bartram, Robert *10:* 42
Bartram, Simon *218:* 8
Bartsch, Jochen *8:* 105; *39:* 38
Bascove, Barbara *45:* 73
Base, Graeme *101:* 15, 16, 17, 18; *162:* 8, 10, 12
Baseman, Gary *174:* 12
Bash, Barbara *132:* 9
Baskin, Leonard *30:* 42, 43, 46, 47; *49:* 125, 126, 128, 129,133; *173:* 120
Bass, Saul *49:* 192
Bassett, Jeni *40:* 99; *64:* 30
Basso, Bill *99:* 139; *189:* 134
Batchelor, Joy *29:* 41, 47, 48
Bate, Norman *5:* 16
Bates, Amy June *188:* 170; *189:* 27, 28
Bates, Leo *24:* 35
Batet, Carmen *39:* 134
Batherman, Muriel *31:* 79; *45:* 185
Battaglia, Aurelius *50:* 44
Batten, John D. *25:* 161, 162
Batten, Mary *162:* 14, 15
Battles, Asa *32:* 94, 95
Bauer, Carla *193:* 6
Bauer, Jutta *150:* 32
Bauernschmidt, Marjorie *15:* 15
Baum, Allyn *20:* 10
Baum, Willi *4:* 24, 25; *7:* 173
Bauman, Leslie *61:* 121
Baumann, Jill *34:* 170
Baumhauer, Hans *11:* 218; *15:* 163, 165, 167
Baxter, Glen *57:* 100
Baxter, Leon *59:* 102
Baxter, Robert *87:* 129
Bayer, Herbert *181:* 16
Bayley, Dorothy *37:* 195
Bayley, Nicola *40:* 104; *41:* 34, 35; *69:* 15; *129:* 33, 34, 35
Baylin, Mark *158:* 233

Baynes, Pauline *2:* 244; *3:* 149; *13:* 133, 135,137, 141; *19:* 18, 19, 20; *32:* 208, 213, 214; *36:* 105, 108; *59:* 12, 13, 14, 16, 17, 18, 20; *100:* 158, 159, 243; *133:* 3, 4
Beach, Lou *150:* 150; *207:* 117, 118
Beame, Rona *12:* 40
Bean, Jonathan *196:* 102
Bear's Heart *73:* 215
Beard, Alex *222:* 40
Beard, Dan *22:* 31, 32
Beard, J.H. *YABC 1:* 158
Bearden, Romare *9:* 7; *22:* 35
Beardshaw, Rosalind *169:* 22; *190:* 22
Beardsley, Aubrey *17:* 14; *23:* 181; *59:* 130, 131
Bearman, Jane *29:* 38
Beaton, Cecil *24:* 208
Beaton, Clare *125:* 28; *208:* 67; *220:* 10, 11, 12
Beauce, J.A. *18:* 103
Beaujard, Sophie *81:* 54
Beccia, Carlyn *189:* 29
Bechtold, Lisze *208:* 29
Beck, Charles *11:* 169; *51:* 173
Beck, Ian *138:* 27; *182:* 150; *190:* 25
Beck, Melinda *203:* 112
Beck, Ruth *13:* 11
Becker, Harriet *12:* 211
Beckerman, Jonathan *208:* 194
Beckett, Sheilah *5:* 5; *33:* 37, 38
Beckhoff, Harry *1:* 78; *5:* 163
Beckhorn, Susan Williams *189:* 32
Beckman, Kaj *45:* 38, 39, 40, 41
Beckman, Per *45:* 42, 43
Beddows, Eric *72:* 70
Bedford, F.D. *20:* 118, 122; *33:* 170; *41:* 220, 221,230, 233
Bee, Joyce *19:* 62
Bee, William *188:* 6
Beeby, Betty *25:* 36
Beech, Carol *9:* 149
Beech, Mark *192:* 122
Beek *25:* 51, 55, 59
Beeke, Tiphanie *177:* 127; *204:* 140; *212:* 178; *218:* 102
Beekman, Doug *125:* 146, 148
Beerbohm, Max *24:* 208
Beeson, Bob *108:* 57
Begin, Mary Jane *82:* 13; *206:* 13
Beha, Philippe *172:* 85
Behr, Joyce *15:* 15; *21:* 132; *23:* 161
Behrens, Hans *5:* 97
Beier, Ellen *135:* 170; *139:* 47; *183:* 164; *221:* 177; *222:* 151
Beingessner, Laura *220:* 14
Beinicke, Steve *69:* 18
Beisner, Monika *46:* 128, 131; *112:* 127
Belden, Charles J. *12:* 182
Belina, Renate *39:* 132
Bell, Corydon *3:* 20
Bell, Graham *54:* 48
Bell, Julia *151:* 214
Bell, Julie *159:* 172; *165:* 18
Bell, Thomas P. *76:* 182
Bellamy, Glen *127:* 15
Beltran, Alberto *43:* 37
Bemelmans, Ludwig *15:* 19, 21; *100:* 27
Ben-Ami, Doron *75:* 96; *84:* 107; *108:* 132; *110:* 63; *159:* 157; *197:* 142
Bendall-Brunello, John *150:* 4; *157:* 163; *185:* 3, 4; *203:* 5
Benda, Wladyslaw T. *15:* 256; *30:* 76, 77; *44:* 182
Bender, Robert *77:* 162; *79:* 13; *160:* 23
Bendick, Jeanne *2:* 24; *68:* 27, 28
Benioff, Carol *121:* 42; *175:* 23
Benner, Cheryl *80:* 11
Bennett, Charles H. *64:* 6
Bennett, Erin Susanne *165:* 216
Bennett, F.I. *YABC 1:* 134
Bennett, James *146:* 240

Bennett, Jill *26:* 61; *41:* 38, 39; *45:* 54
Bennett, Rainey *15:* 26; *23:* 53
Bennett, Richard *15:* 45; *21:* 11, 12, 13; *25:* 175
Bennett, Susan *5:* 55
Benny, Mike *142:* 78; *203:* 13, 14; *207:* 85
Benoit, Elise *77:* 74
Benson, Linda *60:* 130; *62:* 91; *75:* 101; *79:* 156; *134:* 129
Benson, Patrick *68:* 162; *147:* 17, 18, 19, 20
Bentley, Carolyn *46:* 153
Bentley, James *149:* 30
Bentley, Roy *30:* 162
Benton, Jim *172:* 22
Benton, Thomas Hart *2:* 99
Berelson, Howard *5:* 20; *16:* 58; *31:* 50
Berenstain, Jan *12:* 47; *64:* 33, 34, 36, 37, 38, 40, 42, 44; *135:* 25, 28, 31, 35
Berenstain, Stan *12:* 47; *64:* 33, 34, 36, 37, 38, 40, 42, 44; *135:* 25, 28, 31, 35
Berenzy, Alix *65:* 13; *73:* 6; *78:* 115
Berg, Joan *1:* 115; *3:* 156; *6:* 26, 58
Berg, Ron *36:* 48, 49; *48:* 37, 38; *67:* 72
Bergen, David *115:* 44; *207:* 34
Berger, Barbara *77:* 14
Berger, Carin *185:* 6
Berger, Joe *221:* 9
Berger, William M. *14:* 143; *YABC 1:* 204
Bergherr, Mary *74:* 170; *151:* 123
Bergin, Mark *114:* 8, 9; *143:* 95; *160:* 26, 27
Bergstreser, Douglas *69:* 76
Bergum, Constance R. *121:* 14, 15; *208:* 31, 32, 33; *209:* 176
Bering, Claus *13:* 14
Berkeley, Jon *139:* 218
Berkowitz, Jeanette *3:* 249
Berman, Paul *66:* 14
Berman, Rachel *217:* 26
Bernal, Richard *154:* 176
Bernadette
    See Watts, Bernadette
Bernard, Gary *216:* 71
Bernardin, James *112:* 24; *167:* 94
Bernasconi, Pablo *183:* 10, 11
Bernath, Stefen *32:* 76
Berner, Rotraut Susanne *214:* 32
Bernhard, Durga *80:* 13
Bernstein, Michel J. *51:* 71
Bernstein, Ted *38:* 183; *50:* 131
Bernstein, Zena *23:* 46
Berridge, Celia *86:* 63
Berrill, Jacquelyn *12:* 50
Berry, Erick
    See Best, Allena
Berry, Holly *205:* 116; *210:* 49, 50
Berry, William D. *14:* 29; *19:* 48
Berry, William A. *6:* 219
Berson, Harold *2:* 17, 18; *4:* 28, 29, 220; *9:* 10; *12:* 19; *17:* 45; *18:* 193; *22:* 85; *34:* 172; *44:* 120; *46:* 42; *80:* 240
Bertholf, Bret *187:* 9; *189:* 32, 33
Berton, Patsy *99:* 16
Bertschmann, Harry *16:* 1
Besco, Don *70:* 99
Beskow, Elsa *20:* 13, 14, 15
Bess, Clayton *63:* 94
Best, Allena *2:* 26; *34:* 76
Betera, Carol *74:* 68
Bethell, Thomas N. *61:* 169
Bethers, Ray *6:* 22
Betteridge, Deirdre *214:* 34
Bettina
    See Ehrlich, Bettina
Betts, Ethel Franklin *17:* 161, 164, 165; *YABC 2:* 47
Betz, Rudolf *59:* 161
Bewick, Thomas *16:* 40, 41, 43, 44, 45, 47; *54:* 150; *YABC 1:* 107
Beyer, Paul J. III *74:* 24
Bezencon, Jacqueline *48:* 40
Biamonte, Daniel *40:* 90

Bianchi, John *91:* 19
Bianco, Pamela *15:* 31; *28:* 44, 45, 46
Bible, Charles *13:* 15
Bice, Clare *22:* 40
Biedrzycki, David *186:* 170; *219:* 7
Bierman, Don *57:* 184
Biggers, John *2:* 123
Biggs, Brian *192:* 38; *196:* 15; *207:* 170
Bikadoroff, Roxanna *201:* 74
Bileck, Marvin *3:* 102; *40:* 36, 37
Bilibin, Ivan *61:* 8, 9, 12, 13, 14, 15, 151, 152, 154, 162
Billington, Patrick *98:* 71
Billout, Guy *144:* 38, 39
Bimen, Levent *5:* 179
Binch, Caroline *81:* 18; *140:* 15, 16; *144:* 115; *211:* 82
Binder, Hannes *169:* 163
Bing, Christopher *126:* 34
Binger, Bill *121:* 46
Binks, Robert *25:* 150
Binzen, Bill *24:* 47
Birch, Reginald *15:* 150; *19:* 33, 34, 35, 36; *37:* 196,197; *44:* 182; *46:* 176; *YABC 1:* 84; *2:* 34, 39
Birch, Wendy *223:* 70
Birchall, Mark *123:* 188
Bird, Esther Brock *1:* 36; *25:* 66
Birdsong, Keith *167:* 85; *219:* 105
Birkett, Georgie *204:* 121
Birkett, Rachel *78:* 206
Birling, Paul *109:* 30
Birmingham, Christian *132:* 243; *143:* 114; *209:* 58; *220:* 20
Birmingham, Lloyd P. *12:* 51; *83:* 13
Biro, Val *1:* 26; *41:* 42; *60:* 178; *67:* 23, 24; *84:* 242, 243
Bischoff, Ilse *44:* 51
Bishop, Don *199:* 133
Bishop, Gavin *97:* 17, 18; *144:* 42, 44; *216:* 52, 55, 56, 57
Bishop, Kathleen Wong *115:* 67
Bishop, Rich *56:* 43
Bite, I. *60:* 14
Bittinger, Ned *93:* 117; *205:* 115
Bjorklund, Lorence *3:* 188, 252; *7:* 100; *9:* 113; *10:* 66; *19:* 178; *33:* 122, 123; *35:* 36, 37, 38, 39,41, 42, 43; *36:* 185; *38:* 93; *47:* 106; *66:* 194; *YABC 1:* 242
Björkman, Steve *91:* 199; *160:* 110; *198:* 18; *218:* 188; *223:* 20, 21
Blabey, Aaron *214:* 35
Black Sheep *164:* 100
Blackburn, Loren H. *63:* 10
Blackall, Sophie *194:* 140; *209:* 157
Blackford, John *137:* 105; *180:* 36
Blackwell, Basil T. *YABC 1:* 68, 69
Blackwood, Freya *199:* 9
Blackwood, Gary L. *118:* 17
Blades, Ann *16:* 52; *37:* 213; *50:* 41; *69:* 21; *99:* 215
Blair, Jay *45:* 46; *46:* 155
Blaisdell, Elinore *1:* 121; *3:* 134; *35:* 63
Blake, Anne Catharine *189:* 71
Blake, Francis *198:* 4
Blake, Quentin *3:* 170; *10:* 48; *13:* 38; *21:* 180; *26:* 60; *28:* 228; *30:* 29, 31; *40:* 108; *45:* 219; *46:* 165, 168; *48:* 196; *52:* 10, 11, 12,13, 14, 15, 16, 17; *73:* 41, 43; *78:* 84, 86; *80:* 250, 251; *84:* 210, 211, 212; *87:* 177; *96:* 24, 26, 28; *124:* 79; *125:* 32, 34; *181:* 139; *211:* 26, 27
Blake, Robert J. *37:* 90; *53:* 67; *54:* 23; *160:* 28, 29
Blake, William *30:* 54, 56, 57, 58, 59, 60
Blakeslee, Lys *218:* 11, 105
Blanchard, N. Taylor *82:* 140
Blass, Jacqueline *8:* 215
Blazek, Scott R. *91:* 71
Bleck, Cathie *118:* 116
Bleck, Linda *204:* 124

Blegvad, Erik *2:* 59; *3:* 98; *5:* 117; *7:* 131; *11:* 149; *14:* 34, 35; *18:* 237; *32:* 219; *60:* 106; *66:* 16, 17, 18, 19; *70:* 233; *76:* 18; *82:* 106; *87:* 45; *100:* 188; *129:* 125; *132:* 17, 18, 19, 20; *176:* 14; *200:* 100; *YABC 1:* 201
Blessen, Karen *93:* 126
Bliss, Corinne Demas *37:* 38
Bliss, Harry *196:* 27, 28, 29
Blitt, Barry *179:* 199; *187:* 13
Bloch, Lucienne *10:* 12
Blondon, Herve *129:* 48; *183:* 22
Bloom, Lloyd *35:* 180; *36:* 149; *47:* 99; *62:* 117; *68:* 231; *72:* 136; *75:* 185; *83:* 99; *108:* 19
Bloom, Suzanne *172:* 23, 24
Blossom, Dave *34:* 29
Blumenschein, E.L. *YABC 1:* 113, 115
Blumer, Patt *29:* 214
Blundell, Kim *29:* 36
Bluthenthal, Diana Cain *93:* 32; *104:* 106; *177:* 26
Blythe, Benjamin *128:* 7
Blythe, Gary *112:* 52; *181:* 166; *182:* 64; *185:* 7; *186:* 116, 117
Boake, Kathy *176:* 185
Board, Perry *171:* 99
Boardman, Gwenn *12:* 60
Boatwright, Phil *211:* 195
Bober, Richard *125:* 145; *132:* 40
Bobri, Vladimir *30:* 138; *47:* 27
Bock, Vera *1:* 187; *21:* 41
Bock, William Sauts *8:* 7; *14:* 37; *16:* 120; *21:* 141; *36:* 177; *62:* 203
Bodecker, N(iels) M(ogens) *8:* 13; *14:* 2; *17:* 55, 56, 57; *73:* 22, 23, 24
Boehm, Linda *40:* 31
Bogacki, Tomek *138:* 31, 32; *144:* 123; *202:* 13
Bogan, Paulette *197:* 152; *201:* 17
Bogdan, Florentina *107:* 43
Bohdal, Susi *22:* 44; *101:* 20
Bohlen, Nina *58:* 13
Boies, Alex *96:* 53
Bok, Chip *205:* 16
Bolam, Emily *101:* 216; *159:* 12; *205:* 59
Bolian, Polly *3:* 270; *4:* 30; *13:* 77; *29:* 197
Bolle, Frank *87:* 100; *208:* 101
Bollen, Roger *79:* 186; *83:* 16
Bolling, Vickey *114:* 44
Bollinger, Peter *101:* 7; *128:* 198; *172:* 26
Bolognese, Don *2:* 147, 231; *4:* 176; *7:* 146; *17:* 43; *23:* 192; *24:* 50; *34:* 108; *36:* 133; *71:* 24, 25; *103:* 131; *129:* 39, 40
Bolster, Rob *186:* 169
Bolton, A.T. *57:* 158
Bond, Arnold *18:* 116
Bond, Barbara Higgins *21:* 102
Bond, Bruce *52:* 97
Bond, Felicia *38:* 197; *49:* 55, 56; *89:* 170; *90:* 171; *126:* 37
Bond, Higgins *177:* 22, 23; *209:* 175; *220:* 22, 23, 24
Bonn, Pat *43:* 40
Bonner, Hannah *197:* 13, 14
Bonners, Susan *41:* 40; *85:* 36; *94:* 99, 100; *151:* 105, 106
Bono, Mary *184:* 73
Bonsall, Crosby *23:* 6
Boon, Debbie *103:* 6; *144:* 188
Boon, Emilie *86:* 23, 24
Boone, Debbie *165:* 77
Boore, Sara *60:* 73
Bootman, Colin *155:* 13; *159:* 35; *174:* 192; *222:* 128
Booth, Franklin *YABC 2:* 76
Booth, George *191:* 13
Booth, Graham *32:* 193; *37:* 41, 42
Borda, Juliette *102:* 188
Bordier, Georgette *16:* 54
Boren, Tinka *27:* 128
Borges, Jose Francisco *119:* 62

Borja, Robert *22:* 48
Born, Adolf *49:* 63
Bornstein, Ruth *14:* 44; *88:* 45, 46; *107:* 30
Borten, Helen *3:* 54; *5:* 24
Bosin, Blackbear *69:* 104
Bossom, Naomi *35:* 48
Bostock, Mike *83:* 221; *114:* 14; *188:* 205
Boston, Peter *19:* 42
Bosustow, Stephen *34:* 202
Boszko, Ron *75:* 47
Bottner, Barbara *14:* 46
Boucher, Joelle *41:* 138
Boulat, Pierre *44:* 40
Boulet, Susan Seddon *50:* 47
Bouma, Paddy *118:* 25; *128:* 16
Bour, Daniele *66:* 145
Bourke-White, Margaret *15:* 286, 287; *57:* 102
Boutavant, Marc *200:* 136
Boutet de Monvel, M. *30:* 61, 62, 63, 65
Bowen, Betsy *105:* 222
Bowen, Richard *42:* 134
Bowen, Ruth *31:* 188
Bower, Ron *29:* 33
Bowers, David *95:* 38; *115:* 20; *127:* 169, 170; *165:* 57; *207:* 11
Bowers, Tim *185:* 35; *201:* 41; *218:* 13
Bowman, Claire *174:* 177
Bowman, Eric *151:* 23
Bowman, Leslie *85:* 203; *105:* 108; *116:* 76; *128:* 234; *182:* 24, 25
Bowman, Peter *146:* 214, 215; *150:* 115
Bowser, Carolyn Ewing *22:* 253
Boxall, Ed *178:* 28
Boyd, Aaron *158:* 242
Boyd, Patti *45:* 31
Boyle, Eleanor Vere *28:* 50, 51
Boynton, Sandra *57:* 13, 14, 15; *107:* 36, 37; *152:* 12, 13, 14
Bozzo, Frank *4:* 154
Brabbs, Derry *55:* 170
Brace, Eric *132:* 193, 194; *152:* 71; *184:* 195; *197:* 6; *201:* 54
Brackers de Hugo, Pierre *115:* 21
Bradford, June *158:* 138
Bradford, Ron *7:* 157
Bradley, David P. *69:* 105
Bradley, Richard D. *26:* 182
Bradley, William *5:* 164
Brady, Irene *4:* 31; *42:* 37; *68:* 191
Bragg, Michael *32:* 78; *46:* 31
Bragg, Ruth Gembicki *77:* 18
Brainerd, John W. *65:* 19
Braithwaite, Althea *23:* 12, 13; *119:* 16
Brak, Syd *146:* 187
Bralds, Braldt *90:* 28; *91:* 151
Bram, Elizabeth *30:* 67
Bramley, Peter *4:* 3
Brandenberg, Aliki *2:* 36, 37; *24:* 222; *35:* 49, 50, 51,52, 53, 54, 56, 57; *75:* 15, 17; *92:* 205; *113:* 18, 19, 20; *157:* 28; *156:* 111
Brandenburg, Alexa *75:* 19
Brandenburg, Jim *47:* 58; *150:* 212
Brandi, Lillian *31:* 158
Brandon, Brumsic, Jr. *9:* 25
Brannen, Sarah S. *202:* 15; *216:* 199
Bransom, Paul *17:* 121; *43:* 44
Braren, Loretta Trezzo *87:* 193
Brassard, France *186:* 22
Braun, Wendy *80:* 17, 18; *213:* 14
Brautigam, Don *115:* 175, 176
Brazell, Derek *75:* 105; *79:* 9
Breathed, Berkeley *86:* 27, 28, 29; *161:* 13, 14
Breckenreid, Julia *192:* 209
Breen, Steve *186:* 23
Brennan, Steve *83:* 230; *101:* 184
Brenner, Fred *22:* 85; *36:* 34; *42:* 34
Brett, Bernard *22:* 54
Brett, Harold M. *26:* 98, 99, 100
Brett, Jan *30:* 135; *42:* 39; *71:* 31, 32; *130:* 23, 24, 25, 26, 27; *171:* 15, 16
Brewer, Paul *106:* 115; *145:* 202

Brewer, Sally King *33:* 44
Brewster, Patience *40:* 68; *45:* 22, 183; *51:* 20; *66:* 144; *89:* 4; *97:* 30, 31; *212:* 99
Brick, John *10:* 15
Brickman, Robin D. *131:* 88; *142:* 150; *155:* 18; *178:* 109; *184:* 32
Bridge, David R. *45:* 28
Bridgman, L.J. *37:* 77
Bridwell, Norman *4:* 37; *138:* 36, 37, 40
Brierley, Louise *91:* 22; *96:* 165; *183:* 51
Briggs, Harry *172:* 187
Briggs, Raymond *10:* 168; *23:* 20, 21; *66:* 29, 31, 32; *131:* 28, 29; *184:* 15, 16
Brigham, Grace A. *37:* 148
Bright, Robert *24:* 55
Brighton, Catherine *107:* 39; *206:* 23
Brinckloe, Julie *13:* 18; *24:* 79, 115; *29:* 35; *63:* 140; *81:* 131
Brion *47:* 116
Brisley, Joyce L. *22:* 57
Brisson, James F. *110:* 60
Brittingham, Geoffrey *88:* 37
Brix-Henker, Silke *81:* 194
Broadway, Hannah *208:* 104
Brock, Charles E. *15:* 97; *19:* 247, 249; *23:* 224, 225; *36:* 88; *42:* 41, 42, 43, 44, 45; *100:* 189; *YABC 1:* 194, 196, 203
Brock, Emma *7:* 21
Brock, Henry Matthew *15:* 81; *16:* 141; *19:* 71; *34:* 115; *40:* 164; *42:* 47, 48, 49; *49:* 66
Brocksopp, Arthur *57:* 157
Broda, Ron *136:* 180; *174:* 123
Brodkin, Gwen *34:* 135
Brodovitch, Alexi *52:* 22
Bromhall, Winifred *5:* 11; *26:* 38
Bromley, Lizzy *159:* 179
Bronson, Linda *150:* 210; *174:* 133; *203:* 16, 17
Brooke, L. Leslie *16:* 181, 182, 183, 186; *17:* 15, 16, 17; *18:* 194
Brooker, Christopher *15:* 251
Brooker, Kyrsten *111:* 94; *140:* 28; *162:* 111; *175:* 108; *186:* 42, 225; *199:* 12; *201:* 30; *219:* 98
Brooks, Erik *166:* 52; *182:* 30
Brooks, Karen Stormer *186:* 110; *220:* 65
Brooks, Maya Itzna *92:* 153
Brooks, Ron *94:* 15; *197:* 188; *212:* 6, 7, 8, 9
Brooks, S.G. *178:* 127
Broomfield, Maurice *40:* 141
Brotman, Adolph E. *5:* 21
Brown, Buck *45:* 48
Brown, Calef *179:* 18; *210:* 206; *217:* 30, 31
Brown, Christopher *62:* 124, 125, 127, 128
Brown, Craig McFarland *73:* 28; *84:* 65
Brown, Dan *61:* 167; *115:* 183, 184; *116:* 28, 29; *193:* 190; *200:* 21, 23
Brown, David *7:* 47; *48:* 52
Brown, Denise *11:* 213
Brown, Don *172:* 29
Brown, Elbrite *195:* 39; *198:* 5
Brown, Ford Madox *48:* 74
Brown, Hunter *191:* 111, 112
Brown, Judith Gwyn *1:* 45; *7:* 5; *8:* 167; *9:* 182, 190; *20:* 16, 17, 18; *23:* 142; *29:* 117; *33:* 97; *36:* 23, 26; *43:* 184; *48:* 201, 223; *49:* 69; *86:* 227; *110:* 188; *153:* 7
Brown, Kathryn *98:* 26
Brown, Lisa *187:* 175
Brown, Laurie Krasny *99:* 30
Brown, Marc (Tolon) *10:* 17, 197; *14:* 263; *51:* 18; *53:* 11, 12, 13, 15, 16, 17; *75:* 58; *80:* 24, 25, 26; *82:* 261; *99:* 29; *145:* 22, 23, 25, 27; *162:* 198
Brown, Marcia *7:* 30; *25:* 203; *47:* 31, 32, 33, 34, 35, 36, 37, 38, 39, 40, 42, 43, 44; *YABC 1:* 27
Brown, Margery W. *5:* 32, 33; *10:* 3
Brown, Martin *101:* 43
Brown, Mary Barrett *97:* 74
Brown, Palmer *36:* 40

Brown, Paul *25:* 26; *26:* 107
Brown, Richard *61:* 18; *67:* 30
Brown, Rick *78:* 71; *150:* 154
Brown, Robert S. *85:* 33
Brown, Rod *157:* 142
Brown, Ruth *55:* 165; *86:* 112, 113; *105:* 16, 17, 18; *171:* 178
Brown, Trevor *99:* 160; *139:* 247; *189:* 206
Browne, Anthony *45:* 50, 51, 52; *61:* 21, 22, 23, 24, 25; *105:* 21, 22, 23, 25
Browne, Dik *8:* 212; *67:* 32, 33, 35, 37, 39
Browne, Gordon *16:* 97; *64:* 114, 116, 117, 119, 121
Browne, Hablot K. *15:* 65, 80; *21:* 14, 15, 16, 17, 18, 19,20; *24:* 25
Browne, Jane *165:* 222
Browning, Coleen *4:* 132
Browning, Mary Eleanor *24:* 84
Bruce, Robert *23:* 23
Brude, Dick *48:* 215
Bruel, Nick *166:* 41; *205:* 17, 18
Brule, Al *3:* 135
Brumbeau, Jeff *157:* 29
Bruna, Dick *43:* 48, 49, 50; *76:* 27, 28
Brundage, Frances *19:* 244
Brunhoff, Jean de *24:* 57, 58
Brunhoff, Laurent de *24:* 60; *71:* 35, 36, 37
Brunkus, Denise *84:* 50; *123:* 117; *178:* 209; *193:* 99; *204:* 10, 11, 12; *209:* 202
Brunson, Bob *43:* 135
Bryan, Ashley *31:* 44; *72:* 27, 28, 29; *107:* 92; *116:* 192; *132:* 24; *178:* 33, 34, 35; *208:* 83
Bryant, Laura J. *176:* 36; *183:* 168; *214:* 141; *222:* 49, 152
Bryant, Michael *93:* 74
Brychta, Alex *21:* 21
Bryer, Diana *107:* 121
Bryson, Bernarda *3:* 88, 146; *39:* 26; *44:* 185; *131:* 40
Buba, Joy *12:* 83; *30:* 226; *44:* 56
Buchanan, George *166:* 198
Buchanan, Lilian *13:* 16
Buchanan, Rachel *171:* 71
Bucholtz-Ross, Linda *44:* 137
Buchs, Thomas *40:* 38
Buck, Margaret Waring *3:* 30
Buckhardt, Marc *172:* 59
Buckley, Mike *166:* 180
Budwine, Greg *175:* 172
Buehner, Mark *104:* 12, 15; *105:* 160; *119:* 98; *157:* 188; *159:* 39, 40, 43; *192:* 111; *219:* 13, 14, 15, 16; *221:* 17, 18, 19
Buehr, Walter *3:* 31
Buell, Carl *222:* 68
Buff, Conrad *19:* 52, 53, 54
Buff, Mary *19:* 52, 53
Bull, Charles Livingston *18:* 207; *88:* 175, 176
Bullen, Anne *3:* 166, 167
Buller, Jon *205:* 21
Bullock, Kathleen *77:* 24
Bumgarner-Kirby, Claudia *77:* 194
Burbank, Addison *37:* 43
Burchard, Peter Duncan *3:* 197; *5:* 35; *6:* 158, 218; *143:* 17
Burckhardt, Marc *94:* 48; *110:* 89; *196:* 41; *199:* 116
Burger, Carl *3:* 33; *45:* 160, 162
Burgeson, Marjorie *19:* 31
Burgess, Anne *76:* 252
Burgess, Gelett *32:* 39, 42
Burgess, Mark *157:* 31
Burke, Jim *179:* 19; *185:* 63
Burke, Phillip *95:* 117
Burkert, Nancy Ekholm *18:* 186; *22:* 140; *24:* 62, 63,64, 65; *26:* 53; *29:* 60, 61; *46:* 171; *YABC 1:* 46
Burkhardt, Bruce *142:* 86
Burkhardt, Melissa A. *142:* 86
Burleson, Joe *104:* 35; *172:* 139
Burn, Doris *6:* 172
Burn, Jeffrey *89:* 125; *152:* 132

Burn, Ted
  See Burn, Thomas E.
Burn, Thomas E. *151:* 41
Burnard, Damon *115:* 23
Burnett, Lindy *210:* 59
Burnett, Virgil *44:* 42
Burningham, John *9:* 68; *16:* 60, 61; *59:* 28, 29, 30,31, 32, 33, 35; *111:* 18, 19, 21; *160:* 37
Burns, Howard M. *12:* 173
Burns, Jim *47:* 70; *86:* 32; *91:* 197; *123:* 16
Burns, M.F. *26:* 69
Burns, Raymond *9:* 29
Burns, Robert *24:* 106
Burr, Dan *65:* 28; *108:* 134; *164:* 203; *182:* 68
Burr, Dane *12:* 2
Burra, Edward *YABC 2:* 68
Burrell, Galen *56:* 76
Burri, Rene *41:* 143; *54:* 166
Burridge, Marge Opitz *14:* 42
Burris, Burmah *4:* 81
Burroughs, John Coleman *41:* 64
Burroughs, Studley O. *41:* 65
Burton, Marilee Robin *46:* 33
Burton, Virginia Lee *2:* 43; *44:* 49, 51; *100:* 46, 47; *YABC 1:* 24; *147:* 56
Busoni, Rafaello *1:* 186; *3:* 224; *6:* 126; *14:* 5; *16:* 62, 63
Butchkes, Sidney *50:* 58
Butler, Geoff *94:* 20
Butler, Ralph *116:* 212
Butterfield, Ned *1:* 153; *27:* 128; *79:* 63
Butterworth, Ian *184:* 48, 49
Butterworth, Nick *106:* 43, 44; *149:* 34
Buxton, John *123:* 12
Buzelli, Christopher *105:* 149
Buzonas, Gail *29:* 88
Buzzell, Russ W. *12:* 177
Byard, Carole *39:* 44; *57:* 18, 19, 20; *60:* 60; *61:* 93, 96; *69:* 210; *78:* 246; *79:* 227
Byars, Betsy *46:* 35
Byfield, Barbara Ninde *8:* 18
Byfield, Graham *32:* 29
Bynum, Janie *176:* 50
Byrd, Robert *13:* 218; *33:* 46; *158:* 70; *212:* 100
Byrd, Samuel *123:* 104

C

Cabat, Erni *74:* 38
Cabban, Vanessa *138:* 73; *176:* 39; *185:* 65
Cabrera, Jane *103:* 24; *152:* 27; *182:* 33, 34
Caceres, Ana Palmero *198:* 106
Caddy, Alice *6:* 41
Cady, Harrison *17:* 21, 23; *19:* 57, 58
Caffrey, Aileen *72:* 223; *141:* 154
Cairns, Julia *177:* 37
Caldecott, Randolph *16:* 98, 103; *17:* 32, 33, 36, 38, 39; *26:* 90; *100:* 49, 50; *YABC 2:* 172
Calder, Alexander *18:* 168
Calderón, Gloria *179:* 5
Calderon, W. Frank *25:* 160
Caldwell, Ben *105:* 75; *149:* 60; *195:* 61
Caldwell, Clyde *98:* 100; *116:* 39; *208:* 145
Caldwell, Doreen *23:* 77; *71:* 41
Caldwell, John *46:* 225
Call, Greg *126:* 135; *165:* 49; *182:* 105, 163; *197:* 18, 19; *200:* 159; *209:* 166; *212:* 161
Callahan, Kevin *22:* 42
Callahan, Philip S. *25:* 77
Callan, Jamie *59:* 37
Calvert, Rosemary *218:* 96
Calvin, James *61:* 92
Camburn-Bracalente, Carol A. *118:* 22
Cameron, Chad *190:* 144
Cameron, Julia Margaret *19:* 203
Cameron, Scott *99:* 18

Camm, Martin *140:* 208, 209, 210
Campbell, Ann *11:* 43; *123:* 182; *183:* 68
Campbell, Bill *89:* 39
Campbell, Ken *126:* 143; *205:* 162
Campbell, Robert *55:* 120
Campbell, Rod *51:* 27; *98:* 34
Campbell, Walter M. *YABC 2:* 158
Camps, Luis *28:* 120, 121; *66:* 35
Canga, C.B. *187:* 165
Caniglia, Jeremy *201:* 89
Cann, Helen *124:* 50; *141:* 78; *170:* 138; *179:* 22, 23
Cannell, Jon *196:* 43
Cannon, Janell *78:* 25; *128:* 40
Canright, David *36:* 162
Cantone, AnnaLaura *182:* 146; *196:* 80
Canty, Thomas *85:* 161; *92:* 47; *113:* 192; *134:* 60; *185:* 117
Canyon, Christopher *150:* 44; *151:* 112
Caparo, Antonio Javier *204:* 128; *218:* 88; *220:* 114; *221:* 167
Caporale, Wende *70:* 42
Capp, Al *61:* 28, 30, 31, 40, 41, 43, 44
Cappon, Manuela *154:* 64; *218:* 149
Caras, Peter *36:* 64
Caraway, Caren *57:* 22
Caraway, James *3:* 200, 201
Carbe, Nino *29:* 183
Cares, Linda *67:* 176
Carigiet, Alois *24:* 67
Carle, Eric *4:* 42; *11:* 121; *12:* 29; *65:* 32,33, 34, 36; *73:* 63, 65; *163:* 55, 56
Carling, Amelia Lau *164:* 46
Carlino, Angela *168:* 43; *188:* 20
Carlson, Nancy L. *41:* 116; *56:* 25; *90:* 45; *144:* 48, 50; *213:* 24, 25, 26
Carluccio, Maria *175:* 129; *221:* 119
Carmi, Giora *79:* 35; *149:* 40; *208:* 126
Carpenter, Nancy *76:* 128; *86:* 173; *89:* 171; *131:* 186; *134:* 8; *138:* 215; *153:* 204; *159:* 93; *165:* 232; *211:* 134; *216:* 113
Carr, Archie *37:* 225
Carrick, Donald *5:* 194; *39:* 97; *49:* 70; *53:* 156; *63:* 15, 16, 17, 18, 19, 21; *80:* 131; *86:* 151; *118:* 24
Carrick, Malcolm *28:* 59, 60
Carrick, Paul *118:* 26; *194:* 28
Carrick, Valery *21:* 47
Carrier, Lark *71:* 43
Carroll, Jim *88:* 211; *140:* 177; *153:* 99; *195:* 75
Carroll, Lewis
    See Dodgson, Charles L.
Carroll, Michael *72:* 5
Carroll, Pamela *84:* 68; *128:* 214; *199:* 130
Carroll, Ruth *7:* 41; *10:* 68
Carter, Abby *81:* 32; *97:* 121; *102:* 61; *163:* 139; *164:* 125; *184:* 22, 23; *191:* 85; *222:* 51
Carter, Barbara *47:* 167, 169
Carter, David A. *114:* 24, 25; *170:* 42, 43
Carter, Don *124:* 54; *184:* 100; *192:* 43, 44, 45
Carter, Harry *22:* 179
Carter, Helene *15:* 38; *22:* 202, 203; *YABC 2:* 220, 221
Carter, Penny *173:* 91
Cartlidge, Michelle *49:* 65; *96:* 50, 51
Cartwright, Reg *63:* 61, 62; *78:* 26; *143:* 4
Cartwright, Shannon *176:* 81
Carty, Leo *4:* 196; *7:* 163; *58:* 131
Cary *4:* 133; *9:* 32; *20:* 2; *21:* 143
Cary, Page *12:* 41
Casale, Paul *71:* 63; *109:* 122; *136:* 28
Case, Chris *209:* 23
Case, Sandra E. *16:* 2
Caseley, Judith *87:* 36; *159:* 47, 48, 49
Casilla, Robert *78:* 7; *167:* 124; *211:* 41; *212:* 165
Casino, Steve *85:* 193
Cassel, Lili
    See Wronker, Lili Cassel

Cassel-Wronker, Lili
    See Wronker, Lili Cassel
Cassels, Jean *8:* 50; *150:* 119; *173:* 37; *186:* 182
Cassen, Melody *140:* 51
Cassity, Don *104:* 24
Cassler, Carl *75:* 137, 138; *82:* 162
Casson, Hugh *65:* 38, 40, 42, 43
Castellon, Federico *48:* 45, 46, 47, 48
Castle, Jane *4:* 80
Castro, Antonio *84:* 71
Casu, Danny "casroc" *201:* 10
Catalano, Dominic *94:* 79; *163:* 60, 61; *162:* 54
Catalanotto, Peter *63:* 170; *70:* 23; *71:* 182; *72:* 96; *74:* 114; *76:* 194, 195; *77:* 7; *79:* 157; *80:* 28, 67; *83:* 157; *85:* 27; *108:* 11; *113:* 30, 31, 33, 34, 36; *114:* 27, 28, 29; *117:* 53; *124:* 168; *159:* 54, 55; *195:* 19, 20, 21, 22, 24, 174; *200:* 156; *207:* 103; *209:* 184
Catania, Tom *68:* 82
Cather, Carolyn *3:* 83; *15:* 203; *34:* 216
Catlin, George *214:* 172
Catrow, David *117:* 179; *152:* 31, 33; *173:* 24; *206:* 29
Catusanu, Mircea *222:* 53
Cauley, Lorinda Bryan *44:* 135; *46:* 49
Cayard, Bruce *38:* 67
Cazet, Denys *52:* 27; *99:* 39, 40; *163:* 65, 66; *191:* 25, 27, 28
Ceccoli, Nicoletta *181:* 39; *188:* 99; *199:* 118; *209:* 6
Cecil, Randy *127:* 132, 133; *187:* 16, 17; *191:* 168; *209:* 5; *223:* 37, 38
Cellini, Joseph *2:* 73; *3:* 35; *16:* 116; *47:* 103
Cepeda, Joe *90:* 62; *109:* 91; *134:* 172; *159:* 57, 58, 164; *197:* 157; *203:* 69, 95; *215:* 38, 39, 40
Chabrian, Debbi *45:* 55
Chabrian, Deborah *51:* 182; *53:* 124; *63:* 107; *75:* 84; *79:* 85; *82:* 247; *89:* 93; *101:* 197; *212:* 13
Chagnon, Mary *37:* 158
Chalmers, Mary *3:* 145; *13:* 148; *33:* 125; *66:* 214
Chamberlain, Christopher *45:* 57
Chamberlain, Margaret *46:* 51; *106:* 89; *188:* 193; *212:* 16, 17
Chamberlain, Nigel *78:* 140
Chambers, C.E. *17:* 230
Chambers, Dave *12:* 151
Chambers, Jill *134:* 110
Chambers, Mary *4:* 188
Chambliss, Maxie *42:* 186; *56:* 159; *93:* 163, 164; *103:* 178; *186:* 33, 34; *196:* 39; *223:* 182
Champlin, Dale *136:* 124
Chan, Harvey *96:* 236; *99:* 153; *143:* 218; *179:* 144; *211:* 219
Chan, Peter *207:* 21; *221:* 39
Chandler, David P. *28:* 62
Chaney, Howard *139:* 27
Chang, Warren *101:* 209
Chapel, Jody *68:* 20
Chapman, C.H. *13:* 83, 85, 87
Chapman, Frederick T. *6:* 27; *44:* 28
Chapman, Gaye *203:* 133
Chapman, Gaynor *32:* 52, 53
Chapman, Jane *145:* 186; *150:* 56; *166:* 220; *174:* 202; *176:* 43, 44; *179:* 131; *202:* 189; *212:* 20, 21, 22; *216:* 123, 225; *221:* 181, 182
Chapman, Lynne *175:* 31; *197:* 25; *208:* 44
Chapman-Crane, Jeff *220:* 101
Chappell, Warren *3:* 172; *21:* 56; *27:* 125
Charles, Donald *30:* 154, 155
Charlip, Remy *4:* 48; *34:* 138; *68:* 53, 54; *119:* 29, 30; *210:* 63, 64
Charlot, Jean *1:* 137, 138; *8:* 23; *14:* 31; *48:* 151; *56:* 21
Charlot, Martin *64:* 72

Charlton, Michael *34:* 50; *37:* 39
Charmatz, Bill *7:* 45
Chartier, Normand *9:* 36; *52:* 49; *66:* 40; *74:* 220; *145:* 169; *168:* 91; *177:* 108
Chase, Lynwood M. *14:* 4
Chast, Roz *97:* 39, 40; *212:* 25
Chastain, Madye Lee *4:* 50
Chateron, Ann *152:* 19
Chatterton, Martin *68:* 102; *152:* 19
Chau, Tungwai *140:* 35
Chauncy, Francis *24:* 158
Chayka, Doug *145:* 97; *177:* 150; *196:* 46; *212:* 58
Chee, Cheng-Khee *79:* 42; *81:* 224; *180:* 245
Chen, Chih-sien *90:* 226
Chen, Tony *6:* 45; *19:* 131; *29:* 126; *34:* 160
Chen, Wendy *221:* 76
Chen, Yong *183:* 34
Cheney, T.A. *11:* 47
Cheng, Andrea *205:* 28
Cheng, Judith *36:* 45; *51:* 16
Chermayeff, Ivan *47:* 53
Cherry, David *93:* 40
Cherry, Lynne *34:* 52; *65:* 184; *87:* 111; *99:* 46, 47
Chesak, Lina *135:* 118
Chess, Victoria *12:* 6; *33:* 42, 48, 49; *40:* 194; *41:* 145; *69:* 80; *72:* 100; *92:* 33, 34; *104:* 167
Chessare, Michele *41:* 50; *56:* 48; *69:* 145
Chesterton, G.K. *27:* 43, 44, 45, 47
Chestnutt, David *47:* 217
Chesworth, Michael *75:* 24; *152:* 88; *88:* 136; *94:* 25; *98:* 155; *160:* 42; *207:* 23, 24, 25; *214:* 145
Chetham, Celia *134:* 34
Chetwin, Grace *86:* 40
Cheung, Irving *158:* 96
Chevalier, Christa *35:* 66
Chew, Ruth *7:* 46; *132:* 147
Chewning, Randy *92:* 206
Chichester Clark, Emma *72:* 121; *77:* 212; *78:* 209; *87:* 143; *117:* 37, 39, 40; *144:* 138; *156:* 24, 25; *209:* 26
Chifflart *47:* 113, 127
Child, Lauren *119:* 32; *183:* 30, 31
Chin, Alex *28:* 54
Chitwood, Susan Tanner *163:* 16
Cho, Shinta *8:* 126
Chodos-Irvine, Margaret *52:* 102, 103, 107; *152:* 44
Choi, Yangsook *171:* 134; *173:* 135; *178:* 38, 39, 40
Choksi, Nishant *222:* 54
Chollat, Emilie *170:* 203
Chollick, Jay *25:* 175
Choma, Christina *99:* 169
Chomey, Steve *188:* 53
Chorao, Kay *7:* 200, 201; *8:* 25; *11:* 234; *33:* 187; *35:* 239; *69:* 35; *70:* 235; *123:* 174; *193:* 179; *215:* 43, 44, 45, 46
Chorney, Steve *221:* 63
Chow, Frances J. Soo Ping *206:* 36
Chowdhury, Subrata *62:* 130; *162:* 22, 23
Christelow, Eileen *38:* 44; *83:* 198, 199; *90:* 57, 58; *184:* 26
Christensen, Bonnie *93:* 100; *153:* 67; *213:* 29, 30
Christensen, Gardell Dano *1:* 57
Christensen, James C. *140:* 226
Christiana, David *90:* 64; *135:* 13; *171:* 7; *195:* 26, 27
Christiansen, Per *40:* 24
Christie, R. Gregory *116:* 107; *127:* 20, 21; *162:* 179; *164:* 114; *165:* 137; *174:* 157; *179:* 172; *185:* 17, 18, 19; *200:* 2; *204:* 85; *215:* 207; *218:* 57; *220:* 80, 130
Christy, Howard Chandler *17:* 163, 164, 165, 168, 169; *19:* 186, 187; *21:* 22, 23, 24, 25
Christy, Jana *194:* 21
Chronister, Robert *23:* 138; *63:* 27; *69:* 167

Church, Caroline Jayne *179:* 27; *219:* 28, 29
Church, Frederick *YABC 1:* 155
Chute, Marchette *1:* 59
Chwast, Jacqueline *1:* 63; *2:* 275; *6:* 46, 47; *11:* 125; *12:* 202; *14:* 235
Chwast, Seymour *3:* 128, 129; *18:* 43; *27:* 152; *92:* 79; *96:* 56, 57, 58; *146:* 32, 33; *197:* 99
Cieslawksi, Steve *101:* 142; *127:* 116; *158:* 169, 171; *190:* 174; *212:* 85
Cinelli, Lisa *146:* 253
Cirlin, Edgard *2:* 168
Clairin, Georges *53:* 109
Clapp, John *105:* 66; *109:* 58; *126:* 7; *129:* 148; *130:* 165; *195:* 48; *220:* 102
Clark, Brenda *119:* 85; *153:* 55
Clark, David *77:* 164; *134:* 144, 145; *216:* 66, 67
Clark, Emma Chichester
    See Chichester Clark, Emma
Clark, Victoria *35:* 159
Clarke, Greg *169:* 134; *215:* 47, 115
Clarke, Gus *72:* 226; *134:* 31
Clarke, Harry *23:* 172, 173
Clarke, Peter *75:* 102
Claverie, Jean *38:* 46; *88:* 29
Clavis, Philippe Goossens *182:* 167
Clay, Wil *203:* 29
Clayton, Elaine *159:* 60; *209:* 32
Clayton, Robert *9:* 181
Cleary, Brian P. *186:* 37
Cleaver, Elizabeth *8:* 204; *23:* 36
Cleland, T.M. *26:* 92
Clemens, Peter *61:* 125
Clement, Charles *20:* 38
Clement, Gary *186:* 79; *191:* 32
Clement, Janet *182:* 50
Clement, Nathan *200:* 30
Clement, Rod *97:* 42
Clement, Stephen *88:* 3
Clementson, John *84:* 213
Clemesha, David *192:* 49, 50
Cleminson, Kate *221:* 26
Clevin, Jorgen *7:* 50
Clifford, Judy *34:* 163; *45:* 198
Clokey, Art *59:* 44
Clouse, Dennis *187:* 158
Clouse, James *84:* 15
Clouse, Nancy L. *78:* 31; *114:* 90
Clover, Peter *152:* 45
Cneut, Carll *156:* 166; *165:* 67; *197:* 26
Coalson, Glo *9:* 72, 85; *25:* 155; *26:* 42; *35:* 212; *53:* 31; *56:* 154; *94:* 37, 38, 193
Cober, Alan E. *17:* 158; *32:* 77; *49:* 127
Cober-Gentry, Leslie *92:* 111
Cocca-Leffler, Maryann *80:* 46; *136:* 60; *139:* 193; *194:* 31, 33, 34
Cochran, Bobbye *11:* 52
Cochran, Josh *221:* 27
CoConis, Ted *4:* 41; *46:* 41; *51:* 104
Cocozza, Chris *87:* 18; *110:* 173; *111:* 149
Cockroft, Jason *152:* 20
Coerr, Eleanor *1:* 64; *67:* 52
Coes, Peter *35:* 172
Cogancherry, Helen *52:* 143; *69:* 131; *77:* 93; *78:* 220; *109:* 204; *110:* 129; *203:* 92
Coggins, Jack *2:* 69
Cohen, Alix *7:* 53
Cohen, Miriam *155:* 23, 24
Cohen, Nancy R. *165:* 35
Cohen, Santiago *164:* 26; *215:* 52, 199
Cohen, Sheldon *105:* 33, 34; *166:* 46, 47
Cohen, Vincent O. *19:* 243
Cohen, Vivien *11:* 112
Coker, Paul *51:* 172
Colbert, Anthony *15:* 41; *20:* 193
Colby, C.B. *3:* 47
Cole, Babette *58:* 172; *96:* 63, 64; *155:* 29
Cole, Brock *68:* 223; *72:* 36, 37, 38, 192; *127:* 23; *136:* 64, 65; *197:*
Cole, Gwen *87:* 185

Cole, Henry *178:* 120; *181:* 42, 43; *189:* 60; *213:* 35, 36; *222:* 139
Cole, Herbert *28:* 104
Cole, Michael *59:* 46
Cole, Olivia H.H. *1:* 134; *3:* 223; *9:* 111; *38:* 104
Cole, Rachael *209:* 39
Colin, Paul *102:* 59; *123:* 118; *126:* 152; *192:* 129
Colley, Jacqui *202:* 20
Collicott, Sharleen *98:* 39; *143:* 29, 30
Collier, Bryan *126:* 54; *151:* 166; *174:* 16, 17, 18; *204:* 18, 19; *208:* 84; *211:* 143
Collier, David *13:* 127
Collier, John *27:* 179; *208:* 154
Collier, Steven *50:* 52
Collier-Morales, Roberta *168:* 61
Collins, Heather *66:* 84; *67:* 68; *81:* 40; *98:* 192, 193; *129:* 95, 96, 98
Collins, Matt *167:* 90
Collins, Ross *140:* 23, 24; *200:* 36, 37; *209:* 54
Colman, Audrey *146:* 161
Colón, Raul *108:* 112; *113:* 5; *117:* 167; *134:* 112; *146:* 23; *159:* 92; *166:* 73; *180:* 107; *186:* 156; *190:* 6; *193:* 24, 205; *202:* 21, 22, 23; *217:* 68; *220:* 126, 157
Colonna, Bernard *21:* 50; *28:* 103; *34:* 140; *43:* 180; *78:* 150
Comport, Sally Wern *117:* 169; *169:* 104; *190:* 42; *207:* 50
Conahan, Carolyn *215:* 17
Conde, J.M. *100:* 120
Condon, Grattan *54:* 85 Condon, Ken *161:* 44; *195:* 28, 29
Cone, Ferne Geller *39:* 49
Cone, J. Morton *39:* 49
Conklin, Paul *43:* 62
Connelly, Gwen *212:* 30
Connelly, James *198:* 12
Connolly, Howard *67:* 88
Connolly, Jerome P. *4:* 128; *28:* 52
Connolly, Peter *47:* 60
Conoly, Walle *110:* 224
Conover, Chris *31:* 52; *40:* 184; *41:* 51; *44:* 79; *213:* 39
Constantin, Pascale *207:* 159
Contreras, Gerry *72:* 9
Converse, James *38:* 70
Conway *62:* 62
Conway, Michael *69:* 12; *81:* 3; *92:* 108
Cook, Ande *188:* 135
Cook, G.R. *29:* 165
Cook, Joel *108:* 160
Cookburn, W.V. *29:* 204
Cooke, Donald E. *2:* 77
Cooke, Tom *52:* 118
Coomaraswamy, A.K. *50:* 100
Coombs, Charles *43:* 65
Coombs, Deborah *139:* 175
Coombs, Patricia *2:* 82; *3:* 52; *22:* 119; *51:* 32, 33, 34, 35, 36, 37, 38, 39, 40, 42, 43
Cooney, Barbara *6:* 16, 17, 50; *12:* 42; *13:* 92; *15:* 145; *16:* 74, 111; *18:* 189; *23:* 38, 89, 93; *32:* 138; *38:* 105; *59:* 48, 49, 51, 52, 53; *74:* 222; *81:* 100; *91:* 25; *96:* 71, 72, 74; *100:* 149; *YABC2:* 10
Cooper, Elisha *157:* 38, 39
Cooper, Floyd *79:* 95; *81:* 45; *84:* 82; *85:* 74; *91:* 118; *96:* 77, 78; *103:* 149; *144:* 54; *145:* 151; *159:* 196; *176:* 133, 134; *187:* 26, 27, 28, 29; *188:* 22; *199:* 175; *219:* 66
Cooper, Heather *50:* 39
Cooper, Helen *102:* 42, 43, 44
Cooper, Mario *24:* 107
Cooper, Marjorie *7:* 112
Cope, Jane *61:* 201; *108* 52
Copeland, Mark *180:* 12
Copelman, Evelyn *8:* 61; *18:* 25
Copley, Heather *30:* 86; *45:* 57
Corace, Jen *208:* 48

Corbett, Grahame *30:* 114; *43:* 67
Corbino, John *19:* 248
Corcos, Lucille *2:* 223; *10:* 27; *34:* 66
Cordell, Matthew *197:* 93; *199:* 20, 21
Córdova, Amy *220:* 194
Corey, Robert *9:* 34
Corlass, Heather *10:* 7
Cornell, James *27:* 60
Cornell, Jeff *11:* 58
Cornell, Laura *94:* 179; *95:* 25
Corr, Christopher *204:* 98
Corral, Ridrigs *212:* 87
Corrigan, Barbara *8:* 37
Corrigan, Patrick *145:* 149
Corwin, Judith Hoffman *10:* 28
Corwin, Oliver *191:* 119
Cory, Fanny Y. *20:* 113; *48:* 29
Cosentino, Ralph *169:* 32
Cosgrove, Margaret *3:* 100; *47:* 63; *82:* 133
Costabel, Eva Deutsch *45:* 66, 67
Costanza, John *58:* 7, 8, 9
Costello, Chris *86:* 78
Costello, David F. *23:* 55
Côté, Geneviéve *184:* 37, 39; *210:* 256; *211:* 151
Cote, Nancy *126:* 139; *156:* 101; *174:* 101; *182:* 53, 54, 55; *222:* 49
Cottenden, Jeff *190:* 45
Couch, Greg *94:* 124; *110:* 13; *162:* 31; *168:* 149; *199:* 22; *216:* 144
Councell, Ruth Tietjen *79:* 29
Courtney, Cathy *58:* 69, 144; *59:* 15; *61:* 20, 87
Courtney, R. *35:* 110
Counihan, Claire *133:* 106
Cousineau, Normand *89:* 180; *112:* 76
Cousins, Lucy *172:* 53, 54; *205:* 34, 35
Couture, Christin *41:* 209
Covarrubias, Miguel *35:* 118, 119, 123, 124, 125
Coville, Katherine *32:* 57; *36:* 167; *92:* 38
Covington, Neverne *113:* 87
Cowdrey, Richard *169:* 170; *178:* 205; *204:* 22, 23; *215:* 31
Cowell, Cressida *140:* 39
Cowell, Lucinda *77:* 54
Cowles, Rose *203:* 164, 167
Cox *43:* 93
Cox, Charles *8:* 20
Cox, David *56:* 37; *90:* 63; *119:* 38
Cox, Palmer *24:* 76, 77
Cox, Steve *140:* 96
Coxe, Molly *69:* 44
Coxon, Michele *158:* 80
Crabb, Gordon *70:* 39
Crabtree, Judith *98:* 42
Craft, Kinuko *22:* 182; *36:* 220; *53:* 122, 123, 148, 149; *74:* 12; *81:* 129; *86:* 31; *89:* 139; *127:* 27, 28, 29; *132:* 142; *139:* 38
Craig, Daniel *177:* 67; *180:* 11; *185:* 203; *211:* 212
Craig, David *136:* 198; *205:* 37
Craig, Helen *49:* 76; *62:* 70, 71, 72; *69:* 141; *94:* 42, 43, 44; *112:* 53; *135:* 101, 102; *213:* 45, 46, 47, 55, 81, 82
Crane, Alan H. *1:* 217
Crane, H.M. *13:* 111
Crane, Jack *43:* 183
Crane, Jordan *174:* 21
Crane, Walter *18:* 46, 47, 48, 49, 53, 54, 56, 57, 59, 60, 61; *22:* 128; *24:* 210, 217; *100:* 70, 71
Cravath, Lynne Avril *98:* 45; *182:* 58, 59; *216:* 48; *219:* 61; *220:* 124
Crawford, Allen *212:* 181
Crawford, Denise *137:* 213
Crawford, Will *43:* 77
Credle, Ellis *1:* 69
Czekaj, Jef *217:* 44; *218:* 77
Czernecki, Stefan *154:* 104; *178:* 68, 69
Crespi, Francesca *87:* 90

Cressy, Michael *124:* 55; *203:* 132
Crews, Donald *32:* 59, 60; *76:* 42, 43, 44
Crews, Nina *97:* 49
Crichlow, Ernest *74:* 88; *83:* 203
Crilley, Mark *210:* 71
Croft, James *150:* 57
Crofut, Bob *80:* 87; *81:* 47
Crofut, Susan *23:* 61
Croll, Carolyn *80:* 137; *102:* 52
Cross, Peter *56:* 78; *63:* 60, 65
Crossman, David A. *219:* 38
Crowe, Elizabeth *88:* 144
Crowell, Pers *3:* 125
Cruikshank, George *15:* 76, 83; *22:* 74, 75, 76, 77, 78, 79,80, 81, 82, 84, 137; *24:* 22, 23
Crump, Fred H. *11:* 62
Cruz, Ray *6:* 55; *70:* 234; *123:* 173; *172:* 192
Csatari, Joe *44:* 82; *55:* 152; *63:* 25, 28; *102:* 58
Cuetara, Mittie *158:* 85
Cuffari, Richard *4:* 75; *5:* 98; *6:* 56; *7:* 13,84, 153; *8:* 148, 155; *9:* 89; *11:* 19; *12:* 55, 96,114; *15:* 51, 202; *18:* 5; *20:* 139; *21:* 197; *22:* 14, 192; *23:* 15, 106; *25:* 97; *27:* 133; *28:* 196; *29:* 54; *30:* 85; *31:* 35; *36:* 101; *38:* 171; *42:* 97; *44:* 92, 192; *45:* 212, 213; *46:* 36, 198; *50:* 164; *54:* 80, 136, 137, 145; *56:* 17; *60:* 63; *66:* 49, 50; *70:* 41; *71:* 132; *77:* 157; *78:* 58, 149; *79:* 120; *85:* 2, 152
Cugat, Xavier *19:* 120
Cumings, Art *35:* 160
Cummings, Chris *29:* 167
Cummings, Michael *159:* 142
Cummings, Pat *42:* 61; *61:* 99; *69:* 205; *71:* 57,58; *78:* 24, 25; *93:* 75; *107:* 49, 50; *164:* 259; *203:* 45, 46
Cummings, Richard *24:* 119
Cunette, Lou *20:* 93; *22:* 125
Cunningham, Aline *25:* 180
Cunningham, David *11:* 13
Cunningham, Imogene *16:* 122, 127
Cunningham, Kelley *176:* 159
Cupples, Pat *107:* 12; *126:* 109; *182:* 13; *198:* 68; *217:* 21, 22
Curlee, Lynn *98:* 48; *141:* 39; *190:* 48
Currey, Anna *190:* 145; *202:* 130, 132
Curry, John Steuart *2:* 5; *19:* 84; *34:* 36; *144:* 126
Curry, Tom *127:* 131; *185:* 25, 26
Curtis, Bruce *23:* 96; *30:* 88; *36:* 22
Curtis, Neil *167:* 30
Curtis, Stacy *205:* 38
Cusack, Margaret *58:* 49, 50, 51
Cushman, Doug *65:* 57; *101:* 39, 40; *133:* 179; *157:* 45; *186:* 157; *210:* 76, 77
Cutting, Ann *196:* 194
Cyrus, Kurt *132:* 39; *179:* 36, 37
Czechowski, Alicia *95:* 21; *171:* 37
Czernecki, Stefan *117:* 173

D

Dabcovich, Lydia *25:* 105; *40:* 114; *99:* 75, 76
Dacey, Bob *82:* 175; *152:* 65
d'Achille, Gino *127:* 175, 176
Daily, Don *78:* 197; *220:* 154
Dain, Martin J. *35:* 75
Dale, Penny *127:* 224; *151:* 57; *160:* 89; *197:* 75
Dale, Rae *72:* 197
Daley, Joann *50:* 22
Dalton, Anne *40:* 62; *63:* 119
Daly, Deborah M. *74:* 213
Daly, Jim *103:* 60; *150:* 48
Daly, Jude *138:* 118, 119; *213:* 41; *222:* 56, 57
Daly, Nicholas *37:* 53; *76:* 48, 49
Daly, Niki *107:* 15; *114:* 38, 39, 40; *164:* 86; *192:* 53; *198:* 26, 27
Daly, Paul *97:* 205

Dalziel, Brothers *33:* 113
D'Amato, Alex *9:* 48; *20:* 25
D'Amato, Janet *9:* 48; *20:* 25; *26:* 118
D'Amico, Steve *170:* 52
Danalis, Johnny *167:* 27
D'Andrea, Domenick *183:* 108
Daniel, Alan *23:* 59; *29:* 110; *76:* 50, 53, 55, 56; *153:* 76 *115:* 74; *134:* 70
Daniel, Lea *76:* 53, 55; *153:* 76
Daniel, Lewis C. *20:* 216
Daniels, Beau *73:* 4
Daniels, Steve *22:* 16
Daniels, Stewart *56:* 12
Dann, Bonnie *31:* 83
Dann, Penny *82:* 128
Danska, Herbert *24:* 219
Danyell, Alice *20:* 27
Darbyshire, Kristen *218:* 41
Dardik, Helen *208:* 200
Darley, F.O.C. *16:* 145; *19:* 79, 86, 88, 185; *21:* 28,36; *35:* 76, 77, 78, 79, 80, 81; *YABC 2:* 175
Darling, Lois *3:* 59; *23:* 30, 31
Darling, Louis *1:* 40, 41; *2:* 63; *3:* 59; *23:* 30,31; *43:* 54, 57, 59; *121:* 53
Darnell, K.L. *210:* 247
Darrow, David R. *84:* 101
Darrow, Whitney, Jr. *13:* 25; *38:* 220, 221
Darwin, Beatrice *43:* 54
Darwin, Len *24:* 82
Dastolfo, Frank *33:* 179
Dauber, Liz *1:* 22; *3:* 266; *30:* 49
Daugherty, James *3:* 66; *8:* 178; *13:* 27, 28, 161; *18:* 101; *19:* 72; *29:* 108; *32:* 156; *42:* 84; *YABC 1:* 256; *2:* 174
d'Aulaire, Edgar Parin *5:* 51; *66:* 53
d'Aulaire, Ingri Parin *5:* 51; *66:* 53
Davalos, Felipe *99:* 197; *159:* 66; *174:* 163
Davenier, Christine *125:* 88; *127:* 32; *128:* 152; *179:* 39, 40; *216:* 84, 85, 86, 87; *218:* 62, 63
Davick, Linda *151:* 124; *208:* 187
David, Jacques-Louis *193:* 22
David, Jonathan *19:* 37
Davidson, Kevin *28:* 154
Davidson, Raymond *32:* 61
Davie, Helen K. *77:* 48, 49
Davies, Andy Robert *205:* 169
Davies, Lottie *214:* 69
Davis, Allen *20:* 11; *22:* 45; *27:* 222; *29:* 157; *41:* 99; *47:* 99; *50:* 84; *52:* 105
Davis, Bette J. *15:* 53; *23:* 95
Davis, Dimitris *45:* 95
Davis, Eleanor *209:* 33
Davis, Hendon *151:* 122
Davis, Jack E. *145:* 139; *175:* 84, 85; *208:* 102; *210:* 81, 82; *213:* 151
Davis, Jim *32:* 63, 64
Davis, Katie *152:* 52, 53, 54; *208:* 52
Davis, Lambert *110:* 23, 24; *176:* 58
Davis, Marguerite *31:* 38; *34:* 69, 70; *100:* 34; *YABC 1:* 126, 230
Davis, Nelle *69:* 191
Davis, Paul *78:* 214
Davis, Rich *206:* 38
Davis, Stuart *211:* 69
Davis, Yvonne LeBrun *94:* 144
Davisson, Virginia H. *44:* 178
DaVolls, Andy *85:* 53
Dawson, Diane *24:* 127; *42:* 126; *52:* 130; *68:* 104
Dawson, Janine *215:* 198
Dawson, Willow *208:* 54; *216:* 119
Day, Alexandra *67:* 59; *97:* 54; *166:* 65; *169:* 40; *197:* 50, 51, 52, 54
Day, Larry *169:* 88; *185:* 59
Day, Rob *94:* 110; *127:* 24; *197:* 32
Dean, Bob *19:* 211
Dean, David *192:* 55
de Angeli, Marguerite *1:* 77; *27:* 62, 65, 66, 67, 69, 70, 72; *100:* 75, 76; *YABC 1:* 166

DeArmond, Dale *70:* 47
Deas, Michael *27:* 219, 221; *30:* 156; *67:* 134; *72:* 24; *75:* 155; *84:* 206; *88:* 124
Deas, Rich *191:* 87; *193:* 10; *212:* 79
deBarros, Jim *196:* 60
Debon, Nicolas *151:* 60; *177:* 46
de Bosschere, Jean *19:* 252; *21:* 4; *186:* 44, 45
De Bruyn, M(onica) G. *13:* 30, 31
Decker, C.B. *172:* 120; *215:* 94
De Cuir, John F. *1:* 28, 29
Deeter, Catherine *74:* 110; *103:* 150; *137:* 50
Degen, Bruce *40:* 227, 229; *57:* 28, 29; *56:* 156; *75:* 229; *76:* 19; *81:* 36, 37; *92:* 26; *93:* 199; *97:* 56, 58, 59; *124:* 40; *147:* 39, 40, 41; *168:* 23; *205:* 45, 46
De Grazia *14:* 59; *39:* 56, 57
DeGrazio, George *88:* 40
deGroat, Diane *9:* 39; *18:* 7; *23:* 123; *28:* 200, 201; *31:* 58, 59; *34:* 151; *41:* 152; *43:* 88; *46:* 40, 200; *49:* 163; *50:* 89; *52:* 30, 34; *54:* 43; *63:* 70: 136; *71:* 99; *73:* 117,156; *77:* 34; *85:* 48; *86:* 201; *87:* 142; *90:* 72, 73, 143; *95:* 182; *111:* 123; *118:* 160; *126:* 8; *130:* 130; *138:* 93, 94; *169:* 46, 47
de Groot, Lee *6:* 21
Deines, Brian *110:* 139; *220:* 36, 37
DeJohn, Marie *89:* 78
Dekhteryov, B. *61:* 158
de Kiefte, Kees *94:* 107
Delacre, Lulu *36:* 66; *156:* 35; *202:* 10, 53; *209:* 36
Delaney, A. *21:* 78
Delaney, Michael *180:* 16
Delaney, Molly *80:* 43
Delaney, Ned *28:* 68; *56:* 80; *102:* 11
DeLapine, Jim *79:* 21
De La Roche Saint Andre, Anne *75:* 37
de Larrea, Victoria *6:* 119, 204; *29:* 103; *72:* 203; *87:* 199
Delehanty, Joan W. *223:* 165
DeLeon, Melanie *210:* 43
Delessert, Étienne *7:* 140; *46:* 61, 62, 63, 65, 67, 68; *130:* 38, 39, 40, 41, 42; *179:* 46, 47, 48, 49; *YABC 2:* 209
Delezenne, Christine *186:* 126
Del Negro, Janice *196:* 161
Delon, Melanie *216:* 30
DeLorenzo, Christopher *154:* 149
Delulio, John *15:* 54
DeLuna, Tony *88:* 95
Demarest, Chris L. *45:* 68, 69, 70; *73:* 172, 173, 176; *78:* 106; *82:* 48, 49; *89:* 212; *92:* 86; *128:* 57, 58; *175:* 46, 48
De Mejo, Oscar *40:* 67
De Muth, Roger *205:* 184; *221:* 35
Demi *11:* 135; *15:* 245; *66:* 129, 130; *89:* 216; *102:* 66, 68; *210:* 86, 87, 89
Denetsosie, Hoke *13:* 126; *82:* 34
Denise, Christopher *147:* 43, 44; *176:* 101; *193:* 35, 36, 37; *201:* 37
Dennis, Morgan *18:* 68, 69; *64:* 89
Dennis, Wesley *2:* 87; *3:* 111; *11:* 132; *18:* 71, 72, 73, 74; *22:* 9; *24:* 196, 200; *46:* 178; *69:* 94, 96; *129:* 62
Denos, Julia *202:* 26
Denslow, W.W. *16:* 84, 85, 86, 87; *18:* 19, 20, 24; *29:* 211; *100:* 21
Denton, Kady MacDonald *110:* 82; *130:* 70; *181:* 54, 55, 56; *192:* 75
Denton, Phil *220:* 6
Denton, Terry *72:* 163; *174:* 26; *186:* 52; *196:* 83, 84
DePalma, Mary Newell *132:* 114; *139:* 75; *185:* 30, 31; *186:* 121; *213:* 62
dePaola, Tomie *8:* 95; *9:* 93; *11:* 69; 25; *103:* 28: 157; *29:* 80; *39:* 52, 53; *40:* 226; *46:* 187; *59:* 61, 62, 63, 64, 65, 66, 67, 68, 69, 71, 72, 74; *62:* 19; *108:* 63, 67, 68, 70; *155:* 62, 64, 66; *180:* 105; *200:* 47, 48, 49, 50
Deraney, Michael J. *77:* 35; *78:* 148
deRosa, Dee *70:* 48; *71:* 210; *91:* 78

Dervaux, Isabelle *111:* 117
DeSaix, Deborah Durland *180:* 15; *188:* 24
De Saulles, Tony *119:* 39
de Sève, Peter *146:* 261; *207:* 78; *219:* 42
Deshaprabhu, Meera Dayal *86:* 192
Desimini, Lisa *86:* 68; *94:* 47; *96:* 7; *104:* 107; *125:* 194; *131:* 180; *172:* 56; *216:* 89, 90
de St. Menin, Charles *70:* 17
Detmold, Edward J. *22:* 104, 105, 106, 107; *35:* 120; *64:* 5; *YABC 2:* 203
Detrich, Susan *20:* 133
Deutermann, Diana *77:* 175
DeVelasco, Joseph E. *21:* 51
de Veyrac, Robert *YABC 2:* 19
DeVille, Edward A. *4:* 235
de Visser, John *55:* 119
Devito, Bert *12:* 164
Devlin, Harry *11:* 74; *74:* 63, 65; *136:* 77, 78
Dewan, Ted *108:* 73; *157:* 55; *165:* 129
Dewar, Nick *133:* 122
Dewdney, Anna *184:* 43, 44
Dewey, Ariane *7:* 64; *33:* 195; *35:* 208; *68:* 16,17; *75:* 46; *93:* 91; *94:* 197; *109:* 65, 66, 67; *125:* 2, 3, 4, 5; *127:* 188; *143:* 25; *178:* 17, 19, 74; *188:* 166; *202:* 164
Dewey, Jennifer (Owings) *58:* 54; *64:* 214; *65:* 207; *88:* 169; *103:* 45
Dewey, Kenneth *39:* 62; *51:* 23; *56:* 163
de Zanger, Arie *30:* 40
Diakité, Baba Wagué *174:* 28
Diamond, Donna *21:* 200; *23:* 63; *26:* 142; *35:* 83, 84, 85, 86, 87, 88, 89; *38:* 78; *40:* 147; *44:* 152; *50:* 144; *53:* 126; *69:* 46, 47, 48, 201; *71:* 133; *123:* 19
Dias, Ron *71:* 67
Diaz, David *80:* 213; *96:* 83, 84; *108:* 228; *110:* 29; *149:* 106; *150:* 63; *179:* 160; *184:* 95, 97; *189:* 51, 52, 53; *221:* 86
Dibley, Glin *138:* 83; *141:* 128; *211:* 162; *221:* 61
DiCesare, Joe *70:* 38; *71:* 63, 106; *79:* 214; *93:* 147; *116:* 217; *143:* 111; *166:* 57
Dick, John Henry *8:* 181
Dickens, Frank *34:* 131
Dickey, Robert L. *15:* 279
Dickson, Mora *84:* 21
Didier, Sam *166:* 114
Dietz, James *128:* 223; *193:* 136
di Fate, Vincent *37:* 70; *90:* 11; *93:* 60; *109:* 219, 220
Di Fiori, Lawrence *10:* 51; *12:* 190; *27:* 97; *40:* 219; *93:* 57; *130:* 45
Digby, Desmond *97:* 180
Dignan, James *196:* 143
Di Grazia, Thomas *32:* 66; *35:* 241
Dillard, Annie *10:* 32
Dillard, Sarah *136:* 186; *217:* 53
Dillon, Corinne B. *1:* 139
Dillon, Diane *4:* 104, 167; *6:* 23; *13:* 29; *15:* 99; *26:* 148; *27:* 136, 201; *51:* 29, 48, 51, 52, 53, 54,55, 56, 57, 58, 59, 60, 61, 62; *54:* 155; *56:* 69; *58:* 127,128; *61:* 95; *62:* 27; *64:* 46; *68:* 3; *69:* 209; *74:* 89; *79:* 92; *86:* 89; *92:* 28, 177; *93:* 7, 210; *94:* 239, 240; *97:* 167; *106:* 58, 59,61, 64; *107:* 3; *139:* 246; *167:* 77; *189:* 202; *191:* 191; *194:* 45, 46, 48, 49
Dillon, Leo *4:* 104, 167; *6:* 23; *13:* 29; *15:* 99; *26:* 148; *27:* 136, 201; *51:* 29, 48, 51, 52, 53, 54,55, 56, 57, 58, 59, 60, 61, 62; *54:* 155; *56:* 69; *58:* 127,128; *61:* 95; *62:* 27; *64:* 46; *68:* 3; *69:* 209; *74:* 89; *79:* 92; *86:* 89; *92:* 28, 177; *93:* 7, 210; *94:* 239, 240; *97:* 167; *106:* 58, 59,61, 64; *107:* 3; *139:* 246; *167:* 77; *189:* 202; *191:* 191; *194:* 45, 46, 48, 49
Dillon, Sharon Saseen *59:* 179, 188
DiMaccio, Gerald *121:* 80
DiMaggio, Joe *36:* 22
DiMassi, Gina *169:* 17

Dinan, Carol *25:* 169; *59:* 75
Dines, Glen *7:* 66, 67
Dinesen, Thomas *44:* 37
Dinh, Pham Viet *167:* 184
Dinnerstein, Harvey *42:* 63, 64, 65, 66, 67, 68; *50:* 146
Dinsdale, Mary *10:* 65; *11:* 171
Dinyer, Eric *86:* 148; *109:* 163; *110:* 239; *124:* 11; *150:* 69; *170:* 4; *171:* 30
Dion, Nathalie *170:* 124; *213:* 52
DiRocco, Carl *181:* 23
DiSalvo-Ryan, DyAnne *59:* 77; *62:* 185; *117:* 46; *144:* 64; *150:* 153; *186:* 162
Disney, Walt *28:* 71, 72, 73, 76, 77, 78, 79, 80, 81, 87, 88, 89,90, 91, 94
DiTerlizzi, Tony *105:* 7; *147:* 22; *154:* 31, 32, 33; *214:* 74
Divito, Anna *83:* 159
Dixon, Don *74:* 17; *109:* 196
Dixon, Larry *127:* 125
Dixon, Maynard *20:* 165
Doares, Robert G. *20:* 39
Dob, Bob *205:* 14
Dobias, Frank *22:* 162
Dobrin, Arnold *4:* 68
Dobson, Steven Gaston *102:* 103
Docherty, Thomas *218:* 45, 46
Dockray, Tracy *139:* 77
Docktor, Irv *43:* 70
Dodd, Ed *4:* 69
Dodd, Emma *203:* 57
Dodd, Julie *74:* 73
Dodd, Lynley *35:* 92; *86:* 71; *132:* 45, 46, 47
Dodge, Bill *96:* 36; *118:* 7, 8, 9; *133:* 135
Dodgson, Charles L. *20:* 148; *33:* 146; *YABC 2:* 98
Dodson, Bert *9:* 138; *14:* 195; *42:* 55; *54:* 8; *60:* 49; *101:* 125
Dodson, Liz Brenner *105:* 117; *111:* 15
Dohanos, Stevan *16:* 10
Dolce, J. Ellen *74:* 147; *75:* 41
Dolch, Marguerite P. *50:* 64
Dolesch, Susanne *34:* 49
Dollar, Diane *57:* 32
Dolobowsky, Mena *81:* 54
Dolson, Hildegarde *5:* 57
Domanska, Janina *6:* 66, 67; *YABC 1:* 166
Domi *134:* 113
Dominguez, El *53:* 94
Domjan, Joseph *25:* 93
Domm, Jeffrey C. *84:* 69; *135:* 70
Donahey, William *68:* 209
Donahue, Dorothy *76:* 170
Donahue, Vic *2:* 93; *3:* 190; *9:* 44
Donald, Elizabeth *4:* 18
Donalty, Alison *149:* 195, 196, 197
Donato *85:* 59; *149:* 204; *191:* 19
Donato, Michael A. *200:* 143
Doner, Kim *208:* 57
Doney, Todd L.W. *87:* 12; *93:* 112; *98:* 135; *101:* 57; *104:* 40; *118:* 163; *135:* 162, 163; *151:* 18
Donna, Natalie *9:* 52
Donohue, Dorothy *95:* 2; *132:* 30; *176:* 54, 55; *178:* 77, 78, 79
Dooling, Michael *82:* 19; *105:* 55; *106:* 224; *125:* 135; *171:* 46; *172:* 12; *176:* 120; *197:* 89; *220:* 39, 40
Doran, Ben-Ami *128:* 189
Doran, Colleen *211:* 48
Dore, Gustave *18:* 169, 172, 175; *19:* 93, 94, 95, 96, 97, 98,99, 100, 101, 102, 103, 104, 105; *23:* 188; *25:* 197, 199
Doremus, Robert *6:* 62; *13:* 90; *30:* 95, 96, 97; *38:* 97
Dorfman, Ronald *11:* 128
Doriau *86:* 59; *91:* 152
Dorman, Brandon *197:* 35; *204:* 6; *210:* 104; *212:* 95; *216:* 156; *222:* 133
Dormer, Frank W. *200:* 55; *222:* 48
Dorros, Arthur *78:* 42, 43; *91:* 28

Doruyter, Karel *165:* 105
dos Santos, Joyce Audy *57:* 187, 189
Doty, Roy *28:* 98; *31:* 32; *32:* 224; *46:* 157; *82:* 71; *142:* 7
Doucet, Bob *132:* 238; *169:* 159
Dougherty, Charles *16:* 204; *18:* 74
Doughty, Rebecca *177:* 174; *222:* 159
Doughty, Thomas *118:* 31; *140:* 60
Douglas, Aaron *31:* 103
Douglas, Allen *223:* 53
Douglas, Carole Nelson *73:* 48
Douglas, Goray *13:* 151
Dow, Brian *150:* 92
Dowd, Jason *132:* 51, 52; *164:* 244
Dowd, Vic *3:* 244; *10:* 97
Dowden, Anne Ophelia *7:* 70, 71; *13:* 120
Dowdy, Mrs. Regera *29:* 100
Downard, Barry *202:* 32
Downes, Belinda *180:* 29
Downing, Julie *60:* 140; *81:* 50; *86:* 200; *99:* 129
Doyle, Janet *56:* 31
Doyle, Richard *21:* 31, 32, 33; *23:* 231; *24:* 177; *31:* 87
Draper, Angie *43:* 84
Drath, Bill *26:* 34
Drawson, Blair *17:* 53; *126:* 65
Dray, Matt *177:* 47
Drescher, Henrik *105:* 60, 62, 63; *172:* 72
Drescher, Joan *30:* 100, 101; *35:* 245; *52:* 168; *137:* 52
Dressell, Peggy *186:* 41
Drew, Janet *201:* 177
Drew, Patricia *15:* 100
Dronzek, Laura *199:* 28, 29; *207:* 69
Drummond, Allan *209:* 41
Drummond, V.H. *6:* 70
Drury, Christian Potter *105:* 97; *186:* 224
Dubanevich, Arlene *56:* 44
Dubin, Jill *205:* 56; *217:* 25
Dubois, Claude K. *196:* 2
Dubois, Gerard *182:* 9
DuBurke, Randy *187:* 89; *222:* 136
Ducak, Danilo *99:* 130; *108:* 214
Duchesne, Janet *6:* 162; *79:* 8
Duda, Jana *102:* 155; *209:* 134
Dudash, C. Michael *32:* 122; *77:* 134; *82:* 149; *212:* 93, 94
Duer, Douglas *34:* 177
Duewell, Kristina *195:* 76
Duffy, Daniel Mark *76:* 37; *101:* 196; *108:* 147, 148
Duffy, Joseph *38:* 203
Duffy, Pat *28:* 153
Dugan, Karen *181:* 26; *202:* 35
Dugin, Andrej *77:* 60
Dugina, Olga *77:* 60
Duke, Chris *8:* 195; *139:* 164
Duke, Kate *87:* 186; *90:* 78, 79, 80, 81; *192:* 21, 59, 60, 61, 63
Duke, Marion *165:* 87
Dulac, Edmund *19:* 108, 109, 110, 111, 112, 113, 114, 115, 117; *23:* 187; *25:* 152; *YABC 1:* 37; *2:* 147
Dulac, Jean *13:* 64
Dumas, Philippe *52:* 36, 37, 38, 39, 40, 41, 42, 43, 45; *119:* 40, 41, 42
Dunaway, Nancy *108:* 161
Dunbar, James *76:* 63
Dunbar, Polly *181:* 60, 61; *211:* 51, 52, 53; *212:* 42
Duncan, Beverly *72:* 92
Duncan, John *116:* 94
Dunn, H.T. *62:* 196
Dunn, Harvey *34:* 78, 79, 80, 81
Dunn, Iris *5:* 175
Dunn, Phoebe *5:* 175
Dunne, Jeanette *72:* 57, 173, 222
Dunnick, Regan *176:* 51; *178:* 83, 84; *219:* 36
Dunnington, Tom *3:* 36; *18:* 281; *25:* 61; *31:* 159; *35:* 168; *48:* 195; *79:* 144; *82:* 230

Dunn-Ramsey, Marcy *117:* 131
Dunrea, Olivier *59:* 81; *118:* 53, 54; *124:* 43
Duntze, Dorothee *88:* 28; *160:* 76
Dupasquier, Philippe *86:* 75; *104:* 76; *151:* 63
duPont, Lindsay Harper *207:* 39
DuQuette, Keith *90:* 83; *155:* 73, 74
Durand, Delphine *200:* 56
Durham, Sarah *192:* 248
Durney, Ryan *208:* 122
Duroussy, Nathalie *146:* 150
Durrell, Julie *82:* 62; *94:* 62
Dusíková, Maja *223:* 49
Dutz *6:* 59
Duvoisin, Roger *2:* 95; *6:* 76, 77; *7:* 197; *28:* 125; *30:* 101, 102, 103, 104, 105, 107; *47:* 205; *84:* 254
Dyer, Dale *141:* 71
Dyer, Jane *75:* 219; *129:* 28; *147:* 49, 50, 51; *168:* 121; *190:* 4; *191:* 57, 59, 60; *203:* 4
Dyer, Sarah *212:* 40
Dypold, Pat *15:* 37

E

E.V.B.
 See Boyle, Eleanor Vere (Gordon)
Eachus, Jennifer *29:* 74; *82:* 201; *164:* 153
Eadie, Bob *63:* 36
Eagle, Bruce *95:* 119
Eagle, Ellen *82:* 121; *89:* 3
Eagle, Jeremy *141:* 71
Eagle, Michael *11:* 86; *20:* 9; *23:* 18; *27:* 122; *28:* 57; *34:* 201; *44:* 189; *73:* 9; *78:* 235; *85:* 43
Earl-Bridges, Michele *159:* 128
Earle, Edwin *56:* 27
Earle, Olive L. *7:* 75
Earle, Vana *27:* 99
Earley, Lori *132:* 2; *186:* 4; *195:* 8
Early, Margaret *72:* 59
East, Jacqueline *218:* 198
East, Stella *131:* 223
Eastman, P.D. *33:* 57
Easton, Reginald *29:* 181
Eaton, Tom *4:* 62; *6:* 64; *22:* 99; *24:* 124
Ebbeler, Jeffrey *193:* 62; *206:* 45
Ebel, Alex *11:* 89
Eberbach, Andrea *192:* 115
Ebert, Len *9:* 191; *44:* 47
Echevarria, Abe *37:* 69
Echo Hawk, Bunky *187:* 192
Eckersley, Maureen *48:* 62
Eckert, Horst *72:* 62
Ede, Janina *33:* 59
Edens, Cooper *49:* 81, 82, 83, 84, 85; *112:* 58
Edens, John *109:* 115
Edgar, Sarah E. *41:* 97
Edgerton, Perky *195:* 144
Edliq, Emily S. *131:* 107
Edrien *11:* 53
Edwards, Freya *45:* 102
Edwards, George Wharton *31:* 155
Edwards, Gunvor *2:* 71; *25:* 47; *32:* 71; *54:* 106
Edwards, Jeanne *29:* 257
Edwards, Linda Strauss *21:* 134; *39:* 123; *49:* 88, 89
Edwards, Michelle *152:* 62, 63
Edwards, Wallace *170:* 55
Egan, Tim *155:* 76, 77, 78
Egge, David *102:* 71
Eggenhofer, Nicholas *2:* 81
Eggleton, Bob *74:* 40; *81:* 190, 191; *105:* 6; *121:* 183; *149:* 203; *166:* 215
Egielski, Richard *11:* 90; *16:* 208; *33:* 236; *38:* 35; *49:* 91, 92, 93, 95, 212, 213, 214, 216; *79:* 122; *106:* 67, 68, 69; *134:* 135; *144:* 244; *163:* 82, 84; *207:* 125

Ehlert, Lois *35:* 97; *69:* 51; *112:* 7; *113:* 208; *128:* 63, 64, 65; *172:* 77, 79, 80; *220:* 43, 44, 45, 46, 47, 48
Ehrlich, Bettina *1:* 83
Eitan, Ora *160:* 165
Eichenberg, Fritz *1:* 79; *9:* 54; *19:* 248; *23:* 170; *24:* 200; *26:* 208; *50:* 67, 68, 69, 70, 71, 72, 73,74, 75, 77, 79, 80, 81; *60:* 165; *100:* 137; *YABC 1:* 104, 105; *2:* 213
Einsel, Naiad *10:* 35; *29:* 136
Einsel, Walter *10:* 37
Einzig, Susan *3:* 77; *43:* 78; *67:* 155; *129:* 154
Eisner, Will *165:* 82, 83
Eitzen, Allan *9:* 56; *12:* 212; *14:* 226; *21:* 194; *38:* 162; *76:* 218
Eldridge, H. *54:* 109
Eldridge, Harold *43:* 83
Elgaard, Greta *19:* 241
Elgin, Kathleen *9:* 188; *39:* 69
Ellacott, S.E. *19:* 118
Elliot, David *192:* 26; *208:* 62, 63
Elliott, Mark *93:* 69; *105:* 108; *107:* 123; *140:* 53; *165:* 189; *173:* 67; *195:* 95; *203:* 67; *210:* 99; *221:* 57, 70
Elliott, Sarah M. *14:* 58
Ellis, Carson *216:* 210
Ellis, Dianne *130:* 208
Ellis, Jan Davey *88:* 50; *115:* 80
Ellis, Richard *130:* 47, 48
Ellison, Chris *196:* 66; *199:* 131; *207:* 193
Ellison, Pauline *55:* 21
Ellwand, David *213:* 60
Elmer, Richard *78:* 5
Elmore, Larry *90:* 8
Elschner, Géraldine *183:* 38
Elwell, Peter *195:* 150
Elwell, Tristan *110:* 39; *121:* 182; *127:* 46; *137:* 144; *141:* 173; *151:* 236; *158:* 264; *167:* 119, 120, 121; *169:* 20; *190:* 12; *202:* 16
Elzbieta *88:* 80, 81
Ember, Kathi *214:* 147
Emberley, Ed *8:* 53; *70:* 53, 54; *146:* 65, 69, 70; *218:* 50
Emberley, Rebecca *218:* 50
Emberley, Michael *34:* 83; *80:* 72; *119:* 47, 48; *147:* 100; *158:* 115; *189:* 62, 64; *203:* 87, 89
Emerling, Dorothy *104:* 27
Emery, Leslie *49:* 187
Emmett, Bruce *49:* 147; *80:* 175; *101:* 206; *220:* 200
Emry-Perrott, Jennifer *61:* 57
Emshwiller, Ed *174:* 45
Endle, Kate *191:* 167; *207:* 41
Engel, Diana *70:* 57
Engle, Mort *38:* 64
Englebert, Victor *8:* 54
English, Mark *101:* 207; *220:* 201
Enik, Ted *142:* 39
Enos, Randall *20:* 183
Enright, Maginel Wright *19:* 240, 243; *39:* 31, 35, 36
Enrique, Romeo *34:* 135
Ensor, Barbara *180:* 30
Epstein, Stephen *50:* 142, 148
Erdogan, Buket *174:* 179
Erdrich, Louise *141:* 62
Erhard, Walter *1:* 152
Erickson, Jim *196:* 190
Erickson, Phoebe *11:* 83; *59:* 85
Erikson, Mel *31:* 69
Eriksson, Eva *63:* 88, 90, 92, 93; *203:* 99; *207:* 44
Ering, Timothy Basil *131:* 100; *176:* 63, 64; *202:* 29; *204:* 8
Erlbruch, Wolf *181:* 66
Ernst, Lisa Campbell *47:* 147; *95:* 47; *154:* 46, 47, 48; *164:* 88; *212:* 45
Esco, Jo *61:* 103
Escourido, Joseph *4:* 81

Escrivá, Viví *119:* 51; *181:* 36
Essakalli, Julie Klear *200:* 58
Este, Kirk *33:* 111
Estep, David *73:* 57
Estes, Eleanor *91:* 66
Estoril, Jean *32:* 27
Estrada, Pau *74:* 76
Estrada, Ric *5:* 52, 146; *13:* 174
Etchemendy, Teje *38:* 68
Etheredges, the *73:* 12
Etienne, Kirk-Albert *145:* 184
Ets, Marie Hall *2:* 102
Ettlinger, Doris *171:* 98; *186:* 106; *197:* 126; *214:* 125
Eulalie *YABC 2:* 315
Evangelista, Theresa M. *213:* 67
Evans, Greg *73:* 54, 55, 56; *143:* 40, 41
Evans, Katherine *5:* 64
Evans, Leslie *144:* 227; *207:* 57; *214:* 88; *221:* 28
Evans, Shane W. *159:* 142; *160:* 190; *168:* 39; *188:* 88; *189:* 66, 67, 68
Everitt, Betsy *151:* 110
Ewart, Claire *76:* 69; *145:* 59, 60
Ewing, Carolyn *66:* 143; *79:* 52
Ewing, Juliana Horatia *16:* 92
Eyolfson, Norman *98:* 154

F

Fabian, Limbert *136:* 114
Facklam, Paul *132:* 62
Falconer, Ian *125:* 66; *179:* 59
Falconer, Pearl *34:* 23
Falkenstern, Lisa *70:* 34; *76:* 133; *78:* 171; *127:* 16; *191:* 151
Falls, C.B. *1:* 19; *38:* 71, 72, 73, 74
Falter, John *40:* 169, 170
Falwell, Cathryn *118:* 77; *137:* 185; *196:* 71, 72
Fancher, Lou *138:* 219; *141:* 64; *144:* 199; *177:* 51; *214:* 95; *221:* 63
Fanelli, Sara *89:* 63; *126:* 69
Faria, Rosana *150:* 143
Faricy, Patrick *185:* 182; *212:* 61
Farooqi, Musharraf Ali *207:* 46
Farmer, Andrew *49:* 102
Farmer, Peter *24:* 108; *38:* 75
Farnsworth, Bill *93:* 189; *116:* 147; *124:* 8; *135:* 52; *146:* 242, 243, 244; *182:* 176; *186:* 31, 83, 84, 85; *191:* 197; *222:* 2
Farquharson, Alexander *46:* 75
Farrell, David *40:* 135
Farrell, Russell *196:* 38
Farris, David *74:* 42
Fasolino, Teresa *118:* 145
Fatigati, Evelyn *24:* 112
Fatus, Sophie *182:* 74; *190:* 218
Faul-Jansen, Regina *22:* 117
Faulkner, Jack *6:* 169
Faulkner, Matt *161:* 174; *167:* 75
Fava, Rita *2:* 29
Fax, Elton C. *1:* 101; *4:* 2; *12:* 77; *25:* 107
Fay *43:* 93
Fearing, Mark *223:* 142
Fearnley, Jan *153:* 82, 83; *205:* 63, 64, 65
Fearrington, Ann *146:* 80
Federspiel, Marian *33:* 51
Fedorov, Nickolai Ivanovich *110:* 102
Feelings, Tom *5:* 22; *8:* 56; *12:* 153; *16:* 105; *30:* 196; *49:* 37; *61:* 101; *69:* 56, 57; *93:* 74; *105:* 88
Fehr, Terrence *21:* 87
Feiffer, Jules *3:* 91; *8:* 58; *61:* 66, 67, 70, 74, 76,77, 78; *111:* 47, 48, 49, 50; *132:* 122; *157:* 62; *201:* 48, 49, 50
Feigeles, Neil *41:* 242
Feldman, Elyse *86:* 7
Feller, Gene *33:* 130

Fellows, Muriel H. *10:* 42
Felstead, Cathie *116:* 85
Felts, Shirley *33:* 71; *48:* 59
Fennell, Tracy *171:* 69
Fennelli, Maureen *38:* 181
Fenton, Carroll Lane *5:* 66; *21:* 39
Fenton, Mildred Adams *5:* 66; *21:* 39
Ferguson, Peter *177:* 30, 31; *181:* 154; *197:* 4; *199:* 40; *215:* 104; *221:* 66
Ferguson, Walter W. *34:* 86
Fernandes, Eugenie *77:* 67; *205:* 68
Fernandes, Stanislaw *70:* 28
Fernandez, Fernando *77:* 57
Fernandez, Laura *77:* 153; *101:* 117; *131:* 222; *170:* 119; *175:* 182
Ferrari, Alex *188:* 121
Ferrington, Susan *172:* 22
Fetz, Ingrid *11:* 67; *12:* 52; *16:* 205; *17:* 59; *29:* 105; *30:* 108, 109; *32:* 149; *43:* 142; *56:* 29; *60:* 34; *85:* 48; *87:* 146
Fiammenghi, Gioia *9:* 66; *11:* 44; *12:* 206; *13:* 57, 59; *52:* 126, 129; *66:* 64; *85:* 83; *91:* 161; *166:* 169
Fiedler, Joseph Daniel *96:* 42; *113:* 173; *129:* 164; *146:* 17; *159:* 68; *162:* 104
Field, Rachel *15:* 113
Fielding, David *70:* 124
Fieser, Stephen *152:* 36
Fine, Howard *145:* 159; *159:* 64; *165:* 134; *174:* 129; *181:* 68
Fine, Peter K. *43:* 210
Finger, Helen *42:* 81
Fink, Sam *18:* 119
Finlay, Winifred *23:* 72
Finney, Pat *79:* 215
Fiore, Peter *99:* 196; *125:* 139; *144:* 225; *160:* 169; *180:* 72; *212:* 103
Fiorentino, Al *3:* 240
Firehammer, Karla *174:* 202; *221:* 183
Firmin, Charlotte *29:* 75; *48:* 70
Firmin, Peter *58:* 63, 64, 65, 67, 68, 70, 71
Firth, Barbara *81:* 208; *127:* 218; *179:* 62
Fischel, Lillian *40:* 204
Fischer, Hans *25:* 202
Fischer, Scott M. *207:* 37; *217:* 29
Fischer-Nagel, Andreas *56:* 50
Fischer-Nagel, Heiderose *56:* 50
Fisher, Carolyn *154:* 50
Fisher, Chris *79:* 62; *158:* 248; *188:* 195
Fisher, Cynthia *117:* 45; *137:* 118; *195:* 40
Fisher, Jeffrey *142:* 80
Fisher, Leonard Everett *3:* 6; *4:* 72, 86; *6:* 197; *9:* 59; *16:* 151, 153; *23:* 44; *27:* 134; *29:* 26; *34:* 87, 89, 90, 91, 93, 94, 95, 96; *40:* 206; *50:* 150; *60:* 158; *73:* 68, 70, 71, 72, 73; *176:* 71, 72, 73; *208:* 131; *YABC 2:* 169
Fisher, Lois *20:* 62; *21:* 7
Fisher, Valorie *177:* 55; *214:* 92
Fisk, Nicholas *25:* 112
Fitschen, Marilyn *2:* 20, 21; *20:* 48
Fitz-Maurice, Jeff *175:* 2
Fitzgerald, F.A. *15:* 116; *25:* 86, 87
Fitzgerald, Joanne *157:* 153, 154; *198:* 34, 35
Fitzgerald, Royce *205:* 5
Fitzhugh, Louise *1:* 94; *9:* 163; *45:* 75, 78
Fitzhugh, Susie *11:* 117
Fitzpatrick, Jim *109:* 130
Fitzpatrick, Marie-Louise *125:* 69, 70; *189:* 72, 73
Fitzsimmons, Arthur *14:* 128
Fix, Philippe *26:* 102
Flack, Marjorie *21:* 67; *100:* 93; *YABC 2:* 122
Flagg, James Montgomery *17:* 227
Flavin, Teresa *132:* 115; *186:* 119
Flax, Zeona *2:* 245
Fleetwood, Tony *171:* 51
Fleishman, Seymour *14:* 232; *24:* 87
Fleming, Denise *71:* 179; *81:* 58; *126:* 71, 72, 73; *173:* 52, 53
Fleming, Guy *18:* 41

Flesher, Vivienne *85:* 55
Fletcher, Claire *80:* 106; *157:* 159
Flint, Russ *74:* 80
Floate, Helen *111:* 163
Floca, Brian *155:* 88, 89; *190:* 10, 66, 67
Floethe, Richard *3:* 131; *4:* 90
Floherty, John J., Jr. *5:* 68
Flook, Helen *160:* 81
Flora, James *1:* 96; *30:* 111, 112
Florczak, Robert *166:* 51
Florian, Douglas *19:* 122; *83:* 64, 65; *125:* 71, 72, 74, 76; *128:* 130; *177:* 58, 60
Flory, Jane *22:* 111
Flower, Renee *125:* 109
Floyd, Gareth *1:* 74; *17:* 245; *48:* 63; *62:* 35,36, 37, 39, 40, 41; *74:* 245; *79:* 56
Fluchere, Henri A. *40:* 79
Flynn, Alice *183:* 2
Flynn, Barbara *7:* 31; *9:* 70
Fogarty, Thomas *15:* 89
Foley, Greg *190:* 69
Folger, Joseph *9:* 100
Folkard, Charles *22:* 132; *29:* 128, 257, 258
Foott, Jeff *42:* 202
Forberg, Ati *12:* 71, 205; *14:* 1; *22:* 113; *26:* 22; *48:* 64, 65
Ford, George *24:* 120; *31:* 70, 177; *58:* 126; *81:* 103; *107:* 91; *136:* 100; *194:* 47; *208:* 81; *218:* 56
Ford, Gilbert *199:* 10
Ford, H.J. *16:* 185, 186
Ford, Jason *174:* 119
Ford, Pamela Baldwin *27:* 104
Fordham, John *168:* 160, 161
Foreman, Michael *2:* 110, 111; *67:* 99; *73:* 78, 79, 80,81, 82; *93:* 146; *135:* 55, 56, 57; *184:* 58, 59; *216:* 100, 101, 102, 103
Forrester, Victoria *40:* 83
Forsey, Chris *140:* 210
Fortnum, Peggy *6:* 29; *20:* 179; *24:* 211; *26:* 76, 77, 78; *39:* 78; *58:* 19, 21, 23, 27; *YABC 1:* 148
Fortune, Eric *191:* 52
Foster, Brad W. *34:* 99
Foster, Genevieve *2:* 112
Foster, Gerald L. *7:* 78; *198:* 40
Foster, Jon *146:* 18; *198:* 7
Foster, Laura Louise *6:* 79
Foster, Marian Curtis *23:* 74; *40:* 42
Foster, Sally *58:* 73, 74
Fotheringham, Edwin *219:* 32
Foucher, Adele *47:* 118
Foust, Mitch *168:* 50
Fowler, Jim *184:* 190
Fowler, Mel *36:* 127
Fowler, Richard *87:* 219
Fowles, Shelley *165:* 127; *205:* 72
Fox, Charles Phillip *12:* 84
Fox, Christyan *188:* 36
Fox, Jim *6:* 187
Fox, Nathan *208:* 64
Fox-Davies, Sarah *76:* 150; *182:* 63; *199:* 42, 43
Frace, Charles *15:* 118
Frailey, Joy *72:* 108
Frame, Paul *2:* 45, 145; *9:* 153; *10:* 124; *21:* 71; *23:* 62; *24:* 123; *27:* 106; *31:* 48; *32:* 159; *34:* 195; *38:* 136; *42:* 55; *44:* 139; *60:* 39, 40, 41, 42, 43, 44, 46; *73:* 183
Frampton, David *85:* 72; *102:* 33; *139:* 182; *152:* 37; *189:* 171
Francis, Guy *198:* 164
Francois, Andre *25:* 117
Francoise
  See Seignobosc, Francoise
Frank, Lola Edick *2:* 199
Frank, Mary *4:* 54; *34:* 100
Franke, Phil *45:* 91
Frankel, Alona *66:* 70
Frankel, Julie *40:* 84, 85, 202

Frankenberg, Robert *22:* 116; *30:* 50; *38:* 92, 94, 95; *68:* 111
Frankfeldt, Gwen *84:* 223; *110:* 92
Frankland, David *169:* 137; *182:* 164; *201:* 159
Franklin, Ashton *165:* 144
Franklin, John *24:* 22
Franson, Leanne R. *111:* 57, 58; *151:* 7; *223:* 63, 64, 158
Frascino, Edward *9:* 133; *29:* 229; *33:* 190; *48:* 80, 81, 82, 83, 84, 85, 86
Frasconi, Antonio *6:* 80; *27:* 208; *53:* 41, 43, 45, 47,48; *68:* 145; *73:* 226; *131:* 68
Fraser, Betty *2:* 212; *6:* 185; *8:* 103; *31:* 72,73; *43:* 136; *111:* 76
Fraser, Eric *38:* 78; *41:* 149, 151
Fraser, James *171:* 68
Fraser, Mary Ann *137:* 63; *214:* 98
Fraser, F.A. *22:* 234
Frasier, Debra *69:* 60; *112:* 67; *182:* 81, 82, 83
Fraustino, Lisa Rowe *146:* 87
Frazee, Marla *72:* 98; *105:* 79, 80; *151:* 67, 68; *164:* 165; *171:* 190, 191; *187:* 53, 54, 55, 56, 143; *222:* 173
Frazetta, Frank *41:* 72; *58:* 77, 78, 79, 80, 81, 82, 83
Frazier, Craig *177:* 63; *221:* 47
Freas, John *25:* 207
Fredrickson, Mark *103:* 33
Freeland, Michael J. *118:* 115
Freeman, Don *2:* 15; *13:* 249; *17:* 62, 63, 65, 67, 68; *18:* 243; *20:* 195; *23:* 213, 217; *32:* 155; *55:* 129
Freeman, Irving *67:* 150
Freeman, Laura *144:* 111; *200:* 62, 63
Freeman, Pietri *140:* 223
Freeman, Tom *167:* 118
Freeman, Tor *164:* 93
Fregosi, Claudia *24:* 117
Fremaux, Charlotte Murray *138:* 29; *141:* 95
French, Fiona *6:* 82, 83; *75:* 61; *109:* 170; *132:* 79, 80, 81, 82
French, Martin *163:* 4
French, S. Terrell *216:* 106
Frendak, Rodney *126:* 97, 98
Freschet, Gina *175:* 73
Freynet, Gilbert *72:* 221
Fried, Janice *202:* 121
Frieden, Sarajo *213:* 119
Friedman, Judith *43:* 197; *131:* 221
Friedman, Marvin *19:* 59; *42:* 86
Frinta, Dagmar *36:* 42
Frith, Michael K. *15:* 138; *18:* 120
Fritz, Ronald *46:* 73; *82:* 124
Fromm, Lilo *29:* 85; *40:* 197
Frost, A.B. *17:* 6, 7; *19:* 123, 124, 125, 126, 127, 128, 129,130; *100:* 119; *YABC 1:* 156, 157, 160; *2:* 107
Frost, Helen *183:* 51
Frost, Kristi *118:* 113
Frost, Michael *151:* 209; *209:* 44; *212:* 70
Froud, Brian *150:* 82, 83
Froud, Wendy *151:* 237
Fry, Guy *2:* 224
Fry, Rosalie *3:* 72; *YABC 2:* 180, 181
Fry, Rosalind *21:* 153, 168
Fryer, Elmer *34:* 115
Fuchs, Bernie *110:* 10; *162:* 46
Fuchs, Erich *6:* 84
Fuchshuber, Annegert *43:* 96
Fucile, Tony *221:* 48
Fufuka, Mahiri *32:* 146
Fuge, Charles *144:* 91, 93
Fujikawa, Gyo *39:* 75, 76; *76:* 72, 73, 74
Fulford, Deborah *23:* 159
Fuller, Margaret *25:* 189
Fulweiler, John *93:* 99
Funai, Mamoru *38:* 105
Funfhausen, Christian *196:* 30
Funk, Tom *7:* 17, 99
Furchgott, Terry *29:* 86

Furness, William Henry, Jr. *94:* 18
Furukawa, Mel *25:* 42
Fusari, Erika *164:* 227

G

Gaadt, David *78:* 212; *121:* 166; *201:* 171
Gaadt, George *71:* 9
Gaber, Susan *99:* 33; *115:* 57, 58; *164:* 195; *169:* 61, 62, 63; *185:* 50, 51; *188:* 124
Gaberell, J. *19:* 236
Gable, Brian *195:* 68, 69
Gabler, Mirko *99:* 71; *195:* 32
Gabor, Tim *216:* 61
Gackenbach, Dick *19:* 168; *41:* 81; *48:* 89, 90, 91, 92,93, 94; *54:* 105; *79:* 75, 76, 77
Gad, Victor *87:* 161
Gaetano, Nicholas *23:* 209
Gaffney-Kessell, Walter *94:* 219; *174:* 188
Gag, Flavia *17:* 49, 52
Gag, Wanda *100:* 101, 102; *YABC 1:* 135, 137, 138, 141, 143
Gagnon, Cecile *11:* 77; *58:* 87
Gaillard, Jason *200:* 69; *204:* 74
Gal, Laszlo *14:* 127; *52:* 54, 55, 56; *65:* 142; *68:* 150; *81:* 185; *96:* 104, 105
Galazinski, Tom *55:* 13
Galbraith, Ben *200:* 70
Galdone, Paul *1:* 156, 181, 206; *2:* 40, 241; *3:* 42,144; *4:* 141; *10:* 109, 158; *11:* 21; *12:* 118, 210; *14:* 12; *16:* 36, 37; *17:* 70, 71, 72, 73, 74; *18:* 111, 230; *19:* 183; *21:* 154; *22:* 150, 245; *33:* 126; *39:* 136, 137; *42:* 57; *51:* 169; *55:* 110; *66:* 80, 82, 139; *72:* 73; *100:* 84
Gale, Cathy *140:* 22; *143:* 52; *213:* 166
Gall, Chris *176:* 79, 80
Gallagher, Jack *187:* 100
Gallagher, S. Saelig *105:* 154; *198:* 91
Gallagher, Sears *20:* 112Gallagher-Cole, Mernie *206:* 56
Galloway, Ewing *51:* 154
Galouchka, Annouchka Gravel *95:* 55; *182:* 40
Galster, Robert *1:* 66
Galsworthy, Gay John *35:* 232
Galvez, Daniel *125:* 182
Gamble, Kim *112:* 64, 65; *124:* 77; *183:* 40, 42, 43, 56, 57; *187:* 170
Gammell, Stephen *7:* 48; *13:* 149; *29:* 82; *33:* 209; *41:* 88; *50:* 185, 186, 187; *53:* 51, 52, 53, 54, 55, 56,57, 58; *54:* 24, 25; *56:* 147, 148, 150; *57:* 27, 66; *81:* 62, 63; *87:* 88; *89:* 10; *106:* 223; *126:* 2; *128:* 71, 73, 74, 77; *154:* 34; *211:* 210
Gamper, Ruth *84:* 198
Gampert, John *58:* 94
Ganly, Helen *56:* 56
Gannett, Ruth Chrisman *3:* 74; *18:* 254; *33:* 77, 78
Gannon, Ned *205:* 6
Gantschev, Ivan *45:* 32
Garafano, Marie *73:* 33
Garbot, Dave *131:* 106
Garbutt, Bernard *23:* 68
Garcia *37:* 71
Garcia, Geronimo *222:* 73
Garcia, Manuel *74:* 145
Garcia-Franco, Rebecca *173:* 46
Gardiner, Lindsey *178:* 128; *186:* 137
Gardner, Earle *45:* 167
Gardner, Joan *40:* 87
Gardner, Joel *40:* 87, 92
Gardner, John *40:* 87
Gardner, Lucy *40:* 87
Gardner, Richard
   See Cummings, Richard
Gardner, Sally *171:* 177; *177:* 66, 68
Gargiulo, Frank *84:* 158

Garland, Michael *36:* 29; *38:* 83; *44:* 168; *48:* 78, 221, 222; *49:* 161; *60:* 139; *71:* 6, 11; *72:* 229; *74:* 142; *89:* 187; *93:* 183; *104:* 110; *131:* 55; *139:* 209; *168:* 56; *208:* 72, 73, 75
Garland, Peggy *60:* 139
Garland, Sarah *62:* 45; *135:* 67, 68; *171:* 118
Garn, Aimee *75:* 47
Garner, Joan *128:* 170
Garneray, Ambroise Louis *59:* 140
Garnett, Eve *3:* 75
Garnett, Gary *39:* 184
Garns, Allen *80:* 125; *84:* 39; *165:* 231; *209:* 44
Garófoli, Viviana *186:* 123
Garraty, Gail *4:* 142; *52:* 106
Garrett, Agnes *46:* 110; *47:* 157
Garrett, Edmund H. *20:* 29
Garrett, Tom *107:* 194; *215:* 179
Garrick, Jacqueline *67:* 42, 43; *77:* 94
Garrison, Barbara *19:* 133; *104:* 146; *109:* 87
Garro, Mark *108:* 131; *128:* 210
Garvey, Robert *98:* 222
Garza, Carmen Lomas *80:* 211; *182:* 86
Garza, Xavier *184:* 64
Gates, Frieda *26:* 80
Gaughan, Jack *26:* 79; *43:* 185
Gaver, Becky *20:* 61
Gavril, David *211:* 196
Gawing, Toby *72:* 52
Gay, Marie-Louise *68:* 76, 77, 78; *102:* 136; *126:* 76, 78, 81, 83; *127:* 55, 56; *179:* 70, 72, 73, 74
Gay, Zhenya *19:* 135, 136
Gaydos, Tim *62:* 201
Gazsi, Ed *80:* 48
Gazso, Gabriel *73:* 85
Geary, Clifford N. *1:* 122; *9:* 104; *51:* 74
Geary, Rick *142:* 44, 46
Gee, Frank *33:* 26
Geehan, Wayne *157:* 181
Geer, Charles *1:* 91; *3:* 179; *4:* 201; *6:* 168; *7:* 96; *9:* 58; *10:* 72; *12:* 127; *39:* 156,157, 158, 159, 160; *42:* 88, 89, 90, 91; *55:* 111, 116
Geerinck, Manuel *173:* 128
Gehm, Charlie *36:* 65; *57:* 117; *62:* 60, 138
Geis, Alissa Imre *189:* 77
Geisel, Theodor Seuss *1:* 104, 105, 106; *28:* 108, 109, 110,111, 112, 113; *75:* 67, 68, 69, 70, 71; *89:* 127, 128; *100:* 106, 107, 108
Geisert, Arthur *92:* 67, 68; *133:* 72, 73, 74; *165:* 97, 98; *171:* 64, 65
Geldart, William *15:* 121; *21:* 202
Genia *4:* 84
Gentry, Cyrille R. *12:* 66
Genzo, John Paul *136:* 74
George, Jean *2:* 113
George, Lindsay Barrett *95:* 57; *155:* 97, 98
Geraghty, Paul *130:* 60, 61
Gerard, Jean Ignace *45:* 80
Gerard, Rolf *27:* 147, 150
Gerber, Mark *61:* 105
Gerber, Mary Jane *112:* 124; *171:* 56
Gerber, Stephanie *71:* 195
Gerdstein, Mordecai *169:* 105
Gergely, Tibor *54:* 15, 16
Geritz, Franz *17:* 135
Gerlach, Geff *42:* 58
Gerrard, Roy *47:* 78; *90:* 96, 97, 98, 99
Gerritsen, Paula *177:* 69; *217:* 166
Gershinowitz, George *36:* 27
Gerstein, Mordicai *31:* 117; *47:* 80, 81, 82, 83, 84, 85, 86; *51:* 173; *69:* 134; *107:* 122; *142:* 49, 52; *165:* 209; *176:* 119; *178:* 95, 97, 99; *215:* 173; *222:* 76
Gervase *12:* 27
Geter, Tyrone *146:* 249; *150:* 86
Getz, Arthur *32:* 148
Gévry, Claudine *188:* 47
Gewirtz, Bina *61:* 81
Giancola, Donato *95:* 146; *164:* 226

Gibala-Broxholm, Scott *205:* 76; *219:* 186
Gibbons, Gail *23:* 78; *72:* 77, 78, 79; *82:* 182; *104:* 65; *160:* 99, 100; *201:* 59, 60, 62
Gibbs, Tony *40:* 95
Gibran, Kahlil *32:* 116
Gibson, Barbara Leonard *205:* 77; *212:* 151
Gider, Iskender *81:* 193
Giebfried, Rosemary *170:* 135
Giesen, Rosemary *34:* 192, 193
Giffard, Hannah *83:* 70
Giguere, George *20:* 111
Gilbert, John *19:* 184; *54:* 115; *YABC 2:* 287
Gilbert, W.S. *36:* 83, 85, 96
Gilbert, Yvonne *116:* 70; *128:* 84; *149:* 119; *185:* 69; *192:* 25; *195:* 81
Gilchrist, Jan Spivey *72:* 82, 83, 84, 85, 87; *77:* 90; *105:* 89, 91; *130:* 63, 64; *155:* 105, 107; *182:* 67
Giles, Will *41:* 218
Gili, Phillida *70:* 73
Gill, Margery *4:* 57; *7:* 7; *22:* 122; *25:* 166; *26:* 146, 147
Gillen, Denver *28:* 216
Gillette, Henry J. *23:* 237
Gilliam, Stan *39:* 64, 81
Gillies, Chuck *62:* 31
Gilliland, Jillian *87:* 58
Gillman, Alec *98:* 105
Gilman, Esther *15:* 124
Gilman, Phoebe *104:* 70, 71
Gilpin, Stephen *213:* 68
Ginsberg, Sari *111:* 184
Ginsburg, Max *62:* 59; *68:* 194 Girard, Roge *161:* 30
Girouard, Patrick *155:* 100; *218:* 165
Giovanopoulos, Paul *7:* 104; *60:* 36
Giovine, Sergio *79:* 12; *93:* 118; *139:* 118; *205:* 114
Gist, E.M. *206:* 60
Githens, Elizabeth M. *5:* 47
Gladden, Scott *99:* 108; *103:* 160; *193:* 46, 47
Gladstone, Gary *12:* 89; *13:* 190
Gladstone, Lise *15:* 273
Glanzman, Louis S. *2:* 177; *3:* 182; *36:* 97, 98; *38:* 120, 122; *52:* 141, 144; *71:* 191; *91:* 54, 56
Glaser, Byron *154:* 59, 60
Glaser, Milton *3:* 5; *5:* 156; *11:* 107; *30:* 26; *36:* 112; *54:* 141; *151:* 70
Glass, Andrew *36:* 38; *44:* 133; *48:* 205; *65:* 3; *68:* 43, 45; *90:* 104, 105; *150:* 89; *223:* 73, 74
Glass, Marvin *9:* 174
Glasser, Judy *41:* 156; *56:* 140; *69:* 79; *72:* 101
Glattauer, Ned *5:* 84; *13:* 224; *14:* 26
Glauber, Uta *17:* 76
Gleeson, J.M. *YABC 2:* 207
Glegg, Creina *36:* 100
Glienke, Amelie *63:* 150
Gliewe, Unada *3:* 78, 79; *21:* 73; *30:* 220
Gliori, Debi *72:* 91; *138:* 82; *162:* 37; *189:* 79, 81, 82
Glovach, Linda *7:* 105
Gobbato, Imero *3:* 180, 181; *6:* 213; *7:* 58; *9:* 150; *18:* 39; *21:* 167; *39:* 82, 83; *41:* 137, 251; *59:* 177
Goble, Paul *25:* 121; *26:* 86; *33:* 65; *69:* 68, 69; *131:* 79, 80
Goble, Warwick *46:* 78, 79; *194:* 143
Godal, Eric *36:* 93
Godbey, Cory *221:* 154
Godkin, Celia *145:* 84, 86
Godfrey, Michael *17:* 279
Godon, Ingrid *166:* 163; *186:* 99
Goede, Irene *208:* 87
Goembel, Ponder *42:* 124
Goffe, Toni *61:* 83, 84, 85; *89:* 11; *90:* 124; *178:* 118
Goffstein, M.B. *8:* 71; *70:* 75, 76, 77
Golbin, Andre *15:* 125

Gold, Robert *166:* 151, 152
Goldfeder, Cheryl *11:* 191
Goldfinger, Jennifer P. *185:* 71
Goldman, Todd H. *221:* 50, 51
Goldsborough, June *5:* 154, 155; *8:* 92, *14:* 226; *19:* 139; *54:* 165
Goldsmith, Robert *110:* 77
Goldstein, Barry *198:* 147
Goldstein, Leslie *5:* 8; *6:* 60; *10:* 106
Goldstein, Nathan *1:* 175; *2:* 79; *11:* 41, 232; *16:* 55
Goldstrom, Robert *98:* 36; *145:* 51, 52
Golembe, Carla *79:* 80, 81; *136:* 91; *144:* 113; *193:* 53
Golin, Carlo *74:* 112
Gomez, Elena *188:* 122; *191:* 72
Gomez, Elizabeth *127:* 70; *133:* 76
Gomi, Taro *64:* 102; *103:* 74, 76
Gon, Adriano *101:* 112
Gonsalves, Ron *178:* 213; *212:* 196
Gonzalez, Maya Christina *104:* 3; *136:* 92; *215:* 4, 5
Gonzalez, Yolanda *212:* 65
Good, Karen Hillard *212:* 143; *214:* 103
Goodall, John S. *4:* 92, 93; *10:* 132; *66:* 92, 93; *YABC 1:* 198
Goode, Diane *15:* 126; *50:* 183; *52:* 114, 115; *76:* 195; *84:* 94; *99:* 141; *114:* 76, 77, 78; *170:* 99, 101
Goodelman, Aaron *40:* 203
Goodenow, Earle *40:* 97
Goodfellow, Peter *62:* 95; *94:* 202
Goodman, Joan Elizabeth *50:* 86
Goodman, Vivienne *82:* 251; *146:* 181, 182
Goodnow, Patti *117:* 33
Goodrich, Carter *221:* 52, 53
Goodwin, Harold *13:* 74
Goodwin, Philip R. *18:* 206
Goor, Nancy *39:* 85, 86
Goor, Ron *39:* 85, 86
Goossens, Philippe *195:* 71
Gorbachev, Valeri *89:* 96; *112:* 97; *143:* 63, 64; *184:* 66, 67, 68, 101; *222:* 84, 85, 86, 87
Gordon, David *216:* 159
Gordon, Gwen *12:* 151
Gordon, Margaret *4:* 147; *5:* 48, 49; *9:* 79
Gordon, Mike *101:* 62, 63, 64
Gordon, Russell *136:* 204; *137:* 214
Gordon, Walter *138:* 9
Gore, Leonid *89:* 51; *94:* 74; *136:* 8; *158:* 117; *166:* 136; *168:* 36; *170:* 107; *181:* 94; *185:* 73; *222:* 89, 90, 91, 92
Gorecka-Egan, Erica *18:* 35
Gorey, Edward *1:* 60, 61; *13:* 169; *18:* 192; *20:* 201; *29:* 90, 91, 92, 93, 94, 95, 96, 97, 98, 99, 100; *30:* 129; *32:* 90; *34:* 200, *65:* 48; *68:* 24, 25; *69:* 79; *70:* 80, 82, 83, 84; *85:* 136; *127:* 62
Gorman, Mike *222:* 167
Gorsline, Douglas *1:* 98; *6:* 13; *11:* 113; *13:* 104; *15:* 14; *28:* 117, 118; *YABC 1:* 15
Gorton, Julia *108:* 94; *178:* 81, 82
Gosfield, Josh *118:* 165, 166; *149:* 67
Gosner, Kenneth *5:* 135
Gosney, Joy *167:* 142
Gotlieb, Jules *6:* 127
Goto, Scott *115:* 86; *136:* 69; *203:* 77, 78
Gott, Barry *197:* 95; *212:* 102
Gottlieb, Dale *67:* 162; *107:* 16; *149:* 6
Goudey, Ray *97:* 86
Gough, Alan *91:* 57
Gough, Philip *23:* 47; *45:* 90
Gould, Chester *49:* 112, 113, 114, 116, 117, 118
Gould, Jason *151:* 232
Gourbault, Martine *177:* 159
Govern, Elaine R. *26:* 94
Gower, Teri *102:* 184
Gowing, Toby *60:* 25; *63:* 33; *78:* 70, 252; *83:* 228; *86:* 187; *93:* 145; *108:* 133; *110:* 217; *184:* 125

Grabianski *20:* 144
Grabianski, Janusz *39:* 92, 93, 94, 95
Graboff, Abner *35:* 103, 104
Graef, Renée *61:* 188; *72:* 207; *204:* 45; *210:* 249
Grafe, Max *156:* 173; *178:* 237; *192:* 240; *198:* 51
Graham, A.B. *11:* 61
Graham, Bob *101:* 66, 67, 68; *151:* 74, 75; *187:* 65, 67, 68, 70
Graham, Georgia *188:* 3; *190:* 75
Graham, L. *7:* 108
Graham, Margaret Bloy *11:* 120; *18:* 305, 307
Graham, Mark *88:* 208; *159:* 153; *182:* 3
Grahame-Johnstone, Janet *13:* 61
Grahame-Johnstone, Anne *13:* 61
Grainger, Sam *42:* 95
Gralley, Jean *166:* 86
Gramatky, Hardie *1:* 107; *30:* 116, 119, 120, 122, 123
Gran, Julie *168:* 118
Granahan, Julie *84:* 84
GrandPré, Mary *84:* 131; *109:* 199; *118:* 76; *180:* 65; *184:* 70, 71, 180; *192:* 87; *215:* 24
Grandström, Brita *176:* 139
Grandville, J.J. *45:* 81, 82, 83, 84, 85, 86, 87, 88; *47:* 125; *64:* 10
Granger, Paul *39:* 153
Granström, Brita *162:* 35; *167:* 46
Grant, (Alice) Leigh *10:* 52; *15:* 131; *20:* 20; *26:* 119; *48:* 202
Grant, Gordon *17:* 230, 234; *25:* 123, 124, 125, 126; *52:* 69; *YABC 1:* 164
Grant, Melvyn *159:* 186, 187; *170:* 48, 49; *213:* 168, 169
Grant, Michelle *210:* 95
Grant, Renee *77:* 40
Grant, Shirley *109:* 45
Graves, Elizabeth *45:* 101
Graves, Keith *167:* 89; *191:* 74; *216:* 34; *223:* 103
Gray, Harold *33:* 87, 88
Gray, Les *82:* 76; *83:* 232
Gray, Reginald *6:* 69
Greco, Tony *184:* 6
Greder, Armin *76:* 235
Green, Ann Canevari *62:* 48
Green, Eileen *6:* 97
Green, Elizabeth Shippen *139:* 109
Green, Jonathan *86:* 135; *105:* 109; *221:* 73
Green, Ken *111:* 68
Green, Michael *32:* 216
Green, Robina *87:* 138
Green, Jonathan *157:* 105
Greene, Jeffrey *117:* 93
Greenaway, Kate *17:* 275; *24:* 180; *26:* 107; *41:* 222, 232; *100:* 115, 116; *YABC 1:* 88, 89; *2:* 131, 133, 136,138, 139, 141
Greenberg, Melanie Hope *72:* 93; *80:* 125; *101:* 174; *133:* 180; *186:* 189; *214:* 105
Greenseid, Diane *178:* 106, 107
Greenstein, Elaine *150:* 100
Greenwald, Sheila *1:* 34; *3:* 99; *8:* 72
Greger, Carol *76:* 86
Gregorian, Joyce Ballou *30:* 125
Gregory, Emilian *177:* 146; *187:* 10
Gregory, Fran *130:* 4; *140:* 93
Gregory, Frank M. *29:* 107
Greiffenhagen, Maurice *16:* 137; *27:* 57; *YABC 2:* 288
Greiner, Robert *6:* 86
Gretter, J. Clemens *31:* 134
Gretz, Susanna *7:* 114
Gretzer, John *1:* 54; *3:* 26; *4:* 162; *7:* 125; *16:* 247; *18:* 117; *28:* 66; *30:* 85, 211; *33:* 235; *56:* 16
Grey, Mini *166:* 90; *192:* 71
Grey Owl *24:* 41
Gri *25:* 90
Grieder, Walter *9:* 84
Griesbach/Martucci *59:* 3

Grifalconi, Ann *2:* 126; *3:* 248; *11:* 18; *13:* 182; *46:* 38; *50:* 145; *66:* 99, 100, 101, 104, 106; *69:* 38; *70:* 64; *87:* 128; *90:* 53; *93:* 49; *128:* 48; *133:* 79, 81; *210:* 111
Griffin, Gillett Good *26:* 96
Griffin, James *30:* 166
Griffin, John Howard *59:* 186
Griffin, Rachel *131:* 23
Griffith, Gershom *94:* 214
Griffiths, Dave *29:* 76
Griffiths, Dean *168:* 180; *169:* 182
Grimly, Gris *186:* 102; *192:* 112; *197:* 86; *219:* 34
Grimsdell, Jeremy *83:* 75
Grimwood, Brian *82:* 89
Gringhuis, Dirk *6:* 98; *9:* 196
Gripe, Harald *2:* 127; *74:* 98
Grisha *3:* 71
Grobler, Piet *201:* 100
Grohmann, Susan *84:* 97
Gropper, William *27:* 93; *37:* 193
Gros *60:* 199
Grose, Helen Mason *YABC 1:* 260; *2:* 150
Grossman, Nancy *24:* 130; *29:* 101
Grossman, Robert *11:* 124; *46:* 39
Groth, John *15:* 79; *21:* 53, 54; *83:* 230
Grover, Lorie Ann *168:* 59
Grubb, Lisa *160:* 116
Grue, Lisa *187:* 193
Gruelle, Johnny *35:* 107
Gschwind, William *11:* 72
Guarnaccia, Steven *201:* 170, 173
Guay-Mitchell, Rebecca *110:* 95, 96; *135:* 240; *180:* 76; *181:* 71, 73; *216:* 77
Guback, Georgia *88:* 102
Gudeon, Karla *212:* 67
Guerguerion, Claudine *105:* 73
Guevara, Susan *97:* 87; *167:* 49; *194:* 54
Guggenheim, Hans *2:* 10; *3:* 37; *8:* 136
Guhathaakurta, Ajanta *183:* 199
Guida, Lisa Chauncy *172:* 188
Guilbeau, Honore *22:* 69
Guillette, Joseph *137:* 37
Guisewite, Cathy *57:* 52, 53, 54, 56, 57
Gukova, Julia *95:* 104; *154:* 103; *168:* 195
Gundersheimer, Karen *35:* 240; *82:* 100
Gunderson, Nick *57:* 120
Gunnella *192:* 144
Gurney, James *76:* 97; *86:* 32
Gurney, John Steven *75:* 39, 82; *110:* 175; *143:* 67, 68; *169:* 172; *217:* 50, 88
Gusman, Annie *38:* 62
Gustafson, Scott *34:* 111; *43:* 40
Gustavson, Adam *104:* 10; *171:* 183; *176:* 87; *197:* 94; *204:* 35; *219:* 187
Guthridge, Bettina *108:* 79; *186:* 92
Guthrie, R. Dale *64:* 143
Guthrie, Robin *20:* 122
Gutierrez, Akemi *172:* 87; *205:* 135
Gutierrez, Alan *136:* 31, 32
Gutierrez, Rudy *97:* 162; *203:* 79; *216:* 158
Gutmann, Bessie Pease *73:* 93, 94
Gwynne, Fred *41:* 94, 95
Gyberg, Bo-Erik *38:* 131

H

Haas, Irene *17:* 77; *87:* 46; *96:* 117
Hack, Konrad *51:* 127
Hader, Berta H. *16:* 126
Hader, Elmer S. *16:* 126
Haeffele, Deborah *76:* 99
Haemer, Alan *62:* 109
Hafner, Marylin *22:* 196, 216; *24:* 44; *30:* 51; *35:* 95; *51:* 25, 160, 164; *86:* 16; *105:* 196; *121:* 93, 94; *149:* 208, 209; *179:* 82, 83, 84, 115; *190:* 200; *201:* 29; *217:* 91
Hagerty, Sean *62:* 181

Hague, Michael *32:* 128; *48:* 98, 99, 100, 101, 103, 105,106, 107, 108, 109, 110; *49:* 121; *51:* 105; *64:* 14, 15; *79:* 134; *80:* 91, 92; *83:* 135; *100:* 241; *102:* 29; *129:* 101, 103, 104; *185:* 80, 81, 82; *215:* 89
Hair, Jonathan *115:* 135
Halas, John *29:* 41, 47, 48
Haldane, Roger *13:* 76; *14:* 202
Hale, Bruce *203:* 83
Hale, Christy *124:* 124; *84:* 200; *114:* 201; *128:* 2, 3; *146:* 203; *158:* 243; *167:* 99; *179:* 87
Hale, Irina *26:* 97
Hale, James Graham *88:* 207
Hale, Kathleen *17:* 79; *66:* 114, 116, 118
Hale, Nathan *210:* 115, 116; *214:* 179
Haley, Amanda *205:* 82, 83
Haley, Gail E. *43:* 102, 103, 104, 105; *78:* 65, 67; *136:* 106, 107
Hall, Amanda *96:* 110
Hall, August N. *217:* 74
Hall, Chuck *30:* 189
Hall, Douglas *15:* 184; *43:* 106, 107; *86:* 100; *87:* 82; *129:* 72
Hall, H. Tom *1:* 227; *30:* 210
Hall, Melanie *116:* 48, 49; *169:* 77, 78; *219:* 170
Hall, Sydney P. *31:* 89
Hall, Tim *164:* 196; *202:* 41
Hall, Vicki *20:* 24
Hallinan, P.K. *39:* 98
Hallman, Tom *98:* 166
Hally, Greg *101:* 200; *151:* 224
Halperin, Wendy Anderson *96:* 151; *125:* 96, 97, 98, 99; *139:* 22; *140:* 84; *200:* 77, 78; *210:* 157; *215:* 65
Halpern, Joan *10:* 25
Halpern, Shari *174:* 172
Halsey, Megan *96:* 172; *114:* 185; *180:* 8; *185:* 85
Halstead, Virginia *125:* 105
Halverson, Janet *49:* 38, 42, 44
Hallensleben, Georg *134:* 5, 6; *172:* 17
Hallett, Mark *220:* 63
Hamanaka, Sheila *71:* 100
Hamann, Brad *78:* 151
Hamann, Sigune *104:* 115
Hamberger, John *6:* 8; *8:* 32; *14:* 79; *34:* 136; *88:* 78
Hamil, Tom *14:* 80; *43:* 163
Hamilton, Bill and Associates *26:* 215
Hamilton, Helen S. *2:* 238
Hamilton, J. *19:* 83, 85, 87
Hamilton, Laurie *116:* 210
Hamilton, Todd Cameron *84:* 15
Hamlin, Janet *97:* 136; *124:* 90; *137:* 157; *182:* 117
Hamlin, Louise *71:* 135
Hammill, Matt *206:* 65
Hammond, Chris *21:* 37
Hammond, Elizabeth *5:* 36, 203
Hampshire, Michael *5:* 187; *7:* 110, 111; *48:* 150; *51:* 129
Hampson, Denman *10:* 155; *15:* 130
Hampton, Blake *41:* 244
Handford, Martin *64:* 105, 106, 107, 109
Handforth, Thomas *42:* 100, 101, 102, 103, 104, 105, 107
Handville, Robert *1:* 89; *38:* 76; *45:* 108, 109
Hane, Roger *17:* 239; *44:* 54
Haney, Elizabeth Mathieu *34:* 84
Hanke, Ted *71:* 10
Hankinson, Phil *181:* 164
Hanley, Catherine *8:* 161
Hann, Jacquie *19:* 144
Hanna, Cheryl *91:* 133
Hanna, Wayne A. *67:* 145
Hannon, Mark *38:* 37
Hanrahan, Kelly-Anne *203:* 142
Hansen, Gaby *159:* 11; *186:* 25
Hansen, Mia *149:* 76
Hanson, Joan *8:* 76; *11:* 139

Hanson, Peter E. *52:* 47; *54:* 99, 100; *73:* 21; *84:* 79; *116:* 144
Hansson, Gunilla *64:* 111, 112
Harbour, Elizabeth *221:* 68
Hardcastle, Nick *121:* 82; *175:* 185; *222:* 135
Hardy, David A. *9:* 96; *119:* 74
Hardy, Paul *YABC 2:* 245
Hargis, Wes *219:* 70 Haring, Keith *145:* 65
Harlan, Jerry *3:* 96
Harlin, Greg *89:* 194; *103:* 82; *118:* 161; *121:* 167; *182:* 76; *201:* 172; *215:* 76
Harman, Dominic *206:* 48
Harness, Cheryl *106:* 80; *131:* 87; *178:* 111; *200:* 39
Harnischfeger *18:* 121
Harper, Arthur *YABC 2:* 121
Harper, Betty *126:* 90
Harper, Jamie *174:* 71; *214:* 212
Harper, Piers *79:* 27; *105:* 102; *161:* 67
Harrington, Glenn *82:* 18; *94:* 66, 68; *185:* 118
Harrington, Jack *83:* 162
Harrington, Richard *5:* 81
Harris, Andrew N. *191:* 78
Harris, Jim *127:* 130; *183:* 4
Harris, John *83:* 25
Harris, Nick *86:* 177
Harris, Susan Yard *42:* 121
Harrison, Florence *20:* 150, 152
Harrison, Harry *4:* 103
Harrison, Jack *28:* 149
Harrison, Mark *105:* 157; *165:* 190
Harrison, Ted *56:* 73
Harsh, Fred *72:* 107
Harston, Jerry *105:* 143
Hart, Lewis *98:* 115
Hart, Thomas *181:* 165
Hart, William *13:* 72
Hartland, Jessie *171:* 80, 81; *186:* 165; *223:* 58
Hartung, Susan Kathleen *150:* 107, 108; *173:* 106; *175:* 106; *192:* 78; *211:* 19
Hartelius, Margaret *10:* 24
Hartshorn, Ruth *5:* 115; *11:* 129
Harvey, Amanda *145:* 44
Harvey, Bob *48:* 219
Harvey, Gerry *7:* 180
Harvey, Lisa *97:* 21
Harvey, Paul *88:* 74
Harvey, Roland *71:* 88; *123:* 63; *179:* 94; *218:* 94; *219:* 74
Haskamp, Steve *195:* 36
Hassall, Joan *43:* 108, 109
Hassell, Hilton *YABC 1:* 187
Hassett, John *162:* 59
Hasselriis, Else *18:* 87; *YABC 1:* 96
Hastings, Glenn *89:* 183
Hastings, Ian *62:* 67
Hauman, Doris *2:* 184; *29:* 58, 59; *32:* 85, 86, 87
Hauman, George *2:* 184; *29:* 58, 59; *32:* 85, 86, 87
Hausherr, Rosmarie *15:* 29
Hawkes, Kevin *78:* 72; *104:* 198; *105:* 197; *112:* 109; *126:* 87; *144:* 88; *149:* 210; *150:* 110, 135; *156:* 94; *164:* 35; *186:* 18; *190:* 197; *198:* 152; *201:* 70, 71, 72; *220:* 99; *221:* 90, 92, 93
Hawkins, Jacqui *112:* 86; *162:* 64
Hawkinson, John *4:* 109; *7:* 83; *21:* 64
Hawkinson, Lucy *21:* 64
Hawthorne, Mike *140:* 228
Haxton, Elaine *28:* 131
Haydock, Robert *4:* 95
Hayes, Geoffrey *26:* 111; *44:* 133; *91:* 85; *207:* 63
Hayes, Karel *207:* 65
Haynes, Max *72:* 107
Hays, Michael *73:* 207; *83:* 93; *139:* 197; *146:* 202, 250; *202:* 47
Haywood, Carolyn *1:* 112; *29:* 104

Heale, Jonathan *104:* 117
Healy, Daty *12:* 143
Healy, Deborah *58:* 181, 182; *101:* 111
Heap, Sue *102:* 207; *150:* 113, 114; *187:* 84, 85, 87
Hearn, Diane Dawson *79:* 99; *113:* 13; *209:* 71, 72; *211:* 106
Hearon, Dorothy *34:* 69
Heaslip, William *57:* 24, 25
Hechtkopf, H. *11:* 110
Heck, Ed *173:* 81
Hector, Julian *205:* 85
Hedderwick, Mairi *30:* 127; *32:* 47; *36:* 104; *77:* 86; *145:* 91, 93, 95
Heffernan, Phil *146:* 197; *195:* 172; *218:* 123
Hefter, Richard *28:* 170; *31:* 81, 82; *33:* 183
Hehenberger, Shelly *126:* 91
Heigh, James *22:* 98
Heighway, Richard *25:* 160; *64:* 4
Heighway-Bury, Robin *159:* 89
Heine, Helme *67:* 86; *135:* 91, 92
Heinly, John *45:* 113
Hellard, Susan *81:* 21; *204:* 82; *209:* 92
Hellebrand, Nancy *26:* 57
Heller, Linda *46:* 86
Heller, Ruth M. *66:* 125; *77:* 30, 32
Hellmuth, Jim *38:* 164
Helquist, Brett *142:* 203; *146:* 133, 134; *156:* 10; *173:* 25; *180:* 106; *187:* 90, 91; *193:* 12
Helweg, Hans *41:* 118; *50:* 93; *58:* 22, 26
Hemingway, Edward *212:* 71
Hemphill, Helen *179:* 95
Henba, Bobbie *90:* 195
Henderling, Lisa *214:* 65
Henderson, Dave *73:* 76; *75:* 191, 192, 193, 194; *82:* 4
Henderson, D.F. *216:* 77
Henderson, Douglas *103:* 68
Henderson, Kathy *55:* 32; *155:* 118
Henderson, Keith *35:* 122
Henderson, Meryl *127:* 58, 60; *169:* 81
Hendrix, John *187:* 133; *208:* 106, 107, 108; *216:* 115
Hendry, Linda *80:* 104; *83:* 83; *164:* 216
Hengeveld, Dennis *142:* 86
Henkes, Kevin *43:* 111; *108:* 106, 107, 108
Henneberger, Robert *1:* 42; *2:* 237; *25:* 83
Henriquez, Celeste *103:* 137
Henriquez, Elsa *82:* 260
Henriquez, Emile F. *89:* 88; *211:* 56
Henry, Everett *29:* 191
Henry, Matthew *117:* 58
Henry, Paul *93:* 121; *194:* 125
Henry, Rohan *217:* 77
Henry, Thomas *5:* 102
Hensel *27:* 119
Henshaw, Jacqui *141:* 127
Henstra, Friso *8:* 80; *36:* 70; *40:* 222; *41:* 250; *73:* 100, 101
Henterly, Jamichael *93:* 4
Heo, Yumi *89:* 85, 86; *94:* 89, 90; *146:* 40, 137, 138; *163:* 227; *201:* 192
Hepple, Norman *28:* 198
Herbert, Helen *57:* 70
Herbert, Jennifer *189:* 47
Herbert, Wally *23:* 101
Herbster, Mary Lee *9:* 33
Herder, Edwin *182:* 104
Herge
  See Remi, Georges
Hermansen, Pal *133:* 113
Hermanson, Dennis *10:* 55
Hermes, Gertrude *54:* 161
Herr, Margo *57:* 191
Herr, Susan *83:* 163
Herriman, George *140:* 74, 75, 76, 77, 78
Herriman, Lisa *87:* 190
Herring, Michael *121:* 76; *182:* 103
Herrington, Roger *3:* 161

Herscovici, C. *165:* 240

Hescox, Richard *85:* 86; *90:* 30; *139:* 35

Heslop, Mike *38:* 60; *40:* 130

Hess, Lydia J. *85:* 17

Hess, Mark *111:* 146; *113:* 207

Hess, Paul *134:* 47; *166:* 133; *193:* 13

Hess, Richard *42:* 31

Hester, Ronnie *37:* 85

Heuser, Olga J. *121:* 116

Heusser, Sibylle *168:* 195

Heustis, Louise L. *20:* 28

Hewgill, Jodi *201:* 90

Hewitson, Jennifer *74:* 119; *124:* 167

Hewitt, Kathryn *80:* 126; *149:* 105; *184:* 93; *196:* 36

Hewitt, Margaret *84:* 112

Heyduck-Huth, Hilde *8:* 82

Heyer, Carol *74:* 122; *130:* 72, 73; *192:* 35; *203:* 78

Heyer, Hermann *20:* 114, 115

Heyer, Marilee *102:* 108

Heyman, Ken *8:* 33; *34:* 113

Heyne, Ulrike *146:* 151

Heywood, Karen *48:* 114

Hickling, P.B. *40:* 165

Hickman, Stephen *85:* 58; *136:* 33; *171:* 128

Hierstein, Judith *56:* 40; *162:* 168; *212:* 72

Higashi, Sandra *154:* 59, 60

Higginbottom, J. Winslow *8:* 170; *29:* 105, 106

Higgins, Chester *101:* 79

Higham, David *50:* 104

Hilb, Nora *176:* 8

Hild, Anja *215:* 194

Hildebrandt, Greg *8:* 191; *55:* 35, 36, 38, 39, 40, 42, 46; *172:* 110

Hildebrandt, Tim *8:* 191; *55:* 44, 45, 46

Hilder, Rowland *19:* 207

Hill, Eric *66:* 127, 128; *133:* 91

Hill, Gregory *35:* 190

Hill, Pat *49:* 120

Hillenbrand, Will *84:* 115; *92:* 76, 80; *93:* 131; *104:* 168; *128:* 137; *145:* 187; *146:* 184; *147:* 105, 106, 107; *152:* 59; *184:* 179; *195:* 34, 180; *196:* 125; *210:* 122, 123, 124; *217:* 62

Hilliard, Richard *183:* 74

Hillier, Matthew *45:* 205

Hillman, Priscilla *48:* 115

Hills, Tad *113:* 4; *137:* 147; *173:* 83; *208:* 199

Himler, Ronald *6:* 114; *7:* 162; *8:* 17, 84, 125; *14:* 76; *19:* 145; *26:* 160; *31:* 43; *38:* 116; *41:* 44, 79; *43:* 52; *45:* 120; *46:* 43; *54:* 44, 83; *58:* 180; *59:* 38; *68:* 146; *69:* 231; *70:* 98; *71:* 177, 178; *77:* 219; *79:* 212; *83:* 62; *89:* 5; *91:* 160; *92:* 91, 92, 93; *94:* 93; *95:* 69, 174, 194; *99:* 99, 112; *113:* 92; *118:* 114; *137:* 73, 74, 77, 167; *163:* 99; *165:* 138; *178:* 9, 220; *183:* 77, 79, 80, 81; *184:* 80, 83; *215:* 151

Himmelman, John *47:* 109; *65:* 87; *94:* 96, 97; *159:* 85; *221:* 79, 80, 81, 82

Hinds, Bill *37:* 127, 130

Hines, Anna Grossnickle *51:* 90; *74:* 124; *95:* 78, 79,80, 81

Hines, Bob *135:* 149, 150

Hirao, Amiko *203:* 98

Hiroko *99:* 61

Hiroshige *25:* 71

Hirsh, Marilyn *7:* 126

Hiscock, Bruce *137:* 80, 81; *204:* 51, 53

Hissey, Jane *103:* 90; *130:* 81

Hitch, Jeff *99:* 206; *128:* 86

Hitz, Demi *11:* 135; *15:* 245; *66:* 129, 130; *152:* 94, 95

Hnizdovsky, Jacques *32:* 96; *76:* 187

Ho, Kwoncjan *15:* 132

Hoban, Lillian *1:* 114; *22:* 157; *26:* 72; *29:* 53; *40:* 105, 107, 195; *41:* 80; *69:* 107, 108; *71:* 98; *77:* 168; *106:* 50; *113:* 86; *136:* 118

Hoban, Tana *22:* 159; *104:* 82, 83, 85

Hobbie, Jocelyn *190:* 78; *196:* 92

Hobbie, Nathaniel *196:* 92

Hobbs, Leigh *166:* 95

Hoberman, Norman *5:* 82

Hobson, Sally *77:* 185

Hockerman, Dennis *39:* 22; *56:* 23

Hodgell, P.C. *42:* 114

Hodges, C. Walter *2:* 139; *11:* 15; *12:* 25; *23:* 34; *25:* 96; *38:* 165; *44:* 197; *45:* 95; *100:* 57; *YABC 2:* 62, 63

Hodges, David *9:* 98

Hodgetts, Victoria *43:* 132

Hofbauer, Imre *2:* 162

Hoff, Syd *9:* 107; *10:* 128; *33:* 94; *72:* 115,116, 117, 118; *138:* 114, 115

Hoffman, Rosekrans *15:* 133; *50:* 219; *63:* 97

Hoffman, Sanford *38:* 208; *76:* 174; *88:* 160, 161; *151:* 156

Hoffmann, Felix *9:* 109

Hoffnung, Gerard *66:* 76, 77

Hofsinde, Robert *21:* 70

Hogan, Inez *2:* 141

Hogan, Jamie *192:* 94; *198:* 177

Hogarth, Burne *41:* 58; *63:* 46, 48, 49, 50, 52, 53, 54, 55,56

Hogarth, Paul *41:* 102, 103, 104; *YABC 1:* 16

Hogarth, William *42:* 33

Hogenbyl, Jan *1:* 35

Hogner, Nils *4:* 122; *25:* 144

Hogrogian, Nonny *3:* 221; *4:* 106, 107; *5:* 166; *7:* 129; *15:* 2; *16:* 176; *20:* 154; *22:* 146; *25:* 217; *27:* 206; *74:* 127, 128, 129, 149, 152; *127:* 99; *YABC 2:* 84, 94

Hokanson, Lars *93:* 111; *172:* 137; *212:* 88

Hokusai *25:* 71

Hol, Colby *126:* 96

Holberg, Richard *2:* 51

Holbrook, Kathy *107:* 114

Holdcroft, Tina *38:* 109

Holden, Caroline *55:* 159

Holder, Heidi *36:* 99; *64:* 9

Holder, Jim *204:* 163

Holder, Jimmy *151:* 224

Holderness, Grizelda *215:* 107

Hole, Stian *204:* 55

Holiday, Henry *YABC 2:* 107

Holl, F. *36:* 91

Holland, Brad *45:* 59, 159

Holland, Gay W. *128:* 105

Holland, Janice *18:* 118

Holland, Marion *6:* 116

Holland, Richard *216:* 109, 124

Holldobler, Turid *26:* 120

Holliday, Keaf *144:* 236

Holling, Holling C. *15:* 136, 137

Hollinger, Deanne *12:* 116

Holm, Sharon Lane *114:* 84; *115:* 52

Holmes, B. *3:* 82

Holmes, Bea *7:* 74; *24:* 156; *31:* 93

Holmes, Dave *54:* 22

Holmes, Lesley *135:* 96

Holmgren, George Ellen *45:* 112

Holmlund, Heather D. *150:* 140

Holt, Norma *44:* 106

Holt, Pater *151:* 188

Holtan, Gene *32:* 192

Holub, Joan *149:* 72

Holyfield, John *149:* 231

Holz, Loretta *17:* 81

Hom, Nancy *79:* 195

Homar, Lorenzo *6:* 2

Homer, Winslow *128:* 8; *YABC 2:* 87

Honey, Elizabeth *112:* 95, 96; *137:* 93, 94

Honeywood, Varnette P. *110:* 68, 70

Hong, Lily Toy *76:* 104

Honigman, Marian *3:* 2

Honore, Paul *42:* 77, 79, 81, 82

Hood, Alun *69:* 145, 218; *72:* 41; *80:* 226; *87:* 4; *95:* 139

Hood, Susan *12:* 43

Hook, Christian *104:* 103

Hook, Frances *26:* 188; *27:* 127

Hook, Jeff *14:* 137; *103:* 105

Hook, Richard *26:* 188

Hooks *63:* 30

Hooper, Hadley *177:* 145

Hoover, Carol A. *21:* 77

Hoover, Russell *12:* 95; *17:* 2; *34:* 156

Hope, James *141:* 116

Hopkins, Chris *99:* 127

Hopkinson, Leigh *202:* 70

Hopman, Philip *178:* 184

Hoppe, Paul *209:* 85

Hoppin, Augustus *34:* 66

Horacek, Judy *211:* 86

Horacek, Petr *163:* 117; *214:* 113

Horder, Margaret *2:* 108; *73:* 75

Horen, Michael *45:* 121

Horne, Daniel *73:* 106; *91:* 153; *109:* 127; *110:* 232; *164:* 176

Horne, Richard *111:* 80

Horowitz, Dave *204:* 58

Horse, Harry *128:* 195; *169:* 86

Horstman, Lisa *219:* 79

Horton, Anthony *211:* 98

Horvat, Laurel *12:* 201

Horvath, David *192:* 95

Horvath, Ferdinand Kusati *24:* 176

Horvath, Maria *57:* 171

Horwitz, Richard *57:* 174

Hotchkiss, De Wolfe *20:* 49

Hough, Charlotte *9:* 112; *13:* 98; *17:* 83; *24:* 195

Houlihan, Ray *11:* 214

House, Caroline *183:* 121

Housman, Laurence *25:* 146, 147

Houston, James *13:* 107; *74:* 132, 134, 135

Hovland, Gary *88:* 172; *171:* 148

Hoyt, Eleanor *158:* 231

How, W.E. *20:* 47

Howard, Alan *16:* 80; *34:* 58; *45:* 114

Howard, Arthur *165:* 111, 112; *190:* 5

Howard, J.N. *15:* 234

Howard, John *33:* 179

Howard, Kim *116:* 71

Howard, Paul *142:* 126, 129; *144:* 187

Howard, Rob *40:* 161

Howarth, Daniel *170:* 34; *222:* 97, 98

Howe, John *79:* 101; *80:* 150; *115:* 47; *176:* 106; *207:* 32, 35

Howe, Phillip *79:* 117; *175:* 115

Howe, Stephen *1:* 232

Howell, Karen *119:* 123

Howell, Pat *15:* 139

Howell, Troy *23:* 24; *31:* 61; *36:* 158; *37:* 184; *41:* 76, 235; *48:* 112; *56:* 13; *57:* 3; *59:* 174; *63:* 5; *74:* 46; *89:* 188; *90:* 231; *95:* 97; *98:* 130; *99:* 189; *153:* 156, 157, 158; *176:* 104; *199:* 96, 98; *222:* 65

Howes, Charles *22:* 17

Hoyt, Ard *145:* 141; *190:* 82; *207:* 148

Hranilovich, Barbara *127:* 51

Hu, Ying-Hwa *116:* 107; *152:* 236; *173:* 171

Huang, Benrei *137:* 55

Huang, Zhong-Yang *117:* 30, 32; *213:* 18

Hubbard, Woodleigh Marx *98:* 67; *115:* 79; *160:* 138; *214:* 120

Hubbell, Patricia *222:* 31

Hubley, Faith *48:* 120, 121, 125, 130, 131, 132, 134

Hubley, John *48:* 125, 130, 131, 132, 134

Hudak, Michal *143:* 74

Hudnut, Robin *14:* 62

Huerta, Catherine *76:* 178; *77:* 44, 45; *90:* 182; *210:* 202

Huffaker, Sandy *10:* 56

Huffman, Joan *13:* 33

Huffman, Tom *13:* 180; *17:* 212; *21:* 116; *24:* 132; *33:* 154; *38:* 59; *42:* 147

Hughes, Arthur *20:* 148, 149, 150; *33:* 114, 148, 149

Hughes, Darren *95:* 44

Hughes, David *36:* 197
Hughes, Shirley *1:* 20, 21; *7:* 3; *12:* 217; *16:* 163; *29:* 154; *63:* 118; *70:* 102, 103, 104; *73:* 169; *88:* 70; *110:* 118, 119; *159:* 103
Hugo, Victor *47:* 112
Huliska-Beith, Laura *204:* 108; *220:* 137
Hull, Cathy *78:* 29
Hull, Richard *95:* 120; *123:* 175; *172:* 195
Hulsmann, Eva *16:* 166
Hume, Lachie *189:* 93
Hummel, Berta *43:* 137, 138, 139
Hummel, Lisl *29:* 109; *YABC 2:* 333, 334
Humphrey, Henry *16:* 167
Humphreys, Graham *25:* 168
Humphries, Tudor *76:* 66; *80:* 4; *124:* 4, 5
Huneck, Stephen *183:* 88, 89
Hunt, James *2:* 143
Hunt, Jonathan *84:* 120
Hunt, Paul *119:* 104; *129:* 135; *139:* 160; *173:* 112
Hunt, Robert *110:* 206, 235; *147:* 136, 137; *170:* 3; *211:* 76
Hunt, Scott *190:* 143
Hunter, Anne *133:* 190; *178:* 150
Huntington, Amy *180:* 99
Hurd, Clement *2:* 148, 149; *64:* 127, 128, 129, 131, 133, 134,135, 136; *100:* 37, 38
Hurd, Peter *24:* 30, 31,; *YABC 2:* 56
Hurd, Thacher *46:* 88, 89; *94:* 114, 115, 116; *123:* 81, 82, 84; *219:* 82
Hurlimann, Ruth *32:* 99
Hurst, Carol Otis *185:* 92
Hurst, Elise *221:* 98
Hurst, Philip *196:* 79
Hurst, Tracey *192:* 238
Hussar, Michael *114:* 113; *117:* 159
Hustler, Tom *6:* 105
Hutchins, Laurence *55:* 22
Hutchins, Pat *15:* 142; *70:* 106, 107, 108; *178:* 131, 132
Hutchinson, Sascha *95:* 211
Hutchinson, William M. *6:* 3, 138; *46:* 70
Hutchison, Paula *23:* 10
Hutton, Clarke *YABC 2:* 335
Hutton, Kathryn *35:* 155; *89:* 91
Hutton, Warwick *20:* 91
Huyette, Marcia *29:* 188
Hyatt, John *54:* 7
Hyatt, Mitch *178:* 162
Hyde, Maureen *82:* 17; *121:* 145, 146
Hyman, David *117:* 64
Hyman, Miles *210:* 132
Hyman, Trina Schart *1:* 204; *2:* 194; *5:* 153; *6:* 106; *7:* 138, 145; *8:* 22; *10:* 196; *13:* 96; *14:* 114; *15:* 204; *16:* 234; *20:* 82; *22:* 133; *24:* 151; *25:* 79, 82; *26:* 82; *29:* 83; *31:* 37, 39; *34:* 104; *38:* 84, 100, 128; *41:* 49; *43:* 146; *46:* 91, 92, 93, 95, 96, 97, 98, 99, 100, 101, 102, 103, 104, 105,108, 109, 111, 197; *48:* 60, 61; *52:* 32; *60:* 168; *66:* 38; *67:* 214; *72:* 74; *75:* 92; *79:* 57; *82:* 95, 238; *89:* 46; *95:* 91, 92, 93; *100:* 33, 199; *132:* 12; *147:* 33, 35, 36; *167:* 58, 60; *177:* 189, 190; *211:* 188

I

Ibarra, Rosa *147:* 91
Ibatoulline, Bagram *156:* 48; *174:* 33, 82; *202:* 30; *211:* 213
Ichikawa, Satomi *29:* 152; *41:* 52; *47:* 133, 134,135, 136; *78:* 93, 94; *80:* 81; *146:* 143, 145, 146; *208:* 117, 118, 119
Ide, Jacqueline *YABC 1:* 39
Idle, Molly Schaar *223:* 95
Ilsley, Velma *3:* 1; *7:* 55; *12:* 109; *37:* 62; *38:* 184
Imai, Ayano *190:* 85, 86
in den Bosch, Nicole *150:* 204

Inga *1:* 142
Ingman, Bruce *134:* 50; *182:* 91, 92; *214:* 10
Ingpen, Robert *109:* 103, 104; *132:* 138; *137:* 177; *166:* 103; *181:* 140
Ingraham, Erick *21:* 177; *84:* 256; *103:* 66
Inkpen, Mick *99:* 104, 105; *106:* 44
Innerst, Stacy *149:* 104
Innocenti, Roberto *21:* 123; *96:* 122; *159:* 111, 197; *199:* 176
Inoue, Yosuke *24:* 118
Iofin, Michael *97:* 157
Iosa, Ann *63:* 189
Ipcar, Dahlov *1:* 124, 125; *49:* 137, 138, 139, 140, 141, 142,143, 144, 145; *147:* 122, 124, 126
Irvin, Fred *13:* 166; *15:* 143, 144; *27:* 175
Irving, Jay *45:* 72
Irving, Laurence *27:* 50
Isaac, Joanne *21:* 76
Isaacs, Gary *170:* 188
Isadora, Rachel *43:* 159, 160; *54:* 31; *79:* 106, 107,108; *121:* 100, 102; *165:* 116, 117; *204:* 61, 63, 64
Ishmael, Woodi *24:* 111; *31:* 99
Isol *220:* 73
Ives, Ruth *15:* 257
Iwai, Melissa *149:* 233; *183:* 92; *199:* 115
Iwamura, Kazuo *213:* 87

J

Jabar, Cynthia *101:* 201; *210:* 134, 135
Jackness, Andrew *94:* 237
Jackson, Julian *91:* 104, 106
Jackson, Michael *43:* 42
Jackson, Shelley *79:* 71; *99:* 109; *187:* 82
Jacob, Murv *89:* 30
Jacobi, Kathy *62:* 118
Jacobs, Barbara *9:* 136
Jacobs, Lou, Jr. *9:* 136; *15:* 128
Jacobsen, Laura *176:* 98; *177:* 85, 86
Jacobson, Rick *131:* 222; *170:* 119; *222:* 52
Jacobus, Tim *79:* 140; *109:* 126; *129:* 180
Jacques, Robin *1:* 70; *2:* 1; *8:* 46; *9:* 20; *15:* 187; *19:* 253; *32:* 102, 103, 104; *43:* 184; *73:* 135; *YABC 1:* 42
Jaeggi, Yoshiko *186:* 184
Jaffee, Al *66:* 131, 132
Jago *216:* 122
Jagr, Miloslav *13:* 197
Jahn-Clough, Lisa *88:* 114; *152:* 104; *193:* 70, 71
Jahnke, Robert *84:* 24
Jainschigg, Nicholas *80:* 64; *91:* 138; *95:* 63; *99:* 25; *108:* 50; *171:* 41
Jakesavic, Nenad *85:* 102
Jakobsen, Kathy *116:* 83
Jakubowski, Charles *14:* 192
Jambor, Louis *YABC 1:* 11
James, Ann *73:* 50; *82:* 113; *158:* 61; *183:* 44
James, Brian *140:* 91
James, Curtis E. *182:* 93
James, Derek *35:* 187; *44:* 91; *61:* 133; *74:* 2; *80:* 57; *86:* 88; *130:* 30; *179:* 29; *218:* 31
James, Gilbert *YABC 1:* 43
James, Gordon C. *195:* 89
James, Harold *2:* 151; *3:* 62; *8:* 79; *29:* 113; *51:* 195; *74:* 90
James, Kennon *126:* 211
James, Robin *50:* 106; *53:* 32, 34, 35
James, Simon *202:* 73, 74
James, Will *19:* 150, 152, 153, 155, 163
Janosch
  See Eckert, Horst
Janovitch, Marilyn *68:* 168
Janovitz, Marilyn *87:* 187; *130:* 198; *194:* 91
Jansons, Inese *48:* 117
Jansson, Alexander *216:* 59

Jansson, Tove *3:* 90; *41:* 106, 108, 109, 110, 111, 113, 114
Jaques, Faith *7:* 11, 132, 133; *21:* 83, 84; *69:* 114,116; *73:* 170
Jaques, Frances Lee *29:* 224
Jarka, Jeff *221:* 94
Jarrett, Clare *201:* 77
Jarrie, Martin *219:* 86
Jauss, Anne Marie *1:* 139; *3:* 34; *10:* 57, 119; *11:* 205; *23:* 194
Jay, Alison *158:* 97, 98; *183:* 126, 127; *196:* 95, 96, 97, 98; *200:* 72, 73, 74; *212:* 39
Jeffers, Oliver *175:* 111; *213:* 89
Jeffers, Susan *17:* 86, 87; *25:* 164, 165; *26:* 112; *50:* 132, 134, 135; *70:* 111, 112, 113; *137:* 107, 108, 109, 110, 111; *202:* 77, 78
Jefferson, Louise E. *4:* 160
Jenkin-Pearce, Susie *78:* 16
Jenkins, Debra Reid *85:* 202; *114:* 89; *173:* 134
Jenkins, Jean *98:* 79, 102
Jenkins, Leonard *157:* 169; *167:* 128; *189:* 96, 97; *190:* 89
Jenkins, Patrick *72:* 126
Jenkins, Steve *124:* 177; *154:* 90, 91, 92, 93; *185:* 194; *188:* 81, 82, 83, 84, 85, 86; *218:* 67, 69, 70, 71, 72
Jenks, Aleta *73:* 117; *124:* 225
Jenkyns, Chris *51:* 97
Jensen, Bruce *95:* 39
Jensinius, Kirsten *56:* 58
Jeram, Anita *89:* 135; *102:* 122, 123; *129:* 112; *154:* 96, 97, 98; *164:* 154; *203:* 123, 124; *219:* 88, 89, 90, 91
Jernigan, E. Wesley *85:* 92
Jerome, Karen A. *72:* 194
Jeruchim, Simon *6:* 173; *15:* 250
Jeschke, Susan *20:* 89; *39:* 161; *41:* 84; *42:* 120
Jessel, Camilla *29:* 115
Jessell, Tim *159:* 3; *177:* 87; *181:* 95; *205:* 4; *213:* 74; *223:* 187
Jeyaveeran, Ruth *182:* 100
Jiang, Cheng An *109:* 108
Jiang, Wei *109:* 108
Jimenez, Maria *77:* 158; *93:* 127
Jobling, Curtis *138:* 74
Jocelyn, Marthe *118:* 83; *137:* 219; *163:* 119, 120; *198:* 62
Joerns, Consuelo *38:* 36; *44:* 94
John, Diana *12:* 209
John, Helen *1:* 215; *28:* 204
Johns, Elizabeth *127:* 33
Johns, Jasper *61:* 172
Johns, Jeanne *24:* 114
Johnson, Adrian *143:* 50
Johnson, Bruce *9:* 47
Johnson, Cathy *92:* 136; *218:* 112
Johnson, Crockett
  See Leisk, David
Johnson, D. William *23:* 104
Johnson, D.B. *183:* 98, 139
Johnson, David A. *175:* 18; *191:* 91; *218:* 19
Johnson, Gillian *119:* 175; *164:* 217; *215:* 99
Johnson, Harper *1:* 27; *2:* 33; *18:* 302; *19:* 61; *31:* 181; *44:* 46, 50, 95
Johnson, Ingrid *37:* 118
Johnson, James Ralph *1:* 23, 127
Johnson, James David *12:* 195
Johnson, Jane *48:* 136
Johnson, Joel Peter *98:* 18; *128:* 111; *201:* 13; *213:* 189
Johnson, John E. *34:* 133
Johnson, Kevin *72:* 44
Johnson, Kevin Eugene *109:* 215
Johnson, Larry *47:* 56; *123:* 107; *159:* 203
Johnson, Layne *187:* 94; *209:* 63; *222:* 100, 101
Johnson, Margaret S. *35:* 131
Johnson, Meredith Merrell *71:* 181; *83:* 158; *89:* 103; *104:* 88

Johnson, Milton *1:* 67; *2:* 71; *26:* 45; *31:* 107; *60:* 112; *68:* 96

Johnson, Pamela *16:* 174; *52:* 145; *62:* 140; *73:* 116; *85:* 64

Johnson, Paul Brett *83:* 95; *132:* 119

Johnson, Stephen T. *80:* 15; *131:* 35; *141:* 96; *145:* 40; *164:* 187; *175:* 32; *189:* 99, 100; *208:* 43

Johnson, Steve *138:* 219; *141:* 64; *144:* 199; *177:* 51; *214:* 95; *221:* 63

Johnson, William R. *38:* 91

Johnson-Petrov, Arden *115:* 206

Johnston, David McCall *50:* 131, 133

Johnston, Lynne *118:* 85, 87, 89; *216:* 127, 128, 131

Johnstone, Anne *8:* 120; *36:* 89

Johnstone, Janet Grahame *8:* 120; *36:* 89

Jonas, Ann *50:* 107, 108, 109; *135:* 113

Jones, Bob *71:* 5; *77:* 199

Jones, Carol *5:* 131; *72:* 185, 186; *153:* 111, 112

Jones, Chuck *53:* 70, 71

Jones, Curtis *211:* 144

Jones, Davy *89:* 176

Jones, Douglas B. *185:* 192; *202:* 82

Jones, Elizabeth Orton *18:* 124, 126, 128, 129

Jones, Harold *14:* 88; *52:* 50

Jones, Holly *127:* 3

Jones, Jeff *41:* 64

Jones, Laurian *25:* 24, 27

Jones, Margaret *74:* 57

Jones, Noah Z. *182:* 37; *203:* 159

Jones, Randy *131:* 104

Jones, Richard *127:* 222

Jones, Robert *25:* 67

Jones, Wilfred *35:* 115; *YABC 1:* 163

Jordan, Charles *89:* 58

Jordan, Jess *158:* 136; *203:* 111

Jordan, Martin George *84:* 127

Jordan, Richard *84:* 36

Jorgenson, Andrea *91:* 111

Jorisch, Stéphane *153:* 56, 193; *177:* 29; *178:* 138, 139; *187:* 23; *211:* 182

Joseph, James *53:* 88

Joudrey, Ken *64:* 145; *78:* 6

Joyce, William *72:* 131, 132, 133, 134; *73:* 227; *145:* 37

Joyner, Jerry *34:* 138

Joyner, Loraine M. *209:* 17

Joysmith, Brenda *210:* 237

Juan, Ana *175:* 38; *179:* 111, 112; *213:* 9

Jucker, Sita *5:* 93

Judge, Lita *192:* 99

Judkis, Jim *37:* 38

Juhasz, Victor *31:* 67

Jullian, Philippe *22:* 206; *25:* 203

Jung, Tom *91:* 217

Junge, Alexandra *183:* 37

Junge, Walter *67:* 150

Jupo, Frank *7:* 148, 149

Jurisch, Stephane *154:* 105

Justice, Martin *34:* 72

K

Kabatova-Taborska, Zdenka *107:* 153

Kachik, John *165:* 230

Kaczman, James *156:* 98

Kadair, Deborah Ousley *184:* 45, 89

Kahl, David *74:* 95; *97:* 35; *109:* 174; *110:* 213; *198:* 15

Kahl, M.P. *37:* 83

Kahl, Virginia *48:* 138

Kahn, Katherine Janus *90:* 135; *211:* 155; *218:* 75, 76; *220:* 89,90

Kakimoo, Kozo *11:* 148

Kalett, Jim *48:* 159, 160, 161

Kalin, Victor *39:* 186

Kalis, Jennifer *207:* 82; *219:* 62

Kalman, Maira *96:* 131, 132; *137:* 115

Kalmenoff, Matthew *22:* 191

Kalow, Gisela *32:* 105

Kamen, Gloria *1:* 41; *9:* 119; *10:* 178; *35:* 157; *78:* 236; *98:* 82

Kaminsky, Jef *102:* 153

Kandell, Alice *35:* 133

Kane, Henry B. *14:* 90; *18:* 219, 220

Kane, Robert *18:* 131

Kanfer, Larry *66:* 141

Kangas, Juli *200:* 88

Kappes, Alfred *28:* 104

Karalus, Bob *41:* 157

Karas, G. Brian *80:* 60; *99:* 179; *115:* 41; *118:* 50; *136:* 168; *145:* 166; *149:* 245; *159:* 65; *171:* 192; *178:* 142, 143; *202:* 38; *209:* 142; *222:* 106, 107, 108, 109

Karasz, Ilonka *128:* 163

Karlin, Eugene *10:* 63; *20:* 131

Karlin, Nurit *63:* 78; *103:* 110

Karpinski, Tony *134:* 160

Kasamatsu, Shiro *139:* 155

Kasparavicius, Kestutis *139:* 210

Kassian, Olena *64:* 94

Kastner, Jill *79:* 135; *117:* 84, 85

Kasuya, Masahiro *41:* 206, 207; *51:* 100

Kasza, Keiko *191:* 99, 100, 101, 102, 103

Katona, Robert *21:* 85; *24:* 126

Katz, Avi *199:* 55

Katz, Karen *158:* 123

Kauffer, E. McKnight *33:* 103; *35:* 127; *63:* 67

Kaufman, Angelika *15:* 156

Kaufman, Joe *33:* 119

Kaufman, John *13:* 158

Kaufman, Stuart *62:* 64; *68:* 226; *137:* 44

Kaufmann, John *1:* 174; *4:* 159; *8:* 43, 1; *10:* 102; *18:* 133, 134; *22:* 251

Kaye, Graham *1:* 9; *67:* 7, 8

Kaye, M.M. *62:* 95

Kazalovski, Nata *40:* 205

Keane, Bil *4:* 135

Kearney, David *72:* 47; *121:* 83

Keating, Pamel T. *77:* 37

Keats, Ezra Jack *3:* 18, 105, 257; *14:* 101, 102; *33:* 129; *57:* 79, 80, 82, 83, 84, 87

Keegan, Charles *166:* 211

Keegan, Marcia *9:* 122; *32:* 93

Keeler, Patricia A. *81:* 56; *183:* 102, 103

Keely, Jack *119:* 95

Keely, John *26:* 104; *48:* 214

Keen, Eliot *25:* 213

Keep, Richard C. *170:* 122

Keeping, Charles *9:* 124, 185; *15:* 28, 134; *18:* 115; *44:* 194, 196; *47:* 25; *52:* 3; *54:* 156; *69:* 123, 124; *74:* 56; *155:* 9

Keeter, Susan *168:* 46; *183:* 192

Keith, Eros *4:* 98; *5:* 138; *31:* 29; *43:* 220; *52:* 91, 92, 93, 94; *56:* 64, 66; *60:* 37; *79:* 93

Keleinikov, Andrei *65:* 101, 102

Kelen, Emery *13:* 115

Keller, A.J. *62:* 198

Keller, Arthur I. *26:* 106

Keller, Dick *36:* 123, 125

Keller, Holly *45:* 79; *76:* 118, 119, 120, 121; *108:* 137, 138, 140; *157:* 117, 118, 119; *216:* 136

Keller, Katie *79:* 222; *93:* 108

Keller, Laurie *196:* 105, 106

Keller, Ronald *45:* 208

Kelley, Gary *183:* 105; *216:* 78; *217:* 95, 96, 97

Kelley, Marty *211:* 91

Kelley, True *41:* 114, 115; *42:* 137; *75:* 35; *92:* 104, 105; *124:* 62; *130:* 100, 101; *179:* 120, 121, 122; *192:* 251

Kellogg, Steven *8:* 96; *11:* 207; *14:* 130; *20:* ; *201:* 38 58; *29:* 140, 141; *30:* 35; *41:* 141; *57:* 89, 90, 92,93, 94, 96; *59:* 182; *73:* 141; *77:* 129; *130:* 105, 106; *177:* 94, 95, 96, 97; *199:* 57; *217:* 61; *YABC 1:* 65, 73

Kelly, Billy *158:* 143

Kelly, Geoff *97:* 196; *112:* 25

Kelly, Irene *147:* 134; *210:* 144, 145

Kelly, John *194:* 186

Kelly, Joseph *174:* 94

Kelly, Kathleen M. *71:* 109

Kelly, Laura *89:* 217

Kelly, True *163:* 87

Kelly, Walt *18:* 136, 137, 138, 139, 140, 141, 144, 145, 146, 148, 149

Kemble, E.W. *34:* 75; *44:* 178; *YABC 2:* 54, 59

Kemly, Kathleen *209:* 165

Kemp-Welsh, Lucy *24:* 197; *100:* 214

Kendall, Jane *150:* 105; *186:* 109

Kendall, Peter *152:* 85

Kendrick, Dennis *79:* 213

Kennaway, Adrienne *60:* 55, 56; *171:* 88, 89

Kennedy, Anne *212:* 34

Kennedy, Doug *189:* 104

Kennedy, Paul Edward *6:* 190; *8:* 132; *33:* 120

Kennedy, Richard *3:* 93; *12:* 179; *44:* 193; *100:* 15; *YABC 1:* 57

Kent, Jack *24:* 136; *37:* 37; *40:* 81; *84:* 89; *86:* 150; *88:* 77

Kent, Rockwell *5:* 166; *6:* 129; *20:* 225, 226, 227,229; *59:* 144

Kenyon, Tony *81:* 201; *127:* 74

Kepes, Juliet *13:* 119

Kerins, Anthony *76:* 84

Kerr, Judith *24:* 137

Kerr, Phyllis Forbes *72:* 141

Kessler, Leonard *1:* 108; *7:* 139; *14:* 107, 227; *22:* 101; *44:* 96; *67:* 79; *82:* 123

Kest, Kristin *168:* 99; *173:* 23

Kesteven, Peter *35:* 189

Ketcham, Hank *28:* 140, 141, 142

Kettelkamp, Larry *2:* 164

Key, Alexander *8:* 99

Khalsa, Dayal Kaur *62:* 99

Kiakshuk *8:* 59

Kid, Tom *207:* 54

Kidd, Chip *94:* 23

Kidd, Richard *152:* 110

Kidd, Tom *64:* 199; *81:* 189; *185:* 173

Kiddell-Monroe, Joan *19:* 201; *55:* 59, 60; *87:* 174; *121:* 112

Kidder, Harvey *9:* 105; *80:* 41

Kidwell, Carl *43:* 145

Kieffer, Christa *41:* 89

Kiesler, Kate *110:* 105; *136:* 142

Kiff, Ken *40:* 45

Kilaka, John *223:* 107

Kilbride, Robert *37:* 100

Kilby, Don *141:* 144

Kim, David *201:* 79; *202:* 97

Kim, Glenn *99:* 82

Kimball, Anton *78:* 114; *119:* 105

Kimball, Yeffe *23:* 116; *37:* 88

Kimber, Murray *171:* 91

Kimmel, Warren *176:* 112

Kincade, Orin *34:* 116

Kindersley, Barnabas *96:* 110

Kindred, Wendy *7:* 151

King, Colin *53:* 3

King, Robin *10:* 164, 165

King, Stephen Michael *141:* 31; *197:* 191; *218:* 81, 82

King, Tara Calahan *139:* 172

King, Tony *39:* 121

Kingman, Dong *16:* 287; *44:* 100, 102, 104

Kingsley, Charles *YABC 2:* 182

Kingston, Julie *147:* 14

Kingston, Maxine Hong *53:* 92

Kinney, Jeff *187:* 97

Kipling, John Lockwood *YABC 2:* 198

Kipling, Rudyard *YABC 2:* 196

Kipniss, Robert *29:* 59

Kirchherr, Astrid *55:* 23

Kirchhoff, Art *28:* 136

Kirk, Daniel *153:* 115, 116, 117; *173:* 101; *196:* 113, 114, 115, 116

Kirk, David *117:* 88, 89; *161:* 97, 98
Kirk, Ruth *5:* 96
Kirk, Steve *170:* 37
Kirk, Tim *32:* 209, 211; *72:* 89; *83:* 49
Kirmse, Marguerite *15:* 283; *18:* 153
Kirsch, Vincent X. *124:* 207
Kirschner, Ruth *22:* 154
Kirwan, Wednesday *198:* 73
Kish, Ely *73:* 119; *79:* 2
Kitamura, Satoshi *62:* 102; *98:* 91; *101:* 147;
    138: 2; *143:* 83, 85, 86; *201:* 83; *223:* 3, 4
Kiss, Andrew *168:* 115
Kitchel, JoAnn E. *133:* 32
Kitchen, Bert *70:* 126; *193:* 49
Kittelsen, Theodor *62:* 14
Kiuchi, Tatsuro *114:* 71
Kiwak, Barbara *172:* 135
Klahr, Susan *176:* 196
Klapholz, Mel *13:* 35
Klee, Jutte *209:* 136
Klein, Bill *89:* 105
Klein, Robert *55:* 77
Klein, Suzanna *63:* 104
Kleinman, Zalman *28:* 143
Kleven, Elisa *173:* 96, 97; *217:* 100, 102
Kliban, B. *35:* 137, 138
Kline, Michael *127:* 66
Klise, M. Sarah *180:* 117, 118; *181:* 97; *221:*
    100, 102
Knabel, Lonnie *73:* 103; *75:* 187, 228; *194:*
    216
Kneen, Maggie *140:* 139; *221:* 104, 105
Knight, Ann *34:* 143
Knight, Christopher *13:* 125
Knight, Hilary *1:* 233; *3:* 21; *15:* 92, 158, 159;
    16: 258, 259, 260; *18:* 235; *19:* 169; *35:*
    242; *46:* 167; *52:* 116; *69:* 126, 127; *132:*
    129; *YABC 1:* 168, 169, 172
Knorr, Laura *200:* 91
Knorr, Peter *126:* 92, 93
Knotts, Howard *20:* 4; *25:* 170; *36:* 163
Knutson, Barbara *112:* 134; *202:* 108
Knutson, Kimberley *115:* 90
Kobayashi, Ann *39:* 58
Kochalka, James *196:* 120, 121, 122
Kocsis, J.C.
    See Paul, James
Kodman, Stanislawa *201:* 85
Koehler, Hanne Lore *176:* 203
Koehn, Ilse *34:* 198; *79:* 123
Koelsch, Michael *99:* 182; *107:* 164; *109:* 239;
    138: 142; *150:* 94; *176:* 105; *187:* 63; *198:*
    63
Koering, Ursula *3:* 28; *4:* 14; *44:* 5; *64:*
    140,141; *85:* 46
Koerner, Henry
    See Koerner, W.H.D.
Koerner, W.H.D. *14:* 216; *21:* 88, 89, 90, 91;
    23: 211
Koetsch, Mike *166:* 68
Koffler, Camilla *36:* 113
Kogan, Deborah Ray *161:* 101, 102
Koide, Yasuko *50:* 114
Kolado, Karen *102:* 228
Kolesova, Juliana *217:* 81; *222:* 185
Komoda, Kiyo *9:* 128; *13:* 214
Kompaneyets, Marc *169:* 92
Konashevich, Vladimir *61:* 160
Konashevicha, V. *YABC 1:* 26
Konigsburg, E.L. *4:* 138; *48:* 141, 142, 144,
    145; *94:* 129, 130; *126:* 129, 130, 131; *194:*
    95, 98
Kono, Erin Eitter *177:* 99
Kooiker, Leonie *48:* 148
Koonook, Simon *65:* 157
Koontz, Robin Michal *136:* 155
Koopmans, Loek *101:* 121
Kopelke, Lisa *154:* 107
Kopper, Lisa *72:* 152, 153; *105:* 135, 136
Korach, Mimi *1:* 128, 129; *2:* 52; *4:* 39; *5:*
    159; *9:* 129; *10:* 21; *24:* 69

Koren, Edward *5:* 100; *65:* 65, 67
Kosaka, Fumi *164:* 130
Koscielniak, Bruce *99:* 122; *153:* 120, 121,
    122
Koshkin, Alexander *92:* 180
Kossin, Sandy *10:* 71; *23:* 105
Kostin, Andrej *26:* 204
Kosturko, Bob *164:* 56
Kotzky, Brian *68:* 184
Kovacevic, Zivojin *13:* 247
Kovalski, Maryann *58:* 120; *84:* 88; *97:* 124,
    125, 126; *158:* 3; *186:* 80
Kozjan, Drazen *209:* 99
Krahn, Fernando *2:* 257; *34:* 206; *49:* 152
Krall, Dan *218:* 84, 85
Kramer, Anthony *33:* 81
Kramer, David *96:* 162; *109:* 132; *150:* 220
Kramer, Frank *6:* 121
Krantz, Kathy *35:* 83
Kratter, Paul *139:* 65
Kraus, Robert *13:* 217; *65:* 113; *93:* 93, 94
Krause, Jon *176:* 62
Krauss, Trisha *174:* 10
Kredel, Fritz *6:* 35; *17:* 93, 94, 95, 96; *22:*
    147; *24:* 175; *29:* 130; *35:* 77; *YABC 2:* 166,
    300
Kreloff, Eliot *189:* 107, 108; *205:* 182
Krementz, Jill *17:* 98; *49:* 41
Krenina, Katya *117:* 106; *125:* 133; *176:* 117;
    221: 107
Kresin, Robert *23:* 19
Krieger, Salem *54:* 164
Kriegler, Lyn *73:* 29
Krinitz, Esther Nisenthal *193:* 196
Krommes, Beth *128:* 141; *149:* 136; *181:* 100,
    101; *184:* 105; *188:* 125; *208:* 135; *209:* 185
Krone, Mike *101:* 71
Kronheimer, Ann *135:* 119
Krosoczka, Jarrett J. *155:* 142; *200:* 93, 94
Kruck, Gerald *88:* 181
Krudop, Walter Lyon *199:* 19
Krupinski, Loretta *67:* 104; *102:* 131; *161:*
    105, 106
Krupp, Robin Rector *53:* 96, 98
Krush, Beth *1:* 51, 85; *2:* 233; *4:* 115; *9:* 61;
    10: 191; *11:* 196; *18:* 164, 165; *32:* 72; *37:*
    203; *43:* 57; *60:* 102, 103, 107, 108, 109
Krush, Joe *2:* 233; *4:* 115; *9:* 61; *10:* 191; *11:*
    196; *18:* 164, 165; *32:* 72, 91; *37:* 203; *43:*
    57; *60:* 102, 103, 107, 108, 109
Krych, Duane *91:* 43
Krykorka, Vladyana *96:* 147; *143:* 90, 91;
    168: 14
Kubick, Dana *165:* 91; *212:* 104, 105, 212
Kubinyi, Laszlo *4:* 116; *6:* 113; *16:* 118; *17:*
    100; *28:* 227; *30:* 172; *49:* 24, 28; *54:* 23;
    167: 149
Kubricht, Mary *73:* 118
Kucharik, Elena *139:* 31
Kuchera, Kathleen *84:* 5
Kuhn, Bob *17:* 91; *35:* 235
Kulikov, Boris *163:* 185; *185:* 23; *205:* 99,
    100; *217:* 160
Kulka, Joe *188:* 110
Kukalis, Romas *90:* 27; *139:* 37
Kuklin, Susan *63:* 82, 83, 84
Kunhardt, Dorothy *53:* 101
Kunhardt, Edith *67:* 105, 106
Kunstler, Mort *10:* 73; *32:* 143
Kurchevsky, V. *34:* 61
Kurczok, Belinda *121:* 118
Kurelek, William *8:* 107
Kuriloff, Ron *13:* 19
Kurisu, Jane *160:* 120
Kuskin, Karla *2:* 170; *68:* 115, 116; *111:* 116
Kutzer, Ernst *19:* 249
Kuzma, Steve *57:* 8; *62:* 93
Kuznetsova, Berta *74:* 45
Kvasnosky, Laura McGee *93:* 103; *142:* 83;
    182: 108

Kwas, Susan Estelle *179:* 116; *217:* 90
Kyong, Yunmee *165:* 139

L

LaBlanc, Andre *24:* 146
Laboccetta, Mario *27:* 120
LaBrose, Darcie *157:* 134
Labrosse, Darcia *58:* 88; *108:* 77; *178:* 89
LaCava, Vince *95:* 118
Laceky, Adam *32:* 121
Lacis, Astra *85:* 117
Lacome, Julie *174:* 96, 97
La Croix *YABC 2:* 4
Ladd, London *206:* 50
Ladwig, Tim *98:* 212; *117:* 76; *215:* 32; *223:*
    111, 112
La Farge, Margaret *47:* 141
LaFave, Kim *64:* 177; *72:* 39; *97:* 146; *99:*
    172; *106:* 123; *149:* 126; *196:* 128, 129
Lafontaine, Roger *167:* 158
Lafrance, Marie *197:* 109
Lagarrigue, Jerome *136:* 102; *187:* 81
Laimgruber, Monika *11:* 153
Laio, Jimmy *213:* 57
Laite, Gordon *1:* 130, 131; *8:* 209; *31:* 113;
    40: 63; *46:* 117
Laliberté, Louise-Andrée *169:* 98
LaMarche, Jim *46:* 204; *61:* 56; *94:* 69; *114:*
    22; *129:* 163; *162:* 78, 80
Lamb, Jim *10:* 117
Lambase, Barbara *101:* 185; *150:* 221; *166:*
    234
Lambert, J.K. *38:* 129; *39:* 24
Lambert, Sally Anne *133:* 191
Lambert, Saul *23:* 112; *33:* 107; *54:* 136
Lambert, Stephen *109:* 33; *174:* 99
Lambo, Don *6:* 156; *35:* 115; *36:* 146
Lamontagne, Jacques *166:* 227
Lamut, Sonja *57:* 193
Lamut, Sonya *85:* 102
Landa, Peter *11:* 95; *13:* 177; *53:* 119
Landau, Jacob *38:* 111
Landis, Joan *104:* 23; *203:* 32
Landon, Lucinda *79:* 31
Landshoff, Ursula *13:* 124
Landström, Lena *146:* 165, 166
Landström, Olof *146:* 166, 168; *170:* 22
Lane, Daniel *112:* 60
Lane, John R. *8:* 145
Lane, John *15:* 176, 177; *30:* 146
Lane, Nancy *166:* 74
Lang, G.D. *48:* 56
Lang, Gary *73:* 75
Lang, Glenna *221:* 113
Lang, Jerry *18:* 295
Langdo, Bryan *186:* 187; *191:* 113, 114, 115
Lange, Dorothea *50:* 141
Langley, Jonathan *162:* 128
Langner, Nola *8:* 110; *42:* 36
Lanino, Deborah *105:* 148
Lantz, Paul *1:* 82, 102; *27:* 88; *34:* 102; *45:*
    123
Larkin, Bob *84:* 225
Laroche, Giles *126:* 140; *146:* 81; *221:* 116,
    117
LaRochelle, David *171:* 97
Larrecq, John *44:* 108; *68:* 56
Larsen, Suzanne *1:* 13
Larson, Gary *57:* 121, 122, 123, 124, 125,
    126, 127
Larsson, Carl *35:* 144, 145, 146, 147, 148,
    149, 150, 152, 153, 154
Larsson, Karl *19:* 177
Lartitegui, Ana G. *105:* 167
LaRue, Jenna *167:* 20
La Rue, Michael D. *13:* 215
Lasker, Joe *7:* 186, 187; *14:* 55; *38:* 115; *39:*
    47; *83:* 113, 114, 115
Latham, Barbara *16:* 188, 189; *43:* 71

Lathrop, Dorothy *14:* 117, 118, 119; *15:* 109; *16:* 78, 79, 81; *32:* 201, 203; *33:* 112; *YABC 2:* 301
Lattimore, Eleanor Frances *7:* 156
Lauden, Claire *16:* 173
Lauden, George, Jr. *16:* 173
Laune, Paul *2:* 235; *34:* 31
Laure, Jason *49:* 53; *50:* 122
Lauter, Richard *63:* 29; *67:* 111; *77:* 198
Lavallee, Barbara *74:* 157; *92:* 154; *96:* 126; *145:* 193; *166:* 125, 126; *186:* 155; *192:* 172
Lave, Fitz Hugh *59:* 139
Lavis, Steve *43:* 143; *87:* 137, 164, 165; *222:* 161
Layton, Neal *152:* 120, 121; *182:* 65; *187:* 103, 105, 106
Law, Jenny *201:* 31
Lawrason, June *168:* 30
Lawrence, John *25:* 131; *30:* 141; *44:* 198, 200; *214:* 7
Lawrence, Stephen *20:* 195
Lawson, Carol *6:* 38; *42:* 93, 131; *174:* 56; *189:* 89; *209:* 59
Lawson, George *17:* 280
Lawson, Robert *5:* 26; *6:* 94; *13:* 39; *16:* 11; *20:* 100, 102, 103; *54:* 3; *66:* 12; *100:* 144, 145; *YABC 2:* 222, 224, 225, 227, 228, 229, 230, 231, 232, 233, 234, 235, 237, 238, 239, 240, 241
Layfield, Kathie *60:* 194
Lazare, Jerry *44:* 109; *74:* 28
Lazarevich, Mila *17:* 118
Lazarus, Claire *103:* 30
Lazarus, Keo Felker *21:* 94
Lazzaro, Victor *11:* 126
Lea, Bob *166:* 208; *203:* 108
Lea, Tom *43:* 72, 74
Leacroft, Richard *6:* 140
Leaf, Munro *20:* 99
Leake, Donald *70:* 41
Leander, Patricia *23:* 27
Lear, Edward *18:* 183, 184, 185
Lear, Rebecca *149:* 46
Lebenson, Richard *6:* 209; *7:* 76; *23:* 145; *44:* 191; *87:* 153
Le Cain, Errol *6:* 141; *9:* 3; *22:* 142; *25:* 198; *28:* 173; *68:* 128, 129; *86:* 49
Lechon, Daniel *113:* 211
Leder, Dora *129:* 172
Ledger, Bill *181:* 58
Leduc, Bernard *102:* 36
Lee, Alan *62:* 25, 28
Lee, Bryce *99:* 60; *101:* 195; *196:* 53
Lee, Chinlun *181:* 138; *182:* 112
Lee, Declan *191:* 20
Lee, Dom *83:* 118, 120; *93:* 123; *121:* 121, 126; *146:* 174, 175, 206, 207; *174:* 204
Lee, Doris *13:* 246; *32:* 183; *44:* 111
Lee, Hector Viveros *115:* 96
Lee, Ho Baek *200:* 160
Lee, Huy Voun *106:* 106
Lee, Jeanne M. *158:* 56
Lee, Jared *93:* 200; *157:* 229; *215:* 113, 191, 192, 193
Lee, Jody *81:* 121; *82:* 225; *91:* 155; *100:* 182
Lee, Jody A. *127:* 124, 126, 127
   See also Lee, Jody
Lee, Manning de V. *2:* 200; *17:* 12; *27:* 87; *37:* 102, 103, 104; *YABC 2:* 304
Lee, Margaret *213:* 179
Lee, Marie G. *138:* 157
Lee, Paul *97:* 100; *105:* 72, 209; *109:* 177; *128:* 113; *202:* 45
Lee, Robert J. *3:* 97; *67:* 124
Lee, Victor *96:* 228; *105:* 182; *140:* 196; *208:* 191
Lee, Virginia *208:* 139, 140; *218:* 28
Leech, Dorothy *98:* 76
Leech, John *15:* 59
Leedy, Loreen *84:* 142; *128:* 144, 145, 146; *175:* 125, 126, 127

Leeman, Michael *44:* 157
Leeming, Catherine *87:* 39
Lees, Harry *6:* 112
LeFever, Bill *88:* 220, 221
Legenisel *47:* 111
Legrand, Edy *18:* 89, 93
Lehman, Barbara *73:* 123; *170:* 130
Lehrman, Rosalie *2:* 180
Leichman, Seymour *5:* 107
Leick, Bonnie *205:* 104
Leighton, Clare *25:* 130; *33:* 168; *37:* 105, 106, 108,109
Leisk, David *1:* 140, 141; *11:* 54; *30:* 137, 142, 143,144
Leister, Bryan *89:* 45; *106:* 37; *114:* 67; *149:* 236; *222:* 181
Leloir, Maurice *18:* 77, 80, 83, 99
Lemaître, Pascal *144:* 175; *176:* 130; *189:* 135
Lemieux, Michele *100:* 148; *139:* 153
Lemke, Horst *14:* 98; *38:* 117, 118, 119
Lemke, R.W. *42:* 162
Lemon, David Gwynne *9:* 1
LeMoult, Adolph *82:* 116
Lenn, Michael *136:* 89
Lennon, John *114:* 100
Lennox, Elsie *95:* 163; *143:* 160
Lenski, Lois *1:* 144; *26:* 135, 137, 139, 141; *100:* 153, 154
Lent, Blair *1:* 116, 117; *2:* 174; *3:* 206, 207; *7:* 168, 169; *34:* 62; *68:* 217; *133:* 101; *183:* 60
Leonard, David *212:* 149
Leonard, Richard *91:* 128
Leonard, Tom *207:* 95; *219:* 55
Leone, Leonard *49:* 190
Lerner, Carol *86:* 140, 141, 142
Lerner, Judith *116:* 138
Lerner, Sharon *11:* 157; *22:* 56
Leroux-Hugon, Helene *132:* 139
Leslie, Cecil *19:* 244
Lessac, Frané *80:* 182, 207; *96:* 182; *202:* 58; *209:* 104
Lessing, Erich *167:* 52; *173:* 60
Lester, Alison *50:* 124; *90:* 147, 148; *129:* 130; *218:* 91, 93
Lester, Mike *208:* 50
Lethcoe, Jason *191:* 116, 117
Le Tord, Bijou *49:* 156; *95:* 112
Leutz, Emanuel *165:* 27
Levai, Blaise *39:* 130
Levert, Mireille *211:* 101
Levin, Ted *12:* 148
Levine, David *43:* 147, 149, 150, 151, 152; *64:* 11
Levine, Joe *71:* 88; *219:* 74
Levine, Marge *81:* 127
Levinson, David *178:* 232
Levit, Herschel *24:* 223
Levstek, Ljuba *131:* 192; *134:* 216; *149:* 65; *168:* 180
Levy, Jessica Ann *19:* 225; *39:* 191
Levy, Lina *117:* 126
Lewin, Betsy *32:* 114; *48:* 177; *90:* 151; *91:* 125; *92:* 85; *115:* 105; *169:* 110, 111; *178:* 47; *186:* 188; *194:* 201; *222:* 120
Lewin, Ted *4:* 77; *8:* 168; *20:* 110; *21:* 99,100; *27:* 110; *28:* 96, 97; *31:* 49; *45:* 55; *48:* 223; *60:* 20, 119, 120; *62:* 139; *66:* 108; *71:* 12; *72:* 21; *74:* 226; *76:* 139, 140; *77:* 82; *79:* 87; *85:* 49, 177; *86:* 55; *88:* 182; *93:* 28, 29; *94:* 34, 182, 194; *99:* 156; *104:* 8; *115:* 123; *118:* 74; *119:* 114, 116; *131:* 54; *145:* 99; *165:* 151; *177:* 75; *178:* 42; *190:* 30; *192:* 86; *195:* 101, 102; *203:* 52; *222:* 119
Lewis, Allen *15:* 112
Lewis, E.B. *88:* 143; *93:* 109; *119:* 79; *124:* 113; *128:* 49; *151:* 167; *168:* 110; *173:* 121; *174:* 66; *176:* 7; *184:* 150; *185:* 191; *211:* 108, 109, 110, 111; *223:* 17
Lewis, H.B. *170:* 124
Lewis, J. Patrick *162:* 83

Lewis, Jan *81:* 22
Lewis, Kim *136:* 165; *217:* 109, 111
Lewis, Richard W. *52:* 25
Lewis, Robin Baird *98:* 193
Leydon, Rita Floden *21:* 101
Li, Xiojun *187:* 172
Liao, Jimmy *202:* 100
Lichtenheld, Tom *152:* 125, 126; *222:* 160
Lieblich, Irene *22:* 173; *27:* 209, 214
Lieder, Rick *108:* 197; *199:* 58, 59, 60
Lies, Brian *92:* 40; *141:* 101; *150:* 138; *190:* 97, 98, 99,
Liese, Charles *4:* 222
Liew, Sonny *219:* 108
Life, Kay *79:* 49
Lifton, Robert Jay *66:* 154
Lightburn, Ron *86:* 153; *91:* 122
Lightfoot, Norman R. *45:* 47
Lignell, Lois *37:* 114
Lill, Debra *112:* 70
Lilly, Charles *8:* 73; *20:* 127; *48:* 53; *72:* 9,16; *77:* 98; *102:* 94
Lilly, Ken *37:* 224
Lim, John *43:* 153
Limona, Mercedes *51:* 183
Lin, Grace *143:* 217; *162:* 86, 87; *174:* 185
Lincoln, Patricia Henderson *27:* 27; *78:* 127
Lindahn, Ron *84:* 17
Lindahn, Val *84:* 17
Lindberg, Howard *10:* 123; *16:* 190
Lindberg, Jeffrey *64:* 77; *77:* 71; *79:* 54; *80:* 149; *174:* 109; *179:* 52
Linden, Seymour *18:* 200, 201; *43:* 140
Lindenbaum, Pija *144:* 143; *183:* 113
Linder, Richard *27:* 119
Lindman, Maj *43:* 154
Lindsay, Norman *67:* 114
Lindsay, Vachel *40:* 118
Lindstrom, Jack *145:* 118
Line, Les *27:* 143
Linell
   See Smith, Linell
Lionni, Leo *8:* 115; *72:* 159, 160, 161
Lipinsky, Lino *2:* 156; *22:* 175
Lippincott, Gary A. *70:* 35; *119:* 118; *220:* 105, 106, 107
Lippman, Peter *8:* 31; *31:* 119, 120, 160
Lisi, Victoria *89:* 145
Lisker, Emily *169:* 114
Lisker, Sonia O. *16:* 274; *31:* 31; *44:* 113, 114
Lisowski, Gabriel *47:* 144; *49:* 157
Lissim, Simon *17:* 138
Little, Ed *89:* 145; *151:* 53
Little, Harold *16:* 72
Little, Mary E. *28:* 146
Littlewood, Karen *165:* 126; *211:* 112
Litty, Julie *111:* 63
Litzinger, Rosanne *151:* 101; *176:* 118; *196:* 133, 134, 135; *208:* 129; *209:* 147
Liu, Lesley *143:* 72
Lively, Lorna *19:* 216
Livingston, Susan *95:* 22
Liwska, Renata *164:* 113; *199:* 25, 69; *220:* 79
Ljungkvist, Laura *180:* 120
Llerena, Carlos Antonio *19:* 181
Lloyd, Errol *11:* 39; *22:* 178
Lloyd, Megan *77:* 118; *80:* 113; *97:* 75; *117:* 94, 95; *189:* 121, 122; *208:* 128; *211:* 72
Lloyd, Sam *183:* 116, 117
Lo, Beth *165:* 154
Lo, Koon-chiu *7:* 134
Loates, Glen *63:* 76
Lobel, Anita *6:* 87; *9:* 141; *18:* 248; *55:* 85,86, 87, 88, 93, 104; *60:* 67; *78:* 263; *82:* 110; *96:* 157, 159; *101:* 84; *132:* 35; *162:* 93, 94
Lobel, Arnold *1:* 188, 189; *5:* 12; *6:* 147; *7:* 167, 209; *18:* 190, 191; *25:* 39, 43; *27:* 40; *29:* 174; *52:* 127; *55:* 89, 91, 94, 95, 97, 98, 99, 100, 101, 102,103, 105, 107, 108; *60:* 18, 31; *66:* 181, 183; *75:* 57; *82:* 246; *136:* 146
Lobel, Gillian *190:* 21

Locker, Thomas *109:* 134
Lodge, Bernard *107:* 125, 126; *153:* 93
Loeb, Jeph *153:* 177
Lodge, Jo *112:* 119
Loefgren, Ulf *3:* 108
Loescher, Ann *20:* 108
Loescher, Gil *20:* 108
Loew, David *93:* 184; *171:* 120; *211:* 187
Lofting, Hugh *15:* 182, 183; *100:* 161, 162
Lofts, Pamela *60:* 188
Loh, George *38:* 88
Lomberg, Jon *58:* 160
Lonette, Reisie *11:* 211; *12:* 168; *13:* 56; *36:* 122; *43:* 155
Long, Ethan *168:* 146; *178:* 12; *182:* 120, 121; *196:* 124; *223:* 116, 117
Long, Laurel *162:* 135; *190:* 11; *203:* 113, 114
Long, Loren *99:* 176; *172:* 65; *182:* 78; *188:* 114, 115
Long, Melinda *152:* 128
Long, Miles *115:* 174
Long, Sally *42:* 184
Long, Sylvia *74:* 168; *132:* 63; *179:* 134
Longoni, Eduardo *73:* 85
Longtemps, Ken *17:* 123; *29:* 221; *69:* 82
Looser, Heinz *YABC 2:* 208
Lopez, Loretta *190:* 100
López, Rafael *197:* 160; *198:* 85
Lopshire, Robert *6:* 149; *21:* 117; *34:* 166; *73:* 13
Lord, John Vernon *21:* 104; *23:* 25; *51:* 22
Lorenz, Albert *40:* 146; *115:* 127
Loretta, Sister Mary *33:* 73
Lorraine, Walter H. *3:* 110; *4:* 123; *16:* 192; *103:* 119
Los, Marek *146:* 22; *193:* 23
Loss, Joan *11:* 163
Louderback, Walt *YABC 1:* 164
Loughridge, Stuart *214:* 131
Louis, Catherine *212:* 186
Lousada, Sandra *40:* 138
Louth, Jack *149:* 252; *151:* 191, 192
Love, Judy *173:* 43; *196:* 40
Lovelock, Brian *214:* 132, 197
Low, Joseph *14:* 124, 125; *18:* 68; *19:* 194; *31:* 166; *80:* 239
Low, William *62:* 175; *80:* 147; *112:* 194; *150:* 202; *169:* 175; *177:* 110; *192:* 27
Lowe, Vicky *177:* 130
Lowenheim, Alfred *13:* 65, 66
Lowenstein, Sallie *116:* 90, 91
Lowitz, Anson *17:* 124; *18:* 215
Lowrey, Jo *8:* 133
Lubach, Vanessa *142:* 152
Lubell, Winifred *1:* 207; *3:* 15; *6:* 151
Lubin, Leonard B. *19:* 224; *36:* 79, 80; *45:* 128, 129,131, 132, 133, 134, 135, 136, 137, 139, 140, 141; *70:* 95; *YABC2:* 96
Lucas, David *208:* 148
Lucht, Irmgard *82:* 145
Ludwig, Helen *33:* 144, 145
Luebs, Robin *212:* 109
Lufkin, Raymond *38:* 138; *44:* 48
Luhrs, Henry *7:* 123; *11:* 120
Lujan, Tonita *82:* 33
Lupo, Dom *4:* 204
Lustig, Loretta *30:* 186; *46:* 134, 135, 136, 137
Lutes, Jason *210:* 163
Luthardt, Kevin *172:* 125, 126; *217:* 2
Luxbacher, Irene *153:* 145; *219:* 112, 113
Luzak, Dennis *52:* 121; *99:* 142
Lydbury, Jane *82:* 98
Lydecker, Laura *21:* 113; *42:* 53
Lynch, Charles *16:* 33
Lynch, Marietta *29:* 137; *30:* 171
Lynch, P.J. *126:* 228; *129:* 110; *132:* 247; *183:* 64; *207:* 184; *213:* 100, 101, 102
Lyne, Alison Davis *188:* 118, 198
Lyon, Carol *102:* 26
Lyon, Elinor *6:* 154

Lyon, Fred *14:* 16
Lyon, Lea *212:* 110
Lyon, Tammie *175:* 170
Lyons, Oren *8:* 193
Lyster, Michael *26:* 41

M

Maas, Dorothy *6:* 175
Maas, Julie *47:* 61
Macaulay, David *46:* 139, 140, 141, 142, 143, 144, 145, 147, 149, 150; *72:* 167, 168, 169; *137:* 129, 130, 131, 132
MacCarthy, Patricia *69:* 141
Macdonald, Alister *21:* 55
Macdonald, Roberta *19:* 237; *52:* 164
MacDonald, Norman *13:* 99
MacDonald, Ross *201:* 103
MacDonald, Suse *54:* 41; *109* 138; *130:* 156; *193:* 106, 107, 109, 110
Mace, Varian *49:* 159
MacEachern, Stephen *206:* 2
Macguire, Robert Reid *18:* 67
Machetanz, Fredrick *34:* 147, 148
MacInnes, Ian *35:* 59
MacIntyre, Elisabeth *17:* 127, 128
Mack, Jeff *161:* 128; *194:* 119, 120; *219:* 67
Mack, Stan *17:* 129; *96:* 33
Mackay, Donald *17:* 60
MacKaye, Arvia *32:* 119
Mackenzie, Robert *204:* 78
Mackenzie, Stuart *73:* 213
MacKenzie, Garry *33:* 159
Mackie, Clare *87:* 134
Mackinlay, Miguel *27:* 22
MacKinstry, Elizabeth *15:* 110; *42:* 139, 140, 141, 142, 143,144, 145
MacLeod, Lee *91:* 167
Maclise, Daniel *YABC 2:* 257
Macnaughton, Tina *182:* 145; *218:* 106, 107
MacRae, Tom *181:* 112
Madden, Don *3:* 112, 113; *4:* 33, 108, 155; *7:* 193; *78:* 12; *YABC 2:* 211
Maddison, Angela Mary *10:* 83
Madsen, Jim *146:* 259; *152:* 237; *184:* 106; *197:* 21; *202:* 103, 104
Maestro, Giulio *8:* 124; *12:* 17; *13:* 108; *25:* 182; *54:* 147; *59:* 114, 115, 116, 117, 118, 121, 123, 124, 125,126, 127; *68:* 37, 38; *106:* 129, 130, 131, 136, 137, 138
Maffia, Daniel *60:* 200
Maggio, Viqui *58:* 136, 181; *74:* 150; *75:* 90; *85:* 159; *90:* 158; *109:* 184; *193:* 113
Magnus, Erica *77:* 123
Magnuson, Diana *28:* 102; *34:* 190; *41:* 175
Magoon, Scott *181:* 104; *217:* 165; *222:* 126
Magovern, Peg *103:* 123; *218:* 164
Maguire, Sheila *41:* 100
Magurn, Susan *91:* 30
Mahony, Will *37:* 120
Mahony, Will *85:* 116
Mahood, Kenneth *24:* 141
Mahurin, Matt *164:* 225; *175:* 95; *189:* 37; *196:* 14; *209:* 163
Maik, Henri *9:* 102
Maione, Heather *106:* 5; *178:* 8; *189:* 126, 127; *193:* 58
Maisto, Carol *29:* 87
Maitland, Antony *1:* 100, 176; *8:* 41; *17:* 246; *24:* 46; *25:* 177, 178; *32:* 74; *60:* 65, 195; *67:* 156; *87:* 131; *101:* 110
Majewski, Dawn W. *169:* 95
Mak, Kam *72:* 25; *75:* 43; *87:* 186; *97:* 24; *102:* 154; *149:* 195; *186:* 28; *209:* 132
Makie, Pam *37:* 117
Maktima, Joe *116:* 191
Maland, Nick *99:* 77
Male, Alan *132:* 64
Malone, James Hiram *84:* 161

Malone, Nola Langner *82:* 239
Malone, Peter *191:* 121, 122, 123
Malsberg, Edward *51:* 175
Malvern, Corinne *2:* 13; *34:* 148, 149
Manchess, Gregory *165:* 241; *203:* 119
Mancusi, Stephen *63:* 198, 199
Mandelbaum, Ira *31:* 115
Manders, John *138:* 152, 155; *188:* 171; *190:* 92; *199:* 5; *217:* 52; *219:* 35; *219:* 115, 116, 117
Manet, Edouard *23:* 170
Mangiat, Jeff *173:* 127
Mangurian, David *14:* 133
Manham, Allan *42:* 109; *77:* 180; *80:* 227
Manley, Matt *103:* 167; *117:* 98; *172:* 49; *212:* 207
Manna, Giovanni *178:* 44
Manniche, Lise *31:* 121
Manning, Jane *96:* 203
Manning, Jo *63:* 154
Manning, Lawrence *191:* 153
Manning, Maurie J. *211:* 116
Manning, Mick *176:* 139
Manning, Samuel F. *5:* 75
Mantel, Richard *57:* 73; *63:* 106; *82:* 255
Mantha, John *205:* 164; *217:* 117
Maraja *15:* 86; *YABC 1:* 28; *2:* 115
Marcellino, Fred *20:* 125; *34:* 222; *53:* 125; *58:* 205; *61:* 64, 121, 122; *68:* 154, 156, 157, 158, 159; *72:* 25; *86:* 184; *98:* 181; *118:* 129, 130, 131; *149:* 218; *194:* 7
Marchesi, Stephen *34:* 140; *46:* 72; *50:* 147; *66:* 239; *70:* 33; *73:* 18, 114, 163; *77:* 47, 76,147; *78:* 79; *80:* 30; *81:* 6; *89:* 66; *93:* 21,130; *94:* 94; *97:* 66; *98:* 96; *114:* 115, 116
Marchiori, Carlos *14:* 60
Marciano, John Bemelmans *118:* 133; *167:* 110, 111, 112
Marconi, Guilherme *220:* 143
Marcus, Barry David *139:* 248; *145:* 18
Maren, Julie *199:* 73
Margules, Gabriele *21:* 120
Mariana
    See Foster, Marian Curtis
Mariano, Michael *52:* 108
Marino, Dorothy *6:* 37; *14:* 135
Mario, Heide Stetson *101:* 202
Maris, Ron *71:* 123
Maritz, Nicolaas *85:* 123
Mark, Mona *65:* 105; *68:* 205; *116:* 213
Markham, R.L. *17:* 240
Marklew, Gilly *211:* 118
Marks, Alan *104:* 104; *109:* 182; *164:* 92; *185:* 134; *187:* 120, 121, 122; *218:* 114, 115
Marks, Cara *54:* 9
Marks, Colin *203:* 129
Marokvia, Artur *31:* 122
Marquez, Susan *108:* 121; *219:* 95
Marrella, Maria Pia *62:* 116
Marriott, Pat *30:* 30; *34:* 39; *35:* 164, 165, 166; *44:* 170; *48:* 186, 187, 188, 189, 191, 192, 193; *91:* 92
Mars, W.T. *1:* 161; *3:* 115; *4:* 208, 225; *5:* 92, 105, 186; *8:* 214; *9:* 12; *13:* 121; *27:* 151; *31:* 180; *38:* 102; *48:* 66; *62:* 164, 165; *64:* 62; *68:* 229; *79:* 55
Marschall, Ken *85:* 29
Marsh, Christine *3:* 164
Marsh, James *73:* 137
Marsh, Reginald *17:* 5; *19:* 89; *22:* 90, 96
Marshall, Anthony D. *18:* 216
Marshall, Felicia *170:* 190
Marshall, James *6:* 160; *40:* 221; *42:* 24, 25, 29; *51:* 111, 112, 113, 114, 115, 116, 117, 118, 119, 120, 121; *64:* 13; *75:* 126, 127, 128, 129; *102:* 10, 12; *216:* 26, 28
Marshall, Janet *97:* 154
Marstall, Bob *55:* 145; *84:* 153, 170; *104:* 145; *154:* 166, 167, 168

Martchenko, Michael *50:* 129, 153, 155, 156, 157; *83:* 144,145; *154:* 137, 138, 139
Marten, Ruth *129:* 52
Martin, Brad *199:* 186
Martin, Charles E. *70:* 144
Martin, Courtney A. *214:* 28
Martin, David Stone *24:* 232; *62:* 4
Martin, Fletcher *18:* 213; *23:* 151
Martin, Rene *7:* 144; *42:* 148, 149, 150
Martin, Richard E. *51:* 157; *131:* 203
Martin, Ron *32:* 81
Martin, Stefan *8:* 68; *32:* 124, 126; *56:* 33
Martin, Whitney *166:* 137
Martinez, Ed *58:* 192; *72:* 231; *77:* 33; *80:* 214; *167:* 123
Martinez, John *6:* 113; *118:* 13; *139:* 143
Martinez, Sergio *158:* 190; *220:* 156
Martini, Angela *183:* 161
Martiniere, Stephan *171:* 130
Marton, Jirina *95:* 127, 128; *144:* 145
Martorell, Antonio *84:* 6; *97:* 161
Martucci, Griesbach *52:* 106
Marvin, Frederic *83:* 86
Marx, Robert F. *24:* 143
Marzollo, Jean *190:* 127
Masefield, Judith *19:* 208, 209
Masheris, Robert *78:* 51
Masiello, Ralph *186:* 171; *214:* 134
Mason, George F. *14:* 139
Mason, Robert *84:* 96
Masse, Josée *208:* 45; *217:* 19; *221:* 134
Massey, Barbara *68:* 142
Massie, Diane Redfield *16:* 194
Massie, Kim *31:* 43
Massini, Sarah *213:* 79
Mataya, David *121:* 66
Mathers, Petra *119:* 135; *163:* 104; *176:* 143, 144; *187:* 142; *196:* 101
Mathewuse, James *51:* 143
Mathieu, Joseph *14:* 33; *39:* 206; *43:* 167; *56:* 180; *79:* 126; *94:* 147; *185:* 140
Matje, Martin *169:* 177, 178; *172:* 180
Matsubara, Naoko *12:* 121
Matsuda, Shizu *13:* 167
Matsuoka, Mei *192:* 135; *214:* 84
Matte, L'Enc *22:* 183
Mattelson, Marvin *36:* 50, 51
Mattheson, Jenny *180:* 132; *222:* 153
Matthews, Elizabeth *194:* 128; *223:* 35
Matthews, F. Leslie *4:* 216
Matthews, Tina *190:* 130
Mattingly, David *71:* 76, 77; *82:* 64; *91:* 216, 217; *109:* 25
Matulay, Laszlo *5:* 18; *43:* 168
Matus, Greta *12:* 142
Maughan, Bill *181:* 31; *211:* 211
Mauldin, Bill *27:* 23
Mauterer, Erin Marie *119:* 5
Mawicke, Tran *9:* 137; *15:* 191; *47:* 100
Mawson, Matt *74:* 115
Max, Peter *45:* 146, 147, 148, 149, 150
Maxie, Betty *40:* 135
Maxwell, John Alan *1:* 148
May, Steve *204:* 30
Mayan, Earl *7:* 193
Maydak, Michael S. *220:* 117
Mayer, Bill *200:* 138
Mayer, Danuta *117:* 103
Mayer, Marianna *32:* 132
Mayer, Mercer *11:* 192; *16:* 195, 196; *20:* 55, 57; *32:* 129, 130, 132, 133, 134; *41:* 144, 248, 252; *58:* 186; *73:* 140, 142, 143; *137:* 137, 138
Mayforth, Hal *166:* 77
Mayhew, James *85:* 121; *138:* 187; *149:* 140; *204:* 81
Mayhew, Richard *3:* 106
Mayo, Gretchen Will *38:* 81; *84:* 166
Mays, Victor *5:* 127; *8:* 45, 153; *14:* 245; *23:* 50; *34:* 155; *40:* 79; *45:* 158; *54:* 91; *66:* 240

Mazal, Chanan *49:* 104
Maze, Deborah *71:* 83
Mazellan, Ron *75:* 97, 98; *210:* 169
Mazetti, Alan *112:* 72
Mazille, Capucine *96:* 168
Mazza, Adriana Saviozzi *19:* 215
Mazzella, Mary Jo *82:* 165
Mazzetti, Alan *45:* 210
McAfee, Steve *135:* 146; *167:* 176; *191:* 84; *210:* 117; *218:* 34
McAlinden, Paul *112:* 128
McBride, Angus *28:* 49; *103:* 40
McBride, Will *30:* 110
McCaffery, Janet *38:* 145
McCall, Bruce *209:* 119
McCallum, Graham *78:* 78
McCallum, Stephen *141:* 143; *156:* 5; *166:* 228
McCann, Gerald *3:* 50; *4:* 94; *7:* 54; *41:* 121
McCarthy, Dan *174:* 74
McCarthy, Linda *177:* 128; *218:* 104
McCarthy, Meghan *168:* 134; *199:* 74
McCauley, Adam *157:* 36; *184:* 199; *193:* 100; *209:* 122
McCay, Winsor *41:* 124, 126, 128, 129, 130, 131; *134:* 77, 79
McClary, Nelson *1:* 111
McClements, George *196:* 146
McClennan, Connie *210:* 181
McClintock, Barbara *57:* 135; *95:* 130; *146:* 190; *213:* 3, 5, 107, 108
McClintock, Theodore *14:* 141
McCloskey, Robert *1:* 184, 185; *2:* 186, 187; *17:* 209; *39:* 139, 140, 141, 142, 143, 146, 147, 148; *85:* 150, 151; *100:* 172, 173, 174
McClung, Robert *2:* 189; *68:* 166, 167
McClure, Gillian *31:* 132; *150:* 53
McClure, Nikki *218:* 120
McConnel, Jerry *31:* 75, 187
McConnell, Mary *102:* 49
McCord, Kathleen Garry *78:* 236
McCormack, John *66:* 193
McCormick, A.D. *35:* 119
McCormick, Dell J. *19:* 216
McCoy, Glenn *212:* 132
McCrady, Lady *16:* 198; *39:* 127
McCrea, James *3:* 122; *33:* 216
McCrea, Ruth *3:* 122; *27:* 102; *33:* 216
McCue, Lisa *65:* 148, 149; *77:* 54; *80:* 132; *175:* 33; *177:* 133, 135; *212:* 136, 137, 138
McCully, Emily Arnold *2:* 89; *4:* 120, 121, 146, 197; *5:* 2, 129; *7:* 191; *11:* 122; *15:* 210; *33:* 23; *35:* 244; *37:* 122; *39:* 88; *40:* 103; *50:* 30,31, 32, 33, 34, 35, 36, 37; *52:* 89, 90; *57:* 6; *62:* 3; *70:* 195; *86:* 82; *96:* 192; *97:* 93; *110:* 143,144; *117:* 47; *167:* 96; *210:* 175, 176
McCurdy, Michael *13:* 153; *24:* 85; *81:* 160; *82:* 157, 158; *86:* 125; *97:* 92; *117:* 178; *132:* 6; *147:* 159, 160
McCusker, Paul *99:* 19
McDaniel, Jerry *132:* 135
McDaniel, Preston *160:* 206; *170:* 139
McDermott, Beverly Brodsky *11:* 180
McDermott, Gerald *16:* 201; *74:* 174, 175; *163:* 150, 151
McDermott, Mike *96:* 187
McDonald, Jill *13:* 155; *26:* 128
McDonald, Mercedes *169:* 118
McDonald, Ralph J. *5:* 123, 195
McDonnell, Flora *146:* 199, 200
McDonnell, Patrick *179:* 153, 154; *221:* 136, 137, 138
McDonough, Don *10:* 163
McElligott, Matt *196:* 147
McElmurry, Jill *137:* 148; *163:* 141; *202:* 186
McElrath-Eslick, Lori *129:* 145; *142:* 21; *173:* 123; *202:* 194; *204:* 88, 89
McEntee, Dorothy *37:* 124
McEwan, Keith *88:* 116; *165:* 122, 123
McEwen, Katharine *169:* 34

McFall, Christie *12:* 144
McFeely, Daniel *160:* 213
McGaw, Laurie *109:* 243; *143:* 216; *211:* 218
McGee, Barbara *6:* 165
McGee, Marni *163:* 153
McGillvray, Kim *158:* 171; *165:* 213; *186:* 183; *190:* 175
McGinley-Nally, Sharon *131:* 19
McGinnis, Robert *110:* 113; *177:* 80
McGovern, Tara *98:* 171
McGraw, Sheila *83:* 146
McGregor, Barbara *200:* 155
McGregor, Malcolm *23:* 27
McGrory, Anik *193:* 120
McGuire, Robert *204:* 57; *209:* 86
McGuirk, Leslie *152:* 159
McHale, John *138:* 190
McHenry, E.B. *193:* 122
McHugh, Tom *23:* 64
McIntosh, Jon *42:* 56
McKay, Donald *2:* 118; *32:* 157; *45:* 151, 152
McKean, Dave *150:* 71; *174:* 156; *197:* 83, 118
McKeating, Eileen *44:* 58
McKee, David *10:* 48; *21:* 9; *70:* 154, 155; *107:* 139, 140, 141; *134:* 218; *158:* 148, 149, 150, 151
McKee, Diana *109:* 185
McKelvey, Patrick *164:* 141
McKendry, Joe *170:* 136
McKeveny, Tom *164:* 60; *173:* 79
McKie, Roy *7:* 44
McKie, Todd *205:* 181
McKillip, Kathy *30:* 153
McKinney, Ena *26:* 39
McKinnon, James *136:* 75
McKowen, Scott *172:* 63; *202:* 49
McLachlan, Edward *5:* 89
McLaren, Chesley *133:* 53; *213:* 112; *219:* 31
McLaren, Kirsty *123:* 99; *124:* 226
Mclean, Andrew *113:* 117, 118, 120, 121; *172:* 130, 131
Mclean, Janet *172:* 130
McLean, Meg *94:* 196
McLean, Sammis *32:* 197
McLean, Wilson *29:* 30; *113:* 195
McLoughlin, John C. *47:* 149
McLoughlin, Wayne *102:* 230; *134:* 178; *216:* 196
McMahon, Robert *36:* 155; *69:* 169
McManus, Shawn *85:* 71
McMenemy, Sarah *156:* 139 ; *211:* 93
McMillan, Bruce *22:* 184
McMullan, James *40:* 33; *67:* 172; *87:* 142; *99:* 63, 64; *189:* 133; *196:* 51
McMullen, Nigel *147:* 177
McNeely, Tom *162:* 55
McNaught, Harry *12:* 80; *32:* 136
McNaughton, Colin *39:* 149; *40:* 108; *92:* 144, 145, 146; *134:* 104, 106; *211:* 122, 123, 124
McNicholas, Maureen *38:* 148
McNicholas, Shelagh *173:* 61; *191:* 125, 126
McPhail, David *14:* 105; *23:* 135; *37:* 217, 218, 220,221; *47:* 151, 152, 153, 154, 155, 156, 158, 159, 160, 162, 163, 164; *71:* 211; *81:* 139, 140, 142; *86:* 123; *132:* 150; *140:* 129, 131, 132; *183:* 134, 135, 137; *189:* 132; *219:* 121, 122, 123, 124, 125
McPhee, Richard B. *41:* 133
McPheeters, Neal *78:* 132; *86:* 90; *99:* 162; *111:* 141; *142:* 162
McQuade, Jacqueline *124:* 223
McQueen, Lucinda *28:* 149; *41:* 249; *46:* 206; *53:* 103
McQuillan, Mary *153:* 97; *200:* 140
McVay, Tracy *11:* 68
McVicker, Charles *39:* 150
McWilliam, Howard *219:* 135
Mead, Ben Carlton *43:* 75
Meade, Holly *90:* 102; *94:* 101; *149:* 8; *151:* 107

Mecray, John *33:* 62
Meddaugh, Susan *20:* 42; *29:* 143; *41:* 241;
  77: 50; *84:* 173, 174, 175, 176, 177, 178;
  125: 160, 161, 162; *176:* 148, 149, 150, 151
Meehan, Dennis B. *56:* 144
Meents, Len W. *73:* 147, 150
Meers, Tony *99:* 113
Meisel, Paul *98:* 137; *124:* 18; *162:* 180; *179:*
  16; *181:* 62; *194:* 154; *221:* 5
Melanson, Luc *149:* 229; *198:* 97, 98; *221:*
  166
Melendez, Francisco *72:* 180
Melling, David *202:* 199
Melnychuk, Monika *153:* 65
Melo, Esperança *196:* 90
Melo, John *16:* 285; *58:* 203
Meloni, Maria Teresa *98:* 62
Meltzer, Ericka
  See O'Rourke, Ericka
Menasco, Milton *43:* 85
Menchin, Scott *188:* 129
Mendelson, Steven T. *86:* 154
Mendelssohn, Felix *19:* 170
Mendola, Christopher *88:* 223
Meng, Heinz *13:* 158
Merian, Maria Sibylla *140:* 88
Mero, Lee *34:* 68
Merrell, David *205:* 3
Merrill, Frank T. *16:* 147; *19:* 71; *YABC 1:*
  226, 229,273
Merriman, Rachel *98:* 108; *114:* 122; *149:* 142
Merveille, David *200:* 142
Meryman, Hope *27:* 41
Meryweather, Jack *10:* 179
Meseldzija, Petar *168:* 97
Meserve, Jessica *184:* 137; *211:* 127
Messick, Dale *64:* 150, 151, 152
Meth, Harold *24:* 203
Meyer, Herbert *19:* 189
Meyer, Renate *6:* 170
Meyers, Bob *11:* 136
Meyers, Nancy *172:* 124
Meynell, Louis *37:* 76
Micale, Albert *2:* 65; *22:* 185
Miccuci, Charles *82:* 163; *144:* 150
Micich, Paul *164:* 163
Middleton, Jeffrey *177:* 173; *222:* 157
Middleton, Joshua *208:* 146; *219:* 24
Middleton-Sandford, Betty *2:* 125
Mieke, Anne *45:* 74
Mighell, Patricia *43:* 134
Miglio, Paige *101:* 203; *151:* 223; *201:* 118,
  119; *204:* 162
Mikec, Larry *204:* 125
Mikolaycak, Charles *9:* 144; *12:* 101; *13:* 212;
  21: 121; *22:* 168; *30:* 187; *34:* 103, 150; *37:*
  183; *43:* 179; *44:* 90; *46:* 115, 118, 119; *49:*
  25; *78:* 121, 122, 205, 207; *81:* 4
Milelli, Pascal *129:* 66; *135:* 153; *187:* 45
Miles, Elizabeth *117:* 77
Miles, Jennifer *17:* 278
Milgrim, David *158:* 157; *187:* 125, 126, 128;
  223: 124, 125, 126, 127
Milhous, Katherine *15:* 193; *17:* 51
Millais, John E. *22:* 230, 231
Millar, H.R. *YABC 1:* 194, 195, 203
Millard, C.E. *28:* 186
Millard, Kerry *105:* 124; *204:* 93, 94
Miller, Don *15:* 195; *16:* 71; *20:* 106; *31:* 178
Miller, Edna *29:* 148
Miller, Edward *115:* 64; *183:* 140, 141; *218:*
  129, 130, 131
Miller, Frank J. *25:* 94
Miller, Grambs *18:* 38; *23:* 16
Miller, Ian *99:* 128
Miller, Jane *15:* 196
Miller, Marcia *13:* 233
Miller, Marilyn *1:* 87; *31:* 69; *33:* 157
Miller, Mitchell *28:* 183; *34:* 207
Miller, Phil *175:* 150
Miller, Shane *5:* 140

Miller, Virginia *81:* 206
Millman, Isaac *172:* 18
Mills, Elaine *72:* 181
Mills, Judith Christine *130:* 168, 169
Mills, Lauren *92:* 170
Mills, Yaroslava Surmach *35:* 169, 170; *46:*
  114
Millsap, Darrel *51:* 102
Milone, Karen *89:* 169; *222:* 149
Milord, Susan *147:* 163, 164; *200:* 144
Milton, Debbie *162:* 161
Mims, Ashley *170:* 51
Min, Willemien *222:* 62
Miner, Julia *98:* 69
Minor, Wendell *39:* 188; *52:* 87; *56:* 171; *58:*
  116; *62:* 56; *66:* 109; *74:* 93; *78:* 129; *94:*
  67; *117:* 12, 13; *124:* 84, 86; *136:* 121; *164:*
  168, 169; *170:* 71; *199:* 79, 80, 81, 82; *217:*
  63; *223:* 149
Minter, Daniel *176:* 154; *179:* 177
Mirocha, Paul *81:* 133; *192:* 148; *194:* 36
Misako Rocks! *192:* 149, 150
Mitchell, Judith *109:* 117
Mitchell, Mark *91:* 208
Mitchell, Tracy *190:* 15
Mitgutsch, Ali *76:* 161
Mitsuhashi, Yoko *45:* 153
Miyake, Yoshi *38:* 141
Mizumura, Kazue *10:* 143; *18:* 223; *36:* 159
Mochi, Ugo *8:* 122; *38:* 150
Mock, Paul *55:* 83; *123:* 32
Modarressi, Mitra *90:* 236; *126:* 168; *173:*
  165, 166; *200:* 147, 148
Modell, Frank *39:* 152
Mogenson, Jan *74:* 183
Mohn, Susan *89:* 224
Mohr, Mark *133:* 201
Mohr, Nicholasa *8:* 139; *113:* 127
Molan, Christine *60:* 177; *84:* 183
Moldon, Peter L. *49:* 168
Molk, Laurel *92:* 150
Mollica, Gene *197:* 11
Momaday, N. Scott *48:* 159
Mombourquette, Paul *112:* 91; *126:* 142
Monk, Julie *165:* 231; *191:* 96
Monks, Lydia *189:* 136, 137
Monroe, Chris *219:* 133
Monroy, Manuel *199:* 192
Montgomery, Lucy *150:* 126
Montgomery, Michael G. *208:* 159
Montgomery-Higham, Amanda *169:* 131
Monteiel, David *201:* 95
Montiel, David *69:* 106; *84:* 145
Montijo, Rhode *193:* 164
Montresor, Beni *2:* 91; *3:* 138; *38:* 152, 153,
  154,155, 156, 157, 158, 159, 160; *68:* 63
Montserrat, Pep *128:* 135; *181:* 119; *184:* 53
Moon, Carl *25:* 183, 184, 185
Moon, Eliza *14:* 40
Moon, Ivan *22:* 39; *38:* 140
Moore, Adrienne *67:* 147
Moore, Agnes Kay Randall *43:* 187
Moore, Cyd *117:* 107, 108; *159:* 137, 138;
  186: 148, 149, 151; *203:* 15; *214:* 138, 139
Moore, Gustav *127:* 181, 182; *170:* 162, 163
Moore, Jackie *128:* 79
Moore, Janet *63:* 153
Moore, Margie *176:* 156; *221:* 125
Moore, Mary *29:* 160
Moore, Patrick *184:* 121
Moore, Yvette *101:* 11, 12; *154:* 141
Mora, Giovanni *179:* 127; *184:* 11
Mora, Raul Mina *20:* 41
Moraes, Odilon *102:* 144
Morales, Yuyi *154:* 144
Moran, Rosslyn *111:* 26
Moran, Tom *60:* 100
Mordan, C.B. *193:* 115
Mordvinoff, Nicolas *15:* 179
Moreno, René King *169:* 59; *190:* 133, 209;
  212: 52

Morgan, Barbara *169:* 116
Morgan, Jacqui *58:* 57
Morgan, Mary *114:* 133, 134, 135; *123:* 11;
  213: 115, 116, 117
Morgan, Tom *42:* 157
Morgan, Pierr *173:* 148
Morgenstern, Michael *158:* 7, 57; *171:* 103;
  174: 60
Morice, Dave *93:* 142
Morin, Paul *73:* 132; *79:* 130; *88:* 140; *137:*
  143
Moriuchi, Mique *177:* 203
Morozumi, Atsuko *110:* 155; *217:* 126, 127
Morrill, Leslie *18:* 218; *29:* 177; *33:* 84; *38:*
  147; *42:* 127; *44:* 93; *48:* 164, 165, 167,
  168, 169, 170,171; *49:* 162; *63:* 136, 180;
  70: 72; *71:* 70, 91,92; *72:* 228; *80:* 163, 164,
  165; *90:* 121; *121:* 88; *178:* 117
Morrill, Rowena A. *84:* 16; *98:* 163
Morris *47:* 91
Morris, Frank *55:* 133; *60:* 28; *76:* 2
Morris, Harry O. *119:* 138
Morris, Jackie *128:* 194; *144:* 119; *151:* 146;
  202: 126, 127; *204:* 83; *211:* 80; *214:* 163
Morris, Jennifer E. *179:* 157
Morris, Oradel Nolen *128:* 180
Morris, Tony *62:* 146; *70:* 97
Morrison, Bill *42:* 116; *66:* 170; *69:* 40
Morrison, Gordon *87:* 150; *113:* 93; *128:* 181,
  182; *183:* 144, 145, 146
Morrison, Frank *162:* 162; *205:* 156
Morrison, Taylor *159:* 144, 145; *187:* 131
Morrow, Gray *2:* 64; *5:* 200; *10:* 103, 114; *14:*
  175
Morse, Scott *200:* 149, 150
Morton, Lee Jack *32:* 140
Morton, Marian *3:* 185
Mosberg, Hilary *117:* 195; *118:* 164; *149:* 55
Moser, Barry *56:* 68, 117, 118, 119, 120, 121,
  122, 123, 124; *59:* 141; *60:* 160; *79:* 91,
  147, 149, 151, 152; *82:* 81; *90:* 118; *91:* 35;
  95: 210; *97:* 91, 93; *102:* 152; *126:* 4; *128:*
  175; *133:* 141; *138:* 167, 171, 174; *153:*
  205; *174:* 130; *185:* 152, 154; *195:* 163;
  204: 115; *209:* 201
Moser, Cara *90:* 118; *138:* 167
Moses, Grandma *18:* 228
Moses, Will *178:* 170, 171
Moskof, Martin Stephen *27:* 152
Mosley, Francis *57:* 144
Moss, Donald *11:* 184
Moss, Geoffrey *32:* 198
Moss, Marissa *71:* 130; *104:* 127; *163:* 156;
  216: 164, 165, 166
Most, Bernard *48:* 173; *91:* 142, 143; *134:* 120
Mourning, Tuesday *205:* 25; *220:* 68; *221:* 42
Mowll, Joshua *188:* 133
Mowry, Carmen *50:* 62
Moxley, Sheila *96:* 174; *169:* 26; *206:* 16
Moyers, William *21:* 65
Moyler, Alan *36:* 142
Mozley, Charles *9:* 87; *20:* 176, 192, 193; *22:*
  228; *25:* 205; *33:* 150; *43:* 170, 171, 172,
  173, 174; *YABC2:* 89
Mueller, Hans Alexander *26:* 64; *27:* 52, 53
Mugnaini, Joseph *11:* 35; *27:* 52, 53; *35:* 62
Mujica, Rick *72:* 67; *88:* 95; *111:* 53; *180:*
  185; *197:* 70
Mullen, Douglas *180:* 178
Muller, Robin *86:* 161
Muller, Steven *32:* 167
Muller, Jorg *35:* 215; *67:* 138, 139
Mulock, Julie *163:* 112
Mullins, Edward S. *10:* 101
Mullins, Patricia *51:* 68
Multer, Scott *80:* 108
Munari, Bruno *15:* 200
Munch, Edvard *140:* 143
Munowitz, Ken *14:* 148; *72:* 178, 179
Muñoz, Claudio *208:* 161
Munoz, William *42:* 160

Munro, Roxie 58: 134; *136:* 177; *137:* 218; *184:* 133, 134; *223:* 130, 132, 133
Munsinger, Lynn 33: 161; *46:* 126; *71:* 92; *82:* 80; *89:* 218; *92:* 125; *94:* 157, 158, 159, 160; *98:* 196; *103:* 198; *142:* 143; *145:* 133, 134, 136; *153:* 203; *176:* 162; *177:* 140, 141, 142; *189:* 113, 114, 116, 117; *201:* 42; *221:* 148, 149,150
Munson, Russell *13:* 9
Munster, Sebastian *166:* 107
Munzar, Barbara *149:* 75
Murdocca, Salvatore 73: 212; *98:* 132; *111:* 168; *157:* 228; *164:* 257
Murphy, Bill 5: 138; *130:* 170
Murphy, Jill 37: 142; *70:* 166; *142:* 132, 134
Murphy, Kelly *130:* 212; *143:* 119; *176:* 158; *190:* 135
Murphy, Liz *210:* 183; *212:* 157
Murphy, Mary *196:* 158
Murphy, Tom *192:* 40
Murr, Karl 20: 62
Murray, Joe *175:* 37
Murray, Ossie *43:* 176
Mussino, Attilio 29: 131; *100:* 164
Mutchler, Dwight *1:* 25
Myers, Bernice 9: 147; *36:* 75; *81:* 146, 147, 148
Muth, Jon J. *165:* 169; *167:* 109; *190:* 227; *193:* 59
Myers, Christopher *183:* 150; *193:* 139
Myers, Duane O. *99:* 145
Myers, Tim *147:* 168
Myers, V.G. *142:* 41
Myers, Lou *11:* 2

N

Nachreiner, Tom *29:* 182
Nacht, Merle 65: 49
Nadler, Ellis 88: 91
Nagle, Shane *180:* 223
Nagy, Ian *195:* 64
Najaka, Marlies 62: 101
Nakai, Michael 30: 217; *54:* 29
Nakata, Hiroe *157:* 156; *162:* 30; *205:* 124, 125
Nakatani, Chiyoko *12:* 124
Narahashi, Keiko 77: 188; *82:* 213; *115:* 142, 143, 144
Nascimbene, Yan *133:* 128; *173:* 132, 133
Nash, Lesa 87: 135
Nash, Linell 46: 175
Nash, Scott *130:* 36; *188:* 196
Naso, John 33: 183
Nason, Thomas W. *14:* 68
Nasser, Muriel 48: 74
Nast, Thomas 21: 29; *28:* 23; *51:* 132, 133, 134, 135,136, 137, 138, 139, 141
Nasta, Vincent 78: 185
Natale, Vincent 76: 3; *78:* 125; *112:* 47; *166:* 81; *174:* 189; *185:* 212; *197:* 59; *218:* 35
Natchev, Alexi 96: 177
Nathan, Charlott *125:* 151
Nathan, Cheryl *150:* 104; *186:* 112
Natti, Susanna 20: 146; *32:* 141, 142; *35:* 178; *37:* 143; *71:* 49; *93:* 98; *125:* 166, 168; *126:* 228; *151:* 6; *178:* 8; *188:* 106
Navarra, Celeste Scala 8: 142
Naylor, Penelope *10:* 104
Nazz, James *72:* 8
Nebel, M. 45: 154
Neebe, William 7: 93
Needham, Dave *196:* 85
Needler, Jerry *12:* 93
Neel, Alice *31:* 23
Neely, Beth *119:* 184
Neely, Keith R. *46:* 124
Neff, Leland 78: 74

Negri, Rocco 3: 213; *5:* 67; *6:* 91, 108; *12:* 159
Negrin, Fabian *174:* 125; *175:* 15; *223:* 91
Neidigh, Sherry *128:* 53; *204:* 101, 102, 103; *222:* 95
Neilan, Eujin Kim *180:* 241; *200:* 151, 152
Neill, John R. *18:* 8, 10, 11, 21, 30; *100:* 22
Neilsen, Cliff *158:* 131; *177:* 112, 121; *209:* 8; *215:* 150
Neilsen, Terese *116:* 74
Nelson, Craig 62: 151; 153; *183:* 86
Nelson, Gail White 68: 140
Nelson, Jennifer *129:* 152; *199:* 132
Nelson, Kadir *151:* 185; *154:* 146, 147; *157:* 189, 222; *181:* 122, 124; *197:* 155; *213:* 122, 123, 124
Nelson, S.D. *131:* 34; *181:* 126, 127
Ness, Evaline 1: 164, 165; *2:* 39; *3:* 8; *10:* 147; *12:* 53; *26:* 150, 151, 152, 153; *49:* 30, 31, 32; *56:* 30; *60:* 113
Neubecker, Robert *170:* 143; *214:* 157
Neville, Vera 2: 182
Nevins, Daniel *191:* 173
Nevwirth, Allan 79: 168
Newberry, Clare Turlay 1: 170
Newbold, Greg *108:* 125; *145:* 199; *151:* 23; *193:* 178; *197:* 10; *199:* 92, 93
Newfeld, Frank *14:* 121; *26:* 154
Newland, Gillian *220:* 132
Newman, Andy 61: 91; *195:* 63
Newman, Ann 43: 90
Newman, Barbara Johansen *191:* 137, 138
Newsham, Ian *143:* 162
Newsom, Carol 40: 159; *44:* 60; *47:* 189; *65:* 29; *70:* 192; *80:* 36; *85:* 137, 138; *92:* 167; *191:* 82
Newsom, Tom 49: 149; *71:* 13, 62; *75:* 156; *91:* 113
Newton, Jill 83: 105; *200:* 154
Nez, John *218:* 136
Ng, Michael 29: 171
Ng, Simon *167:* 7
Nguyen, Vincent *189:* 49
Nichols, Sandy *219:* 103
Nicholson, William 15: 33, 34; *16:* 48
Nickens, Bessie *104:* 153
Nicklaus, Carol 45: 194; *62:* 132, 133
Nickle, John *181:* 128
Nickless, Will *16:* 139
Nicholas, Corasue *154:* 20
Nicolas *17:* 130, 132, 133; *YABC 2:* 215
Niebrugge, Jane 6: 118
Nielsen, Cliff 95: 207, 208; *105:* 58; *114:* 112; *124:* 12; *125:* 91, 92; *132:* 224; *135:* 187; *136:* 40; *137:* 168; *145:* 54; *149:* 28; *158:* 129; *165:* 64, 158; *168:* 169; *170:* 6; *175:* 114, 116; *187:* 75, 76; *194:* 107; *197:* 172; *201:* 14; *208:* 192; *211:* 186; *216:* 215; *217:* 67
Nielsen, Jon 6: 100; *24:* 202
Nielsen, Kay 15: 7; *16:* 211, 212, 213, 215, 217; *22:* 143; *YABC 1:* 32, 33
Niemann, Christoph *191:* 141
Niemann, Christoph *191:* 141
Nikola-Lisa, W. *180:* 180
Niland, Deborah 25: 191; *27:* 156; *135:* 50; *172:* 143
Niland, Kilmeny 25: 191; *75:* 143
Nino, Alex 59: 145
Ninon *1:* 5; *38:* 101, 103, 108
Nissen, Rie 44: 35
Nithael, Mark *158:* 237
Nivola, Claire A. 78: 126; *140:* 147; *208:* 164
Nixon, K. *14:* 152
Nobati, Eugenia *194:* 118
Noble, Louise 61: 170
Noble, Marty 97: 168; *125:* 171
Noble, Trinka Hakes 39: 162; *84:* 157
Noda, Takayo *168:* 143
Noguchi, Yoshie 30: 99

Nolan, Dennis 42: 163; *67:* 163; *78:* 189; *82:* 225; *83:* 26; *92:* 169, 170; *103:* 166; *111:* 35; *112:* 213; *127:* 171; *166:* 161; *194:* 218
Noll, Sally 82: 171
Nolte, Larry *121:* 63, 65
Nones, Eric Jon 61: 111; *76:* 38; *77:* 177
Noonan, Daniel *100:* 224
Noonan, Julia 4: 163; *7:* 207; *25:* 151; *91:* 29; *95:* 149
Norcia, Ernie *108:* 155; *140:* 47
Nordenskjold, Birgitta 2: 208
Noreika, Robert *173:* 20; *217:* 24
Norling, Beth *149:* 153, 154; *209:* 77
Norman, Elaine 77: 72, 176; *94:* 35; *136:* 63; *178:* 42
Norman, Mary 36: 138, 147
Norman, Michael 12: 117; *27:* 168
Northway, Jennifer 85: 96
Nostlinger, Christiana *162:* 131
Novak, Linda *166:* 205
Novak, Matt *104:* 132, 133; *165:* 173, 174; *204:* 104, 106
Novelli, Luca 61: 137
Novgorodoff, Danica *215:* 133
Nugent, Cynthia *106:* 189; *205:* 126, 127; *209:* 180
Numberman, Neil *220:* 133
Numeroff, Laura Joffe 28: 161; *30:* 177
Nurse, Chris *164:* 91
Nussbaumer, Paul *16:* 219; *39:* 117
Nutt, Ken 72: 69; *97:* 170
Nyce, Helene *19:* 219
Nygren, Tord 30: 148; *127:* 164

O

Oakley, Graham 8: 112; *30:* 164, 165; *84:* 188,189, 190, 191, 192
Oakley, Thornton *YABC 2:* 189
Oberheide, Heide *118:* 37
Obligado, Lilian 2: 28, 66, 67; *6:* 30; *14:* 179; *15:* 103; *25:* 84; *61:* 138, 139, 140, 141, 143
Oblinski, Rafael *190:* 139
Obrant, Susan *11:* 186
O'Brien, Anne Sibley 53: 116, 117; *155:* 115; *213:* 127
O'Brien, John 41: 253; *72:* 12; *89:* 59, 60; *98:* 16; *161:* 185; *169:* 16; *180:* 196
O'Brien, Patrick *193:* 142, 143, 144
O'Brien, Teresa 87: 89
O'Brien, Tim 93: 25; *136:* 94; *164:* 57; *169:* 57; *173:* 55; *175:* 86; *184:* 192; *191:* 134; *193:* 137; *210:* 159
O'Clair, Dennis *127:* 25
O'Connor, George *183:* 153
Odell, Carole 35: 47
Odem, Mel 99: 164; *167:* 84, 87
O'Donohue, Thomas 40: 89
Oechsli, Kelly 5: 144, 145; *7:* 115; *8:* 83, 183; *13:* 117; *20:* 94; *81:* 199
Ofer, Avi *208:* 143
Offen, Hilda 42: 207
Ogden, Bill 42: 59; *47:* 55
Ogg, Oscar 33: 34
Ogle, Nancy Gray *163:* 144
Ohi, Ruth 90: 175, 177; *131:* 63; *135:* 106; *175:* 107; *179:* 55
Ohlsson, Ib 4: 152; *7:* 57; *10:* 20; *11:* 90; *19:* 217; *41:* 246; *82:* 106; *92:* 213
Ohtomo, Yasuo 37: 146; *39:* 212, 213
O'Keefe, Jennifer *136:* 184
O'Kelley, Mattie Lou 36: 150
Olbinski, Rafal *149:* 27; *158:* 77; *203:* 36
Oldland, Nicholas *223:* 136
O'Leary, Chris *208:* 166
Oleynikov, Igor *202:* 134
Oliver, Isaac *171:* 182
Oliver, Jenni 23: 121; *35:* 112
Oliver, Narelle *152:* 192; *197:* 129, 130

Oller, Erika *128:* 186; *134:* 126
Olschewski, Alfred *7:* 172
Olsen, Ib Spang *6:* 178, 179; *81:* 164
Olson, Alan *77:* 229
Olson-Brown, Ellen *183:* 154
Olugebefola, Ademola *15:* 205
O'Malley, Kevin *94:* 180; *106:* 8; *113:* 108; *136:* 70; *157:* 193; *191:* 146; *203:* 78; *217:* 84
O'Neil, Dan IV *7:* 176
O'Neill, Catharine *72:* 113; *84:* 78; *134:* 153
O'Neill, Jean *22:* 146
O'Neill, Martin *187:* 39; *203:* 118
O'Neill, Michael J. *54:* 172
O'Neill, Rose *48:* 30, 31
O'Neill, Steve *21:* 118
Ono, Chiyo *7:* 97
Orbaan, Albert *2:* 31; *5:* 65, 171; *9:* 8; *14:* 241; *20:* 109
Orbach, Ruth *21:* 112
Orback, Craig *197:* 132
Orfe, Joan *20:* 81
Org, Ed *119:* 93
Ormai, Stella *72:* 129
Ormerod, Jan *55:* 124; *70:* 170, 171; *90:* 39; *132:* 172, 173, 174; *147:* 98
Ormsby, Virginia H. *11:* 187
O'Rourke, Ericka *108:* 216; *117:* 194; *111:* 142; *119:* 194; *137:* 152; *150:* 134; *167:* 64; *172:* 164; *188:* 163; *191:* 172; *201:* 15; *203:* 75; *209:* 130; *219:* 99
O'Rourke, Ericka Meltzer
See O'Rourke, Ericka
Orozco, Jose Clemente *9:* 177
Orr, Forrest W. *23:* 9
Orr, N. *19:* 70
Ortiz, Vilma *88:* 158
Osborn, Kathy *152:* 232; *199:* 101, 102; *206:* 67
Osborn, Robert *65:* 49
Osborne, Billie Jean *35:* 209
Osmond, Edward *10:* 111
Ostow, David *223:* 138
O'Sullivan, Tom *3:* 176; *4:* 55; *78:* 195
Otani, June *124:* 42; *156:* 53
Otis, Rebecca *185:* 92
Ottley, Matt *147:* 221; *171:* 133
Otto, Svend *22:* 130, 141; *67:* 188, 189
Oudry, J.B. *18:* 167
Oughton, Taylor *5:* 23; *104:* 136
Overeng, Johannes *44:* 36
Overlie, George *11:* 156
Owens, Carl *2:* 35; *23:* 521
Owens, Gail *10:* 170; *12:* 157; *19:* 16; *22:* 70; *25:* 81; *28:* 203, 205; *32:* 221, 222; *36:* 132; *46:* 40; *47:* 57; *54:* 66, 67, 68, 69, 70, 71, 72, 73; *71:* 100; *73:* 64; *77:* 157; *80:* 32; *82:* 3; *99:* 226
Owens, Mary Beth *113:* 202, 203; *191:* 148, 149
Owens, Nubia *84:* 74
Oxenbury, Helen *3:* 150, 151; *24:* 81; *68:* 174, 175,176; *81:* 209; *84:* 213, 245; *129:* 56; *149:* 159; *184:* 181
Oz, Robin *88:* 167; *185:* 181

P

Padgett, Jim *12:* 165
Page, Gail *205:* 128
Page, Homer *14:* 145
Page, Mark *162:* 70
Paget, Sidney *24:* 90, 91, 93, 95, 97
Paget, Walter *64:* 122
Paillot, Jim *173:* 89
Pajouhesh, Noushin *160:* 121
Pak *12:* 76
Pak, Yu Cha *86:* 174
Paladino, Lance *134:* 30

Palazzo, Tony *3:* 152, 153
Palecek, Josef *56:* 136; *89:* 158
Palen, Debbie *135:* 88; *195:* 148, 149
Palencar, John Jude *84:* 12, 45; *85:* 87; *92:* 187; *99:* 128; *110:* 204; *150:* 122; *171:* 86; *207:* 36
Palin, Nicki *81:* 201; *89:* 161
Palladini, David *4:* 113; *40:* 176, 177, 178, 179, 181,224, 225; *50:* 138; *78:* 186
Pallarito, Don *43:* 36
Palmer, Carol *158:* 230; *195:* 187
Palmer, Heidi *15:* 207; *29:* 102
Palmer, Jan *42:* 153; *82:* 161
Palmer, Judd *153:* 160, 161
Palmer, Juliette *6:* 89; *15:* 208
Palmer, Kate Salley *104:* 143; *154:* 169
Palmer, Lemuel *17:* 25, 29
Palmisciano, Diane *110:* 62; *162:* 26; *202:* 138, 139
Palmquist, Eric *38:* 133
Pamintuan, Macky *214:* 160
Panesis, Nicholas *3:* 127
Panter, Gary *182:* 191
Panton, Doug *52:* 99
Paparone, Pamela *129:* 174
Papas, William *11:* 223; *50:* 160
Papin, Joseph *26:* 113
Papish, Robin Lloyd *10:* 80
Papp, Robert *198:* 41; *205:* 130; *219:* 53
Paradis, Susan *40:* 216
Paraquin, Charles H. *18:* 166
Pardo DeLange, Alex *179:* 128; *211:* 135, 136
Paris, Peter *31:* 127
Parisi, Elizabeth B. *141:* 82; *164:* 57
Park, Nick *113:* 143
Park, Seho *39:* 110
Park, W.B. *22:* 189
Parker, Ant *82:* 87, 88; *104:* 121
Parker, Lewis *2:* 179
Parker, Nancy Winslow *10:* 113; *22:* 164; *28:* 47, 144; *52:* 7; *69:* 153; *91:* 171, 174; *132:* 175
Parker, Robert *4:* 161; *5:* 74; *9:* 136; *29:* 39
Parker, Robert Andrew *11:* 81; *29:* 186; *39:* 165; *40:* 25; *41:* 78; *42:* 123; *43:* 144; *48:* 182; *54:* 140; *74:* 141; *91:* 24; *111:* 115; *151:* 201; *154:* 156; *200:* 163, 164; *211:* 67
Parker-Rees, Guy *149:* 145; *193:* 149, 150
Parkin, Trevor *140:* 151
Parkins, David *114:* 123; *146:* 176; *176:* 168; *192:* 107; *218:* 139, 140, 141, 148
Parkinson, Kathy *71:* 143; *144:* 234
Parkinson, Keith *70:* 66
Parks, Gordon, Jr. *33:* 228
Parlato, Stephen *222:* 137
Parnall, Peter *5:* 137; *16:* 221; *24:* 70; *40:* 78; *51:* 130; *69:* 17, 155; *136:* 22, 23, 24
Parnall, Virginia *40:* 78
Paros, Jennifer *210:* 197
Parow, Lorraine *158:* 127
Parr, Todd *134:* 139, 140; *179:* 163, 164, 165
Parrish, Anne *27:* 159, 160
Parrish, Dillwyn *27:* 159
Parrish, Maxfield *14:* 160, 161, 164, 165; *16:* 109; *18:* 12, 13; *YABC 1:* 149, 152, 267; *2:* 146, 149
Parry, David *26:* 156
Parry, Marian *13:* 176; *19:* 179
Parsons, Garry *197:* 135
Partch, Virgil *45:* 163, 165
Pascal, David *14:* 174
Paschkis, Julie *177:* 153, 154; *220:* 140, 141
Pasquier, J.A. *16:* 91
Pastel, Elyse *201:* 123
Pasternak, Robert *119:* 53
Paterson, Diane *13:* 116; *39:* 163; *59:* 164, 165, 166,167; *72:* 51, 53; *129:* 175; *177:* 156, 157
Paterson, Helen *16:* 93
Patkau, Karen *112:* 123
Paton, Jane *15:* 271; *35:* 176

Patricelli, Leslie *207:* 129
Patrick, John *139:* 190
Patrick, Pamela *90:* 160; *93:* 211; *105:* 12
Patrick, Tom *190:* 103
Patterson, Geoffrey *54:* 75
Patterson, Robert *25:* 118
Patti, Joyce *187:* 145, 146
Patz, Nancy *111:* 40; *154:* 161; *214:* 80
Paul, James *4:* 130; *23:* 161
Paul, Korky *102:* 85
Paull, Grace *24:* 157; *87:* 127
Paulsen, Ruth Wright *79:* 160, 164; *189:* 146
Pavlov, Elena *80:* 49
Payne, Adam S. *135:* 166
Payne, C.F. *145:* 138, 140; *179:* 168
Payne, Joan Balfour *1:* 118
Payne, Tom *170:* 27
Payson, Dale *7:* 34; *9:* 151; *20:* 140; *37:* 22
Payzant, Charles *21:* 147
Peacock, Ralph *64:* 118
Peake, Mervyn *22:* 136, 149; *23:* 162, 163, 164; *YABC2:* 307
Pearson, Larry *38:* 225
Pearson, Tracey Campbell *64:* 163, 164, 167, 168, 169; *118:* 51; *156:* 169, 171, 172; *163:* 140; *219:* 140, 141, 142, 143
Peat, Fern B. *16:* 115
Peck, Anne Merriman *18:* 241; *24:* 155
Peck, Beth *66:* 242; *79:* 166; *80:* 136; *91:* 34; *95:* 9; *101:* 77; *164:* 197; *190:* 170
Peddicord, Jane Ann *199:* 106
Pedersen, Janet *193:* 152; *217:* 57; *218:* 15
Pedersen, Judy *66:* 217; *121:* 36; *172:* 67
Pedersen, Vilhelm *YABC 1:* 40
Pederson, Sharleen *12:* 92
Pedlar, Elaine *161:* 45
Peek, Merle *39:* 168
Peet, Bill *2:* 203; *41:* 159, 160, 161, 162, 163; *78:* 158, 159, 160, 161
Peguero, Adrian *116:* 133
Peguero, Gerard *116:* 133
Pels, Winslow Pinney *55:* 126
Peltier, Leslie C. *13:* 178
Peltzer, Marc *202:* 92
Penberthy, Mark *171:* 78
Pendle, Alexy *7:* 159; *13:* 34; *29:* 161; *33:* 215; *86:* 62
Pendola, Joanne *76:* 203; *81:* 125; *105:* 181; *178:* 152, 153
Pene du Bois, William *4:* 70; *10:* 122; *26:* 61; *27:* 145, 211; *35:* 243; *41:* 216; *68:* 180, 181; *73:* 45
Penfound, David *102:* 185
Pennington, Eunice *27:* 162
Peppe, Mark *28:* 142
Peppe, Rodney *4:* 164, 165; *74:* 187, 188, 189
Pepper, Hubert *64:* 143
Percy, Graham *63:* 2
Pericoli, Matteo *178:* 177
Perini, Ben *173:* 77
Perkins, David *60:* 68
Perkins, Lucy Fitch *72:* 199
Perkins, Lynne Rae *172:* 146; *212:* 153
Perl, Susan *2:* 98; *4:* 231; *5:* 44, 45, 118; *6:* 199; *8:* 137; *12:* 88; *22:* 193; *34:* 54, 55; *52:* 128; *YABC 1:* 176
Perlman, Janet *222:* 141
Perrone, Donna *78:* 166
Perry, Marie Fritz *165:* 180
Perry, Patricia *29:* 137; *30:* 171
Perry, Roger *27:* 163
Perske, Martha *46:* 83; *51:* 108, 147
Persson, Stina *175:* 166
Pesek, Ludek *15:* 237
Petach, Heidi *149:* 166; *200:* 207
Peters, David *72:* 205; *182:* 116
Petersen, Jeff *181:* 95
Petersham, Maud *17:* 108, 147, 148, 149, 150, 151, 152, 153
Petersham, Miska *17:* 108, 147, 148, 149, 150, 151, 152, 153

Peterson, Eric *109:* 125
Peterson, Nisse *99:* 27
Peterson, R.F. *7:* 101
Peterson, Russell *7:* 130
Petie, Haris *2:* 3; *10:* 41, 118; *11:* 227; *12:* 70
Petricic, Dusan *153:* 75, 76, 77; *170:* 12; *172:* 13; *176:* 170; *179:* 56
Petrides, Heidrun *19:* 223
Petrone, Valeria *159:* 160; *171:* 92; *186:* 173; *204:* 49; *216:* 208; *220:* 98
Petrosino, Tamara *177:* 40; *193:* 154, 155
Petruccio, Steven James *67:* 159; *127:* 5
Pettingill, Ondre *64:* 181; *70:* 64; *222:* 167, 168
Peyo *40:* 56, 57
Peyton, K.M. *15:* 212
Pfeifer, Herman *15:* 262
Pfister, Marcus *83:* 165, 166, 167; *146:* 152; *150:* 160; *207:* 132, 134, 135, 136
Pfloog, Jan *124:* 60
Pham, LeUyen *160:* 48; *175:* 154, 156; *179:* 149; *201:* 124, 125, 126, 127; *204:* 28; *208:* 206; *217:* 92
Phelan, Matt *182:* 160; *184:* 222; *215:* 140, 141; *221:* 157
Phillipps, J.C. *218:* 142
Phillips, Craig *70:* 151; *207:* 74; *221:* 159
Phillips, Douglas *1:* 19
Phillips, F.D. *6:* 202
Phillips, Gary R. *223:* 23
Phillips, Louise *133:* 67
Phillips, Matt *184:* 173
Phillips, Thomas *30:* 55
Philpot, Glyn *54:* 46
Phiz
    See Browne, Hablot K.
Piatti, Celestino *16:* 223
Pica, Steve *115:* 181
Picarella, Joseph *13:* 147
Picart, Gabriel *121:* 165; *201:* 169
Pichon, Liz *174:* 139
Pickard, Charles *12:* 38; *18:* 203; *36:* 152
Picken, George A. *23:* 150
Pickens, David *22:* 156
Pickering, Jimmy *195:* 152; *197:* 163
Pien, Lark *222:* 143, 144
Pienkowski, Jan *6:* 183; *30:* 32; *58:* 140, 141, 142,143, 146, 147; *73:* 3; *87:* 156, 157; *131:* 189
Pieper, Christiane *200:* 168
Pignataro, Anna *163:* 220; *223:* 143 Pile, Emma *218:* 156 Pileggi, Steve *145:* 122
Pilkey, Dav *68:* 186; *115:* 164, 166; *166:* 173, 174, 175
Pimlott, John *10:* 205
Pincus, Harriet *4:* 186; *8:* 179; *22:* 148; *27:* 164, 165; *66:* 202
Pini, Wendy *89:* 166
Pinkett, Neil *60:* 8
Pinkney, Brian *81:* 184, 185; *94:* 107; *113:* 146, 147; *117:* 121, 166; *132:* 145; *158:* 108, 191; *160:* 189; *200:* 8
Pinkney, Jerry *8:* 218; *10:* 40; *15:* 276; *20:* 66; *24:* 121; *33:* 109; *36:* 222; *38:* 200; *41:* 165, 166, 167, 168, 169, 170, 171, 173, 174; *44:* 198; *48:* 51; *53:* 20; *56:* 61, 68; *58:* 184; *60:* 59; *61:* 91; *71:* 146, 148, 149; *72:* 17; *73:* 149; *74:* 159,192; *75:* 45; *80:* 206; *81:* 44; *85:* 144; *95:* 50; *107:* 158, 159, 160; *108:* 164; *112:* 114, 115; *133:* 58; *195:* 140
Pinkwater, Daniel Manus *8:* 156; *46:* 180, 181, 182, 185, 188, 189, 190; *151:* 161 *76:* 178, 179, 180; *210:* 203
Pinkwater, Manus
    See Pinkwater, Daniel Manus
Pinkwater, Jill *114:* 160, 161; *158:* 179; *188:* 143, 145, 146
Pinto, Ralph *10:* 131; *45:* 93
Pinto, Sara *200:* 165
Pinon, Mark *74:* 22
Piven, Hanoch *173:* 142

Pistolesi *73:* 211
Pitcairn, Ansel *188:* 10
Pittman, Helena Clare *71:* 151
Pitz, Henry C. *4:* 168; *19:* 165; *35:* 128; *42:* 80; *YABC 2:* 95, 176
Pitzenberger, Lawrence J. *26:* 94
Pitzer, Susanna *181:* 131
Place, François *218:* 42
Plant, Andrew *214:* 166
Player, Stephen *82:* 190
Plecas, Jennifer *84:* 201; *106:* 124; *149:* 168; *205:* 180; *220:* 81
Ploog, Mike *180:* 19
Plowden, David *52:* 135, 136
Plume, Ilse *170:* 149
Plummer, William *32:* 31
Podevin, Jean François *184:* 185
Podwal, Mark *56:* 170, 173; *101:* 154, 155, 157; *149:* 176; *160:* 194
Pogany, Willy *15:* 46, 49; *19:* 222, 256; *25:* 214; *44:* 142, 143, 144, 145, 146, 147, 148
Pohrt, Tom *67:* 116; *104:* 80; *152:* 199; *195:* 154; *199:* 85
Poirson, V.A. *26:* 89
Polacco, Patricia *74:* 195, 196, 197, 198; *123:* 121, 122, 123; *180:* 189, 190, 191, 193, 194; *212:* 168, 170, 171
Polgreen, John *21:* 44
Polhemus, Coleman *210:* 209
Politi, Leo *1:* 178; *4:* 53; *21:* 48; *47:* 173,174, 176, 178, 179, 180, 181
Pollack, Barbara *219:* 60
Pollema-Cahill, Phyllis *123:* 126
Pollen, Samson *64:* 80
Polonsky, Arthur *34:* 168
Polseno, Jo *1:* 53; *3:* 117; *5:* 114; *17:* 154; *20:* 87; *32:* 49; *41:* 245
Pomaska, Anna *117:* 148
Pons, Bernadette *184:* 100
Ponter, James *5:* 204
Poole, Colin *111:* 27
Poortvliet, Rien *6:* 212; *65:* 165, 166, 167
Pope, Kevin *183:* 158
Popp, Wendy *72:* 122; *158:* 68
Poppel, Hans *71:* 154, 155
Porfirio, Guy *76:* 134
Portal, Colette *6:* 186; *11:* 203
Porter, George *7:* 181
Porter, Janice Lee *136:* 175; *164:* 37
Porter, John *113:* 47
Porter, Pat Grant *84:* 112; *125:* 101
Porter, Sue *146:* 246, 247; *213:* 139, 140, 141; *221:* 91
Porter, Walter *124:* 175
Porto, James *221:* 14
Posada, Mia *187:* 151
Posen, Michael *175:* 82
Posthuma, Sieb *150:* 163
Postier, Jim *202:* 140; *204:* 25
Postma, Lidia *79:* 17
Potter, Beatrix *100:* 194, 195; *132:* 179, 180, 181, 182; *YABC 1:* 208, 209, 210, 212, 213
Potter, Giselle *117:* 123; *143:* 44; *144:* 170, 197; *149:* 7; *150:* 165; *187:* 152, 153; *190:* 198; *196:* 152; *200:* 12
Potter, Katherine *104:* 147; *171:* 135; *173:* 136; *217:* 130, 131
Potter, Miriam Clark *3:* 162
Poulin, Stephane *98:* 140, 141
Poullis, Nick *146:* 210
Powell, Constance Buffington *174:* 141
Powell, Gary *151:* 208
Powell, Ivan *67:* 219
Power, Margaret *105:* 122
Powers, Daniel *161:* 173
Powers, Richard M. *1:* 230; *3:* 218; *7:* 194; *26:* 186
Powledge, Fred *37:* 154
Powzyk, Joyce *74:* 214
Poydar, Nancy *96:* 149; *190:* 180, 181, 182
Pracher, Richard *91:* 166

Prachaticka, Marketa *126:* 126
Prange, Beckie *181:* 169
Prap, Lila *177:* 165
Prater, John *103:* 142, 143, 144; *149:* 172
Pratt, Charles *23:* 29
Pratt, Christine Joy *214:* 167
Pratt, George *116:* 208; *212:* 37
Pratt, Pierre *150:* 73; *166:* 183; *168:* 172; *201:* 27; *208:* 171, 172, 173
Prebenna, David *73:* 174
Preiss-Glasser, Robin *123:* 176; *152* 40; *172:* 194
Press, Jenny *116:* 95
Preston, Mark *152:* 162
Pretro, Korinna *91:* 126
Prevost, Mikela *209:* 111
Price, Christine *2:* 247; *3:* 163, 253; *8:* 166
Price, Cynthia *118:* 156
Price, Edward *33:* 34
Price, Garrett *1:* 76; *2:* 42
Price, Hattie Longstreet *17:* 13
Price, Nick *216:* 173; *220:* 7
Price, Norman *YABC 1:* 129
Price, Willard *48:* 184
Priceman, Marjorie *81:* 171; *136:* 169; *156:* 200; *168:* 153, 154; *188:* 45
Priestley, Alice *168:* 33
Priestley, Chris *198:* 144
Primavera, Elise *26:* 95; *58:* 151; *73:* 37; *80:* 79; *86:* 156; *105:* 161; *213:* 157
Primrose, Jean *36:* 109
Prince, Alison *86:* 188, 189
Prince, Leonora E. *7:* 170
Pritchett, Shelley *116:* 148
Prittie, Edwin J. *YABC 1:* 120
Proimos, James *176:* 4; *217:* 132, 133, 134
Proimos, John *173:* 144
Prosmitsky, Jenya *132:* 33
Provensen, Alice *37:* 204, 215, 222; *70:* 176, 177, 178, 180, *71:* 213; *147:* 184; *191:* 190
Provensen, Martin *37:* 204, 215, 222; *70:* 176, 177, 178, 180; *71:* 213; *191:* 190
Pucci, Albert John *44:* 154
Pudlo *8:* 59
Puggaard, Ulla *196:* 25
Pullen, Zachary *211:* 161
Pulver, Harry, Jr. *129:* 159
Pulver, Robin *160:* 4
Punchatz, Don *99:* 57
Purdy, Susan *8:* 162
Pursell, Weimer *55:* 18
Purtscher, Alfons *97:* 6
Puskas, James *5:* 141
Pyk, Jan *7:* 26; *38:* 123
Pyle, Chuck *99:* 149; *191:* 83
Pyle, Howard *16:* 225, 226, 227, 228, 230, 231, 232, 235; *24:* 27; *34:* 124, 125, 127, 128; *59:* 132; *100:* 198

Q

Quackenbush, Robert *4:* 190; *6:* 166; *7:* 175, 178; *9:* 86; *11:* 65, 221; *41:* 154; *43:* 157; *70:* 185, 186; *71:* 137; *85:* 47; *92:* 148; *133:* 154, 164, 169
Qualls, Sean *177:* 167, 168; *193:* 43
Quennell, Marjorie (Courtney) *29:* 163, 164
Quidor, John *19:* 82
Quirk, John *62:* 170
Quirk, Thomas *12:* 81

R

Rackham, Arthur *15:* 32, 78, 214-227; *17:* 105, 115; *18:* 233; *19:* 254; *20:* 151; *22:* 129, 131, 132, 133; *23:* 175; *24:* 161, 181; *26:* 91; *32:* 118; *64:* 18; *100:* 9, 16, 203, 204; *YABC 1:* 25, 45, 55, 147; *2:* 103, 142, 173, 210

Racz, Michael *56:* 134
Raczka, Bob *191:* 155, 156
Radcliffe, Andrew *82:* 215
Rader, Laura *101:* 219; *197:* 147; *203:* 53
Radunsky, Vladimir *177:* 170; *192:* 30
Radzinski, Kandy *212:* 174
Rafilson, Sidney *11:* 172
Raglin, Tim *125:* 24
Raible, Alton *1:* 202, 203; *28:* 193; *35:* 181; *110:* 207
Raine, Patricia *82:* 74; *88:* 154
Ramá, Sue *173:* 45; *185:* 186; *190:* 184
Ramhorst, John *117:* 11
Ramirez, Gladys *177:* 19
Ramirez, Jose *207:* 27
Ramsey, James *16:* 41
Ramsey, Marcy Dunn *82:* 11; *180:* 186
Ramus, Michael *51:* 171
Rand, Paul *6:* 188
Rand, Ted *67:* 9, 10, 121, 123; *74:* 190; *84:* 170; *103:* 170; *112:* 6; *114:* 73; *139:* 168; *143:* 194; *156:* 154; *161:* 9, 10; *200:* 38; *204:* 7
Randazzo, Tony *81:* 98
Randell, William *55:* 54
Rane, Walter *93:* 144; *143:* 109; *184:* 126
Rankin, Joan *163:* 40; *212:* 176
Rankin, Laura *176:* 173, 174; *179:* 150
Ransome, Arthur *22:* 201
Ransome, James E. *74:* 137; *75:* 80; *84:* 181; *94:* 108; *117:* 115; *123:* 128, 129, 130; *158:* 101, 102; *159:* 205; *178:* 188, 189, 190; *216:* 114
Rantz, Don *119:* 184
Rao, Anthony *28:* 126
Raphael, Elaine *23:* 192; *71:* 24, 25
Rappaport, Eva *6:* 190
Raschka, Chris *80:* 187, 189, 190; *97:* 211; *115:* 210; *117:* 151, 152, 153, 154; *143:* 195; *145:* 153; *166:* 190, 191; *170:* 114; *207:* 140, 143, 144, 145; *208:* 82; *220:* 85
Rash, Andy *158:* 178; *162:* 172; *210:* 204; *219:* 145
Raskin, Ellen *2:* 208, 209; *4:* 142; *13:* 183; *22:* 68; *29:* 139; *36:* 134; *38:* 173, 174, 175, 176, 177, 178,179, 180, 181; *60:* 163; *86:* 81
Rathmann, Peggy *93:* 32; *94:* 168; *157:* 212, 214
Ratkus, Tony *77:* 133
Ratzkin, Lawrence *40:* 143
Rau, Margaret *9:* 157
Raverat, Gwen *YABC 1:* 152
Ravid, Joyce *61:* 73
Ravielli, Anthony *1:* 198; *3:* 168; *11:* 143
Ravilious, Robin *77:* 169
Rawlins, Donna *72:* 198; *73:* 15, 129
Rawlins, Janet *76:* 79
Rawlings, Steve *143:* 139; *151:* 54; *208:* 150
Rawlinson, Debbie *75:* 132
Ray, Deborah Kogan *8:* 164; *29:* 238; *50:* 112, 113; *62:* 119; *78:* 191; *203:* 149, 150, 151
Ray, Jane *96:* 166; *97:* 104; *152:* 208; *190:* 221; *196:* 165
Ray, Ralph *2:* 239; *5:* 73
Rayann, Omar *162:* 205; *186:* 29, 30
Rayevsky, Robert *64:* 17; *70:* 173; *80:* 204; *117:* 79; *190:* 187, 188
Raymond, Larry *31:* 108; *97:* 109
Rayner, Hugh *151:* 170
Rayner, Mary *22:* 207; *47:* 140; *72:* 191; *87:* 171, 172; *192:* 104
Rayner, Shoo
See Rayner, Hugh
Raynes, John *71:* 19
Raynor, Dorka *28:* 168
Raynor, Paul *24:* 73
Rayyan, Omar *110:* 222; *112:* 17; *125:* 131
Razzi, James *10:* 127
Read, Alexander D. *20:* 45
Reader, Dennis *71:* 157
Reasoner, Charles *53:* 33, 36, 37

Rebenschied, Shane *203:* 76; *215:* 124
Reczuch, Karen *115:* 132; *145:* 131
Redlich, Ben *163:* 221; *198:* 193
Reddy, Mike *203:* 67
Reed, Joseph *116:* 139
Reed, Lynn Rowe *115:* 173; *171:* 146; *208:* 177; *215:* 144, 145
Reed, Mike *211:* 147; *215:* 131
Reed, Tom *34:* 171
Reeder, Colin *74:* 202; *77:* 113
Rees, Mary *134:* 219
Reese, Bob *60:* 135
Reeve, Philip *171:* 50
Reeves, Eira B. *130:* 173, 174; *141:* 151
Reeves, Rick *181:* 179
Reeves, Rosie *202:* 200
Regan, Dana *117:* 116
Regan, Laura *103:* 198; *153:* 206
Reichert, Renée *169:* 127
Reid, Barbara *82:* 178; *92:* 17; *93:* 169, 170; *222:* 45
Reid, Stephen *19:* 213; *22:* 89
Reim, Melanie *104:* 151; *150:* 98
Reinert, Kirk *89:* 138; *195:* 129
Reinertson, Barbara *44:* 150; *62:* 103
Reiniger, Lotte *40:* 185
Reisberg, Mira *119:* 2
Reisch, Jesse *158:* 130
Reiser, Lynn *81:* 175; *138:* 184; *180:* 200
Reiss, John J. *23:* 193
Relf, Douglas *3:* 63
Relyea, C.M. *16:* 29; *31:* 153
Remi, Georges *13:* 184
Remington, Frederic *19:* 188; *41:* 178, 179, 180, 181, 183,184, 185, 186, 187, 188; *62:* 197
Remkiewicz, Frank *67:* 102; *77:* 171; *80:* 130; *113:* 107; *152:* 116; *152:* 211, 212; *157:* 148; *217:* 120, 138, 139, 140, 141
Rendon, Maria *116:* 141; *192:* 134; *134:* 152
Renfro, Ed *79:* 176
Renier, Aaron *202:* 141; *207:* 119
Renlie, Frank *11:* 200
Reschofsky, Jean *7:* 118
Rethi, Lili *2:* 153; *36:* 156
Rethi *60:* 181
Reusswig, William *3:* 267
Revell, Cindy *195:* 93
Rex, Adam *156:* 172; *169:* 91; *186:* 178, 179; *215:* 103; *223:* 11
Rex, Michael *157:* 147; *191:* 159, 160; *221:* 124
Rey, H.A. *1:* 182; *26:* 163, 164, 166, 167, 169; *69:* 172, 173, 174, 175; *86:* 195, 196, 197; *100:* 211; *YABC 2:* 17
Rey, Luis V. *201:* 162
Reynish, Jenny *222:* 155
Reynolds, Adrian *192:* 159, 160
Reynolds, Doris *5:* 71; *31:* 77
Reynolds, Peter H. *142:* 12; *179:* 175, 176; *202:* 113, 114
Rhead, Louis *31:* 91; *100:* 228
Rhodes, Andrew *38:* 204; *50:* 163; *54:* 76; *61:* 123, 124; *87:* 200
Ribbons, Ian *3:* 10; *37:* 161; *40:* 76
Ricci, Regolo *93:* 22; *164:* 148
Rice, Elizabeth *2:* 53, 214
Rice, Eve *34:* 174, 175; *91:* 172
Rice, James *22:* 210; *93:* 173
Rich, Anna *212:* 180
Rich, Martha *195:* 16
Richards, Chuck *170:* 154
Richards, George *40:* 116, 119, 121; *44:* 179
Richards, Henry *YABC 1:* 228, 231
Richardson, Ernest *2:* 144
Richardson, Frederick *18:* 27, 31
Richardson, John *110:* 88
Richman, Hilda *26:* 132
Richmond, George *24:* 179

Riddell, Chris *114:* 170, 195; *166:* 179; *199:* 164, 166, 167; *218:* 146, 148; *219:* 149, 150, 152, 153
Riddle, Tohby *74:* 204; *151:* 179; *223:* 154, 156
Riding, Peter *63:* 195
Rieniets, Judy King *14:* 28
Riger, Bob *2:* 166
Riggio, Anita *73:* 191; *85:* 63; *137:* 184; *172:* 165
Rigano, Giovanni *219:* 45
Riley, Jon *74:* 70
Riley, Kenneth *22:* 230
Riley, Terry *203:* 100
Riley-Webb, Charlotte *153:* 143
Rinaldi, Angelo *165:* 60, 69
Ringgold, Faith *71:* 162; *114:* 173, 174, 176; *187:* 160, 161, 163
Ringi, Kjell *12:* 171
Rios, Tere
See Versace, Marie
Rioux, Jo *215:* 110
Ripper, Charles L. *3:* 175
Ripplinger, Henry *117:* 31
Ritchie, Scot *217:* 145
Ritchie, William *74:* 183
Ritter, John *175:* 14
Ritz, Karen *41:* 117; *72:* 239; *87:* 125; *102:* 7; *106:* 6
Rivas, Victor *209:* 193
Rivers, Ruth *178:* 193
Rivkin, Jay *15:* 230
Rivoche, Paul *45:* 125
Roach, Marilynne *9:* 158
Robbin, Jodi *44:* 156, 159
Robbins, Frank *42:* 167
Robbins, Ken *147:* 191, 192
Robbins, Ruth *52:* 102
Roberts, Cliff *4:* 126
Roberts, David *154:* 4, 6; *191:* 162; *196:* 184; *197:* 105; *210:* 257
Roberts, Doreen *4:* 230; *28:* 105
Roberts, Jim *22:* 166; *23:* 69; *31:* 110
Roberts, Tony *109:* 195, 214
Roberts, W. *22:* 2, 3
Robertson, M.P. *197:* 153
Robins, Arthur *137:* 172; *151:* 225; *204:* 161
Robinson, Aminah Brenda Lynn *86:* 205; *103:* 55; *159:* 175
Robinson, Charles [1870-1937] *17:* 157, 171, 172, 173, 175, 176; *24:* 207; *25:* 204; *YABC 2:* 308, 309, 310, 331
Robinson, Charles *3:* 53; *5:* 14; *6:* 193; *7:* 150; *7:* 183; *8:* 38; *9:* 81; *13:* 188; *14:* 248, 249; *23:* 149; *26:* 115; *27:* 48; *28:* 191; *32:* 28; *35:* 210; *36:* 37; *48:* 96; *52:* 33; *53:* 157; *56:* 15; *62:* 142; *77:* 41; *111:* 148
Robinson, Jerry *3:* 262
Robinson, Joan G. *7:* 184
Robinson, Lolly *90:* 227
Robinson, T.H. *17:* 179, 181, 182, 183; *29:* 254
Robinson, W. Heath *17:* 185, 187, 189, 191, 193, 195, 197, 199, 202; *23:* 167; *25:* 194; *29:* 150; *YABC 1:* 44; *2:* 183
Rocco, John *187:* 4; *188:* 151; *208:* 180, 181, 182; *213:* 94; *222:* 34
Roche, Christine *41:* 98
Roche, Denis *99:* 184; *180:* 32; *196:* 168
Roche, P.K. *57:* 151, 152
Rocker, Fermin *7:* 34; *13:* 21; *31:* 40; *40:* 190,191
Rocklen, Margot *101:* 181
Rockwell, Anne *5:* 147; *33:* 171, 173; *71:* 166, 167,168; *114:* 183, 184; *194:* 152, 155
Rockwell, Gail *7:* 186
Rockwell, Harlow *33:* 171, 173, 175
Rockwell, Lizzy *114:* 182; *162:* 182; *185:* 189
Rockwell, Norman *23:* 39, 196, 197, 199, 200, 203, 204, 207; *41:* 140, 143; *123:* 47; *YABC 2:* 60

Rockwood, Richard *119:* 75
Rodanas, Kristina *156:* 183, 184; *221:* 127
Rodegast, Roland *43:* 100
Rodgers, Frank *69:* 177
Rodriguez, Albert G. *182:* 50
Rodriguez, Christina *184:* 12
Rodriguez, Edel *204:* 86
Rodriguez, Joel *16:* 65
Rodriguez, Robert *145:* 145; *212:* 33
Rodriguez-Howard, Pauline *177:* 18
Roe, Monika *210:* 94
Roeckelein, Katrina *134:* 223
Roennfeldt, Robert *66:* 243
Roever, J.M. *4:* 119; *26:* 170
Roffey, Maureen *33:* 142, 176, 177
Rogasky, Barbara *46:* 90
Rogé *173:* 160
Rogers, Carol *2:* 262; *6:* 164; *26:* 129
Rogers, Chris M. *150:* 59; *196:* 61
Rogers, Forest *87:* 160; *101:* 76
Rogers, Frances *10:* 130
Rogers, Gregory *104:* 76; *126:* 57; *171:* 26
Rogers, Jacqueline *78:* 249; *80:* 34; *86:* 54
　103: 70; *115:* 72; *129:* 173; *131:* 57, 225;
　143: 211; *153:* 100; *193:* 186; *203:* 51; *213:*
　144, 145, 146; *214:* 142
Rogers, Sherry *191:* 66
Rogers, Walter S. *31:* 135, 138; *67:* 65, 168;
　100: 81
Rogers, William A. *15:* 151, 153, 154; *33:* 35
Rogoff, Barbara *95:* 20
Rohmann, Eric *103:* 152; *198:* 151
Rojankovsky, Feodor *6:* 134, 136; *10:* 183; *21:*
　128,129, 130; *25:* 110; *28:* 42; *68:* 120
Rolfsen, Alf *62:* 15
Rolston, Steve *209:* 154; *223:* 113
Romain, Trevor *134:* 157
Roman, Barbara J. *103:* 171
Romas *114:* 111; *165:* 63
Romano, Robert *64:* 68
Romero, Alejandro *187:* 185
Roos, Maryn *168:* 198
Root, Barry *80:* 212; *90:* 196; *146:* 78; *156:*
　165; *159:* 161; *182:* 18, 172
Root, Kimberly Bulcken *86:* 72; *98:* 21; *108:*
　111; *127:* 114; *159:* 162; *176:* 134; *192:* 163
Roper, Bob *65:* 153
Roraback, Robin *111:* 156
Rorer, Abigail *43:* 222; *85:* 155
Rosales, Melodye *80:* 35
Rosamilia, Patricia *36:* 120
Rose, Carl *5:* 62
Rose, David S. *29:* 109; *70:* 120
Rose, Gerald *68:* 200, 201; *86:* 48
Rose, Ted *93:* 178
Rosen, Elizabeth *205:* 137
Rosenbaum, Jonathan *50:* 46
Rosenberg, Amye *74:* 207, 208
Rosenberry, Vera *87:* 22, 26; *144:* 212, 213;
　158: 120; *219:* 163, 164
Rosenblum, Richard *11:* 202; *18:* 18
Rosenstiehl, Agnès *203:* 153
Rosier, Lydia *16:* 236; *20:* 104; *21:* 109; *22:*
　125; *30:* 151, 158; *42:* 128; *45:* 214; *77:*
　227, 228
Rosing, Jens *85:* 142
Ross
　See Thomson, Ross
Ross, Christine *83:* 172, 173
Ross, Clare Romano *3:* 123; *21:* 45; *48:* 199
Ross, Dave *32:* 152; *57:* 108
Ross, Graham *199:* 4
Ross, Herbert *37:* 78
Ross, John *3:* 123; *21:* 45
Ross, Johnny *32:* 190
Ross, Larry *47:* 168; *60:* 62
Ross, Ruth *109:* 233
Ross, Tony *17:* 204; *56:* 132; *65:* 176, 177,
　179; *90:* 123; *123:* 186, 187, 190; *130:* 188,
　190, 191, 192; *132:* 242; *174:* 159; *176:* 181,
　182, 183; *202:* 198

Rossetti, Dante Gabriel *20:* 151, 153
Rostant, Larry *180:* 221; *194:* 108; *195:* 96;
　197: 12; *207:* 53; *210:* 189
Roth, Arnold *4:* 238; *21:* 133
Roth, Julie Jersild *180:* 206
Roth, Marci *135:* 223
Roth, R.G. *184:* 50
Roth, Rob *105:* 98; *146:* 41
Roth, Robert *176:* 159
Roth, Roger *61:* 128; *190:* 192
Roth, Ruby *216:* 185
Roth, Stephanie *136:* 171, 172
Roth, Susan L. *80:* 38; *93:* 78; *134:* 165, 166;
　181: 145, 146
Rothenberg, Joani Keller *162:* 190, 191
Rothman, Michael *139:* 62; *184:* 34 *Rotman,
Jeffrey L. 145:* 30
Rotondo, Pat *32:* 158
Roughsey, Dick *35:* 186
Rouille, M. *11:* 96
Rounds, Glen *8:* 173; *9:* 171; *12:* 56; *32:* 194;
　40: 230; *51:* 161, 162, 166; *56:* 149; *70:*
　198, 199; *YABC 1:* 1, 2, 3; *112:* 163
Roundtree, Katherine *114:* 88; *168:* 102
Rovetch, Lissa *201:* 164
Rowan, Evadne *52:* 51
Rowe, Eric *111:* 161
Rowe, Gavin *27:* 144; *72:* 47; *88:* 201
Rowe, John *132:* 70, 71; *180:* 126
Rowell, Kenneth *40:* 72
Rowen, Amy *52:* 143
Rowena *116:* 101
Rowland, Andrew *164:* 136
Rowland, Jada *83:* 73
Rowles, Daphne *58:* 24
Roy, Jeroo *27:* 229; *36:* 110
Royo *118:* 32; *144:* 105, 106, 108; *165:* 19;
　166: 166
Rubbino, Salvatore *220:* 147
Rubel, Nicole *18:* 255; *20:* 59; *81:* 66, 67; *95:*
　169, 170; *119:* 60; *135:* 177, 179, 180; *169:*
　68; *181:* 150
Rubel, Reina *33:* 217
Rud, Borghild *6:* 15
Ruddell, Gary *110:* 238; *116:* 207
Rudolph, Norman Guthrie *17:* 13
Rue, Leonard Lee III *37:* 164
Rueda, Claudia *183:* 170, 171
Ruelle, Karen Gray *126:* 193
Ruff, Donna *50:* 173; *72:* 203; *78:* 49; *80:*
　120,121; *93:* 162; *164:* 121
Ruffins, Reynold *10:* 134, 135; *41:* 191, 192,
　193, 194, 195, 196; *125:* 187, 188, 189; *162:*
　197
Ruhlin, Roger *34:* 44
Rui, Paolo *217:* 115
Ruiz, Art *95:* 154; *110:* 91
Rumford, James *193:* 167
Runnerstroem, Bengt Arne *75:* 161
Ruse, Margaret *24:* 155
Rush, Ken *98:* 74
Rush, Peter *42:* 75
Russell, Charles M. *167:* 171
Russell, E.B. *18:* 177, 182
Russell, Jim *53:* 134
Russell, Natalie *218:* 170, 171
Russell, P. Craig *80:* 196; *146:* 102; *162:* 186
Russo, Marisabina *84:* 51; *106:* 164; *151:* 183;
　188: 153, 154, 155, 156
Russo, Susan *30:* 182; *36:* 144
Russon, Mary *87:* 145
Ruth, Greg *183:* 125
Ruth, Rod *9:* 161
Rutherford, Alexa *110:* 108
Rutherford, Jenny *78:* 5
Rutherford, Meg *25:* 174; *34:* 178, 179; *69:*
　73; *72:* 31
Rutland, Jonathan *31:* 126
Ruurs, Margriet *147:* 195
Ruzzier, Sergio *159:* 176, 177; *163:* 184; *210:*
　214, 216

Ryan, Amy *188:* 50
Ryan, Will *86:* 134
Ryden, Hope *8:* 176
Rylant, Cynthia *112:* 170, 172
Rymer, Alta M. *34:* 181
Ryniak, Christopher *178:* 11
Rystedt, Rex *49:* 80

S

Saaf, Chuck *49:* 179
Saaf, Donald *101:* 220; *124:* 180
Sabaka, Donna R. *21:* 172
Sabin, Robert *45:* 35; *60:* 30; *99:* 161; *223:* 29
Sabuda, Robert *170:* 166, 167, 168
Sacker, Amy *16:* 100
Saelig, S.M. *129:* 73; *173:* 59
Saffioti, Lino *36:* 176; *48:* 60; *223:* 26
Saflund, Birgitta *94:* 2
Sagsoorian, Paul *12:* 183; *22:* 154; *33:* 106;
　87: 152
Sahara, Tony *168:* 106; *177:* 181; *178:* 228;
　186: 132; *207:* 89
Sahlberg, Myron *57:* 165
Saidens, Amy *145:* 162; *191:* 131; *210:* 129
Saint Exupery, Antoine de *20:* 157
Saint James, Synthia *152:* 220; *188:* 90; *200:*
　7
Sakai, Komako *213:* 148
Saldutti, Denise *39:* 186; *57:* 178
Sale, Morton *YABC 2:* 31
Sale, Tim *153:* 177
Salerno, Steven *150:* 79; *176:* 188; *202:* 39;
　216: 190
Salter, George *72:* 128, 130
Saltzberg, Barney *135:* 184, 185; *194:* 160
Saltzman, David *86:* 209
Salwowski, Mark *71:* 54
Salzman, Yuri *86:* 12
Sambourne, Linley *YABC 2:* 181
Sampson, Katherine *9:* 197
Samson, Anne S. *2:* 216
San Souci, Daniel *40:* 200; *96:* 199, 200; *113:*
　171; *157:* 149; *170:* 69; *192:* 167, 168; *220:*
　152; *221:* 126
Sancha, Sheila *38:* 185
Sanchez, Enrique O. *155:* 84
Sand, George X. *45:* 182
Sandberg, Lasse *15:* 239, 241
Sanders, Beryl *39:* 173
Sanderson, Ruth *21:* 126; *24:* 53; *28:* 63; *33:*
　67; *41:* 48, 198, 199, 200, 201, 202, 203; *43:*
　79; *46:* 36,44; *47:* 102; *49:* 58; *62:* 121, 122;
　85: 3; *109:* 207, 208, 209, 210; *172:* 157,
　158; *223:* 85
Sandia *119:* 74
Sandin, Joan *4:* 36; *6:* 194; *7:* 177; *12:*
　145,185; *20:* 43; *21:* 74; *26:* 144; *27:* 142;
　28: 224, 225; *38:* 86; *41:* 46; *42:* 35; *59:* 6;
　80: 136; *94:* 188; *140:* 116; *153:* 179, 180;
　197: 168
Sandland, Reg *39:* 215
Sandoz, Edouard *26:* 45, 47
Sanford, John *66:* 96, 97
Sanger, Amy Wilson *205:* 140
Sankey, Tom *72:* 103
Sano, Kazuhiko *153:* 208; *195:* 171; *203:* 21;
　221: 71
Santat, Dan *188:* 160; *221:* 62; *223:* 163
Santiago, Wilfred *210:* 48
Santore, Charles *54:* 139; *200:* 171, 172
Santoro, Christopher *74:* 215
Santos, Jesse J. *99:* 24
Sapieha, Christine *1:* 180
Saport, Linda *123:* 137, 138; *215:* 29
Sara
　See De La Roche Saint Andre, Anne
Sarcone-Roach, Julia *215:* 158
Sardinha, Rick *175:* 151

Sarg, Tony *YABC 2:* 236
Sargent, Claudia *64:* 181
Sargent, Robert *2:* 217
Saris *1:* 33
Sarony *YABC 2:* 170
Saroff, Phyllis V. *202:* 160
Sasaki, Goro *170:* 46
Sasaki, Ellen Joy *216:* 49
Sasek, Miroslav *16:* 239, 240, 241, 242
Sassman, David *9:* 79
Sattler, Jennifer Gordon *218:* 175
Satty *29:* 203, 205
Sauber, Robert *40:* 183; *76:* 256; *78:* 154; *87:* 92
Saunders, Dave *85:* 163, 164, 165
Savadier, Elivia *84:* 50; *145:* 45; *164:* 206
Savage, Naomi *56:* 172
Savage, Steele *10:* 203; *20:* 77; *35:* 28
Savage, Stephen *174:* 182
Savio *76:* 4
Savitt, Sam *8:* 66, 182; *15:* 278; *20:* 96; *24:* 192; *28:* 98
Sawyer, Kem Knapp *84:* 228, 229
Say, Allen *28:* 178; *69:* 182, 183, 232; *110:* 194, 195,196; *161:* 154, 155
Sayles, Elizabeth *82:* 93; *105:* 155; *109:* 116; *180:* 64; *220:* 160, 161
Scabrini, Janet *13:* 191; *44:* 128
Scanlan, Peter *83:* 27; *153:* 165; *187:* 149
Scanlon, Paul *83:* 87
Scannell, Reece *105:* 105
Scarry, Huck *35:* 204, 205
Scarry, Richard *2:* 220, 221; *18:* 20; *35:* 193, 194, 195,196, 197, 198, 199, 200, 201, 202; *75:* 165, 167, 168
Schachner, Judith Byron *88:* 180; *92:* 163; *93:* 102; *142:* 82; *178:* 199, 200; *190:* 140
Schade, Susan *205:* 21
Schaeffer, Mead *18:* 81, 94; *21:* 137, 138, 139; *47:* 128
Schaffer, Amanda *90:* 206
Schallau, Daniel *222:* 164
Schanzer, Rosalyn *138:* 192, 193
Scharl, Josef *20:* 132; *22:* 128
Scheel, Lita *11:* 230
Scheffler, Axel *180:* 23, 24
Scheib, Ida *29:* 28
Schermer, Judith *30:* 184
Schick, Eleanor *82:* 210, 211; *144:* 222
Schick, Joel *16:* 160; *17:* 167; *22:* 12; *27:* 176; *31:* 147, 148; *36:* 23; *38:* 64; *45:* 116, 117; *52:* 5, 85; *104:* 159
Schields, Gretchen *75:* 171, 203
Schindelman, Joseph *1:* 74; *4:* 101; *12:* 49; *26:* 51; *40:* 146; *56:* 158; *73:* 40
Schindler, Edith *7:* 22
Schindler, S.D. *38:* 107; *46:* 196; *74:* 162; *75:* 172, 173; *99:* 133; *112:* 177; *118:* 185, 186; *121:* 71; *136:* 159; *143:* 45; *149:* 120; *156:* 30; *169:* 135; *171:* 161, 162, 163; *172:* 9; *186:* 163; *194:* 109; *195:* 35; *198:* 170, 171, 172
Schlesinger, Bret *7:* 77
Schlossberg, Elisabeth *221:* 161
Schmid, Eleanore *12:* 188; *126:* 196, 197
Schmiderer, Dorothy *19:* 224
Schmidt, Bill *73:* 34; *76:* 220, 222, 224
Schmidt, Elizabeth *15:* 242
Schmidt, George Paul *132:* 122
Schmidt, Karen Lee *54:* 12; *71:* 174; *92:* 56; *94:* 190, 191; *127:* 103
Schmidt, Lynette *76:* 205
Schmitz, Tamara *207:* 147
Schneider, Christine M. *171:* 165
Schneider, Howie *181:* 159
Schneider, Rex *29:* 64; *44:* 171
Schnurr, Edward *170:* 62
Schoberle, Cecile *80:* 200; *92:* 134; *218:* 113
Schoenherr, Ian *32:* 83; *173:* 41

Schoenherr, John *1:* 146, 147, 173; *3:* 39, 139; *17:* 75; *29:* 72; *32:* 83; *37:* 168, 169, 170; *43:* 164, 165; *45:* 160, 162; *51:* 127; *66:* 196, 197, 198; *68:* 83; *72:* 240; *75:* 225; *88:* 176
Scholder, Fritz *69:* 103
Schomburg, Alex *13:* 23
Schongut, Emanuel *4:* 102; *15:* 186; *47:* 218, 219; *52:* 147, 148, 149, 150; *185:* 27
Schoonover, Frank *17:* 107; *19:* 81, 190, 233; *22:* 88,129; *24:* 189; *31:* 88; *41:* 69; *YABC 2:* 282, 316
Schories, Pat *164:* 210
Schottland, Miriam *22:* 172
Schramm, Ulrik *2:* 16; *14:* 112
Schreiber, Elizabeth Anne *13:* 193
Schreiber, Ralph W. *13:* 193
Schreiter, Rick *14:* 97; *23:* 171; *41:* 247; *49:* 131
Schroades, John *214:* 129
Schroeder, Binette *56:* 128, 129
Schroeder, E. Peter *12:* 112
Schroeder, Ted *11:* 160; *15:* 189; *30:* 91; *34:* 43
Schrotter, Gustav *22:* 212; *30:* 225
Schubert, Dieter *101:* 167, 168; *217:* 151, 152, 153, 155
Schubert, Ingrid *217:* 151, 152, 153, 155
Schubert-Gabrys, Ingrid *101:* 167, 168
Schucker, James *31:* 163
Schuett, Stacey *72:* 137; *208:* 204
Schulder, Lili *146:* 29
Schulke, Debra *57:* 167
Schulke, Flip *57:* 167
Schulz, Barbara *167:* 24
Schulz, Charles M. *10:* 137, 138, 139, 140, 141, 142; *118:* 192, 193, 194, 196, 199
Schutzer, Dena *109:* 32
Schwark, Mary Beth *51:* 155; *72:* 175
Schwartz, Amy *47:* 191; *82:* 100; *83:* 178, 179, 180,181; *129:* 107; *131:* 197, 198; *189:* 166, 168
Schwartz, Carol *124:* 41; *130:* 199
Schwartz, Charles *8:* 184
Schwartz, Daniel *46:* 37
Schwartz, Joanie *124:* 170
Schwartzberg, Joan *3:* 208
Schwarz, Viviane *204:* 132
Schweitzer, Iris *2:* 137; *6:* 207
Schweninger, Ann *29:* 172; *82:* 246; *159:* 202; *168:* 166; *211:* 193
Schwinger, Laurence *84:* 44; *91:* 61
Scofield, Penrod *61:* 107; *62:* 160
Scott, Anita Walker *7:* 38
Scott, Art *39:* 41
Scott, Frances Gruse *38:* 43
Scott, Julian *34:* 126
Scott, Roszel *33:* 238
Scott, Sally *87:* 27
Scott, Steve *166:* 230, 231; *171:* 93
Scott, Trudy *27:* 172
Scotton, Rob *214:* 183
Scrace, Carolyn *143:* 95, 96
Scrambly, Crab *198:* 196
Scribner, Joanne *14:* 236; *29:* 78; *33:* 185; *34:* 208; *78:* 75; *164:* 237; *203:* 73
Scrofani, Joseph *31:* 65; *74:* 225
Scroggs, Kirk *187:* 169
Seaman, Mary Lott *34:* 64
Searle, Ronald *24:* 98; *42:* 172, 173, 174, 176, 177, 179; *66:* 73, 74; *70:* 205, 206, 207
Searle, Townley *36:* 85
Sebree, Charles *18:* 65
Sedacca, Joseph M. *11:* 25; *22:* 36
Seder, Jason *108:* 102
Seeger, Laura Vaccaro *172:* 162
Seegmiller, Don *174:* 57
Seely, David *164:* 173
Seeley, Laura L. *97:* 105
Segal, John *178:* 202
Segar, E.C. *61:* 179, 181

Segur, Adrienne *27:* 121
Seibold, J. Otto *83:* 188, 190, 191; *149:* 212, 214, 215, 216; *196:* 177, 179; *215:* 204
Seignobosc, Francoise *21:* 145, 146
Sejima, Yoshimasa *8:* 187
Selig, Sylvie *13:* 199
Seltzer, Isadore *6:* 18; *133:* 59
Seltzer, Meyer *17:* 214
Selven, Maniam *144:* 133
Selway, Martina *169:* 157
Selznick, Brian *79:* 192; *104:* 25; *117:* 175; *126:* 156; *134:* 171; *158:* 76, 78; *169:* 70; *171:* 172, 173; *191:* 106; *192:* 130; *197:* 158; *203:* 35; *205:* 92; *210:* 219, 220, 221, 222
Sempe, Jean-Jacques *47:* 92; *YABC 2:* 109
Sendak, Maurice *1:* 135, 190; *3:* 204; *7:* 142; *15:* 199; *17:* 210; *27:* 181, 182, 183, 185, 186, 187, 189,190, 191, 192, 193, 194, 195, 197, 198, 199, 203; *28:* 181, 182; *32:* 108; *33:* 148, 149; *35:* 238; *44:* 180, 181; *45:* 97, 99; *46:* 174; *73:* 225; *91:* 10, 11 *YABC1:* 167; *113:* 163, 165, 167, 168; *118:* 153; *127:* 161
Senders, Marci *180:* 79
Sengler, Johanna *18:* 256
Senn, Steve *60:* 145
Seredy, Kate *1:* 192; *14:* 20, 21; *17:* 210
Sergeant, John *6:* 74
Serra, Sebastía *212:* 215
Servello, Joe *10:* 144; *24:* 139; *40:* 91; *70:* 130, 131; *146:* 159
Seton, Ernest Thompson *18:* 260-269, 271
Seuss, Dr.
    See Geisel, Theodor
Severin, John Powers *7:* 62
Sewall, Marcia *15:* 8; *22:* 170; *37:* 171, 172, 173; *39:* 73; *45:* 209; *62:* 117; *69:* 185, 186; *71:* 212; *90:* 232; *96:* 127; *102:* 101; *107:* 129; *119:* 176, 177, 178, 180
Seward, James *70:* 35
Seward, Prudence *16:* 243
Sewell, Helen *3:* 186; *15:* 308; *33:* 102; *38:* 189, 190, 191, 192
Seymour, Stephen *54:* 21
Sfar, Joann *182:* 183
Shachat, Andrew *82:* 179
Shadbolt, Robert *203:* 68
Shahn, Ben *39:* 178; *46:* 193
Shalansky, Len *38:* 167
Shanks, Anne Zane *10:* 149
Shannon, David *57:* 137; *107:* 184; *112:* 216; *135:* 12; *152:* 223, 224, 225; *158:* 192; *212:* 159, 160, 163
Sharkey, Niamh *213:* 152
Sharp, Paul *52:* 60
Sharp, William *6:* 131; *19:* 241; *20:* 112; *25:* 141
Sharratt, Nick *102:* 207, 208; *104:* 163; *153:* 198; *175:* 176; *192:* 208; *199:* 141, 142, 143, 184, 187, 188
Shaw, Barclay *74:* 14, 16; *118:* 138
Shaw, Charles *21:* 135; *38:* 187; *47:* 124; *126:* 219
Shaw, Charles G. *13:* 200
Shaw-Smith, Emma *144:* 117
Shea, Edmund *56:* 19
Shearer, Ted *43:* 193, 194, 195, 196
Sheban, Chris *182:* 185; *190:* 102, 104; *202:* 28; *204:* 112, 114; *209:* 150; *210:* 107; *220:* 103
Sheeban, Chris *144:* 190; *158:* 163
Shefcik, James *48:* 221, 222; *60:* 141
Shefelman, Karl *58:* 168
Shefelman, Tom *204:* 137
Shefts, Joelle *48:* 210
Shein, Bob *139:* 189

Shecter, Ben *16:* 244; *25:* 109; *33:* 188, 191; *41:* 77
Shed, Greg *74:* 94; *84:* 204; *129:* 149; *167:* 91; *179:* 192; *223:* 104

Sheinkin, Stephen *204:* 139
Shekerjian, Haig *16:* 245
Shekerjian, Regina *16:* 245; *25:* 73
Sheldon, David *184:* 174; *185:* 204; *211:* 189
Shelley, John *186:* 223
Shemie, Bonnie *96:* 207
Shenton, Edward *45:* 187, 188, 189; *YABC 1:* 218, 219, 221
Shepard, Ernest H. *3:* 193; *4:* 74; *16:* 101; *17:* 109; *25:* 148; *33:* 152, 199, 200, 201, 202, 203, 204, 205, 206,207; *46:* 194; *98:* 114; *100:* 111, 178, 179, 217, 219, 220,221; *YABC 1:* 148, 153, 174, 176, 180, 181
Shepard, Mary *4:* 210; *22:* 205; *30:* 132, 133; *54:* 150, 152, 153, 157, 158; *59:* 108, 109, 111; *100:* 246
Shepherd, Amanda *198:* 14
Shepherd, Irana *171:* 112
Sheppard, Kate *195:* 176
Shepperson, Rob *96:* 153; *177:* 163; *178:* 204; *197:* 34; *205:* 108
Sheridan, Brian *196:* 193
Sherman, Theresa *27:* 167
Sherwan, Earl *3:* 196
Shields, Charles *10:* 150; *36:* 63
Shields, Leonard *13:* 83, 85, 87
Shiffman, Lena *139:* 167; *168:* 136
Shigley, Neil K. *66:* 219
Shillabeer, Mary *35:* 74
Shilston, Arthur *49:* 61; *62:* 58
Shimin, Symeon *1:* 93; *2:* 128, 129; *3:* 202; *7:* 85; *11:* 177; *12:* 139; *13:* 202, 203; *27:* 138; *28:* 65; *35:* 129; *36:* 130; *48:* 151; *49:* 59; *56:* 63, 65, 153
Shimizu, Yuko *215:* 197
Shine, Andrea *104:* 165; *128:* 34
Shinn, Everett *16:* 148; *18:* 229; *21:* 149, 150, 151; *24:* 218
Shinn, Florence Scovel *63:* 133, 135
Shore, Robert *27:* 54; *39:* 192, 193; *YABC 2:* 200
Shortall, Leonard *4:* 144; *8:* 196; *10:* 166; *19:* 227, 228, 229, 230; *25:* 78; *28:* 66, 167; *33:* 127; *52:* 125; *73:* 12, 212
Shortt, T.M. *27:* 36
Shpitalnik, Vladimir *83:* 194
Shropshire, Sandy *170:* 191
Shtainments, Leon *32:* 161
Shulevitz, Uri *3:* 198, 199; *17:* 85; *22:* 204; *27:* 212; *28:* 184; *50:* 190, 191, 192, 193, 194, 195, 196,197, 198, 199, 201; *106:* 181, 182, 183; *165:* 203, 205; *166:* 138
Shulman, Dee *180:* 140
Shupe, Bobbi *139:* 80, 81
Shute, A.B. *67:* 196
Shute, Linda *46:* 59; *74:* 118
Siberell, Anne *29:* 193
Sibley, Don *1:* 39; *12:* 196; *31:* 47
Sibthorp, Fletcher *94:* 111, 112
Sidjakov, Nicolas *18:* 274
Siebel, Fritz *3:* 120; *17:* 145
Siebold, J. Otto *158:* 227
Siegel, Hal *74:* 246
Sieger, Ted *189:* 172
Siegl, Helen *12:* 166; *23:* 216; *34:* 185, 186
Silin-Palmer, Pamela *184:* 102
Sill, John *140:* 194; *141:* 157; *221:* 163; *222:* 171
Sills, Joyce *5:* 199
Silva, Simon *108:* 122
Silver, Maggie *85:* 210
Silveria, Gordon *96:* 44
Silverstein, Alvin *8:* 189
Silverstein, Shel *33:* 211; *92:* 209, 210
Silverstein, Virginia *8:* 189
Silvey, Joe *135:* 203
Simard, Rémy *95:* 156; *221:* 144
Siminovich, Laura *219:* 172
Simmons, Elly *110:* 2; *127:* 69; *134:* 181
Simon, Eric M. *7:* 82
Simon, Hilda *28:* 189

Simon, Howard *2:* 175; *5:* 132; *19:* 199; *32:* 163, 164, 165
Simont, Marc *2:* 119; *4:* 213; *9:* 168; *13:* 238,240; *14:* 262; *16:* 179; *18:* 221; *26:* 210; *33:* 189, 194; *44:* 132; *58:* 122; *68:* 117; *73:* 204, 205, 206; *74:* 221; *126:* 199, 200; *133:* 195; *163:* 40; *164:* 128; *223:* 28
Sims, Agnes *54:* 152
Sims, Blanche *44:* 116; *57:* 129; *75:* 179, 180; *77:* 92; *104:* 192; *152:* 117; *156:* 160; *160:* 70; *168:* 174, 175; *198:* 17
Singer, Edith G. *2:* 30
Singer, Gloria *34:* 56; *36:* 43
Singer, Julia *28:* 190
Singh, Jen *178:* 146
Sinquette, Jaclyn *215:* 83
Siomades, Lorianne *134:* 45; *204:* 48; *217:* 157
Siracusa, Catherine *68:* 135; *82:* 218
Sís, Peter *67:* 179, 181, 183, 184, 185; *96:* 96, 98; *106:* 193, 194, 195; *149:* 224, 226; *180:* 177; *192:* 180, 182; *222:* 64
Sivard, Robert *26:* 124
Sivertson, Liz *116:* 84
Skardinski, Stanley *23:* 144; *32:* 84; *66:* 122; *84:* 108
Slack, Michael *185:* 108; *189:* 173, 174
Slackman, Charles B. *12:* 201
Slade, Christian *193:* 187; *204:* 134
Slade, Paul *61:* 170
Slark, Albert *99:* 212; *205:* 161
Slater, Rod *25:* 167
Slavin, Bill *182:* 14, 15; *196:* 90; *199:* 148, 149, 150; *217:* 20
Sloan, Joseph *16:* 68
Sloane, Eric *1:* 3; *52:* 153, 154, 155, 156, 157, 158, 160
Sloat, Teri *164:* 231
Slobodkin, Louis *1:* 200; *3:* 232; *5:* 168; *13:* 251; *15:* 13, 88; *26:* 173, 174, 175, 176, 178, 179; *60:* 180
Slobodkina, Esphyr *1:* 201
Slonim, David *166:* 167, 168
Small, David *50:* 204, 205; *79:* 44; *95:* 189, 190, 191; *126:* 203, 204; *136:* 119; *143:* 201, 202, 203; *144:* 246; *150:* 5; *161:* 176; *183:* 181, 182, 183, 184; *200:* 211; *212:* 86; *216:* 202, 203, 204
Small, W. *33:* 113
Smalley, Janet *1:* 154
Smath, Jerry *198:* 179, 180
Smedley, William T. *34:* 129
Smee, David *14:* 78; *62:* 30
Smee, Nicola *167:* 156
Smith, A.G., Jr. *35:* 182
Smith, Ali *204:* 66
Smith, Alvin *1:* 31, 229; *13:* 187; *27:* 216; *28:* 226; *48:* 149; *49:* 60
Smith, Andy *188:* 20; *207:* 151
Smith, Anne *194:* 147
Smith, Anne Warren *41:* 212
Smith, Barry *75:* 183
Smith, Brian *200:* 183
Smith, Carl *36:* 41
Smith, Cat Bowman *146:* 39; *164:* 219; *201:* 55, 184
Smith, Craig *97:* 197; *172:* 175; *206:* 40; *215:* 19; *217:* 129; *220:* 145
Smith, Donald A. *178:* 7
Smith, Doris Susan *41:* 139
Smith, Douglas *189:* 159; *213:* 170
Smith, Duane *171:* 152; *208:* 97
Smith, E. Boyd *19:* 70; *22:* 89; *26:* 63; *YABC 1:* 4, 5, 240, 248, 249
Smith, Edward J. *4:* 224
Smith, Elwood H. *157:* 231; *181:* 79; *203:* 160, 161, 162
Smith, Eunice Young *5:* 170
Smith, Gary *113:* 216
Smith, George *102:* 169
Smith, Howard *19:* 196

Smith, J. Gerard *95:* 42
Smith, Jacqueline Bardner *27:* 108; *39:* 197
Smith, Jay J. *61:* 119
Smith, Jeff *93:* 191
Smith, Jessie Willcox *15:* 91; *16:* 95; *18:* 231; *19:* 57, 242; *21:* 29, 156, 157, 158, 159, 160, 161; *34:* 65; *100:* 223; *YABC 1:* 6; *2:* 180, 185, 191, 311, 325
Smith, Jos. A. *52:* 131; *72:* 120; *74:* 151; *84:* 147, 148; *85:* 146; *87:* 96; *94:* 219; *96:* 97; *104:* 33; *108:* 126, 127, 128; *111:* 140; *136:* 145; *181:* 173; *200:* 213; *201:* 94
Smith, Kenneth R. *47:* 182
Smith, Keri *216:* 60
Smith, Kevin Warren *89:* 112
Smith, Kristin *209:* 197
Smith, L.H. *35:* 174
Smith, Lane *76:* 211, 213; *88:* 115; *105:* 202, 203,204, 205; *131:* 207; *160:* 217, 221; *179:* 183, 184, 185, 186; *199:* 122, 123, 124, 126
Smith, Lee *29:* 32
Smith, Linell Nash *2:* 195
Smith, Maggie Kaufman *13:* 205; *35:* 191; *110:* 158; *178:* 226; *190:* 204; *209:* 145
Smith, Mavis *101:* 219
Smith, Moishe *33:* 155
Smith, Philip *44:* 134; *46:* 203
Smith, Ralph Crosby *2:* 267; *49:* 203
Smith, Robert D. *5:* 63
Smith, Sally J. *84:* 55
Smith, Susan Carlton *12:* 208
Smith, Terry *12:* 106; *33:* 158
Smith, Virginia *3:* 157; *33:* 72
Smith, William A. *1:* 36; *10:* 154; *25:* 65
Smith-Moore, J.J. *98:* 147
Smolinski, Dick *84:* 217
Smoljan, Joe *112:* 201
Smollin, Mike *39:* 203
Smyth, Iain *105:* 207
Smyth, M. Jane *12:* 15
Smythe, Fiona *151:* 213
Smythe, Theresa *141:* 37
Snair, Andy *176:* 4
Sneed, Brad *125:* 25; *191:* 175, 176; *211:* 194
Snyder, Andrew A. *30:* 212
Snyder, Jerome *13:* 207; *30:* 173
Snyder, Joel *28:* 163
So, Meilo *162:* 201; *208:* 188
Soentpiet, Chris K. *97:* 208; *110:* 33; *159:* 184; *161:* 10; *163:* 130
Sofia *1:* 62; *5:* 90; *32:* 166; *86:* 43
Sofilas, Mark *93:* 157
Sogabe, Aki *207:* 153; *221:* 110
Sohn, Jiho *182:* 78
Sokol, Bill *37:* 178; *49:* 23
Sokolov, Kirill *34:* 188
Solbert, Ronni *1:* 159; *2:* 232; *5:* 121; *6:* 34; *17:* 249
Solomon, Michael *174:* 115
Solonevich, George *15:* 246; *17:* 47
Soloviov, Michael *223:* 122
Soma, Liana *81:* 118
Soman, David *90:* 122; *102:* 126; *140:* 120; *93:* 188; *188:* 43, 89; *200:* 180, 181
Sommer, Robert *12:* 211
Song, Jae *203:* 27
Soo, Kean *201:* 185
Sorel, Edward *4:* 61; *36:* 82; *65:* 191, 193; *126:* 214
Sorensen, Henri *196:* 58
Sorensen, Henrik *62:* 16
Sorensen, Svend Otto *22:* 130, 141; *67:* 188, 189
Sorra, Kristin *155:* 80
Sosa, Hernan *198:* 66
Sostre, Maria *187:* 36
Sotomayor, Antonio *11:* 215
Souhami, Jessica *112:* 128; *176:* 193
Sousa, Natalie C. *209:* 89
Souza, Diana *71:* 139
Sovak, Jan *115:* 190

Sowards, Ben *215:* 62
Soyer, Moses *20:* 177
Spaenkuch, August *16:* 28
Spafford, Suzy *160:* 228
Spain, Valerie *105:* 76
Spain, Sunday Sahara *133:* 204
Spalenka, Greg *149:* 69; *151:* 228; *184:* 195; *191:* 21; *196:* 12; *198:* 181, 182, 201; *208:* 92
Spanfeller, James *1:* 72, 149; *2:* 183; *19:* 230, 231,232; *22:* 66; *36:* 160, 161; *40:* 75; *52:* 166; *76:* 37
Spangler, Brie *212:* 188
Sparks, Mary Walker *15:* 247
Spears, Rick *182:* 187; *220:* 67
Speidel, Sandra *78:* 233; *94:* 178; *134:* 180; *210:* 67
Speirs, John *67:* 178
Spence, Geraldine *21:* 163; *47:* 196
Spence, Jim *38:* 89; *50:* 102
Spencer, Laurie *113:* 12
Spencer, Mark *57:* 170
Spengler, Kenneth J. *146:* 256
Sperling, Andrea *133:* 182
Spiegel, Beth *184:* 203
Spiegel, Doris *29:* 111
Spiegelman, Art *109:* 227
Spier, Jo *10:* 30
Spier, Peter *3:* 155; *4:* 200; *7:* 61; *11:* 78; *38:* 106; *54:* 120, 121, 122, 123, 124, 125, 126, 127, 128, 129, 130,131, 132, 133, 134
Spilka, Arnold *5:* 120; *6:* 204; *8:* 131
Spirin, Gennady *95:* 196, 197; *113:* 172; *128:* 9; *129:* 49; *134:* 210; *153:* 9; *204:* 143, 144, 145; *220:* 153
Spiro, Ruth *208:* 197
Spivak, I. Howard *8:* 10; *13:* 172
Spohn, David *72:* 233
Spohn, Kate *87:* 195; *147:* 201, 202
Spollen, Christopher J. *12:* 214
Spooner, Malcolm *40:* 142
Spoor, Mike *220:* 92
Spowart, Robin *82:* 228; *92:* 149; *133:* 131; *176:* 163; *177:* 183, 184; *217:* 123, 124
Sprague, Kevin *150:* 60; *196:* 62
Spranger, Nina *201:* 199
Sprattler, Rob *12:* 176
Spring, Bob *5:* 60
Spring, Ira *5:* 60
Springer, Harriet *31:* 92
Spudvilas, Anne *110:* 74; *197:* 192; *199:* 154
Spurll, Barbara *78:* 199; *88:* 141, 142; *99:* 215
Spurrier, Steven *28:* 198
Spuvilas, Anne *85:* 114
Spy
    See Ward, Leslie
Squires, Stuart *127:* 74
St. Aubin, Bruno *179:* 54
St. John, J. Allen *41:* 62
Staake, Bob *209:* 168, 169
Stabin, Victor *101:* 131; *164:* 158
Stadler, John *62:* 33; *204:* 149
Stadnyk, Greg *212:* 55
Staffan, Alvin E. *11:* 56; *12:* 187
Stahl, Ben *5:* 181; *12:* 91; *49:* 122; *71:* 128; *87:* 206; *112:* 107
Stair, Gobin *35:* 214
Stallwood, Karen *73:* 126
Stamaty, Mark Alan *12:* 215
Stammen, JoEllen McAllister *113:* 14
Stampnick, Ken *51:* 142
Stanbridge, Joanne *150:* 91
Stanley, Diane *3:* 45; *37:* 180; *80:* 217, 219
Stanley, Sanna *145:* 228
Star, Lindsay *219:* 39
Starcke, Helmut *86:* 217
Stark, Ken *197:* 102
Starr, Branka *73:* 25
Stasiak, Krystyna *49:* 181; *64:* 194
Staub, Leslie *103:* 54
Stauffer, Brian *220:* 123

Staunton, Ted *112:* 192
Stawicki, Matt *164:* 250
Stead, L. *55:* 51, 56
Steadman, Broeck *97:* 185, 186; *99:* 56; *121:* 48; *208:* 190
Steadman, Henry *211:* 130
Steadman, Ralph *32:* 180; *123:* 143, 145
Stearn, Nick *183:* 26
Stearn, Todd *218:* 179
Steckler, June *90:* 178
Steele, Robert Gantt *169:* 174
Steichen, Edward *30:* 79
Steig, William *18:* 275, 276; *70:* 215, 216, 217, 218; *111:* 173, 174, 175, 176, 177
Stein, David Ezra *211:* 168
Stein, Harve *1:* 109
Steinberg, Saul *47:* 193
Steinel, William *23:* 146
Steiner, Charlotte *45:* 196
Steiner, Joan *110:* 219; *199:* 160, 161
Steirnagel, Michael *80:* 56
Stemp, Eric *60:* 184
Stephens, Alice Barber *66:* 208, 209
Stephens, Charles H. *YABC 2:* 279
Stephens, Pam *198:* 69
Stephens, Pat *126:* 110; *128:* 101
Stephens, William M. *21:* 165
Steptoe, Javaka *151:* 203, 204; *190:* 169; *213:* 163, 164
Steptoe, John *8:* 197; *57:* 9; *63:* 158, 159, 160, 161,163, 164, 165, 166, 167; *96:* 4; *105:* 87
Stern, Simon *15:* 249, 250; *17:* 58; *34:* 192, 193
Sterret, Jane *53:* 27
Stetsios, Debbie *165:* 108, 109
Steven, Kat *158:* 237
Stevens, David *62:* 44
Stevens, Helen *189:* 31; *207:* 83
Stevens, Janet *40:* 126; *57:* 10, 11; *80:* 112; *90:* 221, 222; *109:* 156; *130:* 34; *166:* 202; *176:* 53, 116; *193:* 199, 200, 202; *208:* 127; *212:* 182
Stevens, Mary *11:* 193; *13:* 129; *43:* 95
Stevenson, Harvey *66:* 143; *80:* 201, 221; *153:* 60; *191:* 166
Stevenson, James *42:* 182, 183; *51:* 163; *66:* 184; *71:* 185, 187, 188; *78:* 262; *87:* 97; *113:* 182, 183,184, 185; *161:* 182, 183
Stevenson, Sucie *92:* 27; *104:* 194, 195; *112:* 168; *160:* 202; *194:* 172, 173; *195:* 166
Stewart, April Blair *75:* 210
Stewart, Arvis *33:* 98; *36:* 69; *60:* 118; *75:* 91; *127:* 4
Stewart, Charles *2:* 205
Stewart, Joel *151:* 205; *211:* 170, 171
Stieg, William *172:* 58
Stiles, Fran *26:* 85; *78:* 56; *82:* 150
Stillman, Susan *44:* 130; *76:* 83
Stimpson, Tom *49:* 171
Stimson, James *208:* 46
Stinemetz, Morgan *40:* 151
Stinson, Paul *110:* 86
Stirnweis, Shannon *10:* 164
Stites, Joe *86:* 96
Stobbs, William *1:* 48, 49; *3:* 68; *6:* 20; *17:* 117, 217; *24:* 150; *29:* 250; *60:* 179; *87:* 204, 205,206
Stock, Catherine *37:* 55; *65:* 198; *72:* 7; *99:* 225; *114:* 197, 198, 199; *126:* 3; *145:* 161; *161:* 82; *173:* 149; *208:* 210; *214:* 192,194
Stockman, Jack *113:* 24
Stoeke, Janet Morgan *90:* 225; *136:* 196; *202:* 182, 183
Stoerrle, Tom *55:* 147
Stolp, Jaap *49:* 98
Stolp, Todd *89:* 195
Stone, David L. *87:* 154
Stone, David *9:* 173
Stone, David K. *4:* 38; *6:* 124; *9:* 180; *43:* 182; *60:* 70
Stone, Helen V. *6:* 209

Stone, Helen *44:* 121, 122, 126
Stone, Kazuko G. *134:* 43
Stone, Kyle M. *202:* 185
Stone, Phoebe *86:* 212; *134:* 213; *162:* 188; *205:* 145
Stone, Steve *166:* 213; *208:* 185; *220:* 57,58
Stone, Tony *150:* 34, 35
Storms, Patricia *217:* 163
Storrings, Michael *191:* 108; *216:* 217
Stoud, Virginia A. *89:* 31
Stover, Jill *82:* 234
Stower, Adam *217:* 89
Strachan, Bruce *205:* 146
Stratton, Helen *33:* 151
Stratton-Porter, Gene *15:* 254, 259, 263, 264, 268, 269
Straub, Matt *192:* 176
Straub, Phillip *197:* 22
Streano, Vince *20:* 173
Street, Janet Travell *84:* 235
Streeter, Clive *121:* 2
Strickland, Shadra *209:* 179
Stringer, Lauren *129:* 187; *154:* 172, 173; *161:* 127; *183:* 187, 188
Strodl, Daniel *47:* 95
Strogart, Alexander *63:* 139
Stromoski, Rick *111:* 179; *124:* 161, 190
Strong, Joseph D., Jr. *YABC 2:* 330
Stroyer, Poul *13:* 221
Strugnell, Ann *27:* 38
Struzan, Drew *117:* 6
Stubbs, William *73:* 196
Stubis, Talivaldis *5:* 182, 183; *10:* 45; *11:* 9; *18:* 304; *20:* 127
Stubley, Trevor *14:* 43; *22:* 219; *23:* 37; *28:* 61; *87:* 26
Stuck, Marion *104:* 44
Stuecklen, Karl W. *8:* 34, 65; *23:* 103
Stull, Betty *11:* 46
Stutzman, Mark *119:* 99
Stutzmann, Laura *73:* 185
Suarez, Maribel *162:* 208; *200:* 202
Suave, Gordon *209:* 66
Suba, Susanne *4:* 202, 203; *14:* 261; *23:* 134; *29:* 222; *32:* 30
Sue, Majella Lue *209:* 182; *212:* 146
Sueling, Barbara *98:* 185
Sueling, Gwenn *98:* 186
Sugarman, Tracy *3:* 76; *8:* 199; *37:* 181, 182
Sugimoto, Yugo *170:* 144; *223:* 137
Sugita, Yutaka *36:* 180, 181
Suh, John *80:* 157
Sullivan, Dorothy *89:* 113
Sullivan, Edmund J. *31:* 86
Sullivan, James F. *19:* 280; *20:* 192
Sully, Tom *104:* 199, 200; *182:* 77
Sumichrast, Jozef *14:* 253; *29:* 168, 213
Sumiko *46:* 57
Summers, Leo *1:* 177; *2:* 273; *13:* 22
Summers, Mark *118:* 144
Summers, Mike *190:* 176
Sutton, Judith *94:* 164
Svarez, Juan *56:* 113
Svendsen, Mark *181:* 176
Svolinsky, Karel *17:* 104
Swain, Carol *172:* 182
Swain, Su Zan Noguchi *21:* 170
Swan, Susan *22:* 220, 221; *37:* 66; *60:* 146; *145:* 205; *181:* 168
Swann, Susan *86:* 55
Swanson, Karl *79:* 65; *89:* 186
Swarner, Kristina *203:* 62; *215:* 184
Swayne, Sam *53:* 143, 145
Swayne, Zoa *53:* 143, 145
Swearingen, Greg *152:* 56; *165:* 135; *173:* 2
Sweat, Lynn *25:* 206; *57:* 176; *73:* 184; *168:* 178

Sweet, Darrell K. *60:* 9; *69:* 86; *74:* 15; *75:* 215; *76:* 130, 131; *81:* 96, 122; *82:* 253; *83:* 11; *84:* 14; *85:* 37; *89:* 140; *90:* 6; *91:* 137,139; *95:* 160, 161; *126:* 25; *185:* 175; *195:* 132
Sweet, Darrell K. *1:* 163; *4:* 136; *164:* 175
Sweet, Melissa *71:* 94; *72:* 172; *111:* 82; *139:* 53, 58; *141:* 88; *142:* 231; *155:* 121; *159:* 121, 122; *172:* 185; *188:* 127; *209:* 81; *211:* 174, 175; *218:* 21
Sweet, Ozzie *31:* 149, 151, 152
Sweetland, Robert *12:* 194
Swiatkowska, Gabi *132:* 43; *175:* 139; *180:* 218; *183:* 176
Swope, Martha *43:* 160; *56:* 86, 87, 89
Sylvada, Peter *154:* 174
Sylvester, Natalie G. *22:* 222
Szafran, Gene *24:* 144
Szasz, Susanne *13:* 55, 226; *14:* 48
Szekeres, Cyndy *2:* 218; *5:* 185; *8:* 85; *11:* 166; *14:* 19; *16:* 57, 159; *26:* 49, 214; *34:* 205; *60:* 150, 151, 152, 153, 154; *73:* 224; *74:* 218; *131:* 213, 215
Szpura, Beata *81:* 68; *119:* 65; *168:* 201
Szuc, Jeff *220:* 188

T

Taback, Simms *40:* 207; *52:* 120; *57:* 34; *80:* 241; *104:* 202, 203; *170:* 176, 177; *205:* 183
Taber, Patricia *75:* 124
Tabor, Nancy Maria Grande *89:* 210; *161:* 188
Taddei, Richard *112:* 13, 14
Tadgell, Nicole *150:* 77; *161:* 20; *177:* 186; *209:* 16; *220:* 190, 191
Tadiello, Ed *133:* 200
Tafuri, Nancy *39:* 210; *75:* 199, 200; *92:* 75; *130:* 215, 216, 217
Tailfeathers, Gerald *86:* 85
Tait, Douglas *12:* 220; *74:* 105, 106
Takabayashi, Mari *113:* 112; *130:* 22; *156:* 169
Takahashi, Hideko *136:* 160; *187:* 6; *209:* 152, 187
Takakjian, Portia *15:* 274
Takashima, Shizuye *13:* 228
Talarczyk, June *4:* 173
Talbott, Hudson *84:* 240; *163:* 100; *212:* 191, 192, 193
Tallarico, Tony *116:* 197
Tallec, Olivier *218:* 4
Tallon, Robert *2:* 228; *43:* 200, 201, 202, 203, 204, 205,206, 207, 209
Tamaki, Jillian *201:* 188
Tamas, Szecsko *29:* 135
Tamburine, Jean *12:* 222
Tanaka, Yoko *215:* 187
Tancredi, Sharon *215:* 127
Tandy, H.R. *13:* 69
Tandy, Russell H. *65:* 9; *100:* 30, 131
Tang, Charles *81:* 202; *90:* 192
Tang, Susan *80:* 174; *108:* 158
Tang, You-shan *63:* 100
Tankersley, Paul *69:* 206; *133:* 219
Tannenbaum, Robert *48:* 181
Tanner, Jane *87:* 13; *97:* 37
Tanner, Tim *72:* 192; *84:* 35
Tanobe, Miyuki *23:* 221
Tarabay, Sharif *110:* 149; *113:* 123; *169:* 83
Tarkington, Booth *17:* 224, 225
Tarlow, Phyllis *61:* 198
Tate, Don *159:* 141, 191; *183:* 69; *186:* 120
Tauss, Herbert *95:* 179
Tauss, Marc *117:* 160; *126:* 155; *178:* 221; *197:* 7; *223:* 168
Tavares, Matt *159:* 192, 193; *198:* 188, 189, 190; *199:* 86
Taylor, Ann *41:* 226
Taylor, Dahl *129:* 157

Taylor, Geoff *93:* 156; *197:* 173, 175; *204:* 151, 152
Taylor, Isaac *41:* 228
Taylor, Mike *143:* 99, 100
Teague, Mark *83:* 6; *139:* 241; *170:* 180, 181; *205:* 150, 151
Teale, Edwin Way *7:* 196
Teason, James *1:* 14
Teckentrup, Britta *200:* 191, 192
Teeple, Lyn *33:* 147
Tee-Van, Helen Damrosch *10:* 176; *11:* 182
Teevee, Ningeokuluk *223:* 173
Teicher, Dick *50:* 211
Teichman, Mary *77:* 220; *124:* 208; *127:* 22; *197:* 33
Temertey, Ludmilla *96:* 232; *104:* 43, 45; *109:* 244
Tempest, Margaret *3:* 237, 238; *88:* 200
Temple, Frances *85:* 185, 186, 187
Temple, Herbert *45:* 201
Templeton, Owen *11:* 77
ten Cate, Marijke *183:* 193
Tenggren, Gustaf *18:* 277, 278, 279; *19:* 15; *28:* 86; *YABC2:* 145
Tennent, Julie *81:* 105
Tenneson, Joyce *153:* 166
Tenney, Gordon *24:* 204
Tenniel, John *74:* 234, 235; *100:* 89; *YABC 2:* 99; *153:* 63
Tepper, Matt *116:* 80
Terkel, Ari *103:* 162
Terry, Michael *180:* 209
Terry, Will *131:* 73; *205:* 155; *223:* 105
Teskey, Donald *71:* 51
Tessler, Manya *200:* 193
Thacher, Mary M. *30:* 72
Thackeray, William Makepeace *23:* 224, 228
Thamer, Katie *42:* 187
Tharlet, Eve *146:* 149
Thelwell, Norman *14:* 201
Theobalds, Prue *40:* 23
Theurer, Marilyn Churchill *39:* 195
Thiesing, Lisa *89:* 134; *95:* 202; *156:* 190; *159:* 195
Thiewes, Sam *133:* 114
Thisdale, François *223:* 55
Thistlethwaite, Miles *12:* 224
Thollander, Earl *11:* 47; *18:* 112; *22:* 224
Thomas, Allan *22:* 13
Thomas, Art *48:* 217
Thomas, Eric *28:* 49
Thomas, Harold *20:* 98
Thomas, Jacqui *125:* 95
Thomas, Jan *197:* 180
Thomas, Mark *42:* 136
Thomas, Martin *14:* 255
Thomas, Middy *177:* 114
Thompson, Arthur *34:* 107
Thompson, Carol *85:* 189; *95:* 75; *102:* 86; *147:* 166; *189:* 179, 180, 181; *190:* 84; *207:* 18
Thompson, Colin *95:* 204
Thompson, Ellen *51:* 88, 151; *60:* 33; *67:* 42; *77:* 148; *78:* 75, 219; *79:* 122, 170; *84:* 219; *85:* 97; *87:* 37; *88:* 192, 194; *89:* 80; *93:* 37; *98:* 59; *132:* 14
Thompson, George W. *22:* 18; *28:* 150; *33:* 135
Thompson, John *58:* 201; *102:* 226; *124:* 154; *128:* 228; *129:* 157; *150:* 49; *185:* 160; *191:* 192
Thompson, Julie *44:* 158
Thompson, Katherine *132:* 146
Thompson, K. Dyble *84:* 6
Thompson, Miles *152:* 77
Thompson, Sharon *74:* 113; *158:* 60; *165:* 87
Thomson, Arline K. *3:* 264
Thomson, Bill *186:* 160
Thomson, Hugh *26:* 88
Thomson, Ross *36:* 179

Thorkelson, Gregg *95:* 183, 184; *98:* 58; *165:* 30, 31
Thorn, Lori *189:* 119
Thornberg, Dan *104:* 125
Thornburgh, Rebecca McKillip *143:* 37
Thorne, Diana *25:* 212
Thornhill, Jan *77:* 213
Thorpe, Peter *58:* 109
Thorvall, Kerstin *13:* 235
Threadgall, Colin *77:* 215
Thurber, James *13:* 239, 242, 243, 245, 248, 249
Thurman, Mark *63:* 173; *168:* 116
Tibbles, Jean-Paul *115:* 200
Tibbles, Paul *45:* 23
Tibo, Gilles *67:* 207; *107:* 199, 201
Tichenor, Tom *14:* 207
Tichnor, Richard *90:* 218
Tiegreen, Alan *36:* 143; *43:* 55, 56, 58; *77:* 200; *94:* 216, 217; *121:* 54, 59
Tierney, Tom *113:* 198, 200, 201
Tildes, Phyllis Limbacher *210:* 240
Tilley, Debbie *102:* 134; *133:* 226; *137:* 101; *159:* 96; *190:* 211, 212; *213:* 51
Tillman, Nancy *211:* 129, 178
Tilney, F.C. *22:* 231
Timbs, Gloria *36:* 90
Timmins, Harry *2:* 171
Timmons, Bonnie *194:* 189
Tinkelman, Murray *12:* 225; *35:* 44
Titherington, Jeanne *39:* 90; *58:* 138; *75:* 79; *135:* 161
Tjader, Ella *209:* 14
Tobin, Nancy *145:* 197
Toddy, Irving *172:* 144
Tokunbo, Dimitrea *181:* 183; *187:* 182, 183
Tolbert, Jeff *128:* 69
Toledo, Francisco *197:* 182; *198:* 199
Toledo, Natalia *197:* 182
Tolford, Joshua *1:* 221
Tolkien, J.R.R. *2:* 243; *32:* 215
Tolman, Marije *195:* 43
Tolmie, Ken *15:* 292
Tomei, Lorna *47:* 168, 171
Tomes, Jacqueline *2:* 117; *12:* 139
Tomes, Margot *1:* 224; *2:* 120, 121; *16:* 207; *18:* 250; *20:* 7; *25:* 62; *27:* 78, 79; *29:* 81, 199; *33:* 82; *36:* 186, 187, 188, 189, 190; *46:* 129; *56:* 71; *58:* 183; *70:* 228; *75:* 73, 75; *80:* 80; *83:* 97; *90:* 205
Tommaso, Rich *200:* 198
Tommorow, Tom *223:* 176
Toner, Raymond John *10:* 179
Tong, Gary *66:* 215
Tongier, Stephen *82:* 32
Tooke, Susan *173:* 162
Toothill, Harry *6:* 54; *7:* 49; *25:* 219; *42:* 192
Toothill, Ilse *6:* 54
Topolski, Feliks *44:* 48
Torbert, Floyd James *22:* 226
Torgersen, Don *55:* 157
Torline, Kevin *169:* 171
Tormey, Bertram M. *75:* 3, 4
Torrecilla, Pablo *176:* 207
Torres, Leyla *156:* 199, 201
Torrey, Helen *87:* 41
Torrey, Marjorie *34:* 105
Torrey, Richard *189:* 182; *205:* 24
Toschik, Larry *6:* 102
Totten, Bob *13:* 93
Toy, Julie *128:* 112
Trachok, Cathy *131:* 16
Tracy, Libba *82:* 24
Trago, Keith *158:* 253
Trail, Lee *55:* 157
Trang, To Ngoc *167:* 180
Trang, Winson *89:* 151
Trapani, Iza *116:* 202; *214:* 203
Travers, Bob *49:* 100; *63:* 145
Treatner, Meryl *95:* 180
Tremain, Ruthven *17:* 238

Tresilian, Stuart 25: 53; 40: 212
Trez, Alain 17: 236
Trezzo, Loretta 86: 45
Trier, Walter 14: 96
Trimby, Elisa 47: 199
Trinkle, Sally 53: 27
Triplett, Gina 182: 193; 188: 100; 198: 38
Tripp, F.J. 24: 167
Tripp, Wallace 2: 48; 7: 28; 8: 94; 10: 54,76;
    11: 92; 31: 170, 171; 34: 203; 42: 57; 60:
    157; 73: 182
Trivas, Irene 53: 4; 54: 168; 82: 46, 101
Trnka, Jiri 22: 151; 43: 212, 213, 214, 215;
    YABC 1: 30, 31
Trondheim, Lewis 182: 183
Troughton, Joanna 37: 186; 48: 72
Troyer, Johannes 3: 16; 7: 18
Trudeau, G.B. 35: 220, 221, 222; 48: 119,
    123, 126, 127,128, 129, 133; 168: 189
Trueman, Matthew 165: 208; 183: 191; 220:
    61; 222: 174
Truesdell, Sue 55: 142; 108: 219, 220; 212:
    202; 220: 78
Tryon, Leslie 84: 7; 139: 214; 143: 10; 181:
    10
Tseng, Jean 72: 195; 94: 102; 119: 126; 151:
    106; 173: 138, 139; 200: 158
Tseng, Mou-sien 72: 195; 94: 102; 119: 126;
    151: 106; 173: 138, 139; 200: 158
Tsinajinie, Andy 2: 62
Tsinganos, Jim 180: 142
Tsugami, Kyuzo 18: 198, 199
Tucker, Ezra 156: 31
Tuckwell, Jennifer 17: 205
Tudor, Bethany 7: 103
Tudor, Tasha 18: 227; 20: 185, 186, 187; 36:
    111; 69: 196, 198; 100: 44;
    YABC 2: 46, 314; 160: 234
Tuerk, Hanne 71: 201
Tugeau, Jeremy 199: 170; 203: 96
Tulloch, Maurice 24: 79
Tunis, Edwin 1: 218, 219; 28: 209, 210, 211,
    212
Tunnicliffe, C.F. 62: 176; 177; 178, 179; 181
Turkle, Brinton 1: 211, 213; 2: 249; 3: 226;
    11: 3; 16: 209; 20: 22; 50: 23; 67: 50; 68:
    65; 79: 205, 206, 207; 128: 47; YABC 1: 79
Turnbull, Christopher J. 143: 99, 100
Turner, Gwenda 59: 195
Turner, Helen 203: 154
Turska, Krystyna 12: 103; 31: 173, 174, 175;
    56: 32,34; 100: 66
Tusa, Tricia 72: 242; 111: 180, 181; 157: 165;
    164: 186; 189: 40; 201: 9; 207: 163, 164
Tusan, Stan 6: 58; 22: 236, 237
Tuschman, Richard 219: 100
Tworkov, Jack 47: 207
Tyers, Jenny 89: 220
Tylden-Wright, Jenny 114: 119
Tyrol, Adelaide Murphy 103: 27
Tyrrell, Frances 107: 204
Tzimoulis, Paul 12: 104

U

Uchida, Yoshiko 1: 220
Uderzo 47: 88
Udovic, David 189: 185; 195: 201
Ueno, Noriko 59: 155
Ugliano, Natascia 196: 186
Ulm, Robert 17: 238
Ulrich, George 73: 15; 75: 136, 139; 99: 150
Ulriksen, Mark 101: 58; 182: 43; 210: 243
Unada 84: 67
    See Gliewe, Unada
Underhill, Liz 53: 159
Underwood, Beck 192: 36
Underwood, Clarence 40: 166
Unger, Jim 67: 208

Ungerer, Tomi 5: 188; 9: 40; 18: 188; 29:
    175; 33: 221, 222, 223, 225; 71: 48; 106:
    209, 210, 211, 212
Unwin, Nora S. 3: 65, 234, 235; 4: 237; 44:
    173, 174; YABC 1: 59; 2: 301
Upitis, Alvis 145: 179
Urban, Helle 149: 243
Urbanovic, Jackie 86: 86; 189: 186, 187
Urberuaga, Emilio 219: 110, 175
U'ren, Andrea 213: 177
Uris, Jill 49: 188, 197
Ursell, Martin 50: 51
Utpatel, Frank 18: 114
Utz, Lois 5: 190

V

Vagin, Vladimir 66: 10; 142: 215
Vaillancourt, Francois 107: 199
Vainio, Pirkko 123: 157, 158
Valério, Geraldo 180: 225; 194: 116
Vallejo, Boris 62: 130; 72: 212; 91: 38; 93: 61
Van Abbe, S. 16: 142; 18: 282; 31: 90; YABC
    2: 157, 161
Van Allsburg, Chris 37: 205, 206; 53: 161,
    162, 163, 165,166, 167, 168, 169, 170, 171;
    105: 215, 216, 217, 218; 156: 176, 177, 178
Vance, James 65: 28
Van Der Linde, Henry 99: 17
van der Meer, Ron 98: 204, 205
van der Meer, Atie 98: 204, 205
Vandivert, William 21: 175
Van Dongen, H.R. 81: 97
Van Dusen, Chris W. 173: 169
Vane, Mitch 210: 160; 218: 152
Van Everen, Jay 13: 160; YABC 1: 121
Van Fleet, John 165: 12, 13
Van Frankenhuyzen, Gijsbert 145: 230; 149:
    164; 184: 151; 210: 248
van Genechten, Guido 165: 226
van Haeringen, Annemarie 193: 206
Van Horn, William 43: 218
van Hout, Mies 195: 191; 207: 58
van Kampen, Vlasta 194: 217
van Lawick, Hugo 62: 76, 79
Van Lieshout, Maria 201: 196; 223: 119
Van Loon, Hendrik Willem 18: 285, 289, 291
Van Munching, Paul 83: 85
van Ommen, Sylvia 186: 192
Van Patter, Bruce 183: 195
Van Rynbach, Iris 102: 192
Van Sciver, Ruth 37: 162
VanSeveren, Joe 63: 182
Van Stockum, Hilda 5: 193
Van Vleet, John 213: 180
Van Wassenhove, Sue 202: 193
Van Wely, Babs 16: 50; 79: 16
Van Wright, Cornelius 72: 18; 102: 208; 116:
    107; 152: 236; 173: 170, 171; 199: 185
Van Zyle, Jon 103: 125; 160: 181, 182; 176:
    199, 200; 221: 128
Vardzigulyants, Ruben 90: 54
Varga, Judy 29: 196
Vargo, Kurt 79: 224
Varley, Susan 61: 199; 63: 176, 177; 101: 148;
    134: 220
Varon, Sara 195: 208
Vasconcellos, Daniel 80: 42
Vasiliu, Mircea 2: 166, 253; 9: 166; 13: 58;
    68: 42
Vaughn, Frank 34: 157
Vavra, Robert 8: 206
Vawter, Will 17: 163
Vayas, Diana 71: 61
Vazquez, Carlos 125: 184
Veeder, Larry 18: 4

Velasquez, Eric 45: 217; 61: 45; 63: 110, 111;
    88: 162; 90: 34, 144; 94: 213; 107: 147;
    132: 192; 138: 213; 159: 126; 181: 184;
    184: 96; 191: 16; 192: 234; 208: 37; 214:
    81
Velasquez, Jose A. 63: 73
Velez, Walter 71: 75; 91: 154; 121: 181; 168:
    49; 207: 52
Velthuijs, Max 110: 228, 229
Vendrell, Carme Sole 42: 205
Venezia, Mike 54: 17
Venti, Anthony Bacon 124: 103; 126: 26
Venturo, Piero 61: 194, 195
Ver Beck, Frank 18: 16, 17
Verkaaik, Ben 110: 209
Verling, John 71: 27
Verney, John 14: 225; 75: 8
Vernon, Ursula 204: 157
Verrier, Suzanne 5: 20; 23: 212
Verroken, Sarah 223: 178
Versace, Marie 2: 255
Vess, Charles 215: 201
Vestal, H.B. 9: 134; 11: 101; 27: 25; 34: 158
Vestergaard, Hope 190: 203
Vicatan 59: 146
Vickrey, Robert 45: 59, 64
Victor, Joan Berg 30: 193
Vieceli, Emma 210: 245
Viereck, Ellen 3: 242; 14: 229
Vigna, Judith 15: 293; 102: 194, 195, 196, 197
Vila, Laura 207: 172
Vilato, Gaspar E. 5: 41
Villiard, Paul 51: 178
Vimnera, A. 23: 154
Vincent, Eric 34: 98
Vincent, Felix 41: 237
Vincent, Gabrielle 121: 175
Vip 45: 164
Viskupic, Gary 83: 48
Vitale, Stefano 109: 71, 107; 114: 219, 220;
    123: 106; 138: 232; 180: 228, 229; 212: 38
Vivas, Julie 51: 67, 69; 96: 225; 197: 190;
    199: 71
Voake, Charlotte 114: 221, 222; 180: 232
Vo-Dinh, Mai 16: 272; 60: 191
Vogel, Ilse-Margret 14: 230
Voigt, Erna 35: 228
Vojnar, Kamil 95: 31; 114: 4; 115: 62; 121:
    90; 124: 72; 130: 31; 141: 81; 146: 196;
    150: 123; 158: 5, 6; 158: 154; 171: 119,
    188; 179: 15; 180: 112; 203: 74; 223: 30
Vojtech, Anna 42: 190; 108: 222, 223; 150:
    203; 174: 173
von Buhler, Cynthia 149: 237; 162: 177; 177:
    205; 180: 77; 185: 214, 215, 216
von Roehl, Angela 126: 191
von Schmidt, Eric 8: 62; 50: 209, 210
von Schmidt, Harold 30: 80
Vosburgh, Leonard 1: 161; 7: 32; 15: 295,
    296; 23: 110; 30: 214; 43: 181
Voss, Tom 127: 104
Voter, Thomas W. 19: 3, 9
Vroman, Tom 10: 29
Vulliamy, Clara 72: 65

W

Waber, Bernard 47: 209, 210, 211, 212, 213,
    214; 95: 215, 216, 217; 156: 203, 205, 206,
    207
Wachenje, Benjamin 194: 170
Wack, Jeff 95: 140; 110: 90
Wagner, John 8: 200; 52: 104
Wagner, Ken 2: 59
Wagner, Michael 211: 159
Wahman, Wendy 218: 186
Waide, Jan 29: 225; 36: 139
Wainwright, Jerry 14: 85

Waites, Joan C. *171:* 2
Wakeen, Sandra *47:* 97
Wakiyama, Hanako *171:* 96; *192:* 236; *200:* 16
Waldherr, Kris *81:* 186
Waldman, Bruce *15:* 297; *43:* 178
Waldman, Neil *35:* 141; *50:* 163; *51:* 180; *54:* 78, 77; *77:* 112; *79:* 162; *82:* 174; *84:* 5, 56, 106; *94:* 232, 233, 234; *96:* 41; *111:* 139; *113:* 9; *118:* 30; *142:* 220, 223; *203:* 173, 174
Waldrep, Richard *111:* 147; *198:* 202
Walker, Brian *144:* 128
Walker, Charles *1:* 46; *4:* 59; *5:* 177; *11:* 115; *19:* 45; *34:* 74; *62:* 168; *72:* 218
Walker, Dugald Stewart *15:* 47; *32:* 202; *33:* 112
Walker, Gil *8:* 49; *23:* 132; *34:* 42
Walker, Jeff *55:* 154; *123:* 116
Walker, Jim *10:* 94
Walker, Mort *8:* 213
Walker, Norman *41:* 37; *45:* 58
Walker, Stephen *12:* 229; *21:* 174
Wallace, Beverly Dobrin *19:* 259
Wallace, Cly *87:* 93
Wallace, Ian *53:* 176, 177; *56:* 165, 166; *58:* 4; *98:* 4; *101:* 191; *112:* 124; *141:* 197, 198, 199, 200; *151:* 212; *219:* 180, 182
Wallace, John *105:* 228
Wallace, Nancy Elizabeth *141:* 204; *186:* 195, 197, 199; *222:* 191, 192, 193, 194
Wallenta, Adam *123:* 180
Waller, S.E. *24:* 36
Wallner, Alexandra *15:* 120; *156:* 183
Wallner, John C. *9:* 77; *10:* 188; *11:* 28; *14:* 209; *31:* 56, 118; *37:* 64; *51:* 186, 187, 188, 189, 190, 191,192, 193, 194, 195; *52:* 96; *53:* 23, 26; *71:* 99; *73:* 158; *89:* 215; *141:* 9
Wallner, John *162:* 17
Wallower, Lucille *11:* 226
Walotsky, Ron *93:* 87
Walsh, Ellen Stoll *99:* 209; *147:* 219; *194:* 194, 195, 196
Walsh, Rebecca *158:* 193; *217:* 169, 170
Walsh, Vivian *149:* 215; *158:* 227
Walters, Anita *205:* 163
Walters, Audrey *18:* 294
Walther, Tom *31:* 179
Walton, Garry *69:* 149
Walton, Tony *11:* 164; *24:* 209; *153:* 8; *177:* 73
Waltrip, Lela *9:* 195
Waltrip, Mildred *3:* 209; *37:* 211
Waltrip, Rufus *9:* 195
Wan *12:* 76
Wan, Shelly *212:* 131
Wang, Lin *221:* 179
Wang, Shaoli *216:* 220
Wang, Suling *191:* 183; *213:* 194
Warburton, Sarah *154:* 187
Wappers, G. *121:* 40
Ward, Chad Michael *217:* 121
Ward, Fred *52:* 19
Ward, Helen *72:* 244; *144:* 240, 242
Ward, John *42:* 191; *96:* 54; *97:* 110; *123:* 105; *124:* 71; *173:* 66; *221:* 55
Ward, Keith *2:* 107; *132:* 69
Ward, Leslie *34:* 126; *36:* 87
Ward, Lynd *1:* 99, 132, 133, 150; *2:* 108, 158, 196, 259; *18:* 86; *27:* 56; *29:* 79, 187, 253, 255; *36:* 199,200, 201, 202, 203, 204, 205, 206, 207, 209; *43:* 34; *56:* 28; *60:* 116; *100:* 65
Ward, Peter *37:* 116
Waring, Geoff *172:* 84
Warhola, James *92:* 5; *115:* 85, 87; *118:* 174, 175, 177; *176:* 84; *187:* 189, 190; *223:* 102
Warner, Ben *159:* 171
Warner, Peter *14:* 87
Warner, Sally *214:* 210
Warnes, Tim *175:* 159; *202:* 188; *216:* 224
Warnick, Elsa *113:* 223

Warren, Betsy *2:* 101
Warren, Jim *85:* 81
Warren, Marion Cray *14:* 215
Warshaw, Jerry *30:* 197, 198; *42:* 165
Wasden, Kevin *102:* 162
Washington, Nevin *20:* 123
Washington, Phyllis *20:* 123
Wasserman, Amy L. *92:* 110; *209:* 95
Waterman, Stan *11:* 76
Watkins-Pitchford, D.J. *6:* 215, 217
Watling, James *67:* 210; *78:* 112; *101:* 81; *117:* 189, 190; *127:* 119, 120
Watson, Aldren A. *2:* 267; *5:* 94; *13:* 71; *19:* 253; *32:* 220; *42:* 193, 194, 195, 196, 197, 198, 199, 200, 201; *YABC 2:* 202
Watson, G. *83:* 162
Watson, Gary *19:* 147; *36:* 68; *41:* 122; *47:* 139
Watson, J.D. *22:* 86
Watson, Jesse Joshua *197:* 124; *199:* 181; *202:* 136
Watson, Karen *11:* 26
Watson, Mary *117:* 193
Watson, Richard Jesse *62:* 188, 189; *211:* 201
Watson, Wendy *5:* 197; *13:* 101; *33:* 116; *46:* 163; *64:* 12; *74:* 242, 243; *91:* 21; *142:* 228; *215:* 79
Watt, Mélanie *136:* 206; *193:* 211
Wattenberg, Jane *174:* 200; *185:* 46; *187:* 108
Watterson, Bill *66:* 223, 225, 226
Watts, Bernadette *4:* 227; *103:* 182, 183
Watts, James *59:* 197; *74:* 145; *86:* 124
Watts, John *37:* 149
Watts, Leslie Elizabeth *150:* 207; *165:* 106; *209:* 67
Watts, Stan *116:* 205
Weatherby, Mark Alan *77:* 141
Webb, Jennifer *110:* 79
Webb, Lanny *142:* 175
Webb, Sophie *135:* 214
Webber, Helen *3:* 141
Webber, Irma E. *14:* 238
Weber, Erik *56:* 19, 20
Weber, Florence *40:* 153
Weber, Jill *127:* 227, 228; *189:* 163; *208:* 157; *209:* 190, 191; *216:* 46
Weber, Roland *61:* 204
Weber, Sam *190:* 227
Weber, William J. *14:* 239
Webster, Jean *17:* 241
Weeks, Sarah *162:* 39
Wegman, William *78:* 243
Wegner, Fritz *14:* 250; *20:* 189; *44:* 165; *86:* 62
Weidenear, Reynold H. *21:* 122
Weigel, Jeff *170:* 193
Weihs, Erika *4:* 21; *15:* 299; *72:* 201; *107:* 207, 208
Weil, Lisl *7:* 203; *10:* 58; *21:* 95; *22:* 188,217; *33:* 193
Weiman, Jon *50:* 162, 165; *52:* 103; *54:* 78, 79, 81; *78:* 80; *82:* 107; *93:* 82; *97:* 69; *105:* 179; *193:* 65
Weiner, Greg *215:* 21
Weiner, Sandra *14:* 240
Weiner, Scott *55:* 27
Weinhaus, Karen Ann *53:* 90; *71:* 50; *86:* 124
Weinman, Brad *197:* 20
Weinstock, Robert *204:* 165, 166
Weisgard, Leonard *1:* 65; *2:* 191, 197, 204, 264, 265; *5:* 108; *21:* 42; *30:* 200, 201, 203, 204; *41:* 47; *44:* 125; *53:* 25; *85:* 196, 198, 200, 201; *100:* 139,207; *YABC 2:* 13
Weisman, David *173:* 47
Weiss, Ellen *44:* 202
Weiss, Emil *1:* 168; *7:* 60
Weiss, Harvey *1:* 145, 223; *27:* 224, 227; *68:* 214; *76:* 245, 246, 247
Weiss, Nicki *33:* 229
Weissman, Bari *49:* 72; *90:* 125; *139:* 142
Weitzman, David L. *172:* 199

Welch, Sheila Kelly *130:* 221
Welkes, Allen *68:* 218
Wellington, Monica *99:* 223; *157:* 259, 260, 261; *222:* 197, 198, 199, 200
Welliver, Norma *76:* 94
Wellner, Fred *127:* 53
Wells, Frances *1:* 183
Wells, H.G. *20:* 194, 200
Wells, Haru *53:* 120, 121
Wells, Robert E. *184:* 208
Wells, Rosemary *6:* 49; *18:* 297; *60:* 32; *66:* 203; *69:* 215, 216; *114:* 227; *118:* 149, 150; *156:* 188, 189, 190, 191; *207:* 180, 181, 182, 183
Wells, Rufus III *56:* 111, 113
Wells, Susan *22:* 43
Wendelin, Rudolph *23:* 234
Wengenroth, Stow *37:* 47
Weninger, Brigitte *189:* 192, 194
Werenskiold, Erik *15:* 6; *62:* 17
Werner, Honi *24:* 110; *33:* 41; *88:* 122
Werth, Kurt *7:* 122; *14:* 157; *20:* 214; *39:* 128
Wesson,
West, Harry A. *124:* 38
Westcott, Nadine Bernard *68:* 46; *84:* 49; *86:* 133; *106:* 199; *111:* 78; *113:* 111; *130:* 224; *139:* 54; *158:* 256; *194:* 199
Westerberg, Christine *29:* 226
Westerduin, Anne *105:* 229
Westerman, Johanna *162:* 206
Weston, Martha *29:* 116; *30:* 213; *33:* 85, 100; *53:* 181, 182, 183, 184; *77:* 95; *80:* 152; *119:* 196,197, 198, 199; *127:* 189; *133:* 196; *209:* 199
Wetherbee, Margaret *5:* 3
Wexler, Jerome *49:* 73; *150:* 129
Whalley, Peter *50:* 49
Whamond, Dave *222:* 203
Whatley, Bruce *186:* 93, 95; *207:* 127; *213:* 183, 184
Wheatley, Arabelle *11:* 231; *16:* 276
Wheeler, Cindy *49:* 205
Wheeler, Dora *44:* 179
Wheelright, Rowland *15:* 81; *YABC 2:* 286
Whelan, Michael *56:* 108; *70:* 27, 29, 67, 68, 148; *74:* 18; *84:* 14; *91:* 195, 196; *95:* 147; *98:* 150, 151; *106:* 157; *113:* 218, 220; *116:* 99, 100
Whelan, Patrick *135:* 145
Whistler, Rex *16:* 75; *30:* 207, 208
White, Beth *216:* 139
White, Craig *110:* 130; *119:* 193; *130:* 33; *179:* 31
White, David Omar *5:* 56; *18:* 6
White, Joan *83:* 225
White, Lee *221:* 176; *223:* 188, 189, 190
White, Martin *51:* 197; *85:* 127
Whitear *32:* 26
Whitehead, Beck *86:* 171
Whitehead, Jenny *221:* 16
Whitehead, S.B. *154:* 132
Whithorne, H.S. *7:* 49
Whitman, Candace *208:* 208
Whitney, George Gillett *3:* 24
Whitney, Jean *99:* 53
Whitson, Paul *102:* 161
Whittam, Geoffrey *30:* 191
Whyte, Mary *96:* 127
Wiberg, Harald *38:* 127; *93:* 215
Wick, Walter *77:* 128
Wickstrom, Sylvie *106:* 87; *169:* 180; *214:* 110
Wickstrom, Thor *200:* 205
Widener, Terry *105:* 230; *106:* 7; *163:* 23; *200:* 17; *209:* 195
Wiese, Kurt *3:* 255; *4:* 206; *14:* 17; *17:* 18, 19; *19:* 47; *24:* 152; *25:* 212; *32:* 184; *36:* 211,213, 214, 215, 216, 217, 218; *45:* 161; *100:* 92

Wiesner, David *33:* 47; *51:* 106; *57:* 67; *58:* 55; *64:* 78, 79, 81; *69:* 233; *72:* 247, 248, 249, 251,252, 253, 254; *83:* 134; *104:* 31; *117:* 197, 199, 200, 202; *139:* 223, 224; *151:* 51; *181:* 189, 190
Wiesner, William *4:* 100; *5:* 200, 201; *14:* 262
Wight, Eric *218:* 190
Wiggins, George *6:* 133
Wijngaard, Juan *111:* 36; *114:* 124
Wikkelsoe, Otto *45:* 25, 26
Wikland, Ilon *5:* 113; *8:* 150; *38:* 124, 125, 130; *127:* 162
Wikler, Madeline *114:* 233
Wilbur, C. Keith, M.D. *27:* 228
Wilburn, Kathy *53:* 102; *68:* 234
Wilcox, Cathy *105:* 123
Wilcox, J.A.J. *34:* 122
Wilcox, Lydia *207:* 187
Wilcox, R. Turner *36:* 219
Wild, Jocelyn *46:* 220, 221, 222; *80:* 117
Wilde, George *7:* 139
Wildsmith, Brian *16:* 281, 282; *18:* 170, 171; *66:* 25; *69:* 224, 225, 227; *77:* 103; *83:* 218; *124:* 214,217, 219
Wildsmith, Mike *140:* 229
Wilhelm, Hans *58:* 189, 191; *73:* 157; *77:* 127; *135:* 229, 230, 233, 234; *196:* 209
Wilkin, Eloise *36:* 173; *49:* 208, 209, 210
Wilkinson, Barry *50:* 213
Wilkinson, Gerald *3:* 40
Wilkon, Jozef *31:* 183, 184; *71:* 206, 207, 209; *133:* 222
Wilks, Mike *34:* 24; *44:* 203
Willems, Mo *154:* 245, 246, 247; *180:* 236, 237, 239
Willey, Bee *103:* 129; *139:* 159; *173:* 115
Willhoite, Michael A. *71:* 214
William, Maria *168:* 51
Williams, Berkeley, Jr. *64:* 75
Williams, Ferelith Eccles *22:* 238
Williams, Garth *1:* 197; *2:* 49, 270; *4:* 205; *15:* 198, 302, 304, 307; *16:* 34; *18:* 283, 298, 299, 300, 301; *29:* 177, 178, 179, 232, 233, 241, 242, 243, 244, 245, 248; *40:* 106; *66:* 229, 230, 231, 233, 234; *71:* 192; *73:* 218, 219, 220; *78:* 261; *100:* 251, 252, 255; *136:* 117; *YABC 2:* 15, 16, 19
Williams, J. Scott *48:* 28
Williams, Jennifer *102:* 201
Williams, Jenny *60:* 202; *81:* 21; *88:* 71
Williams, Kent *180:* 18
Williams, Kit *44:* 206, 207, 208, 209, 211, 212
Williams, Marcia *97:* 214; *159:* 208, 209
Williams, Maureen *12:* 238
Williams, Patrick *14:* 218
Williams, Richard *44:* 93; *72:* 229; *74:* 133; *78:* 155, 237; *91:* 178; *110:* 212; *136:* 201, 202, 203; *152:* 115
Williams, Sam *124:* 222; *153:* 11; *177:* 201, 202; *180:* 34; *212:* 49
Williams, Sophy *135:* 236
Williams, Vera B. *53:* 186, 187, 188, 189; *102:* 201, 202, 203; *210:* 65
Williamson, Alex *177:* 180; *205:* 50
Williamson, Mel *60:* 9
Willingham, Fred *104:* 206; *154:* 157
Willis, Adam *181:* 75; *209:* 11
Willmore, J.T. *54:* 113, 114
Wilsdorf, Anne *180:* 122; *189:* 124; *191:* 195
Wilson, Anne *160:* 114
Wilson, Charles Banks *17:* 92; *43:* 73
Wilson, Connie *113:* 194
Wilson, Dagmar *10:* 47
Wilson, Dawn *67:* 161; *81:* 120; *113:* 158
Wilson, Edward A. *6:* 24; *16:* 149; *20:* 220, 221; *22:* 87; *26:* 67; *38:* 212, 214, 215, 216, 217
Wilson, Forrest *27:* 231
Wilson, Gahan *35:* 234; *41:* 136
Wilson, George *76:* 87
Wilson, Helen Miranda *140:* 61

Wilson, Jack *17:* 139
Wilson, Janet *77:* 154; *96:* 114; *99:* 219, 220; *153:* 64 *106:* 122; *130:* 210; *145:* 178; *173:* 64
Wilson, John *22:* 240
Wilson, Maurice *46:* 224
Wilson, Patten *35:* 61
Wilson, Peggy *15:* 4; *84:* 20
Wilson, Phil *181:* 29
Wilson, Rowland B. *30:* 170
Wilson, Sarah *50:* 215
Wilson, Tom *33:* 232
Wilson, W.N. *22:* 26
Wilson-Max, Ken *170:* 196; *180:* 181
Wilton, Nicholas *103:* 52; *183:* 111
Wilwerding, Walter J. *9:* 202
Wimmer, Mike *63:* 6; *70:* 121; *75:* 186; *76:* 21,22, 23; *91:* 114; *97:* 45, 68; *98:* 28; *107:* 130; *146:* 21; *149:* 47; *173:* 126; *193:* 21, 25; *194:* 204, 205
Winborn, Marsha *78:* 34; *99:* 70; *192:* 20
Winch, John *165:* 233
Winchester, Linda *13:* 231
Wind, Betty *28:* 158
Windham, Kathryn Tucker *14:* 260
Windham, Sophie *184:* 212
Winfield, Alison *115:* 78; *214:* 121
Winfield, Wayne *72:* 23
Wing, Gary *64:* 147
Wing, Ron *50:* 85
Wingerter, Linda S. *132:* 199; *174:* 181; *200:* 196
Winick, Judd *124:* 227, 228, 229
Winn-Lederer, Ilene *202:* 91
Winnick, Karen B. *211:* 207
Winslow, Will *21:* 124
Winstead, Rosie *180:* 243
Winsten, Melanie Willa *41:* 41
Winter, Jeanette *151:* 240, 241, 242; *184:* 215, 217, 218, 219
Winter, Milo *15:* 97; *19:* 221; *21:* 181, 203, 204, 205; *64:* 19; *YABC 2:* 144
Winter, Paula *48:* 227
Winter, Susan *163:* 177; *182:* 201
Winters, Greg *70:* 117
Winters, Nina *62:* 194
Wise, Louis *13:* 68
Wiseman, Ann *31:* 187
Wiseman, B. *4:* 233
Wishnefsky, Phillip *3:* 14
Wiskur, Darrell *5:* 72; *10:* 50; *18:* 246
Wisniewski, David *95:* 220, 221
Wisniewski, Robert *95:* 10; *119:* 192
Witschonke, Alan *153:* 149, 150
Witt, Dick *80:* 244
Wittmann, Patrick *162:* 204
Wittman, Sally *30:* 219
Wittner, Dale *99:* 43
Wittwer, Hala *158:* 267; *195:* 80
Woehr, Lois *12:* 5
Wohlberg, Meg *12:* 100; *14:* 197; *41:* 255
Wohnoutka, Mike *88:* 190; *190:* 199; *195:* 218; *205:* 132; *221:* 6
Wojtowycz, David *167:* 168
Woldin, Beth Weiner *34:* 211
Wolf, Elizabeth *133:* 151; *208:* 175
Wolf, J. *16:* 91
Wolf, Janet *78:* 254
Wolf, Linda *33:* 163
Wolfe, Corey *72:* 213
Wolfe, Frances *216:* 227
Wolfe, Gillian *199:* 193
Wolff, Ashley *50:* 217; *81:* 216; *156:* 216, 217; *170:* 57; *174:* 174; *184:* 72; *203:* 181, 182, 183, 184
Wolff, Glenn *178:* 230
Wolff, Jason *213:* 186
Wolfsgruber, Linda *166:* 61
Wondriska, William *6:* 220
Wong, Janet S. *98:* 225; *152:* 43
Wong, Nicole *174:* 13; *214:* 216; *215:* 25

Wonsetler, John C. *5:* 168
Wood, Audrey *50:* 221, 222, 223; *81:* 219, 221; *198:* 206
Wood, Don *50:* 220, 225, 226, 228, 229; *81:* 218, 220; *139:* 239, 240
Wood, Grant *19:* 198
Wood, Heather *133:* 108
Wood, Ivor *58:* 17
Wood, Jakki *211:* 209
Wood, Muriel *36:* 119; *77:* 167; *171:* 55; *187:* 46
Wood, Myron *6:* 220
Wood, Owen *18:* 187; *64:* 202, 204, 205, 206, 208, 210
Wood, Rob *193:* 48
Wood, Ruth *8:* 11
Woodbridge, Curtis *133:* 138; *204:* 113
Wooding, Sharon L. *66:* 237
Woodruff, Liza *132:* 239; *182:* 46, 204
Woodruff, Thomas *171:* 73
Woods, John, Jr. *109:* 142
Woodson, Jack *10:* 201
Woodson, Jacqueline *94:* 242
Woodward, Alice *26:* 89; *36:* 81
Wool, David *26:* 27
Woolley, Janet *112:* 75
Woolman, Steven *106:* 47; *163:* 73
Wooten, Vernon *23:* 70; *51:* 170
Worboys, Evelyn *1:* 166, 167
Word, Reagan *103:* 204
Wormell, Christopher *154:* 251; *202:* 206
Worth, Jo *34:* 143
Worth, Wendy *4:* 133
Wosmek, Frances *29:* 251
Wrenn, Charles L. *38:* 96; *YABC 1:* 20, 21
Wright, Barbara Mullarney *98:* 161
Wright, Cliff *168:* 203
Wright, Dare *21:* 206
Wright-Frierson, Virginia *58:* 194; *110:* 246
Wright, George *YABC 1:* 268
Wright, Joseph *30:* 160
Wronker, Lili Cassel *3:* 247; *10:* 204; *21:* 10
Wu, Donald *200:* 18
Wummer, Amy *154:* 181; *168:* 150; *176:* 85; *201:* 202, 203; *218:* 154
Wyant, Alexander Helwig *110:* 19
Wyatt, David *97:* 9; *101:* 44; *114:* 194; *140:* 20; *167:* 13; *188:* 48
Wyatt, Stanley *46:* 210
Wyeth, Andrew *13:* 40; *YABC 1:* 133, 134
Wyeth, Jamie *41:* 257
Wyeth, N.C. *13:* 41; *17:* 252, 253, 254, 255, 256, 257, 258, 259, 264, 265, 266, 267, 268; *18:* 181; *19:* 80, 191, 200; *21:* 57, 183; *22:* 91; *23:* 152; *24:* 28, 99; *35:* 61; *41:* 65; *100:* 206; *YABC1:* 133, 223; *2:* 53, 75, 171, 187, 317
Wyman, Cherie R. *91:* 42
Wynne, Patricia J. *210:* 260; *223:* 184

X

Xuan, YongSheng *119:* 202, 207, 208; *140:* 36; *187:* 21

Y

Yaccarino, Dan *141:* 208, 209; *147:* 171; *192:* 244, 245; *207:* 168
Yakovetic, Joe *59:* 202; *75:* 85
Yalowitz, Paul *93:* 33; *211:* 92
Yamaguchi, Marianne *85:* 118
Yamasaki, James *167:* 93
Yang, Belle *170:* 198
Yang, Jay *1:* 8; *12:* 239
Yap, Weda *6:* 176

Yaroslava
   See Mills, Yaroslava Surmach
Yashima, Taro *14:* 84
Yates, John *74:* 249, 250
Yates, Kelly *208:* 214
Yayo *178:* 88
Yeatts, Tabatha *215:* 210
Yee, Cora *166:* 233
Yee, Wong Herbert *115:* 216, 217; *172:* 204, 205; *194:* 59
Yelchin, Eugene *204:* 4
Yeo, Brad *135:* 121; *192:* 106
Yerxa, Leo *181:* 195
Yezerski, Thomas F. *162:* 29
Ylla
   See Koffler, Camilla
Yohn, F.C. *23:* 128; *YABC 1:* 269
Yoo, Taeeun *191:* 198
Yorinks, Adrienne *144:* 248; *200:* 214
Yorke, David *80:* 178
Yoshida, Toshi *77:* 231
Yoshikawa, Sachiko *168:* 104; *177:* 28; *181:* 196, 197
Youll, Paul *91:* 218
Youll, Stephen *92:* 227; *118:* 136, 137; *164:* 248; *202:* 92
Young, Amy L. *185:* 218; *190:* 46
Young, Cybéle *167:* 9
Young, Ed *7:* 205; *10:* 206; *40:* 124; *63:* 142; *74:* 250, 251, 252, 253; *75:* 227; *81:* 159; *83:* 98; *94:* 154; *115:* 160; *137:* 162; *YABC 2:* 242; *173:* 174, 175, 176; *205:* 29; *212:* 82; *221:* 72
Young, Mary O'Keefe *77:* 95; *80:* 247; *134:* 214; *140:* 213; *211:* 223, 225
Young, Noela *8:* 221; *89:* 231; *97:* 195
Young, Paul *190:* 222
Young, Selina *153:* 12; *201:* 204, 205
Yuen, Sammy *223:* 46

Yum, Hyewon *211:* 228
Yun, Cheng Mung *60:* 143
Yung, Jennifer *220:* 136

Z

Zacharow, Christopher *88:* 98
Zacks, Lewis *10:* 161
Zadig *50:* 58
Zaffo, George *42:* 208
Zagwyn, Deborah Turney *138:* 227
Zahares, Wade *193:* 219
Zaid, Barry *50:* 127; *51:* 201
Zaidenberg, Arthur *34:* 218, 219, 220
Zalben, Jane Breskin *7:* 211; *79:* 230, 231, 233; *170:* 202
Zallinger, Jean *4:* 192; *8:* 8, 129; *14:* 273; *68:* 36; *80:* 254; *115:* 219, 220, 222
Zallinger, Rudolph F. *3:* 245
Zakrajsek, Molly *177:* 146
Zappa, Ahmet *180:* 250
Zebot, George *83:* 214
Zecca, Katherine *207:* 195
Zeck, Gerry *40:* 232
Zeff, Joe *181:* 98; *221:* 101
Zeifert, Harriet *154:* 265, 267
Zeiring, Bob *42:* 130
Zeldich, Arieh *49:* 124; *62:* 120
Zeldis, Malcah *86:* 239; *94:* 198; *146:* 265, 266
Zelinsky, Paul O. *14:* 269; *43:* 56; *49:* 218-223; *53:* 111; *68:* 195; *102:* 219, 222, 221, 222; *154:* 255, 256, 257; *171:* 141; *185:* 96
Zelvin, Diana *72:* 190; *76:* 101; *93:* 207
Zemach, Kaethe *149:* 250

Zemach, Margot *3:* 270; *8:* 201; *21:* 210, 211; *27:* 204, 205, 210; *28:* 185; *49:* 22, 183, 224; *53:* 151; *56:* 146; *70:* 245, 246; *92:* 74
Zeman, Ludmila *153* 212
Zemsky, Jessica *10:* 62
Zepelinsky, Paul *35:* 93
Zerbetz, Evon *127:* 34; *158:* 109
Zezejl, Daniel *197:* 74
Zhang, Ange *101:* 190; *172:* 41
Zhang, Son Nang *163:* 113; *170:* 206
Ziegler, Jack *84:* 134
Zimdars, Berta *129:* 155
Zimet, Jay *147:* 94; *152:* 74; *196:* 75
Zimic, Tricia *72:* 95
Zimmer, Dirk *38:* 195; *49:* 71; *56:* 151; *65:* 214; *84:* 159; *89:* 26; *147:* 224
Zimmer, Tracie Vaughn *169:* 183
Zimmerman, Andrea *192:* 49, 50
Zimmermann, H. Werner *101:* 223; *112:* 197
Zimnik, Reiner *36:* 224
Zingone, Robin *180:* 134
Zinkeisen, Anna *13:* 106
Zinn, David *97:* 97
Zoellick, Scott *33:* 231
Zollars, Jaime *190:* 190
Zonia, Dhimitri *20:* 234, 235
Zorn, Peter A., Jr. *142:* 157
Zudeck, Darryl *58:* 129; *63:* 98; *80:* 52
Zug, Mark *88:* 131; *204:* 169
Zulewski, Tim *164:* 95
Zuma *99:* 36
Zvorykin, Boris *61:* 155
Zweifel, Francis *14:* 274; *28:* 187
Zwerger, Lisbeth *54:* 176, 178; *66:* 246, 247, 248; *130:* 230, 231, 232, 233; *181:* 92; *194:* 224, 225, 226
Zwinger, Herman H. *46:* 227
Zwolak, Paul *67:* 69, 71, 73, 74

Author Index

The following index gives the number of the volume in which an author's biographical sketch, Autobiography Feature, Brief Entry, or Obituary appears.

This index includes references to all entries in the following series, which are also published by The Gale Group.

YABC—*Yesterday's Authors of Books for Children: Facts and Pictures about Authors and Illustrators of Books for Young People from Early Times to 1960*

CLR—*Children's Literature Review: Excerpts from Reviews, Criticism, and Commentary on Books for Children*

SAAS—*Something about the Author Autobiography Series*

A

Aardema, Verna 1911-2000 .... *107*
  Obituary *119*
  Earlier sketches in SATA *:4, 68*
  See also CLR *17*
  See also SAAS *8*
Aaron, Chester 1923- *216*
  Autobiography Feature *216*
  Earlier sketches in SATA *9, 74*
  See also SAAS *12*
Aaseng, Nate
  See Aaseng, Nathan
Aaseng, Nathan 1953- *172*
  Brief entry *38*
  Earlier sketches in SATA *51, 88*
  See also CLR *54*
  See also SAAS *12*
Abadzis, Nick 1965- *193*
Abalos, Rafael 1956-
  See Abalos, Rafael
Abalos, Rafael 1956- *197*
Abbas, Jailan 1952- *91*
Abbey, Lynn
  See Abbey, Marilyn Lorraine
Abbey, Marilyn Lorraine 1948- *156*
Abbott, Alice
  See Borland, Kathryn Kilby
  and Speicher, Helen Ross S(mith)
Abbott, Jacob 1803-1879 .... *22*
Abbott, Manager Henry
  See Stratemeyer, Edward L.
Abbott, R(obert) Tucker 1919-1995 .... *61*
  Obituary *87*
Abbott, Sarah
  See Zolotow, Charlotte
Abbott, Tony 1952- *205*
  Earlier sketch in SATA *159*
Abdelsayed, Cindy 1962- *123*
Abdul, Raoul 1929- *12*
Abeele, Veronique van den *196*
Abel, Raymond 1911- *12*
Abell, Kathleen 1938- *9*
Abelove, Joan *110*
Abels, Harriette S(heffer) 1926- *50*
Abercrombie, Barbara 1939- *182*
  Earlier sketch in SATA *16*
Abercrombie, Barbara Mattes
  See Abercrombie, Barbara

Abercrombie, Lynn
  See Sorrells, Walter
Abernethy, Robert G(ordon) 1927- *5*
Abisch, Roslyn Kroop 1927- *9*
Abisch, Roz
  See Abisch, Roslyn Kroop
Ablow, Gail 1962- *198*
Abodaher, David J. (Naiph) 1919- *17*
Abolafia, Yossi 1944-
  See Abulafia, Yossi
Abolivier, Aurelie *219*
Abouzeid, Chris *175*
Abrahall, Clare Hoskyns
  See Hoskyns-Abrahall, Clare (Constance Drury)
Abrahams, Hilary (Ruth) 1938- *29*
Abrahams, Peter 1947- *194*
Abrahams, Robert David 1905-1998 .... *4*
Abramovitz, Anita (Zeltner Brooks) 1914- *5*
Abrams, Joy 1941- *16*
Abrams, Lawrence F. *58*
  Brief entry *47*
Abrashkin, Raymond 1911-1960 .... *50*
Abulafia, Yossi 1944- *177*
  Brief entry *46*
  Earlier sketch in SATA *60*
Acampora, Paul *175*
Accardo, Anthony *191*
Acer, David *206*
Achebe, Albert Chinualumogu
  See Achebe, Chinua
Achebe, Chinua 1930- *40*
  Brief entry *38*
  Earlier sketch in SATA *38*
  See also CLR *156*
Acheson, Alison 1964- *222*
Ackerman, Diane 1948- *102*
Ackerman, Eugene (Francis) 1888-1974 ...... *10*
Ackerman, Karen 1951- *126*
Ackerman, Susan Yoder 1945- *92*
Ackison, Wendy Wassink 1956- *103*
Ackley, Peggy Jo 1955- *58*
Ackroyd, Peter 1949- *153*
Acorn, John (Harrison) 1958- *79*
Acredolo, Linda (Potter) 1947- *159*
Acs, Laszlo (Bela) 1931- *42*
  Brief entry *32*
Acuff, Selma Boyd 1924- *45*

Ada, Alma Flor 1938- *222*
  Autobiography Feature *222*
  Earlier sketches in SATA *43, 84, 143, 181*
  See also CLR *62*
Adair, Gilbert 1944- *98*
Adair, Ian 1942- *53*
Adair, Margaret Weeks (?)-1971 .... *10*
Adam, Cornel
  See Lengyel, Cornel Adam
Adam, Mark
  See Alexander, Marc
Adam, Robert 1948- *93*
Adams, Adrienne 1906- *90*
  Earlier sketch in SATA *8*
  See also CLR *73*
Adams, Andy 1859-1935
  See YABC *1*
Adams, Barbara Johnston 1943- *60*
Adams, Bruin
  See Ellis, Edward S.
Adams, Captain Bruin
  See Ellis, Edward S.
Adams, Captain J. F. C.
  See Ellis, Edward S.
Adams, Dale
  See Quinn, Elisabeth
Adams, Daniel
  See Nicole, Christopher (Robin)
Adams, Debra
  See Speregen, Devra Newberger
Adams, Diane 1960- *217*
Adams, Douglas 1952-2001 .... *116*
  Obituary *128*
Adams, Douglas Noel
  See Adams, Douglas
Adams, Edith
  See Shine, Deborah
Adams, Florence 1932- *61*
Adams, Georgie 1945- *216*
Adams, Harriet S(tratemeyer) 1892(?)-1982 .. *1*
  Obituary *29*
Adams, Harrison
  See Rathborne, St. George (Henry)
  and Stratemeyer, Edward L.
Adams, Hazard 1926- *6*
Adams, Hazard Simeon
  See Adams, Hazard
Adams, John Anthony 1944- *67*
Adams, Laurie 1941- *33*

Adams, Lowell
　See Joseph, James (Herz)
Adams, Nicholas
　See Pine, Nicholas
Adams, Nicholas
　See Smith, Sherwood
Adams, Nicholas
　See Doyle, Debra
　and Macdonald, James D.
Adams, Pam 1919- 112
Adams, Pamela
　See Adams, Pam
Adams, Richard 1920- 69
　Earlier sketch in SATA 7
　See also CLR 121
Adams, Richard George
　See Adams, Richard
Adams, Ruth Joyce 14
Adams, Tricia
　See Kite, Pat
Adams, William Taylor 1822-1897 28
Adam Smith, Janet (Buchanan) 1905-1999 .. 63
Adamson, Gareth 1925-1982(?) 46
　Obituary 30
Adamson, George 1906-1989
　Obituary 63
Adamson, George (Worsley) 1913-2005 30
Adamson, Graham
　See Groom, Arthur William
Adamson, Joy(-Friederike Victoria)
　1910-1980 11
　Obituary 22
Adamson, Wendy Writson 1942- 22
Addasi, Maha 1968- 205
Addison, Kenneth 1949(?)-2005 187
Addison, Kenneth L.
　See Addison, Kenneth
Addona, Angelo F. 1925- 14
Addy, Sean 1976- 222
Addy, Sharon Hart 1943- 192
　Earlier sketch in SATA 108
Addy, Ted
　See Winterbotham, R(ussell) R(obert)
Adelberg, Doris
　See Orgel, Doris
Adelson, Leone 1908- 11
Adinolfi, JoAnn 176
Adkins, Jan 1944- 210
　Autobiography Feature 210
　Earlier sketches in SATA 8, 69, 144
　See also CLR 77
　See also SAAS 19
Adler, C. S. 1932- 126
　Earlier sketches in SATA 26, 63, 102
　See also CLR 78
　See also SAAS 15
Adler, Carole Schwerdtfeger
　See Adler, C. S.
Adler, David A. 1947- 178
　Earlier sketches in SATA 14, 70, 106, 151
　See also CLR 108
Adler, Irene
　See Penzler, Otto
　and Storr, Catherine (Cole)
Adler, Irving 1913- 29
　Autobiography Feature 164
　Earlier sketch in SATA 1
　See also CLR 27
　See also SAAS 15
Adler, Larry 1939- 36
Adler, Peggy 22
Adler, Ruth 1915-1968 1
Adlerman, Daniel (Ezra) 1963- 163
　Earlier sketch in SATA 96
Adlerman, Kim
　See Adlerman, Kimberly M(arie)
Adlerman, Kimberly M(arie) 1964- 163
　Earlier sketch in SATA 96

Adoff, Arnold 1935- 96
　Earlier sketches in SATA 5, 57
　See also CLR 7
　See also SAAS 15
Adoff, Jaime 163
Adoff, Jaime Levi
　See Adoff, Jaime
Adorjan, Carol (Madden) 1934- 71
　Earlier sketch in SATA 10
Adrian, Frances
　See Polland, Madeleine A(ngela Cahill)
Adrian, Mary
　See Jorgensen, Mary Venn
Adshead, Gladys L(ucy) 1896-1985 3
Aesop 620(?)B.C.-560(?)B.C. 64
　See also CLR 14
Aesop, Abraham
　See Newbery, John
Affabee, Eric
　See Stine, R.L.
Agapida, Fray Antonio
　See Irving, Washington
Agard, John 1949- 223
　Earlier sketch in SATA 138
Agard, Nadema 1948- 18
Agarwal, Deepa 1947- 141
Agee, Jon 1960- 196
　Earlier sketches in SATA 116, 157
Agell, Charlotte 1959- 214
　Earlier sketches in SATA 99, 150
Agent Orange
　See Moseley, James W(illett)
Aghill, Gordon
　See Garrett, Randall
　and Silverberg, Robert
Agle, Nan Hayden 1905- 3
　See also SAAS 10
Agnew, Edith J(osephine) 1897-1988 11
Agnew, Lincoln 222
Agonito, Joseph 177
Agonito, Rosemary 1937- 177
Aguilar, David 214
Aguilar, David A.
　See Aguilar, David
Ahern, Margaret McCrohan 1921- 10
Ahl, Anna Maria 1926- 32
Ahlberg, Allan 1938- 214
　Brief entry 35
　Earlier sketches in SATA 68, 120, 165
　See also CLR 18
Ahlberg, Janet 1944-1994 120
　Brief entry 32
　Obituary 83
　Earlier sketch in SATA 68
　See also CLR 18
Aho, Julia Kay
　See Kay, Julia
Aichinger, Helga 1937- 4
Aiken, Clarissa (M.) Lorenz 1899-1992 12
　Obituary 109
Aiken, Conrad 1889-1973 30
　Earlier sketch in SATA 3
Aiken, Conrad Potter
　See Aiken, Conrad
Aiken, Joan (Delano) 1924-2004 73
　Autobiography Feature 109
　Obituary 152
　Earlier sketches in SATA 2, 30
　See also CLR 90
　See also SAAS 1
Aillaud, Cindy Lou 1955- 184
Ainsley, Alix
　See Steiner, Barbara A(nnette)
Ainsworth, Catherine Harris 1910- 56
Ainsworth, Norma 1911-1987 9
Ainsworth, Ruth (Gallard) 1908- 73
　Earlier sketch in SATA 7
Ainsworth, William Harrison 1805-1882 24
Aistrop, Jack 1916- 14
Aitken, Amy 1952- 54
　Brief entry 40

Aitken, Dorothy 1916- 10
Aitmatov, Chingiz 1928-2008 56
Aitmatov, Chingiz Torekulovich
　See Aitmatov, Chingiz
Ajhar, Brian 1957- 220
Akaba, Suekichi 1910- 46
Akers, Floyd
　See Baum, L. Frank
Akib, Jamel 181
Aks, Patricia 1926-1994 68
Alagoa, Ebiegberi Joe 1933- 108
Alain
　See Brustlein, Daniel
Alajalov, Constantin 1900-1987
　Obituary 53
Alalou, Ali 203
Alalou, Elizabeth 203
Alan, David
　See Horsfield, Alan
Alan, Robert
　See Silverstein, Robert Alan
Alarcon, Francisco X. 1954- 215
　Earlier sketch in SATA 104
Alarcon, Francisco Xavier
　See Alarcon, Francisco X.
Alarcon, Karen Beaumont
　See Beaumont, Karen
Albert, Burton 1936- 22
Albert, Louise 1928- 157
Albert, Michael 1966- 202
Albert, Richard E. 1909-1999 82
Albert, Susan Wittig 1940- 107
Alberts, Frances Jacobs 1907-1989 14
Albertson, Susan
　See Wojciechowski, Susan
Albion, Lee Smith 29
Alborough, Jez 1959- 149
　Earlier sketch in SATA 86
Albrecht, Lillie (Vanderveer H.)
　1894-1985 12
Albyn, Carole Lisa 1955- 83
Alchemy, Jack
　See Gershator, David
Alcock, Gudrun 1908- 56
　Brief entry 33
Alcock, Vivien (Dolores) 1924-2003 76
　Brief entry 38
　Obituary 148
　Earlier sketch in SATA 45
　See also CLR 26
Alcorn, John 1935- 31
　Brief entry 30
Alcorn, Stephen 1958- 207
　Earlier sketch in SATA 110
Alcott, Louisa May 1832-1888 100
　See also YABC 1
　See also CLR 109
Alda, Arlene 1933- 205
　Brief entry 36
　Earlier sketches in SATA 44, 106, 158
　See also CLR 93
Alden, Isabella (Macdonald) 1841-1930 115
　See also YABC 2
Alden, Sue
　See Francis, Dorothy
Alderman, Clifford Lindsey 1902-1988 3
Alderson, Sue Ann 1940- 59
　Brief entry 48
Alding, Peter
　See Jeffries, Roderic
Aldis, Dorothy (Keeley) 1896-1966 2
Aldiss, Brian W. 1925- 34
Aldiss, Brian Wilson
　See Aldiss, Brian W.
Aldon, Adair
　See Meigs, Cornelia Lynde
Aldous, Allan (Charles) 1911- 27
Aldrich, Ann
　See Meaker, Marijane
Aldrich, Bess Streeter 1881-1954
　See CLR 70

Aldrich, Thomas (Bailey) 1836-1907 .... *114*
    Earlier sketch in SATA *17*
Aldridge, (Harold Edward) James 1918- *87*
Aldridge, Josephine Haskell *14*
Aldridge, Sheila 1974- *192*
Aleas, Richard
    See Appelt, Kathi
Alegria, Malin 1974(?)- *190*
Alegria, Ricardo E(nrique) 1921- *6*
Aleksin, Anatolii Georgievich 1924- *36*
Alenov, Lydia 1948- *61*
Alex, Ben (a pseudonym) 1946- *45*
Alex, Marlee (a pseudonym) 1948- *45*
Alexander, Alma 1963- *217*
Alexander, Anna B(arbara Cooke) 1913- *1*
Alexander, Anne
    See Alexander, Anna B(arbara Cooke)
Alexander, Ellen 1938- *91*
Alexander, Frances (Laura) 1888-1979 .... *4*
Alexander, Janet 1907-1994 .... *97*
    Earlier sketch in SATA *1*
Alexander, Jill S. 1964- *223*
Alexander, Jill Shurbet
    See Alexander, Jill S.
Alexander, Jocelyn Anne Arundel 1930- *22*
Alexander, Linda 1935- *2*
Alexander, Lloyd 1924-2007 .... *135*
    Obituary *182*
    Earlier sketches in SATA *3, 49, 81, 129*
    See also CLR *48*
    See also SAAS *19*
Alexander, Lloyd Chudley
    See Alexander, Lloyd
Alexander, Marc 1929- *117*
Alexander, Martha 1920- *136*
    Earlier sketches in SATA *11, 70*
Alexander, Rae Pace
    See Alexander, Raymond Pace
Alexander, Raymond Pace 1898-1974 .... *22*
Alexander, Robert *200*
Alexander, Rod
    See Pellowski, Michael (Joseph)
Alexander, Sally Hobart 1943- *84*
Alexander, Sue 1933-2008 .... *136*
    Obituary *195*
    Earlier sketches in SATA *12, 89*
    See also SAAS *15*
Alexander, Vincent Arthur 1925-1980
    Obituary *23*
Alexeieff, Alexandre A. 1901-1979 .... *14*
Alger, Horatio, Jr.
    See Stratemeyer, Edward L.
Alger, Horatio, Jr. 1832-1899 .... *16*
    See also CLR *87*
Alger, Leclaire (Gowans) 1898-1969 .... *15*
Aliki
    See Brandenberg, Aliki
Alkema, Chester Jay 1932- *12*
Al-Khalili, Jim 1962- *124*
Alkiviades, Alkis 1953- *105*
Alko, Selina 1968- *218*
Alkouatli, Claire *186*
Allaby, John Michael
    See Allaby, Michael
Allaby, Michael 1933- *167*
Allamand, Pascale 1942- *12*
Allan, Mabel Esther 1915-1998 .... *75*
    Earlier sketches in SATA *5, 32*
    See also CLR *43*
    See also SAAS *11*
Allan, Nicholas 1956- *123*
    Earlier sketch in SATA *79*
Allan-Meyer, Kathleen 1918- *51*
    Brief entry *46*
Allard, Harry
    See Allard, Harry G., Jr.
Allard, Harry G.
    See Allard, Harry G., Jr.
Allard, Harry G., Jr. 1928- *216*
    Earlier sketches in SATA *42, 102*
    See also CLR *85*

Allee, Marjorie Hill 1890-1945 .... *17*
Allen, Adam
    See Epstein, Beryl
    and Epstein, Samuel
Allen, Alex B.
    See Heide, Florence Parry
Allen, Allyn
    See Eberle, Irmengarde
Allen, Betsy
    See Harrison, Elizabeth (Allen) Cavanna
Allen, Bob 1961- *76*
Allen, Gertrude E(lizabeth) 1888-1984 .... *9*
Allen, Grace
    See Hogarth, Grace (Weston Allen)
Allen, Jeffrey (Yale) 1948- *42*
Allen, John
    See Perry, Ritchie (John Allen)
Allen, Jonathan 1957- *177*
    Earlier sketch in SATA *131*
Allen, Jonathan Dean
    See Allen, Jonathan
Allen, Joy 1948- *217*
Allen, Judy (Christina) 1941- *124*
    Earlier sketch in SATA *80*
Allen, Kenneth S. 1913-1981 .... *56*
Allen, Leroy 1912- *11*
Allen, Linda 1925- *33*
Allen, Marjorie 1931- *22*
Allen, Maury 1932-2010 .... *26*
Allen, Merritt Parmelee 1892-1954 .... *22*
Allen, Nancy Kelly 1949- *171*
    Earlier sketch in SATA *127*
Allen, Nina (Stroemgren) 1935- *22*
Allen, Pamela (Kay) 1934- *123*
    Earlier sketches in SATA *50, 81*
    See also CLR *44*
Allen, Raul *205*
Allen, Rodney F. 1938-1999 .... *27*
Allen, Roger MacBride 1957- *105*
Allen, Ruth
    See Peterson, Esther (Allen)
Allen, Samuel W(ashington) 1917- *9*
Allen, T. D.
    See Allen, Terril Diener
Allen, Terril Diener 1908- *35*
Allen, Terry D.
    See Allen, Terril Diener
Allen, Thomas B. 1929- *193*
    Earlier sketches in SATA *45, 140*
Allen, Thomas Benton
    See Allen, Thomas B.
Allen, Tom
    See Allen, Thomas B.
Allende, Isabel 1942- *163*
    See also CLR *99*
Allerton, Mary
    See Govan, (Mary) Christine Noble
Alley, Robert W.
    See Alley, R.W.
Alley, R.W. *211*
    Earlier sketch in SATA *169*
Alley, Zoe B. *214*
Alleyn, Ellen
    See Rossetti, Christina
Allington, Richard L(loyd) 1947- *39*
    Brief entry *35*
Allison, Amy 1956- *138*
Allison, Bob *14*
Allison, Diane Worfolk *78*
Allison, Jennifer *173*
Allison, Linda 1948- *43*
Allison, Margaret
    See Klam, Cheryl
Allman, Barbara 1950- *137*
Allmendinger, David F(rederick), Jr. 1938- . *35*
Allred, Alexandra Powe 1965- *144*
Allred, Gordon T(hatcher) 1930- *10*
Allsop, Kenneth 1920-1973 .... *17*
Allsopp, Sophie *188*
Alma, Ann 1946- *201*

Almedingen, E. M.
    See Almedingen, Martha Edith von
Almedingen, Martha Edith von 1898-1971 .... *3*
Almon, Russell
    See Clevenger, William R.
    and Downing, David A(lmon)
Almond, David 1951- *158*
    Earlier sketch in SATA *114*
    See also CLR *85*
Almond, Linda Stevens 1881(?)-1987
    Obituary *50*
Almquist, Don 1929- *11*
Alonzo, Sandra *199*
Alphin, Elaine Marie 1955- *139*
    Autobiography Feature *139*
    Earlier sketches in SATA *80, 130*
Alsenas, Linas 1979- *186*
Alsop, Mary O'Hara 1885-1980 .... *34*
    Obituary *24*
    Earlier sketch in SATA *2*
Alter, Anna 1974- *206*
    Earlier sketch in SATA *135*
Alter, Judith 1938- *101*
    Earlier sketch in SATA *52*
Alter, Judith MacBain
    See Alter, Judith
Alter, Judy
    See Alter, Judith
Alter, Robert Edmond 1925-1965 .... *9*
Alter, Stephen 1956- *187*
Althea
    See Braithwaite, Althea
Altman, Linda Jacobs 1943- *21*
Altman, Suzanne
    See Orgel, Doris
    and Schecter, Ellen
Alton, Steve *169*
Altschuler, Franz 1923- *45*
Altsheler, Joseph A(lexander) 1862-1919
    See YABC *1*
Alvarez, John
    See del Rey, Lester
Alvarez, Joseph A. 1930- *18*
Alvarez, Julia 1950- *129*
al-Windawi, Thura
    See Windawi, Thura al-
Alyer, Philip A.
    See Stratemeyer, Edward L.
Amado, Elisa *193*
Amann, Janet 1951- *79*
Amato, Carol A. 1942- *92*
Amato, Mary 1961- *178*
    Earlier sketch in SATA *140*
Ambrose, Stephen E. 1936-2002 .... *138*
    Earlier sketch in SATA *40*
Ambrose, Stephen Edward
    See Ambrose, Stephen E.
Ambrus, Gyozo Laszlo 1935- *1*
    See also SAAS *4*
Ambrus, Victor G.
    See Ambrus, Gyozo Laszlo
Amend, Bill 1962- *147*
Amerman, Lockhart 1911-1969 .... *3*
Ames, Evelyn 1908-1990 .... *13*
    Obituary *64*
Ames, Gerald 1906-1993 .... *11*
    Obituary *74*
Ames, Lee J(udah) 1921- *151*
    Earlier sketch in SATA *3*
Ames, Mildred 1919-1994 .... *85*
    Earlier sketches in SATA *22, 81*
Amico, Tom 1960(?)- *176*
Amit, Ofra 1966- *205*
Ammon, Richard 1942- *124*
Amon, Aline 1928- *9*
Amory, Jay
    See Lovegrove, James
Amoss, Berthe 1925- *112*
    Earlier sketch in SATA *5*
Amstutz, Andre 1925- *214*

Anastasio, Dina 1941- 94
  Brief entry 30
  Earlier sketch in SATA 37
Anaya, Rudolfo 1937-
  See CLR 129
Anaya, Rudolfo A.
  See Anaya, Rudolfo
Anaya, Rudolpho Alfonso
  See Anaya, Rudolfo
Anckarsvard, Karin Inez Maria 1915-1969 6
Ancona, George 1929- 208
  Autobiography Feature 208
  Earlier sketches in SATA 12, 85, 145, 192
  See also SAAS 18
Anders, C. J.
  See Bennett, Cherie
Anders, Isabel 1946- 101
Anders, Lou 176
Andersdatter, Karla M. 1938- 34
Andersen, Bethanne 1954- 191
Andersen, Hans Christian 1805-1875 100
  See also YABC 1
  See also CLR 113
Andersen, Ted
  See Boyd, Waldo T.
Andersen, Yvonne 1932- 27
Anderson, Bernice G(oudy) 1894-1997 33
Anderson, Bob 1944- 139
  Earlier sketch in SATA 136
Anderson, Brad 1924- 33
  Brief entry 31
Anderson, Bradley Jay
  See Anderson, Brad
Anderson, Brian 1974- 211
Anderson, C. C.
  See Anderson, Catherine Corley
Anderson, C(larence) W(illiam) 1891-1971 . 11
Anderson, Carolyn Dunn
  See Dunn, Carolyn
Anderson, Catherine C.
  See Anderson, Catherine Corley
Anderson, Catherine Corley 1909-2001 72
  See Lee, Cora
Anderson, Clifford
  See Gardner, Richard (M.)
Anderson, Daryl Shon 1963- 93
Anderson, Dave
  See Anderson, David
Anderson, David 1929- 60
Anderson, Derek 1969- 169
Anderson, Eloise Adell 1927- 9
Anderson, George
  See Groom, Arthur William
Anderson, Grace Fox 1932- 43
Anderson, J(ohn) R(ichard) L(ane)
  1911-1981 15
  Obituary 27
Anderson, Jodi Lynn 182
Anderson, John David 197
Anderson, John L. 1905- 2
Anderson, Joy 1928- 1
Anderson, Kevin J. 1962- 117
  Earlier sketch in SATA 74
Anderson, Kevin James
  See Anderson, Kevin J.
Anderson, Kirsty 1978- 108
Anderson, K.J.
  See Moesta, Rebecca
Anderson, Laurie Halse 1961- 186
  Earlier sketches in SATA 95, 132
  See also CLR 138
Anderson, LaVere Francis Shoenfelt
  1907-1998 27
Anderson, Leone Castell 1923- 53
  Brief entry 49
Anderson, Lisa G. 1963- 108
Anderson, Lonzo
  See Anderson, John L.
Anderson, Lucia (Lewis) 1922- 10
Anderson, Madelyn Klein 1926-2005 28

Anderson, Margaret J(ean) 1931- 27
  See also SAAS 8
Anderson, Marilyn D. 1943- 144
Anderson, Mary 1939- 82
  Earlier sketch in SATA 7
  See also SAAS 23
Anderson, Matthew Tobin
  See Anderson, M.T.
Anderson, Mona 1910-2004 40
Anderson, Mrs. Melvin
  See Anderson, Catherine Corley
Anderson, M.T. 1968- 182
  Earlier sketches in SATA 97, 146
Anderson, Norman Dean 1928- 22
Anderson, Peggy Perry 1953- 179
  Earlier sketch in SATA 84
Anderson, Poul 1926-2001 90
  Autobiography Feature 106
  Brief entry 39
  See also CLR 58
Anderson, Poul William
  See Anderson, Poul
Anderson, Rachel 1943- 86
  Earlier sketch in SATA 34
  See also SAAS 18
Anderson, Rebecca J.
  See Anderson, R.J.
Anderson, Rebecca M.
  See Moesta, Rebecca
Anderson, Rebecca Moesta
  See Moesta, Rebecca
Anderson, Richard
  See Anderson, J(ohn) R(ichard) L(ane)
Anderson, R.J. 1970(?)- 216
Anderson, Sara 173
Anderson, Scoular 201
Anderson, (Tom) Scoular 138
Anderson, Susan 1952- 90
Anderson, Thomas Scoular
  See Anderson, Scoular
Anderson, W. B.
  See Schultz, James Willard
Anderson, Wayne 1946- 202
  Earlier sketches in SATA 56, 147
Andersson, Kenneth 1970- 200
Andre, Evelyn M. 1924- 27
Andre, Evelyn Marie
  See Andre, Evelyn M.
Andreasen, Dan 186
Andreassen, Karl
  See Boyd, Waldo T.
Andreassi, K. Robert
  See DeCandido, Keith R.A.
Andree, Louise
  See Coury, Louise Andree
Andrew, Ian 1962- 166
  Earlier sketch in SATA 116
Andrew, Ian Peter
  See Andrew, Ian
Andrew, Prudence (Hastings) 1924- 87
Andrews, Benny 1930-2006 31
  Obituary 178
Andrews, Eleanor Lattimore
  See Lattimore, Eleanor Frances
Andrews, Elton V.
  See Pohl, Frederik
Andrews, F(rank) Emerson 1902-1978 22
Andrews, J(ames) S(ydney) 1934- 4
Andrews, Jan 1942- 167
  Brief entry 49
  Earlier sketches in SATA 58, 98
Andrews, Julie 1935- 153
  Earlier sketch in SATA 7
  See also CLR 85
Andrews, Laura
  See Coury, Louise Andree
Andrews, Roy Chapman 1884-1960 19
Andrews, Tamra 1959- 129
Andrews, V(irginia) C(leo) 1924(?)-1986
  Obituary 50

Andrews, Wendy
  See Sharmat, Marjorie Weinman
Andrews, William G. 1930- 74
Andrews, William George
  See Andrews, William G.
Andrezel, Pierre
  See Blixen, Karen
Andriani, Renee
  See Williams-Andriani, Renee
Andriola, Alfred J. 1912-1983
  Obituary 34
Andrist, Ralph K. 1914-2004 45
Andronik, Catherine M. 189
Andryszewski, Tricia 1956- 148
  Earlier sketch in SATA 88
Anelli, Melissa 1979- 215
Angel, Ann 1952- 192
Angel, Carl 178
Angel, Marie 1923- 47
Angeles, Peter A. 1931- 40
Angeletti, Roberta 1964- 124
Angeli, Marguerite (Lofft) de
  See de Angeli, Marguerite (Lofft)
Angell, Judie 1937- 78
  Earlier sketch in SATA 22
  See also CLR 33
Angell, Madeline 1919- 18
Angelo, Valenti 1897- 14
Angelou, Maya 1928- 136
  Earlier sketch in SATA 49
  See also CLR 53
Angier, Bradford -1997 12
Angle, Kimberly Greene 203
Angle, Paul M(cClelland) 1900-1975
  Obituary 20
Anglund, Joan Walsh 1926- 2
  See also CLR 94
Ango, Fan D.
  See Longyear, Barry B(rookes)
Angrist, Stanley W(olff) 1933- 4
Anholt, Catherine 1958- 131
  Earlier sketch in SATA 74
Anholt, Laurence 1959- 141
  Earlier sketch in SATA 74
Anita
  See Daniel, Anita
Anmar, Frank
  See Nolan, William F.
Annett, Cora
  See Scott, Cora Annett (Pipitone)
Annie-Jo
  See Blanchard, Patricia
  and Suhr, Joanne
Annixter, Jane
  See Sturtzel, Jane Levington
Annixter, Paul
  See Sturtzel, Howard A(llison)
Anno, Mitsumasa 1926- 157
  Earlier sketches in SATA 5, 38, 77
  See also CLR 122
Anrooy, Francine Van
  See Van Anrooy, Francine
Ansary, Mir Tamim 1948- 140
Anstey, Caroline 1958- 81
Antell, Will D. 1935- 31
Anthony, Barbara
  See Barber, Antonia
Anthony, C. L.
  See Smith, Dorothy Gladys
Anthony, Edward 1895-1971 21
Anthony, John
  See Beckett, Ronald Brymer
  and Ciardi, John (Anthony)
  and Sabini, John Anthony
Anthony, Joseph Patrick 1964- 103
Anthony, Patricia 1947- 109
Anthony, Piers 1934- 129
  Autobiography Feature 129
  Earlier sketch in SATA 84
  See also CLR 118
  See also SAAS 22

Anthony, Susan C(arol) 1953- 87
Anticaglia, Elizabeth 1939- 12
Antieau, Kim 214
Antilles, Kem
  See Moesta, Rebecca
Antle, Nancy 1955- 102
Antolini, Margaret Fishback 1904-1985
  Obituary 45
Anton, Michael J(ames) 1940- 12
Antonacci, Robert J(oseph) 1916- 45
  Brief entry 37
Anvil, Christopher 1925-2009 102
Anzaldua, Gloria (Evanjelina) 1942-2004
  Obituary 154
Aoki, Hisako 1942- 45
Apfel, Necia H(alpern) 1930- 51
  Brief entry 41
Aphrodite, J.
  See Livingston, Carole
Apikuni
  See Schultz, James Willard
Apostolina, M. 184
Apostolina, Michael
  See Apostolina, M.
Apostolou, Christine Hale 1955- 179
  Earlier sketches in SATA 82, 128
Appel, Allen (R.) 1945- 115
Appel, Benjamin 1907-1977 39
  Obituary 21
Appel, Martin 1948- 45
Appel, Martin Eliot
  See Appel, Martin
Appel, Marty
  See Appel, Martin
Appelbaum, Diana Muir Karter 1953- 132
Appelt, Kathi 1954- 190
  Earlier sketches in SATA 83, 129
Apperley, Dawn 1969- 135
Appiah, Peggy 1921-2006 84
  Earlier sketch in SATA 15
  See also SAAS 19
Apple, Margot 214
  Brief entry 42
  Earlier sketches in SATA 64, 152
Applebaum, Stan 1922- 45
Applegate, K.A.
  See Applegate, Katherine
Applegate, Katherine 1956- 196
  Earlier sketches in SATA 109, 162
  See also CLR 90
Applegate, Katherine Alice
  See Applegate, Katherine
Appleton, Victor
  See Barrett, Neal, Jr.
  and Doyle, Debra
  and Stratemeyer, Edward L.
  and Vardeman, Robert E.
Appollo 1969- 214
Appollodorus, Olivier
  See Appollo
Apsler, Alfred 1907-1982 10
Aragones, Sergio 1937- 48
  Brief entry 39
Araujo, Frank P. 1937- 86
Arbo, Cris 1950- 220
  Earlier sketch in SATA 103
Arbuckle, Dorothy Fry 1910-1982
  Obituary 33
Arbuthnot, May Hill 1884-1969 2
Archambault, John 163
  Earlier sketches in SATA 67, 112
Archambault, Matthew 1968- 219
Archbold, Rick 1950- 97
Archer, Colleen Rutherford 1949- 164
Archer, Frank
  See O'Connor, Richard
Archer, Jules 1915- 85
  Earlier sketch in SATA 4
  See also SAAS 5
Archer, Lily 1981- 193
Archer, Marion Fuller 1917- 11

Archer, Nathan
  See Watt-Evans, Lawrence
Archer, Peggy 1947- 199
Archibald, Joe
  See Archibald, Joseph S(topford)
Archibald, Joseph S(topford) 1898-1986 3
  Obituary 47
Ard, William
  See Jakes, John
Ardagh, Philip 1961- 154
Ardai, Charles 1969- 85
Arden, Barbi
  See Stoutenburg, Adrien (Pearl)
Arden, William
  See Lynds, Dennis
Ardizzone, Edward (Jeffrey Irving)
  1900-1979 28
  Obituary 21
  Earlier sketch in SATA 1
  See also CLR 3
Ardley, Neil 1937- 121
  Earlier sketch in SATA 43
Ardley, Neil Richard
  See Ardley, Neil
Arehart-Treichel, Joan 1942- 22
Arena, Felice 1968- 151
Arenella, Roy 1939- 14
Argent, Kerry 1960- 138
Arguelles, Francisco Xavier
  See Stork, Francisco X.
Argueta, Jorge 179
Arihara, Shino 1973- 201
Arkin, Alan 1934- 59
  Brief entry 32
Arkin, Alan Wolf
  See Arkin, Alan
Arksey, Neil 158
Arlen, Leslie
  See Nicole, Christopher (Robin)
Arley, Robert
  See Jackson, Mike
Armer, Alberta (Roller) 1904-1986 9
Armer, Laura Adams 1874-1963 13
Armistead, John 1941- 130
Armitage, David 1943- 155
  Brief entry 38
  Earlier sketch in SATA 99
Armitage, Frank
  See Carpenter, John
Armitage, Ronda (Jacqueline) 1943- 155
  Brief entry 38
  Earlier sketches in SATA 47, 99
Armour, Richard (Willard) 1906-1989 14
  Obituary 61
Armstrong, Alan 1939- 172
Armstrong, Alan W.
  See Armstrong, Alan
Armstrong, George D. 1927- 10
Armstrong, Gerry (Breen) 1929- 10
Armstrong, Jeannette (C.) 1948- 102
Armstrong, Jennifer 1961- 165
  Autobiography Feature 120
  Earlier sketches in SATA 77, 111
  See also CLR 66
  See also SAAS 24
Armstrong, Louise 43
  Brief entry 33
Armstrong, Martin Donisthorpe
  1882-1974 115
Armstrong, Matthew 1975- 188
Armstrong, Matthew S.
  See Armstrong, Matthew
Armstrong, Ralph Richard
  See Armstrong, Richard
Armstrong, Richard 1903-1986 11
Armstrong, William H(oward) 1914-1999 4
  Obituary 111
  See also CLR 117
  See also SAAS 7
Armstrong-Ellis, Carey (Fraser) 1956- 145

Arndt, Ursula (Martha H.) 56
  Brief entry 39
Arneson, D(on) J(on) 1935- 37
Arnett, Caroline
  See Cole, Lois Dwight
Arnett, Jack
  See Goulart, Ron
Arnette, Robert
  See Silverberg, Robert
Arno, Enrico 1913-1981 43
  Obituary 28
Arnold, Ann 1953(?)- 207
Arnold, Caroline 1944- 174
  Brief entry 34
  Earlier sketches in SATA 36, 85, 131
  See also CLR 61
  See also SAAS 23
Arnold, Elizabeth 1944- 164
Arnold, Elliott 1912-1980 5
  Obituary 22
Arnold, Emily 1939- 210
  Autobiography Feature 134
  Earlier sketches in SATA 5, 50, 76, 110, 134
  See also CLR 46
  See also SAAS 7
Arnold, Gillian Clare
  See Cross, Gillian
Arnold, Katya 1947- 168
  Earlier sketches in SATA 82, 115
Arnold, Louise 175
Arnold, Louise Claire
  See Arnold, Louise
Arnold, Marsha Diane 1948- 147
  Earlier sketch in SATA 93
Arnold, Nick 1961- 113
Arnold, Oren 1900-1980 4
Arnold, Susan (Riser) 1951- 58
Arnold, Tedd 1949- 208
  Earlier sketches in SATA 69, 116, 160
Arnoldy, Julie
  See Bischoff, Julia Bristol
Arnosky, James Edward 1946- 189
  Earlier sketches in SATA 70, 118
  See also CLR 93
Arnosky, Jim
  See Arnosky, James Edward
Arnott, Kathleen 1914- 20
Arnov, Boris, Jr. 1926- 12
Arnow, Harriette (Louisa) Simpson
  1908-1986 42
  Obituary 47
Arnsteen, Katy Keck 1934- 68
Arnstein, Helene S(olomon) 1915- 12
Arntson, Herbert E(dward) 1911-1982 12
Aroner, Miriam 82
Aronin, Ben 1904-1980
  Obituary 25
Aronson, Marc 1950- 189
  Autobiography Feature 189
  Earlier sketches in SATA 126, 175
Aronson, Marc Henry
  See Aronson, Marc
Aronson, Sarah 196
Aronson, Virginia 1954- 122
Arora, Shirley (Lease) 1930- 2
Arrasmith, Patrick 176
Arrick, Fran
  See Angell, Judie
Arrigan, Mary 1943- 142
Arrington, Aileen 183
Arrington, Stephen L. 1948- 97
Arrington, Stephen Lee
  See Arrington, Stephen L.
Arrley, Richmond
  See Delany, Samuel R., Jr.
Arrou-Vignod, Jean-Philippe 1958- 218
Arrowood, (McKendrick Lee) Clinton
  1939- 19
Arrowsmith, Pat 1930- 59
Arsenault, Isabelle 1978- 207

Artell, Mike 1948- *183*
  Earlier sketches in SATA *89, 134*
Arthur, Robert (Andrew) 1909-1969
  See Arthur, Robert, (Jr.)
Arthur, Robert, (Jr.) 1909-1969 .... *118*
Arthur, Ruth M(abel) 1905-1979 .... *26*
  Earlier sketch in SATA *7*
Artis, Vicki Kimmel 1945- *12*
Artzybasheff, Boris (Miklailovich)
  1899-1965 .... *14*
Aruego, Ariane
  See Dewey, Ariane
Aruego, Jose 1932- *178*
  Earlier sketches in SATA *6, 68, 125*
  See also CLR *5*
Aruego, Jose Espiritu
  See Aruego, Jose
Arundel, Honor (Morfydd) 1919-1973 .... *4*
  Obituary *24*
  See also CLR *35*
Arundel, Jocelyn
  See Alexander, Jocelyn Anne Arundel
Arvey, Michael 1948- *79*
Arzoumanian, Alik *177*
Asare, Meshack (Yaw) 1945- *139*
  Earlier sketch in SATA *86*
Asaro, Catherine 1955- *165*
  Earlier sketch in SATA *101*
Asaro, Catherine Ann 1955-
  See Asaro, Catherine
Asay, Donna Day 1945- *127*
Asbjornsen, Peter Christen 1812-1885 .... *15*
  See also CLR *104*
Asch, Frank 1946- *154*
  Earlier sketches in SATA *5, 66, 102*
Ash, Jutta 1942- *38*
Ashabranner, Brent 1921- *166*
  Earlier sketches in SATA *1, 67, 130*
  See also CLR *28*
  See also SAAS *14*
Ashabranner, Brent Kenneth
  See Ashabranner, Brent
Ashbless, William
  See Blaylock, James P.
  and Powers, Tim
Ashby, Gil 1958- *146*
Ashby, Gwynneth 1922- *44*
Ashby, Ruth *170*
Ashby, Yvonne 1955- *121*
Ashe, Arthur (Robert, Jr.) 1943-1993 .... *65*
  Obituary *87*
Ashe, Geoffrey (Thomas) 1923- *17*
  Autobiography Feature *125*
Ashe, Mary Ann
  See Lewis, Mary
Asher, Bridget
  See Baggott, Julianna
Asher, Sandra Fenichel
  See Asher, Sandy
Asher, Sandy 1942- *71*
  Autobiography Feature *158*
  Brief entry *34*
  Earlier sketch in SATA *36*
  See also SAAS *13*
Asheron, Sara
  See Moore, Lilian
Ashey, Bella
  See Breinburg, Petronella
Ashford, Daisy
  See Ashford, Margaret Mary
Ashford, Jeffrey
  See Jeffries, Roderic
Ashford, Margaret Mary 1881-1972 .... *10*
Ashland, Monk 1972- *207*
Ashley, Bernard (John) 1935- *155*
  Brief entry *39*
  Earlier sketches in SATA *47, 79*
  See also CLR *4*
Ashley, Elizabeth
  See Salmon, Annie Elizabeth

Ashley, Ray
  See Abrashkin, Raymond
Ashman, Linda 1960- *203*
  Earlier sketch in SATA *150*
Ashton, Lorayne
  See Gottfried, Theodore Mark
Ashton, Warren T.
  See Adams, William Taylor
Asimov, Isaac 1920-1992 .... *74*
  Earlier sketches in SATA *1, 26*
  See also CLR *79*
Asinof, Eliot 1919-2008 .... *6*
Asinof, Eliot Tager
  See Asinof, Eliot
Aska, Warabe
  See Masuda, Takeshi
Asprin, Robert 1946-2008 .... *92*
Asprin, Robert L.
  See Asprin, Robert
Asprin, Robert Lynn
  See Asprin, Robert
Asquith, Cynthia Mary Evelyn (Charteris)
  1887-1960 .... *107*
Asquith, Ros *153*
Astley, Juliet
  See Lofts, Norah (Robinson)
Aston, Dianna Hutts 1964- *176*
Aston, James
  See White, T(erence) H(anbury)
Ata, Te 1895-1995 .... *119*
Atene, Ann
  See Atene, (Rita) Anna
Atene, (Rita) Anna 1922- *12*
Atheling, William, Jr.
  See Blish, James
Atkins, Catherine *160*
Atkins, Jeannine 1953- *172*
  Earlier sketch in SATA *113*
Atkinson, Allen G. 1953(?)-1987 .... *60*
  Brief entry *46*
  Obituary *55*
Atkinson, Elizabeth *215*
Atkinson, M. E.
  See Frankau, Mary Evelyn Atkinson
Atkinson, Margaret Fleming *14*
Atteberry, Kevan J. *186*
Attema, Martha 1949- *156*
  Earlier sketch in SATA *94*
Atticus
  See Davies, Hunter
  and Fleming, Ian
  and Pawle, Gerald Strachan
  and Wilson, (Thomas) Woodrow
Atwater, Florence (Hasseltine Carroll)
  1896-1979 .... *66*
  Earlier sketch in SATA *16*
  See also CLR *19*
Atwater, Montgomery Meigs 1904-1976 ...... *15*
Atwater, Richard (Tupper) 1892-1948 .... *66*
  Brief entry *27*
  Earlier sketch in SATA *54*
  See also CLR *19*
Atwater-Rhodes, Amelia 1984- *170*
  Earlier sketch in SATA *124*
Atwell, Debby 1953- *150*
  Earlier sketch in SATA *87*
Atwood, Ann (Margaret) 1913-1992 .... *7*
Atwood, Margaret 1939- *170*
  Earlier sketch in SATA *50*
Atwood, Margaret Eleanor
  See Atwood, Margaret
Aubrey, Meg Kelleher 1963- *83*
Aubry, Claude B. 1914-1984 .... *29*
  Obituary *40*
Auch, Herm *173*
Auch, Mary Jane *173*
  Earlier sketch in SATA *138*
Auch, M.J.
  See Auch, Mary Jane
Auclair, Joan 1960- *68*
Auel, Jean 1936- *91*

Auel, Jean M.
  See Auel, Jean
Auel, Jean Marie
  See Auel, Jean
Auer, Martin 1951- *77*
Augarde, Steve 1950- *210*
  Earlier sketches in SATA *25, 159*
Augarde, Steven Andre
  See Augarde, Steve
Augelli, John P(at) 1921- *46*
Augustine, Mildred
  See Benson, Mildred
Ault, Phil
  See Ault, Phillip H(alliday)
Ault, Phillip H(alliday) 1914- *23*
Ault, Rosalie Sain 1942- *38*
Ault, Roz
  See Ault, Rosalie Sain
Aung, (Maung) Htin 1909- *21*
Auntie Deb
  See Coury, Louise Andree
Auntie Louise
  See Coury, Louise Andree
Aunt Weedy
  See Alcott, Louisa May
Auseon, Andrew 1976- *217*
  Earlier sketch in SATA *166*
Austen, Carrie
  See Bennett, Cherie
Austen, Catherine 1965- *223*
Austin, Carrie
  See Seuling, Barbara
Austin, Elizabeth S. 1907-1977 .... *5*
Austin, Harry
  See McInerny, Ralph
Austin, Margot 1909(?)-1990 .... *11*
  Obituary *66*
Austin, Michael *178*
Austin, Oliver L(uther), Jr. 1903-1988 .... *7*
  Obituary *59*
Austin, Patricia 1950- *137*
Austin, R. G.
  See Gelman, Rita Golden
  and Lamb, Nancy
Austin, Virginia 1951- *152*
  Earlier sketch in SATA *80*
Auteur, Hillary
  See Gottfried, Theodore Mark
Auth, Tony
  See Auth, William Anthony, Jr.
Auth, William Anthony, Jr. 1942- *192*
Autry, Gloria Diener
  See Allen, Terril Diener
Auvil, Peggy A 1954- *122*
Auvil, Peggy Appleby
  See Auvil, Peggy A
Aveni, Anthony F. 1938- *181*
Aveni, Anthony Francis
  See Aveni, Anthony F.
Averbeck, Jim 1963- *201*
Averill, Esther (Holden) 1902-1992 .... *28*
  Obituary *72*
  Earlier sketch in SATA *1*
Avery, A. A.
  See Montgomery, Rutherford George
Avery, Al
  See Montgomery, Rutherford George
Avery, Gillian 1926- *137*
  Autobiography Feature *137*
  Earlier sketches in SATA *7, 75*
  See also SAAS *6*
Avery, Gillian Elise
  See Avery, Gillian
Avery, Kay 1908- *5*
Avery, Lorraine
  See Older, Effin
  and Older, Jules
Avery, Lynn
  See Cole, Lois Dwight

Avi 1937- *190*
  Earlier sketches in SATA *14, 71, 108, 156*
  See also CLR *68*
Aviles, Martha *218*
Avishai, Susan 1949- *82*
Avril, Francois 1961- *191*
Avril, Lynne
  See Cravath, Lynne W.
Awdry, Christopher Vere 1940- *67*
Awdry, Wilbert Vere 1911-1997 .... *94*
  See also CLR *23*
Axelrod, Amy *131*
Axelsen, Stephen 1953- *165*
Axton, David
  See Koontz, Dean
Ayars, James S(terling) 1898-1986 .... *4*
Aye, A. K.
  See Edwards, Hazel (Eileen)
Ayer, Eleanor H. 1947-1998 .... *121*
  Earlier sketch in SATA *78*
Ayer, Jacqueline 1930- *13*
Ayer, Margaret (?)-1981 .... *15*
Aylesworth, Jim 1943- *213*
  Earlier sketches in SATA *38, 89, 139*
  See also CLR *89*
Aylesworth, Thomas G(ibbons) 1927-1995 .. *88*
  Earlier sketch in SATA *4*
  See also CLR *6*
  See also SAAS *17*
Ayliffe, Alex *190*
Aylward, Marcus
  See Alexander, Marc
Aymar, Brandt 1911- *22*
Ayme, Marcel (Andre) 1902-1967 .... *91*
  See also CLR *25*
Ayres, Becky
  See Hickox, Rebecca (Ayres)
Ayres, Katherine 1947- *187*
Ayres, Pam 1947- *90*
Ayres, Patricia Miller 1923-1985
  Obituary *46*
Aytmatov, Chingiz
  See Aitmatov, Chingiz
Ayto, Russell 1960- *206*
  Earlier sketches in SATA *111, 166*
Azaid
  See Zaidenberg, Arthur
Azar, Penny 1952- *121*
Azarian, Mary 1940- *171*
  Earlier sketch in SATA *112*
Azore, Barbara 1934- *188*

B

Baasansuren, Bolormaa 1982- *216*
Baastad, Babbis Friis
  See Friis-Baastad, Babbis Ellinor
Bab
  See Gilbert, W(illiam) S(chwenck)
Babbis, Eleanor
  See Friis-Baastad, Babbis Ellinor
Babbitt, Lucy Cullyford 1960- *85*
Babbitt, Natalie 1932- *194*
  Earlier sketches in SATA *6, 68, 106*
  See also CLR *141*
  See also SAAS *5*
Babbitt, Natalie Zane Moore
  See Babbitt, Natalie
Babcock, Chris 1963- *83*
Babcock, Dennis 1948- *22*
Babcock, Dennis Arthur
  See Babcock, Dennis
Baber, Carolyn Stonnell 1936- *96*
Baboni, Elena *198*
Baca, Ana 1967- *191*
Baca, Maria 1951- *104*
Baccalario, Pierdomenico 1974- *222*

Bach, Alice (Hendricks) 1942- *93*
  Brief entry *27*
  Earlier sketch in SATA *30*
Bach, Bellamy
  See Windling, Terri
Bach, Mary 1960- *125*
Bach, Richard 1936- *13*
Bach, Richard David
  See Bach, Richard
Bache, Ellyn 1942- *124*
Bachel, Beverly K. 1957- *142*
Bachelet, Gilles 1952- *196*
Bachman, Fred 1949- *12*
Bachman, Richard
  See King, Stephen
Bachrach, Deborah *80*
Backus, James Gilmore 1913-1989
  Obituary *63*
Backus, Jim
  See Backus, James Gilmore
Bacmeister, Rhoda W(arner) 1893-1991 .... *11*
Bacon, Betty
  See Bacon, Elizabeth
Bacon, Elizabeth 1914-2001 .... *3*
  Obituary *131*
Bacon, Joan Chase
  See Bowden, Joan Chase
Bacon, Josephine Dodge (Daskam)
  1876-1961 .... *48*
Bacon, Margaret Frances
  See Bacon, Peggy
Bacon, Margaret Hope 1921- *6*
Bacon, Martha Sherman 1917-1981 .... *18*
  Obituary *27*
  See also CLR *3*
Bacon, Melvin 1950- *93*
Bacon, Melvin L.
  See Bacon, Melvin
Bacon, Peggy 1895-1987 .... *50*
Bacon, R(onald) L(eonard) 1924- *84*
  Earlier sketch in SATA *26*
Baddiel, Ivor 1963- *210*
Baden, Robert 1936- *70*
Baden-Powell, Robert (Stephenson Smyth)
  1857-1941 .... *16*
Badt, Karin L(uisa) 1963- *91*
Bae, Hyun-Joo *186*
Baehr, Kingsley M. 1937- *89*
Baehr, Patricia 1952- *65*
Baehr, Patricia Goehner
  See Baehr, Patricia
Baek, Matthew J. 1971- *202*
Baer, Jill
  See Gilbert, (Agnes) Joan (Sewell)
Baer, Judy 1951- *71*
Baer, Julie 1960- *161*
Baer-Block, Roxanna *172*
Baerg, Harry J(ohn) 1909-1996 .... *12*
Baeten, Lieve 1954- *83*
Bagert, Brod 1947- *191*
  Earlier sketch in SATA *80*
Baggette, Susan K. 1942- *126*
Baggott, Julianna 1969- *197*
Bagnold, Enid 1889-1981 .... *25*
  Earlier sketch in SATA *1*
Baguley, Elizabeth 1959- *199*
Bahlke, Valerie Worth -1994
  See Worth, Valerie
Bahous, Sally 1939- *86*
Bahr, Mary (Madelyn) 1946- *95*
Bahr, Robert 1940- *38*
Bahti, Tom 1926-1972 .... *57*
  Brief entry *31*
Bai, Durga *211*
Baicker-McKee, Carol 1958- *177*
Bailey, Alice Cooper 1890-1978 .... *12*
Bailey, Anne 1958- *71*
Bailey, Bernadine (Freeman) 1901-1995 .... *14*
Bailey, Carolyn Sherwin 1875-1961 .... *14*
Bailey, Debbie 1954- *123*
Bailey, Donna (Veronica Anne) 1938- *68*

Bailey, Jane H(orton) 1916- *12*
Bailey, John (Robert) 1940- *52*
Bailey, Len *193*
Bailey, Linda 1948- *217*
  Earlier sketches in SATA *107, 182*
Bailey, Maralyn Collins (Harrison) 1941- *12*
Bailey, Matilda
  See Radford, Ruby L(orraine)
Bailey, Maurice Charles 1932- *12*
Bailey, Pearl (Mae) 1918-1990 .... *81*
Bailey, Peter 1946- *194*
Bailey, Ralph Edgar 1893-1982 .... *11*
Bailey, Sheila (Lucas) 1960- *155*
Baillie, Allan 1943- *151*
  Earlier sketch in SATA *87*
  See also CLR *49*
  See also SAAS *21*
Baillie, Allan Stuart
  See Baillie, Allan
Baines, John (David) 1943- *71*
Bains, Larry
  See Sabin, Louis
Baird, Alison 1963- *138*
Baird, Bil 1904-1987 .... *30*
  Obituary *52*
Baird, Thomas (P.) 1923-1990 .... *45*
  Brief entry *39*
  Obituary *64*
Baird, William Britton
  See Baird, Bil
Baity, Elizabeth Chesley 1907-1989 .... *1*
Baiul, Oksana 1977- *108*
Bajoria, Paul 1964- *187*
Bakeless, John (Edwin) 1894-1978 .... *9*
Bakeless, Katherine Little 1895-1992 .... *9*
Baker, Alan 1951- *146*
  Earlier sketches in SATA *22, 93*
Baker, Augusta 1911-1998 .... *3*
Baker, Barbara 1947- *192*
Baker, Betty Lou 1928-1987 .... *73*
  Obituary *54*
  Earlier sketch in SATA *5*
Baker, Carin Greenberg 1959- *79*
Baker, Charlotte 1910- *2*
Baker, Christina
  See Kline, Christina Baker
Baker, Christopher W. 1952- *144*
Baker, Deirdre 1955- *195*
Baker, E.D. *190*
Baker, (Mary) Elizabeth (Gillette) 1923- *7*
Baker, Gayle Cunningham 1950- *39*
Baker, James W. 1924- *65*
  Earlier sketch in SATA *22*
Baker, James W. 1926- *122*
Baker, Janice E(dla) 1941- *22*
Baker, Jeanette *178*
Baker, Jeannie 1950- *156*
  Earlier sketches in SATA *23, 88*
  See also CLR *28*
Baker, Jeffrey J(ohn) W(heeler) 1931- *5*
Baker, Jim
  See Baker, James W.
Baker, Keith 1953- *222*
  Earlier sketch in SATA *179*
Baker, Ken 1962- *133*
Baker, Laura Nelson 1911- *3*
Baker, Margaret 1890-1965 .... *4*
Baker, Margaret J(oyce) 1918- *12*
  See also SAAS *8*
Baker, Mary Gladys Steel 1892-1974 .... *12*
Baker, (Robert) Michael (Graham) 1938- *4*
Baker, Nina (Brown) 1888-1957 .... *15*
Baker, Pamela J. 1947- *66*
Baker, Rachel 1904-1978 .... *2*
  Obituary *26*
Baker, Roberta *206*
Baker, Rosalie F. 1945- *166*
Baker, Samm Sinclair 1909-1997 .... *12*
  Obituary *96*
Baker, Sharon Reiss 1962- *207*
Baker, Susan (Catherine) 1942-1991 .... *29*

Baker-Smith, Grahame 223
Balaam
    See Lamb, G(eoffrey) F(rederick)
Balan, Bruce 1959- 113
Balcavage, Dynise 1965- 137
Balch, Glenn 1902-1989 3
    Obituary 83
    See also SAAS 11
Baldacci, David 1960- 184
Baldacci, David G.
    See Baldacci, David
    and Baldacci, David
Balderose, Nancy Ward 1952- 93
Balderson, Margaret 1935- 151
Baldini, Michelle 205
Baldry, Cherith 1947- 167
    Earlier sketch in SATA 72
Balducci, Carolyn 1946- 5
Balducci, Carolyn Feleppa
    See Balducci, Carolyn
Baldwin, Alex
    See Griffin, W. E. B.
Baldwin, Anne Norris 1938- 5
Baldwin, Clara 11
Baldwin, Gordo
    See Baldwin, Gordon C(ortis)
Baldwin, Gordon C(ortis) 1908-1983 12
Baldwin, James 1841-1925 24
Baldwin, James 1924-1987 9
    Obituary 54
Baldwin, Louis 1919- 110
Baldwin, Margaret
    See Weis, Margaret
Baldwin, Stan(ley C.) 1929- 62
    Brief entry 28
Bales, Carol Ann 1940- 57
    Brief entry 29
Balet, Jan (Bernard) 1913- 11
Balgassi, Haemi 1971- 131
Balian, Lorna 1929- 91
    Earlier sketch in SATA 9
Balit, Christina 1961- 212
    Earlier sketches in SATA 102, 159
Ball, Duncan 1941- 73
Ball, Zachary
    See Janas, Frankie-Lee
    and Masters, Kelly R(ay)
Ballantine, Lesley Frost
    See Frost, Lesley
Ballantyne, R(obert) M(ichael) 1825-1894 ... 24
    See also CLR 137
Ballard, James G.
    See Ballard, J.G.
Ballard, James Graham
    See Ballard, J.G.
Ballard, Jane
    See Gorman, Carol
Ballard, J.G. 1930-2009 93
    Obituary 203
Ballard, Jim G.
    See Ballard, J.G.
Ballard, John 1945- 110
Ballard, Lowell C(lyne) 1904-1986 12
    Obituary 49
Ballard, (Charles) Martin 1929- 1
Ballard, Mignon F. 1934- 64
    Brief entry 49
Ballard, Mignon Franklin
    See Ballard, Mignon F.
Ballard, Robert D(uane) 1942- 85
    See also CLR 60
Ballard, Robin 1965- 126
Balliett, Blue 1955- 156
Ballinger, Bryan 1968- 161
Ballouhey, Pierre 1944- 90
Balog, Cyn 221
Balogh, Penelope 1916-1975 1
    Obituary 34
Balouch, Kristen 176
Balow, Tom 1931- 12
Baltazzi, Evan S(erge) 1921- 90

Balterman, Marcia Ridlon 1942- 22
Baltimore, J.
    See Catherall, Arthur
Baltzer, Hans (Adolf) 1900- 40
Balzano, Jeanne (Koppel) 1912- 7
Bambara, Toni Cade 1939-1995 112
Bamfylde, Walter
    See Bevan, Tom
Bamman, Henry A. 1918- 12
Banat, D. R.
    See Bradbury, Ray
Bancroft, Bronwyn 1958- 216
Bancroft, Griffing 1907-1999 6
Bancroft, Laura
    See Baum, L. Frank
Bandel, Betty 1912- 47
Baner, Skulda Vanadis 1897-1964 10
Banerjee, Anjali 174
Banfill, A. Scott 1956- 98
Bang, Betsy 1912- 48
    Brief entry 37
Bang, Garrett
    See Bang, Molly
Bang, Molly 1943- 215
    Earlier sketches in SATA 24, 69, 111, 158
    See also CLR 8
Bang, Molly Garrett
    See Bang, Molly
Bang-Campbell, Monika 1975(?)- 195
    Earlier sketch in SATA 140
Banjo, The
    See Paterson, A(ndrew) B(arton)
Banke, Cecile de
    See de Banke, Cecile
Banks, Erin Bennett 1978- 211
Banks, Kate 1960- 200
    Earlier sketches in SATA 134, 172
Banks, Laura Stockton Voorhees 1908(?)-1980
    Obituary 23
Banks, Lynne Reid
    See Reid Banks, Lynne
Banks, Merry 197
Banks, Michael A. 1951- 101
Banks, Paul 1952- 174
Banks, Sara
    See Harrell, Sara Gordon
Banks, Sara Jeanne Gordon Harrell
    See Harrell, Sara Gordon
Bannatyne-Cugnet, Elizabeth Jo-Anne
    See Bannatyne-Cugnet, Jo
Bannatyne-Cugnet, Jo 1951- 101
Banner, Angela
    See Maddison, Angela Mary
Bannerman, Helen (Brodie Cowan Watson)
    1862(?)-1946 19
    See also CLR 144
Banning, Evelyn I. 1903-1993 36
Bannon, Laura (?)-1963 6
Bannor, Brett 1959- 143
Banta, Susan 181
Bantock, Nick 1950(?)- 95
Banyai, Istvan 193
Barakat, Ibtisam 1963- 186
Barasch, Lynne 1939- 186
    Earlier sketches in SATA 74, 126
Barbalet, Margaret 1949- 77
Barbary, James
    See Baumann, Amy Beeching
    and Beeching, Jack
Barbash, Shepard 1957- 84
Barbauld, Anna Laetitia 1743-1825
    See CLR 160
Barbe, Walter Burke 1926- 45
Barber, Alison 222
Barber, Antonia 1932- 163
    Earlier sketch in SATA 29
Barber, Atiim Kiambu
    See Barber, Tiki
Barber, Lynda
    See Graham-Barber, Lynda

Barber, Lynda Graham
    See Graham-Barber, Lynda
Barber, Richard (William) 1941- 35
Barber, Ronde 1975- 182
Barber, Tiki 1975- 182
Barbera, Joe 1911-2006 51
    Obituary 179
Barbera, Joseph
    See Barbera, Joe
Barbera, Joseph Roland
    See Barbera, Joe
Barberis, Juan C(arlos) 1920- 61
Barbour, Karen 1956- 170
    Earlier sketches in SATA 63, 121
Barbour, Ralph Henry 1870-1944 16
Barclay, Bill
    See Moorcock, Michael
Barclay, Isabel
    See Dobell, I(sabel) M(arian) B(arclay)
Barclay, William Ewert
    See Moorcock, Michael
Barclay, William Ewert
    See Moorcock, Michael
Bardhan-Quallen, Sudipta 1977- 214
    Earlier sketch in SATA 168
Bardoe, Cheryl 181
Bare, Arnold Edwin 1920- 16
Bare, Colleen Stanley 32
Bar-el, Dan 199
Barenholtz, Bernard 1914-1989
    Obituary 64
Bargar, Gary W. 1947-1985 63
Barger, Jan 1948- 147
Barish, Matthew 1907-2000 12
Barkan, Joanne 127
    Earlier sketch in SATA 77
Barker, Albert W. 1900- 8
Barker, Carol (Minturn) 1938- 31
Barker, Cicely Mary 1895-1973 49
    Brief entry 39
    See also CLR 88
Barker, Melvern 1907-1989 11
Barker, S. Omar 1894-1985 10
Barker, Squire Omar
    See Barker, S. Omar
Barker, Will 1913-1983 8
Barkin, Carol 1944- 52
    Earlier sketch in SATA 42
Barklem, Jill 1951- 96
    See also CLR 31
Barkley, Brad 178
Barkley, James Edward 1941- 6
Barks, Carl 1901-2000 37
Barley, Janet Crane 1934- 95
Barlow, Steve 1952- 211
Barnaby, Ralph S(tanton) 1893-1986 9
Barnard, A. M.
    See Alcott, Louisa May
Barnard, Bryn 1956- 169
    Earlier sketch in SATA 115
Barne, Kitty
    See Barne, Marion Catherine
Barne, Marion Catherine 1883-1957 97
Barneda, David 206
Barner, Bob 1947- 136
    Earlier sketch in SATA 29
Barnes, Dawn 1957- 175
Barnes, Derrick 191
Barnes, Derrick D.
    See Barnes, Derrick
Barnes, (Frank) Eric Wollencott 1907-1962 . 22
Barnes, Joyce Annette 1958- 85
Barnes, Laura T. 1958- 119
Barnes, Loutricia
    See Barnes-Svarney, Patricia L(ou)
Barnes, Malcolm 1909(?)-1984
    Obituary 41
Barnes, Michael 1934- 55
Barnes-Murphy, Frances 1951- 88
Barnes-Murphy, Rowan 1952- 88
Barnes-Svarney, Patricia L(ou) 1953- 67

Barnet, Nancy 1954- 84
Barnett, Ivan 1947- 70
Barnett, Lincoln (Kinnear) 1909-1979 36
Barnett, Mac 223
Barnett, Moneta 1922-1976 33
Barnett, Naomi 1927- 40
Barney, Maginel Wright 1881(?)-1966 39
    Brief entry 32
Barnhart, Clarence L(ewis) 1900-1993 48
    Obituary 78
Barnouw, Adriaan Jacob 1877-1968
    Obituary 27
Barnouw, Victor 1915-1989 43
    Brief entry 28
Barnstone, Willis 1927- 20
Barnum, Jay Hyde 1888(?)-1962 20
Barnum, P. T., Jr.
    See Stratemeyer, Edward L.
Barnum, Richard 67
    Earlier sketch in SATA *1*
Barnum, Theodore
    See Stratemeyer, Edward L.
Barnwell, Ysaye M. 1946- 200
Baron, Kathy 1954- 90
Baron, Virginia Olsen 1931- 46
    Brief entry 28
Barr, Donald 1921-2004 20
    Obituary 152
Barr, George 1907-1992 2
Barr, Jene 1922-1985 16
    Obituary 42
Barr, Nevada 1952- 126
    Earlier sketch in SATA *115*
Barragan, Paula 1963- 216
Barrer, Gertrude
    See Barrer-Russell, Gertrude
Barrer-Russell, Gertrude 1921- 27
Barrett, Angela 1955- 223
Barrett, Angela (Jane) 1955- 145
    Earlier sketch in SATA *75*
Barrett, Ethel 87
    Brief entry 44
Barrett, Joyce Durham 1943- 138
Barrett, Judi
    See Barrett, Judith
Barrett, Judith 1941- 204
    Earlier sketch in SATA *26*
    See also CLR *98*
Barrett, Robert T(heodore) 1949- 92
Barrett, Ron 1937- 14
Barrett, Susan (Mary) 1938- 113
Barrett, Tracy 1955- 207
    Earlier sketches in SATA *84, 115, 156*
Barrett, William E(dmund) 1900-1986
    Obituary 49
Barretta, Gene 214
    Earlier sketch in SATA *176*
Barretton, Grandall
    See Garrett, Randall
Barrie, Baronet
    See Barrie, J. M.
Barrie, J. M. 1860-1937 100
    See also YABC *1*
    See also CLR *124*
Barrie, James Matthew
    See Barrie, J. M.
Barringer, William 1940-1996 153
Barrington, Michael
    See Moorcock, Michael
Barris, George 1925- 47
Barrol, Grady
    See Bograd, Larry
Barron, Rex 1951- 84
Barron, T.A. 1952- 192
    Earlier sketches in SATA *83, 126*
    See also CLR *86*
Barron, Thomas Archibald
    See Barron, T.A.
Barron, Tom
    See Barron, T.A.
Barrow, Lloyd H. 1942- 73

Barrows, Annie 1962- 180
Barry, Dan 1958- 177
Barry, Dana (Marie Malloy) 1949- 139
Barry, James P(otvin) 1918- 14
Barry, Katharina Watjen 1936- 4
Barry, Robert 1931- 6
Barry, Robert Everett
    See Barry, Robert
Barry, Scott 1952- 32
Barry, Sheila Anne -2003 91
Barshaw, Ruth McNally 203
Bartell, Susan S. 175
Bartenbach, Jean 1918- 40
Barth, Edna 1914-1980 7
    Obituary 24
Barth, Kelly L. 1964- 152
Barthelme, Donald 1931-1989 7
    Obituary 62
Barth-Grozinger, Inge 1950- 185
Bartholomew, Barbara 1941- 86
    Brief entry 42
Bartholomew, Jean
    See Beatty, Patricia (Robbins)
Bartlett, Alison 153
Bartlett, Philip A. 1
Bartlett, Robert Merrill 1899-1995 12
Bartoletti, Susan Campbell 1958- 173
    Earlier sketches in SATA *88, 129, 135*
Barton, Byron 1930- 126
    Earlier sketches in SATA *9, 90*
Barton, Jill(ian) 1940- 75
Barton, May Hollis 67
    Earlier sketch in SATA *1*
Barton, Pat
    See Arrowsmith, Pat
Bartos-Hoeppner, Barbara 1923- 5
Bartram, Simon 218
    Earlier sketch in SATA *156*
Bartsch, Jochen 1906- 39
Baruch, Dorothy W(alter) 1899-1962 21
Barunga, Albert 1912(?)-1977 120
Baryshnikov, Mikhail 1948- 192
Bas, Rutger
    See Rutgers van der Loeff-Basenau, An(na)
    Maria Margaretha
Base, Graeme 1958- 162
    Earlier sketches in SATA *67, 101*
    See also CLR *22*
Base, Graeme Rowland
    See Base, Graeme
Baseman, Gary 1960- 174
Bash, Barbara 1948- 132
Bashevis, Isaac
    See Singer, Isaac Bashevis
Bashevis, Yitskhok
    See Singer, Isaac Bashevis
Bashista, Adrienne Ehlert 203
Basile, Gloria Vitanza 1929- 180
Baskin, Leonard 1922-2000 120
    Brief entry 27
    Earlier sketch in SATA *30*
Baskin, Nora Raleigh 1961- 189
    Earlier sketch in SATA *129*
Bason, Lillian 1913- 20
Bass, Hester 1956- 223
Bass, L. G.
    See Geringer, Laura
Bassett, Jeni 1959- 64
    Brief entry 43
Bassett, John Keith
    See Keating, Lawrence A.
Bassett, Lisa 1958- 61
Bassil, Andrea
    See Nilsen, Anna
Bastyra, Judy 108
Basye, Dale E. 205
Bataille, Marion 1963- 209
Bat-Ami, Miriam 1950- 150
    Autobiography Feature 150
    Earlier sketches in SATA *82, 122*
Bate, Lucy 1939-1993 18

Bate, Norman (Arthur) 1916- 5
Bateman, Colin 1962- 172
Bateman, Donna M. 190
Bateman, Teresa 1957- 216
    Earlier sketches in SATA *112, 168*
Bates, Amy June 189
Bates, Barbara S(nedeker) 1919- 12
Bates, Betty
    See Bates, Elizabeth
Bates, Dianne 1948- 147
Bates, Elizabeth 1921- 19
Bates, Ivan 175
Bates, Katharine Lee 1859-1929 113
Bates, Martine
    See Leavitt, Martine
Bateson, Catherine 1960- 197
    Earlier sketch in SATA *157*
Batey, Tom 1946- 52
    Brief entry 41
Bath, Kevin P.
    See Bath, K.P.
Bath, K.P. 1959- 171
Batherman, Muriel
    See Sheldon, Muriel
Batson, Larry 1930- 35
Batt, Tanya Robyn 1970- 131
Battaglia, Aurelius 1910- 50
    Brief entry 33
Batten, H(arry) Mortimer 1888-1958 25
Batten, Mary 1937- 162
    Earlier sketches in SATA *5, 102*
Batterberry, Ariane Ruskin 1935- 13
Batterberry, Michael Carver 1932-2010 32
Battle-Lavert, Gwendolyn 1951- 155
    Earlier sketches in SATA *85, 131*
Battles, (Roxy) Edith 1921- 7
Baudouy, Michel-Aime 1909- 7
Bauer, A.C.E. 201
Bauer, Caroline Feller 1935- 98
    Brief entry 46
    Earlier sketch in SATA *52*
    See also SAAS *24*
Bauer, Fred 1934- 36
Bauer, Helen 1900-1988 2
Bauer, Joan 1951- 160
    Earlier sketch in SATA *117*
Bauer, Jutta 1955- 150
Bauer, Marion Dane 1938- 192
    Autobiography Feature 144
    Earlier sketches in SATA *20, 69, 113, 144*
    See also SAAS *9*
Bauer, Michael Gerard 1955(?)- 167
Bauer, Steven 1948- 125
Bauerschmidt, Marjorie 1926- 15
Baughman, Dorothy 1940- 61
Baum, Allyn Z(elton) 1924-1997 98
    Earlier sketch in SATA *20*
Baum, L. Frank
    See Thompson, Ruth Plumly
Baum, L. Frank 1856-1919 100
    Earlier sketch in SATA *18*
    See also CLR *107*
Baum, Louis 1948- 182
    Brief entry 52
    Earlier sketch in SATA *64*
Baum, Louis F.
    See Baum, L. Frank
Baum, Lyman Frank
    See Baum, L. Frank
Baum, Maxie 188
Baum, Willi 1931- 4
Bauman, Beth Ann 1964- 220
Baumann, Amy Beeching 1922- 10
Baumann, Amy Brown Beeching
    See Baumann, Amy Beeching
Baumann, Hans 1914- 2
    See also CLR *35*
Baumann, Kurt 1935- 21
Baumgartner, Barbara 1939- 86
Baurys, Flo 1938- 122

Baurys, Florence
    See Baurys, Flo
Bausum, Ann *173*
Bawden, Nina 1925- *132*
    Earlier sketches in SATA *4, 72*
    See also CLR *51*
    See also SAAS *16*
Bawden, Nina Mary Mabey
    See Bawden, Nina
Baxter, Roberta 1952- *219*
Baxter, Valerie
    See Meynell, Laurence Walter
Bay, Jeanette Graham 1928- *88*
Bayer, Harold
    See Gregg, Andrew K.
Bayer, Jane E. (?)-1985
    Obituary *44*
Bayley, Nicola 1949- *129*
    Earlier sketches in SATA *41, 69*
Baylor, Byrd 1924- *136*
    Earlier sketches in SATA *16, 69*
    See also CLR *3*
Baynes, Pauline 1922-2008 .... *133*
    Obituary *196*
    Earlier sketches in SATA *19, 59*
Baynes, Pauline Diana
    See Baynes, Pauline
Bayoc, Cbabi *186*
Bayrock, Fiona *215*
BB
    See Watkins-Pitchford, Denys James
Beach, Charles
    See Reid, (Thomas) Mayne
Beach, Charles Amory *1*
Beach, Edward L. 1918-2002 .... *12*
    Obituary *140*
Beach, Edward Latimer
    See Beach, Edward L.
Beach, Lisa 1957- *111*
Beach, Lynn
    See Lance, Kathryn
Beach, Stewart T(aft) 1899-1979 .... *23*
Beachcroft, Nina 1931- *18*
Beagle, Peter S. 1939- *130*
    Earlier sketch in SATA *60*
Beagle, Peter Soyer
    See Beagle, Peter S.
Beaglehole, Helen 1946- *117*
Beake, Lesley 1949- *209*
Beale, Fleur *107*
Bealer, Alex W(inkler III) 1921-1980 ...... *8*
    Obituary *22*
Beales, Valerie 1915- *74*
Beals, Carleton 1893-1979 .... *12*
Beals, Frank Lee 1881-1972
    Obituary *26*
Beam, Matt 1970- *187*
Beame, Rona 1934- *12*
Beamer, Charles 1942- *43*
Beamer, George Charles, Jr.
    See Beamer, Charles
Bean, Jonathan 1979- *194*
Bean, Normal
    See Burroughs, Edgar Rice
Beaney, Jan
    See Udall, Jan Beaney
Beaney, Jane
    See Udall, Jan Beaney
Bear, Carolyn
    See Rayban, Chloe
Bear, Greg 1951- *105*
    Earlier sketch in SATA *65*
Bear, Gregory Dale
    See Bear, Greg
Bearanger, Marie
    See Messier, Claire
Beard, Alex 1970- *222*
Beard, Charles A(ustin) 1874-1948 .... *18*
Beard, Dan(iel Carter) 1850-1941 .... *22*
Beard, Darleen Bailey 1961- *96*

Bearden, Romare (Howard) 1914(?)-1988 ... *22*
    Obituary *56*
Beardmore, Cedric
    See Beardmore, George
Beardmore, George 1908-1979 .... *20*
Beardshaw, Rosalind 1969- *190*
Beardsley, Martyn R. 1957- *150*
Bearman, Jane (Ruth) 1917- *29*
Bearn, Emily *220*
Beaton, Clare 1947- *220*
    Earlier sketch in SATA *125*
Beatty, Elizabeth
    See Holloway, Teresa (Bragunier)
Beatty, Hetty Burlingame 1907-1971 ...... *5*
Beatty, Jerome, Jr. 1918- *5*
Beatty, John (Louis) 1922-1975 .... *6*
    Obituary *25*
Beatty, Patricia (Robbins) 1922-1991 ..... *73*
    Obituary *68*
    Earlier sketches in SATA *1, 30*
    See also SAAS *4*
Beaty, Andrea *186*
Beaty, Mary (T.) 1947- *146*
Beaudoin, Sean *210*
Beaumont, Karen 1954- *204*
Beccia, Carlyn *189*
Bechard, Margaret 1953- *164*
    Earlier sketch in SATA *85*
Bechtel, Louise Seaman 1894-1985 .... *4*
    Obituary *43*
Bechtold, Lisze *208*
Beck, Barbara L. 1927- *12*
Beck, Ian 1947- *190*
    Earlier sketch in SATA *138*
    See Beck, Ian Archibald
Beck, Peggy 1949- *171*
Beck, Scott *197*
Becker, Beril 1901-1999 .... *11*
Becker, Bonny *184*
Becker, Deborah Zimmett 1955- *138*
Becker, Helaine 1961- *142*
Becker, John (Leonard) 1901- *12*
Becker, John E(mil) 1942- *148*
Becker, Joyce 1936- *39*
Becker, May Lamberton 1873-1958 .... *33*
Becker, Neesa 1951- *123*
Becker, Shari *174*
Beckerman, Chad W. *198*
Beckett, Sheilah 1913- *33*
Beckhorn, Susan Williams 1953- *189*
Beckles Willson, Robina 1930- *27*
Beckman, Delores 1914-1994 .... *51*
Beckman, Gunnel 1910- *6*
    See also CLR *25*
    See also SAAS *9*
Beckman, Kaj
    See Beckman, Karin
Beckman, Karin 1913- *45*
Beckman, Per (Frithiof) 1913- *45*
Bedard, Michael 1949- *154*
    Earlier sketch in SATA *93*
    See also CLR *35*
Beddor, Frank *194*
Beddows, Eric
    See Nutt, Ken
Bedford, A. N.
    See Watson, Jane Werner
Bedford, Annie North
    See Watson, Jane Werner
Bedford, David *159*
Bedoukian, Kerop 1907-1981 .... *53*
Bee, Jay
    See Brainerd, John W(hiting)
Bee, William *188*
Beebe, B. F.
    See Johnson, B. F.
Beebe, (Charles) William 1877-1962 ...... *19*
Beeby, Betty 1923- *25*
Beech, Mark 1971- *191*
Beech, Webb
    See Griffin, W. E. B.

Beecham, Jahnna *161*
Beechcroft, William
    See Hallstead, William F(inn III)
Beeching, Jack 1922- *14*
Beeke, Tiphanie *219*
    Earlier sketch in SATA *163*
Beeler, Janet
    See Shaw, Janet
Beeler, Nelson F(rederick) 1910-1978 ...... *13*
Beere, Peter 1951- *97*
Beers, Dorothy Sands 1917- *9*
Beers, Lorna 1897-1989 .... *14*
Beers, V(ictor) Gilbert 1928- *130*
    Earlier sketch in SATA *9*
Beeton, Max
    See Redding, Robert Hull
Begay, Shonto 1954- *137*
Begaye, Lisa Shook
    See Beach, Lisa
Begin, Mary Jane 1963- *82*
Begin-Callanan, Mary Jane
    See Begin, Mary Jane
Begley, Kathleen A. 1948- *21*
Begley, Kathleen Anne
    See Begley, Kathleen A.
Beguine, Anna
    See Saintcrow, Lilith
Beha, Eileen *221*
Beha, Philippe *211*
Behan, Leslie
    See Gottfried, Theodore Mark
Behler, Deborah A. 1947- *145*
Behler, John L. 1943-2006 .... *145*
    Obituary *173*
Behler, John Luther
    See Behler, John L.
Behn, Harry 1898-1973 .... *2*
    Obituary *34*
Behnke, Frances L. *8*
Behr, Joyce 1929- *15*
Behrens, June York 1925- *19*
Behrman, Carol H(elen) 1925- *144*
    Earlier sketch in SATA *14*
Beifuss, John, (Jr.) 1959- *92*
Beil, Karen Magnuson 1950- *221*
    Earlier sketch in SATA *124*
Beiler, Edna 1923- *61*
Beingessner, Laura 1965- *220*
Beinicke, Steve 1956- *69*
Beirne, Barbara 1933- *71*
Beiser, Arthur 1931- *22*
Beiser, Germaine 1931- *11*
Belair, Richard L. 1934- *45*
Belaney, Archibald Stansfeld 1888-1938 ...... *24*
    See also CLR *32*
Belasen, Amy 1983- *213*
Belbin, David 1958- *164*
    Earlier sketch in SATA *106*
Belden, Wilanne Schneider 1925- *56*
Belfrage, Sally 1936-1994 .... *65*
    Obituary *79*
Belknap, B. H.
    See Ellis, Edward S.
Belknap, Boynton
    See Ellis, Edward S.
Belknap, Boynton M.D.
    See Ellis, Edward S.
Bell, Anthea 1936- *148*
    Earlier sketch in SATA *88*
Bell, Cathleen Davitt 1971- *203*
Bell, Cece *202*
Bell, Clare (Louise) 1952- *99*
Bell, Corydon Whitten 1894-1980 .... *3*
Bell, David Owen 1949- *99*
Bell, Emerson
    See Stratemeyer, Edward L.
Bell, Emily Mary
    See Cason, Mabel Earp
Bell, Frank
    See Benson, Mildred
Bell, Gertrude (Wood) 1911-1987 .... *12*

Bell, Gina
  See Balzano, Jeanne (Koppel)
Bell, Hilari 1958- *197*
  Earlier sketch in SATA *151*
Bell, Jadrien
  See Golden, Christie
Bell, Janet
  See Clymer, Eleanor
Bell, Janet Cheatham 1937- *127*
Bell, Krista 1950- *215*
  Earlier sketch in SATA *126*
Bell, Krista Anne Blakeney
  See Bell, Krista
Bell, Margaret E(lizabeth) 1898-1990 .... *2*
Bell, Mary Reeves 1946- *88*
Bell, Norman (Edward) 1899- *11*
Bell, Raymond Martin 1907-1999 .... *13*
Bell, Siobhan *177*
Bell, Thelma Harrington 1896-1985 .... *3*
Bell, William 1945- *90*
  See also CLR *91*
Bellairs, John (Anthony) 1938-1991 .... *160*
  Obituary *66*
  Earlier sketches in SATA *2, 68*
  See also CLR *37*
Beller, Susan Provost 1949- *128*
  Earlier sketch in SATA *84*
  See also CLR *106*
Bellingham, Brenda 1931- *99*
  Brief entry *51*
Bello, Rosario de
  See De Bello, Rosario
Belloc, Hilaire 1870-1953 .... *112*
  See also YABC *1*
  See also CLR *102*
Belloc, Joseph Hilaire Pierre Sebastien Rene
  Swanton
  See Belloc, Hilaire
Belloc, Joseph Peter Rene Hilaire
  See Belloc, Hilaire
Belloc, Joseph Pierre Hilaire
  See Belloc, Hilaire
Belloli, Andrea P. A. 1947- *86*
Bell-Rehwoldt, Sheri 1962- *199*
Bellville, Cheryl Walsh 1944- *54*
  Brief entry *49*
Bell-Zano, Gina
  See Balzano, Jeanne (Koppel)
Belpre, Pura 1899-1982 .... *16*
  Obituary *30*
Belting, Natalia Maree 1915-1997 .... *6*
Belton, John Raynor 1931- *22*
Belton, Sandra 1939- *186*
  Earlier sketches in SATA *85, 134*
Belton, Sandra Yvonne
  See Belton, Sandra
Beltran, Alberto 1923- *43*
Beltran-Hernandez, Irene 1945- *74*
Belvedere, Lee
  See Grayland, Valerie (Merle Spanner)
Bemelmans, Ludwig 1898-1962 .... *100*
  Earlier sketch in SATA *15*
  See also CLR *93*
Benander, Carl D. 1941- *74*
Benary, Margot
  See Benary-Isbert, Margot
Benary-Isbert, Margot 1889-1979 .... *2*
  Obituary *21*
  See also CLR *12*
Benasutti, Marion 1908-1992 .... *6*
Benatar, Raquel 1955- *167*
Benchley, Nathaniel (Goddard) 1915-1981 .. *25*
  Obituary *28*
  Earlier sketch in SATA *3*
Benchley, Peter 1940-2006 .... *164*
  Earlier sketches in SATA *3, 89*
Benchley, Peter Bradford
  See Benchley, Peter
Bendall-Brunello, John *185*
Bender, Edna 1941- *92*
Bender, Esther 1942- *88*

Bender, Lucy Ellen 1942- *22*
Bender, Robert 1962- *160*
  Earlier sketch in SATA *79*
Bendick, Jeanne 1919- *135*
  Earlier sketches in SATA *2, 68*
  See also CLR *5*
  See also SAAS *4*
Bendick, Robert L(ouis) 1917- *11*
Benedetto, William R. 1928- *180*
Benedetto, William Ralph
  See Benedetto, William R.
Benedict, Andrew
  See Arthur, Robert, (Jr.)
Benedict, Dorothy Potter 1889-1979 .... *11*
  Obituary *23*
Benedict, Lois Trimble 1902-1967 .... *12*
Benedict, Rex 1920-1995 .... *8*
Benedict, Stewart H(urd) 1924- *26*
Beneduce, Ann Keay *128*
Benet, Laura 1884-1979 .... *3*
  Obituary *23*
Benet, Stephen Vincent 1898-1943
  See YABC *1*
Benet, Sula 1906-1982 .... *21*
  Obituary *33*
Ben-Ezer, Ehud 1936- *122*
Benezra, Barbara (Beardsley) 1921- *10*
Benham, Leslie 1922- *48*
Benham, Lois (Dakin) 1924- *48*
Benham, Mary Lile 1914-1991 .... *55*
Benjamin, E. M. J.
  See Bache, Ellyn
Benjamin, Floella 1949- *206*
Benjamin, Nora
  See Kubie, Nora Gottheil Benjamin
Benjamin, Saragail Katzman 1953- *86*
Benner, Cheryl 1962- *80*
Benner, Judith Ann 1942- *94*
Bennett, Alice
  See Ziner, Florence
Bennett, Cherie 1960- *158*
  Earlier sketch in SATA *97*
Bennett, Dorothea
  See Young, Dorothea Bennett
Bennett, Erin Susanne
  See Banks, Erin Bennett
Bennett, Holly 1957- *181*
Bennett, James (W.) 1942- *153*
  Autobiography Feature *153*
  Earlier sketches in SATA *93, 148*
Bennett, Jay 1912- *87*
  Brief entry *27*
  Earlier sketch in SATA *41*
  See also SAAS *4*
Bennett, Jill (Crawford) 1934- *41*
Bennett, John 1865-1956
  See YABC *1*
Bennett, Penelope (Agnes) 1938- *94*
Bennett, Rachel
  See Hill, Margaret (Ohler)
Bennett, Rainey 1907-1998 .... *15*
  Obituary *111*
Bennett, Richard 1899- *21*
Bennett, Russell H(oradley) 1896- *25*
Bennett, Veronica 1953- *178*
Bennett, William (John) 1943- *102*
Benning, Elizabeth
  See Rice, Bebe Faas
Benny, Mike 1964- *203*
Benson, Elizabeth P(olk) 1924- *65*
Benson, Kathleen 1947- *183*
  Earlier sketches in SATA *62, 111*
Benson, Linda M(aria) 1959- *84*
Benson, Mildred 1905-2002 .... *100*
  Obituary *135*
  Earlier sketches in SATA *1, 65, 67*
Benson, Mildred Augustine Wirt
  See Benson, Mildred
Benson, Mildred Wirt
  See Benson, Mildred

Benson, Millie
  See Benson, Mildred
Benson, Patrick 1956- *147*
Benson, Sally 1900-1972 .... *35*
  Obituary *27*
  Earlier sketch in SATA *1*
Bentley, Judith (McBride) 1945- *89*
  Earlier sketch in SATA *40*
Bentley, Karen
  See Taschek, Karen
Bentley, Nancy (L.) 1946- *78*
Bentley, Nicolas Clerihew 1907-1978
  Obituary *24*
Bentley, Phyllis Eleanor 1894-1977 .... *6*
  Obituary *25*
Bentley, Roy 1947- *46*
Bentley, William (George) 1916- *84*
Bently, Peter 1960- *221*
Benton, Jim 1963- *172*
ben Uzair, Salem
  See Horne, Richard Henry Hengist
Ben-Zvi, Rebeccca Tova
  See O'Connell, Rebecca
Bercaw, Edna Coe 1961- *124*
Berck, Judith 1960- *75*
Berelson, Howard 1940- *5*
Berends, Polly Berrien 1939- *50*
  Brief entry *38*
Berenstain, Jan 1923- *135*
  Earlier sketches in SATA *12, 64, 129*
  See also CLR *150*
  See also SAAS *20*
Berenstain, Janice
  See Berenstain, Jan
Berenstain, Michael 1951- *220*
  Earlier sketch in SATA *45*
Berenstain, Mike
  See Berenstain, Michael
Berenstain, Stan 1923-2005 .... *135*
  Obituary *169*
  Earlier sketches in SATA *12, 64, 129*
  See also CLR *150*
  See also SAAS *20*
Berenstain, Stanley
  See Berenstain, Stan
Berenzy, Alix 1957- *168*
  Earlier sketch in SATA *65*
Beresford, Elisabeth 1928-2010 .... *141*
  Earlier sketches in SATA *25, 86*
  See also SAAS *20*
Berg, Adriane G(ilda) 1948- *152*
Berg, Dave
  See Berg, David
Berg, David 1920-2002 .... *27*
  Obituary *137*
Berg, Elizabeth 1948- *104*
Berg, Jean Horton 1913-1995 .... *6*
Berg, Joan
  See Victor, Joan Berg
Berg, Ron 1952- *48*
Bergaust, Erik 1925-1978 .... *20*
Bergel, Colin J. 1963- *137*
Bergen, Joyce 1949- *95*
Berger, Barbara (Helen) 1945- *77*
Berger, Carin *185*
Berger, Gilda 1935- *88*
  Brief entry *42*
Berger, Joe 1970- *221*
Berger, Josef 1903-1971 .... *36*
Berger, Lou 1950- *213*
Berger, Melvin H. 1927- *158*
  Autobiography Feature *124*
  Earlier sketches in SATA *5, 88*
  See also CLR *32*
  See also SAAS *2*
Berger, Phil 1942-2001 .... *62*
Berger, Samantha 1969- *140*
Berger, Samantha Allison
  See Berger, Samantha
Berger, Terry 1933- *8*
Bergey, Alyce 1934- *45*

Bergey, Alyce Mae
  See Bergey, Alyce
Bergin, Mark 1961- 160
  Earlier sketch in SATA 114
Berglin, Ruth Marie 1970- 181
Bergman, Donna 1934- 73
Bergman, Mara 1956- 196
Bergman, Tamar 1939- 95
Bergren, Lisa T.
  See Bergren, Lisa Tawn
Bergren, Lisa Tawn 200
Bergsma, Jody Lynn 163
Bergstein, Rita M. 211
Bergum, Constance R. 1952- 208
  Earlier sketch in SATA 121
Berk, Ari 208
Berkebile, Fred D(onovan) 1900-1978
  Obituary 26
Berkeley, Jon 1962- 204
Berkes, Marianne 217
  Earlier sketch in SATA 173
Berkey, Barry Robert 1935- 24
Berkowitz, Freda Pastor 1908-1994 12
Berkus, Clara Widess 1909- 78
Berlan, Kathryn Hook 1946- 78
Berlfein, Judy Reiss 1958- 79
Berlin, Eric 1968- 195
Berliner, Don 1930- 33
Berliner, Franz 1930- 13
Berlitz, Charles (L. Frambach) 1914-2003 ... 32
  Obituary 151
Berman, Linda 1948- 38
Berman, Paul (Lawrence) 1949- 66
Berman, Rachel 1946- 217
Berna, Paul 1910-1994 15
  Obituary 78
  See also CLR 19
Bernadette
  See Watts, (Anna) Bernadette
Bernard, Bruce 1928-2000 78
  Obituary 124
Bernard, George I. 1949- 39
Bernard, Jacqueline (de Sieyes) 1921-1983 ... 8
  Obituary 45
Bernard, Patricia 1942- 181
  Earlier sketch in SATA 106
Bernard, Trish
  See Bernard, Patricia
Bernardin, James (B.) 1966- 112
Bernardo, Anilu 184
Bernards, Neal 1963- 71
Bernasconi, Pablo 1973- 183
Bernays, Anne 1930- 32
Berner, Rotraut Susanne 1948- 214
Bernhard, Durga T. 1961- 80
Bernhard, Emery 1950- 80
Bernheimer, Kate 201
Bernier-Grand, Carmen T. 1947- 202
Bernstein, Daryl (Evan) 1976- 81
Bernstein, Joanne E(ckstein) 1943- 15
Bernstein, Jonathan 217
Bernstein, Margery 1933- 114
Bernstein, Nina 1949- 180
Bernstein, Theodore M(enline) 1904-1979 ... 12
  Obituary 27
Berrien, Edith Heal
  See Heal, Edith
Berrill, Jacquelyn (Batsel) 1905- 12
Berrington, John
  See Brownjohn, Alan
Berry, B. J.
  See Berry, Barbara J.
Berry, Barbara J. 1937- 7
Berry, Erick
  See Best, (Evangel) Allena Champlin
Berry, Holly 1957- 210
Berry, James 1924- 110
  Earlier sketch in SATA 67
  See also CLR 143
Berry, Jane Cobb 1915(?)-1979
  Obituary 22

Berry, Joy 1944- 58
  Brief entry 46
Berry, Joy Wilt
  See Berry, Joy
Berry, Julie 1974- 218
Berry, Lynne 190
Berry, William D(avid) 1926- 14
Bersani, Shennen 1961- 164
Berson, Harold 1926- 4
Bertagna, Julie 1962- 151
Bertholf, Bret 189
Bertin, Charles-Francois
  See Berlitz, Charles (L. Frambach)
Bertolet, Paul
  See McLaughlin, Frank
Berton, Pierre (Francis de Marigny)
  1920-2004 99
  Obituary 158
Bertrand, Cecile 1953- 76
Bertrand, Diane Gonzales 1956- 177
  Earlier sketch in SATA 106
Bertrand, Lynne 1963- 164
  Earlier sketch in SATA 81
Beskow, Elsa (Maartman) 1874-1953 20
  See also CLR 17
Bess, Clayton
  See Locke, Robert
Besson, Luc 1959- 199
Best, (Evangel) Allena Champlin 1892-1974 . 2
  Obituary 25
Best, Cari 1951- 200
  Earlier sketches in SATA 107, 149
Best, (Oswald) Herbert 1894-1980 2
Bestall, A(lfred) E(dmeades) 1892-1986 97
  Obituary 48
Betancourt, Jeanne 1941- 148
  Brief entry 43
  Earlier sketches in SATA 55, 96
Beth, Mary
  See Miller, Mary Beth
Bethancourt, T. Ernesto
  See Paisley, Tom
Bethel, Dell 1929- 52
Bethell, Jean (Frankenberry) 1922- 8
Bethers, Ray 1902-1973 6
Bethke, Bruce Raymond 1955- 114
Bethlen, T.D.
  See Silverberg, Robert
Bethune, J. G.
  See Ellis, Edward S.
Bethune, J. H.
  See Ellis, Edward S.
Betteridge, Anne
  See Potter, Margaret
Betteridge, Deirdre 214
Bettina
  See Ehrlich, Bettina Bauer
Bettmann, Otto Ludwig 1903-1998 46
Bettoli, Delana 187
Betts, James
  See Haynes, Betsy
Betz, Eva Kelly 1897-1968 10
Bevan, Tom 1868-1930(?)
  See YABC 2
Bevis, Mary 1939- 202
Bewick, Thomas 1753-1828 16
Beyer, Audrey White 1916- 9
Beyer, Paul J. III 1950- 74
Beynon, John
  See Harris, John (Wyndham Parkes Lucas)
  Beynon
Bezencon, Jacqueline (Buxcel) 1924- 48
Bhatia, Jamunadevi 1919- 48
Bhatia, June
  See Bhatia, Jamunadevi
Bial, Morrison David 1917- 62
Bial, Raymond 1948- 165
  Earlier sketches in SATA 76, 116
Biala
  See Brustlein, Janice Tworkov
Biale, Rachel 1952- 99

Bialk, Elisa
  See Krautter, Elisa (Bialk)
Bianchi, John 1947- 91
Bianchi, Robert S(teven) 1943- 92
Bianco, Margery
  See Bianco, Margery Williams
Bianco, Margery Williams 1881-1944 15
  See also CLR 146
Bianco, Pamela 1906- 28
Bibby, Violet 1908-1996 24
Bible, Charles 1937- 13
Bibo, Bobette
  See Gugliotta, Bobette
Bice, Clare 1909-1976 22
Bickerstaff, Isaac
  See Swift, Jonathan
Bidner, Jenni 1963- 193
Biedrzycki, David 1955- 219
Biegel, Paul 1925- 79
  Earlier sketch in SATA 16
  See also CLR 27
  See also SAAS 18
Biemiller, Carl L(udwig), Jr.) 1912-1979 40
  Obituary 21
Bienenfeld, Florence L(ucille) 1929- 39
Bierhorst, John (William) 1936- 149
  Autobiography Feature 149
  Earlier sketches in SATA 6, 91
  See also SAAS 10
Biggar, Joan R. 1936- 120
Biggar, Joan Rawlins
  See Biggar, Joan R.
Biggle, Lloyd, Jr. 1923-2002 65
Biggs, Brian 1968- 192
Bilal, Abdel W(ahab) 1970- 92
Bilbrough, Norman 1941- 111
Bildner, Phil 173
Bileck, Marvin 1920- 40
Bilibin, Ivan (Iakolevich) 1876-1942 61
Bill, Alfred Hoyt 1879-1964 44
Billam, Rosemary 1952- 61
Billings, Charlene W(interer) 1941- 41
Billingsley, Franny 1954- 132
Billington, Elizabeth T(hain) 1924- 50
  Brief entry 43
Billout, Guy (Rene) 1941- 144
  Earlier sketch in SATA 10
  See also CLR 33
Bilson, Geoffrey 1938-1987 99
Binch, Caroline (Lesley) 1947- 140
  Earlier sketch in SATA 81
Bing, Christopher (H.) 126
Bingham, Caroline 1962- 158
Bingham, Jane M. 1941- 163
Bingham, Jane Marie
  See Bingham, Jane M.
Bingham, Janet 1959- 200
Bingham, Kelly 1967- 207
Bingham, Sam 1944- 96
Bingham, Samuel A.
  See Bingham, Sam
Bingley, Margaret (Jane Kirby) 1947- 72
Binkley, Anne
  See Rand, Ann (Binkley)
Binzen, Bill
  See Binzen, William
Binzen, William 24
Birch, David (W.) 1913-1996 89
Birch, Reginald B(athurst) 1856-1943 19
Birchman, David 1949- 72
Birchmore, Daniel A. 1951- 92
Bird, Carmel 1940- 124
Bird, E(lzy) J(ay) 1911- 58
Birdsall, Jeanne 1952(?)- 170
Birdseye, Tom 1951- 148
  Earlier sketches in SATA 66, 98
Birenbaum, Barbara 1941- 65
Birmingham, Christian 1970- 220
Birmingham, Lloyd P(aul) 1924- 83
  Earlier sketch in SATA 12

Birmingham, Ruth
    See Sorrells, Walter
Birney, Betty G. 1947- *169*
    Earlier sketch in SATA *98*
Biro, B.
    See Biro, B. S.
Biro, B. S. 1921- *1*
    See also CLR *28*
    See also SAAS *13*
Biro, Val
    See Biro, B. S.
Bischoff, Julia Bristol 1899-1970 .... *12*
Bishop, Bonnie 1943- *37*
Bishop, Claire Huchet 1899(?)-1993 .... *14*
    Obituary *74*
    See also CLR *80*
Bishop, Courtney
    See Ruemmler, John D(avid)
Bishop, Curtis (Kent) 1912-1967 .... *6*
Bishop, Elizabeth 1911-1979
    Obituary *24*
Bishop, Gavin 1946- *216*
    Earlier sketches in SATA *97, 144*
Bishop, Kathleen Wong 1954- *120*
Bishop, Kathy
    See Bishop, Kathleen Wong
Bishop, Nic 1955- *161*
    Earlier sketch in SATA *107*
Bisset, Donald 1910-1995 .... *86*
    Earlier sketch in SATA *7*
Bisson, Terry 1942- *99*
Bisson, Terry Ballantine
    See Bisson, Terry
Bitter, Gary G(len) 1940- *22*
Bixby, William (Courtney) 1920-1986 .... *6*
    Obituary *47*
Bjoerk, Christina 1938- *99*
    Earlier sketch in SATA *67*
    See also CLR *22*
Bjork, Christina
    See Bjoerk, Christina
Bjorklund, Lorence F. 1913-1978 .... *35*
    Brief entry *32*
Bjorkman, Lauren *222*
Bjorkman, Steve *223*
    Earlier sketch in SATA *163*
Blabey, Aaron 1975(?)- *214*
Black, Algernon David 1900-1993 .... *12*
    Obituary *76*
Black, Holly 1971- *210*
    Earlier sketch in SATA *147*
Black, Irma Simonton 1906-1972 .... *2*
    Obituary *25*
Black, Kat *217*
Black, Katherine
    See Black, Kat
Black, Mansell
    See Trevor, Elleston
Black, MaryAnn
    See Easley, MaryAnn
Black, Susan Adams 1953- *40*
Blackall, Bernie 1956- *126*
Blackall, Sophie *182*
Blackburn, Claire
    See Altman, Linda Jacobs
Blackburn, John(ny) Brewton 1952- *15*
Blackburn, Joyce Knight 1920- *29*
Blacker, Terence 1948- *194*
Blacker, Tina
    See Louise, Tina
Blackett, Veronica Heath 1927- *12*
Blackie, Jean Cutler 1943- *79*
Blacklin, Malcolm
    See Chambers, Aidan
Blacklock, Dyan 1951- *112*
Blackman, Malorie 1962- *196*
    Earlier sketches in SATA *83, 128*
Blackton, Peter
    See Wilson, Lionel
Blackwood, Alan 1932- *70*
Blackwood, Freya *199*

Blackwood, Gary
    See Blackwood, Gary L.
Blackwood, Gary L. 1945- *169*
    Earlier sketches in SATA *72, 118*
Blade, Alexander
    See Garrett, Randall
    and Hamilton, Edmond
    and Silverberg, Robert
Blades, Ann (Sager) 1947- *69*
    Earlier sketch in SATA *16*
    See also CLR *15*
Bladow, Suzanne Wilson 1937- *14*
Blaine, Chris
    See Gardner, Craig Shaw
Blaine, John
    See Goodwin, Harold L(eland)
Blaine, Marge
    See Blaine, Margery Kay
Blaine, Margery Kay 1937- *11*
Blair, Alison
    See Lerangis, Peter
Blair, Anne Denton 1914-1993 .... *46*
Blair, David Nelson 1954- *80*
Blair, Eric
    See Orwell, George
Blair, Jay 1953- *45*
Blair, Lucile
    See Yeakley, Marjory Hall
Blair, Margaret Whitman 1951- *124*
Blair, Mary 1911-1978 .... *195*
Blair, Pauline Hunter
    See Clarke, Pauline
Blair, Ruth Van Ness 1912-1999 .... *12*
Blair, Shannon
    See Kaye, Marilyn
Blair, Walter 1900-1992 .... *12*
    Obituary *72*
Blaisdell, Bob
    See Blaisdell, Robert
Blaisdell, Robert 1959- *105*
Blake, Bronwyn 1940- *149*
Blake, Francis *198*
Blake, Jon 1954- *171*
    Earlier sketch in SATA *78*
Blake, Olive
    See Supraner, Robyn
Blake, Quentin 1932- *211*
    Earlier sketches in SATA *9, 52, 96, 125*
    See also CLR *31*
Blake, Robert 1949- *42*
Blake, Robert J. *160*
Blake, Walker E.
    See Griffin, W. E. B.
Blake, William 1757-1827 .... *30*
    See also CLR *52*
Blakely, Gloria 1950- *139*
Blakely, Roger K. 1922- *82*
Blakeney, Jay D.
    See Chester, Deborah
Blakeslee, Lys 1985- *218*
Blakey, Nancy 1955- *94*
Blanc, Esther S. 1913-1997 .... *66*
Blanc, Mel 1908-1989
    Obituary *64*
Blanchard, Patricia *125*
Blanchet, M(uriel) Wylie 1891-1961 .... *106*
Blanco, Richard L(idio) 1926- *63*
Bland, E.
    See Nesbit, E.
Bland, Edith Nesbit
    See Nesbit, E.
Bland, Fabian
    See Nesbit, E.
Blane, Gertrude
    See Blumenthal, Gertrude
Blank, Clarissa Mabel 1915-1965 .... *62*
Blankenship, LeeAnn 1944- *181*
Blassingame, Wyatt Rainey 1909-1985 .... *34*
    Obituary *41*
    Earlier sketch in SATA *1*
Blatchford, Claire H. 1944- *94*

Blauer, Ettagale 1940- *49*
Bleck, Linda *207*
Bledsoe, Glen L. 1951- *108*
Bledsoe, Glen Leonard
    See Bledsoe, Glen L.
Bledsoe, Karen E. 1962- *167*
    Earlier sketch in SATA *108*
Bledsoe, Karen Elizabeth
    See Bledsoe, Karen E.
Bledsoe, Lucy Jane 1957- *162*
    Earlier sketch in SATA *97*
Bleeker, Sonia
    See Zim, Sonia Bleeker
Blegen, Daniel M. 1950- *92*
Blegvad, Erik 1923- *132*
    Earlier sketches in SATA *14, 66*
Blegvad, Lenore 1926- *176*
    Earlier sketches in SATA *14, 66*
Blessing, Charlotte *223*
Bley, Anette 1967- *188*
Blish, James 1921-1975 .... *66*
Blish, James Benjamin
    See Blish, James
Blishen, Edward (William) 1920-1996 .... *66*
    Obituary *93*
    Earlier sketch in SATA *8*
Bliss, Corinne Demas 1947- *203*
    Earlier sketches in SATA *37, 131*
Bliss, Frederick
    See Card, Orson Scott
Bliss, Gillian
    See Paton Walsh, Jill
Bliss, Harry 1964- *196*
    Earlier sketch in SATA *156*
Bliss, Reginald
    See Wells, H. G.
Bliss, Ronald G(ene) 1942- *12*
Blitt, Barry *187*
Bliven, Bruce, Jr. 1916-2002 .... *2*
Blixen, Karen 1885-1962 .... *44*
Blizzard, Gladys S. (?)-1992 .... *79*
Blobaum, Cindy 1966- *123*
Bloch, Lucienne 1909-1999 .... *10*
Bloch, Marie Halun 1910-1998 .... *6*
    See also SAAS *9*
Bloch, Robert (Albert) 1917-1994 .... *12*
    Obituary *82*
Bloch, Serge 1956- *213*
Blochman, Lawrence G(oldtree)
    1900-1975 .... *22*
Block, Francesca Lia 1962- *213*
    Earlier sketches in SATA *80, 116, 158*
    See also CLR *116*
    See also SAAS *21*
Block, Irvin 1917- *12*
Blomgren, Jennifer (Alice) 1954- *136*
Blonder, Terry Joyce
    See Golson, Terry
Blood, Charles Lewis 1929- *28*
Bloom, Barbara Lee 1943- *146*
Bloom, Freddy 1914-2000 .... *37*
    Obituary *121*
Bloom, Lloyd 1947- *108*
    Brief entry *43*
Bloom, Suzanne 1950- *172*
Bloomfield, Michaela 1966- *70*
Bloor, Edward 1950- *201*
    Earlier sketches in SATA *98, 155*
Bloor, Edward William
    See Bloor, Edward
Blos, Joan W. 1928- *153*
    Autobiography Feature *153*
    Brief entry *27*
    Earlier sketches in SATA *33, 69, 109*
    See also CLR *18*
    See also SAAS *11*
Blos, Joan Winsor
    See Blos, Joan W.
Blough, Glenn O(rlando) 1907-1995 .... *1*

Blue, Rose 1931- *166*
    Autobiography Feature *117*
    Earlier sketches in SATA *5, 91, 93*
    See also SAAS *24*
Blue, Zachary
    See Stine, R.L.
Bluemle, Elizabeth *209*
Bluggage, Oranthy
    See Alcott, Louisa May
Blumberg, Leda 1956- *59*
Blumberg, Rhoda 1917- *123*
    Earlier sketches in SATA *35, 70*
    See also CLR *21*
Blume, Judy 1938- *195*
    Earlier sketches in SATA *2, 31, 79, 142*
    See also CLR *69*
Blume, Judy Sussman
    See Blume, Judy
Blume, Lesley M.M. 1975- *180*
Blumenthal, Deborah *204*
    Earlier sketch in SATA *161*
Blumenthal, Gertrude 1907-1971
    Obituary *27*
Blumenthal, Shirley 1943- *46*
Blutig, Eduard
    See Gorey, Edward (St. John)
Bly, Janet 1945- *43*
Bly, Janet Chester
    See Bly, Janet
Bly, Stephen A(rthur) 1944- *116*
    Earlier sketch in SATA *43*
Blyler, Allison Lee 1966- *74*
Blythe, Gary 1959- *185*
Blyton, Carey 1932-2002 .... *9*
    Obituary *138*
Blyton, Enid 1897-1968 .... *25*
    See also CLR *31*
Blyton, Enid Mary
    See Blyton, Enid
Bo, Ben
    See Richardson, V.A.
Boardman, Fon Wyman, Jr. 1911-2000 .... *6*
Boardman, Gwenn R.
    See Petersen, Gwenn Boardman
Boase, Wendy 1944-1999 .... *28*
    Obituary *110*
Boatner, Mark Mayo III 1921- *29*
Bobbe, Dorothie de Bear 1905-1975 .... *1*
    Obituary *25*
Bober, Natalie S. 1930- *134*
    Earlier sketch in SATA *87*
    See also SAAS *23*
Bobette, Bibo
    See Gugliotta, Bobette
Bobri, Vladimir V. 1898-1986 .... *47*
    Brief entry *32*
Bobritsky, Vladimir
    See Bobri, Vladimir V.
Bochak, Grayce 1956- *76*
Bock, Hal
    See Bock, Harold I.
Bock, Harold I. 1939- *10*
Bock, William Sauts Netamux'we 1939- *14*
Bodanis, David *179*
Bode, Janet 1943-1999 .... *96*
    Obituary *118*
    Earlier sketch in SATA *60*
Bode, N.E.
    See Baggott, Julianna
Bodecker, N(iels) M(ogens) 1922-1988 .... *73*
    Obituary *54*
    Earlier sketch in SATA *8*
Bodeen, S. A. 1965- *158*
    Earlier sketch in SATA *114*
Boden, Hilda
    See Bodenham, Hilda Morris
Bodenham, Hilda Morris 1901- *13*
Bodett, Thomas Edward 1955- *70*
Bodett, Tom
    See Bodett, Thomas Edward

Bodie, Idella F(allaw) 1925- *89*
    Earlier sketch in SATA *12*
Bodker, Cecil
    See Bodker, Cecil
Bodker, Cecil 1927- *133*
    Earlier sketch in SATA *14*
    See also CLR *23*
Bodsworth, (Charles) Fred(erick) 1918- *27*
Boeckman, Charles 1920- *12*
Boegehold, Betty (Doyle) 1913-1985
    Obituary *42*
Boelts, Maribeth 1964- *200*
    Earlier sketches in SATA *78, 163*
Boerst, William J. 1939- *170*
    Earlier sketch in SATA *121*
Boesch, Mark J(oseph) 1917- *12*
Boesen, Victor 1908- *16*
Bogacki, Tomek 1950- *214*
    Earlier sketch in SATA *138*
Bogaerts, Gert 1965- *80*
Bogan, Paulette 1960- *201*
    Earlier sketch in SATA *129*
Bogart, Jo Ellen 1945- *222*
    Earlier sketch in SATA *92*
    See also CLR *59*
Boggs, Ralph Steele 1901-1994 .... *7*
Bograd, Larry 1953- *89*
    Earlier sketch in SATA *33*
    See also SAAS *21*
Bogue, Gary 1938- *195*
Bogue, Gary L.
    See Bogue, Gary
Bohdal, Susi 1951- *101*
    Earlier sketch in SATA *22*
Bohlen, Nina 1931- *58*
Bohlmeijer, Arno 1956- *94*
Bohner, Charles (Henry) 1927- *62*
Bohnhoff, Maya Kaathryn 1954- *88*
Boie, Kirsten 1950- *221*
Boiger, Alexandra *178*
Boissard, Janine 1932- *59*
Bojunga, Lygia
    See Nunes, Lygia Bojunga
Bojunga-Nunes, Lygia
    See Nunes, Lygia Bojunga
Bok, Arthur
    See Bok, Chip
Bok, Chip 1952- *205*
Bolam, Emily 1969- *206*
Boland, Janice *98*
Bolden, Tonya 1959- *188*
    Earlier sketches in SATA *79, 138*
Bolden, Tonya Wilyce
    See Bolden, Tonya
Boles, Paul Darcy 1916-1984 .... *9*
    Obituary *38*
Bolian, Polly 1925- *4*
Bollen, Roger 1941(?)- *83*
    Brief entry *29*
Bolliger, Max 1929- *7*
Bollinger, Max 1929- *167*
Bollinger, Peter *172*
Bolognese, Don(ald Alan) 1934- *129*
    Earlier sketches in SATA *24, 71*
Bolognese, Elaine 1933- *23*
Bolotin, Norman (Phillip) 1951- *93*
Bolton, Carole 1926- *6*
Bolton, Elizabeth
    See St. John, Nicole
Bolton, Evelyn
    See Bunting, Eve
Bonar, Veronica
    See Bailey, Donna (Veronica Anne)
Bond, B. J.
    See Heneghan, James
Bond, Bruce 1939- *61*
Bond, Felicia 1954- *219*
    Earlier sketches in SATA *49, 126*
Bond, Gladys Baker 1912- *14*
Bond, Higgins 1951- *220*
    Earlier sketches in SATA *83, 177*

Bond, J. Harvey
    See Winterbotham, R(ussell) R(obert)
Bond, (Thomas) Michael 1926- *157*
    Earlier sketches in SATA *6, 58*
    See also CLR *95*
    See also SAAS *3*
Bond, Nancy 1945- *159*
    Autobiography Feature *159*
    Earlier sketches in SATA *22, 82*
    See also CLR *11*
    See also SAAS *13*
Bond, Nancy Barbara
    See Bond, Nancy
Bond, Rebecca 1972- *214*
    Earlier sketch in SATA *130*
Bond, Ruskin 1934- *87*
    Earlier sketch in SATA *14*
Bondie, J. D.
    See Cunningham, Chet
Bondoux, Anne-Laure 1971- *175*
Bone, Ian 1956- *158*
    Earlier sketch in SATA *117*
Bonehill, Captain Ralph
    See Stratemeyer, Edward L.
Bonestell, Chesley 1888-1986
    Obituary *48*
Bonham, Barbara Thomas 1926- *7*
Bonham, Frank 1914-1989 .... *49*
    Obituary *62*
    Earlier sketch in SATA *1*
    See also SAAS *3*
Boniface, William 1963- *182*
    Earlier sketch in SATA *102*
Bonino, Louise
    See Williams, Louise Bonino
Bonk, John J. *189*
Bonn, Pat
    See Bonn, Patricia Carolyn
Bonn, Patricia Carolyn 1948- *43*
Bonner, Hannah *197*
Bonner, Mary Graham 1890-1974 .... *19*
Bonner, Mike 1951- *121*
Bonners, Susan 1947- *85*
    Brief entry *48*
Bonnett-Rampersaud, Louise *173*
Bonning, Tony 1948- *169*
Bonsall, Crosby Barbara (Newell)
    1921-1995 .... *23*
    Obituary *84*
Bonsall, Joseph S. 1948- *119*
Bontemps, Arna 1902-1973 .... *44*
    Obituary *24*
    Earlier sketch in SATA *2*
    See also CLR *6*
Bontemps, Arnaud Wendell
    See Bontemps, Arna
Bonzon, Paul-Jacques 1908-1978 .... *22*
Boock, Paula 1964- *134*
Booher, Dianna Daniels 1948- *33*
Book, Rick 1949- *119*
Book, Rita
    See Holub, Joan
Bookman, Charlotte
    See Zolotow, Charlotte
Boon, Debbie 1960- *103*
Boon, Emilie (Laetitia) 1958- *86*
Boone, Charles Eugene
    See Boone, Pat
Boone, Pat 1934- *7*
Booraem, Ellen *211*
Boorman, Linda 1940- *46*
Boorman, Linda Kay
    See Boorman, Linda
Boorstin, Daniel J(oseph) 1914-2004 .... *52*
Boos, Ben 1971- *206*
Booth, Coe *187*
Booth, Ernest Sheldon 1915-1984 .... *43*
Booth, George 1926- *191*
Booth, Graham (Charles) 1935- *37*
Bootman, Colin *159*

Borden, Louise 1949- *190*
  Autobiography Feature *141*
  Earlier sketches in SATA 68, 104, 141
Bordier, Georgette 1924- *16*
Borgman, James
  See Borgman, Jim
Borgman, James Mark
  See Borgman, Jim
Borgman, Jim 1954- *122*
Borgo, Lacy Finn 1972- *194*
Boring, Mel 1939- *168*
  Earlier sketch in SATA 35
Borja, Corinne 1929- *22*
Borja, Robert 1923- *22*
Borland, Hal
  See Borland, Harold Glen
Borland, Harold Glen 1900-1978 .... *5*
  Obituary *24*
Borland, Kathryn Kilby 1916- *16*
Borlenghi, Patricia 1951- *79*
Born, Adolf 1930- *49*
Bornstein, Ruth Lercher
  See Bornstein-Lercher, Ruth
Bornstein-Lercher, Ruth 1927- *88*
  Autobiography Feature *107*
  Earlier sketch in SATA 14
Borris, Albert *221*
Borski, Lucia Merecka *18*
Borten, Helen Jacobson 1930- *5*
Bortolotti, Dan 1969- *157*
Borton, Elizabeth
  See Trevino, Elizabeth B(orton) de
Borton, Lady 1942- *98*
Borton de Trevino, Elizabeth
  See Trevino, Elizabeth B(orton) de
Bortstein, Larry 1942-2010 .... *16*
Bortz, Alfred B(enjamin) 1944- *139*
  Earlier sketch in SATA 74
Bortz, Fred
  See Bortz, Alfred B(enjamin)
Bosch, Pseudonymous *199*
Bosco, Jack
  See Holliday, Joseph
Bose, Mitali
  See Perkins, Mitali
Boshell, Gordon 1908-1991 .... *15*
Boshinski, Blanche 1922- *10*
Bosman, Paul 1929- *107*
Bosse, Malcolm (Joseph, Jr.) 1926-2002 .... *136*
  Earlier sketch in SATA 35
Bosserman, Charles Phillip
  See Bosserman, Phillip
Bosserman, Phillip 1931- *84*
Bossley, Michele Martin 1969- *219*
Bossom, Naomi 1933- *35*
Bostock, Mike 1962- *114*
Boston, L(ucy) M(aria Wood) 1892-1990 ... *19*
  Obituary *64*
  See also CLR 3
Bostrom, Kathleen (Susan) Long 1954- *139*
Bostrom, Kathy
  See Bostrom, Kathleen (Susan) Long
Boswell, Addie *208*
Boswell, Addie Kay
  See Boswell, Addie
Bosworth, J. Allan 1925- *19*
Bothwell, Jean (?)-1977 .... *2*
Botkin, B(enjamin) A(lbert) 1901-1975 .... *40*
Botsford, Ward 1927-2004 .... *66*
Botting, Douglas (Scott) 1934- *43*
Bottner, Barbara 1943- *170*
  Autobiography Feature *121*
  Earlier sketches in SATA 14, 93
  See also SAAS 26
Bottone, Frank G., Jr. 1969- *141*
Bouchard, David 1952- *213*
  Earlier sketch in SATA 117
Boucher, (Clarence) Carter 1954- *129*
Boudelang, Bob
  See Pell, Ed(ward)
Boughton, Richard 1954- *75*

Boulet, Susan Seddon 1941- *50*
Boulle, Pierre (Francois Marie-Louis)
  1912-1994 .... *22*
  Obituary *78*
Boulton, Jane 1921- *91*
Bouma, Paddy 1947- *128*
Bour, Daniele 1939- *62*
Bourbonniere, Sylvie 1966- *182*
Bourdon, David 1934-1998 .... *46*
Bourgeois, Paulette 1951- *153*
Bourne, Lesley
  See Marshall, Evelyn
Bourne, Miriam Anne 1931-1989 .... *16*
  Obituary *63*
Boutavant, Marc 1970- *200*
Boutet de Monvel, (Louis) M(aurice)
  1850(?)-1913 .... *30*
  See also CLR 32
Bouwman, Heather M.
  See Bouwman, H.M.
Bouwman, H.M. *209*
Bova, Ben 1932- *133*
  Earlier sketches in SATA 6, 68
  See also CLR 96
Bova, Benjamin William
  See Bova, Ben
Bovaird, Anne E(lizabeth) 1960- *90*
Bow, Patricia 1946- *168*
Bowden, Joan Chase 1925- *51*
  Brief entry *38*
Bowe, Julie 1962- *194*
Bowen, Alexandria Russell *97*
Bowen, Andy Russell
  See Bowen, Alexandria Russell
Bowen, Anne 1952- *202*
  Earlier sketch in SATA 170
Bowen, Betty Morgan
  See West, Betty
Bowen, Catherine (Shober) Drinker
  1897-1973 .... *7*
Bowen, David
  See Bowen, Joshua David
Bowen, Fred 1953- *136*
Bowen, Joshua David 1930- *22*
Bowen, Rhys
  See Quin-Harkin, Janet
Bowen, Robert Sydney 1900-1977 .... *52*
  Obituary *21*
Bowermaster, Jon 1954- *135*
  Earlier sketch in SATA 77
Bowers, Terrell L. 1945- *101*
Bowers, Terry
  See Bowers, Terrell L.
Bowers, Tim *218*
  Earlier sketch in SATA 185
Bowie, C. W.
  See Old, Wendie C(orbin)
  and Wirths, Claudine (Turner) G(ibson)
Bowie, Jim
  See Norwood, Victor G(eorge) C(harles)
  and Stratemeyer, Edward L.
Bowkett, Stephen 1953- *67*
Bowler, Jan Brett
  See Brett, Jan
Bowler, Tim 1953- *209*
  Earlier sketch in SATA 149
Bowman, Catherine
  See Smith, Cat Bowman
Bowman, Crystal 1951- *105*
Bowman, James Cloyd 1880-1961 .... *23*
Bowman, John S(tewart) 1931- *16*
Bowman, Kathleen (Gill) 1942- *52*
  Brief entry *40*
Bowman, Leslie
  See Bowman, Leslie W.
Bowman, Leslie W. *182*
Bowsher, Melodie *195*
Boxall, Ed *178*
Boyce, Frank Cottrell *182*
Boyce, George A(rthur) 1898- *19*

Boyd, Candy Dawson 1946- *72*
  See also CLR 50
Boyd, Pauline
  See Schock, Pauline
Boyd, Selma
  See Acuff, Selma Boyd
Boyd, Waldo T. 1918- *18*
Boyden, Linda 1948- *143*
Boyer, Allen B. 1963- *153*
Boyer, Robert E(rnst) 1929- *22*
Boyes, Vivien 1952- *106*
Boyes, Vivien Elizabeth
  See Boyes, Vivien
Boyle, Ann (Peters) 1916- *10*
Boyle, Eleanor Vere (Gordon) 1825-1916 .... *28*
Boyle, Robert H. 1928- *65*
Boylston, Helen Dore 1895-1984 .... *23*
  Obituary *39*
Boyne, John 1971- *181*
Boynton, Sandra (Keith) 1953- *152*
  Brief entry *38*
  Earlier sketches in SATA 57, 107
  See also CLR 105
Boz
  See Dickens, Charles
Braasch, Gary *201*
Bracken, Charles
  See Pellowski, Michael (Joseph)
Brackers de Hugo, Pierre 1960- *115*
Brackett, Dolli Tingle 1911-1993 .... *137*
Brackett, Virginia 1950- *166*
  Earlier sketch in SATA 121
Brackett, Virginia Roberts Meredith
  See Brackett, Virginia
Bradbury, Bianca (Ryley) 1908-1982 .... *56*
  Earlier sketch in SATA 3
Bradbury, Edward P.
  See Moorcock, Michael
Bradbury, Ray 1920- *123*
  Earlier sketches in SATA 11, 64
Bradbury, Ray Douglas
  See Bradbury, Ray
Bradby, Marie *161*
Bradfield, Carl 1942- *91*
Bradford, Ann (Liddell) 1917- *56*
  Brief entry *38*
Bradford, Barbara Taylor 1933- *66*
Bradford, Chris 1974- *215*
Bradford, Karleen 1936- *96*
  Earlier sketch in SATA 48
Bradford, Lois J(ean) 1936- *36*
Bradford, Richard (Roark) 1932-2002 .... *59*
  Obituary *135*
Bradley, Duane
  See Sanborn, Duane
Bradley, Kimberly Brubaker 1967- *179*
Bradley, Marion Zimmer 1930-1999 .... *139*
  Obituary *116*
  Earlier sketch in SATA 90
  See also CLR 158
Bradley, Timothy J. *193*
Bradley, Virginia 1912- *23*
Bradley, Will
  See Strickland, Brad
Bradman, Tony 1954- *152*
  Earlier sketch in SATA 81
Bradshaw, Gillian (Joan) 1949- *118*
Bradshaw, Gillian 1956- *127*
Bradshaw, Gillian Marucha
  See Bradshaw, Gillian
Bradstreet, T. J.
  See Thesman, Jean
Brady, Esther Wood 1905-1987 .... *31*
  Obituary *53*
Brady, Irene 1943- *4*
Brady, Kimberley S. 1953- *101*
Brady, Kimberley Smith
  See Brady, Kimberley S.
Brady, Lillian 1902- *28*
Bragdon, Elspeth MacDuffie 1897-1980 .... *6*
Bragdon, Lillian Jacot *24*

Brager, Bruce L. 1949- *146*
Bragg, Mabel Caroline 1870-1945 .... *24*
Bragg, Michael 1948- *46*
Bragg, Ruth Gembicki 1943- *77*
Brahm, Sumishta 1954- *58*
Brailsford, Frances
  See Wosmek, Frances
Brainerd, John W(hiting) 1918- *65*
Braithwaite, Althea 1940- *23*
  Autobiography Feature *119*
  See also SAAS *24*
Bram, Elizabeth 1948- *30*
Brancato, Robin F. 1936- *97*
  See also CLR *32*
  See also SAAS *9*
Brancato, Robin Fidler
  See Brancato, Robin F.
Branch, Muriel Miller 1943- *152*
  Earlier sketch in SATA *94*
Brand, Christianna
  See Lewis, Mary
Brand, Rebecca
  See Charnas, Suzy McKee
Brande, Robin *194*
Brandel, Marc 1919- *71*
Brandenberg, Alexa (Demetria) 1966- *97*
Brandenberg, Aliki 1929- *157*
  Earlier sketches in SATA *2, 35, 75, 113*
  See also CLR *71*
Brandenberg, Franz 1932- *75*
  Earlier sketches in SATA *8, 35*
Brandenburg, Jim 1945- *87*
Brandhorst, Carl T(heodore) 1898-1988 .... *23*
Brandis, Marianne 1938- *149*
  Earlier sketches in SATA *59, 96*
Brandon, Brumsic, Jr. 1927- *9*
Brandon, Curt
  See Bishop, Curtis (Kent)
Brandreth, Gyles 1948- *28*
Brandreth, Gyles Daubeney
  See Brandreth, Gyles
Brandt, Catharine 1905-1997 .... *40*
Brandt, Keith
  See Sabin, Louis
Brandt, Sue R(eading) 1916- *59*
Branfield, John (Charles) 1931- *11*
Branford, Henrietta 1946-1999 .... *106*
Branley, Franklyn M(ansfield) 1915-2002 .. *136*
  Earlier sketches in SATA *4, 68*
  See also CLR *13*
  See also SAAS *16*
Brannen, Sarah S. *202*
Branscum, Robbie (Tilley) 1937-1997 .... *72*
  Obituary *96*
  Earlier sketch in SATA *23*
  See also SAAS *17*
Bransom, (John) Paul 1885-1979 .... *43*
Brashares, Ann 1967- *188*
  Earlier sketch in SATA *145*
  See also CLR *113*
Brassard, France 1963- *186*
Braswell, E.J.
  See Lynn, Tracy
Braswell, Elizabeth J.
  See Lynn, Tracy
Braswell, Liz
  See Lynn, Tracy
Bratton, Helen 1899-1986 .... *4*
Bratun, Katy 1950- *160*
  Earlier sketch in SATA *83*
Braude, Michael 1936- *23*
Braun, Lilian Jackson 1916(?)- *109*
Brautigan, Richard 1935-1984 .... *56*
Brautigan, Richard Gary
  See Brautigan, Richard
Bray, Libba *203*
  Earlier sketch in SATA *159*
Bray, Martha E.
  See Bray, Libba
Braymer, Marjorie Elizabeth 1911-1988 .... *6*

Brazil, Angela 1869(?)-1947
  See CLR *157*
Breathed, Berke 1957- *161*
  Earlier sketch in SATA *86*
Breathed, Berkeley
  See Breathed, Berke
Breathed, Guy Berkeley
  See Breathed, Berke
Brecht, Edith 1895-1975 .... *6*
  Obituary *25*
Breck, Vivian
  See Breckenfeld, Vivian Gurney
Breckenfeld, Vivian Gurney 1895-1992 .... *1*
Breda, Tjalmar
  See DeJong, David C(ornel)
Bredeson, Carmen 1944- *163*
  Earlier sketch in SATA *98*
Breen, M.E. *216*
Breen, Molly
  See Breen, M.E.
Breen, Steve 1970- *186*
Breinburg, Petronella 1927- *11*
  See also CLR *31*
Breisky, William J(ohn) 1928- *22*
Brenaman, Miriam *172*
Brennan, Caitlin
  See Tarr, Judith
Brennan, Gale (Patrick) 1927- *64*
  Brief entry *53*
Brennan, Herbie 1940- *214*
  Autobiography Feature *214*
  Earlier sketches in SATA *140, 183*
Brennan, J. H.
  See Brennan, Herbie
Brennan, James Herbert
  See Brennan, Herbie
Brennan, Jan
  See Brennan, Herbie
Brennan, Joseph Lomas 1903-2000 .... *6*
Brennan, Linda Crotta 1952- *130*
Brennan, Sarah Rees 1983- *221*
Brennan, Tim
  See Conroy, John Wesley
Brennan-Nelson, Denise *203*
Brenner, Anita 1905-1974 .... *56*
Brenner, Barbara (Johnes) 1925- *124*
  Earlier sketches in SATA *4, 42, 76*
  See also SAAS *14*
Brenner, Fred 1920- *36*
  Brief entry *34*
Brent, Hope 1935(?)-1984
  Obituary *39*
Brent, Stuart 1912-2010 .... *14*
Breskin, Jane
  See Zalben, Jane Breskin
Breslin, Theresa *128*
  Autobiography Feature *128*
  Earlier sketch in SATA *70*
Breslow, Maurice 1935- *72*
Breslow, Maurice A
  See Breslow, Maurice
Breslow, Susan 1951- *69*
Brett, Bernard 1925- *22*
Brett, Grace N(eff) 1900-1975 .... *23*
Brett, Jan 1949- *171*
  Earlier sketches in SATA *42, 71, 130*
  See also CLR *27*
Brett, Jan Churchill
  See Brett, Jan
Brett Bowler, Jan
  See Brett, Jan
Brewer, Heather 1973- *196*
Brewer, James D. 1951- *108*
Brewer, Sally King 1947- *33*
Brewster, Benjamin
  See Folsom, Franklin (Brewster)
Brewster, Hugh 1950- *191*
  Earlier sketch in SATA *95*
Brewster, Patience 1952- *97*
Brewton, John E(dmund) 1898-1982 .... *5*
Breznak, Irene *218*

Brian, Janeen (Paulette) 1948- *141*
Briant, Ed *218*
  Earlier sketch in SATA *180*
Brick, John 1922-1973 .... *10*
Brickman, Robin D. 1954- *155*
Bride, Nadja
  See Nobisso, Josephine
Bridgers, Sue Ellen 1942- *90*
  Autobiography Feature *109*
  Earlier sketch in SATA *22*
  See also CLR *18*
  See also SAAS *1*
Bridges, Laurie
  See Bruck, Lorraine
Bridges, Ruby (Nell) 1954- *131*
Bridges, William (Andrew) 1901-1984 .... *5*
Bridwell, Norman (Ray) 1928- *138*
  Earlier sketches in SATA *4, 68*
  See also CLR *96*
Brier, Howard M(axwell) 1903-1969 .... *8*
Brierley, (Louise) 1958- *59*
Briggs, Katharine Mary 1898-1980 .... *101*
  Obituary *25*
Briggs, Peter 1921-1975 .... *39*
  Obituary *31*
Briggs, Raymond 1934- *184*
  Earlier sketches in SATA *23, 66, 131*
  See also CLR *10*
Briggs, Raymond Redvers
  See Briggs, Raymond
Bright, Paul 1949- *182*
Bright, Robert Sr.) 1902-1988 .... *63*
  Obituary *60*
  Earlier sketch in SATA *24*
Bright, Robert Douglas
  See Bright, Robert Sr.)
Bright, Sarah
  See Shine, Deborah
Brightfield, Richard 1927- *65*
  Brief entry *53*
Brightfield, Rick
  See Brightfield, Richard
Brighton, Catherine 1943- *206*
  Earlier sketches in SATA *65, 107*
Brill, Marlene Targ 1945- *124*
  Earlier sketch in SATA *77*
Brimberg, Stanlee 1947- *9*
Brimner, Larry Dane 1949- *170*
  Autobiography Feature *112*
  Earlier sketch in SATA *79*
Brin, David 1950- *65*
Brin, Ruth Firestone 1921- *22*
Brinckloe, Julie 1950- *13*
Brinckloe, Julie Lorraine
  See Brinckloe, Julie
Brindel, June (Rachuy) 1919- *7*
Brindle, Max
  See Fleischman, Sid
Brindze, Ruth 1903-1984 .... *23*
Brink, Carol Ryrie 1895-1981 .... *100*
  Obituary *27*
  Earlier sketches in SATA *1, 31*
  See also CLR *149*
Brinsmead, H. F(ay)
  See Brinsmead, H(esba) F(ay)
Brinsmead, H. F.
  See Brinsmead, H(esba) F(ay)
Brinsmead, H(esba) F(ay) 1922- *78*
  Earlier sketch in SATA *18*
  See also CLR *47*
  See also SAAS *5*
Briquebec, John
  See Rowland-Entwistle, (Arthur) Theodore
  (Henry)
Brisbane, Henry R.
  See Ellis, Edward S.
Brisco, P. A.
  See Matthews, Patricia
Brisco, Patty
  See Matthews, Patricia
  and Matthews, Clayton (Hartley)

Briscoe, Jill (Pauline) 1935- 56
  Brief entry 47
Brisley, Joyce Lankester 1896-1978 22
  Obituary 84
Brissenden, Connie
  See Brissenden, Constance
Brissenden, Constance 1947- 150
Brisson, Pat 1951- 177
  Autobiography Feature 133
  Earlier sketches in SATA *67, 128, 133*
Britt, Albert 1874-1969
  Obituary 28
Britt, Dell 1934- *1*
Brittain, Bill
  See Brittain, William
Brittain, C. Dale 1948- 82
Brittain, William 1930- 76
  Earlier sketch in SATA *36*
  See also SAAS *7*
Brittingham, Geoffrey (Hugh) 1959- 76
Brittney, L. 209
Britton, Kate
  See Stegeman, Janet Allais
Britton, Louisa
  See McGuire, Leslie (Sarah)
Britton, Rick 1952- 82
Bro, Margueritte (Harmon) 1894-1977 .... *19*
  Obituary 27
Broach, Elise 1963- 173
Broadhead, Helen Cross 1913- 25
Broadway, Hannah 208
Brochmann, Elizabeth 1938- 41
Brock, Betty (Carter) 1923-2003 .... *4*
  Obituary 150
Brock, C(harles) E(dmund) 1870-1938 42
  Brief entry 32
Brock, Delia
  See Ephron, Delia
Brock, Emma L(illian) 1886-1974 8
Brock, H(enry) M(atthew) 1875-1960 42
Brockett, Eleanor Hall 1913-1967 10
Brockman, C(hristian) Frank 1902-1985 26
Brockmeier, Kevin 1972- 176
Broda, Ron 1954- 209
Broderick, Dorothy M. 1929- *5*
Brodeur, Ruth Wallace
  See Wallace-Brodeur, Ruth
Brodie, Sally
  See Cavin, Ruth
Brodsky, Beverly
  See McDermott, Beverly Brodsky
Brody, Wendy
  See Staub, Wendy Corsi
Broekel, Rainer Lothar
  See Broekel, Ray
Broekel, Ray 1923- 38
Broekstra, Lorette 1964- 189
  Earlier sketch in SATA *124*
Brogden, Sherryl
  See Jordan, Sherryl
Broger, Achim
  See Broger, Achim
Broger, Achim 1944- 31
Broida, Marian 154
Brokamp, Marilyn 1920- 10
Broman, Fred
  See Moseley, James W(illett)
Bromhall, Winifred 26
Brommer, Gerald F(rederick) 1927- 28
Brondfield, Jerome 1913-1998 22
Brondfield, Jerry
  See Brondfield, Jerome
Bronner, Stephen Eric 1949- 101
Bronowski, Jacob 1908-1974 55
Bronson, Alice
  See Watkins, Dawn L.
Bronson, Linda 203
Bronson, Lynn
  See Lampman, Evelyn Sibley
Bronson, Wilfrid Swancourt 1894-1985
  Obituary 43

Brook, Judith (Penelope) 1926- 59
  Brief entry 51
Brook, Judy
  See Brook, Judith (Penelope)
Brooke, L(eonard) Leslie 1862-1940 17
  See also CLR *20*
Brooke, William J. 1946- 139
Brooke-Haven, P.
  See Wodehouse, P. G.
Brooker, Kyrsten 199
Brookins, Dana 1931- 28
Brooks, Anita
  See Abramovitz, Anita (Zeltner Brooks)
Brooks, Bill 1939- 59
Brooks, Bruce 1950- 112
  Brief entry 53
  Earlier sketch in SATA *72*
  See also CLR *25*
Brooks, Caryl 1924- 84
Brooks, Charlotte K(endrick) 1918-1998 24
  Obituary 112
Brooks, Erik 1972- 182
  Earlier sketch in SATA *152*
Brooks, George
  See Baum, L. Frank
Brooks, Gwendolyn 1917-2000 .... *6*
  Obituary 123
  See also CLR *27*
Brooks, Gwendolyn Elizabeth
  See Brooks, Gwendolyn
Brooks, Jerome 1931- 23
Brooks, Kevin 1959- 197
  Earlier sketch in SATA *150*
Brooks, Kevin M.
  See Brooks, Kevin
Brooks, Laurie 209
Brooks, Lester 1924- *7*
Brooks, Martha 1944- 134
  Autobiography Feature 134
  Earlier sketches in SATA *68, 121*
Brooks, Maurice (Graham) 1900- 45
Brooks, Polly Schoyer 1912- 12
Brooks, Ron 1948- 212
  Brief entry 33
  Earlier sketch in SATA *94*
Brooks, Ronald George
  See Brooks, Ron
Brooks, Terry 1944- 60
Brooks, Walter R(ollin) 1886-1958 17
Brooks-Hill, Helen (Mason) 1908-1994 59
Broome, Errol 1937- 158
  Earlier sketch in SATA *105*
Brophy, Nannette 1963- 73
Brosnan, James Patrick 1929- 14
Brosnan, Jim
  See Brosnan, James Patrick
Brostoff, Anita 1931- 132
Brothers Grimm
  See Grimm, Jacob Ludwig Karl
  and Grimm, Wilhelm Karl
Brothers Hildebrandt, The
  See Hildebrandt, Greg
  and Hildebrandt, Tim
Broun, Emily
  See Sterne, Emma Gelders
Brouwer, S. W.
  See Brouwer, Sigmund (W.)
Brouwer, Sigmund (W.) 1959- 109
Brow, Thea 1934- 60
Brower, Millicent 8
Brower, Pauline 1929- 22
Browin, Frances Williams 1898-1986 5
Brown, Alexis
  See Baumann, Amy Beeching
Brown, Anne Ensign 1937- 61
Brown, Beverly Swerdlow 97
Brown, Bill
  See Brown, William L(ouis)
Brown, Billye Walker
  See Cutchen, Billye Walker

Brown, Bob
  See Brown, Robert Joseph
Brown, Buck 1936- 45
Brown, Calef 217
  Earlier sketch in SATA *179*
Brown, Cassie 1919-1986 55
Brown, Charlotte Lewis 181
Brown, Conrad 1922- 31
Brown, Craig McFarland 1947- 73
Brown, David
  See Brown, David A(lan)
  and Myller, Rolf
Brown, Dee 1908-2002 110
  Obituary 141
  Earlier sketch in SATA *5*
Brown, Dee Alexander
  See Brown, Dee
Brown, Don 1949- 200
  Earlier sketch in SATA *172*
Brown, Drew T. III 1955- 83
Brown, Drollene P. 1939- 53
Brown, Elbrite 198
Brown, Eleanor Frances 1908-1987 3
Brown, Elizabeth Ferguson 1937- 153
Brown, Elizabeth M(yers) 1915- 43
Brown, Fern G. 1918- 34
Brown, (Robert) Fletch 1923- 42
Brown, Fornan 1901-1996 71
  Obituary 88
Brown, George Earl 1883-1964 11
Brown, George Mackay 1921-1996 35
Brown, Irene Bennett 1932- 3
Brown, Irving
  See Adams, William Taylor
Brown, Ivor (John Carnegie) 1891-1974 5
  Obituary 26
Brown, Jane Clark 1930- 81
Brown, Janet Mitsui 87
Brown, Jo 1964- 170
Brown, Joanne 1933- 147
Brown, Joe David 1915-1976 44
Brown, Joseph E(dward) 1929- 59
  Brief entry 51
Brown, Judith Gwyn 1933- 20
Brown, Kathryn 1955- 168
  Earlier sketch in SATA *98*
Brown, Kathy
  See Brown, Kathryn
Brown, Ken (James) 129
Brown, Kevin 1960- 101
Brown, Laurene Krasny 1945- 99
  Earlier sketch in SATA *54*
Brown, Laurie Krasny
  See Brown, Laurene Krasny
Brown, Lloyd Arnold 1907-1966 36
Brown, Mahlon A.
  See Ellis, Edward S.
Brown, Marc (Tolon) 1946- 145
  Earlier sketches in SATA *10, 53, 80*
  See also CLR *29*
Brown, Marcia (Joan) 1918- 47
  Earlier sketch in SATA *7*
  See also CLR *12*
Brown, Margaret Wise 1910-1952 100
  See also YABC *2*
  See also CLR *107*
Brown, Margery (Wheeler) 78
  Earlier sketch in SATA *5*
Brown, Marion Marsh 1908-2001 6
Brown, Myra Berry 1918- 6
Brown, Palmer 1919- 36
Brown, Pamela (Beatrice) 1924-1989 5
  Obituary 61
Brown, Paul 1942- 221
Brown, Peter 1979- 178
Brown, Rachel W.N. 1947- 203
Brown, Reeve Lindbergh
  See Lindbergh, Reeve
Brown, Richard E. 1946- 61
Brown, Robert Joseph 1907-1989 14

Brown, Roderick (Langmere) Haig-
See Haig-Brown, Roderick (Langmere)
Brown, Rosalie
See Moore, Rosalie (Gertrude)
Brown, Roswell
See Webb, Jean Francis (III)
Brown, Roy (Frederick) 1921-1982 .... *51*
Obituary *39*
Brown, Ruth 1941- *170*
Earlier sketch in SATA *105*
Brown, Scott 1971- *134*
Brown, Sue Ellen 1954- *81*
Brown, Tricia 1954- *114*
Brown, Vinson 1912-1991 .... *19*
Brown, Walter R(eed) 1929- *19*
Brown, Will
See Ainsworth, William Harrison
Brown, William L(ouis) 1910-1964 .... *5*
Browne, Anthony 1946- *163*
Brief entry *44*
Earlier sketches in SATA *45, 61, 105*
See also CLR *156*
Browne, Anthony Edward Tudor
See Browne, Anthony
Browne, Dik
See Browne, Richard Arthur Allen
Browne, Hablot Knight 1815-1882 .... *21*
Browne, Matthew
See Rands, William Brighty
Browne, Nicki M.
See Browne, N.M.
Browne, Nicky Matthews
See Browne, N.M.
Browne, N.M. 1960- *167*
Browne, Richard Arthur Allen 1917-1989 ... *67*
Brief entry *38*
Browne, Vee F. 1956- *214*
Earlier sketch in SATA *90*
Browning, Robert 1812-1889
See YABC *1*
See also CLR *97*
Brownjohn, Alan 1931- *6*
Brownlee, Walter 1930- *62*
Brownlie, Betty 1946- *159*
Brownlow, Kevin 1938- *65*
Brownlow, Mike *183*
Brownridge, William R(oy) 1932- *94*
Broyles, Anne 1953- *201*
Bruce, Dorita Fairlie 1885-1970
Obituary *27*
Bruce, (William) Harry 1934- *77*
Bruce, Mary 1927- *1*
Bruchac, Joseph III
See Bruchac, Joseph
Bruchac, Joseph 1942- *176*
Autobiography Feature *176*
Earlier sketches in SATA *42, 89, 131*
See also CLR *46*
Bruchac, Margaret M.
See Bruchac, Marge
Bruchac, Marge *181*
Bruck, Lorraine 1921- *55*
Brief entry *46*
Bruel, Nick *205*
Earlier sketch in SATA *166*
Bruel, Robert O. 1929-2002 .... *189*
Bruemmer, Fred 1929- *47*
Brugman, Alyssa (F.) 1974- *152*
Brumbeau, Jeff 1955- *157*
Bruna, Dick 1927- *76*
Brief entry *30*
Earlier sketch in SATA *43*
See also CLR *7*
Brunhoff, Jean de 1899-1937 .... *24*
See also CLR *116*
Brunhoff, Laurent de 1925- *150*
Earlier sketches in SATA *24, 71*
See also CLR *116*
Brunkus, Denise *204*
Bruno, Elsa Knight 1935-2009 .... *221*

Brunskill, Elizabeth Ann Flatt
See Flatt, Lizann
Brush, Karen A(lexandra) 1960- *85*
Brussel-Smith, Bernard 1914- *58*
Brust, Steven 1955- *121*
Earlier sketch in SATA *86*
Brust, Steven Karl Zoltan
See Brust, Steven
Brustlein, Daniel 1904- *40*
Brustlein, Janice Tworkov -2000 .... *40*
Obituary *126*
Brutschy, Jennifer 1960- *84*
Bryan, Ashley 1923- *178*
Earlier sketches in SATA *31, 72, 132*
See also CLR *66*
Bryan, Ashley F.
See Bryan, Ashley
Bryan, Dorothy M. 1896(?)-1984
Obituary *39*
Bryan, Jennifer *190*
Bryan, Sean *192*
Bryant, Bernice (Morgan) 1908-1976 .... *11*
Bryant, Jen 1960- *218*
Earlier sketches in SATA *94, 175*
Bryant, Jennifer
See Bryant, Jen
Bryant, Jennifer Fisher
See Bryant, Jen
Bryant, Laura J. *176*
Brychta, Alex 1956- *21*
Brynie, Faith H. 1946- *113*
Brynie, Faith Hickman
See Brynie, Faith H.
Bryson, Bernarda 1903-2004 .... *9*
Buba, Joy Flinsch 1904- *44*
Buchan, Bryan 1945- *36*
Buchan, John 1875-1940
See YABC *2*
Buchan, Stuart 1942-1987
Obituary *54*
Buchanan, Debby 1952- *82*
Buchanan, Deborah Leevonne
See Buchanan, Debby
Buchanan, Jane 1956- *160*
Buchanan, Paul 1959- *116*
Buchanan, Sue 1939- *139*
Buchheimer, Naomi Barnett
See Barnett, Naomi
Buchignani, Walter 1965- *84*
Buchmann, Stephen L. *194*
Buchwald, Art 1925-2007 .... *10*
Buchwald, Arthur
See Buchwald, Art
Buchwald, Emilie 1935- *7*
Buck, Gisela 1941- *101*
Buck, Lewis 1925- *18*
Buck, Margaret Waring 1905-1997 .... *3*
Buck, Nola
See Godwin, Laura
Buck, Pearl S. 1892-1973 .... *25*
Earlier sketch in SATA *1*
Buck, Pearl Sydenstricker
See Buck, Pearl S.
Buck, Siegfried 1941- *101*
Buckalew, Clare B.
See Dunkle, Clare B.
Buckeridge, Anthony (Malcolm)
1912-2004 .... *85*
Earlier sketch in SATA *6*
Buckholtz, Eileen (Garber) 1949- *54*
Brief entry *47*
Buckingham, Royce 1966- *210*
Buckingham, Royce Scott
See Buckingham, Royce
Buckler, Ernest 1908-1984 .... *47*
Buckless, Andrea K. 1968- *117*
Buckley, Helen E(lizabeth) 1918- *90*
Earlier sketch in SATA *2*
Buckley, James, Jr. 1963- *166*
Earlier sketch in SATA *114*
Buckley, Michael *177*

Buckley, Susan *184*
Buckley, Susan Washburn
See Buckley, Susan
Buckley-Archer, Linda *185*
Buckmaster, Henrietta
See Stephens, Henrietta Henkle
Bucks, Brad
See Holub, Joan
Budd, E. S.
See Sirimarco, Elizabeth
Budd, Lillian (Peterson) 1897-1989 .... *7*
Budhos, Marina *173*
Buehler, Stephanie Jona 1956- *83*
Buehner, Caralyn 1963- *219*
Earlier sketches in SATA *104, 159*
Buehner, Mark 1959- *221*
Earlier sketches in SATA *104, 159*
Buehr, Walter Franklin 1897-1971 .... *3*
Buell, Ellen Lewis
See Cash, Ellen Lewis Buell
Buell, Janet 1952- *185*
Earlier sketch in SATA *106*
Buergel, Paul-Hermann H. 1949- *83*
Buettner, Dan 1960- *95*
Buff, Conrad 1886-1975 .... *19*
Buff, Mary (E. Marsh) 1890-1970 .... *19*
Buffett, Jimmy 1946- *110*
Earlier sketch in SATA *76*
Buffie, Margaret 1945- *161*
Earlier sketches in SATA *71, 107*
See also CLR *39*
Bugbee, Emma 1888(?)-1981
Obituary *29*
Bugni, Alice 1951- *122*
Buhhos, Marina Tamar
See Budhos, Marina
Bujold, Lois McMaster 1949- *136*
Bulfinch, Thomas 1796-1867 .... *35*
Bulion, Leslie 1958- *209*
Earlier sketch in SATA *161*
Bull, Angela (Mary) 1936- *45*
Bull, Emma 1954- *190*
Autobiography Feature *103*
Earlier sketch in SATA *99*
Bull, Norman John 1916- *41*
Bull, Peter (Cecil) 1912-1984
Obituary *39*
Bull, Schuyler M. 1974- *138*
Bulla, Clyde R. 1914-2007 .... *139*
Obituary *182*
Earlier sketches in SATA *2, 41, 91*
See also SAAS *6*
Bullard, Lisa 1961- *142*
Buller, Jon *205*
Bullock, Kathleen (Mary) 1946- *77*
Bullock, Robert (D.) 1947- *92*
Bulpin, (Barbara) Vicki *92*
Bulwer-Lytton, Edward 1803-1873 .... *23*
Bulwer-Lytton, Edward George Earle Lytton
See Bulwer-Lytton, Edward
Bumstead, Kathleen Mary 1918-1987 .... *53*
Bundles, A'Lelia Perry 1952- *76*
Bunge, Daniela 1973- *207*
Bunin, Catherine 1967- *30*
Bunin, Sherry 1925- *30*
Bunkers, Suzanne L. 1950- *136*
Bunting, A.E.
See Bunting, Eve
Bunting, Anne Evelyn
See Bunting, Eve
Bunting, Eve 1928- *196*
Earlier sketches in SATA *18, 64, 110, 158*
See also CLR *82*
Bunting, Glenn (Davison) 1957- *22*
Bunyan, John 1628-1688
See CLR *124*
Bupp, Walter
See Garrett, Randall
Burack, Sylvia K. 1916-2003 .... *35*
Obituary *143*
Burbank, Addison (Buswell) 1895-1961 ...... *37*

Burch, Joann J(ohansen) 75
Burch, Robert J(oseph) 1925- 74
　Earlier sketch in SATA 1
　See also CLR 63
Burchard, Peter Duncan 1921- 143
　Earlier sketches in SATA 5, 74
　See also SAAS 13
Burchard, S. H.
　See Burchard, Sue
Burchard, Sue 1937- 22
Burchardt, Nellie 1921- 7
Burckhardt, Marc 1962- 196
Burdett, Lois 117
Burdick, Eugene (Leonard) 1918-1965 22
Burford, Eleanor
　See Hibbert, Eleanor Alice Burford
Burg, Ann E. 1954- 217
Burg, Shana 1968- 204
Burgan, Michael 1960- 167
　Earlier sketch in SATA 118
Burger, Carl 1888-1967 9
Burgess, Ann Marie
　See Gerson, Noel Bertram
Burgess, Barbara Hood 1926- 69
Burgess, Em
　See Burgess, Mary Wyche
Burgess, (Frank) Gelett 1866-1951 32
　Brief entry 30
Burgess, Mark 157
Burgess, Mary Wyche 1916- 18
Burgess, Melvin 1954- 198
　Earlier sketches in SATA 96, 146
Burgess, Michael
　See Gerson, Noel Bertram
Burgess, Robert F(orrest) 1927- 4
Burgess, Starling
　See Tudor, Tasha
Burgess, Thornton Waldo 1874-1965 17
Burgess, Trevor
　See Trevor, Elleston
Burgwyn, Mebane Holoman 1914-1992 7
Burke, David 1927- 46
Burke, Diana G.
　See Gallagher, Diana G.
Burke, Diana Gallagher
　See Gallagher, Diana G.
Burke, Dianne O'Quinn 1940- 89
Burke, Janine 1952- 139
Burke, Jim 1973- 179
Burke, John
　See O'Connor, Richard
Burke, Katie 1953- 168
Burke, Patrick 1958- 114
Burke, Ralph
　See Garrett, Randall
　and Silverberg, Robert
Burkert, Nancy Ekholm 1933- 24
　See also SAAS 14
Burkett, D. Brent 194
Burke-Weiner, Kimberly 1962- 95
Burks, Brian 1955- 95
Burland, Brian (Berkeley) 1931- 34
Burland, C. A.
　See Burland, Cottie (Arthur)
Burland, Cottie (Arthur) 1905-1983 5
Burleigh, Robert 1936- 193
　Earlier sketches in SATA 55, 98, 146
Burlingame, (William) Roger 1889-1967 2
Burman, Alice Caddy 1896(?)-1977
　Obituary 24
Burman, Ben Lucien 1896-1984 6
　Obituary 40
Burn, Doris 1923- 1
Burn, Ted
　See Burn, Thomas E.
Burn, Thomas E. 1940- 150
Burnard, Damon 1963- 115
Burnett, Constance Buel 1893-1975 36
Burnett, Frances Eliza Hodgson
　See Burnett, Frances Hodgson

Burnett, Frances Hodgson 1849-1924 100
　See also YABC 2
　See also CLR 122
Burnett, Lindy 210
Burnett Bossi, Lisa 193
Burney, Anton
　See Hopkins, (Hector) Kenneth
Burnford, Sheila (Philip Cochrane Every)
　1918-1984 3
　Obituary 38
　See also CLR 2
Burnham, Gretchen
　See Sprague, Gretchen
Burnham, Nicole 1970- 161
Burnham, Niki
　See Burnham, Nicole
Burnham, Sophy 1936- 65
Burningham, John 1936- 160
　Earlier sketches in SATA 16, 59, 111
　See also CLR 9
Burningham, Robin Yoko
　See Racoma, Robin Yoko
Burningham, Sarah O'Leary 216
Burns, Diane L. 1950- 81
　See also SAAS 24
Burns, Eloise Wilkin
　See Wilkin, Eloise
Burns, Florence M. 1905-1988 61
Burns, Khephra 1950- 92
Burns, Loree Griffin 193
Burns, Marilyn 1941- 96
　Brief entry 33
Burns, Olive Ann 1924-1990 65
Burns, Paul C. 5
Burns, Ray
　See Burns, Raymond (Howard)
Burns, Raymond (Howard) 1924- 9
Burns, Theresa 1961- 84
Burns, William A. 1909-1999 5
Burr, Dan 1951- 65
Burr, Dan 1960- 219
Burr, Lonnie 1943- 47
Burrell, Roy E(ric) C(harles) 1923- 72
Burroughs, Edgar Rice 1875-1950 41
　See also CLR 157
Burroughs, Jean Mitchell 1908- 28
Burroughs, Polly 1925- 2
Burroway, Janet 1936- 23
Burroway, Janet Gay
　See Burroway, Janet
Burstein, Chaya M(alamud) 1923- 64
Burstein, Fred 1950- 83
Burstein, John 1949- 54
　Brief entry 40
Burstein, Stanley M.
　See Burstein, Stanley Mayer
Burstein, Stanley Mayer 1941- 175
Bursztynski, Sue 1953- 114
Burt, Jesse Clifton 1921-1976 46
　Obituary 20
Burt, Olive Woolley 1894-1981 4
Burtinshaw, Julie 185
Burton, Gennett 1945- 95
Burton, Hester (Wood-Hill) 1913-2000 74
　Earlier sketch in SATA 7
　See also CLR 1
　See also SAAS 8
Burton, Leslie
　See McGuire, Leslie (Sarah)
Burton, Marilee Robin 1950- 82
　Earlier sketch in SATA 46
Burton, Maurice 1898-1992 23
Burton, Rebecca 1970- 183
Burton, Robert (Wellesley) 1941- 22
Burton, Virginia Lee 1909-1968 100
　Earlier sketch in SATA 2
　See also CLR 11
Burton, William H(enry) 1890-1964 11
Busby, Ailie 192
Busby, Cylin 1970- 118

Busby, Edith (A. Lake) (?)-1964
　Obituary 29
Busby, John 1942- 209
Buscaglia, (Felice) Leo(nardo) 1924-1998 ... 65
Buscaglia, Leo F.
　See Buscaglia, (Felice) Leo(nardo)
Busch, Phyllis S. 1909- 30
Bush, Anne Kelleher
　See Kelleher, Anne
Bush, Catherine 1961- 128
Bush, Jenna 1981- 208
Bush, Laura 1946- 208
Bushmiller, Ernest Paul 1905-1982 31
Bushmiller, Ernie
　See Bushmiller, Ernest Paul
Bushnell, Jack 1952- 86
Busoni, Rafaello 1900-1962 16
Buss, Helen M.
　See Clarke, Margaret
Busse, Sarah Martin 194
Busselle, Rebecca 1941- 80
Bustard, Anne 1951- 173
Butcher, Kristin 1951- 140
Butenko, Bohdan 1931- 90
Butler, Beverly Kathleen 1932- 7
Butler, Bill
　See Butler, William Vivian
　and Butler, Ernest Alton
　and Butler, William Huxford
Butler, Charles 1963- 175
　Earlier sketch in SATA 121
Butler, Charles Cadman
　See Butler, Charles
Butler, Dori Hillestad 1965- 207
　Earlier sketch in SATA 164
Butler, Dorothy 1925- 73
Butler, Geoff 1945- 94
Butler, M. Christina 1934- 170
　Earlier sketch in SATA 72
Butler, Octavia 1947-2006 84
　See also CLR 65
Butler, Octavia E.
　See Butler, Octavia
Butler, Octavia Estelle
　See Butler, Octavia
Butler, Vivian
　See Butler, William Vivian
Butler, William
　See Butler, William Vivian
Butler, William Vivian 1927-1987 79
Butterfield, Moira 1960- 219
Butters, Dorothy Gilman
　See Gilman, Dorothy
Butterworth, Emma Macalik 1928- 43
Butterworth, Nick 1946- 149
　Earlier sketch in SATA 106
Butterworth, Oliver 1915-1990 1
　Obituary 66
Butterworth, W. E.
　See Griffin, W. E. B.
Butterworth, William E.
　See Griffin, W. E. B.
Butterworth, William Edmund III
　See Griffin, W. E. B.
Butts, Ed 1951- 177
Butts, Edward P.
　See Butts, Ed
Butts, Ellen R. 1942- 93
Butts, Ellen Rubinstein
　See Butts, Ellen R.
Butzer, C. M. 1974- 212
Buxton, Ralph
　See Silverstein, Alvin
　and Silverstein, Virginia B.
Buzzeo, Toni 1951- 215
　Earlier sketch in SATA 135
Byalick, Marcia 1947- 141
　Earlier sketch in SATA 97
Byard, Carole (Marie) 1941- 57

Byars, Betsy 1928- *223*
  Autobiography Feature *108*
  Earlier sketches in SATA *4, 46, 80, 163*
  See also CLR *72*
  See also SAAS *1*
Byars, Betsy Cromer
  See Byars, Betsy
Byfield, Barbara Ninde 1930-1988 .... *8*
Byman, Jeremy 1944- *129*
Bynum, Janie *133*
Byrd, Elizabeth 1912-1989 .... *34*
Byrd, Nicole
  See Zach, Cheryl (Byrd)
Byrd, Robert (John) 1942- *158*
  Earlier sketches in SATA *33, 112*
Byrd, Tim 1964- *216*
Byrne, Gayle *218*
Byrne, Mary Gregg 1951- *162*

C

C. 3. 3.
  See Wilde, Oscar
C. E. M.
  See Mastrangelo, Charles E(lmer)
Cabaniss, J(ames) Allen 1911-1997 .... *5*
Cabat, Erni 1914- *74*
Cabban, Vanessa 1971- *176*
Cable, Mary 1920- *9*
Cabot, Meg 1967- *217*
  Earlier sketches in SATA *127, 175*
  See also CLR *85*
Cabot, Meggin
  See Cabot, Meg
Cabot, Meggin Patricia
  See Cabot, Meg
Cabot, Patricia
  See Cabot, Meg
Cabral, O. M.
  See Cabral, Olga
Cabral, Olga 1909- *46*
Cabrera, Cozbi A. 1963- *177*
Cabrera, Jane 1968- *182*
  Earlier sketches in SATA *103, 152*
Cabrera, Marcela 1966- *90*
Caddy, Alice
  See Burman, Alice Caddy
Cade, Toni
  See Bambara, Toni Cade
Cadena, Beth *222*
Cadmus and Harmonia
  See Buchan, John
Cadnum, Michael 1949- *165*
  Earlier sketches in SATA *87, 121*
  See also CLR *78*
Caduto, Michael J. 1955- *103*
Cadwallader, Sharon 1936- *7*
Cady, (Walter) Harrison 1877(?)-1970 .... *19*
Caffey, Donna (J.) 1954- *110*
Cagle, Malcolm W(infield) 1918- *32*
Cahn, Rhoda 1922- *37*
Cahn, William 1912-1976 .... *37*
Cain, Arthur H(omer) 1913-1981 .... *3*
Cain, Christopher
  See Fleming, Thomas
Cain, Sheridan 1952- *186*
Caine, Geoffrey
  See Walker, Robert W.
Caines, Jeannette (Franklin) 1938- *78*
  Brief entry *43*
  See also CLR *24*
Cairns, Trevor 1922- *14*
Calabro, Marian 1954- *79*
Caldecott, Moyra 1927- *22*
Caldecott, Randolph (J.) 1846-1886 .... *100*
  Earlier sketch in SATA *17*
  See also CLR *110*
Calder, Charlotte 1952- *125*
Calder, David 1932-1997 .... *105*

Calder, Lyn
  See Calmenson, Stephanie
Calder, Marie D(onais) 1948- *96*
Calderone-Stewart, Lisa
  See Calderone-Stewart, Lisa-Marie
Calderone-Stewart, Lisa-Marie 1958- *123*
Caldwell, Doreen (Mary) 1942- *71*
Caldwell, John C(ope) 1913-1984 .... *7*
Caletti, Deb 1963- *221*
  Earlier sketch in SATA *171*
Calhoun, B. B. 1961- *98*
Calhoun, Chad
  See Barrett, Neal, Jr.
  and Cunningham, Chet
  and Goulart, Ron
Calhoun, Dia 1959- *183*
  Earlier sketch in SATA *129*
Calhoun, Mary
  See Wilkins, Mary Huiskamp
Calhoun, T.B.
  See Bisson, Terry
Cali, Davide 1972- *190*
Calif, Ruth 1922- *67*
Calkins, Franklin
  See Stratemeyer, Edward L.
Call, Greg *197*
Call, Hughie Florence 1890-1969 .... *1*
Callahan, Dorothy M. 1934- *39*
  Brief entry *35*
Callahan, Dorothy Monahan
  See Callahan, Dorothy M.
Callahan, Philip Serna 1923- *25*
Callahan, Sean 1965- *222*
Callan, Jamie 1954- *59*
Callan, Jim 1951- *181*
Callaway, Bernice (Anne) 1923- *48*
Callaway, Kathy 1943- *36*
Callen, Larry
  See Callen, Lawrence Willard, Jr.
Callen, Lawrence Willard, Jr. 1927- *19*
Calley, Karin 1965- *92*
Calmenson, Stephanie 1952- *211*
  Brief entry *37*
  Earlier sketches in SATA *51, 84, 139*
Calonita, Jen *216*
Calvert, Elinor H.
  See Lasell, Elinor H.
Calvert, John
  See Leaf, (Wilbur) Munro
Calvert, Pam 1966- *205*
Calvert, Patricia 1931- *132*
  Earlier sketches in SATA *45, 69*
  See also SAAS *17*
Camburn, Carol A.
  See Camburn-Bracalente, Carol A.
Camburn-Bracalente, Carol A. 1962- *118*
Cameron, Ann 1943- *129*
  Earlier sketches in SATA *27, 89*
  See also SAAS *20*
Cameron, Edna M. 1905-1999 .... *3*
Cameron, Eleanor (Frances) 1912-1996 .... *25*
  Obituary *93*
  Earlier sketch in SATA *1*
  See also CLR *72*
  See also SAAS *10*
Cameron, Elizabeth
  See Nowell, Elizabeth Cameron
Cameron, Elizabeth Jane 1910-1976 .... *32*
  Obituary *30*
Cameron, Ian
  See Payne, Donald Gordon
Cameron, M(alcolm) G(ordon) Graham
  See Graham-Cameron, M(alcolm) G(ordon)
Cameron, M. Graham
  See Graham-Cameron, M(alcolm) G(ordon)
Cameron, Mike Graham
  See Graham-Cameron, M(alcolm) G(ordon)
Cameron, Natalie Russell
  See Russell, Natalie
Cameron, Polly 1928- *2*
Cameron, Scott 1962- *84*

Camp, Charles L. 1893-1975
  Obituary *31*
Camp, Lindsay 1957- *133*
Camp, Madeleine L'Engle
  See L'Engle, Madeleine
Camp, Walter (Chauncey) 1859-1925
  See YABC *1*
Campbell, (Elizabeth) Andrea 1963- *50*
Campbell, Ann R. 1925- *11*
Campbell, Bill 1960- *89*
Campbell, Bruce
  See Epstein, Samuel
Campbell, Camilla 1905-1992 .... *26*
Campbell, Carole R. 1939- *125*
Campbell, Hope 1925- *20*
Campbell, Hugh 1930- *90*
Campbell, Jane
  See Edwards, Jane Campbell
Campbell, Julie
  See Tatham, Julie Campbell
Campbell, Patricia J(ean) 1930- *45*
Campbell, Patty
  See Campbell, Patricia J(ean)
Campbell, Peter A. 1948- *99*
Campbell, R. W.
  See Campbell, Rosemae Wells
Campbell, Robin
  See Strachan, Ian
Campbell, Rod 1945- *98*
  Brief entry *44*
  Earlier sketch in SATA *51*
Campbell, Rosemae Wells 1909- *1*
Campbell, Sarah C. 1966- *207*
Camper, Cathy 1956- *170*
Campion, Nardi Reeder 1917-2007 .... *22*
Campling, Elizabeth 1948- *53*
Campoy, F. Isabel 1946- *181*
  Earlier sketch in SATA *143*
Camps, Luis 1928- *66*
Canales, Viola 1957- *141*
Candell, Victor 1903-1977
  Obituary *24*
Canfield, Dorothea F.
  See Fisher, Dorothy (Frances) Canfield
Canfield, Dorothea Frances
  See Fisher, Dorothy (Frances) Canfield
Canfield, Dorothy
  See Fisher, Dorothy (Frances) Canfield
Canfield, Jack 1944- *164*
Canfield, Jane White 1897-1984 .... *32*
  Obituary *38*
Canfield, Muriel 1935- *94*
Canga, C.B. 1976- *216*
Canga, Chris
  See Canga, C.B.
Caniff, Milton 1907-1988
  Obituary *58*
Caniff, Milton Arthur Paul
  See Caniff, Milton
Cann, Helen 1969- *179*
  Earlier sketch in SATA *124*
Cann, Kate 1954- *152*
  Earlier sketch in SATA *103*
Cannan, Joanna
  See Pullein-Thompson, Joanna Maxwell
Cannell, Jon *196*
Cannell, Jonathan C.
  See Cannell, Jon
Cannon, A.E. *202*
  Earlier sketches in SATA *93, 163*
Cannon, Ann Edwards
  See Cannon, A.E.
Cannon, Bettie (Waddell) 1922- *59*
Cannon, Curt
  See Hunter, Evan
Cannon, Eileen E(mily) 1948- *119*
Cannon, Frank
  See Mayhar, Ardath
Cannon, Janell 1957- *128*
  Earlier sketch in SATA *78*
  See also CLR *120*

Cannon, Marian G. 1923- 85
Cannon, Taffy
    See Cannon, Eileen E(mily)
Cantone, AnnaLaura 182
Cantrell, Julie 1973- 217
Canusi, Jose
    See Barker, S. Omar
Canyon, Christopher 1966- 150
    Earlier sketch in SATA *104*
Caparo, Antonio
    See Caparo, Antonio Javier
Caparo, Antonio Javier 205
Capek, Michael 1947- 142
    Earlier sketch in SATA *96*
Capes, Bernard (Edward Joseph)
    1854-1918 116
Caple, Kathy 193
Caple, Laurie 1958- 201
Caplin, Alfred Gerald 1909-1979 61
    Obituary 21
Caponigro, John Paul 1965- 84
Capote, Truman 1924-1984 91
Capp, Al
    See Caplin, Alfred Gerald
Cappel, Constance 1936- 22
Cappetta, Cynthia 1949- 125
Cappo, Nan Willard 1955- 143
Capps, Benjamin (Franklin) 1922- 9
Cappy Dick
    See Cleveland, George
Captain Kangaroo
    See Keeshan, Robert J.
Captain Wheeler
    See Ellis, Edward S.
Captain Young of Yale
    See Stratemeyer, Edward L.
Capucilli, Alyssa Satin 1957- 203
    Earlier sketches in SATA *115, 163*
Capucine
    See Mazille, Capucine
Carafoli, Marci
    See Balterman, Marcia Ridlon
Caraher, Kim(berley Elizabeth) 1961- 105
Caraker, Mary 1929- 74
Caras, Roger A(ndrew) 1928-2001 12
    Obituary 127
Caravantes, Peggy 1935- 140
Caraway, Caren 1939- 57
Carbone, Elisa 1954- 173
    Earlier sketches in SATA *81, 137*
Carbone, Elisa Lynn
    See Carbone, Elisa
Carbonnier, Jeanne 1894-1974 3
    Obituary 34
Card, Orson Scott 1951- 127
    Earlier sketch in SATA *83*
    See also CLR *116*
Care, Felicity
    See Coury, Louise Andree
Carew, Jan 1925- 51
    Brief entry 40
Carew, Jan Rynveld
    See Carew, Jan
Carey, Benedict 1960- 219
Carey, Bonnie
    See Marshall, Bonnie C.
Carey, Charles W., Jr. 1951- 170
Carey, Ernestine Gilbreth 1908-2006 2
    Obituary 177
Carey, Janet Lee 1954(?)- 185
Carey, Lisa 110
Carey, M. V.
    See Carey, Mary V(irginia)
Carey, Mary V(irginia) 1925-1994 44
    Brief entry 39
Carey, Peter 1943- 94
Carey, Peter Philip
    See Carey, Peter
Carey, Valerie Scho 1949- 60
Carheden, Goorel Kristina
    See Naaslund, Goorel Kristina

Carigiet, Alois 1902-1985 24
    Obituary 47
    See also CLR *38*
Carini, Edward 1923- 9
Carkeet, David 1946- 75
Carle, Eric 1929- 163
    Earlier sketches in SATA *4, 65, 120*
    See also CLR *72*
    See also SAAS *6*
Carleton, Captain L. C.
    See Ellis, Edward S.
Carleton, Captain Latham C.
    See Ellis, Edward S.
Carleton, Latham C.
    See Ellis, Edward S.
Carley, V(an Ness) Royal 1906-1976
    Obituary 20
Carling, Amelia Lau 1949- 164
    Earlier sketch in SATA *119*
Carlisle, Carolyn
    See Hawes, Louise
Carlisle, Clark
    See Holding, James (Clark Carlisle, Jr.)
Carlisle, Olga Andreyev 1930- 35
Carlock, Miriam
    See Eyerly, Jeannette
Carls, Claudia 1978- 198
Carlsen, G(eorge) Robert 1917- 30
Carlsen, Ruth C(hristoffer) 1918- 2
Carlson, Bernice Wells 1910- 8
Carlson, Christopher C. 202
Carlson, Dale (Bick) 1935- 1
Carlson, Daniel (Bick) 1960- 27
Carlson, Kirsten 1968- 192
Carlson, Kirsten M.
    See Carlson, Kirsten
Carlson, Laurie 1952- 173
    Earlier sketch in SATA *101*
Carlson, Laurie Winn
    See Carlson, Laurie
Carlson, Melody 1956- 171
    Earlier sketch in SATA *113*
Carlson, Nancy 1953- 213
    Brief entry 45
    Earlier sketches in SATA *56, 90, 144*
Carlson, Nancy L.
    See Carlson, Nancy
Carlson, Natalie Savage 1906-1997 68
    Earlier sketch in SATA *2*
    See also SAAS *4*
Carlson, Susan Johnston 1953- 88
Carlson, Vada F. 1897- 16
Carlstrom, Nancy White 1948- 215
    Brief entry 48
    Earlier sketches in SATA *53, 92, 156*
Carlton, Keith
    See Robertson, Keith (Carlton)
Carlton, Susan 1960- 195
Carlyon, Richard 55
Carman, Bill
    See Carman, William
Carman, Patrick 1966- 197
    Earlier sketch in SATA *161*
Carman, William 223
Carmer, Carl (Lamson) 1893-1976 37
    Obituary 30
Carmer, Elizabeth Black 1904- 24
Carmi, Giora 1944- 149
    Earlier sketch in SATA *79*
Carmichael, Carrie
    See Carmichael, Harriet
Carmichael, Clay 218
Carmichael, Harriet 40
Carmody, Isobelle 1958- 191
    Earlier sketch in SATA *161*
Carmody, Isobelle Jane
    See Carmody, Isobelle
Carney, Elizabeth 1981- 199
Carney, Jeff 1962- 196
Carney, Mary Lou 1949- 170

Carol, Bill J.
    See Knott, William C(ecil, Jr.)
Caron, Romi
    See Caron-Kyselkova', Romana
Caron-Kyselkova', Romana 1967- 94
Caroselli, Remus F(rancis) 1916- 36
Carpelan, Bo 1926- 8
Carpelan, Bo Gustaf Bertelsson
    See Carpelan, Bo
Carpenter, (John) Allan 1917- 81
    Earlier sketch in SATA *3*
Carpenter, Angelica Shirley 1945- 153
    Earlier sketch in SATA *71*
Carpenter, Frances 1890-1972 3
    Obituary 27
Carpenter, John 1948- 58
Carpenter, John Howard
    See Carpenter, John
Carpenter, Johnny
    See Carpenter, John
Carpenter, Nancy 215
Carpenter, Nancy Sippel
    See Carpenter, Nancy
Carpenter, Patricia (Healy Evans) 1920- 11
Carr, Glyn
    See Styles, (Frank) Showell
Carr, Harriett H(elen) 1899-1977 3
Carr, Jan 1953- 132
    Earlier sketch in SATA *89*
Carr, M. J.
    See Carr, Jan
Carr, Mary Jane 1899-1988 2
    Obituary 55
Carr, Philippa
    See Hibbert, Eleanor Alice Burford
Carr, Roger Vaughan 1937- 95
Carrel, Annette Felder 1929- 90
Carrick, Carol (Hatfield) 1935- 118
    Earlier sketches in SATA *7, 63*
    See also SAAS *18*
Carrick, Donald (F.) 1929-1989 63
    Earlier sketch in SATA *7*
Carrick, Malcolm 1945- 28
Carrick, Paul 1972- 194
Carrier, Lark 1947- 71
    Brief entry 50
Carrier, Roch 1937- 166
    Earlier sketch in SATA *105*
Carrighar, Sally 1898-1985 24
Carrillo, Patricia S.
    See Carrillo, P.S.
Carrillo, P.S. 209
Carrington, G. A.
    See Cunningham, Chet
Carrington, Marsha Gray 1954- 168
    Earlier sketch in SATA *111*
Carris, Joan 1938- 182
    Brief entry 42
    Earlier sketch in SATA *44*
Carris, Joan Davenport
    See Carris, Joan
Carroll, Curt
    See Bishop, Curtis (Kent)
Carroll, Elizabeth
    See Barkin, Carol
    and James, Elizabeth
Carroll, Jaye
    See Carroll, Michael
Carroll, Jenny
    See Cabot, Meg
Carroll, (Archer) Latrobe 1894-1996 7
Carroll, Laura
    See Parr, Lucy
Carroll, Lewis 1832-1898 100
    See also YABC *2*
    See also CLR *108*
Carroll, Michael 1966- 203
Carroll, Raymond 1924- 86
    Brief entry 47
Carruth, Hayden 1921-2008 47
    Obituary 197

Carryl, Charles E. 1841-1920 .... *114*
Carryl, Charles Edward
    See Carryl, Charles E.
Carse, Robert 1902-1971 .... *5*
Carson, J(ohn) Franklin 1920-1981 .... *1*
    Obituary *107*
Carson, Mary Kay 1964- *200*
    Earlier sketch in SATA *150*
Carson, Rachel 1907-1964 .... *23*
Carson, Rachel Louise
    See Carson, Rachel
Carson, Rosalind
    See Chittenden, Margaret
Carson, S. M.
    See Gorsline, (Sally) Marie
Carson, William C. 1928- *154*
Carter, Abby *222*
    Earlier sketch in SATA *184*
Carter, Alden R 1947- *137*
    Earlier sketch in SATA *67*
    See also CLR *22*
    See also SAAS *18*
Carter, Alden Richardson
    See Carter, Alden R
Carter, Andy 1948- *134*
Carter, Angela 1940-1992 .... *66*
    Obituary *70*
Carter, Angela Olive
    See Carter, Angela
Carter, Anne Laurel 1953- *209*
    Earlier sketch in SATA *135*
Carter, Asa Earl
    See Carter, Forrest
Carter, Avis Murton
    See Allen, Kenneth S.
Carter, Bruce
    See Hough, Richard (Alexander)
Carter, Carol S(hadis) 1948- *124*
Carter, David A. 1957- *170*
    Earlier sketch in SATA *114*
Carter, Don 1958- *192*
    Earlier sketch in SATA *124*
Carter, Dorothy Sharp 1921- *8*
Carter, Forrest 1927(?)-1979 .... *32*
Carter, Helene 1887-1960 .... *15*
Carter, (William) Hodding, Jr. 1907-1972 ...... *2*
    Obituary *27*
Carter, James Earl, Jr.
    See Carter, Jimmy
Carter, Jimmy 1924- *79*
Carter, Katharine J(ones) 1905-1984 .... *2*
Carter, Lin(wood Vrooman) 1930-1988 .... *91*
Carter, Mike 1936- *138*
Carter, Nick
    See Avallone, Michael (Angelo, Jr.)
    and Ballard, (Willis) Todhunter
    and Crider, Bill
    and Cassiday, Bruce (Bingham)
    and Chastain, Thomas
    and Dey, Frederic (Merrill) Van Rensselaer
    and Garside, Jack
    and Hayes, Ralph E(ugene)
    and Henderson, M(arilyn) R(uth)
    and Lynds, Dennis
    and Lynds, Gayle (Hallenbeck)
    and Randisi, Robert J.
    and Rasof, Henry
    and Stratemeyer, Edward L.
    and Smith, Martin Cruz
    and Swain, Dwight V(reeland)
    and Vardeman, Robert E.
    and Wallmann, Jeffrey M(iner)
    and White, Lionel
Carter, Peter 1929- *57*
Carter, Phyllis Ann
    See Eberle, Irmengarde
Carter, Samuel (Thomson) III 1904-1988 .... *37*
    Obituary *60*
Carter, William E. 1926-1983 .... *1*
    Obituary *35*

Cartlidge, Michelle 1950- *96*
    Brief entry *37*
    Earlier sketch in SATA *49*
Cartner, William Carruthers 1910- *11*
Cartwright, Ann 1940- *78*
Cartwright, Reg(inald Ainsley) 1938- *64*
Cartwright, Sally 1923- *9*
Carusone, Al 1949- *89*
Carvell, Marlene *172*
Carver, John
    See Gardner, Richard (M.)
Carwell, L'Ann
    See McKissack, Patricia C.
Cary
    See Cary, Louis F(avreau)
Cary, Barbara Knapp 1912(?)-1975
    Obituary *31*
Cary, Kate 1967(?)- *174*
Cary, Louis F(avreau) 1915- *9*
Caryl, Jean
    See Kaplan, Jean Caryl Korn
Casanova, Mary 1957- *186*
    Earlier sketches in SATA *94, 136*
Cascone, A.G.
    See Cascone, Annette
    and Cascone, Gina
Cascone, Annette 1960- *103*
Cascone, Gina 1955- *103*
Case, Chris 1976- *209*
Case, Marshal T(aylor) 1941- *9*
Case, Michael
    See Howard, Robert West
Caseley, Judith 1951- *159*
    Brief entry *53*
    Earlier sketch in SATA *87*
Casewit, Curtis W(erner) 1922-2002 .... *4*
Casey, Barbara (Louise) 1944- *147*
    Earlier sketch in SATA *79*
Casey, Brigid 1950- *9*
Casey, Tina 1959- *141*
Cash, Ellen Lewis Buell 1905-1989
    Obituary *64*
Cash, John Carter 1970- *218*
Cash, Megan Montague *160*
Cashore, Kristin 1976(?)- *206*
Casilla, Robert 1959- *211*
    Earlier sketches in SATA *75, 146*
Cason, Mabel Earp 1892-1965 .... *10*
Cass, Joan E(velyn) *1*
Cass-Beggs, Barbara 1904- *62*
Cassedy, Patrice (Rinaldo) 1953- *149*
Cassedy, Sylvia 1930-1989 .... *77*
    Obituary *61*
    Earlier sketch in SATA *27*
    See also CLR *26*
Cassel, Lili
    See Wronker, Lili Cassel
Cassels, Jean *173*
Cassidy, Anne 1952- *166*
Cassidy, Anne Josephine
    See Cassidy, Anne
Cassidy, Cathy 1962- *183*
Casson, Hugh Maxwell 1910-1999 .... *65*
    Obituary *115*
Cassutt, Michael 1954- *78*
Cassutt, Michael Joseph
    See Cassutt, Michael
Castaldi, Elicia *194*
Castaldo, Nancy Fusco 1962- *151*
    Earlier sketch in SATA *93*
Castaneda, Omar S. 1954- *71*
Castell, Megan
    See Williams, Jeanne
Castellanos, Jane Mollie Robinson
    1913-2001 .... *9*
Castellon, Federico 1914-1971 .... *48*
Castellucci, Cecil 1969- *176*
Castillo, Edmund L. 1924-2005 .... *1*
    Obituary *167*
Castillo, Lauren *195*

Castle, Lee
    See Ogan, George F.
    and Ogan, Margaret E. (Nettles)
Castle, Paul
    See Howard, Vernon (Linwood)
Castle, Robert
    See Hamilton, Edmond
Castrovilla, Selene 1966- *186*
Caswell, Brian 1954- *171*
    Earlier sketch in SATA *97*
Caswell, Deanna *223*
Caswell, Helen (Rayburn) 1923- *12*
Catalano, Dominic 1956- *163*
    Earlier sketch in SATA *76*
Catalano, Grace (A.) 1961- *99*
Catalanotto, Peter 1959- *195*
    Autobiography Feature *113*
    Earlier sketches in SATA *70, 114, 159*
    See also CLR *68*
    See also SAAS *25*
Catanese, P. W. 1961- *179*
Cate, Annette LeBlanc *196*
Cate, Dick
    See Cate, Richard Edward Nelson
Cate, Richard Edward Nelson 1932- *28*
Cather, Willa 1873-1947 .... *30*
    See also CLR *98*
Catherall, Arthur 1906-1980 .... *74*
    Earlier sketches in SATA *3, 4*
Cathon, Laura E(lizabeth) 1908-1991 .... *27*
Catlett, Elizabeth 1919(?)- *82*
Catlin, Wynelle 1930- *13*
Catlow, Nikalas
    See Catlow, Niki
Catlow, Niki 1975- *193*
Cato, Heather *105*
Cato, Sheila *114*
Catran, Ken 1944- *190*
Catrow, David
    See Catrow, David J. III
Catrow, David J. III *206*
    Earlier sketch in SATA *152*
Catt, Louis
    See French, Vivian
Cattell, James 1954- *123*
Catton, (Charles) Bruce 1899-1978 .... *2*
    Obituary *24*
Catusanu, Mircea *222*
Catz, Max
    See Glaser, Milton
Caudell, Marian 1930- *52*
Caudill, Rebecca 1899-1985 .... *1*
    Obituary *44*
Cauley, Lorinda Bryan 1951- *46*
    Brief entry *43*
Caulfield, Peggy F. 1926-1987
    Obituary *53*
Cauman, Samuel 1910-1971 .... *48*
Causley, Charles (Stanley) 1917-2003 .... *66*
    Obituary *149*
    Earlier sketch in SATA *3*
    See also CLR *30*
Cavallaro, Ann (Abelson) 1918- *62*
Cavallo, Diana 1931- *7*
Cavanagh, Helen (Carol) 1939- *98*
    Brief entry *37*
    Earlier sketch in SATA *48*
Cavanah, Frances 1899-1982 .... *31*
    Earlier sketch in SATA *1*
Cavanna, Betty
    See Harrison, Elizabeth (Allen) Cavanna
Cavanna, Elizabeth
    See Harrison, Elizabeth (Allen) Cavanna
Cave, Kathryn 1948- *123*
    Earlier sketch in SATA *76*
Cavendish, Peter
    See Horler, Sydney
Caveney, Philip 1951- *219*
Caveney, Philip Richard
    See Caveney, Philip
Cavin, Ruth 1918-2011 .... *38*

Cavin, Ruth Brodie
　　See Cavin, Ruth
Cavoukian, Raffi 1948- 68
Cawley, Winifred 1915- 13
Cazeau, Charles J(ay) 1931- 65
Cazet, Denys 1938- 191
　　Brief entry 41
　　Earlier sketches in SATA 52, 99, 163
Cazzola, Gus 1934- 73
Cebulash, Mel 1937- 91
　　Earlier sketch in SATA 10
Ceccoli, Nicoletta 181
Cecil, Randy 1968- 223
　　Earlier sketch in SATA 187
Cecka, Melanie 199
Ceder, Georgiana Dorcas -1985 10
Celenza, Anna Harwell 133
Celestino, Martha Laing
　　See Laing, Martha
Cepeda, Joe 215
　　Earlier sketch in SATA 159
Cerf, Bennett (Alfred) 1898-1971 7
Cerf, Christopher (Bennett) 1941- 2
Cermak, Martin
　　See Duchacek, Ivo D(uka)
Cerullo, Mary M. 1949- 145
　　Earlier sketch in SATA 86
Cervon, Jacqueline
　　See Moussard, Jacqueline
Cetin, Frank Stanley 1921- 2
Chabon, Michael 1963- 145
Chabrian, Deborah
　　See Chabrian, Deborah L.
Chabrian, Deborah L. 212
Chaconas, D.J.
　　See Chaconas, Dori
Chaconas, Dori 1938- 208
　　Earlier sketches in SATA 145, 175
Chaconas, Doris J.
　　See Chaconas, Dori
Chadwick, Lester 67
　　Earlier sketch in SATA 1
Chaffee, Allen 3
Chaffin, Lillie D(orton) 1925- 4
Chaikin, Miriam 1924- 152
　　Earlier sketches in SATA 24, 102
Chall, Marsha Wilson 150
Challand, Helen J(ean) 1921- 64
Challans, Mary
　　See Renault, Mary
Chalmers, Mary (Eileen) 1927- 6
　　See also SAAS 14
Chamberlain, Barbara A.
　　See Azore, Barbara
Chamberlain, Margaret 1954- 212
　　Earlier sketch in SATA 46
Chamberlin, Kate 1945- 105
Chamberlin, Mary 1960- 177
Chamberlin, Rich 177
Chamberlin, Richard
　　See Chamberlin, Rich
Chambers, Aidan 1934- 171
　　Earlier sketches in SATA 1, 69, 108
　　See also CLR 151
　　See also SAAS 12
Chambers, Bradford 1922-1984
　　Obituary 39
Chambers, Catherine E.
　　See St. John, Nicole
Chambers, John W. 1933- 57
　　Brief entry 46
Chambers, Kate
　　See St. John, Nicole
Chambers, Margaret Ada Eastwood 1911- 2
Chambers, Peggy
　　See Chambers, Margaret Ada Eastwood
Chambers, Robert W(illiam) 1865-1933 107
Chambliss, Maxie 186
Chan, Gillian 1954- 147
　　Earlier sketch in SATA 102
Chan, Peter 1980(?)- 207

Chance, James T.
　　See Carpenter, John
Chance, John T.
　　See Carpenter, John
Chance, Stephen
　　See Turner, Philip (William)
Chandler, Caroline A(ugusta) 1906-1979 22
　　Obituary 24
Chandler, David P. 1933- 28
Chandler, David Porter
　　See Chandler, David P.
Chandler, Edna Walker 1908-1982 11
　　Obituary 31
Chandler, Jennifer
　　See Westwood, Jennifer
Chandler, Karen 1959- 122
Chandler, Linda S(mith) 1929- 39
Chandler, Pauline 175
Chandler, Robert 1953- 40
Chandler, Ruth Forbes 1894-1978 2
　　Obituary 26
Chandonnet, Ann F. 1943- 92
Chaney, Jill 1932- 87
Chang, Chih-Wei 1966- 111
Chang, Cindy 1968- 90
Chang, Margaret 1941- 71
Chang, Margaret Scrogin
　　See Chang, Margaret
Chang, Raymond 1939- 142
　　Earlier sketches in SATA 71, 142 PEN
Chanin, Michael 1952- 84
Channel, A. R.
　　See Catherall, Arthur
Chapian, Marie 1938- 29
Chapin, Alene Olsen Dalton 1915(?)-1986
　　Obituary 47
Chapin, Tom 1945- 83
Chapman, Allen 67
　　Earlier sketch in SATA 1
Chapman, Cheryl O(rth) 1948- 80
Chapman, (Constance) Elizabeth (Mann)
　　1919- 10
Chapman, Gaye 1970- 200
Chapman, Gaye Coralie
　　See Chapman, Gaye
Chapman, Gaynor 1935- 32
Chapman, Gillian 1955- 120
Chapman, Jane 1970- 212
　　Earlier sketches in SATA 122, 176
Chapman, Jean 104
　　Earlier sketch in SATA 34
　　See also CLR 65
Chapman, John Stanton Higham 1891-1972
　　Obituary 27
Chapman, Lee
　　See Bradley, Marion Zimmer
Chapman, Linda 1969- 223
Chapman, Lynne 1960- 197
Chapman, Lynne F(erguson) 1963- 150
　　Earlier sketch in SATA 94
Chapman, Maristan
　　See Chapman, John Stanton Higham
Chapman, Vera (Ivy May) 1898-1996 33
Chapman, Walker
　　See Silverberg, Robert
Chappell, Audrey 1954- 72
Chappell, Crissa-Jean 198
Chappell, Warren 1904-1991 68
　　Obituary 67
　　Earlier sketch in SATA 6
　　See also SAAS 10
Chapra, Mimi 182
Charbonneau, Eileen 1951- 118
　　Earlier sketch in SATA 84
Charbonnet, Gabrielle 1961- 81
Chardiet, Bernice 1927(?)- 27
Chardiet, Bernice Kroll
　　See Chardiet, Bernice
Charest, Emily MacLachlan 198
Charles, Donald
　　See Meighan, Donald Charles

Charles, Louis
　　See Stratemeyer, Edward L.
Charles, Nicholas
　　See Kuskin, Karla
Charles, Nicholas J.
　　See Kuskin, Karla
Charles, Norma 153
Charles, Veronika Martenova 182
Charlip, Remy 1929- 119
　　Earlier sketches in SATA 4, 68
　　See also CLR 8
Charlot, Jean 1898-1979 8
　　Obituary 31
Charlot, Martin 1944- 64
Charlot, Martin Day
　　See Charlot, Martin
Charlton, Michael (Alan) 1923- 34
Charlton-Trujillo, e.E. 189
Charmatz, Bill 1925-2005 7
Charnas, Suzy McKee 1939- 110
　　Earlier sketch in SATA 61
Charosh, Mannis 1906- 5
Chartier, Normand L. 1945- 66
Chase, Alice
　　See McHargue, Georgess
Chase, Alyssa 1965- 92
Chase, Andra 1942- 91
Chase, Emily
　　See Aks, Patricia
　　and Garwood, Julie
　　and Sachs, Judith
　　and White, Carol
Chase, Mary (Coyle) 1907-1981 17
　　Obituary 29
Chase, Mary Ellen 1887-1973 10
Chase, Paula 214
Chase, Richard 1904-1988 64
　　Obituary 56
Chase, Samantha
　　See Glick, Ruth (Burtnick)
Chast, Roz 1954- 212
　　Earlier sketch in SATA 97
Chastain, Madye Lee 1908-1989 4
Chataway, Carol 1955- 140
Chatterjee, Debjani 1952- 83
Chauncy, Nan(cen Beryl Masterman)
　　1900-1970 6
　　See also CLR 6
Chaundler, Christine 1887-1972 1
　　Obituary 25
Chayka, Doug 196
Chbosky, Stephen 1972- 164
Cheaney, Janie B.
　　See Cheaney, J.B.
Cheaney, J.B. 1950- 188
Chee, Cheng-Khee 1934- 79
Cheese, Chloe 1952- 118
Chekhonte, Antosha
　　See Chekhov, Anton
Chekhov, Anton 1860-1904 90
Chekhov, Anton Pavlovich
　　See Chekhov, Anton
Chelushkin, Kirill 1968- 186
Chen, Anthony 1929- 6
Chen, Chih-Yuan 1975- 216
　　Earlier sketch in SATA 155
Chen, Ju-Hong 1941- 78
Chen, Pauline 1966- 202
Chen, Sara
　　See Odgers, Sally Farrell
Chen, Tony
　　See Chen, Anthony
Chen, Yong 1963- 183
Chen, Yuan-tsung 1932- 65
Chen, Zhiyuan
　　See Chen, Chih-Yuan
Chenault, Nell
　　See Smith, Linell Nash
Chen Chih-Yuan
　　See Chen, Chih-Yuan
Chenery, Janet (Dai) 1923- 25

Cheney, Cora 1916-1999 .... *3*
   Obituary *110*
Cheney, Glenn (Alan) 1951- *99*
Cheney, Lynne V. 1941- *152*
Cheney, Lynne Vincent
   See Cheney, Lynne V.
Cheney, Ted
   See Cheney, Theodore Albert
Cheney, Theodore A. Rees
   See Cheney, Theodore Albert
Cheney, Theodore Albert 1928- *11*
Cheng, Andrea 1957- *205*
   Earlier sketches in SATA *128, 172*
Cheng, Christopher 1959- *173*
   Earlier sketch in SATA *106*
Cheng, Judith 1955- *36*
Cheng, Shan
   See Jiang, Cheng An
Cheripko, Jan 1951- *155*
   Earlier sketch in SATA *83*
Chermayeff, Ivan 1932- *47*
Chernenko, Dan
   See Turtledove, Harry
Chernoff, Dorothy A.
   See Ernst, (Lyman) John
Chernoff, Goldie Taub 1909- *10*
Cherry, Carolyn Janice
   See Cherryh, C.J.
Cherry, Lynne 1952- *99*
   Earlier sketch in SATA *34*
Cherryh, C.J. 1942- *172*
   Earlier sketch in SATA *93*
Cherryholmes, Anne
   See Price, Olive
Cheshire, Simon *172*
Chesler, Bernice 1932-2002 .... *59*
Chess, Victoria (Dickerson) 1939- *92*
   Earlier sketch in SATA *33*
Chessa, Francesca *191*
Chester, Deborah 1957- *85*
Chester, Kate
   See Guccione, Leslie Davis
Chesterton, G. K. 1874-1936 .... *27*
Chesterton, Gilbert Keith
   See Chesterton, G. K.
Chesworth, Michael *207*
   Earlier sketch in SATA *160*
Chetin, Helen 1922- *6*
Chetwin, Grace *86*
   Brief entry *50*
Chevalier, Christa 1937- *35*
Chevalier, Tracy 1962- *128*
Chew, Ruth 1920-2010 .... *7*
Chichester Clark, Emma 1955- *209*
   Earlier sketches in SATA *117, 156, 69*
Chidsey, Donald Barr 1902-1981 .... *3*
   Obituary *27*
Chiefari, Janet D. 1942- *58*
Chien, Catia *193*
Chien-min, Lin
   See Rumford, James
Child, L. Maria
   See Child, Lydia Maria
Child, Lauren 1965- *183*
   Earlier sketches in SATA *119, 160*
Child, Lincoln 1957- *113*
Child, Lincoln B.
   See Child, Lincoln
Child, Lydia Maria 1802-1880 .... *67*
Child, Mrs.
   See Child, Lydia Maria
Child, Philip 1898-1978 .... *47*
Children's Shepherd, The
   See Westphal, Arnold Carl
Childress, Alice 1920-1994 .... *81*
   Earlier sketches in SATA *7, 48*
   See also CLR *14*
Childs, H(alla) Fay (Cochrane) 1890-1971 .... *1*
   Obituary *25*
Chilton, Charles (Frederick William)
   1917- *102*

Chima, Cinda Williams *192*
Chimaera
   See Farjeon, Eleanor
Chin, Jason 1978- *218*
Chin, Richard (M.) 1946- *52*
Chinery, Michael 1938- *26*
Chin-Lee, Cynthia 1958- *102*
Chin-Lee D., Cynthia
   See Chin-Lee, Cynthia
Chippendale, Lisa A. *158*
Chipperfield, Joseph Eugene 1912-1980(?) .. *87*
   Earlier sketch in SATA *2*
Chisholm, P. F.
   See Finney, Patricia
Chislett, Gail (Elaine) 1948- *58*
Chittenden, Elizabeth F. 1903-1999 .... *9*
Chittenden, Margaret 1935- *28*
Chittum, Ida 1918- *7*
Chitwood, Suzanne Tanner 1958- *160*
Chmielarz, Sharon Lee 1940- *72*
Choate, Judith (Newkirk) 1940- *30*
Chocolate, Debbi 1954- *223*
   Earlier sketch in SATA *96*
Chocolate, Deborah H. Newton
   See Chocolate, Debbi
Chodos-Irvine, Margaret *211*
   Earlier sketch in SATA *152*
Choi, Sook Nyul 1937- *73*
   Autobiography Feature *126*
   See also CLR *53*
Choi, Yangsook *178*
Choksi, Nishant 1975- *222*
Choldenko, Gennifer 1957- *182*
   Earlier sketch in SATA *135*
Chorao, Kay 1936- *215*
Chorao, (Ann Mc)Kay (Sproat) 1936- *162*
   Earlier sketches in SATA *8, 69*
Choron, Sandra (Zena Samelson) 1950- *146*
Choung, Eun-hee *199*
Chown, Marcus 1959- *137*
Choyce, Lesley 1951- *165*
   Earlier sketch in SATA *94*
Choyce, Lesley Willis
   See Choyce, Lesley
Chrisman, Arthur Bowie 1889-1953 .... *124*
   See also YABC *1*
Christelow, Eileen 1943- *184*
   Autobiography Feature *120*
   Brief entry *35*
   Earlier sketches in SATA *38, 90*
Christensen, Bonnie 1951- *213*
   Earlier sketches in SATA *110, 157*
Christensen, Gardell Dano 1907-1991 .... *1*
Christensen, Laurie
   See Steding, Laurie
Christesen, Barbara 1940- *40*
Christgau, Alice Erickson 1902-1977 .... *13*
Christian, Mary Blount 1933- *9*
Christiana, David *195*
Christie, Agatha 1890-1976 .... *36*
Christie, Agatha Mary Clarissa
   See Christie, Agatha
Christie, Ann Philippa
   See Pearce, Philippa
Christie, Gregory
   See Christie, R. Gregory
Christie, Philippa
   See Pearce, Philippa
Christie, R. Gregory 1971- *185*
   Earlier sketch in SATA *127*
Christopher, John
   See Youd, Samuel
Christopher, Louise
   See Hale, Arlene
Christopher, Matt(hew Frederick)
   1917-1997 .... *80*
   Obituary *99*
   Earlier sketches in SATA *2, 47*
   See also CLR *119*
   See also SAAS *9*
Christopher, Milbourne 1914(?)-1984 .... *46*

Christy, Howard Chandler 1873-1952 .... *21*
Chrustowski, Rick *176*
Chrystie, Frances N(icholson) 1904-1986 .... *60*
Chu, Daniel 1933- *11*
Chukovsky, Kornei (Ivanovich) 1882-1969 . *34*
   Earlier sketch in SATA *5*
Church, Caroline Jayne *219*
   Earlier sketch in SATA *179*
Church, Richard 1893-1972 .... *3*
Churchill, E(lmer) Richard 1937- *11*
Churchill, Elizabeth
   See Hough, Richard (Alexander)
Chute, B(eatrice) J(oy) 1913-1987 .... *2*
   Obituary *53*
Chute, Marchette (Gaylord) 1909-1994 .... *1*
Chwast, Jacqueline 1932- *6*
Chwast, Seymour 1931- *146*
   Earlier sketches in SATA *18, 96*
Ciardi, John (Anthony) 1916-1986 .... *65*
   Obituary *46*
   Earlier sketch in SATA *1*
   See also CLR *19*
   See also SAAS *26*
Ciccone, Madonna Louise Veronica
   See Madonna
Ciddor, Anna 1957- *213*
Ciment, James D. 1958- *140*
Cirrone, Dorian *182*
Cisneros, Sandra 1954-
   See CLR *123*
Citra, Becky 1954- *137*
Citrin, Michael 1965(?)- *183*
Claflin, Willy 1944- *208*
Clair, Andree *19*
Clampett, Bob 1914(?)-1985 .... *44*
   Obituary *38*
Clampett, Robert
   See Clampett, Bob
Clapp, John 1968- *109*
Clapp, Patricia 1912- *74*
   Earlier sketch in SATA *4*
   See also SAAS *4*
Clare, Ellen
   See Sinclair, Olga
Clare, Helen
   See Clarke, Pauline
Claremont, Chris 1950- *87*
Claremont, Christopher Simon
   See Claremont, Chris
Clark, Ann Nolan 1896-1995 .... *82*
   Obituary *87*
   Earlier sketch in SATA *4*
   See also CLR *16*
   See also SAAS *16*
Clark, Champ 1923-2002 .... *47*
Clark, Christopher (Anthony) Stuart
   See Stuart-Clark, Christopher (Anthony)
Clark, Clara Gillow 1951- *154*
   Earlier sketch in SATA *84*
Clark, David
   See Hardcastle, Michael
Clark, David Allen
   See Ernst, (Lyman) John
Clark, Emma Chichester
   See Chichester Clark, Emma
Clark, Frank J(ames) 1922- *18*
Clark, Garel
   See Garelick, May
Clark, Halsey
   See Deming, Richard
Clark, Joan
   See Benson, Mildred
Clark, Joan 1934- *182*
   Earlier sketches in SATA *59, 96*
Clark, Leonard 1905-1981 .... *30*
   Obituary *29*
Clark, M. R.
   See Clark, Mavis Thorpe
Clark, Margaret (D.) 1943- *126*
Clark, Margaret Goff 1913- *82*
   Earlier sketch in SATA *8*

Clark, Mary Higgins 1929- *46*
Clark, Mavis Thorpe 1909-1999 .... *74*
  Earlier sketch in SATA *8*
  See also CLR *30*
  See also SAAS *5*
Clark, Merle
  See Gessner, Lynne
Clark, Patricia Denise 1921- *117*
Clark, Patricia Finrow 1929- *11*
Clark, Ronald Harry 1904-1999 .... *193*
Clark, Ronald William 1916-1987 .... *2*
  Obituary *52*
Clark, Sherryl 1956- *149*
Clark, Van D(eusen) 1909-1974 .... *2*
Clark, Virginia
  See Gray, Patricia (Clark)
Clark, Walter Van Tilburg 1909-1971 .... *8*
Clarke, Arthur
  See Clarke, Arthur C.
Clarke, Arthur C. 1917-2008 .... *115*
  Obituary *191*
  Earlier sketches in SATA *13, 70*
  See also CLR *119*
Clarke, Arthur Charles
  See Clarke, Arthur C.
Clarke, Clorinda 1917- *7*
Clarke, Elizabeth L. 1934- *103*
Clarke, Greg 1959- *215*
Clarke, Gus 1948- *134*
Clarke, J.
  See Clarke, Judith
Clarke, James Hall
  See Rowland-Entwistle, (Arthur) Theodore
  (Henry)
Clarke, Joan B. 1921- *42*
  Brief entry *27*
Clarke, John
  See Laklan, Carli
  and Sontup, Dan(iel)
Clarke, Judith 1943- *164*
  Earlier sketches in SATA *75, 110*
  See also CLR *61*
Clarke, Julia 1950- *138*
Clarke, Kenneth 1957- *107*
Clarke, Lea
  See Rowland-Entwistle, (Arthur) Theodore
  (Henry)
Clarke, Margaret 1941-
  See CLR *99*
Clarke, Mary Stetson 1911-1994 .... *5*
Clarke, Michael
  See Newlon, (Frank) Clarke
Clarke, Pauline 1921- *131*
  Earlier sketch in SATA *3*
  See also CLR *28*
Clarkson, E(dith) Margaret 1915- *37*
Clarkson, Ewan 1929- *9*
Claudia, Susan
  See Goulart, Ron
  and Johnston, William
Claverie, Jean 1946- *38*
Clay, Patrice 1947- *47*
Clay, Wil *203*
Clayman, Deborah Paula
  See Da Costa, Deborah
Claypool, Jane
  See Miner, Jane Claypool
Clayton, Elaine 1961- *209*
  Earlier sketches in SATA *94, 159*
Clayton, Lawrence (Otto, Jr.) 1945- *75*
Clayton, Sally Pomme *218*
Clayton, Sandra 1951- *110*
Cle, Troy *202*
Clea, Super
  See Hantman, Clea
Cleary, Beverly 1916- *121*
  Earlier sketches in SATA *2, 43, 79*
  See also CLR *72*
  See also SAAS *20*
Cleary, Beverly Atlee Bunn
  See Cleary, Beverly

Cleary, Brian P. 1959- *186*
  Earlier sketches in SATA *93, 132*
Cleaver, Bill
  See Cleaver, William J.
Cleaver, Carole 1934- *6*
Cleaver, Elizabeth (Ann Mrazik)
  1939-1985 .... *23*
  Obituary *43*
  See also CLR *13*
Cleaver, Hylton Reginald 1891-1961 .... *49*
Cleaver, Vera 1919-1993 .... *76*
  Earlier sketch in SATA *22*
  See also CLR *6*
Cleaver, Vera Allen
  See Cleaver, Vera
Cleaver, William J. 1920-1981 .... *22*
  Obituary *27*
  See also CLR *6*
Cleishbotham, Jebediah
  See Scott, Sir Walter
Cleland, Mabel
  See Widdemer, Mabel Cleland
Clem, Margaret H(ollingsworth) 1923- *90*
Clemens, James
  See Rollins, James
Clemens, Samuel
  See Twain, Mark
Clemens, Samuel Langhorne
  See Twain, Mark
Clemens, Virginia Phelps 1941- *35*
Clement, Gary *191*
Clement, Janet *182*
Clement, Nathan 1966- *200*
Clement, Priscilla Ferguson 1942- *171*
Clement, Rod *97*
Clement-Moore, Rosemary *188*
Clements, Andrew 1949- *203*
  Earlier sketches in SATA *104, 158*
Clements, Bruce 1931- *178*
  Earlier sketches in SATA *27, 94*
Clemesha, David *192*
Cleminson, Katie *221*
Clemons, Elizabeth
  See Nowell, Elizabeth Cameron
Clerk, N. W.
  See Lewis, C. S.
Cleveland, Bob
  See Cleveland, George
Cleveland, George 1903(?)-1985
  Obituary *43*
Cleveland-Peck, Patricia *80*
Cleven, Cathrine
  See Cleven, Kathryn Seward
Cleven, Kathryn Seward *2*
Clevenger, William R. 1954- *84*
Clevenger, William Russell
  See Clevenger, William R.
Clevin, Joergen 1920- *7*
Clevin, Jorgen
  See Clevin, Joergen
Clewes, Dorothy (Mary) 1907-2003 .... *86*
  Obituary *138*
  Earlier sketch in SATA *1*
Clifford, David
  See Rosenberg, Eth Clifford
Clifford, Eth
  See Rosenberg, Eth Clifford
Clifford, Harold B(urton) 1893-1988 .... *10*
Clifford, Margaret Cort 1929- *1*
Clifford, Martin
  See Hamilton, Charles (Harold St. John)
Clifford, Mary Louise Beneway 1926- *23*
Clifford, Peggy
  See Clifford, Margaret Cort
Clifford, Rachel Mark
  See Lewis, Brenda Ralph
Clifton, Lucille 1936-2010 .... *128*
  Earlier sketches in SATA *20, 69*
  See also CLR *5*
Clifton, Thelma Lucille
  See Clifton, Lucille

Climo, Shirley 1928- *166*
  Autobiography Feature *110*
  Brief entry *35*
  Earlier sketches in SATA *39, 77*
  See also CLR *69*
Cline-Ransome, Lesa *201*
Clinton, Catherine 1952- *203*
Clinton, Cathryn 1957- *136*
Clinton, Dirk
  See Silverberg, Robert
Clinton, Jon
  See Prince, J(ack) H(arvey)
Clippinger, Carol *193*
Clish, (Lee) Marian 1946- *43*
Clive, Clifford
  See Hamilton, Charles (Harold St. John)
Clokey, Art 1921- *59*
Cloudsley-Thompson, J(ohn) L(eonard)
  1921- *19*
Clouse, Nancy L. 1938- *78*
Clover, Peter 1952- *215*
  Earlier sketch in SATA *152*
Clutha, Janet
  See Frame, Janet
Clutha, Janet Paterson Frame
  See Frame, Janet
Clymer, Eleanor 1906-2001 .... *85*
  Obituary *126*
  Earlier sketch in SATA *9*
  See also SAAS *17*
Clyne, Patricia (Edwards) *31*
Cneut, Carll 1969- *197*
Coalson, Glo 1946- *94*
  Earlier sketch in SATA *26*
Coates, Anna 1958- *73*
Coates, Belle 1896-1986 .... *2*
Coates, Ruth Allison 1915- *11*
Coats, Alice M(argaret) 1905-1976 .... *11*
Coatsworth, Elizabeth (Jane) 1893-1986 .... *100*
  Obituary *49*
  Earlier sketches in SATA *2, 56*
  See also CLR *2*
Cobalt, Martin
  See Mayne, William
Cobb, Jane
  See Berry, Jane Cobb
Cobb, Mary 1931- *88*
Cobb, Vicki 1938- *136*
  Autobiography Feature *136*
  Earlier sketches in SATA *8, 69, 131*
  See also CLR *2*
  See also SAAS *6*
Cobbett, Richard
  See Pluckrose, Henry (Arthur)
Cober, Alan E(dwin) 1935-1998 .... *7*
  Obituary *101*
Cobham, Sir Alan
  See Hamilton, Charles (Harold St. John)
Coburn, Jake 1978- *155*
Cocagnac, Augustin Maurice(-Jean) 1924- *7*
Cocca-Leffler, Maryann 1958- *194*
  Earlier sketches in SATA *80, 136*
Cochran, Bill *187*
Cochran, Bobbye A. 1949- *11*
Cochran, Josh *221*
Cochran, Thomas 1955- *198*
Cochrane, Hamilton E.
  See Cochrane, Mick
Cochrane, Mick 1956- *215*
Cockcroft, Jason *217*
Cockett, Mary *3*
Cocks, Peter *204*
Cocovini, Abby *202*
Coddell, Esme Raji
  See Codell, Esme Raji
Codell, Esme Raji 1968- *160*
Cody, C. S.
  See Waller, Leslie
Cody, Jess
  See Cunningham, Chet
Coe, Anne (E.) 1949- *95*

Coe, Douglas
  See Epstein, Beryl
  and Epstein, Samuel
Coe, Lloyd 1899(?)-1976
  Obituary *30*
Coen, Rena Neumann 1925- *20*
Coerr, Eleanor (Beatrice) 1922- *67*
  Earlier sketch in SATA *1*
Cofer, Judith Ortiz 1952- *164*
  Earlier sketch in SATA *110*
Coffelt, Nancy 1961- *189*
Coffey, Brian
  See Koontz, Dean
Coffin, Geoffrey
  See Mason, F(rancis) van Wyck
Coffin, M. T.
  See Stanley, George Edward
Coffman, Ramon Peyton 1896-1989 .... *4*
Cogan, Karen 1954- *125*
Coggins, Jack (Banham) 1911-2006 .... *2*
Cohen, Barbara 1932-1992 .... *77*
  Obituary *74*
  Earlier sketch in SATA *10*
  See also SAAS *7*
Cohen, Daniel (E.) 1936- *70*
  Earlier sketch in SATA *8*
  See also CLR *43*
  See also SAAS *4*
Cohen, Deborah Bodin 1968- *180*
Cohen, Jan Barger
  See Barger, Jan
Cohen, Jene Barr
  See Barr, Jene
Cohen, Joan Lebold 1932- *4*
Cohen, Judith Love 1933- *78*
Cohen, Miriam 1926-1955 .... *155*
  Earlier sketches in SATA *29, 106*
  See also SAAS *11*
Cohen, Nora *75*
Cohen, Paul 1945- *58*
Cohen, Paul S.
  See Cohen, Paul
Cohen, Peter Zachary 1931- *150*
  Earlier sketch in SATA *4*
Cohen, Robert Carl 1930- *8*
Cohen, Santiago 1954- *215*
Cohen, Sholom 1951- *94*
Cohn, Angelo 1914-1997 .... *19*
Cohn, Diana *194*
Cohn, Rachel 1968- *161*
Coit, Margaret Louise 1922-2003 .... *2*
  Obituary *142*
Colasanti, Susane 1973- *214*
Colato Lainez, Rene 1970- *176*
Colbert, Anthony 1934-2007 .... *15*
Colbert, Nancy A. 1936- *139*
Colby, C(arroll) B(urleigh) 1904-1977 .... *35*
  Earlier sketch in SATA *3*
Colby, Jean Poindexter 1909-1993 .... *23*
Cole, Annette
  See Steiner, Barbara A(nnette)
Cole, Babette 1949- *155*
  Earlier sketches in SATA *61, 96*
Cole, Betsy 1940- *83*
Cole, Brock 1938- *200*
  Earlier sketches in SATA *72, 136*
  See also CLR *18*
Cole, Davis
  See Elting, Mary
Cole, Hannah 1954- *74*
Cole, Henry 1955- *213*
  Earlier sketch in SATA *181*
Cole, Jack -1974
  See Stewart, John
Cole, Jackson
  See Curry, Thomas Albert
  and Germano, Peter B.
  and Heckelmann, Charles N(ewman)
  and Newton, D(wight) B(ennett)
  and Schisgall, Oscar

Cole, Jennifer
  See Zach, Cheryl (Byrd)
Cole, Joanna 1944- *168*
  Brief entry *37*
  Earlier sketches in SATA *49, 81, 120*
  See also CLR *40*
Cole, Lois Dwight 1903-1979 .... *10*
  Obituary *26*
Cole, Michael 1947- *59*
Cole, Samantha
  See Cole, Stephen
Cole, Sheila 1939- *171*
  Earlier sketches in SATA *24, 95*
Cole, Sheila R.
  See Cole, Sheila
Cole, Sheila Rotenberg
  See Cole, Sheila
Cole, Stephen 1971- *161*
Cole, William (Rossa) 1919-2000 .... *71*
  Earlier sketch in SATA *9*
  See also SAAS *9*
Coleman, Andrew
  See Pine, Nicholas
Coleman, Clare
  See Bell, Clare (Louise)
  and Easton, M(alcolm) Coleman
Coleman, Janet Wyman *184*
Coleman, Loren 1947- *164*
Coleman, Loren Elwood, Jr.
  See Coleman, Loren
Coleman, Mary Ann 1928- *83*
Coleman, Michael
  See Jones, Allan Frewin
Coleman, Michael 1946- *199*
  Autobiography Feature *133*
  Earlier sketches in SATA *108, 133*
Coleman, Rowan *187*
Coleman, William L(eRoy) 1938- *49*
  Brief entry *34*
Coleman, Wim 1926- *212*
Coles, Robert (Martin) 1929- *23*
Colfer, Eoin 1965- *197*
  Earlier sketch in SATA *148*
  See also CLR *112*
Colin, Ann
  See Ure, Jean
Collard, Sneed B. III 1959- *184*
  Earlier sketches in SATA *84, 139*
Colledge, Anne 1939- *142*
Colley, Jacqui 1965- *202*
Collicott, Sharleen 1937- *143*
  Earlier sketch in SATA *98*
Collier, Bryan *204*
  Earlier sketches in SATA *126, 174*
Collier, Christopher 1930- *70*
  Earlier sketch in SATA *16*
  See also CLR *126*
Collier, Ethel 1903-1999 .... *22*
Collier, James Lincoln 1928- *166*
  Earlier sketches in SATA *8, 70*
  See also CLR *126*
  See also SAAS *21*
Collier, Jane
  See Collier, Zena
Collier, Kristi *182*
Collier, Steven 1942- *61*
Collier, Zena 1926- *23*
Collings, Gillian 1939- *102*
Collington, Peter 1948- *99*
  Earlier sketch in SATA *59*
Collins, Ace 1953- *82*
Collins, Andrew J.
  See Collins, Ace
Collins, B. R. 1981- *214*
Collins, David R(aymond) 1940-2001 .... *121*
  Earlier sketch in SATA *7*
Collins, Heather 1946- *81*
Collins, Hunt
  See Hunter, Evan
Collins, Michael
  See Lynds, Dennis

Collins, Michael 1930- *58*
Collins, Pat Lowery 1932- *217*
  Earlier sketches in SATA *31, 151*
Collins, Paul 1954- *126*
Collins, Ross 1972- *200*
Collins, Ruth Philpott 1890-1975
  Obituary *30*
Collins, Suzanne *180*
Collins, Yvonne *194*
Collinson, A. S.
  See Collinson, Alan S.
Collinson, Alan S. 1934- *80*
Collinson, Roger (Alfred) 1936- *133*
Collison, Linda 1953- *185*
Collodi, Carlo 1826-1890 .... *100*
  Earlier sketch in SATA *29*
  See also CLR *120*
Colloms, Brenda 1919- *40*
Colman, Hila 1909-2008 .... *53*
  Earlier sketch in SATA *1*
  See also SAAS *14*
Colman, Morris 1899(?)-1981
  Obituary *25*
Colman, Penny (Morgan) 1944- *160*
  Autobiography Feature *160*
  Earlier sketches in SATA *77, 114*
Colman, Warren (David) 1944- *67*
Coloma, Cindy
  See Martinusen-Coloma, Cindy
Colombo, John Robert 1936- *50*
Colon, Raul *156*
Colon, Raul 1952- *202*
Colonius, Lillian 1911-1992 .... *3*
Colorado, Antonio J.
  See Colorado (Capella), Antonio J(ulio)
Colorado (Capella), Antonio J(ulio)
  1903-1994 .... *23*
  Obituary *79*
Colquhoun, Glenn 1964- *165*
Colston, Fifi E. 1960- *150*
Colt, Martin
  See Epstein, Beryl
  and Epstein, Samuel
Colum, Padraic 1881-1972 .... *15*
  See also CLR *36*
Columbus, Chris 1959- *97*
Columbus, Christopher
  See Columbus, Chris
Columella
  See Moore, Clement Clarke
Colver, Anne 1908- *7*
Colvin, James
  See Moorcock, Michael
Colwell, Eileen (Hilda) 1904-2002 .... *2*
Colwyn, Stewart
  See Pepper, Frank S.
Coman, Carolyn 1951- *197*
  Earlier sketch in SATA *127*
Combs, Lisa M.
  See McCourt, Lisa
Combs, Robert
  See Murray, John
Comfort, Jane Levington
  See Sturtzel, Jane Levington
Comfort, Mildred Houghton 1886-1976 .... *3*
Comins, Ethel M(ae) *11*
Comins, Jeremy 1933- *28*
Commager, Henry Steele 1902-1998 .... *23*
  Obituary *102*
Comora, Madeleine *190*
Compere, Mickie
  See Davidson, Margaret
Compestine, Ying Chang 1963- *187*
  Earlier sketch in SATA *140*
Comport, Sally Wern *190*
Compton, Patricia A. 1936- *75*
Comte, The Great
  See Hawkesworth, Eric
Comus
  See Ballantyne, R(obert) M(ichael)

Comyns, Nance
  See Comyns-Toohey, Nantz
Comyns-Toohey, Nantz 1956- 86
Conahan, Carolyn
  See Conahan, Carolyn Digby
Conahan, Carolyn Digby 1961- 216
Conan Doyle, Arthur
  See Doyle, Sir Arthur Conan
Condie, Ally 204
Condie, Allyson B.
  See Condie, Ally
Condit, Martha Olson 1913- 28
Condon, Bill 1949- 142
Condon, Judith 83
Condon, Ken 195
Condy, Roy 1942- 96
Cone, Ferne Geller 1921- 39
Cone, Molly (Lamken) 1918- 151
  Autobiography Feature 151
  Earlier sketches in SATA *1, 28, 115*
  See also SAAS *11*
Cone, Patrick 1954- 89
Coney, Michael G. 1932-2005 61
  Obituary 170
Coney, Michael Greatrex
  See Coney, Michael G.
Coney, Mike
  See Coney, Michael G.
Conford, Ellen 1942- 162
  Earlier sketches in SATA *6, 68, 110*
  See also CLR *71*
Conger, Lesley
  See Suttles, Shirley (Smith)
Conklin, Gladys Plemon 1903- 2
Conklin, Paul S. 1929(?)-2003 43
  Brief entry 33
  Obituary 147
Conkling, Hilda 1910-1986 23
Conlan, Kathleen Elizabeth 1950- 145
Conlan, Kathy
  See Conlan, Kathleen Elizabeth
Conley, Robyn 1963- 125
Conley-Weaver, Robyn
  See Conley, Robyn
Conlon-McKenna, Marita 1956- 71
Conly, Jane Leslie 1948- 164
  Earlier sketches in SATA *80, 112*
Conly, Robert Leslie 1918(?)-1973 23
  See also CLR *2*
Connell, Kirk
  See Chapman, John Stanton Higham
Connell, Tom 206
Connelly, Gwen 1952- 212
Connelly, Marc(us Cook) 1890-1980
  Obituary 25
Connolly, Jerome P(atrick) 1931- 8
Connolly, Pat 1943- 74
Connolly, Peter 1935- 105
  Earlier sketch in SATA *47*
Conover, Chris 1950- 213
  Earlier sketch in SATA *31*
Conquest, Owen
  See Hamilton, Charles (Harold St. John)
Conrad, Joseph 1857-1924 27
Conrad, Pam 1947-1996 133
  Brief entry 49
  Obituary 90
  Earlier sketches in SATA *52, 80*
  See also CLR *18*
  See also SAAS *19*
Conroy, Jack
  See Conroy, John Wesley
Conroy, John Wesley 1899-1990 19
  Obituary 65
Conroy, Robert
  See Goldston, Robert (Conroy)
Constable, Kate 1966- 172
Constant, Alberta Wilson 1908-1981 22
  Obituary 28
Constantin, Pascale 185
Conway, Celeste 210

Conway, David 1970- 213
Conway, Diana C. 1943- 91
Conway, Diana Cohen
  See Conway, Diana C.
Conway, Gordon
  See Hamilton, Charles (Harold St. John)
Cook, Ande 192
Cook, Bernadine 1924- 11
Cook, Fred J(ames) 1911-2003 2
  Obituary 145
Cook, Glen 1944- 171
  Earlier sketch in SATA *108*
Cook, Glen Charles
  See Cook, Glen
Cook, Hugh 1956- 85
Cook, Hugh, Walter Gilbert
  See Cook, Hugh
Cook, Jean Thor 1930- 94
Cook, Joel 1934- 79
Cook, Joseph Jay 1924- 8
Cook, Lisa Broadie 157
Cook, Lyn
  See Waddell, Evelyn Margaret
Cook, Roy
  See Silverberg, Robert
Cook, Sally 207
Cook, Trish 175
Cooke, Ann
  See Cole, Joanna
Cooke, Arthur
  See Lowndes, Robert A(ugustine) W(ard)
Cooke, Barbara
  See Alexander, Anna B(arbara Cooke)
Cooke, David Coxe 1917- 2
Cooke, Donald Ewin 1916-1985 2
  Obituary 45
Cooke, Frank E. 1920- 87
Cooke, Jean (Isobel Esther) 1929- 74
Cooke, John Estes
  See Baum, L. Frank
Cooke, Trish 1962- 129
Cookson, Catherine (McMullen) 1906-1998 .. 9
  Obituary 116
Cooley, Beth 210
Cooley, Elizabeth
  See Cooley, Beth
Cooley, Regina Francoise 1940- 177
Coolidge, Olivia E(nsor) 1908- 26
  Earlier sketch in SATA *1*
Cooling, Wendy 169
  Earlier sketch in SATA *111*
Coombs, Charles I(ra) 1914-1994 43
  Earlier sketch in SATA *3*
  See also SAAS *15*
Coombs, Chick
  See Coombs, Charles I(ra)
Coombs, Jonathan 204
Coombs, Kate 190
Coombs, Patricia 1926- 51
  Earlier sketch in SATA *3*
  See also SAAS *22*
Cooney, Barbara 1917-2000 96
  Obituary 123
  Earlier sketches in SATA *6, 59*
  See also CLR *23*
Cooney, Caroline B. 1947- 218
  Brief entry 41
  Earlier sketches in SATA *48, 80, 113, 130,*
  179
Cooney, Doug 181
Cooney, Nancy Evans 1932- 42
Coontz, Otto 1946- 33
Cooper, Ann (Catharine) 1939- 104
Cooper, Dutch
  See Kuyper, Sjoerd
Cooper, Elisha 1971- 157
  Earlier sketch in SATA *99*
Cooper, Elizabeth Keyser -1992 47
Cooper, Floyd 187
  Earlier sketches in SATA *96, 144*
  See also CLR *60*

Cooper, Gordon 1932- 23
Cooper, Helen 1963- 169
  Earlier sketch in SATA *102*
Cooper, Henry S. F., Jr. 1933- 65
Cooper, Henry Spotswood Fenimore, Jr.
  See Cooper, Henry S. F., Jr.
Cooper, Ilene 1948- 145
  Earlier sketches in SATA *66, 97*
Cooper, James Fenimore 1789-1851 19
  See also CLR *105*
Cooper, John R. 1
Cooper, Kay 1941- 11
Cooper, Lee Pelham 1926- 5
Cooper, Lester (Irving) 1919-1985 32
  Obituary 43
Cooper, Lettice (Ulpha) 1897-1994 35
  Obituary 82
Cooper, Louise 1952-2009 152
Cooper, M.E.
  See Davis, Maggie S.
Cooper, M.E.
  See Lerangis, Peter
Cooper, Melrose
  See Kroll, Virginia L.
Cooper, Michael L. 1950- 181
  Earlier sketches in SATA *79, 117*
Cooper, Patrick 1949- 134
Cooper, Susan 1935- 151
  Earlier sketches in SATA *4, 64, 104*
  See also CLR *161*
  See also SAAS *6*
Cooper, Susan Mary
  See Cooper, Susan
Cope, Jane U(rsula) 1949- 108
Copeland, Helen 1920- 4
Copeland, Mark 1956- 180
Copeland, Paul W. 23
Coplans, Peta 1951- 84
Copley (Diana) Heather Pickering 1918- 45
Coppard, A(lfred) E(dgar) 1878-1957
  See YABC *1*
Copper, Melinda 1952- 172
Copper, Melinda McConnaughey
  See Copper, Melinda
Corace, Jen 208
Coralie
  See Anderson, Catherine Corley
Corbett, Grahame 43
  Brief entry 36
Corbett, Scott 1913- 42
  Earlier sketch in SATA *2*
  See also CLR *1*
  See also SAAS *2*
Corbett, Sue 174
Corbett, W(illiam) J(esse) 1938- 102
  Brief entry 44
  Earlier sketch in SATA *50*
  See also CLR *19*
Corbin, Sabra Lee
  See Malvern, Gladys
Corbin, William
  See McGraw, William Corbin
Corbman, Marjorie 1987- 179
Corby, Dan
  See Catherall, Arthur
Corcoran, Barbara (Asenath) 1911-2003 77
  Autobiography Feature 125
  Earlier sketch in SATA *3*
  See also CLR *50*
  See also SAAS *20*
Corcos, Lucille 1908-1973 10
Cordell, Alexander
  See Graber, Alexander
Cordell, Matthew 1975- 199
Corder, Zizou
  See Young, Louisa
Corella, Joseph
  See Odgers, Sally Farrell
Coren, Alan 1938-2007 32
  Obituary 187
Corey, Dorothy 23

Corey, Shana 1974- 219
Earlier sketch in SATA 133
Corfe, Thomas Howell 1928- 27
Corfe, Tom
See Corfe, Thomas Howell
Corfield, Robin Bell 1952- 74
Corke, Estelle 1969- 220
Corlett, William 1938-2005 46
Brief entry 39
Cormack, M(argaret) Grant 1913- 11
Cormack, Maribelle B. 1902-1984 39
Cormier, Robert 1925-2000 83
Obituary 122
Earlier sketches in SATA 10, 45
See also CLR 55
Cormier, Robert Edmund
See Cormier, Robert
Cornelius, Carol 1942- 40
Cornelius, Kay 1933- 157
Cornell, J.
See Cornell, Jeffrey
Cornell, James (Clayton, Jr.) 1938- 27
Cornell, Jean Gay 1920- 23
Cornell, Jeffrey 1945- 11
Cornell, Laura 189
Cornish, D.M. 1972- 185
Cornish, Sam(uel James) 1935- 23
Cornwall, Nellie
See Sloggett, Nellie
Cornwell, Autumn 195
Corr, Christopher 1955- 189
Correy, Lee
See Stine, G(eorge) Harry
Corrick, James A. 1945- 76
Corrigan, (Helen) Adeline 1909- 23
Corrigan, Barbara 1922- 8
Corrigan, Eireann 1977- 163
Corrin, Sara 1918- 86
Brief entry 48
Corrin, Stephen 86
Brief entry 48
Corsi, Wendy
See Staub, Wendy Corsi
Cort, M. C.
See Clifford, Margaret Cort
Cort, Margaret
See Clifford, Margaret Cort
Corwin, Judith H(offman) 1946- 10
Corwin, Oliver
See Corwin, Oliver J.
Corwin, Oliver J. 206
Cory, Rowena
See Lindquist, Rowena Cory
Cosby, Bill 1937- 110
Earlier sketch in SATA 66
Cosby, William Henry, Jr.
See Cosby, Bill
and Cosby, Bill
Cosentino, Ralph 169
Cosgrave, John O'Hara II 1908-1968
Obituary 21
Cosgrove, Margaret (Leota) 1926- 47
Cosgrove, Stephen E(dward) 1945- 53
Brief entry 40
Coskey, Evelyn 1932- 7
Cosner, Shaaron 1940- 43
Cossi, Olga 1921- 216
Earlier sketches in SATA 67, 102
Costabel, Eva Deutsch 1924- 45
Costabel-Deutsch, Eva
See Costabel, Eva Deutsch
Coste, Marion 1938- 183
Costello, David 174
Costello, David F(rancis) 1904-1990 23
Cte, Genevieve 1964- 184
Cote, Nancy 1952- 182
Cott, Jonathan 1942- 23
Cottam, Clarence 1899-1974 25
Cotten, Cynthia 188
Cottin, Menena 1950- 213
Cottle, Joan 1960- 135

Cottler, Joseph 1899-1996 22
Cottonwood, Joe 1947- 92
Cottrell, Leonard 1913-1974 24
Cottringer, Anne 1952- 150
Earlier sketch in SATA 97
Couch, Greg 199
Coulman, Valerie 1969- 161
Couloumbis, Audrey 173
Counsel, June 1926- 70
Countryman, The
See Whitlock, Ralph
Courlander, Harold 1908-1996 6
Obituary 88
Coursen, Valerie 1965(?)- 102
Courtis, Stuart Appleton 1874-1969
Obituary 29
Courtland, Tyler
See Stevens, Serita
Courtney, Dayle
See Goldsmith, Howard
Coury, Louise Andree 1895(?)-1983
Obituary 34
Cousins, Linda 1946- 90
Cousins, Lucy 1964- 205
Earlier sketch in SATA 172
Cousins, Margaret 1905-1996 2
Obituary 92
Cousteau, Jacques 1910-1997 98
Earlier sketch in SATA 38
Cousteau, Jacques-Yves
See Cousteau, Jacques
Couture, Christin 1951- 73
Couvillon, Jacques 195
Coverly, Dave 1964- 223
Covert, Ralph 1968- 197
Coville, Bruce 1950- 216
Autobiography Feature 155
Earlier sketches in SATA 32, 77, 118, 155
Covington, Dennis 109
Covington, Linda
See Windsor, Linda
Cowan, Catherine 121
Cowan, Rebecca M.
See Moesta, Rebecca
Cowan, Rebecca Moesta
See Moesta, Rebecca
Coward, Fiona 1963- 178
Cowdrey, Richard 1959- 204
Cowell, Cressida 1966- 140
Cowen, Eve
See Werner, Herma
Cowen, Ida 1898-1993 64
Cowie, Leonard W(allace) 1919- 4
Cowles, Kathleen
See Krull, Kathleen
Cowley, Cassia Joy
See Cowley, Joy
Cowley, Joy 1936- 164
Autobiography Feature 118
Earlier sketches in SATA 4, 90
See also CLR 55
See also SAAS 26
Cowley, Marjorie 1925- 111
Cox, (Christopher) Barry 1931- 62
Cox, Clinton 1934- 108
Earlier sketch in SATA 74
Cox, David 1933- 56
Cox, David Dundas
See Cox, David
Cox, Donald William 1921- 23
Cox, Jack
See Cox, John Roberts
Cox, John Roberts 1915-1981 9
Cox, Judy 1954- 198
Earlier sketches in SATA 117, 160
Cox, Marion Monroe 1898-1983
Obituary 34
Cox, Palmer 1840-1924 24
See also CLR 24
Cox, Vic 1942- 88
Cox, Vicki 1945- 158

Cox, Victoria 1945- 44
Cox, Wallace 1924-1973 25
Cox, Wally
See Cox, Wallace
Cox, William R(obert) 1901-1988 46
Brief entry 31
Obituary 57
Coxe, Molly 1959- 101
Earlier sketch in SATA 69
Coxon, Michele 1950- 158
Earlier sketch in SATA 76
Coy, Harold 1902-1986 3
Coy, John 1958- 171
Earlier sketch in SATA 120
Craats, Rennay 1973- 131
Crabtree, Judith 1928- 98
Earlier sketch in SATA 63
Crabtree, Julie 1970- 214
Cracker, Edward E.B.
See Odgers, Sally Farrell
Craft, Elizabeth 1971(?)- 204
Craft, K. Y.
See Craft, Kinuko Y.
Craft, Kinuko Y. 1940- 127
Earlier sketch in SATA 65
Craft, Kinuko Yamabe
See Craft, Kinuko Y.
Craft, Ruth 1935- 87
Brief entry 31
Craig, A. A.
See Anderson, Poul
Craig, Alisa
See MacLeod, Charlotte (Matilda)
Craig, David
See James, Bill
Craig, Helen 1934- 213
Earlier sketches in SATA 46, 49, 94
Craig, Joe 1979- 198
Craig, Joe Alexander
See Craig, Joe
Craig, John Eland
See Chipperfield, Joseph Eugene
Craig, John Ernest 1921- 23
Craig, Kit
See Reed, Kit
Craig, M. F.
See Craig, Mary (Francis) Shura
Craig, M. Jean 17
Craig, M. S.
See Craig, Mary (Francis) Shura
Craig, Margaret (Maze) 1911-1964 9
Craig, Mary
See Craig, Mary (Francis) Shura
Craig, Mary Shura
See Craig, Mary (Francis) Shura
Craig, Mary (Francis) Shura 1923-1991 86
Obituary 65
Earlier sketch in SATA 6
See also SAAS 7
Craig, Ruth 1922- 95
Craik, Mrs.
See Craik, Dinah Maria (Mulock)
Craik, Dinah Maria (Mulock) 1826-1887 34
Crandall, Court 1965- 175
Crandell, Rachel 1943- 152
Crane, Barbara (Joyce) 1934- 31
Crane, Caroline 1930- 11
Crane, Jordan 1973- 174
Crane, M. A.
See Wartski, Maureen (Ann Crane)
Crane, Royston Campbell 1901-1977
Obituary 22
Crane, Stephen 1871-1900
See YABC 2
See also CLR 132
Crane, Stephen Townley
See Crane, Stephen
Crane, Walter 1845-1915 100
Earlier sketch in SATA 18
See also CLR 56
Crane, William D(wight) 1892-1976 1

Author Index

Cranfield, Ingrid 1945- 74
Cranshaw, Stanley
  See Fisher, Dorothy (Frances) Canfield
Crary, Elizabeth (Ann) 1942- 99
  Brief entry 43
Crary, Margaret (Coleman) 1906-1986 9
Craste, Marc 201
Cravath, Lynne Avril
  See Cravath, Lynne W.
Cravath, Lynne W. 1951- 182
  Earlier sketches in SATA *98, 148*
Craven, Thomas 1889-1969 22
Crawford, Brent 1975- 220
Crawford, Charles P. 1945- 28
Crawford, Deborah 1922- 6
Crawford, John E(dmund) 1904-1971 3
Crawford, K(aren) Michael 1959- 155
Crawford, Mel 1925- 44
  Brief entry 33
Crawford, Phyllis 1899- 3
Crawley, Dave 177
Cray, Roberta
  See Emerson, Ru
Crayder, Dorothy 7
Crayder, Teresa
  See Colman, Hila
Crayon, Geoffrey
  See Irving, Washington
Craz, Albert G. 1926- 24
Crebbin, June 1938- 169
  Earlier sketch in SATA *80*
Crecy, Jeanne
  See Williams, Jeanne
Credle, Ellis 1902-1998 1
Creech, Sharon 1945- 172
  Earlier sketches in SATA *94, 139*
  See also CLR *89*
Creeden, Sharon 1938- 91
Creel, Ann Howard 1953- 187
Creighton, (Mary) Helen 1899-1989
  Obituary 64
Creighton, Jill 1949- 96
Crelin, Bob 1959(?)- 221
Crenson, Victoria 1952- 159
  Earlier sketch in SATA *88*
Cresp, Gael 1954- 119
Crespo, George 1962- 82
Cresswell, Helen 1934-2005 79
  Obituary 168
  Earlier sketches in SATA *1, 48*
  See also CLR *18*
  See also SAAS *20*
Cressy, Michael 1955- 124
Cressy, Mike
  See Cressy, Michael
Cretan, Gladys (Yessayan) 1921- 2
Cretzmeyer, Stacy (Megan) 1959- 124
Crew, Gary 1947- 163
  Earlier sketches in SATA *75, 110*
  See also CLR *42*
Crew, Helen (Cecilia) Coale 1866-1941
  See YABC *2*
Crew, Linda (Jean) 1951- 137
  Earlier sketch in SATA *71*
Crews, Donald 1938- 76
  Brief entry 30
  Earlier sketch in SATA *32*
  See also CLR *7*
Crews, Nina 1963- 158
  Earlier sketch in SATA *97*
Crichton, John Michael
  See Crichton, Michael
Crichton, Michael 1942-2008 88
  Obituary 199
  Earlier sketch in SATA *9*
Crider, Allen Billy
  See Crider, Bill
Crider, Bill 1941- 99
Crilley, Mark 1966- 210
  Autobiography Feature 148
  Earlier sketches in SATA *120, 148*

Crimi, Carolyn 1959- 219
  Earlier sketch in SATA *176*
Cripps, Enid Margaret
  See Appiah, Peggy
Crisler, Curtis L. 188
Crisman, Ruth 1914- 73
Crisp, Marta Marie
  See Crisp, Marty
Crisp, Marty 1947- 128
Crispin, A(nn) C(arol) 1950- 86
Crist, James J. 1961- 168
Cristall, Barbara 79
Crist-Evans, Craig 1954- 153
Crocker, Carter 193
Crocker, Nancy 1956- 185
Crofford, Emily (Ardell) 1927- 61
Crofut, William E. III 1934- 23
Croggon, Alison 1962- 194
Croll, Carolyn 1945- 102
  Brief entry 52
  Earlier sketch in SATA *56*
Croman, Dorothy Young
  See Rosenberg, Dorothy
Cromie, Alice Hamilton 1914-2000 24
Cromie, William J(oseph) 1930- 4
Crompton, Anne Eliot 1930- 73
  Earlier sketch in SATA *23*
Crompton, Richmal
  See Lamburn, Richmal Crompton
Cronbach, Abraham 1882-1965 11
Crone, Ruth 1919-2003 4
Cronin, A(rchibald) J(oseph) 1896-1981 47
  Obituary 25
Cronin, Doreen (A.) 125
Cronin, Doreen 1966(?)- 178
  See also CLR *136*
Cronin, Doreen A.
  See Cronin, Doreen
Crook, Beverly Courtney 38
  Brief entry 35
Crook, Connie Brummel 1930- 168
  Earlier sketch in SATA *98*
Crook, Constance
  See Crook, Connie Brummel
Crosby, Alexander L. 1906-1980 2
  Obituary 23
Crosby, Harry C.
  See Anvil, Christopher
Crosby, Margaret
  See Rathmann, Peggy
Crosher, G. R. 14
Cross, Gilbert B. 1939- 60
  Brief entry 51
Cross, Gillian 1945- 178
  Autobiography Feature 178
  Earlier sketches in SATA *38, 71, 110, 165*
  See also CLR *28*
Cross, Gillian Clare
  See Cross, Gillian
Cross, Helen Reeder
  See Broadhead, Helen Cross
Cross, Peter 1951- 95
Cross, Sarah 216
Cross, Shauna 1976(?)- 196
Cross, Tom 1954- 146
Cross, Verda 1914- 75
Cross, Wilbur Lucius III 1918- 2
Crossland, Caroline 1964- 83
Crossley-Holland, Kevin 1941- 165
  Earlier sketches in SATA *5, 74, 120*
  See also CLR *84*
  See also SAAS *20*
Crossley-Holland, Kevin John William
  See Crossley-Holland, Kevin
Crossman, David A. 1951- 219
Crouch, Karen Hillard
  See Good, Karen Hillard
Crouch, Marcus 1913-1996 4
Crout, George C(lement) 1917- 11
Crow, Donna Fletcher 1941- 40

Crow, Francis Luther
  See Luther, Frank
Crow, Kristyn 208
Crowe, Andrew 111
Crowe, Carole 1943- 204
Crowe, Chris 206
Crowe, Ellie 203
Crowe, John
  See Lynds, Dennis
Crowe, (Bettina) Peter Lum 1911- 6
Crowell, Grace Noll 1877-1969 34
Crowell, Pers 1910-1990 2
Crowell, Robert Leland 1909-2001 63
Crowfield, Christopher
  See Stowe, Harriet Beecher
Crowley, Arthur 1945- 38
Crowley, Arthur McBlair
  See Crowley, Arthur
Crowley, John 1942- 140
  Earlier sketch in SATA *65*
Crowley, Suzanne 1963- 196
Crowley, Suzanne Carlisle
  See Crowley, Suzanne
Crownfield, Gertrude 1867-1945
  See YABC *1*
Crowther, James Gerald 1899-1983 14
Crowther, Kitty 1970- 220
Crowther, Robert 1948- 163
Cruikshank, George 1792-1878 22
  See also CLR *63*
Cruise, Robin 1951- 179
Crum, Shutta 192
  Earlier sketch in SATA *134*
Crummel, Susan Stevens 1949- 176
  Earlier sketch in SATA *130*
Crump, Fred H., Jr. 1931- 76
  Earlier sketch in SATA *11*
Crump, J(ames) Irving 1887-1979 57
  Obituary 21
Crump, William D(rake) 1949- 138
Crunden, Reginald
  See Cleaver, Hylton Reginald
Crunk, T.
  See Crunk, Tony
Crunk, Tony 1956- 130
Crutcher, Chris 1946- 196
  Earlier sketches in SATA *52, 99, 153*
  See also CLR *159*
Crutcher, Christopher C.
  See Crutcher, Chris
Cruz, Ray(mond) 1933- 6
Cruz Martinez, Alejandro (?)-1987 74
Crystal, Billy 1947- 154
Crystal, William
  See Crystal, Billy
Ctvrtek, Vaclav 1911-1976
  Obituary 27
Cuate, Melodie A. 219
Cuetara, Mittie 1957- 158
  Earlier sketch in SATA *106*
Cuffari, Richard 1925-1978 66
  Obituary 25
  Earlier sketch in SATA *6*
Cuffe-Perez, Mary 1946- 199
Cullen, Countee 1903-1946 18
Cullen, Lynn 190
Culliford, Pierre 1928-1992 40
  Obituary 74
Cullinan, Bernice E(llinger) 1926- 135
Culp, Louanna McNary 1901-1965 2
Culper, Felix
  See McCaughrean, Geraldine
Cumbaa, Stephen 1947- 72
Cumming, Peter 1951- 168
Cumming, Primrose Amy 1915- 24
Cumming, Robert 1945- 65
Cummings, Betty Sue 1918- 15
  See also SAAS *9*
Cummings, John Michael 1963(?)- 216
Cummings, Mary 1951- 185

Cummings, Parke 1902-1987 2
  Obituary 53
Cummings, Pat 1950- 203
  Earlier sketches in SATA *42, 71, 107*
  See also CLR *48*
  See also SAAS *13*
Cummings, Phil 1957- 123
  Earlier sketch in SATA *74*
Cummings, Priscilla 1951- 170
  Earlier sketch in SATA *129*
Cummings, Richard
  See Gardner, Richard (M.)
Cummins, Julie 200
Cummins, Maria Susanna 1827-1866
  See YABC *1*
Cumpliano, Ina 207
Cuneo, Mary Louise -2001 85
Cunliffe, John Arthur 1933- 86
  Earlier sketch in SATA *11*
Cunliffe, Marcus (Falkner) 1922-1990 37
  Obituary 66
Cunnane, Kelly 175
Cunningham, Bob
  See May, Julian
Cunningham, Captain Frank
  See Glick, Carl (Cannon)
Cunningham, Cathy
  See Cunningham, Chet
Cunningham, Chet 1928- 23
Cunningham, Dale S(peers) 1932- 11
Cunningham, Dru 91
Cunningham, E. V.
  See Fast, Howard
Cunningham, Julia (Woolfolk) 1916- 132
  Earlier sketches in SATA *1, 26*
  See also SAAS *2*
Cunningham, Lawrence J. 1943- 125
Cunningham, Virginia
  See Holmgren, Virginia C(unningham)
Cunxin, Li 1961- 220
Curiae, Amicus
  See Fuller, Edmund (Maybank)
Curie, Eve 1904-2007 1
  Obituary 188
Curlee, Lynn 1947- 190
  Earlier sketches in SATA *98, 141*
Curley, Daniel 1918-1988 23
  Obituary 61
Curley, Marianne 1959- 175
  Earlier sketch in SATA *131*
Currey, Anna 194
Currie, Robin 1948- 120
Currie, Stephen 1960- 132
  Earlier sketch in SATA *82*
Curry, Ann (Gabrielle) 1934- 72
Curry, Jane L(ouise) 1932- 138
  Autobiography Feature 138
  Earlier sketches in SATA *1, 52, 90*
  See also CLR *31*
  See also SAAS *6*
Curry, Peggy Simson 1911-1987 8
  Obituary 50
Curry, Tom 185
Curtis, Bruce (Richard) 1944- 30
Curtis, Chara M(ahar) 1950- 78
Curtis, Christopher Paul 1953- 187
  Earlier sketches in SATA *93, 140*
  See also CLR *68*
Curtis, Gavin 1965- 107
Curtis, Jamie Lee 1958- 144
  Earlier sketch in SATA *95*
  See also CLR *88*
Curtis, Jennifer Keats 185
Curtis, Marci 160
Curtis, Munzee
  See Caseley, Judith
Curtis, Neil 1950-2006 202
Curtis, Patricia 1921- 101
  Earlier sketch in SATA *23*
Curtis, Peter
  See Lofts, Norah (Robinson)

Curtis, Philip (Delacourt) 1920- 62
Curtis, Richard 1937- 29
Curtis, Richard Alan
  See Curtis, Richard
Curtis, Richard Hale
  See Deming, Richard
  and Levinson, Leonard
  and Rothweiler, Paul Roger
Curtis, Stacy 205
Curtis, Wade
  See Pournelle, Jerry
Curtiss, A(rlene) B. 1934- 90
Cusack, Margaret 1945- 58
Cushman, Doug 1953- 210
  Earlier sketches in SATA *65, 101, 157*
Cushman, Jerome 2
Cushman, Karen 1941- 147
  Earlier sketch in SATA *89*
  See also CLR *55*
Cusick, Richie Tankersley 1952- 140
  Earlier sketch in SATA *67*
Cusimano, Maryann K.
  See Love, Maryann Cusimano
Cutbill, Andy 1972- 201
Cutchen, Billye Walker 1930- 15
Cutchins, Judy 1947- 59
Cutler, Daniel S. 1951- 78
Cutler, Daniel Solomon
  See Cutler, Daniel S.
Cutler, Ebbitt 1923- 9
Cutler, Ivor 1923-2006 24
  Obituary 174
Cutler, Jane 1936- 162
  Earlier sketches in SATA *75, 118*
Cutler, May Ebbitt
  See Cutler, Ebbitt
Cutler, Samuel
  See Folsom, Franklin (Brewster)
Cutlip, Kimbra L(eigh-Ann) 1964- 128
Cutrate, Joe
  See Spiegelman, Art
Cutt, W(illiam) Towrie 1898-1981 16
  Obituary 85
Cuyler, Margery 1948- 195
  Earlier sketches in SATA *39, 99, 156*
Cuyler, Margery Stuyvesant
  See Cuyler, Margery
Cuyler, Stephen
  See Bates, Barbara S(nedeker)
Cyrus, Kurt 1954- 179
  Earlier sketch in SATA *132*
Czajkowski, James
  See Rollins, James
Czekaj, Jef 1969- 217
Czernecki, Stefan 1946- 178

D

Dabba Smith, Frank 174
Dabcovich, Lydia 99
  Brief entry 47
  Earlier sketch in SATA *58*
Dace, Dolores B(oelens) 1929- 89
Da Costa, Deborah 193
Daddo, Andrew 1967- 198
Dadey, Debbie 1959- 217
  Earlier sketches in SATA *73, 136*
Dahl, Borghild (Margarethe) 1890-1984 7
  Obituary 37
Dahl, Roald 1916-1990 73
  Obituary 65
  Earlier sketches in SATA *1, 26*
  See also CLR *111*
Dahlberg, Maurine F. 1951- 171
Dahlstedt, Marden (Stewart) 1921-1983 8
  Obituary 110
Dahme, Joanne 206
Dain, Martin J. 1924-2000 35

Dakos, Kalli 1950- 115
  Earlier sketch in SATA *80*
Dale, Anna 1971- 170
Dale, Gary
  See Reece, Colleen L.
Dale, George E.
  See Asimov, Isaac
Dale, Jack
  See Holliday, Joseph
Dale, Kim 1957- 123
Dale, Margaret J(essy) Miller 1911- 39
Dale, Mitzi
  See Hemstock, Gillian
Dale, Norman
  See Denny, Norman (George)
Dale, Penny 1954- 151
  Earlier sketch in SATA *70*
Daley, Michael J. 170
Dalgliesh, Alice 1893-1979 17
  Obituary 21
  See also CLR *62*
Dalkey, Kara 1953- 132
Dalkey, Kara Mia
  See Dalkey, Kara
Dallas, Ruth 1919- 86
Dalmas, John
  See Jones, John R(obert)
Dalton, Alene
  See Chapin, Alene Olsen Dalton
Dalton, Annie 1948- 140
  Earlier sketch in SATA *40*
Dalton, Kit
  See Cunningham, Chet
Dalton, Pamela
  See Johnson, Pamela
Dalton, Sean
  See Chester, Deborah
Dalton, Sheila 1949- 108
D'Aluisio, Faith 1957- 205
Daly, James 217
Daly, Jim
  See Stratemeyer, Edward L.
Daly, Jude 1951- 222
  Earlier sketch in SATA *177*
Daly, Kathleen N(orah) 124
  Brief entry 37
Daly, Maureen 1921-2006 129
  Obituary 176
  Earlier sketch in SATA *2*
  See also CLR *96*
  See also SAAS *1*
Daly, Nicholas
  See Daly, Niki
Daly, Niki 1946- 198
  Earlier sketches in SATA *37, 76, 114, 164*
  See also CLR *41*
  See also SAAS *21*
D'Amato, Alex 1919- 20
D'Amato, Janet (Potter) 1925- 9
Damerow, Gail 1944- 83
Damerow, Gail Jane
  See Damerow, Gail
D'Amico, Carmela 170
D'Amico, Steve 170
Damrell, Liz 1956- 77
Damrosch, Helen
  See Tee-Van, Helen Damrosch
Dana, Barbara 1940- 218
  Earlier sketch in SATA *22*
Dana, Richard Henry, Jr. 1815-1882 26
Danachair, Caoimhin O
  See Danaher, Kevin
Danaher, Kevin 1913-2002 22
Danakas, John 1963- 94
Dandi
  See Mackall, Dandi Daley
D'Andrea, Kate
  See Steiner, Barbara A(nnette)
Dangerfield, Balfour
  See McCloskey, (John) Robert

Author Index

Daniel, Alan 1939- *76*
  Brief entry *53*
Daniel, Anita 1893(?)-1978 .... *23*
  Obituary *24*
Daniel, Anne
  See Steiner, Barbara A(nnette)
Daniel, Becky 1947- *56*
Daniel, Claire 1949- *164*
Daniel, Colin
  See Windsor, Patricia
Daniel, Hawthorne 1890- *8*
Daniel, (Donna) Lee 1944- *76*
Daniel, Rebecca
  See Daniel, Becky
Daniels, Guy 1919-1989 .... *11*
  Obituary *62*
Daniels, Kit
  See Diver, Lucienne
Daniels, Lucy
  See Oldfield, Jenny
Daniels, Max
  See Gellis, Roberta
Daniels, Olga
  See Sinclair, Olga
Daniels, Patricia 1955- *93*
Daniels, Zoe
  See Laux, Constance
Dank, Gloria Rand 1955- *56*
  Brief entry *46*
Dank, Leonard D(ewey) 1929- *44*
Dank, Milton 1920- *31*
Dann, Max 1955- *62*
Danneberg, Julie 1958- *173*
Dantz, William R.
  See Philbrick, Rodman
Danzig, Dianne *213*
Danziger, Paula 1944-2004 .... *149*
  Brief entry *30*
  Obituary *155*
  Earlier sketches in SATA *36, 63, 102*
  See also CLR *20*
Darby, Gene Kegley
  See Darby, Jean (Kegley)
Darby, J. N.
  See Govan, (Mary) Christine Noble
Darby, Jean (Kegley) 1921- *68*
Darby, Patricia (Paulsen) *14*
Darby, Ray(mond) 1912-1982 .... *7*
Darbyshire, Kristen *218*
d'Arcy, Willard
  See Cox, William R(obert)
Dare, Geena
  See McNicoll, Sylvia (Marilyn)
D'arge, Mackie *218*
Darian, Shea 1959- *97*
Daringer, Helen Fern 1892-1986 .... *1*
Darke, Marjorie 1929- *87*
  Earlier sketch in SATA *16*
Darley, F(elix) O(ctavius) C(arr)
  1822-1888 .... *35*
Darling, David J. 1953- *60*
  Brief entry *44*
Darling, Kathy
  See Darling, Mary Kathleen
Darling, Lois (MacIntyre) 1917-1989 .... *3*
  Obituary *64*
Darling, Louis, (Jr.) 1916-1970 .... *3*
  Obituary *23*
Darling, Mary Kathleen 1943- *124*
  Earlier sketches in SATA *9, 79*
Darling, Sandra Louise Woodward
  See Day, Alexandra
Darnell, K(athryn) L(ynne) 1955- *150*
Darroll, Sally
  See Odgers, Sally Farrell
Darrow, Sharon *181*
Darrow, Whitney, (Jr.) 1909-1999 .... *13*
  Obituary *115*
Darwin, Len
  See Darwin, Leonard
Darwin, Leonard 1916- *24*

Dasent, Sir George Webbe 1817-1896 .... *62*
  Brief entry *29*
Dash, Joan 1925- *142*
Daskam, Josephine Dodge
  See Bacon, Josephine Dodge (Daskam)
D'ath, Justin 1953- *174*
  Earlier sketch in SATA *106*
Dauer, Rosamond 1934- *23*
Daugherty, Charles Michael 1914- *16*
Daugherty, James (Henry) 1889-1974 .... *13*
  See also CLR *78*
Daugherty, Richard D(eo) 1922- *35*
Daugherty, Sonia Medwedeff (?)-1971
  Obituary *27*
d'Aulaire, Edgar Parin 1898-1986 .... *66*
  Obituary *47*
  Earlier sketch in SATA *5*
  See also CLR *21*
d'Aulaire, Ingri 1904-1980 .... *66*
  Obituary *24*
  Earlier sketch in SATA *5*
  See also CLR *21*
d'Aulaire, Ingri Mortenson Parin
  See d'Aulaire, Ingri
Dave, Dave
  See Berg, David
Daveluy, Paule Cloutier 1919- *11*
Davenier, Christine 1961- *216*
  Earlier sketches in SATA *127, 179*
Davenport, John 1960- *156*
Daves, Michael 1938- *40*
David, A. R.
  See David, A(nn) Rosalie
David, A(nn) Rosalie 1946- *103*
David, Jonathan
  See Ames, Lee J(udah)
David, Lawrence 1963- *165*
  Earlier sketch in SATA *111*
David, Peter 1956- *72*
David, Peter Allen
  See David, Peter
David, Rosalie
  See David, A(nn) Rosalie
Davidson, Alice Joyce 1932- *54*
  Brief entry *45*
Davidson, Basil 1914-2010 .... *13*
Davidson, (Marie) Diane 1924- *91*
Davidson, Hugh
  See Hamilton, Edmond
Davidson, Jessica 1915-1986 .... *5*
Davidson, Judith 1953- *40*
Davidson, Lionel 1922-2009 .... *87*
Davidson, Margaret 1936- *5*
Davidson, Marion
  See Garis, Howard R.
Davidson, Mary R. 1885-1973 .... *9*
Davidson, Mary S. 1940- *61*
Davidson, Mickie
  See Davidson, Margaret
Davidson, Nicole
  See Jensen, Kathryn
Davidson, R.
  See Davidson, Raymond
Davidson, Raymond 1926- *32*
Davidson, Rosalie 1921- *23*
Davie, Helen K(ay) 1952- *148*
  Earlier sketch in SATA *77*
Davies, Andrew (Wynford) 1936- *27*
Davies, Andy Robert *200*
Davies, Bettilu D(onna) 1942- *33*
Davies, Hunter 1936- *55*
  Brief entry *45*
Davies, Jacqueline 1962- *186*
  Earlier sketch in SATA *155*
Davies, Joan 1934- *50*
  Brief entry *47*
Davies, Nicola 1958- *182*
  Earlier sketches in SATA *99, 150*
Davies, Peter J(oseph) 1937- *52*
Davies, Sumiko 1942- *46*
Davis, (A.) Aubrey 1949- *153*

Davis, Barbara Steincrohn
  See Davis, Maggie S.
Davis, Bette J. 1923- *15*
Davis, Burke 1913- *4*
Davis, Christopher 1928- *6*
Davis, D(elbert) Dwight 1908-1965 .... *33*
Davis, Daniel S(heldon) 1936- *12*
Davis, David R. 1948- *106*
Davis, Donald 1944- *169*
  Earlier sketch in SATA *93*
Davis, Donald D.
  See Davis, Donald
Davis, Eleanor 1983(?)- *209*
Davis, Emma
  See Davis, Maggie S.
Davis, Gibbs 1953- *102*
  Brief entry *41*
  Earlier sketch in SATA *46*
Davis, Grania 1943- *88*
  Brief entry *50*
Davis, H(arold) L(enoir) 1896-1960 .... *114*
Davis, Heather 1970- *221*
Davis, Hubert J(ackson) 1904-1997 .... *31*
Davis, Jack E. *210*
Davis, Jacky *204*
Davis, James Robert 1945- *32*
Davis, Jenny 1953- *74*
Davis, Jim
  See Davis, James Robert
Davis, Julia 1900(?)-1993 .... *6*
  Obituary *75*
Davis, Karen (Elizabeth) 1944- *109*
Davis, Katie 1959(?)- *208*
  Earlier sketch in SATA *152*
Davis, Lambert *176*
Davis, Leslie
  See Guccione, Leslie Davis
Davis, Louise Littleton 1921- *25*
Davis, Maggie S. 1943- *57*
Davis, Marguerite 1889- *34*
Davis, Mary L(ee) 1935- *9*
Davis, Mary Octavia 1901-1976 .... *6*
Davis, Nelle 1958- *73*
Davis, Ossie 1917-2005 .... *81*
  See also CLR *56*
Davis, Paxton 1925-1994 .... *16*
Davis, Rich 1958- *206*
Davis, Robert 1881-1949
  See YABC *1*
Davis, Robin W(orks) 1962- *87*
Davis, Russell Gerard 1922- *3*
Davis, Tanita S. *212*
Davis, Tim(othy N.) 1957- *94*
Davis, Tony 1961- *222*
Davis, Verne Theodore 1889-1973 .... *6*
Davis, Yvonne 1927- *115*
Davol, Marguerite W. 1928- *146*
  Earlier sketch in SATA *82*
DaVolls, Andy (P.) 1967- *85*
DaVolls, Linda 1966- *85*
Davys, Sarah
  See Manning, Rosemary
Dawes, Claiborne 1935- *111*
Dawson, Arthur L. *207*
Dawson, Elmer A. *67*
  Earlier sketch in SATA *1*
Dawson, Imogen (Zoe) 1948- *126*
  Earlier sketch in SATA *90*
Dawson, Janine 1957- *196*
Dawson, Mary 1919- *11*
Dawson, Willow 1975- *208*
Day, A(rthur) Grove 1904-1994 .... *59*
Day, Alexandra 1941- *197*
  Autobiography Feature *197*
  Earlier sketches in SATA *67, 97, 169*
  See also CLR *22*
  See also SAAS *19*
Day, Beth (Feagles) 1924- *33*
Day, Donna
  See Asay, Donna Day
Day, Edward C. 1932- *72*

Day, Jon 1936(?)- 79
Day, Karen 187
Day, Larry 1956- 181
Day, Nancy 1953- 140
Day, Nancy Raines 1951- 148
  Earlier sketch in SATA 93
Day, Shirley 1962- 94
Day, Thomas 1748-1789
  See YABC 1
Day, Trevor 1955- 124
Dazey, Agnes J(ohnston) 2
Dazey, Frank M. 2
Deacon, Alexis 1978- 139
Deacon, Eileen
  See Geipel, Eileen
Deacon, Richard
  See McCormick, (George) Donald (King)
Deadman, Ronald 1919-1988(?)
  Obituary 56
Deak, Erzsi 1959- 152
Dean, Anabel 1915- 12
Dean, Carolee 1962- 148
Dean, Claire 215
Dean, David 1976- 192
Dean, Karen Strickler 1923- 49
Dean, Ruth (Brigham) 1947- 145
Dean, Zoey
  See Bennett, Cherie
de Angeli, Marguerite (Lofft) 1889-1987 ... 100
  Obituary 51
  Earlier sketch in SATA 1, 27
  See also CLR 1
Deans, Karen 195
Deans, Sis Boulos 1955- 136
  Earlier sketch in SATA 78
DeArmand, Frances Ullmann 1904(?)-1984 . 10
  Obituary 38
DeArmond, Dale 1914- 70
DeArmond, Dale Burlison
  See DeArmond, Dale
Deary, Terry 1946- 171
  Brief entry 41
  Earlier sketches in SATA 51, 101
Deaver, Julie Reece 1953- 68
de Banke, Cecile 1889-1965 11
De Bello, Rosario 1923- 89
Debon, Nicolas 186
  Earlier sketch in SATA 151
de Bono, Edward 1933- 66
de Brissac, Malcolm
  See Dickinson, Peter
de Brunhoff, Jean
  See Brunhoff, Jean de
De Brunhoff, Laurent
  See Brunhoff, Laurent de
De Bruyn, Monica G. 1952- 13
De Bruyn, Monica Jean Grembowicz
  See De Bruyn, Monica G.
DeBry, Roger K. 1942- 91
de Camp, Catherine Crook 1907-2000 83
  Earlier sketch in SATA 12
de Camp, L. Sprague 1907-2000 83
  Earlier sketch in SATA 9
de Camp, Lyon Sprague
  See de Camp, L. Sprague
DeCandido, Keith R.A. 112
Dechausay, Sonia E. 94
Decker, C.B. 172
Decker, Cynthia B.
  See Decker, C.B.
Decker, Duane 1910-1964 5
Decker, Timothy 1974- 197
DeClements, Barthe 1920- 131
  Earlier sketches in SATA 35, 71
  See also CLR 23
DeClements, Barthe Faith
  See DeClements, Barthe
de Clercq Zubli, Rita la Fontaine 1929- 199
de Conte, Sieur Louis
  See Twain, Mark
Dedman, Stephen 108

Dee, Barbara 1958- 220
Dee, Catherine 1964- 138
Dee, Ruby
  See Wallace, Ruby Ann
Deeble, Jason 1979- 221
Deedy, Carmen Agra 1960- 196
Deedy, John 1923- 24
Deegan, Paul Joseph 1937- 48
  Brief entry 38
Deem, James M. 1950- 191
  Autobiography Feature 191
  Earlier sketches in SATA 75, 134
Deem, James Morgan
  See Deem, James M.
Deeter, Catherine 1947- 137
DeFelice, Cynthia 1951- 165
  Earlier sketches in SATA 79, 121
DeFelice, Cynthia C.
  See DeFelice, Cynthia
Defoe, Daniel 1660(?)-1731 22
  See also CLR 61
de Fombelle, Timothee
  See Fombelle, Timothee de
DeFord, Deborah H. 123
deFrance, Anthony
  See DiFranco, Anthony (Mario)
Degen, Bruce 1945- 205
  Brief entry 47
  Earlier sketches in SATA 57, 97, 147
DeGering, Etta (Belle) Fowler 1898-1996 7
De Goldi, Kate 1959- 123
De Goldi, Kathleen Domenica
  See De Goldi, Kate
de Goursac, Olivier 1959- 184
De Grazia, Ettore 1909-1982 39
De Grazia, Ted
  See De Grazia, Ettore
deGroat, Diane 1947- 169
  Earlier sketches in SATA 31, 90
deGros, J. H.
  See Villiard, Paul
de Grummond, Lena Young 62
  Earlier sketch in SATA 6
de Hamel, Joan Littledale 1924- 86
De Haven, Tom 1949- 72
de Hugo, Pierre
  See Brackers de Hugo, Pierre
Deines, Brian 1955- 220
Deiss, Joseph Jay 1915- 12
de Jenkins, Lyll Becerra 1925-1997 102
DeJong, David C(ornel) 1905-1967 10
de Jong, Dola
  See de Jong, Dorothea Rosalie
de Jong, Dorothea Rosalie 1911-2003 7
  Obituary 149
DeJong, Meindert 1906-1991 2
  Obituary 68
  See also CLR 73
DeJonge, Joanne E. 1943- 56
Deka, Connie
  See Laux, Constance
de Kay, Ormonde (Jr.) 1923-1998 7
  Obituary 106
DeKeyser, Stacy 1959- 214
de Kiriline, Louise
  See Lawrence, Louise de Kiriline
Dekker, Carl
  See Laffin, John (Alfred Charles)
  and Lynds, Dennis
deKruif, Paul (Henry) 1890-1971 50
  Earlier sketch in SATA 5
Delacre, Lulu 1957- 209
  Earlier sketches in SATA 36, 156
DeLaCroix, Alice 1940- 195
  Earlier sketch in SATA 75
de la Cruz, Melissa 1971- 179
De la Garza, Phyllis 1942- 169
De Lage, Ida 1918- 11
de la Mare, Walter (John) 1873-1956 16
  See also CLR 148
Delaney, Harry 1932- 3

Delaney, Joseph 1945- 172
Delaney, M.C.
  See Delaney, Michael
Delaney, Michael 1955- 180
  Earlier sketch in SATA 96
Delaney, Michael Clark
  See Delaney, Michael
Delaney, Ned 1951- 28
Delaney, Thomas Nicholas III
  See Delaney, Ned
DeLange, Alex Pardo
  See Pardo DeLange, Alex
Delano, Hugh 1933- 20
Delano, Marfe Ferguson 215
Delany, Samuel R., Jr. 1942- 92
Delany, Samuel Ray
  See Delany, Samuel R., Jr.
de la Pena, Matt 205
De La Ramee, Marie Louise 1839-1908 20
de la Roche, Mazo 1879-1961 64
De La Roche Saint Andre, Anne 1950- 75
de Las Casas, Dianne 1970- 221
Delaune, (Jewel) Lynn (de Grummond) 7
DeLaurentis, Louise Budde 1920- 12
del Barco, Lucy Salamanca 1900(?)-1989
  Obituary 64
Delderfield, Eric R(aymond) 1909-1995 14
Delderfield, Ronald Frederick 1912-1972 ... 20
DeLeeuw, Adele (Louise) 1899-1988 30
  Obituary 56
  Earlier sketch in SATA 1
De Leon, Nephtali 1945- 97
Delessert, Etienne 1941- 179
  Brief entry 27
  Earlier sketches in SATA 46, 130
  See also CLR 81
Delgado, James P. 1958- 122
de Lint, Charles 1951- 207
  Earlier sketches in SATA 115, 157
de Lint, Charles Henri Diederick Hofsmit
  See de Lint, Charles
Delmar, Roy
  See Wexler, Jerome (LeRoy)
Del Negro, Janice M. 197
Deloria, Vine, Jr. 1933-2005 21
  Obituary 171
Deloria, Vine Victor, Jr.
  See Deloria, Vine, Jr.
del Rey, Lester 1915-1993 22
  Obituary 76
Delrio, Martin
  See Doyle, Debra
  and Macdonald, James D.
Delton, Judy 1931-2001 77
  Obituary 130
  Earlier sketch in SATA 14
  See also SAAS 9
Delulio, John 1938- 15
Delving, Michael
  See Williams, Jay
de Marcken, Gail 186
Demarest, Chris L. 1951- 175
  Brief entry 44
  Earlier sketches in SATA 45, 82, 128
Demarest, Christopher Lynn
  See Demarest, Chris L.
Demarest, Doug
  See Barker, Will
De Mari, Silvana 1953- 193
Demas, Corinne
  See Bliss, Corinne Demas
Demas, Vida 1927- 9
Dematons, Charlotte 1957- 203
DeMatteis, J.M. 1953- 180
DeMatteis, John Marc
  See DeMatteis, J.M.
De Mejo, Oscar 1911-1992 40
Demers, Dominique 1956- 177
de Messieres, Nicole 1930- 39

Demi 1942- 210
Earlier sketches in SATA *11, 66, 102, 152*
See also CLR *58*
Demijohn, Thom
See Disch, Thomas M.
and Sladek, John
Deming, Richard 1915-1983 24
Deming, Sarah 191
de Monfreid, Dorothee 1973- 189
Demuth, Patricia Brennan 1948- 84
Brief entry 51
De Muth, Roger 1948- 221
Dendinger, Roger E. 1952- 158
Denenberg, Barry 1940- 175
Dengler, Marianna (Herron) 1935- 103
Dengler, Sandy 1939- 54
Brief entry 40
Denim, Sue
See Pilkey, Dav
Denise, Anika 210
Denise, Christopher 1968- 193
Earlier sketch in SATA *147*
Denman, K.L. 1957- 186
Denmark, Harrison
See Zelazny, Roger
Dennard, Deborah 1953- 136
Earlier sketch in SATA *78*
Denney, Diana 1910-2000 25
Obituary 120
Dennis, Morgan 1891(?)-1960 18
Dennis, Wesley 1903-1966 18
Denniston, Elinore 1900-1978
Obituary 24
Denny, Norman (George) 1901-1982 43
Denos, Julia 202
Denslow, Sharon Phillips 1947- 142
Earlier sketch in SATA *68*
Denslow, W(illiam) W(allace) 1856-1915 16
See also CLR *15*
Dent, Grace 1973- 187
Denton, Kady MacDonald 181
Earlier sketches in SATA *66, 110*
See also CLR *71*
Denton, Terry 1950- 186
Denver, Walt
See Redding, Robert Hull
and Sherman, Jory (Tecumseh)
Denzel, Justin F(rancis) 1917-1999 46
Brief entry 38
Denzer, Ann Wiseman
See Wiseman, Ann (Sayre)
DePalma, Mary Newell 1961- 185
Earlier sketch in SATA *139*
De Palma, Toni 199
dePaola, Thomas Anthony 1934- 200
Earlier sketches in SATA *11, 59, 108, 155*
See also CLR *81*
See also SAAS *15*
dePaola, Tomie
See dePaola, Thomas Anthony
deParrie, Paul 1949- 74
DePauw, Linda Grant 1940- 24
DeRan, David 1946- 76
Derby, Ken 1956- 181
Derby, Kenneth R.
See Derby, Ken
Derby, Pat 1942- 172
Derby, Sally 1934- 189
Earlier sketches in SATA *89, 132*
de Regniers, Beatrice Schenk (Freedman)
1914-2000 68
Obituary 123
Earlier sketch in SATA *2*
See also SAAS *6*
Dereske, Jo 1947- 72
Deriso, Christine Hurley 1961- 210
Derleth, August (William) 1909-1971 5
Derman, Martha (Winn) 74
Derman, Sarah Audrey 1915- 11
DeRoberts, Lyndon
See Silverstein, Robert Alan

de Roo, Anne Louise 1931-1997 84
Earlier sketch in SATA *25*
See also CLR *63*
deRosa, Dee 70
Derrick, Lionel
See Cunningham, Chet
Derrickson, Jim 1959- 141
Derry Down Derry
See Lear, Edward
Dervaux, Isabelle 1961- 106
Derwent, Lavinia 14
Desai, Anita 1937- 126
Earlier sketch in SATA *63*
DeSaix, Deborah Durland 188
De Saulles, Tony 1958- 119
Desbarats, Peter 1933- 39
de Selincourt, Aubrey 1894-1962 14
de Seve, Peter 1958- 219
de Seve, Randall 198
Deshpande, Chris 1950- 69
Desimini, Lisa 1964- 216
Earlier sketches in SATA *86, 148*
Desjarlais, John 1953- 71
Desjarlais, John J.
See Desjarlais, John
Desmoinaux, Christel 1967- 149
Earlier sketch in SATA *103*
Desmond, Adrian 1947- 51
Desmond, Adrian J.
See Desmond, Adrian
Desmond, Adrian John
See Desmond, Adrian
Desmond, Alice Curtis 1897-1990 8
Desnoettes, Caroline 183
DeSpain, Pleasant 1943- 87
Desputeaux, Helene 1959- 95
Dessen, Sarah 1970- 172
Earlier sketch in SATA *120*
Detine, Padre
See Olsen, Ib Spang
de Trevino, Elizabeth B.
See Trevino, Elizabeth B(orton) de
de Trevino, Elizabeth Borton
See Trevino, Elizabeth B(orton) de
Detwiler, Susan Dill 1956- 58
Deuker, Carl 1950- 196
Earlier sketches in SATA *82, 150*
Deutsch, Babette 1895-1982 1
Obituary 33
Deutsch, Eva Costabel
See Costabel, Eva Deutsch
Deutsch, Helen 1906-1992 76
Deutsch, Kurt
See Singer, Kurt D.
De Valera, Sinead 1879(?)-1975
Obituary 30
Devaney, John 1926-1994 12
de Varennes, Monique 1947- 168
de Varona, Frank J. 1943- 83
Devereux, Frederick L(eonard), Jr.
1914-1993 9
Devi, Nila
See Woody, Regina Jones
deVinck, Christopher 1951- 85
DeVita, James 195
DeVito, Cara 1956- 80
Devlin, Dorothy Wende
See Devlin, Wende
Devlin, Harry 1918-2001 136
Earlier sketches in SATA *11, 74*
Devlin, Wende 1918-2002 74
Earlier sketch in SATA *11*
Devon, Paddie 1953- 92
Devons, Sonia 1974- 72
Devorah-Leah 111
de Vos, Gail 1949- 122
de Vries, Anke 1936- 222
DeVries, Douglas 1933- 122
De Waard, E(lliott) John 1935- 7
Dewan, Ted 1961- 157
Earlier sketch in SATA *108*

Dewdney, Anna 184
Dewdney, Selwyn (Hanington) 1909-1979 ... 64
DeWeese, Gene
See DeWeese, Thomas Eugene
DeWeese, Jean
See DeWeese, Thomas Eugene
DeWeese, Thomas Eugene 1934- 46
Brief entry 45
Dewey, Ariane 1937- 178
Earlier sketch in SATA *7, 109*
Dewey, Jennifer (Owings) 1941- 103
Brief entry 48
Earlier sketch in SATA *58*
Dewey, Kenneth Francis 1940- 39
Dewin, Howie
See Howie, Betsy
De Wire, Elinor 1953- 180
deWit, Dorothy (May Knowles) 1916-1980 . 39
Obituary 28
Dexter, Alison 1966- 125
Dexter, John
See Bradley, Marion Zimmer
Deyneka, Anita 1943- 24
Deyrup, Astrith Johnson 1923- 24
Dezern, Chad 201
de Zubizarreta, Alma
See Ada, Alma Flor
Dhami, Narinder 1958- 152
Dhondy, Farrukh 1944- 152
Earlier sketch in SATA *65*
See also CLR *41*
Diakite, Baba Wague 1961- 174
Diakite, Penda 1993(?)- 174
Diamond, Arthur 1957- 76
Diamond, Donna 1950- 69
Brief entry 30
Earlier sketch in SATA *35*
Diamond, Petra
See Sachs, Judith
Diamond, Rebecca
See Sachs, Judith
Dias, Earl Joseph 1916- 41
Dias, Ron 1937- 71
Diaz, David 1959(?)- 189
Earlier sketches in SATA *96, 150*
See also CLR *65*
Dibley, Glin 188
DiCamillo, Kate 1964- 202
Earlier sketches in SATA *121, 163*
See also CLR *117*
Di Certo, J(oseph) J(ohn) 1933- 60
DiCianni, Ron 1952- 107
Dick, Trella Lamson 1889-1974 9
Dickens, Charles 1812-1870 15
See also CLR *162*
Dickens, Charles John Huffam
See Dickens, Charles
Dickens, Frank
See Huline-Dickens, Frank William
Dickens, Monica (Enid) 1915-1992 4
Obituary 74
Dickerson, Roy Ernest 1886-1965
Obituary 26
Dickinson, Emily 1830-1886 29
Dickinson, Emily Elizabeth
See Dickinson, Emily
Dickinson, Mary 1949- 48
Brief entry 41
Dickinson, Mary-Anne
See Rodda, Emily
Dickinson, Peter 1927- 150
Earlier sketches in SATA *5, 62, 95*
See also CLR *125*
Dickinson, Peter Malcolm de Brissac
See Dickinson, Peter
Dickinson, Susan 1931- 8
Dickinson, Terence 1943- 102
Dickinson, W(illiam) Croft 1897-1963 13
Dickson, Gordon R. 1923-2001 77
Dickson, Gordon Rupert
See Dickson, Gordon R.

Dickson, Helen
  See Reynolds, Helen Mary Greenwood Campbell
Dickson, Naida 1916- 8
Diehn, Gwen 1943- 80
Dierssen, Andreas 1962- 190
Diesen, Deborah 1967- 200
Dieterich, Michele M. 1962- 78
Dietz, David H(enry) 1897-1984 10
  Obituary 41
Dietz, Lew 1907-1997 11
  Obituary 95
Diffily, Deborah 159
Di Fiori, Larry
  See Di Fiori, Lawrence
Di Fiori, Lawrence 1934- 130
DiFranco, Anthony (Mario) 1945- 42
Digby, Anne 1935- 72
Digges, Jeremiah
  See Berger, Josef
Digman, Kristina 1959- 176
D'Ignazio, Fred 1949- 39
  Brief entry 35
D'Ignazio, Frederick
  See D'Ignazio, Fred
Di Grazia, Thomas (?)-1983 32
Dijkstra, Lida 1961- 195
Dikty, Julian May
  See May, Julian
Dillard, Annie 1945- 140
  Earlier sketch in SATA 10
Dillard, Kristine 1964- 113
Dillard, Polly Hargis 1916- 24
Dillard, Sarah 1961- 217
Diller, Harriett 1953- 78
Dillon, Anna
  See Scott, Michael
Dillon, Barbara 1927- 44
  Brief entry 39
Dillon, Diane 1933- 194
  Earlier sketches in SATA 15, 51, 106
  See also CLR 44
Dillon, Diane Claire
  See Dillon, Diane
Dillon, Eilis 1920-1994 74
  Autobiography Feature 105
  Obituary 83
  Earlier sketch in SATA 2
  See also CLR 26
Dillon, Jana (a pseudonym) 1952- 117
Dillon, Leo 1933- 194
  Earlier sketches in SATA 15, 51, 106
  See also CLR 44
Dillon, Sharon Saseen
  See Saseen, Sharon (Dillon)
Dils, Tracey E. 1958- 83
Dilson, Jesse 1914-1988 24
Dinan, Carolyn 59
  Brief entry 47
Dines, Carol 1956- 175
Dines, (Harry) Glen 1925-1996 7
Dinesen, Isak
  See Blixen, Karen
Dinessi, Alex
  See Schembri, Jim
Dinneen, Betty 1929- 61
Dinnerstein, Harvey 1928- 42
Dinsdale, Tim(othy Kay) 1924-1987 11
Dion, Nathalie 1964- 213
Dionne, Erin 1975- 217
Diop, Birago (Ismael) 1906-1989
  Obituary 64
Diouf, Sylviane A. 168
Diouf, Sylviane Anna
  See Diouf, Sylviane A.
DiPucchio, Kelly 204
  Earlier sketch in SATA 159
Dirk
  See Gringhuis, Richard H.
Dirks, Wilhelmina 1916- 59

Dirks, Willy
  See Dirks, Wilhelmina
Dirtmeister
  See Tomecek, Steve
DiSalvo, DyAnne 1960- 144
  Earlier sketch in SATA 59
DiSalvo-Ryan, DyAnne
  See DiSalvo, DyAnne
Disch, Thomas M. 1940-2008 92
  Obituary 195
  See also CLR 18
  See also SAAS 15
Disch, Thomas Michael
  See Disch, Thomas M.
Disch, Tom
  See Disch, Thomas M.
Disher, Garry 1949- 125
  Earlier sketch in SATA 81
Disney, Walt(er Elias) 1901-1966 28
  Brief entry 27
Ditchfield, Christin 1973- 189
DiTerlizzi, Tony 1969- 214
  Earlier sketch in SATA 154
DiTerlooney, Tiny
  See DiTerlizzi, Tony
Divakaruni, Chitra Banerjee 1956- 222
  Earlier sketch in SATA 160
Di Valentin, Maria (Amelia) Messuri
  1911-1985 7
Diver, Lucienne 1971- 218
Divine, Arthur Durham 1904-1987
  Obituary 52
Divine, David
  See Divine, Arthur Durham
Dixon, Ann 1954- 212
  Earlier sketches in SATA 77, 127
Dixon, Ann Renee
  See Dixon, Ann
Dixon, Dougal 1947- 190
  Earlier sketches in SATA 45, 127
Dixon, Franklin W.
  See Barrett, Neal, Jr.
  and Goulart, Ron
  and Lantz, Francess L(in)
  and Lerangis, Peter
  and McFarlane, Leslie
  and Stanley, George Edward
  and Stratemeyer, Edward L.
Dixon, Jeanne 1936- 31
Dixon, Paige
  See Corcoran, Barbara (Asenath)
Dixon, Peter L(ee) 1931- 6
Dixon, Rachel 1952- 74
Djoleto, (Solomon Alexander) Amu 1929- ... 80
d'lacey, Chris 1949- 165
Doak, Annie
  See Dillard, Annie
Doane, Pelagie 1906-1966 7
Dob, Bob 207
Dobell, I(sabel) M(arian) B(arclay)
  1909-1998 11
Dobie, J(ames) Frank 1888-1964 43
Dobkin, Alexander 1908-1975
  Obituary 30
Dobler, Lavinia G. 1910- 6
Dobrin, Arnold 1928- 4
Dobson, Jill 1969- 140
Dobson, Julia 1941- 48
Dobson, Mary 1954- 117
DoCampo, Valeria 1976- 217
Docherty, James
  See Docherty, Jimmy
Docherty, Jimmy 1976- 204
Docherty, Thomas 1955- 218
Dockery, Wallene T. 1941- 27
Dockray, Tracy 1962- 139
Dockrey, Karen 1955- 103
Doctor, Bernard
  See Doctor, Bernard Aquina
Doctor, Bernard Aquina 1950- 81

Doctor X
  See Nourse, Alan E(dward)
Dodd, Ed(ward Benton) 1902-1991 4
  Obituary 68
Dodd, Emma 1969- 203
Dodd, Lynley (Stuart) 1941- 132
  Earlier sketches in SATA 35, 86
  See also CLR 62
Dodd, Marty 1921- 142
Dodd, Quentin 1972- 137
Dodds, Bill 1952- 78
Dodds, Dayle Ann 1952- 201
  Earlier sketches in SATA 75, 150
Doder, Josh 1968- 187
Dodge, Bertha S(anford) 1902-1995 8
Dodge, Fremont
  See Grimes, Lee
Dodge, Gil
  See Hano, Arnold
Dodge, Mary (Elizabeth) Mapes
  1831(?)-1905 100
  Earlier sketch in SATA 21
  See also CLR 62
Dodgson, Charles Lutwidge
  See Carroll, Lewis
Dodson, Kenneth MacKenzie 1907-1999 11
Dodson, Susan 1941- 50
  Brief entry 40
Doerrfeld, Cori 1964- 214
Dogar, Sharon 1962- 211
Dogyear, Drew
  See Gorey, Edward (St. John)
Doherty, Berlie 1943- 111
  Earlier sketch in SATA 72
  See also CLR 21
  See also SAAS 16
Doherty, Charles Hugh 1913- 6
Doherty, Craig A. 1951- 169
  Earlier sketch in SATA 83
Doherty, Katherine M(ann) 1951- 83
Doherty, Kieran 1945- 164
Dokas, Dara 1968- 216
Dokey, Cameron 1956- 97
Dolan, Edward F(rancis), Jr. 1924- 94
  Brief entry 31
  Earlier sketch in SATA 45
Dolan, Ellen M(eara) 1929-1998 88
Dolan, Sean J. 1958- 74
Dolce, J. Ellen 1948- 75
Dolch, Edward William 1889-1961 50
Dolch, Marguerite Pierce 1891-1978 50
Dollar, Diane (Hills) 1933- 57
Dolson, Hildegarde
  See Lockridge, Hildegarde (Dolson)
Domanska, Janina 1913(?)-1995 68
  Obituary 84
  Earlier sketch in SATA 6
  See also CLR 40
  See also SAAS 18
Dominguez, Angel 1953- 76
Dominguez, Angela N. 1982- 219
Domino, John
  See Averill, Esther (Holden)
Domjan, Joseph (Spiri) 1907-1992 25
Domm, Jeffrey C. 1958- 84
Donahue, Dorothy 178
Donald, Rhonda Lucas 1962- 147
Donalds, Gordon
  See Shirreffs, Gordon D(onald)
Donaldson, Bryna
  See Stevens, Bryna
Donaldson, Gordon 1913-1993 64
  Obituary 76
Donaldson, Joan 1953- 78
Donaldson, Julia 1948- 180
  Earlier sketches in SATA 82, 132
Donaldson, Stephen R. 1947- 121
Donaldson, Stephen Reeder
  See Donaldson, Stephen R.
Doner, Kim 1955- 208
  Earlier sketch in SATA 91

Doney, Todd L. W. 1959- *104*
Dong-Sung, Kim 1970- *195*
Dong-Sung Kim
    See Dong-Sung, Kim
Donkin, Andrew *219*
Donkin, Nance (Clare) 1915- *95*
Donna, Natalie 1934-1979 .... *9*
Donnelly, Elfie 1950-
    See also CLR *104*
Donnelly, Jennifer 1963- *154*
Donnelly, Matt 1972- *148*
Donnio, Sylviane *188*
Donofrio, Beverly 1950- *209*
Donoghue, Emma 1969- *101*
Donohue, Moira Rose 1954- *201*
Donoughue, Carol 1935- *139*
Donovan, Frank (Robert) 1906-1975
    Obituary *30*
Donovan, Gail 1962- *217*
Donovan, John 1928-1992 .... *72*
    Brief entry *29*
    See also CLR *3*
Donovan, Mary Lee 1961- *86*
Donovan, William
    See Berkebile, Fred D(onovan)
Donze, Mary Terese 1911- *89*
Doob, Leonard W(illiam) 1909-2000 .... *8*
Doodler, Todd H.
    See Goldman, Todd Harris
Dooley, Norah 1953- *74*
Dooling, Michael 1958- *220*
    Earlier sketch in SATA *105*
Dor, Ana
    See Ceder, Georgiana Dorcas
Doran, Colleen 1963- *211*
Dore, (Louis Christophe Paul) Gustave
    1832-1883 .... *19*
Doremus, Robert 1913-2010 .... *30*
Doren, Marion (Walker) 1928- *57*
Dorenkamp, Michelle 1957- *89*
Dorflinger, Carolyn 1953- *91*
Dorfman, Joaquin 1979- *180*
Dorfman, Joaquin Emiliano
    See Dorfman, Joaquin
Dorian, Edith M(cEwen) 1900-1983 .... *5*
Dorian, Harry
    See Hamilton, Charles (Harold St. John)
Dorian, Marguerite *7*
Dorin, Patrick C(arberry) 1939- *59*
    Brief entry *52*
Dorman, Brandon *194*
Dorman, Michael 1932- *7*
Dorman, N. B. 1927- *39*
Dormer, Frank W. *200*
Dorris, Michael 1945-1997 .... *75*
    Obituary *94*
    See also CLR *58*
Dorris, Michael A.
    See Dorris, Michael
Dorris, Michael Anthony
    See Dorris, Michael
Dorritt, Susan
    See Schlein, Miriam
Dorros, Alex 1991- *194*
Dorros, Arthur 1950- *168*
    Earlier sketches in SATA *78, 122*
    See also CLR *42*
    See also SAAS *20*
Dorros, Arthur M.
    See Dorros, Arthur
Dorson, Richard M(ercer) 1916-1981 .... *30*
Doss, Helen (Grigsby) 1918- *20*
Doss, Margot Patterson *6*
dos Santos, Joyce Audy 1949- *57*
    Brief entry *42*
Dothers, Anne
    See Chess, Victoria (Dickerson)
Dotlich, Rebecca Kai 1951- *182*
Dottig
    See Grider, Dorothy
Dotts, Maryann J. 1933- *35*

Doty, Jean Slaughter 1929- *28*
Doty, Roy 1922- *28*
Doubtfire, Dianne (Abrams) 1918- *29*
Doucet, Sharon Arms 1951- *144*
    Autobiography Feature *144*
    Earlier sketch in SATA *125*
Dougherty, Charles 1922- *18*
Dougherty, Terri (L.) 1964- *146*
Doughty, Rebecca 1955- *174*
Douglas, Allen *223*
Douglas, Blaise 1960- *101*
Douglas, Carole Nelson 1944- *73*
Douglas, Garry
    See Kilworth, Garry
Douglas, James McM.
    See Griffin, W. E. B.
Douglas, Kathryn
    See Ewing, Kathryn
Douglas, Leonard
    See Bradbury, Ray
Douglas, Lola
    See Zeises, Lara M.
Douglas, Marjory Stoneman 1890-1998 .... *10*
Douglas, Michael
    See Crichton, Michael
Douglas, Michael
    See Bright, Robert Sr.)
Douglas, Shirley Stewart
    See Tepper, Sheri S.
Douglass, Barbara 1930- *40*
Douglass, Frederick 1817(?)-1895 .... *29*
Douglass, Keith
    See Cunningham, Chet
Douty, Esther M(orris) 1909-1978 .... *8*
    Obituary *23*
Dow, Emily R. 1904-1987 .... *10*
Dow, Vicki
    See McVey, Vicki
Dowd, John David 1945- *78*
Dowd, Siobhan 1960-2007 .... *204*
Dowdell, Dorothy (Florence) Karns 1910- ... *12*
Dowden, Anne Ophelia Todd 1907-2007 .... *7*
    Obituary *180*
    See also SAAS *10*
Dowdey, Landon Gerald 1923- *11*
Dowdy, Mrs. Regera
    See Gorey, Edward (St. John)
Dowell, Frances O'Roark 1964- *205*
    Earlier sketch in SATA *157*
Dower, Laura 1967- *185*
Dowling, Terry 1947- *101*
Downard, Barry 1956- *202*
Downer, Ann 1960- *155*
Downer, Marion 1892(?)-1971 .... *25*
Downes, Belinda 1962- *180*
Downey, Fairfax D(avis) 1893-1990 .... *3*
    Obituary *66*
Downey, Lisa *214*
Downey, Lynn 1961- *185*
Downham, Jenny 1964- *192*
Downie, John 1931- *87*
Downie, Mary Alice 1934- *171*
    Earlier sketches in SATA *13, 87*
Downie, Mary Alice Dawe
    See Downie, Mary Alice
Downing, David A(lmon) 1958- *84*
Downing, Johnette *184*
Downing, Julie 1956- *148*
    Earlier sketch in SATA *81*
Downing, Paula E. 1951- *80*
Downing, Warwick
    See Downing, Wick
Downing, Wick 1931- *138*
Dowswell, Paul 1957- *184*
Doyle, A. Conan
    See Doyle, Sir Arthur Conan
Doyle, Sir Arthur Conan 1859-1930 .... *24*
    See also CLR *106*

Doyle, Brian 1935- *156*
    Earlier sketches in SATA *67, 104*
    See also CLR *22*
    See also SAAS *16*
Doyle, Charlotte 1937- *178*
    Earlier sketch in SATA *94*
Doyle, Charlotte Lackner
    See Doyle, Charlotte
Doyle, Conan
    See Doyle, Sir Arthur Conan
Doyle, Debra 1952- *165*
    Earlier sketch in SATA *105*
Doyle, Donovan
    See Boegehold, Betty (Doyle)
Doyle, John
    See Graves, Robert
Doyle, Malachy 1954- *165*
    Earlier sketch in SATA *120*
    See also CLR *83*
Doyle, Richard 1824-1883 .... *21*
Doyle, Sir A. Conan
    See Doyle, Sir Arthur Conan
Dr. A
    See Asimov, Isaac
    and Silverstein, Alvin
    and Silverstein, Virginia B.
Dr. Alphabet
    See Morice, Dave
Dr. Fred
    See Bortz, Alfred B(enjamin)
Dr. Laura
    See Schlessinger, Laura (Catherine)
Dr. Seuss 1904-1991 .... *100*
    Obituary *67*
    Earlier sketches in SATA *1, 28, 75*
    See also CLR *100*
Dr. Zed
    See Penrose, Gordon
Drabble, Margaret 1939- *48*
Drackett, Phil(ip Arthur) 1922- *53*
Draco, F.
    See Davis, Julia
Dracup, Angela 1943- *74*
Dragisic, Patricia *116*
Dragonwagon, Crescent 1952- *186*
    Autobiography Feature *186*
    Earlier sketches in SATA *11, 41, 75, 133*
    See also SAAS *14*
Drake, David 1945- *85*
Drake, David Allen
    See Drake, David
Drake, Frank
    See Hamilton, Charles (Harold St. John)
Drake, Jane 1954- *82*
Drake, Salamanda
    See Barlow, Steve
Drakeford, Dale B 1952- *113*
Drakeford, Dale Benjamin
    See Drakeford, Dale B
Draper, Hastings
    See Jeffries, Roderic
Draper, Sharon
    See Draper, Sharon M.
Draper, Sharon M. 1948- *195*
    Autobiography Feature *146*
    Earlier sketches in SATA *98, 146*
    See also CLR *57*
Draper, Sharon Mills
    See Draper, Sharon M.
Drapier, M. B.
    See Swift, Jonathan
Drawson, Blair 1943- *126*
    Earlier sketch in SATA *17*
Dray, Matt 1967- *177*
Dray, Matthew Frederick
    See Dray, Matt
Dresang, Eliza (Carolyn Timberlake) 1941- . *19*
Drescher, Henrik 1955- *172*
    Earlier sketches in SATA *67, 105*
    See also CLR *20*

Drescher, Joan E(lizabeth) 1939- *137*
    Earlier sketch in SATA *30*
Dressen-McQueen, Stacey *191*
Dreves, Veronica R. 1927-1986
    Obituary *50*
Drew, Patricia 1938- *15*
Drew, Patricia Mary
    See Drew, Patricia
Drewery, Mary 1918- *6*
Drewery, Melanie 1970- *165*
Drewry, Henry N(athaniel) 1924- *138*
Dreyer, Ellen *177*
Drial, J. E.
    See Laird, Jean E(louise)
Drimmer, Frederick 1916-2000 .... *60*
    Obituary *124*
Driskill, J. Lawrence 1920- *90*
Driskill, Larry
    See Driskill, J. Lawrence
Driving Hawk, Virginia
    See Sneve, Virginia Driving Hawk
Dron, Laura
    See Matthews, L. S.
Dronzek, Laura *199*
Drucker, Malka 1945- *214*
    Brief entry *29*
    Earlier sketches in SATA *39, 111*
Drucker, Olga Levy 1927- *79*
Druitt, Tobias
    See Purkiss, Diane
Drummond, Allan 1957- *209*
Drummond, Karona 1965- *220*
Drummond, V(iolet) H(ilda) 1911-2000 .... *6*
Drummond, Walter
    See Silverberg, Robert
Drury, Clare Marie
    See Hoskyns-Abrahall, Clare (Constance
    Drury)
Drury, Roger W(olcott) 1914-1996 .... *15*
Druse, Eleanor
    See King, Stephen
Dryden, Pamela
    See St. John, Nicole
D.T., Hughes
    See Hughes, Dean
Duane, Diane (Elizabeth) 1952- *145*
    Brief entry *46*
    Earlier sketches in SATA *58, 95*
Dubanevich, Arlene 1950- *56*
Dubelaar, Thea 1947- *60*
Dubin, Jill *205*
du Blane, Daphne
    See Groom, Arthur William
Duble, Kathleen Benner 1958- *164*
Dubois, Claude K. 1960- *196*
DuBois, Rochelle Holt *41*
Du Bois, Shirley Graham 1907(?)-1977 .... *24*
    See Graham, Shirley
Du Bois, W. E. B. 1868-1963 .... *42*
Du Bois, William Edward Burghardt
    See Du Bois, W. E. B.
du Bois, William Pene
    See Pene du Bois, William (Sherman)
Duboise, Novella 1911-1999 .... *88*
Dubosarsky, Ursula 1961- *193*
    Earlier sketches in SATA *107, 147*
DuBose, LaRocque (Russ) 1926- *2*
Dubrovin, Vivian 1931- *139*
    Earlier sketch in SATA *65*
DuBurke, Randy *172*
Ducey, Jean Sparks 1915- *93*
Duchacek, Ivo D(uka) 1913-1988
    Obituary *55*
Du Chaillu, Paul (Belloni) 1835(?)-1903 ..... *26*
Ducharme, Dede Fox
    See Ducharme, Lilian Fox
Ducharme, Lilian Fox 1950- *122*
Ducornet, Erica 1943- *7*
Ducornet, Rikki
    See Ducornet, Erica
Duddle, Jonny 1971(?)- *219*

Duden, Jane 1947- *136*
Duder, Tessa 1940- *117*
    Earlier sketch in SATA *80*
    See also CLR *43*
    See also SAAS *23*
Dudley, Helen
    See Hope Simpson, Jacynth
Dudley, Martha Ward 1909(?)-1985
    Obituary *45*
Dudley, Nancy
    See Cole, Lois Dwight
Dudley, Robert
    See Baldwin, James
Dudley, Ruth H(ubbell) 1905-2001 .... *11*
Dudley-Smith, T.
    See Trevor, Elleston
Due, Linnea A. 1948- *64*
Dueck, Adele 1955- *97*
Dueland, Joy V(ivian) *27*
Duerr, Gisela 1968- *89*
Duey, Kathleen 1950- *199*
    Earlier sketch in SATA *132*
Dufault, Joseph Ernest Nephtali
    See James, Will(iam Roderick)
Duff, Annis (James) 1904(?)-1986
    Obituary *49*
Duff, Maggie
    See Duff, Margaret K(app)
Duff, Margaret K(app) 1916-2003 .... *37*
    Obituary *144*
Duffey, Betsy (Byars) 1953- *131*
    Earlier sketch in SATA *80*
Duffie, Charles 1960- *144*
Duffield, Katy S. 1961- *147*
Duffy, Carol Ann 1955- *165*
    Earlier sketch in SATA *95*
Duffy Stone, Heather *217*
Dugan, Jack
    See Griffin, W. E. B.
Dugan, John Kevin
    See Griffin, W. E. B.
Dugan, Karen *202*
Dugan, Karen M.
    See Dugan, Karen
Dugan, Michael (Gray) 1947- *15*
Duggan, Alfred Leo 1903-1964 .... *25*
Duggan, Maurice 1922-1974 .... *40*
    Obituary *30*
Duggan, Maurice Noel
    See Duggan, Maurice
Dugger, Elizabeth L.
    See Kanell, Beth
Duggleby, John 1952- *94*
Dugin, Andrej 1955- *77*
Dugina, Olga 1964- *77*
du Jardin, Rosamond Neal 1902-1963 .... *2*
Duka, Ivo
    See Duchacek, Ivo D(uka)
Duke, Kate 1956- *192*
    Earlier sketches in SATA *90, 148*
    See also CLR *51*
Duke, Will
    See Gault, William Campbell
Dulac, Edmund 1882-1953 .... *19*
Dumas, Alexandre (pere) 1802-1870 .... *18*
    See also CLR *134*
Dumas, Jacqueline 1946- *55*
Dumas, Philippe 1940- *119*
    Earlier sketch in SATA *52*
du Maurier, Daphne 1907-1989 .... *27*
    Obituary *60*
Dumbleton, Mike 1948- *206*
    Earlier sketches in SATA *73, 124*
Dunbar, Fiona 1961- *167*
Dunbar, Joyce 1944- *213*
    Earlier sketches in SATA *76, 112, 162*
Dunbar, Paul Laurence 1872-1906 .... *34*
Dunbar, Polly 1980(?)- *211*
    Earlier sketch in SATA *181*
Dunbar, Robert E(verett) 1926- *32*

Duncan, Alexandra
    See Moore, Ishbel (Lindsay)
Duncan, Alice Faye 1967- *168*
    Earlier sketch in SATA *95*
Duncan, Gregory
    See McClintock, Marshall
Duncan, Jane
    See Cameron, Elizabeth Jane
Duncan, Julia K.
    See Benson, Mildred
Duncan, Lois 1934- *219*
    Autobiography Feature *141*
    Earlier sketches in SATA *1, 36, 75, 133, 141*
    See also CLR *129*
    See also SAAS *2*
Duncan, Norman 1871-1916
    See YABC *1*
Duncan, Terence
    See Nolan, William F.
Duncombe, Frances (Riker) 1900-1994 .... *25*
    Obituary *82*
Dungy, Anthony
    See Dungy, Tony
Dungy, Tony 1955- *206*
Dunham, Montrew 1919- *162*
Dunham, Montrew Goetz
    See Dunham, Montrew
Dunkle, Clare B. 1964- *223*
    Earlier sketch in SATA *155*
Dunlap, Julie 1958- *84*
Dunleavy, Deborah 1951- *133*
Dunlop, Agnes M. R. (?)-1982 .... *87*
Dunlop, Eileen (Rhona) 1938- *76*
    Earlier sketch in SATA *24*
    See also SAAS *12*
Dunmore, Helen 1952- *201*
Dunn, Anne M. 1940- *107*
Dunn, Carolyn 1965- *208*
Dunn, Harvey T(homas) 1884-1952 .... *34*
Dunn, Herb
    See Gutman, Dan
Dunn, John M. (III) 1949- *93*
Dunn, Judy
    See Spangenberg, Judith Dunn
Dunn, Mary Lois 1930- *6*
Dunnahoo, Terry Janson 1927- *7*
Dunne, Jeanette 1952- *72*
Dunne, Kathleen 1933- *126*
Dunne, Marie
    See Clark, Ann Nolan
Dunne, Mary Collins 1914- *11*
Dunne, Mary Jo
    See Dunne, Mary Collins
Dunnett, Kaitlyn
    See Emerson, Kathy Lynn
Dunnett, Margaret (Rosalind) 1909-1977 ..... *42*
Dunnick, Regan *178*
Dunphy, Madeleine 1962- *219*
Dunrea, Olivier 1953- *160*
    Brief entry *46*
    Earlier sketches in SATA *59, 118*
Dunrea, Olivier Jean-Paul Dominique
    See Dunrea, Olivier
Dunstan Muller, Rachel *221*
Dunton, Dorothy 1912- *92*
Dupasquier, Philippe 1955- *151*
    Earlier sketch in SATA *86*
duPont, Lindsay *207*
duPont, Lindsay Harper
    See duPont, Lindsay
DuPrau, Jeanne 1944- *215*
    Earlier sketch in SATA *144*
Dupuy, T(revor) N(evitt) 1916-1995 .... *4*
    Obituary *86*
DuQuette, Keith 1960- *155*
    Earlier sketch in SATA *90*
Duran, Gloria 1924- *171*
Duran, Gloria Bradley
    See Duran, Gloria
Duranceau, Suzanne 1952- *162*
Durand, Delphine 1971- *200*

Durand, Hallie 1964(?)- 216
Durango, Julia 1967- 215
  Earlier sketch in SATA 173
Durant, Alan 1958- 214
  Earlier sketches in SATA 121, 165
Durant, John 1902- 27
Durbin, William 1951- 174
  Earlier sketch in SATA 143
Durell, Ann 1930- 66
Durkee, Sarah 173
Durney, Ryan 205
Durrant, Lynda 1954- 212
  Earlier sketches in SATA 96, 148
Durrant, Sabine 210
Durrell, Gerald (Malcolm) 1925-1995 8
  Obituary 84
Durrell, Julie 1955- 94
Durrett, Deanne 1940- 144
  Earlier sketch in SATA 92
Durst, Sarah Beth 1974- 203
Dusikova, Maja 1946- 223
Du Soe, Robert C. 1892-1958
  See YABC 2
Dussling, Jennifer 1970- 143
  Earlier sketch in SATA 96
DuTemple, Lesley A. 1952- 113
Dutton, Sandra 191
Dutz
  See Davis, Mary Octavia
Duval, Katherine
  See James, Elizabeth
Duval, Kathy 1946- 181
Duvall, Aimee
  See Thurlo, Aimee
  and Thurlo, David
Duvall, Evelyn Millis 1906- 9
Duvall, Jill D. 1932- 102
Duvall, Jill Donovan
  See Duvall, Jill D.
Duvoisin, Roger (Antoine) 1904-1980 30
  Obituary 23
  Earlier sketch in SATA 2
  See also CLR 23
Dwiggins, Don(ald J.) 1913-1988 4
  Obituary 60
Dwight, Allan
  See Cole, Lois Dwight
Dwyer, Deanna
  See Koontz, Dean
Dwyer, K.R.
  See Koontz, Dean
Dyck, Peter J. 1914- 75
Dyer, Alan 1953- 218
Dyer, James (Frederick) 1934- 37
Dyer, Jane 191
  Earlier sketch in SATA 147
Dyer, Sarah 1978- 212
Dyer, Sarah L.
  See Dyer, Sarah
Dyess, John (Foster) 1939- 76
Dygard, Thomas J. 1931-1996 97
  Obituary 92
  Earlier sketch in SATA 24
  See also SAAS 15
Dyke, John 1935- 35

E

E. V. L.
  See Lucas, E(dward) V(errall)
Eagar, Frances (Elisabeth Stuart)
  1940-1978 11
  Obituary 55
Eager, Edward (McMaken) 1911-1964 17
  See also CLR 43
Eager, George 1921- 56
Eager, George B.
  See Eager, George
Eagle, Ellen 1953- 61

Eagle, Kin
  See Adlerman, Daniel (Ezra)
  and Adlerman, Kimberly M(arie)
Eagle, Mike 1942- 11
Eamer, Claire 1947- 222
Earle, Olive L(ydia) 1888-1982 7
Earle, William
  See Johns, W(illiam) E(arle)
Earls, Nick 1963- 156
  Earlier sketch in SATA 95
Early, Jack
  See Scoppettone, Sandra
Early, Jon
  See Johns, W(illiam) E(arle)
Early, Margaret 1951- 72
Earnest, Peter 1934- 222
Earnshaw, Brian 1929- 17
Earnshaw, Micky 1939- 88
Earnshaw, Spencer Wright
  See Earnshaw, Micky
Easley, MaryAnn 94
Eason, Alethea 1957- 197
Eastman, Charles A(lexander) 1858-1939
  See YABC 1
Eastman, P(hilip) D(ey) 1909-1986 33
  Obituary 46
Easton, Kelly 1960- 192
  Earlier sketch in SATA 141
Eastwick, Ivy (Ethel) O(live) 3
Eaton, Anne T(haxter) 1881-1971 32
Eaton, Anthony 1971- 167
Eaton, George L.
  See Verral, Charles Spain
Eaton, Janet
  See Givens, Janet E(aton)
Eaton, Jeanette 1886-1968 24
Eaton, Maxwell III 1981- 199
Eaton, Tom 1940- 22
Ebbeler, Jeff
  See Ebbeler, Jeffrey
Ebbeler, Jeffrey 1974- 206
Ebel, Alex 1927- 11
Eber, Dorothy (Margaret) Harley 1930- 27
Eberhart, Sheri S.
  See Tepper, Sheri S.
Eberle, Irmengarde 1898-1979 2
  Obituary 23
Eble, Diane 1956- 74
Eboch, Chris 113
Eccles Williams, Ferelith 1920- 22
Echeverria-Bis, Olivia 217
Echeverria Gyorkos, Charmaine 216
Echlin, Kim 1955- 166
Eckblad, Edith Berven 1923- 23
Ecke, Wolfgang 1927-1983
  Obituary 37
Eckert, Allan W. 1931- 91
  Brief entry 27
  Earlier sketch in SATA 29
  See also SAAS 21
Eckert, Horst 1931- 72
  Earlier sketch in SATA 8
  See also CLR 26
Ecklar, Julia (Marie) 1964- 112
Eddings, David 1931-2009 91
Eddings, David Carroll
  See Eddings, David
Ede, Janina 1937- 33
Edell, Celeste 12
Edelman, Lily (Judith) 1915-1981 22
Edelson, Edward 1932- 51
Edens, Cooper 1945- 166
  Earlier sketches in SATA 49, 112
Edens, (Bishop) David 1926- 39
Edey, Maitland A(rmstrong) 1910-1992 25
  Obituary 71
Edgerton, Perky 196
Edgeworth, Maria 1768-1849 21
  See also CLR 153
Edgson, Alison 211

Edgy, Wardore
  See Gorey, Edward (St. John)
Edison, Theodore
  See Stratemeyer, Edward L.
Edler, Tim(othy) 1948- 56
Edmiston, Jim 1948- 80
Edmonds, I(vy) G(ordon) 1917- 8
Edmonds, Walter D(umaux) 1903-1998 27
  Obituary 99
  Earlier sketch in SATA 1
  See also SAAS 4
Edmund, Sean
  See Pringle, Laurence
Edsall, Marian (Stickney) 1920- 8
Edwards, Al
  See Nourse, Alan E(dward)
Edwards, Anne 1927- 35
Edwards, Audrey 1947- 52
  Brief entry 31
Edwards, Becky (Jane) 1966- 125
Edwards, Bertram
  See Edwards, Herbert Charles
Edwards, Bronwen Elizabeth
  See Rose, Wendy
Edwards, Cecile Pepin 1916- 25
Edwards, David 1962- 198
Edwards, Dorothy 1914-1982 88
  Obituary 31
  Earlier sketch in SATA 4
Edwards, F. E.
  See Nolan, William F.
Edwards, Frank B. 1952- 93
Edwards, Gunvor 32
Edwards, Harvey 1929- 5
Edwards, Hazel (Eileen) 1945- 135
Edwards, Herbert Charles 1912- 12
Edwards, Jane Campbell 1932- 10
Edwards, Julia
  See Stratemeyer, Edward L.
Edwards, Julie
  See Andrews, Julie
Edwards, Julie Andrews
  See Andrews, Julie
Edwards, June
  See Bhatia, Jamunadevi
Edwards, Linda Strauss 1948- 49
  Brief entry 42
Edwards, Margaret (Alexander) 1902-1988
  Obituary 56
Edwards, Michelle 1955- 152
  Earlier sketch in SATA 70
Edwards, Monica le Doux Newton
  1912-1998 12
Edwards, Olwen
  See Gater, Dilys
Edwards, Page (Lawrence, Jr.) 1941-1999 ... 59
Edwards, Pamela Duncan 189
Edwards, R. T.
  See Goulart, Ron
Edwards, Sally (Cary) 1929- 7
Edwards, Samuel
  See Gerson, Noel Bertram
Edwards, Wallace 1957(?)- 170
Edwardson, Debby Dahl 223
Eeckhout, Emmanuelle 1976- 208
Egan, E. W. 1922- 35
Egan, Edward Welstead
  See Egan, E. W.
Egan, Kerry 175
Egan, Lorraine Hopping 1960- 134
  Earlier sketch in SATA 91
Egan, Tim 1957- 191
  Earlier sketches in SATA 89, 155
Egermeier, Elsie E(milie) 1890-1986 65
Eggenberger, David 1918- 6
Eggleston, Edward 1837-1902 27
Egielski, Richard 1952- 220
  Earlier sketches in SATA 11, 49, 106, 163
Egypt, Ophelia Settle 1903-1984 16
  Obituary 38

Ehlert, Lois 1934- *172*
  Earlier sketches in SATA *35, 69, 128*
  See also CLR 28
Ehlert, Lois Jane
  See Ehlert, Lois
Ehling, Katalin Olah 1941- *93*
Ehrenberg, Pamela 1972- *219*
Ehrenfreund, Norbert 1921- *86*
Ehrenhaft, Daniel 1970- *185*
Ehrenhaft, Daniel Parker
  See Ehrenhaft, Daniel
Ehrhardt, Karen 1963- *184*
Ehrlich, Amy 1942- *217*
  Earlier sketches in SATA *25, 65, 96, 132*
Ehrlich, Bettina Bauer 1903-1985 .... *1*
Ehrlich, Fred *205*
Ehrlich, Fred M.D.
  See Ehrlich, Fred
Ehrlich, H. M.
  See Ziefert, Harriet
Eichenberg, Fritz 1901-1990 .... *50*
  Earlier sketch in SATA *9*
Eichler, Margrit 1942- *35*
Eichner, James A. 1927- *4*
Eidson, Thomas 1944- *112*
Eifert, Virginia (Louise) S(nider) 1911-1966 . *2*
Eige, (Elizabeth) Lillian 1915- *65*
Eiken, J. Melia 1967- *125*
Einhorn, Edward 1970- *204*
Einsel, Naiad *10*
Einsel, Walter 1926- *10*
Einzig, Susan 1922- *43*
Eiseman, Alberta 1925- *15*
Eisenberg, Azriel (Louis) 1903-1985 .... *12*
Eisenberg, Lisa 1949- *155*
  Brief entry *50*
  Earlier sketch in SATA *57*
Eisenberg, Phyllis Rose 1924- *41*
Eisner, Vivienne
  See Margolis, Vivienne
Eisner, Will 1917-2005 .... *165*
  Earlier sketch in SATA *31*
Eisner, William Erwin
  See Eisner, Will
Eitzen, Allan 1928- *9*
Eitzen, Ruth (Carper) 1924- *9*
Ekwensi, C. O. D.
  See Ekwensi, Cyprian
Ekwensi, Cyprian 1921-2007 .... *66*
Ekwensi, Cyprian Odiatu Duaka
  See Ekwensi, Cyprian
Elam, Richard M(ace, Jr.) 1920- *9*
Elborn, Andrew
  See Clements, Andrew
  and Clements, Andrew
Elboz, Stephen 1956- *152*
Eldin, Peter 1939- *154*
Eldon, Kathy 1946- *107*
Eldridge, Marion *199*
Eley, Robin *219*
Elfman, Blossom 1925- *8*
Elgin, Kathleen 1923- *39*
Elia
  See Lamb, Charles
Eliot, A. D.
  See Jewett, Sarah Orne
Eliot, Alice
  See Jewett, Sarah Orne
Eliot, Anne
  See Cole, Lois Dwight
Eliot, Dan
  See Silverberg, Robert
Elish, Dan 1960- *204*
  Earlier sketches in SATA *68, 129*
Elisha, Ron 1951- *104*
Elisofon, Eliot 1911-1973
  Obituary *21*
Elkeles, Simone 1970- *187*
Elkin, Benjamin 1911-1995 .... *3*
Elkins, Dov Peretz 1937- *5*
Ellacott, S(amuel) E(rnest) 1911- *19*

Elleman, Barbara 1934- *147*
Ellen, Jaye
  See Nixon, Joan Lowery
Eller, Scott
  See Holinger, William (Jacques)
  and Shepard, Jim
Ellery, Amanda *216*
Ellestad, Myrvin
  See Ellestad, Myrvin H.
Ellestad, Myrvin H. 1921- *120*
Elliot, Bruce
  See Field, Edward
Elliot, David 1952- *208*
  Earlier sketch in SATA *122*
Elliott, Bruce
  See Field, Edward
Elliott, David 1947- *201*
  Earlier sketch in SATA *163*
Elliott, Don
  See Silverberg, Robert
Elliott, Elizabeth Shippen Green
  See Green, Elizabeth Shippen
Elliott, Janice 1931-1995 .... *119*
Elliott, Joey
  See Houk, Randy
Elliott, Laura Malone 1957- *197*
Elliott, L.M.
  See Elliott, Laura Malone
Elliott, Louise *111*
Elliott, Mark 1949- *210*
Elliott, Odette 1939- *75*
Elliott, Patricia 1946- *176*
Elliott, Sarah M(cCarn) 1930- *14*
Elliott, (Robert) Scott 1970- *153*
Elliott, William
  See Bradbury, Ray
Elliott, Zetta *206*
Ellis, (Mary) Amabel (Nassau Strachey)
  Williams
  See Williams-Ellis, (Mary) Amabel (Nassau
  Strachey)
Ellis, Ann Dee *210*
Ellis, Anyon
  See Rowland-Entwistle, (Arthur) Theodore
  (Henry)
Ellis, Carson 1975- *190*
Ellis, Carson Friedman
  See Ellis, Carson
Ellis, Deborah 1960- *187*
  Earlier sketch in SATA *129*
Ellis, E. S.
  See Ellis, Edward S.
Ellis, Edward S. 1840-1916
  See YABC *1*
Ellis, Edward Sylvester
  See Ellis, Edward S.
Ellis, Ella Thorp 1928- *127*
  Earlier sketch in SATA *7*
  See also SAAS *9*
Ellis, Harry Bearse 1921-2004 .... *9*
Ellis, Herbert
  See Wilson, Lionel
Ellis, Mel(vin Richard) 1912-1984 .... *7*
  Obituary *39*
Ellis, Richard 1938- *130*
Ellis, Sarah 1952- *179*
  Earlier sketches in SATA *68, 131*
  See also CLR *42*
Ellison, Chris *196*
Ellison, Elizabeth Stow 1970- *209*
Ellison, Emily *114*
Ellison, Lucile Watkins 1907(?)-1979 .... *50*
  Obituary *22*
Ellison, Virginia H(owell) 1910- *4*
Ellsberg, Edward 1891-1983 .... *7*
Ellsworth, Loretta 1954- *199*
Ellsworth, Mary Ellen (Tressel) 1940- *146*
Ellwand, David 1965(?)- *213*
Elmer, Robert 1958- *154*
  Earlier sketch in SATA *99*

Elmore, (Carolyn) Patricia 1933- *38*
  Brief entry *35*
El-Moslimany, Ann P(axton) 1937- *90*
Elschner, Geraldine 1954- *183*
Elspeth
  See Bragdon, Elspeth MacDuffie
Elster, Jean Alicia 1953- *150*
Elting, Mary 1906- *88*
  Earlier sketch in SATA *2*
  See also SAAS 20
Elvgren, Jennifer Riesmeyer *179*
Elwart, Joan Potter 1927- *2*
Elwell, Peter *220*
Elwood, Ann 1931- *55*
  Brief entry *52*
Elwood, Roger 1943-2007 .... *58*
Ely, Lesley *212*
Elya, Susan Middleton 1955- *202*
  Earlier sketches in SATA *106, 159*
Elzbieta *88*
Ember, Kathi *190*
Emberley, Barbara A. 1932- *146*
  Earlier sketches in SATA *8, 70*
  See also CLR 5
Emberley, Barbara Anne
  See Emberley, Barbara A.
Emberley, Ed 1931- *146*
  Earlier sketches in SATA *8, 70*
  See also CLR *81*
Emberley, Edward Randolph
  See Emberley, Ed
Emberley, Michael 1960- *189*
  Earlier sketches in SATA *34, 80, 119*
Emberley, Rebecca 1958- *218*
Embry, Margaret Jacob 1919-1975 .... *5*
Emecheta, Buchi 1944- *66*
  See also CLR *158*
Emecheta, Florence Onye Buchi
  See Emecheta, Buchi
Emerson, Alice B.
  See Benson, Mildred
Emerson, Kathy Lynn 1947- *63*
Emerson, Kevin *209*
Emerson, Ru 1944- *107*
  Earlier sketch in SATA *70*
Emerson, Sally 1952- *111*
Emerson, William K(eith) 1925- *25*
Emert, Phyllis R. 1947- *93*
Emert, Phyllis Raybin
  See Emert, Phyllis R.
Emery, Anne (McGuigan) 1907- *33*
  Earlier sketch in SATA *1*
Emmens, Carol Ann 1944- *39*
Emmett, Jonathan 1965- *188*
  Earlier sketch in SATA *138*
Emmons, Della (Florence) Gould 1890-1983
  Obituary *39*
Emory, Jerry 1957- *96*
Emrich, Duncan (Black Macdonald)
  1908-1970(?) *11*
Emshwiller, Carol 1921- *174*
  Autobiography Feature *174*
Emshwiller, Carol Fries
  See Emshwiller, Carol
Emslie, M. L.
  See Simpson, Myrtle L(illias)
Ende, Michael (Andreas Helmuth)
  1929-1995 .... *130*
  Brief entry *42*
  Obituary *86*
  Earlier sketch in SATA *61*
  See also CLR *138*
Enderle, Dotti 1954- *203*
  Earlier sketch in SATA *145*
Enderle, Judith (Ann) Ross 1941- *89*
  Autobiography Feature *114*
  Earlier sketch in SATA *38*
  See also SAAS 26
Endle, Kate *207*
Enell, Trinka (Gochenour) 1951- *79*

Enfield, Carrie
See Smith, Susan Vernon
Engdahl, Sylvia Louise 1933- 4
Autobiography Feature 122
See also CLR 2
See also SAAS 5
Engel, Diana 1947- 70
Engelbreit, Mary 1952- 169
Engelhart, Margaret S. 1924- 59
Engelmann, Kim (V.) 1959- 87
England, George Allan 1877-1936 102
Englart, Mindi Rose 1965- 146
Engle, Eloise
See Paananen, Eloise (Katherine)
Engle, Margarita 1951- 193
Englebert, Victor 1933- 8
English, James W(ilson) 1915- 37
English, Karen 202
Engstrom, Elizabeth 1951- 110
Enright, D(ennis) J(oseph) 1920-2002 25
Obituary 140
Enright, Dominique 194
Enright, Elizabeth (Wright) 1909-1968 9
See also CLR 4
Ensor, Barbara 180
Ensor, Robert (T.) 1922- 93
Enthoven, Sam 1974- 187
Entwistle, (Arthur) Theodore (Henry) Rowland
See Rowland-Entwistle, (Arthur) Theodore
(Henry)
Enys, Sarah L.
See Sloggett, Nellie
Epanya, Christian A(rthur Kingue) 1956- 91
Ephraim, Shelly S(chonebaum) 1952- 97
Ephron, Delia 1944- 197
Brief entry 50
Earlier sketch in SATA 65
Epler, Doris M. 1928- 73
Epp, Margaret A(gnes) 1913- 20
Eppenstein, Louise (Kohn) 1892-1987
Obituary 54
Epple, Anne Orth 1927- 20
Epstein, Anne Merrick 1931- 20
Epstein, Beryl 1910- 31
Earlier sketch in SATA 1
See also CLR 26
See also SAAS 17
Epstein, Beryl M. Williams
See Epstein, Beryl
Epstein, Perle S(herry) 1938- 27
Epstein, Rachel S. 1941- 102
Epstein, Samuel 1909-2000 31
Earlier sketch in SATA 1
See also CLR 26
See also SAAS 17
Erdman, Loula Grace 1905(?)-1976 1
Erdoes, Richard 1912- 33
Brief entry 28
Erdogan, Buket 187
Erdrich, Karen Louise
See Erdrich, Louise
Erdrich, Louise 1954- 141
Earlier sketch in SATA 94
Erickson, Betty J. 1923- 97
Erickson, Betty Jean
See Erickson, Betty J.
Erickson, John R. 1943- 136
Earlier sketch in SATA 70
Erickson, Jon 1948- 141
Erickson, Phoebe 59
Erickson, Russell E(verett) 1932- 27
Erickson, Sabra Rollins 1912-1995 35
Erickson, Walter
See Fast, Howard
Ericson, Walter
See Fast, Howard
Ericsson, Jennifer A. 170
Erikson, Mel 1937- 31
Eriksson, Eva 1949- 207
Ering, Timothy Basil 176

Erlanger, Baba
See Trahey, Jane
Erlbach, Arlene 1948- 160
Earlier sketches in SATA 78, 115
Erlbruch, Wolf 1948- 181
Erlich, Lillian (Feldman) 1910-1983 10
Erlings, Fridrik 1962- 196
Erlingsson, Fri****rik
See Erlings, Fridrik
Ermatinger, James W. 1959- 170
Ernest, William
See Berkebile, Fred D(onovan)
Ernst, (Lyman) John 1940- 39
Ernst, Kathleen
See Ernst, Kathleen A.
Ernst, Kathleen A. 1959- 162
Ernst, Kathryn (Fitzgerald) 1942- 25
Ernst, Lisa Campbell 1957- 212
Brief entry 44
Earlier sketches in SATA 55, 95, 154
Erskine, Kathryn 193
Ervin, Janet Halliday 1923- 4
Erwin, Will
See Eisner, Will
Esbaum, Jill 213
Earlier sketch in SATA 174
Esbensen, Barbara J(uster) 1925-1996 97
Brief entry 53
Earlier sketch in SATA 62
Eschbacher, Roger 160
Eschmeyer, R. E. 1898-1989 29
Escriva, Vivi 182
Eseki, Bruno
See Mphahlele, Es'kia
Esekie, Bruno
See Mphahlele, Es'kia
Eshmeyer, Reinhart Ernst
See Eschmeyer, R. E.
Eskridge, Ann E. 1949- 84
Espeland, Pamela (Lee) 1951- 128
Brief entry 38
Earlier sketch in SATA 52
Espinosa, Laura 203
Espinosa, Leo 203
Espriella, Don Manuel Alvarez
See Southey, Robert
Espy, Willard R(ichardson) 1910-1999 38
Obituary 113
Essakalli, Julie Klear 200
Essrig, Harry 1912- 66
Estep, Irene Compton 5
Esterl, Arnica 1933- 77
Estes, Eleanor (Ruth) 1906-1988 91
Obituary 56
Earlier sketch in SATA 7
See also CLR 70
Estoril, Jean
See Allan, Mabel Esther
Estrada, Pau 1961- 200
Earlier sketch in SATA 74
Etchemendy, Nancy 1952- 166
Earlier sketch in SATA 38
Etchemendy, Nancy Elise Howell
See Etchemendy, Nancy
Etchison, Birdie L(ee) 1937- 38
Etchison, Craig 1945- 133
Etherington, Frank 1945- 58
Eton, Robert
See Meynell, Laurence Walter
Ets, Marie Hall 1893-1984 2
See also CLR 33
Ettlinger, Doris 1950- 173
Eugnia, Maria 222
Eunson, (John) Dale 1904-2002 5
Obituary 132
Evan, Frances Y. 1951- 167
Evanoff, Vlad 1916- 59
Evans, Cambria 1981- 178
Evans, Douglas 1953- 144
Earlier sketch in SATA 93
Evans, Eva (Knox) 1905-1998 27

Evans, Freddi Williams 1957- 211
Earlier sketch in SATA 134
Evans, Greg 1947- 143
Earlier sketch in SATA 73
Evans, Hubert Reginald 1892-1986 118
Obituary 48
Evans, Katherine (Floyd) 1901-1964 5
Evans, Larry
See Evans, Laurence Chubb
Evans, Laurence Chubb 1939- 88
Evans, Lawrence Watt
See Watt-Evans, Lawrence
Evans, Leslie 1953- 214
Evans, Lezlie 180
Evans, Mari 1923- 10
Evans, Mark 19
Evans, Nancy 1950- 65
Evans, Nate 201
Evans, Patricia Healy
See Carpenter, Patricia (Healy Evans)
Evans, (Alice) Pearl 1927- 83
Evans, Shane W. 189
Evans, Shirlee 1931- 58
Evans, Tabor
See Cameron, Lou
and Knott, William C(ecil, Jr.)
and Wallmann, Jeffrey M(iner)
and Whittington, Harry (Benjamin)
Evarts, Esther
See Benson, Sally
Evarts, Hal G., (Jr.) 1915-1989 6
Everett, Gail
See Hale, Arlene
Evernden, Margery 1916- 5
Eversole, Robyn 1971- 74
Eversole, Robyn H.
See Eversole, Robyn
Eversole, Robyn Harbert
See Eversole, Robyn
Evslin, Bernard 1922-1993 83
Brief entry 28
Obituary 77
Earlier sketch in SATA 45
Ewart, Claire 1958- 145
Earlier sketch in SATA 76
Ewart, Franzeska G. 1950- 205
Ewen, David 1907-1985 4
Obituary 47
Ewing, Juliana (Horatia Gatty) 1841-1885 ... 16
See also CLR 78
Ewing, Kathryn 1921- 20
Eyerly, Jeannette 1908-2008 86
Obituary 196
Earlier sketch in SATA 4
See also SAAS 10
Eyerly, Jeannette Hyde
See Eyerly, Jeannette
Eyre, Dorothy
See McGuire, Leslie (Sarah)
Eyre, Frank 1910-1988
Obituary 62
Eyre, Katherine Wigmore 1901-1970 26
Ezzell, Marilyn 1937- 42
Brief entry 38

F

Fabe, Maxene 1943- 15
Faber, Doris (Greenberg) 1924- 78
Earlier sketch in SATA 3
Faber, Harold 1919-2010 5
Fabre, Jean Henri (Casimir) 1823-1915 22
Fabry, Glenn 1961- 205
Facklam, Margaret
See Thomas, Peggy
Facklam, Margery (Metz) 1927- 132
Earlier sketches in SATA 20, 85
Fadden, David Kanietakeron 196

Fadiman, Clifton (Paul) 1904-1999 .... *11*
  Obituary *115*
Fagan, Cary 1957- *186*
Fagan, Deva *220*
Fahs, Sophia Blanche Lyon 1876-1978 ...... *102*
Failing, Barbara Larmon *182*
Fain, Sarah 1971- *204*
Fair, David 1952- *96*
Fair, Sylvia 1933- *13*
Fairfax-Lucy, Brian (Fulke Cameron-Ramsay)
  1898-1974 .... *6*
  Obituary *26*
Fairfield, Flora
  See Alcott, Louisa May
Fairlie, Gerard 1899-1983
  Obituary *34*
Fairman, Joan A(lexandra) 1935- *10*
Faithfull, Gail 1936- *8*
Falcone, L(ucy) M. 1951- *155*
Falconer, Ian 1959- *179*
  Earlier sketch in SATA *125*
  See also CLR *146*
Falconer, James
  See Kirkup, James
Falconer, Lee N.
  See May, Julian
Falkner, Brian 1962- *206*
Falkner, Leonard 1900-1977 .... *12*
Fall, Andrew
  See Arthur, Robert, (Jr.)
Fall, Thomas
  See Snow, Donald Clifford
Faller, Regis 1968- *187*
Falls, C(harles) B(uckles) 1874-1960 .... *38*
  Brief entry *27*
Falstein, Louis 1909-1995 .... *37*
Falvey, David 1982- *222*
Falwell, Cathryn 1952- *196*
Fancher, Lou 1960- *177*
Fanelli, Sara 1969- *126*
  Earlier sketch in SATA *89*
Fanning, Leonard M(ulliken) 1888-1967 .... *5*
Fantaskey, Beth 1965- *217*
Faralla, Dana 1909- *9*
Faralla, Dorothy W.
  See Faralla, Dana
Farb, Peter 1929-1980 .... *12*
  Obituary *22*
Farber, Norma 1909-1984 .... *75*
  Obituary *38*
  Earlier sketch in SATA *25*
Fardell, John 1967- *195*
Fardell, John William
  See Fardell, John
Faria, Rosana *213*
Farish, Terry 1947- *146*
  Earlier sketch in SATA *82*
Farjeon, (Eve) Annabel 1919-2004 .... *11*
  Obituary *153*
Farjeon, Eleanor 1881-1965 .... *2*
  See also CLR *34*
Farley, Carol (J.) 1936- *137*
  Earlier sketch in SATA *4*
Farley, Terri *165*
Farley, Walter (Lorimer) 1915-1989 .... *132*
  Earlier sketches in SATA *2, 43*
Farlow, James O(rville, Jr.) 1951- *75*
Farmer, Jacqueline *210*
Farmer, Nancy 1941- *161*
  Earlier sketches in SATA *79, 117*
Farmer, Patti 1948- *79*
Farmer, Penelope (Jane) 1939- *105*
  Brief entry *39*
  Earlier sketch in SATA *40*
  See also CLR *8*
  See also SAAS *22*
Farmer, Peter 1950- *38*
Farmer, Philip Jose
  See Farmer, Philip Jose
Farmer, Philip Jose 1918-2009 .... *93*
  Obituary *201*

Farmer, Philipe Jos
  See Farmer, Philip Jose
Farnham, Burt
  See Clifford, Harold B(urton)
Farnsworth, Bill 1958- *186*
  Earlier sketches in SATA *84, 135*
Farooqi, Musharraf Ali 1968- *207*
Farquhar, Margaret C(utting) 1905-1988 ...... *13*
Farquharson, Alexander 1944- *46*
Farquharson, Martha
  See Finley, Martha
Farr, Diana *82*
  Earlier sketch in SATA *3*
Farr, Finis (King) 1904-1982 .... *10*
Farr, Richard 1960- *209*
Farrar, Jill
  See Morris, Jill
Farrar, Susan Clement 1917- *33*
Farrell, Ben
  See Cebulash, Mel
Farrell, John 1951- *204*
Farrell, Patrick
  See Odgers, Sally Farrell
Farrell, Sally
  See Odgers, Sally Farrell
Farrer, Vashti *167*
Farrington, Benjamin 1891-1974
  Obituary *20*
Farrington, S(elwyn) Kip, Jr. 1904-1983 ...... *20*
Farris, Christine King 1927- *206*
Farshtey, Greg(ory T.) 1965- *148*
Farthing, Alison 1936- *45*
  Brief entry *36*
Farthing-Knight, Catherine 1933- *92*
Fassler, Joan (Grace) 1931- *11*
Fast, Howard 1914-2003 .... *7*
  Autobiography Feature *107*
Fast, Howard Melvin
  See Fast, Howard
Fasulo, Michael 1963- *83*
Fatchen, Max 1920- *84*
  Earlier sketch in SATA *20*
  See also SAAS *20*
Fate, Marilyn
  See Collins, Paul
Father Goose
  See Ghigna, Charles
Fatigati, Evelyn 1948- *24*
Fatigati, Frances Evelyn
  See Fatigati, Evelyn
Fatio, Louise 1904-1993 .... *6*
Fatus, Sophie 1957- *182*
Faulhaber, Martha 1926- *7*
Faulkner, Anne Irvin 1906- *23*
Faulkner, Frank
  See Ellis, Edward S.
Faulkner, Nancy
  See Faulkner, Anne Irvin
Faulknor, Cliff(ord Vernon) 1913- *86*
Favole, Robert J(ames) 1950- *125*
Fax, Elton Clay 1909-1993 .... *25*
Faxon, Lavinia
  See Russ, Lavinia (Faxon)
Feagles, Anita M.
  See Feagles, Anita MacRae
Feagles, Anita MacRae 1927- *9*
Feagles, Elizabeth
  See Day, Beth (Feagles)
Feague, Mildred H. 1915- *14*
Fearnley, Jan 1965- *205*
  Earlier sketch in SATA *153*
Fearrington, Ann (Peyton) 1945- *146*
Fecher, Constance
  See Heaven, Constance (Christina)
Feder, Chris Welles 1938- *81*
Feder, Harriet K. 1928- *73*
Feder, Paula (Kurzband) 1935- *26*
Federici, Debbie 1965- *175*
Federici, Debbie Tanner
  See Federici, Debbie

Feelings, Muriel 1938- *16*
  See also CLR *5*
  See also SAAS *8*
Feelings, Muriel Lavita Grey
  See Feelings, Muriel
Feelings, Thomas 1933-2003 .... *69*
  Obituary *148*
  Earlier sketch in SATA *8*
  See also CLR *58*
  See also SAAS *19*
Feelings, Tom
  See Feelings, Thomas
Fehler, Gene 1940- *201*
  Earlier sketch in SATA *74*
Fehrenbach, T(heodore) R(eed, Jr.) 1925- *33*
Feiffer, Jules 1929- *201*
  Earlier sketches in SATA *8, 61, 111, 157*
Feiffer, Jules Ralph
  See Feiffer, Jules
Feiffer, Kate 1964- *206*
  Earlier sketch in SATA *170*
Feig, Barbara Krane 1937- *34*
Feig, Paul *221*
Feikema, Feike
  See Manfred, Frederick (Feikema)
Feil, Hila 1942- *12*
Feilen, John
  See May, Julian
Feinberg, Barbara Jane 1938- *123*
  Earlier sketch in SATA *58*
Feinberg, Barbara Silberdick
  See Feinberg, Barbara Jane
Feinstein, John 1956- *195*
  Earlier sketch in SATA *163*
Feldman, Anne (Rodgers) 1939- *19*
Feldman, Elane *79*
Feldman, Eve B. *221*
Feldman, Jody *200*
Felin, M. Sindy *194*
Felix
  See Vincent, Felix
Fell, Derek 1939- *167*
Fell, Derek John
  See Fell, Derek
Fellowes, Julian 1950- *198*
Fellows, Muriel H. *10*
Fellows, Stan 1957- *177*
Fellows, Stanley
  See Fellows, Stan
Felsen, Henry Gregor 1916-1995 .... *1*
  See also SAAS *2*
Felstead, Cathie 1954- *192*
Feltenstein, Arlene 1934- *119*
Feltenstine, Arlene H.
  See Feltenstein, Arlene
Felton, Harold William 1902-1991 .... *1*
Felton, Ronald Oliver 1909- *3*
Felts, Shirley 1934- *33*
Felts, Susannah 1973- *214*
Fenderson, Lewis H., Jr. 1907-1983 .... *47*
  Obituary *37*
Fenner, Carol (Elizabeth) 1929-2002 .... *89*
  Obituary *132*
  Earlier sketch in SATA *7*
  See also SAAS *24*
Fenner, Phyllis R(eid) 1899-1982 .... *1*
  Obituary *29*
Fensham, Elizabeth *169*
Fenten, Barbara D(oris) 1935- *26*
Fenten, D(onald) X. 1932- *4*
Fenton, Carroll Lane 1900-1969 .... *5*
Fenton, Edward 1917-1995 .... *7*
  Obituary *89*
Fenton, Joe *213*
Fenton, Mildred Adams 1899-1995 .... *21*
Fenwick, Patti
  See Grider, Dorothy
Feravolo, Rocco Vincent 1922- *10*
Ferber, Brenda A. 1967- *184*
Ferber, Edna 1887-1968 .... *7*
Fergus, Charles *114*

Ferguson, Alane 1957- *182*
Earlier sketch in SATA *85*
Ferguson, Bob
See Ferguson, Robert Bruce
Ferguson, Cecil 1931- *45*
Ferguson, Peter 1968- *199*
Ferguson, Robert Bruce 1927-2001 .... *13*
Ferguson, Sarah 1959- *180*
Earlier sketches in SATA *66, 110*
Ferguson, Sarah Margaret
See Ferguson, Sarah
Ferguson, Walter (W.) 1930- *34*
Fergusson, Erna 1888-1964 .... *5*
Fermi, Laura 1907-1977 .... *6*
Obituary *28*
Fern, Eugene A. 1919-1987 .... *10*
Obituary *54*
Fern, Tracey E. *202*
Fernandes, Eugenie 1943- *205*
Earlier sketches in SATA *77, 139*
Fernandez, Laura 1960- *171*
Ferraiolo, Jack D. *208*
Ferrari, Maria *123*
Ferrari, Michael *223*
Ferrari, Michael J.
See Ferrari, Michael
Ferreiro, Carmen 1958- *158*
Ferrell, Nancy Warren 1932- *70*
Ferrer, Isabel
See Riu, Isabel Ferrer
Ferri, Giuliano 1965- *197*
Ferrier, Lucy
See Penzler, Otto
Ferris, Helen Josephine 1890-1969 .... *21*
Ferris, James Cody
See McFarlane, Leslie
Ferris, Jean 1939- *202*
Brief entry *50*
Earlier sketches in SATA *56, 105, 149*
Ferris, Jeri Chase 1937- *84*
Ferry, Charles 1927- *92*
Earlier sketch in SATA *43*
See also CLR *34*
See also SAAS *20*
Fetz, Ingrid 1915- *30*
Feydy, Anne Lindbergh
See Sapieyevski, Anne Lindbergh
Fiammenghi, Gioia 1929- *66*
Earlier sketch in SATA *9*
Fiarotta, Noel
See Ficarotta, Noel
Fiarotta, Phyllis
See Ficarotta, Phyllis
Ficarotta, Noel 1944- *15*
Ficarotta, Phyllis 1942- *15*
Fichter, George S. 1922-1993 .... *7*
Ficocelli, Elizabeth *189*
Fidler, Kathleen (Annie) 1899-1980 .... *87*
Obituary *45*
Earlier sketch in SATA *3*
Fiedler, Jean(nette Feldman) *4*
Fiedler, Joseph Daniel *159*
Fiedler, Lisa *185*
Field, Dorothy 1944- *97*
Field, Edward 1924- *109*
Earlier sketch in SATA *8*
Field, Elinor Whitney 1889-1980
Obituary *28*
Field, Eugene 1850-1895 .... *16*
Field, Gans T.
See Wellman, Manly Wade
Field, James 1959- *113*
Field, Peter
See Drago, Harry Sinclair
and Dresser, Davis
and Mann, E(dward) B(everly)
Field, Rachel (Lyman) 1894-1942 .... *15*
See also CLR *21*
Fielding, Kate
See Oldfield, Jenny
Fields, Bryan W. 1958(?)- *188*

Fields, Lisa 1984(?)- *216*
Fields, Terri 1948- *191*
Fields, T.S.
See Fields, Terri
Fienberg, Anna 1956- *183*
Earlier sketch in SATA *112*
Fiery, Ann
See Barrows, Annie
Fife, Dale (Odile Hollerbach) 1901- *18*
Fighter Pilot, A
See Johnston, H(ugh) A(nthony) S(tephen)
Figler, Jeanie 1949- *123*
Figley, Marty Rhodes 1948- *158*
Earlier sketch in SATA *88*
Figueredo, D(anilo) H. 1951- *155*
Figueroa, Pablo 1938- *9*
Fijan, Carol 1918- *12*
Filderman, Diane E(lizabeth) 1959- *87*
Files, Meg 1946- *107*
Fillmore, Parker H(oysted) 1878-1944
See YABC *1*
Filstrup, Chris
See Filstrup, E(dward) Christian
Filstrup, E(dward) Christian 1942- *43*
Filstrup, Janie
See Merrill, Jane
Finbarr, Desmond
See Zobel Nolan, Allia
Finchler, Judy 1943- *93*
Finder, Martin
See Salzmann, Siegmund
Findlay, Jamieson 1958- *169*
Findon, Joanne 1957- *161*
Fine, Anne 1947- *197*
Earlier sketches in SATA *29, 72, 111, 160*
See also CLR *25*
See also SAAS *15*
Fine, Edith Hope *169*
Fine, Howard 1961- *181*
Fine, Jane
See Ziefert, Harriet
Finger, Charles J(oseph) 1869(?)-1941 .... *42*
Fink, William B(ertrand) 1916- *22*
Finke, Blythe Foote 1922- *26*
Finkel, George (Irvine) 1909-1975 .... *8*
Finkelstein, Norman H. 1941- *220*
Earlier sketches in SATA *73, 137*
Finkelstein, Norman Henry
See Finkelstein, Norman H.
Finlay, Alice Sullivan 1946- *82*
Finlay, Winifred Lindsay Crawford
(McKissack) 1910-1989 .... *23*
Finlayson, Ann 1925- *8*
Finley, Martha 1828-1909 .... *43*
See also CLR *148*
Finley, Mary Peace 1942- *83*
Finn, Mary *208*
Finney, Jack 1911-1995 .... *109*
Finney, Patricia 1958- *163*
Finney, Shan 1944- *65*
Finney, Walter Braden
See Finney, Jack
Firer, Ben Zion
See Firer, Benzion
Firer, Benzion 1914- *64*
Fireside, Bryna J. 1932- *73*
Firmin, Charlotte 1954- *29*
Firmin, Peter 1928- *58*
Earlier sketch in SATA *15*
Firth, Barbara *179*
Fischbach, Julius 1894-1988 .... *10*
Fischer, John
See Fluke, Joanne
Fischer, R.J.
See Fluke, Joanne
Fischer, Scott M. 1971- *195*
Fischer-Nagel, Andreas 1951- *56*
Fischer-Nagel, Heiderose 1956- *56*
Fischler, Shirley (Walton) *66*
Fischler, Stan(ley I.) *66*
Brief entry *36*

Fischtrom, Harvey 1933-1974 .... *3*
Fishback, Margaret
See Antolini, Margaret Fishback
Fishbone, Greg R. *195*
Fisher, Aileen (Lucia) 1906-2002 .... *73*
Obituary *143*
Earlier sketches in SATA *1, 25*
See also CLR *49*
Fisher, Barbara 1940- *44*
Brief entry *34*
Fisher, Carolyn 1968- *154*
Fisher, Catherine 1957- *155*
Fisher, Chris 1958- *80*
Fisher, Clavin C(argill) 1912- *24*
Fisher, Cynthia *195*
Fisher, Dorothy (Frances) Canfield 1879-1958
See YABC *1*
See also CLR *71*
Fisher, Gary L. 1949- *86*
Fisher, John 1909-1996 .... *15*
Fisher, John Oswald Hamilton
See Fisher, John
Fisher, Laura Harrison 1934- *5*
Fisher, Leonard Everett 1924- *176*
Autobiography Feature *122*
Earlier sketches in SATA *4, 34, 73, 120*
See also CLR *18*
See also SAAS *1*
Fisher, Lois I. 1948- *38*
Brief entry *35*
Fisher, Margery (Turner) 1913-1992 .... *20*
Obituary *74*
Fisher, Marshall Jon 1963- *113*
Fisher, Nikki
See Strachan, Ian
Fisher, Robert (Tempest) 1943- *47*
Fisher, Suzanne
See Staples, Suzanne Fisher
Fisher, Valorie *214*
Earlier sketch in SATA *177*
Fishman, Cathy Goldberg 1951- *106*
Fisk, Nicholas
See Higginbottom, David
Fisk, Pauline 1948- *160*
Earlier sketch in SATA *66*
Fiske, Tarleton
See Bloch, Robert (Albert)
Fisscher, Catharina G. M. 1958- *142*
Fisscher, Tiny
See Fisscher, Catharina G. M.
Fitch, Clarke
See Sinclair, Upton
Fitch, John IV
See Cormier, Robert
Fitch, Sheree 1956- *178*
Earlier sketch in SATA *108*
Fitschen, Dale 1937- *20*
Fitzalan, Roger
See Trevor, Elleston
Fitzgerald, Captain Hugh
See Baum, L. Frank
FitzGerald, Cathleen 1932-1987
Obituary *50*
Fitzgerald, Dawn *175*
Fitzgerald, Edward Earl 1919-2001 .... *20*
Fitzgerald, F(rancis) A(nthony) 1940- *15*
Fitzgerald, Joanne 1956- *198*
Fitzgerald, John D(ennis) 1907(?)-1988 .... *20*
Obituary *56*
See also CLR *1*
Fitzgerald, Merni Ingrassia 1955- *53*
Fitzgibbon, Terry 1948- *121*
Fitzhardinge, Joan Margaret 1912- *73*
Earlier sketch in SATA *2*
See also CLR *5*
See also SAAS *3*
Fitzhugh, Louise (Perkins) 1928-1974 .... *45*
Obituary *24*
Earlier sketch in SATA *1*
See also CLR *72*
Fitzhugh, Percy Keese 1876-1950 .... *65*

Fitzmaurice, Kathryn *217*
Fitzpatrick, Marie-Louise 1962- *189*
  Earlier sketch in SATA *125*
FitzRalph, Matthew
  See McInerny, Ralph
Fitz-Randolph, Jane (Currens) 1915- *51*
Fitzsimons, Cecilia 1952- *97*
Fitzsimons, Cecilia A.L.
  See Fitzsimons, Cecilia
Flack, Marjorie 1897-1958 .... *100*
  See also YABC *2*
  See also CLR *28*
Flack, Naomi John White -1999 .... *40*
  Brief entry *35*
Flake, Sharon G. *166*
Flanagan, John 1944- *180*
Flanagan, John Anthony
  See Flanagan, John
Flannery, Kate
  See De Goldi, Kate
Flatt, Lizann 1966- *88*
Fleagle, Gail S(hatto) 1940- *117*
Fleetwood, Jenni 1947- *80*
Fleischer, Jane
  See Oppenheim, Joanne
Fleischhauer-Hardt, Helga 1936- *30*
Fleischman, Albert Sidney
  See Fleischman, Sid
Fleischman, John 1948- *145*
Fleischman, Paul 1952- *156*
  Brief entry *32*
  Earlier sketches in SATA *39, 72, 110*
  See also CLR *66*
  See also SAAS *20*
Fleischman, Sid 1920-2010 .... *185*
  Earlier sketches in SATA *8, 59, 96, 148*
  See also CLR *15*
Fleischner, Jennifer 1956- *188*
  Earlier sketch in SATA *93*
Fleisher, Paul 1948- *132*
  Earlier sketch in SATA *81*
Fleisher, Robbin 1951-1977 .... *52*
  Brief entry *49*
Fleishman, Seymour 1918- *66*
  Brief entry *32*
Fleming, A. A.
  See Arthur, Robert, (Jr.)
Fleming, Alice Mulcahey 1928- *9*
Fleming, Candace 1962- *190*
  Earlier sketches in SATA *94, 143*
Fleming, Denise 1950- *173*
  Earlier sketches in SATA *81, 126*
Fleming, Elizabeth P. 1888-1985
  Obituary *48*
Fleming, Ian 1908-1964 .... *9*
Fleming, Ian Lancaster
  See Fleming, Ian
Fleming, Ronald Lee 1941- *56*
Fleming, Sally
  See Walker, Sally M.
Fleming, Stuart
  See Knight, Damon (Francis)
Fleming, Susan 1932- *32*
Fleming, Thomas 1927- *8*
Fleming, Thomas James
  See Fleming, Thomas
Fleming, Virginia (Edwards) 1923- *84*
Flesch, Y.
  See Flesch, Yolande
Flesch, Yolande 1950- *55*
Flesch, Yolande Catarina
  See Flesch, Yolande
Fletcher, Charlie *220*
Fletcher, Charlie May Hogue 1897-1977 .... *3*
Fletcher, Colin 1922-2007 .... *28*
Fletcher, Dirk
  See Cunningham, Chet
Fletcher, George U.
  See Pratt, (Murray) Fletcher
Fletcher, Helen Jill 1910- *13*

Fletcher, Ralph 1953- *195*
  Earlier sketches in SATA *105, 149*
  See also CLR *104*
Fletcher, Ralph J.
  See Fletcher, Ralph
Fletcher, Richard E. 1917(?)-1983
  Obituary *34*
Fletcher, Rick
  See Fletcher, Richard E.
Fletcher, Susan 1951- *181*
  Earlier sketches in SATA *70, 110*
Fletcher, Susan Clemens
  See Fletcher, Susan
Fleur, Paul
  See Pohl, Frederik
Flexner, James Thomas 1908-2003 .... *9*
Flinn, Alex 1966- *198*
  Earlier sketch in SATA *159*
Flint, Helen 1952- *102*
Flint, Russ 1944- *74*
Flitner, David, Jr. 1949- *7*
Flitner, David Perkins
  See Flitner, David, Jr.
Floca, Brian *190*
  Earlier sketch in SATA *155*
Floethe, Louise Lee 1913-1988 .... *4*
Floethe, Richard 1901-1998 .... *4*
Floherty, John Joseph 1882-1964 .... *25*
Flood, Bo
  See Flood, Nancy Bo
Flood, Nancy Bo 1945- *130*
Flood, Pansie Hart 1964- *140*
Flood, William 1942- *129*
Flooglebuckle, Al
  See Spiegelman, Art
Flora, James (Royer) 1914-1998 .... *30*
  Obituary *103*
  Earlier sketch in SATA *1*
  See also SAAS *6*
Flores-Galbis, Enrique 1952- *186*
Florian, Douglas 1950- *177*
  Earlier sketches in SATA *19, 83, 125*
Flory, Jane Trescott 1917- *22*
Flournoy, Valerie 1952- *95*
Flournoy, Valerie Rose
  See Flournoy, Valerie
Flowerdew, Phyllis -1994 .... *33*
Flowers, Pam 1946- *136*
Flowers, Sarah 1952- *98*
Floyd, Gareth 1940- *62*
  Brief entry *31*
Fluchere, Henri 1914-1991 .... *40*
Fluke, Joanne 1943- *88*
Flutsztejn-Gruda, Ilona 1930- *170*
Flynn, Barbara 1928- *9*
Flynn, Jackson
  See Bensen, Donald R.
  and Shirreffs, Gordon D(onald)
Flynn, Nicholas
  See Odgers, Sally Farrell
Flynn, Pat 1968- *214*
Flynn, Patrick
  See Flynn, Pat
Flynn, Rachel 1953- *171*
  Earlier sketch in SATA *109*
Flynn, Warren (G.) 1950- *154*
Fodor, R. V. 1944- *25*
Fodor, Ronald Victor
  See Fodor, R. V.
Fogelin, Adrian 1951- *175*
  Earlier sketch in SATA *129*
Foley, (Anna) Bernice Williams 1902-1987 . *28*
Foley, Greg E. 1969- *190*
Foley, June 1944- *44*
Foley, (Mary) Louise Munro 1933- *106*
  Brief entry *40*
  Earlier sketch in SATA *54*
Foley, Rae
  See Denniston, Elinore
Folke, Will
  See Bloch, Robert (Albert)

Follett, Helen Thomas 1884(?)-1970
  Obituary *27*
Folsom, Franklin (Brewster) 1907-1995 .... *5*
  Obituary *88*
Folsom, Michael (Brewster) 1938-1990 .... *40*
  Obituary *88*
Fombelle, Timothee de 1973- *218*
Fontenot, Mary Alice 1910-2003 .... *91*
  Obituary *209*
  Earlier sketch in SATA *34*
Fontes, Justine *172*
Fontes, Ron 1952- *183*
Foon, Dennis 1951- *119*
Fooner, Michael *22*
Foote, Timothy (Gilson) 1926- *52*
Forberg, Ati
  See Forberg, Beate Gropius
Forberg, Beate Gropius 1925- *22*
Forbes, Anna 1954- *101*
Forbes, Bryan 1926- *37*
Forbes, Cabot L.
  See Hoyt, Edwin P(almer), Jr.
Forbes, Esther 1891-1967 .... *100*
  Earlier sketch in SATA *2*
  See also CLR *147*
Forbes, Graham B. *1*
Forbes, Kathryn
  See McLean, Kathryn (Anderson)
Forbes, Robert
  See Arthur, Robert, (Jr.)
Ford, Albert Lee
  See Stratemeyer, Edward L.
Ford, Barbara *56*
  Brief entry *34*
Ford, Bernette *212*
Ford, Bernette G.
  See Ford, Bernette
Ford, B.G.
  See Ford, Bernette
Ford, Brian J(ohn) 1939- *49*
Ford, Carolyn 1938- *98*
Ford, Carolyn Mott
  See Ford, Carolyn
Ford, Christine 1953- *176*
Ford, David
  See Baldacci, David
  and Baldacci, David
Ford, David B.
  See Baldacci, David
Ford, David Baldacci
  See Baldacci, David
Ford, Elbur
  See Hibbert, Eleanor Alice Burford
Ford, Ellen 1949- *89*
Ford, George (Jr.) *31*
Ford, Hilary
  See Youd, Samuel
Ford, Hildegarde
  See Morrison, Velma Ford
Ford, Jerome W. 1949- *78*
Ford, Jerry
  See Ford, Jerome W.
Ford, John C. 1971- *221*
Ford, Juwanda G(ertrude) 1967- *102*
Ford, Marcia
  See Radford, Ruby L(orraine)
Ford, Nancy K(effer) 1906-1961
  Obituary *29*
Ford, Peter 1936- *59*
Ford, S. M.
  See Uhlig, Susan
Forde, Catherine 1961- *170*
Foreman, Mark *199*
Foreman, Michael 1938- *216*
  Earlier sketches in SATA *2, 73, 129, 135, 184*
  See also CLR *32*
  See also SAAS *21*
Foreman, Wilmoth 1939- *153*
Forest, Antonia 1915-2003 .... *29*
  Obituary *149*

Forest, Dial
    See Gault, William Campbell
Forest, Heather 1948- *185*
    Earlier sketch in SATA *120*
Forester, C. S. 1899-1966 .... *13*
Forester, Cecil Scott
    See Forester, C. S.
Forester, Victoria *214*
Forler, Nan *223*
Forman, Brenda 1936- *4*
Forman, James
    See Forman, James D.
Forman, James D. 1932-2009 .... *70*
    Earlier sketch in SATA *8*
Forman, James Douglas
    See Forman, James D.
Forman, Mark L.
    See Forman, M.L.
Forman, M.L. 1964- *215*
Forman, Ruth 1970- *186*
Forrest, Elizabeth
    See Salsitz, Rhondi Vilott
Forrest, Mary
    See Pausacker, Jenny
Forrest, Sybil
    See Markun, Patricia Maloney
Forrestal, Elaine 1941- *165*
    Earlier sketch in SATA *117*
Forrester, Frank H. 1919(?)-1986
    Obituary *52*
Forrester, Helen
    See Bhatia, Jamunadevi
Forrester, Jade
    See Pausacker, Jenny
Forrester, Marian
    See Schachtel, Roger
Forrester, Sandra 1949- *166*
    Earlier sketch in SATA *90*
Forrester, Victoria 1940- *40*
    Brief entry *35*
Forsee, (Frances) Aylesa -1986 .... *1*
Forsey, Chris 1950- *59*
Forshay-Lunsford, Cin 1965- *60*
Forster, E. M. 1879-1970 .... *57*
Forster, Edward Morgan
    See Forster, E. M.
Forsyth, Kate 1966- *154*
Fort, Paul
    See Stockton, Francis Richard
Forte, Maurizio 1961- *110*
Fortey, Richard 1946- *109*
Fortey, Richard A.
    See Fortey, Richard
Fortey, Richard Alan
    See Fortey, Richard
Forth, Melissa D(eal) *96*
Fortnum, Peggy
    See Nuttall-Smith, Margaret Emily Noel
Fortune, Eric *182*
Forward, Robert L(ull) 1932-2002 .... *82*
Foster, Alan Dean 1946- *70*
Foster, Brad W. 1955- *34*
Foster, Doris Van Liew 1899-1993 .... *10*
Foster, E(lizabeth) C(onnell) 1902- *9*
Foster, Elizabeth 1902- *12*
Foster, Elizabeth 1905-1963 .... *10*
Foster, F. Blanche 1919- *11*
Foster, G(eorge) Allen 1907-1969 .... *26*
Foster, Genevieve (Stump) 1893-1979 .... *2*
    Obituary *23*
    See also CLR *7*
Foster, Gerald L. *198*
Foster, Hal
    See Foster, Harold
Foster, Harold 1892-1982 .... *31*
Foster, Jeanne
    See Williams, Jeanne
Foster, John
    See Foster, John L(ouis)
    and Furcolo, Foster
Foster, John (Thomas) 1925- *8*

Foster, John L(ouis) 1941- *102*
Foster, Juliana *196*
Foster, Laura Louise (James) 1918- *6*
Foster, Leila Merrell 1929- *73*
Foster, Lynne 1937- *74*
Foster, Margaret Lesser 1899(?)-1979
    Obituary *21*
Foster, Marian Curtis 1909-1978 .... *23*
Foster, Mark 1961- *197*
Foster, Sally *58*
Fotheringham, Edwin *201*
Foulds, E. V.
    See Foulds, Elfrida Vipont
Foulds, Elfrida Vipont 1902-1992 .... *52*
Fountas, Angela Jane *180*
Fourie, Corlia 1944- *91*
Fourth Brother, The
    See Aung, (Maung) Htin
Fowke, Edith (Margaret) 1913-1996 .... *14*
Fowles, John 1926-2005 .... *22*
    Obituary *171*
Fowles, John Robert
    See Fowles, John
Fowles, Shelley 1956- *205*
Fox, Aileen 1907-2005 .... *58*
    Obituary *170*
Fox, Aileen Mary
    See Fox, Aileen
Fox, Annie 1950- *175*
Fox, Charles Philip 1913-2003 .... *12*
    Obituary *150*
Fox, Christyan *188*
Fox, Diane *188*
Fox, Eleanor
    See St. John, Wylly Folk
Fox, Fontaine Talbot, Jr. 1884-1964
    Obituary *23*
Fox, Fred 1903(?)-1981
    Obituary *27*
Fox, Freeman
    See Hamilton, Charles (Harold St. John)
Fox, Geoffrey 1941- *73*
Fox, Grace
    See Anderson, Grace Fox
Fox, Helen 1962- *181*
Fox, Larry *30*
Fox, Lorraine 1922-1976 .... *27*
    Earlier sketch in SATA *11*
Fox, Louisa
    See Kroll, Virginia L.
Fox, Mary Virginia 1919- *152*
    Brief entry *39*
    Earlier sketches in SATA *44, 88*
Fox, Mem 1946- *211*
    Earlier sketches in SATA *51, 103, 155*
    See also CLR *80*
Fox, Merrion Frances
    See Fox, Mem
Fox, Michael W(ilson) 1937- *15*
Fox, Norma Diane
    See Mazer, Norma Fox
Fox, Paula 1923- *167*
    Earlier sketches in SATA *17, 60, 120*
    See also CLR *96*
Fox, Robert J. 1927- *33*
Fox, Robert Joseph
    See Fox, Robert J.
Fox-Davies, Sarah 1956- *199*
Foyt, Victoria *187*
Fradin, Dennis
    See Fradin, Dennis Brindell
Fradin, Dennis Brindell 1945- *185*
    Earlier sketches in SATA *29, 90, 135*
Fradin, Judith Bloom 1945- *185*
    Earlier sketches in SATA *90, 152*
Frailey, Paige (Menefee) 1965- *82*
Frame, Janet 1924-2004 .... *119*
Frame, Janet Paterson
    See Frame, Janet

Frame, Paul 1913-1994 .... *60*
    Brief entry *33*
    Obituary *83*
Frances, Miss
    See Horwich, Frances R(appaport)
Franchere, Ruth *18*
Francis, Charles
    See Holme, Bryan
Francis, Dee
    See Haas, Dorothy F.
Francis, Dorothy 1926- *127*
    Earlier sketch in SATA *10*
Francis, Dorothy B.
    See Francis, Dorothy
Francis, Dorothy Brenner
    See Francis, Dorothy
Francis, Jaye
    See Pausacker, Jenny
Francis, Pamela (Mary) 1926- *11*
Franck, Eddie
    See Cooke, Frank E.
Franco, Betsy *223*
    Earlier sketches in SATA *150, 188*
Franco, Eloise (Bauder) 1910- *62*
Franco, Johan (Henri Gustave) 1908-1988 ... *62*
Franco, Marjorie *38*
Francois, Andre 1915-2005 .... *25*
Francoise
    See Seignobosc, Francoise
Frank, Anne 1929-1945 .... *87*
    Brief entry *42*
    See also CLR *101*
Frank, Annelies Marie
    See Frank, Anne
Frank, Daniel B. 1956- *55*
Frank, Emily R.
    See Frank, E.R.
Frank, E.R. 1967- *157*
Frank, Helene
    See Vautier, Ghislaine
Frank, Hillary 1976- *148*
Frank, John *199*
Frank, Josette 1893-1989 .... *10*
    Obituary *63*
Frank, Lucy 1947- *166*
    Earlier sketch in SATA *94*
Frank, Mary 1933- *34*
Frank, R., Jr.
    See Ross, Frank (Xavier), Jr.
Frankau, Mary Evelyn Atkinson 1899-1974 .. *4*
Frankel, Alona 1937- *66*
Frankel, Bernice *9*
Frankel, Edward 1910- *44*
Frankel, Ellen 1951- *78*
Frankel, Julie 1947- *40*
    Brief entry *34*
Frankenberg, Robert 1911- *22*
Frankland, David *207*
Franklin, Cheryl J. 1955- *70*
Franklin, Harold 1926- *13*
Franklin, Kristine L. 1958- *124*
    Earlier sketch in SATA *80*
Franklin, Lance
    See Lantz, Francess L(in)
Franklin, Madeleine
    See L'Engle, Madeleine
Franklin, Madeleine L'Engle
    See L'Engle, Madeleine
Franklin, Madeleine L'Engle Camp
    See L'Engle, Madeleine
Franklin, Max
    See Deming, Richard
Franklin, Steve
    See Stevens, Franklin
Franson, Leanne 1963- *223*
    Earlier sketch in SATA *111*
Franson, Scott E. 1966- *192*
Franzen, Nils-Olof 1916- *10*
Frascino, Edward *48*
    Brief entry *33*
    See also SAAS *9*

Frasconi, Antonio 1919- *131*
  Earlier sketches in SATA *6, 53*
  See also SAAS *11*
Fraser, Betty
  See Fraser, Elizabeth Marr
Fraser, Elizabeth Marr 1928- *31*
Fraser, Eric (George) 1902-1983 .... *38*
Fraser, Mary Ann 1959- *214*
  Earlier sketches in SATA *76, 137*
  See also SAAS *23*
Fraser, Wynnette (McFaddin) 1925- *90*
Frasier, Debra 1953- *182*
  Earlier sketches in SATA *69, 112*
Fraustino, Lisa Rowe 1961- *146*
  Autobiography Feature *146*
  Earlier sketch in SATA *84*
Frazee, Marla 1958- *187*
  Earlier sketches in SATA *105, 151*
Frazer, Megan 1977- *221*
Frazetta, Frank 1928-2010 .... *58*
Frazier, Craig 1955- *221*
  Earlier sketch in SATA *177*
Frazier, Neta (Osborn) Lohnes 1890-1990 ..... *7*
Frazier, Sundee T. 1968- *198*
Frazier, Sundee Tucker
  See Frazier, Sundee T.
Frederic, Mike
  See Cox, William R(obert)
Frederick, Heather Vogel *207*
Fredericks, Anthony D. 1947- *113*
Freed, Alvyn M. 1913-1993 .... *22*
Freedman, Benedict 1919- *27*
Freedman, Claire *185*
Freedman, Deborah 1960- *191*
Freedman, Jeff 1953- *90*
Freedman, Nancy 1920-2010 .... *27*
Freedman, Russell 1929- *175*
  Earlier sketches in SATA *16, 71, 123*
  See also CLR *71*
Freedman, Russell Bruce
  See Freedman, Russell
Freeman, Barbara C. 1906-1999 .... *28*
Freeman, Barbara Constance
  See Freeman, Barbara C.
Freeman, Bill
  See Freeman, William Bradford
Freeman, Don 1908-1978 .... *17*
  See also CLR *90*
Freeman, Ira Maximilian 1905-1987 .... *21*
Freeman, Kimberley
  See Wilkins, Kim
Freeman, Laura *200*
Freeman, Lucy (Greenbaum) 1916-2004 ...... *24*
Freeman, Mae 1907-1985 .... *25*
Freeman, Mae Blacker
  See Freeman, Mae
Freeman, Marcia S. 1937- *102*
Freeman, Marcia Sheehan
  See Freeman, Marcia S.
Freeman, Martha 1956- *201*
  Earlier sketches in SATA *101, 152*
Freeman, Nancy 1932- *61*
Freeman, Peter J.
  See Calvert, Patricia
Freeman, Sarah (Caroline) 1940- *66*
Freeman, Tor 1977- *164*
Freeman, VicToria
  See Freeman, Tor
Freeman, William Bradford 1938- *58*
  Brief entry *48*
Fregosi, Claudia (Anne Marie) 1946- *24*
Freitas, Donna 1972- *205*
French, Allen 1870-1946
  See YABC *1*
French, Dorothy Kayser 1926- *5*
French, Fiona 1944- *132*
  Earlier sketches in SATA *6, 75*
  See also CLR *37*
  See also SAAS *21*

French, Jackie *186*
  Autobiography Feature *139*
  Earlier sketches in SATA *108, 139*
  See French, Jackie Anne
  and French, Jacqueline Anne
French, Kathryn
  See Mosesson, Gloria R(ubin)
French, Martin *176*
French, Michael 1944- *49*
  Brief entry *38*
French, Paul
  See Asimov, Isaac
French, S. Terrell *216*
French, Simon 1957- *147*
  Earlier sketch in SATA *86*
French, Vivian *209*
  Earlier sketch in SATA *165*
Frenette, Liza *126*
Freschet, Gina 1960- *175*
  Earlier sketch in SATA *139*
Frewer, Glyn (M.) 1931- *11*
Frey, Darcy *98*
Freymann, Saxton 1958(?)- *178*
Freymann-Weyr, Garret 1965- *145*
Freymann-Weyr, Rhoda Garret Michaela
  See Freymann-Weyr, Garret
Frick, C. H.
  See Irwin, Constance (H.) Frick
Frick, Constance
  See Irwin, Constance (H.) Frick
Fricke, Aaron 1962- *89*
Fridell, Ron 1943- *124*
Fried, Janice *197*
Friedlander, Joanne K(ohn) 1930- *9*
Friedman, Aimee 1979- *189*
Friedman, D. Dina 1957- *180*
Friedman, Debra 1955- *150*
Friedman, Estelle (Ehrenwald) 1920- *7*
Friedman, Frieda 1905- *43*
Friedman, Ina R(osen) 1926- *136*
  Brief entry *41*
  Earlier sketch in SATA *49*
Friedman, Jerrold David
  See Gerrold, David
Friedman, Judi 1935- *59*
Friedman, Laurie 1964- *219*
  Earlier sketches in SATA *138, 179*
Friedman, Marvin 1930- *42*
  Brief entry *33*
Friedman, Robin 1968- *219*
  Earlier sketch in SATA *162*
Friedmann, Stan 1953- *80*
Friedrich, Otto (Alva) 1929-1995 .... *33*
Friedrich, Priscilla 1927- *39*
Friend, Catherine 1957(?)- *194*
Friend, David Michael 1975- *195*
Friend, Natasha 1972- *184*
Friendlich, Dick
  See Friendlich, Richard J.
Friendlich, Richard J. 1909- *11*
Friermood, Elisabeth Hamilton 1903-1992 .... *5*
Friesen, Bernice (Sarah Anne) 1966- *105*
Friesen, Gayle 1960- *200*
  Earlier sketch in SATA *109*
Friesen, Jonathan 1967(?)- *206*
Friesner, Esther 1951- *207*
  Earlier sketches in SATA *71, 168*
Friesner, Esther M.
  See Friesner, Esther
Friis-Baastad, Babbis Ellinor 1921-1970 .... *7*
Frimmer, Steven 1928- *31*
Frischmuth, Barbara 1941- *114*
Friskey, Margaret (Richards) 1901-1995 .... *5*
Fritts, Mary Bahr
  See Bahr, Mary (Madelyn)
Fritz, Jean (Guttery) 1915- *163*
  Autobiography Feature *122*
  Earlier sketches in SATA *1, 29, 72, 119*
  See also CLR *96*
  See also SAAS *2*
Froehlich, Margaret W(alden) 1930- *56*

Frois, Jeanne 1953- *73*
Froissart, Jean 1338(?)-1410(?) *28*
Froman, Elizabeth Hull 1920-1975 .... *10*
Froman, Robert (Winslow) 1917- *8*
Fromm, Lilo 1928- *29*
Frommer, Harvey 1937- *41*
Frost, A(rthur) B(urdett) 1851-1928 .... *19*
Frost, Elizabeth
  See Frost-Knappman, Elizabeth
Frost, Erica
  See Supraner, Robyn
Frost, Helen 1949- *194*
  Autobiography Feature *194*
  Earlier sketches in SATA *157, 183*
Frost, Helen Marie
  See Frost, Helen
Frost, Lesley 1899-1983 .... *14*
  Obituary *34*
Frost, Robert 1874-1963 .... *14*
  See also CLR *67*
Frost, Robert Lee
  See Frost, Robert
Frost, Shelley 1960- *138*
Frost-Knappman, Elizabeth 1943- *179*
Froud, Brian 1947- *150*
Fry, Annette R(iley) *89*
Fry, Christopher 1907-2005 .... *66*
Fry, Edward Bernard 1925- *35*
Fry, Rosalie Kingsmill 1911-1992 .... *3*
  See also SAAS *11*
Fry, Virginia Lynn 1952- *95*
Frye, Sally
  See Moore, Elaine
Fuchs, Bernie 1932- *162*
  Earlier sketch in SATA *95*
Fuchs, Erich 1916- *6*
Fuchshuber, Annegert 1940- *43*
Fucile, Tony *221*
Fuerst, Jeffrey B. 1956- *143*
Fuertes, Gloria 1918-1998 .... *115*
Fuge, Charles 1966- *144*
  Earlier sketch in SATA *74*
Fujikawa, Gyo 1908-1998 .... *76*
  Brief entry *30*
  Obituary *110*
  Earlier sketch in SATA *39*
  See also CLR *25*
  See also SAAS *16*
Fujita, Tamao 1905-1999 .... *7*
Fujiwara, Kim 1957- *81*
Fujiwara, Michiko 1946- *15*
Fuka, Vladimir 1926-1977
  Obituary *27*
Fulcher, Jennifer
  See Westwood, Jennifer
Fuller, Catherine Leuthold 1916- *9*
Fuller, Edmund (Maybank) 1914- *21*
Fuller, Iola
  See McCoy, Iola Fuller
Fuller, John G(rant, Jr.) 1913-1990 .... *65*
Fuller, Kathleen
  See Gottfried, Theodore Mark
Fuller, Lois Hamilton 1915- *11*
Fuller, Margaret 1810-1850 .... *25*
Fuller, Maud
  See Petersham, Maud
Fuller, Roy (Broadbent) 1912-1991 .... *87*
Fuller, Sarah Margaret
  See Fuller, Margaret
Fults, John Lee 1932- *33*
Funk, Thompson 1911- *7*
Funk, Tom
  See Funk, Thompson
Funke, Cornelia 1958- *209*
  Earlier sketches in SATA *154, 174*
  See also CLR *145*
Funke, Cornelia Caroline
  See Funke, Cornelia
Funke, Lewis 1912-1992 .... *11*
Fuqua, Jonathon Scott 1966- *141*

Furbee, Mary R.
    See Furbee, Mary Rodd
Furbee, Mary Rodd 1954- *138*
Furchgott, Terry 1948- *29*
Furlong, Monica (Mavis) 1930-2003 .... *86*
    Obituary *142*
Furlonger, Patricia
    See Wrightson, Patricia
Furman, Gertrude Lerner Kerman 1909- *21*
Furniss, Tim 1948- *49*
Furrow, Robert 1985- *172*
Furukawa, Toshi 1924- *24*
Fusillo, Archimede 1962- *137*
Futcher, Jane P. 1947- *76*
Futehali, Zahida
    See Whitaker, Zai
Fyleman, Rose (Amy) 1877-1957 .... *21*
Fyson, Jenny Grace
    See Fyson, J.G.
Fyson, J.G. 1904-1998 .... *42*

G

Gaan, Margaret 1914- *65*
Gaber, Susan 1956- *169*
    Earlier sketch in SATA *115*
Gaberman, Judie Angell
    See Angell, Judie
Gabhart, Ann
    See Gabhart, Ann H.
Gabhart, Ann H. 1947- *75*
Gable, Brian 1949- *195*
Gabler, Mirko 1951- *77*
Gabriel, Adriana
    See Rojany, Lisa
Gabrys, Ingrid Schubert
    See Schubert-Gabrys, Ingrid
Gackenbach, Dick 1927- *79*
    Brief entry *30*
    Earlier sketch in SATA *48*
Gadd, Jeremy 1949- *116*
Gaddis, Vincent H. 1913-1997 .... *35*
Gadler, Steve J. 1905-1985 .... *36*
Gaeddert, Lou Ann (Bigge) 1931- *103*
    Earlier sketch in SATA *20*
Gaeddert, Louann
    See Gaeddert, Lou Ann (Bigge)
Gaer, Joseph 1897-1969 .... *118*
Gaer, Yossef
    See Gaer, Joseph
Gaetz, Dayle Campbell 1947- *138*
Gaffney, Timothy R. 1951- *170*
    Earlier sketch in SATA *69*
Gaffron, Norma 1931- *97*
Gaffron, Norma Bondeson
    See Gaffron, Norma
Gag, Flavia 1907-1979
    Obituary *24*
Gag, Wanda (Hazel) 1893-1946 .... *100*
    See also YABC *1*
    See also CLR *150*
Gage, Brian *162*
Gage, Wilson
    See Steele, Mary Q(uintard Govan)
Gagliano, Eugene M. 1946- *150*
Gagliardo, Ruth Garver 1895(?)-1980
    Obituary *22*
Gagnon, Cecile 1936- *58*
Gaillard, Jason 1965- *200*
Gaiman, Neil 1960- *197*
    Earlier sketches in SATA *85, 146*
    See also CLR *109*
Gaiman, Neil Richard
    See Gaiman, Neil
Gainer, Cindy 1962- *74*
Gaines, Ernest J. 1933- *86*
    See also CLR *62*
Gaines, Ernest James
    See Gaines, Ernest J.

Gaither, Gloria 1942- *127*
Gal, Laszlo 1933- *96*
    Brief entry *32*
    Earlier sketch in SATA *52*
    See also CLR *61*
Galbraith, Ben 1980- *200*
Galbraith, Kathryn O. 1945- *219*
    Earlier sketch in SATA *85*
Galbraith, Kathryn Osebold
    See Galbraith, Kathryn O.
Galdone, Paul 1907(?)-1986 .... *66*
    Obituary *49*
    Earlier sketch in SATA *17*
    See also CLR *16*
Galindo, Claudia 1979- *203*
Galinsky, Ellen 1942- *23*
Gall, Chris 1961- *176*
Gallagher, Diana G. 1946- *153*
Gallagher, Lurlene Nora
    See McDaniel, Lurlene
Gallagher-Cole, Mernie 1958- *206*
Gallant, Roy A(rthur) 1924- *110*
    Earlier sketches in SATA *4, 68*
    See also CLR *30*
Gallardo, Evelyn 1948- *78*
Gallaz, Christophe 1948- *162*
    See also CLR *126*
Gallego Garcia, Laura 1977- *173*
Gallico, Paul 1897-1976 .... *13*
Gallico, Paul William
    See Gallico, Paul
Gallo, Donald R. 1938- *112*
    Autobiography Feature *104*
Gallo, Donald Robert
    See Gallo, Donald R.
Galloway, Owateka (S.) 1981- *121*
Galloway, Priscilla 1930- *112*
    Earlier sketch in SATA *66*
Gallup, Joan 1957- *128*
Galouchko, Annouchka Gravel 1960- *95*
Galt, Thomas Franklin, Jr. 1908-1989 .... *5*
Galt, Tom
    See Galt, Thomas Franklin, Jr.
Galvin, Matthew R. 1950- *93*
Galvin, Matthew Reppert
    See Galvin, Matthew R.
Gamble, Kim 1952- *183*
    Earlier sketches in SATA *81, 124*
Gambrell, Jamey *82*
Gamerman, Martha 1941- *15*
Gammell, Stephen 1943- *128*
    Earlier sketches in SATA *53, 81*
    See also CLR *83*
Ganly, Helen (Mary) 1940- *56*
Gannett, Ruth Chrisman (Arens)
    1896-1979 .... *33*
Gannett, Ruth Stiles 1923- *3*
Gannij, Joan *208*
Gannij, Joan Levine
    See Gannij, Joan
Gannon, Ned 1974- *205*
Gannon, Robert Haines 1931- *8*
Gano, Lila 1949- *76*
Gans, Roma 1894-1996 .... *45*
    Obituary *93*
Gant, Matthew
    See Hano, Arnold
Gantner, Susan (Verble) 1939- *63*
Gantos, Jack 1951- *169*
    Earlier sketches in SATA *20, 81, 119*
    See also CLR *85*
Gantos, John Bryan, Jr.
    See Gantos, Jack
Ganz, Yaffa 1938- *61*
    Brief entry *52*
Garafano, Marie 1942- *84*
Garant, Andre J. 1968- *123*
Garbe, Ruth Moore
    See Moore, Ruth (Ellen)
Garber, Esther
    See Lee, Tanith

Garcia, Cristina 1958- *208*
Garcia, Emma 1969- *198*
Garcia, Geronimo 1960- *222*
Garcia, Yolanda P. 1952- *113*
Garcia, Yolanda Pacheco
    See Garcia, Yolanda P.
Gard, Janice
    See Latham, Jean Lee
Gard, Joyce
    See Reeves, Joyce
Gard, Robert Edward 1910-1992 .... *18*
    Obituary *74*
Gard, (Sanford) Wayne 1899-1986
    Obituary *49*
Gardam, Jane 1928- *130*
    Brief entry *28*
    Earlier sketches in SATA *39, 76*
    See also CLR *12*
    See also SAAS *9*
Gardam, Jane Mary
    See Gardam, Jane
Gardella, Tricia 1944- *96*
Garden, Nancy 1938- *147*
    Autobiography Feature *147*
    Earlier sketches in SATA *12, 77, 114*
    See also CLR *51*
    See also SAAS *8*
Gardiner, John Reynolds 1944-2006 .... *64*
    Obituary *174*
Gardiner, Lindsey 1971- *144*
Gardner, Craig Shaw 1949- *99*
Gardner, Dic
    See Gardner, Richard (M.)
Gardner, Graham *159*
Gardner, Hugh 1910-1986
    Obituary *49*
Gardner, Jane Mylum 1946- *83*
Gardner, Jeanne LeMonnier 1925- *5*
Gardner, John, Jr. 1933-1982 .... *40*
    Obituary *31*
Gardner, John Champlin, Jr.
    See Gardner, John, Jr.
Gardner, John E(dward) 1917- *192*
Gardner, Lyn *192*
Gardner, Martin 1914-2010 .... *142*
    Earlier sketch in SATA *16*
Gardner, Miriam
    See Bradley, Marion Zimmer
Gardner, Richard (M.) 1931- *24*
Gardner, Richard A(lan) 1931-2003 .... *13*
    Obituary *144*
Gardner, Sally *177*
Gardner, Sandra 1940- *70*
Gardner, Scot 1968- *143*
Gardner, Sheldon 1934- *33*
Gardner, Ted
    See Gardner, Theodore Roosevelt II
Gardner, Theodore Roosevelt
    See Gardner, Theodore Roosevelt II
Gardner, Theodore Roosevelt II 1934- *84*
Garelick, May 1910-1989 .... *19*
Garfield, James B. 1881-1984 .... *6*
    Obituary *38*
Garfield, Leon 1921-1996 .... *76*
    Obituary *90*
    Earlier sketches in SATA *1, 32*
    See also CLR *21*
Garfinkle, Debra L.
    See Garfinkle, D.L.
Garfinkle, D.L. *187*
Garis, Howard R. 1873-1962 .... *13*
Garis, Howard Roger
    See Garis, Howard R.
Garland, Mark 1953- *79*
Garland, Mark A.
    See Garland, Mark
Garland, Michael 1952- *208*
    Earlier sketch in SATA *168*
Garland, Sarah 1944- *135*
    Earlier sketch in SATA *62*

Garland, Sherry 1948- *145*
  Autobiography Feature *145*
  Earlier sketches in SATA *73, 114*
Garner, Alan 1934- *69*
  Autobiography Feature *108*
  Earlier sketch in SATA *18*
  See also CLR *130*
Garner, David 1958- *78*
Garner, Eleanor Ramrath 1930- *122*
Garner, James Finn 1960(?)- *92*
Garnet, A. H.
  See Slote, Alfred
Garnett, Eve C. R. 1900-1991 .... *3*
  Obituary *70*
Garofoli, Viviana 1970- *186*
Garou, Louis P.
  See Bowkett, Stephen
Garraty, John A. 1920-2007 .... *23*
  Obituary *189*
Garraty, John Arthur
  See Garraty, John A.
Garren, Devorah-Leah
  See Devorah-Leah
Garret, Maxwell R. 1917- *39*
Garretson, Victoria Diane
  See Cox, Victoria
Garrett, Helen 1895- *21*
Garrett, Randall 1927-1987 .... *180*
Garrett, Richard 1920- *82*
Garrigue, Sheila 1931- *21*
Garrison, Barbara 1931- *163*
  Earlier sketch in SATA *19*
Garrison, Frederick
  See Sinclair, Upton
Garrison, Mary 1952- *146*
Garrison, Peter
  See Gardner, Craig Shaw
Garrison, Webb B(lack) 1919-2000 .... *25*
Garrity, Jennifer Johnson 1961- *124*
Garrity, Linda K. 1947- *128*
Garsee, Jeannine *199*
Garst, Doris Shannon 1894-1981 .... *1*
Garst, Shannon
  See Garst, Doris Shannon
Garth, Will
  See Hamilton, Edmond
  and Kuttner, Henry
Garthwaite, Marion H(ook) 1893-1981 .... *7*
Garton, Malinda D(ean) (?)-1976
  Obituary *26*
Garvie, Maureen 1944- *175*
Garvie, Maureen McCallum
  See Garvie, Maureen
Garza, Carmen Lomas 1948- *182*
Garza, Xavier *184*
Gascoigne, Bamber 1935- *62*
Gaskins, Pearl Fuyo 1957- *134*
Gasperini, Jim 1952- *54*
  Brief entry *49*
Gater, Dilys 1944- *41*
Gates, Doris 1901-1987 .... *34*
  Obituary *54*
  Earlier sketch in SATA *1*
  See also SAAS *1*
Gates, Frieda 1933- *26*
Gates, Susan 1950- *153*
Gates, Viola R. 1931- *101*
Gathorne-Hardy, Jonathan G. 1933- *124*
  Earlier sketch in SATA *26*
Gatti, Anne 1952- *103*
Gatty, Juliana Horatia
  See Ewing, Juliana (Horatia Gatty)
Gauch, Patricia Lee 1934- *80*
  Earlier sketch in SATA *26*
  See also CLR *56*
  See also SAAS *21*
Gauch, Sarah *223*
Gaudasinska, Elzbieta 1943- *190*
Gaul, Randy 1959- *63*
Gault, Clare 1925- *36*

Gault, Frank 1926-1982 .... *36*
  Brief entry *30*
Gault, William Campbell 1910-1995 .... *8*
Gauthier, Gail 1953- *203*
  Earlier sketches in SATA *118, 160*
Gaver, Becky
  See Gaver, Rebecca
Gaver, Rebecca 1952- *20*
Gavin, Jamila 1941- *223*
  Earlier sketches in SATA *96, 125*
Gay, Amelia
  See Hogarth, Grace (Weston Allen)
Gay, Francis
  See Gee, H(erbert) L(eslie)
Gay, Kathlyn 1930- *144*
  Earlier sketch in SATA *9*
Gay, Marie-Louise 1952- *179*
  Earlier sketches in SATA *68, 126*
  See also CLR *27*
  See also SAAS *21*
Gay, Michel 1947- *162*
Gay, Zhenya 1906-1978 .... *19*
Gaze, Gillian
  See Barklem, Jill
Gear, Kathleen M. O'Neal
  See Gear, Kathleen O'Neal
Gear, Kathleen O'Neal 1954- *166*
  Earlier sketch in SATA *71*
Gear, W. Michael 1955- *166*
  Earlier sketch in SATA *71*
Geary, Rick 1946- *142*
Geason, Susan 1946- *122*
Gedalof, Robin
  See McGrath, Robin
Gedge, Pauline (Alice) 1945- *101*
Gee, H(erbert) L(eslie) 1901-1977
  Obituary *26*
Gee, Maurice 1931- *101*
  Earlier sketch in SATA *46*
  See also CLR *56*
Gee, Maurice Gough
  See Gee, Maurice
Geehan, Wayne (E.) 1947- *107*
Geer, Charles 1922- *42*
  Brief entry *32*
Geeslin, Campbell 1925- *163*
  Earlier sketch in SATA *107*
Gehman, Mary W. 1923- *86*
Gehr, Mary 1910(?)-1997 .... *32*
  Obituary *99*
Geipel, Eileen 1932- *30*
Geis, Alissa Imre 1976- *189*
Geis, Darlene Stern 1918(?)-1999 .... *7*
  Obituary *111*
Geisel, Helen 1898-1967 .... *26*
Geisel, Theodor Seuss
  See Dr. Seuss
Geisert, Arthur 1941- *171*
  Brief entry *52*
  Earlier sketches in SATA *56, 92, 133*
  See also CLR *87*
  See also SAAS *23*
Geisert, Arthur Frederick
  See Geisert, Arthur
Geisert, Bonnie 1942- *165*
  Earlier sketch in SATA *92*
Geist, Ken *191*
Gelber, Lisa *210*
Geldart, William 1936- *15*
Gelinas, Paul J. 1904-1996 .... *10*
Gellis, Roberta 1927- *128*
Gellis, Roberta Leah Jacobs
  See Gellis, Roberta
Gellman, Marc *112*
Gelman, Amy 1961- *72*
Gelman, Jan 1963- *58*
Gelman, Rita Golden 1937- *131*
  Brief entry *51*
  Earlier sketch in SATA *84*
Gelman, Steve 1934- *3*
Gemignani, Tony 1973- *220*

Gemming, Elizabeth 1932- *11*
Gendel, Evelyn W. 1916(?)-1977
  Obituary *27*
Gennaro, Joseph F., Jr. 1924- *53*
Gennaro, Joseph Francis, Jr.
  See Gennaro, Joseph F., Jr.
Gentieu, Penny *204*
Gentile, Petrina 1969- *91*
Gentle, Mary 1956- *48*
Gentleman, David (William) 1930- *7*
Gentry, Marita *215*
Geoghegan, Adrienne 1962- *143*
George, Barbara
  See Katz, Bobbi
George, Emily
  See Katz, Bobbi
George, Gail
  See Katz, Bobbi
George, Jean
  See George, Jean Craighead
George, Jean C.
  See George, Jean Craighead
George, Jean Craighead 1919- *170*
  Earlier sketches in SATA *2, 68, 124*
  See also CLR *136*
George, Jessica Day 1976- *210*
George, John L(othar) 1916- *2*
George, Kristine O'Connell 1954- *156*
  Earlier sketch in SATA *110*
George, Lindsay Barrett 1952- *206*
  Earlier sketches in SATA *95, 155*
George, S. C. 1898- *11*
George, Sally
  See Orr, Wendy
George, Sidney Charles
  See George, S. C.
George, Twig C. 1950- *114*
George, W(illiam) Lloyd 1900(?)-1975
  Obituary *30*
Georgiou, Constantine 1927- *7*
Georgiou, Theo
  See Odgers, Sally Farrell
Geraghty, Paul 1959- *130*
Gerard, Jean Ignace Isidore 1803-1847 .... *45*
Geras, Adele 1944- *180*
  Autobiography Feature *180*
  Earlier sketches in SATA *23, 87, 129, 173*
  See also SAAS *21*
Geras, Adele Daphne Weston
  See Geras, Adele
Gerber, Carole 1947- *207*
Gerber, Linda *213*
Gerber, Merrill Joan 1938- *170*
  Autobiography Feature *170*
  Earlier sketches in SATA *64, 127*
Gerber, Perren 1933- *104*
Gerberg, Mort 1931- *64*
Gergely, Tibor 1900-1978 .... *54*
  Obituary *20*
Geringer, Laura 1948- *164*
  Earlier sketches in SATA *29, 94*
Gerler, William R(obert) 1917-1996 .... *47*
Gerrard, Jean 1933- *51*
Gerrard, Roy 1935-1997 .... *90*
  Brief entry *45*
  Obituary *99*
  Earlier sketch in SATA *47*
  See also CLR *23*
Gerritsen, Paula 1956- *177*
Gerrold, David 1944- *144*
  Earlier sketch in SATA *66*
Gershator, David 1937- *180*
Gershator, Phillis 1942- *188*
  Earlier sketches in SATA *90, 158*
Gershon, Dann 1955- *187*
Gershon, Gina 1962- *187*
Gerson, Corinne 1927- *37*
Gerson, Mary-Joan *136*
  Earlier sketch in SATA *79*
Gerson, Noel Bertram 1914-1988 .... *22*
  Obituary *60*

Gerstein, Mordicai 1935- *222*
    Brief entry *36*
    Earlier sketches in SATA *47, 81, 142, 178*
    See also CLR *102*
Gertridge, Allison 1967- *132*
Gervais, Bernadette 1959- *80*
Gervay, Susanne *183*
Gesner, Clark 1938-2002 .... *40*
    Obituary *143*
Gessner, Lynne 1919- *16*
Geter, Tyrone *150*
Getz, David 1957- *91*
Getzinger, Donna 1968- *128*
Geus, Mireille 1964- *207*
Gevirtz, Eliezer 1950- *49*
Gevry, Claudine *188*
Gewe, Raddory
    See Gorey, Edward (St. John)
Ghan, Linda (R.) 1947- *77*
Ghent, Natale 1962- *148*
Gherman, Beverly 1934- *123*
    Earlier sketch in SATA *68*
Ghigna, Charles 1946- *153*
    Earlier sketch in SATA *108*
Giacobbe, Beppe 1953- *174*
Giambastiani, Kurt R. A. 1958- *141*
Giannini, Enzo 1946- *68*
Gibala-Broxholm, Scott 1959(?)- *205*
Gibbons, Alan 1953- *198*
    Earlier sketch in SATA *124*
Gibbons, Faye 1938- *103*
    Earlier sketch in SATA *65*
Gibbons, Gail 1944- *201*
    Earlier sketches in SATA *23, 72, 104, 160*
    See also CLR *8*
    See also SAAS *12*
Gibbons, Gail Gretchen
    See Gibbons, Gail
Gibbons, Kaye 1960- *117*
Gibbs, Adrea 1960- *126*
Gibbs, Alonzo (Lawrence) 1915-1992 .... *5*
Gibbs, (Cecilia) May 1877-1969
    Obituary *27*
Gibbs, Tony
    See Gibbs, Wolcott, Jr.
Gibbs, Wolcott, Jr. 1935- *40*
Giblin, James Cross 1933- *197*
    Earlier sketches in SATA *33, 75, 122*
    See also CLR *29*
    See also SAAS *12*
Gibson, Andrew (William) 1949- *72*
Gibson, Barbara L. *205*
Gibson, Barbara Leonard
    See Gibson, Barbara L.
Gibson, Betty 1911- *75*
Gibson, Jo
    See Fluke, Joanne
Gibson, Josephine
    See Hine, Sesyle Joslin
    and Hine, Al(fred Blakelee)
Gibson, Sarah P. 1962- *211*
Gibson, William 1914-2008 .... *66*
    Obituary *199*
Gibson, William Ford
    See Gibson, William
Gidal, Nachum
    See Gidal, Tim Nachum
Gidal, Sonia (Epstein) 1922- *2*
Gidal, Tim Nachum 1909-1996 .... *2*
Gidalewitsch, Nachum
    See Gidal, Tim Nachum
Gideon, Melanie 1963- *175*
Giegling, John A(llan) 1935- *17*
Gifaldi, David 1950- *209*
    Earlier sketch in SATA *76*
Giff, Patricia Reilly 1935- *203*
    Earlier sketches in SATA *33, 70, 121, 160*
Giffard, Hannah 1962- *83*
Gifford, Clive 1966- *198*
Gifford, Griselda 1931- *171*
    Earlier sketch in SATA *42*

Gifford, Kerri 1961- *91*
Gifford, Peggy 1952- *191*
Gilbert, Ann
    See Taylor, Ann
Gilbert, Anne Yvonne 1951- *185*
Gilbert, Barbara Snow 1954- *97*
Gilbert, Catherine
    See Murdock, Catherine Gilbert
Gilbert, Frances
    See Collings, Gillian
Gilbert, Harriett 1948- *30*
Gilbert, (Agnes) Joan (Sewell) 1931- *10*
Gilbert, John (Raphael) 1926- *36*
Gilbert, Nan
    See Gilbertson, Mildred Geiger
Gilbert, Roby Goodale 1966- *90*
Gilbert, Ruth Gallard Ainsworth
    See Ainsworth, Ruth (Gallard)
Gilbert, Sara (Dulaney) 1943- *82*
    Earlier sketch in SATA *11*
Gilbert, Sheri L. *157*
Gilbert, Suzie 1956- *97*
Gilbert, W(illiam) S(chwenck) 1836-1911 ... *36*
Gilbert, Yvonne
    See Gilbert, Anne Yvonne
Gilbertson, Mildred Geiger 1908-1988 .... *2*
Gilbreath, Alice 1921- *12*
Gilbreth, Frank B., Jr. 1911-2001 .... *2*
Gilbreth, Frank Bunker
    See Gilbreth, Frank B., Jr.
Gilchrist, Jan Spivey 1949- *130*
    Earlier sketch in SATA *72*
Gilden, Mel 1947- *97*
Giles, Gail *196*
    Earlier sketch in SATA *152*
Gilfond, Henry *2*
Gilge, Jeanette 1924- *22*
Gili, Phillida 1944- *70*
Gill, Derek (Lewis Theodore) 1919-1997 ...... *9*
Gill, Margery Jean 1925- *22*
Gill, Shelley *176*
Gill, Stephen 1932- *63*
Gillespie, Carol Ann 1951- *158*
Gillett, Mary (Bledsoe) *7*
Gillette, Henry Sampson 1915- *14*
Gillette, J. Lynett 1946- *103*
Gillette, Jan Lynett
    See Gillette, J. Lynett
Gilley, Jeremy 1969- *174*
Gillham, Bill
    See Gillham, W(illiam) E(dwin) C(harles)
Gillham, W(illiam) E(dwin) C(harles)
    1936- *42*
Gilliam, Stan 1946- *39*
    Brief entry *35*
Gilliland, Alexis A. 1931- *72*
Gilliland, Alexis Arnaldus
    See Gilliland, Alexis A.
Gilliland, (Cleburne) Hap 1918- *92*
Gilliland, Judith Heide *180*
Gillmor, Don 1954- *127*
Gilman, Dorothy 1923- *5*
Gilman, Esther 1925- *15*
Gilman, Laura Anne *178*
Gilman, Phoebe 1940-2002 .... *104*
    Obituary *141*
    Earlier sketch in SATA *58*
Gilmore, Iris 1900-1982 .... *22*
Gilmore, Kate 1931- *87*
Gilmore, Mary (Jean Cameron) 1865-1962 . *49*
Gilmore, Rachna 1953- *209*
Gilmore, Susan 1954- *59*
Gilpin, Stephen *213*
    Earlier sketch in SATA *177*
Gilroy, Beryl (Agatha) 1924- *80*
Gilson, Barbara
    See Gilson, Charles James Louis
Gilson, Charles James Louis 1878-1943
    See YABC *2*

Gilson, Jamie 1933- *176*
    Brief entry *34*
    Earlier sketches in SATA *37, 91*
Gimpel, Carolyn
    See Hart, Carolyn
Ginsberg, Blaze 1987- *222*
Ginsburg, Mirra 1909-2000 .... *92*
    Earlier sketch in SATA *6*
    See also CLR *45*
Giovanni, Nikki 1943- *208*
    Earlier sketches in SATA *24, 107*
    See also CLR *73*
Giovanni, Yolanda Cornelia
    See Giovanni, Nikki
Giovanni, Yolande Cornelia
    See Giovanni, Nikki
Giovanni, Yolande Cornelia, Jr.
    See Giovanni, Nikki
Giovanopoulos, Paul (Arthur) 1939- *7*
Gipson, Billie
    See Letts, Billie
Gipson, Fred(erick Benjamin) 1908-1973 ...... *2*
    Obituary *24*
Girard, Linda (Walvoord) 1942- *41*
Giraudon, David 1975- *215*
Girion, Barbara 1937- *78*
    Earlier sketch in SATA *26*
    See also SAAS *14*
Girl, Nerdy
    See Castellucci, Cecil
Girouard, Patrick 1957- *155*
Girzone, Joseph F. 1930- *76*
Girzone, Joseph Francis
    See Girzone, Joseph F.
Gise, Joanne
    See Mattern, Joanne
Gist, E.M. *206*
Gittings, Jo (Grenville) Manton 1919- *3*
Gittings, Robert (William Victor) 1911-1992 . *6*
    Obituary *70*
Givens, Janet E(aton) 1932- *60*
Givner, Joan 1936- *171*
Givner, Joan Mary
    See Givner, Joan
Gladstone, Eve
    See Werner, Herma
Gladstone, Gary 1935- *12*
Gladstone, M(yron) J. 1923- *37*
Glanville, Brian (Lester) 1931- *42*
Glanzman, Louis S. 1922- *36*
Glaser, Byron 1954- *154*
Glaser, Dianne E(lizabeth) 1937- *50*
    Brief entry *31*
Glaser, Isabel Joshlin 1929- *94*
Glaser, Milton 1929- *151*
    Earlier sketch in SATA *11*
Glaser, Shirley *151*
Glaspell, Susan 1882(?)-1948
    See YABC *2*
Glass, Andrew 1949- *223*
    Brief entry *46*
    Earlier sketches in SATA *90, 150*
Glass, Linzi *175*
Glass, Linzi Alex
    See Glass, Linzi
Glasscock, Amnesia
    See Steinbeck, John
Glassman, Bruce 1961- *76*
Glatt, Lisa 1963- *217*
Glauber, Uta (Heil) 1936- *17*
Glazer, Thomas (Zachariah) 1914-2003 .... *9*
Glazer, Tom
    See Glazer, Thomas (Zachariah)
Gleasner, Diana (Cottle) 1936- *29*
Gleason, Judith 1929- *24*
Gleason, Katherine (A.) 1960- *104*
Gleeson, Libby 1950- *142*
    Autobiography Feature *142*
    Earlier sketches in SATA *82, 118*
Gleiter, Jan 1947- *111*

Gleitzman, Morris 1953- *156*
   Earlier sketch in SATA *88*
   See also CLR *88*
Glen, Maggie 1944- *88*
Glendinning, Richard 1917-1988 .... *24*
Glendinning, Sally
   See Glendinning, Sara W(ilson)
Glendinning, Sara W(ilson) 1913-1993 .... *24*
Glenn, John W. *195*
Glenn, Mel 1943- *93*
   Brief entry *45*
   Earlier sketch in SATA *51*
   See also CLR *51*
Glenn, Patricia Brown 1953- *86*
Glenn, Sharlee *159*
Glenn, Sharlee Mullins
   See Glenn, Sharlee
Glennon, Karen M. 1946- *85*
Gles, Margaret Breitmaier 1940- *22*
Glick, Carl (Cannon) 1890-1971 .... *14*
Glick, Ruth (Burtnick) 1942- *125*
Glick, Virginia Kirkus 1893-1980
   Obituary *23*
Gliewe, Unada (Grace) 1927- *3*
Glimmerveen, Ulco 1958- *85*
Glines, Carroll V(ane), Jr. 1920- *19*
Gliori, Debi 1959- *189*
   Earlier sketches in SATA *72, 138*
Globe, Leah Ain 1900- *41*
Glori Ann
   See Blakely, Gloria
Glovach, Linda 1947- *105*
   Earlier sketch in SATA *7*
Glover, Denis (James Matthews) 1912-1980 . *7*
Glubok, Shirley (Astor) *146*
   Autobiography Feature *146*
   Earlier sketches in SATA *6, 68*
   See also CLR *1*
   See also SAAS *7*
Gluck, Felix 1923-1981
   Obituary *25*
Glyman, Caroline A. 1967- *103*
Glynne-Jones, William 1907-1977 .... *11*
Gobbato, Imero 1923- *39*
Gobbletree, Richard
   See Quackenbush, Robert M(ead)
Goble, Dorothy *26*
Goble, Paul 1933- *131*
   Earlier sketches in SATA *25, 69*
   See also CLR *21*
Goble, Warwick (?)-1943 .... *46*
Godden, (Margaret) Rumer 1907-1998 .... *36*
   Obituary *109*
   Earlier sketch in SATA *3*
   See also CLR *20*
   See also SAAS *12*
Gode, Alexander
   See Gode von Aesch, Alexander (Gottfried
   Friedrich)
Gode von Aesch, Alexander (Gottfried
   Friedrich) 1906-1970 .... *14*
Godfrey, Jane
   See Bowden, Joan Chase
Godfrey, Martyn
   See Godfrey, Martyn N.
   and Godfrey, Martyn N.
Godfrey, Martyn N. 1949-2000 .... *95*
   See also CLR *57*
Godfrey, William
   See Youd, Samuel
Godkin, Celia 1948- *145*
   Earlier sketch in SATA *66*
Godkin, Celia Marilyn
   See Godkin, Celia
Godon, Ingrid 1958- *186*
Godwin, Laura 1956- *179*
Godwin, Sam
   See Pirotta, Saviour
Godwin, Sarah Massini
   See Massini, Sarah
Goede, Irene 1966- *208*

Goedecke, Christopher (John) 1951- *81*
Goekler, Susan
   See Wooley, Susan Frelick
Goembel, Ponder *204*
Goertzen, Glenda *172*
Goettel, Elinor 1930- *12*
Goetz, Delia 1898-1996 .... *22*
   Obituary *91*
Goffe, Toni 1936- *61*
Goffstein, Brooke
   See Goffstein, Marilyn Brooke
Goffstein, M. B.
   See Goffstein, Marilyn Brooke
Goffstein, Marilyn Brooke 1940- *70*
   Earlier sketch in SATA *8*
   See also CLR *3*
Goforth, Ellen
   See Francis, Dorothy
Gogol, Sara 1948-2004 .... *80*
Goh, Chan Hon 1969- *145*
Going, Kelly L.
   See Going, K.L.
Going, Kelly Louise
   See Going, K.L.
Going, K.L. *199*
   Earlier sketch in SATA *156*
Golann, Cecil Paige 1921-1995 .... *11*
Golbin, Andree 1923- *15*
Gold, Alison Leslie 1945- *104*
Gold, August 1955- *215*
Gold, Bernice *150*
Gold, Phyllis
   See Goldberg, Phyllis
Gold, Robert S(tanley) 1924- *63*
Gold, Sharlya *9*
Gold, Susan
   See Gold, Susan Dudley
Gold, Susan Dudley 1949- *147*
Goldbach, Veronica 1980- *220*
Goldberg, Grace 1956- *78*
Goldberg, Herbert S. 1926- *25*
Goldberg, Jacob 1943- *94*
Goldberg, Jake
   See Goldberg, Jacob
Goldberg, Myla 1972(?)- *210*
Goldberg, Phyllis 1941- *21*
Goldberg, Stan J. 1939- *26*
Goldberg, Susan 1948- *71*
Goldberg, Whoopi 1955- *119*
Goldberger, Judith M. 1948- *80*
Goldblatt, Stacey 1969(?)- *191*
Golden, Christie 1963- *167*
   Earlier sketch in SATA *116*
Goldentyer, Debra 1960- *84*
Goldfeder, Cheryl
   See Pahz, Cheryl Suzanne
Goldfeder, James
   See Pahz, James Alon
Goldfeder, Jim
   See Pahz, James Alon
Goldfinger, Jennifer P. 1963- *185*
Goldfrank, Helen Colodny 1912- *6*
Goldin, Augusta 1906-1999 .... *13*
Goldin, Barbara Diamond 1946- *129*
   Autobiography Feature *129*
   Earlier sketch in SATA *92*
   See also SAAS *26*
Goldin, David 1963- *101*
Golding, Julia 1969- *188*
Golding, Theresa Martin 1960- *150*
Golding, William 1911-1993
   See CLR *130*
Golding, William Gerald
   See Golding, William
Goldman, Alex J. 1917- *65*
Goldman, E. M. 1943- *103*
Goldman, Eleanor Maureen
   See Goldman, E. M.
Goldman, Elizabeth 1949- *90*
Goldman, Judy 1955- *212*
Goldman, Steven 1964- *207*

Goldman, Todd Harris *221*
Goldring, Ann 1937- *149*
Goldsborough, June 1923- *19*
Goldschmidt, Judy *202*
Goldsmith, Connie 1945- *147*
Goldsmith, Howard 1943- *108*
   Earlier sketch in SATA *24*
Goldsmith, John Herman Thorburn 1903-1987
   Obituary *52*
Goldsmith, Oliver 1730(?)-1774 .... *26*
Goldsmith, Ruth M. 1919- *62*
Goldstein, Nathan 1927- *47*
Goldstein, Philip 1910-1997 .... *23*
Goldston, Robert (Conroy) 1927- *6*
Goldstone, Bruce *183*
Goldstone, Lawrence A.
   See Treat, Lawrence
Goldszmit, Henryk 1878-1942 .... *65*
   See also CLR *152*
Golembe, Carla 1951- *79*
Golenbock, Peter 1946- *99*
Goll, Reinhold W(eimar) 1897-1993 .... *26*
Gollub, Matthew 1960- *134*
   Earlier sketch in SATA *83*
Golson, Terry *213*
Golson, Terry Blonder
   See Golson, Terry
Gomes, Filomena 1965- *183*
Gomez, Elena *191*
Gomez, Elizabeth *133*
Gomez-Freer, Elizabeth
   See Gomez, Elizabeth
Gomi, Taro 1945- *103*
   Earlier sketch in SATA *64*
   See also CLR *57*
Gondosch, Linda 1944- *58*
Gonsalves, Rob 1959- *209*
Gonyea, Mark *194*
Gonzalez, Catherine Troxell 1917-2000 .... *87*
Gonzalez, Christina
   See Gonzalez, Maya Christina
Gonzalez, Gloria 1940- *23*
Gonzalez, Julie 1958- *174*
Gonzalez, Julie Sehers
   See Gonzalez, Julie
Gonzalez, Lucia M. 1957- *202*
Gonzalez, Maya
   See Gonzalez, Maya Christina
Gonzalez, Maya Christina 1964- *175*
   Earlier sketch in SATA *115*
Gonzalez, Rigoberto 1970- *147*
Goobie, Beth 1959- *128*
Good, Alice 1950- *73*
Good, Clare
   See Romano, Clare
Good, Karen Hillard *214*
Goodall, Daphne Machin
   See Machin Goodall, Daphne (Edith)
Goodall, Jane 1934- *111*
Goodall, John S(trickland) 1908-1996 .... *66*
   Obituary *91*
   Earlier sketch in SATA *4*
   See also CLR *25*
Goodbody, Slim
   See Burstein, John
Goode, Diane 1949- *170*
   Earlier sketches in SATA *15, 84, 114*
Goode, Diane Capuozzo
   See Goode, Diane
Goode, Stephen Ray 1943- *55*
   Brief entry *40*
Goodenow, Earle 1913- *40*
Goodhart, Pippa 1958- *196*
   Earlier sketch in SATA *153*
Goodhue, Thomas W. 1949- *143*
Goodin, Sallie (Brown) 1953- *74*
Goodman, Alison 1966- *111*
Goodman, Deborah Lerme 1956- *50*
   Brief entry *49*
Goodman, Elaine 1930- *9*
Goodman, Emily *217*

Goodman, Joan Elizabeth 1950- *162*
  Earlier sketches in SATA *50, 94*
Goodman, Susan E. 1952- *181*
Goodman, Walter 1927-2002 .... *9*
Goodman Koz, Paula *211*
Goodrich, Carter 1959(?)- *221*
Goodrich, Samuel Griswold 1793-1860 .... *23*
Goodsell, Jane Neuberger 1921(?)-1988
  Obituary *56*
Goodweather, Hartley
  See King, Thomas
GoodWeather, Hartley
  See King, Thomas
Goodwin, Hal
  See Goodwin, Harold L(eland)
Goodwin, Harold L(eland) 1914-1990 .... *51*
  Obituary *65*
  Earlier sketch in SATA *13*
Goodwin, William 1943- *117*
Goor, Nancy (Ruth Miller) 1944- *39*
  Brief entry *34*
Goor, Ron(ald Stephen) 1940- *39*
  Brief entry *34*
Goossen, Agnes
  See Epp, Margaret A(gnes)
Goossens, Philippe 1963- *195*
Gootman, Marilyn E. 1944- *179*
Gopnik, Adam 1956- *171*
Gorbachev, Valeri 1944- *222*
  Autobiography Feature *143*
  Earlier sketches in SATA *98, 143, 184*
Gordion, Mark
  See Turtledove, Harry
Gordon, Ad
  See Hano, Arnold
Gordon, Amy 1949- *197*
  Earlier sketches in SATA *115, 156*
Gordon, Bernard Ludwig 1931-2010 .... *27*
Gordon, Colonel H. R.
  See Ellis, Edward S.
Gordon, David
  See Garrett, Randall
Gordon, Donald
  See Payne, Donald Gordon
Gordon, Dorothy 1893-1970 .... *20*
Gordon, Esther S(aranga) 1935- *10*
Gordon, Frederick *1*
Gordon, Gaelyn 1939-1997
  See CLR *75*
Gordon, Garrett
  See Garrett, Randall
Gordon, Gary
  See Edmonds, I(vy) G(ordon)
Gordon, Hal
  See Goodwin, Harold L(eland)
Gordon, Jeffie Ross
  See Enderle, Judith (Ann) Ross
  and Gordon, Stephanie Jacob
Gordon, John
  See Gesner, Clark
Gordon, John (William) 1925- *84*
Gordon, Lew
  See Baldwin, Gordon C(ortis)
Gordon, Margaret (Anna) 1939- *9*
Gordon, Mike 1948- *101*
Gordon, Mildred 1912-1979
  Obituary *24*
Gordon, Selma
  See Lanes, Selma G.
Gordon, Sheila 1927- *88*
  See also CLR *27*
Gordon, Shirley 1921- *48*
  Brief entry *41*
Gordon, Sol 1923- *11*
Gordon, Stephanie Jacob 1940- *89*
  Autobiography Feature *114*
  Earlier sketch in SATA *64*
  See also SAAS *26*
Gordon, Stewart
  See Shirreffs, Gordon D(onald)

Gordons, The
  See Gordon, Mildred
  and Gordon, Gordon
Gore, Leonid *222*
  Earlier sketch in SATA *185*
Gorelick, Molly C(hernow) 1920-2003 .... *9*
  Obituary *153*
Gorey, Edward (St. John) 1925-2000 .... *70*
  Brief entry *27*
  Obituary *118*
  Earlier sketch in SATA *29*
  See also CLR *36*
Gorham, Charles Orson 1868-1936 .... *36*
Gorham, Michael
  See Folsom, Franklin (Brewster)
Gorman, Carol *187*
  Earlier sketch in SATA *150*
Gorman, Jacqueline Laks 1955- *148*
Gorman, Mike *206*
Gormley, Beatrice 1942- *202*
  Brief entry *35*
  Earlier sketches in SATA *39, 127*
Gorog, Judith (Katharine Allen) 1938- *75*
  Earlier sketch in SATA *39*
Gorrell, Gena K. 1946- *170*
Gorsline, Douglas (Warner) 1913-1985 .... *11*
  Obituary *43*
Gorsline, (Sally) Marie 1928- *28*
Gorsline, S. M.
  See Gorsline, (Sally) Marie
Gorton, Julia *218*
Gorton, Kaitlyn
  See Emerson, Kathy Lynn
Gorton, Kathy Lynn
  See Emerson, Kathy Lynn
Goryan, Sirak
  See Saroyan, William
Goschke, Julia 1973- *208*
Goscinny, Rene 1926-1977 .... *47*
  Brief entry *39*
  See also CLR *37*
Goss, Clay(ton E.) 1946- *82*
Goss, Gary 1947- *124*
Goss, Mini 1963- *186*
Goto, Scott *203*
Gott, Barry *197*
Gottesman, S. D.
  See Kornbluth, C(yril) M.
  and Lowndes, Robert A(ugustine) W(ard)
  and Pohl, Frederik
Gottfried, Ted
  See Gottfried, Theodore Mark
Gottfried, Theodore Mark 1928- *150*
  Earlier sketch in SATA *85*
Gottlieb, Gerald 1923- *7*
Gottlieb, William P. 1917-2006 .... *24*
Gottlieb, William Paul
  See Gottlieb, William P.
Goudey, Alice E(dwards) 1898-1993 .... *20*
Goudge, Eileen 1950- *88*
Goudge, Elizabeth (de Beauchamp)
  1900-1984 .... *2*
  Obituary *38*
  See also CLR *94*
Gough, Catherine
  See Mulgan, Catherine
Gough, Philip 1908-1986 .... *45*
Gough, Sue 1940- *106*
Goulart, Ron 1933- *67*
  Earlier sketch in SATA *1*
Goulart, Ronald Joseph
  See Goulart, Ron
Gould, Alberta 1945- *96*
Gould, Chester 1900-1985 .... *49*
  Obituary *43*
Gould, Jean R(osalind) 1909-1993 .... *11*
  Obituary *77*
Gould, Lilian *6*
Gould, Marilyn 1928- *76*
  Earlier sketch in SATA *15*
Gould, Robert *154*

Gould, Steven 1955- *95*
Gould, Steven Charles
  See Gould, Steven
Gourley, Catherine 1950- *190*
  Earlier sketch in SATA *95*
Gourse, Leslie 1939-2004 .... *89*
Govan, (Mary) Christine Noble 1898-1985 ... *9*
Gove, Doris 1944- *72*
Govenar, Alan 1952- *189*
Govenar, Alan Bruce
  See Govenar, Alan
Govern, Elaine 1939- *26*
Gowen, L. Kris 1968- *156*
Graaf, Peter
  See Youd, Samuel
Graber, Alexander 1914-1997 .... *98*
  Earlier sketch in SATA *7*
Graber, George Alexander
  See Graber, Alexander
Graber, Janet 1942- *170*
Graber, Richard (Fredrick) 1927- *26*
Grabianski, Janusz 1928-1976 .... *39*
  Obituary *30*
Graboff, Abner 1919-1986 .... *35*
Grace, Fran(ces Jane) *45*
Grace, N.B.
  See Harper, Suzanne
Grace, Theresa
  See Mattern, Joanne
Gracza, Margaret Young 1928- *56*
Graduate of Oxford, A
  See Ruskin, John
Grady, Denise 1952- *189*
Graeber, Charlotte Towner *106*
  Brief entry *44*
  Earlier sketch in SATA *56*
Graef, Renee 1956- *204*
Graeme, Roderic
  See Jeffries, Roderic
Graf, Michael
  See Graf, Mike
Graf, Mike 1960- *164*
Grafe, Max *198*
Graff, Lisa 1981- *188*
Graff, Polly Anne Colver
  See Colver, Anne
Graff, (S.) Stewart 1908-2009 .... *9*
Graham, Ada 1931- *11*
Graham, Alastair 1945- *74*
Graham, Arthur Kennon
  See Harrison, David L.
Graham, Bob 1942- *187*
  Earlier sketches in SATA *63, 101, 151*
  See also CLR *31*
Graham, Brenda Knight 1942- *32*
Graham, Charlotte
  See Bowden, Joan Chase
Graham, Eleanor 1896-1984 .... *18*
  Obituary *38*
Graham, Ennis
  See Molesworth, Mary Louisa
Graham, Frank, Jr. 1925- *11*
Graham, Georgia 1959- *190*
Graham, Ian 1953- *112*
Graham, John 1926-2007 .... *11*
Graham, Kennon
  See Harrison, David L.
Graham, Larry
  See Graham, Lawrence
Graham, Lawrence 1962- *63*
Graham, Lawrence Otis
  See Graham, Lawrence
Graham, Linda
  See Graham-Barber, Lynda
Graham, Lorenz (Bell) 1902-1989 .... *74*
  Obituary *63*
  Earlier sketch in SATA *2*
  See also CLR *10*
  See also SAAS *5*
Graham, Margaret Bloy 1920- *11*
Graham, Robin Lee 1949- *7*

Graham, Shirley 1896(?)-1977
See Du Bois, Shirley Graham
Graham-Barber, Lynda 1944- *159*
Earlier sketch in SATA *42*
Graham-Cameron, M.
See Graham-Cameron, M(alcolm) G(ordon)
Graham-Cameron, M(alcolm) G(ordon)
1931- *53*
Brief entry *45*
Graham-Cameron, Mike
See Graham-Cameron, M(alcolm) G(ordon)
Grahame, Kenneth 1859-1932 .... *100*
See also YABC *1*
See also CLR *135*
Gralley, Jean *166*
Gramatky, Hardie 1907-1979 .... *30*
Obituary *23*
Earlier sketch in SATA *1*
See also CLR *22*
Grambling, Lois G. 1927- *206*
Earlier sketches in SATA *71, 148*
Grambo, Rebecca L(ynn) 1963- *109*
Grammer, June Amos 1927- *58*
Grand, Samuel 1912-1988 .... *42*
Grandits, John 1949- *192*
GrandPre, Mary 1954- *184*
Grandville, J. J.
See Gerard, Jean Ignace Isidore
Grandville, Jean Ignace Isidore Gerard
See Gerard, Jean Ignace Isidore
Granfield, Linda 1950- *160*
Earlier sketch in SATA *96*
Grange, Peter
See Nicole, Christopher (Robin)
Granger, Margaret Jane 1925(?)-1977
Obituary *27*
Granger, Michele 1949- *88*
Granger, Peggy
See Granger, Margaret Jane
Granowsky, Alvin 1936- *101*
Granstaff, Bill 1925- *10*
Granstrom, Brita 1969- *167*
Earlier sketch in SATA *111*
Grant, Bruce 1893-1977 .... *5*
Obituary *25*
Grant, Cynthia D. 1950- *147*
Earlier sketches in SATA *33, 77*
Grant, Eva 1907-1996 .... *7*
Grant, Evva H. 1913-1977
Obituary *27*
Grant, Gordon 1875-1962 .... *25*
Grant, Gwen(doline Ellen) 1940- *47*
Grant, Judyann Ackerman *211*
Grant, Katie M.
See Grant, K.M.
Grant, K.M. *175*
Grant, (Alice) Leigh 1947- *10*
Grant, Matthew G.
See May, Julian
Grant, Maxwell
See Gibson, Walter B(rown)
and Lynds, Dennis
Grant, Melvyn *183*
Grant, Myrna (Lois) 1934- *21*
Grant, Neil 1938- *154*
Earlier sketch in SATA *14*
Grant, Nicholas
See Nicole, Christopher (Robin)
Grant, Richard 1948- *80*
Grant, Skeeter
See Spiegelman, Art
Grater, Michael 1923- *57*
Gratz, Alan 1972- *212*
Gravel, Fern
See Hall, James Norman
Gravelle, Karen 1942- *166*
Earlier sketch in SATA *78*
Graves, Charles Parlin 1911-1972 .... *4*
Graves, Keith *191*
Earlier sketch in SATA *156*
Graves, Robert 1895-1985 .... *45*

Graves, Robert von Ranke
See Graves, Robert
Graves, Valerie
See Bradley, Marion Zimmer
Gravett, Emily 1972(?)- *189*
Gray, Betsy
See Poole, Gray Johnson
Gray, Caroline
See Nicole, Christopher (Robin)
Gray, Claudia *213*
Gray, Dianne E. *183*
Gray, Elizabeth Janet
See Vining, Elizabeth Gray
Gray, Genevieve S(tuck) 1920-1995 .... *4*
Gray, Harold (Lincoln) 1894-1968 .... *33*
Brief entry *32*
Gray, Jenny
See Gray, Genevieve S(tuck)
Gray, John Lee
See Jakes, John
Gray, Judith A. 1949- *93*
Gray, Judith Anne
See Gray, Judith A.
Gray, Keith *151*
Gray, Kes 1960- *153*
Gray, Les 1929- *82*
Gray, Libba Moore 1937- *83*
Gray, Luli 1945- *149*
Earlier sketch in SATA *90*
Gray, Marian
See Pierce, Edith Gray
Gray, Nicholas Stuart 1922-1981 .... *4*
Obituary *27*
Gray, Nigel 1941- *104*
Earlier sketch in SATA *33*
Gray, (Lucy) Noel (Clervaux) 1898-1983 .... *47*
Gray, Patricia (Clark) *7*
Gray, Patsey
See Gray, Patricia (Clark)
Gray, Rita *184*
Graydon, Shari 1958- *158*
Grayland, V. Merle
See Grayland, Valerie (Merle Spanner)
Grayland, Valerie (Merle Spanner) *7*
Grayson, Devin (Kalile) 1970- *119*
Grayson, Kristine
See Rusch, Kristine Kathryn
Grayson, Paul 1946- *79*
Graystone, Lynn
See Brennan, Joseph Lomas
Great Comte, The
See Hawkesworth, Eric
Greaves, Margaret 1914-1995 .... *87*
Earlier sketch in SATA *7*
Greaves, Nick 1955- *77*
Greban, Quentin 1977- *223*
Gree, Alain 1936- *28*
Green, Adam
See Weisgard, Leonard (Joseph)
Green, Anne Canevari 1943- *62*
Green, Brian
See Card, Orson Scott
Green, Cliff(ord) 1934- *126*
Green, Connie Jordan 1938- *80*
Green, D.
See Casewit, Curtis W(erner)
Green, Elizabeth Shippen 1871-1954 .... *139*
Green, Hannah
See Greenberg, Joanne (Goldenberg)
Green, Jane 1937- *9*
Green, Jessica *211*
Green, John 1977(?)- *170*
Green, Mary Moore 1906- *11*
Green, Morton 1937- *8*
Green, Norma B(erger) 1925- *11*
Green, Phyllis 1932- *20*
Green, Roger (Gilbert) Lancelyn 1918-1987 . *2*
Obituary *53*
Green, (James Le)Roy 1948- *89*
Green, Sheila Ellen 1934- *148*
Earlier sketches in SATA *8, 87*

Green, Timothy 1953- *91*
Greenaway, Kate 1846-1901 .... *100*
See also YABC *2*
See also CLR *111*
Greenbank, Anthony Hunt 1933- *39*
Greenberg, David 1954- *171*
Greenberg, David T.
See Greenberg, David
Greenberg, Harvey R. 1935- *5*
Greenberg, Jan 1942- *211*
Earlier sketches in SATA *61, 125*
Greenberg, Joanne (Goldenberg) 1932- *25*
Greenberg, Melanie Hope 1954- *214*
Earlier sketch in SATA *72*
Greenberg, Polly 1932- *52*
Brief entry *43*
Greenblat, Rodney Alan 1960- *106*
Greenburg, Dan 1936- *175*
Earlier sketch in SATA *102*
Greene, Bette 1934- *161*
Earlier sketches in SATA *8, 102*
See also CLR *140*
See also SAAS *16*
Greene, Carla 1916- *67*
Earlier sketch in SATA *1*
Greene, Carol *102*
Brief entry *44*
Earlier sketch in SATA *66*
Greene, Constance C(larke) 1924- *72*
Earlier sketch in SATA *11*
See also CLR *62*
See also SAAS *11*
Greene, Edgar
See Papademetriou, Lisa
Greene, Ellin 1927- *23*
Greene, Graham 1904-1991 .... *20*
Greene, Graham Henry
See Greene, Graham
Greene, Jacqueline Dembar 1946- *212*
Earlier sketches in SATA *76, 131*
Greene, Laura Offenhartz 1935- *38*
Greene, Meg
See Malvasi, Meg Greene
Greene, Michele 1962- *178*
Greene, Michele Dominguez
See Greene, Michele
Greene, Rhonda Gowler 1955- *160*
Earlier sketch in SATA *101*
Greene, Stephanie 1950- *221*
Earlier sketches in SATA *127, 173*
Greene, Wade 1933- *11*
Greene, Yvonne
See Flesch, Yolande
Greenfeld, Howard (Scheinman) 1928- *140*
Earlier sketch in SATA *19*
Greenfeld, Josh(ua Joseph) 1928- *62*
Greenfield, Eloise 1929- *155*
Earlier sketches in SATA *19, 61, 105*
See also CLR *38*
See also SAAS *16*
Greenhaus, Thelma Nurenberg 1903-1984
Obituary *45*
Greenhut, Josh
See Mercer, Sienna
Greening, Hamilton
See Hamilton, Charles (Harold St. John)
Greenlaw, M. Jean 1941- *107*
Greenleaf, Barbara Kaye 1942- *6*
Greenleaf, Peter 1910-1997 .... *33*
Greenlee, Sharon 1935- *77*
Greeno, Gayle 1949- *81*
Greenseid, Diane 1948- *178*
Earlier sketch in SATA *93*
Greenspun, Adele Aron 1938- *142*
Earlier sketch in SATA *76*
Greenstein, Elaine 1959- *150*
Earlier sketch in SATA *82*
Greenwald, Sheila
See Green, Sheila Ellen
Greenwood, Barbara 1940- *129*
Earlier sketch in SATA *90*

Greenwood, Mark 1958- 202
Greenwood, Pamela D. 1944- 115
Greer, Richard
    See Garrett, Randall
    and Silverberg, Robert
Gregg, Andrew K. 1929- 81
Gregg, Charles T(hornton) 1927- 65
Gregg, Walter H(arold) 1919- 20
Gregor, Arthur 1923- 36
Gregor, Lee
    See Pohl, Frederik
Gregori, Leon 1919- 15
Gregorian, Joyce Ballou 1946-1991 30
    Obituary 83
Gregorich, Barbara 1943- 184
    Earlier sketch in SATA 66
Gregorowski, Christopher 1940- 30
Gregory, Diana (Jean) 1933- 49
    Brief entry 42
Gregory, Harry
    See Gottfried, Theodore Mark
Gregory, Jean
    See Ure, Jean
Gregory, Kristiana 1951- 212
    Earlier sketches in SATA 74, 136
Gregory, Nan 1944- 192
    Earlier sketch in SATA 148
Gregory, Philippa 1954- 122
Gregory, Stephen
    See Penzler, Otto
Gregory, Valiska 1940- 82
Greif, Jean-Jacques 1944- 195
Greisman, Joan Ruth 1937- 31
Grendon, Stephen
    See Derleth, August (William)
Grenville, Pelham
    See Wodehouse, P. G.
Gretz, Susanna 1937- 7
Gretzer, John 18
Grewdead, Roy
    See Gorey, Edward (St. John)
Grey, Carol
    See Lowndes, Robert A(ugustine) W(ard)
Grey, Christopher 191
Grey, Christopher Peter
    See Grey, Christopher
Grey, Jerry 1926- 11
Grey, Mini 205
    Earlier sketch in SATA 166
Greybeard the Pirate
    See Macintosh, Brownie
Grey Owl
    See Belaney, Archibald Stansfeld
Gri
    See Denney, Diana
Gribbin, John 1946- 159
Gribbin, John R.
    See Gribbin, John
Grice, Frederick 1910-1983 6
Grider, Dorothy 1915- 31
Gridley, Marion E(leanor) 1906-1974 35
    Obituary 26
Grieco-Tiso, Pina 1954- 108
Grieder, Walter 1924- 9
Griego, Tony A. 1955- 77
Griese, Arnold A(lfred) 1921- 9
Griessman, Annette 1962- 170
    Earlier sketch in SATA 116
Grieve, James 1934- 146
Grifalconi, Ann 1929- 210
    Earlier sketches in SATA 2, 66, 133
    See also CLR 35
    See also SAAS 16
Griffin, Adele 1970- 195
    Earlier sketches in SATA 105, 153
Griffin, Elizabeth May 1985- 89
Griffin, Gillett Good 1928- 26
Griffin, Judith Berry 34
Griffin, Kitty 1951- 137
Griffin, Peni R. 1961- 193
    Earlier sketches in SATA 67, 99

Griffin, Steven A. 1953- 89
Griffin, Steven Arthur
    See Griffin, Steven A.
Griffin, W. E. B. 1929- 5
Griffith, Connie 1946- 89
Griffith, Gershom 1960- 85
Griffith, Helen V. 1934- 87
    Autobiography Feature 107
    Earlier sketch in SATA 39
Griffith, Helen Virginia
    See Griffith, Helen V.
Griffith, Jeannette
    See Eyerly, Jeannette
Griffith, Saul 1974- 200
Griffiths, Andy 1961- 196
    Earlier sketch in SATA 152
Griffiths, G(ordon) D(ouglas) 1910-1973
    Obituary 20
Griffiths, Helen 1939- 86
    Earlier sketch in SATA 5
    See also CLR 75
    See also SAAS 5
Grigson, Jane (McIntire) 1928-1990 63
Grimes, Lee 1920- 68
Grimes, Nikki 1950- 218
    Earlier sketches in SATA 93, 136, 174
    See also CLR 42
Grimly, Gris 186
Grimm, Jacob Ludwig Karl 1785-1863 22
    See also CLR 112
Grimm, Wilhelm Karl 1786-1859 22
    See also CLR 112
Grimm, William C(arey) 1907-1992 14
Grimm and Grim
    See Grimm, Jacob Ludwig Karl
    and Grimm, Wilhelm Karl
Grimm Brothers
    See Grimm, Jacob Ludwig Karl
    and Grimm, Wilhelm Karl
Grimsdell, Jeremy 1942- 83
Grimshaw, Nigel (Gilroy) 1925- 23
Grimsley, Gordon
    See Groom, Arthur William
Grindley, Jane Sally
    See Grindley, Sally
Grindley, Sally 1953- 148
Gringhuis, Dirk
    See Gringhuis, Richard H.
Gringhuis, Richard H. 1918-1974 6
    Obituary 25
Grinnell, David
    See Wollheim, Donald A(llen)
Grinnell, George Bird 1849-1938 16
Grinspoon, David
    See Grinspoon, David H.
Grinspoon, David H. 1959- 156
Grinspoon, David Harry
    See Grinspoon, David H.
Gripe, Maria 1923- 74
    Earlier sketch in SATA 2
    See also CLR 5
Gripe, Maria Kristina
    See Gripe, Maria
Gritton, Steve 223
Grobler, Piet 1959- 201
Groch, Judith (Goldstein) 1929- 25
Grode, Redway
    See Gorey, Edward (St. John)
Groener, Carl
    See Lowndes, Robert A(ugustine) W(ard)
Groening, Matt 1954- 116
    Earlier sketch in SATA 81
Grohmann, Susan 1948- 84
Grohskopf, Bernice 7
Grol, Lini R(icharda) 1913- 9
Grollman, Earl A. 1925- 22
Groom, Arthur William 1898-1964 10
Grooms, Duffy 1964- 169
Gross, Alan 1947- 54
    Brief entry 43
Gross, Ernie 1913- 67

Gross, Philip 1952- 164
    Earlier sketch in SATA 84
Gross, Philip John
    See Gross, Philip
Gross, Ruth Belov 1929- 33
Gross, Sarah Chokla 1906-1976 9
    Obituary 26
Grosser, Morton 1931- 74
Grosser, Vicky 1958- 83
Grossman, Bill 1948- 126
    Earlier sketch in SATA 72
Grossman, Nancy 1940- 29
Grossman, Patricia 1951- 73
Grossman, Robert 1940- 11
Grossmann-Hensel, Katharina 1973- 219
Grote, JoAnn A. 1951- 113
Groten, Dallas 1951- 64
Groth, John (August) 1908-1988 21
    Obituary 56
Groth-Fleming, Candace
    See Fleming, Candace
Grove, Vicki 1948- 151
    Autobiography Feature 151
    Earlier sketch in SATA 122
Grover, Lorie Ann 1964- 168
Grover, Wayne 1934- 69
Groves, Georgina
    See Symons, (Dorothy) Geraldine
Groves, Maketa 1950- 107
Groves, Seli 77
Grubb, Lisa 160
Gruber, Michael 1940- 173
Gruber, Terry (deRoy) 1953- 66
Gruelle, John 1880-1938 35
    Brief entry 32
    See also CLR 34
Gruelle, Johnny
    See Gruelle, John
Gruenberg, Sidonie Matsner 1881-1974 2
    Obituary 27
Gruhzit-Hoyt, Olga (Margaret) 1922- 127
    Earlier sketch in SATA 16
Grummer, Arnold E(dward) 1923- 49
Grunewalt, Pine
    See Kunhardt, Edith
Grunwell, Jeanne Marie 1971- 147
Grupper, Jonathan 137
Gryski, Camilla 1948- 72
Guarino, Dagmar
    See Guarino, Deborah
Guarino, Deborah 1954- 68
Guay, Georgette (Marie Jeanne) 1952- 54
Guay, Rebecca 209
Guay-Mitchell, Rebecca
    See Guay, Rebecca
Guback, Georgia 88
Guccione, Leslie Davis 1946- 111
    Earlier sketch in SATA 72
Guck, Dorothy 1913-2002 27
Gudeon, Karla 212
Guerny, Gene
    See Gurney, Gene
Guest, Elissa Haden 1953- 218
    Earlier sketch in SATA 125
Guest, Jacqueline 1952- 135
Guevara, Susan 167
    Earlier sketch in SATA 97
Gugler, Laurel Dee 95
Gugliotta, Bobette 1918-1994 7
Guianan, Eve 1965- 102
Guiberson, Brenda Z. 1946- 211
    Earlier sketches in SATA 71, 124
Guibert, Emmanuel 1964- 181
Guile, Melanie 1949- 152
    Earlier sketch in SATA 104
Guillaume, Jeanette G. Flierl 1899-1990 8
Guillot, Rene 1900-1969 7
    See also CLR 22
Guisewite, Cathy 1950- 57
Guisewite, Cathy Lee
    See Guisewite, Cathy

Gulbis, Stephen 1959- 142
Gulley, Judie 1942- 58
Gump, P. Q.
    See Card, Orson Scott
Gundrey, Elizabeth 1924- 23
Gunn, James E. 1923- 35
Gunn, James Edwin
    See Gunn, James E.
Gunn, Robin Jones 1955- 84
Gunnella 1956- 197
Gunning, Monica Olwen 1930- 161
Gunston, Bill
    See Gunston, William Tudor
Gunston, William Tudor 1927- 9
Gunterman, Bertha Lisette 1886(?)-1975
    Obituary 27
Gunther, John 1901-1970
Guravich, Dan 1918- 74
Gurko, Leo 1914- 9
Gurko, Miriam 1910(?)-1988 9
    Obituary 58
Gurney, Gene 1924- 65
Gurney, James 1958- 120
    Earlier sketch in SATA 76
Gurney, John Steven 1962- 143
    Earlier sketch in SATA 75
Gustafson, Sarah R.
    See Riedman, Sarah R(egal)
Gustafson, Scott 1956- 34
Gustavson, Adam 1974- 214
    Earlier sketch in SATA 176
Guthrie, A(lfred) B(ertram), Jr. 1901-1991 .. 62
    Obituary 67
Guthrie, Anne 1890-1979 28
Guthrie, Donna W. 1946- 105
    Earlier sketch in SATA 63
Gutierrez, Akemi 172
Gutierrez, Rudy 203
Gutman, Bill 128
    Brief entry 43
    Earlier sketch in SATA 67
Gutman, Dan 1955- 221
    Earlier sketches in SATA 77, 139, 188
Gutman, Naham 1899(?)-1981
    Obituary 25
Gutmann, Bessie Pease 1876-1960 73
Guy, Geoffrey 1942- 153
Guy, Ginger Foglesong 1954- 171
Guy, Rosa 1925- 122
    Earlier sketches in SATA 14, 62
    See also CLR 137
Guy, Rosa Cuthbert
    See Guy, Rosa
Guy, Susan 1948- 149
Guymer, (Wilhelmina) Mary 1909- 50
Guzman, Lila 1952- 168
Guzman, Rick 1957- 168
Gwaltney, Doris 1932- 181
Gwynne, Fred(erick Hubbard) 1926-1993 41
    Brief entry 27
    Obituary 75
Gwynne, Oscar A.
    See Ellis, Edward S.
Gwynne, Oswald A.
    See Ellis, Edward S.
Gyorkos, Charmaine Echeverria
    See Echeverria Gyorkos, Charmaine

                    H

Haab, Sherri 1964- 169
    Earlier sketch in SATA 91
Haar, Jaap ter
    See ter Haar, Jaap
Haarsma, P.J. 183
Haas, Carolyn Buhai 1926- 43
Haas, Dan 1957- 105

Haas, Dorothy F. 46
    Brief entry 43
    See also SAAS 17
Haas, Irene 1929- 96
    Earlier sketch in SATA 17
Haas, James E. 1943- 40
Haas, James Edward
    See Haas, James E.
Haas, Jessie 1959- 215
Haas, (Katherine) Jessie 1959- 135
    Autobiography Feature 135
    Earlier sketch in SATA 98
Haas, Merle S. 1896(?)-1985
    Obituary 41
Habenstreit, Barbara 1937- 5
Haber, Karen 1955- 78
Haber, Louis 1910-1988 12
Hacker, Randi 1951- 185
Hacker, Randi Dawn
    See Hacker, Randi
Hackett, John Winthrop 1910-1997 65
Hacks, Peter 1928-2003
    Obituary 151
Haddix, Margaret Peterson 1964- 187
    Earlier sketches in SATA 94, 125
Haddon, Mark 1962- 223
    Earlier sketch in SATA 155
Hader, Berta (Hoerner) 1891(?)-1976 16
Hader, Elmer (Stanley) 1889-1973 16
Hadithi, Mwenye
    See Hobson, Bruce
Hadley, Franklin
    See Winterbotham, R(ussell) R(obert)
Hadley, Lee 1934-1995 89
    Brief entry 38
    Obituary 86
    Earlier sketch in SATA 47
    See also CLR 40
    See also SAAS 14
Haeffele, Deborah 1954- 76
Haenel, Wolfram 1956- 89
    See also CLR 64
Hafner, Marylin 1925- 179
    Earlier sketches in SATA 7, 121
Haft, Erin
    See Ehrenhaft, Daniel
Hager, Alan 1940- 176
Hager, Alice Rogers 1894-1969
    Obituary 26
Hager, Betty 1923- 89
Hager, Jenna Bush
    See Bush, Jenna
Hager, Sarah 171
Hager, Thomas 1953- 119
Hager, Tom
    See Hager, Thomas
Hagerup, Klaus 1946- 186
Haggard, H(enry) Rider 1856-1925 16
Haggerty, James J(oseph) 1920- 5
Hagon, Priscilla
    See Allan, Mabel Esther
Hague, Kathleen 1949- 49
    Brief entry 45
Hague, Michael 1948- 185
    Brief entry 32
    Earlier sketches in SATA 48, 80, 129
Hague, Michael R.
    See Hague, Michael
Hague, Susan Kathleen
    See Hague, Kathleen
Hahn, Emily 1905-1997 3
    Obituary 96
Hahn, Hannelore 8
Hahn, James (Sage) 1947- 9
Hahn, Lynn 1949- 9
Hahn, Mary Downing 1937- 208
    Autobiography Feature 157
    Brief entry 44
    Earlier sketches in SATA 50, 81, 138, 157
    See also SAAS 12
Hahn, Michael T. 1953- 92

Hahn, Mona Lynn
    See Hahn, Lynn
Haig, Matt 1975- 221
Haig-Brown, Roderick (Langmere)
    1908-1976 12
    See also CLR 31
Haight, Anne Lyon 1895-1977
    Obituary 30
Haight, Rip
    See Carpenter, John
Haight, Sandy 1949- 79
Haij, Vera
    See Jansson, Tove (Marika)
Hailstone, Ruth 219
Haines, Gail Kay 1943- 11
Haines, Margaret Ann Beck
    See Beck, Peggy
Haining, Peter 1940-2007 14
    Obituary 188
Haining, Peter Alexander
    See Haining, Peter
Hains, Harriet
    See Watson, Carol
Hajdusiewicz, Babs Bell 163
Hakim, Joy 1931- 173
    Earlier sketch in SATA 83
Halacy, D. S., Jr. 1919-2002 36
    See also SAAS 8
Halacy, Dan
    See Halacy, D. S., Jr.
Halam, Ann
    See Jones, Gwyneth A.
Haldane, Roger John 1945- 13
Hale, Arlene 1924-1982 49
Hale, Bruce 1957- 203
    Earlier sketch in SATA 123
Hale, Christy
    See Apostolou, Christine Hale
Hale, Edward Everett 1822-1909 16
Hale, Glenn
    See Walker, Robert W.
Hale, Helen
    See Mulcahy, Lucille Burnett
Hale, Irina 1932- 26
Hale, Kathleen 1898-2000 66
    Obituary 121
    Earlier sketch in SATA 17
Hale, Linda (Howe) 1929- 6
Hale, Lucretia P.
    See Hale, Lucretia Peabody
Hale, Lucretia Peabody 1820-1900 26
    See also CLR 105
Hale, Marian 194
Hale, Nancy 1908-1988 31
    Obituary 57
Hale, Nathan 1976- 210
Hale, Shannon 200
    Earlier sketch in SATA 158
Haley, Amanda 205
Haley, Gail E(inhart) 1939- 161
    Autobiography Feature 161
    Brief entry 28
    Earlier sketches in SATA 43, 78, 136
    See also CLR 21
    See also SAAS 13
Haley, Neale 52
Halfmann, Janet 1944- 208
Hall, Adam
    See Trevor, Elleston
Hall, Adele 1910- 7
Hall, Anna Gertrude 1882-1967 8
Hall, August 207
Hall, Barbara 1961- 68
Hall, Becky 1950- 186
Hall, Beverly B. 1918- 95
Hall, Borden
    See Yates, Raymond F(rancis)
Hall, Brian P(atrick) 1935- 31
Hall, Cameron
    See del Rey, Lester

Hall, Caryl
  See Hansen, Caryl (Hall)
Hall, Donald 1928- 97
  Earlier sketch in SATA *23*
Hall, Donald Andrew, Jr.
  See Hall, Donald
Hall, Douglas 1931- 43
Hall, Elizabeth 1929- 77
Hall, Elvajean 1910-1984 6
Hall, Francie 1940- 166
Hall, James Norman 1887-1951 21
Hall, Jesse
  See Boesen, Victor
Hall, Katy
  See McMullan, Kate
Hall, Kirsten Marie 1974- 67
Hall, Lynn 1937- 79
  Earlier sketches in SATA *2, 47*
  See also SAAS *4*
Hall, Malcolm 1945- 7
Hall, Marcellus 203
Hall, Marjory
  See Yeakley, Marjory Hall
Hall, Melanie W. 1949- 169
  Earlier sketches in SATA *78, 116*
Hall, Patricia 1940- 136
Hall, Rosalys Haskell 1914- 7
Hall, Willis 1929-2005 66
Hallard, Peter
  See Catherall, Arthur
Hallas, Richard
  See Knight, Eric
Hall-Clarke, James
  See Rowland-Entwistle, (Arthur) Theodore
  (Henry)
Hallensleben, Georg 1958- 173
Haller, Dorcas Woodbury 1946- 46
Hallett, Mark 1947- 220
  Earlier sketch in SATA *83*
Halliburton, Richard 1900-1939(?) 81
Halliburton, Warren J. 1924- 19
Halliday, Brett
  See Dresser, Davis
  and Johnson, (Walter) Ryerson
  and Terrall, Robert
Halliday, William R(oss) 1926- 52
Hallin, Emily Watson 1916-1995 6
Hallinan, P. K. 1944- 39
  Brief entry 37
Hallinan, Patrick Kenneth
  See Hallinan, P. K.
Hallman, Ruth 1929- 43
  Brief entry 28
Hallowell, Tommy
  See Hill, Thomas
Hall-Quest, (Edna) Olga W(ilbourne)
  1899-1986 11
  Obituary 47
Halls, Kelly Milner 1957- 220
  Earlier sketch in SATA *131*
Hallstead, William F(inn III) 1924- 11
Hallward, Michael 1889-1982 12
Halperin, Michael 156
Halperin, Wendy Anderson 1952- 200
  Earlier sketches in SATA *80, 125*
Halpern, Julie 1975- 198
Halpin, Brendan 1968- 193
Halpin, Marlene 1927- 88
Halse, Laurie Beth
  See Anderson, Laurie Halse
Halsell, Grace (Eleanor) 1923-2000 13
Halsey, Megan 185
Halsted, Anna Roosevelt 1906-1975
  Obituary 30
Halter, Jon C(harles) 1941- 22
Halverson, Deborah 202
Halvorson, Adeline 218
Halvorson, Marilyn 1948- 123
Hamalian, Leo 1920- 41
Hamberger, John 1934- 14
Hamblin, Dora Jane 1920- 36

Hambly, Barbara 1951- 108
Hambly, Barbara Joan
  See Hambly, Barbara
Hamer, Martyn
  See Eldin, Peter
Hamerstrom, Frances 1907-1998 24
Hamil, Thomas Arthur 1928- 14
Hamill, Ethel
  See Webb, Jean Francis (III)
Hamilton, (John) Alan 1943- 66
Hamilton, Alice
  See Cromie, Alice Hamilton
Hamilton, Anita 1919- 92
Hamilton, Buzz
  See Hemming, Roy G.
Hamilton, Carol (Jean Barber) 1935- 94
Hamilton, Charles (Harold St. John)
  1876-1961 13
Hamilton, Charles 1913-1996 65
  Obituary 93
Hamilton, Clive
  See Lewis, C. S.
Hamilton, Dorothy (Drumm) 1906-1983 12
  Obituary 35
Hamilton, Edith 1867-1963 20
Hamilton, Edmond 1904-1977 118
Hamilton, (Muriel) Elizabeth (Mollie)
  1906- 23
Hamilton, Emma Walton 1962- 177
Hamilton, Franklin
  See Silverberg, Robert
Hamilton, Gail
  See Corcoran, Barbara (Asenath)
  and Dodge, Mary Abigail
Hamilton, Kersten 1958- 204
  Earlier sketch in SATA *134*
Hamilton, K.R.
  See Hamilton, Kersten
Hamilton, Martha 1953- 183
  Earlier sketch in SATA *123*
Hamilton, Mary (E.) 1927- 55
Hamilton, Mollie
  See Kaye, M.M.
Hamilton, Morse 1943-1998 101
  Earlier sketch in SATA *35*
Hamilton, Peter F. 1960- 109
Hamilton, Priscilla
  See Gellis, Roberta
Hamilton, Ralph
  See Stratemeyer, Edward L.
Hamilton, Virginia 1936-2002 123
  Obituary 132
  Earlier sketches in SATA *4, 56, 79*
  See also CLR *127*
Hamilton, Virginia Esther
  See Hamilton, Virginia
Hamilton-Paterson, James 1941- 82
Hamlet, Ova
  See Lupoff, Richard A(llen)
Hamley, D. C.
  See Hamley, Dennis
Hamley, Dennis 1935- 69
  Earlier sketch in SATA *39*
  See also CLR *47*
  See also SAAS *22*
Hamley, Dennis C.
  See Hamley, Dennis
Hamlin, Peter J. 1970- 84
Hamm, Diane Johnston 1949- 78
Hammer, Charles 1934- 58
Hammer, Richard 1928- 6
Hammerman, Gay M(orenus) 1926- 9
Hammill, Matt 1982- 206
Hammond, Andrew 1970- 181
Hammond, Ralph
  See Hammond Innes, Ralph
Hammond, Winifred G(raham) 1899-1992 ... 29
  Obituary 107
Hammond Innes, Ralph 1913-1998 116
Hammontree, Marie (Gertrude) 1913- 13
Hample, Zack 1977- 161

Hampshire, Joyce Gregorian
  See Gregorian, Joyce Ballou
Hampshire, Susan 1942- 98
Hampson, (Richard) Denman 1929- 15
Hampson, Frank 1918(?)-1985
  Obituary 46
Hampton, Wilborn 1940- 196
  Earlier sketch in SATA *156*
Hamre, Leif 1914- 5
Hamsa, Bobbie 1944- 52
  Brief entry 38
Han, Jenny 1981- 175
Han, Lu
  See Stickler, Soma Han
Han, Soma
  See Stickler, Soma Han
Han, Suzanne Crowder 1953- 89
Hancock, Mary A. 1923- 31
Hancock, Sibyl 1940- 9
Hand, Elizabeth 1957- 167
  Earlier sketch in SATA *118*
Handford, Martin (John) 1956- 64
  See also CLR *22*
Handforth, Thomas (Schofield) 1897-1948 .. 42
Handleman, Philip 1951- 222
Handler, Daniel
  See Snicket, Lemony
Handville, Robert (Tompkins) 1924- 45
Hane, Roger 1940-1974
  Obituary 20
Hanel, Wolfram
  See Haenel, Wolfram
Haney, Lynn 1941- 23
Hanff, Helene 1916-1997 97
  Earlier sketch in SATA *11*
Hanft, Josh 1956- 197
Hanft, Joshua E.
  See Hanft, Josh
Hanley, Boniface Francis 1924- 65
Hanlon, Emily 1945- 15
Hann, Jacquie 1951- 19
Hann, Judith 1942- 77
Hanna, Bill
  See Hanna, William (Denby)
Hanna, Cheryl 1951- 84
Hanna, Dan 200
Hanna, Jack (Bushnell) 1947- 74
Hanna, Nell(ie L.) 1908- 55
Hanna, Paul R(obert) 1902-1988 9
Hanna, William (Denby) 1910-2001 51
  Obituary 126
Hannam, Charles 1925- 50
Hannan, Peter 1954- 187
Hannigan, Katherine 170
Hannon, Ezra
  See Hunter, Evan
Hann-Syme, Marguerite 127
Hano, Arnold 1922- 12
Hano, Renee Roth
  See Roth-Hano, Renee
Hanover, Terri
  See Huff, Tanya
Hansen, Ann Larkin 1958- 96
Hansen, Brooks 1965- 104
Hansen, Caryl (Hall) 1929- 39
Hansen, Ian V. 1929- 113
Hansen, Jennifer 1972- 156
Hansen, Joyce 1942- 172
  Autobiography Feature 172
  Brief entry 39
  Earlier sketches in SATA *46, 101*
  See also CLR *21*
  See also SAAS *15*
Hansen, Joyce Viola
  See Hansen, Joyce
Hansen, Mark Victor 112
Hansen, Ron 1947- 56
Hansen, Ronald Thomas
  See Hansen, Ron
Hanser, Richard (Frederick) 1909-1981 13
Hanson, Joan 1938- 8

Hanson, Joseph E. 1894(?)-1971
  Obituary 27
Hanson, Mary Elizabeth *188*
Hanson, Warren 1949- *155*
Hansson, Gunilla 1939- *64*
Hantman, Clea *200*
Hapka, C.A.
  See Hapka, Catherine
Hapka, Catherine *223*
Hapka, Cathy
  See Hapka, Catherine
Harald, Eric
  See Boesen, Victor
Harazin, S. A. *210*
Harbour, Elizabeth 1968- *221*
Harcourt, Ellen Knowles 1890(?)-1984
  Obituary 36
Hard, Charlotte (Ann) 1969- *98*
Hardcastle, Michael 1933- *216*
  Brief entry *38*
  Earlier sketch in SATA *47*
Harding, Lee 1937- *32*
  Brief entry *31*
Hardinge, Frances 1973- *210*
Hardt, Helga Fleischhauer
  See Fleischhauer-Hardt, Helga
Hardwick, Richard Holmes, Jr. 1923- *12*
Hardy, Alice Dale *67*
  Earlier sketch in SATA *1*
Hardy, David A(ndrews) 1936- *9*
Hardy, Janice *222*
Hardy, Jon 1958- *53*
Hardy, LeAnne 1951- *154*
Hardy, Stuart
  See Schisgall, Oscar
Hare, Norma Q(uarles) 1924- *46*
  Brief entry *41*
Harel, Nira 1936- *154*
Harford, Henry
  See Hudson, W(illiam) H(enry)
Hargis, Wes *219*
Hargrave, Leonie
  See Disch, Thomas M.
Hargreaves, (Charles) Roger 1935-1988
  Obituary 56
Hargrove, James 1947- *57*
  Brief entry *50*
Hargrove, Jim
  See Hargrove, James
Harik, Elsa
  See Marston, Elsa
Harik, Elsa M.
  See Marston, Elsa
Harik, Elsa Marston
  See Marston, Elsa
Hariton, Anca I. 1955- *79*
Hark, Mildred
  See McQueen, Mildred Hark
Harkaway, Hal
  See Stratemeyer, Edward L.
Harkins, Philip 1912-1997 .... *6*
  Obituary *129*
Harlan, Elizabeth 1945- *41*
  Brief entry *35*
Harlan, Glen
  See Cebulash, Mel
Harlan, Judith 1949- *135*
  Earlier sketch in SATA *74*
  See also CLR *81*
Harland, Richard 1947- *152*
Harlee, J. V.
  See Leese, Jennifer L.B.
Harler, Ann
  See Van Steenwyk, Elizabeth (Ann)
Harley, Avis *183*
Harley, Bill 1954- *208*
  Earlier sketch in SATA *87*
Harlow, Joan Hiatt 1932- *157*
Harman, Fred 1902(?)-1982
  Obituary 30

Harman, Hugh 1903-1982
  Obituary 33
Harmelink, Barbara (Mary) *9*
Harmer, Mabel 1894-1992 .... *45*
Harmon, Dan
  See Harmon, Daniel E(lton)
Harmon, Daniel E(lton) 1949- *157*
Harmon, Margaret 1906- *20*
Harmon, Michael 1969- *189*
Harmon, Michael B.
  See Harmon, Michael
Harmon, William (Ruth) 1938- *65*
Harnan, Terry 1920- *12*
Harness, Cheryl 1951- *178*
  Earlier sketch in SATA *131*
Harnett, Cynthia (Mary) 1893-1981 .... *5*
  Obituary *32*
Harper, Anita 1943- *41*
Harper, Betty 1946- *126*
Harper, Charise
  See Harper, Charise Mericle
Harper, Charise Mericle *179*
Harper, Elaine
  See Hallin, Emily Watson
Harper, Ellen
  See Noble, Marty
Harper, Jamie *174*
Harper, Jessica 1949- *148*
Harper, Jo 1932- *169*
  Earlier sketch in SATA *97*
Harper, Lee *201*
Harper, Mary Wood
  See Dixon, Jeanne
Harper, Piers 1966- *161*
  Earlier sketch in SATA *105*
Harper, Suzanne *194*
Harper, Wilhelmina 1884-1973 .... *4*
  Obituary 26
Harrah, Madge 1931- *154*
Harrah, Michael 1940- *41*
Harrah, Monique
  See Harrah, Madge
Harrar, George E. 1949- *124*
Harrell, Beatrice Orcutt 1943- *93*
Harrell, Janice 1945- *70*
Harrell, Sara Gordon 1940- *26*
Harrell, Sara Jeanne Gordon
  See Harrell, Sara Gordon
Harries, Joan 1922- *39*
Harrill, Ronald 1950- *90*
Harrington, Denis J(ames) 1932- *88*
Harrington, Evelyn Davis 1911- *5*
Harrington, Janice N. 1956- *187*
Harrington, Lyn
  See Harrington, Evelyn Davis
Harris, Alan 1944- *71*
Harris, Aurand 1915-1996 .... *37*
  Obituary *91*
Harris, Bob
  See Harris, Robert J.
Harris, Carol Flynn 1933- *135*
Harris, Catherine
  See Ainsworth, Catherine Harris
Harris, Christie
  See Harris, Christie (Lucy) Irwin
Harris, Christie (Lucy) Irwin 1907-2002 ...... *74*
  Autobiography Feature *116*
  Earlier sketch in SATA *6*
  See also CLR *47*
  See also SAAS *10*
Harris, Christine 1955- *105*
Harris, Colver
  See Colver, Anne
Harris, David 1942- *118*
Harris, David William
  See Harris, David
Harris, Dorothy Joan 1931- *153*
  Earlier sketch in SATA *13*
Harris, Geraldine 1951- *54*
Harris, Geraldine Rachel
  See Harris, Geraldine

Harris, Jacqueline L. 1929- *62*
Harris, Janet 1932-1979 .... *4*
  Obituary 23
Harris, Jesse
  See Standiford, Natalie
Harris, Joan 1946- *146*
Harris, Joe 1928- *201*
Harris, Joel Chandler 1848-1908 .... *100*
  See also YABC *1*
  See also CLR *128*
Harris, John (Wyndham Parkes Lucas) Beynon
  1903-1969 .... *118*
Harris, Johnson
  See Harris, John (Wyndham Parkes Lucas)
  Beynon
Harris, Jonathan 1921-1997 .... *52*
Harris, Larry Vincent 1939- *59*
Harris, Lavinia
  See St. John, Nicole
Harris, Leon A., Jr. 1926-2000 .... *4*
Harris, Lois V. *199*
Harris, Lorle K(empe) 1912-2001 .... *22*
Harris, Marilyn
  See Springer, Marilyn Harris
Harris, Mark Jonathan 1941- *84*
  Earlier sketch in SATA *32*
Harris, Mary K(athleen) 1905-1966 .... *119*
Harris, Robert J. 1955- *195*
Harris, Robie H. 1940- *203*
  Brief entry *53*
  Earlier sketches in SATA *90, 147*
Harris, Robin
  See Shine, Deborah
Harris, Rosemary (Jeanne) *82*
  Earlier sketch in SATA *4*
  See also CLR *30*
  See also SAAS *7*
Harris, Ruth Elwin 1935- *164*
Harris, Sherwood 1932-2009 .... *25*
Harris, Steven Michael 1957- *55*
Harris, Trudy 1949- *191*
  Earlier sketch in SATA *128*
Harris-Filderman, Diane
  See Filderman, Diane E(lizabeth)
Harrison, C(hester) William 1913-1994 .... *35*
Harrison, Carol
  See Harrison, Carol Thompson
Harrison, Carol Thompson *113*
Harrison, David L. 1937- *186*
  Earlier sketches in SATA *26, 92, 150*
Harrison, Deloris 1938- *9*
Harrison, Edward Hardy 1926- *56*
Harrison, Elizabeth (Allen) Cavanna
  1909-2001 .... *30*
  Earlier sketch in SATA *1*
  See also SAAS *4*
Harrison, Harry 1925- *4*
Harrison, Harry Max
  See Harrison, Harry
Harrison, Mette Ivie 1970- *202*
  Earlier sketch in SATA *149*
Harrison, Michael 1939- *106*
Harrison, Molly (Hodgett) 1909-2002 .... *41*
Harrison, Sarah 1946- *63*
Harrison, Ted
  See Harrison, Edward Hardy
Harsh, Fred (T.) 1925- *72*
Harshaw, Ruth H(etzel) 1890-1968 .... *27*
Harshman, Marc 1950- *109*
  Earlier sketch in SATA *71*
Hart, Alexandra 1939- *14*
Hart, Alison
  See Leonhardt, Alice
Hart, Bruce 1938-2006 .... *57*
  Brief entry *39*
Hart, Carole 1943- *57*
  Brief entry *39*
Hart, Carolyn 1936- *74*
Hart, Carolyn G.
  See Hart, Carolyn

Hart, Carolyn Gimpel
See Hart, Carolyn
Hart, Jan Siegel 1940- 79
Hart, Joyce 1954- 148
Hart, Karen 185
Hart, Lenore 171
Hart, Philip S. 1944- 180
Hart, Virginia 1949- 83
Harte, Bret 1836(?)-1902 26
Harte, Francis Brett
See Harte, Bret
Harter, Debbie 1963- 107
Hartfield, Claire 1957- 147
Hartinger, Brent 1964- 217
Earlier sketches in SATA *145, 174*
Hartland, Jessie 171
Hartley, Ellen (Raphael) 1915-1980 23
Hartley, Fred Allan III 1953- 41
Hartley, William B(rown) 1913-1980 23
Hartling, Peter
See Hartling, Peter
Hartling, Peter 1933- 66
See also CLR *29*
Hartman, Cassie 202
Hartman, Dan 1955- 202
Hartman, Evert 1937- 38
Brief entry 35
Hartman, Jane E. 1928- 47
Hartman, Jane Evangeline
See Hartman, Jane E.
Hartman, Louis F(rancis) 1901-1970 22
Hartman, Rachel 174
Hartman, Victoria 1942- 91
Hartnett, Sonya 1968- 176
Earlier sketches in SATA *93, 130*
Hartry, Nancy 219
Hartshorn, Ruth M. 1928- 11
Hartung, Susan Kathleen 192
Earlier sketch in SATA *150*
Hartwig, Manfred 1950- 81
Harvey, Brett 1936- 61
Harvey, Edith 1908(?)-1972
Obituary 27
Harvey, Gill 189
Harvey, Karen D. 1935- 88
Harvey, Roland 1945- 219
Earlier sketches in SATA *71, 123, 179*
Harvey-Fitzhenry, Alyxandra 1974- 189
Harwick, B. L.
See Keller, Beverly L(ou)
Harwin, Brian
See Henderson, LeGrand
Harwood, Pearl Augusta (Bragdon)
1903-1998 9
Haseley, Dennis 1950- 221
Brief entry 44
Earlier sketches in SATA *57, 105, 157*
Hashmi, Kerri 1955- 108
Haskell, Arnold L(ionel) 1903-1981(?) 6
Haskins, James
See Haskins, James S.
Haskins, James S. 1941-2005 132
Autobiography Feature 132
Earlier sketches in SATA *9, 69, 105*
See also CLR *39*
See also SAAS *4*
Haskins, Jim
See Haskins, James S.
Hasler, Eveline 1933- 181
Hasler, Joan 1931- 28
Hass, Robert 1941- 94
Hassall, Joan 1906-1988 43
Obituary 56
Hassett, Ann 1958- 162
Hassett, John 162
Hassler, Jon 1933-2008 19
Obituary 191
Hassler, Jon Francis
See Hassler, Jon

Hastings, Beverly
See Barkin, Carol
and James, Elizabeth
Hastings, Graham
See Jeffries, Roderic
Hastings, Ian 1912- 62
Hastings, Victor
See Disch, Thomas M.
Haszard, Patricia Moyes 1923-2000 63
Hatch, Lynda S. 1950- 90
Hathaway, Barbara 164
Hathorn, Elizabeth
See Hathorn, Elizabeth Helen
Hathorn, Elizabeth Helen 1943- 156
Autobiography Feature 156
Earlier sketches in SATA *74, 120*
Hathorn, Libby 1943-
See Hathorn, Elizabeth Helen
Hatkoff, Craig 1954- 192
Hatlo, Jimmy 1898-1963
Obituary 23
Hatton, Caroline 1957- 205
Hauff, Wilhelm 1802-1827
See CLR *155*
Haugaard, Erik Christian 1923- 68
Earlier sketch in SATA *4*
See also CLR *11*
See also SAAS *12*
Haugaard, Kay 117
Haugen, Hayley Mitchell 1968- 172
Haugen, Tormod 1945- 66
Hauman, Doris 1898-1984 32
Hauman, George 1890-1961 32
Hauptly, Denis J. 1945- 57
Hauptly, Denis James
See Hauptly, Denis J.
Hauser, Jill Frankel 1950- 127
Hauser, Margaret L(ouise) 1909- 10
Hausherr, Rosmarie 1943- 86
Hausman, Gerald 1945- 180
Earlier sketches in SATA *13, 90, 132*
See also CLR *89*
Hausman, Gerry
See Hausman, Gerald
Hauth, Katherine B. 1940- 99
Hautman, Pete 1952- 173
Earlier sketches in SATA *82, 128*
Hautman, Peter Murray
See Hautman, Pete
Hautzig, Deborah 1956- 106
Earlier sketch in SATA *31*
Hautzig, Esther Rudomin 1930-2009 148
Earlier sketches in SATA *4, 68*
See also CLR *22*
See also SAAS *15*
Havel, Geoff 1955- 152
Havel, Jennifer
See Havill, Juanita
Havelin, Kate 1961- 143
Haven, Paul 1971(?)- 213
Havighurst, Walter (Edwin) 1901-1994 1
Obituary 79
Haviland, Virginia 1911-1988 6
Obituary 54
Havill, Juanita 1949- 155
Earlier sketch in SATA *74*
Hawes, Judy 1913- 4
Hawes, Louise 1943- 180
Earlier sketch in SATA *60*
Hawk, Fran 222
Hawke, Rosanne 1953- 165
Earlier sketch in SATA *124*
Hawke, Rosanne Joy
See Hawke, Rosanne
Hawkes, Kevin 1959- 201
Earlier sketches in SATA *78, 150*
Hawkes, Nigel 1943- 119
Hawkesworth, Eric 1921- 13
Hawking, Lucy 1969- 197
Hawkins, Arthur 1903-1985 19

Hawkins, Colin 1945- 162
Earlier sketch in SATA *112*
Hawkins, Jacqui 162
Earlier sketch in SATA *112*
Hawkins, Jimmy 1941- 188
Hawkins, Laura 1951- 74
Hawkins, (Helena Ann) Quail 1905-2002 6
Obituary 141
Hawkinson, John (Samuel) 1912-1994 4
Hawkinson, Lucy (Ozone) 1924-1971 21
Hawks, Robert 1961- 85
Hawley, Mabel C. 67
Earlier sketch in SATA *1*
Haworth, Danette 207
Haworth-Attard, Barbara 1953- 215
Hawthorne, Captain R. M.
See Ellis, Edward S.
Hawthorne, Nathaniel 1804-1864
See YABC *2*
See also CLR *103*
Hay, Jeff T. 154
Hay, John 1915- 13
Hay, Samantha 213
Hay, Timothy
See Brown, Margaret Wise
Hayashi, Leslie Ann 1954- 115
Hayashi, Nancy 1939- 186
Earlier sketch in SATA *80*
Haycak, Cara 1961- 180
Haycock, Kate 1962- 77
Haycraft, Howard 1905-1991 6
Obituary 70
Haycraft, Molly Costain 1911- 6
Hayden, Gwendolen Lampshire 1904- 35
Hayden, Robert
See Hayden, Robert Earl
Hayden, Robert C(arter), Jr. 1937- 47
Brief entry 28
Hayden, Robert E.
See Hayden, Robert Earl
Hayden, Robert Earl 1913-1980 19
Obituary 26
Hayden, Torey L. 1951- 163
Earlier sketch in SATA *65*
Hayden, Torey Lynn
See Hayden, Torey L.
Hayes, Carlton J(oseph) H(untley)
1882-1964 11
Hayes, Daniel 1952- 109
Earlier sketch in SATA *73*
Hayes, Geoffrey 1947- 207
Earlier sketches in SATA *26, 91*
Hayes, Joe 1945- 131
Earlier sketch in SATA *88*
Hayes, John F. 1904-1980 11
Hayes, Karel 1949- 207
Hayes, Rosemary 158
Hayes, Sarah 1945- 208
Hayes, Sheila 1937- 51
Brief entry 50
Hayes, Will 7
Hayes, William D(imitt) 1913-1976 8
Haynes, Betsy 1937- 94
Brief entry 37
Earlier sketch in SATA *48*
See also CLR *90*
Haynes, David 1955- 97
Haynes, Linda
See Swinford, Betty (June Wells)
Haynes, Mary 1938- 65
Haynes, Max 1956- 72
Hays, Anna Jane 214
Hays, H(offmann) R(eynolds) 1904-1980 26
Hays, Thomas A.
See Hays, Tony
Hays, Thomas Anthony
See Hays, Tony
Hays, Tony 1957- 84

Hays, Wilma Pitchford 1909- *28*
   Earlier sketch in SATA *1*
   See also CLR *59*
   See also SAAS *3*
Hayward, Linda 1943- *185*
   Brief entry *39*
   Earlier sketch in SATA *101*
Haywood, Carolyn 1898-1990 .... *75*
   Obituary *64*
   Earlier sketches in SATA *1, 29*
   See also CLR *22*
Hazelaar, Cor *217*
Hazell, Rebecca (Eileen) 1947- *141*
Hazen, Barbara Shook 1930- *178*
   Earlier sketches in SATA *27, 90*
Hazen, Lynn E. *202*
Head, Gay
   See Hauser, Margaret L(ouise)
Head, Tom 1978- *167*
Headley, Elizabeth
   See Harrison, Elizabeth (Allen) Cavanna
Headley, Justina Chen 1968- *176*
Headstrom, (Birger) Richard 1902-1985 .... *8*
Heady, Eleanor B(utler) 1917-1979 .... *8*
Heagy, William D. 1964- *76*
Heal, Edith 1903-1995 .... *7*
Heal, Gillian 1934- *89*
Heale, Jay (Jeremy Peter Wingfield) 1937- .. *84*
Healey, Brooks
   See Albert, Burton
Healey, Larry 1927- *44*
   Brief entry *42*
Heap, Sue 1954- *187*
   Earlier sketch in SATA *150*
Heaps, Willard A(llison) 1908-1987 .... *26*
Hearn, Diane Dawson 1952- *209*
   Earlier sketch in SATA *79*
Hearn, Emily
   See Valleau, Emily
Hearn, Julie 1958- *212*
   Earlier sketch in SATA *152*
Hearn, Lian
   See Rubinstein, Gillian
Hearn, Sneed
   See Gregg, Andrew K.
Hearne, Betsy 1942- *146*
   Earlier sketches in SATA *38, 95*
Heath, Charles D(ickinson) 1941- *46*
Heath, Veronica
   See Blackett, Veronica Heath
Heaven, Constance (Christina) 1911- *7*
Hebert-Collins, Sheila 1948- *111*
Hecht, George J(oseph) 1895-1980
   Obituary *22*
Hecht, Henri Joseph 1922- *9*
Hechtkopf, Henryk 1910- *17*
Heck, Bessie (Mildred) Holland 1911-1995 . *26*
Heck, Ed 1963- *173*
Heckert, Connie K(aye Delp) 1948- *82*
Hector, Julian *205*
Hedderwick, Mairi 1939- *145*
   Earlier sketches in SATA *30, 77*
Hedges, Sid(ney) G(eorge) 1897-1974 .... *28*
Hedrick, Irene Hope 1920- *175*
Heelan, Jamee Riggio 1965- *146*
Heerboth, Sharon
   See Leon, Sharon
Heffernan, John 1949- *168*
   Earlier sketch in SATA *121*
Heffron, Dorris 1944- *68*
Hefter, Richard 1942- *31*
Hegamin, Tonya C. 1975- *209*
Hegarty, Reginald Beaton 1906-1973 .... *10*
Hehenberger, Shelly 1968- *126*
Heidbreder, Robert 1947- *196*
   Earlier sketch in SATA *130*
Heidbreder, Robert K.
   See Heidbreder, Robert

Heide, Florence Parry 1919- *192*
   Earlier sketches in SATA *32, 69, 118*
   See also CLR *60*
   See also SAAS *6*
Heiderstadt, Dorothy 1907-2001 .... *6*
Heidi Louise
   See Erdrich, Louise
Heidler, David S(tephen) 1955- *132*
Heidler, Jeanne T. 1956- *132*
Heilbroner, Joan Knapp 1922- *63*
Heilbrun, Lois Hussey 1922(?)-1987
   Obituary *54*
Heiligman, Deborah 1958- *193*
   Earlier sketches in SATA *90, 144*
Heilman, Joan Rattner *50*
Heimann, Rolf 1940- *164*
   Earlier sketch in SATA *120*
Hein, Lucille Eleanor 1915-1994 .... *20*
Heine, Helme 1941- *135*
   Earlier sketch in SATA *67*
   See also CLR *18*
Heinlein, Robert A. 1907-1988 .... *69*
   Obituary *56*
   Earlier sketch in SATA *9*
   See also CLR *75*
Heinlein, Robert Anson
   See Heinlein, Robert A.
Heins, Ethel L(eah) 1918-1997 .... *101*
Heins, Paul 1909- *13*
Heintze, Carl 1922- *26*
Heinz, Bill
   See Heinz, W. C.
Heinz, Brian J. 1946- *181*
   Earlier sketch in SATA *95*
Heinz, Brian James
   See Heinz, Brian J.
Heinz, W. C. 1915-2008 .... *26*
Heinz, Wilfred Charles
   See Heinz, W. C.
Heinzen, Mildred
   See Masters, Mildred
Heisel, Sharon E(laine) 1941- *125*
   Earlier sketch in SATA *84*
Heitzmann, William Ray 1948- *73*
Heitzmann, Wm. Ray
   See Heitzmann, William Ray
Helakoski, Leslie *178*
Helberg, Shirley Adelaide Holden 1919- ... *138*
Helfer, Andrew *187*
Helfer, Ralph 1937- *177*
Helfman, Elizabeth S(eaver) 1911-2001 .... *3*
Helfman, Harry Carmozin 1910-1995 .... *3*
Helgerson, Joseph 1950- *181*
Hellard, Susan *182*
Hellberg, Hans-Eric 1927- *38*
Heller, Linda 1944- *46*
   Brief entry *40*
Heller, Mike
   See Hano, Arnold
Heller, Ruth M. 1924- *112*
   Earlier sketch in SATA *66*
Hellman, Hal
   See Hellman, Harold
Hellman, Harold 1927- *4*
Helman, Andrea (Jean) 1946- *160*
   Earlier sketch in SATA *107*
Helmer, Diana Star 1962- *86*
Helmer, Marilyn *160*
   Earlier sketch in SATA *112*
Helps, Racey 1913-1971 .... *2*
   Obituary *25*
Helquist, Brett *187*
   Earlier sketch in SATA *146*
Helweg, Hans H. 1917- *50*
   Brief entry *33*
Helyar, Jane Penelope Josephine 1933- *5*
   Autobiography Feature *138*
   See also SAAS *2*
Hemingway, Edith M. 1950- *223*
Hemingway, Edith Morris
   See Hemingway, Edith M.

Hemingway, Edward 1969(?)- *212*
Hemmant, Lynette 1938- *69*
Hemming, Roy G. 1928-1995 .... *11*
   Obituary *86*
Hemphill, Helen 1955- *179*
Hemphill, Kris (Harrison) 1963- *118*
Hemphill, Martha Locke 1904-1973 .... *37*
Hemphill, Michael *220*
Hemphill, Stephanie *190*
Hemstock, Gillian 1956- *173*
Henba, Bobbie 1926- *87*
Henbest, Nigel 1951- *55*
   Brief entry *52*
Henderley, Brooks *1*
Henderson, Aileen Kilgore 1921- *178*
Henderson, Aileen Mary
   See Fox, Aileen
Henderson, Gordon 1950- *53*
Henderson, Kathy 1949- *155*
   Brief entry *53*
   Earlier sketches in SATA *55, 95*
Henderson, Lauren 1966- *201*
Henderson, LeGrand 1901-1965 .... *9*
Henderson, Nancy Wallace 1916- *22*
Henderson, Zenna (Chlarson) 1917-1983 .... *5*
Hendrickson, Walter Brookfield, Jr. 1936- *9*
Hendrix, John 1976- *208*
Hendry, Diana 1941- *213*
   Earlier sketches in SATA *68, 106*
Hendry, Frances Mary 1941- *171*
   Earlier sketch in SATA *110*
Hendry, Linda (Gail) 1961- *83*
Heneghan, James 1930- *160*
   Earlier sketches in SATA *53, 97*
Henkes, Kevin 1960- *207*
   Earlier sketches in SATA *43, 76, 108, 154*
   See also CLR *108*
Henn, Astrid *214*
Hennessy, Barbara G.
   See Hennessy, B.G.
Hennessy, Barbara Gulbrandsen
   See Hennessy, B.G.
Hennessy, B.G. 1951- *175*
Hennesy, Carolyn 1962- *221*
Henney, Carolee Wells 1928- *102*
Henriod, Lorraine 1925- *26*
Henriquez, Emile F. 1937- *170*
   Earlier sketch in SATA *89*
Henry, April 1959- *174*
Henry, Ernest 1948- *107*
Henry, Joanne Landers 1927- *6*
Henry, Maeve 1960- *75*
Henry, Marguerite 1902-1997 .... *100*
   Obituary *99*
   See also CLR *4*
   See also SAAS *7*
Henry, Marie H. 1935- *65*
Henry, Marilyn 1939- *117*
Henry, Marion
   See del Rey, Lester
Henry, O. 1862-1910
   See YABC *2*
Henry, Oliver
   See Henry, O.
Henry, Rohan *217*
Henry, T. E.
   See Rowland-Entwistle, (Arthur) Theodore (Henry)
Henschel, Elizabeth Georgie *56*
Henson, Heather *206*
Henson, James Maury
   See Henson, Jim
Henson, Jim 1936-1990 .... *43*
   Obituary *65*
Henstra, Friso 1928- *73*
   Earlier sketch in SATA *8*
   See also SAAS *14*
Hentoff, Nat(han Irving) 1925- *133*
   Brief entry *27*
   Earlier sketches in SATA *42, 69*
   See also CLR *52*

Henty, G(eorge) A(lfred) 1832-1902 .... *64*
  See also CLR 76
Heo, Yumi 1964- *206*
  Earlier sketches in SATA *94, 146*
Hepler, Heather *177*
Herald, Kathleen
  See Peyton, Kathleen Wendy
Herb, Angela M. 1970- *92*
Herbert, Cecil
  See Hamilton, Charles (Harold St. John)
Herbert, Don 1917-2007 .... *2*
  Obituary *184*
Herbert, Donald Jeffrey
  See Herbert, Don
Herbert, Frank 1920-1986 .... *37*
  Obituary *47*
  Earlier sketch in SATA *9*
Herbert, Frank Patrick
  See Herbert, Frank
Herbert, Helen (Jean) 1947- *57*
Herbert, Janis 1956- *139*
Herbert, Wally 1934-2007 .... *23*
Herbert, Walter William
  See Herbert, Wally
Herbst, Judith 1947- *74*
Herda, D.J. 1948- *80*
Herge
  See Remi, Georges
Heritage, Martin
  See Horler, Sydney
Herkimer, L(awrence) R(ussell) 1925(?)- *42*
Herlihy, Dirlie Anne 1935- *73*
Herlong, Madaline
  See Herlong, M.H.
Herlong, M.H. *211*
Herman, Charlotte 1937- *203*
  Earlier sketches in SATA *20, 99*
Hermanson, Dennis (Everett) 1947- *10*
Hermes, Jules 1962- *92*
Hermes, Patricia 1936- *191*
  Earlier sketches in SATA *31, 78, 141*
Hermes, Patricia Mary
  See Hermes, Patricia
Hernandez, Natalie Nelson 1929- *123*
Herndon, Ernest *91*
Herold, Ann Bixby 1937- *72*
Herrera, Juan Felipe 1948- *127*
Herrick, Steven 1958- *209*
  Earlier sketches in SATA *103, 156*
Herriman, George (Joseph) 1880-1944 .... *140*
Herriot, James 1916-1995 .... *135*
  Brief entry *44*
  Earlier sketch in SATA *86*
  See also CLR *80*
Herrmanns, Ralph 1933- *11*
Herrold, Tracey
  See Dils, Tracey E.
Herron, Carolivia 1947- *203*
Herron, Edward A(lbert) 1912- *4*
Herschler, Mildred Barger *130*
Hersey, John 1914-1993 .... *25*
  Obituary *76*
Hersey, John Richard
  See Hersey, John
Hershberger, Priscilla (Gorman) 1951- *81*
Hershenhorn, Esther 1945- *151*
Hershey, Kathleen M. 1934- *80*
Hershey, Mary *173*
Hershey, Mary L.
  See Hershey, Mary
Hersom, Kathleen 1911- *73*
Hertz, Grete Janus 1915- *23*
Herxheimer, Sophie 1963- *220*
Herzig, Alison Cragin 1935- *87*
Herzog, Brad 1968- *131*
Heslewood, Juliet 1951- *82*
Hess, Lilo 1916- *4*
Hess, Paul 1961- *134*
Hesse, Hermann 1877-1962 .... *50*

Hesse, Karen 1952- *215*
  Autobiography Feature *113*
  Earlier sketches in SATA *74, 103, 158*
  See also CLR *141*
  See also SAAS 25
Hest, Amy 1950- *193*
  Earlier sketches in SATA *55, 82, 129*
Heuer, Karsten 1968(?)- *202*
Heuer, Kenneth John 1927- *44*
Heuman, William 1912-1971 .... *21*
Heuston, Kimberley 1960- *167*
Heuston, Kimberley Burton
  See Heuston, Kimberley
Hewes, Agnes Danforth 1874-1963 .... *35*
Hewett, Anita 1918-1989 .... *13*
Hewett, Joan 1930- *140*
  Earlier sketch in SATA *81*
Hewett, Richard 1929- *81*
Hewitson, Jennifer 1961- *97*
Hewitt, Margaret 1961- *84*
Hewitt, Sally 1949- *127*
Hext, Harrington
  See Phillpotts, Eden
Hey, Nigel S(tewart) 1936- *20*
Heyduck-Huth, Hilde 1929- *8*
Heyer, Carol 1950- *130*
  Earlier sketch in SATA *74*
Heyer, Marilee 1942- *102*
  Earlier sketch in SATA *64*
Heyerdahl, Thor 1914-2002 .... *52*
  Earlier sketch in SATA *2*
Heyes, (Nancy) Eileen 1956- *150*
  Earlier sketch in SATA *80*
Heyliger, William 1884-1955
  See YABC *1*
Heyman, Ken(neth Louis) 1930- *114*
  Earlier sketch in SATA *34*
Heyward, (Edwin) DuBose 1885-1940 .... *21*
Heywood, Karen 1946- *48*
Hezlep, William (Earl) 1936- *88*
Hiaasen, Carl 1953- *208*
Hibbert, Arthur Raymond
  See Hibbert, Christopher
Hibbert, Christopher 1924-2008 .... *4*
  Obituary *201*
Hibbert, Eleanor Alice Burford 1906-1993 .... *2*
  Obituary *74*
Hickman, Estella (Lee) 1942- *111*
Hickman, Janet 1940- *127*
  Earlier sketch in SATA *12*
Hickman, Martha Whitmore 1925- *26*
Hickman, Pamela 1958- *186*
  Earlier sketch in SATA *128*
Hickock, Will
  See Harrison, C(hester) William
Hickok, Lorena A. 1893-1968 .... *20*
Hickox, Rebecca (Ayres) *116*
Hicks, Barbara Jean 1953- *165*
Hicks, Betty *191*
Hicks, Clifford B. 1920- *50*
Hicks, Eleanor B.
  See Coerr, Eleanor (Beatrice)
Hicks, Harvey
  See Stratemeyer, Edward L.
Hicks, Peter 1952- *111*
Hicyilmaz, Gaye 1947- *157*
  Earlier sketch in SATA *77*
Hieatt, Constance B(artlett) 1928- *4*
Hiebert, Ray Eldon 1932- *13*
Hierstein, Judith *212*
Hierstein, Judy
  See Hierstein, Judith
Higdon, Hal 1931- *4*
Higginbottom, David 1923- *87*
  Earlier sketch in SATA *25*
Higginbottom, J(effrey) Winslow 1945- *29*
Higgins, Dalton *223*
Higgins, F.E. *219*
Higgins, Fiona
  See Higgins, F.E.
Higgins, Joanna 1945- *125*

Higgins, Simon (Richard) 1958- *105*
Higginsen, Vy *79*
High, Linda Oatman 1958- *188*
  Autobiography Feature *188*
  Earlier sketches in SATA *94, 145*
High, Philip E. 1914- *119*
High, Philip Empson
  See High, Philip E.
Higham, David 1949- *50*
Higham, David Michael
  See Higham, David
Higham, Jon Atlas
  See Higham, Jonathan Huw
Higham, Jonathan Huw 1960- *59*
Highet, Helen
  See MacInnes, Helen (Clark)
Hightman, Jason 1971(?)- *189*
Hightman, J.P.
  See Hightman, Jason
Hightower, Florence Cole 1916-1981 .... *4*
  Obituary *27*
Highwater, Jamake (Mamake)
  1942(?)-2001 .... *69*
  Brief entry *30*
  Earlier sketch in SATA *32*
  See also CLR *17*
Hilb, Nora 1953- *178*
Hildebrandt, Greg 1939- *172*
  Brief entry *33*
  Earlier sketch in SATA *55*
Hildebrandt, Tim 1939-2006 .... *55*
  Brief entry *33*
Hildebrandt, Timothy
  See Hildebrandt, Tim
Hildebrandts, The
  See Hildebrandt, Greg
  and Hildebrandt, Tim
Hilder, Rowland 1905-1993 .... *36*
  Obituary *77*
Hildick, E. W.
  See Hildick, Wallace
Hildick, Wallace 1925-2001 .... *68*
  Earlier sketch in SATA *2*
  See also SAAS 6
Hilgartner, Beth 1957- *58*
Hill, Alexis
  See Craig, Mary (Francis) Shura
  and Glick, Ruth (Burtnick)
Hill, Anthony R. 1942- *164*
  Earlier sketch in SATA *91*
Hill, Anthony Robert
  See Hill, Anthony R.
Hill, David 1942- *152*
  Earlier sketch in SATA *103*
Hill, Donna (Marie) 1921- *124*
  Earlier sketch in SATA *24*
Hill, Douglas 1935-2007 .... *78*
  Earlier sketch in SATA *39*
Hill, Douglas Arthur
  See Hill, Douglas
Hill, Elizabeth Starr 1925- *143*
  Earlier sketch in SATA *24*
Hill, Eric 1927- *133*
  Brief entry *53*
  Earlier sketch in SATA *66*
  See also CLR *13*
Hill, Gordon
  See Eldin, Peter
Hill, Grace Brooks *67*
  Earlier sketch in SATA *1*
Hill, Grace Livingston 1865-1947
  See YABC *2*
Hill, Helen M(orey) 1915- *27*
Hill, John
  See Koontz, Dean
Hill, Johnson
  See Kunhardt, Edith
Hill, Judy I. R.
  See Roberts, Judy I.
Hill, Kathleen Louise 1917- *4*

Hill, Kay
    See Hill, Kathleen Louise
Hill, Kirkpatrick 1938- *188*
    Earlier sketches in SATA *72, 126*
Hill, Laban
    See Hill, Laban Carrick
Hill, Laban Carrick *170*
Hill, Lee Sullivan 1958- *96*
Hill, Lorna 1902-1991 .... *12*
Hill, Margaret (Ohler) 1915- *36*
Hill, Meg
    See Hill, Margaret (Ohler)
Hill, Meredith
    See Craig, Mary (Francis) Shura
Hill, Monica
    See Watson, Jane Werner
Hill, Pamela Smith 1954- *112*
Hill, Ralph Nading 1917-1987 .... *65*
Hill, Robert W(hite) 1919-1982 .... *12*
    Obituary *31*
Hill, Ruth A.
    See Viguers, Ruth Hill
Hill, Ruth Livingston
    See Munce, Ruth Hill
Hill, Stuart 1958- *186*
Hill, Susan 1942- *183*
Hill, Susan Elizabeth
    See Hill, Susan
Hill, Susanna Leonard 1965- *193*
Hill, Thomas 1960- *82*
Hillcourt, William 1900-1992 .... *27*
Hillenbrand, Will 1960- *210*
    Earlier sketches in SATA *84, 147*
Hiller, Ilo (Ann) 1938- *59*
Hillerman, Anthony Grove
    See Hillerman, Tony
Hillerman, Tony 1925-2008 .... *6*
    Obituary *198*
Hillert, Margaret 1920- *91*
    Earlier sketch in SATA *8*
Hilliard, Richard *183*
Hillman, Ben 1957- *202*
Hillman, Elizabeth 1942- *75*
Hillman, John 1952- *120*
Hillman, Martin
    See Hill, Douglas
Hillman, Priscilla 1940- *48*
    Brief entry *39*
Hillman, Shane *200*
Hills, C.A.R. 1955- *39*
Hills, Charles Albert Reis
    See Hills, C.A.R.
Hills, Tad *173*
Hilton, Irene Pothus -1979 .... *7*
Hilton, James 1900-1954 .... *34*
Hilton, Margaret Lynette 1946- *105*
    Earlier sketch in SATA *68*
    See also CLR *25*
    See also SAAS *21*
Hilton, Nette
    See Hilton, Margaret Lynette
Hilton, Ralph 1907-1982 .... *8*
Hilton, Suzanne 1922- *4*
Hilton-Bruce, Anne
    See Hilton, Margaret Lynette
Him, George 1937-1982
    Obituary *30*
Himelblau, Linda -2005 .... *179*
Himelstein, Shmuel 1940- *83*
Himler, Ann 1946- *8*
Himler, Ronald 1937- *183*
    Earlier sketches in SATA *6, 92, 137*
Himler, Ronald Norbert
    See Himler, Ronald
Himmelman, John 1959- *221*
    Earlier sketches in SATA *47, 94, 159*
Himmelman, John C.
    See Himmelman, John
Hinckley, Helen
    See Jones, Helen Hinckley

Hind, Dolores (Ellen) 1931- *53*
    Brief entry *49*
Hindin, Nathan
    See Bloch, Robert (Albert)
Hindley, Judy 1940- *179*
    Earlier sketch in SATA *120*
Hinds, P. Mignon *98*
Hinds, Patricia Mignon
    See Hinds, P. Mignon
Hine, Sesyle Joslin 1929- *2*
Hines, Anna Grossnickle 1946- *209*
    Brief entry *45*
    Earlier sketches in SATA *51, 95, 141*
    See also SAAS *16*
Hines, Gary (Roger) 1944- *136*
    Earlier sketch in SATA *74*
Hinman, Bonnie 1950- *216*
Hinojosa, Maria (de Lourdes) 1961- *88*
Hinton, Nigel 1941- *166*
Hinton, S. E. 1950- *160*
    Earlier sketches in SATA *19, 58, 115*
    See also CLR *23*
Hinton, Sam 1917-2009 .... *43*
Hinton, Susan Eloise
    See Hinton, S. E.
Hintz, Martin 1945- *128*
    Brief entry *39*
    Earlier sketch in SATA *47*
Hintz, Stephen V. 1975- *129*
Hippopotamus, Eugene H.
    See Kraus, (Herman) Robert
Hirano, Cathy 1957- *68*
Hirao, Amiko *203*
Hirsch, Karen 1941- *61*
Hirsch, Odo *157*
    Earlier sketch in SATA *111*
Hirsch, Phil 1926- *35*
Hirsch, S. Carl 1913-1990 .... *2*
    See also SAAS *7*
Hirschfelder, Arlene B. 1943- *138*
    Earlier sketch in SATA *80*
Hirschi, Ron 1948- *192*
    Earlier sketches in SATA *56, 95*
Hirschmann, Linda (Ann) 1941- *40*
Hirsh, Marilyn 1944-1988 .... *7*
    Obituary *58*
Hirshberg, Al(bert Simon) 1909-1973 .... *38*
Hiscock, Bruce 1940- *204*
    Earlier sketches in SATA *57, 137*
Hiser, Constance 1950- *71*
Hiser, Iona Seibert -1998 .... *4*
Hislop, Julia Rose Catherine 1962- *74*
Hissey, Jane 1952- *130*
    Autobiography Feature *130*
    Earlier sketches in SATA *58, 103*
Hissey, Jane Elizabeth
    See Hissey, Jane
Hitchcock, Alfred (Joseph) 1899-1980 .... *27*
    Obituary *24*
Hite, Sid 1954- *175*
    Earlier sketches in SATA *75, 136*
Hitte, Kathryn 1919- *16*
Hitz, Demi
    See Demi
Hitzeroth, Deborah L. 1961- *78*
Hnizdovsky, Jacques 1915- *32*
Ho, Louise *185*
Ho, Minfong 1951- *151*
    Earlier sketches in SATA *15, 94*
    See also CLR *28*
Hoagland, Edward (Morley) 1932- *51*
Hoare, Robert J(ohn) 1921-1975 .... *38*
Hoban, Julia *217*
Hoban, Lillian 1925-1998 .... *69*
    Obituary *104*
    Earlier sketch in SATA *22*
    See also CLR *67*
Hoban, Russell 1925- *136*
    Earlier sketches in SATA *1, 40, 78*
    See also CLR *139*

Hoban, Russell Conwell
    See Hoban, Russell
Hoban, Tana 1917(?)-2006 .... *104*
    Obituary *173*
    Earlier sketches in SATA *22, 70*
    See also CLR *76*
    See also SAAS *12*
Hobart, Lois (Elaine) *7*
Hobbie, Holly 1944- *178*
    See also CLR *88*
Hobbie, Jocelyn *190*
Hobbie, Nathaniel *196*
Hobbs, Leigh 1953- *166*
Hobbs, Valerie 1941- *193*
    Autobiography Feature *145*
    Earlier sketches in SATA *93, 145*
    See also CLR *148*
Hobbs, Will 1947- *177*
    Autobiography Feature *127*
    Earlier sketches in SATA *72, 110*
    See also CLR *59*
Hobbs, William Carl
    See Hobbs, Will
Hoberman, Mary Ann 1930- *158*
    Earlier sketches in SATA *5, 72, 111*
    See also CLR *22*
    See also SAAS *18*
Hobson, Bruce 1950- *62*
Hobson, Burton (Harold) 1933- *28*
Hobson, Laura Z(ametkin) 1900-1986 .... *52*
Hobson, Sally 1967- *172*
    Earlier sketch in SATA *84*
Hoce, Charley E. *174*
Hochman, David *202*
Hochschild, Arlie Russell 1940- *11*
Hockaby, Stephen
    See Mitchell, Gladys (Maude Winifred)
Hockenberry, Hope
    See Newell, Hope Hockenberry
Hodge, Deborah 1954- *163*
    Earlier sketch in SATA *122*
Hodge, P. W.
    See Hodge, Paul W(illiam)
Hodge, Paul W(illiam) 1934- *12*
Hodgell, P(atricia) C(hristine) 1951- *42*
Hodges, C. Walter 1909-2004 .... *2*
    Obituary *158*
Hodges, Carl G. 1902-1964 .... *10*
Hodges, Cyril Walter
    See Hodges, C. Walter
Hodges, Elizabeth Jamison *1*
Hodges, Margaret 1911-2005 .... *167*
    Obituary *172*
    Earlier sketches in SATA *1, 33, 75, 117*
    See also SAAS *9*
Hodges, Margaret Moore
    See Hodges, Margaret
Hodgetts, Blake Christopher 1967- *43*
Hodgkins, Fran 1964- *199*
Hodgkinson, Leigh 1975- *202*
Hodgman, Ann 1956- *198*
Hodgson, Harriet (W.) 1935- *84*
Hoehne, Marcia 1951- *89*
Hoellwarth, Cathryn Clinton
    See Clinton, Cathryn
Hoestlandt, Jo 1948- *221*
    Earlier sketch in SATA *94*
Hoestlandt, Jocelyne
    See Hoestlandt, Jo
Hoexter, Corinne K. 1927- *6*
Hoeye, Michael 1947- *136*
Hoff, Carol 1900-1979 .... *11*
Hoff, Mary (King) 1956- *157*
    Earlier sketch in SATA *74*
Hoff, Syd(ney) 1912-2004 .... *138*
    Obituary *154*
    Earlier sketches in SATA *9, 72*
    See also CLR *83*
    See also SAAS *4*
Hoffman, Edwin D. *49*

Hoffman, Elizabeth P(arkinson) 1921-2003
　Obituary *153*
Hoffman, Mary 1945- *211*
　Earlier sketches in SATA *59, 97, 144*
　See also SAAS *24*
Hoffman, Mat 1972- *150*
Hoffman, Nina Kiriki 1955- *160*
Hoffman, Phyllis M. 1944- *4*
Hoffman, Phyllis Miriam
　See Hoffman, Phyllis M.
Hoffman, Rosekrans 1926- *15*
Hoffmann, E(rnst) T(heodor) A(madeus)
　1776-1822 .... *27*
　See also CLR *133*
Hoffmann, Felix 1911-1975 .... *9*
Hoffmann, Heinrich 1809-1894
　See CLR *122*
Hoffmann, Margaret Jones 1910- *48*
Hoffmann, Peggy
　See Hoffmann, Margaret Jones
Hofher, Catherine Baxley 1954- *130*
Hofher, Cathy
　See Hofher, Catherine Baxley
Hofmeyr, Dianne (Louise) *138*
Hofsepian, Sylvia A. 1932- *74*
Hofsinde, Robert 1902-1973 .... *21*
Hogan, Bernice Harris 1929- *12*
Hogan, Inez 1895-1973 .... *2*
Hogan, James P. 1941-2010 .... *81*
Hogan, James Patrick
　See Hogan, James P.
Hogan, Jamie *192*
Hogan, Linda 1947- *132*
Hogan, Mary 1957- *210*
Hogarth, Burne 1911-1996 .... *89*
　Earlier sketch in SATA *63*
Hogarth, Grace (Weston Allen) 1905-1995 .. *91*
Hogarth, Jr.
　See Kent, Rockwell
Hogarth, (Arthur) Paul 1917-2001 .... *41*
Hogg, Garry 1902-1976 .... *2*
Hogg, Gary 1957- *172*
　Earlier sketch in SATA *105*
Hogner, Dorothy Childs *4*
Hogner, Nils 1893-1970 .... *25*
Hogrogian, Nonny 1932- *74*
　Autobiography Feature *127*
　Earlier sketch in SATA *7*
　See also CLR *95*
　See also SAAS *1*
Hoh, Diane 1937- *102*
　Brief entry *48*
　Earlier sketch in SATA *52*
Hoke, Helen
　See Watts, Helen L. Hoke
Hoke, Helen L.
　See Watts, Helen L. Hoke
Hoke, John 1925- *7*
Hoke, John Lindsay
　See Hoke, John
Hokenson, Terry 1948- *193*
Hol, Coby 1943- *126*
Holabird, Katharine 1948- *213*
　Earlier sketches in SATA *62, 135*
Holaday, Bobbie 1922- *153*
Holbeach, Henry
　See Rands, William Brighty
Holberg, Ruth L(angland) 1889-1984 .... *1*
Holbrook, Kathy 1963- *107*
Holbrook, Peter
　See Glick, Carl (Cannon)
Holbrook, Sabra
　See Erickson, Sabra Rollins
Holbrook, Sara *131*
Holbrook, Stewart Hall 1893-1964 .... *2*
Holcomb, Jerry (Leona) Kimble 1927- *113*
Holcomb, Nan
　See McPhee, Norma H.
Holden, Elizabeth Rhoda
　See Lawrence, Louise

Holding, James (Clark Carlisle, Jr.)
　1907-1997 .... *3*
Hole, Stian 1969- *204*
Holeman, Linda 1949- *136*
　Autobiography Feature *136*
　Earlier sketch in SATA *102*
Holinger, William (Jacques) 1944- *90*
Holisher, Desider 1901-1972 .... *6*
Holl, Adelaide Hinkle 1910- *8*
Holl, Kristi
　See Holl, Kristi D.
Holl, Kristi D. 1951- *51*
Holl, Kristi Diane
　See Holl, Kristi D.
Holland, Gay W. 1941- *128*
Holland, Isabelle (Christian) 1920-2002 .... *70*
　Autobiography Feature *103*
　Obituary *132*
　Earlier sketch in SATA *8*
　See also CLR *57*
Holland, Janice 1913-1962 .... *18*
Holland, John L(ewis) 1919- *20*
Holland, Joyce
　See Morice, Dave
Holland, Julia 1954- *106*
Holland, Lynda (H.) 1959- *77*
Holland, Lys
　See Gater, Dilys
Holland, Marion 1908-1989 .... *6*
　Obituary *61*
Holland, Richard 1976- *216*
Holland, Trish *221*
Hollander, John 1929- *13*
Hollander, Nicole 1940(?)- *101*
Hollander, Paul
　See Silverberg, Robert
Hollander, Phyllis 1928- *39*
Hollander, Zander 1923- *63*
Holldobler, Turid 1939- *26*
Holliday, Joe
　See Holliday, Joseph
Holliday, Joseph 1910- *11*
Holling, Holling C(lancy) 1900-1973 .... *15*
　Obituary *26*
　See also CLR *50*
Hollingsworth, Alvin C(arl) 1930- *39*
Hollingsworth, Mary 1947- *166*
　Earlier sketch in SATA *91*
Holloway, Teresa (Bragunier) 1906- *26*
Hollyer, Belinda *204*
Holm, (Else) Anne (Lise) 1922-1998 .... *1*
　See also CLR *75*
　See also SAAS *7*
Holm, Jennifer L. 1968(?)- *183*
　Earlier sketches in SATA *120, 163*
Holm, Matthew 1974- *174*
Holm, Sharon Lane 1955- *114*
　Earlier sketch in SATA *78*
Holman, Felice 1919- *82*
　Earlier sketch in SATA *7*
　See also SAAS *17*
Holm and Hamel
　See Holm, Jennifer L.
Holmberg, Bo R. 1945- *203*
Holme, Bryan 1913-1990 .... *26*
　Obituary *66*
Holmes, Barbara Ware 1945- *127*
　Earlier sketch in SATA *65*
Holmes, Elizabeth 1957- *191*
Holmes, Elizabeth Ann
　See Holmes, Elizabeth
Holmes, John
　See Souster, (Holmes) Raymond
Holmes, Marjorie (Rose) 1910-2002 .... *43*
Holmes, Martha 1961- *72*
Holmes, Mary Tavener 1954- *199*
Holmes, Mary Z(astrow) 1943- *80*
Holmes, Oliver Wendell 1809-1894 .... *34*
Holmes, Peggy 1898- *60*
Holmes, Raymond
　See Souster, (Holmes) Raymond

Holmes, Rick
　See Hardwick, Richard Holmes, Jr.
Holmes, Sara Lewis *186*
Holmgren, Helen Jean 1930- *45*
Holmgren, Sister George Ellen
　See Holmgren, Helen Jean
Holmgren, Virginia C(unningham) 1909- *26*
Holmquist, Eve 1921- *11*
Holt, K.A.
　See Roy, Kari Anne
Holt, Kimberly Willis 1960- *223*
　Earlier sketches in SATA *122, 179*
Holt, Margaret 1937- *4*
Holt, Margaret Van Vechten (Saunders)
　1899-1963 .... *32*
Holt, Michael (Paul) 1929- *13*
Holt, Rackham
　See Holt, Margaret Van Vechten (Saunders)
Holt, Rochelle L.
　See DuBois, Rochelle Holt
Holt, Stephen
　See Thompson, Harlan
Holt, Victoria
　See Hibbert, Eleanor Alice Burford
Holtei, Christa 1953- *214*
Holton, Leonard
　See Wibberley, Leonard
Holtz, Thomas R., Jr. 1965- *203*
Holtze, Sally Holmes 1952- *64*
Holtzman, Jerome 1926-2008 .... *57*
　Obituary *194*
Holub, Joan 1956- *149*
　Earlier sketch in SATA *99*
Holub, Josef 1926- *175*
Holubitsky, Katherine 1955- *165*
　Earlier sketch in SATA *121*
Holyer, Erna Maria 1925- *22*
Holyer, Ernie
　See Holyer, Erna Maria
Holz, Loretta 1943- *17*
Holz, Loretta Marie
　See Holz, Loretta
Homel, David 1952- *97*
Homze, Alma C. 1932- *17*
Honey, Elizabeth 1947- *137*
　Autobiography Feature *137*
　Earlier sketch in SATA *112*
Honeycutt, Natalie 1945- *97*
Hong, Lily Toy 1958- *76*
Hong, Maxine Ting Ting
　See Kingston, Maxine Hong
Honig, Donald 1931- *18*
Honig, Donald Martin
　See Honig, Donald
Honness, Elizabeth H. 1904- *2*
Hoobler, Dorothy 1941- *161*
　Earlier sketches in SATA *28, 109*
Hoobler, Thomas *161*
　Earlier sketches in SATA *28, 109*
Hood, Joseph F. 1925- *4*
Hood, Robert E. 1926- *21*
Hood, Sarah
　See Killough, (Karen) Lee
Hook, Brendan 1963- *105*
Hook, Frances 1912-1983 .... *27*
Hook, Geoffrey R(aynor) 1928- *103*
Hook, Jeff
　See Hook, Geoffrey R(aynor)
Hook, Martha 1936- *27*
Hooker, Richard
　See Heinz, W. C.
Hooker, Ruth 1920-1998 .... *21*
hooks, bell 1952(?)- *170*
　Earlier sketch in SATA *115*
Hooks, William H(arris) 1921- *94*
　Earlier sketch in SATA *16*
Hoon, Patricia Easterly 1954- *90*
Hooper, Byrd
　See St. Clair, Byrd Hooper
Hooper, Mary 1948- *205*
　Earlier sketch in SATA *160*

Hooper, Maureen Brett 1927- 76
Hooper, Meredith 1939- 159
  Earlier sketches in SATA 28, 101
Hooper, Meredith Jean
  See Hooper, Meredith
Hooper, Patricia 1941- 95
Hoopes, Lyn Littlefield 1953- 49
  Brief entry 44
Hoopes, Ned E(dward) 1932- 21
Hoopes, Roy 1922-2009 11
Hoose, Phillip 1947- 215
  Earlier sketch in SATA 137
Hoover, H(elen) M(ary) 1935- 132
  Brief entry 33
  Earlier sketches in SATA 44, 83
  See also SAAS 8
Hoover, Helen (Drusilla Blackburn)
  1910-1984 12
  Obituary 39
Hope, Christopher 1944- 62
Hope, Christopher David Tully
  See Hope, Christopher
Hope, Laura Lee
  See Goulart, Ron
  and Stanley, George Edward
Hope Simpson, Jacynth 1930- 12
Hopf, Alice (Martha) L(ightner) 1904-1988 ... 5
  Obituary 55
Hopkins, A. T.
  See Turngren, Annette
Hopkins, C. M.
  See Hopkins, Cathy
Hopkins, Cathy 1953- 165
Hopkins, Cathy M.
  See Hopkins, Cathy
Hopkins, Clark 1895-1976
  Obituary 34
Hopkins, Ellen 1955- 128
Hopkins, Ellen L.
  See Hopkins, Ellen
Hopkins, Jackie
  See Hopkins, Jackie Mims
Hopkins, Jackie Mims 1952- 178
  Earlier sketch in SATA 92
Hopkins, Joseph G(erard) E(dward) 1909- ... 11
Hopkins, (Hector) Kenneth 1914-1988
  Obituary 58
Hopkins, Lee Bennett 1938- 215
  Earlier sketches in SATA 3, 68, 125, 168
  See also CLR 44
  See also SAAS 4
Hopkins, Lyman
  See Folsom, Franklin (Brewster)
Hopkins, Marjorie 1911-1999 9
Hopkins, Mary R(ice) 1956- 97
Hopkinson, Amanda 1948- 84
Hopkinson, Deborah 1952- 216
  Autobiography Feature 180
  Earlier sketches in SATA 76, 108, 159, 180
  See also CLR 118
Hopman, Philip 1961- 177
Hoppe, Joanne 1932- 42
Hoppe, Matthias 1952- 76
Hoppe, Paul 209
Hopper, Nancy J. 1937- 38
  Brief entry 35
Hopping, Lorraine Jean
  See Egan, Lorraine Hopping
Horacek, Judy 1961- 211
Horaek, Petr 214
  Earlier sketch in SATA 163
Horenstein, Henry 1947- 108
Horgan, Paul (George Vincent O'Shaughnessy)
  1903-1995 13
  Obituary 84
Horlak, E.E.
  See Tepper, Sheri S.
Horler, Sydney 1888-1954 102
Horn, Sandra Ann 1944- 154
Hornblow, Arthur, Jr. 1893-1976 15

Hornblow, Leonora 1920-2005 18
  Obituary 171
Hornblow, Leonora Schinasi
  See Hornblow, Leonora
Horne, Constance 1927- 149
Horne, Richard 1960-2007 169
  Obituary 180
  Earlier sketch in SATA 111
Horne, Richard Henry Hengist
  1802(?)-1884 29
Horner, Althea (Jane) 1926- 36
Horner, Dave 1934- 12
Horner, Jack 1946- 106
Horner, John R.
  See Horner, Jack
Horner, John Robert
  See Horner, Jack
Hornik, Laurie Miller 159
Horniman, Joanne 1951- 167
  Earlier sketch in SATA 98
Hornos, Axel 1907-1994 20
Hornstein, Reuben Aaron 1912- 64
Horowitz, Anthony 1955- 195
  Earlier sketch in SATA 137
Horowitz, Dave 1970- 204
  Earlier sketch in SATA 172
Horowitz, Ruth 1957- 136
Horrocks, Anita 1958- 169
Horse, Harry
  See Horne, Richard
Horsfield, Alan 1939- 153
Horstman, Lisa 1964- 219
Hort, Lenny 179
Horton, James O. 1943- 173
Horton, James Oliver
  See Horton, James O.
Horton, Joan 217
Horton, Madelyn (Stacey) 1962- 77
Horvath, Betty 1927- 4
Horvath, David 1972(?)- 192
Horvath, Polly 1957- 194
  Earlier sketches in SATA 85, 140
  See also CLR 90
Horwich, Frances R(appaport) 1908-2001 11
  Obituary 130
Horwitz, Elinor Lander 45
  Brief entry 33
Horwood, William 1944- 85
Hosford, Dorothy (Grant) 1900-1952 22
Hosford, Jessie 1892-1990 5
Hoshi, Shin'ichi 1926- 101
Hoshino, Felicia 1968- 189
Hoskyns-Abrahall, Clare (Constance
  Drury) 13
Hosler, Danamarie 1978- 184
Hossack, Sylvia 1939- 83
Hossack, Sylvie Adams
  See Hossack, Sylvia
Hosseini, Khaled 1965- 156
Hossell, Karen Price
  See Price, Karen
Hosta, Dar 192
Hostetler, Marian 1932- 91
Houck, Carter 1924- 22
Hough, Charlotte 1924-2008 9
  Obituary 202
Hough, Helen Charlotte
  See Hough, Charlotte
Hough, Judy Taylor 1932- 63
  Brief entry 51
  Earlier sketch in SATA 56
Hough, Richard (Alexander) 1922-1999 17
Houghton, Eric 1930- 7
Houk, Randy 1944- 97
Houlehen, Robert J. 1918- 18
Houlton, Peggy Mann 1925(?)-1990 6
Household, Geoffrey 1900-1988 14
  Obituary 59
Housman, Laurence 1865-1959 25
Houston, Dick 1943- 74

Houston, Gloria 138
  Autobiography Feature 138
  Earlier sketch in SATA 81
Houston, James A(rchibald) 1921-2005 74
  Obituary 163
  Earlier sketch in SATA 13
  See also CLR 3
  See also SAAS 17
Houston, James D. 1933-2009 78
  Obituary 203
Houston, James Dudley
  See Houston, James D.
Houston, James Dudley
  See Houston, James D.
Houston, Jeanne Toyo Wakatsuki
  See Houston, Jeanne Wakatsuki
Houston, Jeanne Wakatsuki 1934- 168
  Autobiography Feature 168
  Earlier sketch in SATA 78
Houston, Juanita C. 1921- 129
Houton, Kathleen
  See Kilgore, Kathleen
Houts, Amy F. 164
Houts, Michelle 219
Hovey, Kate 158
Howard, Alan 1922- 45
Howard, Alyssa
  See Buckholtz, Eileen (Garber)
  and Glick, Ruth (Burtnick)
  and Titchener, Louise
Howard, Arthur 1948- 212
  Earlier sketch in SATA 165
Howard, Arthur Charles
  See Howard, Arthur
Howard, Elizabeth Fitzgerald 1927- 119
  Earlier sketch in SATA 74
Howard, Ellen 1943- 184
  Earlier sketches in SATA 67, 99
Howard, Jane R(uble) 1924- 87
Howard, Norman Barry 1949- 90
Howard, P. M.
  See Howard, Pauline Rodriguez
Howard, Paul 1967- 190
  Earlier sketch in SATA 118
Howard, Pauline Rodriguez 1951- 124
Howard, Prosper
  See Hamilton, Charles (Harold St. John)
Howard, Robert West 1908-1988 5
Howard, Todd 1964- 135
Howard, Tristan
  See Currie, Stephen
Howard, Vernon (Linwood) 1918-1992 40
  Obituary 73
Howard, Warren F.
  See Pohl, Frederik
Howarth, Daniel 222
  Earlier sketch in SATA 188
Howarth, David (Armine) 1912-1991 6
  Obituary 68
Howarth, Lesley 1952- 94
Howe, Deborah 1946-1978 29
Howe, James 1946- 161
  Earlier sketches in SATA 29, 71, 111
  See also CLR 9
Howe, John F. 1957- 79
Howe, Norma 1930- 126
Howe, Peter 1942- 214
Howell, Pat 1947- 15
Howell, S.
  See Styles, (Frank) Showell
Howell, Simmone 1971- 214
Howell, Virginia
  See Ellison, Virginia H(owell)
Howes, Barbara 1914-1996 5
Howie, Betsy 1962- 215
Howie, Diana 1945- 122
Howie, Diana Melson
  See Howie, Diana

Howker, Janni 1957- 72
  Brief entry 46
  See also CLR 14
  See also SAAS 13
Howland, Ethan 1963- 131
Hoy, Linda 1946- 65
Hoy, Nina
  See Roth, Arthur J(oseph)
Hoyle, Geoffrey 1942- 18
Hoyt, Ard 190
Hoyt, Edwin P(almer), Jr. 1923- 28
Hoyt, Erich 1950- 140
  Earlier sketch in SATA 65
Hoyt, Olga
  See Gruhzit-Hoyt, Olga (Margaret)
Hrdlitschka, Shelley 1956- 167
  Earlier sketch in SATA 111
Hrdlitschka, Shelley Joanne
  See Hrdlitschka, Shelley
Hromic, Alma A.
  See Alexander, Alma
Htin Aung, U.
  See Aung, (Maung) Htin
Hu, Ying-Hwa 173
Huang, Benrei 1959- 86
Hubalek, Linda K. 1954- 111
Hubbard, Crystal 209
Hubbard, Margaret Ann
  See Priley, Margaret (Ann) Hubbard
Hubbard, Michelle Calabro 1953- 122
Hubbard, Patricia 1945- 124
Hubbard, Woodleigh Marx 160
  Earlier sketch in SATA 98
Hubbell, Patricia 1928- 186
  Earlier sketches in SATA 8, 132
Hubery, Julia 195
Hubley, Faith Elliot 1924-2001 48
  Obituary 133
Hubley, John 1914-1977 48
  Obituary 24
Huck, Charlotte S. 1922- 136
  Earlier sketch in SATA 82
Hucke, Johannes 1966- 218
Hudak, Michal 1956- 143
Hudson, Cheryl Willis 1948- 160
  Earlier sketch in SATA 81
Hudson, Jan 1954-1990 77
  See also CLR 40
Hudson, Jeffery
  See Crichton, Michael
Hudson, Jeffrey
  See Crichton, Michael
Hudson, (Margaret) Kirsty 1947- 32
Hudson, Margaret
  See Shuter, Jane (Margaret)
Hudson, W(illiam) H(enry) 1841-1922 35
Hudson, Wade 1946- 162
  Earlier sketch in SATA 74
Huelsmann, Eva 1928- 16
Huerlimann, Bettina 1909-1983 39
  Obituary 34
Huerlimann, Ruth 1939- 32
  Brief entry 31
Huff, Barbara A. 1929- 67
Huff, Tanya 1957- 171
  Earlier sketch in SATA 85
Huff, Tanya Sue
  See Huff, Tanya
Huff, T.S.
  See Huff, Tanya
Huff, Vivian 1948- 59
Huffaker, Sandy 1943- 10
Huffman, Tom 24
Huggins, Nathan Irvin 1927-1989 63
Huggins, Peter 1951- 178
Hughes, Carol 1955- 217
  Earlier sketch in SATA 108
Hughes, Dean 1943- 139
  Earlier sketches in SATA 33, 77
  See also CLR 76

Hughes, Eden
  See Griffin, W. E. B.
Hughes, Edward James
  See Hughes, Ted
Hughes, James Langston
  See Hughes, Langston
Hughes, Langston 1902-1967 33
  Earlier sketch in SATA 4
  See also CLR 17
Hughes, Libby 71
Hughes, Matilda
  See MacLeod, Charlotte (Matilda)
Hughes, Monica 1925-2003 162
  Earlier sketches in SATA 15, 70, 119
  See also CLR 60
  See also SAAS 11
Hughes, Monica Ince
  See Hughes, Monica
Hughes, Pat 197
Hughes, Richard (Arthur Warren)
  1900-1976 8
  Obituary 25
Hughes, Sara
  See Saunders, Susan
Hughes, Shirley 1927- 159
  Earlier sketches in SATA 16, 70, 110
  See also CLR 15
Hughes, Susan 1960- 216
Hughes, Ted 1930-1998 49
  Brief entry 27
  Obituary 107
  See also CLR 131
Hughes, Thomas 1822-1896 31
  See also CLR 160
Hughes, Virginia
  See Campbell, Hope
Hughes, Walter (Llewellyn) 1910-1993 26
Hughey, Roberta 1942- 61
Hugo, Pierre Brackers de
  See Brackers de Hugo, Pierre
Hugo, Victor 1802-1885 47
Hugo, Victor Marie
  See Hugo, Victor
Huline-Dickens, Frank William 1931- 34
Huling, Jan 172
Huliska-Beith, Laura 175
Hull, Eleanor (Means) 1913- 21
Hull, Eric Traviss
  See Harnan, Terry
Hull, H. Braxton
  See Jacobs, Helen Hull
Hull, Jesse Redding
  See Hull, Jessie Redding
Hull, Jessie Redding 1932- 51
Hull, Katharine 1921-1977 23
Hull, Lise (E.) 1954- 148
Hull, Maureen 1949- 142
Hulme, Joy N. 1922- 161
  Earlier sketches in SATA 74, 112
Hults, Dorothy Niebrugge 1898-2000 6
Humble, Richard 1945- 60
Hume, Lachie 189
Hume, Lotta Carswell 7
Hume, Ruth Fox 1922-1980 26
  Obituary 22
Hume, Stephen Eaton 1947- 136
Hummel, Berta 1909-1946 43
Hummel, Sister Maria Innocentia
  See Hummel, Berta
Hummon, Marcus 1960- 213
Humphrey, Carol Sue 1956- 167
Humphrey, Henry (III) 1930- 16
Humphrey, Kate
  See Forsyth, Kate
Humphrey, Sandra McLeod 1936- 95
Humphreys, Martha 1943- 71
Humphreys, Susan L.
  See Lowell, Susan
Hundal, Nancy 1957- 128
Huneck, Stephen 1949- 183
  Earlier sketch in SATA 129

Hungerford, Hesba Fay
  See Brinsmead, H(esba) F(ay)
Hungerford, Pixie
  See Brinsmead, H(esba) F(ay)
Hunkin, Tim 1950- 53
Hunkin, Timothy Mark Trelawney
  See Hunkin, Tim
Hunt, Angela Elwell 1957- 159
  Earlier sketch in SATA 75
Hunt, Bernice 1920- 4
Hunt, Charlotte Dumaresq
  See Demi
Hunt, Francesca
  See Holland, Isabelle (Christian)
Hunt, Irene 1907-2001 91
  Earlier sketch in SATA 2
  See also CLR 1
Hunt, Janie Louise 1963- 102
Hunt, Jonathan 1966- 84
Hunt, Joyce 1927- 31
Hunt, Linda 1940- 39
Hunt, Lisa B(ehnke) 1967- 84
Hunt, Mabel Leigh 1892-1971 1
  Obituary 26
Hunt, Morton M(agill) 1920- 22
Hunt, Nigel
  See Greenbank, Anthony Hunt
Hunt, Peter (Leonard) 1945- 76
Hunter, Anne B. 1966- 118
Hunter, Bernice Thurman 1922-2002 85
  Brief entry 45
Hunter, Bobbi Dooley 1945- 89
Hunter, Captain Marcy
  See Ellis, Edward S.
Hunter, Chris
  See Fluke, Joanne
Hunter, Clingham M.D.
  See Adams, William Taylor
Hunter, Edith Fisher 1919- 31
Hunter, Erin
  See Cary, Kate
Hunter, Evan 1926-2005 25
  Obituary 167
Hunter, George E.
  See Ellis, Edward S.
Hunter, Hilda 1921- 7
Hunter, Jana
  See Hunter, Jana Novotny
Hunter, Jana Novotny 190
Hunter, Jim 1939- 65
Hunter, Kristin
  See Lattany, Kristin Hunter
Hunter, Leigh
  See Etchison, Birdie L(ee)
Hunter, Lieutenant Ned
  See Ellis, Edward S.
Hunter, Mel 1927-2004 39
Hunter, Mollie 1922- 139
  Autobiography Feature 139
  Earlier sketches in SATA 2, 54, 106
  See also CLR 25
  See also SAAS 7
Hunter, Ned
  See Ellis, Edward S.
Hunter, Norman (George Lorimer)
  1899-1995 84
  Earlier sketch in SATA 26
Hunter, Ryan Ann
  See Greenwood, Pamela D.
  and Macalaster, Elizabeth G.
Hunter, Sara Hoagland 1954- 98
Hunter Blair, Pauline
  See Clarke, Pauline
Huntington, Amy 1956- 180
  Earlier sketch in SATA 138
Huntington, Geoffrey 145
Huntington, Harriet E(lizabeth) 1909- 1
Huntsberry, William E(mery) 1916- 5

Hurd, Clement (G.) 1908-1988 64
  Obituary 54
  Earlier sketch in SATA 2
  See also CLR 49
Hurd, Edith Thacher 1910-1997 64
  Obituary 95
  Earlier sketch in SATA 2
  See also CLR 49
  See also SAAS 13
Hurd, John Thacher
  See Hurd, Thacher
Hurd, Thacher 1949- 219
  Autobiography Feature 123
  Brief entry 45
  Earlier sketches in SATA 46, 94
Hurley, Jo
  See Dower, Laura
Hurley, Tonya 207
Hurlimann, Bettina
  See Huerlimann, Bettina
Hurlimann, Ruth
  See Huerlimann, Ruth
Hurmence, Belinda 1921- 77
  See also CLR 25
  See also SAAS 20
Hurst, Carol Otis 1933-2007 185
  Earlier sketch in SATA 130
Hurt-Newton, Tania 1968- 84
Hurwin, Davida Wills 1950- 180
Hurwitz, Johanna 1937- 175
  Earlier sketches in SATA 20, 71, 113
  See also SAAS 18
Hurwood, Bernhardt J. 1926-1987 12
  Obituary 50
Husain, Shahrukh 1950- 108
Huser, Glen 1943- 151
Hutchens, Paul 1902-1977 31
Hutchins, Carleen M.
  See Hutchins, Carleen Maley
Hutchins, Carleen Maley 1911-2009 9
  Obituary 206
Hutchins, Hazel J. 1952- 175
  Brief entry 51
  Earlier sketches in SATA 81, 135
  See also SAAS 24
Hutchins, Pat 1942- 178
  Earlier sketches in SATA 15, 70, 111
  See also CLR 20
  See also SAAS 16
Hutchins, Ross Elliott 1906- 4
Hutchison, Linda 1942- 152
Huthmacher, J. Joseph 1929- 5
Hutto, Nelson (Allen) 1904-1985 20
Hutton, Kathryn 1915- 89
Hutton, Sam
  See Jones, Allan Frewin
Hutton, Warwick 1939-1994 20
  Obituary 83
  See also SAAS 17
Huxley, Aldous 1894-1963 63
  See also CLR 151
Huxley, Aldous Leonard
  See Huxley, Aldous
Huxley, Elspeth (Josceline Grant)
  1907-1997 62
  Obituary 95
Hyde, Catherine R.
  See Hyde, Catherine Ryan
Hyde, Catherine Ryan 1955- 141
Hyde, Dayton O(gden) 9
Hyde, Hawk
  See Hyde, Dayton O(gden)
Hyde, Jeannette
  See Eyerly, Jeannette
Hyde, Margaret O. 1917- 139
  Earlier sketches in SATA 1, 42, 76
  See also CLR 23
  See also SAAS 8
Hyde, Margaret Oldroyd
  See Hyde, Margaret O.

Hyde, Shelley
  See Reed, Kit
Hyde, Wayne Frederick 1922- 7
Hylander, Clarence J(ohn) 1897-1964 7
Hyman, Miles 1962- 210
Hyman, Paula Chase
  See Chase, Paula
Hyman, Robin 1931- 12
Hyman, Robin Phiilip
  See Hyman, Robin
Hyman, Trina Schart 1939-2004 95
  Obituary 158
  Earlier sketches in SATA 7, 46
  See also CLR 50
Hymes, Lucia M(anley) 1907-1998 7
Hyndman, Jane Andrews Lee 1912-1978 46
  Obituary 23
  Earlier sketch in SATA 1
Hyndman, Robert Utley 1906-1973 18
Hynes, Pat 98

I

Iannone, Jeanne
  See Balzano, Jeanne (Koppel)
Ibatoulline, Bagram 1965(?)- 174
Ibbitson, John Perrie 1955- 102
Ibbotson, Eva 1925-2010 221
  Earlier sketches in SATA 13, 103, 156
Ibbotson, M. C(hristine) 1930- 5
Icenoggle, Jodi 1967- 168
Icenoggle, Jodi O.
  See Icenoggle, Jodi
Ichikawa, Satomi 1949- 208
  Brief entry 36
  Earlier sketches in SATA 47, 78, 146
  See also CLR 62
Idle, Molly Schaar 223
Iggulden, Hal 1972- 196
Ignoffo, Matthew 1945- 92
Igus, Toyomi 1953- 112
  Earlier sketch in SATA 76
Ihimaera, Witi (Tame) 1944- 148
Ikeda, Daisaku 1928- 77
Ilowite, Sheldon A. 1931- 27
Ilsey, Dent
  See Chapman, John Stanton Higham
Ilsley, Dent
  See Chapman, John Stanton Higham
Ilsley, Velma (Elizabeth) 1918- 12
Imai, Ayano 1980- 190
Imai, Miko 1963- 90
Imershein, Betsy 1953- 62
Immel, Mary Blair 1930- 28
Immell, Myra H. 1941- 92
Impey, Rose 1947- 223
  Earlier sketches in SATA 69, 152
Ingelow, Jean 1820-1897 33
Ingermanson, Randall 1958- 134
Ingermanson, Randy
  See Ingermanson, Randall
Ingersoll, Norman 1928- 79
Ingham, Colonel Frederic
  See Hale, Edward Everett
Ingman, Bruce 1963- 182
  Earlier sketch in SATA 134
Ingman, Nicholas 1948- 52
Ingold, Jeanette 128
Ingpen, Robert 1936- 166
  Earlier sketch in SATA 109
Ingpen, Robert Roger
  See Ingpen, Robert
Ingraham, Erick 1950- 145
Ingraham, Leonard W(illiam) 1913-2003 4
Ingram, Scott 1948- 167
  Earlier sketch in SATA 92
Ingram, W. Scott
  See Ingram, Scott

Ingrams, Doreen 1906-1997 97
  Earlier sketch in SATA 20
Ingrid, Charles
  See Salsitz, Rhondi Vilott
Ingves, Gunilla 1939- 101
Ingves, Gunilla Anna Maria Folkesdotter
  See Ingves, Gunilla
Inkpen, Mick 1952- 154
  Earlier sketch in SATA 99
Innes, (Ralph) Hammond
  See Hammond Innes, Ralph
Innes, Ralph Hammond
  See Hammond Innes, Ralph
Innes, Stephanie 220
Innocenti, Roberto 1940- 159
  Earlier sketch in SATA 96
  See also CLR 126
Innocenti and Gallaz
  See Gallaz, Christophe
  and Innocenti, Roberto
Inns, Chris 212
Inyart, Gene
  See Namovicz, Gene Inyart
Ionesco, Eugene 1909-1994 7
  Obituary 79
Ipcar, Dahlov (Zorach) 1917- 147
  Autobiography Feature 147
  Earlier sketches in SATA 1, 49
  See also SAAS 8
Ireland, Karin 151
  Earlier sketch in SATA 101
Ironside, Jetske 1940- 60
Irvin, Fred 1914- 15
Irvine, Georgeanne 1955- 72
Irvine, Joan 1951- 80
Irving, Alexander
  See Hume, Ruth Fox
Irving, Robert
  See Adler, Irving
Irving, Washington 1783-1859
  See YABC 2
  See also CLR 97
Irwin, Ann(abelle Bowen) 1915-1998 89
  Brief entry 38
  Obituary 106
  Earlier sketch in SATA 44
  See also CLR 40
  See also SAAS 14
Irwin, Constance (H.) Frick 1913-1995 6
Irwin, Hadley
  See Hadley, Lee
  and Irwin, Ann(abelle Bowen)
Irwin, Keith Gordon 1885-1964 11
Isaac, Joanne 1934- 21
Isaacs, Anne 1949- 185
  Earlier sketch in SATA 90
Isaacs, Jacob
  See Kranzler, George G(ershon)
Isaacson, Philip M(arshal) 1924- 87
Isadora, Rachel 1953(?)- 204
  Brief entry 32
  Earlier sketches in SATA 54, 79, 121, 165
  See also CLR 7
Isbell, Rebecca T(emple) 1942- 125
Isham, Charlotte H(ickock) 1912- 21
Ishida, Jui 176
Ish-Kishor, Judith 1892-1972 11
Ish-Kishor, Sulamith 1896-1977 17
Ishmael, Woodi 1914-1995 31
  Obituary 109
Isle, Sue 1963- 105
Isol 1972- 220
Israel, Elaine 1945- 12
Israel, Marion Louise 1882-1973
  Obituary 26
Iterson, S(iny) R(ose) Van
  See Van Iterson, S(iny) R(ose)
Ivanko, John D. 1966- 111
Ivanko, John Duane
  See Ivanko, John D.
Iversen, Jeremy 1980(?)- 174

Iversen, Jeremy Watt
See Iversen, Jeremy
Iverson, Carol (L.) 1941- 145
Iverson, Diane 1950- 122
Iverson, Eric G.
See Turtledove, Harry
Ivery, Martha M. 1948- 124
Ives, David 1951- 173
Ives, Morgan
See Bradley, Marion Zimmer
Ives, Penny 1956- 215
Iwai, Melissa 183
Iwamatsu, Jun Atsushi 1908-1994 81
Earlier sketch in SATA 14
See also CLR 4
Iwamura, Kazuo 1939- 213
Iwasaki (Matsumoto), Chihiro 1918-1974
See CLR 18
Iyengar, Malathi Michelle 1954- 220

J

Jabar, Cynthia 210
Jablonski, Carla 184
Jac, Lee
See Morton, Lee Jack, Jr.
Jacka, Martin 1943- 72
Jackson, Alison 1953- 160
Earlier sketches in SATA 73, 108
Jackson, Anne 1896(?)-1984
Obituary 37
Jackson, Barry
See Jackson, Barry E.
Jackson, Barry E. 200
Jackson, C(aary) Paul 1902-1991 6
Jackson, Caary
See Jackson, C(aary) Paul
Jackson, Charlotte E. (Cobden) 1903(?)-1989
Obituary 62
Jackson, Dave
See Jackson, J. David
Jackson, Donna M. 1959- 206
Jackson, Ellen 1943- 214
Earlier sketches in SATA 75, 115, 167
Jackson, Ellen B.
See Jackson, Ellen
Jackson, Garnet Nelson 1944- 87
Jackson, Geoffrey (Holt Seymour) 1915-1987
Obituary 53
Jackson, Gina
See Fluke, Joanne
Jackson, Guida M. 1930- 71
Jackson, J. David 1944- 91
Jackson, Jacqueline 1928- 65
Jackson, Jacqueline Dougan
See Jackson, Jacqueline
Jackson, Jesse 1908-1983 29
Obituary 48
Earlier sketch in SATA 2
See also CLR 28
Jackson, Marjorie 1928- 127
Jackson, Melanie 1956- 141
Jackson, Mike 1946- 91
Jackson, Neta J. 1944- 91
Jackson, O. B.
See Jackson, C(aary) Paul
Jackson, Rob 1961- 176
Jackson, Robert B(lake) 1926- 8
Jackson, Robert Bradley
See Jackson, Rob
Jackson, Sally
See Kellogg, Jean (Defrees)
Jackson, Shirley 1919-1965 2
Jackson, Woody 1948- 92
Jackson Issa, Kai 205
Jacob, Helen Pierce 1927- 21
Jacobin
See Bisson, Terry
Jacobs, Deborah Lynn 187

Jacobs, Flora Gill 1918-2006 5
Obituary 178
Jacobs, Francine 1935- 150
Brief entry 42
Earlier sketch in SATA 43
Jacobs, Frank 1929- 30
Jacobs, Helen Hull 1908-1997 12
Jacobs, Joseph 1854-1916 25
Jacobs, Judy 1952- 69
Jacobs, Laurie A. 1956- 89
Jacobs, Leah
See Gellis, Roberta
Jacobs, Lee
See Stone, Tanya Lee
Jacobs, Leland Blair 1907-1992 20
Obituary 71
Jacobs, Linda
See Altman, Linda Jacobs
Jacobs, Lou(is), Jr. 1921- 2
Jacobs, Shannon K. 1947- 77
Jacobs, Susan
See Quinn, Susan
Jacobs, William Jay 1933- 89
Earlier sketch in SATA 28
Jacobsen, Laura 177
Jacobson, Daniel 1923- 12
Jacobson, Jennifer
See Jacobson, Jennifer Richard
Jacobson, Jennifer Richard 1958- 170
Jacobson, Morris K(arl) 1906- 21
Jacobson, Rick 170
Jacopetti, Alexandra
See Hart, Alexandra
Jacques, Brian 1939- 176
Earlier sketches in SATA 62, 95, 138
See also CLR 21
Jacques, Robin 1920-1995 32
Brief entry 30
Obituary 86
See also SAAS 5
Jaekel, Susan M. 1948- 89
Jaffe, Michele 179
Jaffe, Michele Sharon
See Jaffe, Michele
Jaffee, Al(lan) 1921- 66
Earlier sketch in SATA 37
Jagendorf, Moritz (Adolf) 1888-1981 2
Obituary 24
Jago 1979- 216
Jahn, Joseph Michael
See Jahn, Michael
Jahn, Michael 1943- 28
Jahn, Mike
See Jahn, Michael
Jahn-Clough, Lisa 1967- 193
Earlier sketches in SATA 88, 152
Jahsmann, Allan Hart 1916- 28
Jakes, John 1932- 62
Jakes, John William
See Jakes, John
James, Andrew
See Kirkup, James
James, Ann 1952- 168
Earlier sketches in SATA 82, 117
James, Betsy 183
James, Bill 1929- 205
James, B.J.
See James, Brian
James, Brian 1976- 212
Earlier sketch in SATA 140
James, Bronte
See Nash, Renea Denise
James, Captain Lew
See Stratemeyer, Edward L.
James, Charlie 1961- 185
James, Curtis E. 182
James, Dynely
See Mayne, William
James, Edwin
See Gunn, James E.

James, Elizabeth 1942- 97
Earlier sketches in SATA 39, 45, 52
James, Emily
See Standiford, Natalie
James, Gordon C. 1973- 195
James, Harry Clebourne 1896-1978 11
James, J. Alison 1962- 146
Earlier sketch in SATA 83
James, Josephine
See Sterne, Emma Gelders
James, Mary
See Meaker, Marijane
James, Matt 201
James, Philip
See del Rey, Lester
and Moorcock, Michael
James, Robin 1953- 50
James, Robin Irene
See James, Robin
James, Simon 1961- 202
James, T. F.
See Fleming, Thomas
James, Tegan
See Odgers, Sally Farrell
James, Will(iam Roderick) 1892-1942 19
Jameson, W. C. 1942- 93
Jamieson, Ian R.
See Goulart, Ron
Jamieson, Victoria 218
Jamiolkowski, Raymond M. 1953- 81
Jane, Mary Childs 1909-1991 6
Jane, Pamela 158
Janeczko, Paul B(ryan) 1945- 155
Earlier sketches in SATA 53, 98
See also CLR 47
See also SAAS 18
Janes, Edward C. 1908-1984 25
Janes, Edward Clarence
See Janes, Edward C.
Janes, J(oseph) Robert 1935- 148
Brief entry 50
Earlier sketch in SATA 101
Janeway, Elizabeth (Hall) 1913-2005 19
Janger, Kathleen N. 1940- 66
Jango-Cohen, Judith 1955- 208
Janice
See Brustlein, Janice Tworkov
Janisch, Heinz 1960- 181
Janosch
See Eckert, Horst
Janover, Caroline (Davis) 1943- 141
Earlier sketch in SATA 89
Janovitz, Marilyn 194
Jansen, Jared
See Cebulash, Mel
Janson, Dora Jane (Heineberg) 1916- 31
Janson, H(orst) W(oldemar) 1913-1982 9
Jansson, Tove (Marika) 1914-2001 41
Earlier sketch in SATA 3
See also CLR 125
Janus, Grete
See Hertz, Grete Janus
Jaques, Faith 1923-1997 97
Earlier sketches in SATA 21, 69
Jaquith, Priscilla 1908- 51
Jaramillo, Mari-Luci 1928- 139
Jarka, Jeff 221
Jarman, Julia 1946- 198
Earlier sketch in SATA 133
Jarman, Rosemary Hawley 1935- 7
Jarrell, Mary Von Schrader 1914- 35
Jarrell, Randall 1914-1965 7
See also CLR 111
Jarrett, Clare 1952- 201
Jarrett, Roxanne
See Werner, Herma
Jarrie, Martin 1953- 219
Jarrow, Gail 1952- 185
Earlier sketch in SATA 84

Jarvis, E.K.
  See Ellison, Harlan
  and Silverberg, Robert
Jarvis, Robin 1963- 181
Jaskol, Julie 1958- 127
Jasner, W. K.
  See Watson, Jane Werner
Jassem, Kate
  See Oppenheim, Joanne
Jauss, Anne Marie 1902(?)-1991 10
  Obituary 69
Javernick, Ellen 1938- 217
  Earlier sketch in SATA *89*
Javins, Marie 1966- 212
Jay, Alison 196
Jayne, Lieutenant R. H.
  See Ellis, Edward S.
Jaynes, Clare
  See Mayer, Jane Rothschild
Jeake, Samuel, Jr.
  See Aiken, Conrad
Jean-Bart, Leslie 1954- 121
Jeapes, Ben 1965- 174
Jecan, Gavriel 1962- 200
Jefferds, Vincent H(arris) 1916- 59
  Brief entry 49
Jefferies, (John) Richard 1848-1887 16
Jeffers, Dawn 189
Jeffers, Oliver 1977- 213
  Earlier sketch in SATA *175*
Jeffers, Susan 1942- 202
  Earlier sketches in SATA *17, 70, 129, 137*
  See also CLR *30*
Jefferson, Sarah
  See Farjeon, (Eve) Annabel
Jeffries, Roderic 1926- 4
Jeffries, Roderic Graeme
  See Jeffries, Roderic
Jenkin-Pearce, Susie 1943- 80
Jenkins, A. M. 1961- 174
Jenkins, Amanda McRaney
  See Jenkins, A. M.
Jenkins, Debra Reid
  See Reid Jenkins, Debra
Jenkins, Emily 1967- 174
  Earlier sketch in SATA *144*
Jenkins, Jean 98
Jenkins, Jerry B. 1949- 149
Jenkins, Jerry Bruce
  See Jenkins, Jerry B.
Jenkins, Leonard 189
Jenkins, Marie M(agdalen) 1909- 7
Jenkins, Martin 1959- 216
Jenkins, M.D.
  See Jenkins, Martin
Jenkins, Patrick 1955- 72
Jenkins, Steve 1952- 218
  Earlier sketches in SATA *154, 188*
Jenkins, William A(twell) 1922-1998 9
Jenkyns, Chris 1924- 51
Jennewein, James 215
Jennewein, Jim
  See Jennewein, James
Jennings, Christopher S. 1971(?)- 201
Jennings, Coleman A(lonzo) 1933- 64
Jennings, C.S.
  See Jennings, Christopher S.
Jennings, Dana Andrew 1957- 93
Jennings, Elizabeth (Joan) 1926-2001 66
Jennings, Gary 1928-1999 9
  Obituary 117
Jennings, Gary Gayne
  See Jennings, Gary
Jennings, Linda 1937- 211
Jennings, Linda M.
  See Jennings, Linda
Jennings, Patrick 1962- 205
  Earlier sketches in SATA *96, 160*
Jennings, Paul 1943- 165
  Earlier sketch in SATA *88*
  See also CLR *40*

Jennings, Richard W. 1945- 185
  Earlier sketch in SATA *136*
Jennings, Robert
  See Hamilton, Charles (Harold St. John)
Jennings, S. M.
  See Meyer, Jerome Sydney
Jennings, Sharon 1954- 95
Jennings, Sharon Elizabeth
  See Jennings, Sharon
Jennison, C. S.
  See Starbird, Kaye
Jennison, Keith Warren 1911-1995 14
Jensen, Kathryn 1949- 81
Jensen, Kristine Mary 1961- 78
Jensen, Niels 1927- 25
Jensen, Vickie (Dee) 1946- 81
Jensen, Virginia Allen 1927- 8
Jenson-Elliott, Cynthia L(ouise) 1962- 143
Jeram, Anita 1965- 219
  Earlier sketches in SATA *71, 102, 154*
Jerman, Jerry 1949- 89
Jernigan, E. Wesley 1940- 85
Jernigan, Gisela (Evelyn) 1948- 85
Jeschke, Susan 1942- 42
  Brief entry 27
Jessel, Camilla (Ruth) 1937- 143
  Earlier sketch in SATA *29*
Jessell, Tim 177
Jessey, Cornelia
  See Sussman, Cornelia Silver
Jewel
  See Kilcher, Jewel
Jewell, Nancy 1940- 109
  Brief entry 41
Jewett, Eleanore Myers 1890-1967 5
Jewett, Sarah Orne 1849-1909 15
Jewett, Theodora Sarah Orne
  See Jewett, Sarah Orne
Jezard, Alison 1919- 57
  Brief entry 34
Jiang, Cheng An 1943- 109
Jiang, Ji-li 1954- 101
Jiang, Zheng An
  See Jiang, Cheng An
Jiler, John 1946- 42
  Brief entry 35
Jimenez, Francisco 1943- 219
  Earlier sketch in SATA *108*
Jinks, Catherine 1963- 207
  Earlier sketches in SATA *94, 155*
Jobb, Jamie 1945- 29
Jobling, Curtis 131
Jocelyn, Ann Henning 1948- 92
Jocelyn, Marthe 1956- 198
  Earlier sketches in SATA *118, 163*
Joerns, Consuelo 44
  Brief entry 33
Joey D
  See Macaulay, Teresa
Johansen, Krista V.
  See Johansen, K.V.
Johansen, K.V 1968- 186
Johansen, K.V. 1968- 186
  Earlier sketch in SATA *129*
Johansson, Philip 163
John, Antony 1972- 206
John, Joyce 59
Johns, Avery
  See Cousins, Margaret
Johns, Elizabeth 1943- 88
Johns, Janetta
  See Quin-Harkin, Janet
Johns, Linda 1945- 173
Johns, W(illiam) E(arle) 1893-1968 55
Johns, Captain W. E.
  See Johns, W(illiam) E(arle)
Johnson, A.
  See Johnson, Annabell
Johnson, A. E.
  See Johnson, Annabell
  and Johnson, Edgar (Raymond)

Johnson, Angela 1961- 188
  Earlier sketches in SATA *69, 102, 150*
  See also CLR *33*
Johnson, Annabel
  See Johnson, Annabell
Johnson, Annabell 1921- 72
  Earlier sketch in SATA *2*
Johnson, Art 1946- 123
Johnson, B. F. 1920- 1
Johnson, Benjamin F., of Boone
  See Riley, James Whitcomb
Johnson, Bettye 1858-1919
  See Rogers, Bettye
Johnson, Caryn
  See Goldberg, Whoopi
Johnson, Caryn E.
  See Goldberg, Whoopi
Johnson, Caryn Elaine
  See Goldberg, Whoopi
Johnson, Charles R. 1925- 11
Johnson, Charlotte Buel
  See von Wodtke, Charlotte Buel Johnson
Johnson, Chuck
  See Johnson, Charles R.
Johnson, Crockett
  See Leisk, David (Johnson)
Johnson, D(ana) William 1945- 23
Johnson, Daniel Shahid 1954- 73
Johnson, David
  See Johnson, David A.
Johnson, David A. 1951- 191
Johnson, D.B. 1944- 183
  Earlier sketch in SATA *146*
Johnson, Dianne 1960- 130
Johnson, Dinah
  See Johnson, Dianne
Johnson, Dolores 1949- 69
Johnson, Donald B.
  See Johnson, D.B.
Johnson, Dorothy M(arie) 1905-1984 6
  Obituary 40
Johnson, E(ugene) Harper 44
Johnson, Edgar (Raymond) 1912-1990 72
  Earlier sketch in SATA *2*
Johnson, Eleanor Murdock 1892-1987
  Obituary 54
Johnson, Elizabeth 1911-1984 7
  Obituary 39
Johnson, Eric W(arner) 1918-1994 ....
  Obituary 82
  Earlier sketch in SATA *8*
Johnson, Evelyne 1922- 20
Johnson, Fred 19(?)-1982 63
Johnson, Gaylord 1884-1972 7
Johnson, Gerald White 1890-1980 19
  Obituary 28
Johnson, Gillian 1963- 215
Johnson, Harper
  See Johnson, E(ugene) Harper
Johnson, Harriett 1908-1987
  Obituary 53
Johnson, James Ralph 1922- 1
Johnson, James Weldon 1871-1938 31
  See also CLR *32*
Johnson, Jane 1951- 48
Johnson, Joan J. 1942- 59
Johnson, John E(mil) 1929- 34
Johnson, Johnny 1901-1995
  See Johnson, (Walter) Ryerson
Johnson, Kathleen Jeffrie 1950- 186
Johnson, La Verne B(ravo) 1925- 13
Johnson, Layne 222
  Earlier sketch in SATA *187*
Johnson, Lee Kaiser 1962- 78
Johnson, Lissa H(alls) 1955- 65
Johnson, Lois Smith 1894-1993 6
Johnson, Lois Walfrid 1936- 130
  Earlier sketches in SATA *22, 91*
Johnson, Margaret S(weet) 1893-1964 35
Johnson, Marguerite Annie
  See Angelou, Maya

Johnson, Mary Frances K. 1929(?)-1979
  Obituary 27
Johnson, Maud Battle 1918(?)-1985
  Obituary 46
Johnson, Maureen 1973- 200
Johnson, Meredith Merrell 1952- 104
Johnson, Milton 1932- 31
Johnson, Neil 1954- 135
  Earlier sketch in SATA 73
Johnson, Pamela 1949- 71
Johnson, Patricia Polin 1956- 84
Johnson, Paul Brett 1947- 132
  Earlier sketch in SATA 83
Johnson, Rebecca L. 1956- 147
  Earlier sketch in SATA 67
Johnson, Rick L. 1954- 79
Johnson, (Walter) Ryerson 1901-1995 10
  Obituary 106
Johnson, Scott 1952- 119
  Earlier sketch in SATA 76
Johnson, Sherrie 1948- 87
Johnson, Shirley K(ing) 1927- 10
Johnson, Siddie Joe 1905-1977
  Obituary 20
Johnson, Spencer 1938- 145
  Brief entry 38
Johnson, Stacie
  See Myers, Walter Dean
Johnson, Stephen T. 1964- 189
  Earlier sketches in SATA 84, 141
Johnson, Steve 1960- 177
Johnson, Sue Kaiser 1963- 78
Johnson, Sylvia A. 166
  Brief entry 52
  Earlier sketch in SATA 104
Johnson, William R. 38
Johnson, William Weber 1909-1992 7
Johnson-Feelings, Dianne
  See Johnson, Dianne
Johnston, Agnes Christine
  See Dazey, Agnes J(ohnston)
Johnston, Annie Fellows 1863-1931 37
Johnston, Dorothy Grunbock 1915-1979 54
Johnston, Ginny 1946- 60
Johnston, H(ugh) A(nthony) S(tephen)
  1913-1967 14
Johnston, Janet 1944- 71
Johnston, Jeffry W. 188
Johnston, Johanna 1914(?)-1982 12
  Obituary 33
Johnston, Julie 1941- 110
  Autobiography Feature 128
  Earlier sketch in SATA 78
  See also CLR 41
  See also SAAS 24
Johnston, Lynn 1947- 216
  Earlier sketch in SATA 118
Johnston, Lynn Beverley
  See Johnston, Lynn
Johnston, Mark 194
Johnston, Norma
  See St. John, Nicole
Johnston, Portia
  See Takakjian, Portia
Johnston, Susan Taylor 1942- 180
  Earlier sketches in SATA 8, 83, 128
Johnston, Tim(othy Patrick) 1962- 146
Johnston, Tony
  See Johnston, Susan Taylor
Joinson, Carla 160
Jolin, Paula 186
Jolivet, Joelle 1965- 221
Jonas, Ann 1932- 135
  Brief entry 42
  Earlier sketch in SATA 50
  See also CLR 74
Jonell, Lynne 1956- 196
  Earlier sketch in SATA 109
Jones, Adrienne 1915-2000 82
  Earlier sketch in SATA 7
  See also SAAS 10

Jones, Allan Frewin 1954- 204
Jones, Annabel
  See Lewis, Mary
Jones, Betty Millsaps 1940- 54
Jones, Carol 1942- 153
  Earlier sketch in SATA 79
Jones, Carrie 1971- 191
Jones, Charles M.
  See Jones, Chuck
Jones, Charlotte Foltz 1945- 122
  Earlier sketch in SATA 77
Jones, Chuck 1912-2002 53
  Obituary 133
Jones, Constance 112
Jones, Constance A.
  See Jones, Constance
Jones, David 1956- 202
Jones, Diana Wynne 1934- 160
  Earlier sketches in SATA 9, 70, 108
  See also CLR 120
  See also SAAS 7
Jones, Douglas B. 202
Jones, Douglas C(lyde) 1924-1998 52
Jones, Elizabeth McDavid 155
Jones, Elizabeth Orton 1910-2005 18
  Obituary 164
Jones, Evan 1915-1996 3
Jones, Frewin
  See Jones, Allan Frewin
Jones, Geraldine
  See McCaughrean, Geraldine
Jones, Gillingham
  See Hamilton, Charles (Harold St. John)
Jones, Gwyneth A. 1952- 159
Jones, Gwyneth Ann
  See Jones, Gwyneth A.
Jones, Harold 1904-1992 14
  Obituary 72
Jones, Helen Hinckley 1903-1991 26
Jones, Helen L(ouise) 1903-1973
  Obituary 22
Jones, Hettie 1934- 42
  Brief entry 27
Jones, Hortense P. 1918- 9
Jones, J. Sydney 1948- 101
Jones, Jasmine
  See Papademetriou, Lisa
Jones, Jennifer (Berry) 1947- 90
Jones, Jessie Mae Orton 1887(?)-1983
  Obituary 37
Jones, John R(obert) 1926- 76
Jones, Jon Sydney
  See Jones, J. Sydney
Jones, Judith
  See James, Bill
Jones, Kimberly K. 1957- 187
Jones, Marcia Thornton 1958- 217
  Earlier sketches in SATA 73, 115
Jones, Martha T(annery) 1931- 130
Jones, Mary Alice 1898(?)-1980 6
Jones, McClure 34
Jones, Noah Z. 182
Jones, Patrick 1961- 210
  Earlier sketch in SATA 136
Jones, Penelope 1938- 31
Jones, Rebecca C(astaldi) 1947- 99
  Earlier sketch in SATA 33
Jones, Robin D(orothy) 1959- 80
Jones, Sanford W.
  See Thorn, John
Jones, Sylvie 185
Jones, Sylvie Michelle
  See Jones, Sylvie
Jones, Terence Graham Parry 1942- 127
  Brief entry 51
  Earlier sketch in SATA 67
Jones, Terry
  See Jones, Terence Graham Parry
Jones, Tim Wynne
  See Wynne-Jones, Tim
Jones, Traci L. 186

Jones, V. M. 1958- 147
Jones, Veda Boyd 1948- 119
Jones, Victoria Mary
  See Jones, V. M.
Jones, Volcano
  See Mitchell, Adrian
Jones, Weyman (B.) 1928- 4
  See also SAAS 11
Jones, William Glynne
  See Glynne-Jones, William
Jonk, Clarence 1906-1987 10
Jonsberg, Barry 1951- 168
Joos, Francoise 1956- 78
Joos, Frederic 1953- 78
Joosse, Barbara 1949- 220
  Earlier sketches in SATA 52, 96, 164
Joosse, Barbara M.
  See Joosse, Barbara
Joosse, Barbara Monnot
  See Joosse, Barbara
Jordan, Alexis Hill
  See Glick, Ruth (Burtnick)
  and Titchener, Louise
Jordan, Anne Devereaux 1943- 80
Jordan, Chris
  See Philbrick, Rodman
Jordan, Deloris 191
Jordan, Devin 221
Jordan, Don
  See Howard, Vernon (Linwood)
Jordan, Hope Dahle 1905-1995 15
Jordan, Jael (Michal) 1949- 30
Jordan, June 1936-2002 136
  Earlier sketch in SATA 4
  See also CLR 10
Jordan, June Meyer
  See Jordan, June
Jordan, Lee
  See Scholefield, Alan
Jordan, Martin George 1944- 84
Jordan, Robert 1948-2007 95
Jordan, Robert K.
  See Jordan, Robert
Jordan, Rosa 1939- 191
Jordan, Roslyn M. 189
Jordan, Sherryl 1949- 122
  Earlier sketch in SATA 71
  See also SAAS 23
Jordan, Shirley 1930- 154
Jordan, Tanis 1946- 84
Jorgensen, Ivar
  See Ellison, Harlan
  and Garrett, Randall
Jorgensen, Mary Venn -1995 36
Jorgensen, Norman 1954- 157
Jorgenson, Ivar
  See Silverberg, Robert
Jorisch, Stephane 178
Joseph, Anne
  See Coates, Anna
Joseph, James (Herz) 1924- 53
Joseph, Joan 1939- 34
Joseph, Joseph M(aron) 1903-1979 22
Joseph, Patrick
  See O'Malley, Kevin
Josephs, Rebecca
  See Talbot, Toby
Josephson, Judith Pinkerton 1943- 198
Josh
  See Twain, Mark
Joshua, Peter
  See Stone, Peter
Joslin, Mary 1953- 176
Joslin, Sesyle
  See Hine, Sesyle Joslin
Joubert, Beverly 1957- 204
Joubert, Dereck 204
Journet, Mireille
  See Marokvia, Mireille
Joyce, Bill
  See Joyce, William

Joyce, J(ames) Avery 1902-1987 .... *11*
  Obituary *50*
Joyce, Peter 1937- *127*
Joyce, William 1957- *118*
  Brief entry *46*
  Earlier sketch in SATA 72
  See also CLR 26
Joyner, Jerry 1938- *34*
Juan, Ana 1961- *179*
Jubb, Sophie *210*
Jubert, Herve *185*
Juby, Susan 1969- *202*
  Earlier sketch in SATA 156
Jucker, Sita 1921- *5*
Judah, Aaron 1923- *118*
Judd, Cyril
  See Kornbluth, C(yril) M.
  and Merril, Judith
  and Pohl, Frederik
Judd, Denis (O'Nan) 1938- *33*
Judd, Frances K.
  See Benson, Mildred
Jude, Conny *81*
Judge, Lita *192*
Judson, Clara Ingram 1879-1960 .... *38*
  Brief entry *27*
Judy, Stephen
  See Tchudi, Stephen N.
Judy, Stephen N.
  See Tchudi, Stephen N.
Juhasz, Victor 1954- *177*
Jukes, Mavis 1947- *219*
  Brief entry *43*
  Earlier sketches in SATA 72, 111
  See also SAAS 12
Jules, Jacqueline 1956- *218*
  Earlier sketches in SATA 148, 183
Julesberg, Elizabeth Rider Montgomery
  1902-1985 .... *34*
  Obituary *41*
  Earlier sketch in SATA 3
Julian, Jane
  See Wiseman, David
Jumpp, Hugo
  See MacPeek, Walter G.
Junco, Martha Aviles
  See Aviles, Martha
Jungman, Ann *165*
Jupo, Frank J. 1904-1981 .... *7*
Jurmain, Suzanne 1945- *169*
  Earlier sketch in SATA 72
Jurmain, Suzanne Tripp
  See Jurmain, Suzanne
Juster, Norton 1929- *220*
  Earlier sketches in SATA 3, 132
  See also CLR 112
Justus, May 1898-1989 .... *1*
  Obituary *106*
Juvenilia
  See Taylor, Ann

K

Kaaberbol, Lene
  See Kaaberbol, Lene
Kaaberbol, Lene 1960- *159*
Kabdebo, Tamas
  See Kabdebo, Thomas
Kabdebo, Thomas 1934- *10*
Kabibble, Osh
  See Jobb, Jamie
Kacer, Kathy 1954- *184*
  Earlier sketch in SATA 142
Kaczman, James *156*
Kadair, Deborah Ousley *184*
Kadefors, Sara 1965- *218*
Kadesch, Robert R(udstone) 1922- *31*

Kadohata, Cynthia 1956(?)- *180*
  Earlier sketch in SATA 155
  See also CLR 121
Kadohata, Cynthia L.
  See Kadohata, Cynthia
Kaempfert, Wade
  See del Rey, Lester
Kaestner, Erich 1899-1974 .... *14*
  See also CLR 153
Kahl, Jonathan (D.) 1959- *77*
Kahl, M(arvin) P(hilip) 1934- *37*
Kahl, Virginia (Caroline) 1919-2004 .... *48*
  Brief entry *38*
  Obituary *158*
Kahn, Joan 1914-1994 .... *48*
  Obituary *82*
Kahn, Katherine Janus 1942- *220*
  Earlier sketches in SATA 90, 167
Kahn, Peggy
  See Katz, Bobbi
Kahn, Roger 1927- *37*
Kahukiwa, Robyn 1940- *134*
Kains, Josephine
  See Goulart, Ron
Kaizuki, Kiyonori 1950- *72*
Kajikawa, Kimiko *212*
Kakimoto, Kozo 1915- *11*
Kalashnikoff, Nicholas 1888-1961 .... *16*
Kalb, Jonah 1926- *23*
Kalbacken, Joan 1925- *96*
Kalechofsky, Roberta 1931- *92*
Kaler, James Otis 1848-1912 .... *15*
Kalis, Jennifer *207*
Kalish, Claire M. 1947- *92*
Kallen, Stuart A. 1955- *126*
  Earlier sketch in SATA 86
Kallen, Stuart Arnold
  See Kallen, Stuart A.
Kallevig, Christine Petrell 1955- *164*
Kalman, Bobbie 1947- *63*
Kalman, Maira 1949- *137*
  Earlier sketch in SATA 96
  See also CLR 32
Kalnay, Francis 1899-1992 .... *7*
Kaloustian, Rosanne 1955- *93*
Kalow, Gisela 1946- *32*
Kalstein, Dave *175*
Kamara, Mariatu *214*
Kamen, Gloria 1923- *98*
  Earlier sketch in SATA 9
Kamerman, Sylvia E.
  See Burack, Sylvia K.
Kamm, Josephine (Hart) 1905-1989 .... *24*
Kammerman, Sylvia K.
  See Burack, Sylvia K.
Kandel, Michael 1941- *93*
Kandell, Alice S. 1938- *35*
Kane, Bob 1916-1998 .... *120*
Kane, Henry Bugbee 1902-1971 .... *14*
Kane, Kim 1973(?)- *221*
Kane, L. A.
  See Mannetti, Lisa
Kane, Robert W. 1910- *18*
Kane, Wilson
  See Bloch, Robert (Albert)
Kanefield, Teri 1960- *135*
Kanell, Beth *215*
Kaner, Etta 1947- *198*
  Earlier sketch in SATA 126
Kanetzke, Howard W(illiam) 1932- *38*
Kangas, Juli 1958- *200*
Kann, Elizabeth *180*
Kann, Victoria *180*
Kanninen, Barbara *196*
Kanninen, Barbara J.
  See Kanninen, Barbara
Kanoza, Muriel Canfield
  See Canfield, Muriel
Kantner, Seth 1965- *179*
Kanzawa, Toshiko
  See Furukawa, Toshi

Kanzler, John 1963- *188*
Kaplan, Andrew 1960- *78*
Kaplan, Anne Bernays
  See Bernays, Anne
Kaplan, Bess 1927- *22*
Kaplan, Boche 1926- *24*
Kaplan, Elizabeth 1956- *83*
Kaplan, Elizabeth A.
  See Kaplan, Elizabeth
Kaplan, Irma 1900- *10*
Kaplan, Jean Caryl Korn 1926- *10*
Kaplow, Robert 1954- *70*
Karageorge, Michael
  See Anderson, Poul
Karas, G. Brian 1957- *222*
  Earlier sketch in SATA 178
Karas, George Brian
  See Karas, G. Brian
Karasz, Ilonka 1896-1981
  Obituary *29*
Karen, Ruth 1922-1987 .... *9*
  Obituary *54*
Kark, Nina Mary
  See Bawden, Nina
Karl, Herb 1938- *73*
Karl, Jean E(dna) 1927-2000 .... *122*
  Earlier sketch in SATA 34
  See also SAAS 10
Karlin, Bernie 1927- *68*
Karlin, Eugene 1918- *10*
Karlin, Nurit *103*
  Earlier sketch in SATA 63
Karlins, Mark 1947- *219*
Karnes, Frances A. 1937- *110*
Karp, Naomi J. 1926- *16*
Karpinski, J. Rick
  See Karpinski, John Eric
Karpinski, John Eric 1952- *81*
Karpinski, Rick
  See Karpinski, John Eric
Karr, Kathleen 1946- *212*
  Earlier sketches in SATA 82, 127
Karr, Phyllis Ann 1944- *119*
Karwoski, Gail 1949- *127*
Karwoski, Gail Langer
  See Karwoski, Gail
Kashiwagi, Isami 1925- *10*
Kaslik, Ibi
  See Kaslik, Ibolya Emma
Kaslik, Ibolya Emma 1973- *185*
Kassem, Lou 1931- *62*
  Brief entry *51*
Kastel, Warren
  See Silverberg, Robert
Kastner, Erich
  See Kaestner, Erich
Kastner, Jill (Marie) 1964- *117*
  Earlier sketch in SATA 70
Kasuya, Masahiro 1937- *51*
Kasza, Keiko 1951- *191*
  Earlier sketch in SATA 124
Kataphusin
  See Ruskin, John
Katchen, Carole 1944- *9*
Katcher, Brian 1975- *203*
Kathryn
  See Searle, Kathryn Adrienne
Kato, Aya 1982- *202*
Katona, Robert 1949- *21*
Katsarakis, Joan Harries
  See Harries, Joan
Katz, Alan *185*
Katz, Avi 1949- *199*
Katz, Avner 1939- *103*
Katz, Bobbi 1933- *217*
  Earlier sketches in SATA 12, 179
Katz, Fred(eric Phillip) 1938- *6*
Katz, Jane B(resler) 1934- *33*
Katz, Karen 1947- *195*
  Earlier sketch in SATA 158

Katz, Marjorie P.
  See Weiser, Marjorie P(hillis) K(atz)
Katz, Susan 1945- 156
Katz, Welwyn Wilton 1948- 96
  Autobiography Feature 118
  Earlier sketch in SATA 62
  See also CLR 45
Katz, William 1940- 98
Katz, William Loren 1927- 13
Kaufman, Bel 57
Kaufman, Jeff 1955- 84
Kaufman, Joe 1911-2001 33
Kaufman, Joseph
  See Kaufman, Joe
Kaufman, Mervyn D. 1932- 4
Kaufmann, Angelika 1935- 15
Kaufmann, John 1931- 18
Kaula, Edna Mason 1906-1987 13
Kaur Khalsa, Dayal
  See Khalsa, Dayal Kaur
Kavaler, Lucy 1930- 23
Kavanagh, Jack 1920- 85
Kavanagh, P(atrick) J(oseph Gregory)
  1931- 122
Kavanaugh, Ian
  See Webb, Jean Francis (III)
Kay, Alan N. 1965- 144
Kay, Elizabeth 1949- 165
Kay, Guy Gavriel 1954- 167
  Earlier sketch in SATA 121
Kay, Helen
  See Goldfrank, Helen Colodny
Kay, Jackie 1961- 165
  Earlier sketch in SATA 97
Kay, Jacqueline Margaret
  See Kay, Jackie
Kay, Julia 205
Kay, Mara 13
Kay, Verla 1946- 210
  Earlier sketch in SATA 120
Kaye, Danny 1913-1987
  Obituary 50
Kaye, Geraldine (Hughesdon) 1925- 85
  Earlier sketch in SATA 10
Kaye, Judy
  See Baer, Judy
Kaye, Marilyn 1949- 110
  Earlier sketch in SATA 56
Kaye, Mary Margaret
  See Kaye, M.M.
Kaye, M.M. 1908-2004 62
  Obituary 152
Kaye, Mollie
  See Kaye, M.M.
Kaye, Peggy 1948- 143
Keach, James P. 1950- 125
Keams, Geri 1951- 117
Keane, Bil 1922- 4
Keane, Dave 1965- 216
Keaney, Brian 1954- 188
  Earlier sketch in SATA 106
Kearney, Meg 1964- 178
Kearny, Jillian
  See Goulart, Ron
Keat, Nawuth 1964- 222
Keating, Bern
  See Keating, Leo Bernard
Keating, Frank 1944- 143
Keating, Lawrence A. 1903-1966 23
Keating, Leo Bernard 1915- 10
Keats, Emma 1899(?)-1979(?) 68
Keats, Ezra Jack 1916-1983 57
  Obituary 34
  Earlier sketch in SATA 14
  See also CLR 35
Keefer, Catherine
  See Ogan, George F.
  and Ogan, Margaret E. (Nettles)
Keefer, Janice Kulyk
  See Kulyk Keefer, Janice

Keegan, Marcia 1943- 104
  Earlier sketch in SATA 9
Keehn, Sally M. 1947- 165
  Earlier sketch in SATA 87
Keel, Frank
  See Keeler, Ronald F(ranklin)
Keeler, Patricia 183
Keeler, Patricia A.
  See Keeler, Patricia
Keeler, Ronald F(ranklin) 1913-1983 47
Keely, Jack 1951- 119
Keen, Martin L. 1913-1992 4
Keenan, Sheila 1953- 95
Keene, Ann T. 1940- 86
Keene, Ann Todd
  See Keene, Ann T.
Keene, Carolyn
  See Benson, Mildred
  and Goulart, Ron
  and Lerangis, Peter
  and McFarlane, Leslie
  and Stanley, George Edward
  and Stratemeyer, Edward L.
Keens-Douglas, Richardo 1953- 154
  Earlier sketch in SATA 95
Keep, Linda Lowery
  See Lowery, Linda
Keep, Richard 1949- 170
Keep, Richard Cleminson
  See Keep, Richard
Keeping, Charles (William James)
  1924-1988 69
  Obituary 56
  Earlier sketch in SATA 9
  See also CLR 34
Keeshan, Robert J. 1927-2004 32
  Obituary 151
Kehlenbeck, Angela 1959- 186
Kehret, Peg 1936- 212
  Autobiography Feature 149
  Earlier sketches in SATA 73, 108, 149
Keillor, Garrison 1942- 58
Keillor, Gary Edward
  See Keillor, Garrison
Keir, Christine
  See Pullein-Thompson, Christine
Keiser, Paige 220
Keister, Douglas 1948- 88
Keith, Doug 1952- 81
Keith, Eros 1942- 52
Keith, Hal 1934- 36
Keith, Harold (Verne) 1903-1998 74
  Earlier sketch in SATA 2
Keith, Robert
  See Applebaum, Stan
Keleinikov, Andrei 1924- 65
Kelemen, Julie 1959- 78
Kelen, Emery 1896-1978 13
  Obituary 26
Kelleam, Joseph E(veridge) 1913-1975 31
Kelleher, Anne 1959- 97
Kelleher, Annette 1950- 122
Kelleher, Daria Valerian 1955- 79
Kelleher, Victor (Michael Kitchener)
  1939- 129
  Brief entry 52
  Earlier sketch in SATA 75
  See also CLR 36
Keller, Beverly L(ou) 91
  Earlier sketch in SATA 13
Keller, Charles 1942- 82
  Earlier sketch in SATA 8
Keller, Debra 1958- 94
Keller, Dick 1923- 36
Keller, Emily 96
Keller, Gail Faithfull
  See Faithfull, Gail
Keller, Holly 1942- 216
  Brief entry 42
  Earlier sketches in SATA 76, 108, 157
  See also CLR 45

Keller, Irene (Barron) 1927-2002 36
  Obituary 139
Keller, Laurie 1961(?)- 196
Kelley, Ann 1941- 217
Kelley, Ellen A. 185
Kelley, Ellen Chavez
  See Kelley, Ellen A.
Kelley, Gary 1945- 217
  Earlier sketch in SATA 183
Kelley, Leo P(atrick) 1928- 32
  Brief entry 31
Kelley, Marty 1971- 211
Kelley, Patrick (G.) 1963- 129
Kelley, Patte 1947- 93
Kelley, True 1946- 179
Kelley, True (Adelaide) 1946- 130
  Brief entry 39
  Earlier sketches in SATA 41, 92
Kelley, True Adelaide
  See Kelley, True
Kellin, Sally Moffet 1932- 9
Kelling, Furn L. 1914-2000 37
Kellogg, Gene
  See Kellogg, Jean (Defrees)
Kellogg, Jean (Defrees) 1916-1978 10
Kellogg, Steven 1941- 177
  Earlier sketches in SATA 8, 57, 130
  See also CLR 6
Kellogg, Steven Castle
  See Kellogg, Steven
Kellow, Kathleen
  See Hibbert, Eleanor Alice Burford
Kelly, C. M. O.
  See Gibbs, (Cecilia) May
Kelly, Clint 1950- 140
Kelly, Eric P(hilbrook) 1884-1960
  See YABC 1
Kelly, Fiona
  See Coleman, Michael
  and Hendry, Frances Mary
  and Jones, Allan Frewin
  and Oldfield, Jenny
  and Welford, Sue
Kelly, Irene 1957- 210
  Earlier sketch in SATA 147
Kelly, Jacqueline 216
Kelly, Jeff
  See Kelly, Jeffrey
Kelly, Jeffrey 1946- 65
Kelly, Joanne (W.) 1934- 87
Kelly, Kate 1958- 91
Kelly, Kathleen M. 1964- 71
Kelly, Katy 1955- 215
  Earlier sketch in SATA 169
Kelly, Lauren
  See Oates, Joyce Carol
Kelly, Laurene 1954- 123
Kelly, Martha Rose 1914-1983 37
Kelly, Marty
  See Kelly, Martha Rose
Kelly, Mij 166
Kelly, Ralph
  See Geis, Darlene Stern
Kelly, Regina Z(immerman) 1898-1986 5
Kelly, Rosalie (Ruth) 43
Kelly, Tom 1961- 191
Kelly, Walt(er Crawford) 1913-1973 18
Kelsey, Alice Geer 1896-1982 1
Kelsey, Elin 1961- 159
Kelsey, Marybeth 216
Kemly, Kathleen 1958- 197
Kemnitz, Thomas Milton, Jr. 1984- 152
Kemnitz, Tom, Jr.
  See Kemnitz, Thomas Milton, Jr.
Kemp, Gene 1926- 75
  Earlier sketch in SATA 25
  See also CLR 29
Kempner, Mary Jean 1913-1969 10
Kempter, Christa 1945- 187
Kempton, Jean Welch 1914- 10
Kenah, Katharine 1949- 182

Kenda, Margaret 1942- *71*
Kendall, Carol (Seeger) 1917- *74*
  Earlier sketch in SATA *11*
  See also SAAS 7
Kendall, Gideon 1966- *215*
Kendall, Katherine
  See Applegate, Katherine
Kendall, Lace
  See Stoutenburg, Adrien (Pearl)
Kendall, Martha E. *87*
Kendall, Russ 1957- *83*
Kenealy, James P. 1927- *52*
  Brief entry *29*
Kenealy, Jim
  See Kenealy, James P.
Kennaway, Adrienne 1945- *171*
  Earlier sketch in SATA *60*
Kennedy, Anne 1955- *198*
Kennedy, Anne Vittur
  See Kennedy, Anne
Kennedy, Brendan 1970- *57*
Kennedy, Dana Forrest 1917- *74*
Kennedy, Dorothy M(intzlaff) 1931- *53*
Kennedy, Doug 1963- *189*
  Earlier sketch in SATA *122*
Kennedy, Frances 1937- *192*
Kennedy, James *214*
Kennedy, John F. 1917-1963 .... *11*
Kennedy, John Fitzgerald
  See Kennedy, John F.
Kennedy, Joseph Charles
  See Kennedy, X. J.
Kennedy, Kim *189*
Kennedy, Marlane 1962- *210*
Kennedy, Pamela (J.) 1946- *87*
Kennedy, Paul E(dward) 1929- *113*
  Earlier sketch in SATA *33*
Kennedy, Richard (Pitt) 1910-1989
  Obituary *60*
Kennedy, (Jerome) Richard 1932- *22*
Kennedy, Robert 1938- *63*
Kennedy, T.A. 1953- *42*
  Brief entry *35*
Kennedy, Teresa
  See Kennedy, T.A.
Kennedy, Teresa A.
  See Kennedy, T.A.
Kennedy, William 1928- *57*
Kennedy, William Joseph
  See Kennedy, William
Kennedy, X. J. 1929- *130*
  Autobiography Feature *130*
  Earlier sketches in SATA *14, 86*
  See also CLR 27
  See also SAAS 22
Kennell, Ruth Epperson 1893-1977 .... *6*
  Obituary *25*
Kennemore, Tim 1957- *220*
  Earlier sketch in SATA *133*
Kennen, Ally *190*
Kennett, David 1959- *206*
  Earlier sketch in SATA *121*
Kennison, Ruth *202*
Kenny, Ellsworth Newcomb 1909-1971
  Obituary *26*
Kenny, Herbert Andrew 1912-2002 .... *13*
Kenny, Jude
  See Daly, Jude
Kenny, Kathryn
  See Bowden, Joan Chase
  and Krull, Kathleen
  and Sanderlin, Owenita (Harrah)
  and Stack, Nicolete Meredith
Kenny, Kevin
  See Krull, Kathleen
Kensinger, George
  See Fichter, George S.
Kensington, Kathryn Wesley
  See Rusch, Kristine Kathryn
Kent, Alexander
  See Reeman, Douglas Edward

Kent, David
  See Lambert, David
Kent, Deborah Ann 1948- *155*
  Brief entry *41*
  Earlier sketches in SATA *47, 104*
Kent, Jack
  See Kent, John Wellington
Kent, John Wellington 1920-1985 .... *24*
  Obituary *45*
Kent, Lisa 1942- *90*
Kent, Mallory
  See Lowndes, Robert A(ugustine) W(ard)
Kent, Margaret 1894- *2*
Kent, Rockwell 1882-1971 .... *6*
Kent, Rose *188*
Kent, Sherman 1903-1986 .... *20*
  Obituary *47*
Kenward, Jean 1920- *42*
Kenworthy, Leonard S. 1912-1991 .... *6*
Kenyon, Karen (Smith) 1938- *145*
Kenyon, Kate
  See Adorjan, Carol (Madden)
  and Ransom, Candice
Kenyon, Ley 1913-1990 .... *6*
Keown, Elizabeth *78*
Kepes, Juliet A(ppleby) 1919-1999 .... *13*
Kephart, Beth 1960- *196*
Kerby, Mona 1951- *202*
  Earlier sketch in SATA *75*
Kerigan, Florence 1896-1984 .... *12*
Kerley, Barbara 1960- *191*
  Earlier sketch in SATA *138*
Kerman, Gertrude
  See Furman, Gertrude Lerner Kerman
Kerns, Thelma 1929- *116*
Kerr, Anne Louise
  See Mackey, Weezie Kerr
Kerr, Bob 1951- *120*
Kerr, Jessica 1901-1991 .... *13*
Kerr, (Anne-)Judith 1923-1970 .... *24*
Kerr, M. E.
  See Meaker, Marijane
Kerr, P.B.
  See Kerr, Philip
Kerr, Philip 1956- *168*
Kerr, Phyllis Forbes 1942- *72*
Kerr, Tom 1950- *77*
Kerrin, Jessica Scott *174*
Kerry, Frances
  See Kerigan, Florence
Kerry, Lois
  See Duncan, Lois
Kershen, (L.) Michael 1982- *82*
Kerven, Rosalind 1954- *83*
Ker Wilson, Barbara 1929- *121*
  Earlier sketches in SATA *20, 70*
  See also SAAS 18
Kerz, Anna 1947- *220*
Keselman, Gabriela 1953- *128*
Kesey, Ken 1935-2001 .... *66*
  Obituary *131*
Kesey, Ken Elton
  See Kesey, Ken
Kesler, Jay 1935- *65*
Kessel, Joyce Karen 1937- *41*
Kessler, Cristina *190*
Kessler, Ethel 1922- *44*
  Brief entry *37*
Kessler, Leonard P. 1921- *14*
Kessler, Liz 1966- *206*
Kest, Kristin 1967- *168*
  Earlier sketch in SATA *118*
Kesteven, G. R.
  See Crosher, G. R.
Ketcham, Hank
  See Ketcham, Henry King
Ketcham, Henry King 1920-2001 .... *28*
  Brief entry *27*
  Obituary *128*
Ketcham, Sallie 1963- *124*

Ketchum, Liza 1946- *132*
  Earlier sketch in SATA *78*
Ketner, Mary Grace 1946- *75*
Kettelkamp, Larry (Dale) 1933- *2*
  See also SAAS 3
Ketteman, Helen 1945- *223*
  Earlier sketches in SATA *73, 115, 167*
Kettle, Peter
  See Glover, Denis (James Matthews)
Kevles, Bettyann Holtzmann 1938- *23*
Key, Alexander (Hill) 1904-1979 .... *8*
  Obituary *23*
Key, Samuel M.
  See de Lint, Charles
Key, Watt 1970- *189*
Keyes, Daniel 1927- *37*
Keyes, Diane *207*
Keyes, Fenton 1915-1999 .... *34*
Keyes, Greg 1963- *116*
Keyes, J. Gregory
  See Keyes, Greg
Keyser, Marcia 1933- *42*
Keyser, Sarah
  See McGuire, Leslie (Sarah)
Khalid, Mohamed Nor
  See Lat
Khalsa, Dayal Kaur 1943-1989 .... *62*
  See also CLR 30
Khan, Hena *214*
Khan, Rukhsana 1962- *165*
  Earlier sketch in SATA *118*
Khanshendel, Chiron
  See Rose, Wendy
Kheirabadi, Masoud 1951- *158*
Khemir, Sabiha *87*
Kherdian, David 1931- *74*
  Autobiography Feature *125*
  Earlier sketch in SATA *16*
  See also CLR 24
Khing, T.T. 1933- *192*
Kibbe, Pat (Hosley) *60*
Kidd, Diana 1933-2000 .... *150*
Kidd, Richard 1952-2008 .... *152*
  Obituary *194*
Kidd, Ronald 1948- *173*
  Earlier sketches in SATA *42, 92*
Kiddell, John 1922- *3*
Kiddell-Monroe, Joan 1908-1972 .... *55*
Kidwell, Carl 1910- *43*
Kiefer, Irene 1926- *21*
Kiefer, Kathleen Balmes 1957- *142*
Kiepper, Shirley Morgan 1933- *10*
Kierstead, Vera M.
  See Kierstead-Farber, Vera M.
Kierstead-Farber, Vera M. 1913- *121*
Kierstead-Farber, Vera May
  See Kierstead-Farber, Vera M.
Kiesel, Stanley 1925- *35*
Kiesler, Kate (A.) 1971- *152*
  Earlier sketch in SATA *90*
Kihn, Greg 1952- *110*
Kikukawa, Cecily H(arder) 1919- *44*
  Brief entry *35*
Kilaka, John 1966- *223*
Kilcher, Jewel 1974- *109*
Kile, Joan 1940- *78*
Kilgore, Kathleen 1946- *42*
Kilian, Crawford 1941- *35*
Killdeer, John
  See Mayhar, Ardath
Killien, Christi 1956- *73*
Killilea, Marie (Lyons) 1913-1991 .... *2*
Killingback, Julia 1944- *63*
Killough, (Karen) Lee 1942- *64*
Kilpatrick, Don *206*
Kilreon, Beth
  See Walker, Barbara (Jeanne) K(erlin)
Kilworth, Garry 1941- *216*
  Earlier sketch in SATA *94*
Kilworth, Garry D.
  See Kilworth, Garry

Kilworth, Garry Douglas
    See Kilworth, Garry
Kim, David 1977- 201
Kim, Helen 1899-1970 98
Kim, Joung Un 1970- 205
Kimball, Gayle 1943- 90
Kimball, Violet T(ew) 1932- 126
Kimball, Yeffe 1914-1978 37
Kimber, Murray 1964- 171
Kimble, Warren 176
Kimbrough, Emily 1899-1989 2
    Obituary 59
Kimeldorf, Martin 1948- 121
Kimeldorf, Martin R.
    See Kimeldorf, Martin
Kimenye, Barbara 1940(?)- 121
Kimmel, Elizabeth Cody 209
    Earlier sketch in SATA 170
Kimmel, Eric A. 1946- 208
    Earlier sketches in SATA 13, 80, 125, 176
Kimmel, Margaret Mary 1938- 43
    Brief entry 33
Kimmelman, Burt 1947- 180
Kimmelman, Leslie 1958- 211
    Earlier sketches in SATA 85, 156
Kincaid, Jamaica 1949-
    See CLR 63
Kincher, Jonni 1949- 79
Kindl, Patrice 1951- 128
    Earlier sketch in SATA 82
    See also CLR 132
Kindred, Wendy (Good) 1937- 7
Kinerk, Robert 199
Kines, Pat Decker 1937- 12
King, Adam
    See Hoare, Robert J(ohn)
King, Alison
    See Martini, Teri
King, (Maria) Anna 1964- 72
King, A.S. 1970- 217
King, Billie Jean 1943- 12
King, Christine
    See Farris, Christine King
King, Christopher (L.) 1945- 84
King, (David) Clive 1924- 144
    Earlier sketch in SATA 28
King, Colin 1943- 76
King, Cynthia 1925- 7
King, Daniel (John) 1963- 130
King, Daren 1972- 197
King, Elizabeth 1953- 83
King, Frank O. 1883-1969
    Obituary 22
King, Frank R. 1904-1999 127
King, Jane
    See Currie, Stephen
King, Jeanette (Margaret) 1959- 105
King, Larry L. 1929- 66
King, Laurie R. 1952- 88
King, Marian 1900(?)-1986 23
    Obituary 47
King, Martin Luther, Jr. 1929-1968 14
King, Mary Ellen 1958- 93
King, Paul
    See Drackett, Phil(ip Arthur)
King, Paula
    See Downing, Paula E.
King, Stephen 1947- 161
    Earlier sketches in SATA 9, 55
    See also CLR 124
King, Stephen Edwin
    See King, Stephen
King, Stephen Michael 218
    Earlier sketch in SATA 157
King, Steve
    See King, Stephen
King, Thomas 1943- 96
King, Thomas Hunt
    See King, Thomas
King, Tony 1947- 39

King, Willie Christine
    See Farris, Christine King
Kingfisher, Rupert 209
Kingman, Dong (Moy Shu) 1911-2000 44
Kingman, Lee
    See Natti, Lee
Kingsland, Leslie William 1912- 13
Kingsley, Charles 1819-1875
    See YABC 2
    See also CLR 77
Kingsley, Emily Perl 1940- 33
Kingsley, Kaza 193
King-Smith, Dick 1922-2011 192
    Brief entry 38
    Earlier sketches in SATA 47, 80, 135
    See also CLR 40
Kingston, Maxine Hong 1940- 53
Kingston, Maxine Ting Ting Hong
    See Kingston, Maxine Hong
Kinney, C. Cle(land) 1915- 6
Kinney, Harrison 1921- 13
Kinney, Jean Stout 1912- 12
Kinney, Jeff 1971- 187
Kinsey, Elizabeth
    See Clymer, Eleanor
Kinsey, Helen 1948- 82
Kinsey-Warnock, Natalie 1956- 167
    Earlier sketches in SATA 71, 116
Kinzel, Dorothy 1950- 57
Kinzel, Dottie
    See Kinzel, Dorothy
Kipling, Joseph Rudyard
    See Kipling, Rudyard
Kipling, Rudyard 1865-1936 100
    See also YABC 2
    See also CLR 65
Kippax, Frank
    See Needle, Jan
Kirby, David 1944- 78
Kirby, David K.
    See Kirby, David
Kirby, David Kirk
    See Kirby, David
Kirby, Margaret
    See Bingley, Margaret (Jane Kirby)
Kirby, Pamela F. 1952- 220
Kirby, Susan E. 1949- 62
Kirk, Connie Ann 1957- 167
Kirk, Daniel 1952- 196
    Earlier sketches in SATA 107, 153
Kirk, David 1955- 161
    Earlier sketch in SATA 117
Kirk, Heather 1949- 166
Kirk, Ruth (Kratz) 1925- 5
Kirkham, Dinah
    See Card, Orson Scott
Kirkland, Will
    See Hale, Arlene
Kirkpatrick, Katherine (Anne) 1964- 113
Kirkup, James 1918-2009 12
Kirkus, Virginia
    See Glick, Virginia Kirkus
Kirkwood, Kathryn
    See Fluke, Joanne
Kirsch, Vincent X. 211
Kirshenbaum, Binnie 79
Kirshner, David S. 1958- 123
Kirtland, G. B.
    See Hine, Sesyle Joslin
    and Hine, Al(fred Blakelee)
Kirwan, Wednesday 198
Kish, Eleanor M(ary) 1924- 73
Kish, Ely
    See Kish, Eleanor M(ary)
Kishida, Eriko 1929- 12
Kisinger, Grace Gelvin (Maze) 1913-1965 .. 10
Kissel, Richard 209
Kissin, Eva H. 1923- 10
Kissinger, Rosemary K.
    See Updyke, Rosemary K.
Kistler, John M. 1967- 160

Kitamura, Satoshi 1956- 201
    Earlier sketches in SATA 62, 98, 143
    See also CLR 60
Kitchen, Bert
    See Kitchen, Herbert Thomas
Kitchen, Herbert Thomas 1940- 70
Kite, L. Patricia
    See Kite, Pat
Kite, Pat 1940- 78
Kitt, Tamara
    See de Regniers, Beatrice Schenk (Freedman)
Kittinger, Jo S(usenbach) 1955- 148
    Earlier sketch in SATA 96
Kituomba
    See Odaga, Asenath (Bole)
Kitzinger, Sheila 1929- 57
Kiwak, Barbara 1966- 103
Kjelgaard, James Arthur 1910-1959 17
    See also CLR 81
Kjelgaard, Jim
    See Kjelgaard, James Arthur
Kjelle, Marylou Morano 1954- 146
Klages, Ellen 1954- 196
Klagsbrun, Francine (Lifton) 36
Klaits, Barrie 1944- 52
Klam, Cheryl 191
Klaperman, Gilbert 1921- 33
Klaperman, Libby Mindlin 1921-1982 33
    Obituary 31
Klass, David 1960- 207
    Earlier sketches in SATA 88, 142
Klass, Morton 1927-2001 11
Klass, Sheila Solomon 1927- 219
    Autobiography Feature 126
    Earlier sketches in SATA 45, 99
    See also SAAS 26
Klause, Annette Curtis 1953- 175
    Earlier sketch in SATA 79
    See also CLR 104
Klaveness, Jan O'Donnell 1939- 86
Kleberger, Ilse 1921- 5
Kleeberg, Irene (Flitner) Cumming 1932- 65
Klein, Aaron E. 1930-1998 45
    Brief entry 28
Klein, Bill 1945- 89
Klein, David 1919-2001 59
Klein, Frederick C. 1938- 154
Klein, Gerda Weissmann 1924- 44
Klein, H(erbert) Arthur 8
Klein, James 1932- 115
Klein, Leonore (Glotzer) 1916- 6
Klein, Lisa 1958- 211
Klein, Lisa M.
    See Klein, Lisa
Klein, Mina C(ooper) 1906-1979 8
Klein, Norma 1938-1989 57
    Earlier sketch in SATA 7
    See also CLR 162
    See also SAAS 1
Klein, Rachel S. 1953- 105
Klein, Robin 1936- 164
    Brief entry 45
    Earlier sketches in SATA 55, 80
    See also CLR 21
Klemin, Diana 65
Klemm, Barry 1945- 104
Klemm, Edward G., Jr. 1910-2001 30
Klemm, Roberta K(ohnhorst) 1884-1975 30
Kleven, Elisa 1958- 217
    Earlier sketches in SATA 76, 173
    See also CLR 85
Klevin, Jill Ross 1935- 39
    Brief entry 38
Kliban, B(ernard) 1935-1990 35
    Obituary 66
Klier, Kimberly Wagner 208
Klimo, Kate 214
Klimowicz, Barbara 1927- 10
Kline, Christina Baker 1964- 101
Kline, James
    See Klein, James

Kline, Jim
  See Kline, Jim
Kline, Lisa Williams 1954- 143
Kline, Suzy 1943- 193
  Autobiography Feature 193
  Brief entry 48
  Earlier sketches in SATA 67, 99, 152
Kliros, Thea 1935- 106
Klise, Kate 221
  Earlier sketch in SATA 181
Klise, M. Sarah 1961- 180
  Earlier sketch in SATA 128
Klots, Alexander Barrett 1903-1989
  Obituary 62
Klug, Ron(ald) 1939- 31
Knaak, Richard A. 1961- 166
  Earlier sketch in SATA 86
Knaak, Richard Allen
  See Knaak, Richard A.
Knapman, Timothy 200
Knapp, Edward
  See Kunhardt, Edith
Knapp, Ron 1952- 34
Knebel, Fletcher 1911-1993 36
  Obituary 75
Kneeland, Linda Clarke 1947- 94
Kneen, Maggie 1957- 221
Knickerbocker, Diedrich
  See Irving, Washington
Knifesmith
  See Cutler, Ivor
Knigge, Robert (R.) 1921(?)-1987 50
Knight, Anne (Katherine) 1946- 34
Knight, Brenda 112
Knight, Christopher G. 1943- 96
Knight, Damon (Francis) 1922-2002 9
  Obituary 139
Knight, David C(arpenter) 1925-1984 14
  See also CLR 38
Knight, Eric 1897-1943 18
Knight, Eric Mowbray
  See Knight, Eric
Knight, Francis Edgar 1905- 14
Knight, Frank
  See Knight, Francis Edgar
Knight, Hilary 1926- 132
  Earlier sketches in SATA 15, 69
Knight, Joan
  See Knight, Joan (MacPhail)
Knight, Joan (MacPhail) 159
  Earlier sketch in SATA 82
Knight, Kathryn Lasky
  See Lasky, Kathryn
Knight, Mallory T.
  See Hurwood, Bernhardt J.
Knight, Ruth Adams 1898-1974
  Obituary 20
Knight, Theodore O. 1946- 77
Knobloch, Dorothea 1951- 88
Knoepfle, John (Ignatius) 1923- 66
Knorr, Laura 1971- 200
Knott, Bill
  See Knott, William C(ecil, Jr.)
Knott, William C(ecil, Jr.) 1927- 3
Knotts, Howard (Clayton, Jr.) 1922- 25
Knowles, Anne 1933- 37
Knowles, Jo 1970- 197
Knowles, Johanna Beth
  See Knowles, Jo
Knowles, John 1926-2001 89
  Obituary 134
  Earlier sketch in SATA 8
  See also CLR 98
Knox, Calvin M.
  See Silverberg, Robert
Knox, (Mary) Eleanor Jessie 1909-2000 59
  Earlier sketch in SATA 30
Knox, Elizabeth 1959- 176
Knox, Elizabeth Fiona
  See Knox, Elizabeth

Knox, James
  See Brittain, William
Knox, Jolyne 1937- 76
Knudsen, James 1950- 42
Knudsen, Michelle 1974- 220
  Earlier sketch in SATA 171
Knudson, Mike 1965- 209
Knudson, R. R.
  See Knudson, Rozanne
Knudson, Richard L(ewis) 1930- 34
Knudson, Rozanne 1932-2008 79
  Earlier sketch in SATA 7
  See also SAAS 18
Knutson, Barbara 1959-2005 166
Knutson, Kimberley 115
Knye, Cassandra
  See Disch, Thomas M.
Kobayashi, Masako Matsuno 1935- 6
Kober, Shahar 1979- 213
Koch, Dorothy Clarke 1924- 6
Koch, Kenneth 1925-2002 65
Koch, Kenneth Jay
  See Koch, Kenneth
Koch, Phyllis (Mae) McCallum 1911- 10
Kochalka, James 1967- 196
Kocsis, J. C.
  See Paul, James
Koda-Callan, Elizabeth 1944- 140
  Earlier sketch in SATA 67
Kodera, Craig 1956- 222
Kodman, Stanislawa 201
Koehler, Phoebe 1955- 85
Koehler-Pentacoff, Elizabeth 1957- 160
  Earlier sketch in SATA 96
Koehn, Ilse
  See Van Zwienen, Ilse Charlotte Koehn
Koeller, Carol 192
Koenig, Viviane 1950- 80
Koering, Ursula 1921-1976 64
Koerner, W(illiam) H(enry) D(avid)
  1878-1938 21
Koertge, Ron 1940- 209
  Earlier sketches in SATA 53, 92, 131
Koestler-Grack, Rachel A. 1973- 156
Koff, Richard Myram 1926- 62
Koffinke, Carol 1949- 82
Kogan, Deborah
  See Kogan Ray, Deborah
Kogan Ray, Deborah 1940- 203
  Earlier sketches in SATA 8, 50, 161
Kogawa, Joy 1935- 99
Kogawa, Joy Nozomi
  See Kogawa, Joy
Kogler, Jennie
  See Kogler, Jennifer Anne
Kogler, Jennifer Anne 1982(?)- 174
Kohara, Kazuno 207
Kohl, Herbert 1937- 47
Kohl, Herbert R.
  See Kohl, Herbert
Kohl, MaryAnn F(aubion) 1947- 144
  Earlier sketch in SATA 74
Kohler, Julilly H(ouse) 1908-1976
  Obituary 20
Kohn, Bernice
  See Hunt, Bernice
Kohn, Rita (T.) 1933- 89
Kohner, Frederick 1905-1986 10
  Obituary 48
Koide, Tan 1938-1986 50
Koike, Kay 1940- 72
Koja, Kathe 1960- 199
  Earlier sketch in SATA 155
Koja, Stephan 198
Kolar, Bob 1960(?)- 206
Kolb, Larry J. 1953- 175
Kolba, St. Tamara 22
Kolibalova, Marketa
  See Kolibalova, Marketa
Kolibalova, Marketa 1953- 126

Koller, Jackie French 1948- 157
  Earlier sketches in SATA 72, 109
  See also CLR 68
Kolodny, Nancy J. 1946- 76
Kolosov, Jacqueline 1967- 199
Komaiko, Leah 1954- 164
  Earlier sketch in SATA 97
Komisar, Lucy 1942- 9
Komoda, Beverly 1939- 25
Komoda, Kiyo 1937- 9
Kompaneyets, Marc 1974- 169
Komroff, Manuel 1890-1974 2
  Obituary 20
Konigsberg, Bill 1970- 207
Konigsburg, E.L. 1930- 194
  Earlier sketches in SATA 4, 48, 94, 126
  See also CLR 81
Konigsburg, Elaine Lobl
  See Konigsburg, E.L.
Koning, Hans 1921-2007 5
  Obituary 182
Koningsberger, Hans
  See Koning, Hans
Konkle, Janet Everest 1917- 12
Kono, Erin Eitter 1973- 177
Konrad, Marla Stewart 218
Konzak, Burt 1946- 151
Koob, Theodora (J. Foth) 1918- 23
Kooiker, Leonie
  See Kooyker-Romijn, Johanna Maria
Koons, James
  See Pernu, Dennis
Koontz, Dean 1945- 165
  Earlier sketch in SATA 92
Koontz, Dean R.
  See Koontz, Dean
Koontz, Dean Ray
  See Koontz, Dean
Koontz, Robin Michal 1954- 136
  Earlier sketch in SATA 70
Kooyker, Leonie
  See Kooyker-Romijn, Johanna Maria
Kooyker-Romijn, Johanna Maria 1927- 48
Kooyker-Romyn, Johanna Maria
  See Kooyker-Romijn, Johanna Maria
Kopelke, Lisa 1963- 154
Kopper, Lisa 1950- 105
  Brief entry 51
Kopper, Lisa Esther
  See Kopper, Lisa
Koppes, Steven N. 1957- 169
Koppes, Steven Nelson
  See Koppes, Steven N.
Korach, Mimi 1922- 9
Koralek, Jenny 1934- 215
  Earlier sketches in SATA 71, 140
Korczak, Janusz
  See Goldszmit, Henryk
Koren, Edward (Benjamin) 1935- 148
  Earlier sketch in SATA 5
Koren, Edward 1935- 206
Korinets, Iurii Iosifovich
  See Korinetz, Yuri (Iosifovich)
Korinetz, Yuri (Iosifovich) 1923- 9
  See also CLR 4
Korman, Bernice 1937- 78
Korman, Gordon 1963- 167
  Brief entry 41
  Earlier sketches in SATA 49, 81, 119
  See also CLR 25
Korman, Gordon Richard
  See Korman, Gordon
Korman, Justine 1958- 70
Kornblatt, Marc 1954- 147
  Earlier sketch in SATA 84
Kornprobst, Jacques 1937- 177
Korte, Gene J. 1950- 74
Korthues, Barbara 1971- 203
Korty, Carol 1937- 15
Koscielniak, Bruce 1947- 153
  Earlier sketches in SATA 67, 99

Koshin, Alexander (A.) 1952- *86*
Kositsky, Lynne 1947- *158*
Koskenmaki, Rosalie
　See Maggio, Rosalie
Koss, Amy Goldman 1954- *158*
　Earlier sketch in SATA *115*
Kossin, Sandy (Sanford) 1926- *10*
Kossman, Nina 1959- *84*
Kostecki-Shaw, Jenny Sue *203*
Kostick, Conor 1964- *186*
Kotzwinkle, William 1938- *146*
　Earlier sketches in SATA *24, 70*
　See also CLR *6*
Kouhi, Elizabeth 1917- *54*
　Brief entry *49*
Kouts, Anne 1945- *8*
Koutsky, Jan Dale 1955- *146*
Kovacs, Deborah 1954- *132*
　Earlier sketch in SATA *79*
Kovalski, Maryann 1951- *175*
　Earlier sketches in SATA *58, 97*
　See also CLR *34*
　See also SAAS *21*
Kowalski, Kathiann M. 1955- *151*
　Earlier sketch in SATA *96*
Koz, Paula G.
　See Goodman Koz, Paula
Kozjan, Drazen *209*
Kraft, Betsy Harvey 1937- *157*
Kraft, Erik P. *193*
Krahn, Fernando 1935- *49*
　Brief entry *31*
　See also CLR *3*
Krakauer, Hoong Yee Lee 1955- *86*
Krakauer, Jon 1954- *108*
Krall, Dan 1970- *218*
Kramer, George
　See Heuman, William
Kramer, Nora 1896(?)-1984 .... *26*
　Obituary *39*
Kramer, Remi (Thomas) 1935- *90*
Krantz, Hazel (Newman) *12*
Kranzler, George G(ershon) 1916- *28*
Kranzler, Gershon
　See Kranzler, George G(ershon)
Krasilovsky, Phyllis 1926- *38*
　Earlier sketch in SATA *1*
　See also CLR *83*
　See also SAAS *5*
Krasne, Betty
　See Levine, Betty K(rasne)
Krasner, Steven 1953- *154*
Krasno, Rena 1923- *104*
Kratman, Tom *175*
Kraus, Joanna Halpert 1937- *87*
Kraus, (Herman) Robert 1925-2001 .... *93*
　Obituary *130*
　Earlier sketches in SATA *4, 65*
　See also SAAS *11*
Krauss, Ruth 1911-1993 .... *30*
　Obituary *75*
　Earlier sketch in SATA *1*
　See also CLR *42*
Krauss, Ruth Ida
　See Krauss, Ruth
Krautter, Elisa (Bialk) 1912(?)-1990 .... *1*
　Obituary *65*
Krautwurst, Terry 1946- *79*
Kray, Robert Clement 1930- *82*
Krech, Bob 1956- *185*
Krech, Robert
　See Krech, Bob
Kredel, Fritz 1900-1973 .... *17*
Kreikemeier, Gregory Scott 1965- *85*
Kreloff, Elliot *189*
Krementz, Jill 1940- *134*
　Earlier sketches in SATA *17, 71*
　See also CLR *5*
　See also SAAS *8*
Kremer, Marcie
　See Sorenson, Margo

Krenina, Katya 1968- *221*
　Earlier sketch in SATA *101*
Krensky, Stephen 1953- *188*
　Brief entry *41*
　Earlier sketches in SATA *47, 93, 136*
Krensky, Stephen Alan
　See Krensky, Stephen
Kresh, Paul 1919-1997 .... *61*
　Obituary *94*
Kress, Nancy 1948- *147*
　Autobiography Feature *147*
　Earlier sketch in SATA *85*
Kricher, John C. 1944- *113*
Krieger, Melanie *96*
Krinitz, Esther Nisenthal 1927-2001 .... *194*
Kripke, Dorothy Karp *30*
Krisher, Trudy 1946- *160*
　Earlier sketch in SATA *86*
Krisher, Trudy B.
　See Krisher, Trudy
Krishnaswami, Uma 1956- *182*
　Earlier sketch in SATA *144*
Kristiansen, Teddy 1964- *210*
Kristiansen, Teddy H.
　See Kristiansen, Teddy
Kristof, Jane 1932- *8*
Kroeber, Theodora (Kracaw) 1897-1979 .... *1*
Kroeger, Mary Kay 1950- *92*
Krohn, Katherine E(lizabeth) 1961- *125*
　Earlier sketch in SATA *84*
Kroll, Francis Lynde 1904-1973 .... *10*
Kroll, Steven 1941- *212*
　Autobiography Feature *135*
　Earlier sketches in SATA *19, 66, 125, 135*
　See also SAAS *7*
Kroll, Virginia L. 1948- *168*
　Earlier sketches in SATA *76, 114*
Kroll, Virginia Louisa
　See Kroll, Virginia L.
Kromhout, Rindert 1958- *189*
Krommes, Beth 1956- *208*
　Earlier sketches in SATA *128, 181*
Kronenwetter, Michael 1943- *62*
Kroniuk, Lisa
　See Berton, Pierre (Francis de Marigny)
Kropp, Paul 1948- *38*
　Brief entry *34*
　See also CLR *96*
Kropp, Paul Stephan
　See Kropp, Paul
Krosoczka, Jarrett J. 1977- *200*
　Earlier sketch in SATA *155*
Krovatin, Christopher 1985- *171*
Krudop, Walter
　See Krudop, Walter Lyon
Krudop, Walter Lyon 1966- *210*
Kruess, James
　See Kruss, James
Kruglik, Gerald *187*
Krull, Kathleen 1952- *184*
　Autobiography Feature *106*
　Brief entry *39*
　Earlier sketches in SATA *52, 80, 149*
　See also CLR *44*
Krumgold, Joseph (Quincy) 1908-1980 .... *48*
　Obituary *23*
　Earlier sketch in SATA *1*
Krupinski, Loretta 1940- *161*
　Earlier sketches in SATA *67, 102*
Krupnick, Karen 1947- *89*
Krupp, E. C. 1944- *123*
　Earlier sketch in SATA *53*
Krupp, Edwin Charles
　See Krupp, E. C.
Krupp, Robin Rector 1946- *53*
Krush, Beth 1918- *18*
Krush, Joe 1918-
　See Krush, Joseph P.
Krush, Joseph P. 1918- *18*
Kruss, James 1926-1997 .... *8*
　See also CLR *9*

Kruusval, Catarina 1951- *201*
Krykorka, Vladyana 1945- *96*
Krystoforski, Andrej 1943- *196*
Kubick, Dana *212*
Kubie, Eleanor Gottheil
　See Kubie, Nora Gottheil Benjamin
Kubie, Nora Benjamin
　See Kubie, Nora Gottheil Benjamin
Kubie, Nora Gottheil Benjamin 1899-1988 . *39*
　Obituary *59*
Kubinyi, Laszlo 1937- *94*
　Earlier sketch in SATA *17*
Kudlinski, Kathleen V. 1950- *213*
　Earlier sketch in SATA *150*
Kuehnert, Stephanie 1979- *205*
Kuenstler, Morton 1927- *10*
Kuh, Charlotte 1892(?)-1985
　Obituary *43*
Kuharski, Janice 1947- *128*
Kuhn, Dwight *199*
Kuijer, Guus 1942- *179*
Kujoth, Jean Spealman 1935-1975
　Obituary *30*
Kuklin, Susan 1941- *163*
　Earlier sketches in SATA *63, 95*
　See also CLR *51*
Kulak, Jeff 1984(?)- *223*
Kulikov, Boris 1966- *205*
　Earlier sketch in SATA *170*
Kulka, Joe *188*
Kulling, Monica 1952- *89*
Kullman, Harry 1919-1982 .... *35*
Kulyk Keefer, Janice 1952- *132*
Kumin, Maxine 1925- *12*
Kumin, Maxine Winokur
　See Kumin, Maxine
Kunhardt, Dorothy (Meserve) 1901-1979 .... *53*
　Obituary *22*
Kunhardt, Edith 1937- *67*
Kunjufu, Jawanza 1953- *73*
Kunstler, Morton
　See Kuenstler, Morton
Kuntz, J(ohn) L. 1947- *91*
Kuntz, Jerry 1956- *133*
Kupferberg, Herbert 1918-2001 .... *19*
Kuratomi, Chizuko 1939- *12*
　See also CLR *32*
Kurczok, Belinda 1978- *121*
Kurelek, William 1927-1977 .... *8*
　Obituary *27*
　See also CLR *2*
Kurian, George 1928- *65*
Kurjian, Judi(th M.) 1944- *127*
Kurland, Gerald 1942- *13*
Kurland, Michael 1938- *118*
　Earlier sketch in SATA *48*
Kurland, Michael Joseph
　See Kurland, Michael
Kuroi, Ken 1947- *120*
Kurokawa, Mitsuhiro 1954- *88*
Kurten, Bjorn (Olof) 1924-1988 .... *64*
Kurtz, Jane 1952- *139*
　Earlier sketch in SATA *91*
　See also CLR *123*
Kurtz, Katherine 1944- *182*
　Earlier sketches in SATA *76, 126*
Kurtz, Katherine Irene
　See Kurtz, Katherine
Kurz, Rudolf 1952- *95*
Kushner, Donn (J.) 1927- *52*
　See also CLR *55*
Kushner, Ellen 1955- *202*
　Earlier sketch in SATA *98*
Kushner, Ellen Ruth
　See Kushner, Ellen
Kushner, Jill Menkes 1951- *62*
Kushner, Lawrence 1943- *169*
　Earlier sketch in SATA *83*
Kushner, Tony 1956- *160*

Kuskin, Karla 1932-2009 .... *164*
　Obituary *206*
　Earlier sketches in SATA *2, 68, 111*
　See also CLR *4*
　See also SAAS *3*
Kuskin, Karla Seidman
　See Kuskin, Karla
Kusugak, Michael 1948- *143*
Kusugak, Michael Arvaarluk
　See Kusugak, Michael
Kutner, Merrily 1948- *196*
Kuttner, Paul 1922- *18*
Kuyper, Sjoerd 1952- *177*
Kuzma, Kay 1941- *39*
Kvale, Velma R(uth) 1898-1979 .... *8*
Kvasnosky, Laura McGee 1951- *182*
　Earlier sketches in SATA *93, 142*
Kwasney, Michelle D. 1960- *162*
Kyle, Benjamin
　See Gottfried, Theodore Mark
Kyle, Elisabeth
　See Dunlop, Agnes M. R.
Kyte, Kathy S. 1946- *50*
　Brief entry *44*

L

L., Barry
　See Longyear, Barry B(rookes)
L., Tommy
　See Lorkowski, Thomas V(incent)
Labatt, Mary 1944- *215*
Labouisse, Eve Curie
　See Curie, Eve
Labouisse, Eve Denise
　See Curie, Eve
Lace, William W. 1942- *126*
Lacey, Joshua
　See Doder, Josh
Lachenmeyer, Nathaniel 1969- *221*
Lachner, Dorothea
　See Knobloch, Dorothea
Lachtman, Ofelia Dumas 1919- *179*
Lackey, Mercedes
　See Lackey, Mercedes R.
Lackey, Mercedes R. 1950- *127*
　Earlier sketch in SATA *81*
Lackey, Mercedes Ritchie
　See Lackey, Mercedes R.
Lacoe, Addie *78*
Lacombe, Benjamin 1982- *198*
Lacome, Julie 1961- *174*
　Earlier sketch in SATA *80*
LaCour, Nina 1982- *222*
Lacy, Leslie Alexander 1937- *6*
Ladd, Cheryl (Jean) 1951- *113*
Ladd, London 1972(?)- *206*
Ladd, Louise 1943- *97*
Ladd, Veronica
　See Miner, Jane Claypool
Laden, Nina 1962- *148*
　Earlier sketch in SATA *85*
Lader, Lawrence 1919-2006 .... *6*
　Obituary *178*
LaDoux, Rita C. 1951- *74*
Ladwig, Tim 1952- *223*
Ladwig, Timothy
　See Ladwig, Tim
Lady, A
　See Taylor, Ann
Lady Mears
　See Tempest, Margaret Mary
Lady of Quality, A
　See Bagnold, Enid
La Farge, Oliver 1901-1963 .... *19*
La Farge, Oliver Hazard Perry
　See La Farge, Oliver
La Farge, Phyllis *14*
LaFave, Kim *196*

LaFaye, A. 1970- *220*
　Earlier sketches in SATA *105, 156*
LaFaye, Alexandria R.T.
　See LaFaye, A.
LaFevers, R.L. *191*
LaFevers, Robin L.
　See LaFevers, R.L.
Laffin, John (Alfred Charles) 1922- *31*
LaFleur, Suzanne 1983- *221*
LaFontaine, Bruce 1948- *176*
　Earlier sketch in SATA *114*
La Fontaine, Jean de 1621-1695 .... *18*
Lafrance, Marie 1955- *197*
Lager, Claude
　See Lapp, Christiane (Germain)
Lager, Marilyn 1939- *52*
Lagercrantz, Rose (Elsa) 1947- *39*
Lagerloef, Selma
　See Lagerlof, Selma
Lagerlof, Selma 1858-1940 .... *15*
　See also CLR *7*
Laguna, Sofie 1968- *158*
LaHaye, Tim 1926- *149*
LaHaye, Timothy F.
　See LaHaye, Tim
Laidlaw, Rob *205*
Laiken, Deirdre S. 1948- *48*
　Brief entry *40*
Laiken, Deirdre Susan
　See Laiken, Deirdre S.
Laimgruber, Monika 1946- *11*
Lain, Anna
　See Lamb, Nancy
Laing, Alexander (Kinnan) 1903-1976 .... *117*
Laing, Martha 1951- *39*
Laird, Christa 1944- *108*
　Autobiography Feature *120*
　See also SAAS *26*
Laird, Elizabeth 1943- *159*
　Earlier sketches in SATA *77, 114*
　See also CLR *65*
Laird, Elizabeth Mary Risk
　See Laird, Elizabeth
Laird, Jean E(louise) 1930- *38*
Laite, Gordon 1925- *31*
Lake, Harriet
　See Taylor, Paula (Wright)
Lakeman, Victoria
　See Forester, Victoria
Lakin, Patricia 1944- *190*
Laklan, Carli 1907-1988 .... *5*
Laliberte, Louise-Andree 1958- *169*
Lalicki, Barbara *61*
Lalicki, Tom 1949- *186*
Lally, Soinbhe 1945- *119*
LaMarche, Jim *162*
Lamb, Albert *187*
Lamb, Beatrice Pitney 1904-1997 .... *21*
Lamb, Charles 1775-1834 .... *17*
Lamb, Elizabeth Searle 1917- *31*
Lamb, G(eoffrey) F(rederick) *10*
Lamb, Harold (Albert) 1892-1962 .... *53*
Lamb, Lynton (Harold) 1907-1977 .... *10*
Lamb, Mary Ann 1764-1847 .... *17*
Lamb, Nancy 1939- *80*
Lamb, Robert (Boyden) 1941- *13*
Lamba, Marie *195*
Lambert, David 1932- *84*
　Brief entry *49*
Lambert, David Compton
　See Lambert, David
Lambert, Janet 1895(?)-1973 .... *25*
Lambert, Martha L. *113*
Lambert, Saul 1928- *23*
Lambert, Stephen *174*
Lamburn, Richmal Crompton 1890-1969 .... *5*
Lamensdorf, Len 1930- *120*
Lamensdorf, Leonard
　See Lamensdorf, Len
Laminack, Lester L. 1956- *163*
　Earlier sketch in SATA *120*

Lammle, Leslie 1965- *213*
Lamont, Priscilla *200*
Lamorisse, Albert (Emmanuel) 1922-1970 ... *23*
Lampert, Emily 1951- *52*
　Brief entry *49*
Lamplugh, Lois 1921- *17*
Lampman, Evelyn Sibley 1907-1980 .... *87*
　Obituary *23*
　Earlier sketch in SATA *4*
Lamprey, Louise 1869-1951
　See YABC *2*
Lampton, Chris
　See Lampton, Christopher F.
Lampton, Christopher
　See Lampton, Christopher F.
Lampton, Christopher F. *67*
　Brief entry *47*
Lamstein, Sarah 1943- *174*
　Earlier sketch in SATA *126*
Lamstein, Sarah Marwil
　See Lamstein, Sarah
Lanagan, Margo 1960- *201*
　Earlier sketch in SATA *163*
Lancaster, Bruce 1896-1963 .... *9*
Lancaster, Matthew 1973(?)-1983
　Obituary *45*
Lance, Kathryn 1943- *76*
Land, Barbara (Neblett) 1923- *16*
Land, Jane
　See Borland, Kathryn Kilby
　and Speicher, Helen Ross S(mith)
Land, Myrick (Ebben) 1922-1998 .... *15*
Land, Ross
　See Borland, Kathryn Kilby
　and Speicher, Helen Ross S(mith)
Landa, Norbert 1952- *218*
Landau, Elaine 1948- *141*
　Earlier sketches in SATA *10, 94*
Landau, Jacob 1917- *38*
Landeck, Beatrice 1904-1978 .... *15*
Landin, Les 1923- *2*
Landis, J. D. 1942- *60*
　Brief entry *52*
Landis, James D.
　See Landis, J. D.
Landis, James David
　See Landis, J. D.
Landis, Jill Marie 1948- *101*
Landman, Tanya *207*
Landmann, Bimba 1968- *176*
Landon, Dena 1978(?)- *168*
Landon, Lucinda 1950- *56*
　Brief entry *51*
Landon, Margaret (Dorothea Mortenson)
　1903-1993 .... *50*
Landowne, Youme 1970- *211*
Landry, Leo *202*
Landshoff, Ursula 1908-1989 .... *13*
Landstrom, Lena 1943- *206*
　Earlier sketch in SATA *146*
Landstrom, Olof 1943- *146*
Landy, Derek 1974- *210*
Lane, Alison Hoffman *215*
Lane, Carolyn 1926-1993 .... *10*
Lane, Connie
　See Laux, Constance
Lane, Dakota 1959- *166*
　Earlier sketch in SATA *105*
Lane, Jerry
　See Martin, Patricia Miles
Lane, John (Richard) 1932- *15*
Lane, Leena *199*
Lane, Margaret 1907-1994 .... *65*
　Brief entry *38*
　Obituary *79*
Lane, Rose Wilder 1887-1968 .... *29*
　Brief entry *28*
Lanes, Selma G. 1929- *3*
Lanes, Selma Gordon
　See Lanes, Selma G.
Lanfredi, Judy 1964- *83*

Lang, Andrew 1844-1912 .... *16*
  See also CLR *101*
Lang, Aubrey *169*
Lang, Glenna 1951- *221*
Lang, Lang 1982- *208*
Lang, Paul 1948- *83*
Lang, Susan S. 1950- *68*
Lang, T.T.
  See Taylor, Theodore
Langart, Darrell T.
  See Garrett, Randall
Langdo, Bryan 1973- *191*
  Earlier sketch in SATA *138*
Lange, John
  See Crichton, Michael
Lange, Karen E. *190*
Lange, Suzanne 1945- *5*
Langley, Andrew 1949- *166*
  Earlier sketch in SATA *104*
Langley, Charles P(itman) III 1949- *103*
Langley, Jonathan 1952- *122*
Langley, Noel 1911-1980
  Obituary *25*
Langley, Wanda *173*
Langner, Nola
  See Malone, Nola Langner
Langone, John (Michael) 1929- *46*
  Brief entry *38*
Langreuter, Jutta 1944- *122*
Langrish, Katherine *177*
Langsen, Richard C. 1953- *95*
Langstaff, John 1920-2005 .... *68*
  Obituary *172*
  Earlier sketch in SATA *6*
  See also CLR *3*
Langstaff, John Meredith
  See Langstaff, John
Langstaff, Launcelot
  See Irving, Washington
Langston, Laura 1958- *186*
Langton, Jane 1922- *200*
  Autobiography Feature *140*
  Earlier sketches in SATA *3, 68, 129, 140*
  See also CLR *33*
  See also SAAS *5*
Lanier, Sidney 1842-1881 .... *18*
Lanier, Sterling E. 1927-2007 .... *109*
Lanier, Sterling Edmund
  See Lanier, Sterling E.
Lanino, Deborah 1964- *123*
Lankford, Mary D. 1932- *112*
  Earlier sketch in SATA *77*
Lannin, Joanne 1951- *121*
Lannin, Joanne A.
  See Lannin, Joanne
Lansdale, Joe R. 1951- *116*
Lansdale, Joe Richard
  See Lansdale, Joe R.
Lansing, Alfred 1921-1975 .... *35*
Lansing, Karen E. 1954- *71*
Lansky, Vicki 1942- *177*
Lanthier, Jennifer 1964- *204*
Lantier-Sampon, Patricia 1952- *92*
Lantz, Fran
  See Lantz, Francess L(in)
Lantz, Francess L(in) 1952-2004 .... *153*
  Autobiography Feature *153*
  Obituary *159*
  Earlier sketches in SATA *63, 109*
Lantz, Paul 1908- *45*
Lantz, Walter 1900-1994 .... *37*
  Obituary *79*
Lanza, Barbara 1945- *101*
Lapp, Christiane (Germain) 1948- *74*
Lappin, Peter 1911-1999 .... *32*
Larbalestier, Justine *178*
Lardy, Philippe 1963- *168*
LaReau, Jenna *181*
LaReau, Kara *181*
Larios, Julie 1949- *178*

Larios, Julie Hofstrand
  See Larios, Julie
Larkin, Amy
  See Burns, Olive Ann
Larkin, Maia
  See Wojciechowska, Maia (Teresa)
Larkspur, Penelope
  See Wyatt, Valerie
Laroche, Giles 1956- *221*
  Earlier sketches in SATA *71, 126*
LaRochelle, David 1960- *171*
  Earlier sketch in SATA *115*
Larom, Henry V. 1903(?)-1975
  Obituary *30*
LaRose, Linda *125*
Larrabee, Lisa 1947- *84*
Larrecq, John M(aurice) 1926-1980 .... *44*
  Obituary *25*
Larrick (Crosby), Nancy 1910-2004 .... *4*
Larsen, Anita 1942- *78*
Larsen, Egon 1904- *14*
Larsen, Rebecca 1944- *54*
Larson, Eve
  See St. John, Wylly Folk
Larson, Gary 1950- *57*
Larson, Hope 1982- *205*
Larson, Ingrid D(ana) 1965- *92*
Larson, Jean Russell 1930- *121*
Larson, Kirby 1954- *181*
  Earlier sketch in SATA *96*
Larson, Norita D. 1944- *29*
Larson, Norita Dittberner
  See Larson, Norita D.
Larson, William H. 1938- *10*
Larsson, Carl (Olof) 1853-1919 .... *35*
LaSalle, Charles A.
  See Ellis, Edward S.
LaSalle, Charles E.
  See Ellis, Edward S.
Lasell, Elinor H. 1929- *19*
Lasell, Fen H.
  See Lasell, Elinor H.
Lasenby, Jack 1931- *172*
  Earlier sketches in SATA *65, 103*
Laser, Michael 1954- *117*
Lash, Joseph P. 1909-1987 .... *43*
Lasher, Faith B. 1921- *12*
Lasker, David 1950- *38*
Lasker, Joe
  See Lasker, Joseph Leon
Lasker, Joseph Leon 1919- *83*
  Earlier sketch in SATA *9*
  See also SAAS *17*
Laski, Marghanita 1915-1988 .... *55*
Laskin, Pamela L. 1954- *75*
Lasky, Kathryn 1944- *210*
  Earlier sketches in SATA *13, 69, 112, 157*
  See also CLR *140*
Lasky Knight, Kathryn
  See Lasky, Kathryn
Lass, Bonnie *131*
Lassalle, C. E.
  See Ellis, Edward S.
Lassiter, Mary
  See Hoffman, Mary
Lassiter, Rhiannon 1977- *157*
Lat 1951- *196*
Latham, Barbara 1896- *16*
Latham, Frank B(rown) 1910-2000 .... *6*
Latham, Jean Lee 1902-1995 .... *68*
  Earlier sketch in SATA *2*
  See also CLR *50*
Latham, Mavis
  See Clark, Mavis Thorpe
Latham, Philip
  See Richardson, Robert S(hirley)
Lathrop, Dorothy P(ulis) 1891-1980 .... *14*
  Obituary *24*
Lathrop, Francis
  See Leiber, Fritz (Reuter, Jr.)
Latimer, Jim 1943- *80*

Latta, Rich
  See Latta, Richard
Latta, Richard 1946- *113*
Latta, Sara L. 1960- *174*
Lattany, Kristin
  See Lattany, Kristin Hunter
Lattany, Kristin (Eggleston) Hunter 1931- . *154*
  Autobiography Feature *154*
  Earlier sketch in SATA *132*
Lattany, Kristin Hunter 1931-2008 .... *132*
  Earlier sketch in SATA *12*
  See also CLR *3*
  See also SAAS *10*
Lattimore, Eleanor Frances 1904-1986 .... *7*
  Obituary *48*
Lattin, Ann
  See Cole, Lois Dwight
Lauber, Patricia (Grace) 1924- *138*
  Earlier sketches in SATA *1, 33, 75*
  See also CLR *16*
Laugesen, Malene *207*
Laugesen, Malene Reynolds
  See Laugesen, Malene
Laugesen, Mary E(akin) 1906-1995 .... *5*
Laughbaum, Steve 1945- *12*
Laughlin, Florence Young 1910-2001 .... *3*
Laughlin, Rosemary 1941- *123*
Launder, Sally *206*
Laure, Ettagale
  See Blauer, Ettagale
Laure, Jason 1940- *50*
  Brief entry *44*
Laurence, Ester Hauser 1935- *7*
Laurence, Jean Margaret Wemyss
  See Laurence, Margaret
Laurence, Margaret 1926-1987
  Obituary *50*
Laurie, Rona 1916- *55*
Laurie, Victoria *218*
Laurin, Anne
  See McLaurin, Anne
Lauritzen, Jonreed 1902-1979 .... *13*
Lauscher, Hermann
  See Hesse, Hermann
Lauture, Denize 1946- *86*
Laux, Connie
  See Laux, Constance
Laux, Constance 1952- *97*
Laux, Dorothy 1920- *49*
Lavallee, Barbara 1941- *166*
  Earlier sketch in SATA *74*
Lavender, David (Sievert) 1910-2003 .... *97*
  Obituary *145*
  Earlier sketch in SATA *64*
Lavender, William D. 1921- *143*
Laverne, Christine *175*
Lavert, Gwendolyn Battle 1951-
  See Battle-Lavert, Gwendolyn
Laverty, Donald
  See Blish, James
  and Knight, Damon (Francis)
Lavigne, Louis-Dominique *107*
Lavine, David 1928- *31*
Lavine, Sigmund Arnold 1908-1986 .... *82*
  Earlier sketch in SATA *3*
  See also CLR *35*
Lavond, Paul Dennis
  See Kornbluth, C(yril) M.
  and Lowndes, Robert A(ugustine) W(ard)
  and Pohl, Frederik
Lawford, Paula Jane 1960- *57*
  Brief entry *53*
Lawhead, Stephen R. 1950- *109*
Lawhead, Steve
  See Lawhead, Stephen R.
Lawler, Janet *222*
Lawlor, Laurie 1953- *137*
  Earlier sketch in SATA *80*
Lawlor, William
  See Lawlor, William T.
Lawlor, William T. 1951- *183*

Lawrence, Ann (Margaret) 1942-1987 .... *41*
Obituary *54*
Lawrence, Caroline 1954- *203*
Lawrence, Iain 1955- *183*
Earlier sketch in SATA *135*
Lawrence, J. T.
See Rowland-Entwistle, (Arthur) Theodore
(Henry)
Lawrence, Jerome 1915-2004 .... *65*
Lawrence, John 1933- *30*
Lawrence, Josephine 1890(?)-1978
Obituary *24*
Lawrence, Louise 1943- *119*
Earlier sketches in SATA *38, 78*
Lawrence, Louise de Kiriline 1894-1992 ..... *13*
Lawrence, Lynn
See Garland, Sherry
Lawrence, Margery H. 1889-1969 .... *120*
Lawrence, Michael 1943- *132*
Lawrence, Mildred Elwood 1907-1997 .... *3*
Lawrence, R(onald) D(ouglas) 1921- *55*
Lawrinson, Julia 1969- *141*
Lawson, Amy
See Gordon, Amy
Lawson, Carol (Antell) 1946- *42*
Lawson, Don(ald Elmer) 1917-1990 .... *9*
Lawson, Joan 1906- *55*
Lawson, Julie 1947- *126*
Earlier sketch in SATA *79*
See also CLR *89*
Lawson, Marion Tubbs 1896-1994 .... *22*
Lawson, Robert 1892-1957 .... *100*
See also YABC *2*
See also CLR *73*
Lawton, Clive A. 1951- *145*
Laxdal, Vivienne 1962- *112*
Laybourn, Emma *193*
Laycock, George (Edwin) 1921- *5*
Layne, Laura
See Knott, William C(ecil, Jr.)
Layne, Steven L. *171*
Layson, Annelex Hofstra 1938(?)- *211*
Layton, Neal 1971- *187*
Earlier sketch in SATA *152*
Layton, Neal Andrew
See Layton, Neal
Lazare, Gerald John 1927- *44*
Lazare, Jerry
See Lazare, Gerald John
Lazarevich, Mila 1942- *17*
Lazarus, Keo Felker 1913-1993 .... *21*
Obituary *129*
Lea, Alec 1907- *19*
Lea, Bob 1952- *203*
Lea, Joan
See Neufeld, John (Arthur)
Leach, Maria 1892-1977 .... *39*
Brief entry *28*
Leacock, Elspeth 1946- *131*
Leacroft, Helen (Mabel Beal) 1919- *6*
Leacroft, Richard (Vallance Becher) 1914- *6*
Leaf, Margaret P. 1909(?)-1988
Obituary *55*
Leaf, (Wilbur) Munro 1905-1976 .... *20*
See also CLR *25*
Leaf, VaDonna Jean 1929- *26*
Leah, Devorah
See Devorah-Leah
Leakey, Richard E(rskine Frere) 1944- *42*
Leal, Ann Haywood *216*
Leander, Ed
See Richelson, Geraldine
Lear, Edward 1812-1888 .... *100*
Earlier sketch in SATA *18*
See also CLR *75*
Lears, Laurie 1955- *127*
Leasor, James 1923-2007 .... *54*
Leasor, Thomas James
See Leasor, James
Leavitt, Jerome E(dward) 1916- *23*
Leavitt, Martine 1953- *170*

LeBar, Mary E(velyn) 1910-1982 .... *35*
LeBlanc, Annette M. 1965- *68*
LeBlanc, L(ee) 1913- *54*
LeBox, Annette 1943- *145*
Lebrun, Claude 1929- *66*
Le Cain, Errol (John) 1941-1989 .... *68*
Obituary *60*
Earlier sketch in SATA *6*
Lechner, Jack *201*
Lechner, John 1966- *200*
Lecourt, Nancy (Hoyt) 1951- *73*
Ledbetter, Suzann 1953- *119*
Leder, Jane Mersky 1945- *61*
Brief entry *51*
Lederer, Muriel 1929- *48*
Lederer, William J. 1912-2009 .... *62*
Lederer, William Julius
See Lederer, William J.
Lee, Amanda
See Baggett, Nancy
and Buckholtz, Eileen (Garber)
and Glick, Ruth (Burtnick)
Lee, Benjamin 1921- *27*
Lee, Betsy 1949- *37*
Lee, Carol
See Fletcher, Helen Jill
Lee, Carol Ann 1969- *185*
Lee, Chinlun *182*
Lee, Cora *223*
See Anderson, Catherine Corley
Lee, Dennis (Beynon) 1939- *102*
Earlier sketch in SATA *14*
See also CLR *3*
Lee, Dom 1959- *146*
Autobiography Feature *121*
Earlier sketch in SATA *83*
See also SAAS *26*
Lee, Doris Emrick 1905-1983 .... *44*
Obituary *35*
Lee, Edward
See Lee, J. Edward
Lee, Elizabeth Rogers 1940- *90*
Lee, Harper 1926- *11*
Lee, Hector Viveros 1962- *115*
Lee, Howard N.
See Goulart, Ron
Lee, Huy Voun 1969- *217*
Earlier sketch in SATA *129*
Lee, Insu *213*
Lee, J. Edward 1953- *130*
Lee, Jared 1943- *215*
Lee, Jared D.
See Lee, Jared
Lee, Jeanne M. 1943- *138*
Lee, John R(obert) 1923-1976 .... *27*
Lee, Jordan
See Scholefield, Alan
Lee, Joseph Edward
See Lee, J. Edward
Lee, Julian
See Latham, Jean Lee
Lee, Linda
See Eyerly, Jeannette
Lee, Liz
See Lee, Elizabeth Rogers
Lee, Lucy
See Talbot, Charlene Joy
Lee, Lyn 1953- *128*
Lee, Manning de Villeneuve 1894-1980 ...... *37*
Obituary *22*
Lee, Marian
See Clish, (Lee) Marian
Lee, Marie G. 1964- *178*
Earlier sketches in SATA *81, 130*
Lee, Marie Myung-Ok
See Lee, Marie G.
Lee, Mary Price 1934- *82*
Earlier sketch in SATA *8*
Lee, Mildred
See Scudder, Mildred Lee

Lee, Nelle Harper
See Lee, Harper
Lee, Richard S. 1927- *82*
Lee, Robert C. 1931- *20*
Lee, Robert Edwin 1918-1994 .... *65*
Obituary *82*
Lee, Robert J. 1921- *10*
Lee, Roy
See Hopkins, Clark
Lee, Sally 1943- *67*
Lee, Suzy *193*
Lee, Tammie
See Townsend, Thomas L.
Lee, Tanith 1947- *185*
Earlier sketches in SATA *8, 88, 134*
Lee, Virginia 1976- *208*
Leech, Ben
See Bowkett, Stephen
Leeds, Contance *188*
Leedy, Loreen 1959- *175*
Brief entry *50*
Earlier sketches in SATA *54, 84, 128*
Leedy, Loreen Janelle
See Leedy, Loreen
Lee-Hostetler, Jeri 1940- *63*
Leekley, Thomas B(riggs) 1910-2001 .... *23*
Leeming, Jo Ann
See Leeming, Joseph
Leeming, Joseph 1897-1968 .... *26*
Leemis, Ralph B. 1954- *72*
Leese, Jennifer L.B. 1970- *163*
Leeson, Muriel 1920- *54*
Leeson, R. A.
See Leeson, Robert (Arthur)
Leeson, Robert (Arthur) 1928- *76*
Earlier sketch in SATA *42*
Lee Tae-Jun 1904-1956(?) *194*
Lee-Tai, Amy 1964- *189*
Leffland, Ella 1931- *65*
Leffler, Silke *197*
Lefler, Irene (Whitney) 1917- *12*
LeFrak, Karen *182*
Le Gallienne, Eva 1899-1991 .... *9*
Obituary *68*
Legg, Gerald 1947- *143*
Legg, Sarah Martha Ross Bruggeman (?)-1982
Obituary *40*
LeGrand
See Henderson, LeGrand
Le Guin, Ursula K. 1929- *194*
Earlier sketches in SATA *4, 52, 99, 149*
See also CLR *91*
Le Guin, Ursula Kroeber
See Le Guin, Ursula K.
Legum, Colin 1919-2003 .... *10*
Lehman, Barbara 1963- *170*
Earlier sketch in SATA *115*
Lehman, Bob *91*
Lehman, Elaine *91*
Lehmann, Debra Lynn
See Vanasse, Deb
Lehn, Cornelia 1920- *46*
Lehne, Judith Logan 1947- *93*
Lehr, Delores 1920- *10*
Lehr, Norma 1930- *71*
Leiber, Fritz (Reuter, Jr.) 1910-1992 .... *45*
Obituary *73*
Leibold, Jay 1957- *57*
Brief entry *52*
Leichman, Seymour 1933- *5*
Leick, Bonnie *205*
Leigh, Nila K. 1981- *81*
Leigh, Tom 1947- *46*
Leigh-Pemberton, John 1911-1997 .... *35*
Leighton, Clare (Veronica Hope)
1899-1989 .... *37*
Leighton, Margaret (Carver) 1896-1987 .... *1*
Obituary *52*
Leijten, Aileen *216*
Leiner, Al(an) 1938- *83*
Leiner, Katherine 1949- *93*

Author Index

Leipold, L. Edmond 1902-1983 .... *16*
Leisk, David (Johnson) 1906-1975 .... *30*
  Obituary *26*
  Earlier sketch in SATA *1*
  See also CLR 98
Leister, Mary 1917- *29*
Leitch, Patricia 1933- *98*
  Earlier sketch in SATA *11*
Leitner, Isabella 1924- *86*
Lekich, John *202*
Leland, Bob 1956- *92*
Leland, Robert E.
  See Leland, Bob
Lematre, Pascal 1967- *176*
Lember, Barbara Hirsch 1941- *92*
LeMieux, A.C. 1954- *125*
  Earlier sketch in SATA *90*
LeMieux, Anne
  See LeMieux, A.C.
LeMieux, Anne Connelly
  See LeMieux, A.C.
Lemieux, Michele 1955- *139*
Lemke, Horst 1922- *38*
Lemna, Don 1936- *216*
Lenain, Thierry 1959- *201*
Lenanton, Carola Mary Anima Oman
  See Oman, Carola (Mary Anima)
Lenard, Alexander 1910-1972
  Obituary *21*
Lendroth, Susan *207*
L'Engle, Madeleine 1918-2007 .... *128*
  Obituary *186*
  Earlier sketches in SATA *1, 27, 75*
  See also CLR 57
  See also SAAS 15
L'Engle, Madeleine Camp Franklin
  See L'Engle, Madeleine
Lengyel, Cornel Adam 1915- *27*
Lengyel, Emil 1895-1985 .... *3*
  Obituary *42*
Lennon, John 1940-1980 .... *114*
Lennon, John Ono
  See Lennon, John
Leno, Jay 1950- *154*
LeNoir, Janice 1941- *89*
Lens, Sidney 1912-1986 .... *13*
  Obituary *48*
Lenski, Lois 1893-1974 .... *100*
  Earlier sketches in SATA *1, 26*
  See also CLR 26
Lent, Blair 1930-2009 .... *133*
  Obituary *200*
  Earlier sketch in SATA *2*
Lent, Henry Bolles 1901-1973 .... *17*
Lent, John 1948- *108*
Leodhas, Sorche Nic
  See Alger, Leclaire (Gowans)
Leokum, Arkady 1916(?)- *45*
Leon, Carol Boyd *212*
Leon, Sharon 1959- *79*
Leonard, Alison 1944- *70*
Leonard, Anna
  See Gilman, Laura Anne
Leonard, Constance (Brink) 1923- *42*
  Brief entry *40*
Leonard, Dutch
  See Leonard, Elmore
Leonard, Elmore 1925- *163*
Leonard, Elmore John, Jr.
  See Leonard, Elmore
Leonard, Jonathan N(orton) 1903-1975 .... *36*
Leonard, Laura 1923- *75*
Leonard, Tom 1955- *207*
Leonetti, Mike 1958- *202*
Leong, Gor Yun
  See Ellison, Virginia H(owell)
Leonhard, Herb *217*
Leonhardt, Alice 1950- *152*
Lerangis, Peter 1955- *171*
  Earlier sketch in SATA *72*
Lerman, Josh *215*

Lerner, Aaron 1920-2007 .... *35*
  Obituary *179*
Lerner, Aaron Bunsen
  See Lerner, Aaron
Lerner, Carol 1927- *86*
  Earlier sketch in SATA *33*
  See also CLR 34
  See also SAAS 12
Lerner, Gerda 1920- *65*
Lerner, Harriet 1944- *101*
Lerner, Marguerite Rush 1924-1987 .... *11*
  Obituary *51*
Lerner, Sharon (Ruth) 1938-1982 .... *11*
  Obituary *29*
Leroe, Ellen 1949- *99*
  Brief entry *51*
  Earlier sketch in SATA *61*
Leroe, Ellen W.
  See Leroe, Ellen
Leroe, Ellen Whitney
  See Leroe, Ellen
Leroux, Gaston 1868-1927 .... *65*
Leroux-Hugon, Helene 1955- *132*
LeRoy, Gen *52*
  Brief entry *36*
Lerrigo, Marion Olive 1898-1968
  Obituary *29*
LeShan, Eda J(oan) 1922-2002 .... *21*
  See also CLR 6
Leshem, Yossi 1947- *222*
LeSieg, Theo.
  See Dr. Seuss
Lesinski, Jeanne M. 1960- *120*
Leslie, Robert Franklin 1911-1990 .... *7*
Leslie, Roger 1961- *168*
Leslie, Roger James
  See Leslie, Roger
Leslie, Sarah
  See McGuire, Leslie (Sarah)
LeSourd, Catherine
  See Marshall, (Sarah) Catherine (Wood)
Lessac, Frane
  See Lessac, Frane
Lessac, Frane 1954- *209*
  Earlier sketches in SATA *61, 148*
Lessem, Dino Don
  See Lessem, Don
Lessem, Don 1951- *182*
  Earlier sketches in SATA *97, 155*
Lesser, Margaret 1899(?)-1979
  Obituary *22*
Lesser, Rika 1953- *53*
Lester, Alison 1952- *218*
  Earlier sketches in SATA *50, 90, 129*
Lester, Helen 1936- *189*
  Earlier sketches in SATA *46, 92, 145*
Lester, Julius 1939- *157*
  Earlier sketches in SATA *12, 74, 112*
  See also CLR 143
Lester, Julius Bernard
  See Lester, Julius
Lester, Mike 1955- *206*
  Earlier sketch in SATA *131*
Le Sueur, Meridel 1900-1996 .... *6*
Leszczynski, Diana *211*
Lethcoe, Jason *191*
Le Tord, Bijou 1945- *95*
  Earlier sketch in SATA *49*
Letts, Billie 1938- *121*
Letts, Elizabeth
  See Alalou, Elizabeth
Leuck, Laura 1962- *192*
  Earlier sketches in SATA *85, 146*
Leutscher, Alfred (George) 1913- *23*
Levai, Blaise 1919- *39*
Levchuk, Lisa *215*
Levenkron, Steven 1941- *86*
Leverich, Kathleen 1948- *103*
LeVert, John 1946- *55*
Levert, Mireille 1956- *211*

LeVert, William John
  See LeVert, John
Levete, Sarah 1961- *153*
Levin, Betty 1927- *201*
  Earlier sketches in SATA *19, 84, 137*
  See also SAAS 11
Levin, Ira 1929-2007 .... *66*
  Obituary *187*
Levin, Ira Marvin
  See Levin, Ira
Levin, Marcia Obrasky 1918- *13*
Levin, Meyer 1905-1981 .... *21*
  Obituary *27*
Levin, Miriam (Ramsfelder) 1962- *97*
Levine, Abby 1943- *54*
  Brief entry *52*
Levine, Anna *212*
Levine, Betty K(rasne) 1933- *66*
Levine, David 1926-2009 .... *43*
  Brief entry *35*
Levine, Edna S(imon) *35*
Levine, Ellen 1939- *190*
Levine, Evan 1962- *77*
  Earlier sketch in SATA *74*
Levine, Gail Carson 1947- *195*
  Earlier sketches in SATA *98, 161*
  See also CLR 85
Levine, I(srael) E. 1923-2003 .... *12*
  Obituary *146*
Levine, Joan Goldman *11*
Levine, Joseph 1910- *33*
Levine, Kristin 1974- *213*
Levine, Marge 1934- *81*
Levine, Rhoda *14*
Levine, Sarah 1970- *57*
Levine, Shar 1953- *131*
Levine-Freidus, Gail
  See Provost, Gail Levine
Levinson, Nancy Smiler 1938- *211*
  Earlier sketches in SATA *33, 80, 140*
Levinson, Riki *99*
  Brief entry *49*
  Earlier sketch in SATA *52*
Levithan, David 1972- *166*
Levitin, Sonia 1934- *192*
  Autobiography Feature *131*
  Earlier sketches in SATA *4, 68, 119, 131*
  See also CLR 53
  See also SAAS 2
Levitt, Sidney (Mark) 1947- *68*
Levon, O. U.
  See Kesey, Ken
Levoy, Myron 1930- *49*
  Brief entry *37*
Levy, Barrie *112*
Levy, Constance 1931- *140*
  Earlier sketch in SATA *73*
  See also SAAS 22
Levy, Elizabeth 1942- *169*
  Earlier sketches in SATA *31, 69, 107*
  See also SAAS 18
Levy, Janice *172*
Levy, Marilyn 1937- *67*
Levy, Nathan 1945- *63*
Levy, Robert 1945- *82*
Lewees, John
  See Stockton, Francis Richard
Lewin, Betsy 1937- *222*
  Autobiography Feature *115*
  Earlier sketches in SATA *32, 90, 169*
Lewin, Hugh 1939- *72*
  Brief entry *40*
  See also CLR 9
Lewin, Ted 1935- *195*
  Autobiography Feature *115*
  Earlier sketches in SATA *21, 76, 119, 165*
Lewis, Alice C. 1936- *46*
Lewis, Alice Hudson 1895(?)-1971
  Obituary *29*
Lewis, Amanda 1955- *80*
Lewis, Anthony 1927- *27*

Lewis, Anthony 1966- 120
Lewis, Barbara A. 1943- 73
Lewis, Beverly 1949- 80
Lewis, Brenda Ralph 1932- 72
Lewis, Brian 1963- 128
Lewis, C. S. 1898-1963 100
    Earlier sketch in SATA 13
    See also CLR 109
Lewis, Claudia (Louise) 1907-2001 5
Lewis, Clive Staples
    See Lewis, C. S.
Lewis, Cynthia Copeland 1960- 111
Lewis, E. M. 123
    Earlier sketch in SATA 20
Lewis, Earl Bradley
    See Lewis, E.B.
Lewis, E.B. 1956- 211
    Earlier sketches in SATA 93, 124, 168
Lewis, Elizabeth Foreman 1892-1958 121
    See also YABC 2
Lewis, Francine
    See Wells, Helen
Lewis, Harry Sinclair
    See Lewis, Sinclair
Lewis, Hilda (Winifred) 1896-1974
    Obituary 20
Lewis, J. Patrick 1942- 205
    Earlier sketches in SATA 69, 104, 162
Lewis, Jack P(earl) 1919- 65
Lewis, Jean 1924- 61
Lewis, Jon Samuel
    See Lewis, J.S.
Lewis, Joseph Anthony
    See Lewis, Anthony
Lewis, J.S. 1972- 203
Lewis, Julinda
    See Lewis-Ferguson, Julinda
Lewis, Kevin 173
Lewis, Kim 1951- 217
    Earlier sketches in SATA 84, 136
Lewis, Linda (Joy) 1946- 67
Lewis, Lucia Z.
    See Anderson, Lucia (Lewis)
Lewis, Marjorie 1929- 40
    Brief entry 35
Lewis, Mary 1907(?)-1988 64
    Obituary 56
Lewis, Mervyn
    See Frewer, Glyn (M.)
Lewis, Michael
    See Untermeyer, Louis
Lewis, Naomi 1911-2009 144
    Earlier sketch in SATA 76
Lewis, Paeony 1960- 173
Lewis, Paul
    See Gerson, Noel Bertram
Lewis, Richard 1935- 3
Lewis, Richard 1956- 209
Lewis, Rob 1962- 72
Lewis, Roger
    See Zarchy, Harry
Lewis, Rose 209
Lewis, Rose A.
    See Lewis, Rose
Lewis, Shannon
    See Llywelyn, Morgan
Lewis, Shari 1934-1998 35
    Brief entry 30
    Obituary 104
Lewis, Sylvan R.
    See Aronson, Virginia
Lewis, Thomas P(arker) 1936- 27
Lewis, Wendy A. 1966- 150
Lewis-Ferguson, Julinda 1955- 85
Lewison, Wendy Cheyette 177
Lewiton, Mina 1904-1970 2
Lew-Vriethoff, Joanne 186
Lexau, Joan M. 130
    Earlier sketches in SATA 1, 36
Ley, Willy 1906-1969 2
Leydon, Rita (Floden) 1949- 21

Leyland, Eric (Arthur) 1911- 37
L'Hommedieu, Dorothy Keasley 1885-1961
    Obituary 29
Li, Xiao Jun 1952- 86
Liao, Jimmy 1958- 202
Liatsos, Sandra Olson 1942- 103
Libby, Alisa M. 189
Libby, Barbara M. 153
Libby, Bill
    See Libby, William M.
Libby, William M. 1927-1984 5
    Obituary 39
Liberty, Gene 1924- 3
Lichtenheld, Tom 208
    Earlier sketch in SATA 152
Lichtman, Wendy 1946- 193
Liddell, Kenneth 1912-1975 63
Lidz, Jane 120
Lieberman, E(dwin) James 1934- 62
Liebers, Arthur 1913-1984 12
Lieblich, Irene 1923- 22
Liers, Emil E(rnest) 1890-1975 37
Lies, Brian 1963- 190
    Earlier sketch in SATA 131
Lieshout, Elle van
    See van Lieshout, Elle
Liestman, Vicki 1961- 72
Lietz, Gerald S. 1918- 11
Liew, Sonny 1974- 219
Life, Kay (Guinn) 1930- 83
Lifton, Betty Jean 1926-2010 118
    Earlier sketch in SATA 6
Lifton, Robert Jay 1926- 66
Lightburn, Ron 1954- 91
Lightburn, Sandra 1955- 91
Lightner, A. M.
    See Hopf, Alice (Martha) L(ightner)
Lightner, Alice
    See Hopf, Alice (Martha) L(ightner)
Lignell, Lois 1911- 37
Liles, Maurine Walpole 1935- 81
Lillegard, Dee 184
Lilley, Stephen R. 1950- 97
Lilley, Stephen Ray
    See Lilley, Stephen R.
Lillington, Kenneth (James) 1916-1998 39
Lilly, Nate 182
Lilly, Ray
    See Curtis, Richard
Lim, John 1932- 43
Liman, Ellen (Fogelson) 1936- 22
Limb, Sue 1946- 203
    Earlier sketch in SATA 158
Limburg, Peter R(ichard) 1929- 13
Lin, Grace 1974- 198
    Earlier sketches in SATA 111, 162
Lincoln, C(harles) Eric 1924-2000 5
Lincoln, Christopher 1952- 208
Lincoln, Hazel 187
Lincoln, James
    See Bates, Katharine Lee
Lindbergh, Anne
    See Sapieyevski, Anne Lindbergh
Lindbergh, Anne Morrow 1906-2001 33
    Obituary 125
Lindbergh, Anne Spencer Morrow
    See Lindbergh, Anne Morrow
Lindbergh, Charles A(ugustus, Jr.)
    1902-1974 33
Lindbergh, Reeve 1945- 163
    Earlier sketch in SATA 116
Lindblom, Steven (Winther) 1946- 94
    Brief entry 39
    Earlier sketch in SATA 42
Linde, Gunnel 1924- 5
Lindenbaum, Pija 1955- 183
    Earlier sketches in SATA 77, 144

Lindgren, Astrid (Anna Emilia Ericsson)
    1907-2002 38
    Obituary 128
    Earlier sketch in SATA 2
    See also CLR 119
Lindgren, Barbro 1937- 207
    Brief entry 46
    Earlier sketches in SATA 63, 120
    See also CLR 86
Lindman, Maj (Jan) 1886-1972 43
Lindo, Elvira 1962- 219
Lindop, Edmund 1925- 5
Lindquist, Jennie Dorothea 1899-1977 13
Lindquist, Rowena Cory 1958- 98
Lindquist, Willis 1908-1988 20
Lindsay, Nicholas Vachel
    See Lindsay, Vachel
Lindsay, Norman Alfred William
    1879-1969 67
    See also CLR 8
Lindsay, Vachel 1879-1931 40
Lindsey, Kathleen D(orothy) 1949- 153
Line, David
    See Davidson, Lionel
Line, Les 1935-2010 27
Lines, Kathleen Mary 1902-1988
    Obituary 61
Linfield, Esther 40
Lingard, Joan (Amelia) 1932- 130
    Autobiography Feature 130
    Earlier sketches in SATA 8, 74, 114
    See also CLR 89
    See also SAAS 5
Link, Martin 1934- 28
Linn, Margot
    See Ziefert, Harriet
Linnea, Sharon 1956- 82
Lion, Melissa 1976- 176
Lionni, Leo(nard) 1910-1999 72
    Obituary 118
    Earlier sketch in SATA 8
    See also CLR 71
Lipinsky de Orlov, Lino S. 1908- 22
Lipkind, William 1904-1974 15
Lipman, David 1931-2008 21
Lipman, Matthew 1923-2010 14
Lipp, Frederick 204
Lippincott, Bertram 1898(?)-1985
    Obituary 42
Lippincott, Gary A. 1953- 220
    Earlier sketches in SATA 73, 119
Lippincott, Joseph W(harton) 1887-1976 17
Lippincott, Sarah Lee 1920- 22
Lippman, Peter J. 1936- 31
Lipsyte, Robert 1938- 198
    Earlier sketches in SATA 5, 68, 113, 161
    See also CLR 76
Lipsyte, Robert Michael
    See Lipsyte, Robert
Lisandrelli, Elaine Slivinski 1951- 94
Lisker, Sonia O. 1933- 44
Lisle, Holly 1960- 208
    Earlier sketch in SATA 98
Lisle, Janet Taylor 1947- 150
    Brief entry 47
    Earlier sketches in SATA 59, 96
    See also SAAS 14
Lisle, Rebecca 162
Lisle, Seward D.
    See Ellis, Edward S.
Lisowski, Gabriel 1946- 47
    Brief entry 31
Liss, Howard 1922-1995 4
    Obituary 84
Lissiat, Amy
    See Thompson, Colin
Lisson, Deborah 1941- 110
    Earlier sketch in SATA 71
List, Ilka Katherine 1935- 6
Liston, Robert A. 1927- 5
Litchfield, Ada B(assett) 1916-1999 5

Litchfield, Jo 1973- *116*
Lithgow, John 1945- *145*
Lithgow, John Arthur
　See Lithgow, John
Litowinsky, Olga 1936- *26*
Litowinsky, Olga Jean
　See Litowinsky, Olga
Littke, Lael J. 1929- *140*
　Earlier sketches in SATA *51, 83*
Little, A. Edward
　See Klein, Aaron E.
Little, Douglas 1942- *96*
Little, (Flora) Jean 1932- *149*
　Earlier sketches in SATA *2, 68, 106*
　See also CLR *4*
　See also SAAS *17*
Little, Lessie Jones 1906-1986 .... *60*
　Obituary *50*
Little, Mary E. 1912-1999 .... *28*
Littlechild, George 1958- *85*
Littledale, Freya (Lota) 1929-1992 .... *74*
　Earlier sketch in SATA *2*
Littlefield, Bill 1948- *83*
Littlefield, Holly 1963- *97*
Littlesugar, Amy 1953- *176*
　Earlier sketch in SATA *122*
Littleton, Mark R. 1950- *142*
　Earlier sketch in SATA *89*
Littlewood, Karin *211*
Littman, Sarah Darer *221*
　Earlier sketch in SATA *175*
Litty, Julie 1971- *181*
Litzinger, Rosanne 1948- *196*
Liu, Cynthea *221*
Lively, Penelope 1933- *164*
　Earlier sketches in SATA *7, 60, 101*
　See also CLR *159*
Lively, Penelope Margaret
　See Lively, Penelope
Liverakos, L. A.
　See Gilman, Laura Anne
Liversidge, (Henry) Douglas 1913- *8*
Livesey, Claire (Warner) 1927- *127*
Livingston, Carole 1941- *42*
Livingston, (M.) Irene 1932- *150*
Livingston, Myra Cohn 1926-1996 .... *68*
　Obituary *92*
　Earlier sketch in SATA *5*
　See also CLR *7*
　See also SAAS *1*
Livingston, Richard R(oland) 1922- *8*
Livo, Norma J. 1929- *76*
Liwska, Renata *199*
Ljungkvist, Laura *180*
Llerena Aguirre, Carlos 1952- *19*
Llerena Aguirre, Carlos Antonio
　See Llerena Aguirre, Carlos
Llewellyn, Claire 1954- *196*
　Earlier sketches in SATA *77, 143*
Llewellyn, Grace 1964- *110*
Llewellyn, Richard
　See Llewellyn Lloyd, Richard Dafydd Vivian
Llewellyn, Sam 1948- *185*
　Earlier sketch in SATA *95*
Llewellyn Lloyd, Richard Dafydd Vivian
　1906-1983 .... *11*
　Obituary *37*
Llewelyn, T. Harcourt
　See Hamilton, Charles (Harold St. John)
Lloyd, Alan
　See Lloyd, A.R.
Lloyd, Alan Richard
　See Lloyd, A.R.
Lloyd, A.R. 1927- *168*
　Earlier sketch in SATA *97*
Lloyd, David
　See Lloyd, David T.
Lloyd, David T. 1954- *167*
Lloyd, E. James
　See James, Elizabeth
Lloyd, Errol 1943- *22*

Lloyd, Hugh
　See Fitzhugh, Percy Keese
Lloyd, James
　See James, Elizabeth
Lloyd, Megan 1958- *189*
　Earlier sketches in SATA *77, 117*
Lloyd, Norman 1909-1980
　Obituary *23*
Lloyd, (Mary) Norris 1908-1993 .... *10*
　Obituary *75*
Lloyd, Saci 1967- *220*
Lloyd, Sam *183*
Lloyd-Jones, Sally 1960- *179*
Lloyd Webber, Andrew 1948- *56*
Llywelyn, Morgan 1937- *109*
Lo, Ginnie *165*
Lo, Malinda 1974- *222*
Lo, Virginia M.
　See Lo, Ginnie
Lobato, Jose Bento Monteiro 1882-1948 ... *114*
Lobel, Anita (Kempler) 1934- *162*
　Earlier sketches in SATA *6, 55, 96*
Lobel, Arnold (Stark) 1933-1987 .... *55*
　Obituary *54*
　Earlier sketch in SATA *6*
　See also CLR *5*
Lobel, Gillian *181*
Lobsenz, Amelia *12*
Lobsenz, Norman M(itchell) 1919- *6*
Lochak, Michele 1936- *39*
Lochlons, Colin
　See Jackson, C(aary) Paul
Locke, Clinton W. *1*
Locke, Elsie (Violet) 1912-2001 .... *87*
Locke, Gary 1963- *197*
Locke, Lucie 1904-1989 .... *10*
Locke, Robert 1944- *63*
　See also CLR *39*
Locker, Thomas 1937- *109*
　Earlier sketch in SATA *59*
　See also CLR *14*
Lockhart, E.
　See Jenkins, Emily
Lockridge, Hildegarde (Dolson)
　1908-1981 .... *121*
　Earlier sketch in SATA *5*
Lockwood, Mary
　See Spelman, Mary
Lodge, Bernard 1933- *215*
　Earlier sketches in SATA *33, 107*
Lodge, Jo 1966- *173*
　Earlier sketch in SATA *112*
Loeb, Jeffrey 1946- *57*
Loeb, Robert H., Jr. 1917- *21*
Loefgren, Ulf 1931- *3*
Loehfelm, Bill 1969- *153*
Loehr, Mallory *184*
Loehr, Patrick 1968(?)- *194*
Loeper, John J(oseph) 1929- *118*
　Earlier sketch in SATA *10*
Loescher, Ann Dull 1942- *20*
Loescher, Gil 1945- *20*
Loescher, Gilburt Damian
　See Loescher, Gil
Loewer, Jean Jenkins
　See Jenkins, Jean
Loewer, (Henry) Peter 1934- *98*
LoFaro, Jerry 1959- *77*
Lofo
　See Heimann, Rolf
Lofthouse, Liz *199*
Lofting, Hugh (John) 1886-1947 .... *100*
　Earlier sketch in SATA *15*
　See also CLR *143*
Lofts, Norah (Robinson) 1904-1983 .... *8*
　Obituary *36*

Logan, Jake
　See Knott, William C(ecil, Jr.)
　and Krepps, Robert W(ilson)
　and Pearl, Jacques Bain
　and Riefe, Alan
　and Rifkin, Shepard
　and Smith, Martin Cruz
Logan, Mark
　See Nicole, Christopher (Robin)
Logan, Rochelle 1954- *169*
Logsted, Greg *221*
Logston, Anne 1962- *112*
Logue, Christopher 1926- *23*
Logue, Mary 1952- *161*
　Earlier sketch in SATA *112*
Logue, Mary Louise
　See Logue, Mary
Loh, Morag 1935- *73*
Lohans, Alison 1949- *101*
Loizeaux, William *185*
Loken, Newton Clayton 1919- *26*
Lomas, Steve
　See Brennan, Joseph Lomas
Lomask, Milton (Nachman) 1909-1991 .... *20*
Lombard, Jenny *178*
Lombino, Salvatore
　See Hunter, Evan
LoMonaco, Palmyra 1932- *102*
London, Jack 1876-1916 .... *18*
　See also CLR *108*
London, Jane
　See Geis, Darlene Stern
London, John Griffith
　See London, Jack
London, Jonathan 1947- *221*
　Earlier sketches in SATA *74, 113, 157*
Lonergan, (Pauline) Joy (MacLean) 1909- ... *10*
Lonette, Reisie (Dominee) 1924- *43*
Long, Cathryn J. 1946- *89*
Long, Earlene (Roberta) 1938- *50*
Long, Emmett
　See Leonard, Elmore
Long, Ethan 1968(?)- *223*
　Earlier sketch in SATA *182*
Long, Helen Beecher *1*
Long, Judith Elaine 1953- *20*
Long, Judy
　See Long, Judith Elaine
Long, Kim 1949- *69*
Long, Laura Mooney 1892-1967
　Obituary *29*
Long, Laurel *203*
Long, Loren 1966(?)- *188*
　Earlier sketch in SATA *151*
Long, Melinda 1960- *152*
Long, Sylvia 1948- *179*
　Earlier sketch in SATA *120*
Longbeard, Frederick
　See Longyear, Barry B(rookes)
Longfellow, Henry Wadsworth 1807-1882 ... *19*
　See also CLR *99*
Longfellow, Layne 1937- *102*
Longfellow, Layne A.
　See Longfellow, Layne
Longman, Harold S. 1919- *5*
Longsworth, Polly 1933- *28*
Longtemps, Kenneth 1933- *17*
Longway, A. Hugh
　See Lang, Andrew
Longyear, Barry B(rookes) 1942- *117*
Look, Lenore *180*
Loomans, Diane 1955- *90*
Loomis, Christine *160*
　Earlier sketch in SATA *113*
Loomis, Jennifer A. 1942- *101*
Loomis, Robert D. *5*
Lopez, Angelo (Cayas) 1967- *83*
Lopez, Barry 1945- *67*
Lopez, Barry Holstun
　See Lopez, Barry
Lopez, Jack 1950- *178*

Lopez, Loretta 1963- *190*
Lopez, Lorraine 1956- *181*
Lopez, Lorraine M.
　See Lopez, Lorraine
Lopez, Rafael 1961(?)- *198*
Lopshire, Robert M(artin) 1927- *6*
Loraine, Connie
　See Reece, Colleen L.
Lorbiecki, Marybeth 1959- *172*
　Earlier sketch in SATA *121*
Lord, Athena V. 1932- *39*
Lord, Beman 1924-1991 .... *5*
　Obituary *69*
Lord, Bette Bao 1938- *58*
　See also CLR *151*
Lord, Cynthia *182*
Lord, Doreen Mildred Douglas
　See Lord, Douglas
Lord, Douglas 1904-1992 .... *12*
Lord, Janet *204*
Lord, John Vernon 1939- *21*
Lord, Michele *201*
Lord, Nancy
　See Titus, Eve
Lord, Patricia C. 1927-1988
　Obituary *58*
Lord, Walter 1917-2002 .... *3*
Lorde, Diana
　See Reno, Dawn E(laine)
Lorenz, Albert 1941- *115*
Lorenzini, Carlo
　See Collodi, Carlo
Lorey, Dean 1967- *193*
Lorimer, Janet 1941- *60*
Loring, Emilie (Baker) 1864(?)-1951 .... *51*
Lorkowski, Thomas V(incent) 1950- *92*
Lorkowski, Tom
　See Lorkowski, Thomas V(incent)
Lorraine, Walter (Henry) 1929- *16*
Lorrimer, Claire
　See Clark, Patricia Denise
Loss, Joan 1933- *11*
Lothrop, Harriet Mulford Stone 1844-1924 . *20*
Lottridge, Celia Barker 1936- *157*
　Earlier sketch in SATA *112*
LoTurco, Laura 1963- *84*
Lotz, Wolfgang 1912-1981 .... *65*
Loughridge, Stuart 1978- *214*
Louie, Ai-Ling 1949- *40*
　Brief entry *34*
Louis, Catherine 1963- *186*
Louis, Pat
　See Francis, Dorothy
Louisburgh, Sheila Burnford
　See Burnford, Sheila (Philip Cochrane Every)
Louise, Anita
　See Riggio, Anita
Louise, Tina 1934- *191*
Lourie, Helen
　See Storr, Catherine (Cole)
Lourie, Peter 1952- *183*
　Earlier sketches in SATA *82, 142*
Lourie, Peter King
　See Lourie, Peter
Love, Ann 1947- *168*
　Earlier sketch in SATA *79*
Love, D. Anne 1949- *180*
　Earlier sketches in SATA *96, 145*
Love, Douglas 1967- *92*
Love, Judith Dufour
　See Love, Judy
Love, Judy *188*
Love, Katherine (Isabel) 1907- *3*
Love, Kathleen Ann
　See Love, Ann
Love, Maryann Cusimano *223*
Love, Sandra (Weller) 1940- *26*
Lovegrove, James 1965- *216*
Lovegrove, J.M.H.
　See Lovegrove, James
Lovejoy, Jack 1937- *116*

Lovelace, Delos Wheeler 1894-1967 .... *7*
Lovelace, Maud Hart 1892-1980 .... *2*
　Obituary *23*
Lovell, Ingraham
　See Bacon, Josephine Dodge (Daskam)
Lovelock, Brian 1956- *214*
Loverseed, Amanda (Jane) 1965- *75*
Lovett, Margaret (Rose) 1915- *22*
Low, Alice 1926- *156*
　Earlier sketches in SATA *11, 76*
Low, Elizabeth Hammond 1898-1991 .... *5*
Low, Joseph 1911-2007 .... *14*
Low, Penelope Margaret
　See Lively, Penelope
Low, William *177*
Lowe, Helen 1961- *206*
Lowe, Jay, Jr.
　See Loeper, John J(oseph)
Lowell, Pamela *187*
Lowell, Susan 1950- *206*
　Earlier sketches in SATA *81, 127*
Lowenstein, Dyno 1914-1996 .... *6*
Lowenstein, Sallie 1949- *116*
Lowery, Linda 1949- *151*
　Earlier sketch in SATA *74*
Lowitz, Anson C. 1901(?)-1978 .... *18*
Lowitz, Sadyebeth Heath 1901-1969 .... *17*
Lowndes, Robert A(ugustine) W(ard)
　1916-1998 .... *117*
Lowrey, Janette Sebring 1892-1986 .... *43*
Lowry, Lois 1937- *177*
　Autobiography Feature *127*
　Earlier sketches in SATA *23, 70, 111*
　See also CLR *72*
　See also SAAS *3*
Lowry, Lois Hammersberg
　See Lowry, Lois
Lowry, Peter 1953- *7*
Lowther, George F. 1913-1975
　Obituary *30*
Loyie, Larry 1933- *150*
Lozansky, Edward D. 1941- *62*
Lozier, Herbert 1915- *26*
Lubar, David 1954- *190*
　Earlier sketch in SATA *133*
Lubell, Cecil 1912-2000 .... *6*
Lubell, Winifred (A. Milius) 1914- *6*
Lubin, Leonard
　See Lubin, Leonard B.
Lubin, Leonard B. 1943-1994 .... *45*
　Brief entry *37*
Lubka, S. Ruth 1948- *154*
Lubner, Susan *185*
Luby, Thia 1954- *124*
Lucado, Max (Lee) 1955- *104*
Lucas, Cedric 1962- *101*
Lucas, David 1966- *208*
Lucas, E(dward) V(errall) 1868-1938 .... *20*
Lucas, Eileen 1956- *113*
　Earlier sketch in SATA *76*
Lucas, George 1944- *56*
Lucas, Jerry 1940- *33*
Lucas, Margeaux *186*
Lucas, Victoria
　See Plath, Sylvia
Lucashenko, Melissa 1967- *104*
Luccarelli, Vincent 1923- *90*
Luce, Celia (Geneva Larsen) 1914- *38*
Luce, Willard (Ray) 1914-1990 .... *38*
Lucht, Irmgard 1937- *82*
Lucke, Deb *202*
Luckett, Dave 1951- *220*
　Earlier sketches in SATA *106, 167*
Luckhardt, Mildred Corell 1898-1990 .... *5*
Ludden, Allen (Ellsworth) 1918(?)-1981
　Obituary *27*
Ludel, Jacqueline 1945- *64*
Ludlow, Geoffrey
　See Meynell, Laurence Walter
Ludlum, Mabel Cleland
　See Widdemer, Mabel Cleland

Ludwig, Helen *33*
Ludwig, Lyndell 1923- *63*
Ludwig, Trudy 1959- *209*
　Earlier sketch in SATA *166*
Luebs, Robin 1949- *212*
Lueders, Edward (George) 1923- *14*
Luenn, Nancy 1954- *79*
　Earlier sketch in SATA *51*
Lufkin, Raymond H. 1897- *38*
Lugard, Flora Louisa Shaw 1852-1929 .... *21*
Luger, Harriett Mandelay 1914- *23*
Luhrmann, Winifred B(ruce) 1934- *11*
Luis, Earlene W. 1929- *11*
Lujan, Jorge *201*
Luke, Pauline *178*
Luke, Pauline R.
　See Luke, Pauline
Lum, Peter
　See Crowe, (Bettina) Peter Lum
Lumry, Amanda (R.) *159*
Lund, Deb *157*
Lund, Doris Herold 1919- *12*
Lunde, Darrin *202*
Lundebrek, Amy 1975- *213*
Lung, Chang
　See Jordan, Robert
Lunge-Larsen, Lise 1955- *184*
　Earlier sketch in SATA *138*
Lunn, Carolyn (Kowalczyk) 1960- *67*
Lunn, Janet (Louise Swoboda) 1928- *110*
　Earlier sketches in SATA *4, 68*
　See also CLR *18*
　See also SAAS *12*
Lunsford, Cin Forshay
　See Forshay-Lunsford, Cin
Lupica, Michael
　See Lupica, Mike
Lupica, Michael Thomas
　See Lupica, Mike
Lupica, Mike 1952- *177*
Lupoff, Dick
　See Lupoff, Richard A(llen)
Lupoff, Richard A(llen) 1935- *60*
Lurie, Alison 1926- *112*
　Earlier sketch in SATA *46*
Lurie, Morris 1938- *72*
Lussert, Anneliese 1929- *101*
Lusted, Marcia Amidon 1962- *143*
Lustig, Arnost 1926- *56*
Lustig, Loretta 1944- *46*
Lutes, Jason 1967- *210*
Luthardt, Kevin 1973- *172*
Luther, Frank 1905-1980
　Obituary *25*
Luther, Rebekah (Lyn) S(tiles) 1960- *90*
Luttmann, Gail
　See Damerow, Gail
Luttrell, Guy L. 1938- *22*
Luttrell, Ida (Alleene) 1934- *91*
　Brief entry *35*
　Earlier sketch in SATA *40*
Luttrell, William (J. III) 1954- *149*
Lutz, John 1939- *180*
Lutz, John Thomas
　See Lutz, John
Lutz, Norma Jean 1943- *122*
Lutzeier, Elizabeth 1952- *72*
Lutzker, Edythe 1904-1991 .... *5*
Luxbacher, Irene 1970- *219*
　Earlier sketch in SATA *153*
Luzadder, Patrick 1954- *89*
Luzzati, Emanuele 1921-2007 .... *7*
Luzzatto, Paola Caboara 1938- *38*
Ly, Many 1977- *208*
Lybbert, Tyler 1970- *88*
Lydon, Michael 1942- *11*
Lyfick, Warren
　See Reeves, Lawrence F.
Lyle, Katie Letcher 1938- *8*

Lynch, Chris 1962- 209
  Earlier sketches in SATA 95, 131, 171
  See also CLR 58
Lynch, Janet Nichols 1952- 221
Lynch, Jay 1945- 204
Lynch, Lorenzo 1932- 7
Lynch, Marietta 1947- 29
Lynch, Patricia (Nora) 1898-1972 9
Lynch, Patrick James
  See Lynch, P.J.
Lynch, P.J. 1962- 213
  Earlier sketches in SATA 79, 122
Lynds, Dennis 1924-2005 47
  Brief entry 37
Lyne, Alison Davis 188
Lyngseth, Joan
  See Davies, Joan
Lynn, Elizabeth A(nne) 1946- 99
Lynn, Mary
  See Brokamp, Marilyn
Lynn, Patricia
  See Watts, Mabel Pizzey
Lynn, Tracy 175
Lyon, Elinor 1921-2008 6
  Obituary 192
Lyon, Elinor Bruce
  See Lyon, Elinor
Lyon, George Ella 1949- 207
  Autobiography Feature 148
  Earlier sketches in SATA 68, 119, 148
Lyon, Lea 1945- 212
Lyon, Lyman R.
  See de Camp, L. Sprague
Lyons, Dorothy M(arawee) 1907-1997 3
Lyons, Grant 1941- 30
Lyons, Marcus
  See Blish, James
Lyons, Mary E. 1947- 195
  Autobiography Feature 195
  Earlier sketches in SATA 93, 142
Lyons, Mary Evelyn
  See Lyons, Mary E.
Lystad, Mary (Hanemann) 1928- 11
Lytle, Elizabeth Stewart 1949- 79
Lytle, Robert A. 1944- 119
Lyttle, Richard B(ard) 1927- 23
Lytton, Deborah 1966- 218
Lytton, Edward G.E.L. Bulwer-Lytton Baron
  See Bulwer-Lytton, Edward
Lytton of Knebworth, Baron
  See Bulwer-Lytton, Edward

                        M

Ma, Wenhai 1954- 84
Maar, Leonard (Frank, Jr.) 1927- 30
Maartens, Maretha 1945- 73
Maas, Selve -1997 14
Maass, Robert 195
Mabie, Grace
  See Mattern, Joanne
Mac
  See MacManus, Seumas
  and Maccari, Ruggero
Macalaster, Elizabeth G. 1951- 115
MacAlister, Katie 159
MacAlister, V. A.
  See McKernan, Victoria
MacAllan, Andrew
  See Leasor, James
MacAodhagain, Eamon
  See Egan, E. W.
MacArthur-Onslow, Annette Rosemary
  1933- 26
Macaulay, David (Alexander) 1946- 137
  Brief entry 27
  Earlier sketches in SATA 46, 72
  See also CLR 14
Macaulay, Teresa 1947- 95

Macauley, Theresa E.
  See Macaulay, Teresa
Macavinta, Courtney 176
MacBeth, George (Mann) 1932-1992 4
  Obituary 70
MacBride, Roger Lea 1929-1995 85
MacCarter, Don 1944- 91
MacClintock, Dorcas 1932- 8
MacCready, Robin Merrow 1959(?)- 190
MacCullough, Carolyn 174
MacDonald, Alan 1958- 192
MacDonald, Amy 1951- 156
  Autobiography Feature 156
  Earlier sketches in SATA 76, 136
MacDonald, Anne Elizabeth Campbell Bard
  -1958
  See MacDonald, Betty
MacDonald, Anne Louise 1955- 217
MacDonald, Anson
  See Heinlein, Robert A.
MacDonald, Betty 1908-1958
  See YABC 1
Macdonald, Blackie
  See Emrich, Duncan (Black Macdonald)
Macdonald, Caroline 1948- 86
  Obituary 111
  See also CLR 60
Macdonald, Dwight 1906-1982 29
  Obituary 33
MacDonald, George 1824-1905 100
  Earlier sketch in SATA 33
  See also CLR 67
MacDonald, Golden
  See Brown, Margaret Wise
Macdonald, Guy 195
Macdonald, James D. 1954- 67
  Earlier sketches in SATA 81, 114, 165, 1
Macdonald, Marcia
  See Hill, Grace Livingston
MacDonald, Margaret Read 1940- 194
  Earlier sketches in SATA 94, 164
Macdonald, Marianne 1934- 113
Macdonald, Mary
  See Gifford, Griselda
Macdonald, Maryann 1947- 189
  Earlier sketch in SATA 72
MacDonald, Ross 1957- 201
Macdonald, Shelagh 1937- 25
MacDonald, Suse 1940- 193
  Brief entry 52
  Earlier sketches in SATA 54, 109
Macdonald, Wendy 217
Macdonald, Wendy M.
  See Macdonald, Wendy
Macdonald, Zillah K(atherine) 1885-1979 ... 11
MacDonnell, Megan
  See Stevens, Serita
MacDougal, John
  See Blish, James
Mace, Elisabeth 1933- 27
Mace, Varian 1938- 49
MacEachern, Stephen 206
MacEwen, Gwendolyn (Margaret)
  1941-1987 50
  Obituary 55
Macfarlan, Allan A. 1892-1982 35
MacFarlane, Iris 1922- 11
MacGill-Callahan, Sheila 1926-2000 78
MacGregor, Carol Lynn 153
MacGregor, Ellen 1906-1954 39
  Brief entry 27
MacGregor-Hastie, Roy (Alasdhair Niall)
  1929- 3
MacGrory, Yvonne 1948- 142
Machado, Ana Maria 1941- 150
MacHale, D.J. 1956- 175
MacHale, Donald James
  See MacHale, D.J.
Machetanz, Frederick 1908- 34
Machin, Sue
  See Williams, Sue

Machin Goodall, Daphne (Edith) 37
Macht, Norm
  See Macht, Norman L.
Macht, Norman L. 1929- 122
Macht, Norman Lee
  See Macht, Norman L.
Macht, Norman Lee
  See Macht, Norman L.
MacInnes, Helen (Clark) 1907-1985 22
  Obituary 44
Macintosh, Brownie 1950- 98
MacIntyre, Elisabeth 1916- 17
MacIntyre, Rod
  See MacIntyre, R.P.
MacIntyre, R.P. 1947- 203
MacIntyre, R.P. 1947- 203
MacIntyre, Wendy 1947- 196
Mack, Jeff 194
Mack, L.V.
  See Kimmelman, Burt
Mack, Stan(ley) 17
Mack, Todd 168
Mack, Tracy 1968- 183
  Earlier sketch in SATA 128
Mackall, Dandi D.
  See Mackall, Dandi Daley
Mackall, Dandi Daley 1949- 218
  Earlier sketches in SATA 118, 177, 182
Mackay, Claire 1930- 97
  Autobiography Feature 124
  Earlier sketch in SATA 40
  See also CLR 43
Mackay, Constance D'Arcy (?)-1966 125
Mackay, Donald 1914-2005 81
  Obituary 173
Mackay, Donald Alexander
  See Mackay, Donald
MacKaye, Percy (Wallace) 1875-1956 32
Mackel, Kathryn 1950- 162
Mackel, Kathy
  See Mackel, Kathryn
MacKellar, William 1914- 4
Macken, JoAnn Early 1953- 201
Macken, Walter 1915-1967 36
Mackenzie, Anna 1963- 212
MacKenzie, Jill (Kelly) 1947- 75
Mackenzie, Robert 1974- 204
Mackey, Ernan
  See McInerny, Ralph
Mackey, Weezie Kerr 188
Mackie, Maron
  See McNeely, Jeannette
Mackin, Edward
  See McInerny, Ralph
MacKinnon, Bernie 1957- 69
MacKinnon Groomer, Vera 1915- 57
MacKinstry, Elizabeth 1879-1956 42
Mackler, Carolyn 1973- 156
MacLachlan, Emily
  See Charest, Emily MacLachlan
MacLachlan, Patricia 1938- 168
  Brief entry 42
  Earlier sketches in SATA 62, 107
  See also CLR 14
MacLane, Jack
  See Crider, Bill
MacLean, Alistair 1922(?)-1987 23
  Obituary 50
MacLean, Alistair Stuart
  See MacLean, Alistair
Maclean, Art
  See Shirreffs, Gordon D(onald)
MacLean, Christine Kole 1962- 177
MacLean, Glynne 1964- 150
MacLean, Jill 1941- 211
MacLeod, Beatrice 1910- 162
  Earlier sketch in SATA 10
MacLeod, Beatrice Beach
  See MacLeod, Beatrice
MacLeod, Charlotte (Matilda) 1922-2005 28
  Obituary 160

Author Index

MacLeod, Doug 1959- 201
  Earlier sketch in SATA 60
MacLeod, Elizabeth 184
  Earlier sketch in SATA 158
MacLeod, Ellen Jane (Anderson) 1916- 14
MacManus, James
  See MacManus, Seumas
MacManus, Seumas 1869-1960 25
MacMaster, Eve (Ruth) B(owers) 1942- 46
MacMillan, Annabelle
  See Quick, Annabelle
MacMillan, Dianne M(arie) 1943- 125
  Earlier sketch in SATA 84
Macnaughton, Tina 218
  Earlier sketch in SATA 182
Macneill, Janet
  See McNeely, Jeannette
MacPeek, Walter G. 1902-1973 4
  Obituary 25
MacPhail, Catherine 1946- 197
  Earlier sketch in SATA 130
MacPherson, Margaret 1908-2001 9
  See also SAAS 4
MacPherson, Thomas George 1915-1976
  Obituary 30
MacPherson, Winnie 1930- 107
MacRae, Tom 1980- 181
Macrae, Travis
  See Feagles, Anita MacRae
MacRaois, Cormac 1944- 72
Macumber, Mari
  See Sandoz, Mari(e Susette)
Macy, Sue 1954- 134
  Earlier sketch in SATA 88
Madaras, Lynda 1947- 151
Madden, Don 1927- 3
Madden, Kerry 1961- 168
Madden-Lunsford, Kerry
  See Madden, Kerry
Maddern, Eric 1950- 166
Maddigan, Beth 1967- 174
Maddison, Angela Mary 1923- 10
  See also CLR 24
Maddock, Reginald (Bertram) 1912-1994 15
Madenski, Melissa (Ann) 1949- 77
Madian, Jon 1941- 9
Madison, Alan 182
Madison, Arnold 1937- 6
Madison, Bennett 220
Madison, Winifred 5
Madonna 1958- 149
Madsen, Gunnar 171
Madsen, Jim 1964- 202
Madsen, Ross Martin 1946- 82
Madsen, Susan A. 1954- 90
Madsen, Susan Arrington
  See Madsen, Susan A.
Maehlqvist, Stefan 1943- 30
Maestro, Betsy (Crippen) 1944- 106
  Brief entry 30
  Earlier sketch in SATA 59
  See also CLR 45
Maestro, Giulio 1942- 106
  Earlier sketches in SATA 8, 59
  See also CLR 45
Maeterlinck, Maurice 1862-1949 66
Magee, Doug 1947- 78
Magee, Wes 1939- 64
Maggio, Rosalie 1943- 69
Magid, Ken(neth Marshall) 65
Magnus, Erica 1946- 77
Magoon, Kekla 1980- 213
Magoon, Scott 222
  Earlier sketch in SATA 182
Magorian, James 1942- 92
  Earlier sketch in SATA 32
Magorian, Michelle 1947- 128
  Earlier sketch in SATA 67
Magorian, Michelle Jane
  See Magorian, Michelle
Magovern, Peg 103

Magsamen, Sandra 1959- 213
Maguire, Anne
  See Nearing, Penny
Maguire, Gregory 1954- 200
  Autobiography Feature 200
  Earlier sketches in SATA 28, 84, 129
  See also SAAS 22
Maguire, Gregory Peter
  See Maguire, Gregory
Maguire, Jack 1920-2000 74
Maguire, Jesse
  See Smith, Sherwood
Maguire, Jessie
  See Smith, Sherwood
Maher, Ramona 1934- 13
Mahlqvist, Stefan
  See Maehlqvist, Stefan
Mahon, Julia C(unha) 1916- 11
Mahony, Elizabeth Winthrop
  See Winthrop, Elizabeth
Mahood, Kenneth 1930- 24
Mahy, Margaret 1936- 171
  Earlier sketches in SATA 14, 69, 119
  See also CLR 155
Mahy, Margaret May
  See Mahy, Margaret
Maiden, Cecil (Edward) 1902-1981 52
Maidoff, Ilka
  See List, Ilka Katherine
Maifair, Linda Lee 1947- 83
Maik, Henri
  See Hecht, Henri Joseph
Maillu, David G(ian) 1939- 111
Maine, Trevor
  See Catherall, Arthur
Mains, Randolph P. 1946- 80
Maione, Heather 189
Maiorano, Robert 1946- 43
Maisner, Heather 1947- 89
Maison, Della
  See Katz, Bobbi
Maitland, Antony Jasper 1935- 25
Maitland, Barbara 102
Mai-Wyss, Tatjana 1972- 187
Maizels, Jennie 210
Major, Kevin (Gerald) 1949- 134
  Earlier sketches in SATA 32, 82
  See also CLR 11
Majure, Janet 1954- 96
Makhijani, Pooja 188
Makie, Pam 1943- 37
Makowski, Silk
  See Sullivan, Silky
Makowski, Silvia Ann
  See Sullivan, Silky
Malam, John 1957- 152
  Earlier sketch in SATA 89
Maland, Nick 195
Malaspina, Ann 1957- 222
Malcolm, Dan
  See Silverberg, Robert
Malcolm, Jahnna N.
  See Beecham, Jahnna
Malcolmson, Anne
  See von Storch, Anne B.
Malcolmson, David 1899-1978 6
Maletta, Dr. Arlene
  See Feltenstein, Arlene
Maley, Carleen
  See Hutchins, Carleen Maley
Mali, Jane Lawrence 1937-1995 51
  Brief entry 44
  Obituary 86
Malkin, Nina 1959(?)- 179
Mallett, Jerry J. 1939- 76
Malley, Gemma 198
Malley, G.R.
  See Malley, Gemma
Mallory, Kenneth 1945- 185
  Earlier sketch in SATA 128

Mallowan, Agatha Christie
  See Christie, Agatha
Malmberg, Carl 1904-1979 9
Malmgren, Dallin 1949- 65
Malo, John W. 1911-2000 4
Malone, James Hiram 1930- 84
Malone, Nola Langner 1930-2003 8
  Obituary 151
Malone, Patricia 1932- 155
Malone, Peter 1953- 191
Maloney, Pat
  See Markun, Patricia Maloney
Malory, Sir Thomas 1410(?)-1471(?) 59
  Brief entry 33
Maltese, Michael 1909(?)-1981
  Obituary 24
Malvasi, Meg Greene 143
Malvern, Corinne 1905-1956 34
Malvern, Gladys (?)-1962 23
Mama G.
  See Davis, Grania
Mammano, Julie 1962- 202
  Earlier sketch in SATA 107
Mamonova, Tatyana 1943- 93
Manchel, Frank 1935- 10
Manchess, Gregory 1955- 203
Manchester, William (Raymond)
  1922-2004 65
Mandabach, Brian 1962(?)- 197
Mandel, Brett H. 1969- 108
Mandel, Peter 1957- 87
Mandel, Sally (Elizabeth) 1944- 64
Mandell, Muriel (Hortense Levin) 1921- 63
Manders, John 1957- 219
  Earlier sketch in SATA 175
Manes, Stephen 1949- 99
  Brief entry 40
  Earlier sketch in SATA 42
Manfred, Frederick (Feikema) 1912-1994 30
Mangin, Marie France 1940- 59
Mangione, Gerlando 1909-1998 6
  Obituary 104
Mangione, Jerre
  See Mangione, Gerlando
Mango, Karin N. 1936- 52
Mangurian, David 1938- 14
Mania, Cathy 1950- 102
Mania, Robert 1952- 102
Mania, Robert C., Jr.
  See Mania, Robert
Maniatty, Taramesha 1978- 92
Maniscalco, Joseph 1926- 10
Manley, Deborah 1932- 28
Manley, Seon 1921- 15
  See also CLR 3
  See also SAAS 2
Mann, Elizabeth 1948- 153
Mann, Josephine
  See Pullein-Thompson, Josephine (Mary
  Wedderburn)
Mann, Kenny 1946- 91
Mann, Pamela 1946- 91
Mann, Patrick
  See Waller, Leslie
Mann, Peggy
  See Houlton, Peggy Mann
Mannetti, Lisa 1953- 57
  Brief entry 51
Mannheim, Grete (Salomon) 1909-1986 10
Manniche, Lise 1943- 31
Manning, Jane K. 185
Manning, Maurie
  See Manning, Maurie J.
Manning, Maurie J. 211
Manning, Maurie Jo
  See Manning, Maurie J.
Manning, Mick 1959- 176
Manning, Rosemary 1911-1988 10
Manning, Sarra 162

Manning-Sanders, Ruth (Vernon)
　1895(?)-1988 73
　Obituary 57
　Earlier sketch in SATA 15
Mannion, Diane
　See Paterson, Diane
Mannis, Celeste Davidson 173
Mannon, Warwick
　See Hopkins, (Hector) Kenneth
Manos, Helen 199
Mansir, A. Richard 1932- 170
Manson, Ainslie Kertland 1938- 115
Manson, Beverlie 1945- 57
　Brief entry 44
Mantchev, Lisa 221
Mantha, John 1960- 217
Manthorpe, Helen 1958- 122
Mantinband, Gerda (B.) 1917- 74
Manton, Jo
　See Gittings, Jo (Grenville) Manton
Manuel, Lynn 1948- 179
　Earlier sketch in SATA 99
Manushkin, Fran 1942- 205
　Earlier sketches in SATA 7, 54, 93, 166
Manushkin, Frances
　See Manushkin, Fran
Man Without a Spleen, A
　See Chekhov, Anton
Many, Paul 1947- 210
Many, Paul A.
　See Many, Paul
Manzano, Sonia 1950- 167
Mapes, Mary A.
　See Ellison, Virginia H(owell)
Maple, Marilyn 1931- 80
Mappin, Strephyn 1956- 109
Mara, Barney
　See Roth, Arthur J(oseph)
Mara, Jeanette
　See Cebulash, Mel
Mara, Rachna
　See Gilmore, Rachna
Marais, Josef 1905-1978
　Obituary 24
Marasmus, Seymour
　See Rivoli, Mario
Marbach, Ethel
　See Pochocki, Ethel (Frances)
Marcal, Annette B.
　See Callaway, Bernice (Anne)
Marcelino
　See Agnew, Edith J(osephine)
Marcellino, Fred 1939-2001 118
　Obituary 127
　Earlier sketch in SATA 68
March, Carl
　See Fleischman, Sid
Marchant, Bessie 1862-1941
　See YABC 2
Marchant, Catherine
　See Cookson, Catherine (McMullen)
Marcher, Marion Walden 1890-1987 10
Marchesi, Stephen 1951- 114
Marchesi, Steve
　See Marchesi, Stephen
　and Older, Effin
　and Older, Jules
Marchetta, Melina 1965- 170
Marciano, John Bemelmans 1970- 167
　Earlier sketch in SATA 118
　See also CLR 93
Marco, Lou
　See Gottfried, Theodore Mark
Marcus, Leonard S. 1950- 187
　Earlier sketch in SATA 133
Marcus, Paul 1953- 82
Marcus, Rebecca B(rian) 1907- 9
Marcuse, Aida E. 1934- 89
Marek, Margot L. 1934(?)-1987
　Obituary 54
Maren, Julie 1970- 199

Margaret, Karla
　See Andersdatter, Karla M.
Margolin, Harriet
　See Ziefert, Harriet
Margolis, Jeffrey A. 1948- 108
Margolis, Leslie 187
Margolis, Richard J(ules) 1929-1991 86
　Obituary 67
　Earlier sketch in SATA 4
Margolis, Vivienne 1922- 46
Mariana
　See Foster, Marian Curtis
Marie, Geraldine 1949- 61
Mariner, Scott
　See Pohl, Frederik
Marino, Dorothy Bronson 1912- 14
Marino, Jan 1936- 114
Marino, Nan 216
Marino, Nick
　See Deming, Richard
Marino, Peter 1960- 179
Mario, Anna
　See Odgers, Sally Farrell
Marion, Henry
　See del Rey, Lester
Maris, Ron 71
　Brief entry 45
Mark, Jan 1943-2006 164
　Obituary 173
　Earlier sketches in SATA 22, 69, 114
　See also CLR 11
Mark, Janet Marjorie
　See Mark, Jan
Mark, Joan T. 1937- 122
Mark, Pauline (Dahlin) 1913-1997 14
Mark, Polly
　See Mark, Pauline (Dahlin)
Mark, Ted
　See Gottfried, Theodore Mark
Markel, Michelle 169
Marker, Sherry 1941- 76
Markert, Jennifer 1965- 83
Markert, Jenny
　See Markert, Jennifer
Markey, Kevin 1965- 215
Markham, Lynne 1947- 102
Markham, Marion M. 1929- 60
Markham, Wendy
　See Staub, Wendy Corsi
Markins, W. S.
　See Jenkins, Marie M(agdalen)
Markle, Sandra 1946- 218
　Brief entry 41
　Earlier sketches in SATA 57, 92, 148, 185
Markle, Sandra L.
　See Markle, Sandra
Marklew, Gilly 211
Marko, Katherine D(olores) 28
Markoosie
　See Patsauq, Markoosie
Marks, Alan 1957- 187
　Earlier sketches in SATA 77, 151
Marks, Burton 1930- 47
　Brief entry 43
Marks, Graham 158
Marks, Hannah K.
　See Trivelpiece, Laurel
Marks, J.
　See Highwater, Jamake (Mamake)
Marks, J(ames) M(acdonald) 1921- 13
Marks, Laurie J. 1957- 68
Marks, Margaret L. 1911(?)-1980
　Obituary 23
Marks, Mickey Klar -1986 12
Marks, Peter
　See Smith, Robert Kimmel
Marks, Rita 1938- 47
Marks, Stan(ley) 14
Marks-Highwater, J.
　See Highwater, Jamake (Mamake)
Markun, Patricia Maloney 1924- 15

Markusen, Bruce (Stanley Rodriguez)
　1965- 141
Marley, Louise 1952- 173
　Earlier sketch in SATA 120
Marlin, Hilda
　See Van Stockum, Hilda
Marlow, Layne 204
Marlow, Max
　See Nicole, Christopher (Robin)
Marlow, Susan K. 1953- 178
Marlowe, Amy Bell 67
　Earlier sketch in SATA 1
Marlowe, Jack
　See Deary, Terry
Marlowe, Tess
　See Glick, Ruth (Burtnick)
Marney, Dean 1952- 90
Marokvia, Artur 1909- 31
Marokvia, Mireille 1908-2008 5
　Obituary 197
Marokvia, Mireille Journet
　See Marokvia, Mireille
Marol, Jean-Claude 1946- 125
Marr, John S(tuart) 1940- 48
Marr, Melissa 1972- 189
Marric, J. J.
　See Butler, William Vivian
　and Creasey, John
Marrin, Albert 1936- 193
　Brief entry 43
　Earlier sketches in SATA 53, 90, 126
　See also CLR 53
Marriott, Alice Lee 1910-1992 31
　Obituary 71
Marriott, Janice 1946- 134
Marriott, Pat(ricia) 1920- 35
Marriott, Zoe 1982- 216
Marriott, Zoe Davina
　See Marriott, Zoe
Marroquin, Patricio
　See Markun, Patricia Maloney
Mars, W. T.
　See Mars, Witold Tadeusz J.
Mars, Witold Tadeusz J. 1912-1985 3
Marsden, Carolyn 1950- 212
　Autobiography Feature 212
　Earlier sketches in SATA 140, 175
Marsden, John 1950- 146
　Earlier sketches in SATA 66, 97
　See also CLR 34
　See also SAAS 22
Marsh, Carole 1946- 127
Marsh, Dave 1950- 66
Marsh, J. E.
　See Marshall, Evelyn
Marsh, James 1946- 73
Marsh, Jean
　See Marshall, Evelyn
Marsh, Joan F. 1923- 83
Marsh, Katherine 1974- 220
Marsh, Paul
　See Hopkins, (Hector) Kenneth
Marsh, Valerie 1954- 89
Marshall, Anthony D(ryden) 1924- 18
Marshall, Bonnie C. 1941- 141
　Earlier sketch in SATA 18
Marshall, Bridget M(ary) 1974- 103
Marshall, (Sarah) Catherine (Wood)
　1914-1983 2
　Obituary 34
Marshall, Douglas
　See McClintock, Marshall
Marshall, Edmund
　See Hopkins, (Hector) Kenneth
Marshall, Edward
　See Marshall, James
Marshall, Evelyn 1897-1991 11
Marshall, Felicity 1950- 116
Marshall, Garry 1934- 60
Marshall, H. H.
　See Jahn, Michael

Author Index

Marshall, James 1942-1992 75
    Earlier sketches in SATA 6, 51
    See also CLR 21
Marshall, James Edward
    See Marshall, James
Marshall, James Vance
    See Payne, Donald Gordon
Marshall, Janet (Perry) 1938- 97
Marshall, Jeff
    See Laycock, George (Edwin)
Marshall, Kim
    See Marshall, Michael (Kimbrough)
Marshall, Michael (Kimbrough) 1948- 37
Marshall, Percy
    See Young, Percy M(arshall)
Marshall, S(amuel) L(yman) A(twood)
    1900-1977 21
Marsoli, Lisa Ann 1958- 101
    Brief entry 53
Marsten, Richard
    See Hunter, Evan
Marston, Elsa 1933- 156
Marston, Hope Irvin 1935- 127
    Earlier sketch in SATA 31
Marszalek, John F. 1939- 167
Marszalek, John Francis, Jr.
    See Marszalek, John F.
Marszalek, John Francis 1939-
    See Marszalek, John F.
Martchenko, Michael 1942- 154
    Earlier sketches in SATA 50, 95
Martel, Aimee
    See Thurlo, Aimee
    and Thurlo, David
Martel, Suzanne 1924- 99
Martignoni, Margaret E. 1908(?)-1974
    Obituary 27
Martin, Ann M. 1955- 192
    Brief entry 41
    Earlier sketches in SATA 44, 70, 126
    See also CLR 32
Martin, Bill, Jr. 1916-2004 145
    Brief entry 40
    Earlier sketches in SATA 40, 67
    See also CLR 97
Martin, Charles E(lmer)
    See Mastrangelo, Charles E(lmer)
Martin, Christopher
    See Hoyt, Edwin P(almer), Jr.
Martin, C.K. Kelly 207
Martin, Claire 1933- 76
Martin, Courtney Autumn 1984- 205
Martin, David Stone 1913-1992 39
Martin, Donald
    See Honig, Donald
Martin, Dorothy 1921- 47
Martin, Dorothy McKay
    See Martin, Dorothy
Martin, Eugene 1
Martin, Eva M. 1939- 65
Martin, Frances M(cEntee) 1906-1998 36
Martin, Francesca 1947- 101
Martin, Fred 1948- 119
Martin, Fredric
    See Christopher, Matt(hew Frederick)
Martin, George Raymond Richard
    See Martin, George R.R.
Martin, George R.R. 1948- 118
Martin, J(ohn) P(ercival) 1880(?)-1966 15
Martin, Jacqueline Briggs 1945- 188
    Earlier sketches in SATA 98, 149
Martin, Jane Read 1957- 84
Martin, Jeremy
    See Levin, Marcia Obrasky
Martin, Les
    See Schulman, L(ester) M(artin)
Martin, Linda 1961- 82
Martin, Lynne 1923- 21
Martin, Marcia
    See Levin, Marcia Obrasky
Martin, Marvin 1926- 126

Martin, Melanie
    See Pellowski, Michael (Joseph)
Martin, Nancy
    See Salmon, Annie Elizabeth
Martin, Patricia 200
Martin, Patricia A.
    See Martin, Patricia
Martin, Patricia Miles 1899-1986 43
    Obituary 48
    Earlier sketch in SATA 1
Martin, Peter
    See Chaundler, Christine
Martin, Rafe 1946- 175
Martin, Rene 1891-1977 42
    Obituary 20
Martin, Rupert (Claude) 1905- 31
Martin, S. R.
    See Mappin, Strephyn
Martin, Stefan 1936- 32
Martin, Vicky
    See Storey, Victoria Carolyn
Martin, Webber
    See Silverberg, Robert
Martin, Wendy
    See Martini, Teri
Martin, William Ivan, Jr.
    See Martin, Bill, Jr.
Martineau, Diane 1940- 178
Martineau, Harriet 1802-1876
    See YABC 2
Martinet, Jeanne 1958- 80
Martinez, Agnes 167
Martinez, Arturo O. 1933- 192
Martinez, Claudia Guadalupe 1978- 214
Martinez, Ed(ward) 1954- 98
Martinez, Elizabeth Coonrod 1954- 85
Martinez, Victor 1954- 95
Martini, Angela 1972(?)- 223
Martini, Teri 1930- 3
Martini, Therese
    See Martini, Teri
Martino, Alfred C. 1964- 174
Martinson, Janis
    See Herbert, Janis
Martinusen, Cindy
    See Martinusen-Coloma, Cindy
Martinusen, Cindy McCormick
    See Martinusen-Coloma, Cindy
Martinusen-Coloma, Cindy 1970- 218
Marton, Jirina 1946- 144
    Earlier sketch in SATA 95
Marton, Pierre
    See Stone, Peter
Martson, Del
    See Lupoff, Richard A(llen)
Martyr, Paula (Jane)
    See Lawford, Paula Jane
Maruki, Toshi 1912-2000 112
    See also CLR 19
Marvin, Isabel R(idout) 1924- 84
Marx, Patricia Windschill
    See Marx, Trish
Marx, Robert F(rank) 1936- 24
Marx, Trish 1948- 202
    Earlier sketches in SATA 112, 160
Marzani, Carl (Aldo) 1912-1994 12
Marzollo, Jean 1942- 190
    Autobiography Feature 190
    Earlier sketches in SATA 29, 77, 130
    See also SAAS 15
Masefield, John (Edward) 1878-1967 19
Masiello, Ralph 1961- 214
Masoff, Joy 1951- 118
Mason, Adrienne 1962- 163
Mason, Cherie 170
Mason, Edwin A. 1905-1979
    Obituary 32
Mason, Ernst
    See Pohl, Frederik
Mason, F(rancis) van Wyck 1901-1978 3
    Obituary 26

Mason, Frank W.
    See Mason, F(rancis) van Wyck
Mason, George Frederick 1904-2000 14
Mason, Miriam E(vangeline) 1900-1973 2
    Obituary 26
Mason, Prue 195
Mason, Simon 1962- 178
Mason, Tally
    See Derleth, August (William)
Mason, Van Wyck
    See Mason, F(rancis) van Wyck
Mass, Wendy 1967- 196
    Earlier sketch in SATA 158
Mass, William
    See Gibson, William
Masse, Josee 221
Masselman, George 1897-1971 19
Massey, Misty 212
Massie, Dianne Redfield 1938- 125
    Earlier sketch in SATA 16
Massie, Elizabeth 108
Massini, Sarah 213
Masson, Sophie 1959- 179
    Earlier sketch in SATA 133
Masters, Anthony (Richard) 1940-2003 112
    Obituary 145
Masters, Kelly R(ay) 1897-1987 3
Masters, Mildred 1932- 42
Masters, William
    See Cousins, Margaret
Masters, Zeke
    See Bensen, Donald R.
    and Goulart, Ron
Mastrangelo, Charles E(lmer) 1910-1995 70
    Earlier sketch in SATA 69
Masuda, Takeshi 1944- 56
Matas, Carol 1949- 194
    Autobiography Feature 112
    Earlier sketch in SATA 93
    See also CLR 52
Matchette, Katharine E. 1941- 38
Math, Irwin 1940- 42
Mathabane, Mark 1960- 123
Mather, Kirtley F(letcher) 1888-1978 65
Mathers, Petra 1945- 176
    Earlier sketch in SATA 119
    See also CLR 76
Matheson, Richard (Christian) 1953- 119
Matheson, Shirlee Smith 1942- 155
Mathews, Eleanor
    See Mathews, Ellie
Mathews, Ellie 1946(?)- 193
Mathews, Janet 1914-1992 41
Mathews, Judith
    See Goldberger, Judith M.
Mathews, Louise
    See Tooke, Louise Mathews
Mathiesen, Egon 1907-1976
    Obituary 28
Mathieu, Joe 1949- 185
    Brief entry 36
    Earlier sketches in SATA 43, 94
Mathieu, Joseph P.
    See Mathieu, Joe
Mathis, Sharon Bell 1937- 58
    Earlier sketch in SATA 7
    See also CLR 147
    See also SAAS 3
Matlin, Marlee 1965- 181
Matlin, Marlee Beth
    See Matlin, Marlee
Matloff, Gregory 1945- 73
Matott, Justin 1961- 109
Matranga, Frances Carfi 1922- 78
Matray, James I. 1948- 161
Matray, James Irving
    See Matray, James I.
Matson, Emerson N(els) 1926- 12
Matsui, Tadashi 1926- 8
Matsuno, Masako
    See Kobayashi, Masako Matsuno

Matsuoka, Mei 1981- 192
Matte, (Encarnacion) L'Enc 1936- 22
Mattern, Joanne 1963- 122
Mattheson, Jenny 180
Matthew, James
  See Barrie, J. M.
Matthews, Aline
  See De Wire, Elinor
Matthews, Andrew 1948- 138
Matthews, Caitlin 1952- 122
Matthews, Cecily 1945- 221
Matthews, Downs 1925- 71
Matthews, Elizabeth 1978- 194
Matthews, Ellen
  See Bache, Ellyn
Matthews, Ellen 1950- 28
Matthews, Harold Downs
  See Matthews, Downs
Matthews, Jacklyn Meek
  See Meek, Jacklyn O'Hanlon
Matthews, John (Kentigern) 1948- 116
Matthews, L. S. 183
Matthews, Laura S.
  See Matthews, L. S.
Matthews, Liz
  See Pellowski, Michael (Joseph)
Matthews, Morgan
  See Pellowski, Michael (Joseph)
Matthews, Nicola
  See Browne, N.M.
Matthews, Patricia 1927-2006 28
Matthews, Patricia Anne
  See Matthews, Patricia
Matthews, Tina 1961- 190
Matthews, Tom L.
  See Lalicki, Tom
Matthews, William Henry III 1919- 45
  Brief entry 28
Matthiessen, Peter 1927- 27
Mattingley, Christobel (Rosemary) 1931- 85
  Earlier sketch in SATA *37*
  See also CLR *24*
  See also SAAS *18*
Matulay, Laszlo 1912- 43
Matus, Greta 1938- 12
Matzigkeit, Philip 220
Maugham, W. S.
  See Maugham, W. Somerset
Maugham, W. Somerset 1874-1965 54
Maugham, William S.
  See Maugham, W. Somerset
Maugham, William Somerset
  See Maugham, W. Somerset
Maurer, Diane Philippoff
  See Maurer-Mathison, Diane V(ogel)
Maurer, Diane Vogel
  See Maurer-Mathison, Diane V(ogel)
Maurer-Mathison, Diane V(ogel) 1944- 89
Mauser, Pat Rhoads
  See McCord, Patricia
Mauser, Patricia Rhoads
  See McCord, Patricia
Maves, Mary Carolyn 1916- 10
Maves, Paul B(enjamin) 1913-1994 10
Mavor, Salley 1955- 125
Mawicke, Tran 1911- 15
Max 1906-1989
  See Diop, Birago (Ismael)
Max, Peter 1939- 45
Maxon, Anne
  See Best, (Evangel) Allena Champlin
Maxwell, Arthur S. 1896-1970 11
Maxwell, B.E. 1957- 211
Maxwell, Bruce E.
  See Maxwell, B.E.
Maxwell, Edith 1923- 7
Maxwell, Gavin 1914-1969 65
Maxwell, Katie
  See MacAlister, Katie
Maxwell, William (Keepers, Jr.) 1908-2000
  Obituary 128

Maxwell-Hyslop, Miranda 1968- 154
May, Charles Paul 1920- 4
May, Elaine Tyler 1947- 120
May, J. C.
  See May, Julian
May, Julian 1931- 11
May, Robert Lewis 1905-1976
  Obituary 27
May, Robert Stephen 1929-1996 46
May, Robin
  See May, Robert Stephen
Mayall, Beth 171
Mayberry, Florence V(irginia) Wilson 10
Maybury, Richard J. 1946- 72
Maybury, Rick
  See Maybury, Richard J.
Maydak, Michael S. 1952- 220
Mayer, Agatha
  See Maher, Ramona
Mayer, Albert Ignatius, Jr. 1906-1994
  Obituary 29
Mayer, Ann M(argaret) 1938- 14
Mayer, Bill 200
Mayer, Danuta 1958- 117
Mayer, Hannelore Valencak 1929- 42
Mayer, Jane Rothschild 1903-2001 38
Mayer, Marianna 1945- 132
  Earlier sketches in SATA *32, 83*
Mayer, Mercer 1943- 137
  Earlier sketches in SATA *16, 32, 73, 129*
  See also CLR *11*
Mayerson, Charlotte Leon 36
Mayerson, Evelyn Wilde 1935- 55
Mayfield, Katherine 1958- 118
Mayfield, Sue 1963- 146
  Earlier sketch in SATA *72*
Mayhar, Ardath 1930- 38
Mayhew, James 1964- 204
  Earlier sketches in SATA *85, 149*
Maynard, Olga 1920- 40
Mayne, William 1928-2010 122
  Earlier sketches in SATA *6, 68*
  See also CLR *123*
  See also SAAS *11*
Mayne, William James Carter
  See Mayne, William
Maynes, J. O. Rocky, Jr.
  See Maynes, J. Oscar, Jr.
Maynes, J. Oscar, Jr. 1929- 38
Mayo, Gretchen Will 1936- 163
  Earlier sketch in SATA *84*
Mayo, Margaret 1935- 165
  Earlier sketches in SATA *38, 96*
Mayo, Margaret Mary
  See Mayo, Margaret
Mayr, Diane 1949- 197
Mays, Lucinda L(a Bella) 1924- 49
Mays, (Lewis) Victor (Jr.) 1927- 5
Mazellan, Ron 210
Mazer, Anne 1953- 192
  Earlier sketches in SATA *67, 105*
Mazer, Harry 1925- 167
  Earlier sketches in SATA *31, 67, 105*
  See also CLR *16*
  See also SAAS *11*
Mazer, Norma Fox 1931-2009 198
  Earlier sketches in SATA *24, 67, 105, 168*
  See also CLR *23*
  See also SAAS *1*
Mazille, Capucine 1953- 96
Mazo, Michael 223
Mazza, Adriana 1928- 19
Mazzio, Joann 1926- 74
Mbugua, Kioi Wa 1962- 83
McAfee, Carol 1955- 81
McAllister, Amanda
  See Dowdell, Dorothy (Florence) Karns
  and Hager, Jean
  and Meaker, Eloise
McAllister, Angela 182

McAllister, Margaret I. 1956- 169
  Earlier sketch in SATA *117*
McAllister, M.I.
  See McAllister, Margaret I.
McArdle, Paula 1971- 198
McArthur, Nancy 96
McAvoy, Jim 1972- 142
McBain, Ed
  See Hunter, Evan
McBain, Georgina 189
McBratney, Sam 1943- 203
  Earlier sketches in SATA *89, 164*
  See also CLR *44*
McBrier, Michael
  See Older, Effin
  and Older, Jules
McCafferty, Jim 1954- 84
McCaffery, Janet 1936- 38
McCaffrey, Anne 1926- 152
  Autobiography Feature 152
  Earlier sketches in SATA *8, 70, 116*
  See also CLR *130*
  See also SAAS *11*
McCaffrey, Anne Inez
  See McCaffrey, Anne
McCaffrey, Mary
  See Szudek, Agnes S(usan) P(hilomena)
McCain, Becky Ray 1954- 138
McCain, Murray (David, Jr.) 1926-1981 7
  Obituary 29
McCall, Bruce 1935(?)- 209
McCall, Edith (Sansom) 1911- 6
McCall, Virginia Nielsen 1909-2000 13
McCall, Wendell
  See Pearson, Ridley
McCall Smith, Alexander
  See Smith, Alexander McCall
McCallum, Phyllis
  See Koch, Phyllis (Mae) McCallum
McCallum, Stephen 1960- 91
McCampbell, Darlene Z. 1942- 83
McCann, Edson
  See del Rey, Lester
  and Pohl, Frederik
McCann, Gerald 1916- 41
McCann, Helen 1948- 75
McCannon, Dindga 41
McCants, William D. 1961- 82
McCarter, Neely Dixon 1929- 47
McCarthy, Agnes 1933- 4
McCarthy, Colin (John) 1951- 77
McCarthy, Mary 1951- 203
McCarthy, Meghan 199
  Earlier sketch in SATA *168*
McCarthy, Ralph F. 1950- 139
McCarthy-Tucker, Sherri N. 1958- 83
McCarty, Peter 1966- 182
McCarty, Rega Kramer 1904-1986 10
McCaslin, Nellie 1914-2005 12
McCaughrean, Geraldine 1951- 173
  Earlier sketches in SATA *87, 139*
  See also CLR *38*
McCaughren, Tom 1936- 75
McCauley, Adam 1965- 209
  Earlier sketch in SATA *128*
McCay, (Zenas) Winsor 1869-1934 134
  Earlier sketch in SATA *41*
McClafferty, Carla Killough 1958- 137
McClary, Jane Stevenson 1919-1990
  Obituary 64
McCleery, Patsy R. 1925- 133
  Earlier sketch in SATA *88*
McClelland, Susan 214
McClements, George 196
McClintock, Barbara 1955- 213
  Earlier sketches in SATA *57, 95, 146*
McClintock, Marshall 1906-1967 3
McClintock, May Garelick
  See Garelick, May
McClintock, Mike
  See McClintock, Marshall

McClintock, Norah *178*
McClintock, Theodore 1902-1971 .... *14*
McClinton, Leon 1933- *11*
McCloskey, Kevin 1951- *79*
McCloskey, (John) Robert 1914-2003 .... *100*
  Obituary *146*
  Earlier sketches in SATA *2, 39*
  See also CLR *7*
McCloy, James F(loyd) 1941- *59*
McClung, Robert M(arshall) 1916- *135*
  Earlier sketches in SATA *2, 68*
  See also CLR *11*
  See also SAAS *15*
McClure, Gillian Mary 1948- *31*
McClure, Nikki *218*
McColley, Kevin 1961- *80*
  See also SAAS *23*
McConduit, Denise Walter 1950- *89*
McConnell, James Douglas Rutherford
  1915-1988 .... *40*
  Obituary *56*
McCord, Anne 1942- *41*
McCord, David (Thompson Watson)
  1897-1997 .... *18*
  Obituary *96*
  See also CLR *9*
McCord, Jean 1924- *34*
McCord, Pat Mauser
  See McCord, Patricia
McCord, Patricia 1943- *159*
  Earlier sketch in SATA *37*
McCord, Patricia Sue Rhoads Mauser
  See McCord, Patricia
McCormack, Caren McNelly *217*
McCormick, Brooks
  See Adams, William Taylor
McCormick, Dell J. 1892-1949 .... *19*
McCormick, (George) Donald (King)
  1911-1998 .... *14*
McCormick, Edith (Joan) 1934- *30*
McCormick, Kimberly A. 1960- *153*
McCormick, Patricia 1956- *181*
  Earlier sketch in SATA *128*
McCourt, Edward (Alexander) 1907-1972
  Obituary *28*
McCourt, Lisa 1964- *214*
  Earlier sketches in SATA *117, 159*
McCourt, Malachy 1931- *126*
McCoy, Glenn 1965- *212*
McCoy, Iola Fuller *3*
McCoy, J(oseph) J(erome) 1917- *8*
McCoy, Karen Kawamoto 1953- *82*
McCoy, Lois (Rich) 1941- *38*
McCrady, Lady 1951- *16*
McCrea, James (Craig, Jr.) 1920- *3*
McCrea, Ruth (Pirman) 1921- *3*
McCreigh, James
  See Pohl, Frederik
McCrumb, Sharyn 1948- *109*
McCue, Lisa 1959- *212*
  Earlier sketches in SATA *65, 177*
McCue, Lisa Emiline
  See McCue, Lisa
McCullen, Andrew
  See Arthur, Robert, (Jr.)
McCullers, Carson 1917-1967 .... *27*
McCullers, Lula Carson Smith
  See McCullers, Carson
McCulloch, Derek (Ivor Breashur) 1897-1967
  Obituary *29*
McCulloch, John Tyler
  See Burroughs, Edgar Rice
McCulloch, Sarah
  See Ure, Jean
McCullough, David 1933- *62*
McCullough, David Gaub
  See McCullough, David
McCullough, Frances Monson 1938- *8*
McCullough, Sharon Pierce 1943- *131*
McCully, Emily Arnold
  See Arnold, Emily

McCune, Dan
  See Haas, Dorothy F.
McCunn, Ruthanne Lum 1946- *63*
McCurdy, Michael (Charles) 1942- *147*
  Earlier sketches in SATA *13, 82*
McCusker, Paul 1958- *220*
McCutcheon, Elsie (Mary Jackson) 1937- ... *60*
McCutcheon, John 1952- *97*
McDaniel, Becky Bring 1953- *61*
McDaniel, Lurlene 1944- *218*
  Earlier sketches in SATA *71, 146*
McDaniels, Pellom III 1968- *121*
McDaniels, Preston 1952- *192*
McDearmon, Kay *20*
McDermott, Beverly Brodsky 1941- *11*
McDermott, Eleni *156*
McDermott, Gerald (Edward) 1941- *163*
  Earlier sketches in SATA *16, 74*
  See also CLR *9*
McDermott, Michael 1962- *76*
McDevitt, Jack 1935- *155*
  Earlier sketch in SATA *94*
McDevitt, John Charles
  See McDevitt, Jack
McDole, Carol
  See Farley, Carol (J.)
McDonald, Collin 1943- *79*
McDonald, Gerald D(oan) 1905-1970 .... *3*
McDonald, Jamie
  See Heide, Florence Parry
McDonald, Janet 1953-2007 .... *204*
  Earlier sketch in SATA *148*
McDonald, Jill (Masefield) 1927-1982 .... *13*
  Obituary *29*
McDonald, Joyce 1946- *164*
  Earlier sketch in SATA *101*
McDonald, Lucile Saunders 1898-1992 .... *10*
McDonald, Mary Ann 1956- *84*
McDonald, Megan 1958- *202*
  Autobiography Feature *151*
  Earlier sketches in SATA *67, 99, 148, 151*
  See also CLR *94*
McDonald, Meme 1954- *112*
McDonald, Mercedes 1956- *169*
  Earlier sketch in SATA *97*
McDonald, Rae A. 1952- *201*
McDonell, Chris 1960- *138*
McDonnell, Christine 1949- *115*
  Earlier sketch in SATA *34*
McDonnell, Flora (Mary) 1963- *146*
  Earlier sketch in SATA *90*
McDonnell, Kathleen 1947- *186*
McDonnell, Lois Eddy 1914-2001 .... *10*
McDonnell, Patrick 1956- *221*
  Earlier sketch in SATA *179*
McDonough, Yona Zeldis 1957- *73*
McDowell, Marilyn Taylor *217*
McElligott, Matt 1968- *196*
  Earlier sketch in SATA *135*
McElligott, Matthew
  See McElligott, Matt
McElmeel, Sharron L. 1942- *128*
McElmurry, Jill *198*
  Earlier sketch in SATA *159*
McElrath, William N. 1932- *65*
McElrath-Eslick, Lori 1960- *204*
  Earlier sketch in SATA *96*
McEntee, Dorothy (Layng) 1902- *37*
McEvoy, Anne *214*
McEwen, Katharine *183*
McEwen, Robert (Lindley) 1926-1980
  Obituary *23*
McFadden, Kevin Christopher
  See Pike, Christopher
McFall, Christie 1918- *12*
McFall, Gardner 1952- *183*
McFarlan, Donald M(aitland) 1915- *59*
McFarland, Henry "Hammer"
  See McFarland, Henry O.
McFarland, Henry O. 1934- *143*
McFarland, Kenton D(ean) 1920- *11*

McFarland, Martha
  See Smith-Ankrom, M. E.
McFarlane, Leslie 1902-1977 .... *100*
  Earlier sketches in SATA *31, 1, 65, 67*
  See also CLR *118*
McFarlane, Leslie Charles
  See McFarlane, Leslie
McFarlane, Peter 1940- *95*
McFarlane, Peter William
  See McFarlane, Peter
McFarlane, Sheryl P. 1954- *86*
McFarlane, Todd 1961- *117*
McGaw, Jessie Brewer 1913-1997 .... *10*
McGee, Barbara 1943- *6*
McGee, Marni *163*
McGhee, Alison 1960- *196*
McGhee, Alison R.
  See McGhee, Alison
McGhee, Holly M.
  See Durand, Hallie
McGiffin, (Lewis) Lee (Shaffer) 1908-1978 ... *1*
McGill, Alice *159*
McGill, Marci
  See Balterman, Marcia Ridlon
McGill, Marci Ridlon
  See Balterman, Marcia Ridlon
McGill, Ormond 1913- *92*
McGinley, Jerry 1948- *116*
McGinley, Phyllis 1905-1978 .... *44*
  Obituary *24*
  Earlier sketch in SATA *2*
McGinnis, Lila S(prague) 1924- *44*
McGinty, Alice B. 1963- *202*
  Earlier sketch in SATA *134*
McGivern, Justin 1985- *129*
McGivern, Maureen Daly
  See Daly, Maureen
McGivern, Maureen Patricia Daly
  See Daly, Maureen
McGough, Elizabeth (Hemmes) 1934- *33*
McGovern, Ann 1930- *132*
  Earlier sketches in SATA *8, 69, 70*
  See also CLR *50*
  See also SAAS *17*
McGowen, Thomas E. 1927- *109*
  Earlier sketch in SATA *2*
McGowen, Tom
  See McGowen, Thomas E.
McGrady, Mike 1933- *6*
McGrath, Barbara Barbieri 1953- *169*
  Earlier sketch in SATA *108*
McGrath, Robin 1949- *121*
McGrath, Thomas (Matthew) 1916-1990 ..... *41*
  Obituary *66*
McGraw, Eloise Jarvis 1915-2000 .... *67*
  Obituary *123*
  Earlier sketch in SATA *1*
  See also SAAS *6*
McGraw, William Corbin 1916-1999 .... *3*
McGreal, Elizabeth
  See Yates, Elizabeth
McGregor, Barbara 1959- *82*
McGregor, Craig 1933- *8*
McGregor, Iona 1929- *25*
McGrory, Anik *193*
McGuffey, Alexander Hamilton 1816-1896 . *60*
McGuigan, Mary Ann 1949- *106*
McGuire, Edna 1899- *13*
McGuire, Leslie (Sarah) 1945- *94*
  Brief entry *45*
  Earlier sketch in SATA *52*
McGuire, Robert *187*
McGuirk, Leslie (A.) 1960- *152*
McGurk, Slater
  See Roth, Arthur J(oseph)
McHargue, Georgess 1941- *77*
  Earlier sketch in SATA *4*
  See also CLR *2*
  See also SAAS *5*
McHenry, E.B. 1963(?)- *193*

McHugh, (Berit) Elisabet 1941- *55*
   Brief entry *44*
McIlvaine, Jane
   See McClary, Jane Stevenson
McIlwraith, Maureen Mollie Hunter
   See Hunter, Mollie
McInerney, Judith W(hitelock) 1945- *49*
   Brief entry *46*
McInerny, Ralph 1929-2010 .... *93*
McInerny, Ralph Matthew
   See McInerny, Ralph
McKaughan, Larry (Scott) 1941- *75*
McKay, Donald 1895- *45*
McKay, Hilary 1959- *208*
   Earlier sketches in SATA *92, 145*
   See also SAAS *23*
McKay, Hilary Jane
   See McKay, Hilary
McKay, Lawrence, Jr. 1948- *114*
McKay, Robert W. 1921- *15*
McKay, Sharon E. 1954- *165*
McKay, Simon
   See Nicole, Christopher (Robin)
McKean, Dave 1963- *197*
McKean, David Jeff
   See McKean, Dave
McKeating, Eileen 1957- *81*
McKee, David (John) 1935- *158*
   Earlier sketches in SATA *70, 107*
   See also CLR *38*
McKee, Tim 1970- *111*
McKeever, Marcia
   See Laird, Jean E(louise)
McKellar, Danica 1975- *213*
McKelvey, Carole A. 1942- *78*
McKelvy, Charles 1950- *124*
McKendrick, Melveena (Christine) 1941- *55*
McKendry, Joe 1972- *170*
McKenna, Colleen O'Shaughnessy 1948- .. *136*
   Earlier sketch in SATA *76*
McKenzie, Dorothy Clayton 1910-1981
   Obituary *28*
McKenzie, Ellen Kindt 1928- *80*
McKernan, Victoria 1957- *171*
McKie, Robin *112*
McKillip, Patricia A. 1948- *174*
   Earlier sketches in SATA *30, 80, 126*
McKillip, Patricia Anne
   See McKillip, Patricia A.
McKim, Audrey Margaret 1909-1999 .... *47*
McKimmie, Chris *194*
McKinley, Jennifer Carolyn Robin
   See McKinley, Robin
McKinley, Robin 1952- *195*
   Brief entry *32*
   Earlier sketches in SATA *50, 89, 130*
   See also CLR *127*
McKinney, Barbara Shaw 1951- *116*
McKinney, Nadine 1938- *91*
McKinty, Adrian *186*
McKissack, Fredrick L. 1939- *162*
   Brief entry *53*
   Earlier sketches in SATA *73, 117*
   See also CLR *55*
McKissack, Fredrick Lemuel
   See McKissack, Fredrick L.
McKissack, Patricia C. 1944- *195*
   Earlier sketches in SATA *51, 73, 117, 162*
   See also CLR *129*
McKissack, Patricia L'Ann Carwell
   See McKissack, Patricia C.
McKissack and McKissack
   See McKissack, Fredrick L.
   and McKissack, Patricia C.
McKown, Robin (?)-1976 .... *6*
McKy, Katie 1956- *184*
McLaren, Chesley *213*
McLaren, Clemence 1938- *158*
   Earlier sketch in SATA *105*
McLaughlin, Frank 1934- *73*
McLaughlin, Lauren *209*

McLaurin, Anne 1953- *27*
McLean, Andrew 1946- *172*
   Earlier sketch in SATA *113*
McLean, J. Sloan
   See Gillette, Virginia M(ary)
   and Wunsch, Josephine (McLean)
McLean, Jacqueline
   See Kolosov, Jacqueline
McLean, Janet 1946- *113*
McLean, Kathryn (Anderson) 1909-1966 .... *9*
McLean, Virginia Overton 1946- *90*
McLean-Carr, Carol 1948- *122*
McLeish, Kenneth 1940-1997 .... *35*
McLenighan, Valjean 1947- *46*
   Brief entry *40*
McLennan, Connie *171*
McLennan, Will
   See Wisler, G(ary) Clifton
McLeod, Bob 1951- *173*
McLeod, Chum 1955- *95*
McLeod, Emilie Warren 1926-1982 .... *23*
   Obituary *31*
McLeod, Kirsty
   See Hudson, (Margaret) Kirsty
McLeod, Margaret Vail
   See Holloway, Teresa (Bragunier)
McLerran, Alice 1933- *137*
   Earlier sketch in SATA *68*
McLimans, David 1949- *182*
McLoughlin, John C. 1949- *47*
McMahon, Bob 1956- *208*
McManus, Patrick F. 1933- *46*
McManus, Patrick Francis
   See McManus, Patrick F.
McMeekin, Clark
   See McMeekin, Isabel McLennan
McMeekin, Isabel McLennan 1895-1973 .... *3*
McMenemy, Sarah 1965- *156*
McMillan, Bruce 1947- *192*
   Earlier sketches in SATA *22, 70, 129*
   See also CLR *47*
McMillan, Naomi
   See Grimes, Nikki
McMorey, James L.
   See Moyer, Terry J.
McMorrow, Annalisa 1969- *104*
McMullan, Jim 1934- *150*
   Earlier sketch in SATA *87*
McMullan, K. H.
   See McMullan, Kate
McMullan, Kate 1947- *189*
   Brief entry *48*
   Earlier sketches in SATA *52, 87, 132*
McMullan, Kate Hall
   See McMullan, Kate
McMullan, Margaret 1960- *203*
McMurtrey, Martin A(loysias) 1921- *21*
McNabb, Linda 1963- *147*
McNair, Kate *3*
McNair, Sylvia 1924-2002 .... *74*
McNamara, Margaret C(raig) 1915-1981
   Obituary *24*
McNaught, Harry *32*
McNaughton, Colin 1951- *211*
   Earlier sketches in SATA *39, 92, 134*
   See also CLR *54*
McNaughton, Janet 1953- *162*
   Earlier sketch in SATA *110*
McNeal, Laura *194*
McNeal, Tom *194*
McNeely, Jeannette 1918- *25*
McNeer, May (Yonge) 1902-1994 .... *81*
   Earlier sketch in SATA *1*
McNeese, Tim 1953- *139*
McNeill, Janet
   See Alexander, Janet
McNicholas, Shelagh *191*
McNickle, D'Arcy 1904-1977
   Obituary *22*
McNickle, William D'Arcy
   See McNickle, D'Arcy

McNicoll, Sylvia (Marilyn) 1954- *113*
   See also CLR *99*
McNulty, Faith 1918-2005 .... *168*
   Earlier sketches in SATA *12, 84, 139*
McPhail, David 1940- *219*
   Brief entry *32*
   Earlier sketches in SATA *47, 81, 140, 183*
McPhail, David M.
   See McPhail, David
McPhail, David Michael
   See McPhail, David
McPhee, Norma H. 1928- *95*
McPhee, Peter 1957- *214*
McPhee, Richard B(yron) 1934- *41*
McPherson, James M. 1936- *141*
   Earlier sketch in SATA *16*
McPherson, James Munro
   See McPherson, James M.
McQueen, Lucinda 1950- *58*
   Brief entry *48*
McQueen, Mildred Hark 1908-1978 .... *12*
McQuillan, Mary *200*
McRae, Russell (William) 1934- *63*
McShean, Gordon 1936- *41*
Mc Swigan, Marie 1907-1962 .... *24*
McTavish, Sandy
   See Eyerly, Jeannette
McVeity, Jen *148*
McVey, Vicki 1946- *80*
McVicker, Charles (Taggart) 1930- *39*
McVicker, Chuck
   See McVicker, Charles (Taggart)
McVoy, Terra Elan *220*
McWhirter, A(lan) Ross 1925-1975 .... *37*
   Obituary *31*
McWhirter, Norris (Dewar) 1925-2004 .... *37*
McWilliam, Howard 1977- *219*
McWilliams, Karen 1943- *65*
Mdurvwa, Hajara E. 1962- *92*
Meacham, Margaret 1952- *203*
   Earlier sketch in SATA *95*
Meachum, Virginia 1918- *133*
   Earlier sketch in SATA *87*
Mead, Alice 1952- *146*
   Earlier sketch in SATA *94*
Mead, Margaret 1901-1978
   Obituary *20*
Mead, Russell (M., Jr.) 1935- *10*
Mead, Stella (?)-1981
   Obituary *27*
Meade, Ellen
   See Roddick, Ellen
Meade, Holly *207*
Meade, Marion 1934- *127*
   Earlier sketch in SATA *23*
Meader, Stephen W(arren) 1892-1977 .... *1*
Meadmore, Susan
   See Sallis, Susan (Diana)
Meadow, Charles T(roub) 1929- *23*
Meadowcroft, Enid LaMonte
   See Wright, Enid Meadowcroft (LaMonte)
Meadows, Daisy
   See Chapman, Linda
Meadows, Graham (W.) 1934- *161*
Meadows, Michelle *202*
Meaker, M. J.
   See Meaker, Marijane
Meaker, Marijane 1927- *160*
   Autobiography Feature *111*
   Earlier sketches in SATA *20, 61, 99*
   See also CLR *29*
   See also SAAS *1*
Meaker, Marijane Agnes
   See Meaker, Marijane
Means, Florence Crannell 1891-1980 .... *1*
   Obituary *25*
   See also CLR *56*
Mearian, Judy Frank 1936- *49*
Mebus, Scott 1974- *216*
Mecca, Judy Truesdell 1955- *127*
Mechling, Lauren 1978(?)- *194*

Mechling, Lauren 1978(?)- *194*
Mechner, Jordan 1964- *205*
Medary, Marjorie 1890-1980 .... *14*
Meddaugh, Susan 1944- *176*
  Earlier sketches in SATA *29, 84, 125*
Medearis, Angela Shelf 1956- *123*
  Earlier sketch in SATA *72*
Medearis, Mary 1915- *5*
Medina, Jane 1953- *167*
  Earlier sketch in SATA *122*
Medina, Meg 1963- *212*
Medina, Nico 1982- *193*
Medlicott, Mary 1946- *88*
Mee, Charles L., Jr. 1938- *72*
  Earlier sketch in SATA *8*
Meehan, Kierin *218*
Meehl, Brian *204*
Meek, Jacklyn O'Hanlon 1933- *51*
  Brief entry *34*
Meek, S(terner St.) P(aul) 1894-1972
  Obituary *28*
Meeker, Clare Hodgson 1952- *96*
Meeker, Oden 1919(?)-1976 .... *14*
Meeker, Richard
  See Brown, Fornan
Meeks, Esther MacBain *1*
Meggs, Libby Phillips 1943- *130*
Mehdevi, Alexander (Sinclair) 1947- *7*
Mehdevi, Anne (Marie) Sinclair 1947- *8*
Meidell, Sherry 1951- *73*
Meier, Minta 1906- *55*
Meighan, Donald Charles 1929- *30*
Meigs, Cornelia Lynde 1884-1973 .... *6*
  See also CLR *55*
Meilach, Dona Z(weigoron) 1926- *34*
Meilman, Philip W(arren) 1951- *79*
Meinstereifel, Ronald L. 1960- *134*
Meisel, Paul *184*
Meister, Cari *204*
Melanson, Luc *198*
Melcher, Daniel 1912-1985
  Obituary *43*
Melcher, Frederic Gershom 1879-1963
  Obituary *22*
Melcher, Marguerite Fellows 1879-1969 ...... *10*
Meldrum, Christina *206*
Melendez, Francisco 1964- *72*
Melhuish, Eva *199*
Melin, Grace Hathaway 1892-1973 .... *10*
Mellersh, H(arold) E(dward) L(eslie)
  1897- *10*
Melling, David *186*
Melmed, Laura Krauss *212*
Melmoth, Sebastian
  See Wilde, Oscar
Melnikoff, Pamela (Rita) *97*
Meltzer, Amy 1968- *202*
Meltzer, Milton 1915-2009 .... *201*
  Autobiography Feature *124*
  Earlier sketches in SATA *1, 50, 80, 128*
  See also CLR *13*
  See also SAAS *1*
Melville, Anne
  See Potter, Margaret
Melville, Herman 1819-1891 .... *59*
Melwood, Mary
  See Lewis, E. M.
Melzack, Ronald 1929- *5*
Memling, Carl 1918-1969 .... *6*
Menchin, Scott *188*
Mendel, Jo
  See Bond, Gladys Baker
  and Gilbertson, Mildred Geiger
Mendelson, Steven T. 1958-1995 .... *86*
Mendelson-Stevens, Serita Deborah
  See Stevens, Serita
Mendes, Valerie 1939- *157*
Mendez, Raymond A. 1947- *66*
Mendez, Simon 1975- *215*
Mendonca, Susan
  See Smith, Susan Vernon

Mendoza, George 1934- *41*
  Brief entry *39*
  See also SAAS *7*
Menendez, Shirley (C.) 1937- *146*
Meng, Cece *194*
Meng, Heinz (Karl) 1924- *13*
Mennen, Ingrid 1954- *85*
Menotti, Gian Carlo 1911-2007 .... *29*
  Obituary *180*
Menuhin, Sir Yehudi 1916-1999 .... *40*
  Obituary *113*
Menville, Douglas 1935- *64*
Menzel, Barbara Jean 1946- *63*
Menzel, Peter 1948- *207*
Mercati, Cynthia *164*
Mercati, Cynthia J.
  See Mercati, Cynthia
Mercer, Charles (Edward) 1917-1988 .... *16*
  Obituary *61*
Mercer, Jessie *21*
Mercer, Sienna *192*
Meredith, Arnold
  See Hopkins, (Hector) Kenneth
Meredith, David William
  See Miers, Earl Schenck
Meringoff, Laurene Krasny
  See Brown, Laurene Krasny
Meriwether, Louise 1923- *52*
  Brief entry *31*
Merlin, Arthur
  See Blish, James
Merlin, Christina
  See Heaven, Constance (Christina)
Merrell, Billy 1982- *222*
Merriam, Eve 1916-1992 .... *73*
  Earlier sketches in SATA *3, 40*
  See also CLR *14*
Merrill, Jane 1946- *42*
Merrill, Jane Merrill
  See Merrill, Jane
Merrill, Jean (Fairbanks) 1923- *82*
  Earlier sketch in SATA *1*
  See also CLR *52*
Merrill, Phil
  See Merrill, Jane
Merriman, Alex
  See Silverberg, Robert
Merriman, Rachel 1971- *149*
  Earlier sketch in SATA *98*
Merrit, Elizabeth
  See Goudge, Eileen
Merski, Patricia K.
  See Merski, P.K.
Merski, P.K. *172*
Mertz, Barbara
  See Peters, Elizabeth
Mertz, Barbara Gross
  See Peters, Elizabeth
Merveille, David *200*
Merz, Jennifer J. *196*
Meschel, Susan V. 1936- *83*
Meserve, Jessica *211*
Messenger, Charles (Rynd Milles) 1942- *59*
Messick, Dale 1906-2005 .... *64*
  Brief entry *48*
Messier, Claire 1956- *103*
Messieres, Nicole de
  See de Messieres, Nicole
Messinger, Carla *198*
Messmer, Otto 1892(?)-1983 .... *37*
Mesta, Gabriel
  See Moesta, Rebecca
Metaxas, Eric 1963- *211*
Metcalf, Doris H(unter) *91*
Metcalf, Suzanne
  See Baum, L. Frank
Metos, Thomas H(arry) 1932- *37*
Metter, Bert(ram Milton) 1927- *56*
Metzenthen, David 1958- *167*
  Earlier sketch in SATA *106*
Meunier, Brian 1954- *195*

Meyer, Barbara 1939- *77*
Meyer, Carolyn 1935- *142*
  Autobiography Feature *142*
  Earlier sketches in SATA *9, 70, 118*
  See also SAAS *9*
Meyer, Carolyn Mae
  See Meyer, Carolyn
Meyer, Edith Patterson 1895-1993 .... *5*
Meyer, F(ranklyn) E(dward) 1932- *9*
Meyer, Jean Shepherd *11*
Meyer, Jerome Sydney 1895-1975 .... *3*
  Obituary *25*
Meyer, June
  See Jordan, June
Meyer, Kerstin 1966- *190*
Meyer, L.A. 1942- *221*
  Earlier sketches in SATA *12, 144*
Meyer, Louis A.
  See Meyer, L.A.
Meyer, Renate 1930- *6*
Meyer, Stephenie 1973- *193*
  See also CLR *142*
Meyer, Susan E. 1940- *64*
Meyerhoff, Jenny 1972- *208*
Meyers, Susan 1942- *164*
  Earlier sketches in SATA *19, 108*
Meynell, Laurence Walter 1899-1989
  Obituary *61*
Meynier, Yvonne (Pollet) 1908- *14*
Mezey, Robert 1935- *33*
Micale, Albert 1913- *22*
Michael, James
  See Scagnetti, Jack
Michael, Jan 1947- *216*
Michael, Livi 1960- *172*
Michael, Manfred
  See Winterfeld, Henry
Michael, Olivia
  See Michael, Livi
Michaelis, Antonia 1979- *215*
Michaels, Barbara
  See Peters, Elizabeth
Michaels, Jamie *195*
Michaels, Joanne Louise
  See Teitelbaum, Michael
Michaels, Kristin
  See Williams, Jeanne
Michaels, Molly
  See Untermeyer, Louis
Michaels, Neal
  See Teitelbaum, Michael
Michaels, Rune *194*
Michaels, Ski
  See Pellowski, Michael (Joseph)
Michaels, Steve 1955- *71*
Michaels, William M. 1917- *77*
Michalak, Jamie 1973- *217*
Michel, Anna 1943- *49*
  Brief entry *40*
Michel, Francois 1948- *82*
Michelin, Linda *183*
Michelson, Richard *198*
  Earlier sketch in SATA *173*
Micich, Paul *74*
Mickelson, Scott 1963- *213*
Micklish, Rita 1931- *12*
Micklos, John, Jr. 1956- *173*
  Earlier sketch in SATA *129*
Micklos J., John, Jr. 1956-
  See Micklos, John, Jr.
Micucci, Charles (Patrick, Jr.) 1959- *144*
  Earlier sketch in SATA *82*
Middleton, Haydn 1955- *152*
  Earlier sketch in SATA *85*
Miers, Earl Schenck 1910-1972 .... *1*
  Obituary *26*
Migdale, Lawrence 1951- *89*
Miglio, Paige 1966- *201*
Mikaelsen, Ben 1952- *173*
  Earlier sketches in SATA *73, 107*

Mikaelsen, Benjamin John
   See Mikaelsen, Ben
Miklowitz, Gloria D. 1927- *129*
   Earlier sketches in SATA *4, 68*
   See also SAAS *17*
Mikolaycak, Charles 1937-1993 .... *78*
   Obituary *75*
   Earlier sketch in SATA *9*
   See also SAAS *4*
Mild, Warren (Paul) 1922- *41*
Milelli, Pascal 1965- *135*
Miles, Betty 1928- *78*
   Earlier sketch in SATA *8*
   See also SAAS *9*
Miles, Miska
   See Martin, Patricia Miles
Miles, (Mary) Patricia 1930- *29*
Miles, Patricia A.
   See Martin, Patricia Miles
Miles, Victoria 1966- *188*
Milgrim, David *223*
   Earlier sketches in SATA *158, 187*
Milgrom, Harry 1912-1978 .... *25*
Milhous, Katherine 1894-1977 .... *15*
Milich, Zoran *174*
Milios, Rita 1949- *79*
Militant
   See Sandburg, Carl
Millais, Raoul 1901- *77*
Millar, Barbara F. 1924- *12*
Millar, Margaret (Ellis Sturm) 1915-1994 .... *61*
   Obituary *79*
Millard, Glenda *203*
Millard, Kerry *204*
Millbank, Captain H. R.
   See Ellis, Edward S.
Millen, C(ynthia) M. 1955- *114*
Miller, Albert G(riffith) 1905-1982 .... *12*
   Obituary *31*
Miller, Alice Ann 1958- *150*
Miller, Alice P(atricia McCarthy) *22*
Miller, Allan 1978- *216*
Miller, Christopher 1976- *215*
Miller, Debbie 1951- *160*
   Earlier sketch in SATA *103*
Miller, Debbie S.
   See Miller, Debbie
Miller, Deborah Uchill 1944- *61*
Miller, Don 1923- *15*
Miller, Doris R.
   See Mosesson, Gloria R(ubin)
Miller, Eddie
   See Miller, Edward
Miller, Edna Anita 1920- *29*
Miller, Edward 1905-1974 .... *8*
Miller, Edward 1964- *218*
   Earlier sketch in SATA *183*
Miller, Elizabeth 1933- *41*
Miller, Ellanita 1957- *87*
Miller, Eugene 1925- *33*
Miller, Frances A. 1937- *52*
   Brief entry *46*
Miller, Heather Lynn 1971- *214*
Miller, Helen M(arkley) -1984 .... *5*
Miller, Helen Topping 1884-1960
   Obituary *29*
Miller, Jane (Judith) 1925-1989 .... *15*
Miller, Jewel 1956- *73*
Miller, John
   See Samachson, Joseph
Miller, Judi *117*
Miller, Karen 1949- *210*
Miller, Karen Hokanson
   See Miller, Karen
Miller, Kate 1948- *193*
Miller, Kirsten 1973- *185*
Miller, Louise (Rolfe) 1940- *76*
Miller, M. L. *85*
Miller, Madge 1918- *63*
Miller, Margaret J.
   See Dale, Margaret J(essy) Miller

Miller, Marilyn (Jean) 1925- *33*
Miller, Marvin *65*
Miller, Mary
   See Northcott, (William) Cecil
Miller, Mary Beth 1942- *9*
Miller, Mary Beth 1964- *185*
Miller, Maryann 1943- *73*
Miller, Natalie 1917-1976 .... *35*
Miller, Pat 1951- *214*
Miller, Robert H. 1944- *91*
Miller, Ron 1947- *185*
Miller, Ruth White
   See White, Ruth
Miller, Sandra
   See Miller, Sandy
Miller, Sandra Peden
   See Miller, Sandy
Miller, Sandy 1948- *41*
   Brief entry *35*
Miller, Sarah 1969- *175*
Miller, Virginia
   See Austin, Virginia
Miller, William R. 1959- *116*
Miller Brothers
   See Miller, Allan
Milligan, Bryce 1953- *170*
Milligan, Spike
   See Milligan, Terence Alan
Milligan, Terence Alan 1918-2002 .... *29*
   Obituary *134*
   See also CLR *92*
Millington, Ada
   See Deyneka, Anita
Millman, Isaac 1933- *140*
Mills, Adam
   See Stanley, George Edward
Mills, Claudia 1954- *191*
   Brief entry *41*
   Earlier sketches in SATA *44, 89, 145*
Mills, Elaine (Rosemary) 1941- *72*
Mills, G. Riley *196*
Mills, Joyce C. 1944- *102*
Mills, Judith Christine 1956- *130*
Mills, Yaroslava Surmach 1925-2008 .... *35*
Millspaugh, Ben P. 1936- *77*
Millstead, Thomas E. *30*
Millward, Gwen *202*
Milne, A. A. 1882-1956 .... *100*
   See also YABC *1*
   See also CLR *108*
Milne, Alan Alexander
   See Milne, A. A.
Milne, Lorus J. *5*
   See also CLR *22*
   See also SAAS *18*
Milne, Margery *5*
   See also CLR *22*
   See also SAAS *18*
Milne, Terry
   See Milne, Theresa Ann
Milne, Theresa Ann 1964- *84*
Milnes, Irma McDonough 1924- *101*
Milonas, Rolf
   See Myller, Rolf
Milone, Karen
   See Dugan, Karen
Milone-Dugan, Karen
   See Dugan, Karen
Milord, Susan 1954- *200*
   Earlier sketches in SATA *74, 147*
Milotte, Alfred G(eorge) 1904-1989 .... *11*
   Obituary *62*
Milstein, Linda 1954- *80*
Milton, Ann *134*
Milton, Hilary (Herbert) 1920- *23*
Milton, John R(onald) 1924- *24*
Milton, Joyce 1946- *101*
   Brief entry *41*
   Earlier sketch in SATA *52*
Milusich, Janice *216*

Milverton, Charles A.
   See Penzler, Otto
Milway, Alex 1978- *215*
Milway, Katie Smith 1960- *203*
Minahan, John A. 1956- *92*
Minar, Barbra (Goodyear) 1940- *79*
Minard, Rosemary 1939- *63*
Minarik, Else Holmelund 1920- *127*
   Earlier sketch in SATA *15*
   See also CLR *33*
Miner, Jane Claypool 1933- *103*
   Brief entry *37*
   Earlier sketch in SATA *38*
Miner, Lewis S. 1909-1971 .... *11*
Mines, Jeanette 1948- *61*
Mines, Jeanette Marie
   See Mines, Jeanette
Minier, Nelson
   See Stoutenburg, Adrien (Pearl)
Minnitt, Ronda Jacqueline
   See Armitage, David
Minor, Wendell 1944- *199*
   Earlier sketches in SATA *78, 109, 164*
Minter, Daniel 1961- *176*
Mintonye, Grace *4*
Miranda, Anne 1954- *109*
   Earlier sketch in SATA *71*
Miranda, Inaki 1983(?)- *207*
Mirocha, Paul *192*
Mirsky, Jeannette 1903-1987 .... *8*
   Obituary *51*
Mirsky, Reba Paeff 1902-1966 .... *1*
Misako Rocks! *192*
Misenta, Marisol
   See Innes, Stephanie
Mishica, Clare 1960- *91*
Miskovits, Christine 1939- *10*
Miss Frances
   See Horwich, Frances R(appaport)
Miss Read
   See Saint, Dora Jessie
Mister Rogers
   See Rogers, Fred McFeely
Mitchard, Jacquelyn 1956- *219*
   Earlier sketches in SATA *98, 168*
Mitchell, Adrian 1932-2008 .... *166*
   Obituary *200*
   Earlier sketch in SATA *104*
Mitchell, Allison
   See Griffin, W. E. B.
Mitchell, Betty Jo
   See Mitchell, B.J.
Mitchell, B.J. 1931- *120*
Mitchell, Clyde
   See Ellison, Harlan
   and Silverberg, Robert
Mitchell, Cynthia 1922- *29*
Mitchell, (Sibyl) Elyne (Keith) 1913- *10*
Mitchell, Gladys (Maude Winifred)
   1901-1983 .... *46*
   Obituary *35*
Mitchell, Jay
   See Roberson, Jennifer
Mitchell, Joyce Slayton 1933- *142*
   Brief entry *43*
   Earlier sketch in SATA *46*
Mitchell, K. L.
   See Lamb, Elizabeth Searle
Mitchell, Kathy 1948- *59*
Mitchell, Lori 1961- *128*
Mitchell, Margaree King 1953- *84*
Mitchell, Marianne 1947- *145*
Mitchell, Rhonda *89*
Mitchell, Saundra 1974(?)- *217*
Mitchell, Stephen 1943- *199*
Mitchell, Susan
   See Mitchell, Susan K.
Mitchell, Susan K. 1972- *210*
Mitchell, Todd 1974- *191*
Mitchell, Yvonne 1925-1979
   Obituary *24*

Mitchelson, Mitch
See Mitchelson, Peter Richard
Mitchelson, Peter Richard 1950- *104*
Mitchison, Naomi (Margaret Haldane)
1897-1999 .... *24*
Obituary *112*
Mitchnik, Helen 1901-1982 .... *41*
Brief entry *35*
Mitchum, Hank
See Knott, William C(ecil, Jr.)
and Murray, Stuart A. P.
and Newton, D(wight) B(ennett)
and Sherman, Jory (Tecumseh)
Mitgutsch, Ali 1935- *76*
Mitsuhashi, Yoko *45*
Brief entry *33*
Mitton, Jacqueline 1948- *162*
Earlier sketches in SATA *66, 115*
Mitton, Simon 1946- *66*
Mitton, Tony 1951- *203*
Earlier sketches in SATA *104, 149*
Miura, Taro 1968- *181*
Mizner, Elizabeth Howard 1907- *27*
Mizumura, Kazue *18*
Mlynowski, Sarah 1977(?)- *180*
Mobin-Uddin, Asma *216*
Earlier sketch in SATA *172*
Mobley, Joe A. 1945- *91*
Moche, Dinah (Rachel) L(evine) 1936- *44*
Brief entry *40*
Mochi, Ugo (A.) 1889-1977 .... *38*
Mochizuki, Ken 1954- *146*
Earlier sketch in SATA *81*
See also SAAS *22*
Modarressi, Mitra 1967- *200*
Earlier sketch in SATA *126*
Modell, Frank B. 1917- *39*
Brief entry *36*
Modesitt, Jeanne 1953- *217*
Earlier sketches in SATA *92, 143*
Modesitt, L.E., Jr. 1943- *164*
Earlier sketch in SATA *91*
Modesitt, Leland Exton, Jr.
See Modesitt, L.E., Jr.
Modrell, Dolores 1933- *72*
Moe, Barbara 1937- *20*
Moe, Jorgen (Ingebretsen) 1813-1882
See CLR *104*
Moed-Kass, Pnina *169*
Moerbeek, Kees 1955- *98*
Moeri, Louise 1924- *93*
Earlier sketch in SATA *24*
See also SAAS *10*
Moesta, Rebecca 1956- *182*
Moffett, Jami 1952- *84*
Moffett, Mark W. 1957(?)- *203*
Moffett, Martha (Leatherwood) 1934- *8*
Mogensen, Suzanne A(ncher) 1946- *129*
Mohammed, Khadra *197*
Mohanty, Raja *223*
Mohn, Peter B(urnet) 1934- *28*
Mohn, Viola Kohl 1914- *8*
Mohr, Nicholasa 1938- *97*
Autobiography Feature *113*
Earlier sketch in SATA *8*
See also CLR *22*
See also SAAS *8*
Mok, Esther 1953- *93*
Molan, Christine 1943- *84*
Molarsky, Osmond 1909- *16*
Moldon, Peter L(eonard) 1937- *49*
Mole, John 1941- *103*
Earlier sketch in SATA *36*
See also CLR *61*
Molesworth, Mary Louisa 1839-1921 .... *98*
Molin, Charles
See Mayne, William
Molina, Silvia 1946- *97*
Molk, Laurel 1957- *162*
Earlier sketch in SATA *92*
Mollel, Tololwa M. 1952- *88*

Molloy, Anne Baker 1907-1999 .... *32*
Molloy, Michael (John) 1940- *162*
Molloy, Paul (George) 1924- *5*
Moloney, James 1954- *202*
Autobiography Feature *144*
Earlier sketches in SATA *94, 144*
Molski, Carol *215*
Momaday, N. Scott 1934- *48*
Brief entry *30*
Momaday, Navarre Scott
See Momaday, N. Scott
Monaco, Octavia 1963- *169*
Monagle, Bernie 1957- *121*
Moncure, Jane Belk 1926- *23*
Monjo, F(erdinand) N(icholas III)
1924-1978 .... *16*
See also CLR *2*
Monk, Isabell 1952- *136*
Monks, Lydia *189*
Monroe, Chris 1962- *219*
Monroe, Christine
See Monroe, Chris
Monroe, Lyle
See Heinlein, Robert A.
Monroe, Marion
See Cox, Marion Monroe
Monroy, Manuel 1970- *196*
Monsell, Helen Albee 1895-1971 .... *24*
Monson-Burton, Marianne 1975- *139*
Montana, Bob 1920-1975
Obituary *21*
Montanari, Eva 1977- *209*
Montecalvo, Janet *177*
Montenegro, Laura Nyman 1953- *95*
Montero, Gloria 1933- *109*
Montes, Marisa 1951- *144*
Montgomerie, Norah (Mary) 1913- *26*
Montgomery, Constance
See Cappel, Constance
Montgomery, Elizabeth
See Julesberg, Elizabeth Rider Montgomery
Montgomery, Elizabeth Rider
See Julesberg, Elizabeth Rider Montgomery
Montgomery, Hugh (Edward) 1962- *146*
Montgomery, L. M. 1874-1942 .... *100*
See also YABC *1*
See also CLR *145*
Montgomery, Lucy Maud
See Montgomery, L. M.
Montgomery, Michael G. 1952- *208*
Montgomery, Raymond A. (Jr.) 1936- *39*
Montgomery, Rutherford George 1894-1985 . *3*
Montgomery, Sy 1958- *184*
Autobiography Feature *132*
Earlier sketches in SATA *114, 132*
Montgomery, Vivian *36*
Monthei, Betty *179*
Montijo, Rhode *179*
Montileaux, Donald F. 1948- *183*
Montpetit, Charles 1958- *101*
Montresor, Beni 1926-2001 .... *38*
Earlier sketch in SATA *3*
See also SAAS *4*
Montserrat, Pep *181*
Monty Python
See Chapman, Graham
and Cleese, John (Marwood)
and Gilliam, Terry
and Idle, Eric
and Jones, Terence Graham Parry
and Palin, Michael
Moodie, Craig 1956- *172*
Moodie, Fiona 1952- *133*
Moody, Minerva
See Alcott, Louisa May
Moody, Ralph Owen 1898-1982 .... *1*
Moon, Carl 1879(?)-1948 .... *25*
Moon, Grace (Purdie) 1877(?)-1947 .... *25*
Moon, Lily
See Warnes, Tim

Moon, Nicola 1952- *147*
Earlier sketch in SATA *96*
Moon, Pat 1946- *113*
Moon, Sheila 1910-1991 .... *5*
Obituary *114*
Moon, Sheila Elizabeth
See Moon, Sheila
Mooney, Bel 1946- *95*
Mooney, Bill 1936- *122*
Mooney, Elizabeth C(omstock) 1918-1986
Obituary *48*
Mooney, William
See Mooney, Bill
Moor, Emily
See Deming, Richard
Moorcock, Michael 1939- *166*
Earlier sketch in SATA *93*
Moorcock, Michael John
See Moorcock, Michael
Moorcock, Michael John
See Moorcock, Michael
Moore, Anne Carroll 1871-1961 .... *13*
Moore, Cheri
See Ladd, Cheryl (Jean)
Moore, Clement Clarke 1779-1863 .... *18*
Moore, Cyd 1957- *186*
Earlier sketches in SATA *83, 133*
Moore, Don W. 1905(?)-1986
Obituary *48*
Moore, Elaine 1944- *86*
Moore, Eva 1942- *103*
Earlier sketch in SATA *20*
Moore, Ishbel (Lindsay) 1954- *140*
Moore, Jack (William) 1941- *46*
Brief entry *32*
Moore, Janet Gaylord 1905-1992 .... *18*
Moore, Jim 1946- *42*
Moore, John Travers 1908- *12*
Moore, Lilian 1909-2004 .... *137*
Obituary *155*
Earlier sketch in SATA *52*
See also CLR *15*
Moore, Liz
See Moore, M. Elizabeth
Moore, M. Elizabeth 1959- *156*
Moore, Margaret R(umberger) 1903- *12*
Moore, Margie *176*
Moore, Marianne 1887-1972 .... *20*
Moore, Marianne Craig
See Moore, Marianne
Moore, Patrick (Alfred Caldwell) 1923- *49*
Brief entry *39*
See also SAAS *8*
Moore, Patrick 1959- *184*
Moore, Perry *193*
Moore, Peter 1963- *175*
Moore, Peter G.
See Moore, Peter
Moore, Raina 1970- *212*
Moore, Ray (S.) 1905(?)-1984
Obituary *37*
Moore, Regina
See Dunne, Mary Collins
Moore, Rosalie (Gertrude) 1910-2001 .... *9*
Moore, Ruth (Ellen) 1908-1989 .... *23*
Moore, Ruth Nulton 1923- *38*
Moore, S(arah) E. *23*
Moore, Sarah Margaret
See Hodges, Margaret
Moore, Stephanie Perry 1969(?)- *214*
Moore, Tara 1950- *61*
Moore, Yvette 1958- *154*
Earlier sketches in SATA *69, 70*
Moores, Dick
See Moores, Richard (Arnold)
Moores, Richard (Arnold) 1909-1986
Obituary *48*
Mooser, Stephen 1941- *75*
Earlier sketch in SATA *28*
Mora, Francisco X(avier) 1952- *90*

Mora, Pat 1942- *186*
  Earlier sketches in SATA *92, 134*
  See also CLR *58*
Mora, Patricia
  See Mora, Pat
Morais, Flavio *207*
Morales, Yuyi *180*
  Earlier sketch in SATA *154*
Moran, Tom 1943- *60*
Moranville, Sharelle Byars *196*
  Earlier sketch in SATA *152*
Moray Williams, Ursula 1911-2006 .... *3*
  Obituary *177*
  See also SAAS *9*
Mordecai, Martin *220*
Morden, Simon 1966(?)- *211*
Mordhorst, Heidi 1964- *222*
Mordvinoff, Nicolas 1911-1973 .... *17*
More, Caroline
  See Cone, Molly (Lamken)
  and Strachan, Margaret Pitcairn
Moreau, Jean-Pierre
  See Jarrie, Martin
Moreno, Rene King *190*
Moreton, Andrew Esq.
  See Defoe, Daniel
Morey, Charles
  See Fletcher, Helen Jill
Morey, Walt(er Nelson) 1907-1992 .... *51*
  Obituary *70*
  Earlier sketch in SATA *3*
  See also SAAS *9*
Morgan, Alfred P(owell) 1889-1972 .... *33*
Morgan, Alison (Mary) 1930- *85*
  Earlier sketch in SATA *30*
Morgan, Anne 1954- *121*
Morgan, Christopher 1956- *199*
Morgan, Clay 1950- *198*
Morgan, Douglas
  See Macdonald, James D.
Morgan, Ellen
  See Bumstead, Kathleen Mary
Morgan, Geoffrey 1916- *46*
Morgan, Helen (Gertrude Louise)
  1921-1990 .... *29*
Morgan, Jane
  See Cooper, James Fenimore
  and Franklin, Jane (Morgan)
  and Moren, Sally M(oore)
Morgan, Lenore H. 1908-1976 .... *8*
Morgan, Mary 1957- *213*
  Earlier sketches in SATA *81, 114*
Morgan, McKayla
  See Basile, Gloria Vitanza
Morgan, Michaela
  See Basile, Gloria Vitanza
Morgan, Nicola 1961- *161*
Morgan, Nina 1953- *110*
Morgan, Pierr 1952- *122*
  Earlier sketch in SATA *77*
Morgan, Robin (Evonne) 1941- *80*
Morgan, Roxanne
  See Gentle, Mary
Morgan, Sarah (Nicola) 1959- *68*
Morgan, Shirley
  See Kiepper, Shirley Morgan
Morgan, Stacy T(owle) 1959- *104*
Morgan, Stevie
  See Davies, Nicola
Morgan, Tom 1942- *42*
Morgan, Wendy
  See Staub, Wendy Corsi
Morgan-Vanroyen, Mary
  See Morgan, Mary
Morgenstern, Susie Hoch 1945- *133*
Mori, Hana 1909-1990(?) *88*
Mori, Kyoko 1957- *122*
  Autobiography Feature *126*
  See also CLR *64*
  See also SAAS *26*
Moriarty, Jaclyn 1968- *162*

Moriarty, William J. 1930- *127*
Morice, Dave 1946- *93*
Morin, Isobel V. 1928- *110*
Morine, Hoder
  See Conroy, John Wesley
Morley, Taia *199*
Morley, Wilfred Owen
  See Lowndes, Robert A(ugustine) W(ard)
Morningstar, Mildred (Whaley) 1912-1997 .. *61*
  Obituary *114*
Morozumi, Atsuko *217*
  Earlier sketch in SATA *110*
Morpurgo, Michael 1943- *184*
  Earlier sketches in SATA *93, 143*
  See also CLR *51*
Morrah, Dave
  See Morrah, David Wardlaw, Jr.
Morrah, David Wardlaw, Jr. 1914-1991 .... *10*
Morreale-de la Garza, Phyllis
  See De la Garza, Phyllis
Morressy, John 1930-2006 .... *23*
Morrill, Leslie H(olt) 1934-2003 .... *48*
  Brief entry *33*
  Obituary *148*
  See also SAAS *22*
Morris, Carla *210*
Morris, Carla D.
  See Morris, Carla
Morris, Chris(topher Crosby) 1946- *66*
Morris, Deborah 1956- *91*
Morris, Desmond 1928- *14*
Morris, Desmond John
  See Morris, Desmond
Morris, Don 1954- *83*
Morris, Gerald 1963- *207*
  Earlier sketches in SATA *107, 150*
Morris, Gerald Paul
  See Morris, Gerald
Morris, Gilbert (Leslie) 1929- *104*
Morris, Jackie *202*
  Earlier sketch in SATA *151*
Morris, Janet (Ellen) 1946- *66*
Morris, Jay
  See Tatham, Julie Campbell
Morris, (Margaret) Jean 1924- *98*
Morris, Jeffrey
  See Morris, Jeffrey Brandon
Morris, Jeffrey B.
  See Morris, Jeffrey Brandon
Morris, Jeffrey Brandon 1941- *92*
Morris, Jennifer E. 1969- *179*
Morris, Jill 1936- *165*
  Earlier sketch in SATA *119*
Morris, Juddi *85*
Morris, Judy K. 1936- *61*
Morris, Oradel Nolen *128*
Morris, Robert A(da) 1933- *7*
Morris, William 1913-1994 .... *29*
Morrison, Angela *218*
Morrison, Bill 1935- *66*
  Brief entry *37*
Morrison, Chloe Anthony Wofford
  See Morrison, Toni
Morrison, Dorothy Nafus *29*
Morrison, Frank 1971- *185*
Morrison, Gordon 1944- *183*
  Earlier sketches in SATA *87, 128*
Morrison, Joan 1922- *65*
Morrison, Lillian 1917- *108*
  Earlier sketch in SATA *3*
Morrison, Lucile Phillips 1896- *17*
Morrison, Martha A. 1948- *77*
Morrison, Meighan 1966- *90*
Morrison, P.R. *196*
Morrison, Richard
  See Lowndes, Robert A(ugustine) W(ard)
Morrison, Robert
  See Lowndes, Robert A(ugustine) W(ard)
Morrison, Roberta
  See Webb, Jean Francis (III)

Morrison, Susan Dudley
  See Gold, Susan Dudley
Morrison, Taylor 1971- *187*
  Earlier sketches in SATA *95, 159*
Morrison, Toni 1931- *144*
  Earlier sketch in SATA *57*
  See also CLR *99*
Morrison, Velma Ford 1909- *21*
Morrison, Wilbur Howard 1915- *64*
Morrison, William
  See Samachson, Joseph
Morriss, James E(dward) 1932- *8*
Morrissey, Dean *183*
Morrow, Barbara Olenyik 1952- *167*
Morrow, Betty
  See Bacon, Elizabeth
Morrow, Sue Anne 1966- *218*
Morse, C. Scott
  See Morse, Scott
Morse, Carol
  See Yeakley, Marjory Hall
Morse, C.S.
  See Morse, Scott
Morse, Dorothy B(ayley) 1906-1979
  Obituary *24*
Morse, Flo 1921- *30*
Morse, Scott 1973- *200*
Morse, Tony 1953- *129*
Mort, Vivian
  See Cromie, Alice Hamilton
Mortensen, Denise Dowling *179*
Mortensen, Lori 1955- *221*
Mortimer, Anne 1958- *206*
  Earlier sketch in SATA *116*
Mortimer, Mary H.
  See Coury, Louise Andree
Morton, Alexandra (Hubbard) 1957- *144*
Morton, Anthony
  See Arthur, Robert, (Jr.)
Morton, Christine
  See Morton-Shaw, Christine
Morton, Jane 1931- *50*
Morton, Joseph C. 1932- *156*
Morton, Lee Jack, Jr. 1928- *32*
Morton, Miriam 1918(?)-1985 .... *9*
  Obituary *46*
Morton-Shaw, Christine 1957- *211*
Mosatche, Harriet 1949- *122*
Mosatche, Harriet S.
  See Mosatche, Harriet
Moscow, Alvin 1925- *3*
Mosel, Arlene (Tichy) 1921-1996 .... *7*
Moseley, James W(illett) 1931- *139*
Moseng, Elisabeth 1967- *90*
Moser, Barry 1940- *185*
  Earlier sketches in SATA *56, 79, 138*
  See also CLR *49*
  See also SAAS *15*
Moser, Don(ald Bruce) 1932- *31*
Moser, Laura *194*
Moser, Lisa *192*
Moses, Sheila P. 1961- *168*
Moses, Will 1956- *178*
  Earlier sketch in SATA *120*
Mosesson, Gloria R(ubin) *24*
Mosher, Richard 1949- *120*
Moskin, Marietta D(unston) 1928- *23*
Moskof, Martin Stephen 1930- *27*
Mosley, Francis 1957- *57*
Moss, Don(ald) 1920- *11*
Moss, Elaine (Dora) 1924- *57*
  Brief entry *31*
Moss, Jeff(rey) 1942-1998 .... *73*
  Obituary *106*
Moss, Marissa 1959- *216*
  Earlier sketches in SATA *71, 104, 163*
  See also CLR *134*
Moss, Miriam 1955- *202*
  Earlier sketches in SATA *76, 140*
Moss, Thylias 1954- *108*

Moss, Thylias Rebecca Brasier
  See Moss, Thylias
Most, Bernard 1937- *134*
  Brief entry *40*
  Earlier sketches in SATA *48, 91*
Mosz, Gosia 1972- *194*
Mott, Evelyn Clarke 1962- *133*
  Earlier sketch in SATA *75*
Motz, Lloyd 1909-2004 .... *20*
Mould, Chris *205*
Mould, Edwin
  See Whitlock, Ralph
Moulton, Mark Kimball *212*
Mouly, Francoise *155*
Mountain, Robert
  See Montgomery, Raymond A. (Jr.)
Mountfield, David
  See Grant, Neil
Mourlevat, Jean-Claude 1952- *187*
Mourning, Tuesday *206*
Moussard, Jacqueline 1924- *24*
Mowat, Claire 1933- *123*
Mowat, Claire Angel Wheeler
  See Mowat, Claire
Mowat, Farley 1921- *55*
  Earlier sketch in SATA *3*
  See also CLR *20*
Mowat, Farley McGill
  See Mowat, Farley
Mowll, Joshua 1970(?)- *188*
Mowry, Jess 1960- *131*
  Autobiography Feature *131*
  Earlier sketch in SATA *109*
  See also CLR *65*
Moxley, Sheila 1966- *96*
Moyer, Terry J. 1937- *94*
Moyes, Patricia
  See Haszard, Patricia Moyes
Moyler, Alan (Frank Powell) 1926- *36*
Mozelle, Shirley *179*
Mozley, Charles 1915- *43*
  Brief entry *32*
Mphahlele, Es'kia 1919-2008 .... *119*
  Obituary *198*
Mphahlele, Ezekiel
  See Mphahlele, Es'kia
Mphahlele, Zeke
  See Mphahlele, Es'kia
Mr. McGillicuddy
  See Abisch, Roslyn Kroop
Mr. Sniff
  See Abisch, Roslyn Kroop
Mr. Tivil
  See Lorkowski, Thomas V(incent)
Mr. Wizard
  See Herbert, Don
Mraz, David 1947- *219*
Mrs. Fairstar
  See Horne, Richard Henry Hengist
Muchamore, Robert 1972- *175*
Muchmore, Jo Ann 1937- *103*
Mude, O.
  See Gorey, Edward (St. John)
Mudgeon, Apeman
  See Mitchell, Adrian
Mueller, Jorg 1942- *67*
  See also CLR *43*
Mueller, Miranda R. *201*
Mueller, Virginia 1924- *28*
Muggs
  See Watkins, Lois
Muir, Diana
  See Appelbaum, Diana Muir Karter
Muir, Frank (Herbert) 1920-1998 .... *30*
Muir, Helen 1937- *65*
Muirhead, Margaret *220*
Mukerji, Dhan Gopal 1890-1936 .... *40*
  See also CLR *10*
Mulcahy, Lucille Burnett *12*
Mulford, Philippa G. 1948- *112*
  Earlier sketch in SATA *43*

Mulford, Philippa Greene
  See Mulford, Philippa G.
Mulgan, Catherine 1931- *24*
Mulila, Vigad G.
  See Maillu, David G(ian)
Mull, Brandon 1974- *190*
Mullen, Michael 1937- *122*
Muller, Billex
  See Ellis, Edward S.
Muller, Birte 1973- *214*
Muller, Jorg
  See Mueller, Jorg
Muller, (Lester) Robin 1953- *86*
Mullin, Caryl Cude 1969- *130*
Mullins, Edward S(wift) 1922- *10*
Mullins, Hilary 1962- *84*
Mulock, Dinah Maria
  See Craik, Dinah Maria (Mulock)
Mulvihill, William Patrick 1923- *8*
Mumford, Ruth
  See Dallas, Ruth
Mumy, Bill 1954- *112*
Mun
  See Leaf, (Wilbur) Munro
Munari, Bruno 1907-1998 .... *15*
  See also CLR *9*
Munce, Ruth Hill 1898- *12*
Mundy, Simon 1954- *64*
Mundy, Simon Andrew James Hainault
  See Mundy, Simon
Munger, Nancy *170*
Munowitz, Ken 1935-1977 .... *14*
Munoz, Claudio *208*
Munoz, William 1949- *92*
  Earlier sketch in SATA *42*
Munro, Alice 1931- *29*
Munro, Alice Anne
  See Munro, Alice
Munro, Eleanor 1928- *37*
Munro, Roxie 1945- *223*
  Earlier sketches in SATA *58, 136, 184*
Munsch, Bob
  See Munsch, Robert (Norman)
Munsch, Robert (Norman) 1945- *120*
  Brief entry *48*
  Earlier sketches in SATA *50, 83*
  See also CLR *19*
Munsinger, Lynn 1951- *221*
  Earlier sketches in SATA *33, 94, 177*
Munson, Derek 1970- *139*
Munson, R. W.
  See Karl, Jean E(dna)
Munson-Benson, Tunie 1946- *15*
Munsterberg, Peggy 1921- *102*
Muntean, Michaela *182*
Munthe, Nelly 1947- *53*
Munves, James (Albert) 1922- *30*
Munzer, Martha E. 1899-1999 .... *4*
Murawski, Darlyne A. *193*
Murch, Mel
  See Manes, Stephen
Murdoch, David H(amilton) 1937- *96*
Murdoch, Patricia 1957- *192*
Murdock, Catherine Gilbert *185*
Murhall, J(acqueline) J(ane) 1964- *143*
Murphy, Barbara Beasley 1933- *130*
  Earlier sketch in SATA *5*
Murphy, Claire Rudolf 1951- *137*
  Earlier sketch in SATA *76*
Murphy, E(mmett) Jefferson 1926- *4*
Murphy, Elizabeth Ann Maureen
  See Murphy, Liz
Murphy, Jill 1949- *214*
  Earlier sketches in SATA *37, 70, 142*
  See also CLR *39*
Murphy, Jill Frances
  See Murphy, Jill
Murphy, Jim 1947- *185*
  Brief entry *32*
  Earlier sketches in SATA *37, 77, 124*
  See also CLR *53*

Murphy, Joseph E., Jr. 1930- *65*
Murphy, Kelly 1977- *190*
  Earlier sketch in SATA *143*
Murphy, Liz 1964- *210*
Murphy, Louise 1943- *155*
Murphy, Mary 1961- *196*
Murphy, Pat
  See Murphy, E(mmett) Jefferson
Murphy, Patricia J. 1963- *132*
Murphy, Rita *180*
Murphy, Robert (William) 1902-1971 .... *10*
Murphy, Shirley Rousseau 1928- *126*
  Earlier sketches in SATA *36, 71*
  See also SAAS *18*
Murphy, Stuart J. 1942- *157*
  Earlier sketch in SATA *115*
Murphy, Thomas Basil, Jr. 1935- *191*
Murphy, Tim
  See Murphy, Jim
Murphy, Tom
  See Murphy, Thomas Basil, Jr.
Murray, John 1923- *39*
Murray, Kirsty 1960- *165*
  Earlier sketch in SATA *108*
Murray, Marguerite 1917- *63*
Murray, Marian *5*
Murray, Martine 1965- *125*
Murray, (Judith) Michele (Freedman)
  1933-1974 .... *7*
Murray, Ossie 1938- *43*
Murray, Peter
  See Hautman, Pete
Murrow, Liza Ketchum
  See Ketchum, Liza
Musgrave, Florence 1902-1999 .... *3*
Musgrove, Margaret W(ynkoop) 1943- *124*
  Earlier sketch in SATA *26*
Musgrove, Marianne *207*
Mussey, Virginia Howell
  See Ellison, Virginia H(owell)
Mussey, Virginia T.H.
  See Ellison, Virginia H(owell)
Mussi, Sarah *206*
Mutel, Cornelia F. 1947- *74*
Muth, Jon J. *206*
  Earlier sketch in SATA *165*
Mutz
  See Kuenstler, Morton
Mwangi, Meja 1948- *174*
My Brother's Brother
  See Chekhov, Anton
Myers, Anna *220*
  Earlier sketch in SATA *160*
Myers, Arthur 1917- *91*
  Earlier sketch in SATA *35*
Myers, Bernice *81*
  Earlier sketch in SATA *9*
Myers, Caroline Elizabeth Clark
  1887-1980 .... *28*
Myers, Christopher 1975- *183*
  See also CLR *97*
Myers, Edward 1950- *172*
  Earlier sketch in SATA *96*
Myers, Elisabeth P(erkins) 1918- *36*
Myers, (Mary) Hortense (Powner)
  1913-1987 .... *10*
Myers, Jack 1913-2006 .... *83*
  Obituary *178*
Myers, Jack Edgar
  See Myers, Jack
Myers, Lou 1915-2005 .... *81*
  Obituary *171*
Myers, Louis
  See Myers, Lou
Myers, R.E. 1924- *119*
Myers, Robert Eugene
  See Myers, R.E.
Myers, Tim 1953- *176*
  Earlier sketch in SATA *147*
Myers, Timothy Joseph
  See Myers, Tim

Myers, Walter Dean 1937- *193*
  Brief entry *27*
  Earlier sketches in SATA *41, 71, 109, 157*
  See also CLR *110*
  See also SAAS *2*
Myers, Walter M.
  See Myers, Walter Dean
Myller, Rolf 1926-2006 .... *27*
  Obituary *175*
Myra, Harold L(awrence) 1939- *46*
  Brief entry *42*
Myracle, Lauren 1969- *204*
  Earlier sketch in SATA *162*
Myrus, Donald (Richard) 1927- *23*
Mysterious Traveler, The
  See Arthur, Robert, (Jr.)

N

Na, An *149*
Naaslund, Goorel Kristina 1940- *170*
Nadel, Laurie 1948- *74*
Naden, Corinne J. 1930- *166*
  Earlier sketch in SATA *79*
Nadimi, Suzan *188*
Nagda, Ann Whitehead *199*
Nagel, Andreas Fischer
  See Fischer-Nagel, Andreas
Nagel, Heiderose Fischer
  See Fischer-Nagel, Heiderose
Nagle, Shane *176*
Nahoko, Uehashi
  See Uehashi, Nahoko
Naidoo, Beverley 1943- *180*
  Earlier sketches in SATA *63, 135*
  See also CLR *29*
Nails, Jennifer *213*
Nakae, Noriko 1940- *59*
Nakata, Hiroe *205*
Nakatani, Chiyoko 1930-1981 .... *55*
  Brief entry *40*
  See also CLR *30*
Nally, Susan W. 1947- *90*
Namioka, Lensey 1929- *157*
  Autobiography Feature *116*
  Earlier sketches in SATA *27, 89*
  See also CLR *48*
  See also SAAS *24*
Namovicz, Gene Inyart 1927- *6*
Nance, Andrew *210*
Nanji, Shenaaz 1954- *204*
  Earlier sketch in SATA *131*
Nanogak Agnes 1925- *61*
Napier, Mark
  See Laffin, John (Alfred Charles)
Napoli, Donna Jo 1948- *190*
  Earlier sketches in SATA *92, 137*
  See also CLR *51*
  See also SAAS *23*
Napp, Daniel 1974- *204*
Narahashi, Keiko 1959- *115*
  Earlier sketch in SATA *79*
Narayan, R. K. 1906-2001 .... *62*
Narayan, Rasipuram Krishnaswami
  See Narayan, R. K.
Nascimbene, Yan 1949- *173*
  Earlier sketch in SATA *133*
Nash, Bruce M(itchell) 1947- *34*
Nash, Frederic Ogden
  See Nash, Ogden
Nash, Linell
  See Smith, Linell Nash
Nash, Mary (Hughes) 1925- *41*
Nash, Ogden 1902-1971 .... *46*
  Earlier sketch in SATA *2*
Nash, Renea Denise 1963- *81*
Nast, Elsa Ruth
  See Watson, Jane Werner

Nast, Thomas 1840-1902 .... *51*
  Brief entry *33*
Nastick, Sharon 1954- *41*
Natale, Vince *196*
Natalini, Sandro 1970- *222*
Natarajan, Srividya *187*
Nathan, Adele (Gutman) 1900(?)-1986
  Obituary *48*
Nathan, Amy *155*
  Earlier sketch in SATA *104*
Nathan, Dorothy (Goldeen) (?)-1966 .... *15*
Nathan, Robert (Gruntal) 1894-1985 .... *6*
  Obituary *43*
Nathanson, Laura Walther 1941- *57*
Nation, Kaleb 1988- *222*
Natti, Lee 1919- *67*
  Earlier sketch in SATA *1*
  See also SAAS *3*
Natti, Susanna 1948- *125*
  Earlier sketch in SATA *32*
Nau, Thomas *186*
Naughtie, Eleanor
  See Updale, Eleanor
Naughton, Bill
  See Naughton, William John (Francis)
Naughton, James Franklin 1957- *85*
Naughton, Jim
  See Naughton, James Franklin
Naughton, William John (Francis)
  1910-1992 .... *86*
Navarra, John Gabriel 1927- *8*
Naylor, Penelope 1941- *10*
Naylor, Phyllis 1933-
  See Naylor, Phyllis Reynolds
Naylor, Phyllis Reynolds 1933- *209*
  Autobiography Feature *152*
  See also CLR *135*
  See also SAAS *10*
Nazarian, Nikki
  See Nichols, Cecilia Fawn
Nazaroff, Alexander I(vanovich) 1898-1981 .. *4*
Nazoa, Aquiles 1920-1976 .... *198*
Neal, Harry Edward 1906-1993 .... *5*
  Obituary *76*
Neal, Michael
  See Teitelbaum, Michael
Nearing, Penny 1916- *47*
  Brief entry *42*
Nebel, Gustave E. *45*
  Brief entry *33*
Nebel, Mimouca
  See Nebel, Gustave E.
Nee, Kay Bonner *10*
Needham, Kate 1962- *95*
Needle, Jan 1943- *98*
  Earlier sketch in SATA *30*
  See also CLR *43*
  See also SAAS *23*
Needleman, Jacob 1934- *6*
Neel, David 1960- *82*
Neel, Preston 1959- *93*
Neff, Henry H. 1973- *221*
Negri, Rocco 1932- *12*
Negrin, Fabian 1963- *189*
Neidigh, Sherry 1956- *204*
Neier, Aryeh 1937- *59*
Neigoff, Anne *13*
Neigoff, Mike 1920- *13*
Neilan, Eujin Kim 1969- *200*
Neilson, Frances Fullerton (Jones)
  1910-2001 .... *14*
Neimark, Anne E. 1935- *145*
  Earlier sketch in SATA *4*
Neimark, Paul G. 1934- *80*
  Brief entry *37*
Neitzel, Shirley 1941- *134*
  Earlier sketch in SATA *77*
Nell
  See Hanna, Nell(ie L.)
Nelscott, Kris
  See Rusch, Kristine Kathryn

Nelson, Blake 1960- *177*
Nelson, Catherine Chadwick 1926- *87*
Nelson, Cordner 1918-2009 .... *54*
  Brief entry *29*
Nelson, Cordner Bruce
  See Nelson, Cordner
Nelson, D.A. 1970- *215*
Nelson, Dawn Ann
  See Nelson, D.A.
Nelson, Drew 1952- *77*
Nelson, Esther L. 1928- *13*
Nelson, Jim A.
  See Stotter, Mike
Nelson, Julie L. 1970- *117*
Nelson, Kadir *213*
  Earlier sketches in SATA *154, 181*
Nelson, Kris
  See Rusch, Kristine Kathryn
Nelson, Lawrence E(rnest) 1928-1977
  Obituary *28*
Nelson, Marilyn 1946- *60*
  Autobiography Feature *180*
Nelson, Mary Carroll 1929- *23*
Nelson, O. Terry 1941- *62*
Nelson, Peter 1953- *73*
Nelson, Peter N.
  See Nelson, Peter
Nelson, R. A. *197*
Nelson, Richard K(ing) 1941- *65*
Nelson, Robin Laura 1971- *141*
Nelson, Roy Paul 1923- *59*
Nelson, S.D. *181*
Nelson, Sharlene (P.) 1933- *96*
Nelson, Suzanne 1976- *184*
Nelson, Ted (W.) 1931- *96*
Nelson, Theresa 1948- *143*
  Autobiography Feature *143*
  Earlier sketch in SATA *79*
Nelson, Vaunda Micheaux 1953- *220*
Nemeth, Sally *187*
Neri, G. *197*
Neri, Greg
  See Neri, G.
Neri, Gregory
  See Neri, G.
Nerlove, Miriam 1959- *53*
  Brief entry *49*
Nesbit, E. 1858-1924 .... *100*
  See also YABC *1*
  See also CLR *70*
Nesbit, Edith
  See Nesbit, E.
Nesbit, Troy
  See Folsom, Franklin (Brewster)
Nespojohn, Katherine V(eronica) 1912-1975 . *7*
Ness, Evaline (Michelow) 1911-1986 .... *26*
  Obituary *49*
  Earlier sketch in SATA *1*
  See also CLR *6*
  See also SAAS *1*
Ness, Patrick 1971- *207*
Nestor, Larry 1940- *149*
Nestor, William P(rodromos) 1947- *49*
Nethery, Mary *93*
Neubecker, Robert *214*
  Earlier sketch in SATA *170*
Neuberger, Julia (Babette Sarah) 1950- *142*
  Earlier sketch in SATA *78*
Neufeld, John (Arthur) 1938- *131*
  Autobiography Feature *131*
  Earlier sketches in SATA *6, 81*
  See also CLR *52*
  See also SAAS *3*
Neuhaus, David 1958- *83*
Neumeyer, Peter F(lorian) 1929- *13*
Neurath, Marie (Reidemeister) 1898-1986 ..... *1*
Neuschwander, Cindy 1953- *157*
  Earlier sketch in SATA *107*
Neusner, Jacob 1932- *38*
Neville, Charles
  See Bodsworth, (Charles) Fred(erick)

Neville, Emily Cheney 1919- *1*
  See also SAAS 2
Neville, Mary
  See Woodrich, Mary Neville
Nevins, Albert (Francis) J(erome)
  1915-1997 .... *20*
Nevius, Carol 1955- *186*
Newberger, Devra
  See Speregen, Devra Newberger
Newberry, Clare Turlay 1903-1970 .... *1*
  Obituary *26*
Newbery, John 1713-1767 .... *20*
  See also CLR 147
Newbery, Linda 1952- *184*
  Earlier sketch in SATA *142*
Newbigging, Martha *198*
Newbold, Greg *199*
Newcomb, Ellsworth
  See Kenny, Ellsworth Newcomb
Newcombe, Eugene A. 1923-1990 .... *45*
  Brief entry *33*
Newcombe, Jack
  See Newcombe, Eugene A.
Newcome, Robert 1955- *91*
Newcome, Zita 1959- *88*
Newell, Crosby
  See Bonsall, Crosby Barbara (Newell)
Newell, Edythe W(eatherford) 1910-1989 .... *11*
Newell, Hope Hockenberry 1896-1965 .... *24*
Newfeld, Frank 1928- *26*
Newgarden, Mark 1959- *194*
Newland, Gillian *220*
Newlon, (Frank) Clarke 1905(?)-1982 .... *6*
  Obituary *33*
Newman, Barbara Johansen *191*
Newman, C.J.
  See Newman, Coleman J.
Newman, Coleman J. 1935- *82*
Newman, Daisy 1904-1994 .... *27*
  Obituary *78*
Newman, Gerald 1939- *46*
  Brief entry *42*
Newman, Jerry
  See Newman, Coleman J.
Newman, Leslea 1955- *134*
  Earlier sketches in SATA *71, 128*
Newman, Margaret
  See Potter, Margaret
Newman, Marjorie *146*
Newman, Matthew (Harrison) 1955- *56*
Newman, Nanette 1934- *162*
Newman, Robert (Howard) 1909-1988 .... *87*
  Obituary *60*
  Earlier sketch in SATA *4*
Newman, Shirlee P(etkin) *144*
  Earlier sketches in SATA *10, 90*
Newsom, Carol 1948- *92*
  Earlier sketch in SATA *40*
Newsom, Tom 1944- *80*
Newth, Mette 1942- *140*
Newton, David E(dward) 1933- *67*
Newton, James R(obert) 1935- *23*
Newton, Jill 1964- *200*
Newton, Robert 1965- *191*
Newton, Suzanne 1936- *77*
  Earlier sketch in SATA *5*
Newton, Vanessa
  See Newton, Vanessa Brantley
Newton, Vanessa Brantley 1962(?)- *206*
Ney, John 1923- *43*
  Brief entry *33*
Nez, John *218*
  Earlier sketch in SATA *155*
Nez, John Abbott
  See Nez, John
Ng, Franklin *82*
Nguyen, Vincent *187*
Nichol, B(arrie) P(hillip) 1944-1988 .... *66*
Nicholas, Louise D.
  See Watkins, Dawn L.
Nicholls, Judith (Ann) 1941- *61*

Nicholls, Sally 1983- *209*
Nichols, Cecilia Fawn 1906-1987 .... *12*
Nichols, Grace 1950- *164*
  Earlier sketch in SATA *98*
Nichols, Janet (Louise) 1952- *67*
Nichols, Judy 1947- *124*
Nichols, Leigh
  See Koontz, Dean
Nichols, Michael 1952- *215*
Nichols, Nick
  See Nichols, Michael
Nichols, Paul
  See Hawks, Robert
Nichols, Peter
  See Youd, Samuel
Nichols, (Joanna) Ruth 1948- *15*
  See also CLR 149
Nichols, Travis *206*
Nicholson, C. R.
  See Nicole, Christopher (Robin)
Nicholson, Christina
  See Nicole, Christopher (Robin)
Nicholson, Joyce Thorpe 1919- *35*
Nicholson, Lois P. 1949- *88*
Nicholson, Robin
  See Nicole, Christopher (Robin)
Nicholson, William *180*
Nicholson, William 1872-1949
  See CLR 76
Nickel, Barbara 1966- *188*
Nickell, Joe 1944- *167*
  Earlier sketch in SATA *73*
Nickelsburg, Janet 1893-1983 .... *11*
Nickerson, Betty 1922- *14*
Nickerson, Elizabeth
  See Nickerson, Betty
Nickl, Barbara (Elisabeth) 1939- *56*
Nicklaus, Carol *62*
  Brief entry *33*
Nickle, John *181*
Nickless, Will 1902-1979(?) *66*
Nic Leodhas, Sorche
  See Alger, Leclaire (Gowans)
Nicol, Ann
  See Turnbull, Ann
Nicolas
  See Mordvinoff, Nicolas
Nicolay, Helen 1866-1954
  See YABC *1*
Nicole, Christopher (Robin) 1930- *5*
Nicoll, Helen 1937- *87*
Nicolson, Cynthia Pratt 1949- *141*
Ni Dhuibhne, Eilis 1954- *91*
Niehaus, Paddy Bouma
  See Bouma, Paddy
Nields, Nerissa 1967- *166*
Nielsen, Kay (Rasmus) 1886-1957 .... *16*
  See also CLR *16*
Nielsen, Laura F. 1960- *93*
Nielsen, Laura Farnsworth
  See Nielsen, Laura F.
Nielsen, Nancy J. 1951- *77*
Nielsen, Susin 1964- *195*
Nielsen, Virginia
  See McCall, Virginia Nielsen
Nielsen-Fernlund, Susin
  See Nielsen, Susin
Niemann, Christoph 1970- *191*
Nieuwsma, Milton J(ohn) 1941- *142*
Nightingale, Sandy 1953- *76*
Nikolajeva, Maria 1952- *127*
Nikola-Lisa, W. 1951- *180*
  Earlier sketch in SATA *71*
Niland, Deborah 1951- *172*
  Earlier sketch in SATA *27*
Niland, Kilmeny *75*
Nilsen, Anna 1948- *174*
  Earlier sketch in SATA *96*
Nilsson, Eleanor 1939- *117*
  Earlier sketch in SATA *81*
  See also SAAS 23

Nilsson, Per 1954- *159*
Nimmo, Jenny 1944- *144*
  Earlier sketch in SATA *87*
  See also CLR 44
Nishimura, Kae *196*
Niven, Larry 1938- *171*
  Earlier sketch in SATA *95*
Niven, Laurence Van Cott
  See Niven, Larry
Niven, Laurence VanCott
  See Niven, Larry
Nivola, Claire A. 1947- *208*
  Earlier sketches in SATA *84, 140*
Nix, Garth 1963- *210*
  Earlier sketches in SATA *97, 143*
  See also CLR 68
Nixon, Hershell Howard 1923- *42*
Nixon, Joan Lowery 1927-2003 .... *115*
  Obituary *146*
  Earlier sketches in SATA *8, 44, 78*
  See also CLR 24
  See also SAAS 9
Nixon, K.
  See Nixon, Kathleen Irene (Blundell)
Nixon, Kathleen Irene (Blundell)
  1894-1988(?) *14*
  Obituary *59*
Nobati, Eugenia 1968- *201*
Nobisso, Josephine 1953- *121*
  Earlier sketch in SATA *78*
Noble, Iris (Davis) 1922-1986 .... *5*
  Obituary *49*
Noble, Marty 1947- *125*
  Earlier sketch in SATA *97*
Noble, Trinka Hakes 1944- *197*
  Brief entry *37*
  Earlier sketch in SATA *123*
Nobleman, Marc Tyler 1972- *203*
Noda, Takayo 1961- *168*
Nodelman, Perry 1942- *101*
Nodset, Joan L.
  See Lexau, Joan M.
Noel Hume, Ivor 1927- *65*
Noestlinger, Christine
  See Nostlinger, Christine
Noguere, Suzanne 1947- *34*
Nolan, Dennis 1945- *166*
  Brief entry *34*
  Earlier sketches in SATA *42, 92*
Nolan, Han 1956- *157*
  Earlier sketch in SATA *109*
Nolan, Janet 1956- *191*
  Earlier sketch in SATA *145*
Nolan, Jeannette Covert 1897-1974 .... *2*
  Obituary *27*
Nolan, Lucy *215*
Nolan, Paul T(homas) 1919- *48*
Nolan, William F. 1928- *88*
  Brief entry *28*
Nolan, William Francis
  See Nolan, William F.
Nolen, Jerdine 1953- *157*
  Earlier sketch in SATA *105*
Noll, Amanda *219*
Noll, Sally 1946- *82*
Noonan, Brandon 1979- *184*
Noonan, Diana 1960- *146*
Noonan, Julia 1946- *148*
  Earlier sketches in SATA *4, 95*
Norac, Carl 1960- *166*
Norcross, John
  See Conroy, John Wesley
Nordan, Robert W(arren) 1934-2004 .... *133*
Nordhoff, Charles Bernard 1887-1947 .... *23*
Nordlicht, Lillian *29*
Nordstrom, Ursula 1910-1988 .... *3*
  Obituary *57*
Nordtvedt, Matilda 1926- *67*
Norling, Beth 1969- *149*
Norman, Charles 1904-1996 .... *38*
  Obituary *92*

Norman, Geoffrey 223
Norman, Howard
  See Norman, Howard A.
Norman, Howard A. 1949- 81
Norman, James
  See Schmidt, James Norman
Norman, Jay
  See Arthur, Robert, (Jr.)
Norman, Lilith 1927- 120
  Earlier sketch in SATA 86
Norman, Mary 1931- 36
Norman, Steve
  See Pashko, Stanley
Norment, Lisa 1966- 91
Norris, Gunilla Brodde 1939- 20
North, Andrew
  See Norton, Andre
North, Anthony
  See Koontz, Dean
North, Captain George
  See Stevenson, Robert Louis
North, Captain George
  See Stevenson, Robert Louis
North, Howard
  See Trevor, Elleston
North, Joan 1920- 16
North, Milou
  See Erdrich, Louise
North, Robert
  See Withers, Carl A.
North, Sara
  See Bonham, Barbara Thomas
  and Hager, Jean
North, Sherry 201
North, Sterling 1906-1974 45
  Obituary 26
  Earlier sketch in SATA 1
Northcott, (William) Cecil 1902-1987
  Obituary 55
Northeast, Brenda V(ictoria) 1948- 106
Northmore, Elizabeth Florence 1906-1974 . 122
Norton, Alice Mary
  See Norton, Andre
Norton, Andre 1912-2005 91
  Earlier sketches in SATA 1, 43
  See also CLR 50
Norton, Browning
  See Norton, Frank R. B(rowning)
Norton, Frank R. B(rowning) 1909-1989 10
Norton, Mary 1903-1992 60
  Obituary 72
  Earlier sketch in SATA 18
  See also CLR 140
Nosredna, Trebor
  See Anderson, Bob
Nostlinger, Christine 1936- 162
  Brief entry 37
  Earlier sketch in SATA 64
  See also CLR 12
Nourse, Alan E(dward) 1928-1992 48
  See also CLR 33
Novak, Matt 1962- 204
  Brief entry 52
  Earlier sketches in SATA 60, 104, 165
Novelli, Luca 1947- 61
Novgorodoff, Danica 1982(?)- 215
Nowell, Elizabeth Cameron 12
Noyes, Deborah 1965- 194
  Earlier sketch in SATA 145
Nugent, Cynthia 1954- 205
Nugent, Nicholas 1949- 73
Numberman, Neil 1981(?)- 220
Numeroff, Laura 1953- 206
  Earlier sketches in SATA 28, 90, 142
  See also CLR 85
Numeroff Joffe, Laura
  See Numeroff, Laura
Nunes, Lygia Bojunga 1932- 154
  Earlier sketch in SATA 75
Nunn, Laura (Donna) Silverstein 1968- 124

Nurenberg, Thelma
  See Greenhaus, Thelma Nurenberg
Nurnberg, Maxwell 1897-1984 27
  Obituary 41
Nussbaumer, Paul (Edmund) 1934- 16
Nutt, Ken 1951- 163
  Earlier sketch in SATA 97
Nuttall-Smith, Margaret Emily Noel 1919- .. 26
Nuygen, Mathieu 1967- 80
Nuzum, K. A. 195
Nuzum, Kathy A.
  See Nuzum, K. A.
Nwapa, Flora (Nwanzuruaha) 1931-1993
  See CLR 162
Nyberg, (Everett Wayne) Morgan 1944- 87
Nyce, (Nellie) Helene von Strecker
  1885-1969 19
Nyce, Vera 1862-1925 19
Nye, Naomi Shihab 1952- 198
  Earlier sketches in SATA 86, 147
  See also CLR 59
Nye, Robert 1939- 6
Nyeu, Tao 206
Nyikos, Stacy A. 1969- 164
Nystrom, Carolyn 1940- 130
  Earlier sketch in SATA 67

O

O. Henry
  See Henry, O.
Oakes, Elizabeth H. 1964- 132
Oakes, Vanya 1909-1983 6
  Obituary 37
Oakley, Don(ald G.) 1927- 8
Oakley, Graham 1929- 84
  Earlier sketch in SATA 30
  See also CLR 7
Oakley, Helen (McKelvey) 1906- 10
Oaks, J. Adams 220
Oana, Katherine 1929- 53
  Brief entry 37
Oates, Eddie H. 1943- 88
Oates, Joyce Carol 1938- 159
Oates, Stephen B(aery) 1936- 59
Obed, Ellen Bryan 1944- 74
Oberle, Joseph 1958- 69
Oberman, Sheldon 1949-2004 85
  Autobiography Feature 114
  Obituary 153
  See also CLR 54
  See also SAAS 26
Obligado, Lilian (Isabel) 1931- 61
  Brief entry 45
Obrant, Susan 1946- 11
O'Brian, E.G.
  See Clarke, Arthur C.
O'Brien, Anne Sibley 1952- 213
  Brief entry 48
  Earlier sketches in SATA 53, 80
O'Brien, E.G.
  See Clarke, Arthur C.
O'Brien, Esse Forrester 1895(?)-1975
  Obituary 30
O'Brien, Johnny 222
O'Brien, Patrick 1960- 193
O'Brien, Robert C.
  See Conly, Robert Leslie
O'Brien, Thomas C. 1938-2010 29
O'Brien, Thomas Clement
  See O'Brien, Thomas C.
O'Callaghan, Julie 1954- 113
O'Callahan, Jay 1938- 88
O'Carroll, Ryan
  See Markun, Patricia Maloney
Ochiltree, Dianne 1953- 117
Ockham, Joan Price
  See Price, Joan

O'Connell, Margaret F(orster) 1935-1977 30
  Obituary 30
O'Connell, Peg
  See Ahern, Margaret McCrohan
O'Connell, Rebecca 1968- 212
  Earlier sketch in SATA 130
O'Connor, Barbara 1950- 193
  Earlier sketch in SATA 154
O'Connor, Francine M(arie) 1930- 90
O'Connor, Genevieve A. 1914- 75
O'Connor, George 183
O'Connor, Ian 1965- 188
O'Connor, Jane 1947- 186
  Brief entry 47
  Earlier sketches in SATA 59, 103, 150
O'Connor, Karen 1938- 89
  Earlier sketch in SATA 34
O'Connor, Patrick
  See Wibberley, Leonard
O'Connor, Richard 1915-1975
  Obituary 21
O'Conor, Jane 1958- 78
Odaga, Asenath (Bole) 1937- 130
  Earlier sketch in SATA 67
  See also SAAS 19
O Danachair, Caoimhin
  See Danaher, Kevin
Odanaka, Barbara 159
O'Daniel, Janet 1921- 24
O'Day, Cathy
  See Crane, Barbara (Joyce)
O'Dell, Scott 1898-1989 134
  Earlier sketches in SATA 12, 60
  See also CLR 126
Odenwald, Robert P(aul) 1899-1965 11
Odgers, Sally
  See Odgers, Sally Farrell
Odgers, Sally Farrell 1957- 139
  Earlier sketch in SATA 72
Odone, Jamison 1980- 209
O'Donnell, Dick
  See Lupoff, Richard A(llen)
  and Thompson, Don(ald Arthur)
O'Donnell, Liam 1970- 209
Odriozola, Elena 186
Oechsli, Kelly 1918-1999 5
Oesterle, Virginia Rorby
  See Rorby, Ginny
Ofek, Uriel 1926- 36
  See also CLR 28
Ofer, Avi 1975- 207
Offenbacher, Ami 1958- 91
Offill, Jenny 1968- 211
Offit, Sidney 1928- 10
Ofosu-Appiah, L(awrence) H(enry) 1920- ... 13
Ogan, George F. 1912-1983 13
Ogan, M. G.
  See Ogan, George F.
  and Ogan, Margaret E. (Nettles)
Ogan, Margaret E. (Nettles) 1923-1979 13
Ogburn, Charlton (Jr.) 1911-1998 3
  Obituary 109
Ogburn, Jacqueline K. 162
Ogilvie, Elisabeth May 1917-2006 40
  Brief entry 29
  Obituary 176
Ogilvy, Gavin
  See Barrie, J. M.
Ogilvy, Ian 1943- 177
Ogilvy, Ian Raymond
  See Ogilvy, Ian
Ogle, Lucille Edith 1904-1988
  Obituary 59
Ogletree, Charles J. 1952- 175
O'Green, Jennifer
  See Roberson, Jennifer
O'Green, Jennifer Roberson
  See Roberson, Jennifer
O'Hagan, Caroline 1946- 38
O'Hanlon, Jacklyn
  See Meek, Jacklyn O'Hanlon

O'Hara, Elizabeth
  See Ni Dhuibhne, Eilis
O'Hara, Kenneth
  See Morris, (Margaret) Jean
O'Hara, Mary
  See Alsop, Mary O'Hara
O'Hara (Alsop), Mary
  See Alsop, Mary O'Hara
O'Hare, Jeff(rey A.) 1958- 105
Ohi, Ruth 1964- 95
Ohiyesa
  See Eastman, Charles A(lexander)
Ohlsson, Ib 1935- 7
Ohmi, Ayano 1959- 115
Ohtomo, Yasuo 1946- 37
o huigin, sean 1942- 138
  See also CLR 75
Oiseau
  See Moseley, James W(illett)
Oke, Janette 1935- 97
O'Keefe, Susan Heyboer 176
  Earlier sketch in SATA 133
O'Keeffe, Frank 1938- 99
O'Kelley, Mattie Lou 1908-1997 97
  Earlier sketch in SATA 36
Okimoto, Jean Davies 1942- 103
  Earlier sketch in SATA 34
Okomfo, Amasewa
  See Cousins, Linda
olafsdottir, Gudrun Elin
  See Gunnella
Olaleye, Isaac O. 1941- 96
  See also SAAS 23
Olcott, Frances Jenkins 1872(?)-1963 19
Old, Wendie C(orbin) 1943- 154
Old Boy
  See Hughes, Thomas
Oldenburg, E(gbert) William 1936-1974 35
Older, Effin 1942- 114
Older, Jules 1940- 156
  Earlier sketch in SATA 114
Oldfield, Jenny 1949- 140
Oldfield, Margaret J(ean) 1932- 56
Oldfield, Pamela 1931- 86
Oldham, June 70
Oldham, Mary 1944- 65
Oldland, Nicholas 1972- 223
Olds, Elizabeth 1896-1991 3
  Obituary 66
Olds, Helen Diehl 1895-1981 9
  Obituary 25
Oldstyle, Jonathan
  See Irving, Washington
O'Leary, Brian (Todd) 1940- 6
O'Leary, Chris 208
O'Leary, Patsy B. 1937- 97
O'Leary, Patsy Baker
  See O'Leary, Patsy B.
Oleynikov, Igor 1953- 202
Oliphant, B.J.
  See Tepper, Sheri S.
Oliver, Burton
  See Burt, Olive Woolley
Oliver, Chad
  See Oliver, Symmes C.
Oliver, John Edward 1933- 21
Oliver, Lin 202
Oliver, Marilyn Tower 1935- 89
Oliver, Mark 1960- 214
Oliver, Narelle 1960- 197
  Earlier sketch in SATA 152
Oliver, Shirley (Louise Dawkins) 1958- 74
Oliver, Symmes C. 1928-1993 101
Oliviero, Jamie 1950- 84
Olmsted, Lorena Ann 1890-1989 13
Olney, Ross R. 1929- 13
Olschewski, Alfred (Erich) 1920- 7
Olsen, Barbara 148
Olsen, Carol 1945- 89
Olsen, Ib Spang 1921- 81
  Earlier sketch in SATA 6

Olsen, Violet (Mae) 1922-1991 58
Olson, Arielle North 1932- 67
Olson, David J. 1974- 198
Olson, Gene 1922- 32
Olson, Gretchen 187
Olson, Helen Kronberg 48
Olson, Kay Melchisedech 1948- 175
Olson, Marianne
  See Mitchell, Marianne
Olson-Brown, Ellen 1967- 183
Olten, Manuela 1970- 197
Olugebefola, Ademole 1941- 15
Oluonye, Mary N(kechi) 1955- 111
Om
  See Gorey, Edward (St. John)
O'Malley, Donough 208
O'Malley, Kevin 1961- 191
  Earlier sketch in SATA 157
Oman, Carola (Mary Anima) 1897-1978 35
O'Mara, Carmel 1965- 166
O'Mara-Horwitz, Carmel
  See O'Mara, Carmel
O'Meara, Walter (Andrew) 1897-1989 65
Ommanney, F(rancis) D(ownes) 1903-1980 . 23
Omololu, Cynthia Jaynes 222
O Mude
  See Gorey, Edward (St. John)
Oneal, Elizabeth 1934- 82
  Earlier sketch in SATA 30
  See also CLR 13
O'Neal, Katherine Pebley 1957- 204
O'Neal, Reagan
  See Jordan, Robert
O'Neal, Regan
  See Jordan, Robert
Oneal, Zibby
  See Oneal, Elizabeth
O'neill, Alexis 1949- 220
O'Neill, Amanda 1951- 111
O'Neill, Catharine 203
O'Neill, Gerard K(itchen) 1927-1992 65
O'Neill, Judith (Beatrice) 1930- 34
O'Neill, Mary L(e Duc) 1908(?)-1990 2
  Obituary 64
O'Neill, Reagan
  See Jordan, Robert
Onslow, Annette Rosemary MacArthur
  See MacArthur-Onslow, Annette Rosemary
Onslow, John 1906-1985
  Obituary 47
Onyefulu, Ifeoma 1959- 157
  Earlier sketches in SATA 81, 115
Opie, Iona (Margaret Balfour) 1923- 118
  Earlier sketches in SATA 3, 63
  See also SAAS 6
Opie, Peter (Mason) 1918-1982 118
  Obituary 28
  Earlier sketches in SATA 3, 63
Oppel, Kenneth 1967- 199
  Earlier sketches in SATA 99, 153
Oppel, Kenneth Kerry
  See Oppel, Kenneth
Oppenheim, Joanne 1934- 174
  Earlier sketches in SATA 5, 82, 136
Oppenheim, Shulamith Levey 1928- 177
Oppenheimer, Joan L(etson) 1925- 28
Oppong, Joseph Ransford 1953- 160
Optic, Oliver
  See Adams, William Taylor
  and Stratemeyer, Edward L.
Oram, Hiawyn 1946- 101
  Earlier sketch in SATA 56
Orbach, Ruth Gary 1941- 21
Orback, Craig 197
Orczy, Emma
  See Orczy, Baroness Emmuska
Orczy, Emma Magdalena Rosalia Maria Josefa
  See Orczy, Baroness Emmuska
Orczy, Emmuska
  See Orczy, Baroness Emmuska
Orczy, Baroness Emmuska 1865-1947 40

Orde, A.J.
  See Tepper, Sheri S.
O'Reilly, Jackson
  See Jordan, Robert
Orenstein, Denise Gosliner 1950- 157
Orgad, Dorit 1936- 199
Orgel, Doris 1929- 148
  Earlier sketches in SATA 7, 85
  See also CLR 48
  See also SAAS 19
Orgill, Roxane 198
Oriolo, Joe
  See Oriolo, Joseph D.
Oriolo, Joseph D. 1913-1985
  Obituary 46
Orlean, Susan 1955- 209
Orleans, Ilo 1897-1962 10
Orlev, Uri 1931- 135
  Earlier sketch in SATA 58
  See also CLR 30
  See also SAAS 19
Ormai, Stella 57
  Brief entry 48
Ormerod, Jan 1946- 210
  Brief entry 44
  Earlier sketches in SATA 55, 70, 132
  See also CLR 20
Ormerod, Janette Louise
  See Ormerod, Jan
Ormes, Jackie
  See Ormes, Zelda J.
Ormes, Zelda J. 1914-1986
  Obituary 47
Ormondroyd, Edward 1925- 14
Ormsby, Virginia H(aire) 1906-1990 11
Orona-Ramirez, Kristy 1964- 189
Orozco, Jose-Luis 1948- 179
Orr, Katherine S(helley) 1950- 72
Orr, Wendy 1953- 206
  Earlier sketches in SATA 90, 141
Orris
  See Ingelow, Jean
Orth, Richard
  See Gardner, Richard (M.)
Ortiz Cofer, Judith
  See Cofer, Judith Ortiz
Orwell, George 1903-1950 29
  See also CLR 68
Orwin, Joanna 1944- 141
Os, Eric van
  See van Os, Erik
Osborn, Elinor 1939- 145
Osborn, Jacob 1981(?)- 215
Osborn, Kathy 1955(?)- 199
Osborn, Lois D(orothy) 1915- 61
Osborne, Charles 1927- 59
Osborne, Chester G(orham) 1915-1987 11
Osborne, David
  See Silverberg, Robert
Osborne, George
  See Silverberg, Robert
Osborne, Leone Neal 1914-1996 2
Osborne, Linda Barrett 1949- 215
Osborne, Mary Pope 1949- 144
  Earlier sketches in SATA 41, 55, 98
  See also CLR 88
Osceola
  See Blixen, Karen
Osgood, William E(dward) 1926- 37
O'Shaughnessy, Darren
  See Shan, Darren
O'Shaughnessy, Ellen Cassels 1937- 78
O'shaughnessy, Tam 1951- 221
O'Shea, Catherine Patricia Shiels
  See O'Shea, Pat
O'Shea, Pat 1931-2007 87
  See also CLR 18
Osmond, Edward 1900- 10
Ossoli, Sarah Margaret
  See Fuller, Margaret

Ostendorf, (Arthur) Lloyd, (Jr.) 1921-2000 .. *65*
  Obituary *125*
Osterweil, Adam 1972- *217*
Ostow, Micol 1976- *223*
  Earlier sketch in SATA *170*
Otfinoski, Steven 1949- *116*
  Earlier sketch in SATA *56*
Otis, James
  See Kaler, James Otis
O'Toole, Thomas 1941- *71*
O'Trigger, Sir Lucius
  See Horne, Richard Henry Hengist
Otten, Charlotte
  See Otten, Charlotte F.
Otten, Charlotte F. 1926- *98*
Otten, Charlotte Fennema
  See Otten, Charlotte F.
Ottley, Matt 1962- *171*
  Earlier sketch in SATA *102*
Ottley, Reginald Leslie 1909-1985 .... *26*
  See also CLR *16*
Otto, Margaret Glover 1909-1976
  Obituary *30*
Otto, Svend
  See Soerensen, Svend Otto
Ouellet, Debbie 1954- *219*
Oughton, Jerrie (Preston) 1937- *131*
  Earlier sketch in SATA *76*
Oughton, (William) Taylor 1925- *104*
Ouida
  See De La Ramee, Marie Louise
Ousley, Odille 1896-1976 .... *10*
Outcalt, Todd 1960- *123*
Overmyer, James E. 1946- *88*
Overton, Jenny (Margaret Mary) 1942- *52*
  Brief entry *36*
Owen, Ann
  See Qualey, Marsha
Owen, Annie 1949- *75*
Owen, Caroline Dale
  See Snedeker, Caroline Dale (Parke)
Owen, Clifford
  See Hamilton, Charles (Harold St. John)
Owen, Dilys
  See Gater, Dilys
Owen, (Benjamin) Evan 1918-1984 .... *38*
Owen, (John) Gareth 1936-2002 .... *162*
  Earlier sketch in SATA *83*
  See also CLR *31*
  See also SAAS *14*
Owen, James A. *185*
Owens, Bryant 1968- *116*
Owens, Dana Elaine
  See Queen Latifah
Owens, Gail 1939- *54*
Owens, Mary Beth *191*
Owens, Thomas S(heldon) 1960- *86*
Owens, Tom
  See Owens, Thomas S(heldon)
Oxenbury, Helen 1938- *149*
  Earlier sketches in SATA *3, 68*
  See also CLR *70*
Oxendine, Bess Holland 1933- *90*
Oz, Frank (Richard) 1944- *60*
Ozer, Jerome S. 1927- *59*

P

Paananen, Eloise (Katherine) 1923-1993 .... *9*
Pace, Lorenzo 1943- *131*
Pace, Mildred Mastin 1907- *46*
  Brief entry *29*
Pachter, Hedwig (?)-1988 .... *63*
Pack, Janet 1952- *77*
Pack, Robert 1929- *118*
Packard, Edward 1931- *148*
  Earlier sketches in SATA *47, 90*
Packer, Kenneth L. 1946- *116*

Packer, Vin
  See Meaker, Marijane
Pad, Peter
  See Stratemeyer, Edward L.
Page, Eileen
  See Heal, Edith
Page, Eleanor
  See Coerr, Eleanor (Beatrice)
Page, Gail 1950- *205*
Page, Jake 1936- *81*
Page, James Keena, Jr.
  See Page, Jake
Page, Lou Williams 1912-1997 .... *38*
Page, Mary
  See Heal, Edith
Page, Robin 1943- *154*
Pagliarulo, Antonio 1977(?)- *212*
Pagnucci, Susan 1944- *90*
Pahlen, Kurt 1907-2003
  Obituary *147*
Pahz, Cheryl
  See Pahz, Cheryl Suzanne
Pahz, Cheryl Suzanne 1949- *11*
Pahz, James Alon 1943- *11*
Paice, Margaret 1920- *10*
Paige, Harry W(orthington) 1922- *41*
  Brief entry *35*
Paige, Richard
  See Koontz, Dean
Paige, Robin
  See Albert, Susan Wittig
Paine, Penelope Colville 1946- *87*
Paine, Roberta M. 1925- *13*
Paisley, Tom 1932- *11*
  See also CLR *3*
Palatini, Margie *207*
  Earlier sketches in SATA *134, 174*
Palazzo, Anthony D.
  See Palazzo, Tony
Palazzo, Tony 1905-1970 .... *3*
Palder, Edward L. 1922- *5*
Palecek, Josef 1932- *56*
Palecek, Libuse 1937- *89*
Palen, Debbie *195*
Palin, Michael 1943- *67*
Palin, Michael Edward
  See Palin, Michael
Palladini, David (Mario) 1946- *40*
  Brief entry *32*
Pallas, Norvin 1918-1983 .... *23*
Pallister, John C(lare) 1891-1980
  Obituary *26*
Pallotta, Gerard Larry
  See Pallotta, Jerry
Pallotta, Jerry 1953- *186*
Pallotta-Chiarolli, Maria 1960- *117*
Palmer, Bernard (Alvin) 1914-1998 .... *26*
Palmer, C. Everard 1930- *14*
Palmer, (Ruth) Candida 1926- *11*
Palmer, Cyril Everard
  See Palmer, C. Everard
Palmer, Don
  See Benson, Mildred
Palmer, Hap 1942- *68*
Palmer, Heidi 1948- *15*
Palmer, Helen Marion
  See Geisel, Helen
Palmer, Jessica 1953- *120*
Palmer, Judd 1972- *153*
Palmer, Juliette 1930- *15*
Palmer, Kate Salley 1946- *97*
Palmer, Maria
  See Strachan, Ian
Palmer, Maria
  See Brennan, Herbie
Palmer, Robin 1909-2000 .... *43*
Palmero Caceres, Ana *198*
Palmisciano, Diane *202*
Paltrowitz, Donna 1950- *61*
  Brief entry *50*

Paltrowitz, Donna Milman
  See Paltrowitz, Donna
Paltrowitz, Stuart 1946- *61*
  Brief entry *50*
Pamela, Todd 1950- *124*
Pamintuan, Macky *214*
  Earlier sketch in SATA *178*
Panagopoulos, Janie Lynn *149*
Panati, Charles 1943- *65*
Panchyk, Richard 1970- *138*
Panetta, George 1915-1969 .... *15*
Panetta, Joseph N. 1953- *96*
Pang, YaWen Ariel *206*
Panik, Sharon 1952- *82*
Panowski, Eileen Thompson 1920- *49*
Pansy
  See Alden, Isabella (Macdonald)
Pantell, Dora (Fuchs) *39*
Panter, Carol 1936- *9*
Paolini, Christopher 1983- *157*
  See also CLR *102*
Papademetriou, Lisa *175*
Paparone, Pam *185*
Paparone, Pamela
  See Paparone, Pam
Papas, Bill
  See Papas, William
Papas, William 1927-2000 .... *50*
Papashvily, George 1898-1978 .... *17*
Papashvily, Helen (Waite) 1906-1996 .... *17*
Pape, D. L.
  See Pape, Donna (Lugg)
Pape, Donna (Lugg) 1930- *82*
  Earlier sketch in SATA *2*
Paperny, Myra (Green) 1932- *51*
  Brief entry *33*
Papp, Robert 1967- *205*
Paradis, Adrian A(lexis) 1912- *67*
  Earlier sketch in SATA *1*
  See also SAAS *8*
Paradis, Marjorie Bartholomew
  1886(?)-1970 .... *17*
Paradiz, Valerie 1963- *176*
Paratore, Coleen
  See Paratore, Coleen Murtagh
Paratore, Coleen Murtagh 1958- *200*
Pardo DeLange, Alex *211*
Parenteau, Shirley 1935- *199*
  Brief entry *40*
  Earlier sketch in SATA *47*
Parish, Margaret 1927-1988 .... *73*
  Obituary *59*
  Earlier sketch in SATA *17*
  See also CLR *22*
Parish, Margaret Holt
  See Holt, Margaret
Parish, Peggy
  See Parish, Margaret
Park, Barbara 1947- *123*
  Brief entry *35*
  Earlier sketches in SATA *40, 78*
  See also CLR *34*
Park, Bill
  See Park, W(illiam) B(ryan)
Park, Frances 1955- *171*
Park, Ginger *173*
Park, Janie Jaehyun *150*
Park, Jordan
  See Kornbluth, C(yril) M.
  and Pohl, Frederik
Park, Linda Sue 1960- *200*
  Earlier sketches in SATA *127, 173*
  See also CLR *84*
Park, Nick 1958- *113*
Park, Rosina Ruth Lucia
  See Park, Ruth
Park, Ruth 1917(?)-2010 .... *93*
  Earlier sketch in SATA *25*
  See also CLR *51*
Park, W(illiam) B(ryan) 1936- *22*
Parke, Marilyn 1928- *82*

Parker, Barbara Keevil 1938- *157*
Parker, Daniel
   See Ehrenhaft, Daniel
Parker, Elinor Milnor 1906- *3*
Parker, Julie F. 1961- *92*
Parker, Kim 1963- *174*
Parker, Kristy 1957- *59*
Parker, Lois M(ay) 1912-1996 .... *30*
Parker, Margot M. 1937- *52*
Parker, Marjorie Blain 1960- *205*
   Earlier sketch in SATA *145*
Parker, Mary Jessie 1948- *71*
Parker, Nancy Winslow 1930- *132*
   Earlier sketches in SATA *10, 69*
   See also SAAS *20*
Parker, Richard 1915-1990 .... *14*
Parker, Robert
   See Boyd, Waldo T.
   and Parker, Robert Andrew
Parker, Robert Andrew 1927- *200*
Parker, Steve 1954- *213*
Parker, Tom S. *215*
Parker, Toni Trent 1947-2005 .... *142*
   Obituary *169*
Parker-Rees, Guy *193*
Parker-Rock, Michelle *214*
Parkes, Lucas
   See Harris, John (Wyndham Parkes Lucas)
   Beynon
Parkhill, John
   See Cox, William R(obert)
Parkins, David 1955- *218*
   Earlier sketch in SATA *176*
Parkinson, Curtis *219*
Parkinson, Ethelyn M(inerva) 1906-1999 ..... *11*
Parkinson, Kathryn N. 1954- *71*
Parkinson, Kathy
   See Parkinson, Kathryn N.
Parkinson, Siobhan
   See Parkinson, Siobhan
Parkinson, Siobhan 1954- *178*
Parks, Deborah A. 1948- *133*
   Earlier sketch in SATA *91*
Parks, Edd Winfield 1906-1968 .... *10*
Parks, Gordon 1912-2006 .... *108*
   Obituary *175*
   Earlier sketch in SATA *8*
Parks, Gordon Roger Alexander
   See Parks, Gordon
Parks, Peggy J. 1951- *143*
Parks, PJ
   See Parks, Peggy J.
Parks, Rosa 1913-2005 .... *83*
   Obituary *169*
Parks, Rosa Louise Lee
   See Parks, Rosa
Parks, Van Dyke 1943- *62*
Parlato, Stephen 1954- *222*
Parley, Peter
   See Goodrich, Samuel Griswold
Parlin, John
   See Graves, Charles Parlin
Parme, Fabrice 1966- *191*
Parnall, Peter 1936- *69*
   Earlier sketch in SATA *16*
   See also SAAS *11*
Paros, Jennifer *210*
Parotti, Phillip (Elliott) 1941- *109*
Parr, Ann 1943- *144*
Parr, Danny
   See Parr, Ann
Parr, Letitia (Evelyn) 1906-1985(?) *37*
Parr, Lucy 1924- *10*
Parr, Todd *179*
   Earlier sketch in SATA *134*
Parrish, Anne 1888-1957 .... *27*
Parrish, Mary
   See Cousins, Margaret
Parrish, Maxfield
   See Parrish, (Frederick) Maxfield
Parrish, (Frederick) Maxfield 1870-1966 ..... *14*

Parry, Marian 1924- *13*
Parry, Rosanne *212*
Parson Lot
   See Kingsley, Charles
Parsons, Alexandra 1947- *92*
Parsons, Ellen
   See Dragonwagon, Crescent
Parsons, Garry *197*
Parsons, Martin 1951- *116*
Parsons, Martin Leslie
   See Parsons, Martin
Parsons, Tom
   See MacPherson, Thomas George
Parsons-Yazzi, Evangeline *172*
Partch, Virgil Franklin II 1916-1984 .... *39*
   Obituary *39*
Parton, Dolly 1946- *94*
Parton, Dolly Rebecca
   See Parton, Dolly
Partridge, Benjamin W., Jr. 1915-2005 .... *28*
   Obituary *163*
Partridge, Benjamin Waring, Jr.
   See Partridge, Benjamin W., Jr.
Partridge, Cora Cheney
   See Cheney, Cora
Partridge, Elizabeth *216*
   Earlier sketch in SATA *134*
Partridge, Jenny (Lilian) 1947- *52*
   Brief entry *37*
Pasachoff, Naomi 1947- *147*
Pascal, David 1918- *14*
Pascal, Francine 1938- *143*
   Brief entry *37*
   Earlier sketches in SATA *51, 80*
   See also CLR *25*
Paschal, Nancy
   See Trotter, Grace V(iolet)
Paschkis, Julie 1957- *220*
   Earlier sketch in SATA *177*
Pascudniak, Pascal
   See Lupoff, Richard A(llen)
Pashko, Stanley 1913-1982 .... *29*
Passailaigue, Thomas E.
   See Paisley, Tom
Pastel, Elyse *201*
Pateman, Robert 1954- *84*
Patent, Dorothy Hinshaw 1940- *162*
   Autobiography Feature *162*
   Earlier sketches in SATA *22, 69, 120*
   See also CLR *19*
   See also SAAS *13*
Paterson, A(ndrew) B(arton) 1864-1941 .... *97*
Paterson, Banjo
   See Paterson, A(ndrew) B(arton)
Paterson, Diane 1946- *177*
   Brief entry *33*
   Earlier sketch in SATA *59*
Paterson, John (Barstow) 1932- *114*
Paterson, Katherine 1932- *204*
   Earlier sketches in SATA *13, 53, 92, 133*
   See also CLR *127*
Paterson, Katherine Womeldorf
   See Paterson, Katherine
Patience, John 1949- *90*
Patneaude, David 1944- *159*
   Earlier sketch in SATA *85*
Paton, Alan 1903-1988 .... *11*
   Obituary *56*
Paton, Alan Stewart
   See Paton, Alan
Paton, Jane (Elizabeth) 1934- *35*
Paton, Priscilla 1952- *98*
Paton Walsh, Gillian
   See Paton Walsh, Jill
Paton Walsh, Jill 1937- *190*
   Autobiography Feature *190*
   Earlier sketches in SATA *4, 72, 109*
   See also CLR *128*
   See also SAAS *3*
Patricelli, Leslie *207*

Patrick, Susan
   See Clark, Patricia Denise
Patron, Susan 1948- *182*
   Earlier sketch in SATA *76*
Patsauq, Markoosie 1942-
   See CLR *23*
Patschke, Steve 1955- *125*
Patten, Brian 1946- *152*
   Earlier sketch in SATA *29*
Patterson, Charles 1935- *59*
Patterson, Geoffrey 1943- *54*
   Brief entry *44*
Patterson, James 1947- *197*
   Earlier sketch in SATA *164*
Patterson, James B.
   See Patterson, James
Patterson, Lillie G. -1999 .... *88*
   Earlier sketch in SATA *14*
Patterson, Nancy Ruth 1944- *148*
   Earlier sketch in SATA *72*
Patterson, Valerie O. *223*
Pattison, Darcy (S.) 1954- *126*
   Earlier sketch in SATA *72*
Pattou, Edith *164*
Patz (Blaustein), Nancy *154*
Paul, Aileen 1917- *12*
Paul, Alison *196*
Paul, Ann Whitford 1941- *209*
   Earlier sketches in SATA *76, 110, 168*
Paul, David (Tyler) 1934-1988
   Obituary *56*
Paul, Dominique 1973- *184*
Paul, Elizabeth
   See Crow, Donna Fletcher
Paul, Hamish Vigne Christie 1951- *151*
   See also CLR *87*
Paul, James 1936- *23*
Paul, Korky
   See Paul, Hamish Vigne Christie
Paul, Robert
   See Roberts, John G(aither)
Paul, Tessa 1944- *103*
Pauley, Kimberly 1973- *208*
Pauli, Hertha (Ernestine) 1909-1973 .... *3*
   Obituary *26*
Paull, Grace A. 1898- *24*
Paulsen, Gary 1939- *189*
   Earlier sketches in SATA *22, 50, 54, 79, 111,
   158*
   See also CLR *82*
Paulson, Jack
   See Jackson, C(aary) Paul
Pauquet, Gina Ruck
   See Ruck-Pauquet, Gina
Pausacker, Jenny 1948- *72*
   See also SAAS *23*
Pausewang, Gudrun 1928- *165*
   Earlier sketch in SATA *104*
Pavel, Frances 1907- *10*
Paver, Michelle *215*
   Earlier sketch in SATA *170*
Paxton
   See Barr, Nevada
Paxton, Thomas R. 1937- *70*
Paxton, Tom
   See Paxton, Thomas R.
Paye, Won-Ldy *185*
Payne, Alan
   See Jakes, John
Payne, Bernal C., Jr. 1941- *60*
Payne, C. Douglas
   See Payne, C.D.
Payne, C.D. 1949- *133*
Payne, C.F. 1956- *179*
Payne, Chris Fox
   See Payne, C.F.
Payne, Donald Gordon 1924- *37*
Payne, Emmy
   See West, Emily Govan
Payne, Nina *135*

Payne, Rachel Ann
    See Jakes, John
Payson, Dale 1943- 9
Payzant, Charles 18
Paz, A.
    See Pahz, James Alon
Paz, Natalia Toledo
    See Toledo, Natalia
Paz, Zan
    See Pahz, Cheryl Suzanne
Peace, Mary
    See Finley, Mary Peace
Peacock, Louise 210
Peacock, Shane 1957- 192
Peake, Mervyn 1911-1968 23
Peale, Norman Vincent 1898-1993 20
    Obituary 78
Pearce, Ann Philippa
    See Pearce, Philippa
Pearce, Emily Smith 1975- 199
Pearce, Jacqueline 1962- 146
Pearce, Margaret 104
Pearce, Philippa 1920-2006 129
    Obituary 179
    Earlier sketches in SATA *1, 67*
    See also CLR *9*
Peare, Catherine Owens 1911- 9
Pearle, Ida 207
Pearsall, Shelley 1966- 190
Pearson, Gayle 1947- 119
    Earlier sketch in SATA *53*
Pearson, Jean Mary
    See Gardam, Jane
Pearson, Kit 1947- 77
    Autobiography Feature 117
    See also CLR *26*
Pearson, Mary E. 1955- 211
    Earlier sketch in SATA *134*
Pearson, Ridley 1953- 182
Pearson, Susan 1946- 166
    Brief entry 27
    Earlier sketches in SATA *39, 91*
Pearson, Tracey Campbell 1956- 219
    Earlier sketches in SATA *64, 155*
Pease, (Clarence) Howard 1894-1974 2
    Obituary 25
Peavy, Linda 1943- 54
Peck, Anne Merriman 1884-1976 18
Peck, Beth 1957- 190
    Earlier sketch in SATA *79*
Peck, Jan 159
Peck, Jeanie J. 1967- 147
Peck, Marshall III 1951- 92
Peck, Richard 1934- 190
    Autobiography Feature 110
    Earlier sketches in SATA *18, 55, 97, 110, 158*
    See also CLR *142*
    See also SAAS *2*
Peck, Richard Wayne
    See Peck, Richard
Peck, Robert Newton 1928- 156
    Autobiography Feature 108
    Earlier sketches in SATA *21, 62, 111*
    See also CLR *45*
    See also SAAS *1*
Peck, Sylvia 1953- 133
Peck-Whiting, Jeanie J.
    See Peck, Jeanie J.
Peddicord, Jane Ann 199
Pedersen, Janet 193
Pederson, Sharleen
    See Collicott, Sharleen
Pedler, Caroline 197
Peebles, Anne
    See Galloway, Priscilla
Peek, Merle 1938- 39
Peel, John 1954- 79
Peel, Norman Lemon
    See Hirsch, Phil
Peeples, Edwin A(ugustus, Jr.) 1915-1994 6
Peers, Judi 1956- 119

Peers, Judith May West
    See Peers, Judi
Peet, Bill
    See Peet, William Bartlett
Peet, Creighton B. 1899-1977 30
Peet, Mal 171
Peet, Malcolm
    See Peet, Mal
Peet, William Bartlett 1915-2002 78
    Obituary 137
    Earlier sketches in SATA *2, 41*
    See also CLR *12*
Peguero, Leone 116
Pelaez, Jill 1924- 12
Pelham, David 1938- 70
Pelikan, Judy 1941- 219
Pell, Ed(ward) 1950- 157
Pelletier, Andrew T. 195
Pelletier, Andrew Thomas
    See Pelletier, Andrew T.
Pellowski, Anne 1933- 20
Pellowski, Michael (Joseph) 1949- 151
    Brief entry 48
    Earlier sketch in SATA *88*
Pellowski, Michael Morgan
    See Pellowski, Michael (Joseph)
Pelta, Kathy 1928- 18
Peltier, Leslie C(opus) 1900-1980 13
Pemberton, Bonnie 191
Pemberton, John Leigh
    See Leigh-Pemberton, John
Pembury, Bill
    See Groom, Arthur William
Pemsteen, Hans
    See Manes, Stephen
Pendennis, Arthur Esquir
    See Thackeray, William Makepeace
Pender, Lydia Podger 1907- 61
Pendery, Rosemary (Schmitz) 7
Pendle, Alexy 1943- 29
Pendle, George 1906-1977
    Obituary 28
Pendleton, Don
    See Cunningham, Chet
    and Garside, Jack
    and Jagninski, Tom
    and Krauzer, Steven M(ark)
    and Obstfeld, Raymond
Pendleton, Thomas 1965- 206
Pendziwol, Jean E. 1965- 177
Pene du Bois, William (Sherman)
    1916-1993 68
    Obituary 74
    Earlier sketch in SATA *4*
    See also CLR *1*
Penn, Audrey 1947- 212
Penn, Audrey 1950- 22
Penn, Ruth Bonn
    See Rosenberg, Eth Clifford
Pennac, Daniel 1944- 155
Pennage, E. M.
    See Finkel, George (Irvine)
Penner, Fred 1946- 169
    Earlier sketch in SATA *67*
Penner, Frederick Ralph Cornelius
    See Penner, Fred
Penney, Grace Jackson 1904-2000 35
Penney, Ian 1960- 76
Penney, Sue 1957- 152
    Earlier sketch in SATA *102*
Pennington, Eunice 1923- 27
Pennington, Lillian Boyer 1904-2003 45
Pennypacker, Sara 1951- 187
Penrose, Gordon 1925- 66
Penson, Mary E. 1917- 78
Penzler, Otto 1942- 38
Pepe, Phil 1935- 20
Pepe, Philip
    See Pepe, Phil

Peppe, Rodney (Darrell) 1934- 74
    Earlier sketch in SATA *4*
    See also SAAS *10*
Pepper, Frank S. 1910-1988
    Obituary 61
Percy, Charles Henry
    See Smith, Dorothy Gladys
Percy, Rachel 1930- 63
Perdrizet, Marie-Pierre 1952- 79
Perenyi, Constance 1954- 93
Perenyi, Constance Marie
    See Perenyi, Constance
Perera, Hilda 1926- 105
Perera, Thomas Biddle 1938- 13
Peretti, Frank E. 1951- 141
    Earlier sketch in SATA *80*
Perez, L. King 1940- 199
Perez, Lana
    See Perez, Marlene
Perez, Lucia Angela 1973- 182
Perez, Marlene 170
Pericoli, Matteo 1968- 178
Perkins, Al(bert Rogers) 1904-1975 30
Perkins, Dan
    See Tomorrow, Tom
Perkins, Lucy Fitch 1865-1937 72
Perkins, Lynne Rae 1956- 212
    Earlier sketches in SATA *131, 172*
Perkins, (Richard) Marlin 1905-1986 21
    Obituary 48
Perkins, Mitali 1963- 188
    Earlier sketch in SATA *88*
Perks, Anne-Marie 1955- 122
Perl, Erica S. 222
    Earlier sketch in SATA *188*
Perl, Lila 72
    Earlier sketch in SATA *6*
Perl, Susan 1922-1983 22
    Obituary 34
Perlman, Janet 1954- 222
Perlman, Rhea 1948- 183
Perlmutter, O(scar) William 1920-1975 8
Pernu, Dennis 1970- 87
Perrault, Charles 1628-1703 25
    See also CLR *134*
Perret, Delphine 1980- 190
Perret, Gene (Richard) 1937- 76
Perriman, Cole
    See Perrin, Pat
Perriman, Cole
    See Coleman, Wim
Perrin, Pat 212
Perrine, Mary 1913-1976 2
Perrins, Lesley 1953- 56
Perrow, Angeli 1954- 121
Perry, Andrea 1956- 190
    Earlier sketch in SATA *148*
Perry, Barbara Fisher
    See Fisher, Barbara
Perry, Elizabeth 1959- 174
Perry, Elizabeth Goodwin
    See Perry, Elizabeth
Perry, John 1967- 223
Perry, Marie Fritz 165
Perry, Patricia 1949- 30
Perry, Phyllis J(ean) 1933- 152
    Earlier sketches in SATA *60, 101*
Perry, Ritchie (John Allen) 1942- 105
Perry, Roger 1933- 27
Perry, Steve(n Carl) 1947- 76
Pershall, Mary K. 1951- 172
    Earlier sketch in SATA *70*
Pershing, Marie
    See Schultz, Pearle Henriksen
Perske, Robert 1927- 57
Persun, Morgan Reed
    See Watkins, Dawn L.
Perversi, Margaret 213
Petach, Heidi 149
Peter
    See Stratemeyer, Edward L.

Peters, Alexander
  See Hollander, Zander
Peters, Andrew Fusek 1965- *169*
  Earlier sketch in SATA *107*
Peters, Bernadette 1948- *212*
Peters, Caroline
  See Betz, Eva Kelly
Peters, David
  See David, Peter
Peters, Elizabeth 1927- *49*
Peters, Emma
  See Price, Karen
Peters, Gabriel
  See Matott, Justin
Peters, Julie Anne 1952- *197*
  Earlier sketches in SATA *82, 128*
Peters, Linda
  See Catherall, Arthur
Peters, Lisa Westberg 1951- *161*
  Earlier sketches in SATA *74, 115*
Peters, Patricia 1953- *84*
Peters, Russell M. 1929- *78*
Peters, S. H.
  See Henry, O.
  and Proffitt, Nicholas
Petersen, David 1946- *109*
  Earlier sketch in SATA *62*
Petersen, Gwenn Boardman 1924- *12*
Petersen, P(eter) J(ames) 1941- *118*
  Brief entry *43*
  Earlier sketches in SATA *48, 83*
Petersen, Palle 1943- *85*
Petersham, Maud 1890-1971 .... *17*
  See also CLR *24*
Petersham, Maud Sylvia Fuller
  See Petersham, Maud
Petersham, Miska 1888-1960 .... *17*
  See also CLR *24*
Peterson, Cris 1952- *174*
  Earlier sketches in SATA *84, 145*
Peterson, Dawn 1934- *86*
Peterson, Esther (Allen) 1934- *35*
Peterson, Hans 1922- *8*
Peterson, Harold L(eslie) 1922-1978 .... *8*
Peterson, Helen Stone 1910- *8*
Peterson, Jean Sunde 1941- *108*
Peterson, Jeanne Whitehouse 1939- *159*
  Earlier sketch in SATA *29*
Peterson, Kathleen B. 1951- *119*
Peterson, Lorraine 1940- *56*
  Brief entry *44*
Peterson, Mary *215*
Peterson, Shelley 1952- *146*
Peterson, Will
  See Cocks, Peter
Petie, Haris
  See Petty, Roberta
Petricic, Dusan 1946- *176*
Petrides, Heidrun 1944- *19*
Petrie, Catherine 1947- *52*
  Brief entry *41*
Petrone, Valeria *186*
Petrosino, Tamara *193*
Petroski, Catherine (Ann Groom) 1939- *48*
Petrovich, Michael B(oro) 1922- *40*
Petrovskaya, Kyra
  See Wayne, Kyra Petrovskaya
Petruccio, Steven James 1961- *67*
Petrucha, Stefan 1959- *213*
Petry, Ann 1908-1997 .... *5*
  Obituary *94*
  See also CLR *12*
Petry, Ann Lane
  See Petry, Ann
Pettit, Jayne 1932- *108*
Petty, J.T. 1977- *189*
Petty, Kate 1951-2007 .... *204*
Petty, Roberta 1915- *10*
Pevsner, Stella *131*
  Earlier sketches in SATA *8, 77*
  See also SAAS *14*

Peyo
  See Culliford, Pierre
Peyton, K. M.
  See Peyton, Kathleen Wendy
Peyton, Kathleen Wendy 1929- *157*
  Earlier sketches in SATA *15, 62*
  See also CLR *3*
  See also SAAS *17*
Pfanner, (Anne) Louise 1955- *68*
Pfeffer, Susan Beth 1948- *180*
  Earlier sketches in SATA *4, 83*
  See also CLR *11*
  See also SAAS *17*
Pfeffer, Wendy 1929- *204*
  Earlier sketches in SATA *78, 142*
Pfeiffer, Janet (B.) 1949- *96*
Pfister, Marcus *207*
  Earlier sketches in SATA *83, 150*
  See also CLR *42*
Pfitsch, Patricia Curtis 1948- *148*
Pfitzenmaier, Audrey 1959- *220*
Pflieger, Pat 1955- *84*
Pham, LeUyen 1973- *201*
  Earlier sketch in SATA *175*
Phelan, Mary Kay 1914- *3*
Phelan, Matt 1970- *215*
  Earlier sketch in SATA *172*
Phelan, Terry Wolfe 1941- *56*
Phelps, Ethel Johnston 1914-1984 .... *35*
Philbrick, Rodman 1951- *163*
Philbrick, W. Rodman
  See Philbrick, Rodman
Philbrick, W.R.
  See Philbrick, Rodman
Philbrook, Clem(ent E.) 1917- *24*
Phillipps, J.C. *218*
Phillipps, Julie Christine
  See Phillipps, J.C.
Phillips, Aileen Paul
  See Paul, Aileen
Phillips, Betty Lou
  See Phillips, Elizabeth Louise
Phillips, Bob 1940- *95*
Phillips, Douglas A. 1949- *161*
Phillips, Elizabeth Louise *58*
  Brief entry *48*
Phillips, Irv(ing W.) 1905-2000 .... *11*
  Obituary *125*
Phillips, Jack
  See Sandburg, Carl
Phillips, Leon
  See Gerson, Noel Bertram
Phillips, Loretta (Hosey) 1893-1987 .... *10*
Phillips, Louis 1942- *102*
  Earlier sketch in SATA *8*
Phillips, Mark
  See Garrett, Randall
  and Janifer, Laurence M(ark)
Phillips, Mary Geisler 1881-1964 .... *10*
Phillips, Michael
  See Nolan, William F.
Phillips, (Woodward) Prentice 1894-1981 .... *10*
Phillpotts, Eden 1862-1960 .... *24*
Phin
  See Thayer, Ernest Lawrence
Phipson, Joan
  See Fitzhardinge, Joan Margaret
Phiz
  See Browne, Hablot Knight
Phleger, Fred B. 1909-1993 .... *34*
Phleger, Marjorie Temple 1908(?)-1986 .... *1*
  Obituary *47*
Piaget, Jean 1896-1980
  Obituary *23*
Piatti, Celestino 1922- *16*
Picard, Barbara Leonie 1917- *89*
  Earlier sketch in SATA *2*
  See also SAAS *10*
Pichon, Liz *174*
Pickard, Charles 1932- *36*

Pickering, James Sayre 1897-1969 .... *36*
  Obituary *28*
Pickering, Jimmy *195*
Pickering, Robert B. 1950- *93*
Pielichaty, Helena 1955- *142*
Pien, Lark *222*
Pienkowski, Jan (Michal) 1936- *131*
  Earlier sketches in SATA *6, 58*
  See also CLR *6*
Pierce, Edith Gray 1893-1977 .... *45*
Pierce, Katherine
  See St. John, Wylly Folk
Pierce, Meredith Ann 1958- *127*
  Brief entry *48*
  Earlier sketch in SATA *67*
  See also CLR *20*
Pierce, Ruth (Ireland) 1936- *5*
Pierce, Sharon
  See McCullough, Sharon Pierce
Pierce, Tamora 1954- *187*
  Brief entry *49*
  Earlier sketches in SATA *51, 96, 153*
Pierce, Terry *178*
Pierik, Robert 1921- *13*
Piernas-Davenport, Gail *199*
Piers, Robert
  See Anthony, Piers
Pig, Edward
  See Gorey, Edward (St. John)
Pignataro, Anna 1965- *223*
Pike, Aprilynne *218*
Pike, Bob
  See Pike, Robert W.
Pike, Christopher 1954(?)- *156*
  Earlier sketch in SATA *68*
  See also CLR *29*
Pike, Deborah 1951- *89*
Pike, E(dgar) Royston 1896-1980 .... *22*
  Obituary *56*
Pike, R. William 1956- *92*
Pike, Robert
  See Pike, Robert W.
Pike, Robert W. 1931- *102*
Pike, Robert Wilson
  See Pike, Robert W.
Pilarski, Laura 1926- *13*
Pilgrim, Anne
  See Allan, Mabel Esther
Pilkey, Dav 1966- *166*
  Earlier sketches in SATA *68, 115*
  See also CLR *160*
Pilkey, David Murray, Jr.
  See Pilkey, Dav
Pilkington, Francis Meredyth 1907-1993 .... *4*
Pilkington, Roger (Windle) 1915-2003 .... *10*
  Obituary *144*
Pilutti, Deb *208*
Pin, Isabel 1975- *183*
Pinchot, David 1914(?)-1983
  Obituary *34*
Pincus, Harriet 1938- *27*
Pinczes, Elinor J(ane) 1940- *81*
Pine, Nicholas 1951- *91*
Pine, Tillie S(chloss) 1896-1999 .... *13*
Pini, Richard (Alan) 1950- *89*
Pini, Wendy 1951- *89*
Pinkerton, Kathrene Sutherland (Gedney)
  1887-1967
  Obituary *26*
Pinkett, Jada
  See Smith, Jada Pinkett
Pinkney, Andrea Davis 1963- *160*
  Earlier sketch in SATA *113*
Pinkney, Brian 1961- *206*
  Earlier sketches in SATA *74, 148*
  See also CLR *54*
Pinkney, Gloria Jean 1941- *212*
  Earlier sketch in SATA *85*
Pinkney, J. Brian
  See Pinkney, Brian

Pinkney, Jerry 1939- *198*
   Autobiography Feature *198*
   Brief entry *32*
   Earlier sketches in SATA *41, 71, 107, 151*
   See also CLR *43*
   See also SAAS *12*
Pinkney, John *97*
Pinkney, Sandra L. *193*
   Earlier sketch in SATA *128*
Pinkwater, D. Manus
   See Pinkwater, Daniel
Pinkwater, Daniel 1941- *210*
   Earlier sketches in SATA *8, 46, 76, 114, 158*
   See also CLR *4*
   See also SAAS *3*
Pinkwater, Daniel M.
   See Pinkwater, Daniel
Pinkwater, Daniel Manus
   See Pinkwater, Daniel
Pinkwater, Jill *188*
Pinkwater, Manus
   See Pinkwater, Daniel
Pinner, Joma
   See Werner, Herma
Pinto, Sara *200*
Pioneer
   See Yates, Raymond F(rancis)
Piowaty, Kim Kennelly 1957- *49*
Piper, Roger
   See Fisher, John
Pirner, Connie White 1955- *72*
Piro, Richard 1934- *7*
Pirot, Alison Lohans
   See Lohans, Alison
Pirotta, Saviour *184*
Pirsig, Robert M(aynard) 1928- *39*
Pita
   See Rendon, Maria
Pitcher, C.
   See Pitcher, Caroline
Pitcher, Caroline 1948- *214*
   Earlier sketch in SATA *128*
Pitcher, Caroline Nell
   See Pitcher, Caroline
Pitman, (Isaac) James 1901-1985
   Obituary *46*
Pitre, Felix 1949- *84*
Pitrone, Jean Maddern 1920- *4*
Pittman, Helena Clare 1945- *71*
Pitz, Henry C(larence) 1895-1976 .... *4*
   Obituary *24*
Pitzer, Susanna 1958- *181*
Piven, Hanoch 1963- *173*
Pixley, Marcella *194*
Pizer, Vernon 1918- *21*
Place, Marian T(empleton) 1910- *3*
Place, Robin (Mary) 1926- *71*
Plaidy, Jean
   See Hibbert, Eleanor Alice Burford
Plain, Belva 1919-2010 .... *62*
Plaine, Alfred R. 1898(?)-1981
   Obituary *29*
Plant, Andrew *214*
Plath, Sylvia 1932-1963 .... *96*
Platt, Chris 1959- *185*
Platt, Kin 1911- *86*
   Earlier sketch in SATA *21*
   See also SAAS *17*
Platt, Randall 1948- *95*
Platt, Randall Beth
   See Platt, Randall
Platt, Richard 1953- *218*
   Earlier sketches in SATA *120, 166*
Playfellow, Robin
   See Ellis, Edward S.
Playsted, James
   See Wood, James Playsted
Plecas, Jennifer 1966- *149*
   Earlier sketch in SATA *84*
Plimpton, George 1927-2003 .... *10*
   Obituary *150*

Plimpton, George Ames
   See Plimpton, George
Plomer, William Charles Franklin
   1903-1973 .... *24*
Plotz, Helen Ratnoff 1913-2000 .... *38*
Plourde, Lynn 1955- *218*
   Earlier sketches in SATA *122, 168*
Plowden, David 1932- *52*
Plowden, Martha Ward 1948- *98*
Plowhead, Ruth Gipson 1877-1967 .... *43*
Plowman, Stephanie 1922- *6*
Pluckrose, Henry (Arthur) 1931- *141*
   Earlier sketch in SATA *13*
Plum, J.
   See Wodehouse, P. G.
Plum, Jennifer
   See Kurland, Michael
Plumb, Charles P. 1900(?)-1982
   Obituary *29*
Plume, Ilse *170*
   Brief entry *43*
Plumme, Don E.
   See Katz, Bobbi
Plummer, Margaret 1911- *2*
Plum-Ucci, Carol *184*
Pochocki, Ethel (Frances) 1925- *76*
Podendorf, Illa (E.) 1903(?)-1983 .... *18*
   Obituary *35*
Podwal, Mark 1945- *160*
   Earlier sketch in SATA *101*
Podwal, Mark H.
   See Podwal, Mark
Poe, Edgar Allan 1809-1849 .... *23*
Poe, Ty (Christopher) 1975- *94*
Pogany, William Andrew 1882-1955 .... *44*
   Brief entry *30*
Pogany, Willy
   See Pogany, William Andrew
Pogue, Carolyn 1948- *223*
Pohl, Frederik 1919- *24*
Pohlmann, Lillian (Grenfell) 1902-1997 .... *11*
Pohrt, Tom 1953- *195*
   Earlier sketches in SATA *67, 152*
Pointon, Robert
   See Rooke, Daphne
Points, Larry G. 1945- *177*
   Earlier sketch in SATA *133*
Points, Larry Gene
   See Points, Larry G.
Pokeberry, P.J.
   See Mitchell, B.J.
POLA
   See Watson, Pauline
Polacco, Patricia 1944- *212*
   Earlier sketches in SATA *74, 123, 180*
   See also CLR *40*
Polacco, Patricia Ann
   See Polacco, Patricia
Polak, Monique 1960- *178*
Polatnick, Florence T. 1923- *5*
Polcovar, Jane 1948- *211*
Polder, Markus
   See Kruss, James
Polese, Carolyn 1947- *58*
Polese, James 1914- *87*
Polette, Nancy (Jane) 1930- *42*
Polhamus, Jean Burt 1928- *21*
Polhemus, Coleman *210*
Policoff, Stephen Phillip 1948- *77*
Polikoff, Barbara G. 1929- *162*
   Earlier sketch in SATA *77*
Polikoff, Barbara Garland
   See Polikoff, Barbara G.
Polisar, Barry Louis 1954- *134*
   Earlier sketch in SATA *77*
Politi, Leo 1908-1996 .... *47*
   Obituary *88*
   Earlier sketch in SATA *1*
   See also CLR *29*
Polking, Kirk 1925- *5*
Pollack, Jill S. 1963- *88*

Pollack, Merrill S. 1924-1988
   Obituary *55*
Polland, Barbara K(ay) 1939- *44*
Polland, Madeleine A(ngela Cahill) 1918- ... *68*
   Earlier sketch in SATA *6*
   See also SAAS *8*
Pollema-Cahill, Phyllis 1958- *123*
Pollock, Bruce 1945- *46*
Pollock, Mary
   See Blyton, Enid
Pollock, Penny 1935- *137*
   Brief entry *42*
   Earlier sketch in SATA *44*
Pollowitz, Melinda Kilborn 1944- *26*
Polner, Murray 1928- *64*
Polonsky, Arthur 1925- *34*
Polseno, Jo *17*
Pomaska, Anna 1946- *117*
Pomerantz, Charlotte 1930- *177*
   Earlier sketches in SATA *20, 80*
Pomeroy, Pete
   See Roth, Arthur J(oseph)
Pon, Cindy 1973- *216*
Pond, Alonzo W(illiam) 1894-1986 .... *5*
Pontiflet, Ted 1932- *32*
Poole, Gray Johnson 1906- *1*
Poole, Josephine
   See Helyar, Jane Penelope Josephine
Poole, (Jane Penelope) Josephine
   See Helyar, Jane Penelope Josephine
Poole, Lynn 1910-1969 .... *1*
Poole, Peggy 1925- *39*
Poortvliet, Rien 1932- *65*
   Brief entry *37*
Pope, Elizabeth Marie 1917-1992 .... *38*
   Brief entry *36*
Pope, Kevin 1958- *183*
Popescu, Christine
   See Pullein-Thompson, Christine
Poploff, Michelle 1956- *67*
Popp, K. Wendy *91*
Poppel, Hans 1942- *71*
Porfirio, Guy 1958- *197*
Portal, Colette 1936- *6*
Porte, Barbara Ann 1943- *152*
   Brief entry *45*
   Earlier sketches in SATA *57, 93*
Porter, A(nthony) P(eyton) 1945- *68*
Porter, Connie (Rose) 1959(?)- *129*
   Earlier sketch in SATA *81*
Porter, Donald Clayton
   See Gerson, Noel Bertram
Porter, Eleanor H(odgman) 1868-1920
   See CLR *110*
Porter, Gene Stratton
   See Stratton-Porter, Gene
Porter, Janice Lee 1953- *108*
   Earlier sketch in SATA *68*
Porter, Katherine Anne 1890-1980 .... *39*
   Obituary *23*
Porter, Kathryn
   See Swinford, Betty (June Wells)
Porter, Pamela 1956- *193*
Porter, Sheena 1935- *24*
   See also SAAS *10*
Porter, Sue
   See Limb, Sue
Porter, Sue 1951- *213*
   Earlier sketch in SATA *76*
Porter, Tracey *191*
Porter, William Sydney
   See Henry, O.
Portis, Antoinette *189*
Porto, Tony 1960- *153*
Portteus, Eleanora Marie Manthei (?)-1983
   Obituary *36*
Posada, Mia *187*
Posell, Elsa Z(eigerman) -1995 .... *3*
Posesorski, Sherie *216*
Posten, Margaret L(ois) 1915- *10*
Postgate, Daniel 1964- *216*

Posthuma, Sieb 1960- *150*
Postier, Jim 1965- *202*
Potok, Chaim 1929-2002 .... *106*
  Obituary *134*
  Earlier sketch in SATA *33*
  See also CLR *92*
Potok, Herbert Harold
  See Potok, Chaim
Potok, Herman Harold
  See Potok, Chaim
Potter, Alicia *216*
Potter, Beatrix 1866-1943 .... *132*
  Earlier sketch in SATA *100*
  See also YABC *1*
  See also CLR *73*
Potter, Ellen 1973- *218*
Potter, Giselle *187*
  Earlier sketch in SATA *150*
Potter, Helen Beatrix
  See Potter, Beatrix
Potter, Katherine *217*
Potter, Margaret 1926-1998 .... *21*
  Obituary *104*
Potter, Marian 1915- *9*
Potter, Miriam Clark 1886-1965 .... *3*
Poulin, Stephane 1961- *98*
  See also CLR *28*
Poulton, Kimberly 1957(?)- *136*
Pournelle, Jerry 1933- *161*
  Earlier sketches in SATA *26, 91*
Pournelle, Jerry Eugene
  See Pournelle, Jerry
Povelite, Kay 1955- *102*
Pow, Tom 1950- *163*
Powe-Allred, Alexandra
  See Allred, Alexandra Powe
Powell, A. M.
  See Morgan, Alfred P(owell)
Powell, Consie *174*
Powell, E. Sandy 1947- *72*
Powell, E.S.
  See Powell, E. Sandy
Powell, Pamela 1960- *78*
Powell, Patricia Hruby 1951- *136*
Powell, Randy 1956- *118*
Powell, Richard Stillman
  See Barbour, Ralph Henry
Powell, Robert (Stephenson Smyth) Baden
  See Baden-Powell, Robert (Stephenson Smyth)
Powell, Stephanie 1953- *93*
Power, Margaret (M.) 1945- *125*
  Earlier sketch in SATA *75*
Powers, Anne
  See Schwartz, Anne Powers
Powers, Bill 1931- *52*
  Brief entry *31*
Powers, Daniel 1959- *164*
Powers, J. L. *195*
Powers, Jessica
  See Powers, J. L.
Powers, Jessica Lynn
  See Powers, J. L.
Powers, Margaret
  See Heal, Edith
Powers, Tim 1952- *107*
Powers, Timothy Thomas
  See Powers, Tim
Powledge, Fred 1935- *37*
Poydar, Nancy *190*
Poynter, Margaret 1927- *27*
Prachaticka, Marketa
  See Kolibalova, Marketa
Prachatika, Marketa
  See Kolibalova, Marketa
Prager, Arthur *44*
Prager, Ellen J. 1962- *136*
Prange, Beckie *172*
Prap, Lila 1955- *177*
Praprotnik-Zupancic, Lilijana
  See Prap, Lila

Pratchett, Terence David John
  See Pratchett, Terry
Pratchett, Terry 1948- *185*
  Earlier sketches in SATA *82, 139*
  See also CLR *64*
Prater, John 1947- *149*
  Earlier sketches in SATA *72, 103*
Prato, Rodica *184*
Pratt, Christine Joy *214*
Pratt, (Murray) Fletcher 1897-1956 .... *102*
Pratt, Kristin Joy 1976- *87*
Pratt, Pierre 1962- *208*
  Earlier sketches in SATA *95, 166*
Preiss, Byron 1953-2005 .... *166*
  Brief entry *42*
  Earlier sketch in SATA *47*
Preiss, Byron Cary
  See Preiss, Byron
Preller, James 1961- *209*
  Earlier sketch in SATA *88*
Prelutsky, Jack 1940- *171*
  Earlier sketches in SATA *22, 66, 118*
  See also CLR *115*
Prentice, Amy
  See Kaler, James Otis
Prescott, Casey
  See Morris, Chris(topher Crosby)
Presnall, Judith (Ann) Janda 1943- *96*
Pressler, Mirjam 1940- *155*
Preston, Douglas 1956- *113*
Preston, Edna Mitchell *40*
Preston, Lillian Elvira 1918- *47*
Preus, Margi *209*
Preussler, Otfried 1923- *24*
Prevert, Jacques 1900-1977
  Obituary *30*
Prevert, Jacques Henri Marie
  See Prevert, Jacques
Prevost, Guillaume 1964- *192*
Prevost, Mikela *203*
Price, Beverley Joan 1931- *98*
Price, Charlie *187*
Price, Christine (Hilda) 1928-1980 .... *3*
  Obituary *23*
Price, Garrett 1896-1979
  Obituary *22*
Price, Jennifer
  See Hoover, Helen (Drusilla Blackburn)
Price, Joan 1931- *124*
Price, Jonathan (Reeve) 1941- *46*
Price, Karen 1957- *125*
Price, Kathy Z. 1957- *172*
Price, Lucie Locke
  See Locke, Lucie
Price, Olive 1903-1991 .... *8*
Price, Susan 1955- *128*
  Earlier sketches in SATA *25, 85*
Price, Willard 1887-1983 .... *48*
  Brief entry *38*
Price-Groff, Claire *127*
Priceman, Marjorie 1958- *168*
  Earlier sketches in SATA *81, 120*
Prichard, Katharine Susannah 1883-1969 ..... *66*
Prideaux, Tom 1908-1993 .... *37*
  Obituary *76*
Priestley, Alice 1962- *95*
Priestley, Chris 1958- *198*
Priestley, Lee (Shore) 1904-1999 .... *27*
Priestly, Doug 1954- *122*
Priestly, Douglas Michael
  See Priestly, Doug
Prieto, Mariana Beeching 1912-1999 .... *8*
Priley, Margaret (Ann) Hubbard 1909-1992
  Obituary *130*
Primavera, Elise 1954- *185*
  Brief entry *48*
  Earlier sketches in SATA *58, 109*
Prime, Derek (James) 1931- *34*
Prince, Alison (Mary) 1931- *86*
  Earlier sketch in SATA *28*
Prince, April Jones 1975- *180*

Prince, J(ack) H(arvey) 1908- *17*
Prince, Joshua *188*
Prince, Maggie *102*
Prineas, Sarah *204*
Pringle, Eric *138*
Pringle, Laurence 1935- *201*
  Autobiography Feature *201*
  Earlier sketches in SATA *4, 68, 104, 154*
  See also CLR *57*
  See also SAAS *6*
Pringle, Laurence Patrick
  See Pringle, Laurence
Prinz, Yvonne 1960- *175*
Prior, Natalie Jane 1963- *106*
Pritchett, Elaine H(illyer) 1920- *36*
Pritchett, Laura 1971- *178*
Pritchett, Laura Rose
  See Pritchett, Laura
Pritts, Kim Derek 1953- *83*
Prochazkova, Iva 1953- *68*
Proctor, Everitt
  See Montgomery, Rutherford George
Proeysen, Alf 1914-1970 .... *67*
  See also CLR *24*
Professor Scribbler
  See Hollingsworth, Mary
Proimos, James 1955- *217*
  Earlier sketch in SATA *173*
Prose, Francine 1947- *198*
  Earlier sketches in SATA *101, 149*
Prosek, James 1975- *216*
Protopopescu, Orel *186*
Protopopescu, Orel Odinov
  See Protopopescu, Orel
Provensen, Alice 1918- *147*
  Earlier sketches in SATA *9, 70*
  See also CLR *11*
Provensen, Martin 1916-1987 .... *70*
  Obituary *51*
  Earlier sketch in SATA *9*
  See also CLR *11*
Provensen, Martin Elias
  See Provensen, Martin
Provenzo, Eugene (F., Jr.) 1949- *142*
  Earlier sketch in SATA *78*
Provist, d'Alain 1906-1989
  See Diop, Birago (Ismael)
Provost, Gail Levine 1944- *65*
Provost, Gary (Richard) 1944-1995 .... *66*
Proysen, Alf
  See Proeysen, Alf
Pruett, Candace (J.) 1968- *157*
Pryor, Bonnie H. 1942- *69*
Pryor, Boori (Monty) 1950- *112*
Pryor, Helen Brenton 1897-1972 .... *4*
Pryor, Michael 1957- *153*
Pucci, Albert John 1920- *44*
Pudney, John (Sleigh) 1909-1977 .... *24*
Pugh, Ellen (Tiffany) 1920- *7*
Pullein-Thompson, Christine 1925-2005 ...... *82*
  Obituary *172*
  Earlier sketch in SATA *3*
Pullein-Thompson, Diana
  See Farr, Diana
Pullein-Thompson, Joanna Maxwell
  1898-1961 .... *82*
Pullein-Thompson, Josephine (Mary Wedderburn) *82*
  Earlier sketch in SATA *3*
Pullen, Zachary *189*
Pullman, Philip 1946- *198*
  Earlier sketches in SATA *65, 103, 150*
  See also CLR *84*
  See also SAAS *17*
Pullman, Philip Nicholas
  See Pullman, Philip
Pulver, Harry, Jr. 1960- *129*
Pulver, Robin 1945- *208*
  Earlier sketches in SATA *76, 133*
Puner, Helen W(alker) 1915-1989 .... *37*
  Obituary *63*

Purdy, Carol 1943- *120*
  Earlier sketch in SATA *66*
Purdy, Susan G(old) 1939- *8*
Purkiss, Diane 1961- *194*
Purmell, Ann 1953- *206*
  Earlier sketch in SATA *147*
Purnell, Idella 1901-1982 .... *120*
Purscell, Phyllis 1934- *7*
Purtill, Richard L. 1931- *53*
Pushker, Gloria 1927- *162*
  Earlier sketch in SATA *75*
Pushker, Gloria Teles
  See Pushker, Gloria
Pushkin, Aleksandr Sergeevich
  See Pushkin, Alexander
Pushkin, Alexander 1799-1837 .... *61*
Putnam, Alice 1916- *61*
Putnam, Arthur Lee
  See Alger, Horatio, Jr.
Putnam, Peter B(rock) 1920-1998 .... *30*
  Obituary *106*
Puttapipat, Niroot *199*
Puttock, Simon *178*
Puvilland, Alex *205*
Puvilland, Alexandre
  See Puvilland, Alex
Puybaret, Eric 1976- *195*
Pyle, Howard 1853-1911 .... *100*
  Earlier sketch in SATA *16*
  See also CLR *117*
Pyle, Katharine 1863-1938 .... *66*
Pyne, Mable Mandeville 1903-1969 .... *9*
Pyrnelle, Louise-Clarke 1850-1907 .... *114*

Q

Quackenbush, Robert M(ead) 1929- *133*
  Autobiography Feature *133*
  Earlier sketches in SATA *7, 70*
  See also CLR *122*
  See also SAAS *7*
Qualey, Marsha 1953- *124*
  Earlier sketch in SATA *79*
Qualls, Sean *177*
Quammen, David 1948- *7*
Quark, Jason
  See Eldin, Peter
Quarles, Benjamin 1904-1996 .... *12*
Quarles, Benjamin Arthur
  See Quarles, Benjamin
Quatermass, Martin
  See Carpenter, John
Quattlebaum, Mary 1958- *185*
  Earlier sketches in SATA *88, 134*
Quay, Emma *173*
  Earlier sketch in SATA *119*
Queen, Ellery
  See Deming, Richard
  and Dannay, Frederic
  and Davidson, Avram (James)
  and Fairman, Paul W.
  and Flora, Fletcher
  and Holding, James (Clark Carlisle, Jr.)
  and Hoch, Edward D.
  and Kane, Henry
  and Lee, Manfred B.
  and Marlowe, Stephen
  and Powell, (Oval) Talmage
  and Sheldon, Walter J(ames)
  and Sturgeon, Theodore (Hamilton)
  and Tracy, Don(ald Fiske)
  and Vance, Jack
Queen Latifah 1970- *185*
Quennell, Marjorie Courtney 1884-1972 ...... *29*
Quentin
  See Sheldon, David
Quentin, Brad
  See Bisson, Terry

Quest, (Edna) Olga W(ilbourne) Hall
  See Hall-Quest, (Edna) Olga W(ilbourne)
Quick, Annabelle 1922-1986 .... *2*
Quigg, Jane (Hulda) (?)-1986
  Obituary *49*
Quigley, Sarah 1976- *220*
Quill, Monica
  See McInerny, Ralph
Quin-Harkin, Janet 1941- *165*
  Earlier sketches in SATA *18, 90, 119*
Quin-Harkin, Janet Elizabeth
  See Quin-Harkin, Janet
Quinlan, Susan E. 1954- *88*
Quinlan, Susan Elizabeth
  See Quinlan, Susan E.
Quinn, Elisabeth 1881-1962 .... *22*
Quinn, Pat 1947- *130*
Quinn, Patrick 1950- *73*
Quinn, Rob 1972- *138*
Quinn, Susan 1940- *30*
Quinn, Susan Taft
  See Quinn, Susan
Quinn, Theodora K.
  See Kroeber, Theodora (Kracaw)
Quinn, Vernon
  See Quinn, Elisabeth
Quirk, Anne (E.) 1956- *99*
Quixley, Jim 1931- *56*
Quyth, Gabriel
  See Jennings, Gary

R

Ra, Carol F. 1939- *76*
Raab, Evelyn 1951- *129*
Rabb, Margo 1972- *188*
Rabb, M.E.
  See Rabb, Margo
Rabe, Berniece (Louise) 1928- *148*
  Autobiography Feature *148*
  Earlier sketches in SATA *7, 77*
  See also SAAS *10*
Rabe, Olive H(anson) (?)-1968 .... *13*
Rabin, Staton 1958- *162*
  Earlier sketch in SATA *84*
Rabinowich, Ellen 1946- *29*
Rabinowitz, Sandy 1954- *52*
  Brief entry *39*
Rachlin, Carol K(ing) 1919- *64*
Rachlin, Harvey 1951- *47*
Rachlin, Harvey Brant
  See Rachlin, Harvey
Rachlin, Nahid *64*
Rachlis, Eugene (Jacob) 1920-1986
  Obituary *50*
Rackham, Arthur 1867-1939 .... *100*
  Earlier sketch in SATA *15*
  See also CLR *57*
Racoma, Robin Yoko 1953- *207*
Raczka, Bob 1963- *191*
  Earlier sketch in SATA *163*
Radencich, Marguerite C. 1952-1998 .... *79*
Rader, Laura *197*
Radford, Ruby L(orraine) 1891-1971 .... *6*
Radin, Ruth Yaffe 1938- *107*
  Brief entry *52*
  Earlier sketch in SATA *56*
Radlauer, David 1952- *28*
Radlauer, Edward 1921- *15*
Radlauer, Ruth Shaw 1926- *98*
  Earlier sketch in SATA *15*
Radley, Gail 1951- *112*
  Earlier sketch in SATA *25*
Radunsky, Vladimir *177*
Radzinski, Kandy 1948- *212*
Rae, Gwynedd 1892-1977 .... *37*
Raebeck, Lois 1921- *5*
Rael, Elsa Okon 1927-
  See CLR *84*

Raffi
  See Cavoukian, Raffi
Raftery, Gerald (Bransfield) 1905-1986 .... *11*
Ragan-Reid, Gale 1956- *90*
Rahaman, Vashanti 1953- *98*
Rahn, Joan Elma 1929- *27*
Rai, Bali 1971- *152*
Raible, Alton (Robert) 1918- *35*
Raiff, Stan 1930- *11*
Raines, Shirley C(arol) 1945- *128*
Rainey, W. B.
  See Blassingame, Wyatt Rainey
Rake, Jody 1961- *157*
Rallison, Janette 1966- *183*
Ralston, Jan
  See Dunlop, Agnes M. R.
Rama, Sue *190*
Ramal, Walter
  See de la Mare, Walter (John)
Ramanujan, A(ttipat) K(rishnaswami)
  1929-1993 .... *86*
Rame, David
  See Divine, Arthur Durham
Ramirez, Jose 1967- *198*
Ramirez, Orlando L. 1972- *194*
Ramos, Jorge 1958- *205*
Ramstad, Ralph L. 1919- *115*
Ramthun, Bonnie *214*
Rana, Indi
  See Rana, Indira Higham
Rana, Indira Higham 1944- *82*
Rana, J.
  See Bhatia, Jamunadevi
Ranadive, Gail 1944- *10*
Rand, Ann (Binkley) *30*
Rand, Gloria 1925- *156*
  Earlier sketch in SATA *101*
Rand, Paul 1914-1996 .... *6*
Randall, Carrie
  See Ransom, Candice
Randall, David 1972- *167*
Randall, Florence Engel 1917-1997 .... *5*
Randall, Janet
  See Young, Janet Randall
  and Young, Robert W(illiam)
Randall, Robert
  See Garrett, Randall
  and Silverberg, Robert
Randall, Ruth (Elaine) Painter 1892-1971 ..... *3*
Randell, Beverley
  See Price, Beverley Joan
Randle, Kristen D. 1952- *92*
  Autobiography Feature *119*
  See also SAAS *24*
Randle, Kristen Downey
  See Randle, Kristen D.
Randolph, Boynton M.D.
  See Ellis, Edward S.
Randolph, Ellen
  See Rawn, Melanie
Randolph, Geoffrey
  See Ellis, Edward S.
Randolph, J. H.
  See Ellis, Edward S.
Randolph, Lieutenant J. H.
  See Ellis, Edward S.
Rands, William Brighty 1823-1882 .... *17*
Raney, Ken 1953- *74*
Rankin, Joan 1940- *212*
  Earlier sketches in SATA *88, 148*
Rankin, Laura 1953(?)- *176*
Ranney, Agnes V. 1916-1985 .... *6*
Ransom, Candice 1952- *222*
  Brief entry *49*
  Earlier sketches in SATA *52, 89, 135, 183*
Ransom, Jeanie Franz 1957- *187*
Ransome, Arthur (Michell) 1884-1967 .... *22*
  See also CLR *8*
Ransome, James E. 1961- *178*
  Earlier sketches in SATA *76, 123*
  See also CLR *86*

Rant, Tol E.
  See Longyear, Barry B(rookes)
Rao, Rohitash *218*
Raphael, Elaine
  See Bolognese, Elaine
Raposo, Joseph Guilherme 1938-1989
  Obituary *61*
Rapp, Adam 1968- *148*
Rappaport, Doreen *211*
  Earlier sketch in SATA *151*
Rappaport, Eva 1924- *6*
Rappoport, Ken 1935- *167*
  Earlier sketch in SATA *89*
Rarick, Carrie 1911-2002 .... *41*
Raschka, Chris 1959- *207*
  Earlier sketches in SATA *80, 117, 166*
Raschka, Christopher
  See Raschka, Chris
Rascol, Sabina I. *159*
Rash, Andy *219*
  Earlier sketch in SATA *162*
Raskin, Edith Lefkowitz 1908-1987 .... *9*
Raskin, Ellen 1928-1984 .... *139*
  Earlier sketches in SATA *2, 38*
  See also CLR *12*
Raskin, Joseph 1897-1982 .... *12*
  Obituary *29*
Rathjen, Carl Henry 1909-1984 .... *11*
Rathmann, Peggy 1953- *157*
  Earlier sketch in SATA *94*
  See also CLR *77*
Ratliff, Thomas M. 1948- *118*
Ratner, Sue Lynn
  See Alexander, Sue
Rattigan, Jama Kim 1951- *99*
Ratto, Linda Lee 1952- *79*
Rattray, Simon
  See Trevor, Elleston
Ratz de Tagyos, Paul 1958- *198*
  Earlier sketch in SATA *76*
Rau, Dana Meachen 1971- *218*
  Earlier sketches in SATA *94, 167*
Rau, Margaret 1913- *168*
  Earlier sketch in SATA *9*
  See also CLR *8*
Rauch, Mabel Thompson 1888-1972
  Obituary *26*
Raucher, Herman 1928- *8*
Raude, Karina *199*
Rauh, Sherry
  See North, Sherry
Raum, Elizabeth 1949- *155*
Raut, Radhashyam *222*
Raven, Margot Theis *184*
RavenWolf, Silver 1956- *155*
Ravielli, Anthony 1916-1997 .... *3*
  Obituary *95*
Ravilious, Robin 1944- *77*
Ravishankar, Anushka 1961- *200*
Rawding, F(rederick) W(illiam) 1930- *55*
Rawlings, Marjorie Kinnan 1896-1953 ... *100*
  See also YABC *1*
  See also CLR *63*
Rawlins, Donna 1956- *206*
Rawlinson, Julia *212*
  Earlier sketch in SATA *175*
Rawls, (Woodrow) Wilson 1913-1984 ..... *22*
  See also CLR *81*
Rawlyk, George Alexander 1935- *64*
Rawn, Melanie 1954- *98*
Rawn, Melanie Robin
  See Rawn, Melanie
Rawson, Katherine 1955- *190*
Ray, Carl 1943-1978 .... *63*
Ray, Deborah
  See Kogan Ray, Deborah
Ray, Delia 1963- *179*
  Earlier sketch in SATA *70*
Ray, Irene
  See Sutton, Margaret Beebe

Ray, Jane 1960- *196*
  Earlier sketches in SATA *72, 152*
Ray, JoAnne 1935- *9*
Ray, Mary (Eva Pedder) 1932- *127*
  Earlier sketch in SATA *2*
Ray, Mary Lyn 1946- *154*
  Earlier sketch in SATA *90*
Rayban, Chloe 1944- *167*
Rayevsky, Robert 1955- *190*
  Earlier sketch in SATA *81*
Raymond, James Crossley 1917-1981
  Obituary *29*
Raymond, Robert
  See Alter, Robert Edmond
Rayner, Catherine *204*
Rayner, Hugh *151*
Rayner, Mary 1933- *87*
  Earlier sketch in SATA *22*
  See also CLR *41*
Rayner, Shoo
  See Rayner, Hugh
Rayner, William 1929- *55*
  Brief entry *36*
Raynor, Dorka *28*
Raynor, Gemma 1985- *216*
Rayson, Steven 1932- *30*
Rayyan, Omar 1968- *216*
Razzell, Arthur (George) 1925- *11*
Razzell, Mary (Catherine) 1930- *102*
Razzi, James 1931- *10*
Read, Elfreida 1920- *2*
Read, Nicholas 1956- *146*
Read, Piers Paul 1941- *21*
Reade, Deborah 1949- *69*
Reader, Dennis 1929- *71*
Reading, Richard P(atrick) 1962- *161*
Readman, Jo 1958- *89*
Ready, Kirk L(ewis) 1943- *39*
Reaney, James 1926-2008 .... *43*
Reaney, James Crerar
  See Reaney, James
Reardon, Joyce
  See Pearson, Ridley
Reaver, Chap 1935-1993 .... *69*
  Obituary *77*
Reaver, Herbert R.
  See Reaver, Chap
Reaves, J. Michael
  See Reaves, (James) Michael
Reaves, (James) Michael 1950- *99*
Reber, Deborah *189*
Recorvits, Helen *191*
Redding, Robert Hull 1919- *2*
Redekopp, Elsa *61*
Redlich, Ben 1977- *181*
Redsand, Anna 1948- *184*
Redway, Ralph
  See Hamilton, Charles (Harold St. John)
Redway, Ridley
  See Hamilton, Charles (Harold St. John)
Reece, Colleen L. 1935- *116*
Reece, Gabrielle 1970- *108*
Reed, Amy 1979- *223*
Reed, Betty Jane 1921- *4*
Reed, Dallas
  See Pendleton, Thomas
Reed, E.
  See Evans, Mari
Reed, Gwendolyn E(lizabeth) 1932- *21*
Reed, Kit 1932- *184*
  Autobiography Feature *184*
  Earlier sketches in SATA *34, 116*
Reed, Lynn Rowe *215*
  Earlier sketch in SATA *171*
Reed, Mike 1951- *211*
Reed, Neil 1961- *99*
Reed, Talbot Baines 1852-1893
  See CLR *76*
Reed, Thomas (James) 1947- *34*
Reed, William Maxwell 1871-1962 .... *15*

Reeder, Carolyn 1937- *97*
  Earlier sketch in SATA *66*
  See also CLR *69*
Reeder, Colin (Dawson) 1938- *74*
Reeder, Colonel Red
  See Reeder, Russell P(otter), Jr.
Reeder, Russell P(otter), Jr. 1902-1998 ... *4*
  Obituary *101*
Reeder, Stephanie Owen 1951- *102*
Reed-Jones, Carol 1955- *112*
Reef, Catherine 1951- *223*
  Earlier sketches in SATA *73, 128, 189*
Reekie, Jocelyn (Margaret) 1947- *145*
Reeman, Douglas Edward 1924- *63*
  Brief entry *28*
Rees, Celia 1949- *124*
Rees, David (Bartlett) 1936-1993 .... *69*
  Obituary *76*
  Earlier sketch in SATA *36*
  See also SAAS *5*
Rees, Douglas 1947- *169*
Rees, Ennis (Samuel, Jr.) 1925-2009 ...... *3*
Rees, (George) Leslie (Clarence)
  1905-2000 .... *105*
  Obituary *135*
Reese, Bob
  See Reese, Robert A.
Reese, Carolyn Johnson 1938- *64*
Reese, Della 1931(?)- *114*
Reese, Lyn
  See Reese, Carolyn Johnson
Reese, Robert A. 1938- *60*
  Brief entry *53*
Reese, (John) Terence 1913-1996 .... *59*
Reeve, Joel
  See Cox, William R(obert)
Reeve, Kirk 1934- *117*
Reeve, Philip *201*
  Earlier sketch in SATA *170*
Reeve, Rosie *188*
  Earlier sketch in SATA *186*
Reeves, Faye Couch 1953- *76*
Reeves, James
  See Reeves, John Morris
Reeves, Jeni 1947- *111*
Reeves, John Morris 1909-1978 .... *87*
  Earlier sketch in SATA *15*
Reeves, Joyce 1911- *17*
Reeves, Lawrence F. 1926- *29*
Reeves, Ruth Ellen
  See Ranney, Agnes V.
Regan, Dian Curtis 1950- *149*
  Autobiography Feature *149*
  Earlier sketches in SATA *75, 133*
Regehr, Lydia 1903-1991 .... *37*
Reger, James P. 1952- *106*
Reggiani, Renee 1925- *18*
Rehm, Karl M. 1935- *72*
Reibstein, Mark *211*
Reich, Ali
  See Katz, Bobbi
Reich, Susanna 1954- *214*
  Earlier sketch in SATA *113*
Reiche, Dietlof 1941- *159*
Reichert, Edwin C(lark) 1909-1988
  Obituary *57*
Reichert, Mickey Zucker
  See Reichert, Miriam Zucker
Reichert, Miriam Zucker 1962- *85*
Reichert, Renee *172*
Reichhold, Jane(t E.) 1937- *147*
Reid, Alastair 1926- *46*
Reid, Barbara 1922- *21*
Reid, Barbara (Jane) 1957- *93*
  See also CLR *64*
Reid, Desmond
  See Moorcock, Michael
  and McNeilly, Wilfred (Glassford)
Reid, Eugenie Chazal 1924- *12*
Reid, John Calvin *21*
Reid, (Thomas) Mayne 1818-1883 .... *24*

Reid, Meta Mayne 1905-1991 58
  Brief entry 36
Reid, Robin (Nicole) 1969- 145
Reid Banks, Lynne 1929- 165
  Earlier sketches in SATA 22, 75, 111
  See also CLR 86
Reider, Katja 1960- 126
Reid Jenkins, Debra 1955- 87
Reiff, Stephanie Ann 1948- 47
  Brief entry 28
Reig, June 1933- 30
Reigot, Betty Polisar 1924- 55
  Brief entry 41
Reilly, Joan 195
Reim, Melanie (K.) 1956- 104
Reinach, Jacquelyn (Krasne) 1930-2000 28
Reiner, Carl 1922- 151
Reiner, William B(uck) 1910-1976 46
  Obituary 30
Reinfeld, Fred 1910-1964 3
Reinhardt, Dana 1971- 175
Reinhart, Matthew 1971- 197
  Earlier sketch in SATA 161
Reiniger, Lotte 1899-1981 40
  Obituary 33
Reinsma, Carol 1949- 91
Reinstedt, Randall A. 1935- 101
Reinstedt, Randy
  See Reinstedt, Randall A.
Reisberg, Mira 1955- 82
Reisberg, Veg
  See Reisberg, Mira
Reiser, Lynn 1944- 180
  Earlier sketches in SATA 81, 138
Reiser, Lynn Whisnant
  See Reiser, Lynn
Reisgies, Teresa (Maria) 1966- 74
Reiss, Johanna 1929(?)- 18
  See also CLR 19
Reiss, Johanna de Leeuw
  See Reiss, Johanna
Reiss, John J. 23
Reiss, Kathryn 1957- 144
  Earlier sketch in SATA 76
Reit, Seymour Victory 1918-2001 21
  Obituary 133
Reit, Sy
  See Reit, Seymour Victory
Relf, Patricia 1954- 134
  Earlier sketch in SATA 71
Remark, Erich Paul
  See Remarque, Erich Maria
Remarque, Erich Maria 1898-1970
  See CLR 159
Remi, Georges 1907-1983 13
  Obituary 32
  See also CLR 114
Remington, Frederic S(ackrider)
  1861-1909 41
Remkiewicz, Frank 1939- 217
  Earlier sketches in SATA 77, 152
Rempt, Fiona 1973- 198
Remy, Georges
  See Remi, Georges
Renaud, Anne 1957- 211
Renaud, Bernadette 1945- 66
Renault, Mary 1905-1983 23
  Obituary 36
Rendell, Joan 28
Rendina, Laura (Jones) Cooper 1902- 10
Rendon, Marcie R. 1952- 97
Rendon, Maria 1965- 116
Renee, Janina 1956- 140
Renfro, Ed 1924- 79
Renick, Marion (Lewis) 1905-1983 1
Renier, Aaron 1977- 202
Renken, Aleda 1907- 27
Renlie, Frank H. 1936- 11
Rennert, Richard Scott 1956- 67
Rennison, Louise 1951- 149
Reno, Dawn E(laine) 1953- 130

Rensie, Willis
  See Eisner, Will
Renton, Cam
  See Armstrong, Richard
Renvoize, Jean 5
Resau, Laura 1973- 190
Resciniti, Angelo G. 1952- 75
Resnick, Michael David
  See Resnick, Mike
Resnick, Mike 1942- 159
  Earlier sketches in SATA 38, 106
Resnick, Seymour 1920- 23
Retla, Robert
  See Alter, Robert Edmond
Rettig, Liz 199
Rettstatt, Chris
  See Ashland, Monk
Reuter, Bjarne (B.) 1950- 142
  Earlier sketch in SATA 68
Reuter, Carol (Joan) 1931- 2
Revena
  See Wright, Betty Ren
Revsbech, Vicki
  See Liestman, Vicki
Rex, Adam 186
Rex, Michael 191
Rey, H. A. 1898-1977 100
  Earlier sketches in SATA 1, 26, 69
  See also CLR 93
Rey, Hans Augusto
  See Rey, H. A.
Rey, Luis V. 1955- 201
Rey, Margret 1906-1996 86
  Obituary 93
  Earlier sketch in SATA 26
  See also CLR 93
Rey, Margret Elisabeth
  See Rey, Margret
Reyher, Becky
  See Reyher, Rebecca Hourwich
Reyher, Rebecca Hourwich 1897-1987 18
  Obituary 50
Reynish, Jenny 222
Reynold, Ann
  See Bernardo, Anilu
Reynolds, Aaron 1970- 197
Reynolds, Adrian 1963- 192
Reynolds, C. Buck 1957- 107
Reynolds, Dickson
  See Reynolds, Helen Mary Greenwood Camp-
  bell
Reynolds, Helen Mary Greenwood Campbell
  1884-1969
  Obituary 26
Reynolds, Jan 1956- 180
Reynolds, John
  See Whitlock, Ralph
Reynolds, Madge
  See Whitlock, Ralph
Reynolds, Malvina 1900-1978 44
  Obituary 24
Reynolds, Marilyn 1935- 121
  See also SAAS 23
Reynolds, Marilyn M.
  See Reynolds, Marilyn
Reynolds, Marilynn 1940- 141
  Earlier sketch in SATA 80
Reynolds, Pamela 1923- 34
Reynolds, Peter H. 1961- 128
Reynolds, Peter J. 1961- 179
Reynolds, Susan 179
Rhine, Richard
  See Silverstein, Alvin
  and Silverstein, Virginia B.
Rhoades, Diane 1952- 90
Rhodes, Bennie (Loran) 1927- 35
Rhodes, Donna McKee 1962- 87
Rhodes, Frank Harold Trevor 1926- 37
Rhue, Morton
  See Strasser, Todd
Rhyne, Nancy 1926- 66

Rhynes, Martha E. 1939- 141
Ribbons, Ian 1924- 37
  Brief entry 30
  See also SAAS 3
Ricciuti, Edward R(aphael) 1938- 10
Rice, Alice (Caldwell) Hegan 1870-1942 63
Rice, Bebe Faas 1932- 89
Rice, Charles D(uane) 1910-1971
  Obituary 27
Rice, Dale R. 1948- 42
Rice, Dale Richard
  See Rice, Dale R.
Rice, Dick
  See Rice, R. Hugh
Rice, Earle (Wilmont), Jr. 1928- 151
  Earlier sketch in SATA 92
Rice, Edward 1918-2001 47
  Brief entry 42
Rice, Elizabeth 1913-1976 2
Rice, Eve 1951- 91
  Earlier sketch in SATA 34
Rice, Eve Hart
  See Rice, Eve
Rice, Inez 1907- 13
Rice, James 1934- 93
  Earlier sketch in SATA 22
Rice, John F. 1958- 82
Rice, R. Hugh 1929- 115
Rice, Richard H.
  See Rice, R. Hugh
Rich, Anna 1956- 212
Rich, Barbara
  See Graves, Robert
Rich, Elaine Sommers 1926- 6
Rich, Josephine Bouchard 1912- 10
Rich, Louise Dickinson 1903-1991 54
  Obituary 67
Rich, Naomi 217
Richard, Adrienne 1921- 5
  See also SAAS 9
Richard, James Robert
  See Bowen, Robert Sydney
Richards, Chuck 1957- 170
Richards, Frank
  See Hamilton, Charles (Harold St. John)
Richards, Hilda
  See Hamilton, Charles (Harold St. John)
Richards, Jackie 1925- 102
Richards, Jean 1940- 135
Richards, Justin 169
Richards, Kay
  See Baker, Susan (Catherine)
Richards, Laura E(lizabeth Howe) 1850-1943
  See YABC 1
  See also CLR 54
Richards, Leigh
  See King, Laurie R.
Richards, Marlee
  See Brill, Marlene Targ
Richards, Norman 1932- 48
Richards, R(onald) C(harles) W(illiam)
  1923- 59
  Brief entry 43
Richards, Walter Alden (Jr.) 1907-1988
  Obituary 56
Richardson, Andrew (William) 1986- 120
Richardson, Carol 1932- 58
Richardson, Frank Howard 1882-1970
  Obituary 27
Richardson, Grace Lee
  See Dickson, Naida
Richardson, Jean (Mary) 59
Richardson, Judith Benet 1941- 77
Richardson, Nigel 1957- 187
Richardson, Robert S(hirley) 1902-1981 8
Richardson, Sandy 1949- 116
Richardson, V.A. 189
Richardson, Willis 1889-1977 60
Richelson, Geraldine 1922- 29
Richemont, Enid 1940- 82

Richler, Mordecai 1931-2001 98
  Brief entry 27
  Earlier sketch in SATA 44
  See also CLR 17
Richman, Sophia 1941- 142
Rich-McCoy, Lois
  See McCoy, Lois (Rich)
Richmond, Robin 1951- 75
Richoux, Pat(ricia) 1927- 7
Richter, Alice 1941- 30
Richter, Conrad (Michael) 1890-1968 3
Richter, Hans Peter 1925-1993 6
  See also CLR 21
  See also SAAS 11
Richter, Jutta 1955- 184
Rickard, Graham 1949- 71
Rico, Don(ato) 1917-1985
  Obituary 43
Riddell, Chris 1962- 219
  Earlier sketches in SATA 114, 166
Riddell, Christopher Barry
  See Riddell, Chris
Riddell, Edwina 1955- 82
Ridden, Brian 1934- 123
  See Ridden, Brian John
Riddle, Tohby 1965- 223
  Earlier sketches in SATA 74, 151
Riddleburger, Sam 202
Riddles, Libby 1956- 140
Ride, Sally 1951- 219
Ride, Sally Kristen
  See Ride, Sally
Rideout, Sandy 194
Ridge, Antonia (Florence) (?)-1981 7
  Obituary 27
Ridge, Martin 1923-2003 43
Ridley, Philip 171
  Earlier sketch in SATA 88
Ridlon, Marci
  See Balterman, Marcia Ridlon
Riedman, Sarah R(egal) 1902-1995 1
Riehecky, Janet 1953- 164
Ries, Lori 185
Riesenberg, Felix, Jr. 1913-1962 23
Rieu, E(mile) V(ictor) 1887-1972 46
  Obituary 26
Riffenburgh, Beau 1955- 175
Rigg, Sharon
  See Creech, Sharon
Riggenbach, Holly
  See Black, Holly
Riggio, Anita 1952- 148
  Earlier sketch in SATA 73
Riggs, Shannon 190
Riggs, Sidney Noyes 1892-1975
  Obituary 28
Riggs, Stephanie 1964- 138
Riglietti, Serena 1969- 189
Rigney, James Oliver, Jr.
  See Jordan, Robert
Rikhoff, Jean 1928- 9
Rikki
  See Ducornet, Erica
Riley, James A. 1939- 97
Riley, James Whitcomb 1849-1916 17
Riley, Jocelyn 1949- 60
  Brief entry 50
Riley, Jocelyn Carol
  See Riley, Jocelyn
Riley, Linda Capus 1950- 85
Riley, Martin 1948- 81
Rimbauer, Steven
  See Pearson, Ridley
Rimes, (Margaret) LeAnn 1982- 154
Rinaldi, Ann 1934- 202
  Brief entry 50
  Earlier sketches in SATA 51, 78, 117, 161
  See also CLR 46
Rinard, Judith E(llen) 1947- 140
  Earlier sketch in SATA 44
Rinck, Maranke 1976- 214

Rinder, Lenore 1949- 92
Ring, Elizabeth 1920- 79
Ringdahl, Mark
  See Longyear, Barry B(rookes)
Ringgold, Faith 1930- 187
  Earlier sketches in SATA 71, 114
  See also CLR 30
Ringi, Kjell (Arne Soerensen) 1939- 12
Rinkoff, Barbara Jean (Rich) 1923-1975 4
  Obituary 27
Rinn, Miriam 1946- 127
Riordan, James 1936- 95
Riordan, Rick 208
  Earlier sketch in SATA 174
Rios, Tere
  See Versace, Marie Teresa Rios
Ripken, Cal, Jr. 1960- 215
  Earlier sketch in SATA 114
Ripken, Calvin Edward, Jr.
  See Ripken, Cal, Jr.
Ripley, Catherine 1957- 82
Ripley, Elizabeth Blake 1906-1969 5
Ripper, Charles L(ewis) 1929- 3
Ripper, Chuck
  See Ripper, Charles L(ewis)
Rippin, Sally 220
Riq
  See Atwater, Richard (Tupper)
Rish, David 1955- 110
Riskind, Mary 1944- 60
Rissinger, Matt 1956- 93
Rissman, Art
  See Sussman, Susan
Rissman, Susan
  See Sussman, Susan
Ritchie, Barbara Gibbons 14
Ritchie, Scot 1954- 217
Ritter, Felix
  See Kruss, James
Ritter, John H. 1951- 215
  Earlier sketches in SATA 129, 137
Ritter, Lawrence S(tanley) 1922-2004 58
  Obituary 152
Ritthaler, Shelly 1955- 91
Ritts, Paul 1920(?)-1980
  Obituary 25
Ritz, Karen 1957- 202
  Earlier sketch in SATA 80
Riu, Isabel Ferrer 1969- 222
Rivera, Geraldo (Miguel) 1943- 54
  Brief entry 28
Rivers, Elfrida
  See Bradley, Marion Zimmer
Rivers, Karen 1970- 131
Riverside, John
  See Heinlein, Robert A.
Rivkin, Ann 1920- 41
Rivoli, Mario 1943- 10
Roach, Marilynne K. 1946- 9
Roach, Marilynne Kathleen
  See Roach, Marilynne K.
Roach, Portia
  See Takakjian, Portia
Robb, Don 1937- 194
Robb, Laura 1937- 95
Robberecht, Thierry 1960- 182
Robbins, Frank 1917-1994(?) 42
  Brief entry 32
Robbins, Jacqui 221
Robbins, Ken 1945- 219
  Brief entry 53
  Earlier sketches in SATA 94, 147
Robbins, Raleigh
  See Hamilton, Charles (Harold St. John)
Robbins, Ruth 1917(?)- 14
Robbins, Tony
  See Pashko, Stanley
Robbins, Wayne
  See Cox, William R(obert)
Robel, S. L.
  See Fraustino, Lisa Rowe

Roberson, Jennifer 1953- 72
Roberson, John R(oyster) 1930- 53
Robert, Adrian
  See St. John, Nicole
Roberts, Bethany 202
  Earlier sketch in SATA 133
Roberts, Bruce (Stuart) 1930- 47
  Brief entry 39
Roberts, Charles G(eorge) D(ouglas)
  1860-1943 88
  Brief entry 29
  See also CLR 33
Roberts, David
  See Cox, John Roberts
Roberts, David 1970- 191
Roberts, Diane 1937- 184
Roberts, Elizabeth 1944- 80
Roberts, Elizabeth Madox 1886-1941 33
  Brief entry 27
  See also CLR 100
Roberts, Jim
  See Bates, Barbara S(nedeker)
Roberts, Jody 218
Roberts, John G(aither) 1913-1993 27
Roberts, Judy I. 1957- 93
Roberts, Katherine 1962- 152
Roberts, Ken 223
  See Lake, Kenneth R(obert)
Roberts, M. L.
  See Mattern, Joanne
Roberts, Marion 1966- 212
Roberts, Nancy Correll 1924- 52
  Brief entry 28
Roberts, Priscilla 1955- 184
Roberts, Terence
  See Sanderson, Ivan T(erence)
Roberts, Willo Davis 1928-2004 150
  Autobiography Feature 150
  Obituary 160
  Earlier sketches in SATA 21, 70, 133
  See also CLR 95
  See also SAAS 8
Robertson, Barbara (Anne) 1931- 12
Robertson, Don 1929-1999 8
  Obituary 113
Robertson, Dorothy Lewis 1912- 12
Robertson, Ellis
  See Ellison, Harlan
  and Silverberg, Robert
Robertson, James I., Jr. 1930- 182
Robertson, James Irvin
  See Robertson, James I., Jr.
Robertson, Janet (E.) 1935- 68
Robertson, Jennifer Sinclair 1942-1998 12
Robertson, Jenny
  See Robertson, Jennifer Sinclair
Robertson, Keith (Carlton) 1914-1991 85
  Obituary 69
  Earlier sketch in SATA 1
  See also SAAS 15
Robertson, Mark
  See Robertson, M.P.
Robertson, M.P. 1965- 197
Robertson, Stephen
  See Walker, Robert W.
Robertus, Polly M. 1948- 212
  Earlier sketch in SATA 73
Robeson, Kenneth
  See Dent, Lester
  and Goulart, Ron
Robeson, Kenneth
  See Johnson, (Walter) Ryerson
Robinet, Harriette Gillem 1931- 104
  Earlier sketch in SATA 27
  See also CLR 64
Robins, Deri 1958- 166
  Earlier sketch in SATA 117
Robins, Patricia
  See Clark, Patricia Denise
Robins, Rollo, Jr.
  See Ellis, Edward S.

Robins, Seelin
  See Ellis, Edward S.
Robinson, Adjai 1932- 8
Robinson, Aminah Brenda Lynn 1940- 159
  Earlier sketch in SATA 77
Robinson, Barbara (Webb) 1927- 84
  Earlier sketch in SATA 8
Robinson, C(harles) A(lexander), Jr.
  1900-1965 36
Robinson, Charles 1870-1937 17
Robinson, Charles 1931- 6
Robinson, Dorothy W. 1929- 54
Robinson, Elizabeth Keeler 1959- 204
Robinson, Eve
  See Tanselle, Eve
Robinson, Glen 1953- 92
Robinson, Glendal P.
  See Robinson, Glen
Robinson, Jan M. 1933- 6
Robinson, Jean O. 1934- 7
Robinson, Joan (Mary) G(ale Thomas)
  1910-1988 7
Robinson, Kim Stanley 1952- 109
Robinson, Lee 1948- 110
Robinson, Lloyd
  See Silverberg, Robert
Robinson, Lynda S(uzanne) 1951- 107
Robinson, Marileta 1942- 32
Robinson, Maudie Millian Oller 1914- 11
Robinson, Maurice R(ichard) 1895-1982
  Obituary 29
Robinson, Nancy K(onheim) 1942-1994 91
  Brief entry 31
  Obituary 79
  Earlier sketch in SATA 32
Robinson, Ray 1920- 23
Robinson, Raymond Kenneth
  See Robinson, Ray
Robinson, Shari
  See McGuire, Leslie (Sarah)
Robinson, Sharon 1950- 197
  Earlier sketch in SATA 162
Robinson, Spider 1948- 118
Robinson, Sue
  See Robinson, Susan Maria
Robinson, Susan Maria 1955- 105
Robinson, Susan Patricia
  See Gates, Susan
Robinson, Suzanne
  See Robinson, Lynda S(uzanne)
Robinson, T(homas) H(eath) 1869-1950 17
Robinson, Tim 1963- 205
Robinson, (Wanda) Veronica 1926- 30
Robinson, W(illiam) Heath 1872-1944 17
Robison, Bonnie 1924- 12
Robison, Nancy L(ouise) 1934- 32
Robles, Harold E. 1948- 87
Robottom, John 1934- 7
Robson, Eric 1939- 82
Roca, Francois 1971- 200
Rocco, John 1967- 188
Roche, A. K.
  See Abisch, Roslyn Kroop
  and Kaplan, Boche
Roche, Denis 1967- 196
  Earlier sketch in SATA 99
Roche, Denis Mary
  See Roche, Denis
Roche, Luane 1937- 170
Roche, P(atricia) K. 1935- 57
  Brief entry 34
Roche, Terry
  See Poole, Peggy
Rochman, Hazel 1938- 105
Rock, Lois
  See Joslin, Mary
Rock, Maxine 1940- 108
Rocker, Fermin 1907- 40
Rocklin, Joanne 1946- 134
  Earlier sketch in SATA 86

Rockwell, Anne F. 1934- 194
  Earlier sketches in SATA 33, 71, 114, 162
  See also SAAS 19
Rockwell, Anne Foote
  See Rockwell, Anne F.
Rockwell, Bart
  See Pellowski, Michael (Joseph)
Rockwell, Harlow 1910-1988 33
  Obituary 56
Rockwell, Lizzy 1961- 185
Rockwell, Norman (Percevel) 1894-1978 23
Rockwell, Thomas 1933- 70
  Earlier sketch in SATA 7
  See also CLR 6
Rockwood, Joyce 1947- 39
Rockwood, Roy
  See McFarlane, Leslie
  and Stratemeyer, Edward L.
Rodanas, Kristina 1952- 155
Rodari, Gianni 1920-1980
  See CLR 24
Rodd, Kathleen Tennant
  See Rodd, Kylie Tennant
Rodd, Kylie Tennant 1912-1988 57
  Obituary 55
  Earlier sketch in SATA 6
Rodda, Emily 1948- 146
  Earlier sketch in SATA 97
  See also CLR 32
Roddenberry, Eugene Wesley 1921-1991 45
  Obituary 69
Roddenberry, Gene
  See Roddenberry, Eugene Wesley
Roddick, Ellen 1936- 5
Roddie, Shen 153
Roddy, Lee 1921- 57
Rodenas, Paula 73
Rodgers, Frank 1944- 69
Rodgers, Mary 1931- 130
  Earlier sketch in SATA 8
  See also CLR 20
Rodman, Emerson
  See Ellis, Edward S.
Rodman, Eric
  See Silverberg, Robert
Rodman, Maia
  See Wojciechowska, Maia (Teresa)
Rodman, Mary Ann 185
Rodman, (Cary) Selden 1909-2002 9
Rodowsky, Colby 1932- 164
  Earlier sketches in SATA 21, 77, 120
  See also SAAS 22
Rodowsky, Colby F.
  See Rodowsky, Colby
Rodriguez, Alejo 1941- 83
Rodriguez, Alex 1975- 189
Rodriguez, Christina 1981- 177
Rodriguez, Edel 1971- 196
Rodriguez, Luis J. 1954- 125
Rodriguez, Rachel 180
Rodriguez, Rachel Victoria
  See Rodriguez, Rachel
Roeder, Virginia Marsh 1926- 98
Roehrig, Catharine H. 1949- 67
Roennfeldt, Robert 1953- 78
Roessel-Waugh, C. C.
  See Waugh, Carol-Lynn Rossel
  and Waugh, Charles G(ordon)
Roets, Lois F. 1937- 91
Roever, J(oan) M(arilyn) 1935- 26
Rofes, Eric 1954-2006 52
Rofes, Eric Edward 1954-2006
  See Rofes, Eric
Roffey, Maureen 1936- 33
Rogak, Lisa 1962- 80
Rogak, Lisa Angowski
  See Rogak, Lisa
Rogan, S. Jones 199
Rogan, Sally Jones
  See Rogan, S. Jones

Rogasky, Barbara 1933- 144
  Earlier sketch in SATA 86
Rogers, (Thomas) Alan (Stinchcombe)
  1937- 81
  Earlier sketch in SATA 2
Rogers, Bettye 1858-1919 103
Rogers, Cindy 1950- 89
Rogers, Emma 1951- 74
Rogers, Frances 1888-1974 10
Rogers, Fred McFeely 1928-2003 33
  Obituary 138
Rogers, Gregory 1957- 211
Rogers, Hal
  See Sirimarco, Elizabeth
Rogers, Jacqueline 1958- 213
Rogers, Jean 1919- 55
  Brief entry 47
Rogers, Matilda 1894-1976 5
  Obituary 34
Rogers, Pamela 1927- 9
Rogers, Paul 1950- 98
  Earlier sketch in SATA 54
Rogers, Robert
  See Hamilton, Charles (Harold St. John)
Rogers, Sherry 193
Rogers, W(illiam) G(arland) 1896-1978 23
Rohan, M. S.
  See Rohan, Michael Scott
Rohan, Michael Scott 1951- 98
Rohan, Mike Scott
  See Rohan, Michael Scott
Rohmann, Eric 1957- 171
  See also CLR 100
Rohmer, Harriet 1938- 56
Rohrer, Doug 1962- 89
Rojan
  See Rojankovsky, Feodor (Stepanovich)
Rojankovsky, Feodor (Stepanovich)
  1891-1970 21
Rojany, Lisa 94
Rokeby-Thomas, Anna E(lma) 1911- 15
Roland, Albert 1925-2002 11
Roland, Mary
  See Lewis, Mary
Roleff, Tamara L. 1959- 143
Rolerson, Darrell A(llen) 1946- 8
Roll, Winifred 1909-1998 6
Rollins, Charlemae Hill 1897-1979 3
  Obituary 26
Rollins, James 1961- 216
Rollock, Barbara T(herese) 1924- 64
Rolston, Steve 1978- 209
Romack, Janice Reed
  See LeNoir, Janice
Romain, Trevor 134
Romanenko, Vitaliy 1962- 101
Romano, Christy
  See Romano, Christy Carlson
Romano, Christy Carlson 1984- 210
Romano, Clare 1922- 111
  Earlier sketch in SATA 48
Romano, Louis G. 1921- 35
Romano, Melora A. 1966- 118
Romano, Ray 1957- 170
Romano, Raymond
  See Romano, Ray
Romijn, Johanna Maria Kooyker
  See Kooyker-Romijn, Johanna Maria
Romyn, Johanna Maria Kooyker
  See Kooyker-Romijn, Johanna Maria
Rong, Yu 1970- 174
Rongen, Bjoern 1906- 10
Rongen, Bjorn
  See Rongen, Bjoern
Ronson, Mark
  See Alexander, Marc
Rood, Ronald (N.) 1920- 12
Rook, Sebastian
  See Jeapes, Ben
Rooke, Daphne 1914-2009 12

Rooke, Daphne Marie
  See Rooke, Daphne
Rooney, Ronnie 1970- 212
Roop, Connie 1951- 167
  Brief entry 49
  Earlier sketches in SATA *54, 116*
Roop, Constance Betzer
  See Roop, Connie
Roop, Peter 1951- 167
  Brief entry 49
  Earlier sketches in SATA *54, 116*
Roop, Peter G.
  See Roop, Peter
Roop, Peter Geiger
  See Roop, Peter
Roos, Stephen 1945- 128
  Brief entry 41
  Earlier sketches in SATA *47, 77*
Roosa, Karen 1961- 218
Roose-Evans, James 1927- 65
Roosevelt, Eleanor 1884-1962 50
Root, Barry 182
Root, Betty 84
Root, Kimberly Bulcken 192
Root, Phyllis 1949- 184
  Brief entry 48
  Earlier sketches in SATA *55, 94, 145*
Root, Shelton L., Jr. 1923-1986
  Obituary 51
Roper, Laura (Newbold) Wood 1911-2003 .. 34
  Obituary 150
Roper, Robert 1946- 142
  Earlier sketch in SATA *78*
Roraback, Robin (Ellan) 1964- 111
Rorby, Ginny 1944- 94
Rorer, Abigail 1949- 85
Rosaler, Maxine 208
Rosamel, Godeleine de 1968- 151
Roscoe, D(onald) T(homas) 1934- 42
Rose, Anne 8
Rose, Deborah Lee 1955- 185
  Earlier sketches in SATA *71, 124*
Rose, Elizabeth (Jane Pretty) 1933- 68
  Brief entry 28
Rose, Florella
  See Carlson, Vada F.
Rose, Gerald (Hembdon Seymour) 1935- 68
  Brief entry 30
Rose, Malcolm 1953- 168
  Earlier sketch in SATA *107*
Rose, Nancy A.
  See Sweetland, Nancy A(nn)
Rose, Ted 1940- 93
Rose, Wendy 1948- 12
Rosen, Elizabeth 1961- 205
Rosen, Lillian (Diamond) 1928- 63
Rosen, Marvin 1933- 161
Rosen, Michael 1946- 181
  Brief entry 40
  Earlier sketches in SATA *48, 84, 137*
  See also CLR *45*
Rosen, Michael J. 1954- 199
  Earlier sketch in SATA *86*
Rosen, Michael Wayne
  See Rosen, Michael
Rosen, Sidney 1916- 1
Rosen, Winifred 1943- 8
Rosenbaum, Maurice 1907-1987 6
Rosenberg, Amye 1950- 74
Rosenberg, Dorothy 1906- 40
Rosenberg, Eth Clifford 1915- 92
  See also SAAS *22*
Rosenberg, Jane 1949- 58
Rosenberg, Liz 1958- 129
  Earlier sketch in SATA *75*
Rosenberg, Maxine B(erta) 1939- 93
  Brief entry 47
  Earlier sketch in SATA *55*
Rosenberg, Nancy (Sherman) 1931- 4
Rosenberg, Sharon 1942- 8

Rosenberry, Vera 1948- 219
  Earlier sketches in SATA *83, 144*
Rosenblatt, Arthur
  See Rosenblatt, Arthur S.
Rosenblatt, Arthur S. 1938- 68
  Brief entry 45
Rosenblatt, Lily 1956- 90
Rosenbloom, Joseph 1928- 21
Rosenblum, Richard 1928- 11
Rosenburg, John M. 1918- 6
Rosenfeld, Dina 1962- 99
Rosenstiehl, Agnes 1941- 203
Rosenthal, Amy Krouse 1965- 222
  Earlier sketch in SATA *177*
Rosenthal, Betsy R. 1957- 178
Rosenthal, Harold 1914-1999 35
Rosenthal, M(acha) L(ouis) 1917-1996 59
Rosenthal, Marc 1949- 193
Rosenthal, Mark A(lan) 1946- 64
Rosing, Norbert 1953- 196
Rosman, Steven M 1956- 81
Rosman, Steven Michael
  See Rosman, Steven M
Rosoff, Meg 1956- 209
  Earlier sketch in SATA *160*
Ross, Alan
  See Warwick, Alan R(oss)
Ross, Christine 1950- 172
  Earlier sketch in SATA *83*
Ross, Clare
  See Romano, Clare
Ross, Dana Fuller
  See Cockrell, Amanda
  and Gerson, Noel Bertram
Ross, Dave
  See Ross, David
Ross, David 1896-1975 49
  Obituary 20
Ross, David 1949- 133
  Earlier sketch in SATA *32*
Ross, Deborah J.
  See Wheeler, Deborah
Ross, Diana
  See Denney, Diana
Ross, Edward S(hearman) 1915- 85
Ross, Eileen 1950- 115
Ross, Frank (Xavier), Jr. 1914- 28
Ross, Jane 1961- 79
Ross, John 1921- 45
Ross, Judy 1942- 54
Ross, Katharine Reynolds
  See Ross, Kathy
Ross, Kathy 1948- 169
  Earlier sketch in SATA *89*
Ross, Kent 1956- 91
Ross, Lillian Hammer 1925- 72
Ross, Michael Elsohn 1952- 170
  Earlier sketches in SATA *80, 127*
Ross, Pat(ricia Kienzle) 1943- 53
  Brief entry 48
Ross, Ramon R(oyal) 1930- 62
Ross, Stewart 1947- 134
  Earlier sketch in SATA *92*
  See also SAAS *23*
Ross, Tom 1958- 84
Ross, Tony 1938- 176
  Earlier sketches in SATA *17, 65, 130*
Ross, Wilda 1915- 51
  Brief entry 39
Rossel, Seymour 1945- 28
Rossell, Judith 1953- 187
Rossel-Waugh, C. C.
  See Waugh, Carol-Lynn Rossel
Rossetti, Christina 1830-1894 20
  See also CLR *115*
Rossetti, Christina Georgina
  See Rossetti, Christina
Rossi, Joyce 1943- 116
Rossotti, Hazel Swaine 1930- 95
Rostkowski, Margaret I. 1945- 59
Roth, Arnold 1929- 21

Roth, Arthur J(oseph) 1925-1993 43
  Brief entry 28
  Obituary 75
  See also SAAS *11*
Roth, Carol 222
Roth, David 1940- 36
Roth, Julie Jersild 180
Roth, Matthue 1978(?)- 174
Roth, Roger 190
Roth, Ruby 1983(?)- 216
Roth, Stephanie 202
Roth, Susan L. 181
  Earlier sketch in SATA *134*
Rothberg, Abraham 1922- 59
Roth-Hano, Renee 1931- 85
Rothkopf, Carol Z. 1929- 4
Rothman, Joel 1938- 7
Rotner, Shelley 1951- 169
  Earlier sketch in SATA *76*
Rottman, S.L. 1970- 157
  Earlier sketch in SATA *106*
Rottman, Susan Lynn
  See Rottman, S.L.
Roueche, Berton 1911-1994 28
Roughsey, Dick 1921(?)-1985 35
  See also CLR *41*
Roughsey, Goobalathaldin
  See Roughsey, Dick
Rounds, Glen (Harold) 1906-2002 112
  Obituary 141
  Earlier sketches in SATA *8, 70*
Rourke, Constance Mayfield 1885-1941
  See YABC *1*
Rouss, Sylvia 211
Rovetch, Gerda 1925(?)- 202
Rovetch, L. Bob
  See Rovetch, Lissa
Rovetch, Lissa 201
Rowan, Deirdre
  See Williams, Jeanne
Rowe, Jennifer
  See Rodda, Emily
Rowe, John A. 1949- 198
  Earlier sketch in SATA *146*
Rowe, Viola Carson 1903-1969
  Obituary 26
Rowh, Mark 1952- 90
Rowland, Florence Wightman 1900-1997 8
  Obituary 108
Rowland-Entwistle, (Arthur) Theodore (Henry)
  1925- 94
  Earlier sketch in SATA *31*
Rowling, J.K. 1965- 174
  Earlier sketch in SATA *109*
  See also CLR *112*
Rowling, Joanne Kathleen
  See Rowling, J.K.
Rowsome, Frank (Howard), Jr. 1914-1983 .. 36
Roy, Gabrielle 1909-1983 104
Roy, Jacqueline 1954- 74
Roy, James 1968- 218
Roy, Jennifer
  See Roy, Jennifer Rozines
Roy, Jennifer Rozines 1967- 178
Roy, Jessie Hailstalk 1895-1986
  Obituary 51
Roy, Kari Anne 1977(?)- 221
Roy, Liam
  See Scarry, Patricia (Murphy)
Roy, Ron(ald) 1940- 110
  Brief entry 35
  Earlier sketch in SATA *40*
Roybal, Laura 1956- 85
Roybal, Laura Husby
  See Roybal, Laura
Royds, Caroline 1953- 55
Royston, Angela 1945- 169
  Earlier sketch in SATA *120*
Rozakis, Laurie E. 1952- 84
Rozen, Anna 1960- 206
Rubbino, Salvatore 1970- 220

Rubel, David 1961- 223
Rubel, Nicole 1953- 181
  Earlier sketches in SATA 18, 95, 135
Rubin, Eva Johanna 1925- 38
Rubin, Susan Goldman 1939- 182
  Earlier sketches in SATA 84, 132
Rubin, Vicky 1964- 193
Rubinetti, Donald 1947- 92
Rubinstein, Gillian 1942- 158
  Autobiography Feature 116
  Earlier sketches in SATA 68, 105
  See also CLR 35
  See also SAAS 25
Rubinstein, Gillian Margaret
  See Rubinstein, Gillian
Rubinstein, Patricia -2003
  See Forest, Antonia
Rubinstein, Patricia Giulia Caulfield Kate
  See Forest, Antonia
Rubinstein, Robert E(dward) 1943- 49
Rublowsky, John M(artin) 1928- 62
Rubright, Lynn 1936- 171
Ruby, Laura 181
  Earlier sketch in SATA 155
Ruby, Lois 1942- 184
  Autobiography Feature 105
  Brief entry 34
  Earlier sketches in SATA 35, 95
Ruby, Lois F.
  See Ruby, Lois
Ruchlis, Hy(man) 1913-1992 3
  Obituary 72
Ruckdeschel, Liz 214
Rucker, Mike 1940- 91
Ruckman, Ivy 1931- 93
  Earlier sketch in SATA 37
Ruck-Pauquet, Gina 1931- 40
  Brief entry 37
Ruddell, Deborah 1949- 210
Ruditis, Paul 190
Rudley, Stephen 1946- 30
Rudolph, Marguerita 1908- 21
Rudomin, Esther
  See Hautzig, Esther Rudomin
Rue, Leonard Lee III 1926- 142
  Earlier sketch in SATA 37
Rueda, Claudia 183
Ruedi, Norma Paul
  See Ainsworth, Norma
Ruelle, Karen Gray 1957- 209
  Earlier sketches in SATA 84, 126
Ruemmler, John D(avid) 1948- 78
Ruepp, Krista 1947- 143
Ruffell, Ann 1941- 30
Ruffins, Reynold 1930- 125
  Earlier sketch in SATA 41
Rugg, Jim 206
Ruggles, Lucy
  See Williams, Kathryn
Rugoff, Milton 1913- 30
Ruhen, Olaf 1911-1989 17
Rui, Paolo 1962- 217
Rukeyser, Muriel 1913-1980
  Obituary 22
Rumbaut, Hendle 1949- 84
Rumford, James 1948- 193
  Earlier sketch in SATA 116
Rumsey, Marian (Barritt) 1928- 16
Rumstuckle, Cornelius
  See Brennan, Herbie
Runholt, Susan 216
Runnerstroem, Bengt Arne 1944- 75
Runyan, John
  See Palmer, Bernard (Alvin)
Runyon, Brent 217
Runyon, Catherine 1947- 62
Ruoff, A. LaVonne Brown 1930- 76
Rupp, Rebecca 185
Rusch, Elizabeth 1966- 198
Rusch, Kris
  See Rusch, Kristine Kathryn

Rusch, Kristine Kathryn 1960- 113
Rush, Alison 1951- 41
Rush, Peter 1937- 32
Rushdie, Ahmed Salman
  See Rushdie, Salman
Rushdie, Salman 1947-
  See CLR 125
Rushford, Patricia H(elen) 1943- 134
Rushmore, Helen 1898-1994 3
Rushmore, Robert (William) 1926-1986 8
  Obituary 49
Ruskin, Ariane
  See Batterberry, Ariane Ruskin
Ruskin, John 1819-1900 24
Russ, Lavinia (Faxon) 1904-1992 74
Russell, Charlotte
  See Rathjen, Carl Henry
Russell, Ching Yeung 1946- 107
Russell, Don(ald Bert) 1899-1986
  Obituary 47
Russell, Franklin (Alexander) 1926- 11
Russell, Gertrude Barrer
  See Barrer-Russell, Gertrude
Russell, Helen Ross 1915- 8
Russell, James 1933- 53
Russell, Jim
  See Russell, James
Russell, Joan Plummer 1930- 139
Russell, Natalie 1972- 218
Russell, P(hilip) Craig 1951- 162
  Earlier sketch in SATA 80
Russell, Patrick
  See Sammis, John
Russell, Paul (Gary) 1942- 57
Russell, Sarah
  See Laski, Marghanita
Russell, Sharman Apt 1954- 123
Russell, Solveig Paulson 1904-1985 3
Russo, Marisabina 1950- 188
  Earlier sketches in SATA 106, 151
Russo, Monica J. 1950- 83
Russo, Susan 1947- 30
Russon, Penni 1974- 179
Rutgers van der Loeff, An
  See Rutgers van der Loeff-Basenau, An(na)
    Maria Margaretha
Rutgers van der Loeff-Basenau, An(na) Maria
  Margaretha 1910- 22
Ruth, Rod 1912-1987 9
Rutherford, Douglas
  See McConnell, James Douglas Rutherford
Rutherford, Meg 1932- 34
Ruthin, Margaret
  See Catherall, Arthur
Rutkoski, Marie 1977- 219
Rutledge, Jill Zimmerman 1951- 155
Rutz, Viola Larkin 1932- 12
Ruurs, Margriet 1952- 215
  Earlier sketches in SATA 97, 147
Ruzicka, Rudolph 1883-1978
  Obituary 24
Ruzzier, Sergio 1966- 210
  Earlier sketch in SATA 159
Ryan, Betsy
  See Ryan, Elizabeth (Anne)
Ryan, Cheli Duran 20
Ryan, Darlene 1958- 176
Ryan, Elizabeth (Anne) 1943- 30
Ryan, Jeanette
  See Mines, Jeanette
Ryan, John 1921-2009 22
Ryan, John Gerald Christopher
  See Ryan, John
Ryan, Margaret 1950- 166
  Earlier sketch in SATA 78
Ryan, Mary E. 1953- 61
Ryan, Mary Elizabeth
  See Ryan, Mary E.
Ryan, Pam Munoz 1951- 197
  Earlier sketch in SATA 134
Ryan, Patrick 1957- 138

Ryan, Peter (Charles) 1939- 15
Ryan-Lush, Geraldine 1949- 89
Rybakov, Anatoli (Naumovich) 1911-1998 .. 79
  Obituary 108
Rybakov, Anatolii (Naumovich)
  See Rybakov, Anatoli (Naumovich)
Rybolt, Thomas R. 1954- 62
Rybolt, Thomas Roy
  See Rybolt, Thomas R.
Rybolt, Tom
  See Rybolt, Thomas R.
Rydberg, Ernest E(mil) 1901-1993 21
Rydberg, Lou(isa Hampton) 1908- 27
Rydell, Katy 1942- 91
Rydell, Wendell
  See Rydell, Wendy
Rydell, Wendy 4
Ryden, Hope 91
  Earlier sketch in SATA 8
Ryder, Joanne (Rose) 1946- 163
  Brief entry 34
  Earlier sketches in SATA 65, 122
  See also CLR 37
Ryder, Pamela
  See Lamb, Nancy
Rye, Anthony
  See Youd, Samuel
Rylant, Cynthia 1954- 195
  Brief entry 44
  Earlier sketches in SATA 50, 76, 112, 160
  See also CLR 86
  See also SAAS 13
Rymer, Alta May 1925- 34
Rymond, Lynda Gene 199

                        S

S. L. C.
  See Twain, Mark
S., Svend Otto
  See Soerensen, Svend Otto
Saaf, Donald W(illiam) 1961- 124
Saal, Jocelyn
  See Sachs, Judith
Sabbeth, Carol (Landstrom) 1957- 125
Saberhagen, Fred 1930-2007 89
  Obituary 184
  Earlier sketch in SATA 37
Saberhagen, Fred T.
  See Saberhagen, Fred
Saberhagen, Fred Thomas
  See Saberhagen, Fred
Saberhagen, Frederick Thomas
  See Saberhagen, Fred
Sabin, Edwin L(egrand) 1870-1952
  See YABC 2
Sabin, Francene 27
Sabin, Lou
  See Sabin, Louis
Sabin, Louis 1930- 27
Sabre, Dirk
  See Laffin, John (Alfred Charles)
Sabuda, Robert (James) 1965- 120
  Earlier sketch in SATA 81
Sabuda, Robert 1965- 170
Sabuda, Robert James
  See Sabuda, Robert
Sachar, Louis 1954- 154
  Brief entry 50
  Earlier sketches in SATA 63, 104
  See also CLR 161
Sachs, Elizabeth-Ann 1946- 48
Sachs, Judith 1947- 52
  Brief entry 51
Sachs, Marilyn 1927- 164
  Autobiography Feature 110
  Earlier sketches in SATA 3, 68
  See also CLR 2
  See also SAAS 2

Sachs, Marilyn Stickle
See Sachs, Marilyn
Sackett, S(amuel) J(ohn) 1928- 12
Sackson, Sid 1920- 16
Sacre, Antonio 1968- 152
Saddler, Allen
See Richards, R(onald) C(harles) W(illiam)
Saddler, K. Allen
See Richards, R(onald) C(harles) W(illiam)
Sadie, Stanley 1930-2005 14
Sadie, Stanley John
See Sadie, Stanley
Sadiq, Nazneen
See Sheikh, Nazneen
Sadler, Catherine Edwards 1952- 60
Brief entry 45
Sadler, Marilyn (June) 1950- 79
Sadler, Mark
See Lynds, Dennis
Saffer, Barbara 144
Sagan, Carl 1934-1996 58
Obituary 94
Sagan, Carl Edward
See Sagan, Carl
Sage, Angie 1952- 197
Sage, Juniper
See Brown, Margaret Wise
and Hurd, Edith Thacher
Sagsoorian, Paul 1923- 12
Said, S.F. 1967- 174
Saidman, Anne 1952- 75
Saint, Dora Jessie 1913- 10
St. Anthony, Jane 175
St. Antoine, Sara L. 1966- 84
St. Clair, Byrd Hooper 1905-1976
Obituary 28
St. Crow, Lili
See Saintcrow, Lilith
Saintcrow, Lilith 1976- 221
Saint-Exupery, Antoine de 1900-1944 20
See also CLR 142
Saint-Exupery, Antoine Jean Baptiste Marie
Roger de
See Saint-Exupery, Antoine de
St. George, Judith 1931- 161
Earlier sketches in SATA 13, 99
See also CLR 57
See also SAAS 12
St. George, Judith Alexander
See St. George, Judith
St. James, Blakely
See Gottfried, Theodore Mark
and Platt, Charles
St. James, Blakely
See Griffin, W. E. B.
St. James, Sierra
See Rallison, Janette
Saint James, Synthia 1949- 152
Earlier sketch in SATA 84
St. John, Lauren 1966- 214
St. John, Nicole 143
Autobiography Feature 143
Earlier sketches in SATA 29, 89
See also CLR 46
See also SAAS 7
St. John, Patricia Mary 1919-1993
Obituary 79
St. John, Philip
See del Rey, Lester
St. John, Wylly Folk 1908-1985 10
Obituary 45
St. Max, E. S.
See Ellis, Edward S.
St. Meyer, Ned
See Stratemeyer, Edward L.
St. Mox, E. A.
See Ellis, Edward S.
St. Myer, Ned
See Stratemeyer, Edward L.
St. Tamara
See Kolba, St. Tamara

Saito, Michiko
See Fujiwara, Michiko
Sakai, Komako 1966- 213
Sakaki, Ichiro 1969- 192
Sakamoto, Miki 198
Sakers, Don 1958- 72
Sakharnov, S.
See Sakharnov, Svyatoslav
Sakharnov, Svyatoslav 1923- 65
Sakharnov, Svyatoslav Vladimirovich
See Sakharnov, Svyatoslav
Saksena, Kate 148
Sakurai, Gail 1952- 153
Earlier sketch in SATA 87
Salamanca, Lucy
See del Barco, Lucy Salamanca
Salas, Laura Purdie 1966- 216
Salassi, Otto R(ussell) 1939-1993 38
Obituary 77
Salat, Cristina 82
Saldana, Rene, Jr. 186
Saldutti, Denise 1953- 39
Sale, Tim 1956- 153
Salem, Kay 1952- 92
Salerno, Steven 176
Salinger, J.D. 1919-2010 67
See also CLR 18
Salinger, Jerome David
See Salinger, J.D.
Salisbury, Graham 1944- 195
Earlier sketches in SATA 76, 108, 161
Salisbury, Joyce E(llen) 1944- 138
Salkey, (Felix) Andrew (Alexander)
1928-1995 118
Earlier sketch in SATA 35
Salley, Coleen 166
Sallis, Susan (Diana) 1929- 55
Salmieri, Daniel 1983- 208
Salmon, Annie Elizabeth 1899- 13
Salmon, Dena K. 1959(?)- 219
Salonen, Roxane Beauclair 1968- 184
Salsi, Lynn 1947- 130
Salsitz, R. A. V.
See Salsitz, Rhondi Vilott
Salsitz, Rhondi Vilott 115
Salten, Felix
See Salzmann, Siegmund
Salter, Cedric
See Knight, Francis Edgar
Salter, Sydney 220
Saltman, Judith 1947- 64
Saltzberg, Barney 1955- 194
Earlier sketch in SATA 135
Saltzman, David (Charles Laertes)
1967-1990 86
Salvadori, Mario (George) 1907-1997 97
Earlier sketch in SATA 40
Salwood, F.K.
See Kilworth, Garry
Salzer, L. E.
See Wilson, Lionel
Salzman, Marian 1959- 77
Salzmann, Siegmund 1869-1945 25
Samachson, Dorothy (Mirkin) 1914-1997 3
Samachson, Joseph 1906-1980 3
Obituary 52
Sammis, John 1942- 4
Sampson, Emma (Keats) Speed 1868-1947 . 68
Sampson, Fay (Elizabeth) 1935- 151
Brief entry 40
Earlier sketch in SATA 42
Sampson, Michael 1952- 143
Earlier sketch in SATA 95
Samson, Anne S(tringer) 1933- 2
Samson, Joan 1937-1976 13
Samson, Suzanne M. 1959- 91
Samuels, Barbara 199
Samuels, Charles 1902-1982 12
Samuels, Cynthia K(alish) 1946- 79
Samuels, Gertrude 1910(?)-2003 17
Obituary 147

Sanborn, Duane 1914-1996 38
Sancha, Sheila 1924- 38
Sanchez, Alex 1957- 151
Sanchez, Anita 1956- 209
Sanchez, Sonia 1934- 136
Earlier sketch in SATA 22
See also CLR 18
Sanchez-Silva, Jose Maria 1911- 132
Earlier sketch in SATA 16
See also CLR 12
Sand, George X. 45
Sandak, Cass R(obert) 1950-2001 51
Brief entry 37
Sandberg, (Karin) Inger 1930- 15
Sandberg, Karl C. 1931- 35
Sandberg, Lasse (E. M.) 1924- 15
Sandburg, Carl 1878-1967 8
See also CLR 67
Sandburg, Carl August
See Sandburg, Carl
Sandburg, Charles
See Sandburg, Carl
Sandburg, Charles A.
See Sandburg, Carl
Sandburg, Helga 1918- 3
See also SAAS 10
Sandell, Lisa Ann 1977- 175
Sandemose, Iben 1950- 211
Sander, Heather L. 1947- 157
Sanderlin, George 1915- 4
Sanderlin, Owenita (Harrah) 1916- 11
Sanders, Betty Jane
See Monthei, Betty
Sanders, Nancy I. 1960- 141
Earlier sketch in SATA 90
Sanders, Scott Russell 1945- 109
Earlier sketch in SATA 56
Sanders, Winston P.
See Anderson, Poul
Sanderson, Irma 1912- 66
Sanderson, Ivan T(erence) 1911-1973 6
Sanderson, Margaret Love
See Keats, Emma
and Sampson, Emma (Keats) Speed
Sanderson, Ruth 1951- 172
Earlier sketches in SATA 41, 109
Sanderson, Ruth L.
See Sanderson, Ruth
Sanders-Wells, Linda 220
Sand-Eveland, Cyndi 211
Sandin, Joan 1942- 197
Earlier sketches in SATA 12, 94, 153
Sandison, Janet
See Cameron, Elizabeth Jane
Sandler, Martin W. 216
Earlier sketch in SATA 160
Sandom, J. Gregory
See Welsh, T.K.
Sandom, J.G.
See Welsh, T.K.
Sandoz, Mari(e Susette) 1900-1966 5
Sanford, Agnes (White) 1897-1976 61
Sanford, Doris 1937- 69
Sanford, Rose
See Simmonds, Posy
Sanger, Amy Wilson 1967- 205
Sanger, Marjory Bartlett 1920- 8
San Jose, Christine 1929- 167
Sankey, Alice (Ann-Susan) 1910- 27
San Souci, Daniel 192
Earlier sketch in SATA 96
San Souci, Robert D. 1946- 220
Earlier sketches in SATA 40, 81, 117, 158
See also CLR 43
Santamaria, Benjamin 1955- 184
Santat, Dan 188
Santesson, Hans Stefan 1914(?)-1975
Obituary 30
Santiago, Esmeralda 1948- 129
Santopolo, Jill 214
Santore, Charles 1935- 200

Santoro, C.
   See Santoro, Christopher
Santoro, Christopher 218
Santos, Helen
   See Griffiths, Helen
Santrey, Louis
   See Sabin, Louis
Santucci, Barbara 1948- 130
Sapergia, Barbara 1943- 181
Sapet, Kerrily 1972- 214
Sapieyevski, Anne Lindbergh 1940-1993 81
   Brief entry 32
   Earlier sketches in SATA 35, 78
Saport, Linda 1954- 123
Sapp, Allen 1929- 151
Sarac, Roger
   See Caras, Roger A(ndrew)
Sarah, Duchess of York
   See Ferguson, Sarah
Sarasin, Jennifer
   See Sachs, Judith
Sarcone-Roach, Julia 215
Sardinha, Rick 192
Sarg, Anthony Frederick
   See Sarg, Tony
Sarg, Tony 1882-1942
   See YABC 1
Sargent, Pamela 1948- 78
   Earlier sketch in SATA 29
Sargent, Robert 1933- 2
Sargent, Sarah 1937- 44
   Brief entry 41
Sargent, Shirley 1927-2004 11
Sarnoff, Jane 1937- 10
Saroff, Phyllis V. 202
Saroyan, William 1908-1981 23
   Obituary 24
Sarton, Eleanor May
   See Sarton, May
Sarton, May 1912-1995 36
   Obituary 86
Sasaki, Chris 182
Sasaki, Ellen Joy 206
Saseen, Sharon (Dillon) 1949- 59
Sasek, Miroslav 1916-1980 16
   Obituary 23
   See also CLR 4
Sasso, Sandy Eisenberg 1947- 162
   Earlier sketches in SATA 86, 116
Sathre, Vivian 1952- 133
   Earlier sketch in SATA 79
Satterfield, Charles
   See del Rey, Lester
   and Pohl, Frederik
Sattgast, L. J.
   See Sattgast, Linda J.
Sattgast, Linda J. 1953- 91
Sattler, Helen Roney 1921-1992 74
   Earlier sketch in SATA 4
   See also CLR 24
Sattler, Jennifer
   See Sattler, Jennifer Gordon
Sattler, Jennifer Gordon 218
Sauer, Julia Lina 1891-1983 32
   Obituary 36
Sauer, Tammi 1972- 223
Sauerwein, Leigh 1944- 155
Saul, Carol P. 1947- 117
   Earlier sketch in SATA 78
Saul, John III
   See Saul, John
Saul, John 1942- 98
Saul, John W.
   See Saul, John
Saul, John W. III
   See Saul, John
Saul, John Woodruff III
   See Saul, John
Saul, (Ellen) Wendy 1946- 42
Saulnier, Karen Luczak 1940- 80

Saunders, Caleb
   See Heinlein, Robert A.
Saunders, Dave 1939- 85
Saunders, Julie 1939- 85
Saunders, (William) Keith 1910-1994 12
Saunders, Rubie (Agnes) 1929- 21
Saunders, Steven
   See Jones, Allan Frewin
Saunders, Susan 1945- 96
   Brief entry 41
   Earlier sketch in SATA 46
Saunders-Smith, Gail 1952- 169
Sauvain, Philip Arthur 1933- 111
Savadier, Elivia 1950- 164
   Earlier sketch in SATA 79
Savage, Alan
   See Nicole, Christopher (Robin)
Savage, Blake
   See Goodwin, Harold L(eland)
Savage, Candace 1949- 142
Savage, Deborah 1955- 76
Savage, Jeff 1961- 97
Savage, Katharine James 1905-1989
   Obituary 61
Savage, Stephen 1965- 194
Savage, Thomas 1915-2003
   Obituary 147
Savageau, Cheryl 1950- 96
Savery, Constance (Winifred) 1897-1999 1
Saville, Andrew
   See Taylor, Andrew
Saville, (Leonard) Malcolm 1901-1982 23
   Obituary 31
Saviozzi, Adriana
   See Mazza, Adriana
Savitt, Sam 1917-2000 8
   Obituary 126
Savitz, Harriet May 1933-2008 72
   Earlier sketch in SATA 5
   See also SAAS 26
Sawicki, Mary 1950- 90
Sawyer, (Frederick) Don(ald) 1947- 72
Sawyer, Kem Knapp 1953- 84
Sawyer, Robert J. 1960- 149
   Earlier sketch in SATA 81
Sawyer, Robert James
   See Sawyer, Robert J.
Sawyer, Ruth 1880-1970 17
   See also CLR 36
Saxby, H.M.
   See Saxby, (Henry) Maurice
Saxby, (Henry) Maurice 1924- 71
Saxon, Andrew
   See Arthur, Robert, (Jr.)
Saxon, Antonia
   See Sachs, Judith
Say, Allen 1937- 161
   Earlier sketches in SATA 28, 69, 110
   See also CLR 135
Sayers, Frances Clarke 1897-1989 3
   Obituary 62
Sayles, Elizabeth 1956- 220
   Earlier sketches in SATA 108, 163
Saylor-Marchant, Linda 1963- 82
Sayre, April Pulley 1966- 191
   Earlier sketches in SATA 88, 131
Sazer, Nina 1949- 13
Scabrini, Janet 1953- 13
Scagell, Robin 1946- 107
Scagnetti, Jack 1924- 7
Scaletta, Kurtis 1968- 215
Scamander, Newt
   See Rowling, J.K.
Scamell, Ragnhild 1940- 180
   Earlier sketch in SATA 77
Scanlon, Marion Stephany 11
Scannel, John Vernon
   See Scannell, Vernon
Scannell, Vernon 1922-2007 59
   Obituary 188

Scarborough, Elizabeth
   See Scarborough, Elizabeth Ann
Scarborough, Elizabeth Ann 1947- 171
   Earlier sketch in SATA 98
Scarf, Maggi
   See Scarf, Maggie
Scarf, Maggie 1932- 5
Scariano, Margaret M. 1924- 86
Scarlett, Susan
   See Streatfeild, Noel
Scarry, Huck
   See Scarry, Richard McClure, Jr.
Scarry, Patricia (Murphy) 1924- 2
Scarry, Patsy
   See Scarry, Patricia (Murphy)
Scarry, Richard (McClure) 1919-1994 75
   Obituary 90
   Earlier sketches in SATA 2, 35
   See also CLR 41
Scarry, Richard McClure, Jr. 1953- 35
Schachner, Judith Byron 1951- 178
   Earlier sketch in SATA 88
Schachner, Judy
   See Schachner, Judith Byron
Schachtel, Roger 1949- 38
Schachtel, Roger Bernard
   See Schachtel, Roger
Schade, Susan 189
Schaedler, Sally 116
Schaefer, Carole Lexa 173
Schaefer, Jack (Warner) 1907-1991 66
   Obituary 65
   Earlier sketch in SATA 3
Schaefer, Lola M. 1950- 183
   Earlier sketches in SATA 91, 144
Schaeffer, Mead 1898- 21
Schaeffer, Susan Fromberg 1941- 22
Schaer, Brigitte 1958- 112
Schallau, Daniel 1966- 222
Schaller, George
   See Schaller, George B.
Schaller, George B. 1933- 30
Schaller, George Beals
   See Schaller, George B.
Schanzer, Rosalyn (Good) 1942- 138
   Earlier sketch in SATA 77
Schatell, Brian 66
   Brief entry 47
Schechter, Betty (Goodstein) 1921- 5
Schechter, Simone
   See Elkeles, Simone
Schecter, Ellen 1944- 85
Scheeder, Louis 1946- 141
Scheer, Julian (Weisel) 1926-2001 8
Scheffer, Victor B(lanchard) 1906- 6
Scheffler, Axel 1957- 180
Scheffler, Ursel 1938- 81
Scheffrin-Falk, Gladys 1928- 76
Scheidl, Gerda Marie 1913- 85
Scheier, Michael 1943- 40
   Brief entry 36
Schell, Mildred 1922- 41
Schell, Orville (Hickok) 1940- 10
Scheller, Melanie 1953- 77
Schellie, Don 1932- 29
Schembri, Jim 1962- 124
Schembri, Pamela 1969- 195
Schemm, Mildred Walker 1905-1998 21
   Obituary 103
Schenker, Dona 1947- 133
   Earlier sketch in SATA 68
Scher, Paula 1948- 47
Scherer, Jeffrey 194
Scherf, Margaret 1908-1979 10
Schermer, Judith (Denise) 1941- 30
Schertle, Alice 1941- 192
   Earlier sketches in SATA 36, 90, 145
Schick, Alice 1946- 27
Schick, Eleanor 1942- 144
   Earlier sketches in SATA 9, 82

Schick, Joel 1945- *31*
  Brief entry *30*
Schields, Gretchen 1948- 75
Schiff, Ken(neth Roy) 1942- 7
Schiller, Andrew 1919- 21
Schiller, Barbara (Heyman) 1928- 21
Schiller, Pamela (Byrne) *127*
Schindel, John 1955- *213*
  Earlier sketches in SATA *77, 115*
Schindelman, Joseph 1923- *67*
  Brief entry *32*
Schindler, S.D. 1952- *198*
  Brief entry *50*
  Earlier sketches in SATA *75, 118, 171*
Schindler, Steven D.
  See Schindler, S.D.
Schinto, Jeanne 1951- 93
Schisgall, Oscar 1901-1984 .... *12*
  Obituary *38*
Schlaepfer, Gloria G. 1931- *154*
Schlee, Ann 1934- 44
  Brief entry 36
Schleichert, Elizabeth 1945- 77
Schlein, Miriam 1926-2004 .... *130*
  Obituary *159*
  Earlier sketches in SATA *2, 87*
  See also CLR *41*
Schlesinger, Arthur M., Jr. 1917-2007 .... *61*
  Obituary *181*
  See Schlesinger, Arthur Meier
Schlesinger, Arthur Meier 1888-1965
Schlessinger, Laura (Catherine) 1947- *160*
  Earlier sketch in SATA *110*
Schlitz, Laura Amy *184*
Schloat, G. Warren, Jr. 1914-2000 .... *4*
Schlossberg, Elisabeth *221*
Schmatz, Pat *197*
Schmid, Eleonore 1939- *126*
  Earlier sketches in SATA *12, 84*
Schmid, Susan Maupin *208*
Schmiderer, Dorothy 1940- *19*
Schmidt, Annie M. G. 1911-1995 .... *67*
  Obituary *91*
  See also CLR *22*
Schmidt, C.A. *196*
Schmidt, Diane 1953- *70*
Schmidt, Elizabeth 1915- *15*
Schmidt, Gary D. 1957- *193*
  Earlier sketches in SATA *93, 135*
Schmidt, James Norman 1912-1983 .... *21*
Schmidt, Karen Lee 1953- *185*
  Earlier sketch in SATA *94*
Schmidt, Lynette 1952- *76*
Schmitz, Tamara *207*
Schneider, Antonie 1954- *167*
  Earlier sketch in SATA *89*
Schneider, Christine M. 1972(?)- *171*
  Earlier sketch in SATA *120*
Schneider, Dick
  See Schneider, Richard H.
Schneider, Elisa
  See Kleven, Elisa
Schneider, Herman 1905-2003 7
  Obituary *148*
Schneider, Howie -2007 .... *181*
Schneider, Josh 1980- *196*
Schneider, Laurie
  See Adams, Laurie
Schneider, Nina 1913-2007 2
  Obituary *186*
Schneider, Nina Zimet
  See Schneider, Nina
Schneider, Rex 1937- 44
Schneider, Richard H. 1922- *171*
Schneider, Richard Henry
  See Schneider, Richard H.
Schneider, Robyn 1986- *187*
Schnirel, James R. 1931- *14*
Schnitter, Jane T. 1958- 88
Schnitzlein, Danny *134*

Schnur, Steven 1952- *144*
  Earlier sketch in SATA *95*
Schnurre, Wolfdietrich 1920-1989
  Obituary *63*
Schoberle, Cecile 1949- 80
Schock, Pauline 1928- *45*
Schoell, William 1951- *160*
Schoen, Barbara (Taylor) 1924-1993 .... *13*
Schoenherr, Ian *177*
Schoenherr, John 1935-2010 66
  Earlier sketch in SATA *37*
  See also SAAS *13*
Schoenherr, John Carl
  See Schoenherr, John
Schofield, Sandy
  See Rusch, Kristine Kathryn
Scholastica, Sister Mary
  See Jenkins, Marie M(agdalen)
Scholefield, A. T.
  See Scholefield, Alan
Scholefield, Alan 1931- 66
Scholefield, Edmund O.
  See Griffin, W. E. B.
Scholey, Arthur 1932- 28
Scholz, Jackson Volney 1897-1986
  Obituary *49*
Schon, Nick 1955- *223*
Schone, Virginia 22
Schongut, Emanuel 1936- *184*
  Brief entry 36
  Earlier sketch in SATA *52*
Schoonover, Frank (Earle) 1877-1972 24
Schoor, Gene 1921- 3
Schories, Pat 1952- *164*
  Earlier sketch in SATA *116*
Schorr, Melissa 1972- *194*
Schorr, Melissa Robin
  See Schorr, Melissa
Schott, Jane A. 1946- *172*
Schotter, Roni *190*
  Earlier sketches in SATA *105, 149*
Schraff, Anne E(laine) 1939- 92
  Earlier sketch in SATA *27*
Schram, Penninah 1934- *219*
  Earlier sketch in SATA *119*
Schrank, Joseph 1900-1984
  Obituary *38*
Schrecengost, Maity 1938- *118*
Schrecengost, S. Maitland
  See Schrecengost, Maity
Schreck, Karen
  See Schreck, Karen Halvorsen
Schreck, Karen Halvorsen 1962- *185*
Schrecker, Judie 1954- 90
Schreiber, Elizabeth Anne (Ferguson)
  1947- *13*
Schreiber, Ralph W(alter) 1942- *13*
Schreiner, Samuel A(gnew), Jr. 1921- *70*
Schroades, John *214*
Schroeder, Alan 1961- 98
  Earlier sketch in SATA *66*
Schroeder, Binette
  See Nickl, Barbara (Elisabeth)
Schroeder, Russell (K.) 1943- *146*
Schroeder, Ted 1931(?)-1973
  Obituary 20
Schubert, Dieter 1947- *217*
  Earlier sketches in SATA *62, 101*
Schubert, Ingrid 1953- *217*
Schubert, Leda 1950(?)- *181*
Schubert-Gabrys, Ingrid 1953- *101*
  Earlier sketch in SATA *62*
Schuelein-Steel, Danielle
  See Steel, Danielle
Schuelein-Steel, Danielle Fernande
  See Steel, Danielle
Schuerger, Michele R. *110*
Schuett, Stacey 1960- *168*
  Earlier sketch in SATA *75*
Schulke, Flip Phelps Graeme 1930- 57
Schulman, Arlene 1961- *105*

Schulman, Janet 1933- *208*
  Earlier sketches in SATA *22, 137*
Schulman, L(ester) M(artin) 1934- *13*
Schulte, Elaine L(ouise) 1934- *36*
Schultz, Betty K(epka) 1932- *125*
Schultz, Gwendolyn 21
Schultz, James Willard 1859-1947
  See YABC *1*
Schultz, Pearle Henriksen 1918- 21
Schulz, Charles M. 1922-2000 .... *10*
  Obituary *118*
Schulz, Charles Monroe
  See Schulz, Charles M.
Schumacher, Julie 1958- *191*
Schumaker, Ward 1943- 96
Schuman, Michael A. 1953- *134*
  Earlier sketch in SATA *85*
Schur, Maxine
  See Schur, Maxine Rose
Schur, Maxine Rose 1948- *135*
  Autobiography Feature *135*
  Brief entry *49*
  Earlier sketches in SATA *53, 98*
Schurfranz, Vivian 1925- *13*
Schutzer, A. I. 1922- *13*
Schuyler, Pamela R. 1948- *30*
Schwabach, Karen *185*
Schwager, Tina 1964- *110*
Schwandt, Stephen (William) 1947- *61*
Schwark, Mary Beth 1954- *51*
Schwartz, Alvin 1927-1992 56
  Obituary *71*
  Earlier sketch in SATA *4*
  See also CLR *89*
Schwartz, Amy 1954- *189*
  Brief entry *41*
  Earlier sketches in SATA *47, 83, 131*
  See also CLR *25*
  See also SAAS *18*
Schwartz, Anne Powers 1913-1987 .... *10*
Schwartz, Carol 1954- 77
Schwartz, Charles W(alsh) 1914- 8
Schwartz, David M. 1951- *110*
  Earlier sketch in SATA *59*
Schwartz, David Martin
  See Schwartz, David M.
Schwartz, Elizabeth Reeder 1912- 8
Schwartz, Ellen 1949- *117*
Schwartz, Jerome L.
  See Lawrence, Jerome
Schwartz, Joanne 1960- *220*
Schwartz, Joel L. 1940- 54
  Brief entry *51*
Schwartz, Joyce R. 1950- 93
Schwartz, Julius 1907-2004 .... *45*
Schwartz, Perry 1942- 75
Schwartz, Sheila (Ruth) 1929- 27
Schwartz, Stephen (Lawrence) 1948- 19
Schwartz, Virginia Frances 1950- *184*
  Earlier sketch in SATA *131*
Schwarz, Silvia Tessa Viviane
  See Schwarz, Viviane
Schwarz, Viviane 1977- *204*
Schwarz, (Silvia Tessa) Viviane 1977- *141*
Schweitzer, Byrd Baylor
  See Baylor, Byrd
Schweitzer, Iris 59
  Brief entry 36
Schweninger, Ann 1951- *168*
  Earlier sketches in SATA *29, 98*
Schwerin, Doris H(alpern) 1922- 64
Schy, Yael *197*
Scieszka, Jon 1954- *199*
  Earlier sketches in SATA *68, 105, 160*
  See also CLR *107*
Scillian, Devin *199*
  Earlier sketch in SATA *128*
Scioscia, Mary (Hershey) 1926- 63
Sciurba, Katie 1957- *196*
Scofield, Penrod 1933- 62
  Obituary *78*

Scoggin, Margaret C(lara) 1905-1968 .... *47*
    Brief entry *28*
Scoltock, Jack 1942- *141*
    Earlier sketch in SATA *72*
Scoppettone, Sandra 1936- *92*
    Earlier sketch in SATA *9*
Scot, Michael
    See Rohan, Michael Scott
Scot-Bernard, P.
    See Bernard, Patricia
Scotland, Jay
    See Jakes, John
Scott, Alastair
    See Allen, Kenneth S.
Scott, Ann Herbert 1926- *140*
    Autobiography Feature *140*
    Brief entry *29*
    Earlier sketches in SATA *56, 94*
Scott, Bill
    See Scott, William N(eville)
Scott, Bill 1920(?)-1985
    Obituary *46*
Scott, Cora Annett (Pipitone) 1931- *11*
Scott, Dan
    See Barker, S. Omar
Scott, Elaine 1940- *198*
    Earlier sketches in SATA *36, 90, 164*
Scott, Elizabeth 1972- *194*
Scott, Jack Denton 1915-1995 .... *83*
    Earlier sketch in SATA *31*
    See also CLR *20*
    See also SAAS *14*
Scott, Jane (Harrington) 1931- *55*
Scott, Jessica
    See De Wire, Elinor
Scott, John 1912-1976 .... *14*
Scott, John Anthony 1916- *23*
Scott, John M(artin) 1913- *12*
Scott, Mary
    See Mattern, Joanne
Scott, Melissa 1960- *109*
Scott, Michael 1959- *211*
Scott, Michael Peter
    See Scott, Michael
Scott, Mike
    See Scott, Michael
Scott, Richard
    See Rennert, Richard Scott
Scott, Roney
    See Gault, William Campbell
Scott, Sally 1909-1978 .... *43*
Scott, Sally 1948- *44*
Scott, Sally Elisabeth
    See Scott, Sally
Scott, W. N.
    See Scott, William N(eville)
Scott, Sir Walter 1771-1832
    See YABC *2*
    See also CLR *154*
Scott, Warwick
    See Trevor, Elleston
Scott, William N(eville) 1923- *87*
Scotti, Anna
    See Coates, Anna
Scotton, Rob 1960- *214*
    Earlier sketch in SATA *177*
Scribner, Charles, Jr. 1921-1995 .... *13*
    Obituary *87*
Scribner, Joanne L. 1949- *33*
Scribner, Kimball 1917- *63*
Scrimger, Richard 1957- *164*
    Earlier sketch in SATA *119*
Scrimsher, Lila Gravatt 1897-1974
    Obituary *28*
Scroder, Walter K. 1928- *82*
Scroggs, Kirk *187*
Scruggs, Sandy 1961- *89*
Scudder, Brooke 1959- *154*
Scudder, Mildred Lee 1908- *6*
    See also SAAS *12*
Scull, Marie-Louise 1943-1993 .... *77*

Scuro, Vincent 1951- *21*
Seabrooke, Brenda 1941- *148*
    Earlier sketches in SATA *30, 88*
Seaman, Augusta Huiell 1879-1950 .... *31*
Seamands, Ruth 1916- *9*
Searcy, Margaret Zehmer 1926- *54*
    Brief entry *39*
Searight, Mary W(illiams) 1918- *17*
Searle, Kathryn Adrienne 1942- *10*
Searle, Ronald (William Fordham) 1920- *70*
    Earlier sketch in SATA *42*
Sears, Stephen W. 1932- *4*
Seaskull, Cecil
    See Castellucci, Cecil
Sebastian, Lee
    See Silverberg, Robert
Sebestyen, Igen
    See Sebestyen, Ouida
Sebestyen, Ouida 1924- *140*
    Earlier sketch in SATA *39*
    See also CLR *17*
    See also SAAS *10*
Sebrey, Mary Ann 1951- *62*
Sechrist, Elizabeth Hough 1903-1991 .... *2*
Sederman, Marty *211*
Sedges, John
    See Buck, Pearl S.
Sedgwick, Marcus 1968- *197*
    Earlier sketch in SATA *160*
Seed, Cecile Eugenie 1930- *86*
    Earlier sketch in SATA *8*
    See also CLR *76*
Seed, Jenny
    See Seed, Cecile Eugenie
Seed, Sheila Turner 1937(?)-1979
    Obituary *23*
Seeger, Elizabeth 1889-1973
    Obituary *20*
Seeger, Laura Vaccaro *200*
    Earlier sketch in SATA *172*
Seeger, Pete 1919- *139*
    Earlier sketch in SATA *13*
Seeger, Peter R.
    See Seeger, Pete
Seeley, Laura L. 1958- *71*
Seever, R.
    See Reeves, Lawrence F.
Sefozo, Mary 1925- *82*
Sefton, Catherine
    See Waddell, Martin
Segal, John *178*
Segal, Joyce 1940- *35*
Segal, Lore 1928- *163*
    Earlier sketches in SATA *4, 66*
    See also SAAS *11*
Segal, Lore Groszmann
    See Segal, Lore
Segar, E(lzie) C(risler) 1894-1938 .... *61*
Segovia, Andres 1893(?)-1987
    Obituary *52*
Seguin, Marilyn W(eymouth) 1951- *91*
Seguin-Fontes, Marthe 1924- *109*
Seibold, J. Otto 1960- *196*
    Earlier sketches in SATA *83, 149*
    See also SAAS *22*
Seidel, Ross *95*
Seidelman, James Edward 1926- *6*
Seiden, Art(hur) *107*
    Brief entry *42*
Seidensticker, John 1944- *200*
Seidler, Ann (G.) 1925- *131*
Seidler, Tor 1952- *149*
    Brief entry *46*
    Earlier sketches in SATA *52, 98*
Seidman, Karla
    See Kuskin, Karla
Seidman, Laurence Ivan 1925- *15*
Seigel, Kalman 1917-1998 .... *12*
    Obituary *103*
Seignobosc, Francoise 1897-1961 .... *21*
Seinfeld, Jerry 1954- *146*

Seitz, Jacqueline 1931- *50*
Seixas, Judith S. 1922- *17*
Sejima, Yoshimasa 1913- *8*
Selberg, Ingrid (Maria) 1950- *68*
Selden, George
    See Thompson, George Selden
Selden, Neil R(oy) 1931- *61*
Self, Margaret Cabell 1902-1996 .... *24*
Selfors, Suzanne 1963- *193*
Selick, Henry 1952- *183*
Selig, Sylvie 1942- *13*
Selkirk, Jane
    See Chapman, John Stanton Higham
Sellers, Naomi
    See Flack, Naomi John White
Sellier, Marie 1953- *212*
Selman, LaRue W. 1927- *55*
Selsam, Millicent E(llis) 1912-1996 .... *29*
    Obituary *92*
    Earlier sketch in SATA *1*
    See also CLR *1*
Seltzer, Meyer 1932- *17*
Seltzer, Richard 1946- *41*
Seltzer, Richard Warren, Jr.
    See Seltzer, Richard
Selvadurai, Shyam 1965(?)- *171*
Selway, Martina 1940- *169*
    Earlier sketch in SATA *74*
Selzer, Adam 1980- *192*
Selznick, Brian 1966- *210*
    Earlier sketches in SATA *79, 117, 171*
Semel, Nava 1954- *107*
Semloh
    See Holmes, Peggy
Sendak, Jack 1924(?)-1995 .... *28*
Sendak, Maurice 1928- *165*
    Earlier sketches in SATA *1, 27, 113*
    See also CLR *131*
Sendak, Maurice Bernard
    See Sendak, Maurice
Sender, Ruth M(insky) 1926- *62*
Sengler, Johanna 1924- *18*
Senisi, Ellen B. 1951- *116*
Senisi, Ellen Babinec
    See Senisi, Ellen B.
Senn, J(oyce) A(nn) 1941- *115*
Senn, Steve 1950- *60*
    Brief entry *48*
Sensel, Joni 1962- *204*
Serafini, Frank *201*
Serage, Nancy 1924- *10*
Seredy, Kate 1899-1975 .... *1*
    Obituary *24*
    See also CLR *10*
Serfozo, Mary 1925- *194*
Seroff, Victor I(lyitch) 1902-1979 .... *12*
    Obituary *26*
Serra, Sebastia 1966- *202*
Serraillier, Ian (Lucien) 1912-1994 .... *73*
    Obituary *83*
    Earlier sketch in SATA *1*
    See also CLR *2*
    See also SAAS *3*
Serros, Michele *175*
Serros, Michele M.
    See Serros, Michele
Servello, Joe 1932- *10*
Service, Pamela F. 1945- *222*
    Earlier sketch in SATA *64*
Service, Robert
    See Service, Robert W.
Service, Robert W. 1874(?)-1958 .... *20*
Serwadda, W(illiam) Moses 1931- *27*
Serwer-Bernstein, Blanche L(uria)
    1910-1997 .... *10*
Sescoe, Vincent E. 1938- *123*
Seskin, Steve 1953- *211*
Seth, Mary
    See Lexau, Joan M.
Seton, Anya 1904(?)-1990 .... *3*
    Obituary *66*

Seton, Ernest (Evan) Thompson 1860-1946 . *18*
  See also CLR *59*
Seton-Thompson, Ernest
  See Seton, Ernest (Evan) Thompson
Seuling, Barbara 1937- *220*
  Autobiography Feature *220*
  Earlier sketches in SATA *10, 98, 145, 193*
  See also SAAS *24*
Seuss, Dr.
  See Dr. Seuss
Severn, Bill
  See Severn, William Irving
Severn, David
  See Unwin, David S.
Severn, William Irving 1914- *1*
Sewall, Marcia 1935- *119*
  Earlier sketches in SATA *37, 69*
Seward, Prudence 1926- *16*
Sewell, Anna 1820-1878 .... *100*
  Earlier sketch in SATA *24*
  See also CLR *17*
Sewell, Helen (Moore) 1896-1957 .... *38*
Sexton, Anne 1928-1974 .... *10*
Sexton, Anne Harvey
  See Sexton, Anne
Seymour, Alta Halverson *10*
Seymour, Jane 1951- *139*
Seymour, Tres 1966- *164*
  Earlier sketch in SATA *82*
Sfar, Joann 1971- *182*
Shachtman, Tom 1942- *49*
Shackleton, C.C.
  See Aldiss, Brian W.
Shader, Rachel
  See Sofer, Barbara
Shadow, Jak
  See Sutherland, Jon
Shadyland, Sal
  See Cooper, Louise
Shafer, Audrey *183*
Shafer, Robert E(ugene) 1925- *9*
Shaffer, Terea 1968- *79*
Shahan, Sherry 1949- *216*
  Earlier sketches in SATA *92, 134*
Shahn, Ben(jamin) 1898-1969
  Obituary *21*
Shahn, Bernarda Bryson
  See Bryson, Bernarda
Shaik, Fatima *114*
Shalant, Phyllis 1949- *150*
Shan, Darren 1972- *199*
  Earlier sketches in SATA *129, 168*
Shan, D.B.
  See Shan, Darren
Shanahan, Lisa *199*
Shanberg, Karen
  See Shragg, Karen (I.)
Shane, Harold Gray 1914-1993 .... *36*
  Obituary *76*
Shange, Ntozake 1948- *157*
Shanks, Ann Zane (Kushner) *10*
Shannon, David 1959- *152*
  Earlier sketch in SATA *107*
  See also CLR *87*
Shannon, George 1952- *202*
  Earlier sketches in SATA *35, 94, 143*
Shannon, George William Bones
  See Shannon, George
Shannon, Jacqueline *63*
Shannon, Margaret
  See Silverwood, Margaret Shannon
Shannon, Monica 1905(?)-1965 .... *28*
Shannon, Terry
  See Mercer, Jessie
Shannon, Terry Miller 1951- *148*
Shapiro, Irwin 1911-1981 .... *32*
Shapiro, Jody Fickes 1940- *193*
Shapiro, Karen Jo 1964- *186*
Shapiro, Michelle 1961- *196*
Shapiro, Milton J. 1926- *32*

Shapiro, Tricia
  See Andryszewski, Tricia
Shapiro, Zachary 1970- *213*
Shapp, Charles M(orris) 1906-1989
  Obituary *61*
Shapp, Martha Glauber 1910- *3*
Sharenow, Robert *193*
Sharfman, Amalie *14*
Sharkey, Niamh *213*
Sharma, Partap 1939- *15*
Sharma, Rashmi
  See Singh, Rashmi Sharma
Sharman, Alison
  See Leonard, Alison
Sharmat, Marjorie Weinman 1928- *133*
  Earlier sketches in SATA *4, 33, 74*
Sharmat, Mitchell 1927- *127*
  Earlier sketch in SATA *33*
Sharp, Anne Wallace 1947- *144*
Sharp, Luke
  See Alkiviades, Alkis
Sharp, Margery 1905-1991 .... *29*
  Obituary *67*
  Earlier sketch in SATA *1*
  See also CLR *27*
Sharp, Zerna A. 1889-1981 .... *27*
  Obituary *27*
Sharpe, Jon
  See Duncan, Alice
  and Knott, William C(ecil, Jr.)
  and Messman, Jon
Sharpe, Mitchell R(aymond) 1924- *12*
Sharpe, Susan 1946- *71*
Sharratt, Nick 1962- *199*
  Earlier sketches in SATA *104, 153*
Shasha, Mark 1961- *80*
Shattuck, Roger 1923-2005 .... *64*
  Obituary *174*
Shattuck, Roger Whitney
  See Shattuck, Roger
Shaw, Arnold 1909-1989 .... *4*
  Obituary *63*
Shaw, Carolyn V. 1934- *91*
Shaw, Charles (Green) 1892-1974 .... *13*
Shaw, Evelyn S. 1927- *28*
Shaw, Flora Louisa
  See Lugard, Flora Louisa Shaw
Shaw, Janet 1937- *146*
  Earlier sketch in SATA *61*
  See also CLR *96*
Shaw, Janet Beeler
  See Shaw, Janet
Shaw, Liane 1959- *222*
Shaw, Lisa
  See Rogak, Lisa
Shaw, Margret 1940- *68*
Shaw, Mary 1965- *180*
Shaw, Nancy 1946- *162*
  Earlier sketch in SATA *71*
Shaw, Ray *7*
Shaw, Richard 1923- *12*
Shawn, Frank S.
  See Goulart, Ron
Shay, Art
  See Shay, Arthur
Shay, Arthur 1922- *4*
Shay, Lacey
  See Shebar, Sharon Sigmond
Shea, Bob *188*
Shea, George 1940- *54*
  Brief entry *42*
Shea, Pegi Deitz 1960- *172*
  Earlier sketches in SATA *77, 137*
Shearer, Alex 1949- *204*
Shearer, John 1947- *43*
  Brief entry *27*
  See also CLR *34*
Shearer, Ted 1919- *43*
Shearing, Leonie 1972- *184*
Sheban, Chris *182*
Shebar, Sharon Sigmond 1945- *36*

Shecter, Ben 1935- *16*
Shedd, Warner 1934- *147*
  Earlier sketch in SATA *87*
Sheedy, Alexandra Elizabeth 1962- *39*
  Earlier sketch in SATA *19*
Sheehan, Ethna 1908-2000 .... *9*
Sheehan, Patty 1945- *77*
Sheehan, Sean 1951- *154*
  Earlier sketch in SATA *86*
Sheen, Barbara 1949- *143*
Shefelman, Janice 1930- *205*
  Earlier sketches in SATA *58, 129*
Shefelman, Janice Jordan
  See Shefelman, Janice
Shefelman, Tom 1927- *204*
  Earlier sketch in SATA *58*
Sheffer, H. R.
  See Abels, Harriette S(heffer)
Sheffield, Charles 1935-2002 .... *109*
Sheffield, Janet N. 1926- *26*
Sheikh, Nazneen 1944- *101*
Sheinkin, Steve 1968- *204*
Sheinmel, Courtney 1977- *211*
Shekerjian, Regina Tor *16*
Shelby, Anne 1948- *85*
  Autobiography Feature *121*
  See also SAAS *26*
Sheldon, Ann
  See Antle, Nancy
Sheldon, Ann *67*
  Earlier sketch in SATA *1*
Sheldon, Aure 1917-1976 .... *12*
Sheldon, David *185*
Sheldon, Deyan *181*
Sheldon, John
  See Bloch, Robert (Albert)
Sheldon, Muriel 1926- *45*
  Brief entry *39*
Shell, Barry 1951- *176*
Shelley, Frances
  See Wees, Frances Shelley
Shelley, John 1959- *202*
Shelley, Mary
  See Shelley, Mary Wollstonecraft
Shelley, Mary Wollstonecraft 1797-1851 ..... *29*
  See also CLR *133*
Shelton, William Roy 1919-1995 .... *5*
  Obituary *129*
Shemie, Bonnie (Jean Brenner) 1949- *96*
Shemin, Margaretha (Hoeneveld) 1928- *4*
Shen, Michele 1953- *173*
Shenker, Michele
  See Shen, Michele
Shenton, Edward 1895-1977 .... *45*
Shepard, Aaron 1950- *187*
  Earlier sketches in SATA *75, 113*
Shepard, Ernest Howard 1879-1976 .... *100*
  Obituary *24*
  Earlier sketches in SATA *3, 33*
  See also CLR *27*
Shepard, James R.
  See Shepard, Jim
Shepard, Jim 1956- *164*
  Earlier sketch in SATA *90*
Shepard, Mary
  See Knox, (Mary) Eleanor Jessie
Shephard, Esther 1891-1975 .... *5*
  Obituary *26*
Shepherd, Amanda *201*
Shepherd, Donna Walsh
  See Walsh Shepherd, Donna
Shepherd, Elizabeth *4*
Shepherd, Irana *173*
Shepherd, Roni
  See Shepherd, Irana
Sheppard, Kate *195*
Shepperson, Rob *178*
Sherburne, Zoa (Lillian Morin) 1912-1995 .... *3*
  See also SAAS *18*
Sherk-Savage, Candace
  See Savage, Candace

Sherlock, Patti *71*
Sherman, D(enis) R(onald) 1934- *48*
　Brief entry *29*
Sherman, Diane (Finn) 1928- *12*
Sherman, Elizabeth
　See Friskey, Margaret (Richards)
Sherman, Harold (Morrow) 1898-1987 .... *37*
　Obituary *137*
Sherman, Josepha *163*
　Earlier sketch in SATA *75*
Sherman, Michael
　See Lowndes, Robert A(ugustine) W(ard)
Sherman, Nancy
　See Rosenberg, Nancy (Sherman)
Sherman, Pat *174*
Sherman, Peter Michael
　See Lowndes, Robert A(ugustine) W(ard)
Sherrard, Valerie (Anne) 1957- *141*
Sherrod, Jane
　See Singer, Jane Sherrod
Sherry, Clifford J. 1943- *84*
Sherry, (Dulcie) Sylvia 1932- *122*
　Earlier sketch in SATA *8*
Sherwan, Earl 1917- *3*
Sherwood, Jonathan
　See London, Jonathan
Sheth, Kashmira *186*
Shetterly, Will 1955- *78*
　Autobiography Feature *106*
Shetterly, William Howard
　See Shetterly, Will
Shiefman, Vicky 1942- *22*
Shields, Brenda Desmond (Armstrong)
　1914- *37*
Shields, Carol Diggory *174*
Shields, Charles 1944- *10*
Shields, Gillian *203*
Shiels, Barbara
　See Adams, Barbara Johnston
Shiffman, Lena 1957- *101*
Shiina, Makoto 1944- *83*
Shimin, Symeon 1902-1984 .... *13*
Shimko, Bonnie 1941- *191*
Shine, Andrea 1955- *104*
Shine, Deborah 1932- *71*
Shinn, Everett 1876-1953 .... *21*
Shinn, Sharon 1957- *164*
　Earlier sketch in SATA *110*
Shippen, Katherine B(inney) 1892-1980 .... *1*
　Obituary *23*
　See also CLR *36*
Shippey, T. A. 1943- *143*
Shippey, Thomas Alan
　See Shippey, T. A.
Shipton, Eric Earle 1907-1977 .... *10*
Shipton, Jonathan 1948- *215*
Shipton, Paul 1963- *196*
Shiraz, Yasmin *173*
Shirer, William L(awrence) 1904-1993 .... *45*
　Obituary *78*
Shirley, Debra *203*
Shirley, Gayle C 1955- *96*
Shirley, Gayle Corbett
　See Shirley, Gayle C
Shirley, Jean 1919- *70*
Shirreffs, Gordon D(onald) 1914-1996 .... *11*
Shirts, Morris A(lpine) 1922- *63*
Shlichta, Joe 1968- *84*
Shmurak, Carole B. 1944- *118*
Sholokhov, Mikhail 1905-1984
　Obituary *36*
Sholokhov, Mikhail Aleksandrovich
　See Sholokhov, Mikhail
Shore, Diane Z. *215*
　Earlier sketch in SATA *179*
Shore, Diane ZuHone
　See Shore, Diane Z.
Shore, June Lewis *30*
Shore, Nancy 1960- *124*
Shore, Robert 1924- *39*
Short, Michael 1937- *65*

Short, Roger
　See Arkin, Alan
Shortall, Leonard W. *19*
Shortt, Tim(othy Donald) 1961- *96*
Shotwell, Louisa Rossiter 1902-1993 .... *3*
Shoulders, Michael 1954- *216*
Shoup, Barbara 1947- *156*
　Earlier sketch in SATA *86*
　See also SAAS *24*
Shoveller, Herb *184*
Showalter, Jean B(reckinridge) *12*
Showell, Ellen Harvey 1934- *33*
Showers, Paul C. 1910-1999 .... *92*
　Obituary *114*
　Earlier sketch in SATA *21*
　See also CLR *6*
　See also SAAS *7*
Shpakow, Tanya 1959(?)- *94*
Shpitalnik, Vladimir 1964- *83*
Shragg, Karen (I.) 1954- *142*
Shreeve, Elizabeth 1956- *156*
Shreve, Susan
　See Shreve, Susan Richards
Shreve, Susan Richards 1939- *152*
　Brief entry *41*
　Earlier sketches in SATA *46, 95*
Shriver, Jean Adair 1932- *75*
Shriver, Maria 1955- *134*
Shriver, Maria Owings
　See Shriver, Maria
Shrode, Mary
　See Hollingsworth, Mary
Shtainmets, Leon *32*
Shub, Elizabeth 1915(?)-2004 .... *5*
Shuken, Julia 1948- *84*
Shulevitz, Uri 1935- *165*
　Earlier sketches in SATA *3, 50, 106*
　See also CLR *61*
Shulman, Alix Kates 1932- *7*
Shulman, Dee 1957- *146*
Shulman, Irving 1913-1995 .... *13*
Shulman, Lisa *202*
Shulman, Mark 1962- *184*
Shulman, Max 1919-1988
　Obituary *59*
Shulman, Milton 1913-2004
　Obituary *154*
Shulman, Neil B(arnett) 1945- *89*
Shumsky, Zena
　See Collier, Zena
Shura, Mary Francis
　See Craig, Mary (Francis) Shura
Shusterman, Neal 1962- *201*
　Autobiography Feature *140*
　Earlier sketches in SATA *85, 121, 140*
Shuter, Jane (Margaret) 1955- *151*
　Earlier sketch in SATA *90*
Shuttlesworth, Dorothy Edwards *3*
Shwartz, Susan (Martha) 1949- *94*
Shyer, Christopher 1961- *98*
Shyer, Marlene Fanta *13*
Siberell, Anne *29*
Sibley, Don 1922- *12*
Siburt, Ruth 1951- *121*
Siculan, Daniel 1922- *12*
Siddon, Barbara
　See Bradford, Barbara Taylor
Sidgwick, Ethel 1877-1970 .... *116*
Sidjakov, Nicolas 1924- *18*
Sidman, Joyce 1956- *181*
　Earlier sketch in SATA *145*
Sidney, Frank
　See Warwick, Alan R(oss)
Sidney, Margaret
　See Lothrop, Harriet Mulford Stone
Siebert, Diane 1948- *189*
Siegal, Aranka 1930- *88*
　Brief entry *37*
Siegel, Beatrice *36*
Siegel, Helen
　See Siegl, Helen

Siegel, Robert 1939- *39*
Siegel, Robert Harold
　See Siegel, Robert
Siegel, Siena Cherson 1967(?)- *185*
Siegelson, Kim L. 1962- *114*
Sieger, Ted 1958- *189*
Siegl, Helen 1924- *34*
Siepmann, Mary Aline
　See Wesley, Mary (Aline)
Sierra, Judy 1945- *195*
　Earlier sketches in SATA *104, 162*
Sieswerda, Paul L. 1942- *147*
Sievert, Terri
　See Dougherty, Terri (L.)
Sigsawa, Keiichi 1972- *211*
Silas
　See McCay, (Zenas) Winsor
Silcock, Sara Lesley 1947- *12*
Silin-Palmer, Pamela *184*
Sill, Cathryn 1953- *221*
　Earlier sketches in SATA *74, 141*
Sill, John 1947- *222*
　Earlier sketches in SATA *74, 140*
Sillitoe, Alan 1928-2010 .... *61*
Sills, Leslie (Elka) 1948- *129*
Silly, E. S.
　See Kraus, (Herman) Robert
Silsbe, Brenda 1953- *73*
Silva, Joseph
　See Goulart, Ron
Silvano, Wendi 1962- *223*
Silver, Jago
　See Jago
Silver, Maggie *216*
Silver, Ruth
　See Chew, Ruth
Silverberg, Robert 1935- *91*
　Autobiography Feature *104*
　Earlier sketch in SATA *13*
　See also CLR *59*
Silverman, Erica 1955- *222*
　Earlier sketches in SATA *78, 112, 165*
Silverman, Janis L. 1946- *127*
Silverman, Mel(vin Frank) 1931-1966 .... *9*
Silverman, Robin L. 1954- *96*
Silverman, Robin Landew
　See Silverman, Robin L.
Silverstein, Alvin 1933- *124*
　Earlier sketches in SATA *8, 69*
　See also CLR *25*
Silverstein, Herma 1945- *106*
Silverstein, Robert Alan 1959- *124*
　Earlier sketch in SATA *77*
Silverstein, Shel 1932-1999 .... *92*
　Brief entry *27*
　Obituary *116*
　Earlier sketch in SATA *33*
　See also CLR *96*
Silverstein, Sheldon Allan
　See Silverstein, Shel
Silverstein, Virginia B. 1937- *124*
　Earlier sketches in SATA *8, 69*
　See also CLR *25*
Silverstein, Virginia Barbara Opshelor
　See Silverstein, Virginia B.
Silverthorne, Elizabeth 1930- *35*
Silverwood, Margaret Shannon 1966- *137*
　Earlier sketch in SATA *83*
Silvey, Diane F. 1946- *135*
Sim, David 1953- *162*
Sim, Dorrith M. 1931- *96*
Simak, Clifford D(onald) 1904-1988
　Obituary *56*
Simard, Remy 1959- *168*
Siminovich, Lorena 1976(?)- *219*
Simmie, Lois (Ann) 1932- *106*
Simmonds, Posy 1945- *130*
　See also CLR *23*
Simmonds, Rosemary Elizabeth
　See Simmonds, Posy
Simmons, Andra 1939- *141*

Simmons, Elly 1955- *134*
Simmons, Michael 1970- *185*
Simms, Laura 1947- *117*
Simner, Janni Lee *113*
Simon, Charlie May
  See Fletcher, Charlie May Hogue
Simon, Francesca 1955- *111*
Simon, Gabriel 1972- *118*
Simon, Hilda Rita 1921- *28*
  See also CLR *39*
Simon, Howard 1903-1979 .... *32*
  Obituary *21*
Simon, Joe
  See Simon, Joseph H.
Simon, Joseph H. 1913- *7*
Simon, Martin P(aul William) 1903-1969 .... *12*
Simon, Mina Lewiton
  See Lewiton, Mina
Simon, Norma (Feldstein) 1927- *129*
  Earlier sketches in SATA *3, 68*
Simon, Seymour 1931- *202*
  Earlier sketches in SATA *4, 73, 138*
  See also CLR *63*
Simon, Shirley (Schwartz) 1921- *11*
Simon, Solomon 1895-1970 .... *40*
Simonetta, Linda 1948- *14*
Simonetta, Sam 1936- *14*
Simons, Barbara B(rooks) 1934- *41*
Simont, Marc 1915- *126*
  Earlier sketches in SATA *9, 73*
Simpson, Colin 1908-1983 .... *14*
Simpson, Harriette
  See Arnow, Harriette (Louisa) Simpson
Simpson, Jacynth Hope
  See Hope Simpson, Jacynth
Simpson, Lesley 1963- *150*
Simpson, Margaret 1943- *128*
Simpson, Myrtle L(illias) 1931- *14*
Sims, Blanche *168*
  Earlier sketch in SATA *75*
Sims, Blanche L.
  See Sims, Blanche
Simundsson, Elva 1950- *63*
Sinclair, Clover
  See Gater, Dilys
Sinclair, Emil
  See Hesse, Hermann
Sinclair, Jeff 1958- *77*
Sinclair, Olga 1923- *121*
Sinclair, Rose
  See Smith, Susan Vernon
Sinclair, Upton 1878-1968 .... *9*
Sinclair, Upton Beall
  See Sinclair, Upton
Singer, A.L.
  See Lerangis, Peter
Singer, Arthur 1917-1990 .... *64*
Singer, Isaac
  See Singer, Isaac Bashevis
Singer, Isaac Bashevis 1904-1991 .... *27*
  Obituary *68*
  Earlier sketch in SATA *3*
  See also CLR *1*
Singer, Jane Sherrod 1917-1985 .... *4*
  Obituary *42*
Singer, Julia 1917- *28*
Singer, Kurt D. 1911-2005 .... *38*
  Obituary *172*
Singer, Marilyn 1948- *201*
  Autobiography Feature *158*
  Brief entry *38*
  Earlier sketches in SATA *48, 80, 125, 158*
  See also CLR *48*
  See also SAAS *13*
Singer, Muff 1942-2005 .... *104*
  Obituary *160*
Singer, Nicky 1956- *194*
Singer, Susan (Mahler) 1941- *9*
Singh, Rashmi Sharma 1952- *90*
Singleton, Linda Joy 1957- *166*
  Earlier sketch in SATA *88*

Singleton, L.J.
  See Singleton, Linda Joy
Singleton, Sarah 1966- *214*
Sinykin, Sheri
  See Sinykin, Sheri Cooper
Sinykin, Sheri Cooper 1950- *142*
  Autobiography Feature *142*
  Earlier sketches in SATA *72, 133*
Sinykin, Sheril Terri Cooper
  See Sinykin, Sheri Cooper
Siomades, Lorianne *217*
Sipiera, Paul P., (Jr.) 1948- *144*
  Earlier sketch in SATA *89*
Siracusa, Catherine (Jane) 1947- *82*
Sirett, Dawn (Karen) 1966- *88*
Sirimarco, Elizabeth 1966- *158*
Sirof, Harriet 1930- *94*
  Earlier sketch in SATA *37*
Sirois, Allen L. 1950- *76*
Sirvaitis (Chernyaev), Karen (Ann) 1961- ... *79*
Sis, Peter 1949- *192*
  Earlier sketch in SATA *149*
  See also CLR *110*
Sisson, Rosemary Anne 1923- *11*
Sister Mary Terese
  See Donze, Mary Terese
Sita, Lisa 1962- *87*
Sitarski, Anita *200*
Sitomer, Alan Lawrence *174*
Sitomer, Harry 1903-1985 .... *31*
Sitomer, Mindel 1903-1987 .... *31*
Sittenfeld, Curtis 1975(?)- *164*
Sive, Helen R(obinson) 1951- *30*
Sivulich, Sandra (Jeanne) Stroner 1941- *9*
Siy, Alexandra *193*
Skarmeta, Antonio 1940- *57*
Skeers, Linda 1958- *207*
Skelly, James R(ichard) 1927- *17*
Skelton, Matthew 1971- *185*
Skinner, Constance Lindsay 1877-1939
  See YABC *1*
Skinner, Cornelia Otis 1901-1979 .... *2*
Skipper, G. C. 1939- *46*
  Brief entry *38*
Sklansky, Amy E(dgar) 1971- *145*
Sklansky, Amy E. 1971- *204*
Skofield, James *95*
  Brief entry *44*
Skold, Betty Westrom 1923- *41*
Skorpen, Liesel Moak 1935- *3*
Skott, Maria
  See Nikolajeva, Maria
Skrypuch, Marsha Forchuk 1954- *134*
Skultety, Nancy Laney 1960- *175*
Skurzynski, Gloria 1930- *145*
  Autobiography Feature *145*
  Earlier sketches in SATA *8, 74, 122*
  See also SAAS *9*
Skurzynski, Gloria Joan
  See Skurzynski, Gloria
Skutch, Robert 1925- *89*
Skye, Maggie
  See Werner, Herma
Skye, Obert *200*
  Earlier sketch in SATA *170*
Slack, Michael 1969- *189*
Slackman, Charles B. 1934- *12*
Slade, Arthur G. 1967- *221*
  Earlier sketches in SATA *106, 149*
Slade, Arthur Gregory
  See Slade, Arthur G.
Slade, Christian 1974- *193*
Slade, Richard 1910-1971 .... *9*
Slangerup, Erik Jon 1969- *130*
Slate, Joseph 1928- *174*
  Earlier sketches in SATA *38, 122*
Slate, Joseph Frank
  See Slate, Joseph
Slater, Dashka 1963- *179*
Slater, David Michael 1970- *212*

Slater, Ray
  See Lansdale, Joe R.
Slaughter, Hope 1940- *84*
Slaughter, Jean
  See Doty, Jean Slaughter
Slaughter, Tom 1955- *152*
Slavicek, Louise Chipley 1956- *144*
Slavin, Bill 1959- *199*
  Earlier sketches in SATA *76, 148*
Slaymaker, Melissa Eskridge 1958- *158*
Slayton, Fran Cannon *221*
Sleator, William 1945- *208*
  Earlier sketches in SATA *3, 68, 118, 161*
  See also CLR *128*
Sleator, William Warner III
  See Sleator, William
Slegers, Liesbet 1975- *154*
Sleigh, Barbara 1906-1982 .... *86*
  Obituary *30*
  Earlier sketch in SATA *3*
Slepian, Jan 1921- *85*
  Brief entry *45*
  Earlier sketch in SATA *51*
  See also SAAS *8*
Slepian, Janice B.
  See Slepian, Jan
Slicer, Margaret O. 1920- *4*
Slier, Debby
  See Shine, Deborah
Sloan, Brian 1966- *172*
Sloan, Carolyn 1937- *116*
  Earlier sketch in SATA *58*
Sloan, Glenna 1930- *120*
Sloan, Glenna Davis
  See Sloan, Glenna
Sloane, Eric 1910(?)-1985 .... *52*
  Obituary *42*
Sloane, Todd 1955- *88*
Sloat, Teri 1948- *164*
  Earlier sketches in SATA *70, 106*
Slobodkin, Florence Gersh 1905-1994 .... *5*
  Obituary *107*
Slobodkin, Louis 1903-1975 .... *26*
  Earlier sketch in SATA *1*
Slobodkina, Esphyr 1908-2002 .... *1*
  Obituary *135*
  See also SAAS *8*
Sloggett, Nellie 1851-1923 .... *44*
Slonim, David 1966- *207*
Sloss, Lesley Lord 1965- *72*
Slote, Alfred 1926- *72*
  Earlier sketch in SATA *8*
  See also CLR *4*
  See also SAAS *21*
Slote, Elizabeth 1956- *80*
Small, Charlie
  See Ward, Nick
Small, David 1945- *216*
  Brief entry *46*
  Earlier sketches in SATA *50, 95, 126, 183*
  See also CLR *53*
Small, Ernest
  See Lent, Blair
Small, Mary 1932- *165*
Small, Terry 1942- *75*
Smallcomb, Pam 1954- *159*
Smallman, Steve *197*
Smalls, Irene
  See Smalls-Hector, Irene
Smalls-Hector, Irene 1950- *146*
  Earlier sketch in SATA *73*
  See also CLR *103*
Smallwood, Norah (Evelyn) 1910(?)-1984
  Obituary *41*
Smaridge, Norah (Antoinette) 1903-1994 ...... *6*
Smath, Jerry 1933- *198*
Smee, Nicola 1948- *167*
  Earlier sketch in SATA *76*
Smiley, Virginia Kester 1923- *2*
Smit, Noelle 1972- *199*

Smith, Alexander McCall 1948- *179*
  Earlier sketch in SATA *73*
Smith, Andrew 1959- *209*
Smith, Andrew Anselmo
  See Smith, Andrew
Smith, Andy J. 1975- *207*
Smith, Anne Warren 1938- *41*
  Brief entry *34*
Smith, Barry (Edward Jervis) 1943- *75*
Smith, Beatrice S(chillinger) *12*
Smith, Betsy Covington 1937- *55*
  Earlier sketch in SATA *43*
Smith, Betty (Wehner) 1904-1972 .... *6*
Smith, Bradford 1909-1964 .... *5*
Smith, Brenda 1946- *82*
Smith, C. Pritchard
  See Hoyt, Edwin P(almer), Jr.
Smith, Caesar
  See Trevor, Elleston
Smith, Cat Bowman 1939- *201*
Smith, Charles R., Jr. 1969- *203*
  Earlier sketch in SATA *159*
Smith, Craig 1955- *172*
  Earlier sketches in SATA *81, 117*
Smith, Cynthia Leitich 1967- *215*
  Earlier sketch in SATA *152*
Smith, D. James 1955- *176*
Smith, Danna *216*
Smith, Danna Kessimakis
  See Smith, Danna
Smith, Datus C(lifford), Jr. 1907-1999 .... *13*
  Obituary *116*
Smith, Debra 1955- *89*
Smith, Derek 1943- *141*
Smith, Dick King
  See King-Smith, Dick
Smith, D.J.
  See Smith, D. James
Smith, Dodie
  See Smith, Dorothy Gladys
Smith, Doris Buchanan 1934-2002 .... *75*
  Obituary *140*
  Earlier sketch in SATA *28*
  See also SAAS *10*
Smith, Dorothy Gladys 1896-1990 .... *82*
  Obituary *65*
Smith, Dorothy Stafford 1905- *6*
Smith, Duane 1974- *202*
Smith, E(lmer) Boyd 1860-1943
  See YABC *1*
Smith, E(dric) Brooks 1917- *40*
Smith, Elwood H. 1941- *203*
Smith, Emily Wing 1980- *215*
Smith, Emma 1923- *52*
  Brief entry *36*
Smith, (Katherine) Eunice (Young)
  1902-1993 .... *5*
Smith, Frances C(hristine) 1904-1986 .... *3*
Smith, Gary R. 1932- *14*
Smith, Geof 1969- *102*
Smith, George Harmon 1920- *5*
Smith, Gordon 1951- *184*
Smith, Greg Leitich *152*
Smith, H(arry) Allen 1907-1976
  Obituary *20*
Smith, Helene 1937- *142*
Smith, Hope Anita *202*
Smith, Howard E(verett), Jr. 1927- *12*
Smith, Hugh L(etcher) 1921-1968 .... *5*
Smith, Imogene Henderson 1922- *12*
Smith, Jacqueline B. 1937- *39*
Smith, Jada Pinkett 1971- *161*
Smith, James Noel 1950- *193*
Smith, Janet (Buchanan) Adam
  See Adam Smith, Janet (Buchanan)
Smith, Janice Lee 1949- *155*
  Earlier sketch in SATA *54*
Smith, Jean
  See Smith, Frances C(hristine)
Smith, Jean Pajot 1945- *10*

Smith, Jeff 1958- *161*
  Earlier sketch in SATA *93*
Smith, Jeff Allen
  See Smith, Jeff
Smith, Jenny 1963- *90*
Smith, Jessie
  See Kunhardt, Edith
Smith, Jessie Willcox 1863-1935 .... *21*
  See also CLR *59*
Smith, Joan (Mary) 1933- *54*
  Brief entry *46*
Smith, Johnston
  See Crane, Stephen
Smith, Jos A. 1936- *181*
  Earlier sketches in SATA *73, 120*
Smith, Joseph Arthur
  See Smith, Jos A.
Smith, Judie R. 1936- *80*
Smith, Kirsten 1970- *210*
Smith, Lafayette
  See Higdon, Hal
Smith, Lane 1959- *179*
  Earlier sketches in SATA *76, 131*
  See also CLR *47*
Smith, Lee
  See Albion, Lee Smith
Smith, Lendon H(oward) 1921- *64*
Smith, Lillian H(elena) 1887-1983
  Obituary *32*
Smith, Linda 1949- *177*
Smith, Linell Nash 1932- *2*
Smith, Lucia B. 1943- *30*
Smith, Maggie 1965- *190*
Smith, Margaret Emily Noel Nuttall
  See Nuttall-Smith, Margaret Emily Noel
Smith, Marion Hagens 1913- *12*
Smith, Marion Jaques 1899-1987 .... *13*
Smith, Mary Ellen *10*
Smith, Marya 1945- *78*
Smith, Mike
  See Smith, Mary Ellen
Smith, Nancy Covert 1935- *12*
Smith, Norman F. 1920- *70*
  Earlier sketch in SATA *5*
Smith, Patricia Clark 1943- *96*
Smith, Pauline C.
  See Arthur, Robert, (Jr.)
Smith, Pauline C(oggeshall) 1908-1994 .... *27*
Smith, Philip Warren 1936- *46*
Smith, R. Alexander McCall
  See Smith, Alexander McCall
Smith, Rebecca 1946- *123*
Smith, Robert Kimmel 1930- *77*
  Earlier sketch in SATA *12*
Smith, Robert Paul 1915-1977 .... *52*
  Obituary *30*
Smith, Roland 1951- *193*
  Earlier sketches in SATA *115, 161*
Smith, Rosamond
  See Oates, Joyce Carol
Smith, Ruth Leslie 1902- *2*
Smith, Samantha 1972-1985
  Obituary *45*
Smith, Sandra Lee 1945- *75*
Smith, Sarah Stafford
  See Smith, Dorothy Stafford
Smith, Sharon 1947- *82*
Smith, Sherri L. 1971- *156*
Smith, Sherwood 1951- *206*
  Autobiography Feature *206*
  Earlier sketches in SATA *82, 140*
Smith, Shirley Raines
  See Raines, Shirley C(arol)
Smith, Susan Carlton 1923- *12*
Smith, Susan Mathias 1950- *43*
  Brief entry *35*
Smith, Susan Vernon 1950- *48*
  Brief entry *45*
Smith, Tim(othy R.) 1945- *151*
Smith, Ursula 1934- *54*
Smith, Vian (Crocker) 1920-1969 .... *11*

Smith, Wanda VanHoy 1926- *65*
Smith, Ward
  See Goldsmith, Howard
Smith, William A. 1918- *10*
Smith, William Jay 1918- *154*
  Autobiography Feature *154*
  Earlier sketches in SATA *2, 68*
  See also SAAS *22*
Smith, Winsome 1935- *45*
Smith, Z.Z.
  See Westheimer, David
Smith-Ankrom, M. E. 1942- *130*
Smith-Griswold, Wendy 1955- *88*
Smith-Rex, Susan J. 1950- *94*
Smithsen, Richard
  See Pellowski, Michael (Joseph)
Smithson, Ryan 1985- *216*
Smits, Teo
  See Smits, Theodore R(ichard)
Smits, Theodore R(ichard) 1905-1996 .... *45*
  Brief entry *28*
Smolinski, Dick 1932- *86*
Smothers, Ethel Footman 1944- *149*
  Earlier sketch in SATA *76*
Smucker, Anna Egan 1948- *209*
Smucker, Barbara 1915-2003 .... *130*
  Earlier sketches in SATA *29, 76*
  See also CLR *10*
  See also SAAS *11*
Smucker, Barbara Claassen
  See Smucker, Barbara
Smyth, Iain 1959- *105*
Snedeker, Caroline Dale (Parke) 1871-1956
  See YABC *2*
Sneed, Brad *191*
Sneider, Marian 1932-2005 .... *197*
Snell, Nigel (Edward Creagh) 1936- *57*
  Brief entry *40*
Snellgrove, L(aurence) E(rnest) 1928- *53*
Snelling, Dennis (Wayne) 1958- *84*
Sneve, Virginia Driving Hawk 1933- *95*
  Earlier sketch in SATA *8*
  See also CLR *2*
Snicket, Lemony 1970- *215*
  Earlier sketches in SATA *126, 187*
  See also CLR *79*
Sniegoski, Thomas E. *195*
Sniegoski, Tom
  See Sniegoski, Thomas E.
Snodgrass, Mary Ellen 1944- *75*
Snodgrass, Quentin Curtius
  See Twain, Mark
Snodgrass, Thomas Jefferson
  See Twain, Mark
Snook, Barbara (Lillian) 1913-1976 .... *34*
Snow, Alan 1959- *190*
Snow, Carol 1965- *208*
Snow, Donald Clifford 1917-1979 .... *16*
Snow, Dorothea J(ohnston) 1909- *9*
Snow, Richard F(olger) 1947- *52*
  Brief entry *37*
Snyder, Anne 1922-2001 .... *4*
  Obituary *125*
Snyder, Bernadette McCarver 1930- *97*
Snyder, Carol 1941- *35*
Snyder, Gerald S(eymour) 1933- *48*
  Brief entry *34*
Snyder, Jerome 1916-1976
  Obituary *20*
Snyder, Laurel 1974- *209*
Snyder, Midori 1954- *106*
Snyder, Paul A. 1946- *125*
Snyder, Zilpha Keatley 1927- *163*
  Autobiography Feature *163*
  Earlier sketches in SATA *1, 28, 75, 110*
  See also CLR *121*
  See also SAAS *2*
Snyderman, Reuven K. 1922- *5*
So, Meilo *162*
Sobel, June 1950- *149*

Soble, Jennie
  See Cavin, Ruth
Sobol, Donald J. 1924- *132*
  Earlier sketches in SATA *1, 31, 73*
  See also CLR *4*
Sobol, Harriet Langsam 1936- *47*
  Brief entry *34*
Sobol, Richard *211*
Sobol, Rose 1931- *76*
Sobott-Mogwe, Gaele 1956- *97*
Soderlind, Arthur E(dwin) 1920- *14*
Soentpiet, Chris K. 1970- *159*
  Earlier sketch in SATA *97*
Soerensen, Svend Otto 1916- *67*
Sofer, Barbara 1949- *109*
Sofer, Rachel
  See Sofer, Barbara
Softly, Barbara Frewin 1924- *12*
Sogabe, Aki *207*
Soglow, Otto 1900-1975
  Obituary *30*
Sohl, Frederic J(ohn) 1916- *10*
Sohr, Daniel 1973- *190*
Sokol, Bill
  See Sokol, William
Sokol, William 1923- *37*
Sokolov, Kirill 1930- *34*
Solbert, Romaine G. 1925- *2*
Solbert, Ronni
  See Solbert, Romaine G.
Solheim, James *133*
Solomon, Heather M. *188*
Solomon, Joan 1930- *51*
  Brief entry *40*
Solomons, Ikey Esquir
  See Thackeray, William Makepeace
Solonevich, George 1915-2003 .... *15*
Solot, Mary Lynn 1939- *12*
Solov'ev, Mikhail
  See Soloviov, Michael
Soloviov, Michael 1972- *222*
Soman, David 1965- *200*
Somerlott, Robert 1928-2001 .... *62*
Somers, Kevin *205*
Somervill, Barbara A(nn) 1948- *140*
Sommer, Angela
  See Sommer-Bodenburg, Angela
Sommer, Carl 1930- *175*
  Earlier sketch in SATA *126*
Sommer, Elyse 1929- *7*
Sommer, Robert 1929- *12*
Sommer-Bodenburg, Angela 1948- *113*
  Earlier sketch in SATA *63*
Sommerdorf, Norma 1926- *131*
Sommerdorf, Norma Jean
  See Sommerdorf, Norma
Sommerfelt, Aimee 1892-1975 .... *5*
Son, John *160*
Sones, Sonya *131*
Sonneborn, Ruth (Cantor) 1899-1974 .... *4*
  Obituary *27*
Sonnenblick, Jordan 1969- *223*
  Earlier sketch in SATA *185*
  See also CLR *144*
Sonnenmark, Laura A. 1958- *73*
Soo, Kean *201*
Sopko, Eugen 1949- *58*
Sorel, Edward 1929- *126*
  Brief entry *37*
  Earlier sketch in SATA *65*
Sorensen, Henri 1950- *115*
  Earlier sketch in SATA *77*
Sorensen, Svend Otto
  See Soerensen, Svend Otto
Sorensen, Virginia 1912-1991 .... *2*
  Obituary *72*
  See also SAAS *15*
Sorenson, Jane 1926- *63*
Sorenson, Margo 1946- *96*
Sorley Walker, Kathrine *41*
Sorra, Kristin *185*

Sorrells, Walter *177*
Sorrentino, Joseph N. 1937- *6*
Sortor, June Elizabeth 1939- *12*
Sortor, Toni
  See Sortor, June Elizabeth
Sosa, Hernan 1977- *203*
Soskin, V. H.
  See Ellison, Virginia H(owell)
Soto, Gary 1952- *174*
  Earlier sketches in SATA *80, 120*
  See also CLR *38*
Sotomayor, Antonio 1902-1985 .... *11*
Souci, Robert D. San
  See San Souci, Robert D.
Soudley, Henry
  See Wood, James Playsted
Souhami, Jessica *176*
Soule, Gardner (Bosworth) 1913-2000 .... *14*
Soule, Jean Conder 1919- *10*
Souster, (Holmes) Raymond 1921- *63*
South, Sheri Cobb 1959- *82*
Southall, Ivan 1921-2008 .... *134*
  Autobiography Feature *134*
  Earlier sketches in SATA *3, 68*
  See also CLR *2*
  See also SAAS *3*
Southall, Ivan Francis
  See Southall, Ivan
Southey, Robert 1774-1843 .... *54*
Southgate, Vera *54*
Souza, Janet
  See Tashjian, Janet
Sovak, Jan 1953- *115*
Sowden, Celeste
  See Walters, Celeste
Sowter, Nita *69*
Spafford, Suzy 1945- *160*
Spagnoli, Cathy 1950- *134*
  Earlier sketch in SATA *79*
Spain, Sahara Sunday 1991- *133*
Spain, Susan Rosson *185*
Spalding, Andrea 1944- *150*
  Earlier sketch in SATA *101*
Spalenka, Greg 1958- *198*
Spanfeller, James J. 1930- *19*
  See also SAAS *8*
Spanfeller, Jim
  See Spanfeller, James J.
Spangenberg, Judith Dunn 1942- *5*
Spangler, Brie *212*
Spanyol, Jessica 1965- *206*
  Earlier sketch in SATA *137*
Spar, Jerome 1918- *10*
Sparks, Barbara 1942- *78*
Sparks, Beatrice (Mathews) 1918- *44*
  Brief entry *28*
  See also CLR *139*
Sparks, Mary W. 1920- *15*
Spaulding, Douglas
  See Bradbury, Ray
Spaulding, Leonard
  See Bradbury, Ray
Spaulding, Norma *107*
Speare, Elizabeth George 1908-1994 .... *62*
  Obituary *83*
  Earlier sketch in SATA *5*
  See also CLR *8*
Spearing, Judith (Mary Harlow) 1922- *9*
Spears, Rick *182*
Speck, Katie *196*
Speck, Nancy 1959- *104*
Specking, Inez 1890-1960(?) *11*
Speed, Nell
  See Keats, Emma
  and Sampson, Emma (Keats) Speed
Speed, Nell (Ewing) 1878-1913 .... *68*
Speer, Bonnie Stahlman 1929- *113*
Speer-Lyon, Tammie L. 1965- *89*
Speicher, Helen Ross S(mith) 1915- *8*
Speir, Nancy 1958- *210*
  Earlier sketch in SATA *81*

Spellman, John W(illard) 1934- *14*
Spellman, Roger G.
  See Cox, William R(obert)
Spelman, Cornelia Maude 1946- *144*
  Earlier sketch in SATA *96*
Spelman, Mary 1934- *28*
Spelvin, George
  See Lerangis, Peter
  and Phillips, David Atlee
Spence, Cynthia
  See Eble, Diane
Spence, Eleanor (Rachel) 1928- *21*
  See also CLR *26*
Spence, Geraldine 1931- *47*
Spencer, Ann 1918- *10*
Spencer, Britt *206*
Spencer, Cornelia
  See Yaukey, Grace S(ydenstricker)
Spencer, Donald D(ean) 1931- *41*
Spencer, Elizabeth 1921- *14*
Spencer, Leonard G.
  See Garrett, Randall
  and Silverberg, Robert
Spencer, William 1922- *9*
Spencer, Zane A(nn) 1935- *35*
Spengler, Margaret *223*
Sper, Emily 1957- *142*
Speregen, Devra Newberger 1964- *84*
Sperling, Dan(iel Lee) 1949- *65*
Sperry, Armstrong W. 1897-1976 .... *1*
  Obituary *27*
Sperry, Raymond
  See Garis, Howard R.
Sperry, Raymond, Jr. *1*
Spetter, Jung-Hee 1969- *134*
Spicer, Dorothy Gladys -1975 .... *32*
Spiegel, Beth *184*
Spiegelman, Art 1948- *158*
  Earlier sketch in SATA *109*
Spiegelman, Judith M. *5*
Spielberg, Steven 1947- *32*
Spier, Peter (Edward) 1927- *54*
  Earlier sketch in SATA *4*
  See also CLR *5*
Spilhaus, Athelstan (Frederick) 1911-1998 .. *13*
  Obituary *102*
Spilka, Arnold 1917- *6*
Spillane, Frank Morrison
  See Spillane, Mickey
Spillane, Mickey 1918-2006 .... *66*
  Obituary *176*
Spinelli, Eileen 1942- *186*
  Earlier sketches in SATA *38, 101, 150*
Spinelli, Jerry 1941- *195*
  Earlier sketches in SATA *39, 71, 110, 158*
  See also CLR *82*
Spink, Reginald (William) 1905-1994 .... *11*
Spinka, Penina Keen 1945- *72*
Spinner, Stephanie 1943- *132*
  Earlier sketches in SATA *38, 91*
Spinossimus
  See White, William, Jr.
Spiotta-DiMare, Loren *173*
Spires, Ashley 1978- *183*
Spires, Elizabeth 1952- *215*
  Earlier sketches in SATA *71, 111*
Spiridellis, Gregg 1971(?)- *199*
Spirin, Gennadii
  See Spirin, Gennady
Spirin, Gennadij
  See Spirin, Gennady
Spirin, Gennady 1948- *204*
  Earlier sketches in SATA *95, 134*
  See also CLR *88*
Spiro, Ruth *208*
Spivak, Dawnine *101*
Spizman, Robyn Freedman *194*
Spohn, David 1948- *72*
Spohn, Kate 1962- *147*
  Earlier sketch in SATA *87*
Spollen, Christopher 1952- *12*

Spooner, Michael (Tim) 1954- 92
Spoor, Mike 218
Spowart, Robin 1947- 177
  Earlier sketch in SATA 82
Spradlin, Michael P. 204
Sprague, Gretchen 1926-2003 27
Spranger, Nina 1969- 203
Sprengel, Artie
  See Lerangis, Peter
Sprigge, Elizabeth (Miriam Squire)
  1900-1974 10
Spring, (Robert) Howard 1889-1965 28
Springer, Margaret 1941- 78
Springer, Marilyn Harris 1931- 47
Springer, Nancy 1948- 222
  Earlier sketches in SATA 65, 110, 172
Springstubb, Tricia 1950- 78
  Brief entry 40
  Earlier sketch in SATA 46
Spudvilas, Anne 1951- 199
  Earlier sketch in SATA 94
Spurll, Barbara 1952- 78
Spurr, Elizabeth 172
Spykman, E(lizabeth) C(hoate) 1896-1965 .. 10
  See also CLR 35
Spyri, Johanna (Heusser) 1827-1901 100
  Earlier sketch in SATA 19
  See also CLR 115
Squires, Janet 215
Squires, Phil
  See Barker, S. Omar
Srba, Lynne 98
Sreenivasan, Jyotsna 1964- 101
S-Ringi, Kjell
  See Ringi, Kjell (Arne Soerensen)
Staake, Bob 1957- 209
Stacey, Cherylyn 1945- 96
Stacy, Donald
  See Pohl, Frederik
Stadler, John 204
Stadtler, Bea 1921- 17
Stafford, Jean 1915-1979
  Obituary 22
Stafford, Liliana 1950- 141
Stafford, Paul 1966- 116
Stahl, Ben(jamin) 1910-1987 5
  Obituary 54
Stahl, Hilda 1938-1993 48
  Obituary 77
Stahler, David, Jr. 218
  Earlier sketch in SATA 162
Staines, Bill 1949- 213
Stainton, Sue 187
Stair, Gobin (John) 1912- 35
Stalder, Valerie 27
Stamaty, Mark Alan 1947- 12
Stambler, Irwin 1924- 5
Stampler, Ann Redisch 209
Standiford, Natalie 1961- 169
  Earlier sketch in SATA 81
Stanek, Lou Willett 1931- 63
Stang, Judit 1921-1977 29
Stang, Judy
  See Stang, Judit
Stangl, (Mary) Jean 1928- 67
Stanhope, Eric
  See Hamilton, Charles (Harold St. John)
Stankevich, Boris 1928- 2
Stanley, Diane 1943- 213
  Brief entry 32
  Earlier sketches in SATA 37, 80, 115, 164
  See also CLR 46
  See also SAAS 15
Stanley, Elizabeth 1947- 206
Stanley, George Edward 1942- 67
  Earlier sketches in SATA 53, 111, 157, 1
Stanley, Jerry 1941- 127
  Earlier sketch in SATA 79
Stanley, Mandy 165
Stanley, Robert
  See Hamilton, Charles (Harold St. John)

Stanley, Sanna 1962- 145
Stanli, Sue
  See Meilach, Dona Z(weigoron)
Stanstead, John
  See Groom, Arthur William
Stanton, Karen 1960- 190
Stanton, Schuyler
  See Baum, L. Frank
Staples, Suzanne Fisher 1945- 207
  Earlier sketches in SATA 70, 105, 151
  See also CLR 137
Stapleton, Marjorie (Winifred) 1932- 28
Stapp, Arthur D(onald) 1906-1972 4
Starbird, Kaye 1916- 6
  See also CLR 60
Stark, Evan 1942- 78
Stark, James
  See Goldston, Robert (Conroy)
Stark, Ken 1943- 199
Stark, Ulf 1944- 124
Starke, Ruth (Elaine) 1946- 129
Starkey, Marion L(ena) 1901-1991 13
Starr, Ward
  See Manes, Stephen
Starret, William
  See McClintock, Marshall
Starr Taylor, Bridget 1959- 99
Stasiak, Krystyna 49
Staub, Frank 1949- 116
Staub, Frank Jacob
  See Staub, Frank
Staub, Wendy Corsi 1964- 114
Stauffacher, Sue 1961- 199
  Earlier sketch in SATA 155
Stauffer, Don
  See Berkebile, Fred D(onovan)
Staunton, Schuyler
  See Baum, L. Frank
Staunton, Ted 1956- 167
  Earlier sketch in SATA 112
Stead, Judy 210
Stead, Rebecca 1968(?)- 188
Steadman, Ralph 1936- 123
  Earlier sketch in SATA 32
Steadman, Ralph Idris
  See Steadman, Ralph
Stearman, Kaye 1951- 118
Stearn, Ted 1961- 218
Stearns, Monroe (Mather) 1913-1987 5
  Obituary 55
Steckler, Arthur 1921-1985 65
Steding, Laurie 1953- 119
Steel, Danielle 1947- 66
Steel, Danielle Fernande
  See Steel, Danielle
Steele, Addison II
  See Lupoff, Richard A(llen)
Steele, Alexander 1958- 116
Steele, Henry Maxwell
  See Steele, Max
Steele, Mary 1930- 94
Steele, Mary Q(uintard Govan) 1922-1992 .. 51
  Obituary 72
  Earlier sketch in SATA 3
Steele, Max 1922-2005 168
  Earlier sketch in SATA 10
Steele, Philip 1948- 140
  Earlier sketch in SATA 81
Steele, William O(wen) 1917-1979 51
  Obituary 27
  Earlier sketch in SATA 1
Steelhammer, Ilona 1952- 98
Steelsmith, Shari 1962- 72
Stefanik, Alfred T. 1939- 55
Steffanson, Con
  See Cassiday, Bruce (Bingham)
  and Goulart, Ron
Steffens, Bradley 1955- 166
  Earlier sketch in SATA 77
Steffensmeier, Alexander 1977- 195

Stegeman, Janet Allais 1923- 49
  Brief entry 49
Steggall, Susan 1967- 182
Steig, William 1907-2003 111
  Obituary 149
  Earlier sketches in SATA 18, 70
  See also CLR 103
Steig, William H.
  See Steig, William
Stein, David Ezra 211
  Earlier sketch in SATA 180
Stein, Janet 1955- 218
Stein, M(eyer) L(ewis) 1920- 6
Stein, Mathilde 1969- 195
Stein, Mini 2
Stein, R(ichard) Conrad 1937- 154
  Earlier sketches in SATA 31, 82
Stein, Wendy 1951- 77
Steinbeck, John 1902-1968 9
Steinbeck, John Ernst
  See Steinbeck, John
Steinberg, Alfred 1917-1995 9
Steinberg, David 1962- 200
Steinberg, D.J.
  See Steinberg, David
Steinberg, Fannie 1899-1990 43
Steinberg, Fred J. 1933- 4
Steinberg, Phillip Orso 1921- 34
Steinberg, Rafael (Mark) 1927- 45
Steinberg, Saul 1914-1999 67
Steincrohn, Maggie
  See Davis, Maggie S.
Steiner, Barbara A(nnette) 1934- 83
  Earlier sketch in SATA 13
  See also SAAS 13
Steiner, Charlotte 1900-1981 45
Steiner, George 1929- 62
Steiner, Joan 199
  Earlier sketch in SATA 110
Steiner, Jorg
  See Steiner, Jorg
Steiner, Jorg 1930- 35
Steiner, K. Leslie
  See Delany, Samuel R., Jr.
Steiner, Stan(ley) 1925-1987 14
  Obituary 50
Steins, Richard 1942- 79
Stem, Jacqueline 1931- 110
Stemple, Heidi E.Y. 1966- 214
Stemple, Jason 179
Steneman, Shep 1945- 132
Stengel, Joyce A. 1938- 158
Stephanie, Gordon
  See Gordon, Stephanie Jacob
Stephens, Alice Barber 1858-1932 66
Stephens, Casey
  See Wagner, Sharon B.
Stephens, Henrietta Henkle 1909-1993 6
Stephens, J.B.
  See Lynn, Tracy
Stephens, Mary Jo 1935- 8
Stephens, Rebecca 1961- 141
Stephens, Reed
  See Donaldson, Stephen R.
Stephens, Suzanne
  See Kirby, Susan E.
Stephens, William M(cLain) 1925- 21
Stephensen, A. M.
  See Manes, Stephen
Stephenson, Lynda 1941- 179
Stephenson, Lynda A.
  See Stephenson, Lynda
Stepp, Ann 1935- 29
Stepto, Michele 1946- 61
Steptoe, Javaka 1971- 213
  Earlier sketch in SATA 151
Steptoe, John (Lewis) 1950-1989 63
  Earlier sketch in SATA 8
  See also CLR 12

Sterling, Brett
   See Bradbury, Ray
   and Hamilton, Edmond
   and Samachson, Joseph
Sterling, Dorothy 1913-2008 83
   Autobiography Feature 127
   Obituary 200
   Earlier sketch in SATA *1*
   See also CLR *1*
   See also SAAS *2*
Sterling, Helen
   See Watts, Helen L. Hoke
Sterling, Philip 1907-1989 8
   Obituary 63
Sterling, Shirley (Anne) 1948- 101
Stern, Ellen Norman 1927- 26
Stern, Judith M. 1951- 75
Stern, Madeleine
   See Stern, Madeleine B.
Stern, Madeleine B. 1912-2007 14
Stern, Madeleine Bettina
   See Stern, Madeleine B.
Stern, Maggie 1953- 156
Stern, Philip Van Doren 1900-1984 13
   Obituary 39
Stern, Simon 1943- 15
Sterne, Emma Gelders 1894- 6
Steurt, Marjorie Rankin 1888-1978 10
Stevens, April 1963- 208
Stevens, Bryna 1924- 65
Stevens, Carla M(cBride) 1928- 13
Stevens, Chambers 1968- 128
Stevens, Diane 1939- 94
Stevens, Franklin 1933- 6
Stevens, Greg
   See Cook, Glen
Stevens, Gwendolyn 1944- 33
Stevens, Helen 209
Stevens, Jan Romero 1953- 95
Stevens, Janet 1953- 193
   Earlier sketches in SATA *90, 148*
Stevens, Kathleen 1936- 49
Stevens, Leonard A. 1920- 67
Stevens, Lucile Vernon 1899-1994 59
Stevens, Margaret Dean
   See Aldrich, Bess Streeter
Stevens, Patricia Bunning 1931- 27
Stevens, Peter
   See Geis, Darlene Stern
Stevens, Serita 1949- 70
Stevens, Serita Deborah
   See Stevens, Serita
Stevens, Serita Mendelson
   See Stevens, Serita
Stevens, Shira
   See Stevens, Serita
Stevenson, Anna (M.) 1905- 12
Stevenson, Augusta 1869(?)-1976 2
   Obituary 26
Stevenson, Burton Egbert 1872-1962 25
Stevenson, Drew 1947- 60
Stevenson, Emma 207
Stevenson, Harvey 1960- 148
   Earlier sketch in SATA *80*
Stevenson, James 1929- 195
   Brief entry 34
   Earlier sketches in SATA *42, 71, 113, 161*
   See also CLR *17*
Stevenson, Janet 1913- 8
Stevenson, Robert Louis 1850-1894 100
   See also YABC *2*
   See also CLR *107*
Stevenson, Robert Louis Balfour
   See Stevenson, Robert Louis
Stevenson, Sucie
   See Stevenson, Sucie
Stevenson, Sucie 1956- 194
   Earlier sketch in SATA *104*
Stewart, A(gnes) C(harlotte) 15
Stewart, Amber 181

Stewart, Chantal 1945- 173
   Earlier sketch in SATA *121*
Stewart, Charles
   See Zurhorst, Charles (Stewart, Jr.)
Stewart, Eleanor
   See Porter, Eleanor H(odgman)
Stewart, Elisabeth J(ane) 1927- 93
Stewart, Elizabeth Laing 1907- 6
Stewart, Gail B. 1949- 141
Stewart, George Rippey 1895-1980 3
   Obituary 23
Stewart, Jennifer J. 1960- 128
Stewart, Jennifer Jenkins
   See Stewart, Jennifer J.
Stewart, Joel 211
   Earlier sketch in SATA *151*
Stewart, John 1920- 14
Stewart, Mary (Florence Elinor) 1916- 12
Stewart, Mary Rainbow
   See Stewart, Mary (Florence Elinor)
Stewart, Melissa 1968- 209
   Earlier sketches in SATA *111, 167*
Stewart, Paul 1955- 199
   Earlier sketches in SATA *114, 163*
Stewart, Robert Neil 1891-1972 7
Stewart, Sarah 143
Stewart, Scott
   See Zaffo, George J.
Stewart, Trenton Lee 1970- 216
Stewart, W(alter) P. 1924- 53
Stewart, Whitney 1959- 167
   Earlier sketch in SATA *92*
Stewig, John Warren 1937- 162
   Earlier sketches in SATA *26, 110*
Stickler, Soma Han 1942- 128
Stidworthy, John 1943- 63
Stiegemeyer, Julie 180
Stier, Catherine 198
Stiles, Martha Bennett 108
   Earlier sketch in SATA *6*
Still, James 1906-2001 29
   Obituary 127
Stille, Darlene R. 1942- 170
   Earlier sketch in SATA *126*
Stille, Darlene Ruth
   See Stille, Darlene R.
Stillerman, Marci 104
Stillerman, Robbie 1947- 12
Stilley, Frank 1918- 29
Stilton, Geronimo 158
Stimpson, Gerald
   See Mitchell, Adrian
Stimson, James 1964- 213
Stine, Catherine 165
Stine, G(eorge) Harry 1928-1997 136
   Earlier sketch in SATA *10*
Stine, Jovial Bob
   See Stine, R.L.
Stine, R.L. 1943- 194
   Earlier sketches in SATA *31, 76, 129*
   See also CLR *111*
Stine, Robert Lawrence
   See Stine, R.L.
Stinetorf, Louise (Allender) 1900-1992 10
Stinson, Kathy 1952- 98
Stirling, Arthur
   See Sinclair, Upton
Stirling, Ian 1941- 77
Stirling, Nora B(romley) 1900-1997 3
Stirnweis, Shannon 1931- 10
Stobbs, William 1914-2000 17
   Obituary 120
Stock, Carolmarie 1951- 75
Stock, Catherine 1952- 214
   Earlier sketches in SATA *65, 114, 158*
Stockdale, Susan 1954- 206
   Earlier sketch in SATA *98*
Stockham, Peter (Alan) 1928- 57
Stockton, Francis Richard 1834-1902 44
   Brief entry 32

Stockton, Frank R.
   See Stockton, Francis Richard
Stockwell-Moniz, Marc J. 1954- 164
Stoddard, Edward G. 1923- 10
Stoddard, Hope 1900-1987 6
Stoddard, Sandol 1927- 98
   Earlier sketch in SATA *14*
Stoehr, Shelley 1969- 107
Stoeke, Janet Morgan 1957- 202
   Earlier sketches in SATA *90, 136*
Stohner, Anu 1952- 179
Stoiko, Michael 1919- 14
Stojic, Manya 1967- 156
Stoker, Abraham
   See Stoker, Bram
Stoker, Bram 1847-1912 29
Stokes, Cedric
   See Beardmore, George
Stokes, Jack (Tilden) 1923- 13
Stokes, Olivia Pearl 1916- 32
Stolarz, Laurie Faria 1972- 203
Stolz, Mary 1920-2006 133
   Obituary 180
   Earlier sketches in SATA *10, 71*
   See also SAAS *3*
Stolz, Mary Slattery
   See Stolz, Mary
Stone, Alan
   See Svenson, Andrew E(dward)
Stone, David K(arl) 1922- 9
Stone, David Lee 1978- 166
Stone, Eugenia 1879-1971 7
Stone, Gene
   See Stone, Eugenia
Stone, Helen V(irginia) 6
Stone, Idella Purnell
   See Purnell, Idella
Stone, Ikey
   See Purnell, Idella
Stone, Irving 1903-1989 3
   Obituary 64
Stone, Jeff 178
Stone, Jon 1931-1997 39
   Obituary 95
Stone, Josephine Rector
   See Dixon, Jeanne
Stone, Kyle M. 1972- 202
Stone, Lesley
   See Trevor, Elleston
Stone, Peter 1930-2003 65
   Obituary 143
Stone, Phoebe 205
   Earlier sketch in SATA *134*
Stone, Raymond 1
Stone, Rosetta
   See Dr. Seuss
Stone, Tanya Lee 1965- 217
   Earlier sketch in SATA *182*
Stonehouse, Bernard 1926- 140
   Earlier sketches in SATA *13, 80*
Stones, (Cyril) Anthony 1934- 72
Stong, Phil(ip Duffield) 1899-1957 32
Stoops, Erik D(aniel) 1966- 142
   Earlier sketch in SATA *78*
Stoppelmoore, Cheryl Jean
   See Ladd, Cheryl (Jean)
Stops, Sue 1936- 86
Storace, Patricia 193
Storad, Conrad J. 1957- 119
Storey, Margaret 1926- 9
Storey, Victoria Carolyn 1945- 16
Stork, Francisco
   See Stork, Francisco X.
Stork, Francisco X. 1953- 210
Storme, Peter
   See Stern, Philip Van Doren
Storms, Patricia 1963- 217
Storr, Catherine (Cole) 1913-2001 87
   Obituary 122
   Earlier sketch in SATA *9*

Story, Josephine
　　See Loring, Emilie (Baker)
Stotko, Mary-Ann 1960- *154*
Stott, Ann *219*
Stott, Dorothy (M.) 1958- *99*
　　Earlier sketch in SATA *67*
Stott, Dot
　　See Stott, Dorothy (M.)
Stotter, Mike 1957- *108*
Stout, William 1949- *132*
Stoutenburg, Adrien (Pearl) 1916-1982 .... *3*
Stoutland, Allison 1963- *130*
Stover, Allan C(arl) 1938- *14*
Stover, Jill (Griffin) 1958- *82*
Stover, Marjorie Filley 1914- *9*
Stowe, Harriet Beecher 1811-1896
　　See YABC *1*
　　See also CLR *131*
Stowe, Harriet Elizabeth Beecher
　　See Stowe, Harriet Beecher
Stowe, Leland 1899-1994 .... *60*
　　Obituary *78*
Stowe, Rosetta
　　See Ogan, George F.
　　and Ogan, Margaret E. (Nettles)
Stower, Adam *195*
Strachan, Bruce 1959- *205*
Strachan, Ian 1938- *85*
Strachan, Linda *167*
Strachan, Margaret Pitcairn 1908-1998 .... *14*
Strahinich, H. C.
　　See Strahinich, Helen C.
Strahinich, Helen C. 1949- *78*
Strait, Treva Adams 1909-2002 .... *35*
Strand, Mark 1934- *41*
Strange, Philippa
　　See Coury, Louise Andree
Stranger, Joyce
　　See Wilson, Joyce M.
Strangis, Joel 1948- *124*
Strannigan, Shawn 1956- *93*
Strannigan, Shawn Alyne
　　See Strannigan, Shawn
Strasnick, Lauren *222*
Strasser, Todd 1950- *215*
　　Earlier sketches in SATA *41, 45, 71, 107, 153*
　　See also CLR *11*
Stratemeyer, Edward L. 1862-1930 .... *100*
　　Earlier sketches in SATA *1, 67*
　　See Adams, Harrison
Stratford, Philip 1927- *47*
Stratton, Allan 1951- *178*
Stratton, J. M.
　　See Whitlock, Ralph
Stratton, Thomas
　　See Coulson, Robert S(tratton)
　　and DeWeese, Thomas Eugene
Stratton-Porter, Gene 1863-1924 .... *15*
　　See also CLR *87*
Strauss, Gwen 1963- *77*
Strauss, Joyce 1936- *53*
Strauss, Linda Leopold 1942- *127*
Strauss, Susan (Elizabeth) 1954- *75*
Strayer, E. Ward
　　See Stratemeyer, Edward L.
Streano, Vince(nt Catello) 1945- *20*
Streatfeild, Mary Noel
　　See Streatfeild, Noel
Streatfeild, Noel 1897(?)-1986 .... *20*
　　Obituary *48*
　　See also CLR *83*
Street, Janet Travell 1959- *84*
Street, Julia Montgomery 1898-1993 .... *11*
Streissguth, Thomas 1958- *116*
Strelkoff, Tatiana 1957- *89*
Stren, Patti 1949- *88*
　　Brief entry *41*
　　See also CLR *5*
Strete, Craig Kee 1950- *96*
　　Earlier sketch in SATA *44*

Stretton, Barbara (Humphrey) 1936- *43*
　　Brief entry *35*
Strickland, Brad 1947- *200*
　　Earlier sketches in SATA *83, 137, 142*
Strickland, Craig (A.) 1956- *102*
Strickland, Dorothy S(alley) 1933- *89*
Strickland, Michael R. 1965- *144*
　　Earlier sketch in SATA *83*
Strickland, Shadra *209*
Strickland, Tessa *173*
Strickland, William Bradley
　　See Strickland, Brad
Striegel, Jana 1955- *140*
Striegel-Wilson, Jana
　　See Striegel, Jana
Striker, Lee
　　See Clark, Margaret (D.)
Striker, Susan 1942- *63*
Stringer, Lauren 1957- *183*
　　Earlier sketch in SATA *129*
Stroeyer, Poul 1923- *13*
Stromoski, Rick 1958- *111*
Strong, Charles
　　See Epstein, Beryl
　　and Epstein, Samuel
Strong, David
　　See McGuire, Leslie (Sarah)
Strong, Jeremy 1949- *175*
　　Earlier sketches in SATA *36, 105*
Strong, J.J.
　　See Strong, Jeremy
Strong, Pat
　　See Hough, Richard (Alexander)
Strong, Stacie 1965- *74*
Stroud, Bettye 1939- *165*
　　Earlier sketch in SATA *96*
Stroud, Jonathan 1970- *213*
　　Earlier sketches in SATA *102, 159*
　　See also CLR *134*
Stroyer, Poul
　　See Stroeyer, Poul
Strug, Kerri 1977- *108*
Stryer, Andrea Stenn 1938- *192*
Stryker, Daniel
　　See Morris, Chris(topher Crosby)
　　and Stump, Jane Barr
Stuart, David
　　See Hoyt, Edwin P(almer), Jr.
Stuart, Derek
　　See Foster, John L(ouis)
Stuart, Forbes 1924- *13*
Stuart, Ian
　　See MacLean, Alistair
Stuart, Jesse (Hilton) 1906-1984 .... *2*
　　Obituary *36*
Stuart, Ruth McEnery 1849(?)-1917 .... *116*
Stuart, Sheila
　　See Baker, Mary Gladys Steel
Stuart-Clark, Christopher (Anthony) 1940- .. *32*
Stubis, Talivaldis 1926- *5*
Stubley, Trevor (Hugh) 1932- *22*
Stuchner, Joan Betty *209*
Stucky, Naomi R. 1922- *72*
Stucley, Elizabeth
　　See Northmore, Elizabeth Florence
Stultifer, Morton
　　See Curtis, Richard
Sture-Vasa, Mary
　　See Alsop, Mary O'Hara
Sturges, Philemon *174*
Sturtevant, Katherine 1950- *180*
　　Earlier sketch in SATA *130*
Sturton, Hugh
　　See Johnston, H(ugh) A(nthony) S(tephen)
Sturtzel, Howard A(llison) 1894-1985 .... *1*
Sturtzel, Jane Levington 1903-1996 .... *1*
Stutley, D(oris) J(ean) 1959- *142*
Stutson, Caroline 1940- *104*
Stuve-Bodeen, Stephanie
　　See Bodeen, S. A.
Stux, Erica 1929- *140*

Styles, (Frank) Showell 1908- *10*
Stynes, Barbara White *133*
Suarez, Maribel 1952- *201*
Suba, Susanne *4*
Suber, Melissa *213*
Subond, Valerie
　　See Grayland, Valerie (Merle Spanner)
Sudbery, Rodie 1943- *42*
Sudyka, Diana *208*
Sue, Majella Lue *209*
Suen, Anastasia 1956(?)- *157*
Sufrin, Mark 1925- *76*
Sugarman, Joan G. 1917- *64*
Sugarman, Tracy 1921- *37*
Sugita, Yutaka 1930- *36*
Suhl, Yuri (Menachem) 1908-1986 .... *8*
　　Obituary *50*
　　See also CLR *2*
　　See also SAAS *1*
Suhr, Joanne *129*
Suid, Murray 1942- *27*
Sullivan, Edward T. *206*
Sullivan, George (Edward) 1927- *147*
　　Earlier sketches in SATA *4, 89*
Sullivan, Jacqueline Levering *203*
Sullivan, Jody
　　See Rake, Jody
Sullivan, Kathryn A. 1954- *141*
Sullivan, Mary Ann 1954- *63*
Sullivan, Mary W(ilson) 1907- *13*
Sullivan, Pat
　　See Messmer, Otto
Sullivan, Paul 1939- *106*
Sullivan, Sarah G. 1953- *179*
Sullivan, Silky 1940- *101*
Sullivan, Sue
　　See Sullivan, Susan E.
Sullivan, Susan E. 1962- *123*
Sullivan, Thomas Joseph, Jr. 1947- *16*
Sullivan, Tom
　　See Sullivan, Thomas Joseph, Jr.
Sully, Tom 1959- *104*
Suma, Nova Ren *223*
Sumichrast, Jozef 1948- *29*
Sumiko
　　See Davies, Sumiko
Summerforest, Ivy B.
　　See Kirkup, James
Summers, Barbara 1944- *182*
Summers, Cassia Joy
　　See Cowley, Joy
Summers, James L(evingston) 1910-1973 .... *57*
　　Brief entry *28*
Summertree, Katonah
　　See Windsor, Patricia
Summy, Barrie *208*
Sun, Chyng Feng 1959- *90*
Sunderlin, Sylvia (S.) 1911-1997 .... *28*
　　Obituary *99*
Sung, Betty Lee *26*
Supeene, Shelagh Lynne 1952- *153*
Supplee, Suzanne *204*
Supraner, Robyn 1930- *101*
　　Earlier sketch in SATA *20*
Supree, Burt(on) 1941-1992 .... *73*
Surface, Mary Hall 1958- *126*
Surge, Frank 1931- *13*
Susac, Andrew 1929- *5*
Susi, Geraldine Lee 1942- *98*
Sussman, Cornelia Silver 1914-1999 .... *59*
Sussman, Irving 1908-1996 .... *59*
Sussman, Michael 1953- *217*
Sussman, Michael B.
　　See Sussman, Michael
Sussman, Susan 1942- *48*
Sutcliff, Rosemary 1920-1992 .... *78*
　　Obituary *73*
　　Earlier sketches in SATA *6, 44*
　　See also CLR *138*
Sutcliffe, Jane 1957- *138*
Sutherland, Colleen 1944- *79*

Sutherland, Efua (Theodora Morgue)
  1924-1996 25
Sutherland, Jon 1958- 167
Sutherland, Jonathan D.
  See Sutherland, Jon
Sutherland, Jonathan David
  See Sutherland, Jon
Sutherland, Margaret 1941- 15
Sutherland, Zena Bailey 1915-2002 37
  Obituary 137
Suttles, Shirley (Smith) 1922- 21
Sutton, Ann (Livesay) 1923- 31
Sutton, Eve(lyn Mary) 1906-1992 26
Sutton, Felix 1910(?)-1973 31
Sutton, Jane 1950- 52
  Brief entry 43
Sutton, Larry M(atthew) 1931- 29
Sutton, Margaret Beebe 1903-2001 1
  Obituary 131
Sutton, Myron Daniel 1925- 31
Sutton, Roger 1956- 93
Sutton, Sally 1973- 214
Suzanne, Jamie
  See Hawes, Louise
  and Lantz, Francess L(in)
  and Singleton, Linda Joy
  and Zach, Cheryl (Byrd)
Suzuki, David 1936- 138
Suzuki, David Takayoshi
  See Suzuki, David
Svendsen, Mark 1962- 181
  Earlier sketch in SATA 120
Svendsen, Mark Nestor
  See Svendsen, Mark
Svenson, Andrew E(dward) 1910-1975 2
  Obituary 26
Swaab, Neil 1978- 191
Swaim, Jessica 1950- 202
Swain, Carol 1962- 172
Swain, Gwenyth 1961- 134
  Earlier sketch in SATA 84
Swain, Ruth
  See Swain, Ruth Freeman
Swain, Ruth Freeman 1951- 161
  Earlier sketch in SATA 119
Swain, Su Zan (Noguchi) 1916- 21
Swallow, Pamela Curtis 178
Swamp, Jake 1941- 98
Swan, Susan 1944- 108
  Earlier sketch in SATA 22
Swann, Brian (Stanley Frank) 1940- 116
Swann, E.L.
  See Lasky, Kathryn
Swann, Ruth Rice 1920- 84
Swanson, Diane 1944- 203
Swanson, Helen M(cKendry) 1919- 94
Swanson, June 1931- 76
Swanson, Susan Marie 209
Swanson, Wayne 1942- 167
Swarner, Kristina 1965- 215
Swarthout, Glendon (Fred) 1918-1992 26
Swarthout, Kathryn 1919- 7
Swayne, Sam(uel F.) 1907- 53
Swayne, Zoa (Lourana) 1905- 53
Sweat, Lynn 1934- 168
  Earlier sketch in SATA 57
Swede, George 1940- 67
Sweeney, James B(artholomew) 1910-1999 . 21
Sweeney, Joyce 1955- 167
  Earlier sketches in SATA 65, 68, 108
Sweeney, Joyce Kay
  See Sweeney, Joyce
Sweeney, Karen O'Connor
  See O'Connor, Karen
Sweeney, Matthew (Gerard) 1952- 156
Sweet, Melissa 1956- 211
  Earlier sketch in SATA 172
Sweet, Sarah C.
  See Jewett, Sarah Orne
Sweetland, Nancy A(nn) 1934- 48
Swenson, Allan A(rmstrong) 1933- 21

Swenson, May 1919-1989 15
Swentzell, Rina 1939- 79
Swiatkowska, Gabi 1971(?)- 180
Swift, Bryan
  See Knott, William C(ecil, Jr.)
Swift, David
  See Kaufmann, John
Swift, Hildegarde Hoyt 1890(?)-1977
  Obituary 20
Swift, Jonathan 1667-1745 19
  See also CLR 161
Swift, Merlin
  See Leeming, Joseph
Swiger, Elinor Porter 1927- 8
Swinburne, Laurence (Joseph) 1924- 9
Swinburne, Stephen R. 1952- 188
  Earlier sketch in SATA 150
Swinburne, Steve
  See Swinburne, Stephen R.
Swindells, Robert (Edward) 1939- 150
  Brief entry 34
  Earlier sketches in SATA 50, 80
  See also SAAS 14
Swinford, Betty (June Wells) 1927- 58
Swinford, Bob
  See Swinford, Betty (June Wells)
Swithen, John
  See King, Stephen
Switzer, Ellen 1923- 48
Swope, Sam 156
Swope, Samuel
  See Swope, Sam
Sybesma, Jetske
  See Ironside, Jetske
Sydney, Frank
  See Warwick, Alan R(oss)
Sydor, Colleen 1960- 207
Sykes, Julie 1963- 202
Sylvada, Peter 1964- 202
Sylvester, Natalie G(abry) 1922- 22
Syme, (Neville) Ronald 1913-1992 87
  Earlier sketch in SATA 2
Symes, R. F. 77
Symes, Ruth Louise 1962- 179
Symons, (Dorothy) Geraldine 1909- 33
Symons, Stuart
  See Stanley, George Edward
Symynkywicz, Jeffrey B. 1954- 87
Symynkywicz, Jeffrey Bruce
  See Symynkywicz, Jeffrey B.
Synge, (Phyllis) Ursula 1930- 9
Sypher, Lucy Johnston 1907- 7
Szasz, Suzanne (Shorr) 1915-1997 13
  Obituary 99
Szekeres, Cyndy 1933- 157
  Autobiography Feature 157
  Earlier sketches in SATA 5, 60, 131
  See also SAAS 13
Szekessy, Tanja 98
Szpura, Beata 1961- 93
Szuc, Jeff 1975- 220
Szudek, Agnes S(usan) P(hilomena) 57
  Brief entry 49
Szulc, Tad 1926-2001 26
Szydlow, Jarl
  See Szydlowski, Mary Vigliante
Szydlowski, Mary Vigliante 1946- 94
Szymanski, Lois 1957- 91

T

Taback, Simms 1932- 170
  Brief entry 36
  Earlier sketches in SATA 40, 104
  See also CLR 100
Taber, Gladys (Bagg) 1899-1980
  Obituary 22
Tabor, Nancy Maria Grande 1949- 161
  Earlier sketch in SATA 89

Tabrah, Ruth Milander 1921- 14
Tacang, Brian 213
Tackach, James 1953- 123
Tackach, James M.
  See Tackach, James
Tadgell, Nicole 1969- 220
  Earlier sketch in SATA 177
Tafolla, Carmen 1951- 220
Tafolla, Mary Carmen
  See Tafolla, Carmen
Tafuri, Nancy 1946- 192
  Autobiography Feature 192
  Earlier sketches in SATA 39, 75, 130
  See also CLR 74
  See also SAAS 14
Tagg, Christine Elizabeth 1962- 138
Tagliaferro, Linda 173
Taha, Karen T(erry) 1942- 156
  Earlier sketch in SATA 71
Tai, Sharon O. 1963- 153
Tait, Douglas 1944- 12
Takabayashi, Mari 1960- 156
  Earlier sketch in SATA 115
Takahashi, Hideko 209
Takahashi, Rumiko 1957- 163
Takakjian, Portia 1930- 15
Takashima, Misako
  See Misako Rocks!
Takashima, Shizuye 1928- 13
Takayama, Sandi 1962- 106
Takeda, Pete(r M.) 1964- 148
Tal, Eve 1947- 176
Talbert, Marc (Alan) 1953- 154
  Autobiography Feature 154
  Earlier sketches in SATA 68, 99
Talbot, Charlene Joy 1928- 10
Talbot, Toby 1928- 14
Talbott, Hudson 1949- 212
  Earlier sketches in SATA 84, 131
Talifero, Gerald 1950- 75
Talker, T.
  See Rands, William Brighty
Tallarico, Tony 1933- 116
Tallcott, Emogene 10
Tallec, Olivier 1970- 197
Tallis, Robyn
  See Smith, Sherwood
Tallon, Robert 1939- 43
  Brief entry 28
Talmadge, Marian 14
Tamaki, Jillian 1980- 201
Tamar, Erika 1934- 150
  Earlier sketches in SATA 62, 101
Tamarin, Alfred H. 1913-1980 13
Tamburine, Jean 1930- 12
Tames, Richard (Lawrence) 1946- 102
  Earlier sketch in SATA 67
Tamminga, Frederick W(illiam) 1934- 66
Tammuz, Benjamin 1919-1989
  Obituary 63
Tan, Amy 1952- 75
Tan, Amy Ruth
  See Tan, Amy
Tan, Shaun 1974- 198
Tanaka, Beatrice 1932- 76
Tanaka, Shelley 214
  Earlier sketch in SATA 136
Tanaka, Yoko 1947- 215
Tang, Charles 1948- 81
Tang, Greg 172
Tang, You-Shan 1946- 53
Tania B.
  See Blixen, Karen
Tankard, Jeremy 1973- 191
Tannen, Mary 1943- 37
Tannenbaum, Beulah Goldstein 1916- 3
Tannenbaum, D(onald) Leb 1948- 42
Tanner, Jane 1946- 74
Tanner, Louise S(tickney) 1922-2000 9
Tanobe, Miyuki 1937- 23
Tanselle, Eve 1933- 125

Tapio, Pat Decker
  See Kines, Pat Decker
Tapp, Kathy Kennedy 1949- 88
  Brief entry 50
Tarbescu, Edith 1939- 107
Tarkington, (Newton) Booth 1869-1946 17
Tarpley, Natasha A(nastasia) 1971- 147
Tarr, Judith 1955- 149
  Earlier sketch in SATA 64
Tarry, Ellen 1906-2008 16
  See also CLR 26
  See also SAAS 16
Tarshis, Jerome 1936- 9
Tarshis, Lauren 187
Tarsky, Sue 1946- 41
Taschek, Karen 1956- 185
Tashjian, Janet 1956- 151
  Earlier sketch in SATA 102
Tashjian, Virginia A. 1921-2008 3
Tasker, James 1908- 9
Tate, Don(ald E.) 159
Tate, Eleanora E. 1948- 191
  Earlier sketches in SATA 38, 94
  See also CLR 37
Tate, Eleanora Elaine
  See Tate, Eleanora E.
Tate, Ellalice
  See Hibbert, Eleanor Alice Burford
Tate, Joan 1922- 86
  Earlier sketch in SATA 9
  See also SAAS 20
Tate, Mary Anne
  See Hale, Arlene
Tate, Nikki 134
Tate, Richard
  See Masters, Anthony (Richard)
Tate, Suzanne 1930- 91
Tatham, Betty 142
Tatham, Campbell
  See Elting, Mary
Tatham, Julie
  See Tatham, Julie Campbell
Tatham, Julie Campbell 1908-1999 80
Tavares, Matt 198
  Earlier sketch in SATA 159
Tavares, Victor 1971- 176
Taves, Isabella 1915- 27
Tayleur, Karen 1961- 213
Taylor, Alastair 1959- 130
Taylor, Andrew 1951- 70
Taylor, Andrew John Robert
  See Taylor, Andrew
Taylor, Ann 1782-1866 41
  Brief entry 35
Taylor, Audilee Boyd 1931- 59
Taylor, Barbara J. 1927- 10
Taylor, Ben
  See Strachan, Ian
Taylor, Brooke 205
Taylor, Carl 1937-2010 14
Taylor, Cheryl Munro 1957- 96
Taylor, Cora (Lorraine) 1936- 103
  Earlier sketch in SATA 64
  See also CLR 63
Taylor, Dave 1948- 78
Taylor, David
  See Taylor, Dave
Taylor, David 1900-1965 10
Taylor, Debbie A. 1955- 169
Taylor, Eleanor 1969- 206
Taylor, Elizabeth 1912-1975 13
Taylor, Florance Walton
  See Taylor, Florence M(arian Tompkins)
Taylor, Florence M(arian Tompkins)
  1892-1983 9
Taylor, Gage 1942-2000 87
Taylor, Geoff 1946- 204
Taylor, G.P. 1958(?)- 216
  Earlier sketch in SATA 156
Taylor, Graham Peter
  See Taylor, G.P.
Taylor, Greg 1951- 221

Taylor, Herb(ert Norman, Jr.) 1942-1987 22
  Obituary 54
Taylor, J. David
  See Taylor, Dave
Taylor, Jane 1783-1824 41
  Brief entry 35
Taylor, Jerry D(uncan) 1938- 47
Taylor, John Robert
  See Taylor, Andrew
Taylor, Judy
  See Hough, Judy Taylor
Taylor, Kenneth N. 1917-2005 26
Taylor, Kenneth Nathaniel
  See Taylor, Kenneth N.
Taylor, Kim 180
Taylor, L(ester) B(arbour), Jr. 1932- 27
Taylor, Lois Dwight Cole
  See Cole, Lois Dwight
Taylor, Louise Todd 1939- 47
Taylor, Margaret 1950- 106
Taylor, Mark 1927- 32
  Brief entry 28
Taylor, Mildred D. 1943- 135
  See also CLR 144
  See also SAAS 5
Taylor, Mildred Delois
  See Taylor, Mildred D.
Taylor, Paula (Wright) 1942- 48
  Brief entry 33
Taylor, Peter Lane 210
Taylor, Robert Lewis 1912-1998 10
Taylor, Sean 1965- 192
Taylor, Sydney (Brenner) 1904(?)-1978 28
  Obituary 26
  Earlier sketch in SATA 1
Taylor, Theodore 1921-2006 128
  Obituary 177
  Earlier sketches in SATA 5, 54, 83
  See also CLR 30
  See also SAAS 4
Taylor, William 1938- 164
  Earlier sketches in SATA 78, 113
  See also CLR 63
Taylor-Butler, Christine 1959- 218
Tazewell, Charles 1900-1972 74
Tchana, Katrin
  See Tchana, Katrin Hyman
Tchana, Katrin H.
  See Tchana, Katrin Hyman
Tchana, Katrin Hyman 1963- 177
  Earlier sketch in SATA 125
Tchekhov, Anton
  See Chekhov, Anton
Tchen, Richard 120
Tchudi, Stephen N. 1942- 55
Teague, Bob
  See Teague, Robert
Teague, Mark 1963- 205
  Earlier sketches in SATA 68, 99, 170
Teague, Mark Christopher
  See Teague, Mark
Teague, Robert 1929- 32
  Brief entry 31
Teal, Val 1902-1997 10
  Obituary 114
Teal, Valentine M.
  See Teal, Val
Teale, Edwin Way 1899-1980 7
  Obituary 25
Teasdale, Sara 1884-1933 32
Tebbel, John (William) 1912-2004 26
Teckentrup, Britta 1969- 200
Tedesco, P.R.
  See Naylor, Phyllis Reynolds
Teensma, Lynne Bertrand
  See Bertrand, Lynne
Tee-Van, Helen Damrosch 1893-1976 10
  Obituary 27
Teevee, Ningeokuluk 1963- 223
Tegner, Bruce 1928- 62

Teitelbaum, Michael 1953- 116
  Earlier sketch in SATA 59
Tejima
  See Tejima, Keizaburo
Tejima, Keizaburo 1931- 139
  See also CLR 20
Telander, Todd (G.) 1967- 88
Teleki, Geza 1943- 45
Telemaque, Eleanor Wong 1934- 43
Telescope, Tom
  See Newbery, John
Tellis, Annabel 1967- 191
Temkin, Sara Anne Schlossberg 1913-1996 . 26
Temko, Florence 13
Tempest, Margaret Mary 1892-1982
  Obituary 33
Templar, Maurice
  See Groom, Arthur William
Temple, Arthur
  See Northcott, (William) Cecil
Temple, Charles 1947- 79
Temple, Frances (Nolting) 1945-1995 85
Temple, Herbert 1919- 45
Temple, Paul
  See McConnell, James Douglas Rutherford
Temple, William F(rederick) 1914-1989 107
Tenggren, Gustaf 1896-1970 18
  Obituary 26
Tennant, Kylie
  See Rodd, Kylie Tennant
Tennant, Veronica 1947- 36
Tenneshaw, S.M.
  See Beaumont, Charles
  and Garrett, Randall
  and Silverberg, Robert
Tenniel, John 1820-1914 74
  Brief entry 27
  See also CLR 146
Tepper, Sheri S. 1929- 113
Terada, Alice M. 1928- 90
Terban, Marvin 1940- 54
  Brief entry 45
Teresi, Judith M.
  See Goldberger, Judith M.
ter Haar, Jaap 1922- 6
  See also CLR 15
Terhune, Albert Payson 1872-1942 15
Terkel, Susan N(eiburg) 1948- 103
  Earlier sketch in SATA 59
Terlouw, Jan (Cornelis) 1931- 30
Terrazzini, Daniela Jaglenka 218
Terrell, John Upton 1900-1988
  Obituary 60
Terrill, Beth 198
Terrill, Elizabeth
  See Terrill, Beth
Terris, Susan 1937- 77
  Earlier sketch in SATA 3
Terry, Luther L(eonidas) 1911-1985 11
  Obituary 42
Terry, Margaret
  See Dunnahoo, Terry Janson
Terry, Walter 1913-1982 14
Terry, Will 1966- 205
Terzian, James P. 1915- 14
Tessendorf, K(enneth) C(harles) 1925-2003 . 75
  Obituary 142
Tessler, Manya 200
Tessler, Stephanie Gordon
  See Gordon, Stephanie Jacob
Testa, Dom 208
Tester, Sylvia Root 1939- 64
  Brief entry 37
Tether, (Cynthia) Graham 1950- 46
  Brief entry 36
Tetzner, Lisa 1894-1963 169
Thach, James Otis 195
Thacher, Mary McGrath 1933- 9
Thackeray, William Makepeace 1811-1863 .. 23
Thaler, Michael C.
  See Thaler, Mike

Thaler, Mike 1936- 215
  Brief entry 47
  Earlier sketches in SATA *56, 93*
Thaler, Shmuel 1958- 126
  Earlier sketch in SATA *72*
Thamer, Katie 1955- 42
Thane, Elswyth 1900-1984(?) *32*
Tharp, Louise (Marshall) Hall 1898-1992 ...... *3*
  Obituary 129
Tharp, Tim 1957- 189
Thayer, Ernest Lawrence 1863-1940 60
Thayer, Jane
  See Woolley, Catherine
Thayer, Marjorie 1908-1992 74
  Brief entry 37
Thayer, Peter
  See Wyler, Rose
Thelwell, Norman 1923-2004 14
Themerson, Stefan 1910-1988 65
Thermes, Jennifer 1966- 155
Theroux, Paul 1941- 109
  Earlier sketch in SATA *44*
Theroux, Paul Edward
  See Theroux, Paul
Thesman, Jean 124
  Earlier sketch in SATA *74*
The Tjong-Khing
  See Khing, T.T.
Thieda, Shirley Ann 1943- *13*
Thiele, Colin 1920-2006 125
  Earlier sketches in SATA *14, 72*
  See also CLR *27*
  See also SAAS *2*
Thiele, Colin Milton
  See Thiele, Colin
Thiesing, Lisa 1958- 159
  Earlier sketch in SATA *95*
Thimmesh, Catherine 189
Thiry, Joan (Marie) 1926- 45
Thisdale, Francois 1964- 222
Thistlethwaite, Miles 1945- 12
Thollander, Earl 1922- 22
Thomas, Abigail 1941- 112
Thomas, Andrea
  See Hill, Margaret (Ohler)
Thomas, Art(hur Lawrence) 1952- 48
  Brief entry 38
Thomas, Carroll
  See Ratliff, Thomas M.
  and Shmurak, Carole B.
Thomas, Dylan 1914-1953 60
Thomas, Dylan Marlais
  See Thomas, Dylan
Thomas, Egbert S.
  See Ellis, Edward S.
Thomas, Estelle Webb 1899-1982 26
Thomas, Frances 1943- 171
  Earlier sketch in SATA *92*
Thomas, Garen 213
Thomas, H. C.
  See Keating, Lawrence A.
Thomas, Ianthe 1951- 139
  Brief entry 42
  See also CLR *8*
Thomas, J. F.
  See Fleming, Thomas
Thomas, Jan 1958- 197
Thomas, Jane Resh 1936- 171
  Earlier sketches in SATA *38, 90*
Thomas, Jerry D. 1959- 91
Thomas, Joan Gale
  See Robinson, Joan (Mary) G(ale Thomas)
Thomas, Joyce Carol 1938- 210
  Autobiography Feature 137
  Earlier sketches in SATA *40, 78, 123, 137*
  See also CLR *19*
  See also SAAS *7*
Thomas, Lee
  See Floren, Lee
  and Pendleton, Thomas
Thomas, Lowell Jackson, Jr. 1923- 15

Thomas, Margaret
  See Thomas, Peggy
Thomas, Meredith 1963- 119
Thomas, Michael
  See Wilks, Michael Thomas
Thomas, Middy 1931- 191
Thomas, Patricia 1934- 199
  Earlier sketch in SATA *51*
Thomas, Peggy 174
Thomas, Rob 1965- 97
Thomas, Scott 1959- 147
Thomas, Velma Maia 1955- 171
Thomas, Vernon (Arthur) 1934- 56
Thomas, Victoria
  See DeWeese, Thomas Eugene
  and Kugi, Constance Todd
Thomasma, Kenneth R. 1930- 90
Thomason, Mark 215
Thomassie, Tynia 1959- 92
Thompson, Brenda 1935- 34
Thompson, Carol 1951- 189
  Earlier sketch in SATA *85*
Thompson, China
  See Lewis, Mary
Thompson, Colin 1942- 198
  Earlier sketches in SATA *95, 163*
Thompson, David H(ugh) 1941- 17
Thompson, Eileen
  See Panowski, Eileen Thompson
Thompson, George Selden 1929-1989 73
  Obituary 63
  Earlier sketch in SATA *4*
  See also CLR *8*
Thompson, Harlan 1894-1987 10
  Obituary 53
Thompson, Hilary 1943- 56
  Brief entry 49
Thompson, Joanna Maxwell Pullein
  See Pullein-Thompson, Joanna Maxwell
Thompson, Julian F(rancis) 1927- 155
  Brief entry 40
  Earlier sketches in SATA *55, 99*
  See also CLR *24*
  See also SAAS *13*
Thompson, K(athryn Carolyn) Dyble
  1952- 82
Thompson, Kate 1956- 204
Thompson, Kay 1912(?)-1998 16
  See also CLR *22*
Thompson, Lauren 1962- 200
  Earlier sketches in SATA *132, 174*
Thompson, Lauren Stevens
  See Thompson, Lauren
Thompson, Megan Lloyd
  See Lloyd, Megan
Thompson, Richard 1951- 184
Thompson, Ruth Plumly 1891-1976 66
Thompson, Sharon 1952- 119
Thompson, Sharon Elaine
  See Thompson, Sharon
Thompson, Stith 1885-1976 57
  Obituary 20
Thompson, Vivian L(aubach) 1911- *3*
Thomson, Bill 1963- 187
Thomson, Celia
  See Lynn, Tracy
Thomson, David (Robert Alexander)
  1914-1988 40
  Obituary 55
Thomson, Melissa 1979- 205
Thomson, Pat 1939- 122
  Earlier sketch in SATA *77*
Thomson, Peggy 1922- 31
Thomson, Sarah L. 212
  Earlier sketch in SATA *178*
Thon, Melanie Rae 1957- 132
Thong, Roseanne 174
Thor, Annika 1950- 222
Thorburn, John
  See Goldsmith, John Herman Thorburn
Thorn, John 1947- 59

Thorndyke, Helen Louise
  See Benson, Mildred
Thorne, Ian
  See May, Julian
Thorne, Jean Wright
  See May, Julian
Thornhill, Jan 1955- 148
  Earlier sketch in SATA *77*
Thornton, Hall
  See Silverberg, Robert
Thornton, W. B.
  See Burgess, Thornton Waldo
Thornton, Yvonne S. 1947- 96
Thornton, Yvonne Shirley
  See Thornton, Yvonne S.
Thorpe, E(ustace) G(eorge) 1916- 21
Thorpe, J. K.
  See Nathanson, Laura Walther
Thorvall, Kerstin 1925- 13
Thorvall-Falk, Kerstin
  See Thorvall, Kerstin
Thrasher, Crystal (Faye) 1921- 27
Threadgall, Colin 1941- 77
Three Little Pigs
  See Lantz, Francess L(in)
Thum, Gladys 1920- 26
Thum, Marcella 28
  Earlier sketch in SATA *3*
Thundercloud, Katherine
  See Witt, Shirley Hill
Thurber, James 1894-1961 13
Thurber, James Grover
  See Thurber, James
Thurlo, Aimee 161
Thurlo, David 161
Thurman, Judith 1946- 33
Thurman, Mark (Gordon Ian) 1948- 63
Thwaite, Ann (Barbara Harrop) 1932- 14
Tibbetts, Peggy 127
Tibbles, Jean-Paul 1958- 115
Tibo, Gilles 1951- 107
  Earlier sketch in SATA *67*
Tiburzi, Bonnie 1948- 65
Ticheburn, Cheviot
  See Ainsworth, William Harrison
Tichenor, Tom 1923-1992 14
Tichnor, Richard 1959- 90
Tichy, William 1924- 31
Tickle, Jack
  See Chapman, Jane
Tidholm, Anna-Clara 1946- 223
Tiegreen, Alan F. 1935- 94
  Brief entry 36
Tierney, Frank M. 1930- 54
Tierney, Tom 1928- 113
Tiffault, Benette W. 1955- 77
Tildes, Phyllis Limbacher 1945- 210
Tiller, Ruth L. 1949- 83
Tilley, Debbie 190
Tillman, Nancy 211
Tilly, Nancy 1935- 62
Tilton, Madonna Elaine 1929- 41
Tilton, Rafael
  See Tilton, Madonna Elaine
Timberlake, Amy 156
Timberlake, Carolyn
  See Dresang, Eliza (Carolyn Timberlake)
Timmers, Leo 1970- 190
Timmins, William F(rederick) 10
Tinbergen, Niko(laas) 1907-1988
  Obituary 60
Tincknell, Cathy 194
Tiner, John Hudson 1944- 32
Tingle, Dolli (?)-
  See Brackett, Dolli Tingle
Tingle, Rebecca 174
Tingle, Tim 208
Tingum, Janice 1958- 91
Tinkelman, Murray 1933- 12
Tinkham, Kelly A. 188
Tinkle, (Julien) Lon 1906-1980 36

Tinling, Marion (Rose) 1904- 140
Tipene, Tim 1972- 141
Tippett, James S(terling) 1885-1958 66
Tirone Smith, Mary-Ann 1944- 143
Titlebaum, Ellen 195
Titler, Dale M(ilton) 1926- 35
  Brief entry 28
Titmarsh, Michael Angelo
  See Thackeray, William Makepeace
Titus, Eve 1922- 2
Tjia, Sherwin 1975- 204
Tjong Khing, The 1933- 76
Tobias, Katherine
  See Gottfried, Theodore Mark
Tobias, Tobi 1938- 82
  Earlier sketch in SATA 5
  See also CLR 4
Tocci, C. Lee 1958- 220
Tocci, Cynthia Lee
  See Tocci, C. Lee
Todd, Anne Ophelia
  See Dowden, Anne Ophelia Todd
Todd, Barbara 1961- 173
Todd, Barbara K(eith) 1917- 10
Todd, Chuck 195
Todd, H(erbert) E(atton) 1908-1988 84
  Earlier sketch in SATA 11
Todd, Loreto 1942- 30
Todd, Pamela 212
Todd, Peter
  See Hamilton, Charles (Harold St. John)
Toews, Miriam 1964- 165
Tofel, Richard J. 1957- 140
Toft, Kim Michelle 1960- 170
Tokunbo, Dimitrea 187
Tolan, Stephanie S. 1942- 142
  Earlier sketches in SATA 38, 78
Toland, John (Willard) 1912-2004 38
Tolbert, Steve 1944- 143
Toledo, Francisco 1940- 198
Toledo, Natalia 1967- 197
Tolkien, J. R. R. 1892-1973 100
  Obituary 24
  Earlier sketches in SATA 2, 32
  See also CLR 152
Tolkien, John Ronald Reuel
  See Tolkien, J. R. R.
Toll, Emily
  See Cannon, Eileen E(mily)
Toll, Nelly S. 1935- 78
Tolland, W. R.
  See Heitzmann, William Ray
Tolles, Martha 1921- 76
  Earlier sketch in SATA 8
Tolliver, Ruby C(hangos) 1922- 110
  Brief entry 41
  Earlier sketch in SATA 55
Tolmie, Kenneth Donald 1941- 15
Tolstoi, Lev
  See Tolstoy, Leo
Tolstoy, Leo 1828-1910 26
Tolstoy, Count Leo
  See Tolstoy, Leo
Tolstoy, Leo Nikolaevich
  See Tolstoy, Leo
Tomalin, Ruth 29
Tomaselli, Rosa
  See Pausacker, Jenny
Tomecek, Steve 172
Tomes, Margot (Ladd) 1917-1991 70
  Brief entry 27
  Obituary 69
  Earlier sketch in SATA 36
Tomey, Ingrid 1943- 77
Tomfool
  See Farjeon, Eleanor
Tomic, Tomislav 1977- 202
Tomkins, Jasper
  See Batey, Tom
Tomline, F. Latour
  See Gilbert, W(illiam) S(chwenck)

Tomlinson, Heather 192
Tomlinson, Jill 1931-1976 3
  Obituary 24
Tomlinson, Reginald R(obert) 1885-1979(?)
  Obituary 27
Tomlinson, Theresa 1946- 165
  Earlier sketch in SATA 103
  See also CLR 60
Tommaso, Rich 1970(?)- 200
Tomorrow, Tom 1961- 223
Tompert, Ann 1918- 139
  Earlier sketches in SATA 14, 89
Tompkins, Troy
  See Cle, Troy
Toner, Raymond John 1908-1986 10
Tong, Gary S. 1942- 66
Tong, Paul 188
Took, Belladonna
  See Chapman, Vera (Ivy May)
Tooke, Louise Mathews 1950- 38
Tooke, Susan 173
Toonder, Martin
  See Groom, Arthur William
Toothaker, Roy Eugene 1928- 18
Tooze, Ruth (Anderson) 1892-1972 4
Topaz, Ksenia 212
Topek, Susan Remick 1955- 78
Topping, Audrey R(onning) 1928- 14
Tor, Regina
  See Shekerjian, Regina Tor
Torbert, Floyd James 1922- 22
Torgersen, Don Arthur 1934- 55
  Brief entry 41
Torley, Luke
  See Blish, James
Torrecilla, Pablo 1967- 206
Torres, Andres Segovia
  See Segovia, Andres
Torres, Daniel 1958- 102
Torres, John A. 1965- 163
  Earlier sketch in SATA 94
Torres, John Albert
  See Torres, John A.
Torres, Laura 1967- 146
  Earlier sketch in SATA 87
Torres, Leyla 1960- 155
Torrey, Rich
  See Torrey, Richard
Torrey, Richard 189
Torrie, Malcolm
  See Mitchell, Gladys (Maude Winifred)
Toten, Teresa 1955- 99
Totham, Mary
  See Breinburg, Petronella
Touponce, William F. 1948- 114
Tournier, Michel 1924- 23
Tournier, Michel Edouard
  See Tournier, Michel
Towle, Wendy 1963- 79
Towne, Mary
  See Spelman, Mary
Townley, Rod
  See Townley, Roderick
Townley, Roderick 1942- 177
Townsend, Brad W. 1962- 91
Townsend, John Rowe 1922- 132
  Autobiography Feature 132
  Earlier sketches in SATA 4, 68
  See also CLR 2
  See also SAAS 2
Townsend, Michael 1981- 194
Townsend, Sue 1946- 93
  Brief entry 48
  Earlier sketch in SATA 55
Townsend, Susan Lilian
  See Townsend, Sue
Townsend, Thomas L. 1944- 59
Townsend, Tom
  See Townsend, Thomas L.
Townsend, Wendy 1962- 201
Townson, Hazel 134

Toye, William Eldred 1926- 8
Traherne, Michael
  See Watkins-Pitchford, Denys James
Trahey, Jane 1923-2000 36
  Obituary 120
Trapani, Iza 1954- 214
  Earlier sketches in SATA 80, 116
Trapp, Maria Augusta von
  See von Trapp, Maria Augusta
Travers, P(amela) L(yndon) 1899-1996 100
  Obituary 90
  Earlier sketches in SATA 4, 54
  See also CLR 93
  See also SAAS 2
Travis, Lucille 133
  Earlier sketch in SATA 88
Treadgold, Mary 1910-2005 49
Trease, (Robert) Geoffrey 1909-1998 60
  Obituary 101
  Earlier sketch in SATA 2
  See also CLR 42
  See also SAAS 6
Treat, Lawrence 1903-1998 59
Tredez, Alain 1926- 17
Tredez, Denise 1930- 50
Treece, Henry 1912-1966 2
  See also CLR 2
Tregarthen, Enys
  See Sloggett, Nellie
Tregaskis, Richard 1916-1973 3
  Obituary 26
Treherne, Katie Thamer 1955- 76
Trell, Max 1900-1996 14
  Obituary 108
Tremain, Ruthven 1922- 17
Trembath, Don 1963- 168
  Earlier sketch in SATA 96
Tremens, Del
  See MacDonald, Amy
Trent, Robbie 1894-1988 26
Trent, Timothy
  See Malmberg, Carl
Treseder, Terry Walton 1956- 68
Tresilian, (Cecil) Stuart 1891-(?) 40
Tresselt, Alvin 1916-2000 7
  See also CLR 30
Trevino, Elizabeth B(orton) de 1904- 29
  Earlier sketch in SATA 1
  See also SAAS 5
Trevor, Elleston 1920-1995 28
Trevor, Frances
  See Teasdale, Sara
Trevor, Glen
  See Hilton, James
Trevor, (Lucy) Meriol 1919-2000 113
  Obituary 122
  Earlier sketch in SATA 10
Trewellard, J.M. 195
Trewellard, Juliet
  See Trewellard, J.M.
Trez, Alain
  See Tredez, Alain
Trez, Denise
  See Tredez, Denise
Trezise, Percy 1923-
  See CLR 41
Trezise, Percy James
  See Trezise, Percy
Triggs, Tony D. 1946- 70
Trimble, Marshall I(ra) 1939- 93
Trimby, Elisa 1948- 47
  Brief entry 40
Tring, A. Stephen
  See Meynell, Laurence Walter
Tripp, Eleanor B(aldwin) 1936- 4
Tripp, Janet 1942- 108
Tripp, Jenny 188
Tripp, John
  See Moore, John Travers
Tripp, Nathaniel 1944- 101

Tripp, Paul 1916-2002 8
  Obituary 139
Tripp, Valerie 1951- 168
  Earlier sketch in SATA 78
Tripp, Wallace (Whitney) 1940- 31
Trivelpiece, Laurel 1926- 56
  Brief entry 46
Trivett, Daphne Harwood 1940- 22
Trivizas, Eugene 1946- 84
Trnka, Jiri 1912-1969 43
  Brief entry 32
Trollope, Anthony 1815-1882 22
Trost, Lucille W(ood) 1938- 149
  Earlier sketch in SATA 12
Trott, Betty 1933- 91
Trotter, Deborah W. 184
Trotter, Grace V(iolet) 1900-1991 10
Trottier, Maxine 1950- 175
  Earlier sketch in SATA 131
Troughton, Joanna (Margaret) 1947- 37
Trout, Kilgore
  See Farmer, Philip Jose
Trout, Richard E. 123
Trudeau, Garretson Beekman
  See Trudeau, G.B.
Trudeau, Garry
  See Trudeau, G.B.
Trudeau, Garry B.
  See Trudeau, G.B.
Trudeau, G.B. 1948- 168
  Earlier sketch in SATA 35
Trueit, Trudi
  See Trueit, Trudi Strain
Trueit, Trudi Strain 1963- 179
Trueman, Matthew 183
Trueman, Terry 1947- 178
  Earlier sketch in SATA 132
Truesdell, Judy
  See Mecca, Judy Truesdell
Truesdell, Sue
  See Truesdell, Susan G.
Truesdell, Susan G. 212
  Brief entry 45
  Earlier sketch in SATA 108
Trumbauer, Lisa (Trutkoff) 1963- 149
Truss, Jan 1925- 35
Truss, Lynne 1955(?)- 194
Tryon, Leslie 194
  Earlier sketch in SATA 139
Tubb, Jonathan N. 1951- 78
Tubb, Kristin O'Donnell 1971- 209
Tubby, I. M.
  See Kraus, (Herman) Robert
Tucker, Allan James
  See James, Bill
Tucker, Caroline
  See Nolan, Jeannette Covert
Tucker, James
  See James, Bill
Tudor, Edward
  See Browne, Anthony
Tudor, Tasha 1915-2008 160
  Obituary 205
  Earlier sketches in SATA 20, 69
  See also CLR 13
Tuerk, Hanne 1951- 71
Tugeau, Jeremy 199
Tulloch, Richard 1949- 180
  Earlier sketch in SATA 76
Tulloch, Richard George
  See Tulloch, Richard
Tulloch, Shirley 169
Tully, John (Kimberley) 1923- 14
Tumanov, Vladimir A. 1961- 138
Tung, Angela 1972- 109
Tunis, Edwin (Burdett) 1897-1973 28
  Obituary 24
  Earlier sketch in SATA 1
  See also CLR 2
Tunis, John R(oberts) 1889-1975 37
  Brief entry 30

Tunnell, Michael
  See Tunnell, Michael O.
Tunnell, Michael O. 1950- 157
  Earlier sketch in SATA 103
Tunnell, Michael O'Grady
  See Tunnell, Michael O.
Tunnicliffe, C(harles) F(rederick)
  1901-1979 62
Turck, Mary C. 1950- 144
Turk, Hanne
  See Tuerk, Hanne
Turk, Ruth 1917- 82
Turkle, Brinton 1915- 79
  Earlier sketch in SATA 2
Turlington, Bayly 1919-1977 5
  Obituary 52
Turnbull, Agnes Sligh 1888-1982 14
Turnbull, Ann 1943- 160
  Earlier sketch in SATA 18
Turnbull, Ann Christine
  See Turnbull, Ann
Turnbull, Susan 222
Turner, Alice K. 1940- 10
Turner, Ann 1945- 188
  Autobiography Feature 188
  Earlier sketches in SATA 14, 77, 113, 178
Turner, Ann Warren
  See Turner, Ann
Turner, Bonnie 1932- 75
Turner, Elizabeth 1774-1846
  See YABC 2
Turner, Glennette Tilley 1933- 183
  Earlier sketch in SATA 71
Turner, Josie
  See Crawford, Phyllis
Turner, Megan Whalen 1965- 174
  Earlier sketch in SATA 94
Turner, Pamela S. 1957- 211
Turner, Philip (William) 1925- 83
  Earlier sketch in SATA 11
  See also CLR 89
  See also SAAS 6
Turner, Robyn 1947- 77
Turner, Sheila R.
  See Seed, Sheila Turner
Turngren, Annette 1902(?)-1980
  Obituary 23
Turngren, Ellen (?)-1964 3
Turska, Krystyna (Zofia) 1933- 31
  Brief entry 27
Turteltaub, H. N.
  See Turtledove, Harry
Turtledove, Harry 1949- 166
  Earlier sketch in SATA 116
Turtledove, Harry Norman
  See Turtledove, Harry
Tusa, Tricia 1960- 207
  Earlier sketches in SATA 72, 111
Tusiani, Joseph 1924- 45
Twain, Mark 1835-1910 100
  See also YABC 2
  See also CLR 156
Tweit, Susan J 1956- 94
Tweit, Susan Joan
  See Tweit, Susan J
Tweton, D. Jerome 1933- 48
Twinem, Neecy 1958- 92
Twohill, Maggie
  See Angell, Judie
Tworkov, Jack 1900-1982 47
  Obituary 31
Tyche
  See Papademetriou, Lisa
Tyers, Jenny 1969- 89
Tyers, Kathy 1952- 82
Tyler, Anne 1941- 173
  Earlier sketches in SATA 7, 90
Tyler, Linda
  See Tyler, Linda W(agner)
Tyler, Linda W(agner) 1952- 65
Tyler, Vicki 1952- 64

Tyne, Joel
  See Schembri, Jim
Tyrrell, Frances 1959- 107

U

Ubell, Earl 1926-2007 4
  Obituary 182
Uchida, Yoshiko 1921-1992 53
  Obituary 72
  Earlier sketch in SATA 1
  See also CLR 56
  See also SAAS 1
Udall, Jan Beaney 1938- 10
Uden, (Bernard Gilbert) Grant 1910- 26
Uderzo, Albert 1927-
  See CLR 37
Udovic, David 1950- 189
Udry, Janice May 1928- 152
  Earlier sketch in SATA 4
Uegaki, Chieri 1969- 211
  Earlier sketch in SATA 153
Uehashi, Nahoko 1962- 215
Ueno, Noriko
  See Nakae, Noriko
Ugliano, Natascia 196
Uhlberg, Myron 174
Uhlig, Richard 1970- 195
Uhlig, Susan 1955- 129
Ulam, S(tanislaw) M(arcin) 1909-1984 51
Ullman, Barb Bentler 210
Ullman, James Ramsey 1907-1971 7
Ulm, Robert 1934-1977 17
Ulmer, Louise 1943- 53
Ulmer, Wendy K. 1950- 201
Ulrich, Maureen 1958- 206
Ulriksen, Mark 1957- 210
Ulyatt, Kenneth 1920- 14
Umansky, Kaye 1946- 188
  Earlier sketch in SATA 158
Unada
  See Gliewe, Unada (Grace)
Uncle Carter
  See Boucher, (Clarence) Carter
Uncle Eric
  See Maybury, Richard J.
Uncle Gus
  See Rey, H. A.
Uncle Mac
  See McCulloch, Derek (Ivor Breashur)
Uncle Ray
  See Coffman, Ramon Peyton
Uncle Shelby
  See Silverstein, Shel
Underhill, Alice Mertie (Waterman)
  1900-1971 10
Underhill, Liz 1948- 53
  Brief entry 49
Underwood, Deborah 1962- 206
Unger, Harlow G. 1931- 75
Unger, Harlow Giles
  See Unger, Harlow G.
Unger, Jim 1937- 67
Ungerer, (Jean) Thomas 1931- 106
  Earlier sketches in SATA 5, 33
  See also CLR 77
Ungerer, Tomi 1931-
  See Ungerer, (Jean) Thomas
Unkelbach, Kurt 1913-1992 4
Unnerstad, Edith (Totterman) 1900-1982 3
  See also CLR 36
Unobagha, Uzo 139
Unrau, Ruth 1922- 9
Unstead, R(obert) J(ohn) 1915-1988 12
  Obituary 56
Unsworth, Walt(er) 1928- 4
Untermeyer, Bryna Ivens 1909-1985 61

Untermeyer, Louis 1885-1977 .... *37*
　Obituary *26*
　Earlier sketch in SATA *2*
Unwin, David S. 1918-2010 .... *14*
Unwin, David Storr
　See Unwin, David S.
Unwin, Nora S(picer) 1907-1982 .... *3*
　Obituary *49*
Unzner, Christa 1958- *141*
　Earlier sketch in SATA *80*
Unzner-Fischer, Christa
　See Unzner, Christa
Updale, Eleanor 1953- *175*
Updyke, Rosemary K. 1924- *103*
Upitis, Alvis *109*
Urbain, Cat 1956- *211*
Urbain, Catherine
　See Urbain, Cat
Urban, Helle (Denise) 1957- *149*
Urban, Linda *199*
Urbanovic, Jackie *189*
Urbeuaga, Emilio 1954- *219*
Urbigkit, Cat 1965- *196*
Urdahl, Catherine *215*
Ure, Jean 1943- *192*
　Autobiography Feature *192*
　Earlier sketches in SATA *48, 78, 129*
　See also CLR *34*
　See also SAAS *14*
U'Ren, Andrea 1968- *213*
　Earlier sketch in SATA *142*
Uris, Leon 1924-2003 .... *49*
　Obituary *146*
Uris, Leon Marcus
　See Uris, Leon
Ursu, Anne *177*
Ury, Allen B. 1954- *98*
Uschan, Michael V. 1948- *129*
Usher, Margo Scegge
　See McHargue, Georgess
Usher, Mark David
　See Usher, M.D.
Usher, M.D. 1966- *221*
Uslan, Michael E. 1951- *169*
Uston, Ken(neth Senzo) 1935-1987 .... *65*
Uttley, Alice Jane 1884-1976 .... *88*
　Obituary *26*
　Earlier sketch in SATA *3*
Uttley, Alison
　See Uttley, Alice Jane
Utz, Lois (Marie) 1932-1986 .... *5*
　Obituary *50*

V

Vaeth, J. Gordon 1921- *17*
Vaeth, Joseph Gordon
　See Vaeth, J. Gordon
Vagin, Vladimir (Vasilevich) 1937- *142*
Vail, Rachel 1966- *201*
　Earlier sketches in SATA *94, 163*
Vainio, Pirkko 1957- *123*
　Earlier sketch in SATA *76*
Valen, Nanine 1950- *21*
Valencak, Hannelore
　See Mayer, Hannelore Valencak
Valens, Amy 1946- *70*
Valens, E(vans) G(ladstone), Jr. 1920-1992 ... *1*
Valentine, Johnny *72*
Valerio, Geraldo 1970- *180*
Valgardson, W. D. 1939- *151*
　Earlier sketch in SATA *101*
Valgardson, William Dempsey
　See Valgardson, W. D.
Valleau, Emily 1925- *51*
Vamos, Samantha R. *215*
Van Abbe, Salaman 1883-1955 .... *18*

Van Allsburg, Chris 1949- *156*
　Earlier sketches in SATA *37, 53, 105*
　See also CLR *113*
Van Anrooy, Francine 1924- *2*
Van Anrooy, Frans
　See Van Anrooy, Francine
Vanasse, Deb 1957- *170*
Van Buren, David *203*
Van Camp, Katie 1981- *222*
Vance, Cynthia *207*
Vance, Eleanor Graham 1908-1985 .... *11*
Vance, Gerald
　See Garrett, Randall
　and Silverberg, Robert
Vance, Marguerite 1889-1965 .... *29*
Vance-Abrams, Cynthia
　See Vance, Cynthia
VanCleave, Janice 1942- *116*
　Autobiography Feature *123*
　Earlier sketch in SATA *75*
Vandenburg, Mary Lou 1943- *17*
Vander Boom, Mae M. *14*
Vander-Els, Betty 1936- *63*
van der Heide, Iris 1970- *183*
van der Linde, Laurel 1952- *78*
van der Linden, Martijn 1979- *214*
van der Meer, Ron 1945- *98*
van de Ruit, John 1975- *199*
Van der Veer, Judy 1912-1982 .... *4*
　Obituary *33*
Vanderwal, Andrew H. 1956- *219*
Vanderwerff, Corrine 1939- *117*
Vander Zee, Ruth *199*
　Earlier sketch in SATA *159*
Vande Velde, Vivian 1951- *211*
　Earlier sketches in SATA *62, 95, 141*
　See also CLR *145*
Vandivert, Rita (Andre) 1905-1986 .... *21*
Van Draanen, Wendelin *207*
　Earlier sketch in SATA *122*
Van Dusen, Chris *173*
Van Duyn, Janet 1910- *18*
Van Dyne, Edith
　See Baum, L. Frank
　and Sampson, Emma (Keats) Speed
　and van Zantwijk, Rudolf (Alexander
　Marinus)
Vane, Mitch
　See Vane, Mitchelle
Vane, Mitchelle *176*
van Frankenhuyzen, Gijsbert 1951- *132*
Van Genechten, Guido 1957- *165*
van Haeringen, Annemarie *193*
Van Hook, Beverly 1941- *99*
Van Hook, Beverly H.
　See Van Hook, Beverly
Van Hook, Beverly Hennen
　See Van Hook, Beverly
Van Horn, William 1939- *43*
van Hout, Mies 1962- *178*
Van Iterson, S(iny) R(ose) *26*
Van Kampen, Vlasta 1943- *163*
　Earlier sketch in SATA *54*
Van Laan, Nancy 1939- *214*
　Earlier sketch in SATA *105*
van Lawick-Goodall, Jane
　See Goodall, Jane
Van Leeuwen, Jean 1937- *211*
　Autobiography Feature *141*
　Earlier sketches in SATA *6, 82, 132, 141*
　See also SAAS *8*
van Lhin, Erik
　See del Rey, Lester
van Lieshout, Elle 1963- *217*
van Lieshout, Maria *201*
Van Loon, Hendrik Willem 1882-1944 .... *18*
van Ommen, Sylvia 1978- *186*
VanOosting, James 1951- *170*
Van Orden, M(erton) D(ick) 1921- *4*
van Os, Erik 1963- *217*
Van Patter, Bruce *183*

Van Reek, Wouter *204*
Van Rensselaer, Alexander (Taylor Mason)
　1892-1962 .... *14*
Van Riper, Guernsey, Jr. 1909-1995 .... *3*
van Rossum, Heleen 1962- *174*
Van Rynbach, Iris 1952- *102*
Vansant, Rhonda Joy Edwards 1950- *92*
Van Steenwyk, Elizabeth (Ann) 1928- *89*
　Earlier sketch in SATA *34*
Van Stockum, Hilda 1908-2006 .... *5*
　Obituary *179*
van Straaten, Harmen 1961- *218*
　Earlier sketch in SATA *195*
Van Tuyl, Barbara 1940- *11*
van Vogt, A(lfred) E(lton) 1912-2000 .... *14*
　Obituary *124*
Van Wassenhove, Sue 1951- *202*
Van Woerkom, Dorothy (O'Brien)
　1924-1996 .... *21*
Van Wormer, Joe
　See Van Wormer, Joseph Edward
Van Wormer, Joseph Edward 1913-1998 ...... *35*
Van Wright, Cornelius *173*
Van Zwienen, Ilse Charlotte Koehn
　1929-1991 .... *34*
　Brief entry *28*
　Obituary *67*
Van Zyle, Jon 1942- *176*
　Earlier sketch in SATA *84*
Varela, Barry *180*
Varga, Judy
　See Stang, Judit
Varley, Dimitry V. 1906-1984 .... *10*
Varley, Susan 1961- *134*
　Earlier sketch in SATA *63*
Varon, Sara *195*
Vasileva, Tatiana
　See Wassiljewa, Tatjana
Vasiliev, Valery 1949- *80*
Vasilieva, Tatiana
　See Wassiljewa, Tatjana
Vasiliu, Mircea 1920- *2*
Vass, George 1927- *57*
　Brief entry *31*
Vaughan, Carter A.
　See Gerson, Noel Bertram
Vaughan, Harold Cecil 1923- *14*
Vaughan, Marcia (K.) 1951- *159*
　Earlier sketches in SATA *60, 95*
Vaughan, Richard 1947- *87*
Vaughan, Sam(uel) 1928- *14*
Vaughn, Ruth 1935- *14*
Vaught, Susan 1965- *195*
Vaupel, Robin *198*
Vautier, Ghislaine 1932- *53*
Vavra, Robert James 1935- *8*
Vecsey, George Spencer 1939- *9*
Vedral, Joyce L(auretta) 1943- *65*
Vega, Denise *216*
　Earlier sketch in SATA *174*
Vega, Denise B.
　See Vega, Denise
Vega, Diego
　See Adkins, Jan
Veglahn, Nancy (Crary) 1937- *5*
Vejjajiva, Jane 1963- *189*
Velasquez, Eric *192*
Velasquez, Gloria 1949- *113*
Velasquez, Gloria 1949-
　See Velasquez, Gloria
Velthuijs, Max 1923-2005 .... *110*
　Obituary *160*
　Earlier sketch in SATA *53*
Venable, Alan (Hudson) 1944- *8*
Venezia, Mike 1945- *150*
Ventura, Anthony
　See Pellowski, Michael (Joseph)
Ventura, Piero (Luigi) 1937- *61*
　Brief entry *43*
　See also CLR *16*

Vequin, Capini
  See Quinn, Elisabeth
Verba, Joan Marie 1953- *78*
Verboven, Agnes 1951- *103*
verDorn, Bethea (Stewart) 1952- *76*
Vere, Ed *197*
Verissimo, Erico (Lopes) 1905-1975 .... *113*
Verne, Jules 1828-1905 .... *21*
  See also CLR *88*
Verne, Jules Gabriel
  See Verne, Jules
Verner, Gerald 1897(?)-1980
  Obituary *25*
Verney, John 1913-1993 .... *14*
  Obituary *75*
Verniero, Joan C. 1949- *181*
Vernon, (Elda) Louise A(nderson) 1914- *14*
Vernon, Rosemary
  See Smith, Susan Vernon
Vernon, Ursula *204*
Vernor, D.
  See Casewit, Curtis W(erner)
Verr, Harry Coe
  See Kunhardt, Edith
Verral, Charles Spain 1904-1990 .... *11*
  Obituary *65*
Verrillo, Erica 1953- *199*
Verrillo, Erica F.
  See Verrillo, Erica
Verroken, Sarah 1982- *223*
Verrone, Robert J. 1935(?)-1984
  Obituary *39*
Versace, Marie Teresa Rios 1917- *2*
Vertreace, Martha M(odena) 1945- *78*
Vesey, A(manda) 1939- *62*
Vesey, Mark (David) 1958- *123*
Vesey, Paul
  See Allen, Samuel W(ashington)
Vess, Charles 1951- *215*
Vestergaard, Hope *178*
Vestly, Anne-Cath(arina) 1920-2008 .... *14*
  See also CLR *99*
Vevers, (Henry) Gwynne 1916-1988 .... *45*
  Obituary *57*
Viator, Vacuus
  See Hughes, Thomas
Viau, Nancy *208*
Vicar, Henry
  See Felsen, Henry Gregor
Vick, Helen Hughes 1950- *88*
Vicker, Angus
  See Felsen, Henry Gregor
Vickers, Sheena 1960- *94*
Vickery, Kate
  See Kennedy, T.A.
Victor, Edward 1914- *3*
Victor, Joan Berg 1942- *30*
Vidrine, Beverly Barras 1938- *188*
  Earlier sketch in SATA *103*
Vieceli, Emma 1979- *210*
Viereck, Ellen K. 1928- *14*
Viereck, Phillip 1925- *3*
Viertel, Janet 1915- *10*
Vigliante, Mary
  See Szydlowski, Mary Vigliante
Vigna, Judith 1936- *102*
  Earlier sketch in SATA *15*
Viguers, Ruth Hill 1903-1971 .... *6*
Vila, Laura *207*
Vilela, Fernando 1973- *216*
Villareal, Ray *187*
Villasenor, Edmund
  See Villasenor, Victor E.
Villasenor, Edmundo
  See Villasenor, Victor E.
Villasenor, Victor
  See Villasenor, Victor E.
Villasenor, Victor E. 1940- *171*
Villasenor, Victor Edmundo
  See Villasenor, Victor E.

Villiard, Paul 1910-1974 .... *51*
  Obituary *20*
Villiers, Alan (John) 1903-1982 .... *10*
Vilott, Rhondi
  See Salsitz, Rhondi Vilott
Vincent, Amy
  See Gray, Claudia
Vincent, Eric Douglas 1953- *40*
Vincent, Erin 1969- *188*
Vincent, Felix 1946- *41*
Vincent, Gabrielle 1928-2000 .... *121*
  Earlier sketch in SATA *61*
  See also CLR *13*
Vincent, Mary Keith
  See St. John, Wylly Folk
Vincent, Rachel 1978- *222*
Vincent, William R.
  See Heitzmann, William Ray
Vinegar, Tom
  See Gregg, Andrew K.
Vinest, Shaw
  See Longyear, Barry B(rookes)
Vinge, Joan (Carol) D(ennison) 1948- *113*
  Earlier sketch in SATA *36*
Vining, Elizabeth Gray 1902-1999 .... *6*
  Obituary *117*
Vinson, Kathryn 1911-1995 .... *21*
Vinton, Iris 1906(?)-1988 .... *24*
  Obituary *55*
Viola, Herman J(oseph) 1938- *126*
Viorst, Judith 1931- *172*
  Earlier sketches in SATA *7, 70, 123*
  See also CLR *90*
Vip
  See Partch, Virgil Franklin II
Vipont, Charles
  See Foulds, Elfrida Vipont
Vipont, Elfrida
  See Foulds, Elfrida Vipont
Viramontes, Helena Maria 1954-
  See CLR *285*
Viscott, David S(teven) 1938-1996 .... *65*
Visser, W(illem) F(rederik) H(endrik)
  1900-1968 .... *10*
Vitale, Stefano 1958- *180*
  Earlier sketch in SATA *114*
Vivas, Julie 1947- *96*
Vivelo, Jackie 1943- *63*
Vivelo, Jacqueline J.
  See Vivelo, Jackie
Vivelo, Jacqueline Jean
  See Vivelo, Jackie
Vivian, Siobhan 1979(?)- *215*
Vizzini, Ned 1981- *179*
  Earlier sketch in SATA *125*
Vlahos, Olivia 1924- *31*
Vlasic, Bob
  See Hirsch, Phil
Voake, Charlotte *180*
  Earlier sketch in SATA *114*
Voake, Steve 1961- *178*
Vo-Dinh, Mai 1933- *16*
Vogel, Carole Garbuny 1951- *105*
  Earlier sketch in SATA *70*
Vogel, Ilse-Margret 1918- *14*
Vogel, John H., Jr. 1950- *18*
Vogt, Esther Loewen 1915-1999 .... *14*
Vogt, Gregory L. *94*
Vogt, Marie Bollinger 1921- *45*
Vohwinkel, Astrid 1969- *207*
Voight, Virginia Frances 1909-1989 .... *8*
Voigt, Cynthia 1942- *160*
  Brief entry *33*
  Earlier sketches in SATA *48, 79, 116*
  See also CLR *141*
Voigt, Erna 1925- *35*
Voigt-Rother, Erna
  See Voigt, Erna
Vojtech, Anna 1946- *108*
  Earlier sketch in SATA *42*
Vollstadt, Elizabeth Weiss 1942- *121*

Volponi, Paul *175*
Volting, Dr. R.E.
  See Lerangis, Peter
Von Ahnen, Katherine 1922- *93*
von Buhler, Cynthia *185*
Vondra, J. Gert
  See Vondra, Josef
Vondra, Josef 1941- *121*
Vondra, Josef Gert
  See Vondra, Josef
Von Gunden, Kenneth 1946- *113*
Von Hagen, Victor Wolfgang 1908-1985 ...... *29*
von Klopp, Vahrah
  See Malvern, Gladys
von Schmidt, Eric 1931-2007 .... *50*
  Brief entry *36*
  Obituary *181*
von Storch, Anne B. 1910- *1*
von Trapp, Maria Augusta 1905-1987 .... *16*
von Wodtke, Charlotte Buel Johnson
  1918-1982 .... *46*
von Ziegesar, Cecily 1970- *161*
Vos, Ida 1931-2006 .... *121*
  Earlier sketch in SATA *69*
  See also CLR *85*
Vosburgh, Leonard (W.) 1912- *15*
Votaw, Carol 1961- *201*
Voyle, Mary
  See Manning, Rosemary
Vrettos, Adrienne Maria *187*
Vriens, Jacques 1946- *151*
Vugteveen, Verna Aardema
  See Aardema, Verna
Vulture, Elizabeth T.
  See Gilbert, Suzie
Vuong, Lynette Dyer 1938- *110*
  Earlier sketch in SATA *60*

W

Waas, Uli
  See Waas-Pommer, Ulrike
Waas-Pommer, Ulrike 1949- *85*
Waber, Bernard 1924- *155*
  Brief entry *40*
  Earlier sketches in SATA *47, 95*
  See also CLR *55*
Wachtel, Shirley Russak 1951- *88*
Wachter, Oralee (Roberts) 1935- *61*
  Brief entry *51*
Waddell, Evelyn Margaret 1918- *10*
Waddell, Martin 1941- *129*
  Autobiography Feature *129*
  Earlier sketches in SATA *43, 81, 127*
  See also CLR *31*
  See also SAAS *15*
Waddy, Lawrence 1912-2010 .... *91*
Waddy, Lawrence Heber
  See Waddy, Lawrence
Wade, Mary Dodson 1930- *151*
  Earlier sketch in SATA *79*
Wade, Suzanne
  See Kirby, Susan E.
Wade, Theodore E., Jr. 1936- *37*
Wademan, Peter John 1946- *122*
Wademan, Spike
  See Wademan, Peter John
Wadsworth, Ginger 1945- *223*
  Earlier sketches in SATA *103, 157*
Wagenheim, Kal 1935- *21*
Wagner, Michele R. 1975- *157*
Wagner, Sharon B. 1936- *4*
Wagoner, David (Russell) 1926- *14*
Wahl, Jan (Boyer) 1933- *132*
  Earlier sketches in SATA *2, 34, 73*
  See also SAAS *3*
Wahl, Mats 1945- *186*
Wahman, Wendy *218*
Waide, Jan 1952- *29*

Wainscott, John Milton 1910-1981 .... *53*
Wainwright, Debra *218*
Wainwright, Richard M. 1935- *91*
Wainwright, Ruth
    See Symes, Ruth Louise
Wait, Lea 1946- *137*
Waite, Judy *174*
Waite, Judy Bernard
    See Bernard, Patricia
Waite, Michael
    See Waite, Michael P.
Waite, Michael P. 1960- *101*
Waite, P(eter) B(usby) 1922- *64*
Waites, Joan C. *187*
Waitley, Douglas 1927- *30*
Wakefield, Jean L.
    See Laird, Jean E(louise)
Wakin, Daniel (Joseph) 1961- *84*
Wakin, Edward 1927- *37*
Wakiyama, Hanako 1966- *192*
Walck, Henry Z. 1908(?)-1984
    Obituary *40*
Walden, Amelia Elizabeth *3*
Walden, Mark *188*
Waldherr, Kris 1963- *76*
Waldman, Bruce 1949- *15*
Waldman, Neil 1947- *203*
    Earlier sketches in SATA *51, 94, 142*
Waldrep, Richard *198*
Waldron, Ann Wood 1924-2010 .... *16*
Waldron, Kathleen Cook *176*
Wales, Dirk 1931- *205*
Walgren, Judy 1963- *118*
Walker, Addison
    See Walker, Mort
Walker, Addison Mort
    See Walker, Mort
Walker, Alice 1944- *31*
Walker, Alice Malsenior
    See Walker, Alice
Walker, Anna *223*
Walker, Barbara (Jeanne) K(erlin) 1921- *80*
    Earlier sketch in SATA *4*
Walker, Barbara M(uhs) 1928- *57*
Walker, (James) Braz(elton) 1934-1983 .... *45*
Walker, David 1965- *197*
Walker, David G(ordon) 1926- *60*
Walker, David Harry 1911-1992 .... *8*
    Obituary *71*
Walker, Diana 1925- *9*
Walker, Diane Marie Catherine
    See Walker, Kate
Walker, Dick
    See Pellowski, Michael (Joseph)
Walker, Frank 1931-2000 .... *36*
Walker, Holly Beth
    See Bond, Gladys Baker
Walker, Kate 1950- *165*
    Earlier sketch in SATA *82*
Walker, Kathrine Sorley
    See Sorley Walker, Kathrine
Walker, Lou Ann 1952- *66*
    Brief entry *53*
Walker, Louise Jean 1891-1976
    Obituary *35*
Walker, Mary Alexander 1927- *61*
Walker, Mildred
    See Schemm, Mildred Walker
Walker, Mort 1923- *8*
Walker, Pamela 1948- *142*
    Earlier sketch in SATA *24*
Walker, Paul Robert 1953- *154*
Walker, Robert W. 1948- *66*
Walker, Sally M. 1954- *221*
    Earlier sketch in SATA *135*
Walker, Stephen J. 1951- *12*
Walker-Blondell, Becky 1951- *89*
Wallace, Barbara Brooks 1922- *136*
    Earlier sketches in SATA *4, 78*
    See also CLR *150*
    See also SAAS *17*

Wallace, Beverly Dobrin 1921- *19*
Wallace, Bill 1947- *169*
    Brief entry *47*
    Earlier sketches in SATA *53, 101*
Wallace, Carol 1948- *218*
Wallace, Daisy
    See Cuyler, Margery
Wallace, Ian 1950- *219*
    Earlier sketches in SATA *53, 56, 141*
    See also CLR *37*
Wallace, John 1966- *155*
    Earlier sketch in SATA *105*
Wallace, John A(dam) 1915-2004 .... *3*
    Obituary *155*
Wallace, Karen 1951- *188*
    Earlier sketches in SATA *83, 139*
Wallace, Nancy Elizabeth 1948- *222*
    Earlier sketches in SATA *141, 186*
Wallace, Nigel
    See Hamilton, Charles (Harold St. John)
Wallace, Paula S. *153*
Wallace, Rich 1957- *196*
    Earlier sketches in SATA *117, 158*
Wallace, Robert 1932-1999 .... *47*
    Brief entry *37*
Wallace, Ruby Ann 1923(?)- *77*
Wallace, William Keith
    See Wallace, Bill
Wallace-Brodeur, Ruth 1941- *169*
    Brief entry *41*
    Earlier sketches in SATA *51, 88*
Wallenta, Adam 1974- *123*
Waller, Leslie 1923-2007 .... *20*
Walley, Byron
    See Card, Orson Scott
Wallis, Diz 1949- *77*
Wallis, G. McDonald
    See Campbell, Hope
Wallner, Alexandra 1946- *156*
    Brief entry *41*
    Earlier sketches in SATA *51, 98*
Wallner, John C. 1945- *133*
    Earlier sketches in SATA *10, 51*
Wallower, Lucille *11*
Walrod, Amy 1973(?)- *182*
Walsh, Ann 1942- *176*
    Earlier sketch in SATA *62*
Walsh, Ellen Stoll 1942- *194*
    Earlier sketches in SATA *49, 99, 147*
Walsh, George Johnston 1889-1981 .... *53*
Walsh, Gillian Paton
    See Paton Walsh, Jill
Walsh, Jill Paton
    See Paton Walsh, Jill
Walsh, Joanna 1970- *182*
Walsh, Lawrence 1942- *170*
Walsh, Marissa 1972- *195*
Walsh, Mary Caswell 1949- *118*
Walsh, Mitzy
    See Walsh, Marissa
Walsh, Rebecca *217*
Walsh, Suella *170*
Walsh, V. L.
    See Walsh, Vivian
Walsh, Vivian 1960- *120*
Walsh Shepherd, Donna 1948- *78*
Walter, Frances V. 1923- *71*
Walter, Mildred Pitts 1922- *133*
    Brief entry *45*
    Earlier sketch in SATA *69*
    See also CLR *61*
    See also SAAS *12*
Walter, Villiam Christian
    See Andersen, Hans Christian
Walter, Virginia
    See Walter, Virginia A.
Walter, Virginia A. *134*
Walters, Audrey 1929- *18*
Walters, Celeste 1938- *126*
Walters, Eric 1957- *205*
    Earlier sketches in SATA *99, 155*

Walters, Eric Robert
    See Walters, Eric
Walters, Gregory 1964- *213*
Walters, Helen B. (?)-1987
    Obituary *50*
Walters, Hugh
    See Hughes, Walter (Llewellyn)
Walther, Thomas A. 1950- *31*
Walther, Tom
    See Walther, Thomas A.
Waltner, Elma 1912-1987 .... *40*
Waltner, Willard H. 1909- *40*
Walton, Darwin McBeth 1926- *119*
Walton, Fiona L. M. 1959- *89*
Walton, Richard J. 1928- *4*
Walton, Rick 1957- *204*
    Earlier sketches in SATA *101, 151*
Waltrip, Lela (Kingston) 1904-1995 .... *9*
Waltrip, Mildred 1911- *37*
Waltrip, Rufus (Charles) 1898-1988 .... *9*
Walworth, Nancy Zinsser 1917- *14*
Wang, Gabrielle *212*
Wang, Lin 1973- *221*
Wang, Shaoli *216*
Wangerin, Walter, Jr. 1944- *98*
    Brief entry *37*
    Earlier sketch in SATA *45*
Waniek, Marilyn Nelson 1946-
    See Nelson, Marilyn
Wannamaker, Bruce
    See Moncure, Jane Belk
Warbler, J. M.
    See Cocagnac, Augustin Maurice(-Jean)
Warburg, Sandol Stoddard
    See Stoddard, Sandol
Warburton, Tom 1968(?)- *218*
Ward, David 1967- *213*
Ward, E. D.
    See Gorey, Edward (St. John)
    and Lucas, E(dward) V(errall)
Ward, Ed
    See Stratemeyer, Edward L.
Ward, Helen 1962- *206*
    Earlier sketches in SATA *72, 144*
Ward, Jay 1920-1989
    Obituary *63*
Ward, Jennifer 1963- *146*
Ward, John (Stanton) 1917- *42*
Ward, Jonas
    See Ard, William
    and Cox, William R(obert)
    and Garfield, Brian (Francis Wynne)
Ward, Lynd (Kendall) 1905-1985 .... *36*
    Obituary *42*
    Earlier sketch in SATA *2*
Ward, Martha (Eads) *5*
Ward, Melanie
    See Curtis, Richard
    and Lynch, Marilyn
Ward, Nicholas John
    See Ward, Nick
Ward, Nick 1955- *190*
Ward, Tom
    See Stratemeyer, Edward L.
Wardell, Dean
    See Prince, J(ack) H(arvey)
Wardlaw, Lee 1955- *115*
    Earlier sketch in SATA *79*
Ware, Cheryl 1963- *101*
Ware, Chris 1967- *140*
Ware, Leon (Vernon) 1909-1976 .... *4*
Wargin, Kathy-jo 1964- *210*
    Earlier sketch in SATA *145*
Warhola, James 1955- *187*
Warner, Frank A. *67*
    Earlier sketch in SATA *1*
Warner, Gertrude Chandler 1890-1979 .... *9*
    Obituary *73*
Warner, J(ohn) F. 1929- *75*
Warner, Lucille Schulberg *30*

Warner, Matt
See Fichter, George S.
Warner, Oliver (Martin Wilson) 1903-1976 . 29
Warner, Sally 1946- 214
Earlier sketch in SATA 131
Warner, Sunny (B.) 1931- 108
Warnes, Tim 1971- 216
Earlier sketches in SATA 116, 166
Warnes, Timothy
See Warnes, Tim
Warnick, Elsa 1942- 113
Warren, Andrea 1946- 98
Warren, Betsy
See Warren, Elizabeth Avery
Warren, Billy
See Warren, William Stephen
Warren, Cathy 1951- 62
Brief entry 46
Warren, Elizabeth
See Supraner, Robyn
Warren, Elizabeth Avery 1916- 46
Brief entry 38
Warren, Jackie M. 1953- 135
Warren, Joshua P(aul) 1976- 107
Warren, Joyce W(illiams) 1935- 18
Warren, Mary Phraner 1929- 10
Warren, Robert Penn 1905-1989 46
Obituary 63
Warren, Scott S. 1957- 79
Warren, William Stephen 1882-1968 9
Warrick, Patricia Scott 1925- 35
Warriner, John 1907(?)-1987
Obituary 53
Warsh
See Warshaw, Jerry
Warshaw, Jerry 1929- 30
Warshaw, Mary 1931- 89
Warshofsky, Fred 1931- 24
Warshofsky, Isaac
See Singer, Isaac Bashevis
Wartski, Maureen (Ann Crane) 1940- 50
Brief entry 37
Warwick, Alan R(oss) 1900-1973 42
Wa-sha-quon-asin
See Belaney, Archibald Stansfeld
Wa-Sha-Quon-Asin
See Belaney, Archibald Stansfeld
Washburn, Bradford 1910-2007 38
Obituary 181
Washburn, Henry Bradford, Jr.
See Washburn, Bradford
Washburn, Jan(ice) 1926- 63
Washburn, Lucia 193
Washburne, Carolyn Kott 1944- 86
Washburne, Heluiz Chandler 1892-1970 10
Obituary 26
Washington, Booker T. 1856-1915 28
Washington, Donna L. 1967- 159
Earlier sketch in SATA 98
Wasserman, Robin 1978- 207
Wasserstein, Wendy 1950-2006 94
Obituary 174
Wassiljewa, Tatjana 1928- 106
Watanabe, Etsuko 1968- 219
Watanabe, Shigeo 1928- 131
Brief entry 32
Earlier sketch in SATA 39
See also CLR 8
Waters, John F(rederick) 1930- 4
Waters, Summer
See Sykes, Julie
Waters, Tony 1958- 75
Waterton, Betty 1923- 99
Brief entry 34
Earlier sketch in SATA 37
Waterton, Betty Marie
See Waterton, Betty
Watkins, Dawn L. 126
Watkins, Gloria Jean
See hooks, bell

Watkins, Lis
See Watkins, Liselotte
Watkins, Liselotte 1971- 215
Watkins, Lois 1930- 88
Watkins, Peter 1934- 66
Watkins, Yoko Kawashima 1933- 93
Watkins-Pitchford, Denys James
1905-1990 87
Obituary 66
Earlier sketch in SATA 6
See also SAAS 4
Watling, James 1933- 117
Earlier sketch in SATA 67
Watson, Aldren A(uld) 1917- 42
Brief entry 36
Watson, Amy Zakrzewski 1965- 76
Watson, B. S.
See Teitelbaum, Michael
Watson, Carol 1949- 78
Watson, C.G. 193
Watson, Clyde 1947- 68
Earlier sketch in SATA 5
See also CLR 3
Watson, Helen Orr 1892-1978
Obituary 24
Watson, James 1936- 106
Earlier sketch in SATA 10
Watson, Jane Werner 1915- 54
Earlier sketch in SATA 3
Watson, Jesse Joshua 199
Watson, John H.
See Farmer, Philip Jose
Watson, Mary 1953- 117
Watson, N. Cameron 1955- 81
Watson, Nancy Dingman 32
Watson, Pauline 1925- 14
Watson, Richard F.
See Silverberg, Robert
Watson, Richard Jesse 1951- 211
Earlier sketch in SATA 62
Watson, Sally (Lou) 1924- 3
Watson, Sasha 211
Watson, Wendy (McLeod) 1942- 142
Earlier sketches in SATA 5, 74
Watson Taylor, Elizabeth 1915- 41
Watt, Melanie 1975- 193
Earlier sketch in SATA 136
Watt, Thomas 1935- 4
Wattenberg, Jane 174
Watterson, Bill 1958- 66
Watt-Evans, Lawrence 1954- 121
Watts, (Anna) Bernadette 1942- 103
Earlier sketch in SATA 4
Watts, Ephraim
See Horne, Richard Henry Hengist
Watts, Franklin (Mowry) 1904-1978 46
Obituary 21
Watts, Helen L. Hoke 1903-1990
Obituary 65
Watts, Irene N(aemi) 1931- 111
Earlier sketch in SATA 56
Watts, Isaac 1674-1748 52
Watts, James K(ennedy) M(offitt) 1955- 59
Watts, Jeri Hanel 1957- 170
Watts, Julia 1969- 103
Watts, Leander 1956- 146
Watts, Leslie Elizabeth 1961- 168
Watts, Mabel Pizzey 1906-1994 11
Watts, Nigel 1957-1999 121
Waugh, C. C. Roessel
See Waugh, Carol-Lynn Rossel
and Waugh, Charles G(ordon)
Waugh, Carol-Lynn Rossel 1947- 41
Waugh, Dorothy -1996 11
Waugh, Sylvia 1935- 169
Waugh, Virginia
See Sorensen, Virginia
Wax, Wendy A. 1963- 219
Earlier sketches in SATA 73, 163

Wayland, April Halprin 1954- 143
Earlier sketch in SATA 78
See also SAAS 26
Wayland, Patrick
See O'Connor, Richard
Wayne, (Anne) Jenifer 1917-1982 32
Wayne, Kyra Petrovskaya 1918- 8
Wayne, Richard
See Decker, Duane
Wayshak, Deborah Noyes
See Noyes, Deborah
Waystaff, Simon
See Swift, Jonathan
Weales, Gerald (Clifford) 1925- 11
Weary, Ogdred
See Gorey, Edward (St. John)
Weatherford, Carole Boston 1956- 181
Earlier sketch in SATA 138
Weatherill, Cat 203
Weatherly, Lee 1967- 192
Weatherly, Myra 1926- 130
Weatherly, Myra S.
See Weatherly, Myra
Weaver, Brian M.
See Numberman, Neil
Weaver, Harriett E. 1908-1993 65
Weaver, John L. 1949- 42
Weaver, Robyn
See Conley, Robyn
Weaver, Robyn M.
See Conley, Robyn
Weaver, Tess 197
Weaver, Ward
See Mason, F(rancis) van Wyck
Weaver, Will 1950- 217
Earlier sketches in SATA 88, 109, 161
Weaver, William Weller
See Weaver, Will
Weaver-Gelzer, Charlotte 1950- 79
Webb, Christopher
See Wibberley, Leonard
Webb, Jacqueline
See Pearce, Margaret
Webb, Jacquelyn
See Pearce, Margaret
and Pearce, Margaret
Webb, Jean Francis (III) 1910-1991 35
Webb, Kaye 1914- 60
Webb, Lois Sinaiko 1922- 82
Webb, Margot 1934- 67
Webb, Sharon 1936-2010 41
Webb, Sophie 1958- 135
Webber, Andrew Lloyd
See Lloyd Webber, Andrew
Webber, Desiree Morrison 1956- 170
Webber, Irma E(leanor Schmidt)
1904-1995 14
Weber, Alfons 1921- 8
Weber, Bruce 1942- 120
Earlier sketch in SATA 73
Weber, Debora 1955- 58
Weber, EdNah New Rider 1919(?)- 168
Weber, Elka 1968- 219
Weber, Jill 1950- 209
Earlier sketch in SATA 127
Weber, Judith E(ichler) 1938- 64
Weber, Ken(neth J.) 1940- 90
Weber, Lenora Mattingly 1895-1971 2
Obituary 26
Weber, Lisa K. 217
Weber, Lori 1959- 220
Weber, Michael 1945- 87
Weber, Sandra 1961- 158
Weber, William J(ohn) 1927- 14
Webster, Alice Jane Chandler 1876-1916 17
Webster, David 1930- 11
Webster, Frank V. 67
Earlier sketch in SATA 1
Webster, Gary
See Garrison, Webb B(lack)

Webster, James 1925-1981 .... *17*
   Obituary *27*
Webster, Jean
   See Webster, Alice Jane Chandler
Wechsler, Doug *189*
Wechsler, Herman J. 1904-1976
   Obituary *20*
Wechter, Nell (Carolyn) Wise 1913-1989 .. *127*
   Earlier sketch in SATA *60*
Weck, Thomas L. 1942- *62*
Wedd, Kate
   See Gregory, Philippa
Weddle, Ethel Harshbarger 1897-1996 .... *11*
Wedekind, Annie *204*
Weeks, Sarah *194*
   Earlier sketch in SATA *158*
Weems, David B(urnola) 1922- *80*
Wees, Frances Shelley 1902-1982 .... *58*
Weevers, Peter 1944- *59*
Wegen, Ronald 1946-1985 .... *99*
Wegman, William (George) 1943- *135*
   Earlier sketches in SATA *78, 129*
Wegner, Fritz 1924- *20*
Wehrman, Vicki *223*
Weidhorn, Manfred 1931- *60*
Weidt, Maryann N. 1944- *85*
Weigel, Jeff 1958- *170*
Weigelt, Udo 1960- *201*
   Earlier sketch in SATA *168*
Weihs, Erika 1917-2010 .... *107*
   Earlier sketch in SATA *15*
Weik, Mary Hays 1898(?)-1979 .... *3*
   Obituary *23*
Weil, Ann Yezner 1908-1969 .... *9*
Weil, Lisl 1910- *7*
Weilerstein, Sadie Rose 1894-1993 .... *3*
   Obituary *75*
Weill, Cynthia 1959- *167*
Wein, Elizabeth E. 1964- *151*
   Earlier sketch in SATA *82*
Wein, Elizabeth Eve
   See Wein, Elizabeth E.
Wein, Hallie
   See Zobel Nolan, Allia
Weinberg, Larry
   See Weinberg, Lawrence (E.)
Weinberg, Lawrence (E.) *92*
   Brief entry *48*
Weinberger, Tanya 1939- *84*
Weiner, Sandra 1922- *14*
Weingarten, Lynn *217*
Weingarten, Violet (Brown) 1915-1976 .... *3*
   Obituary *27*
Weingartner, Charles 1922- *5*
Weinheimer, Beckie 1958- *186*
Weinstein, Bruce 1960- *220*
Weinstein, Bruce M.
   See Weinstein, Bruce
Weinstein, Ellen Slusky 1959- *200*
Weinstein, Muriel Harris *215*
Weinstein, Nina 1951- *73*
Weinstock, Robert 1967- *204*
Weir, Bob 1947- *76*
Weir, Diana (R.) Loiewski 1958- *111*
Weir, Joan S(herman) 1928- *99*
Weir, LaVada *2*
Weir, Rosemary (Green) 1905-1994 .... *21*
Weir, Wendy 1949- *76*
Weis, Margaret 1948- *164*
   Earlier sketches in SATA *38, 92*
Weisberger, Bernard A(llen) 1922- *21*
Weisburd, Stefi 1957- *202*
Weiser, Marjorie P(hillis) K(atz) 1934- *33*
Weisgard, Leonard (Joseph) 1916-2000 .... *85*
   Obituary *122*
   Earlier sketches in SATA *2, 30*
   See also SAAS *19*
Weiss, Adelle 1920- *18*
Weiss, Ann E(dwards) 1943- *69*
   Earlier sketch in SATA *30*
   See also SAAS *13*

Weiss, Edna
   See Barth, Edna
Weiss, Ellen 1953- *44*
Weiss, Harvey 1922- *76*
   Earlier sketch in SATA *1, 27*
   See also CLR *4*
   See also SAAS *19*
Weiss, Jaqueline Shachter 1926- *65*
Weiss, Malcolm E. 1928- *3*
Weiss, Margaret Edith
   See Weis, Margaret
Weiss, Miriam
   See Schlein, Miriam
Weiss, Mitch 1951- *183*
   Earlier sketch in SATA *123*
Weiss, Nicki 1954- *86*
   Earlier sketch in SATA *33*
Weiss, Renee Karol 1923- *5*
Weissberger, Ela 1930- *181*
Weissberger, Ela Stein
   See Weissberger, Ela
Weissenborn, Hellmuth 1898-1982
   Obituary *31*
Weissman, Elissa Brent *217*
Weitzman, David L. 1936- *172*
   Earlier sketch in SATA *122*
Wekesser, Carol A. 1963- *76*
Welber, Robert *26*
Welch, Amanda (Jane) 1945- *75*
Welch, D'Alte Aldridge 1907-1970
   Obituary *27*
Welch, Holly *206*
Welch, Jean-Louise
   See Kempton, Jean Welch
Welch, Pauline
   See Bodenham, Hilda Morris
Welch, Ronald
   See Felton, Ronald Oliver
Welch, Sheila Kelly 1945- *130*
Welch, Willy 1952- *93*
Weldin, Frauke 1969- *188*
Welford, Sue 1942- *75*
Weller, George 1907-2002 .... *31*
   Obituary *140*
Weller, George Anthony
   See Weller, George
Welling, Peter J. 1947- *135*
Wellington, Monica 1957- *222*
   Earlier sketches in SATA *67, 99, 157*
Wellman, Alice 1900-1984 .... *51*
   Brief entry *36*
Wellman, Manly Wade 1903-1986 .... *6*
   Obituary *47*
Wellman, Paul I. 1898-1966 .... *3*
Wellman, Paul Iselin
   See Wellman, Paul I.
Wellman, Sam 1939- *122*
Wellman, Samuel
   See Wellman, Sam
Wells, H. G. 1866-1946 .... *20*
   See also CLR *133*
Wells, Helen
   See Campbell, Hope
Wells, Helen 1910-1986 .... *49*
   Earlier sketch in SATA *2*
Wells, Herbert George
   See Wells, H. G.
Wells, J. Wellington
   See de Camp, L. Sprague
Wells, June
   See Swinford, Betty (June Wells)
Wells, Robert
   See Welsch, Roger L(ee)
Wells, Robert E. *184*
Wells, Rosemary 1943- *207*
   Earlier sketches in SATA *18, 69, 114, 156*
   See also CLR *69*
   See also SAAS *1*
Wells, Susan (Mary) 1951- *78*
Wels, Byron G(erald) 1924-1993 .... *9*
Welsbacher, Anne 1955- *89*

Welsch, Roger L(ee) 1936- *82*
Welsh, David
   See Hills, C.A.R.
Welsh, Mary Flynn 1910(?)-1984
   Obituary *38*
Welsh, T.K. 1956- *184*
Weltner, Linda R(iverly) 1938- *38*
Welton, Jude 1955- *143*
   Earlier sketch in SATA *79*
Welty, S. F.
   See Welty, Susan F.
Welty, Susan F. 1905- *9*
Wemmlinger, Raymond *190*
Wendelin, Rudolph 1910-2000 .... *23*
Weninger, Brigitte 1960- *189*
Wentworth, Robert
   See Hamilton, Edmond
Werlin, Nancy 1961- *161*
   Earlier sketches in SATA *87, 119*
Werner, Elsa Jane
   See Watson, Jane Werner
Werner, Herma 1926- *47*
   Brief entry *41*
Werner, Jane
   See Watson, Jane Werner
Werner, K.
   See Casewit, Curtis W(erner)
Wersba, Barbara 1932- *58*
   Autobiography Feature *103*
   Earlier sketch in SATA *1*
   See also CLR *78*
   See also SAAS *2*
Werstein, Irving 1914(?)-1971 .... *14*
Werth, Kurt 1896-1983 .... *20*
Wesley, Alison
   See Barnes, Michael
Wesley, Kathryn
   See Rusch, Kristine Kathryn
Wesley, Mary (Aline) 1912-2002 .... *66*
Wesley, Valerie Wilson 1947- *168*
   Earlier sketch in SATA *106*
West, Andrew
   See Arthur, Robert, (Jr.)
West, Anna 1938- *40*
West, Barbara
   See Price, Olive
West, Betty 1921- *11*
West, Bruce 1951- *63*
West, C. P.
   See Wodehouse, P. G.
West, Dorothy
   See Benson, Mildred
West, Emily Govan 1919- *38*
West, Emmy
   See West, Emily Govan
West, James
   See Withers, Carl A.
West, Jerry
   See Svenson, Andrew E(dward)
West, (Mary) Jessamyn 1902-1984
   Obituary *37*
West, John
   See Arthur, Robert, (Jr.)
West, Owen
   See Koontz, Dean
West, Ward
   See Borland, Harold Glen
Westall, Robert (Atkinson) 1929-1993 .... *69*
   Obituary *75*
   Earlier sketch in SATA *23*
   See also CLR *13*
   See also SAAS *2*
Westaway, Jane 1948- *121*
Westcott, Nadine Bernard 1949- *130*
Westera, Marleen 1962- *187*
Westerberg, Christine 1950- *29*
Westerduin, Anne 1945- *105*
Westerfeld, Scott 1963- *161*
Westervelt, Virginia Veeder 1914-2005 .... *10*
Westheimer, David 1917-2005 .... *14*
   Obituary *170*

Westheimer, David Kaplan
   See Westheimer, David
Westmacott, Mary
   See Christie, Agatha
Westman, Barbara 70
Westman, Paul (Wendell) 1956- 39
Westmoreland, William C. 1914-2005 63
Westmoreland, William Childs
   See Westmoreland, William C.
Weston, Allen
   See Hogarth, Grace (Weston Allen)
   and Norton, Andre
Weston, Carol 1956- 135
Weston, Carrie 190
Weston, John (Harrison) 1932- 21
Weston, Martha 1947- 119
   Earlier sketch in SATA 53
Weston, Robert Paul 209
Westphal, Arnold Carl 1897- 57
Westrup, Hugh 102
Westwood, Jennifer 1940-2008 10
   Obituary 192
Wexler, Jerome (LeRoy) 1923- 14
Weyland, Jack 1940- 81
Weyn, Suzanne 1955- 220
   Earlier sketches in SATA 63, 101, 164
Weyr, Garret
   See Freymann-Weyr, Garret
Wezyk, Joanna 1966- 82
Whaley, Joyce Irene 1923- 61
Whalin, W. Terry 1953- 93
Whamond, Dave 222
Wharf, Michael
   See Weller, George
Wharmby, Margot 63
Wharton, Edith 1862-1937
   See CLR 136
Wharton, Edith Newbold Jones
   See Wharton, Edith
Wharton, Thomas 1963- 223
Whatley, Bruce 1954- 213
   Earlier sketch in SATA 177
Wheatley, Arabelle 1921- 16
Wheatley, Nadia 1949- 147
Wheeler, Cindy 1955- 49
   Brief entry 40
Wheeler, Deborah 1947- 83
Wheeler, Janet D. 1
Wheeler, Jill C. 1964- 136
   Earlier sketch in SATA 86
Wheeler, Jody 1952- 148
   Earlier sketch in SATA 84
Wheeler, Lisa 1963- 200
   Earlier sketch in SATA 162
Wheeler, Opal 1898- 23
Whelan, Elizabeth M(urphy) 1943- 14
Whelan, Gloria 1923- 178
   Earlier sketches in SATA 85, 128
   See also CLR 90
Whelan, Gloria Ann
   See Whelan, Gloria
Whipple, A(ddison) B(eecher) C(olvin)
   1918- 64
Whipple, Cal
   See Whipple, A(ddison) B(eecher) C(olvin)
Whisp, Kennilworthy
   See Rowling, J.K.
Whistler, Reginald John 1905-1944 30
Whistler, Rex
   See Whistler, Reginald John
Whitaker, Zai 183
Whitcher, Susan (Godsil) 1952- 96
Whitcomb, Jon 1906-1988 10
   Obituary 56
Whitcomb, Laura 1958- 214
   Earlier sketch in SATA 171
White, Anne Terry 1896-1980 2
White, Bessie (Felstiner) 1892(?)-1986
   Obituary 50
White, Carolyn 1948- 130

White, Dale
   See Place, Marian T(empleton)
White, Dori 1919- 10
White, E. B. 1899-1985 100
   Obituary 44
   Earlier sketches in SATA 2, 29
   See also CLR 107
White, Eliza Orne 1856-1947
   See YABC 2
White, Elwyn Brooks
   See White, E. B.
White, Florence M(eiman) 1910- 14
White, Laurence B(arton), Jr. 1935- 10
White, Lee 223
   Earlier sketch in SATA 176
White, Martin 1943- 51
White, Nancy 1942- 126
White, Ramy Allison 67
   Earlier sketch in SATA 1
White, Robb 1909-1990 83
   Earlier sketch in SATA 1
   See also CLR 3
   See also SAAS 1
White, Ruth 1942- 186
   Autobiography Feature 186
   Earlier sketches in SATA 39, 117, 165
White, Ruth C.
   See White, Ruth
White, T(erence) H(anbury) 1906-1964 12
   See also CLR 139
White, Tekla N. 1934- 115
White, Timothy (Thomas Anthony)
   1952-2002 60
White, Tom 1923- 148
White, William, Jr. 1934- 16
Whitehead, Don(ald) F. 1908-1981 4
Whitehead, Jenny 1964- 191
Whitehead, Kathy 1957- 176
Whitehouse, Arch
   See Whitehouse, Arthur George Joseph
Whitehouse, Arthur George Joseph
   1895-1979 14
   Obituary 23
Whitehouse, Elizabeth S(cott) 1893-1968 35
Whitehouse, Jeanne
   See Peterson, Jeanne Whitehouse
Whitelaw, Nancy 1933- 166
   Earlier sketch in SATA 76
Whitesel, Cheryl Aylward 162
Whiting, Sue 1960- 205
Whiting, Susan Allana
   See Whiting, Sue
Whitinger, R. D.
   See Place, Marian T(empleton)
Whitley, Mary Ann
   See Sebrey, Mary Ann
Whitley, Peggy 1938- 140
Whitlock, Pamela 1921(?)-1982
   Obituary 31
Whitlock, Ralph 1914-1995 35
Whitman, Alice
   See Marker, Sherry
Whitman, Candace 1958- 208
Whitman, Sylvia (Choate) 1961- 135
   Earlier sketch in SATA 85
Whitman, Walt 1819-1892 20
Whitman, Walter
   See Whitman, Walt
Whitmore, Arvella 1922- 125
Whitmore, Benette 1955- 203
Whitney, Alex(andra) 1922- 14
Whitney, David C(harles) 1921- 48
   Brief entry 29
Whitney, Kim Ablon 162
Whitney, Phyllis A. 1903-2008 30
   Obituary 189
   Earlier sketch in SATA 1
   See also CLR 59
Whitney, Phyllis Ayame
   See Whitney, Phyllis A.
Whitney, Sharon 1937- 63

Whitney, Thomas P. 1917-2007 25
   Obituary 189
Whitney, Thomas Porter
   See Whitney, Thomas P.
Whittington, Mary K(athrine) 1941- 75
Whitworth, John 1945- 123
Whybrow, Ian 202
   Earlier sketch in SATA 132
Whyte, Mal(colm Kenneth, Jr.) 1933- 62
Whyte, Mary 1953- 148
   Earlier sketch in SATA 94
Whyte, Ron 1942(?)-1989
   Obituary 63
Whytock, Cherry 177
Wiater, Stanley 1953- 84
Wibbelsman, Charles J(oseph) 1945- 59
Wibberley, Leonard 1915-1983 45
   Obituary 36
   Earlier sketch in SATA 2
   See also CLR 3
Wibberley, Leonard Patrick O'Connor
   See Wibberley, Leonard
Wiberg, Harald (Albin) 1908- 93
   Brief entry 40
Wick, Walter 1953- 148
Wickberg, Susan
   See Rottman, S.L.
Wickens, Elaine 86
Wicker, Ireene 1905(?)-1987
   Obituary 55
Wickstrom, Sylvie 1960- 169
Wickstrom, Thor 1960- 200
Widdemer, Mabel Cleland 1902-1964 5
Widener, Terry 1950- 209
   Earlier sketch in SATA 105
Widerberg, Siv 1931- 10
Wiebe, Rudy 1934- 156
Wiebe, Rudy Henry
   See Wiebe, Rudy
Wieler, Diana (Jean) 1961- 109
Wiener, Lori 1956- 84
Wier, Ester (Alberti) 1910-2000 3
Wiese, Kurt 1887-1974 36
   Obituary 24
   Earlier sketch in SATA 3
   See also CLR 86
Wiesel, Elie 1928- 56
Wiesel, Eliezer
   See Wiesel, Elie
Wiesner, David 1956- 181
   Earlier sketches in SATA 72, 117, 139
   See also CLR 84
Wiesner, Portia
   See Takakjian, Portia
Wiesner, William 1899-1984 5
Wiggers, Raymond 1952- 82
Wiggin, Eric E. 1939- 167
   Earlier sketch in SATA 88
Wiggin, Eric Ellsworth 1939-
   See Wiggin, Eric E.
Wiggin (Riggs), Kate Douglas (Smith)
   1856-1923
   See YABC 1
   See also CLR 52
Wiggins, VeraLee (Chesnut) 1928-1995 89
Wight, Eric 1974- 218
Wight, James Alfred
   See Herriot, James
Wignell, Edel 1936- 69
Wijnberg, Ellen 85
Wikland, Ilon 1930- 93
   Brief entry 32
Wikler, Madeline 1943- 114
Wilber, Donald N(ewton) 1907-1997 35
Wilbur, C. Keith 1923- 27
Wilbur, Frances 1921- 107
Wilbur, Helen L. 1948- 204
Wilbur, Richard 1921- 108
   Earlier sketch in SATA 9
Wilbur, Richard Purdy
   See Wilbur, Richard

Wilburn, Kathy 1948- 68
Wilcox, Charlotte 1948- 72
Wilcox, Leah 1975(?)- 207
Wilcox, R(uth) Turner 1888-1970 36
Wilcox, Roger
  See Collins, Paul
Wild, Jocelyn 1941- 46
Wild, Kate 1954- 192
Wild, Margaret 1948- 197
  Earlier sketch in SATA *151*
Wild, Robin (Evans) 1936- 46
Wild, Robyn 1947- 117
Wilde, D. Gunther
  See Hurwood, Bernhardt J.
Wilde, Oscar 1854(?)-1900 24
  See also CLR *114*
Wilde, Oscar Fingal O'Flahertie Willis
  See Wilde, Oscar
Wilder, Buck
  See Smith, Tim(othy R.)
Wilder, Laura Elizabeth Ingalls
  See Wilder, Laura Ingalls
Wilder, Laura Ingalls 1867-1957 100
  Earlier sketches in SATA *15, 29*
  See also CLR *111*
Wildsmith, Brian 1930- 124
  Earlier sketches in SATA *16, 69*
  See also CLR *52*
  See also SAAS *5*
Wiles, Deborah 171
Wilhelm, Doug 1952- 190
Wilhelm, Hans 1945- 196
  Autobiography Feature 196
  Earlier sketches in SATA *58, 135*
  See also CLR *46*
  See also SAAS *21*
Wilkie, Katharine E(lliott) 1904-1980 31
Wilkin, Eloise 1904-1987 49
  Obituary 54
Wilkins, Frances 1923- 14
Wilkins, Kim 147
Wilkins, Marilyn (Ruth) 1926- 30
Wilkins, Marne
  See Wilkins, Marilyn (Ruth)
Wilkins, Mary Huiskamp 1926- 2
  See also CLR *42*
Wilkins, Mary Huiskamp Calhoun
  See Wilkins, Mary Huiskamp
Wilkins, Rose 180
Wilkinson, (Thomas) Barry 1923- 50
  Brief entry 32
Wilkinson, Beth 1925- 80
Wilkinson, Brenda 1946- 91
  Earlier sketch in SATA *14*
  See also CLR *20*
Wilkinson, (John) Burke 1913-2000 4
Wilkinson, Carole 1950- 210
Wilkinson, Sylvia 1940- 56
  Brief entry 39
Wilkon, Jozef 1930- 133
  Earlier sketches in SATA *31, 71*
Wilkowski, Sue 193
Wilks, Michael Thomas 1947- 44
Wilks, Mike
  See Wilks, Michael Thomas
Will
  See Lipkind, William
Willard, Barbara (Mary) 1909-1994 74
  Earlier sketch in SATA *17*
  See also CLR *2*
  See also SAAS *5*
Willard, Elizabeth Kimmel
  See Kimmel, Elizabeth Cody
Willard, Mildred Wilds 1911-1978 14
Willard, Nancy 1936- 191
  Brief entry 30
  Earlier sketches in SATA *37, 71, 127*
  See also CLR *5*
Willcox, Isobel 1907-1996 42

Willems, Mo 180
  Earlier sketch in SATA *154*
  See also CLR *114*
Willett, Edward 1959- 115
Willett, Edward C.
  See Willett, Edward
Willey, Bee 184
Willey, Margaret 1950- 86
Willey, Robert
  See Ley, Willy
Willhoite, Michael A. 1946- 71
William, Kate
  See Armstrong, Jennifer
Williams, Alex 1969- 209
Williams, Arlene 171
Williams, Barbara 1925- 107
  Earlier sketch in SATA *11*
  See also CLR *48*
  See also SAAS *16*
Williams, Barbara 1937- 62
Williams, Beryl
  See Epstein, Beryl
Williams, Brian (Peter) 1943- 54
Williams, Carol Lynch 1959- 212
  Earlier sketch in SATA *110*
Williams, Charles
  See Collier, James Lincoln
Williams, Clyde C. 1881-1974 8
  Obituary 27
Williams, Coe
  See Harrison, C(hester) William
Williams, Colleen Madonna Flood 1963- .. 156
Williams, Cynthia G. 1958- 123
Williams, Dar 1967- 168
Williams, Donna Reilly 1945- 83
Williams, Dorothy
  See Williams, Marcia
Williams, Dorothy Snowden
  See Williams, Dar
Williams, Eric (Ernest) 1911-1983 14
  Obituary 38
Williams, Ferelith Eccles
  See Eccles Williams, Ferelith
Williams, Frances B.
  See Browin, Frances Williams
Williams, Garth (Montgomery) 1912-1996 .. 66
  Obituary 90
  Earlier sketch in SATA *18*
  See also CLR *57*
  See also SAAS *7*
Williams, Guy R(ichard) 1920- 11
Williams, Hawley
  See Heyliger, William
Williams, Helen 1948- 77
Williams, J. R.
  See Williams, Jeanne
Williams, J. Walker
  See Wodehouse, P. G.
Williams, Jay 1914-1978 41
  Obituary 24
  Earlier sketch in SATA *3*
  See also CLR *8*
Williams, Jeanne 1930- 5
Williams, Jenny 1939- 60
Williams, Karen Lynn 1952- 99
  Earlier sketch in SATA *66*
Williams, Kathryn 1981- 222
Williams, Kit 1946(?)- 44
  See also CLR *4*
Williams, L. E.
  See Williams, Laura E.
Williams, Laura E.
  See Williams, Laura Ellen
Williams, Laura Ellen 180
Williams, Leslie 1941- 42
Williams, Linda 1948- 59
Williams, Louise Bonino 1904(?)-1984
  Obituary 39
Williams, Lynn
  See Hale, Arlene

Williams, Marcia 1945- 159
  Earlier sketches in SATA *71, 97*
Williams, Marcia Dorothy
  See Williams, Marcia
Williams, Margery
  See Bianco, Margery Williams
Williams, Mark
  See Arthur, Robert, (Jr.)
Williams, Mark London 1959- 140
Williams, Maureen 1951- 12
Williams, Michael
  See St. John, Wylly Folk
Williams, Patrick J.
  See Griffin, W. E. B.
Williams, Paulette Linda
  See Shange, Ntozake
Williams, Pete
  See Faulknor, Cliff(ord Vernon)
Williams, S. P.
  See Hart, Virginia
Williams, Sam 177
  Earlier sketch in SATA *124*
Williams, Selma R(uth) 1925- 14
Williams, Sherley Anne 1944-1999 78
  Obituary 116
Williams, Sheron 1955- 77
Williams, Shirley
  See Williams, Sherley Anne
Williams, Slim
  See Williams, Clyde C.
Williams, Sophy 1965- 135
Williams, Sue 1948-2007 208
Williams, Susan
  See Beckhorn, Susan Williams
Williams, Suzanne
  See Williams, Suzanne Morgan
Williams, Suzanne 1953- 202
  Earlier sketch in SATA *71*
Williams, Suzanne M.
  See Williams, Suzanne Morgan
Williams, Suzanne Morgan 1949- 207
Williams, Ursula Moray
  See Moray Williams, Ursula
Williams, Vera B(aker) 1927- 102
  Brief entry 33
  Earlier sketch in SATA *53*
  See also CLR *9*
Williams-Andriani, Renee 1963- 98
Williams-Ellis, (Mary) Amabel (Nassau
  Strachey) 1894-1984 29
  Obituary 41
Williams-Garcia, Rita 1957- 160
  Earlier sketch in SATA *98*
  See also CLR *36*
Williamson, Gwyneth 1965- 109
Williamson, Henry (William) 1895-1977 37
  Obituary 30
Williamson, Joanne S(mall) 1926- 122
  Earlier sketch in SATA *3*
Williamson, Kate T. 1979- 215
Williamson, Melanie 196
Willis, Charles
  See Clarke, Arthur C.
Willis, Connie 1945- 110
  See also CLR *66*
Willis, Cynthia Chapman 215
Willis, Jeanne 1959- 195
  Earlier sketches in SATA *61, 123*
Willis, Jeanne Mary
  See Willis, Jeanne
Willis, Meredith Sue 1946- 101
Willis, Nancy Carol 1952- 139
  Earlier sketch in SATA *93*
Willis, Paul J. 1955- 113
Willms, Russ 95

Willoughby, Lee Davis
 See Avallone, Michael (Angelo, Jr.)
 and Brandner, Gary (Phil)
 and Deming, Richard
 and DeAndrea, William L(ouis)
 and Laymon, Richard (Carl)
 and Streib, Dan(iel Thomas)
 and Toombs, John
 and Webb, Jean Francis (III)
Willson, Robina Beckles
 See Beckles Willson, Robina
Wilma, Dana
 See Faralla, Dana
Wilsdorf, Anne 1954- *191*
Wilson, April *80*
Wilson, Barbara Ker
 See Ker Wilson, Barbara
Wilson, Beth P(ierre) *8*
Wilson, Budge 1927- *55*
 Brief entry *51*
Wilson, Carletta 1951- *81*
Wilson, Carter 1941- *6*
Wilson, Charles Morrow 1905-1977 .... *30*
Wilson, Christopher B. 1910(?)-1985
 Obituary *46*
Wilson, Darryl B(abe) 1939- *90*
Wilson, Diane Lee *172*
Wilson, Dirk
 See Pohl, Frederik
Wilson, Dorothy Clarke 1904-2003 .... *16*
Wilson, Edward A(rthur) 1886-1970 .... *38*
Wilson, Ellen (Janet Cameron) (?)-1976 .... *9*
 Obituary *26*
Wilson, Eric (H.) 1940- *34*
 Brief entry *32*
Wilson, Erica *51*
Wilson, Forrest 1918- *27*
Wilson, Gahan 1930- *35*
 Brief entry *27*
Wilson, Gina 1943- *85*
 Brief entry *34*
 Earlier sketch in SATA *36*
Wilson, (Leslie) Granville 1912- *14*
Wilson, Hazel (Hutchins) 1898-1992 .... *3*
 Obituary *73*
Wilson, J(erry) M. 1964- *121*
Wilson, Jacqueline 1945- *199*
 Brief entry *52*
 Earlier sketches in SATA *61, 102, 153*
Wilson, John 1922- *22*
Wilson, John 1951- *182*
Wilson, John Alexander
 See Wilson, John
Wilson, Johnniece Marshall 1944- *75*
Wilson, Jonathan 1950- *181*
Wilson, Joyce M. *84*
 Earlier sketch in SATA *21*
 See also SAAS *24*
Wilson, Karma *221*
 Earlier sketch in SATA *174*
Wilson, Leslie 1952- *166*
Wilson, Linda Miller 1936- *116*
Wilson, Lionel 1924-2003 .... *33*
 Brief entry *31*
 Obituary *144*
Wilson, Marjorie
 See Wilson, Budge
Wilson, Martin 1973- *205*
Wilson, Maurice (Charles John) 1914- *46*
Wilson, Nancy Hope 1947- *138*
 Earlier sketch in SATA *81*
Wilson, Nathan D.
 See Wilson, N.D.
Wilson, N.D. 1978- *194*
Wilson, Nick
 See Ellis, Edward S.
Wilson, Phil 1948- *181*
Wilson, Ron(ald William) 1941- *38*
Wilson, Sarah 1934- *208*
 Earlier sketches in SATA *50, 142*

Wilson, Tom 1931- *33*
 Brief entry *30*
Wilson, Troy 1970- *169*
Wilson, Walt(er N.) 1939- *14*
Wilson-Max, Ken 1965- *170*
 Earlier sketch in SATA *93*
Wilton, Elizabeth 1937- *14*
Wilton, Hal
 See Pepper, Frank S.
Wilwerding, Walter Joseph 1891-1966 .... *9*
Wimmer, Mike 1961- *194*
 Earlier sketch in SATA *70*
Winborn, Marsha (Lynn) 1947- *75*
Winch, John 1944- *165*
 Earlier sketch in SATA *117*
Winchester, James H(ugh) 1917-1985 .... *30*
 Obituary *45*
Winchester, Stanley
 See Youd, Samuel
Windawi, Thura al- 1983(?)- *165*
Winders, Gertrude Hecker -1987 .... *3*
Windham, Basil
 See Wodehouse, P. G.
Windham, Kathryn T(ucker) 1918- *14*
Windham, Sophie *184*
Windling, Terri 1958- *151*
Windrow, Martin
 See Windrow, Martin Clive
Windrow, Martin C.
 See Windrow, Martin Clive
Windrow, Martin Clive 1944- *68*
Windsor, Claire
 See Hamerstrom, Frances
Windsor, Linda 1950- *124*
Windsor, Patricia 1938- *78*
 Earlier sketch in SATA *30*
 See also SAAS *19*
Wineman-Marcus, Irene 1952- *81*
Winer, Yvonne 1934- *120*
Winerip, Michael *175*
Winfield, Arthur M.
 See Stratemeyer, Edward L.
Winfield, Edna
 See Stratemeyer, Edward L.
Winfield, Julia
 See Armstrong, Jennifer
Wing, Natasha 1960- *200*
 Earlier sketch in SATA *82*
Wingerter, Linda S. 1973(?)- *207*
Winget, Susan *211*
Winick, Judd 1970- *124*
Winks, Robin William 1930-2003 .... *61*
Winn, Alison
 See Wharmby, Margot
Winn, Chris 1952- *42*
Winn, Janet Bruce 1928- *43*
Winn, Marie 1936(?)- *38*
Winnick, Karen B. 1946- *211*
Winnick, Karen B(eth) B(inkoff) 1946- *51*
Winn-Lederer, Ilene *198*
Winslow, Barbara 1947- *91*
Winstead, Rosie *180*
Winston, Clara 1921-1983 .... *54*
 Obituary *39*
Winston, Richard 1917-1979 .... *54*
Winston, Sherri 1964(?)- *201*
Winter, Janet 1926- *126*
Winter, Jeanette 1939- *184*
 Earlier sketch in SATA *151*
Winter, Jonah 1962- *179*
Winter, Milo (Kendall) 1888-1956 .... *21*
Winter, Paula Cecelia 1929- *48*
Winter, R. R.
 See Winterbotham, R(ussell) R(obert)
Winter, Susan *182*
Winterbotham, R(ussell) R(obert)
 1904-1971 .... *10*
Winterbotham, Russ
 See Winterbotham, R(ussell) R(obert)
Winterfeld, Henry 1901-1990 .... *55*

Winters, J. C.
 See Cross, Gilbert B.
Winters, Jon
 See Cross, Gilbert B.
Winters, Katherine
 See Winters, Kay
Winters, Kay 1936- *153*
 Earlier sketch in SATA *103*
Winters, Nina 1944- *62*
Winters, Paul A. 1965- *106*
Winterson, Jeanette 1959- *190*
Winterton, Gayle
 See Adams, William Taylor
Winthrop, Elizabeth 1948- *164*
 Autobiography Feature *116*
 Earlier sketches in SATA *8, 76*
 See also CLR *89*
Winton, Ian (Kenneth) 1960- *76*
Winton, Tim 1960- *98*
Wintz-Litty, Julie
 See Litty, Julie
Wirt, Ann
 See Benson, Mildred
Wirt, Mildred A.
 See Benson, Mildred
Wirtenberg, Patricia Z. 1932-2007 .... *10*
Wirtenberg, Patricia Zarrella
 See Wirtenberg, Patricia Z.
Wirth, Beverly 1938- *63*
Wirths, Claudine (Turner) G(ibson)
 1926-2000 .... *104*
 Earlier sketch in SATA *64*
Wise, Bill 1958- *191*
Wise, Lenny
 See Wise, Leonard
Wise, Leonard 1940- *167*
Wise, Leonard A.
 See Wise, Leonard
Wise, Leonard Allan
 See Wise, Leonard
Wise, William 1923- *163*
 Earlier sketch in SATA *4*
Wise, Winifred E. *2*
Wiseman, Ann (Sayre) 1926- *31*
Wiseman, B(ernard) 1922-1995 .... *4*
Wiseman, David 1916- *43*
 Brief entry *40*
Wiseman, Eva 1947- *210*
Wishinsky, Frieda 1948- *166*
 Earlier sketches in SATA *70, 112*
Wisler, G(ary) Clifton 1950- *103*
 Brief entry *46*
 Earlier sketch in SATA *58*
Wismer, Donald (Richard) 1946- *59*
Wisner, Bill
 See Wisner, William L.
Wisner, William L. 1914(?)-1983 .... *42*
Wisnewski, David 1953-2002
 See Wisniewski, David
Wisniewski, David 1953-2002 .... *95*
 Obituary *139*
 See also CLR *51*
Wister, Owen 1860-1938 .... *62*
Witham, (Phillip) Ross 1917- *37*
Withers, Carl A. 1900-1970 .... *14*
Withers, Pam 1956- *182*
Withrow, Sarah 1966- *199*
 Earlier sketch in SATA *124*
Witt, Dick 1948- *80*
Witt, Shirley Hill 1934- *17*
Wittanen, Etolin 1907- *55*
Wittels, Harriet Joan 1938- *31*
Wittig, Susan
 See Albert, Susan Wittig
Wittlinger, Ellen 1948- *189*
 Autobiography Feature *128*
 Earlier sketches in SATA *83, 122*
Wittman, Sally (Anne Christensen) 1941- *30*
Witty, Paul 1898-1976 .... *50*
 Obituary *30*
Wodehouse, P. G. 1881-1975 .... *22*

Wodehouse, Pelham Grenville
  See Wodehouse, P. G.
Wodge, Dreary
  See Gorey, Edward (St. John)
Woelfle, Gretchen 1945- 145
Wohlberg, Meg 1905-1990 41
  Obituary 66
Wohlrabe, Raymond A. 1900-1977 4
Wohnoutka, Mike 195
Wojciechowska, Maia (Teresa) 1927-2002 ... 83
  Autobiography Feature 104
  Obituary 134
  Earlier sketches in SATA 1, 28
  See also CLR 1
  See also SAAS 1
Wojciechowski, Susan 126
  Earlier sketch in SATA 78
Wojnarowski, Adrian 1970- 190
Wojtusik, Elizabeth 208
Wolcott, Patty 1929- 14
Wold, Allen L. 1943- 64
Wold, Jo Anne 1938- 30
Woldin, Beth Weiner 1955- 34
Wolf, Allan 1963- 192
Wolf, Bernard 1930- 102
  Brief entry 37
Wolf, Erica (Van Varick) 1978- 156
Wolf, Gita 1956- 101
Wolf, J. M.
  See Wolf, Joan M.
Wolf, Janet 1957- 78
Wolf, Joan M. 1966- 193
Wolf, Sallie 1950- 205
  Earlier sketch in SATA 80
Wolfe, Art 1952- 76
Wolfe, Burton H. 1932- 5
Wolfe, Frances 216
Wolfe, Gene 1931- 165
  Earlier sketch in SATA 118
Wolfe, Gene Rodman
  See Wolfe, Gene
Wolfe, Gillian 199
Wolfe, Louis 1905-1985 8
  Obituary 133
Wolfe, Rinna (Evelyn) 1925- 38
Wolfenden, George
  See Beardmore, George
Wolfer, Dianne 1961- 167
  Autobiography Feature 117
  Earlier sketch in SATA 104
Wolff, Alexander (Nikolaus) 1957- 137
  Earlier sketch in SATA 63
Wolff, Ashley 1956- 203
  Earlier sketches in SATA 50, 81, 155
Wolff, Diane 1945- 27
Wolff, Ferida 1946- 164
  Earlier sketch in SATA 79
Wolff, Jason 1972- 213
Wolff, Jennifer Ashley
  See Wolff, Ashley
Wolff, Nancy 202
Wolff, Robert Jay 1905-1977 10
Wolff, Sonia
  See Levitin, Sonia
Wolff, Virginia Euwer 1937- 137
  Earlier sketch in SATA 78
  See also CLR 62
Wolfman, Judy 1933- 138
Wolfson, Evelyn 1937- 62
Wolitzer, Hilma 1930- 31
Wolkoff, Judie (Edwards) 93
  Brief entry 37
Wolkstein, Diane 1942- 138
  Earlier sketches in SATA 7, 82
Wollheim, Donald A(llen) 1914-1990
  Obituary 69
Wolny, P.
  See Janeczko, Paul B(ryan)
Wolters, Richard A. 1920-1993 35
Wondriska, William 1931- 6

Wong, Jade Snow 1922-2006 112
  Obituary 175
Wong, Janet S. 1962- 210
  Earlier sketches in SATA 98, 148
  See also CLR 94
Wong, Nicole 214
Woo, Howie 1974- 207
Wood, Addie Robinson
  See Wiggin, Eric E.
Wood, Anne (Savage) 1937- 64
Wood, Audrey 198
  Brief entry 44
  Earlier sketches in SATA 50, 81, 139
  See also CLR 26
Wood, Catherine
  See Etchison, Birdie L(ee)
Wood, David 1944- 212
  Earlier sketch in SATA 87
Wood, Don 1945- 50
  Brief entry 44
  See also CLR 26
Wood, Douglas 1951- 180
  Earlier sketches in SATA 81, 132
Wood, Douglas Eric
  See Wood, Douglas
Wood, Edgar A(llardyce) 1907-1998 14
Wood, Esther
  See Brady, Esther Wood
Wood, Frances Elizabeth 34
Wood, Frances M. 1951- 97
Wood, Jacqueline
  See Wood, Jakki
Wood, Jakki 1957- 211
Wood, James Playsted 1905- 1
Wood, Jenny 1955- 88
Wood, John Norris 1930- 85
Wood, June Rae 1946- 120
  Earlier sketch in SATA 79
  See also CLR 82
Wood, Kerry
  See Wood, Edgar A(llardyce)
Wood, Kim Marie 134
Wood, Laura N.
  See Roper, Laura (Newbold) Wood
Wood, Linda C(arol) 1945- 59
Wood, Marcia 1956- 80
Wood, Marcia Mae
  See Wood, Marcia
Wood, Nancy
  See Wood, Nancy C.
Wood, Nancy C. 1936- 178
  Earlier sketch in SATA 6
Wood, Nuria
  See Nobisso, Josephine
Wood, Owen 1929- 64
Wood, Phyllis Anderson 1923- 33
  Brief entry 30
Wood, Richard 1949- 110
Wood, Tim(othy William Russell) 1946- 88
Wood, Wallace 1927-1981
  Obituary 33
Woodard, Carol 1929- 14
Woodburn, John Henry 1914- 11
Woodbury, David Oakes 1896-1981 62
Woodford, Peggy 1937- 25
Woodhouse, Barbara (Blackburn)
  1910-1988 63
Woodhull, Ann Love 194
Wooding, Chris 1977- 166
Wooding, Sharon
  See Wooding, Sharon L(ouise)
Wooding, Sharon L(ouise) 1943- 66
Woodman, Allen 1954- 76
Woodrich, Mary Neville 1915- 2
Woodruff, Elvira 1951- 211
  Earlier sketches in SATA 70, 106, 162
Woodruff, Joan Leslie 1953- 104
Woodruff, Liza 1971(?)- 182
Woodruff, Marian
  See Goudge, Eileen
Woodruff, Noah 1977- 86

Woods, George A(llan) 1926-1988 30
  Obituary 57
Woods, Geraldine 1948- 111
  Brief entry 42
  Earlier sketch in SATA 56
Woods, Harold 1945- 56
  Brief entry 42
Woods, Lawrence
  See Lowndes, Robert A(ugustine) W(ard)
Woods, Margaret 1921- 2
Woods, Nat
  See Stratemeyer, Edward L.
Woods, Titania
  See Weatherly, Lee
Woodson, Jack
  See Woodson, John Waddie Jr.
Woodson, Jacqueline 1964- 189
  Earlier sketches in SATA 94, 139
  See also CLR 49
Woodson, Jacqueline Amanda
  See Woodson, Jacqueline
Woodson, John Waddie Jr. 1913- 10
Woodtor, Dee
  See Woodtor, Delores Parmer
Woodtor, Dee Parmer 1945(?)-2002
  See Woodtor, Delores Parmer
Woodtor, Delores Parmer 1945-2002 93
Wood-Trost, Lucille
  See Trost, Lucille W(ood)
Woodward, (Landon) Cleveland 1900-1986 . 10
  Obituary 48
Woodworth, Chris 1957- 168
Woodworth, Viki 1952- 127
Woody, Regina Jones 1894-1983 3
Woodyadd, Charlotte
  See Hough, Charlotte
Woog, Adam 1953- 125
  Earlier sketch in SATA 84
Wooldridge, Connie Nordhielm 1950- 143
  Earlier sketch in SATA 92
Wooldridge, Frosty 1947- 140
Wooldridge, Rhoda 1906-1988 22
Wooley, Susan Frelick 1945- 113
Woolf, Paula 1950- 104
Woolfe, Angela 1976- 169
Woolley, Catherine 1904-2005 3
  Obituary 166
Woolman, Steven 1969-2004 163
  Earlier sketch in SATA 90
Woolsey, Janette 1904-1989 3
  Obituary 131
Worcester, Donald E(mmet) 1915- 18
Word, Reagan 1944- 103
Work, Virginia 1946- 57
  Brief entry 45
Worline, Bonnie Bess 1914- 14
Wormell, Christopher 1955- 154
  Earlier sketch in SATA 103
Wormell, Mary 1959- 96
Wormser, Richard 1933- 106
  Autobiography Feature 118
  See also SAAS 26
Wormser, Sophie 1897-1979 22
Worth, Richard
  See Wiggin, Eric E.
Worth, Richard 1945- 59
  Brief entry 46
Worth, Valerie 1933-1994 81
  Earlier sketches in SATA 8, 70
  See also CLR 21
Worthington, Leonie 1956- 200
Wortis, Avi
  See Avi
Wortis, Edward Irving
  See Avi
Wosmek, Frances 1917- 29
Woychuk, Denis 1953- 71
Wrede, Patricia C(ollins) 1953- 146
  Earlier sketch in SATA 67
Wriggins, Sally Hovey 1922- 17
Wright, Alexandra 1979- 103

Wright, Betty Ren 1927- *109*
  Brief entry *48*
  Earlier sketch in SATA *63*
Wright, Cliff 1963- *168*
  Earlier sketch in SATA *76*
Wright, Courtni
  See Wright, Courtni C(rump)
Wright, Courtni C(rump) 1950- *84*
Wright, Courtni Crump
  See Wright, Courtni C(rump)
Wright, Dare 1914(?)-2001 .... *21*
  Obituary *124*
Wright, David K. 1943- *112*
  Earlier sketch in SATA *73*
Wright, Elinor
  See Lyon, Elinor
Wright, Enid Meadowcroft (LaMonte)
  1898-1966 .... *3*
Wright, Esmond 1915-2003 .... *10*
Wright, Frances Fitzpatrick 1897-1982 .... *10*
Wright, J. B.
  See Barkan, Joanne
Wright, Johanna *220*
Wright, Judith 1915-2000 .... *14*
  Obituary *121*
Wright, Judith Arundell
  See Wright, Judith
Wright, Katrina
  See Gater, Dilys
Wright, Kenneth
  See del Rey, Lester
Wright, Kit 1944- *87*
Wright, Leslie B(ailey) 1959- *91*
Wright, Michael 1954- *198*
Wright, Nancy Means *38*
Wright, R(obert) H(amilton) 1906- *6*
Wright, Rachel *220*
  Earlier sketch in SATA *134*
Wright, Susan Kimmel 1950- *97*
Wrightfrierson
  See Wright-Frierson, Virginia (Marguerite)
Wright-Frierson, Virginia (Marguerite)
  1949- *110*
  Earlier sketch in SATA *58*
Wrightson, Alice Patricia
  See Wrightson, Patricia
Wrightson, Patricia 1921-2010 .... *112*
  Obituary *215*
  Earlier sketches in SATA *8, 66*
  See also CLR *154*
  See also SAAS *4*
Wroble, Lisa A. 1963- *134*
Wrongo, I.B.
  See Katz, Alan
Wronker, Lili
  See Wronker, Lili Cassel
Wronker, Lili Cassel 1924- *10*
Wryde, Dogear
  See Gorey, Edward (St. John)
Wu, Donald *212*
Wu, Elizabeth
  See Wu, Liz
Wu, Liz *184*
Wu, Norbert 1961- *155*
  Earlier sketch in SATA *101*
Wulf, Linda Press *205*
Wulffson, Don 1943- *155*
  Earlier sketches in SATA *32, 88*
Wulffson, Don L.
  See Wulffson, Don
Wummer, Amy 1955- *201*
Wunderli, Stephen 1958- *79*
Wunsch, Josephine (McLean) 1914- *64*
Wunsch, Marjory 1942- *220*
  Earlier sketch in SATA *82*
Wuorio, Eva-Lis 1918- *34*
  Brief entry *28*
Wurts, Janny 1953- *98*
Wyatt, B. D.
  See Robinson, Spider
Wyatt, David 1968- *185*

Wyatt, Jane
  See Bradbury, Bianca (Ryley)
Wyatt, Melissa 1963- *177*
Wyatt, Valerie *209*
Wyeth, Betsy James 1921- *41*
Wyeth, N(ewell) C(onvers) 1882-1945 .... *17*
  See also CLR *106*
Wyler, Rose 1909-2000 .... *18*
  Obituary *121*
Wylie, Betty Jane *48*
Wylie, Laura
  See Matthews, Patricia
Wylie, Laurie
  See Matthews, Patricia
Wyllie, Stephen *86*
Wyman, Andrea *75*
Wyman, Carolyn 1956- *83*
Wymer, Norman (George) 1911- *25*
Wynard, Talbot
  See Hamilton, Charles (Harold St. John)
Wyndham, John
  See Harris, John (Wyndham Parkes Lucas)
  Beynon
Wyndham, Lee
  See Hyndman, Jane Andrews Lee
Wyndham, Robert
  See Hyndman, Robert Utley
Wynne, Patricia J. *210*
Wynne-Jones, Tim 1948- *186*
  Autobiography Feature *136*
  Earlier sketches in SATA *67, 96, 136*
  See also CLR *58*
Wynne-Jones, Timothy
  See Wynne-Jones, Tim
Wynter, Edward (John) 1914- *14*
Wynyard, Talbot
  See Hamilton, Charles (Harold St. John)
Wyss, Johann David Von 1743-1818 .... *29*
  Brief entry *27*
  See also CLR *92*
Wyss, Thelma Hatch 1934- *202*
  Earlier sketches in SATA *10, 140*

X

Xavier, Father
  See Hurwood, Bernhardt J.
Xuan, YongSheng 1952- *116*
  Autobiography Feature *119*

Y

Yaccarino, Dan *192*
  Earlier sketch in SATA *141*
Yadin, (Rav-Aloof) Yigael 1917-1984 .... *55*
Yaffe, Alan
  See Yorinks, Arthur
Yagher, Kevin 1962- *143*
Yakovetic, (Joseph Sandy) 1952- *59*
Yakovetic, Joe
  See Yakovetic, (Joseph Sandy)
Yamada, Utako 1963- *188*
Yamaguchi, Marianne (Illenberger) 1936- *7*
Yamaka, Sara 1978- *92*
Yamanaka, Lois-Ann 1961- *166*
Yamasaki, Katie *206*
Yancey, Diane 1951- *138*
  Earlier sketch in SATA *81*
Yancey, Richard *193*
Yancey, Rick
  See Yancey, Richard
Yang, Belle 1960- *170*
Yang, James 1960- *190*
Yang, Jay 1941- *12*
Yang, Mingyi 1943- *72*
Yarbrough, Camille 1938- *79*
  See also CLR *29*

Yarbrough, Ira 1910(?)-1983
  Obituary *35*
Yaroslava
  See Mills, Yaroslava Surmach
Yarrow, Peter 1938- *195*
Yashima, Taro
  See Iwamatsu, Jun Atsushi
Yates, Elizabeth 1905-2001 .... *68*
  Obituary *128*
  Earlier sketch in SATA *4*
  See also SAAS *6*
Yates, Janelle K(aye) 1957- *77*
Yates, John 1939- *74*
Yates, Kelly 1971- *208*
Yates, Louise 1983(?)- *218*
Yates, Philip 1956- *212*
  Earlier sketches in SATA *92, 149*
Yates, Raymond F(rancis) 1895-1966 .... *31*
Yaukey, Grace S(ydenstricker) 1899-1994 ... *80*
  Earlier sketch in SATA *5*
Yazzie, Johnson 1946- *205*
Ye, Ting-xing 1952- *106*
Yeahpau, Thomas M. 1975- *187*
Yeakley, Marjory Hall 1908- *21*
Yeatman, Linda 1938- *42*
Yeatts, Tabatha 1970- *215*
Yee, Brenda Shannon *133*
Yee, Lisa 1959- *218*
  Earlier sketch in SATA *160*
Yee, Paul 1956- *211*
  Earlier sketches in SATA *67, 96, 143*
  See also CLR *44*
Yee, Tammy *206*
Yee, Wong Herbert 1953- *172*
  Earlier sketches in SATA *78, 115*
Yeh, Chun-Chan 1914- *79*
Ye Junjian
  See Yeh, Chun-Chan
Yelchin, Eugene 1956- *196*
Yenawine, Philip 1942- *85*
Yensid, Retlaw
  See Disney, Walt(er Elias)
Yeo, Wilma (Lethem) 1918-1994 .... *81*
  Earlier sketch in SATA *24*
Yeoman, John 1934- *80*
  Earlier sketch in SATA *28*
  See also CLR *46*
Yep, Kathleen S. *203*
Yep, Laurence 1948- *213*
  Earlier sketches in SATA *7, 69, 123, 176*
  See also CLR *132*
Yep, Laurence Michael
  See Yep, Laurence
Yepsen, Roger B(ennet), Jr. 1947- *59*
Yerian, Cameron John *21*
Yerian, Margaret A. *21*
Yerxa, Leo 1947- *181*
Yetska
  See Ironside, Jetske
Yezerski, Thomas F. 1969- *190*
Yin *194*
Ylvisaker, Anne 1965(?)- *172*
Yoder, Carolyn P. 1953- *149*
Yoder, Carolyn Patricia
  See Yoder, Carolyn P.
Yoder, Dorothy Meenen 1921- *96*
Yoder, Dot
  See Yoder, Dorothy Meenen
Yoder, Walter D. 1933- *88*
Yohalem, Eve *219*
Yolen, Jane 1939- *194*
  Autobiography Feature *111*
  Earlier sketches in SATA *4, 40, 75, 112, 158*
  See also CLR *149*
  See also SAAS *1*
Yolen, Jane Hyatt
  See Yolen, Jane
Yonezu, Yusuke *196*
Yonge, Charlotte 1823-1901 .... *17*
Yonge, Charlotte Mary
  See Yonge, Charlotte

Yoo, Paula 1969(?)- *174*
Yoo, Taeeun *191*
Yoon, Salina 1972- *204*
Yorinks, Adrienne 1956- *171*
Yorinks, Arthur 1953- *200*
　Earlier sketches in SATA *33, 49, 85, 144*
　See also CLR *20*
York, Alison
　See Nicole, Christopher (Robin)
York, Andrew
　See Nicole, Christopher (Robin)
York, Carol Beach 1928- *77*
　Earlier sketch in SATA *6*
York, Rebecca
　See Buckholtz, Eileen (Garber)
　and Glick, Ruth (Burtnick)
York, Simon
　See Heinlein, Robert A.
Yoshida, Toshi 1911- *77*
Yoshikawa, Sachiko *181*
Yost, Edna 1889-1971
　Obituary *26*
Youd, C. S.
　See Youd, Samuel
Youd, Samuel 1922- *135*
　Brief entry *30*
　Earlier sketch in SATA *47*
　See also CLR *2*
　See also SAAS *6*
Youme
　See Landowne, Youme
Young, Amy L. *185*
Young, Anne Mortimer
　See Mortimer, Anne
Young, Bob
　See Young, Robert W(illiam)
　and Young, James Robert
Young, Carol 1945- *102*
Young, Catherine
　See Olds, Helen Diehl
Young, Clarence
　See Garis, Howard R.
　and Stratemeyer, Edward L.
Young, Collier
　See Bloch, Robert (Albert)
Young, Dan 1952- *126*
Young, Dianne 1959- *88*
Young, Dorothea Bennett 1924- *31*
Young, Ed 1931- *211*
　Earlier sketches in SATA *10, 74, 122, 173*
　See also CLR *27*
Young, Ed Tse-chun
　See Young, Ed
Young, Edward
　See Reinfeld, Fred
Young, E.L. 1973- *219*
Young, Elaine L.
　See Schulte, Elaine L(ouise)
Young, Emma L.
　See Young, E.L.
Young, James
　See Graham, Ian
Young, Jan
　See Young, Janet Randall
Young, Janet 1957- *188*
Young, Janet Randall 1919-1994 .... *3*
Young, Janet Ruth
　See Young, Janet
Young, Jeff C. 1948- *132*
Young, John
　See Macintosh, Brownie
Young, Judy 1956- *207*
　Earlier sketch in SATA *155*
Young, Judy (Elaine) Dockrey 1949- *72*
Young, Karen Romano 1959- *168*
　Earlier sketch in SATA *116*
Young, Ken 1956- *86*
Young, Lois Horton 1911-1981 .... *26*
Young, Louisa *161*
Young, Louise B. 1919- *64*
Young, Margaret B. 1922-2009 .... *2*

Young, Margaret Buckner
　See Young, Margaret B.
Young, Mary 1940- *89*
Young, Miriam 1913-1974 .... *7*
Young, Noela 1930- *89*
Young, (Rodney Lee) Patrick (Jr.) 1937- *22*
Young, Percy M(arshall) 1912-2004 .... *31*
　Obituary *154*
Young, Richard Alan 1946- *72*
Young, Robert W(illiam) 1916-1969 .... *3*
Young, Ross B. 1955- *150*
Young, Ruth 1946- *67*
Young, Sara
　See Pennypacker, Sara
Young, Scott A. 1918-2005 .... *5*
Young, Scott Alexander
　See Young, Scott A.
Young, Selina 1971-2006 .... *201*
Young, Vivien
　See Gater, Dilys
Younger, Barbara 1954- *108*
Youngs, Betty 1934-1985 .... *53*
　Obituary *42*
Younkin, Paula 1942- *77*
Yount, Lisa (Ann) 1944- *124*
　Earlier sketch in SATA *74*
Yourgrau, Barry *179*
Yuditskaya, Tatyana 1964- *75*
Yum, Hyewon *211*
Yumoto, Kazumi 1959- *153*

Z

Zach, Cheryl (Byrd) 1947- *98*
　Brief entry *51*
　Earlier sketch in SATA *58*
　See also SAAS *24*
Zacharias, Gary L. 1946- *153*
Zaffo, George J. (?)-1984 .... *42*
Zagarenski, Pamela 1969(?)- *183*
Zagwyn, Deborah Turney 1953- *138*
　Earlier sketch in SATA *78*
Zahares, Wade *193*
Zahn, Timothy 1951- *156*
　Earlier sketch in SATA *91*
Zaid, Barry 1938- *51*
Zaidenberg, Arthur 1908(?)-1990 .... *34*
　Obituary *66*
Zalben, Jane Breskin 1950- *170*
　Earlier sketches in SATA *7, 79, 120*
　See also CLR *84*
Zallinger, Jean (Day) 1918- *115*
　Earlier sketches in SATA *14, 80*
Zallinger, Peter Franz 1943- *49*
Zambreno, Mary Frances 1954- *140*
　Earlier sketch in SATA *75*
Zanderbergen, George
　See May, Julian
Zappa, Ahmet 1974- *180*
Zappa, Ahmet Emuukha Rodan
　See Zappa, Ahmet
Zappler, Lisbeth 1930- *10*
Zarchy, Harry 1912-1987 .... *34*
Zarin, Cynthia 1959- *192*
　Earlier sketch in SATA *108*
Zaring, Jane (Thomas) 1936- *40*
Zarins, Joyce Audy
　See dos Santos, Joyce Audy
Zaslavsky, Claudia 1917- *36*
Zaugg, Sandra L. 1938- *118*
Zaugg, Sandy
　See Zaugg, Sandra L.
Zaunders, Bo 1939- *137*
Zawadzki, Marek 1958- *97*
Zebra, A.
　See Scoltock, Jack
Zebrowski, George 1945- *67*
Zebrowski, George T.
　See Zebrowski, George

Zecca, Katherine *207*
Zeck, Gerald Anthony 1939- *40*
Zeck, Gerry
　See Zeck, Gerald Anthony
Zed, Dr.
　See Penrose, Gordon
Zei, Alki 1925- *24*
　See also CLR *6*
Zeier, Joan T(heresa) 1931- *81*
Zeinert, Karen 1942-2002 .... *137*
　Earlier sketch in SATA *79*
Zeises, Lara M. 1976- *184*
　Earlier sketch in SATA *145*
Zelazny, Roger 1937-1995 .... *57*
　Brief entry *39*
Zelazny, Roger Joseph
　See Zelazny, Roger
Zeldis, Malcah 1931- *146*
　Earlier sketch in SATA *86*
Zelinsky, Paul O. 1953- *154*
　Brief entry *33*
　Earlier sketches in SATA *49, 102*
　See also CLR *55*
Zellan, Audrey Penn
　See Penn, Audrey
Zemach, Harve
　See Fischtrom, Harvey
Zemach, Kaethe 1958- *149*
　Brief entry *39*
　Earlier sketch in SATA *49*
Zemach, Margot 1931-1989 .... *70*
　Obituary *59*
　Earlier sketch in SATA *21*
Zemach-Bersin, Kaethe
　See Zemach, Kaethe
Zeman, Ludmila 1947- *153*
Zepeda, Gwendolyn 1971- *206*
Zephaniah, Benjamin 1958- *189*
　Earlier sketches in SATA *86, 140*
Zephaniah, Benjamin Obadiah Iqbal
　See Zephaniah, Benjamin
Zephaniah, Benjamin Pbadiah Iqubal
　See Zephaniah, Benjamin
Zerman, Melvyn Bernard 1930-2010 .... *46*
Zettner, Pat 1940- *70*
Zevin, Gabrielle *176*
Zhang, Christopher Zhong-Yuan 1954- *91*
Zhang, Song Nan 1942- *170*
　Earlier sketch in SATA *85*
Ziefert, Harriet 1941- *205*
　Earlier sketches in SATA *101, 154*
Ziegler, Jack (Denmore) 1942- *60*
Ziemienski, Dennis (Theodore) 1947- *10*
Ziliox, Marc
　See Fichter, George S.
Zillah
　See Macdonald, Zillah K(atherine)
Zim, Herbert S(pencer) 1909-1994 .... *30*
　Obituary *85*
　Earlier sketch in SATA *1*
　See also CLR *2*
　See also SAAS *2*
Zim, Sonia Bleeker 1909-1971 .... *2*
　Obituary *26*
Zima, Gordon 1920- *90*
Zimelman, Nathan 1921- *65*
　Brief entry *37*
Zimmer, Dirk 1943- *147*
　Earlier sketch in SATA *65*
Zimmer, Tracie Vaughn *169*
Zimmerman, Andrea 1950- *192*
　Earlier sketch in SATA *123*
Zimmerman, Andrea Griffing
　See Zimmerman, Andrea
Zimmerman, H. Werner 1951- *101*
Zimmerman, Heinz Werner
　See Zimmerman, H. Werner
Zimmerman, Naoma 1914-2004 .... *10*
Zimmermann, Arnold E. 1909- *58*
Zimmermann, Karl 1943- *211*

Zimmermann, Karl R.
  See Zimmermann, Karl
Zimmett, Debbie
  See Becker, Deborah Zimmett
Zimmy
  See Stratemeyer, Edward L.
Zimnik, Reiner 1930- 36
  See also CLR 3
Zindel, Bonnie 1943- 34
Zindel, Lizabeth 187
Zindel, Paul 1936-2003 102
  Obituary 142
  Earlier sketches in SATA *16, 58*
  See also CLR 85
Ziner, Feenie
  See Ziner, Florence
Ziner, Florence 1921- 5
Zingara, Professor
  See Leeming, Joseph
Zinger, Yitskhok
  See Singer, Isaac Bashevis
Zink, Michelle 1969- 220
Zion, Eugene 1913-1975 18
Zion, Gene
  See Zion, Eugene

Zobel, Allia
  See Zobel Nolan, Allia
Zobel Nolan, Allia 218
Zoehfeld, Kathleen Weidner 1954- 193
Zohorsky, Janet R. 1958- 148
Zolkower, Edie Stoltz 171
Zolkowski, Cathy (A.) 1969- 121
Zollars, Jaime 191
Zolotow, Charlotte 1915- 138
  Earlier sketches in SATA *1, 35, 78*
  See also CLR 77
Zolotow, Charlotte Gertrude Shapiro
  See Zolotow, Charlotte
Zolotow, Ellen
  See Dragonwagon, Crescent
Zonderman, Jon 1957- 92
Zonia, Dhimitri 1921- 20
Zonta, Pat 1951- 143
Zubrowski, Bernard 1939- 90
  Earlier sketch in SATA *35*
Zubrowski, Bernie
  See Zubrowski, Bernard
Zucker, Miriam S.
  See Reichert, Miriam Zucker
Zuckerman, Amy 217

Zuckerman, Linda 190
Zudeck, Darryl 1961- 61
Zug, Mark 204
Zupa, G. Anthony
  See Zeck, Gerald Anthony
Zupancic, Lilijana Praprotnik
  See Prap, Lila
Zurbo, Matt(hew) 1967- 98
Zurhorst, Charles (Stewart, Jr.) 1913-1989 .. 12
Zurlo, Tony 1941- 145
Zuromskis, Diane
  See Stanley, Diane
Zuromskis, Diane Stanley
  See Stanley, Diane
Zusak, Markus 1975- 149
Zwahlen, Diana 1947- 88
Zweifel, Frances W. 1931- 14
Zwerger, Lisbeth 1954- 194
  Earlier sketches in SATA *66, 130*
  See also CLR 46
  See also SAAS 13
Zwinger, Ann (H.) 1925- 46
Zymet, Cathy Alter 1965- 121